Four Nails

Four Nails

Poems by Gaylord Brewer

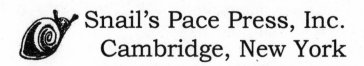 Snail's Pace Press, Inc.
Cambridge, New York

The Snail's Pace Press, Inc.
85 Darwin Road
Cambridge, New York 12816
snail@poetic.com

Darby Penney, Publisher
Ken Denberg, Editor
Stuart Bartow, Consulting Editor
Donna Prescott, Consulting Editor

The Snail's Pace Press, Inc. is a member of the Council
of Literary Magazines and Presses (CLMP).

Special thanks to Siena College and its Greyfriar Living
Literature Series.

Cover art: "Tumbler, 10.98.II," monotype, 12"x 12",
by Steven Swanson
Back cover photograph: Jack ("King") Pressly III
Cover design: Darby Penney

ISBN 0-9575273-3-3

ACKNOWLEDGMENTS

The poems in section II were written during two residencies in 2000: in June at the Chateau de Lavigny (Switzerland) and in October at the Tyrone Guthrie Centre (Ireland). Thanks to my hosts and caretakers. The rest were written in Tennessee.

My gratitude to the editors of the journals where the following poems appeared:

Asheville Poetry Review: "Look for Me under Your Boot-Soles"
Eclipse: "Souvenirs from the New Spain"
Natural Bridge: "The Standard of Forgiveness"
North Dakota Quarterly: "Making Ourselves at Home"
Pacific Review: "First Sex, Age Five"
Poem: "Cleaning Mussels"
Quarterly West: "More Mountains"
River Styx: "For the Woman at the Seafood Restaurant in Spiddle, Ireland"
Shades of December: "Westminster Cemetery," "A Widow of the World"
Sierra Nevada College Review: "Nosferatu, Nostradamus"
Smartish Pace: "A Midlands Adventure," "The World Etiquette of Cool"
Sundog: The Southeast Review: "A History of Text," "Poem for My Wedding," "Poppy"

Thanks to the Middle Tennessee State University Faculty Research and Creative Activities Committee for the Non-Instructional Assignment that allowed for the completion of this book. Thanks also to Kate Gale and Mark Cull at Red Hen Press for their continued support and encouragement.

Passages by Cesare Pavese are taken from *The Burning Brand: Diaries 1935-1950* (New York: Walker & Co., 1961), translated by A. E. Murch (with Jeanne Malli).

for C & J—
still the matter

CONTENTS

I

II

III

I became insane, with long intervals of horrible sanity.

—*Edgar Allan Poe*

the kingdom of theft had arrived
and we were the thieves.

—*Pablo Neruda*

One nail drives out another. But four nails make a cross.

—*Cesare Pavese*

1939, 1st January:

My active work, now organized on a practical basis, should no longer be chaotic; a life of sensible seclusion will follow, and all my energy be devoted to creation.

Remember that the self-confidence of 30th December, '37 was an illusion, and that six months later I was still raving. Remember.

29th April:

A good starting point is to modify one's own past.

14th October:

What is better than finding we are a hero when we've been up to a bit of devilment, on a country road in the morning, as the heavy carts go by?

—*Cesare Pavese*

The Fourth Man

What something bristles the neck
with claws you attribute to night air?
What queasiness beyond the Ferris wheel
and human dots reduced to profit,
frantic melodies across the zither,
the confused accounts of closest friends.

Truth worse than the wrong body buried,
than a sulky actress with false papers.
You thought Harry Lime was your answer
to everything, that his cherubic grin
could ignite the lights of a speeding
ambulance, phrase a dapper explanation

for this new world malevolence of winners.
But then he abandoned the living again,
left the doorway as empty as a magician's
closet, the cat meowing in circles
while laughing shoes disappeared.
And still sometimes a twinge in the small

of your spine, a wind licking up
your calves as you frown over the wet bricks
of the square. In fact more every day
you swear you can almost hear the torrent
of sewer beneath it all, taste the greater
wrong, an enormous shadow in a homburg

dividing this whole city you so dearly loved.
That Vienna's gone. And the chill,
the tongue of insinuation just escaped
forever between bruised, smiling lips,
that was me, old man, helping fates unfold,
lingering in an overcoat amid the rubble,

making Lime seem as grotesque
and innocent as a peasant hawking balloons.
The guards haven't a clue. But the child
who speaks no English, who cries for
a father, he knows my name. Keep looking
where you shouldn't, and *I'll* find *you*.

How Lovely, How Lethal

Her mourning suit of stilettos,
nylon, and black gauze.
She stepped out of it easily enough.
Any chump could see I was the one
who needed protecting.
A jewel-studded Luger from the purse.
Me on my knees, trying to hold
my guts in. "You killed my partner
and now you've killed me."
She sneered, lit a cigarette.
Pressed the gun against a slender thigh.
Our forever was a fist of smoke.

Nosferatu, Nostradamus

The principle of fear is eternally
darkness, spread from a Romanian catacomb,
an alleyway in Minsk, or by thoughts
of fevered men, anywhere the claw may open
its five encrusted points of virtue.
Theirs is a colorless world,
same as everyone's, their métier
the 400 intonations to gray, one for each
pirouette of death. Two exceptions:
the yellow eyes of the Seer,
the single crimson tooth of He Who Hungers.

This night has lasted longer
than anyone alive remembers—the old man
cradling a tureen of cabbage soup,
the child who can't stop sobbing,
the crone who turns suddenly from the window,
spits, and crosses a filthy apron.
Out there gallops the unstoppable future
under greasy lamplight,
from the steaming nostrils of a nag,
in the stain of an unnatural kiss.
They've heard the tales of a black castle,
of robed men with chants and torches.
Of a coffin and a book embossed in gold.
They too believe in premonition, and they too
crave the hot, bitter pulse of life.

Note to My Apprentice

And why does my skeleton pursue me
if my soul has fallen away?
—Neruda

Bones be my occupation. I hunt these
hills to reclaim splinters of history.
Crouched, I comb forgotten foreheads,
rub weathered sockets free of soil
and leaf, hair and accumulated darknesses.
In the shed, with gleaming utensils of my own
design, I extract any rattling debris.
This, too, requires a surgeon's touch.
Bleach softens bone for a while, then whitens
to an intimation of shell on uncrossed sand,
smoothes to a chorus of eternity.
Some skulls harden with wear, grow as durable
as their stony smiles, while others
dissolve in your gaze, as thin and crushed
as eggshell, fissures of accident or attack.

Your thoughts too may worm that way
when bones become your passion,
when the pale cornice of disclosure
edging from brush jump-starts a hollow heart.
You too may discover yourself
distracted as you cup your lover's face
or when, with probing fingers, you explore
the shape of your own unyielding future.
These habits burn trails in the territory
of recognition. And always, teeth come last—
bicuspids and molars often intact,
less often the crown, and, if you have labored
a pure and faithful season, perhaps
one fine arching canine curved like a claw.
Glue these in and your day is done.

The Play Left Unfinished

My thought was for light to rise
on an open casket
turned from the audience.
This, the altar of the stage
to which characters
arrived. There would be tough country
humor, recognitions,
even a child returned too late
from a far and ambiguous distance.
I wrote scenes of such,
choreographing mourners
across the soft glow of curtain,
opening mouths
with great authority.

The second act, the dominion
of the ghosts, killed my play.
I couldn't hear them
or sort their jumble of motivations.
I saw only a gray mime
of imprecise movement,
the arc of a sleeve, a lean wrist,
powder and black mascara,
bodies turning toward some private purpose.
I gave up on the dead,
buried the pages in the Trunk
of Failed Attempts. *Necropolis County*.
I just couldn't finish that play.
But I will.

Eve of the Dead, 1971

There I am now, you see, kneeling
in a booth in the kitchen, by the cutting block
squared on thick legs, beneath the loop
of rope concealing a skeleton
of attic stairs. My mother, my adoring mother
straightens black synthetic whiskers and tightens
my patch. I am Bluebeard, I tell
everyone, half-understanding my own joke
of hidden riches exchanged for hidden terrors.
There is my father, my kind brusque father
barely forty in a crewcut and white T-shirt.
Look at the size of those forearms,
the cobra erupted from the skull's socket,
the knife stabbing mom's name through a plump heart!
He is frying eggs and pork brains
in a skillet, not even thinking yet,
perhaps, of winter work. And I am ready,
bursting with ready for the neighborhood of demons
and demimondes, so ready my whole short life
seems pointed to this night, to the taking
of every lit door, while my oldest brother,
in shadow, steers our campaign
clear of its riskier invitations. We're living
in the bigger house for almost a year now,
the house with the gazebo and French doors, bay windows
across the back, hanging lamps and a fountain
in the living room, and my parents are as happy
as they're ever likely to be.
But what I want, what I want dearly
at the moment—and when else is there?—
is to kick the screen door open and hit the streets,
is for my sack, empty of everything
but the beautiful danger I already imagine myself
bringing, to bulge fat around each sweet prize
I deserve so will demand, and thank you.

Captain Kingfish

Our good Captain wore a red beard, monocle
and white sailor's cap, came out rolled
in a double-breasted yachting jacket.
Oceanic Burl Ives or piscine Santa, he waddled
among the tables unfurling magic,

dealing cards with his photo as we drowned
fried cod in ketchup and mashed coleslaw
under spoons. The Captain I wasn't sure about
but couldn't argue the positive mojo
of his mystical card—sure bet

to produce a few coins under a pillow.
How many more teeth, after all, could one spare
with the string-and-doorknob routine?
I found his trick most effective announced
before bed; it stirred up

the money gods. So hey, the magic didn't last.
With timing, I could still summon an encore
quarter or two. I suspected
even then the great man was full of bologna,
and his job, let's admit, peculiar.

And think of our folks, from whom
this ample fairy took complicity for granted.
How many scrawny kids awoke from dreams
of green, kicked pillows aside to find
only the fat smile, a dog-eared monocle,

and—big deal—another lesson we already knew.

Say Uncle

—for Mike & Rod

I parachute in, boots first
in the snow. My tiger-skin bag rattles
with bottles and Asian secrets.
I give thumbs-up to the sky.
Nieces leap from the house squealing my name;
I toss each a dazzling box
as they get their feet wet dancing.

Inside, my brothers huddle
by the electric logs with their mugs
of holiday decaf. They try hard not to look
out the steaming window
as the girls erect a snowman in my image
and as a single angelic choir
begin to sing.

Look for Me under Your Boot-Soles

Was it where they lost me
that I found myself?
        —Neruda

My mother looks for me in photographs
affixed in books—held by a hospital blanket,
potato arms at the screaming melon of my face.
She turns the page to a kid oozing
from his shirt, betrayed outside a new school.
She diverts wet eyes to a box of sparrows,
then back to black and white. She knew
before she started her baby was going, gone.

My brothers, they wisely prefer not to look.
When they collect the practice bats
and rope them snug and heavy in a canvas bag,
when they lock the door and parade with family
beneath a garland of Sunday bells,
when they grill bun and burger with impunity,
they'd just as soon I didn't appear, a genie
in black hood and suspenders, and I don't.

My oldest friend looks for me at night flat
on his back. Bleary eyes search heaven
for the compass of my sword. His lip curls
with a finely formed insult, unflung.
The familiar bars of Symphony #1 (for ice
and bottle) caress the ear, and he flops to
his feet. To other friends, I'm an unwritten
diary, a cribsheet denied, a burned map.

Once a year my wife looks for me as courtesy,
jumps the bed with a needle of antique brooch
and stitches the pillowy lumps beneath
our hand-pieced quilt. She calls in French,
cuddles under a snore before my silent answer.
Behind a screen, the dog points all day
to the spot he saw me last. Night drops like
a shot partridge and the tail quits wagging.

A Walk with Billy Collins in St. Petersburg

The smoky women of the Nevskiy Prospekt have tripped
lesser talents, but we keep on moving.
We hoof it past the Church of the Spilled Blood,
without missing a beat angle between buses
circling the Hermitage. If it were only raining,

like yesterday, we could speak of clouds
and turn the collars of our fleece jackets.
If only winter, we could discourse on snow.
We settle for architecture, the pleasure of marriage
and dogs, the daily ordeal of lunch.

I risk a joke about Pushkin's fatal duel; it dies.
But when Billy adjusts his Yankees cap and frowns
across the Neva, I discreetly unfold my Woody Hayes
"O" and put it on. What surer sign
could these people possibly be waiting for?

Billy eyes me sideways and, like the magician
that he most certainly is, pours a pony of vodka
from his suddenly unzipped pocket.
"Here's your torch, soldier," he says, and who am I
to argue? I take a drink and run with it.

A Poem by Me

Somehow a poem by me, its caresses
of winter light, its crow calls
and leaning barns, is different from others.
Somehow, when my poem drives into sunset,
its horizon divides the road of your life;
when my poem's mother weeps,
the past squeezes your heart like a dish towel.
Anyone can tell the difference
in my poem's sibling tension, the tincture
of its wounded loves, its mortgages
and great peeling frescoes, all indefinable.

You can rest easy when my poem rubs
its tired, emblematic feet or licks its ankle,
forgive in yourself its wicked pulse.
You can mimic with wet lips
my poem's endless cycle
of human comedy, so singularly outfitted.

The farce of my poem's mistakes
grants everyone a warming halo
of strength, its deflated snapshots
an exhalation of regret.
In my poem no one escapes,
yet, somehow, all emerge gentle and true.
When my name's at the top you know
to expect something tasty,
that even on my poem's stormiest day
the balloon will go up,
the guillotine fall, and spring lilies
part again in a honeyed womb of appreciation.

That's just how it is in a poem by me,
the flaccid world made languid,
a fire burning the belly of the soul,
carved from granite with a blade
forged of poppies; the way it's all in there.
Until at last, tireless but resigned
in its crusade of earthly witness,
my poem eases the steely jaws of truth
and whispers to you, its favorite reader,
to go now, beat it till next time.
And like a troll grown iridescent wings, you do.

Solicitor

I carried my shiny bachelors degree into the cinder block
building, showed it around in mild embarrassment,
and after an hour with pay of learning something useful
I was ready to sell *TV Guide*. A supervisor escorted me,
prompts in hand, to a vacant station in the telephone bank.

The first week's salary was guaranteed, then, of course,
we'd all be surprised if commissions didn't exceed wages.
The classier magazines, too, would be added to my list
as I got my sea legs. Of course, the booth would eavesdrop
on calls at its discretion, check accuracy, offer guidance.

For two hours I aimed at trustworthy confidence, conveying
a warm and convivial vocal swagger, and I never once
finished the sales text. "Hello, Sir/Madam, how are you
this evening? If I may briefly ask you . . ." Pages of this.
One woman listened for a while to my sweaty mumbling,

then finally interrupted, "Honey, I can't feed my kids."
The more merciful—bloodless "phone busters" we'd been
warned of in training—simply hung up and went back
to dinner. 4 to 8 o'clock was our slice of bread and butter.
I apologized a lot, covered the mouthpiece, averted eyes

from colleagues selling *People* and *Good Housekeeping*
right and left. Only an imbecile couldn't move *TV Guide*,
the weekly everybody had to have. Halfway into the shift,
when I stood, put on my jacket, and walked briskly
past the control office, I didn't find nerve to ask

for money due me. But once out in the early evening
of early summer, I felt immediately better. I could sense
the bodies in that building, dialing for their lives,
talking, hustling, hoping. On the other end, all those
poor fish with saggy doors and a thousand kids, televisions

blasting unguided, cans of dinner boiling on greasy stoves,
all dodging to slip the hook. I walked to my crappy car
and got in. It started. At the nearest Starvin Marvin,
I bought three dollars of regular and their biggest cigar.
I lit that mother and rattled toward the sunset, feeling,

by then, loose, easy, strong, cleansed by rebellion.
I was twenty. The sky was orange. I sucked on the cigar
and its tip flared. I had all summer to cruise in
and consider the options. My dad had told me I could
live at home until I was 40, and I'd be a fool not to.

First Sex, Age 5

Don't try to tell me it wasn't sex
and hot, don't start in
with what's natural or what's good for you.
Tracy, seven, I never liked her
much but what's *like* got to do with it?

The undershirt discarded, the rose panties
squeezed deep between her tiny buns
where I'd stuffed them.
Lacy socks, stumbling pirouettes,
a riveted male audience.

And a first draft of glorious glorious shame
in my parched mouth. Every sense
—well, almost—taut to the possibility
of a garage door hauled open
and the lashing light of afternoon.

Parents, the truths you deny would curl
gray hair. Lock them in a basement,
lock them in the shed. Some randy little monster
only dimly aware what he's got
hands around will come fiddling with a key.

Cleaning Mussels

Endure their briny effluvia.
Raise each ebony bivalve
to running water,
burnish away all grit,
all residue of sea possible.
Discard the crushed and broken.
Detach each coarse
beard with whatever force
necessary. Ice the survivors.
Tap parted shells,
allowing the rest a moment
to pull themselves together.

Most won't. Discard the dead.

Westminster Cemetery

Each year at midnight we gather
in the sanctuary, at an eastern window
in attitude of iron gates.
Each year, he comes to the grave.
That instant his figure appears
in black coat and scarf, seemingly
of naught but winter air, stuns us silent.
We hurry for the north
window, where if heavens oblige
a tomb is dimly visible.
Since before we were children, he comes
with a dozen crimson roses
to the grave. We huddle at the narrow
aperture, the pitted glass obscure
with our humid exhortations.
No one impedes him, no one approaches,
yet we are certain he knows of us.
Two years preceding he looked to the chapel,
and, we were certain, perceptibly
touched his brim. Some of our group
glimpsed perhaps some possible
identity. The day following, the curator
received this word: "Dear Sir, the city
makes traditions of us both.
Some must end and others take their place.
The torch will be passed."

The next year we saw no one, all night
suffered the plaintive moan of old shutters,
devils swirled in snow.
In the morning, a dozen white roses
lay prostrate on the stone.

A Widow of the World

She holds a sack of oranges
to her breast. Small Virginia
follows beside,
a box of bread in two arms,
eight fingers cupping the edge.
At a stall for apples
she tallies again
the centimes locked in her purse.
One should have pecans
when a husband's ghost visits
its body after a year,
visits its sons. One should.
She sees an aunt in a dark dress
in the crowd.
They speak, touch palms.
So tomorrow there would be apples,
and pecans, two packages,
for her reunited family.
On the second bus they find
seats in the rear, with a window.
A straw hat nods above
the snores of an old man.

And lawyers prepare the defense.

Poppy

Not the girl in the magazine
requesting erotic lessons,
but last flower of a hot season,
so fine in disposition
yellow petals brush unfelt
across the calluses of fingertips.
Alone, quiescent in glass,
it withdraws from the initiative
of evening, and is closed.

1942, 14th August:

In the little train I was thinking that the fields I saw speeding past, the tree-curtains, the houses, the little out-of-the-way corners, the reminders of former days, all would have served to make a memory, a past. Though the hour was commonplace and, in truth, boring, to find it again one day would no longer have been boring.

1949, 27th February:

In reality, the one thing that touches me, moves and inspires me, is the magic of nature, a glance fixed upon the hill. When that theme is not in mind, when instead I have a human subject, a game of city life and morality, that is when my imagination flags.

1950, 14th January:

Thinking again of the sisters D., I know that I have lost a great opportunity of playing the fool. Rome grows more colorful as I look back.

—*Cesare Pavese*

Making Ourselves at Home

First, many thanks for accommodating
us in such elegance.
A few simple revisions will make
us comfortable. Ivory walls have to go.

Anything less luminous, more
in accord with the soul, should be fine—
then perhaps a dark residue
of field smeared on doors and jambs,

some greasy effect of alleyways flung
randomly at high ceilings, that kind of touch.
We'll be breathing easier already.
Mirrors need breaking—the bureau to reflect

two faces, the closet-length to remind
of bodies divided against themselves.
Fourteen years of cherished doom
for her and me and us and you.

Sunflower curtains must come down
immediately. These will make fine shrouds,
funeral gowns trailing to the future.
Or we'll burn them in a pile with the rest—

silk lampshades and settee, carved
oak desk—although we admired its scars!—
library in German, all those little intrusions.
We're ordinary folks; no fuss necessary.

Plus, we're qualified to do most work
ourselves—carpet paths of thistle
and char we need to find our way in the dark
are a trademark, statues of bone and glue

with a black rose in each mouth
symbols of an artisan's craft
that demands a lifetime.
What a splendid crashing from porcelain

figurines—those glazed and dusted
couples so enamored!—as we clear the mantel
for our own pieces. Then a ripping
surrender of canvas to blade,

leaving only frames of tourniquets
to enlighten. More antidote to this deadly
peacefulness. Sorry. But notice how the place
is taking shape, none of it

losing you a penny? We even supply
nightly entertainment—jagged sobs
in down comforter, bottles pinwheeled onto
pavement stones. We never travel

without our music! Whatever the cost
to make this dive livable, don't worry,
don't think about it, don't miss a wink's sleep.
We always pay cash, and we pay as we go.

The Riviera

They delivered, fresh friends,
pitched me to a beach
as I insisted. Even teenagers
had abandoned lust by then,
were splintering for lonely cars.
Night's fires were ash.
At the edge of the sea,
separate from human voices
unintelligible to me, I
was nowhere, or anywhere.
A casino perching on the water
lured easily, another dazzling
phantom desolate inside.
I donated the last coins
of my pocket. Nothing mattered.
No trains ran till morning.
Past midnight, I lay on stones,
my knickknacks a lump
under my head under a moon,
banal and blazing and indifferent.
My fingers picked a stone
the size of an egg,
a hole for a center. Signs
of eternity, essence eroded.
Smoothed, hardened, imperturbable,
meaningless. I nested it
in the sack, careful of
the cigarettes they had given.
I got up stiff and started walking.
Lord, how I wanted the magic.
Hugging a thin jacket
of cleverness, I kept
moving against the shore.
The ocean's gibberish
didn't teach any song

I couldn't sing already—
I whispered myself
between towns, boarded,
dismal, one sick globe of light
to the next. Each hour I allowed
five minutes' rest and a smoke,
rationing for daylight.
A rat on the beach dismissed me,
returned enterprising
to shadows. What the fuck
was I doing out there,
pushing mile after mile
over rotted pilings, dead fish,
past stinking abandoned boats?
Slouched and stumbling
on sticks of legs toward a
semblance of arrival,
there was no stopping, no refund.
I was responsible and if
I suffered for it, better still.
No luxury of collapse.
The sky a world later
began to pink and one
solitary driver then another
edged me to the side. I kept
going—what choice now?—
until I could find some way back
to the place of wanting
at that time my only home.

More Mountains

This too is a failure
as an articulation of stone
always must be.
Kneeled in yellow wildflowers,
intimate with caterpillars
and beetles,
I studied the glyphs of snow.
Behind me, a great bowled kerf
opened at 2400 meters;
below, an alien promenade
thrust recklessly.

To have Neruda's grinning
exuberance then,
a squint of Jeffers' reverence
as they concocted
their attempts.
Red trails crossed the map
like perambulating ants.
Otherwise I was on my own,
separate, blind
to compassion. I strained again
against all things human,

hoping humility
to preserve me. Nonsense.
That's not at all what happened.
It was just that a mist
arrived, luxuriously,
and I watched
the stones wound
in a curtain of cream
until there remained
only the awful evanescence
and the threat of descent.

The *Godfather* Elegies

I. Hospital Vigil

It begins at the bed of a parent.
This time, my mother's.
I sit beside her, joking,
belittling frailty, then quietly.
I hold her soft hand
and think hard for us
concerning threats
to the family. This illness,
another warning shot. Last year
the old man's light stroke.
She'll recover from
the hospital, toughen up
with sunshine and rest
and our own recipes. But the future
drops away from us
like steps precipitous down a mountain.
My father enters. For a tired smile
I give him the chair.
His recent weight loss
has carved ten years on his face,
his body seems lost in itself.
Since morning,
fighting doctors and bureaucrats,
waiting on unreturned calls.
Not so long ago, a man
was a king. He built a family
on muscle and skill
and his given word. The world changed.

It's my world. Or I'm determined
to make it so, to bow it to my purpose
or destroy it
to honor this aging couple
I adore. After a different kind
of war, service to authority
I no longer believed nor trusted,
I returned to wait
until this danger to us passed.
Decorated in his fashion,
the youngest son had come home.
Where were the others?

II. "Never Ask Me about My Business"

My fiancée has learned not
to question about family, personal
affairs of my life
that do not involve her. She loves me,
and my severe privacy
is the price of that devotion.
When I look away
here is what I see: a single room
of chiseled rock, seared
from hillsides by an acid
of generations. Below, I stare across
the sea, wild groves
planted by ancestors and abandoned
when they gave up land for boats.
I fashioned myself after
old ways to find there were no old ways
and this circle could not be closed.
During long evenings of summer
hawks hunt
the valley once
our livelihood. My fiancée's never been
to the island. I've never invited her.

III. Brothers

One is hot-tempered, leaps first.
The other cultivates a quiet soul.
My cold certainties
unnerve them
so at gatherings they mock me.
I love them and for my parents' sake
would not betray them
for all the temptations of the living.
They could say the same of me
and mean it
but have their own children
demanding devotion, support, legacy.
Sibling blood is lateral,
a seasonal stream. We trickle apart
and hope for the best.

IV. "You Broke My Heart"

Neither brother
carries a stone in his chest
nor do veins rattle
with reptilian blood
warming for movement.
Already I run the family
from behind the passive curtain
of my face.
There are no contenders,
and one day too late
they'll see the truth. How do you
like your heroes, mademoiselle?

V. Passage

I sit outside with my father
in autumn.
He leans over tomato plants,
touching each red bulb,
inspecting merits or deficiencies.
Less and less he offers advice.
All's been said,
and now we wait together
in the sad, luxurious afternoon.
The season's fruit ripens and falls.
He knows now that I am
the one when the crisis comes.
His life, his bones
he sacrificed
for education to make me
legitimate in a world
he could not enter.
I feel his uncertainty about choices,
tenets he took for granted.
He hears me silently,
Whose destiny arrives on schedule?

VI. Sequel

I don't laugh much anymore.
Perhaps I never did,
but photographs expose me as happy.
I am pedigreed beyond belief
from a family to be reckoned with.
My record is irreproachable
and only beginning.
By contrast, the priest is powerless
in pontiff's rags. The police
are savage lackeys.

Politicians, grocery clerks collecting
a bill. My silk tie
gleams like the devil's tooth.
Its small knot is hard
as an acorn.
The New World cries out
for the absolution I offer.

I live and die by what I had to do.
Let God judge, if he's there.

I'll See You Again

So sudden the taxi's arrival,
an abrupt end to it, no more time
for kisses, for blessings,
just here we are, releasing her
fingers, then a tumble into morning
with the red-faced cabby,
hauling luggage from trunk

to the curb of the station.
Day cold on my cheek, my hand
that had reached to touch
the shirt across his thin shoulder.
Quickly they were merged and away,
bound for a plane, return to
the country of their life together.

I waited on the walk, breathing,
standing however a man does
as wind flipped at my open jacket.
I wasn't an inch closer to keeping
anything I didn't want to lose,
just the opposite. I peered
into the immense space opening

in front of me. Then I did
what mind and body could manage:
hoisted the heavy bag, hoped
for their safety and for myself
only that rain would hold
until I arrived north,
to the place where I was going.

Four Little Foxes

Lounging above a fresh-cut field
with stork and heron,
eagles easing in wakes
of nipping crow, I was already grateful.
I had taken more than I'd given.
Then, to be offered
a sudden gift of fox, upwind,
emerged casually from wheat stalks,
roving, scratching a haunch—
my unswatted flies were no price.

And that same day,
the evening stroll through vineyards
to an edge of forest—
again I had behaved badly
in human company—to see another!
Tawny, slim, ears peaked, the broad tail.
It sniffed new cuttings,
pawed, muzzled, lifted a clenched
unmoving prize. Then upfield
another, and further on,
emboldened by fresh kill,
an incredible third! Man,
you can have your churches
and trinities, your cruel cities of art,
your campaigns for applause—
to me this was holiness.
These animals destroyed me.
I can't overstate the moment,
standing in grace, still but unhidden
—too close, not close enough—
one wild lean miracle entreating another
until, alerted to
a dark silhouette, each turned
and bound for its abiding wood.

A Midlands Adventure

Poor fellow—Petey may have been
his name—had merely grown up
hiking the valley, parceling trails
by breath, working a few acres
for berries and vegetables
and unpretentious herbs.
All he'd done was live there
for years with his brothers, tend
the portion under care.
So that's what he knew—nothing.
Now, having refilled wood bins
and completed a morning's work
on his holiday, coerced into
this walking tour of flora and fauna
on a dismal Sunday afternoon.
It couldn't be delayed—
the writers were flying tomorrow
for Paris, for Pittsburgh,
for the Yukon—
and they hadn't collected all
data necessary to render verse
radiant with local expertise.
They had a few more questions.
So women slashed umbrellas
through slapping weeds, tottered
over rudely slippery rocks.
Each carried pen and cloth notebook,
scribbled incessantly, collected
leaves, twigs, and blossoms
to privately affix that evening.
Is that a Swillowing Mimosa, Petey,
like Hardy used to build a swing
for his consumptive wife?
Are those Nanny's Tears
of Gideon's Trumpet? Which poison

branch did Boswell report
Sir Earl Humphrey coaxing to blaze,
asphyxiating children
and horses on Feast of Gloucester?
Petey squinted past us, skyward.
He gamely tried a few bushes
—Ladies, me mother she always
called it Pissy Widow—but destroyed
each time under interrogation
he finally slumped
ahead in dejected rubber boots,
saggy pants, blue slicker.
The bastard never stood a chance.
How old is that Scarlet Maple?
Was it mature when Keats arrived?
Ah, he could tell—by hacking it down
and counting rings!
By then I absolutely loved the guy.
Hair hung plastered to his face
like a pork chop, but he didn't cry.
He gestured toward rubble
obviously intended as a highlight,
mumbled vaguely of invasion.
The writers kept writing.
Journals bulged with wet samplings.
Finally, they could go no further
in their shoes in such unaccommodating
weather. Our tour ended.
The women were politely disgusted:
they'd have to look up
facts required for authenticity.
What the reader expected,
the disciplined artist supplied.
So we slogged to the castle:
three for tea in the drawing room,
me to my secluded single malt
and Petey, almost certainly, to his.

Walk with Me

Beyond the Bog Garden
past the Lodge at White Gates
further to Paddy Cross.
All the way to Maggie's Farm

if you feel spry.
Never mind the weather.
When eyeballs ache like ice
they tell us we're alive.

There're slickers in the hall.
I'll take your hand
beneath the empty rookery,
then lead to Tomb Brae

where the old man's said to lie.
(His wife died young,
she bore no children.)
We'll circle back, legs humming,

snuggled in our boots,
to Cordoo Pass and Crappah
Private School, south again
to Lynch's Cottage.

Along the way, we'll conjure
Cootehill and Ballybay,
the laughing drunk whose best
mate passed that morning,

sing songs we've hardly heard.
For now, there's a pint
at the Black Kesh, local girls
sneering round the cig machine,

the whole place for sale.
Coming back late, good
and trembling together,
perhaps through heavy soup

we'll spy the shape of a man
still among reeds,
clutch each other close as
(it seemed to weary eyes

we'll swear) he turns to a bird
and lofts, wings silent,
into the dark above O'Hanlon's Hill.

For the Woman at the Seafood Restaurant in Spiddle, Ireland

Outstretched behind a bar mirror
for glass or silver, hungrily at work
and turning, I suppose, with no resemblance
to a dancer across the clamorous room.
That was that. Good company now distraction.
I twisted my neck again and again
over my left shoulder until muscles burned,
obviously, openly, for glimpses of you.
Perhaps it was partly drink, partly
my marriage in less than a month,
but that evening and into following days
you figured in every image I held of the world.
You approached our table only once,
as I looked back and, startled to see you
hurrying for us, arms bent beneath
appetizers, pulled my eyes forward in a rush.
I breathed you in obliquely—peninsula
of nose and chin, field of one cheek,
lake of breast beneath a white shirt.
I smelled the heat off your body,
felt certain however childishly that
some palpable reality had passed between us.
I won't try to describe you any more.
I sat still. I ate the oysters.
Lemon on my tongue, pepper sauce
reddening my lips, cool wet bodies swallowed.
There's no name allowed for it.
This loneliness that can arch like a mouth
without explanation, the harrowing
margins of possibility. I've walked streets

for months, straddled continents like the newly
dead riding a nightmare, a cracked
human glass insisting to be shattered.
I won't see you again. To return the next
morning for your name was too foolish
even for me, even now, even the way I've been.

Ode to a Woman's Calf

Crossed over a pedestal of knee,
you taunt with an ideal
of perfection. Luscious minaret
eliciting prayer,
flirtatious consort
swaying just perceptibly
to your body's muscular music.
The foot is a fun time,
scarlet whimsy of nails,
black buds flowering from slipper.
But, ah, sleek imperative
of ankle, guideline of shin
over and again
to a downy dream of hinder flesh.
Tapered island to graze,
sinuous inverted vase,
angelic stalactite
exposed from caverns of womanhood.
Drumstick for nibbling.
Dark alabaster trouble,
slenderly dangerous
flame of grail and riot,
proof and dismissal of godly profusion,
insurrectionist, ruiner of lives.
You, golden calf,
neither meek nor harmless be you,
arbiter of the world you model.

The World Etiquette of Cool

The answer's not in unisex perfume,
not hanging in the sleeves
of an ankle-length lambskin coat,
not in satin blazers, team colors,
or firing the eyes of a rattlesnake tattoo.
Sweat and bark all day, do your reps,
you still can't buy it in a gym,
learn it on a bass or fiddle, shade it
through a pair of Raybans.
All industry earns you is embarrassment.
It's nothing to do with fashion
or attitude, a cashmere scarf from Uruguay,
adoring the mirror above your bed,
shaken or stirred or learning French.
Forget James Dean stroking a cigarette.
Dying's only a fraction of it,
but more than stripped abs, a hot trigger,
and daddy's four-wheel-drive.

You'll catch a glimpse of the real thing
only once, maybe, when I swagger by
in a scowl and baggy shorts,
head shaved and gut proud,
aces and jokers tumbling from every pocket.
Don't try to follow the trail, child,
my woods get dark. Go to the clubhouse
and enjoy the rest of your little life.
Truth's for suckers. As for cool, we have
what the gods imparted. To you, none.

A History of Text

When power was lost for good,
cord cold, screen blank,
he sharpened lead
with a carving knife
and addressed the page by hand.

When candles and oil were reserved
for the rich, he wrote
during daylight,
huddled at night beside fires
of memory.

When words were dismissed,
he traced figures in mud:
his boyhood dog, a bird, a mountain,
men with spears and hats, a boat
he had sailed in dream.
The Sun. From plants he crushed
dyes of red, blue, yellow,
consecrated with stick and leaf
the ruins of the house he had built.

When parched earth cracked raw
to bone beneath him, the man, feverish
with purpose, piled stone
upon stone, each configuration
higher than the last, each announcing
to the sky his plaintive desire,
"Acknowledge me. Here is what I believed,
here is why."

Souvenirs from the New Spain

A goat nailed to the trunk
of a gnarled olive,
totem for buzzards.
Wildflower and skin-hungry
thistle delivering insidious
message.
An eagle drifting the Sierra Norte,
limp reward
locked in beak. Sheep paths
designated by droppings,
the bell-clang of a leader.
Cork sheared.
Streambeds, cracked.
Flies vibrating with ambition.
Inquisitive steers, calves nuzzling,
cranes nested
on a tile roof.
Horses painted in dust.
Sagging bitch a playground for parasites.
Stain of vines warm in bottle,
sun a slaughterhouse,
maps discarded,
late table set,
someone crying, someone silent.
Everything marked by the knife.

Triptych

In the left panel a glowing lawn,
just a bit unkempt, angled by long shadows
of lonely cypress. In the right,
an elbow of garden path, spotted pears
nodding in apparent reach, an empty bench.
The center panel remains obscured
by a linen shade taller than a man.
Beneath it, a sphere of light so brilliant
even a study of the drape intoxicates.
Surely, such a color was never before possible.
Whether this completes our Georgian scene
is uncertain, likely irrelevant.
It could in theory recreate anything,
even the road out, the one you'll learn again
at dawn when, following a sleepless night,
you draw the gauze and step inside.

1947, 1st January:
At the end of '38 I was hard-pressed and working at full stretch; when '46 began, I was contemptuous, rich and rather bitter. This time it is different—I am hard-pressed and rich, but I feel a driving power that throbs louder than the voice of my work and predicts, not fresh works, but sordid realities.

16th August (at Forte dei Marmi):
Autumn, this most mild and tender of seasons, takes over from the previous one and then establishes itself with fearful quakings, tremendous storms, darkness at morning, whirlwinds and a massacre of leaves. All this violence is the price of maturity.

7th December:
So many alarming things have been said and written about our life, our world, our culture, that to see the sun, the clouds, to go out into the street and find grass, dogs, pebbles, moves you like a great boon, like a gift from God, like a dream. But a dream that endures, that actually exists.

—*Cesare Pavese*

How I Would Return

From sunset red on the sierra
floor, failing past Garrucha
and the cold sea,

from rutted paths followed
through desert to silence answered
across the wind's shoulders.

From swallows
slashing citadels
of Moorish kings not in mockery

nor in reverence,
from the tribulation of legs,
the bile of my own

youth raised in my own throat,
from Lorca's phantom
into cheerless November dusk,

from the old quarter
for Jews, from hunting after war
and praying to fail again,

and failing again.
From the leer of Gypsy caves
and the castanet of coin.

From the ocean eel
floating on a blue plate of oil,
from the fish engorged

by it own tail
and imparted to delicate teeth,
from a table for one

toasted without tears or laughter,
from vines thick
and broken as a man's wrist,

from nothing, a worn coat,
a vow named but not believed,
to travel descended

in air, cross the world
with eyes two bruises of coal,
with breath a boisterous smoke,

cross marked stones
to the season's last moth
lacerated by fire, to you

at my door, starved, sleepless,
rank of life and death
like that I would return.

Hell-Bent

I blaze then like a giant
in the suddenly contracted room,
arm raised behind me
among the shadows of my home.
In hand the legacy
of father's oiled leather strop.

My black shirt.
My toxic breath. "Get your ass
in there with your mother."
Beneath me a son I've borne,
puny and indignant, awaiting
my first weakness.

"Boy, don't make me tell you again."

When I'm Gone

Nearly every night, as I close the book
and reach for the lamp, I think of you
cuddling our dog in the queen-size bed,
under the big comforter, between the feather
pillows your parents sent.
I can almost hear your breath
and the dog's snore since he's gotten older.

But since as I try for sleep
it is only afternoon where you are,
I then think of you coming home from classes,
striding over each stone, mail in one hand,
groceries in the other, juggling keys.
The dog yelping, maybe the message
light blinking. You'll have soup
or pasta and cheese for dinner, play *Jeopardy*.
For me, by then, it'll be late.

I think of you throughout the day, my day,
and often I think of the man I'll be
when I get back. How in winter
we'll walk hoping for deer, and if there's snow
how the dog will furrow with his pink nose.
Afterwards I'll make hot whiskeys. We'll talk
like we haven't in years.

When I'm gone I wonder why I'm gone. I live
quietly inside each day and I don't drink as much.
The calendar is a metronome of calm
and anticipation.

But really, these trips amount to only
a small portion of our lives.
Most of the time it is otherwise.
Most times, like now for instance, I am home.
And everything's different.

68

Being a Good Man

I'm sick of lugging this satchel
of bones from office
to woods, alphabetizing each knuckle,
burying hip joint or femur.
I get older; the bag gets heavier.

And this black hat pulled low
across my eyes like a coffin lid,
I don't care anymore for
its rakish angle. I'd like to launch it
into some heavenly wind.

My clogs are out of fashion,
two soggy boats shuffling over a swamp
of bile. What's the point
in silk socks with hearts
when all the world's immutable mud?

And who can stand one more hour
in this morgue laughingly called my study,
steel drawers and shadow,
corpses of books stuffed to ceiling?
I need a tailor, an architect,

fellows who enjoy the trade
who'll abide no more deathly nonsense.
A cutaway tux, track lighting.
Barring that I'll wallow in blood.
I'll kill us both every day of our lives.

Poem for My Wedding

Those who respond to our requests
with"I'll try" intend to deny us, and
call on us to join in the hypocrisy.
                    —David Mamet

I'll try to be forthright or silent.
I'll try to be faithful and discrete
and never humiliate you.
I'll try to enjoy the present
without dismissing
lost years or neglecting our future.
I'll try to make decent money
to give you some security and fun.
I'll try to remember to laugh.
I'll try to be good in bed
and keep the house from collapsing.
I'll try to pretend your family is mine.
I'll try to watch my drinking.
I'll try to be moderate
in both deed and spoken opinion.
I will try to maintain harmony,
regardless of my beliefs.
I'll try to accommodate your friends
and try to achieve at their pace.
I'll try to move through the world
as some version of a man, albeit revised
from the model I was taught.
I'll try not to destroy myself
and drag you with me.
I'll try not to sabotage our vows
beginning the first day.
I'll try to love you and keep on
loving you while we're alive, until we die.

The Black Bed

For days afterwards, this still
holding me: I didn't want it.
Wakefulness, the lurid responsibility,
to face any of morning's claims.
You pressed behind
and I could tell even from that place,
by the brush of your thighs
against me, you were naked.
My sweet bride of two weeks.
Offering comfort. From what?
In the bed where we had made love
on Sunday. An old darkness arrived,
paralyzing. I gripped the pillow
like a raft, like a child.
You knew I was awake, I knew,
but I didn't dare speak or acknowledge.
Finally I did sit up, after you'd
gone, felt I had betrayed
something crucial, irreplaceable,
and struggled to recover it.
The day rose before me
like a brutal field of stone.
Who has any right to behave such a way?
My body tilted for the door.
Everything falling, clashing, gleaning.

Anniversary

Later, we will plant the cherry
our postman brought us bare-rooted
in a plastic shroud.

We will split November earth
and there, between flower bed
and porch, where my wife has prepared
black mulch, we will plant.
A self-pollinating hybrid requiring
no companion. Reportedly its bloom
is bountiful and fruit,
diameter of a quarter, tartly sweet.

This needn't bear special meaning,
neither a memory of March
when we fixed another to the same spot
and sky cracked into storm,
pummeled us as we slopped in mud
up to our ankles. Forget what you may
have read, about fruit trees
thirsting after water. Forget the lies.

This afternoon we'll dig
because it is time to do so
before ground hardens permanently
into winter, and, roots sunk in sand
to irrigate, we'll bury a new,
dormant twig because I killed the first.

Subtext Nancy

When he touched a doorknob he felt Nancy's
face, her soft cheekbones, so he opened
his way very carefully.

As he mowed grass he enjoyed Nancy reclining
on a cloud. When he raised a beer
her long legs propelled her around his bottle.

His dog's coat even shown like Nancy's
new blonde curls, and he petted and combed
that dog effusively.

Staring into her eyes was easiest of all:
he just closed his own at any time
and smiled into the hazel world of Nancy.

A tree swaying in an August breeze,
bales of hay, the paperweight at work,
a rooster pecking a stop sign,
sunflower, mailbox, crickets, a watermark
beside a book, two plates in a drying rack,
songs and paintings and lampshades,
candle stubs and cushions and clocks,
even his own fingers and toes,
every lucky thing held the shape
and smell and taste of Nancy Nancy Nancy.

Of course, he didn't keep the hair
he found on the blanket. That would be
pathetic! And at night, when he heard
his heart and felt it kick against the sheet
as in on some angelic concentrate
of caffeine, as if it wanted out on its own,
well that was uncontrollable,
just the body talking.

And driving his car at sunset—
what's wrong with that?—Tony Bennett
explaining the subtleties of the predicament
as he rushed between friends' houses,
he couldn't ever know, really, whether Nancy
saw his face anywhere at all.
But here was the logic he could find no way
to refute: with her all around,
in the sky and in his socks and on his toothbrush,
with all that beauty to make him a new man,
how could she not?

Dig You Up, Track You Down

Sometimes, I must admit, I think of you
when I am stranded in winter.
I can't tell, then, if I love you
or perhaps wish you harm, or both.

I hear you passing through the amber mist
of a foreign life, your sighs,
your razored accusations. Sometimes,
I brush earth from your face

with fingertips torn and sullied;
your bloodless grin gives hands nothing.
But then I put you back from where you came
and will forever be, kiss good-bye

with a soft impress of boot.

You Haven't Met?

Good sweet god christ, how fine
the one approaching on the sidewalk,
in the lobby, down the aisle
in the sudden slanted light of evening.
So slender, the daring hair,
complexion pale as cream or rugged as fire,
a rakish collar. Those oceanic eyes.
So you're living in the city now . . .

Forget the second act of the play,
the last hall of exhibition,
the overcooked bird like a chary sacrifice
you're trying still to swallow.
You'll recall the denouement as gratitude
for dark, for a seat to burrow in,
a few fuming minutes to rewrite your story.
Now it's all about thinking so loud
how can your dearly beloved possibly pretend
not to hear the wheel spinning,
it's raising the tissue of your
constructed life to a sweaty lip,
it's the odor of fingertips invoking
the native dance of some misplaced country,
luckless chance, fate's fisted flower,
and the long careful night dropping over you
like a hood.

Work

The work makes us animals.
One year ages us ten.
Necks stiffen, backs bow.
Breath rattles from a cage.
The strongest of us
stands against
wind, tears frozen in his beard,
hands two raw bludgeons
of useless pain.
We blink to clear red vision.
This is our duty signed for.
Daily we pray
for the failure of light.
Inside, arms and legs tremble.
Faces lower over plates.
If we dream, we dream of lives
mended, of youth.
Of labor completed at last.

Landscaping

We don't despise you, stone,
strewn at hard angles
dense to compromise,

how your dentures stab
our steel claw. Hammers plunge
only in frustration

across your skull
imprisoning soil,
the earth we sweat to divide

from earth to save it.
We explain a desire to plant,
sink new roots,

nurture the wild garden
like a separated religion.
We are men,

educating our bones
against your bruising argument,
gray template

stoic to intent,
exploding blooms of dust
in narrowed human eyes.

Primate Behavior

Our smiles stitched, touch calculated.
Sex a husk of intimacy, love itself
a bird only rumored to persist
in savaged underbrush.
What else remains to cut and burn?

A simple meal collected without pleasure,
offered without interest.
We squint through a canopy of protection
toward memory of sky, or to the ground,
small eyes always averting.

We hear engines grinding.
Our mouths are tired, our minds sharp
only for the claw. The hour of isolation
falters. We mangle growth.
This game alone we undertake with joy.

Interior trails are ragged, explicit,
meant to lead the young to our shame.
Moments apart we sweeten
with anticipation of the next attack.
These are fruits of the jungle,

to crack on a rock and share.
Our noxious breath blackens the afternoon,
our chins and palms grow sticky.
Spirit withdraws. We hear the engines
closer. There is no stopping them.

We endure the last routine of day,
refuse all tonic of forgiveness
and swing swift together beneath branches
flaked by disease, into a storm
of insects and the pattern of our night.

The Standard of Forgiveness

They rise according to their own
schedules, too tired to resume another
night's calculated parries.
He grinds the coffee, walks the dog,
rips a fistful of dandelions.

Early sun burns off frost, feels good
against the ballast of eyelids.
The man fingers tips of hackberry leaves.
Forty years, maybe thirty, he'd be dead.
He comes inside, pours a cup

over two teaspoons of lowfat milk.
His wife has finished sit-ups
and the dishes, floats a buoy of interest
about his day. She slept poorly,
dreamed of her favorite childhood doll

drowned in a pitcher of water,
of family reunion in a hospital corridor.
What was the point of mentioning it?
She stepped on the scales this morning
and had gained another pound.

Rescue

You, snapper, so sublimely
inhuman, what do you care for efforts
to lift you from certain slaughter. You,
who never asked to be spared.

You don't bother to contain yourself
as I clamp two hands
and rush for your median of choice.
Your black shell as wide as a serving bowl,
your tail as thick as a sow's.

You'd love nothing better than to claw
to a drop on pavement,
or to shut that iron vice through a finger.
My god you stink, you'd make a sewer
seem like roses. What bowel of earth
did you crawl from to cross me?

I stand in a ditch holding firm
as trucks blaze toward daily business.
You crook your head, only half-withdrawn,
reduce me through a rheumy eye.
One clean lunge with that parted hook
is all you'd require to educate this hero.

I put you down not quite gently.
My machine purrs to me, and I run for it.
I'll wash my hands three times and still
carry the odor of you.

Scrub Cedar and Sinkholes

Not a lost country lyric
exposing rough and tumble love,
albeit not so far from that.
Instead, a man's thorny acres
where this evening
he watches the sun diminish,
reviews the sky's palette of color.

Nothing exceptional, a man
with his dog sniffing breeze,
both feeling a dry kiss of winter.
Unseen nearby, the road heard,
drivers racing from hours
parceled and sold.

But the man is home. Inside,
guns whiten beneath dust.
He could trace a name there,
his to engage or abandon.
Better though to leave them,
askew in a cold corner
of a dark room in a log house
on unrelenting land in the state
where he lives, voluntarily.

Now he rubs his face,
raises a collar toward the first star.
A window ignites. He turns
for the door, and the dog follows.

Morning

Begin again. Let the black hat fall
disregarded from its mirror.

Let the blue-tailed skink bask on stone,
trust spindly legs for quickness.

Let yellow teeth graze a border of skin
between pet and predator.

Tongue today's hot and briny
porridge, living mouthfuls
of yeast, the exclamations of caraway,
the astonished, showered greens.

If not, what were you then
and what can you hope to be
when a dark stranger turns for your door?

Dress yourself in hammer,
long-handled ax, and wrecking bar.

When the sun blasts its bugle
of homecoming, why the air's cold salute?
Who murdered the last tulip standing,
and for what reward?

Rural Song

I've been spending the season
outside, trading hours for lungs of cold air
as I dabble at the property. Painting windows,
repairing yard with rye and fescue.
A strange time. No office runs or telephone,
for once my own death as intriguing to me
as that of my loved ones.
I admire this long slant of autumn light,
the sensual amber hues of it, light paid for
with truncated days.

Sun reclines blazing and brief in the south.
It's light that casts romantically
across a house of logs, across a life
that for the moment suits me.
A bird, unidentified, flaps hard for the west.
That lucky old orb lies already behind cedars.
Show me that river. Take me across. But not yet.
My shoulders hum with good exhaustion
of work. My face feels flush. A second
bird appears, wings pumping, gliding

and pumping again. Dedicated to its
instinctive compass. Another, then several
more follow. And I recognize this exotic
traveler as no more than a robin.
In the light, its breast is a handful of fire. More
come and keep coming, individual in purpose.
So intent, crossing overhead, silent
in empty sky and not at all trite or common.
Urgent against an impinging dark.
Each extraordinary.

A Note for Historians

When the dog and I were lonely
we slept with curtains up, so all night
thunder advised our failing.
But the next day, February 25th, 78°F,
I read on the porch in short sleeves.
That Sunday Feeling, we called it,
two purple crocuses, even hyacinths
from the year before stabbing
through for a chance. Maples budded red,
ruts of green across the yard we kept.

Weightier matters existed,
but I noticed that we were alive,
marked the day and its passing leisure.
We felt fine—hollow, full of expectations.
We weren't just fools, I don't think.
Anyway, I wanted to tell you
and wish you safe travel. We were here.

Mr. Domestyk

—for Charles Bronson

He doesn't speak often, prefers squinted eyes
talk. Holding his good dog to a leash,
he surveys the neighborhood's every indiscretion.
The barbecue fork deadly, if necessary.
He's all-vigilant, morose, understands
that life's a dirty business. If only he could
save his wife and daughter, not take the streets
again, a sad human shadow propelled by loss
to an assignment without mercy or end.
He is the lightning rod to fate's unjust cloud.
But if one must pay, another must collect.
Ad exec, insurance salesman, architect,
these are the thin covers the world won't allow.

When some punks growl past in a roadster,
whooping it up and tossing bottles,
the whole street thumping under their swagger,
Mr. Domestyk looks up from his coals. He points
a finger, smiles grimly, and drops the trigger.

Colophon

Four Nails was set in a computer version of Bookman, designed by Ed Benguiat in 1975. His version of the typeface was based on an 1860 design by Alexander Phemister for the Miller & Richard foundry in Scotland. The Bookman typeface was designed to be an alternative text face to Caslon; Phemister's Bookman had slighter serifs, shorter ascenders and descenders, and a more prominent vertical stress. Benguiat added new weights to create a more modern, straightforward look to the typeface. *Four Nails* was printed by A&M Printers in Cambridge, New York.

Other Poetry Titles from the Snail's Pace Press

Field Guide to the Ineffable: Poems on Marcel Duchamp
by Grace Bauer
   These highly original, intelligent poems based on the life
and work of French surrealist Marcel Duchamp are witty and
surprising. The poems evoke not only the spirit of Duchamp,
but the best of contemporary American poetry. Grace Bauer's
previous collections include *The Women at The Well* (Portals
Press), *Where You've Seen Her* (Pennywhistle Press) and *The
House Where I've Never Lived* (Anabiosis Press).
32 pages, perfect-bound   sold out

Green Tombs to Jupiter by Barry Ballard
   Barry Ballard's lyrical blank verse sonnets inhabit con-
temporary settings and tell stories with precise imagery and
metaphor. His poems have appeared in *American Literary
Review, Midwestern Quarterly, Paris/Atlantic,* and *Barbaric
Yawp,* among many others.
32 pages, perfect-bound   sold out

Fishbone by Aimee Nezhukumatathil
   From pickpockets to peacocks, elephant rides to electro-
cuted oysters, Aimee Nezukamatathil's debut collection
teases the uncommon out of the commonplace, the miracu-
lous out of the mundane. The poet was the was the 2000-01
Diane Middlebrook Poetry Fellow at the Wisconsin Institute
for Creative Writing.
32 pages, perfect-bound $7.95/$9.00 post-paid

The Snail's Pace Press, Inc.
85 Darwin Road
Cambridge, New York 12816
snail@poetic.com

C, the third letter in the English alphabet, was also the third letter in the Phoenician, Hebrew, and Greek alphabets. The Phoenicians and Hebrews called it *gimel*. The Greeks called it *gamma*.

The Phoenician *gimel* looked like this:

Some scholars say that the *gimel* represented the head and neck of a camel. Others say it meant "corner" or "throwing stick."

The *gamma* looked like this:

But until about the middle of the 4th century B.C., when the eastern Greek alphabet became the standard one, there were different versions of the letter in different parts of the country. The western Greeks, for instance, had a letter form that looks quite familiar to us:

All these early forms of C had one thing in common. They were pronounced G as in *game*. Another ancient people called the Etruscans gave the letter < the K sound as in *cat*. The Etruscans ruled in Rome during the 6th century B.C.

The Romans adapted the Greek alphabet during a time when they were very much influenced by the Etruscans. So at first the Roman C had two sounds: the G sound and the K sound. Since this was very confusing, the Romans later introduced the letter G for words beginning with the G sound and kept the C for words that began with the K sound. They made the new letter simply by adding a bar to the lower end of C.

The Romans also rounded the C when they adapted the Greek alphabet, and they brought it in its present form to Britain and the nations of western Europe. The Roman alphabet actually contained three letters that were used for the K sound: C, K, and Q. That is why we have words like *cat, king,* and *quiet,* all beginning with the same sound.

In English, C generally has the "hard" (as in *cat*) sound before A, O, and U, as in *candy, cow,* and *cup.* The hard C is also used before all consonants except H.

The combination CH is pronounced so many different ways (as in *chilly, chemistry,* and *chaperone*) that it might almost be a separate letter. In the alphabets of some languages, such as Welsh and Spanish, CH has a place of its own. In English dictionaries it is simply placed alphabetically between CE and CI.

The "soft" C, as in *circle,* is used before E, I, and Y (*cent, cinnamon, cypress*). In French, words with this soft C sound are numerous. Conquerors from France added this sound to English. Also from France came the combination QU, replacing the Old English CW and giving us words like *queen* instead of *cwen* and *quick* instead of *cwic.*

C is "silent," or unspoken, before the letter T in some words, such as *indict.* In other words, such as *trick,* the C and K give exactly the same sound. The C is merely extra.

In a series, C is the third member. In chemistry, C stands for the element carbon.

C is also an abbreviation: C for 100 (from the Latin *centum*), C for Celsius (in many thermometers), *c.* for chapter, and *c.* for *circa,* a Latin word meaning "about."

Reviewed by MARIO PEI
Author, *The Story of Language*
See also ALPHABET.

CABINET OFFICERS. See PRESIDENCY OF THE UNITED STATES.

CABLES. See TELEGRAPH AND CABLES.

CABOT, JOHN (1451?–1498) AND SEBASTIAN (1480?–1557?)

In 1497 an Italian sea captain sailing under the English flag touched the coast of North America. John Cabot may have been the first European to set foot on the North American continent after the Viking explorer Leif Ericson, who had landed there five centuries before. Cabot's discovery became the basis for the English claim to North America.

John Cabot

John Cabot's Italian name was Giovanni Caboto. He was born in Genoa, probably in 1451. Later his family moved to Venice, where Cabot became a merchant. On one of his trading voyages, he visited Mecca, in what is now Saudi Arabia. Mecca was a great trade center where products from Europe and Asia were bought and sold. But the overland journey to obtain spices and other goods from the East was long and slow. Like Columbus, Cabot believed that the earth was a globe and that Asia could be more easily reached by sailing west across the Atlantic Ocean.

Cabot tried to get Spain or Portugal to back an ocean voyage to Cathay (China). But Spain had already sent Columbus, and Portu-

gal had plans for a voyage to Asia around the southern tip of Africa. Cabot then went to England. There he obtained the backing of a group of merchants and of the English king, Henry VII. The merchants provided Cabot with a ship. King Henry gave him a royal charter, granting him the right to claim for England any new lands that he found.

Cabot sailed from Bristol late in May, 1497, with a crew of 18, on a small ship named the *Matthew*. On June 24, he landed somewhere on the coast of North America—probably Newfoundland or Cape Breton Island, in what is now Canada. Cabot was sure he had reached the northeast coast of Asia, and he sailed back to England to report his find.

Encouraged by the news, Henry VII gave Cabot a small fleet and sent him on another voyage in 1498. This voyage is shrouded in mystery. It is believed that Cabot first sailed back to Newfoundland and then went south as far as the Chesapeake Bay before storms wrecked most of his ships. One ship may have reached the Caribbean Sea. For many years it was believed that Cabot survived this voyage and died in England the following year. But because of more recent evidence, historians now believe that Cabot perished when his ship went down in a storm.

Sebastian Cabot

Sebastian Cabot, son of John Cabot, was born in Venice around 1480 and may have sailed with his father on the first voyage to America. At any rate, Sebastian later falsely claimed credit for both of his father's voyages. The record was finally set straight in the 1800's, when historians found documents that proved the voyages were made by John Cabot.

But Sebastian did have a worthy career as an explorer, navigator, and business promoter. In the early 1550's, he helped found the Company of Merchant Adventurers (later the Muscovy Company) in England. The company sent ships in search of a northeast passage to Asia. One ship reached Russia and helped to open trade between England and that country. Sebastian Cabot died about 1557.

HENRY I. KURTZ
Author, *John and Sebastian Cabot*

See also EXPLORATION AND DISCOVERY.

THE NEW
BOOK OF KNOWLEDGE

C
volume
3

THE NEW
BOOK OF
KNOWLEDGE

GROLIER
INCORPORATED
DANBURY, CONN.

ISBN 0–7172–0515–0 (set)
Library of Congress Catalog Card Number: 83–12746

The publishers wish to thank the following for permission to use copyrighted material:
Holt, Rinehart and Winston, Inc., Laurence Pollinger Limited, and Jonathan Cape Limited for excerpt
from ''Chicago'' from *Chicago Poems* by Carl Sandburg, copyright 1916 by Holt, Rinehart and Winston,
Inc., renewed 1944 by Carl Sandburg.

CACTUS

A cactus (plural, cacti) is a remarkable example of the way plants have adapted to extreme conditions. Cacti have the basic structures and processes of plants. But the work done by leaves in most other plants goes on in the stems and branches of cacti. And in the hot, dry regions where cacti are among the few green plants, their spine-covered branches and stems and their absence of leaves have allowed them to survive.

The distant ancestors of the cactus had leaves and grew like the more familiar plants of today. But during millions of years the earth's climate changed. Those parts of the Americas where the cactus ancestors grew became hotter and drier. Gradually these regions turned into desert or near desert. All this time the cactus ancestors were adapting to the changing conditions.

For example, as the climate became drier the roots of cacti gradually spread out, closer to the surface of the ground. That is why cacti quickly absorb water from the earth after a rainfall.

The water taken in through the roots of a cactus is stored in its spongy or hollow stem. The outer layer of the plant is thick and waxy, preventing the escape of water. The outer skin is also ribbed. Some cacti have ribs that fold and expand like an accordion, depending on how much water is contained within the stem.

Although most cacti are leafless, they carry on the normal food-making activities of plants. The leaves of other plants are thin structures that contain many breathing pores; in the course of the food-making process, water is given off to the air through these pores. But in cacti the stems and branches have taken over the work of the leaves. The thick skins have few pores, and the water is retained.

There are still some members of the cactus family that have leaves and stems like more familiar plants—the lemon vine of the West Indies is one. In most cacti the leaves have developed into spines, needles, or hairs. These growths now serve to protect the cacti—which are often the only green plants in an area—from animals.

The true cacti are native only to the Western Hemisphere. They grow mainly in the dry

Cacti in the Arizona desert. Between a pair of saguaro plants (1A and 1B) stand an organ-pipe cactus (2), cholla (3), and prickly pear (4). The ocotillo (5) is a desert shrub.

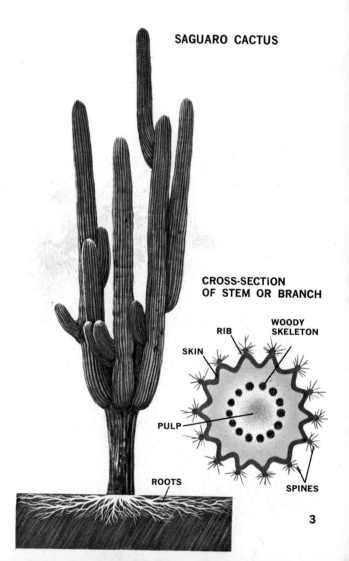

SAGUARO CACTUS

CROSS-SECTION OF STEM OR BRANCH

RIB

WOODY SKELETON

SKIN

PULP

ROOTS

SPINES

3

The large blossoms of an organ-pipe cactus bloom at night.

lands of South America, Central America, and the southwestern United States. Mexico has the greatest number and variety of cacti. A few cacti have extended their ranges as far north as Canada.

In South Africa, Madagascar, and Sri Lanka there is the mistletoe cactus, a small plant that grows on trees. Probably the seeds of these plants were carried from the Americas by birds. Cacti have been introduced to many parts of the world by people. (The African deserts have native plants that resemble cacti, but these are actually daisies and milkweeds that have adapted to desert life.)

▶ KINDS OF CACTI

Today there are perhaps 1,500 species of cacti. They are divided into several groups, depending on their shapes. As a family, the cacti belong to the succulents (from the Latin *succulentus*, meaning "juicy"). The succulents include the many kinds of plants that store large amounts of water.

The Prickly Pears. The prickly pears are probably the best known of all the cacti. There are about 250 species. They grow mainly in the United States and Mexico, but they have been introduced into many other countries.

The prickly pear bears a sweet, juicy fruit that looks like a pear. This fruit is what gives these plants their name. Their flowers are often large and colorful, varying from bright red to yellow.

Barrel Cacti. These thick, heavy cacti are from a few centimeters to over 3.5 meters (about 12 feet) tall and up to a meter in diameter. Their trunklike bodies have ribs with hooked spines. In spring they have yellow flowers. One kind, the bisnaga, may grow almost 3 meters (about 9 feet) tall and have a diameter of well over a meter. Bisnagas this large are probably over 1,000 years old.

All barrel cacti store in their trunks the water collected by their roots. By cutting off the top of a barrel cactus and pounding the pulp inside with a stick or a rock, a person can obtain liquid. In emergencies this can be drunk as water.

The Saguaro. The saguaro, the largest of the cacti, may grow as high as 12 meters (40 feet). Large ones may be over 200 years old. Saguaros grow in the southwestern United States. The blossom is the state flower of Arizona.

Most large saguaros contain one or more holes in which woodpeckers make their homes. Tiny desert owls also live in these holes, where they are safe from most enemies.

At certain times the saguaro sprouts side branches. A relative of the saguaro is called the organ-pipe cactus because its many branches make it look like a church organ.

Peyote Cactus. This cactus grows in the southwestern United States and Mexico. A narcotic drug, mescaline, is obtained from the plant.

Night-blooming Cereus. Closely related to the saguaro and the organ-pipe cactus is the night-blooming cereus. This cactus looks like a tangle of dead sticks. But one night in early summer it bursts into a mass of white blooms. It is often cultivated for its flowers.

Hedgehog Cacti. These cacti are also known as strawberry cacti because their red fruits resemble strawberries. Indians once considered this fruit a delicacy. The fruits are covered with spines that give the plants their common name, hedgehog cacti.

These cacti are small, at most about 15 centimeters (6 inches) tall. Often grown in rock gardens, they bloom in various colors.

Pincushion Cacti. These are among the most widely grown of all household plants. Their natural range is from Mexico to Canada. They have spiral rows of "warts" tipped with clusters of spines, which are often as colorful as their large flowers.

ROSS E. HUTCHINS
Author, *This Is a Flower*

See also PLANTS.

Julius Caesar entering Rome in triumph after a victory.

CAESAR, GAIUS JULIUS (100?—44 B.C.)

Gaius Julius Caesar was one of the greatest men of history. He conquered Gaul, a vast land that covered what is today France and Belgium. And he laid the foundation for the Roman Empire, which ruled the world for over 450 years.

Caesar was born in Rome about 100 B.C. His family were nobles. But his uncle Marius had been a great leader of the plebians—the common people. As a boy Caesar saw many civil wars between the plebians and the nobles. When he was about 18 the nobles, led by Sulla, defeated Marius' plebians. Sulla became ruler of Rome.

Sulla distrusted Caesar because he was Marius' nephew. Besides, Caesar's wife Cornelia was the daughter of one of Sulla's enemies. Sulla demanded that Caesar divorce Cornelia. But Caesar loved his wife deeply, and he refused. To escape Sulla's anger, he fled from Rome. Only when Sulla died 2 years later did Caesar return to Rome.

To further his career, Caesar went to Greece to study oratory (the art of public speaking). But while crossing the Aegean Sea, he was captured by pirates. They demanded a ransom of 20 talents (about $20,000) for his life. Caesar laughed and said he was worth 50 talents. He told the pirates that he would return some day and put them all to death. The pirates thought this a good joke. However, as soon as the ransom was paid, Caesar gathered ships, captured the pirates, and cut their throats.

Caesar was ambitious. He set out to win the favor of the plebians, who elected him to several political offices. He delighted the people with chariot races and gladiator fights. Soon he was one of the most popular men in Rome. In 61 B.C. he was sent to govern Spain, a Roman province.

When he returned to Rome, Caesar formed an alliance with Crassus and Pompey—the two most powerful men in Rome. Crassus had money. Pompey controlled the army. And Caesar had the support of the people. Caesar used the alliance to have himself elected consul, one of the two heads of the Roman Republic.

▶ HE CONQUERS GAUL

But Caesar knew he needed military fame, too. He looked far to the north of Rome, beyond the Alps. There lay the rich land of the Gauls.

Though he had little military experience, Caesar soon showed his genius as a general. The Gauls greatly outnumbered the Romans, but Caesar led his soldiers to victory after victory. He inspired them to great bravery, and the soldiers loved him. They remained loyal to him until his death.

Once, when a battle seemed lost, Caesar dashed into the thick of the fighting. He wore no helmet so that his men would recognize him. The Roman soldiers took courage and won the battle.

During the next 9 years Caesar conquered all of Gaul and doubled the size of the Roman territories. He pushed the fierce German tribes back across the Rhine River. Twice he invaded Britain.

Though most of the Romans praised Caesar, the nobles of the senate feared his power and his popularity with the people. His old ally, Pompey, was jealous of Caesar. He joined with Caesar's enemies in the senate. They ordered Caesar to give up his army and return to Rome alone.

Under Roman law a general was forbidden to enter Rome with his army. But Caesar suspected a trick. With a single legion (about 5,000 men plus cavalry) he marched to the Rubicon. This was a small river that separated Gaul and Rome. If he crossed the river with his army, the senate would declare him a traitor. Caesar paused for a moment—and then crossed the Rubicon.

▶ RULER OF ROME

Within 6 weeks Caesar was the ruler of Rome. Pompey fled to Greece. Caesar followed and defeated him. When Pompey escaped to Egypt, Caesar pursued him, only to find that Pompey had been murdered by the Egyptians.

In Egypt, Caesar met Cleopatra. He fell in love with her and made her queen of

Why were the Roman emperors called Caesars?

Following the death of Julius Caesar in 44 B.C., his great-nephew (and adopted son), Octavius, took Caesar's name and added it to his own. Octavius, after defeating Mark Antony for control of the Roman world, became the first Roman emperor in 27 B.C. He received the title Augustus, meaning "majestic" or "dignified." Later emperors kept the name Caesar as well as the title Augustus. During the reign of Hadrian (A.D. 117–138), the Emperor's heir was given the title Caesar to distinguish him from the Emperor, who was called Caesar Augustus.

Because of the widespread influence of the Latin language, both the German word for emperor ("kaiser") and the Russian word ("czar") are derived from "Caesar."

Egypt. But news of a rebellion in Asia Minor demanded his attention. After a swift victory, he sent his famous victory message: *Veni, vidi, vici,* "I came, I saw, I conquered."

In 45 B.C. Caesar returned to Rome in triumph. He was declared dictator, and in his honor the name of the 5th month of the year was changed to Julius—our modern July.

Though he was without pity in battle, Caesar could be generous to a defeated enemy. After he became dictator, he appointed some of his old enemies to positions of power. He gave Roman citizenship to many of the conquered Gauls.

Caesar then turned to the problem of the calendar. The old Roman calendar was almost 3 months out of date. With the aid of Egyptian astronomers, Caesar planned a new one. It lasted for over 1,600 years. The calendar we use today was developed in 1582, but it is only slightly different from Caesar's.

On March 15 (the ides of March), 44 B.C., Caesar planned to attend a meeting of the senate. His wife Calpurnia (Cornelia had been dead many years) begged her husband not to go. She told Caesar of a dream in which she saw him murdered. Caesar agreed to postpone the meeting, but his friend Brutus persuaded him to go. Soon after entering the senate, Caesar was attacked by his enemies. As he fell dying he saw Brutus among the murderers. Caesar's last words were: *"Et tu, Brute!"* ("You, too, Brutus!").

Reviewed by KENNETH S. COOPER
George Peabody College

CAIRO

Cairo is an old city; Cairo is a new city. Cairo is where the past and the present live together.

With a population of about 8,000,000, Cairo is the capital and the largest city of the Arab Republic of Egypt. It is also the largest city in Africa. Cairo is located on the banks of the world's longest river, the Nile, at the crossroads of the East and the West. Both the East and the West can be seen in the habits, the color, the sights, and the sounds of this Egyptian metropolis.

On a summer's day the sun blazes down on the streets of Cairo and on a huge statue of Ramses II. This ancient statue stands in a busy square and looms over the main railway station like a colossus. Against it the station looks new and very much a part of the world of today. It is alive with the noise and bustle of modern times and transportation. In the traffic-filled square there is the statue—massive and quiet in the Egyptian sun. Its face and figure are of the distant past, a past that stretches back more than 3,000 years to the time when Ramses II was the ruler of Egypt.

There are broad, sparkling streets, ultra-modern department stores, theaters, movie houses, and even movie studios. Over 100 films are produced every year in this Hollywood on the Nile. The movies made here are distributed all over the Arab world.

Cairo is a city of culture—of art, of libraries, and of many fine museums, including the Museum of Modern Art, the Museum of Islamic Art, and the Coptic Museum. The Egyptian Museum is considered to be the greatest museum of its kind in the world. It contains priceless Egyptian relics, including the statue of Chephren, the pharaoh who built the second pyramid at Giza. This statue is regarded as one of the finest pieces of Egyptian sculpture in existence. In the history-filled halls of the museum are the treasures of King Tutankhamen.

Cairo has schools, universities, parks, and

Cairo, capital of the Arab Republic of Egypt, is situated on the mighty Nile River.

Above: In the old quarter of Cairo, brassworkers make and sell their wares in bazaars. Below: The mosque of Mehemet Ali, first ruler of modern Egypt.

dense motor traffic. Many new schools have been built in recent years—kindergartens, technical preparatory schools, trade schools, physical-training institutes, and special institutes for music, ballet, and theater. In Cairo all children must begin school at the age of 6. There are no tuition fees in any institution, from the primary school to the university.

Of Cairo's four universities, Al-Azhar is the best known. It was established in the 10th century and has been called the oldest university in the world. Al-Azhar was modernized in 1961 and for the first time in its long history began to accept women as students.

Shops of all kinds line the city's sidewalks. Along the bustling streets, shopkeepers in traditional long, flowing Arab dress greet friends in Western clothes. Ninety percent of the people are of the Muslim faith. Beautiful mosques with domed roofs and slender, graceful minarets reach up to the sky. When the call to prayer is heard, many of the devout pause in reverence and pray.

In the bazaars, brassworkers hammer and fashion plates of elaborate design. Weavers work with the same sure skill as their forebears did before them. In the crowded, narrow streets of this quarter—scarcely wider than alleys—are donkey carts, mules, and, occasionally, a camel.

A short distance from the city stands one of the Seven Wonders of the World. This is what ancient people called the Great Pyramid at Giza. Two other pyramids and the Sphinx stand nearby. The pyramids were built as kings' tombs. The Sphinx is a huge statue with the body of a lion and a human head.

Cairo is a center of government, trade, commerce, and culture. It is a city that is constantly growing and expanding. But this expansion has placed severe strains upon housing, transportation, and other services.

▶ HISTORY

Cairo's name comes from the Arabic Al-Qahira, which means "the victorious." The present city, which is the fourth on the site, dates back to 969. Jauhar, who was a general for the Fatimid dynasty of Tunis, conquered Egypt and established the city of Al-Qahira. In 1517 the city was captured by the Turks. It remained under Turkish rule until 1798, when the French, led by Napoleon, defeated the Turks. The Turks recaptured the city with the help of the British in 1801. In 1882, after the battle of Tel el Kebir, the English were again in Cairo. They did not fully give up their control of the city until 1936.

During World War II Cairo was the scene of several historic conferences. In 1943 President Franklin D. Roosevelt and Prime Minister Winston Churchill met there with the leaders of China and Turkey.

After the revolution of July 23, 1952, Egypt became a republic with Cairo as its capital. The city is often thought of as the capital of the entire Arab world.

Reviewed by CONSULATE GENERAL
OF THE ARAB REPUBLIC OF EGYPT

CALCULATORS

Counting things is an everyday part of life. People learned thousands of years ago that they could count and do arithmetic more quickly and easily with the help of pebbles, knotted cords, their own fingers, or other devices. One simple, ancient counting device, the abacus, is still used in many countries.

About 300 years ago scientists began to build machines, called calculators, that worked with levers, gears, and other moving parts. The machines were cranked by hand at first, and later by electric motors. These calculating machines solved problems in arithmetic much faster than people could do them. But the machines were bulky, noisy, and far slower than today's electronic calculators.

The work of an electronic calculator depends on the flow of electrical currents. In the early models, transistors controlled the currents. A transistor may be as small as a pencil eraser, but thousands of them are needed in even the simplest calculator. So the early models were large and costly.

Small, low-priced calculators were made possible by the development of a device that is an improvement on the transistor. It is the integrated circuit, or I.C., and it saves a great deal of space. For example, some kinds of I.C.'s, only 6 millimeters (¼ inch) on a side, can do the work of 6,000 transistors.

Hundreds of kinds of electronic calculators are available. There are desk models the size of this book, or bigger. For personal use there are mini-calculators, which fit comfortably in the hand. Other models are even smaller.

Every calculator has a keyboard. The operator presses the keys to feed a problem, say 6 × 7 =   , into the machine. The answer, 42, appears almost instantly in the form of small lighted numerals in a display window on the calculator. Some machines also print both the problem and the answer on a paper tape.

All calculators can be used for doing addition, subtraction, multiplication, and division —the basic functions of arithmetic. Some schools are using calculators in the classroom. Once students have learned to do the basic functions with paper and pencil, they can save a great deal of time by working out problems on a basic calculator, which may be bought for less than $10. Shoppers find basic calcu-

Pocket calculator.

lators useful for checking prices and taxes, totaling purchases, and keeping their checkbooks in balance.

A basic calculator can be used to solve any arithmetic problem. However, there are more advanced, more expensive calculators that can solve certain mathematical problems more quickly and conveniently. For example, calculators may be used to find square roots, to calculate profit and selling price, and also to figure interest.

One type of calculator can be used for quickly changing units of measurement from the system used in the United States to the metric system, or vice versa.

Some calculators can store numbers for use in future calculations. These numbers can be "forgotten" and others stored as needed. This ability to store numbers is called memory.

Some scientists, accountants, and mathematicians use advanced calculators costing several hundred dollars or more. Users of such calculators can preset or program them to solve long, complicated problems quickly. With simpler calculators, such problems require many time-consuming steps.

JAMES D. GATES
National Council of Teachers of Mathematics

See also COMPUTERS.

CALCULUS. See MATHEMATICS.

CALCUTTA

Calcutta is a city that stays in the memory of visitors long after they have returned home. They will remember a city that swirls with the life of the East—the teeming, colorful life of India. The strange, musical names will come softly back to them—Chowringhee Road, the Maidan, and the Dhakuria Lakes. Then they will remember the Strand, the Esplanade, and the Victoria Memorial— names of the West—because Calcutta is also of the West. Many people from the Western countries live and work there.

Calcutta is a great port city and is also the capital of West Bengal State. The city lies along the east bank of the Hooghly River in northeastern India—130 kilometers (80

miles) north of the Bay of Bengal. The Hooghly River, one of several branches of the Ganges River, is the only waterway of the Ganges Delta that permits oceangoing ships to come such a distance inland.

Across the river from Calcutta is Howrah, one of the main industrial sections of the metropolitan area. Connecting the two cities is the famed Howrah Bridge, one of the largest cantilever bridges in the world.

Because of its port, nearness to minerals, and excellent transportation services, greater Calcutta has become the most important manufacturing district of India. The city is known for its many paper mills, iron foundries, steel plants, tanneries, and printing presses. It is also the world's largest producer of materials made from jute.

▶ DAILY LIFE

Huge and sprawling, with a metropolitan population of about 7,000,000, Calcutta is a city of contrasts. There are wide streets with large white houses and green lawns. There is block after block of office and apart-

A view of the harbor at Calcutta, one of India's busiest ports.

ment buildings, nearly all of them with balconies overlooking the busy streets. And there are narrow, winding streets where the people live huddled together in slum buildings. For this city, like many other large cities of the world, has a desperate housing shortage.

The center of Calcutta is the Maidan. This is a huge park that borders on the Hooghly River. In the Maidan, Calcutta has its sports events, its soccer games, cricket matches, and horse racing. Entire families play and picnic in the park. Overlooking a small lake in the park is the Victoria Memorial. This white marble building was built in 1905 to honor Queen Victoria of England. It is a rich storehouse of Indian history.

Along the north side of the Maidan is the Esplanade, which extends to Dalhousie Square, the heart of Calcutta's business district. Along the east side of the park is Chowringhee Road, the main thoroughfare of Calcutta. The wide avenue is lined with fashionable shops, modern restaurants, movie houses, clubs, and office buildings. Near Chowringhee Road is one of the largest markets in all Asia. Here the usual and the unusual are offered for sale. One can buy nearly any kind of food, clothing, or hardware as well as such unusual purchases as live bears, deer, snakes, and birds of many varieties.

Calcutta's zoo has one of the finest collections of animals in the entire East. The zoo is spread over a large area and has many interesting exhibits. In the Botanical Gardens of Calcutta stands the Great Banyan Tree. This tree is about 27 meters (88 feet) high and has over 600 roots reaching into the ground. The Great Banyan spreads out so far that more than 200 people can sit comfortably in its shade.

Calcutta is a center of intellectual activity, for many of India's scholars live in this vital city. The National Library, once the residence of the viceroys, has a notable collection of books and documents. The University of Calcutta, established in 1857, enrolls many thousands of students. It has trained many teachers and leaders who are now working in different parts of India, bringing education to people who want and need it badly.

▶ HISTORY

Many Indian cities go back far in time, but Calcutta began less than 300 years ago. It was founded in 1690 by Job Charnock, who was an agent of the East India Company. There were three small villages in the area, and Charnock chose one of them for a British trade settlement. It was then named Kalikata. Because of its excellent trade position and its importance as headquarters for the British administration, Calcutta grew in size and significance. In 1833 it became the capital of British India. In 1912 the capital was transferred to Delhi. During World War II Calcutta was an important base for the China-Burma-India theater. It served as a supply and transport center.

DAVID FIRMAN
Towson State University
Reviewed by THE CONSULATE GENERAL OF INDIA

CALENDAR, HISTORY OF THE

People rely on clocks and calendars to keep track of time. Clocks measure small units of time—seconds, minutes, and hours. Calendars take up where clocks leave off. They help us keep track of days, weeks, months, and years.

Time as measured by clocks is man-made. There are 60 seconds in a minute, 60 minutes in an hour, and 24 hours in a day because it is convenient to have it that way. But most units of time measured by a calendar are not just "made up." They have to do with certain celestial events. A day is the amount of time it takes the earth to rotate once on its axis. A month is approximately the time it takes the moon to complete its full cycle (from new moon to new moon). A year is based on the time it takes the earth to travel once around the sun. The 7-day week of our present-day calendar is taken from the ancient Hebrew calendar. This division of time is mentioned in the Bible. The Hebrews got the idea of a 7-day week from the Babylonians. Some people believe that the Babylonians chose a

The people who lived on the Greek island of Crete around 1600 B.C. used this round, clay calendar. Scientists do not yet know the meaning of the symbols on the calendar.

division of 7 days to represent the seven heavenly bodies (the sun, the moon, and five planets) that are visible to the naked eye, which they worshiped as gods.

At first men kept track of time by noting natural events—the rising of the sun, the length of shadows, the phase of the moon, or the position of a bright star or group of stars. When civilization grew complicated, more exact ways of measuring time were needed. The trouble was that the units of time based on the movements of the moon and sun didn't divide evenly into one another. It takes a little less than 365¼ days for the earth to make one revolution around the sun. And a month is about 29½ days long. Because there wasn't an even number of days in a month or in a year, adjustments had to be made.

▶ THE ROMAN CALENDAR

We took our calendar from the Romans. Very early in their history, the Romans began basing their calendar on the idea that 12 lunar months make a year. Each lunar month (from new moon to new moon) is about 29½ days, so the Roman year came to 354 days. But the true solar year (the time it takes the earth to circle the sun) is just under 365¼ days. The Romans made up for the difference by adding an extra month every few years.

When Julius Caesar ruled Rome, he found that the calendar was wrong by 80 days. The calendar said it was spring but the season was really midwinter. Caesar asked the advice of a mathematician, Sosigenes, who told him the real year was almost 365¼ days long. So Caesar ordered that each year should be 365 days, with an extra day added in February every fourth year (leap year) to make the calendar come out right. Leap years would always be divisible by four. Caesar also gave up the lunar month and set a month's length at 30 or 31 days. Only February remained less than 30 days long.

Caesar started his new calendar (called the Julian calendar) in 46 B.C. This year was referred to as the year of confusion. Some people believe he moved New Year's Day from March 1 to January 1. He added 2 months between November and December, and another after February. As a result, the year 46 B.C. lasted 445 days. After that, however, his 365-day calendar ran so smoothly that it kept time with the seasons for many centuries.

▶ POPE GREGORY CHANGES THE CALENDAR

But there was still a small mistake in this Julian calendar. The sun's year is really 11 minutes and 14 seconds shorter than the 365¼-day year recommended by Sosigenes. In 1600 years this added up to 10 days, so that the vernal equinox, the first day of spring (when the sun has reached the celestial equator and day and night are equal in length), occurred earlier and earlier. By 1582 it fell on March 11 instead of March 21. Pope Gregory XIII took the advice of the astronomer Christopher Clavius. He corrected the mistake by dropping 10 days, so that the day after October 4, 1582, was October 15. To keep the error from happening again, he decreed that century years (the first year in each century), even though divisible by four, should not have the extra day in February unless they could be divided by 400. Thus, A.D. 1900 was not a leap year, but A.D. 2000 will be.

Catholic countries adopted the Gregorian calendar (named for Pope Gregory), but

The page for the month of July from a 15th-century French calendar made for the Duc de Berry. Each page of the calendar was decorated with a painting of life in the French countryside.

Protestant and Greek Orthodox countries did not. One hundred and seventy years later England and her American colonies found that their calendar had slipped away from the sun's time by 11 days. They dropped these days in 1752, adopting the Gregorian calendar. Thus Washington's birthday is February 22 (New Style), but he was really born on February 11 (Old Style). Russia did not change its calendar until 1918, and Rumania not until 1924. That is why you may find two different dates given for some historical events.

People are still trying to reform the calendar, but so far we continue to use the Roman calendar as it was improved by Pope Gregory XIII.

Reviewed by CATHARINE BARRY
American Museum of Natural History

CALHOUN, JOHN C. (1782–1850)

John Caldwell Calhoun, the South's leading statesman in the years before the Civil War, was born on March 18, 1782, near Abbeville, South Carolina. He graduated from Yale College and then studied law. In 1810 he was elected to Congress. At that time the United States and Great Britain were quarreling over the rights of American ships. Calhoun became a leader of the war hawks, a group who believed the matter could be settled only by war. The War of 1812 followed.

In 1817 President Monroe made Calhoun secretary of war. In 1824 he was elected vice-president under John Quincy Adams. When Andrew Jackson became president in 1829, Calhoun again became vice-president.

Calhoun was a stern-looking man, tall and thin, with icy blue eyes. He seldom laughed, and his only interest was politics. Early in his career he had fought for a strong federal government. But loyalty to his state changed Calhoun's views. He became a defender of states' rights against the federal government.

In 1828 Congress passed a tariff (a tax on imported goods) that hurt the South. To protest this Tariff of Abominations, Calhoun wrote the *South Carolina Exposition*. In it he said that if the federal government overstepped its power in passing a law, the people could refuse to obey it. Calhoun's theory became known as nullification. And when Congress passed a new tariff in 1832, South Carolina nullified it. President Jackson threatened to send soldiers to make the state obey. But the crisis was avoided by a compromise.

In 1832 Calhoun left the vice-presidency to enter the Senate. For the rest of his life (except for 1 year as President Tyler's secretary of state), he served as senator from South Carolina. His great talents were devoted to the interests of the South.

Calhoun made his last appearance in the Senate in 1850. The Senate was debating the Compromise of 1850, which dealt with the problem of slavery in the western states. Though very ill, Calhoun insisted on protesting the compromise. A month later, on March 31, 1850, Calhoun died. Almost his last words were, "The South, the poor South."

See also COMPROMISE OF 1850.

CALIFORNIA

He had the words cut into a brass plate. The words declared that he, Francis Drake, was claiming this new land for Queen Elizabeth I of England. The date was June 17, 1579. The place was near San Francisco, probably Point Reyes.

The brass plate was fixed to a post near the shore. Drake looked out over the quiet waters of the Pacific Ocean. His men had rested. His ship, the *Golden Hind,* had been repaired. He would set sail again, this time westward across the Pacific. He would complete his circling of the earth. Someday he would return here and establish an English colony.

But Drake did not return. More than 350 years passed. Then one day in 1937 a strange, blackened metal plate was brought to the University of California at Berkeley. It had been found in the area. Historians and scientists studied it. Some of them declared it to be the brass plate left by Drake and his men in 1579. It is now a prized possession of the University, where it is displayed in Bancroft Library.

STATE FLAG.

STATE TREE: California redwood.

STATE BIRD: California valley quail.

STATE FLOWER: Golden poppy.

In the early 1840's California was a sleepy territory of Mexico. But the sleepiness was only on the surface. Underneath, the territory was simmering. Great things were about to happen.

For some time traders and trappers from the United States had been coming to California. Some came overland, across deserts and mountains. They battled heat and cold to reach journey's end. Many others, especially Yankee traders, came by ship. They set sail from ports on the Atlantic Ocean or the Gulf of Mexico and made the long voyage around Cape Horn at the southern tip of South America. Months later they landed in California. Many who came to trade remained as settlers. Californians welcomed the settlers, even though their rulers in Mexico did not.

From its capital city, deep in the heart of Mexico, the Republic of Mexico held a loose control over California. In June, 1846, American settlers overthrew Mexico's control. They declared California an independent republic. But a short time later news came that the United States had gone to war with Mexico over possession of Texas. Immediately California declared itself a part of the United States. Mexico officially gave up its claim to California in 1848 as a result of the Mexican War.

About that time people began to hear about a dazzling chance for wealth in far western United States. Gold was discovered in the foothills of the Sierra Nevada. By 1849 a great gold rush was bringing thousands of fortune hunters to California.

Much gold was found, but many gold seekers did not gain sudden wealth. Within a few years they settled down to more ordinary ways of making a living, such as farming or storekeeping.

Since gold-rush days California has continued to be a magic name for many Americans. It has been a state of opportunity, where rich natural resources awaited the coming of people who would develop them. California has gained fame for its varied products, such as redwood, motion pictures, canned tuna, sportswear, fruit, and airplanes. It is no less famous for its mild winter climate. Many persons have migrated to seek health in California. Others have been attracted by the outdoor way of life.

Its great variety of natural surroundings makes California an exciting place. It has long shorelines, towering mountains, dense forests, and immense deserts. Human activities have added to the variety. People have developed vast irrigated farms and have built cities and factories. They have constructed world-

CALIFORNIA

CAPITAL: Sacramento.

STATEHOOD: September 9, 1850; the 31st state.

SIZE: 411,049 km² (158,706 sq mi); rank, 3rd.

POPULATION: 23,667,565 (1980 census); rank, 1st.

ORIGIN OF NAME: From the name of an imaginary island in a Spanish novel of about the year 1500. Explorers gave the name to the peninsula of Lower California because in their eyes it resembled the imaginary island.

ABBREVIATIONS: Calif.; CA.

NICKNAME: The Golden State.

STATE SONG: "I Love You, California."

STATE MOTTO: "Eureka" (I have found it), referring to the finding of gold in California.

STATE SEAL: Thirty-one small stars around the top part of the seal stand for the number of states after California joined the Union. Below the stars is the state motto. In the right foreground sits Minerva, Roman goddess of wisdom, who sprang full grown from the brain of Jupiter, even as California became a state without first having been a territory. The grizzly bear at Minerva's feet is the state animal. Mountains, ships, a gold miner, wheat, and grapes show special features or products of the state.

STATE FLAG: The present state flag is known as the Bear Flag. It was used by the settlers in California when they revolted against Mexico in 1846. The grizzly bear was a symbol of independence. The lone star and the words "California Republic" show that California was not part of the Union when the flag was first used.

famous dams, canals, bridges, and freeways to help join together the people and the resources of this far-flung state.

▶THE LAND

California, one of the Pacific States, occupies the southwest corner of mainland United States. It is the third largest state in the nation. Only Alaska and Texas have greater areas. California contains the lowest point (Death Valley) in the Western Hemisphere and the highest point (Mount Whitney) in the first 48 mainland states.

Landforms

California's landforms provide spectacular scenery. In the middle of the state is the Central Valley, a great alluvial plain, about 650 kilometers (400 miles) long and 80 kilometers (50 miles) wide. This valley is walled on all sides by mountain ranges.

The Coast Ranges are on the west, and the Sierra Nevada is on the east. The Coast Ranges include beautiful San Francisco Bay. The name Sierra Nevada is Spanish for "snowy mountain range." In this range are such scenic splendors as Lake Tahoe, Mount Whitney, and the Yosemite Valley.

To the north of the Central Valley are the Klamath Mountains and the Cascade Range. The Cascades include towering Mount Shasta as well as Lassen Peak, a volcano that has erupted in this century (1914–21).

South of the Central Valley are the Transverse Ranges and the Peninsular Ranges. The Transverse Ranges run west to east across the state. The Peninsular Ranges include most of the Los Angeles lowlands and the group of Channel Islands south of Los Angeles.

Parts of a great region known as the Basin and Range Region enter northeastern and southeastern California. The northeast part of this region contains a high lava plateau known as the Modoc Plateau. The southeast part is made up of desert basins separated by bold, bare mountain ranges. Death Valley and the Mojave and the Colorado deserts are in this section.

Mountains. Nearly half of California is mountainous. It is impossible to cross the state without encountering mountain ranges. Main highways and railroads are usually located in the lowest mountain passes. Even so,

there are many long grades. Donner Pass in the Sierra Nevada, one of the most heavily traveled passes, is more than 2,100 meters (7,000 feet) above sea level.

California's highest mountains were once covered by glaciers. Remains of them still exist. Palisade Glacier, on North Palisade peak, is the southernmost glacier in the United States. Glaciers helped carve spectacular alpine landforms such as Yosemite Valley. Their erosion left thousands of small lakes scattered through the Sierra Nevada.

Mountains are important to California in various ways. From them come water and waterpower, lumber, and minerals. Several peaks are used for radar and for television transmitting stations. Large astronomical observatories are located on Mounts Hamilton, Wilson, and Palomar. Mountains make enjoyable places for recreation, too.

Other Areas. California also has vast level areas. The largest of these are the Central Valley and the Mojave and the Colorado deserts. Many smaller lowlands are found all along the coastal areas and in the Basin and Range Region and the Modoc Plateau.

Rivers, Lakes, and Coastal Waters

Most of the large rivers are in the northern half of the state. The major river systems are the Sacramento and the San Joaquin, both in the Central Valley. They carry runoff water from the mountains out to San Francisco Bay.

The major river in southern California is the Colorado, on the Arizona border. It flows

LANDFORMS

Mount Shasta (*above*) is one of California's highest peaks. The lowest point in the Western Hemisphere is in Death Valley (*below*), a desert basin in southeastern California.

into the Gulf of California. Many of the other rivers in the south are dry for much of the year.

California has thousands of lakes. Some are freshwater lakes. Others are saline, or salty. The largest freshwater lakes are Lake Tahoe, which California shares with Nevada, and Clear Lake, in the Coast Ranges north of San Francisco. Salt lakes are found in the desert areas. These include the Salton Sea, in the Colorado Desert, and Mono Lake, east of Yosemite National Park. Shasta Lake, an artificial lake on the Sacramento River, is California's largest reservoir.

The Pacific Ocean, largest body of water in the world, forms California's western border. The general coastline is 1,352 kilometers (840 miles). The total shoreline, including sounds, bays, and offshore islands, is more than 5,500 kilometers (3,400 miles).

Climate

In the summer a high-pressure center, called the Pacific High, hangs over California. This is a great mass of calm air that keeps away storms and rain. California summers are

Smelting plants, such as this one near San Francisco (*above*), supply metals for California's many manufactured goods. Oranges (*below*) are an important product of California.

almost without rain, except for occasional thunderstorms in the mountains and deserts.

During the winter the Pacific High moves southward and opens the way for storms from the Pacific Ocean to pass over the state. Storms are strongest in northern California, where practically all the rainfall occurs from October through April. The Klamath Mountains and the northern Coast Ranges are the state's wettest areas. Inland from the mountains it is dry, partly because the air loses moisture in crossing the mountains. At high elevations there are heavy snowfalls in winter. In southern California almost all the rain falls between November and March. But parts of the south hardly get any rain.

Winter temperatures are mild in California, particularly in the Colorado Desert, the Central Valley, and the coastal sections from San Francisco to San Diego. Western California is protected in winter by mild air from the ocean and by the state's mountains, which block cold waves from the northern interior states.

In summer the coastline is usually cool and cloudy, and the Pacific Ocean is often chilly, even in August. The desert areas of the southeast are extremely hot in summer.

Natural Resources

California's wealth comes from both its shoreline and its land. The shoreline provides harbors and good locations for cities, fishing ports, and coastal resorts. The land provides minerals, forests, grazing areas, and rich agricultural districts.

California has passed laws dealing with air and water quality, land use, management of solid waste, noise control, pesticides, and radiation. Land developers are required to make studies and let the public know how their proposed developments are likely to affect the environment. The coastal zone is protected by special laws.

Grazing Land. More of California's land is used for pasturing sheep and cattle than for any other purpose. The Coast Ranges and the edges of the Central Valley are the most important grazing areas.

Forests. About one fifth of California is forested. Most of the trees are conifers that are commercially valuable. The best-known tree, the coast redwood, forms one of the world's tallest and densest forests. California supplies nearly all the nation's redwood.

The Douglas fir is the most plentiful tree. It grows inland, beyond the coast redwoods, in the northern part of the state. The ponderosa pine is found still farther inland. California's giant sequoia is the world's largest tree. Related to the coast redwood, the sequoia grows only in scattered groves in the Sierra Nevada. It is protected from commercial harvest.

Minerals. Little gold has been mined in California for many years, but other minerals have taken its place. Petroleum wells yield "black gold." The deserts near Death Valley contain large deposits of borax. More than 40 minerals are commercially produced.

Soils. California has many kinds of soils. They range from rock-strewn mountain soils to the rich alluvial soils in the Central Valley. The main agricultural problem is not lack of fertile soils but lack of water.

Water. The Sacramento and the San Joaquin river systems are major sources of irrigation water. The Central Valley Project transfers water from the Sacramento Valley to the dry San Joaquin Valley. Water is released from Shasta Lake into the Sacramento River. It is pumped out of the river near the head of San Francisco Bay. It then moves south in a canal to irrigate the San Joaquin Valley between Stockton and Fresno. Water that comes out of the Sierra Nevada into the San Joaquin River is moved south in a canal to Bakersfield to irrigate the southern San Joaquin Valley.

Other long canals and aqueducts carry water to where it is needed. San Diego gets most of its supply by means of the Colorado River Aqueduct. Los Angeles obtains water from both the Colorado and the Owens rivers. Part of the Colorado River is diverted through the All-American Canal to irrigate the fertile Imperial Valley of the Colorado Desert.

The California Water Project includes a huge system of dams and aqueducts. It transports water from northern California as far south as San Diego. The most important structure in the system is the Oroville Dam on the Feather River, northeast of Sacramento. The California Aqueduct, a major part of the project, carries water from the northern Sierra Nevada to the southern San Joaquin Valley.

▶ THE PEOPLE AND THEIR WORK

When Europeans first arrived in California, they found a large population of Indians. Today about 90,000 Indians live in California. There are 76 Indian reservations. Some of them are quite small. But only about 15 percent of the Indians live on reservations. The city of Palm Springs occupies half of the Agua Caliente Indian Reservation.

The great majority of Californians are of European descent, although relatively few people migrated there directly from Europe. Spanish is the most common language after English. Most Spanish-speaking Californians came from Mexico or Latin America fairly recently. The state also has a sizable population of Asian descent.

In recent decades many people have moved to California from other states. The black population grew rapidly after World War II, when there was a heavy migration from rural areas of the South.

Where the People Live

California is very unevenly populated. Most Californians, including many farmers, live in towns and cities. The most densely populated area is the Los Angeles lowlands. Most of the valleys, except in the desert, are well populated, but most mountainous areas are not. Recently, some inland rural counties have been the fastest-growing areas of the state.

Industries and Products

Half of all California workers have jobs in offices and stores. One reason is that businesses serving the whole western United States have their home offices in California. These include banking, transportation, construction, insurance, oil, and publishing.

Even so, it is also true that California ranks first among the 50 states in value of

---

THE LAND

LOCATION: Latitude—32° 32′ N to 42° N. **Longitude**—114° 08′ W to 124° 34′ W.
Oregon to the north, Nevada on the east, Arizona to the southeast, Lower California (Mexico) to the south, the Pacific Ocean on the west.

ELEVATION: Highest—Mount Whitney, 4,421 m (14,494 ft). **Lowest**—Death Valley, 86 m (282 ft) below sea level.

LANDFORMS: Klamath Mountains, Coast Ranges, Transverse Ranges, and Peninsular Ranges bordering the Pacific Coast; the Central Valley in center of state; Cascade Range and the Sierra Nevada east of the Central Valley; Basin and Range Region in the northeast and the southeast.

SURFACE WATERS: Major rivers—Sacramento and its tributaries, the Pit, Feather, and American; Klamath and its branch, the Trinity; Eel; San Joaquin; Colorado. **Largest freshwater lakes**—Clear Lake, Lake Tahoe. **Largest reservoir**—Shasta Lake.

CLIMATE: Average temperatures of selected cities—Los Angeles, 13°C (56°F) in January and 23°C (73°F) in July; San Francisco, 11°C (51°F) in January and 15°C (59°F) in July. **Rainfall**—Average exceeds 2,800 mm (110 in) yearly in parts of Klamath Mountains, less than 50 mm (2 in) in Death Valley. Heaviest annual average snowfall, 1,130 cm (446 in), Alpine County. **Growing season**—From 365 days to about 260 days in main agricultural districts; fewer than 80 days in the higher Sierra Nevada and Cascades.

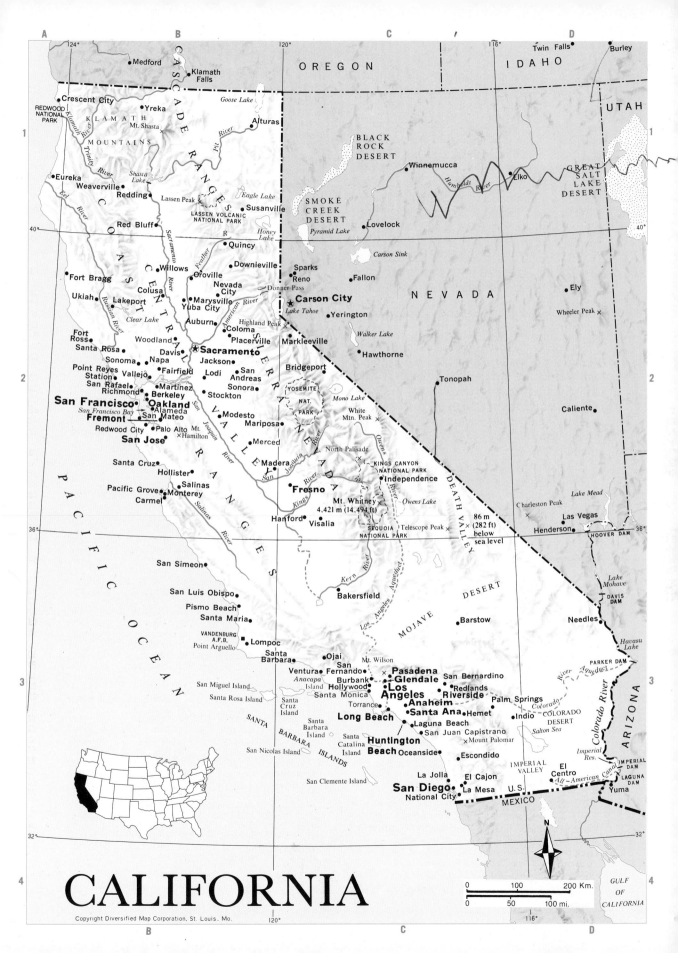

CALIFORNIA

agricultural products and of manufactured goods. It ranks high in value of mineral production.

Agriculture. The farm output each year exceeds the value of all the gold ever mined in the state. Agriculture, in turn, stimulates other industries through the materials that it uses. These materials include fuel, fertilizer, farm machinery, and packing containers.

Because of its unusual climate, California can grow many fruits and vegetables all year long. Grapes, oranges, and peaches are the leading fruits, and tomatoes and lettuce are the leading vegetables. California accounts for nearly all the nation's output of almonds, apricots, avocados, artichokes, Brussels sprouts, dates, figs, garlic, nectarines, olives, persimmons, plums, and walnuts.

In order of value, the chief agricultural products are cattle and calves, milk, grapes, and greenhouse and nursery products. Cotton is also important. It is grown mainly in the San Joaquin and Imperial valleys, where summers are long and hot and there is ample irrigation water. The Central Valley, of which the San Joaquin Valley is a part, contains most of the state's rich agricultural areas.

Manufacturing. Automobiles, aircraft, and other transportation equipment rank first in value among the state's manufactured products. California's aircraft industry was well established by the early 1920's. Airplane manufacturers Glenn Martin, Donald Douglas, and others pioneered in its early development.

California's farms supply raw materials for the many factories that prepare canned and frozen fruits and vegetables. The Pacific Ocean yields a rich harvest of fish. California is the second ranking state, after Alaska, in value of catch, and the canning of seafood forms one small part of the state's extensive food processing industry.

Other Industries. The motion picture industry in California is nearly as old as the aircraft industry. The phonograph record, radio broadcasting, and television industries owe their beginnings partly to motion picture production.

Activities related to space and ocean exploration and to national defense are California's newest major contribution to the nation. Vandenberg Air Force Base on the California coast is second only to Florida's Cape Canaveral for launching of spacecraft. It is one of many military bases in the state.

Mining. The most important mineral by far is petroleum. It comes from fields in the central and southern parts of the state and also from offshore wells in the ocean. Petroleum has been especially useful for the production of electricity in California, for coal is scarce. Petroleum is used to make fuels for motor vehicles and jet aircraft and for many chemical products, such as detergents.

Borax is another major mineral. Much of the world's supply comes from the deserts near Death Valley. Borax is a white powder used for cleansing and for making glassware and other products. A great deal of mining is done for the construction industry. Sand, gravel, and limestone are needed for cement and concrete. Gypsum goes into the making of wallboard.

WHAT CALIFORNIA PRODUCES

MANUFACTURED GOODS: Transportation equipment, including motor vehicles, aircraft, and guided missiles; electric and electronic equipment, chiefly communications equipment; processed foods; nonelectrical machinery; fabricated metal products; products of printing and publishing; chemicals and related products; refined petroleum; precision instruments; lumber and wood products; stone, clay, and glass products; clothing.

AGRICULTURAL PRODUCTS: Cattle and calves, milk, grapes, greenhouse and nursery products, cotton, lettuce, tomatoes, eggs, hay, almonds, oranges.

MINERALS: Petroleum, cement, natural gas, sand and gravel, boron minerals, stone, lime, asbestos, clays, gypsum, tungsten, gold, silver.

POPULATION

TOTAL: 23,667,565 (1980 census). **Density**—58.5 persons to each square kilometer (151.4 persons to each square mile).

GROWTH SINCE 1850

Year	Population	Year	Population
1850	92,597	1940	6,907,387
1870	560,247	1950	10,586,223
1890	1,213,398	1970	19,971,069
1910	2,377,549	1980	23,667,565

Gain Between 1970 and 1980—18.5 percent.

CITIES: Population of California's 15 largest cities according to the 1980 census.

Los Angeles	2,966,850	Fresno	218,202
San Diego	875,538	Santa Ana	204,023
San Francisco	678,974	Riverside	170,591
San Jose	629,546	Huntington	
Long Beach	361,334	Beach	170,505
Oakland	339,337	Stockton	149,779
Sacramento	275,741	Glendale	139,060
Anaheim	219,311	Fremont	131,945

Transportation and Communication

California's vast size and its many mountains have been a problem in unifying the state. But modern transportation and communication have helped to bring the separate areas close together.

Water. California relies greatly on water transportation. Lumber, petroleum, and other heavy cargo move by ship between such ports as Eureka, San Francisco, Los Angeles, and San Diego. Ocean vessels also call at the ports of Sacramento and Stockton.

Land Transportation. California's historic trails have become its highways. Highway 101 follows most of El Camino Real (The Royal Highway), which connected Spanish missions from San Francisco to San Diego. Interstate 15 follows the Old Spanish Trail, used by gold seekers in 1849. Interstate 5 is sometimes called California's Main Street. It runs the length of the state.

Railroads help carry California's fruits and vegetables to other parts of the country. Automobiles, fully loaded truck trailers, and ocean-going containers are carried piggyback on railroad flatcars.

Airlines. Great distances between towns plus good flying weather encouraged air travel to develop early in California. Regular air service between California and the East began in 1927. Now many smaller California cities are linked by scheduled flights. Flights across the Pacific are handled at the busy Los Angeles and San Francisco airports.

Radio, Television, and Newspapers. California has more than 400 AM and FM radio stations and about 50 television stations. The number of newspapers exceeds 900, of which about 125 are dailies.

▶ EDUCATION

California spends almost a third of its budget on education. It is known for the excellence of its free public schools, from kindergarten through college.

Schools and Colleges

During the 1840's American settlers in California began to think seriously of schools. The settlers' first school was founded in 1846 in what had once been the stable of the Santa Clara mission. The teacher spoke no Spanish, and the pupils no English.

The first state constitution, drawn up in 1849, provided for free elementary schools but not for taxes to support them. The situation was corrected in 1866. State funds for high schools did not come until 1903. A few years later funds were made available for 2-year colleges. These junior, or community, colleges now total more than 100. They are an important part of the public school system.

The state-supported University of California, founded in 1868, has nine campuses throughout the state. The central office is in Berkeley. The California State University and College System is made up of 19 different institutions.

California has many private colleges and universities, as well as a large number of professional, technical, and business colleges. Three of the best-known private institutions of higher learning are Stanford University, near Palo Alto; the University of Southern California, at Los Angeles; and California Institute of Technology, at Pasadena.

Libraries, Museums, and the Arts

In 1899 a workable public library system was set up under the guidance of the state librarian, James Gillis. Among its features were traveling book collections and a loan service among libraries. Today there are more than 200 public libraries with nearly 4,000 branches. Rural areas are served by book-mobiles.

There are several noted research libraries. The University of California library at Berkeley has the largest collection of books in the state. The library of the Huntington Library, Art Gallery, and Botanical Gardens at San Marino has a large collection of manuscripts in the fields of English and American history and literature. The Hoover Institution on War, Revolution, and Peace at Stanford University has important documents and books on world affairs, especially since 1900. It was founded by President Herbert Hoover.

Most of California's high schools have orchestras and music groups, as do many communities. The little town of Ojai has a yearly musical festival that is world-famous. The Hollywood Bowl in Los Angeles and Stern Grove in San Francisco hold outdoor concerts. San Francisco has a municipal opera company and a symphony orchestra.

Left, Fisherman's Wharf in San Francisco. Yosemite Falls (*center*) are the highest waterfalls in the country. At right is a view of Disneyland in Anaheim.

California has many museums. The Southwest Museum at Los Angeles and the State Museum at Sacramento exhibit Indian tools and crafts. The George C. Page Museum, a branch of the Los Angeles County Museum, has a fine collection of Ice Age fossils. The California Academy of Sciences in San Francisco maintains a natural history museum, a planetarium, and an aquarium. The California Palace of the Legion of Honor is one of San Francisco's major art museums. The Oakland Museum features California's art, ecology, and history. San Diego has one of the world's finest zoos.

▶ PLACES OF INTEREST

California has a large share of the nation's wonders, as well as many recreation areas.

National Areas

National forests cover about a fifth of the state. National areas that provide places for recreation on or near the water are Point Reyes National Seashore and Golden Gate, Whiskeytown-Shasta-Trinity, and Santa Monica Mountains national recreation areas. The following are the other national areas:

Channel Islands National Park, off Los Angeles, includes Santa Barbara, Anacapa, and other islands that shelter marine life.

Kings Canyon National Park, in the Sierra Nevada, is known for summit peaks of the High Sierra and for canyons of the Kings River.

Lassen Volcanic National Park, in the Cascade Range, has lava fields and other remains of the eruptions of Lassen Peak.

Redwood National Park, along the northwest coast, contains dense forests and long beaches.

Sequoia National Park adjoins Kings Canyon National Park. It includes Mount Whitney and groves of ancient giant sequoias.

Yosemite National Park, also in the Sierra Nevada, is the largest and best known of California's national parks. It has spectacular waterfalls, gorges, and groves of giant sequoias.

Cabrillo National Monument in San Diego is a memorial to the discoverer of San Diego Bay.

Death Valley National Monument covers a vast and colorful area of the Mojave Desert. It includes the lowest point in the Western Hemisphere. The northeastern corner of the monument extends into Nevada.

Devils Postpile National Monument, east of Yosemite, is so named because of its many blue-gray basalt pillars.

Eugene O'Neill National Historic Site, in Danville, preserves the house where Eugene O'Neill wrote some of his best-known plays.

Fort Point National Historic Site, in San Francisco, is the largest fortification on the western coast of North America. It has been restored to its mid-19th century condition.

Joshua Tree National Monument, in the desert near Palm Springs, preserves a fine stand of Joshua trees, a branched treelike yucca.

Lava Beds National Monument, in northern California, contains unusual remains of volcanic activity. The area was the scene of the Modoc War (1872–73), last of California's Indian wars.

Muir Woods National Monument, north of San Francisco, is a virgin redwood forest named for the great naturalist John Muir. Nearby is his home, designated the **John Muir National Historic Site**.

Pinnacles National Monument, east of Monterey, includes caves and spirelike rock formations.

State Parks

California's state park system includes about 200 different areas. The following list shows the variety:

Anza-Borrego Desert State Park covers huge tracts of mountains, canyons, and deserts, east of San Diego.

Calaveras Big Trees State Park, in Calaveras County, has fine specimens of Sierra redwoods. Calaveras County itself lives in literature as the setting of Mark Twain's story "The Celebrated Jumping Frog of Calaveras County."

Columbia Historic State Park, north of Sonora, includes a complete early mining community. Among the interesting buildings is an original Wells Fargo express office.

Hearst San Simeon State Historical Monument, near San Simeon, was the estate of publisher William Randolph Hearst. It includes a huge Spanish mansion and a Roman temple.

La Purísima Concepción Mission, near Lompoc, has been completely restored. The buildings, gardens, furniture, and handicrafts give an authentic example of a typical California mission.

Pismo Beach State Park, Pismo Beach, is one of the many beach parks. It is known for its famous clams and sand dunes.

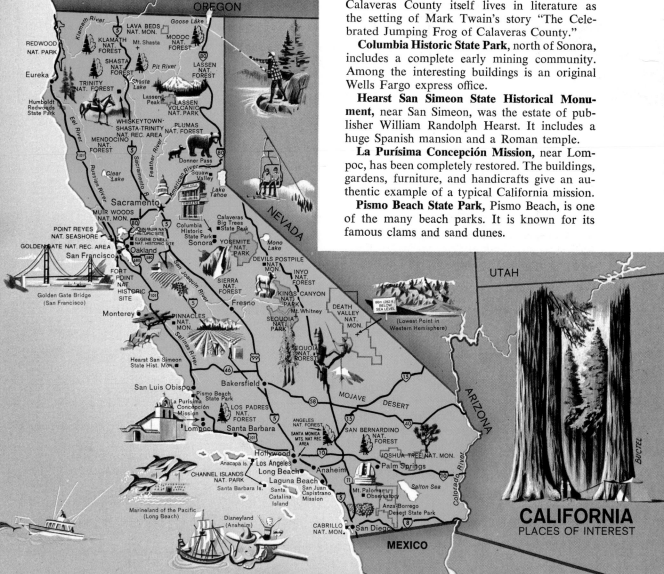

CALIFORNIA
PLACES OF INTEREST

Other Attractions

The following are among the many other places that attract thousands of visitors:

Disneyland in Anaheim is one of the world's most famous amusement parks. It is divided into five sections. They are Adventureland, Fantasyland, Frontierland, Tomorrowland, and Main Street, U.S.A.

Laguna Beach, south of Santa Ana in Orange County, is a noted artists' colony.

Mount Palomar Observatory, near San Diego, has one of the world's largest telescopes, the Hale telescope.

The Pacific Crest Trail for hikers runs from Canada to Mexico, mainly through national forests and parks. In California it winds through the Sierra Nevada.

Sea World, at San Diego's Mission Bay, offers displays of sea life and live shows featuring whales, porpoises, sharks, and sea turtles.

Annual Events

California has many interesting yearly events. The following are some of the best known:

January—Tournament of Roses and Rose Bowl Football Game, Pasadena.

February—Chinese New Year, San Francisco.

April—Easter Sunrise Services, Hollywood Bowl, Los Angeles.

May—Jumping Frog Jubilee, Angels Camp, Calaveras County.

August—Old Spanish Days Festival, Santa Barbara.

September—Los Angeles County Fair, Pomona.

October—Grand National Livestock Exposition, Horse Show, and Rodeo, San Francisco.

November—International Film Festival, San Francisco.

▶ CITIES

The great majority of Californians live in urban places. The following are the state's most important cities:

Sacramento

Sacramento, the state capital, was once a trade center for the gold mines, with riverboat service direct to San Francisco. Its levees, old buildings, and huge shade trees resemble those of towns along the southern Mississippi. Sacramento is the rail and highway crossroads for northern California, and its new harbor handles oceangoing commerce. Its shopping district serves the far-flung Sacramento Valley and Sierra Nevada foothills. Sacramento has canning factories, military installations, and a rocket fuel plant.

Los Angeles

Los Angeles, largest city in the state, is the center of many leading California industries, such as motion pictures, television, clothing, furniture, space, petroleum, fish, and automobiles. The Los Angeles and Long Beach harbors are the chief ports of southwestern United States. An article on Los Angeles is included in Volume L.

San Francisco

San Francisco is a famous center for tourists. Its hills, skyscrapers, bridges, cable cars, and bay make a colorful scene. The dazzling whiteness of its houses is often softened by gray fog. Visitors are attracted by its famous hotels and restaurants, its cool summer climate, and its many places of interest, such as Fisherman's Wharf, Golden Gate Park, and Chinatown.

San Francisco grew up around its harbor. San Francisco Bay, including the ports of Richmond, Oakland, and Redwood City, is the leading West Coast harbor and a shipbuilding center. Trans-Pacific radio and telephone facilities are concentrated in the Bay area. Army headquarters for the western states are at the Presidio of San Francisco. The city has a large financial and office

COUNTIES

Telegraph Hill, one of the highest points in the city, is at upper right in the view above of San Francisco. A network of freeways (*below*) connects Los Angeles' sprawling suburbs.

district, which serves most of the West. An article on San Francisco is included in Volume S.

San Diego

San Diego, on the coast near the Mexican border, owes much of its growth to its mild climate and its fine harbor. Its chief industry is the manufacture of aerospace equipment. Other industries build ships, manufacture oceanographic equipment, and process fish. The city is a hub of naval activities. An article on San Diego appears in Volume S.

▶ GOVERNMENT

The executive branch of the state government includes the governor and other executive officers. All are elected for 4-year terms. The legislative branch is made up of two houses—the Senate and the Assembly. Members of the legislature meet each year on the first Monday after January 1. The judicial branch is headed by the state Supreme Court.

By means of petition, California citizens can propose legislation. If approved by voters

at election, the proposal becomes law without requiring action by the legislature.

▶ **FAMOUS PEOPLE**

The following are representative of the many persons who helped build California:

Father Junípero Serra (1713–84) was one of the famous Spanish missionaries in America. In 1769 he led a group of Spanish soldiers and friars into California. He started the first Franciscan mission at San Diego. For 15 years he built missions, 9 in all, and baptized more than 6,000 Indians. He died at the mission of San Carlos near Monterey.

John Augustus Sutter (1803–80) was born Johann August Suter in Baden, a region of southwest Germany. In 1839 he came to California and founded a colony on the site of what is now Sacramento. He called the colony New Helvetia. Here he welcomed settlers from the United States as they began arriving in the 1840's. Discovery of gold on Sutter's property brought on the gold rush of 1849.

Leland Stanford (1824–93), born in New York, was one of California's pioneer merchants and railroad builders. He was one of the founders of the Central Pacific Railroad and a director and president of the Southern Pacific. Stanford is also remembered as the governor who helped keep California in the Union at the time of the Civil War and as a U.S. senator. He and his wife founded Stanford University in honor of their son, Leland Stanford, Jr.

Walt Disney (1901–1966) was born in Chicago and came to California in 1923. An artist, he was a pioneer in the technique of making animated cartoons. His cartoons and nature movies won him many awards. Disneyland was built in 1955.

Because of California's immense immigration, many of its famous persons are not native sons and daughters. Many persons, especially those in the entertainment and business worlds, have made California their home. One of the best-known adopted Californians is President Ronald Reagan, who pursued an acting career in the state and later served as its governor. A biography of President Reagan is included in Volume R.

Robert Frost was born in San Francisco, as were writers Gertrude Atherton, Jack London, Kathleen Norris, and Lincoln Steffens. Salinas was the birthplace of John Steinbeck, and Fresno, of William Saroyan. Mark Twain, Bret Harte, and Robert Louis Stevenson were among famous authors who once lived and wrote in California. Biographies of Robert Frost, Jack London, John Steinbeck, Robert Louis Stevenson, and Mark Twain are included in Volumes F, L, S, and T.

Other noted persons who were born in the state are General George S. Patton (San Gabriel), aviator and army officer James Doolittle (Alameda), publisher William Randolph Hearst (San Francisco), artist-designer Millard O. Sheets (Pomona), and the baseball-playing DiMaggio brothers (Martinez).

Richard M. Nixon (Yorba Linda) was a U.S. representative and senator before serving as vice-president and then as president of the United States. A biography of President Nixon is included in Volume N. Earl Warren (Los Angeles) served as governor of California and as chief justice of the United States. Edmund Gerald (Pat) Brown and Edmund Gerald (Jerry) Brown, Jr., (both San Francisco) gained prominence as governors of California.

▶ **HISTORY**

There were many Indians in California as long ago as 10,000 B.C. Their camp sites have been traced back to that date. At the time of Columbus, most of the tribes were peaceful hunters and food gatherers. They were poorly prepared to fight off the first Spanish conquistadors.

Spanish and Mexican Rule

Spanish explorers reached California about 50 years after Columbus' first voyage to the New World. Most early explorations were made by ships from Mexico. Of these the voyage of Juan Rodríguez Cabrillo was especially important. From it came the first knowledge of southern California's coastline, people, and climate. Spaniards of that day had little interest in climate and the Indians showed no signs of wealth. For the next two centuries, California lay neglected.

The Spanish finally decided to colonize California when it seemed that the Russians or the English might get there first. Settlers moved north from Mexico in 1769 to found San Diego. Within a dozen years mission settlements were built at Los Angeles, San Francisco, San Jose, and Monterey. The purpose of the missions was to introduce Christianity and Spanish culture to the Indians. Throughout the early period the missions were also a source of food and other goods.

Mexico declared its independence from Spain and took control of California in 1822. The Mexican rulers ordered that the missions be abandoned. Their lands were converted into great cattle ranchos. Life was pleasant for rancheros and their large families during the Mexican period. But conditions soon changed.

Mexican authority was weak. Traders and trappers from the United States began to come in. Many of them became settlers. They learned Spanish and married into California families. Most of the later settlers, such as John Sutter, took up farmlands in the Central Valley away from the inhabited areas. Various presidents of the United States tried to buy California from Mexico. Finally, in 1848, the United States obtained California as a result of the Mexican War.

The Gold Rush and Later

Thousands of gold seekers poured into the area in 1849. By 1850 the population was sufficient for California to become a state without first having been a territory. The supply of gold declined after 1852. Many miners turned to farming. Then followed a long tug of war between the cattle ranchers and the farmers for possession of the land. In the 1860's agriculture began to surpass gold as California's chief source of wealth. At first wheat and barley were the leading crops. They did not need irrigation, and they could be shipped long distances without spoiling. Then irrigation systems were built, and citrus fruits became an important crop.

One of California's greatest needs was transportation for its products to the East. In 1869 the first railroad—the Central Pacific—forged its link with the Union Pacific in Utah. Since that time the Panama Canal, highways, and air service have brought California still closer to the rest of the nation.

Government Reforms

During the gold rush and for many years afterward, lawlessness was a problem in both the mines and the towns. Newcomers arrived faster than police and courts could be established. There was much corruption in state and local governments.

It was not until 1911, under Governor Hiram Johnson, that political housecleaning began. The state legislature was deliberately weakened by giving more power to the voters themselves. Voters could propose laws and pass legislative acts by means of elections.

IMPORTANT DATES

1542	Juan Rodríguez Cabrillo explored San Diego Bay and other coastal places for Spain.
1579	Francis Drake claimed the land for England.
1769	First Franciscan mission founded at San Diego.
1822	California became a province of Mexico.
1826	Trappers led by Jedediah Smith became the first Americans to reach California overland.
1839	John A. Sutter established a colony on the Sacramento River.
1841	Sutter purchased Fort Ross from the Russians; first overland wagon train, the Bidwell-Bartleson party, reached California.
1846	California declared itself a republic in the brief Bear Flag Revolt; war broke out between the United States and Mexico.
1848	James W. Marshall discovered gold at Sutter's sawmill; United States formally acquired California by treaty with Mexico.
1849	Gold rush began; state constitution drafted and ratified at Monterey.
1850	California admitted to the Union on September 9 as 31st state.
1854	Sacramento became state capital.
1857	First overland stage reached California.
1860	First Pony Express mail reached California.
1861	First transcontinental telegraph line completed, ending the need for the Pony Express.
1868	University of California founded.
1869	First transcontinental railroad completed.
1906	Earthquake and fire devastated San Francisco.
1908	First commercial motion picture produced in California.
1913	Los Angeles Aqueduct completed.
1932	Olympic Games held in California (Los Angeles) for the first time.
1935	Boulder (now Hoover) Dam completed.
1936	San Francisco–Oakland Bay Bridge completed.
1937	Golden Gate Bridge opened.
1945	United Nations founded at San Francisco.
1968	Richard M. Nixon became the first Californian elected president of the United States.
1971	A severe earthquake hit the Los Angeles area.
1977	Rose Elizabeth Bird became the first woman chief justice of the state Supreme Court.
1978	Voters overwhelmingly passed Proposition 13, a measure that reduced property taxes.
1981	Former California governor Ronald Reagan took office as president of the United States.

Depression Years and World War II

During the Depression of the 1930's, newcomers to California were fewer and poorer than usual. But still they came. Many plans were offered for improving economic conditions. Among the plans were Upton Sinclair's EPIC (End Poverty in California) and Dr. Francis Townsend's old-age pension idea.

In spite of the depression, San Francisco completed its opera house and its two great bridges, the Golden Gate and the San Francisco–Oakland Bay bridges. It also held a world's fair. In the Los Angeles area the movie industry built huge studios to make the new "talkie" motion pictures.

California's location on the West Coast laid it open to direct attack during World War II. But only one Japanese submarine actually fired on the shoreline. Military installations and war industries brought a flood of people to California. Such major industries as the making of steel and synthetic rubber came to California for the first time.

The Future

California faces many challenges. As the population grows, the natural resources decrease. Oil, fish, water, and forests are less abundant. So are open land and scenic recreation areas.

California lies atop one of the most active earthquake zones in the world. San Francisco suffered its famous earthquake in 1906. And in 1971 the Los Angeles area was shaken by a severe quake that resulted in 64 deaths and caused damage estimated at more than $1,000,000,000. The second of two major quakes to hit the state in 1979 caused at least $25,000,000 in property damage. Californians are trying to devise ways to minimize the damage from future earthquakes. Meanwhile, newcomers keep arriving, bringing skill and energy to their adopted home.

RODNEY STEINER
California State University—Long Beach
Reviewed by JOEL SPLANSKY
California State University—Long Beach

CALORIES. See NUTRITION.

CALVIN, JOHN (1509–1564)

John Calvin was a leader of the Reformation, the religious movement that swept Europe in the 16th century and divided the Christian world into Catholic and Protestant churches.

Calvin was born at Noyon, France, on July 10, 1509. At the age of 14 he was sent to the University of Paris. There he devoted himself to the study of Latin, philosophy, and logic—the science of correct reasoning. In 1528 he went to the city of Orléans to study law. The logic of law appealed to Calvin and influenced his religious thinking in later years.

In 1531 Calvin returned to Paris. It was about this time that he turned to the new Protestant faith. Because of his religious beliefs, he was forced to flee from Paris and, finally, from France. For several years he wandered from city to city. During these years he began to write his great work, *Institutes of the Christian Religion*. In 1536 Calvin went to Geneva, Switzerland. Except for one short period, he lived there for the rest of his life.

Though frail and sickly, Calvin had an iron will. Under his strong leadership Geneva became the center of Protestantism. The Church wrote the city's laws and governed every part of its daily life. The laws were strict. Genevans were expected to be thrifty, hardworking, and serious. Dancing and singing—except hymns—were forbidden. And the punishment for disobedience was severe.

Calvin's religion was stern. People, he believed, were sinful and could receive salvation only through God's grace. But only the few chosen by God (the "elect") would receive grace. And long ago God had already decided who would be among the elect. This was Calvin's doctrine of predestination.

Calvin died on May 27, 1564. By that time, his ideas had spread to much of western Europe. The Puritans who left England to settle in the American colonies were followers of Calvin. They called their churches Congregationalist, Presbyterian, Evangelical, or Reformed.

Reviewed by HUGH T. KERR
Princeton Theological Seminary

See also PROTESTANTISM; REFORMATION.

CAMBODIA
(KAMPUCHEA)

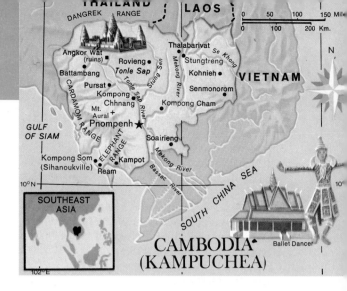

CAMBODIA
(KAMPUCHEA)

Ballet Dancer

The abandoned city and temple ruins of Angkor are symbols of Cambodia's great past and of its present. Angkor was once the magnificent capital of a great empire that ruled much of Southeast Asia until it was weakened by frequent wars and foreign conquests 500 years ago. Today the once peaceful and fertile land has again been reduced to ruin—by foreign invasion and civil war. The country was closed to the rest of the world between 1975 and 1979, when it was ruled by the Cambodian Communist Party (Khmer Rouge). Later, it had two rival governments. For many years, very little accurate information about Cambodia was available. Today we know that the great ruins of Angkor still stand. But they have been looted by vandals and damaged by war.

▶ THE PEOPLE

Cambodia is not so densely populated as most Southeast Asian countries. The population in 1970 was estimated to be more than 8,000,000. But war and economic disruption reduced this figure. It is estimated that as many as 2,000,000 people were killed or died

from other causes during the period of Khmer Rouge rule. (This number includes most of the doctors, teachers, technicians, and monks in the country.) And only a huge international relief effort saved many Cambodians from starvation in 1979.

Most of the people are of Khmer stock, often known as Cambodians. There is a large Vietnamese minority. The other minority groups, including Chinese, Chams, and Thais, have been greatly reduced in size. The main language of Cambodia is Khmer. Vietnamese is also spoken. Traditionally, French was the language of intellectuals, professionals, and government officials.

The practice of religion was forbidden by the Khmer Rouge. But Buddhism was later restored as the major religion of the country.

The Khmer Rouge also abolished education and burned almost all books. Schools have since been reopened to train a new generation of doctors, teachers, technicians, government officials, and religious leaders.

Special efforts are being made to preserve the traditional songs and dances of the Cambodian court. These ancient arts have been admired throughout the world.

▶ THE LAND

Cambodia is part of mainland Southeast Asia. It shares borders with Thailand, Laos, and Vietnam. Most of the country is a saucer-shaped basin surrounded on three sides by a rim of hills and mountains. This rim begins in southwestern Cambodia with the Elephant Range. Along the western side is the Cardamom Range. In the north the rim consists of

---

FACTS AND FIGURES

KAMPUCHEA is the official name of the country.

CAPITAL: Pnompenh.

LOCATION: Southeast Asia. **Latitude**—10° N to 15° N. **Longitude**—102° 31′ E to 108° E.

AREA: 181,035 km² (69,898 sq mi).

POPULATION: 6,700,000 (estimate).

LANGUAGE: Khmer, or Cambodian (official), Vietnamese, French.

GOVERNMENT: Communist republic. **Head of state**— president. **International co-operation**—United Nations.

ECONOMY: Agricultural products—rice, fruit, vegetables, corn, soybeans, sugarcane, rubber, kapok, pepper, poultry. **Industries and products**—processing of agricultural products, fishing, lumbering, handicrafts. **Chief minerals**—iron ore, copper, coal. **Chief imports**— textiles, foodstuffs, machinery, electrical equipment, pharmaceuticals, chemicals, fertilizers. **Monetary unit**—riel.

the Dangrek Range, which forms part of the boundary between Cambodia and Thailand. The hills of eastern Cambodia, usually called the Moi Plateaus, slope westward from the Annamese Cordillera in Vietnam toward the Mekong River.

Cutting through the hills north of the Cardamom Range is a lowland area that stretches from the Chao Phraya (Menam) River in Thailand to the Mekong River. A railroad running through this lowland region once connected Pnompenh, Cambodia's capital, with Bangkok, the capital of Thailand.

The Mekong River

One of the most important features of Cambodia is the Mekong River. It flows through the country for more than 600 kilometers (400 miles) before it enters Vietnam and eventually empties into the South China Sea. It is the main avenue of transportation in Cambodia and the main source of water for irrigation and human use. Water from the mountains flows either directly into the Mekong or into a large, shallow lake called the Tonle Sap ("great lake"). The area near the lake and the Mekong is the heart of Cambodia. This region has traditionally had the largest population, the most productive rice fields, and the greatest amount of commercial fishing. It is also the site of the past and present capitals and the largest cities of Cambodia.

Climate

Cambodia has a tropical climate. The rainy season starts between mid-April and May and ends between mid-October and November. During this period the central basin receives moderately heavy rainfall. For the rest of the year there is very little rainfall, and the Mekong River supplies the additional water needed for irrigation. January is the coolest month, and April the warmest. Cambodia has an average yearly temperature varying between 21 and 35°C (70 and 95°F).

▶ THE ECONOMY

Before the war of the 1970's, almost 90 percent of the Cambodian people worked as farmers. Most of them lived in small villages, raising poultry and growing rice, vegetables, and fruits on small farms for their own use. The major food crop for export was rice. It was produced in surplus on small farms, especially in the rich farming areas of the Mekong River valley and the basin of the Tonle Sap. The second most important commercial crop was rubber, grown on plantations that the French had started near the Vietnamese border. Corn, soybeans, sugarcane, kapok, and pepper were also grown. Some Cambodians were engaged in fishing on the Tonle Sap and in coastal waters. Others were involved in mining iron ore, copper, and coal and in lumbering. There was little industrial development. Most of the industries were in larger towns, where farm products were processed for export.

The war period (1970–75) disrupted agriculture. Cambodia became dependent on imported rice to feed the refugees who moved from the war-torn rural areas to the cities. Following the fall of the government in 1975, the victorious Communist forces, known as the Khmer Rouge, moved vast numbers of city people out into the country. This action was taken partly because there were no supplies of rice to feed the large city population and partly to return the people to the land, where they could grow food crops and restore the nation's agriculture. Individual private farms were reorganized into collective farms, in which everyone worked together on the land. The members of some of these farms lived together in barracks. By 1978, Cambodia was once again self-sufficient in rice. But renewed civil war in 1978 again destroyed dikes and disrupted farming. Refugees once more fled the war-torn countryside. By the end of 1979, the Cambodian nation, which once exported rice to its neighbors, faced widespread famine.

▶ CITIES

The largest and most important city in Cambodia is Pnompenh. As the capital city and the center of transportation, trade, and industry, it had a prewar population of about 500,000. During the war years from 1970 to 1975, refugees swelled the population of Pnompenh to over 3,000,000. But after the new government moved people to rural areas, Pnompenh was reduced to a city of fewer than 200,000. Most of these people worked on farms in the adjoining countryside. During the daytime, while people were in the fields, there were fewer than 20,000 people in this city, which once teemed with activity. When a new

Angkor Wat, a temple completed in the 12th century, was dedicated to the Hindu god Vishnu.

Because of the lack of plumbing in the small villages, water has to be carried to the homes.

government took over Pnompenh in 1979, it allowed people to return to the city and encouraged the revival of industry. The population of Pnompenh slowly returned to its prewar level. The second largest city is Battambang, located in western Cambodia. Kompong Som, Cambodia's deepwater port on the Gulf of Siam, has been rebuilt.

▶ HISTORY AND GOVERNMENT

Funan, a Hindu-influenced kingdom established about the 1st century A.D., ruled what is now Cambodia for over 400 years. During the 6th century, the Khmer people gained power and established their control over what is today Cambodia. In the next 800 years they extended their control over their neighbors. By the 14th century the Khmer Empire was the most powerful in mainland Southeast Asia. During this period the Khmer culture and arts flourished. The magnificent monuments of Angkor, on the north shore of Tonle Sap, were once Southeast Asia's most famous tourist attraction. They were built during the 12th and 13th centuries and include the city of Angkor Thom and the temple of Angkor Wat. Other remains of the Khmer civilization are scattered throughout the former empire.

After many invasions by neighboring kingdoms, the Khmer Empire declined. Between the 14th and 19th centuries, Cambodia lost much of its territory in wars with the Thais and the Vietnamese. In 1864 the French established a protectorate in what remained of Cambodia and added it to the colony of French Indochina, which included Vietnam and Laos. Cambodia declared its independence from France in 1945, when the Japanese ended French power in Indochina. But after World War II, the French returned to claim their colony. King Norodom Sihanouk waged a campaign for complete independence, which came in 1953. Sihanouk turned the throne over to his father in 1955 and became premier upon his father's death in 1960. As the major political leader in Cambodia for the next 15 years, Prince Sihanouk maintained the neutrality of Cambodia in the struggles between Communist and anti-Communist forces in neighboring Vietnam.

Despite Sihanouk's efforts, Cambodia was unable to escape involvement in the Vietnam War. North Vietnamese and Vietcong troops established bases in Cambodia. Sihanouk was overthrown in 1970, and Cambodia became the Khmer Republic, led by the head of the armed forces, General Lon Nol.

The Lon Nol government followed an anti-Communist policy rather than Sihanouk's neutral policies. South Vietnamese and United States troops invaded Cambodian territory to attack North Vietnamese and Vietcong bases there. This led Cambodia into a long period of civil war that disrupted the economy and drove millions of refugees into the cities. Finally, in 1975, Communist forces (the Khmer Rouge) defeated the Lon Nol government, which was backed by the United States. At this time the country was renamed Democratic Kampuchea.

The new government attempted to establish a revolutionary, self-sufficient society that would not be dependent on foreign trade or aid. The Khmer Rouge has been accused of using great brutality in changing the Cambodian society and economy. Money and personal property were abolished. Children over the age of 6 were not allowed to live with their parents. The cities were emptied to provide labor for agricultural production. People in the countryside were moved to other areas and forced to work long hours on large communal farms, even if they were old or ill. Thousands of refugees fled to Thailand and Vietnam.

Cambodia and Vietnam are ancient enemies, and the two countries became involved in a border war. China supported the Khmer Rouge, while the Soviet Union backed Vietnam. Late in 1978, Vietnamese forces and Cambodian exiles invaded Cambodia. They drove the Khmer Rouge out of Pnompenh in 1979 and installed a new government headed by Heng Samrin, a former high official in the Khmer Rouge. They renamed the country the People's Republic of Kampuchea.

The new government gradually gained control of most of the war-torn country. But Cambodia faced mass starvation. Nations from all over the world sent food and other aid. By 1981, most Cambodians had enough to eat. People were allowed to rejoin their families and return home. Farming revived, money was reintroduced, and shops reopened.

But the complete rebuilding of this shattered land remains an enormous task. It is complicated by the fact that the Khmer Rouge still claims to be the official government of Cambodia, and it holds the Cambodian seat in the United Nations. The Khmer Rouge has kept this seat because many countries object to the Vietnamese presence in Cambodia. The Khmer Rouge and other guerrilla groups continue to fight the Vietnamese, particularly in the mountains along the Thai border.

L. A. PETER GOSLING
Center for South and Southeast Asian Studies
University of Michigan

CAMELS

The Arabian camel is a desert animal. If necessary, it can go without food for days at a time. The hump of the camel's back is fat. The fat serves as stored food. The camel can also go without water for long periods of time. But scientists are just beginning to understand how it does this.

The camel is also suited in other ways to desert life. Its broad, padded feet stay on top of sand as the camel walks. When sand blows, the camel can shut its nostrils into slits. And it has thick pads on its knees. It kneels comfortably on these.

The Arabian camel is sometimes called the ship of the desert. Used as a beast of burden, it can carry 270 kilograms (600 pounds). Somewhat smaller camels are raised for riding. One-humped camels are sometimes called dromedaries.

Arabian camels are mostly raised in the deserts of North Africa and Arabia. They all have one hump. They eat the leaves of desert plants. They belong to the big group of animals called hoofed mammals.

Another kind of camel lives on the dry, cold plains of central Asia. This is the Bactrian camel. It has two humps on its back. It also has long hair. The Bactrian camel can carry a pack over deep snow in weather that is below −18°C (0°F). It can stay alive on scrub plants that few other animals would eat. People of the Asian plains raise the camel for milk, meat, hides, and hair for making cloth.

The camel's closest relatives are four animals of South America: the guanaco, vicuña, llama, and alpaca.

Reviewed by ROBERT M. MCCLUNG
Author, science books for children

See also HOOFED MAMMALS.

CAMERAS. See PHOTOGRAPHY.

Bactrian camels have two humps on their backs.

CAMEROON

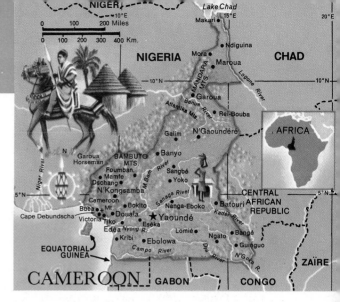

In 1471 a Portuguese sailor and explorer named Fernão do Po anchored his fleet at the mouth of the Wouri River on the west coast of Africa near what is today the port of Douala. Attracted by the masses of shrimp in the water, the sailors named the river *Rio dos Camarões* (Portuguese for "river of the shrimps"). Soon after, the Spanish arrived. They changed the name to *Camarones* (the Spanish word for "shrimps"). Eventually the name was applied not only to the river but also to the land surrounding it. In English the name became Cameroon.

▶ THE PEOPLE

People of nearly 200 ethnic groups live in modern Cameroon. In the south are people of mostly Bantu and semi-Bantu origin. Thousands of Pygmies live in the deep forests of the south and southwest. Most of the groups of the north are Muslims of Sudanese origin. Protestantism, Catholicism, and animism are the other religions that are practiced.

Because many different groups have settled in Cameroon over the centuries, more than 100 languages and dialects are spoken. People must sometimes learn three or more languages in order to understand their neighbors in adjoining villages.

The Europeans who colonized Africa

brought their languages, too. In the first half of the 20th century Cameroon had three colonial governments and three different languages. Grandparents had to learn German. Their children learned some French and some English. And now all must learn French and English as well as their local languages.

Education is compulsory and free through the primary grades. There are secondary schools, teacher-training institutions, and a university, the University of Yaoundé.

More and more young people are moving out of their villages and into such towns as Douala and Yaoundé, hoping to find work.

Marriage customs differ from those in some other parts of Africa. According to law and to custom, a Cameroon girl chooses or takes part in the selection of her future husband. Some marriages are free. In others, a man or woman gives a price in money or goods for a mate.

▶ THE LAND

Cameroon is situated on the western coast of Africa. Its Atlantic coastline is a dense mangrove swamp, with Douala its main port. Kribi, on the coast, and Garoua, on the Benue River, are also good ports. Southern Cameroon is mountainous, with lush tropical rain forests. The hilly Adamawa plateau occupies most of central Cameroon. Farther north the plateau flattens out into semi-arid grasslands.

Rainfall is heavy in the south except for two short dry seasons, from December to February and from July to September. The village of Debundscha is one of the wettest places in the world. The north has a long, rainy, tropi-

---

FACTS AND FIGURES

UNITED REPUBLIC OF CAMEROON is the official name of the country.

CAPITAL: Yaoundé.

LOCATION: West Equatorial Africa. **Latitude**—2° N to 14° N. **Longitude**—9° 15' E to 16° 05' E.

AREA: 475,442 km² (183,569 sq mi).

POPULATION: 8,100,000 (estimate).

LANGUAGE: French and English (both official), numerous local languages and dialects.

GOVERNMENT: Republic. **Head of government**—president. **International co-operation**—United Nations, Organization of African Unity (OAU).

NATIONAL ANTHEM: "O Cameroon, Cradle of Our Forefathers."

ECONOMY: Agricultural products—cassava, millet, peanuts, cacao, bananas, coffee, palm kernels. **Industrial products**—peanut and palm oil, soap, lumber, tobacco, aluminum, chemicals. **Chief exports**—cacao, bananas, cotton, coffee, aluminum, palm kernels. **Chief imports**—foodstuffs, machinery, textiles, vehicles, petroleum, manufactured goods. **Currency unit**—franc CFA (African Financial Community).

Shopping is done at outdoor stores and market stalls in Yaoundé, the capital of Cameroon.

cal summer, but it has a dry season lasting from November to April. Many different animals live in Cameroon's dense forests and on its rugged plateaus.

▶ THE ECONOMY

Most of the people are farmers, who produce enough food for their needs. They grow cassava, millet, corn, and taro in the north, and millet, corn, and peanuts in the south. The major cash crops are cacao, bananas, cotton, coffee, and palm kernels. Cattle are raised in the north and are a symbol of wealth. But they cannot survive in the humid south because of the disease-carrying tsetse fly.

Cameroon has deposits of bauxite, iron ore, and limestone. Aluminum, processed foods, and chemicals are the major manufactures.

▶ HISTORY AND GOVERNMENT

Before the first European protectorate was established in the 19th century, movement of peoples in Cameroon was widespread. The Bantu were continually being pushed into the rain forests of the southwest by warlike groups from the north.

When the Europeans began to colonize Africa in the 1880's, the British and the Germans reached for Cameroon. The Germans got there first and ruled the country with an iron hand from 1884 to 1914. They set up vast plantations and emphasized the growing of cash crops such as bananas, palm kernels, and peanuts. When Germany was defeated at the end of World War I, it lost all of its African colonies. Under the Treaty of Versailles, June 28, 1919, Britain and France divided this former German colony between them.

In 1960, after a decade of unrest, the eastern part received its independence. A parliamentary Republic of Cameroon was established. The following year British Cameroons, which was composed of the Northern and Southern Cameroons, held a referendum under the guidance of the United Nations. Northern Cameroon became part of Nigeria on June 1, 1961. Southern Cameroon joined the Republic of Cameroon to form the Federal Republic of Cameroon on October 1, 1961. In 1972, Cameroon changed its official name to the United Republic of Cameroon.

The president and the members of the legislature, which is called the National Assembly, are elected for 5-year terms. In 1975, the constitution was revised to provide for a prime minister, who is appointed by the president. Ahmadou Ahidjo, who had served as president of Cameroon since 1960, retired from office late in 1982.

SANFORD GRIFFITH
Author, *Cameroon*
Reviewed by BENOIT BINDZI
Former Ambassador of the United Republic
of Cameroon to the United Nations

CAMP FIRE

Camp Fire, Inc.—a nonprofit, nationwide youth organization—is the oldest organization of its kind in the United States. It was founded as Camp Fire Girls, and it still places emphasis on helping young girls realize their fullest potential. But today it is no longer just for girls. Camp Fire is for everyone. Infants, senior citizens, and all members of a family or community now participate in traditional and newly designed Camp Fire activities. Boys across the country are Camp Fire members.

Camp Fire was founded by Luther Halsey Gulick, M.D., and Charlotte Vetter Gulick. Dr. Gulick was a national leader in health, physical education, and recreation for youth. In 1909 the Gulicks—who were the parents of several children—started one of the first girls' camps in the country. It was there, at Camp Sebago-Wohelo in Maine, that much of the early program of Camp Fire Girls was formulated.

The Gulicks' chief aim was to help lead girls into happy, healthy womanhood through a program of fun, friendship, and high ideals. They were committed to providing girls with an out-of-school experience that would enrich their lives, develop skills, offer fun and adventure, and enhance their appreciation of the world around them.

Camp Fire has its own emblem, picturing logs and flames. Camp Fire's watchword is Wohelo, made up of the first letters of "work,"

This Blue Bird member of Camp Fire wears a sash with badges showing her awards.

"health," and "love," on which the entire program is based. The name Camp Fire was chosen because the hearth, with its fire, has symbolized the home from early times. "Camp" was added to suggest the outdoors.

Today Camp Fire—preserving the tradition of warm companionship, leadership, and individualism—is a multipurpose, multiprogram organization serving approximately 750,000 members in more than 35,000 communities. In 1975, Camp Fire adopted new programs and goals. Under the new programs, membership has been expanded to

Members around a campfire. Outdoor activities are a popular part of Camp Fire programs.

include youth of both sexes from birth to age 21. Adults can also become members.

Camp Fire continues to provide the traditional club programs in small groups divided by age. Children who become members of a group at age 6 are called Blue Birds. Older children become members of Adventure clubs and then of Discovery clubs. Those in high school usually belong to Horizon clubs. Each group has its own program suited to the needs of its age level. Clubs focus on learning by doing and on developing a positive self-image, responsibility, and creativity. They also teach how to plan and make decisions and how to appreciate and work with others.

Camp Fire encourages local councils to design programs and activities geared to the individual needs of the youth and communities they serve. All programs must meet national policies and standards. Local Camp Fire people are members of the regional chartered council and are also affiliates of the national organization.

Many new needs have resulted in new club programs. Camping and outdoor activities continue to be a popular basic program. But many Camp Fire councils are adding such activities as day camps in minority communities, tutorial programs, a six-week summer recrea-

tion program, a "Safety Town" program, a self-defense awareness program, and special programs for disabled children. Often children with disabilities are included in regular Camp Fire programs. Programs are funded by membership dues, contributions, and fund-raising activities.

Camp Fire provides opportunities for adults as well as young people to participate as club members or as individual members who take part in council programs. In addition, a majority of the councils offer family membership.

Camp Fire members wear costumes of navy blue and white with red touches. At special times they wear ceremonial robes that are copied from those of the American Indians and are trimmed with colored beads. The Camp Fire uniforms are designed for both girls and boys.

From the start the Camp Fire Girls program was welcomed by churches and synagogues, schools and community centers, and civic organizations interested in the welfare of youth. Today these bodies arrange sponsorship, meeting places, and camping facilities for the Camp Fire program. They make certain that the groups will always be led by qualified persons. Leaders are unpaid. Many groups are formed in neighborhoods and meet

Left: Two young members are shown visiting Camp Fire National Headquarters in Kansas City, Missouri. Right: Camp Fire members march in a parade.

Camp Fire members wear different uniforms according to age. From left to right are representatives of Adventure, Discovery, and Horizon clubs and of the Blue Birds.

in homes. All groups have from one to five adult sponsors.

Trained adults, both volunteer and professional, are the backbone of the agency nationally and locally. Camp Fire's national professional staff is headed by the national executive director. The national organization develops Camp Fire programs, as well as training programs for the adults who direct Camp Fire activities in local communities. Among the materials and services provided from the national offices are program books and related literature, the quarterly magazine *Camp Fire Leadership,* and training sources, surveys, and studies.

Camp Fire is one of the largest organizations of its kind in the United States. It is not organized on an international basis. But there are registered, active Camp Fire groups in other countries that have requested the program. There is a Camp Fire program in England, for example.

If you are interested in becoming a member of Camp Fire, you may apply to the local council in your town, or you may write to the office of the national headquarters. The address is Camp Fire, Inc., 4601 Madison Avenue, Kansas City, Missouri 64112.

Reviewed by PUBLIC RELATIONS DEPARTMENT
Camp Fire, Inc.

Camping is popular all over the world.

CAMPING

Camping in a variety of forms has become increasingly popular. Millions of people each year turn to the great outdoors for relaxation. There are many beautiful places—fine lakes and streams, lush mountain trails, and vast wilderness areas that can be enjoyed only by those who camp. People everywhere are returning to the outdoor life.

Today's camper may be a backpacker—a camper whose equipment is carried on the back. Or the camper may be a "trailerite," who goes with family or friends to a state park in a trailer or mobile home. Backpacker or trailerite, each is camping, and camping is now a part of our way of life.

Why? One reason is that leisure time is on the increase and families are seeking new ways to enjoy their surroundings. Parents are looking for projects to involve the whole family. Money is a second reason for camping's increased popularity. A vacation with motel and restaurant expenses can put a big dent in a budget. So an investment in camping equipment that can be reused seems to many people to be a worthwhile expenditure.

Then there is the current trend to venture forth into the unknown—to be pioneers and to live close to and with nature. Whatever their reasons, campers by the millions are rediscovering their natural surroundings.

▶ CAMPSITE SELECTION

Selecting the right campsite is important wherever and however you camp. The trailerite should check park facilities and reserve the necessary parking space in advance. Campsites with showers, toilets, recreational areas, shopping places, and electrical outlets are available. For the large mobile homes, plumbing hookups are possible.

Finding the right campsite for the backpacker is equally important. Check the area carefully. Keep away from cliffs and deep gullies. In wooded areas stay clear of standing dead trees or trees with large dead branches that can fall down. Avoid areas with poisonous plants such as poison ivy, poison oak, or sumac. Avoid rocky ledges that in some areas are homes of poisonous snakes. The best campsite has open areas with some trees for shade and level ground for pitching tents or making shelter. Drinking water and wood suitable for cooking fires should be nearby.

▶ PLACES TO CAMP

You can find out about campsites from state and federal park departments and from Scout and camping organizations. Road maps from gasoline companies and pamphlets from automobile associations list public and privately owned campsites.

▶ THE BACKPACKER AND PACKING

If your camping trip is going to include a few days of hiking you must be sure to take the time to plan it most carefully. The backpacker has to be ready for all weather and emergencies. Since your first camping will probably be during warm days of summer, take clothing that will protect you from the sun, rain, insects, and brush. This means a hooded poncho, a sweater or jacket, shorts or long trousers, plus underwear, extra socks, handkerchiefs, and pajamas. Sturdy shoes worn over wool socks make a good combination. If your shoes are large enough, it's best to wear two pairs of socks—a lightweight cotton pair, with wool socks over them. If you are to be camping long, be sure to include a change of clothing and an extra pair of camp shoes, such as sneakers.

Packing your things is really quite simple. A pack is a bagful of bags. Put extra clothing, such as underwear and socks, in one or more bags. Plastic bags are excellent. Force the air out after putting items in, then seal the bag with a rubber band or the wire twist that is supplied with some types of plastic bags. Toilet articles, such as soap, towels, toothbrush, and toothpaste, go into another bag. Food should be packed in plastic bags or containers.

Your pack should weigh no more than about one quarter of your own weight. Be sure to place soft, flat items so that they form a cushion against your back. Put items you'll need last at the bottom. Heavier items should be near the top. A flashlight and first aid kit

All the backpacker's camping gear is carried on the back. The pack serves as a suitcase.

should be in a pocket of the pack. A raincoat or poncho goes in last.

Pack straps should be wide enough that they do not cut your shoulders. Pack-strap pads help make straps more comfortable. Do not let equipment dangle outside the pack. This is the sign of a tenderfoot—an inexperienced camper. Keep the pack high up on your shoulders and close to your back. If your sleeping bag or blankets won't fit inside, make a horseshoe roll covered by your ground cloth, and fasten it over the pack. Be sure your pack is waterproof so that none of your equipment gets wet. Have a list of items you need, and check them off as you include them. Food should be divided so that each camper carries

Nearby water and trees to provide shade are necessary features of a good campsite.

BACKYARD TENT

BAKER TENT

EXPLORER TENT

The backyard tent is lightweight and simple to pitch. The Baker tent will fit in a pack. The Explorer tent is another easily pitched tent with adequate space inside.

his or her share. The same goes for equipment. This evens out the load each camper carries. The bigger, stronger campers should carry more than the smaller campers. But all campers should carry their own personal belongings.

▶ SHELTER

You can start learning to put up a tent at home. For backyard camping a tent can be made from a piece of canvas, plastic, or cloth that sheds water. It should be about 3 meters (10 feet) on each side. Hang it over a length of rope, and string it between two trees or posts. This kind of tent is also used by experienced campers because it is lightweight and easy to carry when camping in the wilderness. There are other ways of pitching (putting up) this kind of tent. Actually there are many kinds of tents. Some are made of lightweight material and are used when all equipment must be carried in a pack. Others are larger and heavier. These are generally used when camping in one place for long periods of time. The tent to use is the one that serves best for the kind of camping you plan.

When insects, such as mosquitoes, are plentiful, it is best to have the openings of the tent covered by mosquito netting. There should be no gap between the bottom of the tent and the ground. The best protection is to have a sewn-in floor made of a waterproof fabric.

The location of your tent on the campsite is important. Your tent should be placed on high ground that slopes away from the tent area. The open side of the tent should face away from the direction of possible storms and wind. Stay out from under individual large trees, since lightning may strike such trees. Check the ground area before putting up the tent. Remove all stones and sticks. Never sweep or rake up the leaves on your campsite except on the spot where your cooking fire is made. The natural ground cover keeps the campsite from getting muddy; but more important, grass, leaves, and small twigs on the ground keep the soil from washing away when rain falls.

Knowing how to drive tent stakes may help you to keep your tent up. Longer stakes are needed in loose ground. They should be driven in at an angle away from the tent. Where there is packed dirt or thick sod, stakes will hold if driven in straight or slanted toward the tent.

Once in a while it rains so hard that water may run under your tent. Usually this happens because the ground slopes into the tent. Under such conditions it may be necessary to stop the water by making a ditch at the uphill edge

CAMPING EQUIPMENT

Planning ahead is an important part of camping. Campers should bring along clothing and equipment that will ensure their safety and comfort.

of your tent and directing it around the tent to drain downhill. Remember, do not ditch unless necessary; then always replace the soil and stamp it down well.

There are times when those who camp, hunt, or fish must find emergency shelter. Protection may be found under an overhanging rock ledge or a large fallen tree. The leeward side (side opposite the wind) of a cliff, large boulder, or dense woods will give protection.

▶CAMP BEDS

Sleeping under a tent is wonderful if you are warm and comfortable. A sleeping bag is snug and warm. Next best are wool blankets folded into an envelope and pinned together. Your bed at home is comfortable because it has padding and springs that fit your body. In camp you can make the ground you lie on fit in the same way. If dry leaves, grass, or pine needles are plentiful, they may be collected and shaped to make the ground comfortable. A waterproof ground cloth of plastic or rubber fabric is placed over the bedding material and tucked in to help keep the ground bed together. Experienced campers often carry a lightweight cloth bag large enough to serve as a mattress. This is stuffed with leaves or grass so that it makes a comfortable pad.

Always cover your ground bed with a waterproof ground cloth to keep dampness away from your sleeping bag or blankets.

▶CAMP TOOLS AND FIRES

A knife and an ax, plus matches or other means of lighting a fire, are the camper's best friends. Keep your knife in your pocket or in its sheath when walking or running. Never throw a knife or an ax. Be sure the ax handle is tight. Have a good sheath for your ax, and keep the blade covered when carrying it. When using a knife or an ax, keep other campers at a safe distance. When looking for firewood, remember that deadwood burns best. The lower branches of standing trees are often dead. If they break off with a snap, you may be sure they will burn.

Before you start to cook a meal, prepare all the wood you will need for the fire. Collect the following: (1) Several handfuls of small twigs about 20 centimeters (8 inches) long. (2) A small armful of sticks about as thick as your index finger and as long as your forearm. (3) An armful of wood the size of your wrist and as long as your forearm. Split these in half.

While you gather wood for the fire, watch for material to use for tinder, such as dry weeds, dry outside bark of wild grapevines, red cedar, and dry pine needles. The outside bark of dead white, gray, or yellow birch makes good tinder. Never take this bark from a live tree. Wood shavings made with your knife can be a substitute for twigs and tinder.

Experienced campers often use fire starters. A candle stub can be used. Newspapers rolled tightly, tied with string, cut into pieces 5 centimeters (2 inches) long, and soaked in melted paraffin make a good fire starter. Five or six matches tied in a bundle and dipped in paraffin also make fine fire starters. Paraffin-dipped matches will light in wet weather.

With all this material ready, you can lay your fire. The fireplace should be out in the open. It is best to have it located near your tent. Pick the spot, and scrape away all leaves and ground cover right down to bare dirt. This area should be about 1.5 meters (5 feet) on each side. In rocky country several flat rocks in a circle can serve as a fireplace.

When the fireplace is set to use, lay a small finger-sized stick across a few stones. Put some tinder under this stick, and lay a handful of twigs over the stick. Now add a few larger twigs, and light the tinder. Your wood should start to burn quickly. Add larger sticks of wood as the fire burns brighter.

Cooking fires should be kept small. The high flames of a newly started fire may be used to bring liquids (such as soups, and water for cooking vegetables) to a boil. When the fire burns lower, leaving a bed of hot coals, meat can be broiled, and stews can simmer slowly. Never leave your fire unattended. Have a pail of water nearby in case a sudden gust of wind takes it out of control. Always put out your fire when you leave it or break camp. Put it **dead out** with water, as follows: Spread out burning sticks. Sprinkle sticks and hot coals with water. Turn over the burning sticks, and sprinkle again. Repeat stirring and sprinkling until there is no heat in the coals. The wet, cool ashes can be scattered when breaking camp. Cover the bare ground around the fire spot with the leaves and humus that were removed before making your fireplace.

The following hints will help you to become a better fire builder. Always carry waterproof matches in a container in a pocket. Take along several fire starters in case of really wet weather. A few pieces of birchbark in your pack will save the day. Remember that even in rainy weather, the inside wood of larger sticks is usually dry and can produce dry shavings for tinder. The experienced camper always prepares a supply of firewood so it's ready ahead of each meal. A piece of plastic over the supply of cut wood will protect it from rain. It is good camper courtesy to leave a neatly stacked supply of wood for the next campers.

▶ CAMP MEALS AND COOKING

Nothing tastes better than food cooked in camp. Cooking utensils for simple camp meals include a frying pan, several cooking pots, and spoons. A roll of heavy-duty aluminum foil can be used instead of pots for cooking a number of delicious camp meals.

The fire should be started 15 or 20 minutes before the meal is cooked. Immediately put on

A good fire is made with dry tinder, small twigs and sticks, and a supply of wood.

Before starting to cook, the camper should have at hand all the things that will be needed.

a pot holding about 5 liters (5 quarts) of water. Have a pair of canvas gloves with leather palms for picking up hot pots.

One handy trick with soap will save a lot of time and work. Let a bar of soap soften in a little water. Before putting any pot on the fire, use the softened soap to coat the outside of the pot. The cleanup job will be much easier with the coating of soap.

A square of plastic or canvas as a ground tablecloth will give you a clean work space as you prepare food for cooking.

Your first camp meals should be very simple. Try bacon and eggs for breakfast. Both of these should be cooked over low heat. Put the bacon in a frying pan. Brown it gently; then remove it from the pan, and let it drain on a piece of paper or the heel of your loaf of bread. Break the eggs into the hot bacon fat. Cook gently, basting them with the bacon fat until the yolks are cooked. While the eggs are cooking, spear a piece of bread on a sharp stick to toast. Brown the bread on both sides, and butter it.

To make hot chocolate, empty an individual package of cocoa into a camper's cup, and add hot water. Other items that add variety to breakfast include cereals, pancakes, sausage, ham, and perhaps fried potatoes. Eggs can be cooked in many different ways.

A hearty lunch can be made of sandwiches of canned meat, jelly, peanut butter, or cheese. A cup of bouillon or soup hits the spot in cool weather. For dessert you can have fruit.

For supper use a simple recipe that can be put together in one cooking pot. Try a quick camp stew. The following recipe makes one portion:

100 g (¼ lb) stew beef	1 potato
1 small onion	1 piece celery
1 carrot	salt and pepper to taste

Select a pot large enough to hold ingredients. Cut the meat into small cubes about the size of the end of your thumb. Put a little fat in the pot, and heat it over the fire. Now add the diced meat. Let it brown on all sides. Of course, you will have to stir it once in a while. Meanwhile peel and wash potatoes and onions, and scrape the carrots. Dice all of these into small cubes like the meat. Add the diced onions and celery to the browning beef, and stir once in a while until the onions are golden brown. Next add a little water, cover the pot, and let the mixture simmer for 30 minutes or until the meat is almost tender. Add the carrots and potatoes with just a little water. Let the whole mixture simmer slowly until the vegetables are cooked. This will take about another half hour.

▶ SANITATION, HEALTH, AND SAFETY IN CAMP

Every campsite becomes a tiny new home or community. You must have the same protection for your health and safety as at home—simple sanitary facilities for the disposal of waste food (garbage) and waste water as well as body waste. Public camping areas have these facilities. When making camp in other places, be sure to plan for disposal of waste. Locate a spot near your fire but not where you and your friends usually walk.

Burn all waste such as paper and plastic wrappings. Glass jars and empty tin cans that have been flattened should be put in a plastic container and carried in your pack to a trash can.

Wet garbage should be dried over sticks on your fire and burned. When parks and forests have garbage pails, dispose of your kitchen waste in them. Never bury garbage or other kitchen waste, as animals will dig it up.

Body waste should be disposed of in a latrine (toilet). Organized camping areas generally have these conveniences. In backwoods and wilderness areas, you'll have to dig your own latrine. Locate it in a secluded area away from your campsite and its water supply. A latrine for overnight camping with several friends may be a hole about 45 centimeters (18 inches) deep and 30 centimeters (1 foot) across. Pile the dirt nearby. Drive a stake in the ground to hold the paper roll. Make a paddle to cover the waste after each use. Fill the hole with dirt before leaving the campsite. Mound the dirt, and stamp it down.

Safe drinking water is important. State and federal campsites have good water supplies. To make sure water is safe for drinking, boil it for two or three minutes. It tastes better if it is poured from one pot to another several times. This puts air back into the water and improves its flavor.

Water-purification tablets may be purchased from drugstores or camp-equipment suppliers. Two kinds are available. Halazone tablets and tablets containing iodine are used most commonly. Make sure they are fresh. Follow directions on the bottle.

Good campers know enough about first aid to take care of such things as cuts, blisters, scratches, burns, sunburn, and insect bites. A few simple first aid supplies in your kit are very important. Put the following in a small plastic box: two or three sterile compresses, six adhesive bandages, a small bottle of antiseptic, a small tube of burn ointment, insect repellent, a roll of sterile gauze, adhesive tape, and a needle. Always carry one or two adhesive bandages and some change for emergencies. With change you can call home collect wherever you can get to a telephone. You could also call the operator to get help in case of an emergency.

Getting lost in the woods may be one emergency a camper has to face. It can be an adventure or a tragedy, depending on how well prepared you may be. To make sure you don't get lost, learn about the country you camp in by studying a map. Locate your camping area on it so that you can identify the streams, roads, high points, and other landmarks. Always carry a map with you. Never go camping or far away from your campsite alone. It's best to have three in the party. If one becomes sick or hurt, that leaves one to take care of the injured camper and one to go for help. Each of you should have some things in your pockets to help meet emergencies. Include a small compass, waterproof matches, a pocketknife, and some lightweight, strong string. You should also have a few small fishhooks, with barbs protected, in case you have to fish for food; a small whistle for signaling; a fire starter; and your pocket supply of toilet paper. If you do get lost— keep calm, sit down, relax, and begin to figure things out. Get out your map, locate landmarks, and with the help of your compass, which always should be carried in your pocket, lay out a route to the nearest trail or road. There is really no reason to be afraid. If you aren't sure of a way out, stay where you are, and set up an emergency camp. Get a fire started to keep you warm or to send up a smoke signal. Blow your whistle once in a while, and wait for the searching party and remember—be calm.

Swimming on camping trips is great fun. Do it safely. Always swim with a friend. Don't dive into strange water. Don't swim directly after a meal. Learn how to row a boat and paddle a canoe; then follow the rules for their use. Don't abandon a capsized boat to swim to shore. It's better to hang on until rescued.

Good campers always leave a clean campsite. In fact, it is hard to tell where a good camper has set up camp. All the holes have been filled, and the fireplace is cleaned. Leaves have been scattered back over the ground so that the soil won't wash away in the rain.

RUSSELL A. TURNER
National Director of Camping
Boy Scouts of America

See also BIRDS (Bird Watching); BOATS AND BOATING; BOY SCOUTS; CAMP FIRE; CANOEING; FIRST AID; GIRL GUIDES AND GIRL SCOUTS; PLANTS, POISONOUS.

CAMPING, ORGANIZED

Planning and taking a trip with friends or members of your family is just one of the ways you can enjoy camping. Thousands of young people take part in another form of camping. They attend organized camps. You may have heard these spoken of as summer camps.

Organized camping is popular all over the world. In the United States alone there are about 10,000 organized camps.

▶ **DIFFERENT KINDS OF CAMPS**

There are many kinds of camps. Travel and trip camps travel from one camping location to another. Travel camps may go by car, plane, bus, ship, canoe, or sailboat. Or the campers may travel on foot or on horseback. Such experiences usually last at least two weeks and can continue for as long as eight weeks. Because of the nature of the activities and the strain of day-to-day traveling, such camps are usually designed for teenagers.

Family camps are camps that have facilities and programs for the entire family. Some camps provide dining room services, but in others, families prepare their own meals. Housing may range from cabins to campsites for recreational vehicles or tents.

Children's camps are designed to suit children of different needs, tastes, and ages, so there are many different kinds. There are organized camps for boys, for girls, and for boys and girls together. Many are resident camps, in which the campers spend from a week to the entire summer. There are some organized camps, known as day camps, in which the campers spend the day and go home each night.

Some camps are in the mountains; some are on rivers or near lakes. Others are at the seashore. Some are in farm or ranch country. Each of these camps offers different activities. A camp in the mountains might specialize in hiking and backpacking. A seashore camp could teach sailing. A ranch could offer horseback riding.

A camp may offer a special activity that has nothing to do with its location. There are camps for children who have a particular interest in science or music. Part of each day is devoted to these subjects. There are camps for those who wish to learn a foreign language.

In a camp where French is taught, for example, many of the activities of camp are carried on in that language. Some camps offer tutoring in various subjects. There are work camps, in which boys and girls work together all summer on a large project. They might build an entire building, from foundation to chimney, or do conservation projects or gardening. There are also camps for those who have special physical needs, such as children who have diabetes, who are overweight, or who are disabled.

In many organized camps, groups of six or eight campers sleep in small wooden cabins or bunkhouses. Tents may also be used.

Some camps are owned by one person or a group of people and are run as a business. Others are run by nonprofit organizations, such as clubs, churches, and community groups.

An organized camp has a director, who is in charge, and a staff of counselors, who teach different aspects of camping and look after the health and safety of the campers. Usually a counselor lives in the tent or bunk with each small group of campers.

▶ **CAMP ACTIVITIES**

The camp day is arranged so that there are periods of strenuous play and periods of quiet activity. The list of activities may include swimming, canoeing, fishing, tennis, baseball, basketball, soccer, archery, nature study, hiking, riding, weaving, woodworking, pottery making, and painting.

On rainy days, games and handicraft projects may be organized in the camp's recreation hall or some other large building. Special events take place in the course of the camp season, too. The campers may put on musicals, building the sets and making the costumes themselves. Or a group especially interested in mountaineering or canoeing may go on a two- or three-day trip with a counselor. In sailing camps, regattas or races may be held. In ranch camps, there may be rodeos.

It is easy to see why girls and boys who have attended an organized camp cannot wait for summer. Yet camp can mean much more than just fun and outdoor activities. Camp offers a chance to learn new and satisfying skills. It offers a chance to grow in independence and to learn the give and take of living with others.

ARMAND B. BALL, JR.
American Camping Association

CANADA

Canada is the largest country in the Western Hemisphere and the second-largest country in the world. If the early French settlers had known this, they might not have given the country its Indian name. "Canada," or *kanata,* in the language of the Iroquois means "a village"!

Today Canada is a self-governing confederation composed of 10 provinces and two territories. The provinces, from east to west, are Newfoundland (which includes Labrador); the three Maritime Provinces—Nova Scotia, New Brunswick, and Prince Edward Island; Quebec; Ontario; the three Prairie Provinces—Manitoba, Saskatchewan, and Alberta; and British Columbia. The territories are the Yukon Territory and the Northwest Territories.

Canada is a member of the Commonwealth of Nations. Ottawa, Ontario, is the capital city and the seat of the federal government.

▶ THE PEOPLE

The majority of Canadians are of British or French origin. The English-speaking population is larger than the French and is distributed throughout all Canada. In 1969 the Official Languages Act was passed, making French and English the official languages of Canada. All government and legal business is conducted in both languages.

Most French Canadians live in the province of Quebec. But there are also large numbers in New Brunswick, northern and eastern Ontario, and Manitoba. Many descendants of the Acadians, the original *habitants* (early settlers) of New France, live in Nova Scotia and other parts of the Maritime Provinces, as well as in Louisiana, in the United States.

The French-speaking *Québecois* (people of Quebec), in particular, are different from other Canadians in a number of ways. Most of the families are descended from the French

FACTS AND FIGURES

CANADA is the official name of the country.

CAPITAL: Ottawa, province of Ontario.

LOCATION: Northern North America. **Latitude**—41° 43′ N to 83° 07′ N. **Northernmost land point**—Cape Columbia, on Ellesmere Island. **Southernmost land point**—Middle Island, off Pelee Island in Lake Erie. **Longitude**—52° 37′ W to 141° W.

PROVINCES AND TERRITORIES: Alberta, British Columbia, Manitoba, New Brunswick, Newfoundland, Nova Scotia, Ontario, Prince Edward Island, Quebec, Saskatchewan, Northwest Territories, Yukon Territory.

LARGEST METROPOLITAN AREAS: Toronto (Ontario), Montreal (Quebec), Vancouver (British Columbia), Ottawa-Hull (Ontario-Quebec), Edmonton (Alberta), Calgary (Alberta), Winnipeg (Manitoba), Hamilton (Ontario).

PHYSICAL FEATURES: Area—9,976,185 km² (3,851,809 sq mi). **Highest point**—Mount Logan in the Yukon Territory. **Lowest point**—sea level. **Chief rivers**—Mackenzie-Peace, Yukon, Fraser, St. Lawrence, Nelson, North and South Saskatchewan, Churchill, Kootenay, St. John. **Chief mountain peaks**—Mount Logan, Mount St. Elias, Lucania, King, Steele, Wood, Vancouver. **Chief lakes**—Superior, Erie, Ontario, Huron, Winnipeg, Great Slave, Winnepegosis, Great Bear, Nipigon, Athabasca, Manitoba, Reindeer. **Chief bays**—Hudson, Baffin, James, Fundy. **National parks**—Banff (first national park, 1885), Jasper, Waterton Lakes, Wood Buffalo, Yoho, Kootenay, Mount Revelstoke, Glacier, Elk Island, Pacific Rim, Kluane, Nahanni, Pukaskwa, La Mauricie, Forillon, Auyuittuq (Baffin Island), Kouchibouguac, Kejimkujik, Gros Morne, Prince Albert, Riding Mountain, Point Pelee, Georgian Bay Islands, St. Lawrence Islands, Fundy, Prince Edward Island, Cape Breton Highlands, Terra Nova.

POPULATION: 24,343,181 (1981 census).

LANGUAGE: English and French.

RELIGION: Christian—91%, other—9%.

GOVERNMENT: Constitutional monarchy within the Commonwealth of Nations. **Titular head of state**—British monarch, represented by the governor-general. **Actual head of government**—prime minister.

NATIONAL ANTHEM: "O Canada."

MOTTO: *A Mari usque ad Mare* ("From Sea to Sea").

NATIONAL SYMBOL: Maple leaf.

FLAG: Large red maple leaf on a square field of white between two red borders. (On February 15, 1965, this flag replaced the Canadian ensign.)

NATIONAL HOLIDAY: Dominion Day, July 1 (commemorates passing of the British North America Act in 1867).

ECONOMY: Agricultural products—livestock, dairy products, wheat, tobacco, barley, vegetables, flaxseed, potatoes. **Industries and products**—wood pulp and paper, metal smelting and refining, iron and steel, motor vehicles, printing and publishing, sawmills, petroleum refining, meat packing, machinery, aircraft. **Chief minerals**—petroleum and natural gas, copper, nickel, iron ore, zinc, asbestos. **Chief exports**—newsprint, wheat, lumber, metals, chemicals, cars. **Chief imports**—motor vehicle parts, aircraft, automobiles, machinery, chemicals, crude petroleum. **Monetary unit**—Canadian dollar.

who first settled Canada. They have kept the language as well as the religion, culture, and traditions of their forebears. In all the French-speaking parts of Canada, the predominant faith is Roman Catholic. But churches of various branches of the Protestant faith and of many other religions can also be found in the larger cities. Montreal, for instance, has one of the largest groups of Jewish residents in Canada.

The population of Canada increased about 75 percent between the years 1951 and 1981. This great increase resulted not only from the birth of many babies but also from the arrival in Canada of people from other parts of the world. Between the years 1951 and 1981, more than 4,000,000 people immigrated to Canada from other countries. The largest numbers of immigrants have come from the British Isles, Germany, Hungary, Italy, the Netherlands, and the United States. Many of these new Canadians have settled in Ontario and are making their living in that industrial

province. But many families from the Ukraine and other eastern European countries, as well as a number from Finland and the United States, have immigrated to the western provinces. These people are drawn to Canada's far west by the rich farmlands and cattle ranches and by the many jobs connected with the oil and other mineral industries.

The Indian population in Canada also has been increasing in recent years. Today there are some 300,000 Indians, living mainly on about 2,200 reserves throughout the country. If this increase continues, as is expected, there will soon be as many Indians living in Canada as there were when the French explorer Jacques Cartier reached the shores of Newfoundland in 1534.

Most of the 22,500 Inuit (formerly called Eskimo) live in the Northwest Territories and in northern Labrador and northern Quebec. The Inuit are being encouraged to give up their old way of life and to join the fishing and handicraft co-operatives that have been estab-

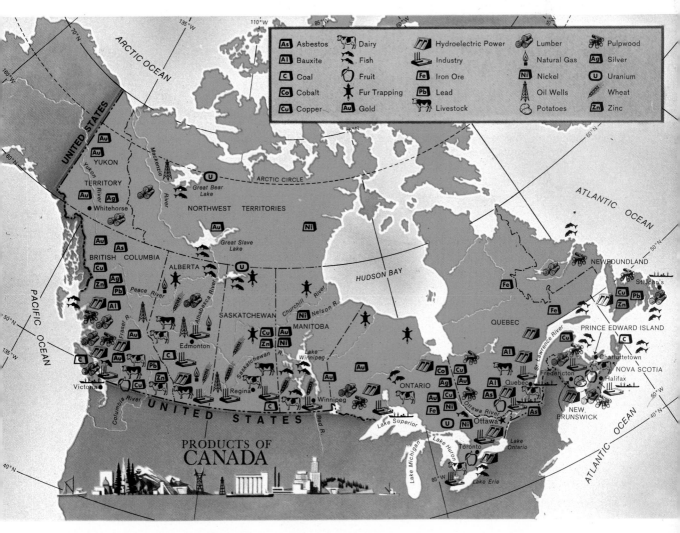

PRODUCTS OF CANADA

lished by the government. Many also are employed at weather and radar stations in the far north.

THE LAND

Canada occupies almost the entire northern half of the North American continent. It is less than half the size of the Soviet Union. But Canada is more than 600,000 square kilometers (230,000 square miles) larger than the United States, including Alaska and Hawaii. It is bordered on the south by the United States and four of the Great Lakes, on the east by the Atlantic Ocean, on the west by the Pacific Ocean, and on the north by the Arctic Ocean.

The population of this enormous land is small—less than one ninth that of the United States. Most of the people live in the southern half of the country, within about 300 kilometers (190 miles) of the Canada–United States border. There are about 40 times as many people living in the Montreal area as there are in the Yukon and Northwest Territories combined. The bleak and barren northland is the home of a few people, including the Inuit, but much of it is uninhabited.

Landforms

Why do so few people live in such a huge country? The main reasons are that much of the land is too rugged for cultivation, and the severe climate makes comfortable living hard.

Canada contains six major landform regions. These are (1) the Appalachian Highlands, (2) the Great Lakes-St. Lawrence Lowland, (3) the Canadian Shield, (4) the Interior Plains, (5) the Cordillera, and (6) the Arctic Islands.

The Appalachian Highlands cover the island of Newfoundland, the Maritime Provinces, and the Gaspé Peninsula of Quebec. Most of the island of Newfoundland consists of low but rugged mountains that have been scarred by the moving ice of eroding glaciers. Numerous bogs and shallow lakes lie in the center of the island. On Avalon Peninsula in southeastern Newfoundland the land is level, and the soil is suitable for cultivation.

Large parts of Nova Scotia and New Brunswick have a rough land surface with many hills and valleys. Prince Edward Island has a level land surface covered with rich, red soil.

The entire island is fertile farmland. Other good farming areas in the Maritime Provinces lie along the southern shores of Northumberland Strait and in the valley of the St. John River off the Bay of Fundy.

The coastlines of Newfoundland and the Maritime Provinces are deeply indented with bays and inlets that provide splendid harbors for the fishing fleets. The famous fishing ground known as the Grand Banks lies off the southeastern coast of Newfoundland.

The Great Lakes–St. Lawrence Lowland lies between the Appalachian Highlands and the Canadian Shield in the southern part of Quebec and Ontario. This is the smallest landform region in Canada, but it is the most heavily populated and the most industrialized. The Lowland is divided into two parts by a wedge of the Canadian Shield that crosses the St. Lawrence River between Ontario and New York State. The wedge contains countless small islands called the Thousand Islands. The broad, level plains in the western part of the region are known as the Great Lakes Lowland. The largest portion of this lowland lies between Lake Huron, Lake Erie, and Lake Ontario. This whole area is excellent farm country. The valley of the St. Lawrence River in the eastern lowland is equally good for farming. Numerous waterfalls from the Laurentian hills provide hydroelectric power for the many industries in this region.

The Canadian Shield, Canada's largest landform region, covers half the land area of the country. This vast expanse of rocks, forests, lakes, and swamps is one of the oldest regions on earth. Some of the rocks that lie on the surface are more than 2,000,000,000 (billion) years old.

The Shield extends over most of northern and eastern Canada, and encircles Hudson Bay like a jagged horseshoe. From the tops of the highest hills the surrounding countryside looks like a sea of rocky waves. Most of the soil in the Shield has been carried away by glaciers of the Ice Age. Farming therefore is difficult. Except for a clay belt in central Ontario and Quebec, little of the region is suitable for cultivation.

Huge deposits of nickel, zinc, copper, and other minerals are located under the surface of the Shield, making the area a treasure chest of mineral wealth.

The Interior Plains extend across large parts of the Prairie Provinces and a segment of northeast British Columbia. They are part of the Great Plains of North America that stretch from the Gulf of Mexico to the Arctic Ocean. The Interior Plains lie on three different levels, rising like steps toward the west. The eastern plains chiefly consist of broad, sweeping prairies and fertile farmlands. This is Canada's wheat belt. Large parts of the area were once covered by ancient glacial lakes. In the southern prairies, where the land is dry, rivers have been dammed to provide irrigation for farms and cattle ranches. In the western prairies the land becomes gently rolling, rising gradually until it merges with the foothills of the Rocky Mountains in western Alberta. Rivers cut through the plains, exposing seams of coal. Rich deposits of crude oil, natural gas, and phosphates lie beneath the plains.

The Cordillera is Canada's westernmost landform. It consists of towering mountain ranges separated by deep valleys and high plateaus. The southwest corner of Alberta, most of British Columbia (including Vancouver Island and the Queen Charlotte Islands), the western part of the Northwest Territories, and all of the Yukon Territory lie within the Cordillera. The most important mountain ranges are the Rocky Mountains and the Coast Mountains. The Rockies form the eastern rim of the Cordillera. The Coast Mountains border the mainland of British Columbia and extend north into the Yukon Territory. Mount Logan in the southwest corner of the Yukon Territory is Canada's highest mountain. Other rugged but lower mountain ranges lie between the Rockies and the Coast Mountains. These interior ranges include the Columbia, the Purcell, the Selkirk, and the Cariboo. The northern section of the Rockies extends into the Mackenzie Mountains in the Northwest Territories. The Columbia Mountains are separated from the Rockies by a remarkable valley known as the Rocky Mountain Trench. The Trench extends for nearly 1,600 kilometers (1,000 miles)—from the state of Montana into the Yukon Territory. It is the source of five great rivers—the Columbia, Fraser, Kootenay, Liard, and Peace.

The western rim of the Cordillera is composed of a submerged mountain chain sometimes referred to as the Insular Mountains. These mountains cover almost all of Vancouver Island and the Queen Charlotte Islands, which lie off the mainland of British Columbia. A natural waterway called the Inside Passage separates the islands from the mainland. Long, narrow inlets, called fiords, extend from the Inside Passage deep into the forest-covered coastal mountains.

The Arctic Islands, or Arctic Archipelago, lie almost entirely within the Arctic Circle. The islands cover more than 1,300,000 square kilometers (500,000 square miles), or about one seventh of the land area of Canada. The largest islands are Baffin, Ellesmere, and Victoria. Baffin is about 507,400 square kilometers (190,900 square miles) in area. Cape Columbia at the tip of Ellesmere Island is Canada's northernmost point. It is about 800 kilometers (500 miles) from the North Pole.

Many peaks on Baffin and Ellesmere islands are more than 1,800 meters (6,000 feet) high. Massive glaciers move slowly down the sides of the mountains to the sea. When they reach the frigid waters, huge chunks of ice break off the edges of the glaciers and form icebergs.

Coal and iron deposits have been found in the barren, ice-covered Arctic Islands, and exploration for oil and gas has begun. But so far the main resources of these lonely islands are furs and fish.

Rivers and Lakes

Canada contains one third of all the fresh water on earth. Many of the rivers and lakes are linked together in large river systems that drain different areas of the country. Geographers call these areas drainage basins. The most important drainage basins are (1) the Atlantic Basin, (2) the Hudson Bay Basin, (3) the Pacific Basin, and (4) the Arctic Basin.

The Atlantic Basin contains the St. Lawrence River, its tributaries, and the five Great Lakes. These waters drain most of southeastern Canada through the Gulf of St. Lawrence into the Atlantic Ocean.

The Ottawa, St. Maurice, and Saguenay rivers are tributaries of the St. Lawrence. Other important rivers in the Atlantic Basin include the Niagara, the Detroit, and the St. Marys. The Niagara River, which connects Lake Erie with Lake Ontario, is the site of the spectacular Niagara Falls. The St. Lawrence

Seaway, the world's longest navigable inland waterway, connects the Atlantic Ocean with the Great Lakes.

Other important rivers in eastern Canada are the Hamilton, which flows across Labrador into the Atlantic Ocean, and the St. John, which flows through New Brunswick into the Bay of Fundy. The famous Reversing Falls is located at the harbor of Saint John where the river meets the bay. The falls is a natural phenomenon caused when the bay waters force the river to reverse its flow at high tide.

The Hudson Bay Basin is the area drained by the rivers flowing into Hudson Bay and by the lakes that connect the rivers. The basin covers the southern half of the Interior Plains and a large part of the Canadian Shield. The main rivers are the North and South Saskatchewan and the Nelson. The North and South Saskatchewan begin in the Rocky Mountains in western Alberta and flow east across the plains until they run together in central Saskatchewan. From this point on, the single Saskatchewan River continues east until it reaches enormous Lake Winnipeg in Manitoba. The Nelson River begins at the northern end of the lake and flows northeast into Hudson Bay. Chief tributary rivers in the Saskatchewan-Nelson system include the Bow, the Oldman, and the Red Deer. The Red River of the North flows into Lake Winnipeg. The Severn and the Churchill flow directly into Hudson Bay. The largest lakes in the system are Winnipeg, Manitoba, and Winnipegosis.

The Pacific Basin is drained by the rivers that begin in the Rockies and the Coast Mountains of British Columbia and flow into the Pacific Ocean. The principal river is the Fraser. It begins in the Rockies and winds southwest until it empties into the Pacific waters at Vancouver. Chief tributaries of the Fraser are the Nechako, Chilcotin, and Thompson rivers. The Kootenay and the Okanagan rivers are major tributaries of the Columbia, which also has its source in the Rocky Mountains. The Columbia River is longer than the Fraser, but most of its course is in the United States. It flows south across the Canada-United States border through the states of Washington and Oregon and finally reaches the Pacific.

Rising in the northern interior of British Columbia are the Stikine, Skeena, and Nass rivers, as well as many lesser streams.

The Yukon River starts in the Yukon Territory and flows northwest through Alaska into the Bering Sea. But it is usually considered a part of the Pacific Basin.

The Arctic Basin is the most extensive of the four major drainage basins. It contains Canada's longest river, the Mackenzie, and its mighty tributaries—the Athabasca, Peace, and Liard rivers. The Great Bear, Great Slave, and Athabasca lakes are also part of the Mackenzie system. Together these waters drain an area of about 2,300,000 square kilometers (900,000 square miles) in the northlands. Eventually they empty into the Arctic seas.

Coastal Waters

Many waters penetrate the coasts of Canada and surround the offshore islands.

Hudson Bay is the largest of these waters; it cuts an enormous part out of the northeastern mainland. Together with James Bay, its southern extension, Hudson Bay covers an area that is more than twice as large as France. The bay is connected with the Atlantic Ocean by Hudson Strait and with the Arctic Ocean by Foxe Channel.

The Gulf of St. Lawrence off the eastern coast is a large inlet of the Atlantic Ocean. The gulf lies at the mouth of the St. Lawrence River and is almost encircled by the Maritime Provinces, the island of Newfoundland, and southeastern Quebec. An extension of the gulf is Northumberland Strait, which separates Prince Edward Island from Nova Scotia and New Brunswick.

The Bay of Fundy is another large inlet of the Atlantic Ocean. The bay lies between Nova Scotia and New Brunswick. Its tides are probably the highest in the world. At high tide the waters of the bay sometimes rise to a height of 15 meters (50 feet).

The Inside Passage, on the western coast of Canada, is a natural waterway that runs from Seattle, Washington, to Skagway, Alaska—a distance of about 1,600 kilometers (1,000 miles). The mountainous coastline of British Columbia is indented by hundreds of fiords leading off from the Inside Passage. Lying between the state of Washington and Vancouver Island is Juan de Fuca Strait.

Typical of the isolated communities that lie within the Arctic Circle is this Hudson's Bay Company trading post, at Spence Bay on Boothia Peninsula.

Oil derricks rise above Alberta's sweeping plains.

A cool, pine-fringed lake in the Rocky Mountains.

Tiny fishing villages called "outports" line the rocky, wind-swept coasts of Newfoundland.

CANADA

In addition to these major coastal waters, there are countless bays, channels, sounds, and other inlets, which give Canada one of the most irregular coastlines in the world. If the jagged coastline were laid out in a straight line, it would measure nearly 97,000 kilometers (60,000 miles), or more than twice the distance around the world at the equator.

Climate

Canada for the most part is a land of long, cold winters and short, moderately warm summers. But within the country's distant boundaries there are many different climates. The differences in climate are caused by (1) the nearness of large bodies of water, (2) the position of the mountains, (3) the direction of the prevailing winds, (4) the altitude, and (5) the latitude.

The climate in the extreme northern parts of Canada—the Yukon, the Northwest Territories, and the Arctic Islands—is bleak and bitter cold. Temperatures in the winter drop many degrees below −18°C (0°F), and in the Arctic Islands darkness lasts for several months. No trees grow in these far-off lands, but lichen and moss cover large surfaces of the frozen plain. Flowers appear in the summer, and for several months the sun does not set. Only 10 to 25 centimeters (4 to 10 inches) of snow fall during the winter months. But the snow remains on the ground and covers the landscape for nine to ten months of the year.

The climate in northern Manitoba, Ontario, and Quebec is less severe but similar to that in the far northlands. This is chiefly because of Hudson Bay. For more than half the year the huge bay is filled with drifting ice. As a result, the surrounding lands remain fairly cold even in the summer.

A more moderate climate prevails in the Maritime Provinces and in southwest Newfoundland. But the coastline is chilled by the icy Labrador Current, which sweeps down from the Arctic. Strong winds from the Atlantic Ocean lash the coasts in spring and early summer, and there is much heavy fog and rain.

The climate of southern Quebec and Ontario is like that of the northeastern United States. The southern part of Ontario is a peninsula bounded by the Great Lakes. It lies in the same latitude as the state of Michigan.

Summers are warm and humid. Winters are cold, with annual snowfalls averaging about 165 centimeters (65 inches). Harrington Harbour, in eastern Quebec, holds a record of more than 500 centimeters (200 inches) of annual snowfall.

The oceans are too far away to influence directly the climate in the midland of Canada. The winters are much colder, and the summers are much hotter in the deep Interior Plains than they are on either coast. The western mountains cut off the rain-bearing winds from the Pacific Ocean. The Prairie Provinces therefore have little rain, and sections of Alberta and Saskatchewan are partly arid. These two provinces are the only ones that do not border on salt water. Snow arrives in the Interior Plains in early November and remains until April. Winter temperatures average about −15°C (5°F) but can drop as low as −34°C (−30°F). Frequently a severe cold wave is broken by a warm wind called the chinook. The chinook is a mass of dry, warm air that descends from the Rocky Mountains. The air loses its moisture in the form of rain on the western side of the mountains. The dry air grows warmer as it sinks down the eastern slopes of the Rockies and across the plains. As a result, the temperature may rise sharply in a few hours, and cattle may nibble the grass under the melting snow.

The climate on the west coast of Vancouver Island and in southwest British Columbia is the mildest—and wettest—in Canada. Weather stations on western Vancouver Island record an average annual rainfall of more than 2,500 millimeters (100 inches). Those on the mainland record an average of more than 1,500 millimeters (60 inches). More rain falls in this area in a single winter month than the Prairie Provinces receive during an entire year. In contrast to the freezing bleakness of the far north, flowers bloom in Vancouver gardens in early March. Very little snow falls along the coast. But the heavy snow that falls in the nearby mountains makes skiing and tobogganing possible during most of the winter.

Natural Resources

Few countries in the world have such an abundance of natural resources as Canada. The most important of these resources are forests, minerals, soils, waterpower, fish, and fur-bearing animals. Not every resource is found in every province, but on the whole the riches of Canada are fairly distributed.

Forests. Canada's forests cover about 4,000,000 square kilometers (1,600,000 square miles) or approximately half of the land surface of the country. Over half of the forests are productive, meaning that they provide the timber that is used for making lumber, pulp and paper, and countless other wood products. Newsprint, for example, is made from pulpwood, and more than 50 percent of all the newsprint in the world is produced in Canada. Quebec is the center of pulpwood production. The wide belt of softwood trees— spruce, balsam fir, tamarack, and others—that supply timber for pulpwood stretches across Canada from the Pacific to the Atlantic.

The forests of British Columbia supply most of Canada's lumber. The most valuable tree in these forests is the towering Douglas fir. Others are the western hemlock, western red cedar, and Sitka spruce.

The forests are valuable in other ways, too. They help prevent erosion of farmlands, provide homes for wild animals, and offer recreation to thousands of people.

Minerals. Canada's wealth of minerals is scattered throughout the country, but the largest mineral concentration is in the Canadian Shield. Copper, iron ore, gold, zinc, lead, silver, cobalt, titanium, and uranium are mined in quantity. Ontario is the world's largest source of nickel, and Quebec produces 85 percent of Canada's asbestos. The mines of Alberta yield an abundance of coal, and Labrador and Quebec are rich in iron ore.

Canada is the world's leading producer of nickel and platinum and the second most important producer of uranium. It ranks third in the production of aluminum, gold, cobalt, and zinc and fifth in the production of lead. The Kootenay district in southeastern British Columbia has one of the most active lead and zinc centers in operation. The aluminum plant at Kitimat in the Coast Mountains is one of the most productive in North America. Vast deposits of crude oil and natural gas lie deep beneath the surface of the Interior Plains. Approximately 11 percent of Canada's oil comes from Saskatchewan. More than 85 percent comes from Alberta. Oil production in Alberta has increased steadily since the oil strike at Leduc field near Edmonton in 1947. The Athabasca tar sands, located along the Athabasca River in northeastern Alberta, contain rich oil reserves. Geologists estimate that these sands contain as much oil as all the known reserves of the world. But the process of removing the thick, tarry oils from the sands is expensive. Two plants are now in operation, and others have been planned.

As a result of the discovery of new mineral locations, new communities have been established. Typical of these settlements is Uranium City in northwestern Saskatchewan. Construction of the town began in 1952. Today Uranium City ranks as a leading uranium production center. It is a busy, bustling frontier town where the people live on streets that bear such names as Nuclear Avenue, Fission Avenue, and Uranium Road.

Soils. Only 7 percent of Canada's total land area contains soils that are rich enough for cultivation. The tundra—that vast area of treeless plains in the far north—consists of barren, weathered rock with hardly any soil covering. The Canadian Shield is almost totally lacking in soils of good quality. Much of it has layers of permanently frozen ground called permafrost. The slopes of the western mountains are too steep and too rugged for soil formation. But in the rest of Canada there are areas that contain good agricultural soils, where farm products are produced in abundance. These areas are the following: the fertile river valleys in southern British Columbia and the Peace River district in the extreme northeast corner of that province; the grasslands that stretch eastward from the Rocky Mountains across Alberta, Saskatchewan, and southern Manitoba; and the Great Lakes-St. Lawrence Lowlands. In addition, good soils exist in the Maritime Provinces around the Bay of Fundy and over the entire surface of Prince Edward Island.

Waterpower. Many of the rivers and lakes of Canada are abundant sources of hydroelectric power. More than 60 percent of the country's electrical energy comes from its waters. They provide the basis for numerous growing industries. The development of Canada's hyroelectric power is still far from complete, but the amount that has been developed has already influenced the economy of the nation.

The rivers of British Columbia, Alberta, Manitoba, and Ontario and Quebec in the Canadian Shield are excellent sources of hydroelectric power. These rivers flow down the sides of mountains or race down rocky slopes and thus create many rapids and waterfalls. Such swift-running water is necessary for the development of power.

The largest hydroelectric plant is at Churchill Falls on the Churchill River in Labrador. This plant serves the mining district around Schefferville and Labrador City. Other major plants are at Niagara Falls and along the Saguenay River in Quebec and Shawinigan Falls near Trois Rivières. Important plants have been built in Manitoba, especially along the Nelson River, and also in northern British Columbia on the Peace River. Other plants, which sell electricity to the United States, are found along the Kootenay and Columbia rivers. There is a huge power development along the west coast of British Columbia near Kitimat. This serves a large aluminum smelter.

Fish. Two of the world's most productive fishing grounds lie off Canada's east and west coasts. One of these—off the southeastern shores of Newfoundland—is the famous Grand Banks. This is a great shelf of submerged land that extends into the Atlantic Ocean for more than 650 kilometers (400 miles). It is a feeding ground for countless schools of cod, haddock, herring, mackerel, Atlantic salmon, and lobster. Fishing the Grand Banks has been a major occupation since the early 17th century.

The coastal waters off British Columbia and the inlets of the Inside Passage are famous for salmon, halibut, and shellfish. Salmon is the most valuable fish in the Pacific fisheries. The salmon catch comprises five species—sockeye, pink, coho, chum, and spring. The salmon run begins in the spring, when the fish return from the ocean to their native streams to spawn and then die. The salmon-fishing season lasts until October. Most of the salmon are caught near the mouths of the streams. Unfortunately, the salmon industry has been seriously affected by the development of hydroelectric power projects along the Columbia River. Efforts to solve the problem include the removal of obstacles, such as landslides, from the streams and the use of fish ladders to encourage the salmon to swim over dams. These dams have made it difficult for the salmon to return to their spawning grounds. Even with such efforts, the salmon runs are decreasing. And the problem, which is due also to overfishing, is still far from being solved.

Canada has taken measures to protect its fishing industry from foreign competition by establishing a limit of 200 nautical miles off its coasts. In this way, Canada also hopes to protect and rebuild some of its depleted fish stocks.

Canada's inland lakes yield great numbers of freshwater fish—trout, whitefish, pickerel, perch, sturgeon, pike, and many others. Altogether, about 900,000,000 kilograms (2,000,000,000 [billion] pounds) of fish and shellfish are taken from Canadian coastal and inland waters every year. Canada ranks as one of the leading fish-exporting countries in the world.

Wild Animals. Today in the vast Canadian wilderness some Indians and Inuit continue to make their living by fur trapping. Fox, raccoon, coyote, and lynx are important furs taken in the wild. Mink are raised on fur farms in almost every province.

The remote, unsettled areas of Canada, as well as the parks and wildlife sanctuaries, abound with a variety of wildlife. Elk, moose, deer, and black and grizzly bears in the huge parks are unconcerned about visitors. Bighorn sheep, standing guard on mountain crags, gaze down with mild curiosity on passing trains and automobiles. Beavers lead their busy lives along woodland streams. Foxes and wolves make their dens in the deep forests. Coyotes, gophers, and many kinds of waterfowl live on the prairies. Herds of caribou and reindeer graze on the carpets of lichen and moss that are scattered over the icy northlands. Buffalo, which once ranged the prairies by the hundreds of thousands, are now protected in Wood Buffalo National Park, in Alberta and the Northwest Territories. Polar bears raise their young on the ice-packed northern coasts, and seals and walruses share the Arctic waters.

▶ **INDUSTRIES AND PRODUCTS**

Canada's pioneer industries were fur trapping, fishing, and logging. These industries are still important, but agriculture and the manufacture of forest products are the chief contributors to the nation's economy today. Mining and smelting are also notable, followed by the development of hydroelectric power.

Agriculture. Ninety percent of Canada's agricultural wealth comes from the Great Lakes–St. Lawrence Lowland and the Interior Plains. Other fertile areas are in the lowlands of the Maritime Provinces and in the river valleys of British Columbia. Parts of the Appalachian Highlands and the clay belt of the Canadian Shield contain small farmlands.

Most grain crops, especially wheat, are grown in the Prairie Provinces. The wheat belt stretches from the Peace River district, in northeastern British Columbia, through Alberta and southern Saskatchewan, into southwestern Manitoba. Saskatchewan is the leading wheat-producing province.

To conserve moisture in relatively dry soil, the same piece of land is not planted every year but is left to lie fallow for one year out of every three. On the dry fringes of the wheat belt, crop growing must rely on dry-farming methods. Some irrigated crops—such as alfalfa, sugar beets, and vegetables for canning—are produced also. The wheat farms in Saskatchewan and the beef-cattle ranches in Alberta often cover large areas.

Farm products worth more than $1,000,000,000 are exported every year to the United States, Britain, and other countries. The reason for the large export is that Canadian farms produce more than is necessary to meet the needs of the Canadians themselves. Many grain crops are grown to provide feed for livestock. The raising of livestock—dairy and beef cattle, sheep, hogs, and poultry—earns more income for the individual Canadian farmer than the sale of grain. The most important dairy-farming areas are in the Great Lakes–St. Lawrence Lowland and in the lower Fraser River valley of British Columbia. The Great Lakes–St. Lawrence Lowland and the southern interior of British Columbia are the chief fruit- and vegetable-growing centers in Canada. Prince Edward Island—Canada's "garden province"—is covered with small farms where vegetables, tobacco, and fruits flourish.

Mining. Canada is a leading world producer of nickel and asbestos. Most of the asbestos is mined in eastern Quebec. The greatest part of the world's nickel comes from the Sudbury mines in Ontario and the Thompson mines in Manitoba. Copper is another important mineral found in Canada. It is produced in mines scattered throughout the southern half of the Canadian Shield, between Saskatchewan and Newfoundland. Geologists believe that Canada contains the largest reserves of uranium on earth. Uranium is produced chiefly around Elliot Lake in northern Ontario, and most of the uranium is exported to the United States. Iron mines extend from northern Quebec into Labrador and west and east of Lake Superior. Most of the iron ore is exported to United States mills on Lake Erie. There are more than 50 active gold mines, mostly in Ontario and Quebec. Zinc and lead also are important. The largest zinc and lead smelter in the Commonwealth is at Trail, British Columbia.

Manufacturing. Canada's many natural resources provide the raw materials used to manufacture countless products. The making of pulp and paper products—especially newsprint—is the leading manufacturing industry. Other important industries include the manufacture of petroleum products and petrochemicals, metal smelting and refining, food and beverage processing, meat packing, and the production of transportation equipment and electrical apparatus. About 80 percent of Canada's manufactured goods are produced in the provinces of Ontario and Quebec.

▶**TRANSPORTATION AND COMMUNICATIONS**

Considering Canada's huge size and small population, the transportation and communications systems are remarkable.

Railways. Canada's first transcontinental railway, the Canadian Pacific, was completed in 1885. This great railway was built to link the eastern provinces with the new province of British Columbia on the western side of the Rockies. Today there are two transcontinental systems, the Canadian Pacific Railway and the Canadian National Railways. The two systems cover almost 72,000 kilometers (45,000 miles). The Canadian National is publicly owned and is one of the largest employers in Canada. Both systems also operate hotels and steamship lines.

In addition to the major rail systems, there are numerous feeder lines. They extend to the

In spring, logs are driven downstream to paper mill.

Magnesium mine (*above*) near the Quebec-Ontario border typifies industrial growth in eastern Canada. Fishing (*right*) is a major industry in the Maritime Provinces. Here a day's catch is being handled.

Wheat fields in the Prairie Provinces stretch to the horizon.

En route to Pacific coast, a Canadian National Railways train skirts lake in Rocky Mountains.

Pontooned planes, called "otter aircraft," carry people and supplies to remote northern areas.

Eisenhower Lock on the St. Lawrence Seaway, the longest inland waterway in the world.

Peace River district in British Columbia and Alberta, to Hay River on Great Slave Lake in the Northwest Territories, to Churchill in Manitoba, and to Schefferville in Quebec. Railways have faced competition from other means of transportation, but they are still vital to the development of natural resources in isolated areas.

Roadways. Although many places in Canada's northlands still cannot be reached by automobile, there is a far-flung network of motor routes in the more settled areas. More than 800,000 kilometers (500,000 miles) of roads stretch from the Atlantic to the Pacific and from southern Ontario to Alaska. The roads range from small gravel side roads to great concrete superhighways. Automobile ferries connect inhabited islands with the Canadian mainland. The Trans-Canada Highway extends from St. John's, Newfoundland, to Victoria, British Columbia—a distance of approximately 8,000 kilometers (5,000 miles). The Mackenzie Highway runs north from Grimshaw, Alberta, to Yellowknife, on Great Slave Lake in the Northwest Territories. Roads starting from Edmonton, Alberta, and the city of Vancouver meet the Alaska Highway at its starting point in Dawson Creek, British Columbia. The Alaska Highway runs through the Yukon Territory to Fairbanks, Alaska. The Dempster Highway opened in 1979. It connects Dawson City in the Yukon to Inuvik in the Northwest Territories. Every year thousands of vehicles travel these scenic highways.

Airways. Canada's two giant commercial airlines are Air Canada and Canadian Pacific. Both are international carriers. Air Canada provides service between major Canadian cities, the United States, the Caribbean, and Europe. Canadian Pacific airliners fly to Japan, Hawaii, Mexico, South America, Australia, and over the North Pole to Europe. Canadian Pacific employs more people than any other Canadian company. Besides the two commercial airlines, there are five regional lines and many small companies. In the far north—off the route of any large aircraft—bush pilots carry mail and supplies to fur trappers, geologists, and other workers. Helicopters are used for exploring and mapping.

Canada's international airports are points of entry for many of the world's great airlines.

The headquarters of the International Civil Aviation Organization and the International Air Transport Association both are located in Montreal.

Overseas Shipping. Every year, more than 90,000 vessels of foreign and Canadian registry sail in and out of Canada's ports and harbors. Montreal and Halifax are the main Atlantic ports. Vancouver, Victoria, and Prince Rupert are the chief ports on the Pacific. Sailing through the St. Lawrence Seaway, oceangoing vessels now can enter the ports of Toronto, Hamilton, Sarnia, and Thunder Bay on the Great Lakes. During the nine months of the year when it is ice-free, the seaway makes it possible for these inland ports to engage in direct overseas trade.

Communications. Despite the distances that lie between the settled areas, Canadians are closely linked by telephone and telegraph and by radio, television, and newspapers. Direct dialing now is in effect between all Canadian cities and towns. The first transatlantic telephone cable—a combined project of Canada, the United States, and Britain—was laid in 1956.

The Canadian Broadcasting Corporation (CBC) operates two radio networks and two television networks. One of each of the networks is in English and the other in French. The CBC is a publicly owned national service, responsible to the federal government. Besides the CBC stations, there are about 300 independent stations operating across the country from Newfoundland to Vancouver Island. The independent stations serve as outlets for the national radio programs. Educational programs are an important feature of the national network, and the CBC News Service maintains news centers in most of the key cities.

A large variety of television programs, both live and taped, are relayed by the CBC and by several independent outlets. The National Film Board produces documentary films for Canadian television.

In the early 1970's, federal legislation was passed requiring that a certain amount of all the material shown on Canadian television and broadcast over the radio should be from Canadian sources exclusively. This ruling about Canadian content has helped to boost the opportunities for Canadian writers, producers, and performers.

Daily newspapers are published in all the major cities. Newspapers in Canada are published in both English and French. A number of papers also appear in other languages.

► EDUCATION

The vast majority of Canadians can read and write. Each province or territory is responsible for the elementary and secondary education of its children. The federal government provides schools for Indians and for children of Armed Forces members serving in Europe.

School attendance is compulsory until the age of 15 or 16, depending on the particular province. Most Canadian schools are co-educational. In the province of Quebec, the school system formerly was divided between Roman Catholic and non-Roman Catholic schools. Roman Catholic schools were predominant. But in 1977, the province enacted a law dividing Quebec schools along language lines instead of religious lines. The school system was re-organized into French-language schools and English-language schools. The law requires the children of most immigrants entering Quebec to attend French-language schools. This new system reflects the recent trend toward French-Canadian nationalism in Quebec. In the province of Newfoundland, children attend schools run by Catholic or Protestant school boards.

Permanent schools have been built recently in lightly populated areas of northern Ontario. These schools replace the mobile classrooms (made of converted railway cars) that were used to take teachers from community to community. There are over 70 schools in the Northwest Territories and 20 schools in the Yukon.

Universities and Colleges

Some 600,000 students are enrolled in Canada's more than 350 colleges and universities. The larger universities offer a wide range of subjects and grant doctorates as well as master's and bachelor's degrees. Teacher training was formerly provided by separate teachers' colleges. But now teachers are trained in colleges of education that are within universities. During the 1960's, community colleges offering a variety of programs were established throughout the provinces. Some institutions are supported by provincial grants, some by both provincial and federal grants, and others by religious orders. Still others rely on private endowment.

The largest university in all Canada is the University of Toronto, which has several affiliated colleges and is noted for its medical school. The Université de Montréal is the largest in French Canada. Laval, in Quebec City, is the oldest French-language university in North America. It was founded as a seminary in 1663. Other important institutions are McGill University in Montreal, also well known for its medical school; Queen's at Kingston, Ontario; and the universities of Alberta, Manitoba, Saskatchewan, and British Columbia.

► CULTURAL ACTIVITIES

For about 300 years most Canadians were too busy building a nation to think about the arts. There was a vast wilderness to explore. There were natural resources to develop, towns to build, and western lands to settle. After the Dominion of Canada was formed in 1867, the scattered provinces still had to be tied together physically, economically, and politically. One by one new provinces joined the federation, and by World War I, Canada was no longer a frontier nation. The people finally had enough time to look at their own culture.

Canadians are now aware that there is a culture shared by all the citizens of their country. This awareness has resulted from a population expansion and the growth of cities across the country. There has also been a great increase in radio, television, and other types of public communication. Even the crafts and customs brought by settlers from Scandinavia, Hungary, the Ukraine, Italy, and other parts of Europe have become part of the Canadian way of life. The National Arts Centre in Ottawa has greatly influenced Canada's cultural development in recent times.

The Canada Council was established by the federal government in 1957, and a fund was set up to aid the arts, humanities, and social sciences. In 1978 the council was divided into the Arts Council and the Humanities and Social Sciences Council. These councils help symphony orchestras, composers, playwrights, choreographers, painters, writers, art galleries, and museums.

Theater and Ballet

In 1953 the director Tyrone Guthrie and businessman Thomas Patterson launched the now famous Stratford Shakespearean Festival in Stratford, Ontario. The Stratford Festival Theatre is built on the banks of the Avon River. In 1962, the Shaw Festival opened at Niagara-on-the-Lake, near Niagara Falls, Ontario. It features the plays of the dramatist George Bernard Shaw.

Montreal is the main center of French-Canadian theater. Le Theatre du Nouveau Monde was the first Canadian group to take part in the annual International Theater Festival held in Paris, France. Another group, Le Patriote, presents contemporary plays in French. Quebec City now has French theater that is comparable in importance to the French theater in Montreal.

The main center of English-speaking theater in Canada is Toronto. Theatrical groups there include the Tarragon Theatre, the Saint Lawrence Centre, the Royal Alexandra Theatre, and the Young People's Theatre, which presents plays for children. The O'Keefe Centre, built in Toronto in 1960, seats 3,200 people. Both English and French companies tour throughout Canada.

The National Theatre School was founded in 1960 in Montreal. Classes are conducted in both French and English. Students receive professional training in acting, stage production, and stage design. Leading Canadian actors and actresses include Genevieve Bujold, Hume Cronyn, Christopher Plummer, Kate Reid, and Donald Sutherland.

Canada has several ballet companies and a national ballet school. The National Ballet of Canada, in Toronto, is the largest company. It performs throughout the world. Les Grands Ballets Canadiens of Montreal, a French company, performs both on the stage and on television. Canada's oldest dance company is the Royal Winnipeg Ballet.

Music

The National Arts Centre in Ottawa opened in 1969. It has a combined opera house and concert hall with 2,300 seats and two theaters. The center has its own symphony orchestra and two theater companies.

Montreal's cultural center is the Place des Arts. Its first building—La Grande Salle, with

A performance of *Twelfth Night* at the Shakespeare Festival at Stratford.

3,000 seats—opened in 1963. The center presents concerts, operas, and symphonies. An addition, built in 1977, provides rehearsal facilities and meeting rooms for the Montreal Symphony.

Canada has many symphony orchestras. In 1978 the Toronto Symphony became the first Western orchestra to visit the People's Republic of China. Choral singing is well represented in Canada. The most prominent society is the Toronto Mendelssohn Choir, which tours the country and goes abroad. There are also annual music festivals in Winnipeg, Stratford, Vancouver, and Montreal. A group called Les Jeunesses Musicales du Canada in Quebec presents music to young audiences, as does the Festival Concert Society in western Canada.

Canadians prominent in the world of music include the conductors Elmer Isler, Nicholas Goldschmidt, and Mario Bernardi and singers John Vickers, Maureen Forrester, and Judith Forst. Other well-known musicians and composers are Maurice Blackburn, Claude Champagne, Gabrielle Charpentier, Harry Freedman, Andre Gagnon, Glenn Gould, Clermont Pepin, Oscar Peterson, Murray Schafer, Harry Somers, and John Weinzweig.

Folk Music. Canada has a rich collection of both traditional folk songs from Britain and France and native folk songs that grew out of the Canadian frontier. Canada's two foremost collectors, Helen Creighton and Edith Fowke, have found many traditional British, Scottish, and Irish folk songs in Ontario and New Brunswick. Nearly 5,000 English-language songs have been found in Nova Scotia. And there are dozens of different versions of the many traditional songs of French Canada, most

The Canadian wilderness is vividly portrayed in Tom Thomson's *Spring Ice.*

of which have been collected by Marius Barbeau. Modern Canadian singers such as Anne Murray and Gordon Lightfoot are steeped in the Canadian folk tradition.

Opera. Canada has five major opera companies. These are the Canadian Opera Company in Toronto, the Vancouver Opera Association in Vancouver, the Edmonton Opera Company in Edmonton, the Southern Alberta Opera in Calgary, and the Manitoba Opera Association in Winnipeg.

Literature

Like writers everywhere, Canadian authors often write about the areas where they grew up or spent a good deal of time. Small prairie towns are depicted in W. O. Mitchell's *Who Has Seen the Wind* and Margaret Laurence's *A Jest of God.* The Ontario countryside is featured in Mazo de la Roche's "Jalna" series and in Stephen Leacock's books. L. M. Montgomery's *Anne of Green Gables* is set in rural Prince Edward Island. Morley Callaghan and Hugh Garner have written about Toronto, and Hugh MacLennan and Mordecai Richler, about Montreal.

The writings of 19th century poets and novelists such as Archibald Lampman, Susanna Moodie, and Ralph Conner were mainly descriptive, focusing on the land itself and on life in the pioneer settlements and growing towns. But gradually the central theme of Canadian literature emerged—the struggle of the individual to survive in a hostile world. This theme has been explored in both French and English by writers as diverse as poets E. J. Pratt, Earle Birney, and Saint-Denys-Garneau; novelists Gabrielle Roy, Roch Carrier, Marie-Claire Blais, Alice Munro, and Marian Engels; and children's author Sheila Burnford.

Another feature of Canadian literature is the versatility of its writers. Margaret Atwood is not only a major novelist but also one of the country's leading poets. Dennis Lee, who is best known for his children's book *Alligator Pie,* is also a poet. Leonard Cohen is at once poet, novelist, songwriter, and performer. Anne Hébert and Earle Birney are acclaimed for their novels as well as their poetry. Poet James Reaney is also an important playwright. Robertson Davies' long career has produced essays both humorous and literary, as well as award-winning plays and novels. Farley Mowat has distinguished himself as a writer of adult nonfiction dealing mainly with the plight of the native peoples and the endangered environment, as well as a writer of books for children such as *Lost in the Barrens* and *The Dog Who Wouldn't Be.* Besides being one of Canada's best-known television personalities, Pierre Berton is the author of several books of social criticism. Berton has also written on aspects of Canadian history, as in *Klondike* and *The National Dream,* a history of the Canadian Pacific Railway.

Painting and Folk Art

Tom Thomson, who died in 1917, influenced the work of a group of young Toronto painters called the Group of Seven. His work *The West Wind* is one of the best-known Canadian paintings. In the 1930's, 40 landscape artists formed the Canadian Group of Painters. Paul Kane painted the western plains, and on the Pacific coast Emily Carr painted Indians and British Columbia forest scenes. Other noted Canadian painters are Alexander Colville and Jack Humphrey in New Brunswick; Jean Paul Lemieux, Paul Emile Borduas, and Jean Dallaire in Quebec; and Jack Nichols and William Ogilvie in Ontario.

The oldest folk art is that of the Indians and the Inuit. Indian art, particularly along the west coast, has included "bird cage" baskets, colorful Chilkat blankets woven of goat's wool and cedar bark, and elaborate totem poles. These crafts have almost died out, but examples of them are found in several museums. The Inuit do carvings of polished gray-green stone and walrus ivory that are much in demand today.

▶CITIES

Until the beginning of the 20th century, most Canadians lived on farms or in small villages. Today more than three fourths of the people live in cities and larger towns. Most of the largest cities are located in the fertile and heavily industrialized Great Lakes–St. Lawrence Lowland. But cities throughout the country are growing, and suburbs are spreading far beyond city limits.

Canada's two largest cities are in the two largest provinces—Toronto, in Ontario, and Montreal, in Quebec. Metropolitan Toronto, with nearly 3,000,000 people, is Canada's largest city. It lies on the northern shore of Lake Ontario and is a busy Great Lakes port. It is Canada's major city for business and

Skyscrapers in Montreal's Place Ville-Marie loom above the Cathédrale Marie-Reine-du-Monde.

finance. Toronto's stock exchange ranks next to New York's in the number of its transactions. Montreal, founded in 1642 by Roman Catholic missionaries, is located on the St. Lawrence Seaway about 1,600 kilometers (1,000 miles) from the Atlantic Ocean. Montreal is the largest port in Canada and one of the world's largest inland seaports. It is also an industrial and financial center. Over 2,800,000 people live in the metropolitan area of this predominantly French city.

Other important cities in Ontario are Ottawa, the national capital; Hamilton; London; and Windsor. Quebec, the capital city of Quebec province, is the unofficial capital of French Canada and a stronghold of French-Canadian life.

Other important eastern cities are the busy seaports of the Maritime Provinces—Halifax, Nova Scotia; Saint John, New Brunswick; and Charlottetown, Prince Edward Island. The port of St. John's on the island of Newfoundland is one of North America's oldest towns.

Vancouver, the huge seaport on the coast of British Columbia, is another major city. Vancouver's magnificent harbor is the second largest in Canada and one of the busiest on

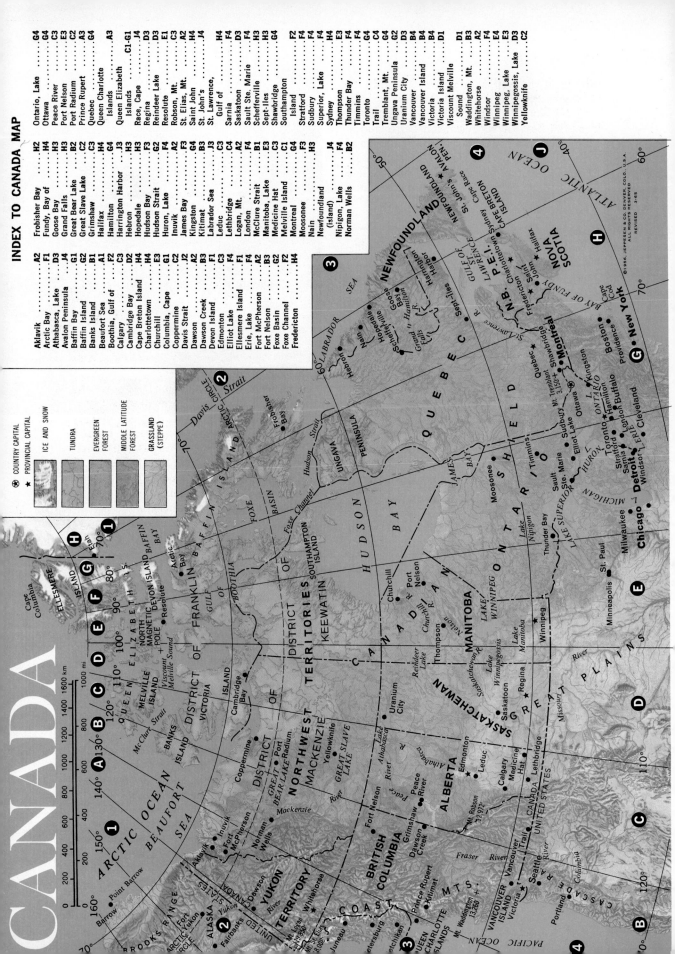

INDEX TO CANADA MAP

Aklavik	A2
Arctic Bay	F1
Athabasca, Lake	D3
Avalon Peninsula	J4
Baffin Bay	G1
Baffin Island	G2
Banks Island	B1
Beaufort Sea	A1
Boothia, Gulf of	F2
Calgary	C3
Cambridge Bay	D2
Cape Breton Island	H4
Charlottetown	H4
Churchill	E3
Columbia, Cape	G1
Coppermine	C2
Davis Strait	J2
Dawson	A2
Dawson Creek	B3
Devon Island	F1
Edmonton	C3
Elliot Lake	F4
Ellesmere Island	F1
Erie, Lake	F4
Fort McPherson	A2
Fort Nelson	B3
Foxe Basin	G2
Foxe Channel	F2
Fredericton	H4

Frobisher Bay	H2
Fundy, Bay of	H4
Goose Bay	H3
Grand Falls	H3
Great Bear Lake	B2
Great Slave Lake	C2
Grimshaw	C3
Halifax	H4
Hamilton	G4
Harrington Harbor	J3
Hebron	H3
Hopedale	H3
Hudson Bay	F3
Hudson Strait	G2
Huron, Lake	F4
Inuvik	A2
James Bay	F3
Kingston	G4
Kitimat	B3
Labrador Sea	J3
Leduc	C3
Lethbridge	C4
Logan, Mt.	A2
London	F4
McClure Strait	B1
Medicine Hat	C3
Melville Island	C1
Montreal	G4
Moosonee	F3
Nain	H3

Newfoundland (island)	J4
Nipigon, Lake	F4
Norman Wells	B2

Ontario, Lake	G4
Ottawa	G4
Peace River	C3
Port Nelson	E3
Port Radium	C2
Prince Rupert	A3
Quebec	G4
Queen Charlotte Islands	A3
Queen Elizabeth Islands	C1-G1
Race, Cape	J4
Regina	D3
Reindeer Lake	D3
Resolute	E1
Robson, Mt.	C3
St. Elias, Mt.	A2
Saint John	H4
St. John's	J4
St. Lawrence, Gulf of	H4
Sarnia	F4
Saskatoon	D3
Sault Ste. Marie	F4
Schefferville	H3
Sept-Iles	H3
Shawbridge	G4
Southampton Island	F2
Stratford	F4
Sudbury	F4
Superior, Lake	F4
Sydney	H4
Thompson	E3
Thunder Bay	F4
Timmins	F4
Toronto	G4
Trail	C4
Tremblant, Mt.	G4
Ungava Peninsula	G2
Uranium City	D3
Vancouver	B4
Vancouver Island	B4
Victoria	B4
Victoria Island	D1
Viscount Melville Sound	D1
Waddington, Mt.	B3
Whitehorse	A2
Windsor	F4
Winnipeg	E4
Winnipeg, Lake	E3
Winnipegosis, Lake	D3
Yellowknife	C2

© 1956, JEPPESEN & CO. DENVER, COLO., U.S.A.
ALL RIGHTS RESERVED
REVISED 3-65

the west coast of North America. Victoria, the capital of British Columbia, lags far behind Vancouver in population but is renowned for its beauty and its mild climate.

Winnipeg, the capital of Manitoba and a transportation center, has a metropolitan population of about 580,000. More than 650,000 people live in the metropolitan area of Edmonton, the capital of Alberta and an important oil center. Calgary, with some 590,000 people in its metropolitan area, is the site of the annual Stampede, a famous rodeo. Calgary is also the administrative center of Alberta's oil industry. In Regina, capital of Saskatchewan, there are more than 160,000 people. Saskatoon, beautifully located high above the Saskatchewan River, is the seat of the provincial university.

▶ **SPORTS AND RECREATION**

The spirit of Canada is very much the spirit of the rugged outdoors. Every summer thousands of Canadians camp among the tall pine, spruce, or birch trees. They take advantage of the numerous lakes and rivers and the long stretches of sandy beaches along the coasts for swimming, sailing, and fishing. In the winter, many Canadians flock to the ski slopes and to the skating rinks that can be found even in the downtown areas of major cities. Cross-country skiing has become increasingly popular.

The system of national and provincial parks has been a major factor in preserving the country's best recreational land for the benefit of the general public. Some parks—such as Quetico Provincial Park in Ontario—are set aside as wilderness areas, where no development is allowed. Other parks have been developed under government supervision and provide camping and boating facilities. Accommodations range from simple cabins to the luxury hotels of Banff and Jasper national parks. In the parks all wildlife is protected.

Canadians know and enjoy most of the sports that are popular in other countries. They are enthusiastic spectators, and many also participate in individual and team sports.

The Canada Games. One of the most important amateur events is the Canada Games. Their purpose is to stimulate interest in amateur sports and to strengthen understanding among athletes. The Games also help prepare athletes for international competition. They are held at various places across Canada on a two-year schedule, alternating winter and summer games.

Ice Hockey. Ice hockey began in Canada, and today it attracts more players and spectators than any other sport. Leagues are organized throughout the country. About 550,000 players are enrolled in the Canadian Amateur Hockey Association. The Allan Cup and the Memorial Cup are awarded annually to the Senior and Junior champions, respectively.

Professional hockey draws thousands of spectators to big-city arenas and millions to their television sets. Excitement is high at the end of the season, when the two best teams of the National Hockey League (NHL) emerge from a series of play-offs to compete for the Stanley Cup. There are seven Canadian teams in the NHL—the Vancouver Canucks, Calgary Flames, Edmonton Oilers, Winnipeg Jets, Toronto Maple Leafs, Montreal Canadiens, and Quebec Nordiques.

Football. Canadian football resembles the United States game but differs in some ways. Amateur football is played in high schools, universities, and various amateur leagues throughout Canada. The professional Canadian Football League (CFL) is composed of nine teams, divided into Eastern and Western conferences. The champions of each conference compete annually for the Grey Cup.

Curling. Curling is constantly attracting more players, both men and women. A tournament, called a bonspiel, is held annually in each province. The winners then compete for the national championship. The Macdonald's Brier, which decides the best men's rink (team), has become one of Canada's outstanding sports events.

Lacrosse. Once called Canada's national game, lacrosse no longer arouses great interest nationally. But it is still played by many amateurs across the country and is enjoying a revival in high schools and universities. Junior and senior teams compete annually for the Minto Cup and the Mann Cup.

Soccer. Soccer has been gaining rapidly in popularity at both amateur and professional levels. There are teams from Toronto, Vancouver, Montreal, and Edmonton in the professional North American Soccer League (NASL).

THOMAS R. WEIR
University of Manitoba

An early map of Canada includes a picture of Cartier and his settlers in the new land.

CANADIAN HISTORY

In 1497 an Italian explorer, John Cabot, set out in an English ship, the *Matthew,* to find a western route to Asia. Instead he discovered a region that would one day form part of Canada. The waters around Cabot's "New Found Land" teemed with fish that could be caught in baskets lowered over the ship's sides. Cabot had stumbled upon the cod fisheries of the Grand Banks—the great underwater plateau off Newfoundland.

Throughout the 16th century fishermen from England, France, Spain, and Portugal ventured in ever-growing numbers to fish in Newfoundland's waters. The French and English set up permanent bases on shore. They salted and dried the cod so it wouldn't spoil on the voyage to Europe. French fishing stations spread out toward the Gulf of St. Lawrence. The English tended to remain in eastern Newfoundland. Sir Humphrey Gilbert, an English explorer, formally claimed that territory for the Crown in 1583.

Trading with the local Indians developed at the fishing stations. In exchange for pots, axes, knives, and other implements, the natives offered various furs, particularly beaver pelts. Soon shiploads of beaver skins were bound for Europe. As the fur trade developed, it spread inland, eventually reaching both the Arctic and the Pacific coasts.

▶ **NEW FRANCE**

On his second trip to the New World in 1535, the French explorer Jacques Cartier sailed up the St. Lawrence River in what is thought to be the first interior exploration of the river. He was stopped by rapids just west of the present city of Montreal. But Cartier's achievement gave France one of the main gateways to the continent. The mighty St. Lawrence River led to the Great Lakes and the heartland of America. The first efforts to set up a colony on the St. Lawrence, in 1541, ended in failure. The hardships of the wilderness, together with troubles at home, discouraged France for a time from further attempts to colonize New France.

Although no settlement was made on what Cartier called the greatest river of Canada, fur traders followed him. Before 1600 the fur trade was flourishing at Tadoussac, on the lower St. Lawrence. The king of France offered generous fur-trading privileges to anyone who founded a permanent colony.

Samuel de Champlain made his first visit to New France in 1603. The next year he returned as part of a fur-trading expedition. In 1605 he founded Port Royal in a region called Acadia. This colony, in a basin off the Bay of Fundy, later became Annapolis Royal, Nova Scotia. Champlain soon saw that Port Royal was not well situated for controlling the rich fur trade along the St. Lawrence. In 1608 he founded Quebec on that river. It soon replaced Tadoussac as the hub of the fur trade and became the heart of New France. Meanwhile restless Champlain kept pushing westward. By 1615 he had canoed up the Ottawa River and reached the Great Lakes. He sent hardy young men into the wilderness to live and trade among the Indians. These adventurers, known as *coureurs de bois* (forest runners), ranged the forests, traded for fur, and cemented French relationships with the Indians.

The Iroquois Almost Destroy New France

Champlain made friends among the Indians, but he also made a powerful enemy— the Iroquois. Champlain helped the Algonkins and Hurons fight the Iroquois, their bitter foes. And the Five (later Six) Nations of the Iroquois were the most powerful tribes in the territory.

The Quebec settlement grew slowly. And when Champlain died in 1635, it still had fewer than 200 inhabitants. Zealous Catholics saw the colony as a springboard for spreading Christianity among the Indians. In 1642 they established Montreal as an Indian mission center. Jesuits braved the wilds, setting up missions for converting the Huron Indians in the unknown reaches of the Great Lakes country.

Meanwhile, the Iroquois had become involved in the fur trade, dealing with Dutch settlers in the Hudson Valley. This pitted the Iroquois against the Hurons, who worked with the French in the race to gain sources of furs. Iroquois and Huron fought to control the flow of trade, and in 1648 the Iroquois launched an all-out war against their rivals. For two years the frontiers were aflame as Iroquois warriors slaughtered the Hurons, destroyed mission villages, and killed Jesuits.

Once they had crushed the Hurons, the Iroquois turned on the French, raiding Montreal and farms near Quebec. The colonists sent desperate pleas for help to France.

New France was barely surviving, and only the king could help.

New France Grows

Before 1660, France had been involved in a series of wars in Europe. But it had won over its enemies and was the most powerful nation on the Continent. King Louis XIV could turn his attention to the plight of his colonies and rebuild his overseas empire. In 1663 he made New France a province of France and appointed a royal governor and an intendant (business manager) for the province. Troops were sent to subdue the Iroquois. Money and settlers were sent to the colony, and an era of peace, plenty, and expansion began.

Jean Talon, the first intendant, guided the colonists in starting industries. Settlers flocked to farms in **seigneuries**. These were large tracts of land along the St. Lawrence granted by the king to **seigneurs** (landlords), who rented them to **habitants** (settlers). Rents were low, and the scheme was so successful that by 1672 more than 6,000 people lived in the St. Lawrence colony.

Long-neglected Port Royal, in Acadia, was also improved, and the fishing industry boomed. Meanwhile, the fur trade, nearly wiped out during the Iroquois War, enjoyed a revival and again expanded westward. French explorers and traders pushed beyond the Great Lakes to the Lake of the Woods, in the southwest corner of present Ontario. To the southwest Father Jacques Marquette and Louis Jolliet traveled to the Mississippi River and journeyed as far as the Arkansas. Robert Cavelier, Sieur de La Salle, who opened the Ohio and the Illinois country, went on to the mouth of the Mississippi in 1682. New western posts like Fort Frontenac (now called Kingston) and Niagara arose. By 1700 the French had built a vast inland empire, stretching from Quebec to the Gulf of Mexico.

War with the English

The expansion of New France brought further conflict. The Iroquois now made war on western tribes, who had allied themselves with the French. They also unleashed their anger toward French settlers and in 1689 destroyed the little village of Lachine, near Montreal. But more important, the Iroquois made an alliance with the English, who had taken New York and the Hudson Valley from the Dutch.

Across North America, English and French interests were locked in a grim rivalry for the future of the continent. In the far north the English followed the route to Hudson Bay, which Henry Hudson had sailed in 1609. By 1670 the Hudson's Bay Company was established. And the French fur traders began to feel the competition of this active rival. English and French fishermen clashed in the Newfoundland and Acadian fishing grounds, regions claimed by the English. To the south, British colonists traded in the vast territories west of the Appalachian Mountains, which the French considered their own.

Early in 1689 the rivalry between the English and the French broke into open warfare both in Europe and in North America. In North America the French and their Indian allies made war on the English and their allies, the Iroquois. The war extended from Hudson Bay, where French and English fur traders contended for mastery, down to the frontiers of New York and New England. The English failed in an attempt to take Quebec by sea. But the conflict had not ended.

In 1702, war erupted again between France and England. It dragged on for 11 years until ended by the Treaty of Utrecht (1713). In that treaty the French gave up the mainland of Acadia (Nova Scotia), most of Newfoundland, and the Hudson Bay territory.

France tried to help New France both militarily and economically in the years that followed. But New France did not grow much during this peaceful period. Its growth was dangerously slow compared to that of the English colonies in North America. Few settlers were willing to migrate from France, and New France's economy depended mostly on the fur trade.

In spite of all the bloodshed of the past, Britain and France had not settled their rivalry for supremacy in the New World. The final struggle took place in the 1750's, when a war called the French and Indian War began. (This war was connected to a war in Europe known as the Seven Years War, 1756–63.) The French fought bravely and skillfully, but the British had much greater resources. At first the French, led by a brilliant soldier, the Marquis de Montcalm, successfully repulsed the English. But the tide turned against the French in 1758. Louisburg fell, then forts Frontenac and Niagara. The powerful British Navy kept reinforcements from reaching New France. In 1759 the British Army under General James Wolfe attacked the main French stronghold of Quebec. In September, Quebec fell during a battle that took the lives of both Montcalm and Wolfe. The next year the remaining French forces surrendered at Montreal. By the Treaty of Paris in 1763, New France was handed over to the British, and a new era began for that vast region.

Richard Montgomery (foreground), an American general, died at the siege of Quebec, 1775.

▶ BRITISH CANADA

The French colony on the St. Lawrence was reorganized in 1763 as the British province of Quebec. But for its approximately 60,000 inhabitants, life stayed much the same on their seigneurial farms and under the spiritual guidance of the Roman Catholic Church. The British rulers took for granted that Quebec, like any other British province in America, would be settled by English-speaking colonists enjoying an English system of government. But a flood of English settlers never went north to Quebec. They preferred to go west rather than to live among their recent enemies in Quebec. But some migrated from New England to Nova Scotia.

A small group of merchants and fur traders went to the St. Lawrence from Britain and the American colonies. Concentrating around Montreal, they soon took over the St. Lawrence fur trade and made it more profitable than ever. Although these Montreal merchants ruled Quebec's commerce, they were too few to transform Quebec into an English-speaking province. The British-appointed governor, James Murray, sympathized with the French Canadians against the merchants, who demanded English law and a legislative body they could control.

Murray's successor, Sir Guy Carleton, did more than sympathize with the French Canadians. He recognized the French character of Quebec. This recognition was made official by the Quebec Act of 1774, in which the British Parliament granted the people of Quebec rights as French Canadians. The act introduced English criminal law but kept French civil law and the seigneurial system. It also recognized the age-old right of the Catholic Church to collect tithes (regular donations) from its members.

Canada During the Revolutionary War

The Quebec Act angered the Montreal merchants. But it added to Quebec the lands westward to the Ohio and Mississippi rivers, the regions in which they did much of their fur trading. Resentment against Carleton's measure spread to the 13 original British colonies. The colonists now saw the West they wanted to settle as part of a French-speaking Catholic province under the French law and land system. American colonists listed the Quebec Act among the Intolerable Acts, which led to the Revolutionary War in America. Early in that war they tried to take Quebec. But Carleton successfully defended the city and defeated the Americans during the winter of 1775. British sea power prevented further American attacks. The presence of the Royal Navy, based at Halifax, Nova Scotia, also helped prevent New Englanders there from joining the American cause.

Factors other than the presence of the Royal Navy kept Canadians out of the Revolutionary War. Canadians in Newfoundland and Hudson Bay were too far from the trouble to get involved in it. In Quebec the French Canadians stayed quiet largely because of the Quebec Act, which the Americans had loudly denounced for favoring the French and the Catholics. The Catholic French Canadians were not attracted by the thought of being absorbed into a large Protestant, English-speaking republic. The Montreal merchants knew that their fur trade depended on the British market. The Americans were also their rivals for the West. The colonists in Nova Scotia wanted to remain neutral in the war. But they found themselves increasingly dependent on Britain for trade. By the time the conflict ended, they were firmly on the British side.

Britain finally recognized the independence of the United States in 1783. Some 40,000 loyalists—people who had remained loyal to the king during the Revolution—fled to Canada. About 30,000 of these took the sea route to Nova Scotia. So many of them moved to the open lands across the Bay of Fundy, near St. John, that a separate province, New Brunswick, was set up in 1784. The remaining 10,000 fleeing loyalists marched overland to Quebec province. They settled around Lake Ontario, near Niagara, and on the upper St. Lawrence, beyond the French-occupied areas. In 1791 this influx brought on the division of the St. Lawrence Valley into two separate provinces. To the west was English-speaking Upper Canada, later to become Ontario, with the English law and land system its settlers desired. In the east was Lower Canada, mainly French in language and tradition, with its French laws and the rights granted by the Quebec Act.

Portrait of the great explorer Sir Alexander Mackenzie.

Farms Forests, Fish, and Furs

By 1800 the British colonies in America consisted of Upper and Lower Canada, the three coastal, or Maritime, provinces, and Newfoundland. To the west stretched a vast, untamed territory known simply as the Northwest. The colonies were thriving, especially Upper Canada, where many American frontier farmers had followed the loyalists and settled on the fertile land. By 1812 there were some 90,000 people inhabiting this rich region, most of them engaged in wheat farming.

The splendid pine forests of the Ottawa Valley provided timber for the growing lumber industry. Timber was sent down the river by raft to the ports of Montreal and Quebec for shipment overseas. Wheat and flour were shipped to British markets. Lumbering also gained importance in New Brunswick. Farming flourished on Prince Edward Island. Fishing was the mainstay of Nova Scotia and Newfoundland. Lumber was so plentiful that the shipbuilding industry grew in Nova Scotia. Soon Canada was involved in a prosperous trade with the British West Indies. Sturdy Nova Scotia schooners sailed the seas to many ports, carrying dried codfish, tanned hides, and other products, which were exchanged for rum, molasses, and sugar.

In the broad land northwest of the Great Lakes, the fur trade ruled supreme. Since the 1780's the leading Montreal fur merchants had pooled their interests in the North West Company to carry on an inland trade. The members of this St. Lawrence company—Nor'-Westers—as they were called—competed for western furs with the older Hudson's Bay Company. The older company kept fairly close to its posts around the great bay. But the Nor'Westers pressed forward from their western base at Fort William, on Lake Superior. They went beyond Rupert's Land, an area claimed by the Hudson's Bay Company. They reached the distant Athabaska country and even across the Rockies to the Pacific slopes.

In 1789, Nor'Wester Alexander Mackenzie went down the river that bears his name to the Arctic. Four years later he traveled by way of the Peace and Fraser rivers to the Pacific. Indeed, Mackenzie, Simon Fraser, and David Thompson explored much of the western half of British North America in the service of the North West Company. The Hudson's Bay Company also began an aggressive westward advance. Backed by the Hudson's Bay Company, Lord Selkirk even founded a little settlement on the plains at the Red River in 1812. This settlement would grow into Canada's first western province, Manitoba. But there was fierce competition between the two fur companies until 1821, when they merged under the name Hudson's Bay Company.

Earlier, the War of 1812 between Britain and the United States had broken out in the east. Forces from the United States tried to invade Canada at several points. They were stopped by a few regiments of British regulars, helped by a combination of loyalists, French-Canadian soldiers, fur traders, and Indians. Many Americans who had settled in Upper Canada fought against their former country. They felt that their own lands and properties were in danger. They were Americans no longer—they were Canadians.

▶ SELF-GOVERNMENT AND CONFEDERATION

After the war of 1812, another era of progress began for Canada. In the years 1815–50, almost 1,000,000 immigrants arrived from Britain to settle in the Canadian colonies. Together with the great migration came an upsurge in wheat production and in the lumber industry. Steamships plied the rivers and lakes. Canals were dug to improve the St. Lawrence waterways. On the Atlantic coast the Maritime provinces enjoyed tremendous prosperity as the days of the sailing ships reached their highest point. Vessels built in Nova Scotia roamed the seas. Some of the world's finest clipper ships were launched from the New Brunswick shipyards.

But the rapid growth of the country brought with it many problems. Now that the colonies were doing well, the people demanded more say in the government. These demands became so insistent that brief rebellions erupted during 1837 in both Upper and Lower Canada. William Lyon Mackenzie led the Upper Canada rebellion, but it never gained popular support. The insurrection in Lower Canada led by Louis Joseph Papineau had the sympathy of French Canadians. But it was opposed by the church, and it soon collapsed.

The two uprisings caused the British to send John George Lambton, first earl of Durham, with orders to investigate the causes of the discontent. In 1839, Lord Durham's report recommended that the colonists be given control of their own affairs by being granted responsible self-government. He also recommended that the two Canadas be united in one province, which was done in 1841. But it took nearly 10 years until responsible government was fully established, largely through the work of such leaders of the Reform and Liberal parties as Robert Baldwin and Louis Lafontaine, in the Province of Canada, and Joseph Howe, in Nova Scotia.

The 1850's were marked by another era of prosperity. New avenues of trade were opened by the Reciprocity Treaty of 1854 with the United States. At the same time a railroad-building boom exploded throughout Canada. By 1860 the Grand Trunk Railway ran across the province of Canada, and there was constant talk of an Intercolonial Railway, serving as a link to the Maritime provinces and their Atlantic ports.

This helped raise the question of a general union of the colonies, which might be able to afford great railways. Quarrels between French and English in Canada also called for a better form of union. Thus at Charlottetown in September, 1864, Canadian and Maritime representatives discussed a plan for a broad federal union called a confederation. They agreed, and the plan was fully worked out at a large conference in Quebec in October. But it ran into strong opposition in the Maritimes, where local provincial loyalties were strong. Prince Edward Island and Newfoundland pulled out completely. Then, in 1866, the United States ended its 12-year-old Reciprocity Treaty. The provinces had to draw together to find new trade among themselves, and the Maritimes wanted the Intercolonial Railway that was promised with Confederation. The plan went through at last. In 1867 the British North America Act was passed. Upper and Lower Canada became Ontario and Quebec. These two provinces were united with Nova Scotia and New Brunswick to found the modern Canadian nation.

▶ THE CANADIAN NATION

After Confederation, the federal government for years was in the hands of John A. Macdonald, one of Canada's greatest prime ministers and nation builders. His first task was to complete the Confederation. In the east he brought in Prince Edward Island in 1873. (Newfoundland did not join until 1949.) In the north and west his government carried through the transfer to Canada of the lands owned by the Hudson's Bay Company. This was accomplished by 1870, and the next year British Columbia was added to the union. But in the Red River colony in present-day Manitoba, many inhabitants objected to being handed over to Canada in this transfer of land. They wanted a choice in the matter. For that reason they backed Louis Riel, leader of the métis (people who had both French and Indian ancestors), in a movement to block the transfer. It was scarcely a rebellion. All Riel and his supporters wanted was a chance to make terms for the colony's entry into Canada. The result was that the Red River colony was raised to full provincial status as the province of Manitoba. Unfortunately, during this Red River uprising, Riel had executed a Canadian, Thomas Scott, who had resisted his authority. That act had in it the seeds of future troubles.

Building the Canadian Pacific

Macdonald's next task was to link and fill in this huge but half-empty Canadian union by building a railway to the Pacific. Serious scandal in the granting of a charter for the new Canadian Pacific Railway Company drove him and his Conservative Party from office in 1873. The Liberal government was able to build only bits and pieces of the railway line. When Macdonald came back to power in 1878, it was barely started.

The next few years saw the railway go forward under great difficulty—partly because the economy was depressed between 1874 and 1879. In all Canada there were only about 4,000,000 people to support one of the world's longest railroad lines. Great natural obstacles created engineering problems that had to be overcome. These obstacles included the muskeg swamps and rock above Lake Superior and the walls of western mountains beyond the plains. But the will of Macdonald and the energy of Cornelius Van Horne, the builder, kept the Canadian Pacific Railway pushing ahead. It was finished late in 1885 just as new calamities beset Canada.

The Northwest Rebellion of 1885

The Indians and métis of the Saskatchewan Valley had worried as settlement moved westward. Many of these people were hunters, and they feared for their way of life. Once again they turned to Louis Riel. This time he led them in a bloody uprising known as the Northwest Rebellion. Troops were rushed out to put down the rebellion and restore order. Riel was sentenced to death for his acts, and Canadian opinion was divided over the sentence. In Quebec the people saw Riel as a French-Canadian hero, the champion of the downtrodden, French-speaking métis. In Ontario, Riel was looked upon as a traitor and the murderer of Thomas Scott. There, the sentence was thought to be just. The execution of Riel late in 1885 left a deep scar in French-Canadian feelings.

The Riel affair, along with the continuing economic depression, strained Canadian unity. Between 1885 and 1896, Canadian politics centered on conflicts between the central government and assertive and dissatisfied provinces. Economic difficulties increased the demands for more provincial rights. The Canadian Pacific Railway did not attract much traffic because too few settlers went west. Partly as a result, the Conservatives lost power to the Liberals in the election of 1896.

The Golden Age of Wilfrid Laurier

Strangely enough, under Wilfrid Laurier, a brilliant French Canadian, the Liberals continued Macdonald's policies. Montreal and Toronto factories boomed. Settlers flowed to the plains over the Canadian Pacific Railway. Their huge new grain crops went east to market. Laurier's government even backed two new transcontinental railways. In 1905, two new western provinces—Alberta and Saskatchewan—were created. Large-scale mining developed in northern Ontario, Quebec, and British Columbia. Between 1896 and 1914, hydroelectric plants and paper mills arose in central Canada. The city of Vancouver grew rapidly on the Pacific coast. So did Winnipeg, Edmonton, and Regina on the prairies. Some 2,500,000 immigrants entered Canada from Europe and the United States.

A change also took place in Canada's foreign relations as Laurier tried to increase Canada's control over its foreign affairs. Laurier's party lost power in 1911. But Robert Borden, his Conservative successor, did not change the trend toward more Canadian activity in foreign affairs. Under Borden's leadership, Canada entered World War I (1914–18). Borden won for Canada the right to sign the Treaty of Versailles (1919), which ended the war, and to join the League of Nations. Canada had found its place among the nations of the world.

Depression, War, and Peace

Borden's policies in Canada itself were less successful. The French Canadians had opposed the military draft, and this opposition left a deep split between the English and the French. Borden retired in 1920, and the Liberals came to power the next year. It was the task of the new Liberal prime minister, Mackenzie King, to re-establish national unity. King was an unusually skillful politician. He accomplished this task over a career that lasted until 1948. King also advanced Canada's status within the British Empire. In 1926, the dominions of the empire (including Canada) were recognized as free and equal partners in what is now the Commonwealth of Nations. The British Parliament passed the Statute of Westminster in 1931, making Canadian independence a practical reality.

Like most other countries, Canada was shaken by the depression of 1930–35. Farmers were hurt by low wheat prices and a severe drought. Industrial workers were also affected, and unemployment was widespread.

When World War II broke out in September, 1939, Canada rallied to Britain's side. The Canadian war effort was a great one. Canadian troops participated in the Sicilian and Italian campaigns and in the Normandy invasion. The Navy patrolled the North Atlantic convoy routes and fought desperate battles with lurking Nazi U-boats. In the air, Canadian pilots flew missions from the Battle of Britain in 1940 until the last bombs fell on Berlin in May, 1945.

Canada also made a great effort economically during the war, and tremendous industrial development took place. Mackenzie King's government prevented disunion of the kind that had occurred after World War I.

Following the war, Canada enjoyed a period of great prosperity. Rich deposits of oil, natural gas, uranium, and iron ore were discovered and developed. Canadian industry flourished, and the national government (still Liberal) was strong and confident. Under Louis S. St. Laurent, who succeeded Mackenzie King, Canada joined the North Atlantic Treaty Organization. At the same time, St. Laurent's government promoted the St. Lawrence Seaway and the development of hydroelectric and nuclear power. Canada received more than a million immigrants.

In 1957, the St. Laurent government was defeated. The Progressive Conservative Party (formerly the Conservative Party), led by John G. Diefenbaker, took power. During this period, economic development started to slow down. There was growing unrest in the French-Canadian province of Quebec, where a separatist movement developed. The separatists demanded that Quebec break away from Canada and form an independent French-speaking nation. The Liberals regained power under Lester B. Pearson in 1963. Pearson tried to deal with the problem of Quebec. He tried to show that reasonable demands by the French-speaking people of Quebec could be satisfied within a united Canada. Pearson also strengthened Quebec's representation in his own cabinet and party.

One of Pearson's French-speaking ministers, Pierre Elliott Trudeau, succeeded him as prime minister in 1968. Trudeau's aim was to prove that French-Canadian culture could flourish in a united Canada. He worked for a bilingual and bicultural country.

In 1976, the separatist Parti Québécois (Quebec Party) won control of the government of Quebec. The party promised to hold a referendum in which the people could vote on the question of Quebec's future. Meanwhile, the Trudeau government, weakened by economic problems, was defeated in an election in May, 1979. A Progressive Conservative government led by Charles Joseph (Joe) Clark came to power but was soon defeated in Parliament. In a federal election held in February, 1980, Trudeau and the Liberals regained power. Then, in May, the people of Quebec voted against separation from Canada.

But relations between Quebec and the federal government remained strained. The oil-rich western provinces also demanded more power. And less prosperous provinces, such as Nova Scotia, sought greater federal aid. Trudeau was unable to resolve completely the problem of how to share power between the provinces and the federal government. But he did achieve one of his major goals—a truly Canadian constitution.

Canada had enjoyed self-rule since the passage in 1867 of the British North America Act, which served as Canada's written constitution. But all amendments to the act had to be approved by the British Parliament because the provinces and the federal government could never agree on a formula for amending the constitution in Canada. After a long struggle, the federal government and all the provinces except Quebec agreed on a revised constitution. It provided for future amendments to be made in Canada alone. The British Parliament approved the Canada Act (which includes the revisions to the constitution) in March, 1982. In April of that year, Canada finally gained full authority over its own constitution.

The government of Quebec, still officially separatist, was unhappy. But Quebec soon turned its attention to a worsening economy. Other provinces did the same, as economic problems once again became an important political issue.

J. M. S. CARELESS
University of Toronto
Reviewed by ROBERT BOTHWELL
University of Toronto

The Canadian Parliament meets in this building on Parliament Hill in Ottawa, Ontario.

CANADIAN GOVERNMENT

The government of Canada is a federation that was established in 1867. In some ways it is similar to the federal union of the United States. The federal government of Canada takes care of national business, such as defense, trade, and international relations. Below the federal government are the ten provinces. Each province has its own government to take care of local matters such as highways, power, lands and forests, and education. There are also two sparsely populated territories in the north—the Yukon and the Northwest Territories. They are governed by councils whose members are elected by the people.

▶THE CONSTITUTION

Because Canada has a parliamentary system of government, much of its constitution is unwritten and based on custom. A written document, the British North American Act of 1867, provided the framework for the federation. This document (now called the Constitu-

tion Act of 1867) could be amended only in Britain. The Canada Act of 1982, passed by the British Parliament, gives Canada full authority over its constitution. In a section called the Constitution Act of 1982, it also sets out revisions to the constitution.

Among the revisions is the Charter of Rights and Freedoms. It guarantees broad rights that Canadians have long enjoyed, such as freedom of speech and worship and the right to due process of law. It also lists specific rights, such as the right to use—and receive education in—English or French. The revised constitution also affirms the rights of Canada's native peoples. It provides for equalizing public services between the richer and poorer provinces, and it strengthens provincial ownership of natural resources. The amending process is complicated. But in most cases, amendments must be approved by the Canadian Parliament and seven provinces that together contain at least half the population.

THE CENTRAL GOVERNMENT

Canada is a constitutional monarchy with a parliamentary system of government copied from that of Britain. The official head of state in Canada is Queen Elizabeth II of Britain, who is also Queen of Canada. The governor-general is the Queen's personal representative in Canada and the official head of the Canadian Parliament. But the governor-general has very limited powers.

The federal Parliament in Canada is made up of two houses, the House of Commons and the Senate. The head of government is the prime minister, who chooses a cabinet to help run the government. Every cabinet member is expected to be a member of Parliament. The system of government in Canada is often called responsible government. This is because the cabinet sits in Parliament and is directly responsible to it. The cabinet holds power only as long as a majority of the House of Commons ''has confidence'' in it (that is, votes with it).

The Houses of Parliament

The Canadian Senate has 102 members. Senators represent entire provinces, with the exception of those from Quebec, who represent districts of the province. Each province has a set number of senators. Canadian senators are not elected. They are appointed to serve until age 75 by the governor-general on the advice of the prime minister. The Canadian Senate generally does little more than give advice and make minor changes in bills.

The House of Commons is much more important than the Senate. Members of the Commons are elected directly by the voters. General elections must be held at the end of every five years. But they may also be held whenever the issues demand it. Parliaments are usually dissolved before the full five-year period expires. When a government loses its majority support in a general election, a change of government occurs. If a government is defeated by a ''no confidence'' vote in the Commons—which seldom happens—an election is usually held soon afterward to allow the voters to choose a new government.

Elections

Before each election a list of all eligible voters is drawn up. On election day the voters go to the nearest poll, or voting place. Behind a screen they mark an X on the ballot paper beside the name of the person they wish to elect. The ballot paper is then folded and dropped into a sealed box, which is not opened until the votes are to be counted. By voting for candidates of the political party of their choice—the Liberal, Conservative, or any of several smaller parties—Canadian voters determine which party will run the government until the next elections are held.

Canada is governed by the party that wins a majority of parliamentary seats in an election. The leader of that party becomes the prime minister. The governor-general asks the victorious leader to form a government by selecting a cabinet from the leader's own party. The party with the second largest number of seats is called Her Majesty's Loyal Opposition. If no single party gets a majority, the party with the largest number of elected seats must get one of the smaller parties to vote with it in supporting a prime minister and running the government.

PROVINCIAL GOVERNMENT

Canada's provincial legislatures, or parliaments, work very much like the federal Parliament. But the provinces all have one-house legislatures. Therefore, they have no upper house equivalent to the federal senate.

The Queen's representative in each province, called the lieutenant governor, is appointed by the federal government. In each province the system of responsible government, political parties, elections, cabinet ministers, and civil services is almost the same as in the federal government.

MUNICIPAL GOVERNMENT

Below the provincial government comes the third type of government in Canada—municipal government. The municipal government deals with local problems, such as water supply, schools, and snow removal. There are two basic kinds of municipal government—urban (for cities, towns, and villages) and rural (or country) municipalities, which are called counties, townships, parishes, or districts. Each municipality is governed by a council and a mayor, or reeve, elected every year or second year. Municipalities have their own civil service.

THE COURTS

In the parliamentary system of government, the executive branch (the cabinet) and the legislative branch (the parliament, or assembly) are really combined in one body, because members of the cabinet are also members of parliament. The third branch of government (the judiciary, or system of law courts) is separate from the executive and legislative branches. All judges in Canada are appointed by either the federal government or the provincial governments.

There are two main types of laws administered in Canadian courts—criminal laws, which cover crimes affecting persons, and civil laws, which are concerned with such matters as debts and ownership of land. Criminal laws can be made only by the federal Parliament, and these laws form the criminal code that applies to all parts of Canada. Civil laws are passed mostly by the provincial legislatures, and they may be slightly different in different provinces. In Quebec, French civil law is used, but the other provinces follow English civil law, which is quite different from the French.

The most important court in Canada is the Supreme Court, established in 1875. It is a federal court that hears appeals and also decides disputes between the federal and provincial governments. The Federal Court of Canada, formerly the Exchequer Court, deals with cases involving money, taxes, trademarks, and other such matters. A branch of this court is the Admiralty Court, which decides cases concerning ships or shipping.

Each province has its own supreme court, sometimes called the Court of Queen's Bench. Provincial supreme courts hear appeals from lower courts. But important cases often go directly to the supreme court without being tried in lower courts. Below these provincial supreme courts are the division courts, which try only civil cases, and the circuit courts (also called county or district courts), which can try all less important criminal or civil cases within their county or district. Finally, at the bottom of this pyramid of courts, we find the magistrates, or justices of the peace, who hear minor cases.

A member of the famous Royal Canadian Mounted Police.

LAW ENFORCEMENT

The famous Mounties—the Royal Canadian Mounted Police—are the police of the federal government. They work in all parts of Canada. Except in Ontario and Quebec, which have provincial police, the Mounties also enforce provincial laws. They even enforce municipal laws in towns that do not have their own police.

Most cities and larger towns have their own police to keep law and order within the boundaries of the municipality. Small villages may have only one constable. But in great cities like Montreal and Toronto, the police departments employ thousands of men and women, including experts in special fields of crime detection.

JOHN S. MOIR
University of Toronto

See also PARLIAMENTS; PRIME MINISTER.

CANADIAN ARMED FORCES

The Army is the oldest service in Canada. It began with the arrival of the first French colonists in Canada. Both Port Royal in 1605 and Quebec in 1608 were rudely fortified with a stockade, moat, and several cannon. In 1627 Governor Montmagny enrolled the people of Quebec in a home guard. This force was the forerunner of the Canadian Armed Forces.

The enemy during the first years of Canada's existence was the Iroquois Confederacy. By becoming friendly with the Hurons and Algonkins, Samuel de Champlain, the father of Canada, involved his country in an Indian war that continued on and off for nearly a century. To meet the Iroquois scourge, the Canadians organized home guards in Quebec, Three Rivers, and Montreal, the three principal settlements.

When Canada came under the direct control of France in 1663, a regiment of regular troops, the Carignan-Salières regiment, was sent to Canada. After defeating the Indians, the regiment returned to France. Four companies, however, remained in Canada. These troops, because they were administered by France's Department of Marine and Colonies, became known as the Marine Infantry. In 1672 a militia was organized. Because the population was scattered, the basic unit was the company rather than the regiment. There was usually a militia company, under the command of a captain, for each parish. All able-bodied men in the parish were liable for service.

Both the Canadian Militia and the Marine Infantry fought in the various wars against the Iroquois and the Anglo-American colonists of New England, New York, and Virginia. Copying the tactics of the Indians, the Canadians became adept in the war of raids and ambushes. Canadian operations were marked by speed, physical endurance, and individual initiative.

In the Seven Years War between Britain and France in North America, the Canadians bore the brunt of the fighting against Edward Braddock and Sir William Johnson in 1755. But when both the British and French sent reinforcements of regulars to the American colonies, the character of the war changed.

A Canadian soldier, taking part in the U.N. peacekeeping mission in Cyprus, patrols a rooftop.

Militiamen took part in the battle at Oswego (1756) and Ticonderoga (1758), won by the French, and Louisbourg (1758) and Quebec (1759), won by the British. But in all these battles, militiamen were in the minority. The battles were largely engagements between the French and British regular troops sent in from overseas.

Helping the British

When the Indian Rebellion led by Chief Pontiac occurred in 1763, the British appealed to the militia to provide troops for the suppression of the Indians. During the American Revolution, a few Canadian militia helped defend Quebec against the assault by generals Richard Montgomery and Benedict Arnold in 1775. Others accompanied John Burgoyne and Barry St. Leger on their offensive against the Americans in 1777. However, the majority of Canadians preferred neutrality.

After the conclusion of peace between Britain and the American colonies in 1783, the several British North American provinces reorganized their militia forces. There were some differences in the militia bills of the various provinces, but fundamentally they were the same. They required all able-bodied men between 16 and 60 to enroll and undergo training. At the same time fencible (defensive) regiments were formed in New Brunswick, Nova Scotia, Newfoundland, and Lower and Upper Canada. These units were in many ways similar to the old Marine Infantry. They were regular troops, whose task was to supplement the regular British garrisons in North America.

Canadian militia and fencible regiments took part in the War of 1812. The British regulars did most of the fighting, but militia and fencibles fought in almost every engagement of the war.

Federation

After the War of 1812, the Canadian defense forces changed considerably. The fencible regiments were disbanded, and the militia was allowed to fall into disorder. Militiamen were mustered (called together) only once a year, and even then the men only talked and drank and did no training. Therefore the more serious men began to form volunteer units and to do their own training. The change from a compulsory to a volunteer militia received official recognition in the Militia Act of 1855. The new volunteer regiments were quite popular, and their numbers grew rapidly.

When the various British North American provinces came together in a federation in 1867, the administration of the armed forces was given to the central government. In 1871 the British garrison regiments withdrew from Canada. To take their place, the Canadian Government authorized the raising of Canadian regular forces.

The newly organized forces were called upon to show their mettle in 1885 at the time of the North West Rebellion. The Canadians suppressed the Indians and métis after little more than a month's fighting. In 1899 Canadian troops were sent to South Africa to assist the British against the Boers.

The World Wars

At the outbreak of war between Great Britain and Germany in 1914, Canadian troops were sent overseas. The existing militia organization was not used. Instead the minister of militia and defense authorized the formation of a number of special battalions. These troops took part in the great battles in Flanders and Ypres (1915), Somme, Vimy Ridge, and Passchendaele (1917) and in the fighting of the last 100 days (1918). The Canadian Army Corps, under Sir Arthur Currie, resisted all efforts to use Canadian troops as reinforcements for British divisions.

During the years between World Wars I and II, little change was made in the Canadian Army, except to bring it into line with new technical developments.

When war began again in 1939 between Great Britain and Germany, Canada immediately sent troops to England. On this occasion the existing militia and regular regiments were mobilized. A Canadian military headquarters was established in London, and two Canadian corps were formed into the First Canadian Army under Lieutenant-General A. G. L. McNaughton and, later, General H. D. G. Crerar. Canadian troops took part in the landing in Sicily, 1943, the campaign in Italy, 1943–4, the Normandy landing (1944), the clearing of the English Channel coasts of France and Belgium (1944), and the liberation of Holland (1945).

▶ THE NAVY, 1763–1945

During the Seven Years' War, both French and English built ships of war on Lake Ontario. In neither case, however, were these ships of sufficient size to form an independent naval force. They were merely assisting the French and British armies in North America.

After the defeat of the French in 1763, the British Government resolved to maintain naval control of the Great Lakes. Orders were issued forbidding the building of any private vessels for service on the Great Lakes. Only government vessels that could serve as both cargo vessels and ships of war were allowed to sail. This government monopoly was known as the Provincial Marine. At the start it was under the control of the British Admiralty; later it became the responsibility of the quartermaster-general's department of the Army. At first the Admiralty provided officers and men, but in time an increasing number of Canadians were employed. The Provincial Marine gave the British naval superiority on the Great Lakes during the Revolutionary War. By 1780 no less than 14 vessels made up the Provincial Marine on the Great Lakes.

In 1788 the British Government gave up its shipping monopoly. As the number of privately owned vessels increased those of the Provincial Marine were allowed to fall into disuse. On the outbreak of the War of 1812, only the *Royal George,* a 23-gun corvette, was fit for service.

Because of the weakness of the Provincial Marine, the naval establishment on the Great Lakes was transferred to the Royal Navy in 1813. At once an active program of shipbuilding was undertaken at the naval base at Kingston. As a result, the British, despite the loss of the Battle of Lake Erie in 1813, were able to dominate Lake Huron and Lake Ontario during the war.

After the War of 1812, the ships of the lake fleet were either sunk or disposed of by sale. No new vessels were built, owing to the Rush-Bagot Agreement of 1817. In this agreement Great Britain and the United States undertook to limit their naval armament on the Great Lakes.

An Independent Navy

The Canadians did not take an interest in naval affairs again until the onset of the rivalry between the British and German navies in the early 20th century. In 1909 the Canadian House of Commons accepted a resolution approving the organization of a Canadian naval service. In the following year the government of Sir Wilfrid Laurier introduced a naval service bill establishing a naval service, a naval reserve, and a naval college. The bill passed Parliament, and two cruisers, the *Niobe* and the *Rainbow,* were acquired as the nucleus of the Royal Canadian Navy.

The general election of 1911 resulted in the defeat of the Laurier government. The new prime minister was Robert Borden. Instead of pushing ahead with the construction of a navy, Borden proposed to contribute $35,000,000 to assist the British Admiralty in building three new dreadnoughts (a type of battleship). Borden's bill was defeated in the Senate. The result was that Canada entered World War I in 1914 without making a contribution to the British Navy and without an adequate navy of its own. However, the *Niobe* and the *Rainbow* were helpful to the British during the war.

At the end of the war, the existing vessels were decommissioned. In 1920 a cruiser and two destroyers were acquired, but in 1922 the cruiser was placed in reserve and the naval college was closed. In 1929 the two destroyers were replaced with more modern craft, and in 1930 two more were built by order of the Canadian Government. In 1937 and 1938 four destroyers of the "river" class were commissioned. Several new mine sweepers were also built, as well as a three-masted training schooner, the *Venture*. When Canada entered World

Units of the Royal Canadian Navy Atlantic Fleet cruise on the St. Lawrence River.

War II in 1939, it was with 13 commissioned ships, including 6 destroyers. During the war, the Royal Canadian Navy grew enormously. By 1945, it had 375 ships armed for offensive action and about 600 local harbor craft. The navy's main wartime task was to escort convoys between Halifax and Britain.

▶ THE AIR FORCE, 1918–45

It was not until 1918 that the Canadian Air Force was organized. Meanwhile, many Canadians joined the British Royal Flying Corps, later the Royal Air Force. During World War II, the Royal Canadian Air Force grew into the fourth largest air force among the Allied nations. In Canada it was responsible for the vast British Commonwealth Air Training plan. In Europe there were 48 Canadian squadrons, including bombers, fighters, and reconnaissance planes.

In the years between the two world wars, Canada turned its attention to the problem of staying neutral in case of a war between the United States and Japan. The Canadian defense department was also concerned with preparing a force that could be sent overseas in the event of a war in Europe involving Britain. In 1940 it looked to many as if Britain would be overrun by the Germans, and even North America seemed in danger of attack at that time. Canada and the United States began to co-ordinate their defense planning. This was done with the help of the Permanent Joint Board on Defence, made up of members from both nations. During the war, the two nations took part in such joint ventures as the building of the Alaska Highway and airfields along the North West Staging Route (an air route to Russia). After the war, co-operation continued. U.S. officers were selected for special staff training in Canada, and Canadians went to the United States.

▶ INTERNATIONAL CO-OPERATION

Following the rise of the Soviet Union as a threat to Canada and the United States, the two countries built three radar lines across Canada. The most northerly of these, the Distant Early Warning (DEW) Line, crosses the northern mainland of Canada. After the completion of these lines in the mid-1950's, Canada became part of the North American Air Defense Organization (NORAD).

In addition to co-operating with the United States through NORAD, Canada is a member of the North Atlantic Treaty Organization (NATO). Canadian troops have been stationed in Europe since 1951. Canadian vessels have also been assigned to NATO, and Canada is responsible for antisubmarine defense of the North West Atlantic zone.

As a member of the United Nations, Canada sent troops in 1950 to Korea, where they fought as part of the United Nations forces. In more recent years, Canadian troops have been committed to U.N. peacekeeping operations in many parts of the world, including Egypt, Israel, Indochina, Kashmir, and the Congo (now Zaïre). The most demanding peacekeeping task has been in Cyprus, where Canadians have been stationed since 1963.

▶ UNIFICATION OF THE ARMED SERVICES, 1967

Three factors explain the decision of the Canadian Government to unite the Canadian armed services—the desire to eliminate costly duplication caused by the three-service system (army, navy, and air force), the hope of achieving an organization more suited to the role Canadian troops might be expected to play in future U.N. operations, and the need to simplify the command structure.

Tentative steps had been taken to unify the armed services in the 1920's and 1930's. But nothing had actually been done before the outbreak of World War II. After 1945, the Canadian forces were brought under a single ministry. The Royal Military College of Canada was re-organized into a three-service system. Then, in 1964, a single Defence Staff was established under one chief. Three years later, steps were taken to abolish the three separate services. All soldiers, sailors, and flyers became members of the Canadian Armed Forces. The old rank structure was assimilated largely into that of the army (with the exception of the senior naval ranks), and a new uniform was adopted. The familiar badges and insignia were retained, and various corps and regiments retained their distinctive identity.

The forces were not unified without opposition, especially from naval officers who were steeped in British naval traditions. But most Canadians have come to accept the new service.

GEORGE F. G. STANLEY
Formerly, Royal Military College of Canada

CANALS

Canals are channels or ditches filled with water. Sometimes they are natural channels, but most often they have been made by people. The earliest canals were probably dug to bring water from rivers or lakes to irrigate dry land. Other canals were used to drain water away from swampy cities and towns.

Early in history, people found another important use for canals—transportation. A canal can be used to join two cities. It can give an inland city access to the sea. It can provide an inland waterway in a country that has few rivers.

Natural bodies of water, such as rivers, lakes, or seas, can be connected by canals to provide shorter or safer water routes. Canals are also sometimes built in rivers that are too swift or too shallow for boats to use.

There are two main types of canals that are used for transportation: ship canals and barge canals. Ship canals are used by large seagoing vessels. Barge canals are used by cargo-carrying barges and small ships.

Canals may be built all on one level, or they may go from one level to another by means of **locks.** Locks are sections of a canal with watertight gates at each end. The gates can be opened and closed to let water in or out and let boats through.

A ship going from a lower to a higher level in a canal first sails into a lock through its open lower gates. The gates are shut behind it. Water is allowed to flow into the lock through small openings until the level of water in the lock is as high as the water in the upper level of the canal. Then the upper gates are opened, and the ship proceeds on

its way. If ships must be lifted a great distance, more than one lock is used. Sometimes a whole series of locks is used, one after the other, like steps in a staircase.

If a ship is descending to a lower level, the process is simply reversed. The lock is filled with water and the upper gate is opened. The ship enters the lock, and the water is let out through small openings in the lower gate. The lower gate is opened, and the ship sails on.

Except in very small locks, the lock is always filled or emptied through small openings in the gates or through pipes in the bottom of the lock. If the gates themselves were opened to let water in or out, the water would rush in or out with terrific force. The ship might be dashed against the side of the lock and damaged. The banks of the canal might also be washed out by the rush of water.

▶HISTORY OF CANALS

One of the earliest known canals for transportation was built by the Egyptians nearly 4,000 years ago. It connected the Nile River with the Red Sea. Ships could travel from the Mediterranean to the Red Sea by sailing along the Nile and through the canal. The canal was destroyed hundreds of years ago. Today the Suez Canal, which follows a different route, connects the Mediterranean and Red seas directly.

One of the greatest canal systems in the world is the Grand Canal of China. Including its side branches, it covers more than 1,900 kilometers (1,200 miles). It links China's most important rivers. The Grand Canal was begun before 500 B.C. Work on it continued, on and off, for hundreds of years.

The lock on the North Canal at Marquion, in the northernmost tip of France.

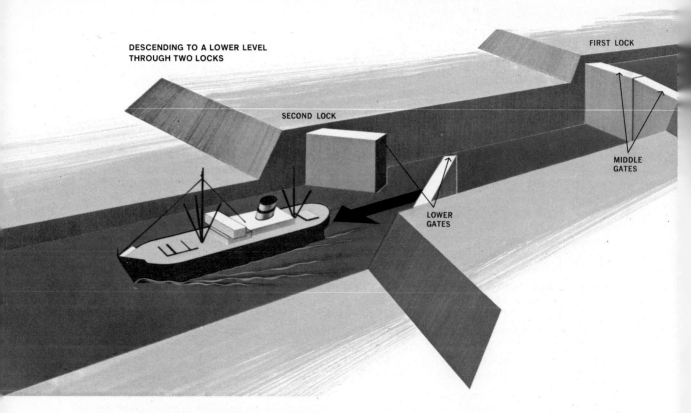

DESCENDING TO A LOWER LEVEL
THROUGH TWO LOCKS

FIRST LOCK

SECOND LOCK

MIDDLE
GATES

LOWER
GATES

In ancient Europe the Romans were the first great canal builders. The Roman canals were mostly built for irrigation and drainage, but some were used for transportation.

Until the development of locks, canals could only be built on one level. This limited the number of places where canals could be built. The first step in the development of locks was to build dams along rapidly falling streams. In this way a series of deep, quiet ponds on different levels was created. Boats were hauled over the sloping faces of the dams. Sometimes cargoes were carried around the dam and loaded onto other boats for the next stage of the journey.

The next improvement in locks was the invention of sluice gates. These were gates in the dams that were raised and lowered vertically, like windows. The first gates of this type were used on China's Grand Canal in A.D. 984. Sluice gates were being used in Europe by 1300. At first sluice gates were not built in pairs, as they were later. There was only one gate for boats to pass through. Because there was no second gate to hold back the water in a part of the canal, each time the one gate was opened, water rushed out and was wasted. The current was often so strong

that boats going upstream had to be hauled through by windlasses. The true lock, with upstream and downstream gates, was developed around A.D. 1400.

The modern type of lock gate, known as the miter gate, was invented by Leonardo da Vinci at the end of the 15th century. This type of gate has two halves and swings open like a double door. The halves form a slight angle when they are closed, like a shallow V. The V points upstream, so that the force of the water tends to push the gates closed. This guards against accidental loss of water by leaving the gates open.

The first sizable American canal was the Erie Canal, begun in 1817 and completed in 1825. Completion of the Erie Canal made New York City the port through which the products of the Great Lakes region flowed to Europe.

The success of the Erie Canal led to a great spurt of canal building. The "canal fever" was particularly strong in Ohio and Indiana. Unfortunately for the canal promoters, railroads were being perfected at the same time. Railroads could carry freight nearly as cheaply as canal barges—and much faster. By the middle of the 19th century, railroads

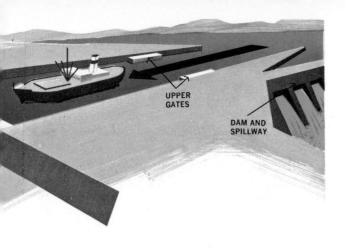

UPPER
GATES

DAM AND
SPILLWAY

The ship enters the first lock through the upper gates, which close behind it. Then, water from the first lock flows into the second lock until the water levels in both locks are the same. The middle gates are then opened, and the ship moves into the second lock as the middle gates close behind it. Water then flows out of the second lock until the water level inside the lock is the same as that outside. Finally, the lower gates are opened, and the ship leaves the locks.

had captured most of the canals' traffic. Today most of these old canals are abandoned.

In their heyday the old canals presented a colorful picture. The passenger and freight barges were pulled by sturdy teams of mules or horses that walked along a path on the canal bank. Steam power was not used because it was feared that the churning paddle wheels would wash out the banks of the canals. Boats were usually lined up at the locks waiting their turn to pass through. A favorite pastime of the workers who drove the teams was fighting to see who would go through the lock first. The canal barges were slow and often crowded and uncomfortable. But they were much more pleasant to ride than the bone-rattling, dusty stagecoaches of that period.

The barge canals that remain in operation have been widened, deepened, and otherwise improved. Instead of straining teams of mules and horses, diesel engines power the barges.

The 19th century saw some bold ventures in the building of ship canals. Probably the most famous of these canals is the Suez Canal, built by a French company between 1859 and 1869. The Suez Canal enabled ships to go from Europe to the Far East without making the long voyage around Africa.

The Panama Canal, considered one of the engineering marvels of the 20th century, was completed by the United States Government in 1914. It links the Atlantic and Pacific oceans, eliminating the long and dangerous trip around the southern tip of South America.

The longest ship canal system in North America is the St. Lawrence Seaway. It is a combination of canals, artificial lakes, natural lakes, and rivers that have been deepened by dredging. A joint project of the United States and Canada, the seaway permits large ocean-going ships to reach the Great Lakes.

▶ CANAL DESIGN

Canals are planned to follow the easiest and least expensive route. They are built to use as little water as possible. Water supply is always a problem for canals. Often special reservoirs are constructed to supply the canals with water. To reduce the amount of water needed and to cut down construction costs, canals are made as narrow as possible. But this also limits the size of ships or barges that can use the canals. Sometimes canals are so narrow that ships cannot pass each other. Such narrow canals have special wide basins where ships can pass. The stretches in between the basins are one-way. Only one ship can use them at a time.

After a canal has been built, it must be kept up. Otherwise, it would soon become unusable. Silting up, or becoming filled with soil, is one of the main problems in canal maintenance. Caving in of banks is another serious problem. The banks are often lined with concrete or masonry to prevent cave-ins. Large sheets of plastic are sometimes used to line canals. Soil is removed from canal bottoms by dredges.

Water leaking out through the soil beneath the canal is also a problem. To prevent this, the bottom of the canal is usually lined with clay. Rock, earth, or concrete is packed on top of the clay to form a tight seal.

▶ CANALS IN THE FUTURE

There have been many advances in air and ground transportation, but canals will continue to be an important means of transportation. Water is still the cheapest means of transportation for heavy products like automobiles, machinery, and oil. Sand and gravel,

SOME WELL-KNOWN CANALS OF THE WORLD

CANAL	COUNTRY	YEAR COMPLETED	APPROX. LENGTH	OTHER FACTS
Albert	Belgium	1939	130 km (81 mi)	Lets barge traffic cross Belgium from east to west.
Amsterdam-Rhine	Netherlands	1952	72 km (45 mi)	Links Amsterdam to Rhine River.
Canal du Midi	France	1681	241 km (150 mi)	Connects Atlantic Ocean and Mediterranean Sea; has three aqueducts and one tunnel.
Corinth	Greece	1893	6.3 km (4 mi)	Cut through solid rock; 80 m (261 ft) deep at one point. Swift tidal currents limit its usefulness.
Erie (now New York State Barge)	U.S.A. (N.Y. State)	1825 (remodeled 1903–18)	845 km (525 mi)	Links Lake Erie and Atlantic Ocean by way of the Hudson River; extension to Lake Champlain.
Grand	China	Around A.D. 620	More than 1,900 km (1,200 mi)	Links China's major river systems; one of the earliest known canals.
Houston Ship Channel	U.S.A. (Texas)	1914	80 km (50 mi)	Makes inland city of Houston a deepwater port by connecting it with Gulf of Mexico.
Kiel	Germany	1895	98 km (61 mi)	Connects Baltic and North seas. Strategically important in World Wars I and II.
Manchester Ship	United Kingdom	1894	56 km (35 mi)	Connects the inland city of Manchester with the Irish Sea.
Panama	Panama	1914	82 km (51 mi)	Connects Atlantic and Pacific oceans.
St. Lawrence Seaway	U.S.A. and Canada	1959	3,800 km (2,350 mi) including Great Lakes	Allows oceangoing vessels to reach Duluth, Minnesota, at head of Great Lakes.
Sault Ste. Marie ("Soo Canals")	U.S.A. and Canada	1855 1895	2.6 km (1⅝ mi) 2.3 km (1⅖ mi)	Two separate, parallel canals, one in each country. Link Lake Superior with Lake Huron. Considered part of the St. Lawrence Seaway.
Suez	Egypt	1869	172 km (107 mi)	Links Mediterranean and Red seas.

timber, and grains are also transported most economically by water.

In many places, barge canals are being modernized and expanded. Increasingly powerful towboats have been developed. Some are able to haul as many as 50 barges at a time.

Ship canals such as the St. Lawrence Seaway and the Sacramento Canal in California have turned inland cities into busy ports and have contributed greatly to the industrial development of regions bordering on them. One problem with ship canals is that they cannot handle supertankers. Present canals and locks are too small for these ships.

GEORGE N. BEAUMARIAGE, JR.
California State University—Sacramento

See also ERIE CANAL; PANAMA CANAL AND ZONE; SAINT LAWRENCE RIVER AND SEAWAY; SHIPS AND SHIPPING; SUEZ CANAL; TRANSPORTATION.

CANARIES. See BIRDS AS PETS.

Which canal took its boats over a mountain by rail?

In the 1830's the Pennsylvania Canal used this method to get its boats over the Allegheny Mountains. The mountains were too high and too steep for the use of locks. The canal boats were specially built so that they could be unbolted into sections. Each section was loaded onto a special carriage that ran on tracks. The tracks ran down into the canal at each side of the range of mountains, so that the boat sections could be quickly and easily floated on and off the carriages. Stationary steam engines pulled the boats up the mountains by cables and lowered them on the other side. Five mountain ridges had to be crossed in this way before the boats reached water again— a distance of 59 kilometers (36½ miles). Locomotives were used to haul the boats over the few level stretches of track. At the far side of the mountains, the boats were put back together to finish their journey by water. The Pennsylvania Canal ran from Columbia, on the Susquehanna River, to Pittsburgh. The mountain stretch—between Hollidaysburg and Johnstown—is commemorated today by the Allegheny Portage Railroad National Historic Site.

CANBERRA

Canberra, the capital city of Australia, is located in the southeastern part of the country. Canberra is a young city, still growing and still unfinished. From the very beginning—from the moment the leaders of Australia decided upon the idea—Canberra was planned and built to take its place as the nation's capital.

The people of Australia call their capital city the Garden City. The region where the city was built was once a vast, treeless plain that looked drearily toward a mountain wall. Today it is a city of many trees, lawns, fountains, and rolling green fields. Canberra has impressive white government buildings, pleasant houses, and inspiring statues and memorials. In the spring the air is filled with the fragrance of flowers.

Canberra is about 580 meters (1,900 feet) above sea level and about 110 kilometers (70 miles) inland from the Pacific Ocean. It has a temperate climate. January is the hottest month, and July is the coolest. Two of Australia's largest cities are not far off—Sydney to the northeast and Melbourne to the southwest. The capital city has rail, highway, and air connections with Adelaide, Brisbane, Perth, and other important cities of Australia. During the 1960's the number of people living in the city more than doubled. Today Canberra has a population of more than 245,000.

Like the United States capital—the city of Washington in the District of Columbia—Canberra is a part of a federal district. When the six Australian colonies decided to become a federation in 1901, they agreed to build their capital in a separate territory. After much discussion, land was chosen in New South Wales. It is called the Australian Capital Territory. Canberra now covers 31 square kilometers (12 square miles) of the Capital Territory.

▶ THE PARLIAMENT CITY

It is in Canberra that the leaders of Australia gather to make the laws of the land. Since 1927 the Senate and the House of Representatives have met at Parliament House. Set amid beautiful gardens, Parliament House is one of the best-known buildings in Australia. While Parliament is in session, a flag is flown above each of the two chambers. At night the flags are replaced by lights—a red light for the Senate and a green light for the House of Representatives. As soon as a chamber adjourns, the light above it is switched off.

A new parliament house is under construction on Capital Hill. It is scheduled for completion in time for the Australian Bicentennial in 1988. The High Court of Australia also meets in Canberra. The modern court building, on the shores of Lake Burley Griffin, is another noted Canberra landmark.

The old Parliament House looks out across the valley of the Molonglo River to the Austra-

The Academy of Science, a building that expresses Canberra's modern spirit.

The statue *Ethos*, which stands in City Square, symbolizes the spirit of the community.

lian War Memorial. This large white stone structure is seen by more than 250,000 persons every year. It has a Pool of Reflection, a Hall of Memory, and many galleries of war relics. The Memorial was built as the nation's tribute to those who fought in all of Australia's wars. Another site that is much visited is the Australian-American Memorial. This magnificent memorial is a tall shaft of gleaming metal with the heroic figure of an eagle at its top. It marks the contribution made by the people of the United States to the defense of Australia in World War II.

▶CULTURE AND EDUCATION

Canberra, the Garden City, is also a city of culture and education. The design of the city planners called for the building of a first-rate university on a site between the Civic Center and Black Mountain. In 1945 their dream was realized. Today the Australian National University is one of the principal centers of nuclear research in the country. Its School of Medical Research is ranked among the world's best. Some of the other noted in-

stitutions in Canberra are the National Library, which has an extensive collection of books; the Institute of Anatomy, which has two large museums; and the Royal Military College, where the future leaders of the Australian Army are trained. The Australian National Gallery in Canberra was opened to the public in 1982.

The best-equipped observatory in the Southern Hemisphere is located on the top of Mount Stromlo. It is the headquarters of the Department of Astronomy of the Australian National University. European and American universities also operate observatories on Mount Stromlo.

Canberra's schools are new, modern, and attractive. Primary education and secondary education are provided by many government and private schools. There are a number of preschool centers. Here youngsters under 5 years of age come to play and receive informal training. These centers have been very successful, and they are heartily supported by the people of Canberra.

▶HISTORY

Canberra started out as a sprawling village on a sprawling plain. At the end of the last century it was just a cluster of scattered houses on sheep-grazing land. But the planners of the nation's capital saw a city where none yet existed. In 1911 a worldwide competition was launched. Architects from many countries were invited to submit their designs for a capital city. A young architect from Chicago, Illinois, hesitantly decided to enter the competition. His name was Walter Burley Griffin, and his design won.

There were many delays in the actual building of Canberra. Two world wars and a depression blocked the fulfillment of its founders' dream. It was only after the end of World War II, in 1945, that the city's real expansion began.

Canberra was officially named in 1913 by Lady Denman, the wife of Lord Denman (Thomas Denman), who was then governor-general. The name Canberra is believed to have come from an Australian aboriginal word meaning "meeting place."

Reviewed by SHARYN KALNINS
Australian Capital Territory
Schools Authority

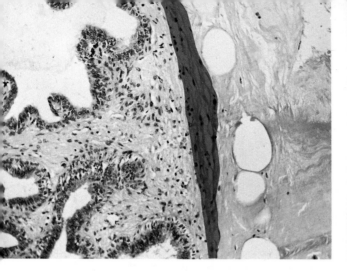

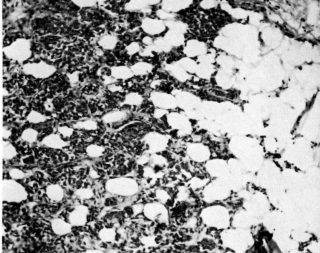

Left: Cell nuclei (black dots) in benign growth are small. Wall of cells (marked in red) surrounds growth. Above: Cancer cells have big nuclei, no wall.

CANCER AND CANCER RESEARCH

Our bodies are made up of many different types of tissue, such as nerve, bone, and muscle. Each kind of tissue is in turn made up of tiny units called cells. The human body contains many different kinds of cells.

Most of these cells are constantly dividing. That is how the body makes more of itself. It explains why young people grow. It explains how the body repairs injuries and replaces worn-out tissue.

Sometimes, though, the process of cell division gets out of hand. Cells are produced that are not needed, and these produce more unneeded cells. And as these new "wild" cells continue to divide, they form a larger and larger mass of new tissue called a **tumor**.

Some tumors are **benign**. They are not of use to the body, and they may interfere with its normal work. But benign tumors are not necessarily harmful. They are surrounded by a skinlike membrane that limits their growth and keeps their cells from spreading into other parts of the body.

Other tumors are **malignant**. They are not contained by a membrane. They grow and spread rapidly, and they invade normal tissue. The malignant cells destroy normal cells or interfere with their work. Such tumors are cancers.

Cancer, then, is an uncontrolled growth and spread of body cells. It can occur in all kinds of animals. It can also occur in plants. But researchers are chiefly concerned with cancer in people because of its threat to health and life.

Cancer can occur in any kind of cell. Since there are many different kinds of cells, there are many different kinds of cancer. In humans alone there are more than one hundred different kinds of cancer. So cancer is not one disease but a large family of diseases.

▶ TYPES OF CANCER

There are three main types of cancers: carcinomas, sarcomas, and the leukemias and lymphomas.

The **carcinomas** include most kinds of human cancers, such as cancer of the skin and the skinlike linings of the lungs, stomach, and

The cell with the large dark nucleus is a cancer cell. Other cells, with small nuclei, are normal.

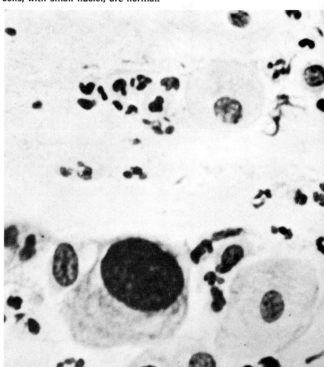

Does cancer occur in plants?

Knoblike growths or tumors are sometimes seen on the stems and trunks of trees. These tumors may be up to 15 centimeters (6 inches) or more in diameter. Some of the tumors are like the cancers of animals. The cells of the plant tumors grow and divide rapidly, forming large masses of tissue. The tumor tissue may invade normal tissues, interfering with their work. In time the normal tissues may be destroyed.

Scientists have made a very important finding in a type of plant tumor called the crown gall tumor. Growth in normal plant cells is controlled by substances called hormones. The hormones are produced by cells that may be far from the cells whose growth is controlled. The growth of animal cells is also controlled by hormones produced in other parts of the body. But the tumor cells in the crown gall tumor make their own hormones. They can live and grow without depending on hormones from another part of the plant. It is not yet known whether this finding applies to animal tumors as well.

intestines. They also include cancer of the internal organs and glands.

Sarcoma is the name given to cancers in the connective tissue, such as bone, cartilage, and fat.

The **leukemias** and **lymphomas** are cancers that involve cells of the bone marrow, the bloodstream, and the lymphatic system. (Vessels in the lymphatic system carry lymph, the fluid that fills the spaces between the body cells.)

How Cancers Spread

Some cancers grow by spreading out from the original site. In fact, that is how cancer got its name. The ancient Greeks called it *karkinos*—meaning "crab"—because of the clawlike spread of an invading cancer. The Romans gave it the Latin name for crab—*cancer*.

Cancer may also spread when malignant cells break off from the original growth. The cells travel to different parts of the body through the bloodstream or the lymph vessels. The new colonies of cancer formed in this way are called **metastases**; cancer that spreads this way is said to have metastasized.

The metastasized cells still resemble the normal cells of the tissue from which they came. This is how an expert can tell which part of the body cancer cells come from. Treatment of cancer is much more likely to be successful before the spreading process has begun. That is why early detection of cancer is important.

▶ **THE CANCER PROBLEM TODAY**

Cancer has become a common disease only in modern times. This is mainly because people are living longer. Ninety per cent of cancers occur in people over 40 years old. A long time ago few people lived to that age. The increase in cancer is also partly the result of chemicals such as cigarette smoke.

In the United States cancer is now a leading cause of death, second only to heart disease. In the late 1970's it was responsible for up to 400,000 deaths each year.

Can cancer be cured? Today about one third of all cancer patients are cured. In some cases a surgical operation is done. Other patients are treated by **radiation** with carefully measured doses of X rays. In another kind of radiation treatment the patient is exposed to measured doses of radioactive cobalt or some other radioactive isotope. Still other patients receive **chemotherapy** (treatment with drugs). Hundreds of institutions throughout the world conduct cancer research. The purposes of this work are to prevent new cases of cancer, detect cancer in its early stages, improve the present treatment of cancer, and find new ways of curing it.

▶ PREVENTING CANCER

There are evidently many different agents, or **carcinogens**, that can bring on cancer. Some of these are large, uncontrolled doses of X rays, the sun's ultraviolet rays, and certain chemicals. The removal of some of these agents from the environment may be one way to prevent cancer.

Chemicals that Cause Cancer

Chemicals that cause cancer are called chemical carcinogens. In 1775 Percival Pott, a London surgeon, observed that many chimney sweeps developed cancer. He believed that the soot from the chimneys was the cause of the cancer. Many chemical carcinogens have been discovered since Pott's time. The chemicals may not actually cause the cancer. However, they seem to affect living cells in such a way that cancers develop.

In 1915 scientists used coal tar to produce cancer in rabbits, and 15 years later other scientists found the chief carcinogen in coal tar.

Since 1930 scientists have identified over 400 chemicals that cause cancer in laboratory animals. As a result, steps have been taken to protect workers who are exposed to coal tar, soot, asbestos, dyes, and other materials commonly used in industry.

Chemicals are often added to foods as coloring or flavoring or as a preservative. Many governments try to make sure that such chemicals are not carcinogens. But the methods for finding out which chemicals cause cancer do not always give clear answers. As a result, there is disagreement about the banning of some of these chemicals. The case of cyclamates, a kind of artificial sweetener, was one example of government banning of chemicals. The U.S. Government banned cyclamates because laboratory tests had shown that very large doses caused cancer in rats.

Chemical damage to tissue is a factor in cancer. Above: Smoking machine is used to gather cigarette smoke much as human lungs do. Below: Tobacco tars condensed from the smoke are painted on the shaved skin of mice. In such tests, the tobacco tars produced skin cancer in the mice.

Smoking and Cancer

Cancer of the lung was a rare disease in 1930. But by the 1970's a drastic change had occurred. Lung cancer had become the leading cause of death from cancer among males in the United States. Lung cancer was

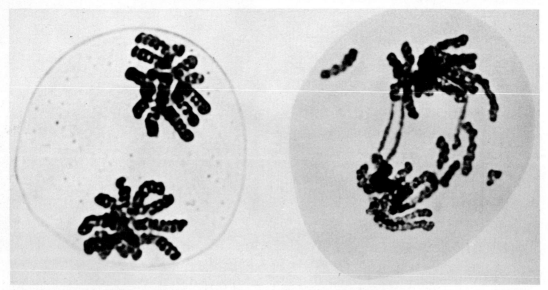

Plant cell at left is about to divide. The chromosomes in its nucleus have split into two groups. Chromosomes are made up of molecules that control the development of the cell. The chromosomes of the cell at right have been exposed to damaging doses of X rays. Chromosomes look tangled and frayed. Such a cell may die. If it lives it may pass on its altered heredity. It may even produce cancer.

also on the increase in other countries. The American Cancer Society blames cigarette smoking for three out of every four lung cancer deaths. The death rate from lung cancer is 10 times as high among cigarette smokers as among those who have never smoked. Among those who smoke two or more packs of cigarettes per day, the rate is 20 times as high as among nonsmokers.

These findings are supported by laboratory results. The tars in tobacco have been found to contain known chemical carcinogens. In spite of the mounting evidence of the connection between smoking and lung cancer, the number of cigarettes sold continues to rise. Many scientists feel that research is needed to learn more about the reasons why people smoke.

The study of the occurrence of cancer in different groups of people is called **cancer epidemiology**. The research on lung cancer in smokers and nonsmokers is an example of such a study. Other studies of this kind have shown that intestinal cancer occurs in the United States more often than in Africa. On the other hand, cancer of the liver is more common in Africa. Another such example is breast cancer. It is the most common form of cancer among women in the United States. Yet it is comparatively rare in Japan. If

scientists can discover the reasons for such differences they may be on the way to preventing new cases of cancer.

Air Pollution and Cancer

Power plants, factories, and motor vehicles burn fuel in order to operate. Wastes result from the burning. The wastes are discharged into the air, mainly over cities. Some of the wastes are carcinogens. Studies have shown that the cancer rate among city-dwellers is only slightly higher than the rate among persons living in rural areas. However, 20 years or more of exposure to some carcinogens may be needed before cancer develops. It may be that the full effects of air pollution have not yet been felt.

Radiation and Cancer

Several kinds of rays, or radiations, can cause cancer. The most common of these are the ultraviolet rays present in sunlight. Seafarers and other persons who are constantly out-of-doors are exposed to large doses of ultraviolet. They may develop cancer of the skin on unprotected areas, such as the face or the back of the hands.

Prolonged exposure to X rays can also cause cancer. These powerful rays were discovered in 1895 by Wilhelm Roentgen (1845–

1923). Roentgen was always careful in using the rays. But some later workers, who were not so careful, developed cancers of the skin or bone from long exposure to the rays.

Today the danger of X rays is recognized. Unnecessary use of X rays is forbidden by law. New types of equipment are designed to protect both the doctor and the patient. The smallest possible amounts of radiation should be used in making chest or dental X rays, for example. The benefits of careful medical use of X rays far outweigh the possible risks.

Exposure to radioactive elements, such as radium, can also cause cancer. Scientists are studying the risks that may come with the use of nuclear energy in industry, and from the explosion of atomic bombs.

Heredity and Cancer

Many cancers cannot be traced to outside agents. Researchers are thus forced to look for causes within the body itself. One major area of research concerns heredity. Living organisms inherit their basic physical makeup through their cells. Suppose something is wrong in the parents' cells. Can this be passed on to future generations?

Much research on this question has been done with mice in laboratories. Scientists have bred closely related mice for generation after generation. These inbred mice produce groups in which all members are as alike as identical twins. This is a great help in comparing what happens to different groups. (Also, cancers and other tissues can be transplanted from one animal to another, because these mice are like identical twins.) In some strains 90 to 100 percent of the mice develop certain types of cancer, usually at about the same age. In other strains, cancer is almost unknown. Thus it seems that mice can inherit cancer or a tendency toward it.

Studies of human beings have not proved anything so definite. Some types of tumors do seem to run in families. But if one member of a family has cancer, this does not mean that other members will develop the same disease. Much more research is needed to learn the relation between cancer and heredity.

Viruses and Cancer

Viruses are the smallest germs known. They grow only within living cells. Viruses were

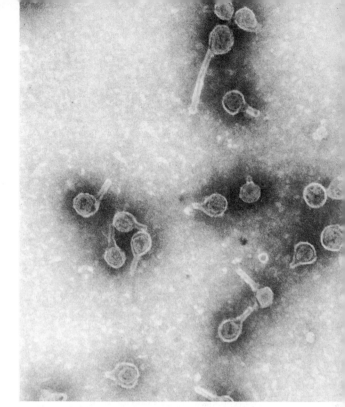

Paddle-shaped objects are Rauscher viruses, magnified 45,000 times by electron microscope. These viruses are known to cause leukemia in mice.

first shown to exist around 1900. Soon after, Dr. Peyton Rous, an American physician, showed that certain types of cancer in chickens were caused by a virus. Since that time, many other cancer-causing viruses have been discovered. It has been proved that viruses cause cancer in mice, hamsters, monkeys, and other mammals.

No virus has been proved to cause cancer in humans. However, most researchers think that such a proof is not far off. In fact, some of them believe that most or all cancers are caused by viruses. They think that chemicals, radiation, and other carcinogens do not actually cause cancer. Instead, the carcinogens "wake up," or activate, viruses that are already within the cell. Support for this theory comes from research on certain viruses that cause other, less serious diseases in man. It is known that these viruses are within the body cells. But they do not make themselves felt until they are activated by some outside agent.

One of the suspected viruses is the Epstein-Barr or **EB virus**. It has been found in humans suffering from a type of cancer called Burkitt's tumor. However, finding the virus in the cells

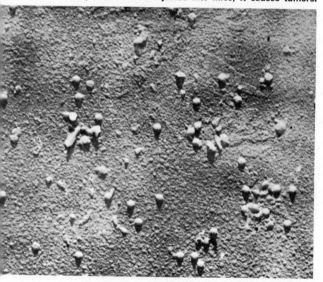

Above are some of the 30,000 carefully tended mice used in a single laboratory for the study of possible cancer-causing compounds. Below: Polyoma virus magnified many times. When injected into mice, it causes tumors.

is not proof that the virus causes the cancer. It may be that the EB virus grows in cells that are already cancerous. Of course, cancer researchers cannot simply inject the virus into healthy persons to find out whether it causes the cancer.

It seems very likely that at least some cancers are caused by viruses. For this reason many scientists are trying to find out how viruses might bring on the disease.

When viruses were discovered it was believed that they were much like bacteria, only smaller. However, bacteria can reproduce by themselves. Viruses can reproduce only after they have invaded a living cell.

A virus is made up of a substance called nucleic acid, wrapped in a coating of protein. Nucleic acids are of two types: deoxyribonucleic acid (DNA), and ribonucleic acid (RNA). The cells of living things, such as the cells that make up our bodies, contain DNA and RNA. The DNA acts as a kind of blueprint. It determines the structure of the cell and what substances the cell will manufacture.

When a virus enters a living cell, the nucleic acid of the virus slips out of its protein coat. It becomes an invisible part of the cell. It may order the cell to make new viruses. That is what happens in such diseases as polio and influenza. Hundreds of new viruses may be produced. They are released from the cell and go on to infect other cells.

Sometimes, however, the virus's nucleic acid does not order the cell to make more viruses. Instead, the nucleic acid seems to become a part of the living cell's DNA. In this way a virus could perhaps change a normal cell into a cancerous one.

Scientists have developed vaccines for use against disease-causing viruses. The vaccines used against polio and measles are examples. If viruses play a part in human cancers, it may be possible to develop vaccines against these viruses, too. But it is clear that making a cancer vaccine will be much more difficult than scientists once believed. Much research will be needed before that goal is reached.

Mutations and Cancer

Before a cell divides, its DNA replicates, or makes an exact copy of itself. When the cell divides, each of the two new cells receives one of the copies. The DNA, along with protein material, makes up the chromosomes in the nucleus of the cell. The new cells are exactly like each other, and like the original cell. That is because the DNA in their chromosomes is identical.

If the DNA of a new cell is damaged, the new cell may not exactly resemble the cell it came from. If the DNA of the new cell is severely damaged in some way the cell will die. But if the DNA is changed only slightly, one or more of the cell's characteristics may change. Such a change is called a **mutation**. The changed cell is a **mutant**. The change is permanent. When the mutant cell divides, copies of its changed DNA will appear in each of the new cells. And these cells, in turn, will pass on the mutation when they divide.

Many scientists believe that cancer cells may be mutants. That is, the DNA of these cells may have been changed in a special way. This belief is supported by the action of some carcinogens, such as X rays and certain chemicals. These agents can cause cancer, but they can also cause mutations that are not cancerous.

▶ **DETECTING CANCER IN ITS EARLY STAGES**

Cancer in an early stage may not be noticed This is because the cancer often does not cause pain or show itself in any other way. However, early cancers are often detected by doctors during regular physical examinations.

A simple test that would reveal hidden cancer anywhere in the body could save thousands of lives each year. Such a test has not yet been found. But there are tests that detect particular types of cancers. The Papanicolaou test, for example, is used for detecting cancer in a part of the womb called the cervix. Cells are constantly discarded from the outer and inner surfaces of the body. Cancer cells present on any surface are discarded too, like normal cells. A trained medical worker can pick out the cancer cells under a microscope. The "Pap test," as it is often called, can detect cancer of the cervix when it is almost 100 percent curable. Scientists are working on ways of using this same method of detection for other forms of cancer.

▶ **IMPROVING CANCER TREATMENT**

Surgical operation is one of the methods used for treating cancer. The surgeon's aim is to remove the cancer tissue completely. However, surgery is not always possible. Then the doctor must look for some other method of treatment.

Radiation is one such method. X rays and radioactive isotopes are used to kill the cancer cells. Researchers and engineers have designed equipment to pinpoint the cancer target, while doing minimum damage to the normal tissue.

Still another promising method is chemotherapy. This is the use of drugs to fight disease. One new approach uses a combination of chemotherapy and radiation. The drug makes the cancer cells more susceptible to radiation. At one time chemotherapy was thought of as a way of prolonging a patient's life and easing pain. Recently, however, patients with different kinds of cancers—even widespread ones—have been cured by the use of drugs. These cures have made scientists hopeful that many cancers—perhaps even most of them—will be cured by chemotherapy in the future.

Immunotherapy is also a promising but still experimental method for the treatment of cancer. It is based on the principle that the body recognizes and attacks "foreign" cells—disease bacteria, for example. This is called the immune reaction. Some cancer cells are different enough from normal cells to trigger the body's immune reaction. In using immunotherapy, doctors try to strengthen this reaction. Immunotherapy has given good results with some cancer patients, but it is still in its very early stages.

▶ **FINDING NEW CURES FOR CANCER**

Many scientists are searching for new cures for cancer. In one huge program, thousands of chemicals are being tested for their effect on cancer in laboratory animals. Some of the chemicals are related to substances that are known to act against cancer. Other chemicals are tested because they are related to substances found in living cells. Still other chemicals are chosen at random. The testing program is slow and very costly, but it has brought results. Most of the drugs now used to treat cancer were found in this way.

Other scientists around the world are studying cells. They believe that knowing everything possible about normal cells is the key to understanding and controlling the abnormal cells of cancer.

The cost of cancer research is enormous. Hundreds of thousands of skilled, trained people are needed. The equipment they use is expensive. But nearly all scientists agree that a vast program of basic research is needed if cancer is ever to be defeated.

HELENA CURTIS
Reviewed by T. GERALD DELANEY
Sloan-Kettering Institute for Cancer Research

See also BODY CHEMISTRY; CELL; GENETICS; VIRUSES.

CANDLES

When you blow out the candles on your birthday cake, you are following a very old custom. People used to believe that by blowing out birthday candles they were blowing away all the bad luck of past years. That is why there is a candle for every year.

How the first candle came about is not known. Perhaps, as primitive man was roasting animals, he poked the carcass with a stick to test its tenderness. The stick covered with animal fat was easy to light and burned brightly. Thus, the torch was created. An improvement was made by dipping twigs in resin, pitch, or oil to make the light last longer. Later, bundles of fat-dipped reeds took the place of twigs and were called rushlights.

The early Egyptians made candles. Their funeral services were lighted and possibly perfumed by cone-shaped lumps of wax or tallow (animal fat) stuck in holders. Bands of material that would burn were wound around the candles to keep the hot tallow or wax from spreading into a shapeless mass. The Egyptians may also have used wicks.

Candle making slowly became an established art. The early Roman Catholic Church made special beeswax candles for their services. By the 13th century candles were in general use. In Paris and other cities candle makers traveled from door to door restocking each household's supply of candles.

▶ CANDLE MANUFACTURE

Although machines that make hundreds of candles at a time have generally replaced the craftsman, the basic steps have not changed over the centuries.

First the manufacturer must prepare the wicks. Wicks are braided cotton fibers that soak up the melted wax. Braiding helps the wick to bend toward the flame and be completely burnt away. Wicks are also pickled (treated in a chemical solution) to make them suck up less wax and not drown the flame. Pickling the wick also stops it from smoldering and becoming too short to relight. Since all waxes melt at different temperatures, wicks must vary in thickness.

An important rule in candle making is: the wider the candle, the thicker the wick. A wick that is too small will cause dripping, and one that is too large will smoke.

The wicks are covered with wax in three different ways—dipping, molding, and rolling.

Dipping. The old-time candle maker dipped his candles over and over in hot tallow. He needed a steady hand and a skilled eye to turn out a smooth, slender candle. Today candles are dipped automatically, and many candles can be made in exactly the same shape at the same time.

Dipping machines are structures that look like bird cages but are actually frames strung with hundreds of wicks. The frames are dipped in a tank of melted wax kept at a temperature of 150 degrees Fahrenheit. One hundred and fifty degrees is generally a good temperature because less dipping is needed. After the wicks have cooled, they are dipped again.

To form a standard-size ¾-inch-diameter candle, the wick must be dipped 24 to 30 times, depending on the temperature of the room and the wax. Smooth, rhythmic dipping is necessary to make the wax cling evenly to the wick. If the candles are dipped too quickly or not cooled long enough, they will become blistered.

All dipped candles are tapered in shape. Many people think that tapering is caused by the wax's flowing from the top to the bottom of the wick as it is dipped. This is not true. The candle will naturally form in a tapered shape because the bottom goes into the hot wax first and comes out last. In this way, the bottom takes on a thicker coat of wax. Many manufacturers also dip the lower end of the candle more often to give the candle a more noticeable taper.

Molding. The difference between dipped candles and molded candles is very simple. Instead of dipping the candle in hot wax, the wax is poured into molds. In some machines cold water around the molds speeds the natural hardening of the wax. The wicks are already strung through the bottom of the mold from bobbins underneath. When the wax has set, pistons push the candles out. More wicks unroll from the bobbins, and fresh wax for a new candle is poured in. Dinner candles, birthday candles, and novelty shapes such as Christmas trees, snowmen, and Halloween pumpkins can all be fashioned in molds.

At left, wax is poured into a candle-molding machine. Strings beneath machine are actually wicks. At right, cagelike frames strung with wicks are dipped in molten wax.

Rolling. The third method of candle making is very similar to wrapping dough around a filling. The wax is kneaded and rolled into a sheet. Then it is wound around the wick until the candle is the right size. Many candles were made in this way in colonial times. Beeswax is the best wax for these candles, since it will not crack when it is rolled out. The candles have borrowed their name from the bees as well as using their wax. They are called honeycomb candles because the wax looks like the tiny cells in a honeycomb.

Candle Wax

Often the tallow used to make early candles gave off a disagreeable odor. Beeswax has no smell and lasts well. Spermaceti wax from the sperm whale has the same good qualities. By the Revolutionary War, whalers were bringing in spermaceti along with whale oil for lamps. But these waxes were scarce and therefore expensive. Not many people could afford to light their homes with beeswax or spermaceti candles.

In the 19th century chemists discovered how to make stearic acid from cheap animal fats. This hard, white, wax-like substance became a leading candle material because of its cheapness and abundance.

Plant waxes, such as carnauba, from a palm tree, and bayberry wax, have been used for candles. Bayberry gives off a pleasing smell and makes pretty holiday candles. A few other waxes go into candles today, but most of the candles are made with petroleum or refining paraffin waxes. The waxes are treated to make them stay hard.

The delicate colors of candles come from aniline or oil dyes. Usually the dye is added to the batch of hot wax just before the candles are ready for the last coat. Sometimes the dye is added to the wax before the candles are dipped or molded at all.

Many of us think of candles as just decorations. Yet when a power failure from storms or earthquakes takes place, we still need candlelight. Many hospitals keep a large stock of candles for emergencies. Churches burn candles as part of their services. Long-lasting candles are burned as memorials.

Candles have many uses, but perhaps their greatest appeal is that they add warmth and cheer. A dinner table lighted by candles becomes gayer. A Christmas candle shining in a window is a sign of goodwill toward all.

RALPH A. AJELLO
President, The Candle Craftsman

See also LIGHTING.

CANDY AND CANDYMAKING

People have always liked sweets. Egyptian wall paintings and lists of supplies for the court show that the Egyptians knew how to make desserts over 4,000 years ago. Cooks in the Egyptian king's court mixed honey, flour, almonds, dates, and figs into sweet cakes.

The soldiers of Alexander the Great (356–323 B.C.) enjoyed a Persian treat called *kand*. *Kand* were pieces of sweet reed flavored with honey and spices. The word "candy" may have come from *kand* or from the Arabic word for "sugar," *qand*.

The story of candy is closely tied to sugar. Huge sugar castles were the high point of 13th-century Venetian banquets. These castles were so beautiful that trumpeters called the people out to admire them as they were carried to the banquet halls. By the 18th century the wealthy had a choice of sugar-coated chocolates, candied ginger, bonbons, and gumdrops.

The introduction of the revolving steam pan from France paved the way for mass production. This pan, which looks like the drum on a concrete mixer, coats candy by tumbling the pieces in sugar syrup. The old coating method was similar to shaking popcorn in a pan over a flame. About the same time a mill for powdering sugar improved candy taste.

Toward the end of the 1800's, penny candies came on the American scene. Among the favorites were such tempters as candy corn, nonpareil drops (chocolate discs covered with white sugar "seeds"), licorice whips, eggs filled with fancy cream, and marshmallow bananas.

In 1911 the first candy bars—almond nougat or chocolate-coated marshmallows with peanuts—were peddled at baseball games. The candy bar soon became a leading confectionery item. Candy has been a part of soldiers' rations since World War I.

The simplest kind of candy is hard candy, which contains sugar, corn syrup, and water. Clear candies that break when they are bitten are hard because almost all of the moisture has been cooked out. The more crunchy grained variety comes from beating the mixture to form large sugar crystals and to fold in air bubbles.

Another way to make hard candy is by pulling it on a hook or on a rotary pulling machine until the candy has turned cloudy and stiff. The pulled candy is rolled into a large 50- to 125-pound candy "log." Colors are folded into separate pieces, and then worked into the log. To make a striped stick, red, yellow, or green pieces are laid over and around the candy. The log is then twisted to pull the strips into the desired pattern.

The last step is to wrap the log in a "jacket" to give the candy its shiny, glazed look. This jacket is a piece of the mixture laid aside before pulling. The log is then spun around while a thin strand is drawn off the head end and fed into a machine that will cut and shape lollipops, fruit drops, or sticks.

Puffy marshmallows are made by whipping air into a sugar and corn syrup mixture after some form of gelatin has been added. The nougat—a cross between hard candy and the marshmallow—is prepared by cooking marshmallow ingredients at a higher temperature. Some areas in Europe specialize in nougat made with honey, and beehives dot the country around the nougat-producing centers.

Caramels are an American discovery. To make a caramel, the candymaker cooks the ingredients into a thick syrup. Caramels have a high milk content, which gives them a smooth flavor. English toffee, a cousin of the caramel, has more fat and is cooked at a higher temperature. Fats keep these candies moist and prevent them from sticking to the teeth.

The family of jellies, such as gumdrops, spice drops, and fruit jellies, ranges from soft and tender to hard, gummy, or chewy. Apricots, oranges, and berries are just a few of the fruits that flavor jellies. These brilliantly colored candies all have a sugar and corn syrup base. Starch, gelatin, pectin (a natural substance in fruits), or agar-agar (a form of gelatin from a seaweed) makes the jellies elastic.

Cream centers have a fondant base. Fondant is a mixture of sugar, corn syrup, and liquid. The mixture is cooked and beaten to break up the sugar crystals. Smooth, creamy candy needs careful beating and cooking. If the batch is warm, the crystals will remain large and gritty tasting, no matter how long the candy is beaten. Many flavorings—chocolate, butter, fruit—give the creams a different taste. The centers are coated in a number of ways. Some candies are hand dipped with a dipping fork. A candy with a liquid fruit center is made by dropping fruit such as a cherry into a mold. Fondant is then poured over the fruit. After the solid center has passed through the enrober, or chocolate-coating machine, the fruit's juices melt the fondant.

The enrober is one of the most ingenious candy-making machines. Candy centers arranged on a belt of wire mesh pass over a pool of melted chocolate, which is forced up through the mesh to coat the undersides of the centers. Then the centers move under a spray of melted chocolate. A typical candy-bar enrobing line moves so swiftly that some 150 bars per minute arrive at the automatic wrapping machines at the end of the line. These wrapping machines take 1 minute to wrap 130 candy bars, to cut and wrap 750 pieces of caramel, or to seal 80 bags of orange slices.

Candy was once a delicacy for the favored few, but now modern industry has made low-priced candy available to all.

DOUGLAS S. STEINBERG
President, National Confectioners Association
See also CHOCOLATE AND COCOA; SUGAR.

CANNING. See FOOD PRESERVATION AND PROCESSING.

CANOEING

The first canoes were most likely dugouts. These were big logs hollowed out by burning and by scraping with stone tools. The word "canoe" comes from the West Indian name for a dugout. Pacific Coast Indians built ocean-sailing canoes out of giant cedar logs. Natives of some of the South Pacific islands still make and use dugout canoes to which they fasten an outrigger (a shaped log joined by spars projecting from the side of the boat) to keep from being tipped over in heavy seas. Dugouts are also found today on many tropical lakes and streams. In swamps of the southern United States dugouts are called pirogues.

Early canoes were also made by stretching animal skins over a light framework of flexible wood. The skins were waterproofed with a substance like pine pitch. The Eskimo kayak, a kind of canoe, has a framework of wood or bone covered with sealskins sewed together. The top is almost completely covered to protect the paddler from the elements.

American Indians of the northeastern woodlands made canoes of birch bark stretched over a cedar frame. The sheets of bark were sewed together, and the seams were waterproofed. The result was a very light-weight canoe, easy to handle on inland water and easy to carry overland from one stream to another. The canoes we use today are descendants of this birchbark canoe.

▶ **CANOES FOR SPORT AND FUN**

For a long time the canoe used for sport and pleasure in North America had a flexible wooden framework. This was covered with canvas that was filled, painted, and varnished. Then the demand for a sturdy lightweight craft that requires little or no maintenance made the aluminum canoe the most popular kind today. Aluminum canoes are light and strong and resist corrosion and rot. Other materials used in making canoes include fiberglass, reinforced plastic, and rubber.

Canoeing on lakes and rivers has become a popular recreational activity.

To help your partner get into the canoe, hold the canoe steady with your paddle. Your partner steps into the center of the canoe and then carefully sits down.

Most canoes used for recreation are 4.6 to 5.2 meters (15 to 17 feet) long. But some are shorter and others longer than this. The choice of a canoe for size and sturdiness depends greatly upon its intended use. A canoe designed for large bodies of water is long and wide and has a rounded bottom. Craft used on streams are shorter and more flat-bottomed.

Today's canoes are so built that a sporty sailing assembly can be readily attached. The rig consists of a sail, mast, boom, rudder for steering, and leeboards for stability.

▶ LEARNING CANOE SKILLS

Many young people learn about canoeing at summer camp. The beginner usually starts with instructions in the proper way to hold the paddle and in the basic paddling strokes. Paddles are usually made of ash or spruce for strength and lightness. They come in lengths from 1.4 to 1.8 meters (4½ to 6 feet). The correct paddle is one that reaches from the ground to your chin. A stern (rear) paddler usually prefers one that reaches to the eyes.

The grip, or knob, of the paddle is designed to fit easily into the palm of one hand while the other hand holds the shaft a short distance above the blade. When paddling from the right side, it is the right hand that is nearest the blade. The opposite is true when paddling from the left side.

Some canoeists prefer a kneeling position, especially for paddling on rough or fast water. But this position becomes uncomfortable and tiring after a time, and recreation canoes usually have seats.

The first stroke to learn is the simple bow stroke. The paddler reaches forward with the blade, dips it into the water, and pulls it back

To get into a canoe from the water, take hold of the side. Reach across the canoe to the far side. Roll into a sitting position as you ease yourself into the canoe.

along the side of the canoe. Although this is known as the bow stroke, it is the basic stroke used by both the bow and stern paddler when two persons are paddling.

The stern paddler, who is responsible for steering the canoe, ends the bow stroke with an outward sweep of the paddle. For balance, safety, and keeping on course, the stern paddler usually paddles on the opposite side of the canoe from the bow paddler. Strokes should be timed with those of the bow paddler. This does not apply to a canoeist who has mastered more complicated strokes.

The bow paddler must learn additional strokes, for it is sometimes necessary to control the direction of the canoe from the bow.

To some, the most thrilling adventure with a canoe is provided by the challenge of "white water." This is the swift and foamy state of rivers and streams during the spring months, when the water is high and fast. The control of a canoe under these conditions requires the greatest skill, co-ordination, and experience. There must be complete co-ordination between the bow and stern paddlers. Regular meets or contests are held under the direction of the American Whitewater Affiliation.

▶ SAFETY

Anyone who goes out in a canoe should be a good swimmer. The canoeist must be secure in the water at all times, must know how to launch and dock a canoe, and should be able to get in and out of a canoe correctly. Skill in handling a canoe properly when alone is essential.

Occasionally a strong wind or a careless boater will cause a canoe to capsize and be swamped. Unless the canoe has been badly damaged, it will float on or just below the surface of the water and may be entered and propelled to shore. The canoeist must first recover the paddle and place it securely under the thwarts before attempting to enter the canoe. It is important to know how to climb into the canoe from the water when the canoe is swamped and filled with water, as well as when it is fully afloat.

A life jacket is an essential piece of safety equipment. Every person in a canoe, even experts, should carry one. If your canoe capsizes, your life jacket will keep you afloat. Many canoeists wear their life jackets at all

The stern paddler reaches forward, dips the blade into the water, and pulls back along the side of the canoe. At the end of each stroke, the stern paddler gives the paddle a little outward twist, using a J stroke. This helps to keep the canoe on a straight course.

times. Some experts do not wear their jackets all the time. But they keep them close by so that they can grab them quickly and put them on in times of danger, such as when they are approaching rapids on a river.

Norma T. Riley
Cortland (New York) Public School System
Joseph K. Riley
Formerly, Grumman Boats

See also Boats and Boating; Camping; Sailing; Transportation.

CAPE TOWN

Cape Town is the oldest city in the Republic of South Africa. It is the country's legislative capital, while Pretoria serves as the administrative capital, and Bloemfontein the judicial capital.

Cape Town, also the capital of the Cape of Good Hope Province, lies between the green wall of Table Mountain and the blue water of Table Bay. Its harbor is one of the most beautiful in all the world. In the 1870's the English writer Anthony Trollope described the harbor as "one of the most picturesque things to be seen on the face of the earth."

Cape Town is an important port city located near the Cape of Good Hope at the southern tip of Africa. Ships traveling between the Indian Ocean and the Atlantic Ocean by the southern route usually stop at Cape Town.

There they take on cargoes of wool, dried and fresh fruits, wine, brandy, and hides. Or they unload automobiles, machinery, and cotton cloth and clothing. Large quantities of diamonds and gold are also exported from Cape Town.

Cape Town is an industrial city as well as a port. Among Cape Town's industries are ship building, printing, engraving, and the manufacture of cement, asbestos, fertilizers, paints, and electrical appliances.

Cape Town is a modern city. It has fine restaurants, stores, and theaters. Yet in many ways Cape Town has the leisurely atmosphere of a small European town. One feels this especially when wandering in one of the city's many beautiful parks or botanical gardens on a mild spring day, or when coming upon one of the fine 18th-century houses—that may now stand next to a tall, modern office building.

The climate is pleasant—cool in the winter, hot and dry in the summer. Cape Town is noted as a resort, and people come from all over South Africa to spend their vacations there. During the summer months the wide beaches are crowded with bathers.

City Hall in Cape Town. The building contains offices, council chamber, library, main concert hall, and banquet hall. Its clock tower is a famous landmark.

The main thoroughfare of Cape Town is Adderley Street. It was named for a man who fought successfully in the British House of Commons to keep the Cape from becoming an English convict settlement in the 19th century. Before that, under the Dutch, the street was called the Heerengracht, or "Gentleman's Walk." In the old days the smartly dressed Cape Towners used to come to this street to stroll and see the latest in fashion. Today Adderley Street is busy and humming with the sounds of automobile traffic. Stores, banks, and office buildings line the street. The Gentleman's Walk is gone. In its place is the main avenue of a large 20th-century city.

Because Cape Town is the legislative capital of South Africa, the Houses of Parliament and other important government buildings are located there. The Prime Minister of the Republic of South Africa lives on the outskirts of Cape Town. His home is called the Groote Schuur, which is Dutch for "Great Barn." It is an old and lovely house filled with finely carved furniture and antiques. The house was built by the famous English empire builder Cecil Rhodes, who gave it to the government.

Cape Town is a city of culture and education. It has many schools and colleges. Its most famous educational institution is the University of Cape Town. This is the oldest university in the country, and was founded in 1829 as the South African College. It is public, co-educational, and has an excellent medical school.

The people of the city enjoy fine music and are proud of their municipal symphony orchestra. Cape Town has several theaters and a number of good art galleries. Places of special cultural interest are the South African Museum, the National Art Gallery, and the South African Public Library, which was founded in 1818.

The oldest building in Cape Town, and in all of South Africa, is the Castle. This is an old Dutch fort that was begun in 1666. Many South Africans visit the Castle because it is a link with the early days of South African history.

▶ HISTORY

Since earliest times brave sailors had tried to sail around Africa. In the 15th century the

Tall modern buildings line Adderley Street, Cape Town's main thoroughfare.

Portuguese first reached the Indies by way of the Cape. But it was the Dutch who made the first real settlement at what is now Cape Town.

In April, 1652, three small ships sailed into Table Bay and anchored. On one of these ships was Jan van Riebeeck, a surgeon of the Dutch East India Company. The company decided that a half-way station was needed where ships could stop and get supplies before going around the Cape of Good Hope. Jan van Riebeeck founded that first settlement.

In 1806 Cape Town passed from Dutch to British rule. In 1910 the city was made the legislative capital of South Africa. Today the settlement that Jan van Riebeeck founded is a thriving city with a metropolitan population of over 1,000,000 people.

Reviewed by D. C. REZELMAN
Information Service of South Africa

CAPE VERDE

Cape Verde is a crescent-shaped archipelago of 15 islands located in the Atlantic Ocean west of Senegal.

The volcanic soils of the islands are fertile, but water is so scarce that Cape Verdeans (the name is also spelled Cape Verdian) are among the world's chief sufferers from drought and famine. Because of poor living conditions and a severe unemployment problem, many Cape Verdeans live and work abroad.

▶ THE PEOPLE

Cape Verde has a total population of about 300,000. Most of the people live on the islands of São Tiago and São Vicente. Praia, located on São Tiago, is the capital of the country. It has a population of about 21,500. Mindêlo, on São Vicente island, the largest town in the archipelago and its chief seaport, has approximately 30,000 people.

About 70 percent of the population are mulattoes, people of mixed Portuguese and West African descent. Only a few thousand Europeans live on the islands, and the remainder of the people are Africans. For the most part, the mulatto population is descended from African slaves imported by the early Portuguese settlers who first colonized the uninhabited islands.

The fusion of the traditions of the two main population groups has resulted in a unique and colorful culture, with sing-song dialects and a varied folklore. Each island, however, has developed its own customs and traditions. The people speak several different dialects made up of Portuguese and various African tongues. The dominant language of the islands is Verdean creole. Most of the people practice Roman Catholicism.

The Cape Verdeans have one of the highest literacy rates in all Africa. There are many schools located throughout the islands.

▶ THE LAND

The Cape Verde archipelago consists of ten islands and five smaller islets. The total land

Mindêlo on São Vicente is Cape Verde's largest town and its chief seaport.

Tiago, Santo Antão, São Vicente, São Nicolau, Sal, Boa Vista, Fogo, Maio, Brava, and Santa Luzia.

The islands are volcanic in origin and for the most part arid and mountainous. Pico do Fogo, the only active crater on the islands, is located on Fogo island.

Because of the islands' volcanic origin, the soils are generally rich. Climatic conditions in the archipelago, however, are not as favorable. The hot and usually dry climate results from the trade winds, which blow westward from the Sahara. Rain is scarce, and the islands often have droughts that last for several years. The moister southwesterly winds blow from August to October, with the greatest amount of precipitation falling on the more southerly islands.

▶ THE ECONOMY

The erratic rainfall and the erosion of the soil caused by the high winds have made it nearly impossible for the people on several of the islands to grow their own food. The drier islands are sparsely populated. They are used mainly for grazing goats and sheep. The islands that receive more moisture have a variety of crops. Coconut palms fringe the coasts, and sugarcane, bananas, corn, oranges, pineapples, and coffee are grown on the higher slopes of the mountains. Most of the crops are grown for local consumption. Surplus foodstuffs are exported to Guinea-Bissau and Portugal.

The Cape Verdeans have tried several ways to solve their water problem. For many years water was transported in tanker vessels from Santo Antão to Mindêlo on São Vicente island. But then water became scarce on Santo Antão. In 1971 a desalinization plant (where salt is removed from seawater), a reservoir, and a distribution system were built on São Vicente by the Portuguese Government.

Although agriculture is the most important economic activity, some industry has been developed. Cement, cigarettes, and pottery are manufactured on the islands, and salt and lime are processed. Cold-storage facilities at Mindêlo handle and freeze up to 8,000 metric tons of tuna brought in annually by Portuguese, Japanese, and other fishing vessels. Many Cape Verdeans have traditionally made their living from fishing.

FACTS AND FIGURES

REPUBLIC OF CAPE VERDE is the official name of the country.

CAPITAL: Praia.

LOCATION: Atlantic Ocean west of Senegal. **Latitude**—14° 48' N to 17° 12' N. **Longitude**—22° 42' W to 25° 22' W.

PHYSICAL FEATURES: Area—4,033 km² (1,557 sq mi). **Highest point**—Pico do Fogo, 2,829 m (9,281 ft). **Lowest point**—sea level.

POPULATION: 303,000 (estimate).

LANGUAGE: Verdean creole, Portuguese, various African dialects.

RELIGION: Roman Catholicism.

GOVERNMENT: Republic. **Head of state**—president. **Head of government**—premier. **International co-operation**—United Nations, Organization of African Unity (OAU).

ECONOMY: Agricultural products—bananas, coffee, sugarcane, corn, citrus fruits, sweet potatoes, beans, sisal, vegetables. **Industries and products**—canned and frozen fish, refined sea salt, beverages, cement. **Chief mineral**—salt. **Chief exports**—bananas, coffee, tuna, salt. **Chief imports**—foodstuffs, manufactured goods, machinery, petroleum products. **Monetary unit**—escudo.

▶ HISTORY AND GOVERNMENT

The islands of the archipelago were uninhabited when they were first sighted by Europeans in 1460. By 1462 the Portuguese sailors were followed by the first settlers. By 1466 the residents of São Tiago were trading in slaves and merchandise with the Guinea coast. For decades the island was a transshipment point in the slave trade between West Africa and the Western Hemisphere.

After 1851 the island of São Vicente became one of the world's busiest refueling stations for ships. Later it became the terminus of one of the first transatlantic underwater communications cables.

Cape Verde remained under Portuguese rule for more than 500 years. In 1974 a coup toppled the government of Portugal. The new Portuguese leaders granted full independence to Cape Verde in 1975. Cape Verde and Guinea-Bissau considered plans for joining together as a single country. But the government that took control of Guinea-Bissau in 1980 did not approve the plans.

RICHARD J. HOUK
De Paul University

CAPILLARY ACTION. See LIQUIDS.

CAPITALISM

Capitalism is an economic system in which most of the industries and businesses in a country are owned privately, rather than by the government. Capitalists are people who use their own wealth (or other people's money) to make more wealth. The extra money they make is their profit. Some capitalists manufacture things to sell at a profit. Some are store owners who sell goods at a profit. Others are financiers or investors who lend their money in the hope of getting more back.

No matter what their business, the aim of capitalists is to make a profit. But this does not mean that they can charge very high prices or sell bad goods. If they do, they will probably lose business to others who sell better goods or have lower prices. Competition forces capitalists to sell the best possible goods at the lowest possible price. Competition is an important feature of capitalism. The profits made by individual capitalists in free competition benefit the economy of a whole country. As capitalists make profits they can expand their businesses and put more people to work.

▶ EARLY CAPITALISM

In the Middle Ages, Europe had a feudal agricultural system. Land belonged to the church and to the nobles and was worked mainly by serfs. Few people were free to own and control their own businesses except in the cities.

As early as the 13th century, guilds of craftsmen, merchants, and traders slowly began to gain economic and political power. By the 16th century, merchants were investing large sums of money at home and abroad. Great trading companies, such as the East India Company in England, sent ships to India. They financed expeditions to open up colonies in the New World. In Europe the new middle class of tradesmen and craftsmen as well as the noble families bought spices, silks, and other luxuries that merchants brought back from the East. The merchants competed fiercely for this market.

By the 18th century, capitalists had large amounts of money (capital) ready to invest. The invention of the steam engine gave them their opportunity. Factories sprang up like mushrooms, first in England, then in other western European countries, and later in the United States. A great change took place, from home manufacture to mass production in factories using machinery. This change is known as the Industrial Revolution. It is only since the Industrial Revolution that capitalism has become the great force it is today.

▶ THE NEED FOR REFORM

In the early stages of the Industrial Revolution, many people believed that capitalism would work best if capitalists were left free to do as they pleased. They believed that governments should follow a hands-off policy toward business.

But factory owners often abused their power, and workers suffered. The working day was long, 10 or 12 hours being common. Women and children worked for very low pay. Factories were badly lighted, poorly ventilated, and dirty. Workers were not protected from dangerous machinery.

Reformers cried out against these conditions. The political economist Karl Marx, one of the founders of Communism, wrote books claiming that capitalism must die of its own cruelty and greed. Even before Marx, trade unions had begun to develop. Members of these unions also criticized the brutal side of capitalism. But they believed that the bad working conditions could be improved without overthrowing capitalism. Though at one time unions were illegal, they slowly grew stronger. With strength came acceptance by governments and employers. By hard bargaining, union leaders have got fair wages and decent working conditions for workers.

Laws have also modified the capitalist system. In the late 19th century some capitalists built monopolies and trusts. These companies were so huge and powerful that they did away with almost all competition. The Sherman Antitrust Act (1890) outlawed monopolies, and President Theodore Roosevelt, while in office (1901–09), enforced the law so strongly that he was called "the Trust Buster."

Still later, during the great depression of the 1930's, President Franklin Delano Roosevelt introduced a broad social welfare program as part of his New Deal. Today social security and unemployment insurance give people in the United States security they did not have before. Government agencies were set up to help prevent another great depression.

Today in many capitalist countries, governments own some businesses and regulate many more. For example, the British Government owns the Bank of England and runs the National Health Service. In the United States the government runs the space program. It regulates many companies that supply services or products needed for public health or convenience, such as water, electricity, and natural gas. Government has an important role to play in the capitalist system. Most people in democratic capitalist countries believe that government should protect free enterprise. They also want government to see that businesses are run in a way that does not harm workers and consumers.

Reviewed by MARCUS NADLER
New York University

See also COMMUNISM; SOCIALISM.

CARAVAGGIO, MICHELANGELO MERISI DA (1571–1610)

The stormy life of the painter Michelangelo Merisi began in northern Italy near Milan. At 13 he was apprenticed to a local artist, but his career began in Rome when he was about 21. It was then that he became known as Caravaggio, after the hometown of his father.

Caravaggio at first painted small still-life pictures—fruits and flowers—and simple pictures of ordinary boys who were sometimes dressed to look like figures from ancient myths. Caravaggio's talent soon attracted the attention of a wealthy patron, Cardinal del Monte, who became his protector.

In 1599, Caravaggio began painting large religious pictures for churches in Rome. These paintings seemed to show contemporary people acting out biblical stories. Showing religious figures as ordinary people was so shocking at that time that some of Caravaggio's paintings were rejected by the priests. But other people thought that he was the greatest painter of his time—an opinion shared by art historians today.

Caravaggio had a violent temper. He liked to gamble and fight, and he was in constant trouble with the police. In 1606 he killed a man and had to flee from Rome. He went to Naples, where he continued to paint and then went to Malta to join the Knights of Saint John of Jerusalem, a military and religious order. But he got into trouble and again had to escape. After painting in Sicily and Naples, Caravaggio heard that he was about to be pardoned by the pope. He set out for Rome, only to die on the way, on July 18, 1610.

HOWARD HIBBARD
Author, *Caravaggio*

In the *Entombment* (1602–04), the most classic work of Caravaggio, the body of Jesus Christ is lowered into the tomb, while his mother grieves. Caravaggio's religious art was often dramatic and very dark, with brilliant highlights. This deeply emotional painting is also called the *Deposition*. Vatican Museums, Rome.

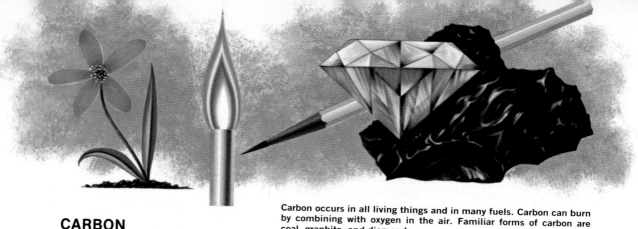

Carbon occurs in all living things and in many fuels. Carbon can burn by combining with oxygen in the air. Familiar forms of carbon are coal, graphite, and diamonds.

CARBON

Carbon is a common element (chemical symbol, C) that all of us have seen. It occurs in several forms, and the best known is probably coal. That immediately tells you something about this form of carbon: It can burn. When coal burns, it combines with the oxygen in the air and forms a gas called carbon dioxide.

Most of the common substances that burn also contain carbon; that is, they have carbon atoms in their structure. When such materials as wood, gasoline, or paper burn, carbon dioxide is produced. The food we eat also contains carbon atoms in its structure. Within our bodies this food undergoes a process somewhat like slow burning—and the air we breathe out contains carbon dioxide.

It is possible to heat wood while keeping oxygen away from it. Without oxygen the wood cannot burn. But the part of the wood that is not carbon is driven off as gases. What remains is called charcoal. It is almost pure carbon. When charcoal is used to make a fire, it burns without a flame. It lasts longer and burns hotter than wood.

Ordinary coal can be similarly treated, for it is not wholly made of carbon. If coal is heated to drive off other materials, the remains are chiefly carbon. This form is called coke.

When coke or charcoal is heated with iron ore, the carbon takes part in a process that removes oxygen from the ore. As a result the metal (iron) is left. Pure iron is not very hard. But if a small amount of carbon is added, the mixture is steel. Steel is much harder than pure iron. The manufacture of iron and steel uses more carbon than any other industry.

Carbon has many varied uses. Powdered charcoal can be formed in such a way as to be full of tiny holes. The charcoal then serves as a filter. As air is drawn through the holes, the charcoal traps gases and chemicals. Such charcoal is put in the gasmasks used by soldiers and fire fighters.

There is a soft kind of carbon that flakes off if scraped across paper. It leaves a black mark behind. This form of carbon is called graphite. What most people call the "lead" in a pencil is really graphite.

Another form of carbon is not black but is as transparent as glass. This is diamond. Diamond forms when carbon is heated to a high temperature and squeezed under great pressure. Scientists now know how to make tiny diamonds in the laboratory, but all big diamonds occur naturally. They form deep in the earth, over millions of years, and are brought near the surface by shifting in the rock. Diamond is the hardest substance known. Diamond powder will cut the hardest steel.

Like all other substances, carbon is made up of atoms. But carbon atoms are unusual in that they can combine with one another and form long, complicated molecules. These chainlike and ringlike molecules become the core of compounds formed when other kinds of atoms are attached to the carbon atoms. That is why carbon exists in many forms and compounds.

Complicated carbon compounds occur in all living bodies. All the important substances that make up the human body contain carbon atoms. Life as we know it would be impossible without carbon.

ISAAC ASIMOV
Boston University School of Medicine

See also ELEMENTS.

CARBON MONOXIDE POISONING. See POISONS AND ANTIDOTES.

CARD GAMES

No one is sure who first invented playing cards. But records show that people in China and India around A.D. 900 had playing cards. In the earliest times cards were used for telling fortunes as well as for playing games.

The cards of the Far East were divided into suits, or groups. Each suit had its own special markings. This system of dividing the pack into suits has come down to our day.

Playing cards had made their way to Italy, France, Germany, and Spain by the 14th century. The early Italian cards were picture cards called tarots. There were 22 in a deck. The 22nd card in a tarot deck was called the fool. The joker, or extra card, in today's pack developed from this card.

After a while, 56 number cards were added to the tarot pack to make a pack of 78 cards. In some parts of Europe a game called tarok is still played with 78 cards.

The pack of 52 cards we use today was originally called the French pack. It was adopted by the English. In French the four suits were called *pique, coeur, carreau,* and *trèfle.* In English they became spade, heart, diamond, and club. In each suit there are three face, or picture, cards: a king (K), a queen (Q), and a jack (J), sometimes called the knave. They are still pictured in the costumes worn in the times of Henry VII and Henry VIII, 15th- and 16th-century kings of England. There are 10 spot cards, numbered from 10 through 1. The one spot is called the ace (A). The two, or two spot, may also be called a deuce. The three, or three spot, is sometimes called a trey.

Over 200 years ago the rules for card games and other games of skill were written down by Edmond Hoyle, an English lawyer who enjoyed playing cards in coffeehouses. In 1742 he published *A Short Treatise on the Game of Whist.* The rules for other games were added to it in later editions.

The first playing cards were painted by hand. Later, cards were printed from woodcuts. The design was carved on a block of wood that was covered with ink and pressed against paper. Then color was added.

Originally cards had no index numbers in the corners. You had to look at the face of each card to see what you held in your hand.

But in the late 1800's, index numbers were placed in the corners. Then it became possible to hold cards in a fan shape and see every card at a glance.

The modern mass printing of cards on pasteboard began in the 1800's, although cards were printed on pasteboard as long as 300 years ago. Pasteboard is made of sheets of paper pasted together. The advantage of cards made of pasteboard is that it is impossible to see through them even when they are held under a strong light.

Cards in the late 1800's were a little wider than they are today. In most of the popular games, players had to hold only five cards in their hands at once. But in the 1900's, bridge became popular, and players had to hold 13 cards at a time. A slightly narrower card was introduced.

▶CONTRACT BRIDGE

Contract bridge is played by millions of people. Some treat it more as a science than as a pastime. Its history goes back to the game of whist, which originated in England sometime in the early 1500's.

The Players, the Deal, and the Game. There are four players—two partners on each side. The partners sit opposite each other at the table. All gains or losses are charged to the partnerships.

A standard deck of 52 cards is used, dealt clockwise one at a time. At the conclusion of the deal, each player has 13 cards.

Contract bridge is divided into two major parts: (1) the bidding and (2) the play.

Bidding. Bidding is a method of estimating the number of tricks that can be won in the play. Beginning with the dealer, each player in turn bids for the right to determine the trump suit (a suit any card of which takes any card of the other suits). The dealer may pass or bid. If a bid is made, the dealer offers to win a certain number of tricks. The player on the left may pass or bid. The auction continues until there are three passes in a row. The player making the highest bid wins the contract, and the partners must gain the specified number of tricks during the play.

In bidding, sound estimates cannot be made without a knowledge of the value of high cards. For the purpose of valuing a hand, the Goren system is shown here. Numbers relating to the value are assigned to each of the high cards, as follows:

Ace	4 points
King	3 points
Queen	2 points
Jack	1 point

Since there are four suits—spades, hearts, diamonds, and clubs—the entire pack contains 40 points.

To open the bidding, more than 10 points (average hand) is needed since the bidder is undertaking to win more tricks than his opponents.

If the hand is played at no-trump (no suit is designated as trumps), only high cards are counted. But if trumps are mentioned, the distribution of short suits (three cards or less) forms a part of the count.

Opening the Bidding. With 13 points the bidding may be opened, but with 14 points the bidding must be opened.

For the purpose of opening the bidding, the high cards are counted first and then distribution points are added—1 point for each doubleton (two cards of a suit only), 2 points for each singleton (one card of a suit only), and 3 points for a void (none of a suit).

Spades:	A 7 6 5 3	(4)
Hearts:	A Q 9 6 3	(6)
Diamonds:	5	(2)
Clubs:	8 2	(1)

This hand is worth 13 points.

The suit selected for bidding must be what is called a biddable suit. If it is only four cards long (you have only four cards in this suit), it must contain 4 high-card points to be biddable. Some examples are:

    K Q 5 4   K J 6 5   A 8 7 6

Any five-card suit is biddable, and there is no high-card requirement.

    Q 9 7 6 4   10 8 7 6 3   J 9 4 3 2

Experience has shown that it takes the equivalent of two opening bids to produce game. Since an opening bid is about 13 points, 26 points divided between the partnership should produce a game.

The Rank of Suits. Suits rank in the following order: spades, hearts, diamonds, and clubs. This means that in order to mention clubs over any of the other suits, the level of the auction must be increased. If you wish to bid one spade when your partner has bid one heart, one diamond, or one club, the level of

the contract need not be increased since spades is the highest-ranking suit. When a player wishes to designate no-trumps, he need not increase the level, because no-trump is higher ranking than any of the suits.

Choice of Suits to Open. When you have more than one biddable suit, length determines the choice. With two five-card suits, bid the higher-ranking suit, not necessarily the stronger of the two. If you have more than one four-card suit, look for the shortest suit in your hand and bid first the suit that ranks below that. For example:

Spades:	6 2
Hearts:	A 8 7 6
Diamonds:	A K Q 4
Clubs:	8 9 2

Bid one heart, the suit below the doubleton. If partner bids two clubs, your rebid is two diamonds, permitting partner to return to two hearts without increasing the level of the auction.

No-trump Bidding. No-trump bidding differs somewhat from suit bidding. Here high cards predominate and distributional points are not counted.

No-trump openings should be made on hands that are more or less evenly divided. Your suits should be divided into one of the following patterns:

    4 3 3 3   4 3 3 2   or   5 3 3 2

If you have a singleton or two doubletons, you should not open the bidding with no-trump.

An opening bid of one no-trump contains 16, 17, or 18 high-card points.

An opening bid of two no-trump contains 22, 23, or 24 high-card points.

The opening bid of three no-trump contains 25, 26, or 27 high-card points.

Twenty-six points will normally produce three no-trump, 33 points will normally produce six no-trump, and 37 points will normally produce seven no-trump. These points will usually be divided between the partnership's hands.

Responding. If your partner bids one of a suit and you have 6 or more points, you should keep the bidding alive. This is because partner's opening bid of one of a suit could contain 20 points, which together with your 6 would produce the necessary 26 points for game.

With a weak hand you may keep the bidding open in one of three ways:

(1) **by bidding one no-trump,**
(2) **by bidding one of another suit,**
(3) **by raising partner from one to two of his suit.**

No-trump Response. If your partner has bid one of a suit and you have at least 6 points, you may show your suit if you can do so at the level of one. For example, if partner opens with one diamond, you may bid one heart with 6 points. But if you are unable to show a suit at the level of one because it is a lower-ranking suit than your partner's, you should bid one no-trump to keep the bidding open. Note that if partner opens with one heart, you may not bid two diamonds with less than 10 points.

The one no-trump response announces 6 to 10 high-card points. In no-trump bidding short suits do not count.

Single Raise. When you have support for partner's suit, you may raise him with 7 to 10 points. Here are some examples of support:

5 4 3 2   A 7 5   K 9 2   Q 3 2   J 10 2

If you have less strength than this in partner's suit, you should look for some other response.

In valuing your hand as "dummy" (in support of partner's suit), count your high cards and add your dummy points according to the following table:

Add 1 point for a doubleton.
Add 3 points for a singleton.
Add 5 points for a void.

HAND A		HAND B	
Spades: 5 4 3		Spades: 6	(3)
Hearts: A 8 6 2	(4)	Hearts: A 8 4 2	(4)
Diamonds: Q 9 6 5	(2)	Diamonds: Q 6 4 2	(2)
Clubs: 3 2	(1)	Clubs: K 4 3 2	(3)

Your partner has opened with one heart. Hand A is worth 7 points and qualifies for a raise to two hearts. Hand B is worth 12 points and is too strong for an immediate raise. Bid two clubs first and raise hearts next time.

Jump Raise. Partner has opened with one spade. You hold:

Spades:	A 7 6 2	(4)
Hearts:	4	(3)
Diamonds:	J 10 4 3	(1)
Clubs:	K Q 9 3	(5)

You have adequate support for partner's suit and your hand is worth 13 points. Partner is presumed to have at least 13 points, so that your partnership is assured of 26 and you should reach a game contract. You announce this to partner by making a double raise (two over partner's bid). This is a demand for game.

To justify a double raise, you should have at least four of partner's trumps and a point count of 13, 14, 15, or 16, including high cards and distribution.

Forcing Bids. One of the basic principles of contract bridge is that when the opener starts with one of a suit and responder names any new suit, opener must bid again.

When responder jumps the bid, in a suit or in no-trump, he shows a strong hand and opener must keep on bidding until game is reached.

If it takes 26 points to produce a game and partner needs 13 to open the bidding, you should make some distinct effort to reach game when your hand is the equivalent of an opening bid (13 points).

The Play. One of the contracting players is called the declarer. The declarer is always that member of the partnership who first mentions the trump suit in which the hand is to be played.

When the bidding ends, the player to the left of the declarer places one of his 13 cards face up on the table. This is known as the opening lead, which starts the play of the hand. The opening leader may play any card. All players must follow suit if they can do so. If a player cannot follow suit, he may play any card in his hand without restriction.

After the opening lead the partner of the declarer spreads his 13 cards upon the table and this hand becomes the dummy. The declarer chooses each card that is to be played from the dummy, but the defending players play their own hands. The play, like the bidding, is clockwise. When each player has played, there will be four cards on the table. These are called a trick. Of the four cards played to the trick, one card will have winning rank and will capture that trick. The player whose card won the trick has the right to lead to the next trick. The process is continued until all 13 cards have been played.

To illustrate the mechanics of trick-taking, let us assume that the bidding has been completed and play is about to begin. South is the declarer. For purposes of identification, the players are referred to by the names of the four directions—North, East, South, and West. As with the points of the compass, North is opposite South, East is opposite West.

The first play, known as the opening lead, has been made by the player to the declarer's (South's) left.

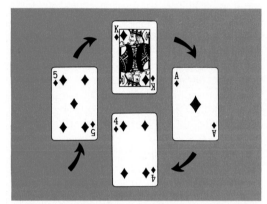

Note that a card has been played by each of the four players in clockwise rotation, starting with West. The four cards are at the moment face up on the table and are about to be picked up by East. These four cards (a trick) belong to East and West. They have won the first trick because East played the highest card of the trick and therefore captured the others.

Play then proceeds to trick number two. Inasmuch as East won the first trick, he plays first (that is, he leads) to the next trick.

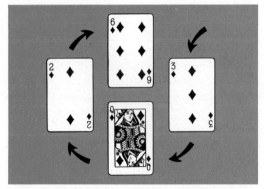

Observe that East led the three of diamonds to trick two. South played the queen of diamonds, West the deuce of diamonds, and North the six of diamonds. The queen of diamonds was the highest card played to this trick and therefore captured the other three cards. South gathers up the four cards and places the trick face down in front of him. Play proceeds in this manner until all the cards have been played. Consequently, there will always be exactly 13 tricks in each hand.

A player may not put down his card until it is his turn to play. If West is the leader, East may not play until after North has played, and South must wait for East to play before he puts down his card.

The leader to each trick has his own complete choice as to which card to play. The other three players must follow suit if possible. If a player has no cards of that suit, he is at liberty to play any card he chooses.

Winning Tricks by Using Trumps (Ruffing). Every card of the trump suit has a superior trick-taking power. It is known as the ruffing power (or trumping power), and a player may exercise it whenever he is unable to follow suit.

A player who has no cards of the suit that has been led may ruff by playing any card of the trump suit. If he is the only one who has played a trump, he wins the trick regardless of the size of his trump. In other words, the deuce of trumps will capture the ace of some other suit that has been led.

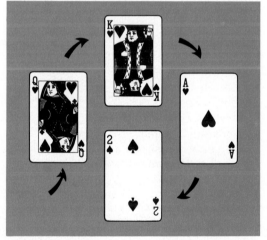

Spades are trumps. West leads the queen of hearts; North attempts to capture with the king of hearts; East beats this with the ace of hearts. South, who has no hearts, wins the trick with the deuce of spades, which is a trump.

If more than one player uses a trump on any particular trick, the player who contributes the highest trump wins the trick. In other words, a trump can be captured by a higher-ranking trump.

When a player is unable to follow suit, he may trump or he may play a card of some other suit. If he plays a card of some other suit, he is said to have made a discard. The discard has no trick-taking power; therefore the rank of the discard does not matter. Any trick that does not contain a trump is won by the hand that plays the highest card of the suit led.

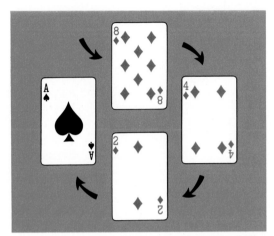

Hearts are trumps. North leads the eight of diamonds. East and South follow suit. West has no diamonds and also has no trumps. He discards the ace of spades. North's eight of diamonds wins the trick.

When a trump is led, the other three players must follow suit if they are able. In other words, the follow-suit rule applies to trumps as well as to the other suits.

Remember that a player may not ruff if he is able to follow suit.

Scoring. In bidding offensively the most important goal is the scoring of a game. "Game" in this sense is a technical term. You achieve a game when your side has scored 100 or more points for fulfilling your own bids. These are sometimes called below-the-line points because that is where they are recorded on the score pad. Only the points that you score by making your own contracts may be counted toward game. Points won defensively are recorded above the line on the score pad.

Game may be scored either in one hand or by the accumulation of the necessary points over several hands. For fulfilled contracts points are awarded as follows.

If spades or hearts are trumps, you score 30 points for each trick you bid. If diamonds or clubs are trumps, you score 20 points for each trick over your book (the first six tricks). If the contract is no-trump, you score 40 points for the first trick over your book and 30 points for each additional trick that you take.

	800				
500	60				
50	100				
60	30				
60	70				
40					
	120				
100					
810	1180				
	-810				
	370				

All points other than tricks are scored above the line.

When a side scores a game by making 100 such points, that game is over and that side starts again in an effort to make another game.

A game can be made in one hand if you bid and make three no-trump ($40 + 30 + 30 = 100$), five clubs or diamonds ($5 \times 20 = 100$), or four spades or hearts ($4 \times 30 = 120$). Any extra tricks above those contracted for are recorded above the line and do not count in scoring toward game.

Bonuses. When a side scores two games, it is said to have won the "rubber" and receives a designated bonus. If your side wins two games before your opponents win one, your bonus is 700 points. If you win the rubber (two games) but your opponents have won a game, your bonus is 500 points.

When you bid for all the tricks and make them, you win the bonus for a "grand slam."

When you bid for all but one of the tricks and are successful, you receive the bonus for a "small slam." You must fulfill your contract in order to be eligible for the bonus.

A player holding any four of the honors in the trump suit (ace, king, queen, jack, ten) wins a bonus of 100 points. If he holds all five honors, the bonus is 150 points.

The only bonuses available to defenders are for "setting" their opponents (preventing them from making their contract). When declarer fails to make his contract, he loses an amount per trick depending upon whether he is doubled or vulnerable. The term "vulnerable" means that your side has won a game. If you are vulnerable, the points lost for failing to make contracts increase but some of the bonuses are increased. The term "double" means that one of the opponents believes that the contract will fail and is willing to double that value of the contract in order to increase the rewards for the penalty tricks. Doubling also affects the value of overtricks. The scoring table reflects the advantages and disadvantages of being vulnerable or doubled or both.

▶ HEARTS

Hearts is based on an 18th-century game called reverse, said to be of Spanish origin. Sometime after 1850 reverse gave way to the basic game of hearts.

The Game. In the basic form of hearts the full pack of 52 cards is dealt. The best game is four-handed, but from three to six persons may play. Some of the low cards (not hearts) are removed from the pack, so that each player is dealt the same number of cards.

The object of the game is to avoid winning any tricks that contain hearts. The hand to the left of the dealer leads, and each player must follow suit if he can. If lacking any card in a suit led, a player may discard any card in his hand. The rank of the cards is A, K, Q, J, 10, 9, 8, 7, 6, 5, 4, 3, 2. The winner of the hand is the player who has collected the least amount of hearts.

Black Lady. The most popular version of the game today is black lady, in which the queen of spades counts 13 and each heart

counts 1. Before the opening lead, each player passes any three cards from his hand to the player on his left. When the opening lead is won by the highest card in that suit, the winner of the trick leads the next trick, and so on until all 13 tricks are played out.

Each heart taken in a trick counts 1, and the queen of spades counts 13. However, if one player "shoots the moon" (wins the queen of spades and all 13 hearts), each of the other players gets 26 points. Each player's points are posted on a score sheet until one of the players reaches or exceeds 100 points. The player with the lowest score is then declared the winner.

▶ RUMMY

Rummy is believed to be an American adaptation of a Spanish game called conquian, which was introduced from Mexico in the middle of the 19th century.

Number of players. From two to six may play, each for himself. Four to six make a better game than two or three.

The Deal. A regular pack, consisting of 52 cards, is used. The dealer distributes cards one at a time, face down, in clockwise rotation, beginning with the player at his left. Each player receives ten cards when two play, seven cards when three or four play, and six cards when five or six play.

The undealt remainder of the pack is placed face down in the center of the table, and becomes the stock. The top card of the stock is turned face up and placed beside it; this up card starts the discard pile.

When two play, the winner deals the next hand. When more than two play, the turn to deal rotates clockwise.

Object of Play. A player tries to get rid of all his cards by melding them. To meld, he must form some or all of his hand into matched sets. A matched set may be made up of either (1) three or four cards of the same rank, as seven of spades, seven of hearts, seven of clubs, and seven of diamonds; or (2)

three or more cards of the same suit in sequence, as queen, jack, and 10 of spades. (In basic rummy the ace is 1, in sequence with the deuce (2), but not with the king.)

The Play. The hand to the left of the dealer plays first, and thereafter the turn to play rotates clockwise. Each player must begin his turn with a draw and end it with a discard. After his draw and before his discard, he may, if able and willing, meld any number of cards.

In drawing, the player always has the choice of taking either the top card of the stock or of the discard pile. He adds his card to his hand. He may discard any card then in his hand, placing the card face up on the up card of the discard pile. If he draws from the discard pile, he may not discard the same card in the same turn. The discard pile is kept squared up, and previous discards may not be examined.

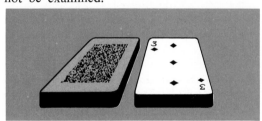

In melding, the player may lay down one or more matched sets, each of three or more cards; he may lay off any number of cards on melds already on the table—opponents' melds as well as his own.

The player who goes out first by getting rid of all cards in his hand wins the deal. If no player goes out by the time the last card of the stock is drawn, the discard pile is turned over (without shuffling) to form a new stock, and play continues. The next player in turn after the last card is drawn has a choice between the discard and the top of the new stock.

The winner scores points for the value of the cards remaining in other players' hands, whether they form matched sets or not. Face cards count 10 each; aces, 1; and spot cards

count at index value. When a player goes out, every player shows his full hand.

If a player "goes rummy" by melding his entire hand in one turn, having made no previous meld, he gets double the number of points from every other player.

There are many kinds of rummy. Two of these, canasta and gin rummy, are popular.

Canasta

Canasta, a form of rummy, originated in Uruguay and became popular in Argentina before spreading to North America.

Number of Players. From two to six persons may play. The game is best with four, in two partnerships. Six may play in partnerships of three on a side, partners competing alternately.

The Pack. Shuffle together two regular packs of 52 cards plus four jokers, making 108 cards in all.

Wild and Special Cards. The four jokers and all eight deuces are wild. A wild card may be designated to be of any rank, as the owner chooses. All treys (three spots) are special cards, the red treys being different from the black treys.

Value of Cards. Each card has a point value as follows:

Joker	50	Each 7, 6, 5, 4	5
Deuce	20	Black 3	5
Ace	20	Red 3	100
Each K, Q, J, 10, 9, 8	10		

When one side has all four treys, they count 200 each.

The Deal. When two play, each player receives 15 cards; when three play, 13 cards; when four or more play, 11 cards.

The remainder of the pack forms the stock. The top card of the stock is turned face up beside it; this up card starts the discard pile. The turn to deal rotates clockwise.

Object of Play. The object is twofold: (1) to score points by melding and (2) to meld all one's cards and also form at least one canasta, which is seven or more of a kind. Cards may be melded in matched sets or added to previous melds of the same player or partnership.

A matched set comprises three or more cards of the same rank. Wild cards may be used to fill sets and to increase them in size, subject to these limitations: Every canasta must include at least four natural cards and may not include more than three wild cards, but additional wild cards may be added to a completed canasta.

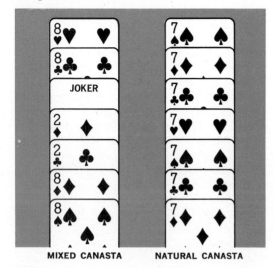

MIXED CANASTA   NATURAL CANASTA

Red treys are melded individually as drawn. Red treys are never thrown in the pack. They are melded, and another card is drawn in its place. They also count against a player if no other meld is made. Wild cards (jokers or deuces) may not be melded in sets apart from natural cards; black treys may be melded in sets only when a player is going out.

A set of seven or more cards is a canasta. A natural canasta includes no wild cards; one that contains any wild card is mixed.

If the up card is a red trey or a wild card, another card must be turned upon it from the stock and the discard pile is frozen.

When the discard pile is frozen, a player may take it only to meld the top card with a natural pair from his hand. For example, if the top card is a king, the pile may be taken only by showing a pair of kings from the hand.

Order of Play. The hand to the left of the dealer plays first, and the turn rotates clockwise. Each player begins his turn with a draw and ends it with a discard. After his draw and before his discard, he may meld any number of cards.

In drawing, a player may take the top card of the stock or the top card and all others in the discard pile, provided that he melds this card in the same turn.

After the initial meld the pack, *when not frozen,* may be taken with a pair corresponding to the top discard card, or with a wild card and one of the same card.

Once a pack has been frozen, which may be done by any player playing a joker, the pack may be taken only with a pair.

The black treys have a special function. They are called stop cards, and may never be taken by a player with a pair of them.

Minimum Count. The initial meld by a player or partnership must have a minimum count, according to the accumulated score of the side for all previous deals.

MINIMUM COUNT TABLE

ACCUMULATED SCORE	MINIMUM SCORE
Minus	No minimum
0–1495	50
1500–2995	90
3000 or more	120

Once a side has made its initial meld, consisting of one or more matched sets, there is no count requirement for additional melds by the same player or any of his partners.

Going Out. To go out in making the initial meld, a player must meld a canasta.

When a player goes out by getting rid of all cards from his hand, his side wins the bonus for going out and play ends.

A player may go out only if the melds of his side, including his final meld, include at least one canasta. Failing this requirement, he must keep at least one card in his hand. All melds of the same rank made by a partnership are put together to build up canastas.

A player goes out with a concealed hand if he melds all his cards at one turn, having made no other melds. He may not lay off a card. His melds must include a complete canasta, but he needs no minimum point value.

The game is over when one side reaches a score of 5000 or more.

Scoring. When play ends, each player or partnership determines its net score for the deal by taking all appropriate items of the following schedule:

For going out	100
For concealed hand	100
For each red trey	100
For all four treys	800
For each natural canasta	500
For each mixed canasta	300
Total values for all cards melded	——
Total	——
Total value of all cards remaining in hand	——
Difference; net score, plus or minus	——

Gin Rummy

This game was invented in 1909 by Elwood T. Baker of Brooklyn, New York, a whist teacher. The game was popular from 1927 to 1930; then it was rarely played until 1940, when the motion picture colony and the radio world adopted it and gave it the publicity that made it a fad game.

Number of Players. Gin rummy is a two-handed game and is hardly ever played in any other form.

The Pack. A regular pack of 52 cards is used.

Rank of Cards. The rank of the cards is K, Q, J, 10, 9, 8, 7, 6, 5, 4, 3, 2, A.

Value of Cards. Face cards count 10 each; aces, 1; other cards, their spot value.

The Deal. The dealer distributes 10 cards one at a time, face down, alternately to his opponent and to himself.

The pack is then placed face down in the center of the table, becoming the stock. The top card of the stock is turned face up and placed beside it; this up card starts the discard pile.

The winner of a hand deals the next hand. The winner of a game deals the first hand of the next game.

Object of Play. The object of play is to reduce one's count of unused cards to less than the count of one's opponent by forming matched sets consisting of three or four cards of the same rank or three or more cards of the same suit in sequence.

The Play. The nondealer plays first, and the turn to play alternates thereafter. In each turn a player must draw either the up card (top card of the discard pile) or the top card of the stock, and then must discard one card (which may not be an up card he has drawn in the same turn) face up on the discard pile.

On the first play, if the nondealer does not wish to take the up card he must so announce, and the dealer may have the first turn by drawing the up card; if the dealer does not wish the up card, the nondealer draws the top card of the stock and play proceeds.

A player may knock (indicate he is going out) in any turn after drawing and before discarding if the value of the unmatched cards in his hand, after he discards, will be 10 points or less. However, he is not required to knock. If he decides to knock, he discards one

card face down and spreads his hand, which is arranged into matched sets and unmatched cards. The opponent then spreads his hand, removes from it any unmatched sets, and lays off whatever cards he has that match the knocker's matched sets.

The point values of the two players' unmatched cards are then compared, and the result of the hand is scored.

Scoring. If the knocker's count is less than his opponent's, the knocker wins the hand; the difference in counts is scored to his credit.

If the opponent ties or beats the knocker, he has undercut him; he wins the hand and scores 25 points plus the difference in counts.

If the knocker has a count of zero (has all 10 of his cards matched in sets), he is gin; his opponent may not lay off, and the knocker wins the hand even if the opponent also has a count of zero; the knocker receives 25 points plus the difference in counts.

A running total of each player's score is kept, with a line drawn under his score every time he wins a hand. (Example: A player wins the first hand by 11 points; he scores 11 and draws a line under it. The same player wins the next hand by 14 points; he writes down 25 and draws another line.)

Game. The player first scoring 100 points or more wins the game. He adds to his score 100 points game bonus.

If the loser has not won a hand during that game, the winner adds an additional 100-point shutout bonus.

Each player then adds to his score 25 points for every hand he has won (called a line or box bonus).

The two players' total scores then are determined, and the player with the higher score wins the difference between the two scores.

Hollywood Gin. A popular version of gin rummy is one in which two players play three games simultaneously. The first hand won by a player counts for game number 1; his second winning hand begins game number 2, and is also credited toward game number 1; the third and any future wins are recorded on all three games. When either player wins a game, that game is closed. The scores that follow are registered in the remaining games.

CHARLES H. GOREN
International authority on card games

CAREERS. See VOCATIONS.

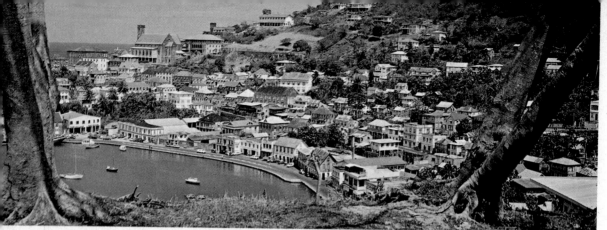

Two harbors illustrate the sharp contrasts found on Caribbean islands. St. George's *(above)* is in hilly Grenada. Willemstad *(below)*, in Curaçao, is quite low and flat.

The gate of the "Iron Market" in Port-au-Prince, capital of Haiti, is a famous tourist attraction.

CARIBBEAN SEA AND ISLANDS

South of the United States, starting at a point about 160 kilometers (100 miles) from the tip of Florida, lie the Caribbean islands, known also as the Antilles. The Antilles form an arc stretching about 3,220 kilometers (2,000 miles) east and south to the coast of Venezuela. Between this arc of islands and the mainland of North, South, and Central America lies the Caribbean Sea. An arm of the Atlantic Ocean, the Caribbean covers an area of about 1,942,500 square kilometers (750,000 square miles). The Panama Canal connects the Caribbean with the Pacific Ocean, making the sea a major waterway.

Named for the Carib Indians who once inhabited the smaller islands, the sea is known for its clear blue color. The temperature of the water rarely falls below 24° C (75° F). Beautiful tropical fish and fascinating marine life, including many kinds of coral, thrive in the mild waters. Swimming, fishing, and snorkeling are popular sports.

There are several hundred islands in the Caribbean. The four largest, known as the Greater Antilles, are Cuba, Hispaniola (Haiti

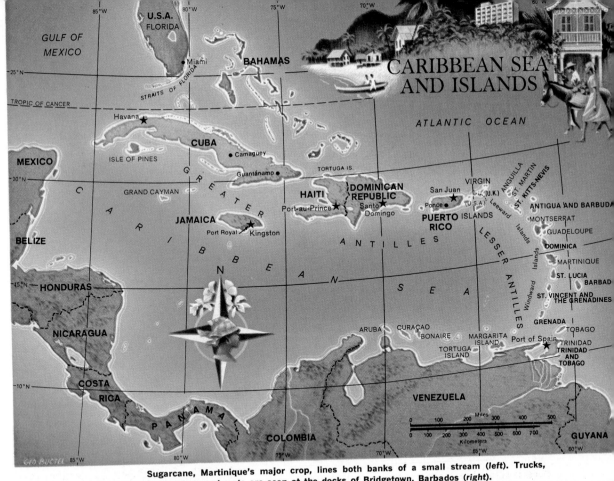

CARIBBEAN SEA
AND ISLANDS

Sugarcane, Martinique's major crop, lines both banks of a small stream (*left*). Trucks, buses, cars, and carts are seen at the docks of Bridgetown, Barbados (*right*).

A sunbather relaxes on one of Tobago's many beaches.

and the Dominican Republic), Jamaica, and Puerto Rico. These comprise more than 90 percent of the land area and are the home of over 80 percent of the inhabitants. East and south are the Lesser Antilles, which are made up of the Leeward and the Windward islands. Except for fall hurricanes, which sometimes cause great damage, the climate throughout the area is pleasant. Temperatures average about 21 to 29°C (70 to 85°F).

Tourism is a major source of income. Sugarcane, spices, limes, bananas, oranges, cacao, and coffee are among the products grown, and most of these are exported. In the Virgin Islands and the Dominican Republic, cattle raising is a major industry. Aruba, Curaçao, and Trinidad produce petroleum, and Jamaica has large deposits of bauxite, a chief source of aluminum.

PRINCIPAL ISLANDS IN THE CARIBBEAN

GREATER ANTILLES

Cuba (ind.), Hispaniola—Haiti (ind.) and Dominican Republic (ind.), Jamaica (ind.), Puerto Rico (U.S.).

LESSER ANTILLES

Anguilla (Br.), Antigua and Barbuda (ind.), Dominica (ind.), Guadeloupe (Fr.), Martinique (Fr.), St. Kitts—Nevis (ind.), St. Lucia (ind.), St. Martin (Fr.-Neth.), St. Vincent and the Grenadines (ind.).

Virgin Islands (U.S.)

| St. Croix | St. John | St. Thomas |

Virgin Islands (Br.)

| Tortola | Anegada | Peter Island | Salt Island |

OTHER ISLANDS

Aruba (Neth.), Barbados (ind.), Bonaire (Neth.), Curaçao (Neth.), Grenada (ind.), Margarita (Venez.), Trinidad and Tobago (ind.), Tortuga (Venez.).

KEY

Br.—British; Fr.—French; ind.—independent; Neth.—Netherlands; U.S.—United States; Venez.—Venezuela.

▶ HISTORY

Christopher Columbus discovered Hispaniola and Cuba on his first voyage in 1492. Believing he had reached India, he called the inhabitants Indians.

Columbus returned to Spain with exciting stories of gold in the lands he had discovered. The Spanish monarchs, King Ferdinand and Queen Isabella, eager to enrich their treasury, arranged to send colonists to the new territory. On September 25, 1493, 17 ships carrying over 1,000 settlers began the second voyage across the seas to Hispaniola.

The early years were filled with difficulties. Food was scarce, sickness became widespread, and hostility between the displaced Indians and the disappointed Spaniards increased. In 1502 Ferdinand and Isabella sent a Spanish governor, Don Nicolás de Ovando, to the New World. Under Don Nicolás, the colony on Hispaniola began to flourish. Settlements grew up on neighboring islands, and Spain established a strong foothold in the area.

But many of the governor's methods were harsh. Workers were needed for farming and cattle raising, and the Indians were forced into service. Unable to withstand the cruel treatment by their masters, the Indians of the Caribbean region were almost wiped out within a few generations.

As the colonies prospered, more European nations began to take an interest in the area, and for 300 years foreign powers vied for control. In the 17th century the French settled Martinique and Guadeloupe, and the

English started a colony on Barbados. The Dutch captured Curaçao from the Spanish, and the Danes settled St. Thomas. When piracy became common, pirate crews, often with the approval of their governments, plundered Spanish ships and sacked Spanish settlements. Laborers were needed to work the land, and slaves were imported from Africa. Soon there were many more blacks than Europeans on most of the islands. During the 18th and 19th centuries, as Spain's control continued to decline, France and Britain became leading Caribbean powers.

The 20th century has brought additional changes. The United States bought St. Thomas, St. Croix, and St. John (the Virgin Islands) from Denmark in 1917. Trinidad and Tobago joined in 1962 to become the nation of Trinidad and Tobago. Barbados became independent in 1966. The following year the West Indies Associated States was created, and Antigua, Dominica, Grenada, St. Kitts–Nevis–Anguilla, St. Lucia, and St. Vincent achieved self-government under the United Kingdom. By 1981 all but St. Kitts–Nevis and Anguilla had taken their place among the independent countries of the world.

History as well as geography has made the islands of the Caribbean wonderful places to visit. The traveler can enjoy the French influence in Martinique, the English influence in Jamaica and Barbados, or the Dutch influence in Curaçao. Spanish culture remains in Cuba, Puerto Rico, and the Dominican Republic. The Danes have left their mark in the Virgin Islands. Each island reflects a bit of its own unique history. Today many people throughout the region have gained control over their own political and economic affairs.

Reviewed by A. Curtis Wilgus
Author, *Historical Atlas of Latin America*

See also ANTIGUA AND BARBUDA; BARBADOS; CUBA; DOMINICA; DOMINICAN REPUBLIC; GRENADA; HAITI; JAMAICA; PUERTO RICO; SAINT KITTS–NEVIS; SAINT LUCIA; SAINT VINCENT AND THE GRENADINES; TRINIDAD AND TOBAGO.

CARILLONS. See BELLS AND CARILLONS.

CARNEGIE, ANDREW (1835–1919)

Andrew Carnegie built the steel industry in the United States and became rich. But he believed a wealthy person's money belonged to the community in which it was earned. In the last 18 years of his life, he shared much of his fortune with other people.

He was born in Dunfermline, Scotland, on November 25, 1835. When he was 13, the family moved to the United States and settled in Pittsburgh, Pennsylvania.

In 1850 Carnegie went to work for the Pittsburgh telegraph office, first as a messenger and later as an operator. Thomas Scott, the superintendent of the Pennsylvania Railroad's western division, hired him as his personal clerk in 1853. Six years later, Carnegie himself became superintendent. During the Civil War, Scott served as assistant secretary of war, and Carnegie helped him set up railroads and a telegraph system for the Union Army.

Meanwhile, Carnegie began to invest in different businesses—oil fields, ironworks, and companies that made locomotives and sleeping cars. In 1865 he resigned from the railroad to concentrate on iron and steel manufacturing. He foresaw that the United States would need more and more steel, and he became known as the Steel King. In 1901 he sold his steel empire. It became part of the United States Steel Corporation.

Carnegie once declared, "He who dies rich, dies disgraced." He used his fortune to help other people. He founded the Carnegie Institute of Pittsburgh, which has a library, a museum of fine arts, and a museum of natural history. He also founded a school of technology (now part of Carnegie-Mellon University, in Pittsburgh). Through the Carnegie Corporation of New York, he gave large sums to establish free libraries and to further education. Much of Carnegie's wealth went to promote world peace, through the Carnegie Endowment for International Peace. And he set up the Carnegie Institute of Washington to fund scientific research.

Carnegie died on August 11, 1919, shortly after the end of World War I.

Reviewed by GERALD KURLAND
Author, *Andrew Carnegie*

CARNIVALS

What do you think of when you hear the word "carnival"? Do you think of a traveling show that comes to town with exciting rides and games of chance? An entertainment put on by the local volunteer fire department or some other community organization to raise money? Or a yearly celebration like the Mardi Gras in New Orleans or the winter carnival in Quebec City? All of these are carnivals, and they aim to provide fun for people.

The word "carnival" comes from the Latin words *carnem levare*, "to put aside flesh [meat]." It seems closely related also to the Latin expression *carne vale!* ("flesh, farewell!") The carnival had its origin hundreds of years ago in the feasting and merrymaking just before the beginning of Lent. (Lent is the long period of penance before Easter during which Christians may fast and eat no meat.)

▶ MARDI GRAS AND SIMILAR CARNIVALS

Pre-Lenten carnivals are still held each year in many towns and cities of Europe and the Americas where the people are mostly Catholic. Among the most famous carnivals are those of Nice, France; Munich, West Germany; and Rio de Janeiro, Brazil. Carnivals generally include parades of costumed revelers and colorful floats, street dancing, and fancy dress balls. There may also be fireworks and "battles" with flowers or confetti.

The carnival season begins officially on Twelfth Night (January 6). But most of the celebrating occurs just before the beginning of Lent on Ash Wednesday. The French call the last day of the carnival Mardi Gras, which means "Fat Tuesday" (from the custom of using up all fats on the day before Lent).

Mardi Gras is celebrated with a carnival in several cities of the United States that were founded by French or Spanish settlers. The most famous is the festival in New Orleans, Louisiana. There the term "Mardi Gras" stands for the two-week carnival period before Lent.

Special organizations, called krewes, prepare the festivities of Mardi Gras in New Orleans. The first, the Mystic Krewe of Comus, was formed in 1857. Its purpose was to celebrate Mardi Gras with good taste. Invitation to membership in a krewe is considered an honor.

The most famous events of Mardi Gras are the parades (with floats and marchers in colorful costumes) and the balls. Each procession and ball has a different theme. An important part of the Mardi Gras is the appearance of Rex, king of the carnival. He is chosen for his outstanding leadership in the community. But his identity is supposed to be kept secret.

▶ TRAVELING CARNIVALS

Carnivals that move from town to town originated in the United States in the late 1890's. Today they sometimes operate in connection with fairs or in amusement parks. To raise money, fire departments, churches, and schools often sponsor the visit of a traveling carnival. Groups similar to American carnivals now tour in many other countries, including the Soviet Union. In Britain, traveling carnivals are known as fun fairs.

Early carnivals in the United States all traveled by railroad. Since good highways are plentiful today, most carnivals now travel in trucks. Traveling carnivals always play outdoors, and their season runs from early spring to late fall. In the southern United States, a few carnivals play winter dates.

The "front end" of the show lot is the main entrance. It is lined with concessions. Here are refreshment stands, with everything from cotton candy to frankfurters, and games of skill and chance, with prizes for the winners— giant stuffed pandas, perhaps.

At the "back end" of the lot are the rides and often a huge fun house. Children's rides may include small fire engines, a merry-go-round, carts, and boats. At major carnivals, where many people attend, there may be up to 75 rides for adults. The Giant Wheel, Sky Fighter, and Octopus are just a few. Many rides are manufactured in the United States. Others are imported from Europe.

When a carnival is not on the road, it is in winter quarters, usually in the same part of the country where it plays. Here equipment is repaired and repainted and made ready for the spring opening. The canvas tents are mended, and the concession booths are repainted and repaired. When the show comes out in the spring, it will look brand new.

Carnivals bring special amusements to many fairs, such as this state fair at Phoenix, Arizona.

Vast crowds attend the New Orleans Mardi Gras.

The Winter Carnival in Quebec.

Carnival life is not easy. The lots are often muddy and washed out by summer downpours. Or they are dry, and dust may cover the concession stands and rides. The usual routine consists of unpacking and setting up, working the stands, repacking and loading up, and moving to the next town. A carnival usually moves once a week. The people of these traveling shows take great pride in what they do. People of a carnival are a closely knit group. Often entire families work for the same show. The ownership and management of almost all large carnivals has been passed on from one generation to the next.

Carnivals are very popular because of the wide variety of entertainment that they offer.

More individual tickets are sold each year to carnivals and carnival attractions than to any other live entertainment in the United States. Totals of ticket sales are close to those of movie ticket sales. Very few of the hundreds of smaller fairs could exist without the attraction of a carnival. Even large state fairs depend on carnivals to increase the number of visitors.

Traveling carnivals continue to thrive because they furnish a type of entertainment in which people can take part directly.

JOSEPH W. MCKENNON
Curatorial Consultant
Ringling Museum of the Circus

See also CIRCUS.

CAROLS

Carols are songs associated with the Christmas season. Since Christmas is a season of joy and good cheer, most carols are joyous and cheerful in character. They have lilting rhythms and gay melodies. They are easy to sing and easy to remember. Carols may have either religious or secular words. Many express a mixture of religious feelings and hearty merriment. Some of the oldest songs we know are Christmas carols.

Carols began as dance songs. In the Middle Ages the word "carol" meant to dance in a ring while singing. This explains the lively character of so many of the old carols. Not all carols have been about Christmas. The earliest were songs celebrating May Day and the seasons of the year. Carols dating from the 15th century in England dealt with a variety of subjects—even politics. Many of the old French carols consisted of religious words sung to popular tunes of the day. Some of them even began with the same words as the popular songs. (In France a Christmas carol is called a *noël*.)

The oldest English carol that is still sung regularly today is "The Boar's Head." It was first published in England in 1521. "The Boar's Head" is part of a traditional festival in England at Queen's College, Oxford. It is chanted while a boar's head is carried in a procession. Two other English carols, "Wassail Song" and "Down in Yon Forest," are among the oldest songs of any kind that we know. The first is a drinking song; the second was sung by wandering troubadours in the Middle Ages. The most popular of the old English carols today is probably "God Rest Ye Merry, Gentlemen." There are several different versions of this lovely carol; some of them date from the 1500's. "The First Noel," one of the oldest of all carols, may have come from France. However, some scholars believe it to be of English origin. It has a serene and radiant melody that describes the first Christmas Eve, when a star from the east shone over Bethlehem. We do not know the names of the composers of any of these old carols.

The composers of carols that were written in more recent times are known. One of the most beautiful of all religious melodies is *Adeste Fideles* ("O Come, All Ye Faithful").

Both the words and music probably were written by an English music teacher named John Francis Wade (1711–86?) and published in 1751. The words to the stirring "Hark! The Herald Angels Sing!" are those of the English hymn writer Charles Wesley (1707–88). They were later adapted to a melody of Felix Mendelssohn's. Another English hymn writer, Isaac Watts (1674–1748), wrote the popular carol "Joy to the World." It was arranged to the music of George Frederick Handel by the American composer Lowell Mason (1792–1872). A minister in Philadelphia named Phillips Brooks (1835–93) wrote "O, Little Town of Bethlehem" in 1868 after a visit to Christ's birthplace. His church organist, Lewis Redner, composed the melody. Edmund H. Sears (1810–76), another American minister, wrote the words of "It Came Upon a Midnight Clear" in 1849. The music is by Richard S. Willis (1819–1900), an American composer and writer.

In Germany and Austria a carol is called a *Weihnachtslied* ("Christmas Eve song"). The beautiful German carol "Lo, How a Rose E'er Blooming," by Michael Praetorius (1571–1621), is a well-known favorite outside Germany. The most popular of all Christmas carols is perhaps "Silent Night, Holy Night!" (*Stille Nacht, Heilige Nacht!*). Joseph Mohr, pastor of a little church in Oberndorf, Austria, wrote the words on Christmas Eve, 1818. The organist of his church, Franz Gruber, composed the music the same evening and played it at the midnight Mass. It was played on a guitar that evening because the organ had mice in its bellows. A concert troupe called the Strasser Children later carried the carol to all parts of Europe. Today it is sung throughout the world wherever Christmas is celebrated.

Among the most recent Christmas songs, Irving Berlin's "White Christmas" (1942) has achieved the status of a modern Christmas carol. In America songs like "Jingle Bells" and "Rudolph the Red-Nosed Reindeer" are so strongly associated with Christmas that they too are often thought of as carols.

DAVID EWEN
Music Historian

CARPENTRY. See WOODWORKING.
CARPETBAGGERS. See RECONSTRUCTION PERIOD.
CARPETS. See RUGS AND CARPETS.

CARROLL, LEWIS (1832–1898)

Alice's Adventures in Wonderland has been read and loved by children for over 100 years. It was written by Charles Lutwidge Dodgson, who used the pen name Lewis Carroll.

As a boy, Charles delighted in entertaining his ten brothers and sisters. His father was the vicar of Daresbury, in western England, when Charles was born, on January 27, 1832. The family moved to Croft in 1843. Taught by his father until he was 12 years old, Charles then attended Richmond Grammar School and, later, Rugby. He spent a year preparing for Oxford and entered Christ Church College there in 1851. He remained at Christ Church the rest of his life, teaching mathematics and acting as a church deacon. But he was not a brilliant lecturer. A bad stammer was a severe handicap to him, and he was most at ease with children.

One day, July 4, 1862, Dodgson and his friend Robinson Duckworth took Lorina, Alice, and Edith Liddell, daughters of the dean, for a picnic up the Isis River. Alice, aged 10, begged for a story, and Dodgson began telling a tale about Alice's adventures underground.

At the end of the day, Alice said, "Oh, Mr. Dodgson, I wish you would write out Alice's adventures for me." Three years later to the day, he sent her *Alice's Adventures in Wonderland*. It was not the first book published by Dodgson, but it was the first by Lewis Carroll. Dodgson published works on mathematics, games, and college interests under his own name and children's stories and verse under the name Lewis Carroll.

Dodgson was also a pioneer in British amateur photography and was the outstanding photographer of children in the 19th century. He spent much time on his mathematical books and the games he invented. But his masterpieces were his imaginative works— *Alice's Adventures in Wonderland* (1865), *Through the Looking-Glass* (1872), and *The Hunting of the Snark* (1876). He died on January 14, 1898, of a severe bronchial cold.

See also ALICE IN WONDERLAND.

CARSON, KIT (1809–1868)

Fur trapper and scout, soldier and Indian fighter, Kit Carson was the first great hero of the American Far West.

Christopher (Kit was a nickname) Carson was born in Kentucky on December 24, 1809. While he was still a baby, his parents moved to Missouri. Life on the Missouri frontier was too busy to allow time for school, and Carson never learned how to read or write until he was in his 50's.

When he was 15, Kit was apprenticed to a saddle maker. A year later he ran away to join a wagon train heading west and settled in Taos, New Mexico. Kit looked out of place next to the big, tough fur trappers of the West. He was a rather short, slender man, with long blond hair and blue eyes. But he was as strong and quick as a panther. Within a few years he had made a reputation as a daring trapper and hunter. Kit was also well known to the Indians. They called him the Little Chief.

In 1842, Carson met Lieutenant John C. Frémont. Congress had sent Frémont to explore the Rocky Mountains to see if there was a safe path for settlers to cross. Frémont hired Carson to guide him over the rugged, unmapped Rockies. Between 1842 and 1845 Carson guided three expeditions across the mountains to California.

When the Mexican War broke out in 1846, Carson acted as an army scout and carried dispatches back East. Once he saved an American army that had been surrounded by Mexicans. Escaping from the circle of enemy soldiers, Kit brought back reinforcements just in time.

Later Carson became United States Indian agent in Taos. He was an excellent choice for the job. The Indians respected Carson's honesty and fairness.

During the Civil War, Carson organized and commanded the 1st New Mexico Volunteers, who fought on the Union side. By the end of the war, he had risen to the rank of brigadier general. A few years later, on May 23, 1868, he died at the age of 58.

See also FRÉMONT, JOHN CHARLES.

JAMES EARL CARTER, JR. (1924–)

39TH PRESIDENT OF THE UNITED STATES

CARTER, JAMES EARL, JR. When we think of Abraham Lincoln, we see him as a poor boy of the frontier, studying by candlelight, working in a country store, splitting logs, striving to make something of himself. We may wonder at his ability to travel from a log cabin to the White House. His story has helped form the American dream—that a person coming from a modest background can attain spectacular success.

James Earl (Jimmy) Carter, Jr., achieved that dream. His roots were in the southwestern part of Georgia, where members of his family had struggled to make a living for 150 years. He was the first Carter to finish high school. People who knew him well said that Carter's strongest trait was his humility—he never forgot his humble beginnings or the people who helped him become president of the United States.

▶ EARLY YEARS

Carter was born in the little town of Plains, Georgia (population about 670), on October 1, 1924. He was the first child of James Earl Carter and Lillian Gordy Carter. Later two daughters, Gloria and Ruth, and another son, William, were born to the Carters. The elder Carter was the manager of a grocery store. In time he was able to acquire some farmland of his own in Archery, just outside Plains.

When Jimmy was not going to school, he was working on the farm. He sold peanuts as a sideline and saved the money he earned. Of his childhood, Carter later said: "In general, the early years of my life on the farm were full and enjoyable, isolated but not lonely. We always had enough to eat—no economic hardship but no money to waste."

Jimmy was a good student and an avid reader. His mother encouraged his reading. The family would read at the dinner table, and Carter and his own family later continued this practice. "What this shows," a Carter aide once said, "is Carter's insistence on using every moment to good advantage."

Jimmy grew up with blacks. His father felt that blacks and whites should not mix, but his mother's attitude was completely different. Apparently his mother's example was the stronger. Years later, when he became governor of Georgia, Carter said in his inaugural address: "The time for racial discrimination is over. No poor, rural, weak or black person should ever have to bear the additional burden of being deprived of the opportunity of

Left: Jimmy Carter, aged 16, at a Future Farmers of America camp. Above: Graduation day at Annapolis. Rosalynn and his mother attach his ensign's bars.

an education, a job, or simple justice." He was generally well received by blacks, and a number of black leaders supported his campaign for the presidency.

▶ NAVAL OFFICER AND BUSINESSMAN

Jimmy graduated from high school with very high marks. From his first days at school, he had wanted to attend the United States Naval Academy at Annapolis. An uncle whom he idolized had been in the Navy. At the same time, it meant a chance for a college education, for there was very little money in the family.

Carter received an appointment to the Naval Academy in 1942. But first he spent a year at the Georgia Institute of Technology in Atlanta, taking courses that would help him to pass the entrance examinations to Annapolis. He entered the academy in 1943 and at first was homesick. He adapted to the strict discipline, did well in his studies, ran track and cross-country, and played on the lightweight football team. He graduated in 1946 in the upper 10 percent of his class. Soon after, he married Rosalynn Smith, whose family lived near Plains. He had met her in his last year at the Naval Academy. The Carters had four children: John, James Earl 3rd (Chip), Jeffrey, and Amy.

Carter spent seven years in the Navy, attaining the rank of lieutenant senior grade. During part of that time he worked with Admiral Hyman G. Rickover in the nuclear submarine program. Carter's ambition then was to become an admiral. But when his father died in 1953, Carter felt that it was necessary to return to the family farm.

▶ HIS POLITICAL CAREER BEGINS

Carter's interest in politics can be traced at least in part to his father, who had served a year in the Georgia state legislature. In 1962, Carter ran for the state Senate. He lost by a few votes. But when violations of voting rules were discovered, he challenged the results and was declared the winner.

In 1966, Carter first declared himself a candidate for the U.S. House of Representatives but then decided to try for the Democratic nomination for governor of Georgia. He lost in the primary election, but he made a good showing. Carter devoted himself to his business and to civic affairs until 1970. Then he tried again for the governorship. He defeated a former governor of the state in the primary and won the election easily.

Carter's first order of business was to streamline Georgia's state government. He moved quickly to reduce the number of state agencies from 300 to 22, with the goal of increasing efficiency.

▶ CAMPAIGN FOR THE PRESIDENCY

Carter announced his candidacy for the presidency late in 1974. He campaigned tire-

Carter prospered as a Georgia peanut farmer.

The Carter family in 1976. Seated: Mrs. Carter; President Carter; Amy; Jeffrey's wife, Annette; and Jeffrey. At rear (left to right): James, 3rd and his wife, Caron; John and his wife, Judy.

IMPORTANT DATES IN THE LIFE OF JAMES EARL CARTER, JR.

1924	Born at Plains, Georgia, October 1.
1946	Graduated from the United States Naval Academy; married Rosalynn Smith.
1947–1953	Served in the United States Navy.
1963–1967	Served in the Georgia state Senate.
1971–1975	Served as governor of Georgia.
1976	Elected president of the United States.
1979	Egyptian-Israeli treaty signed. SALT II signed.

lessly, sought the support of Democratic leaders, and built an efficient political staff. His soft southern drawl and wide smile became familiar across the country.

Carter was sometimes accused of changing his position on important and controversial issues to gain votes. Still, his appeal was obvious. He entered 29 primary contests across the nation and won 17 of them. By the time of the Democratic National Convention in New York in the summer of 1976, he had already won enough delegates to assure his nomination. The only question that remained was whom he would pick as the vice-presidential candidate. He chose Walter F. Mondale, a liberal senator from Minnesota. In the election, Carter defeated the Republican candidate, President Gerald R. Ford. Carter received 297 electoral votes, and Ford had 240.

▶ THE WHITE HOUSE YEARS

The new President adopted a casual style. Carter chose to walk instead of ride down Pennsylvania Avenue after his inauguration. On one occasion, he dressed casually in a sweater to address the nation on television. And he requested that the presidential theme, "Hail to the Chief," not be played every time he entered a public place. Many people welcomed this simplicity. But others were critical of Carter's style, which sometimes seemed less than forceful. They wondered how he would deal with the country's serious problems. And while Democrats held a majority in Congress, Congress did not always support Carter's proposals.

In the United States, Carter's administration faced major problems in the areas of energy supply and the economy. Soon after taking office, Carter declared what he called the "moral equivalent of war" on rising costs and tight supplies of oil. He asked Congress to create a new Department of Energy. And he proposed legislation to reduce oil consumption, increase U.S. oil production, and encourage the use of other energy sources. Congress approved the new department and, after much debate, some of the legislation.

Inflation soon became the leading economic problem. In 1978, Carter called for voluntary limits on wage and price increases. The limits had little effect. Later, controls were

President Carter with his vice-president, Walter F. Mondale of Minnesota.

Egyptian President Anwar el-Sadat, President Carter, and Israeli Prime Minister Menahem Begin at 1978 summit.

imposed on credit. The government hoped that by discouraging borrowing, it would lessen the rate of inflation.

In foreign policy, Carter often stressed moral principles. His goals, he said, were peace, arms control, economic co-operation, and the advancement of human rights. His efforts toward peace in the Middle East were widely acclaimed. In the fall of 1978, the leaders of Egypt and Israel met with him at Camp David, Maryland, and agreed on basic principles for a peace treaty. A treaty was signed in 1979. But negotiations on details of the peace made slow progress.

Carter concluded new treaties with Panama, giving that country control of the Panama Canal by the year 2000. These treaties were controversial, but they were ratified by the U.S. Senate in 1978. Diplomatic relations with the People's Republic of China were established early in 1979. And in June, 1979, Carter signed a new strategic arms limitation treaty with the Soviet Union. But this treaty met with strong opposition in Congress.

Meanwhile, a new gasoline shortage and continuing economic problems had brought Carter's popularity to an all-time low by July, 1979. In a televised speech, Carter said that the United States was facing a "crisis of confidence." He promised to provide strong leadership, and he outlined a new energy program. Then, at the end of 1979, two events tested Carter's leadership. In November, Iranian militants seized the U.S. embassy in Teheran and held the Americans there hostage. And in December, the Soviet Union sent troops into Afghanistan to put down a rebellion against that country's Communist government.

To free the hostages, the United States attempted to negotiate with Iran. (Iran's leaders had come to power in a revolution earlier in the year, and they supported the militants.) Carter also halted trade with Iran and called on other countries to do likewise, and he appealed to the United Nations and the World Court. When these measures were not successful, Carter ordered military action in April, 1980, to rescue the hostages. But the mission was called off when equipment broke down.

As a result of the Soviet action in Afghanistan, Carter asked Congress to delay consideration of the new arms treaty. He limited trade with the Soviet Union and called for a boycott of the 1980 Olympic Games, which were held in Moscow.

Support for the President was strong at the start of these crises. But as 1980 wore on, there seemed to be little progress toward solving them. And economic problems continued—the United States entered a recession, and unemployment rose. Opinion polls showed Carter's popularity falling.

In the election of November, 1980, Carter faced Ronald W. Reagan, a Republican and a former governor of California. Representative John B. Anderson of Illinois was also in the race, as an independent. Reagan won the election. Carter then continued his efforts to obtain the release of the hostages. On January 20th, 1981, the day he left office, the hostages were set free.

GODFREY SPERLING, JR.
The Christian Science Monitor

CARTIER, JACQUES (1491–1557)

Like many early explorers who sailed to the New World, Jacques Cartier hoped to find a short route to Asia. Though he never found a route to the riches of the East, Cartier discovered the St. Lawrence River and established the first French settlement in North America.

Cartier was born in the French seaport of St. Malo in 1491—a year before Columbus sailed for America. Little is known about his early life except that he became a skillful sailor and navigator. He is believed to have sailed to the coast of Canada in 1524 and to Brazil in 1528.

Earlier, the Portuguese explorer Ferdinand Magellan had reached the Pacific Ocean by sailing around the southern tip of South America. But many geographers believed that a shorter passage to Asia could be found by sailing northwest—around North America. (No one then knew how vast the North American continent was.) In 1534 King Francis I of France sent Cartier to find this Northwest Passage.

Cartier sailed into the Gulf of St. Lawrence through the Strait of Belle Isle, north of Newfoundland. After exploring the coasts of western Newfoundland, Prince Edward Island, and New Brunswick, he stopped at the Gaspé Peninsula. There Cartier erected a cross and claimed all the land for King Francis. He met friendly Indians and took two of them back to France with him. The Indians told of a land rich in gold and silver, called the kingdom of the Saguenay. They said this land could be reached by way of the Ottawa River.

Cartier believed that this river might be the Northwest Passage. So in 1535 he returned to North America with three ships. He sailed up the mighty St. Lawrence River past the Indian village of Stadacona, the site of modern Quebec city. He reached the Indian village of Hochelaga. There he climbed a steep hill hoping to see the mythical kingdom of the Saguenay. Cartier called the hill Mont Réal (Mount Royal). Today the city of Montreal stands on the site of Hochelaga.

Cartier's interest was kept alive by more tales of gold and silver mines to the west. But bad weather forced him to return to Stadacona, where he spent the winter. The men had no fresh fruits and vegetables, and many of them died of scurvy (a disease caused by lack of vitamin C). When Cartier returned to France the next spring, he had to leave one ship behind because he had lost so many men.

Though Cartier had failed to find the Northwest Passage, the French government was excited by his reports of gold and silver. They decided to establish a colony in New France. In 1541 an expedition of 10 ships set out under the Sieur de Roberval, with Cartier as pilot. Roberval turned back, but Cartier continued. A few miles above Stadacona, Cartier built a fort and named it Cap Rouge. He spent the winter collecting what he thought were gold and diamonds. When spring came he hurried back to France. But the "gold" and "diamonds" proved to be worthless, and the government refused to spend any more money on New France. Cartier returned to sailing and trading. On September 1, 1557, he died at St. Malo.

Cartier's settlement lasted only a year, but it was the beginning of the French empire in North America.

JOHN S. MOIR
University of Toronto

JACQUES CARTIER'S VOYAGES
TO NORTH AMERICA

CARTOONS

Have you ever watched someone looking at a magazine? What feature attracts attention first? If the magazine contains cartoons, the reader will probably look at them before reading the stories or articles. People often do the same when reading a newspaper. The comic strips may be amusing, but the editorial cartoon can bring a frown instead of a smile.

Because they are usually entertaining and because it takes only a moment to look at them, cartoons are read by nearly everyone. Cartoons have a message, funny or serious. Cartoonists know that just about every reader of the publication in which their work is printed will react to their message. Cartoons may make us laugh, but they can also make us think about important matters.

▶ THE HISTORY OF CARTOONS

The founder of the modern cartoon was the English artist William Hogarth (1697–1764). There were others before him—others who drew pictures that made fun of silly customs and behavior—but it was with Hogarth that the art of cartooning began. Hogarth was interested in human nature—in the character and attitudes of people. His drawings ridiculed drunkenness, the stupidity of spoiled youngsters, the custom of parents arranging marriages for their children, and crooked elections, to name only a few. The characteristics that Hogarth described are called universal, for they existed not only in England but everywhere, not only in the 18th century but always. Unfortunately, crime and evil exist everywhere and at all times.

Cartoons in Print: Magazines and Journals

Another English artist, Thomas Rowlandson (1756–1827), continued the work of Hogarth. Rowlandson worked mainly in etchings. These are prints made from drawings that have been etched (burned with acid) into copper. His cartoons were printed in large quantities and sent all over England. They were fancy and humorous. Rowlandson exaggerated human features to make people look ridiculous. Known as a caricature, this type of cartoon suggests what people might look like if their appearances matched their behavior.

Early in the 19th century, publishers of

HAZEL by Ted Key

"Dinner!"

THE SATURDAY EVENING POST

European journals began inserting cartoons, such as those of Rowlandson, into each issue. Journals were similar to many modern magazines, combining editorial opinion with features on current events and articles of literary criticism. These journals gave birth to the editorial political cartoon, which we are accustomed to today in our daily newspapers.

Honoré Daumier. The first—and perhaps the greatest—political cartoonist to publish his work regularly in a journal was Honoré Daumier (1808–79). Daumier was an outstanding painter and sculptor, but to the citizens of France he was known and admired only for his funny and bitter attacks on people with power. When his keen mind detected corruption in government or the misuse of power, he drew a cartoon to expose the evil. He once drew a caricature of the king that was so savage (but true) that he was sent to jail for six months, and cartoons that attacked the government were outlawed. But Daumier had made his mark on journalism. The edi-

"It reassures me always, that justice keeps her eyes open . . ."

torial cartoon was becoming a regular feature of many journals and magazines in all parts of the world.

Thomas Nast. *Harper's Weekly* was an American magazine that resembled European journals. It was widely read for its honest discussions of the affairs of the United States. A popular feature of *Harper's* was the political cartoons of Thomas Nast (1840–1902). Nast's attacks on crooked politicians were ruthless, and he helped to put an end to the career of Boss Tweed, head of a New York City political organization. The still-familiar symbols of the political parties—an elephant for the Republicans, a donkey for the Democrats—were Nast's creations and first appeared in *Harper's*.

In their crooked political dealings, Boss Tweed and his Tammany ring in New York City completely disregarded the ideals of good government. Tweed was so brazen that even after the authorities proved his corruption, he sneered, "What are you going to do about it?" In this famous cartoon Thomas Nast shows Tweed as a Roman emperor enjoying the cruel murder of the republic. "Americus" refers to the Americus fire company where Tweed got his start.

THE TAMMANY TIGER LOOSE.—"What are you going to do about it?"
(The first use of the famous Tiger symbol)

Toward the end of the 19th century, there were several humor magazines being published, especially in the United States, that contained numerous cartoons. *Puck* and *Judge* were the most read, and the old *Life* became as popular around the turn of the century. *Life* was unusual because most of its humor dealt with everyday life rather than politics.

Newspapers and the Daily Cartoon

Early in the 1900's, the political cartoon began to disappear from the humor magazines. New printing and engraving methods made drawing faster for cartoonists. Cartoons could now be drawn on paper rather than scratched on metal printing plates. High-speed printing presses were developed, and the number and size of daily newspapers increased. Political cartoonists went to work for the newspapers because their cartoons could appear every day and be more up-to-date. By the 1950's, work by well-known cartoonists such as Bill Mauldin and Herblock (Herbert Block) was popular around the United States.

"You're all fired!"

127

The Humorous Cartoon

The cartoon that described a funny, everyday situation instead of a political one became very important to magazines. Many magazines earn most of their money through the advertisements printed within their pages. A company that advertised a product never wanted its advertisement to appear in the back pages of the magazine, for it was felt that readers did not glance through these pages. To attract readers to the back of the issue, magazines began printing cartoons next to the advertisements.

Many cartoon characters have become as familiar as Nast's elephant and donkey. Comic books have been made of the adventures of many characters, such as Carl Anderson's *Henry* and Marge Henderson's *Little Lulu*. Charles Addams' weird and mysterious characters have been made into popular rag dolls. Ted Key's *Hazel,* the bossy maid familiar to many magazine readers, was given a second life in a television series.

Comic strips have also introduced characters well known to almost everyone. Comic strips may find humor in political situations —as in Garry Trudeau's *Doonesbury*—or in everyday situations—as in Charles Schulz's *Peanuts*. Comic strips like *Dick Tracy,* created by Chester Gould, tell a long story with a new episode every day. Like daily cartoons, comic strips were made popular in newspapers.

▶ HOW THE CARTOONIST WORKS

Most editorial cartoonists work in newspaper offices. They must think fast and work fast to keep up with the daily news. Their methods of working vary, but usually they sketch several ideas each day. The editor selects one, and the cartoonist quickly prepares a final copy, which appears in the next edition of the paper.

In contrast, the cartoonist who draws for magazines often works on a free-lance basis— at home or in a studio, selling ideas to any magazine that will buy them. A cartoonist who is not well known will probably submit only rough copies to an editor. If the editor decides to buy one, the rough is returned to the cartoonist, who makes a finished copy on heavy board. Cartoonists today work in many materials—pen, brush and ink, pencil, or watercolor.

Today the cartoon occupies an important place in almost all types of publications. In fact, it is difficult to find any newspaper or popular magazine that does not contain a cartoon of some kind.

TED KEY
Creator, *Hazel* Cartoons

CARTOONS, ANIMATED. See ANIMATED CARTOONS.

CARVER, GEORGE WASHINGTON (1864–1943)

George Washington Carver was one of America's greatest agricultural scientists. He was born near Diamond Grove, Missouri. The exact birthdate is not known. His parents were slaves of Moses Carver. While George was still a baby, his father died and his mother was kidnapped. He remained with the Carvers and took their name.

As a young boy, he showed his love of growing things by caring for sick plants. The neighbors called him the plant doctor. He began his schooling in a nearby town. Through hard work and the help of others, he was able to continue his education.

In 1894, Carver became the first black student to graduate from the Iowa State Agricultural College in Ames. Two years later he earned his master's degree in agricultural science there. He taught at the college, becoming its first black teacher.

In 1896, Carver was invited by Booker T. Washington to become head of the agricultural department at Tuskegee Institute, then a new black college in Alabama. With the help of his students, Carver built a laboratory.

For nearly 50 years, Carver taught at Tuskegee and worked in his laboratory, seeking ways to help Southern farmers. He showed the cotton farmers how such crops as peanuts and sweet potatoes would enrich soil worn out by years of cotton planting.

Carver also discovered new uses for these plants. From peanuts he made butter, coffee, ink, and soap. From sweet potatoes he made flour, cereals, glue, dyes, and rubber. He also made synthetic marble from wood shavings and paint from Alabama clay. Carver gave his discoveries to the world, asking no profit for himself. In recognition, he received many awards and honors.

Carver died on January 5, 1943. His birthplace is a national monument. The Carver Museum at Tuskegee has exhibits of his work. Also at Tuskegee is the Carver Research Foundation, which he founded in 1940.

DANIEL S. DAVIS
Author, *Struggle for Freedom: The History of Black Americans*

CARVING. See SCULPTURE; WOOD CARVING.

CASSATT, MARY (1844–1926)

Mary Cassatt was the foremost American woman painter of the 19th century. She was also the only American to exhibit paintings with the French impressionists—artists who revolutionized painting by using bright colors, small brushstrokes, and informal subjects.

Cassatt was born on May 22, 1844, in Allegheny City (now a part of Pittsburgh), Pennsylvania. She knew early that she wanted to be a painter. In 1861, she enrolled at the Pennsylvania Academy of the Fine Arts. Several years later, she went to Europe to study the old masters in churches and museums.

In 1872, Cassatt had a painting accepted for the Paris Salon, the official exhibition sponsored by the French Academy of Fine Arts. A year later, she settled permanently in Paris. She soon became aware of the impressionists, especially of Edgar Degas, who became her teacher and lifelong friend. The work of the impressionists was not approved by the Academy. But it appealed to Cassatt. She stopped entering works for the Salon and exhibited with the impressionists.

Cassatt made women her main subject. In her work, we see women in their everyday lives. They take tea and talk. They go to the opera. They weave and knit and read quietly in the garden. And always, they enjoy and care for their children, especially the babies.

The taste of Cassatt's time was for highly idealized mothers and children. In contrast, Cassatt painted people as she saw them, often plain and awkward. But her truth reveals a beauty that has endured. Cassatt's work became popular in Paris, and she was the first impressionist to support herself by her art.

Mary Cassatt never married. She died in her country house outside Paris on June 14, 1926. In recent years, her work has gained increasing recognition in the United States.

FRANK GETLEIN
Author, *Mary Cassatt*

CASTLES. See FORTS AND FORTIFICATIONS.

Mother About to Wash Her Sleepy Child **(1880), by Cassatt.**

Fidel Castro, the leader of Cuba and the head of its Communist Party. He is known as a powerful speaker.

CASTRO, FIDEL (1926–)

Fidel Castro Ruz, a fiery speaker and firm believer in the idea of revolution, took power in Cuba in 1959. Under him, Cuba became the first socialist country in the Americas.

Castro once said that he was a "professional revolutionary" because he could not stand injustice. Yet he was not personally a victim of injustice. He was born on August 13, 1926, at Mayarí, in eastern Cuba. His parents were well-to-do farmers, and he was free to roam the family plantation. He attended the Mayarí parish school and Jesuit schools in Santiago de Cuba and Havana. At school, he excelled in debating, and he won a national award in athletics.

At 19, Castro entered the University of Havana to study law. He quickly became involved in politics. In 1947 he took part in an unsuccessful attempt to overthrow Rafael Trujillo, the dictator of the Dominican Republic. The following year, he married Mirta Díaz Balart, a fellow student. Their son, Fidelito, was born in 1949. The marriage ended in divorce about five years later.

Castro became a lawyer in 1950, and he ran for parliament in 1952. But on March 10, before the election, Fulgencio Batista seized power in a military coup. Castro began to organize opposition to Batista. His plan was to storm the Moncada army post, on the outskirts of Santiago, and launch a revolution.

The attack on Moncada, on July 26, 1953, failed. Most of Castro's followers survived but were captured, tortured, and later killed by Batista's police. Castro was tried and jailed. But his defense speech (later published under the title "History Will Absolve Me") was so eloquent that he became the symbol of the opposition. He was set free in 1955, under a general amnesty, and went to Mexico. There he formed a group called the 26th of July Movement and planned his return to Cuba—as head of an army of liberation.

That "army," made up of about 80 men, landed on Cuba's southeastern coast on December 2, 1956. They met immediate resistance from Batista's forces. The rebels who survived fought hit-and-run battles for almost two years, until they had enough recruits to face Batista's forces in the open. When they did, they won. Batista fled Cuba on January 1, 1959.

Castro became prime minister in February. Most Cubans supported him, but many, especially the wealthy, fled. Castro had come to power as a nationalist, but he soon began to move toward Communism. The United States had extensive business interests in Cuba, and Castro opposed this. He nationalized foreign companies and signed a trade agreement with the Soviet Union. In 1961 the United States ended trade and diplomatic relations with Cuba and also backed a group of Cuban exiles in an unsuccessful attempt to overthrow Castro, at the Bay of Pigs.

As head of government and of the Communist Party, Castro transformed Cuba into a socialist state. The government runs industry and agriculture. Health services and education are free, and illiteracy has been almost wiped out. But Cuba depends on Soviet aid, and food and consumer goods are in short supply. The press is censored, and dissent is not allowed. Hundreds of thousands of Cubans have left the island. To his opponents, Castro is a tyrant. But to his supporters, he remains a great revolutionary leader.

Castro's open support of revolution in other countries has made him a figure in world politics. Cuba has trained revolutionaries from countries in Africa and Latin America, and Cuban troops have fought in conflicts in several African countries.

JOHN GERASSI
City University of New York, Queens College
See also CUBA.

CATARACTS. See BLIND, EDUCATION OF THE.
CATERPILLARS. See BUTTERFLIES AND MOTHS.

St. Basil's Cathedral, Moscow (*above left*), begun in 1554, shows a strong Byzantine influence. The cathedral at Rheims, France, begun in 1211, is in the Gothic style.

CATHEDRALS

Cathedrals are Christianity's most glorious contribution to the art of building. Those who planned and built the world's great cathedrals spared no effort to make the structures worthy expressions of their faith and sources of pride to the community.

During the Middle Ages all of Western Europe was Roman Catholic, and each community had its own church. These churches were grouped into districts called dioceses. Each diocese was under the jurisdiction of a bishop. This system still exists today. The principal church of the diocese contained the throne of the bishop. In Latin the name of this church was *ecclesia cathedralis,* or "cathedral church." In English it has been shortened to cathedral.

▶ CONSTRUCTION AND STYLES OF CATHEDRALS

Most European cathedrals were constructed with the floor plan in the general shape of a cross. The long part of the cross is the **nave** and serves as the assembly room for the congregation. The two arms of the cross are the **transepts,** and the fourth part, containing the altar and choir, is the **apse.** The section where the four parts meet is the **crossing.** Towers or domes were often built over the crossing.

Cathedrals have been built in nearly every architectural style. But most of the very famous European cathedrals were either Byzantine, Romanesque, Gothic, or Renaissance.

Byzantine. In the first centuries A.D., the center of Christianity was Asia, not Europe, and the first great Christian empire was centered in the city of Byzantium (later Constantinople; now Istanbul, Turkey). Architecture in the Byzantine Empire was a combination of styles that came from the Middle East and from ancient Rome. Hagia Sophia, one of the first Byzantine cathedrals, is a masterpiece of styles combined from East and West.

Romanesque. Gradually the Christian center moved to Europe. Rome had become entirely Christian, and the barbarians from

European countries north of Italy were slowly being converted. Northern art began to influence traditional Roman art, and a new style, called Romanesque, was born. An early Romanesque cathedral (11th century) at Pisa, Italy, contains many decorative features that are clearly Byzantine. But St. Ambrogio's Cathedral, begun only 25 years later, is purely Romanesque and contains little Eastern influence.

Gothic. By the 12th century the Germanic peoples from the North—Germans, Goths, Franks, Lombards—dominated European Christianity. Their cathedrals had an upward thrust, as though reaching toward heaven. Architecture was the main artistic tool for religious expression in the period.

Most of Europe's very famous cathedrals are in the Gothic style. Because there are so many Gothic cathedrals throughout Europe— every country had its own kind of Gothic style —this type of building has become associated with cathedrals. In fact, St. John the Divine, the world's largest Gothic cathedral, was built not during the Middle Ages but in the 19th and 20th centuries, not in Europe but in New York City, and it is not Roman Catholic but Episcopal.

Renaissance. In the 14th century a new spirit began to grow in Italy. People were encouraged to investigate ideas and to experiment with new discoveries. This period was called the Renaissance, which means

The Cathedral of Milan (*above*) was begun in 1386 and took centuries to complete. It shows the development of the Gothic style. The Cathedral of Pisa (*below*), with its famous leaning bell tower, was begun in 1063. It is an example of Italian Romanesque architecture.

rebirth, because it was felt that scientific reasoning had been dormant since the classical age of Greece and Rome had ended.

Renaissance architects looked back to the pre-Christian architecture of Greece and Rome. They combined qualities of old and new architecture. St. Peter's in Rome (which is not officially a cathedral since it is not the seat of the bishop) is an outstanding example of a Renaissance building. Its interior reflects the attention paid to fine structural detail, and the dome, designed by the great Michelangelo, is a masterpiece in itself.

▶ **MODERN CATHEDRALS**

Most 20th-century cathedrals are modern versions of the Gothic style. However, when the Gothic cathedral at Coventry, England, was destroyed by bombs in World War II, the Episcopal church leaders decided to replace it with a truly modern structure. The new Coventry Cathedral recalls the glories of many past architectural styles, but for the most part it is purely modern—one of the few cathedrals in the world that belong only to our time.

Reviewed by AARON H. JACOBSEN
Author, *The Medieval Sketchbook*

See also ARCHITECTURE; GOTHIC ART AND ARCHITECTURE; STAINED-GLASS WINDOWS.

CATHOLIC CHURCH. See ROMAN CATHOLIC CHURCH.

Above: The new Cathedral of Coventry, England, completed in 1962. Below: A detail of one of the cathedral's stained-glass windows.

CATS

Attacking from ambush, an African lion charges a band of antelope and strikes one down with a single sledgehammer blow of its paw. Padding silently through the Indian jungle, a Bengal tiger stalks an unsuspecting deer. Crouched on a limb, a South American jaguar tenses its muscles, then springs at a passing tapir.

Like all members of the cat family, these three big cats are expert trackers and hunters. They must be if they are to eat. They belong to the order Carnivora—the meat-eating mammals.

Cats vary in size from beasts smaller than the domestic tabby to Siberian tigers weighing 270 kilograms (600 pounds) or more. Their coats come in many colors and many striking patterns. In the wild, cats range throughout most of the temperate regions of the world, except for Australia, Madagascar, and some of the Pacific islands.

▶ HIGHLY SPECIALIZED BEASTS OF PREY

No matter where they live, no matter what their size and appearance—all cats are alike in many ways. All have bodies adapted for hunting and killing. All are highly specialized beasts of prey.

In the front of its mouth the cat has four long, pointed, canine teeth—deadly weapons for biting and tearing flesh. On the sides of its jaws are knife-edged teeth that shear against each other, cutting easily through tough hide and muscle.

On its feet the cat has a murderous arsenal of needle-sharp, curved claws—five on each front foot and four on each hind foot. When not in use, the claws are hidden in protective pockets, or sheaths, in each paw.

Following its prey, the cat moves silently, for the bottom of each foot is cushioned with a soft pad. Like all successful hunters, it is equipped with keen senses. Its hearing and sense of smell are highly developed. Its whiskers connect with nerves and serve as delicate instruments of touch. The keen eyes are directed forward, as ours are. This allows the hunter to focus both eyes on the same object at the same time and to judge its distance.

The cat's eyes are also adapted for seeing in the dark, since it does most of its hunting at night. During the day the pupils contract to slits, or very small openings. But at night they open wide, letting in every bit of light possible. The backs of the eyes are coated with a substance like polished silver. It reflects every bit of light that comes into the eye. That is why a cat's eyes shine like glowing lanterns if you point a flashlight toward them at night.

▶ CATS USUALLY HUNT ALONE

The cat usually stalks its prey, creeping ever closer until it is near enough to charge. Sometimes it lies hidden, waiting for its unsuspecting prey to approach. Then, leaping forward with tremendous bounds, the cat springs onto the quarry's back.

Dinner won, the hungry hunter eats its fill. It often covers or hides any remaining meat, to save for a future meal. Then the cat grooms itself carefully with its rasplike tongue. Cats like to keep themselves clean.

Some people object to cats because they kill other animals for food. But such meat-eating hunters fulfill a vital need in the natural world. They serve as one of the important checks in the balance of nature. Without them we might soon be overrun with rodents, hoofed mammals, and other plant eaters.

Lithe and beautiful, cats are always popular exhibits in zoos, where they sometimes live 15 or 20 years.

Cats are usually solitary animals, living and hunting alone most of the time. The male cat may stay with his mate for some weeks or months, but generally he leaves before the young are born. With the smaller species of cats, the young are usually born about 2 months after mating. But big cats like the lion or tiger carry their unborn young about 3½ months.

▶ HOW CATS TAKE CARE OF THEIR YOUNG

The female mountain lion is a typical cat mother. Her den may be a shallow cave or a sheltered ledge. Here her cubs are born, generally during early spring in northern areas. She usually has two to four cubs at a time.

At birth cubs are about 20 centimeters (10 inches) long and weigh very little. Their soft fur is light brown with dark spots. A

The tiger's markings frame a bold face. Its piercing gaze may stay with you even after you turn the page.

Treed mountain lion in Arizona snarls at hunters.

cub's eyes do not open fully before 2 weeks.

The mother mountain lion nurses and washes her cubs. She guards them from enemies. She leaves them only when she must hunt food for herself.

Until they are nearly 2 months old, the cubs' only food is their mother's milk. They get their first taste of flesh by playing with bones and scraps of meat that the mother brings home from her hunting trips. Growing bigger and stronger all the time, the cubs play like domestic kittens. They pounce on pebbles and insects; they practice stalking each other. By the time they are 3 months old, they are usually weaned. Now the mother lion takes them on real hunting trips.

The growing cubs stay with their mother for at least 6 months and often for a much longer time. When they finally face the world on their own, they are accomplished hunters.

▶ TRUE CATS AND SABER-TOOTHED "TIGERS"

The cat family branched off from the earliest meat-eating forms of mammals some 30,000,000 years ago. Cats then developed along two lines—into the true, or typical, cats we know today and into the saber-toothed cats. The saber-toothed cats developed enormous canine teeth, flattened like daggers, in their upper jaws. Springing onto their victims, the saber-toothed cats killed by stabbing again and again with these weapons.

These cats, sometimes called saber-toothed tigers, reached their greatest development about a million years ago, during the Pleistocene epoch. It was during this time that *Smilodon*, a great saber-toothed cat as large as a lion, roamed North America. This and all other saber-toothed cats became extinct during the Ice Age. Only the true cats survived.

▶ THE LION, "KING OF BEASTS"

The male lion is known as the king of beasts because of his dignified appearance, his deep roar, and his regal-looking mane. But even a lion will avoid a rampaging elephant or an ill-tempered rhinoceros. Inhabiting open plains and grasslands, lions prey upon zebra, antelope, and smaller game.

Unlike most cats, lions are social beasts. They live together in groups called prides. Family-sized or larger, the band usually consists of one or more adult males, several females, and young of various ages. Often the members work together in hunting. Sometimes a male acts as a driver, working his way around a herd of antelope and stampeding them toward the spot where his mate lies in ambush. If his mate is caring for the cubs, the male lion often hunts for all of them.

Occasionally lions develop a taste for human flesh and become very dangerous. These are often old or disabled beasts, unable to catch their usual prey.

In former times the lion ranged from Greece to Asia Minor, Persia, and India as well as throughout most of Africa. Now lions are found only in Africa, with the exception of a very few that still survive in the Gir forest of western India.

The male lion is the only wild cat with a mane.

▶ THE ROYAL BENGAL TIGER AND ITS RELATIVES

Tigers chiefly inhabit the forests of Asia. These great beasts, with their tawny, black-striped orange coats, are perhaps the most striking and beautiful of all the cats. Tigers appear to be leaner and more lithe than lions. But the two species are very closely related and breed together in captivity. If the father is a lion, the offspring are called ligers; if a tiger, they are called tigons. The tigers usually seen in zoos and circuses are Indian or Bengal tigers. Weighing around 180 kilograms (400 pounds), they are about the same size as an average lion.

The largest tigers are those of northern Asia. The Siberian tiger can weigh as much as 300 kilograms (660 pounds) and be as long as 3.5 meters (12 feet). The smallest tigers inhabit Malaysia and some of the islands of Indonesia. Whatever their size, all tigers are accomplished swimmers and seem to enjoy taking frequent dips.

Lion cubs relax in a tree.

An Indian leopard suns itself. Leopards are often considered the fiercest and most dangerous cats.

Above: A jaguar swims in the Amazon River. Many cats are at home in water and are excellent swimmers. The jaguar is an expert fisher. Below: The cheetah is the fastest of all mammals.

Tigers hunt by night, usually stalking deer, wild pigs, and other hoofed animals. In many areas they prey on livestock, finding cattle and goats easier victims than wild animals. Sometimes a tiger will raid the same village again and again, terrorizing it and the surrounding area. As with lions, tigers may sometimes claim human victims.

▶ DIFFERENT KINDS OF LEOPARDS

The handsome leopard is also known as a panther. It is a much smaller cat than the lion or tiger. But the leopard has the reputation of being the fiercest and most dangerous cat of all. The leopard has a splashy yellow coat decorated with small black spots. The spots are arranged in groups of five around a dark center. In certain areas, especially in Malaysia, black leopards are common. The blacks are simply color varieties and may occur in the same litter with normally colored offspring. The leopard's range includes most of Africa and southern Asia.

Unlike most of the other big cats, the leopard is a skillful climber. It will often lie hidden on a tree branch waiting for prey to pass beneath. Fearless and savage if cornered, the leopard will attack people.

Two other kinds of medium-sized cats, also called leopards, are found in Asia. These are known as the snow leopard and clouded leopard, although neither is a true leopard. The snow leopard, sometimes called the ounce, inhabits cold, mountainous areas north of the Himalayas. It is nearly the same size as the common leopard. But its silvery gray fur is long and soft and marked with round clusters of darker spots. Its tail is long and full.

The other so-called leopard is the slightly smaller clouded leopard of Southeast Asia. Its coat is a rich, tawny color, marked with a variety of spots and stripes.

▶ THE JAGUAR IS THE BIGGEST NEW WORLD CAT

When seen in a zoo, the brightly spotted jaguar is often mistaken for a leopard. Somewhat heavier than its Old World cousin, the jaguar has a bigger head, a stockier body, and larger clusters of black spots. It almost never preys upon humans. Once the jaguar wandered as far north as Arizona, New Mexico, and California. But with the advance of human settlement, it has practically disappeared from these areas. It now ranges from Mexico southward through most of South America.

The jaguar inhabits jungle, plains, and open country, dining on deer, tapir, peccary, fish, and even alligator. Expert fishers, the cats will sometimes lie on a limb over a jungle pool and scoop their dinner out of the water with their sharp claws. In some areas jaguars take such a toll of the domestic stock, especially pigs, that ranchers hire professional hunters to control them.

▶ THE MOUNTAIN LION HAS MANY NAMES

The other big cat of the New World is the mountain lion. It has a wide range, extending from British Columbia to Patagonia. A shy, secretive beast, it has tawny fur with lighter underparts. The mountain lion is more slender than the jaguar.

Its usual prey is deer and smaller animals. But the mountain lion also kills sheep and other livestock when it gets the chance. For this reason people have mercilessly hunted it, and the cat has totally disappeared in many areas.

When settlers came to North America, mountain lions ranged throughout wooded areas of the eastern part of the continent as well as in the West. They were known by a variety of names—puma, cougar, catamount, painter, American lion, Indian devil, and others. Trapped, hunted, and killed wherever it was found, the mountain lion has long since disappeared from most eastern areas. At present it is rapidly being exterminated in the West as well.

A few specimens still hide out in the Florida Everglades. And in recent years there have been reports of individual mountain lions sighted in other eastern areas, from Nova Scotia to the southern Appalachians. It is to be hoped that at least a few of these big eastern cats will survive as a reminder of America's pioneer past.

▶ THE CHEETAH, FASTEST OF ALL MAMMALS

The cheetah differs from most other cats in several ways. It has very long, slender legs and claws that cannot be drawn in and hidden. Fastest of all land animals, it can run almost 110 kilometers (70 miles·) an hour when pursuing prey. It inhabits various parts of eastern Africa and southern Asia.

In India full-grown cheetahs are sometimes captured in snares to be tamed and trained as hunting animals. Taken on a hunt, the animals are hooded, like trained falcons. When the quarry (black buck or other antelope) is sighted, the hoods are removed and the cheetahs released. They usually stalk their prey until they are only a short distance away. Then they spring forward and close the gap in a whirlwind finish that the antelope are unable to match.

▶ CATS WITH BOBBED TAILS AND TUFTED EARS

The lynxes differ from other cats in having short tails, luxurious side ruffs, and ears with tufts on their tips. Two species, the Canada lynx and the bobcat, inhabit North America. The Canada lynx is the most northward ranging of all the New World cats. It roams Canada and Alaska and is sometimes found as far south as Oregon, Colorado, and New York. It has a short, black-tipped tail and big broad feet that act as snowshoes when the lynx pursues its favorite prey, the snowshoe rabbit. The lynx has long, soft fur that is gray-brown and blotched with darker spots.

The bobcat is also called the bay lynx and wildcat. It is smaller than its northern cousin, the Canada lynx. The bobcat's coat is darker and redder, and it has a white-tipped tail. Its legs and feet are also more slender. Ranging from southern Canada to Mexico, the bobcat lives in a great variety of habitats. It ranges from forests to farmlands, from mountain areas to southwestern deserts.

Other forms of lynxes, similar to the American species, are found in Europe and northern Asia. Still another related species, the caracal, ranges from India to Arabia and over most of Africa. Chocolate-colored, it has enormous ears tipped with long, black tufts. It is sometimes trained as a hunting animal, like the cheetah.

The serval is another medium-sized cat with a fairly short tail. It lives in Africa, south of the Sahara. Its color is golden brown, thickly dotted with dark spots.

▶ THE SMALLER NEW WORLD CATS

The ocelot looks like a gaily coated, oversized house cat. It is the best known of the smaller New World cats. Its

Above: This wildcat was born in captivity in Britain. Its name does not seem to fit its gentle appearance. Below left: The bobcat, or wildcat, is known from Canada to Mexico. Below right: The ocelot looks more like a large house cat than a forest animal.

tawny or yellowish coat is decorated with spots, stripes, and whorls of dark brown and black. It wanders from Mexico to Paraguay. Usually found in forests, the ocelot roams at night. It invades farms and villages to feed on poultry and other small farm animals. Another small, spotted cat is the margay. It looks like a small edition of the ocelot and is found over much of the same range.

With a slender, lithe body and short legs, the small jaguarundi is one of the strangest and least known of all the New World cats. An expert fisher and swimmer, the jaguarundi is sometimes called the otter-cat. It ranges from Arizona to Paraguay and may be reddish or dark gray in color. The red form is sometimes called the eyra.

Still other kinds of small cats inhabit South America. Very little is known about most of them.

▶ **SMALLER CATS FROM THE OLD WORLD**

A bewildering array of small cats live in Asia and Africa. Some of them are spotted. Others are striped, mottled, or all one hue. They come with a confusing variety of names, too—wildcat, bush cat, jungle cat, desert cat, spotted cat, leopard cat, and tiger cat, among others. Very little is known about many of them.

One of the better-known Asian species is the Indian leopard cat. This handsome little animal is about the size of a house cat. Others are the long-haired Pallas cat, or manul, which may figure in the ancestry of the Persian cat; the Malaysian marbled cat, which looks like a small clouded leopard; and the richly colored golden cat.

▶ **ORIGINS OF THE DOMESTIC CAT**

Best known of the small African wildcats is the Kaffir cat, *Felis lybica*. This species is considered to be the ancestor of our common house cat. The ancient Egyptians tamed this species and gave it a place of honor in their civilization. From Egypt the domestic cat eventually found its way to Europe, where it may have interbred with the European wildcat. Gradually the house cat spread throughout the world.

ROBERT M. MCCLUNG
Author, science books for children

CATS, DOMESTIC

It is often said that the cat is a very independent animal. This is not true. The cat, like all domesticated animals, enjoys the companionship and affection of people.

Ordinary cats that you see on the street, in stores, and in many homes are the so-called alley cats. Cats that have been carefully bred are called pedigreed cats. A pedigree is a written record of a cat's mother and father and grandmother and grandfather. It can go even further back than the cat's great-great-grandparents.

Pedigreed cats are divided into two main classes—short-haired breeds and long-haired breeds. Commonly recognized short-haired breeds are Abyssinian, Burmese, Manx, Russian Blue, Siamese, and Domestic Shorthair. Commonly recognized long-haired breeds are Persian and Himalayan.

Standards for each breed are established by the association interested in the particular breed. Standards are set for color and shape of the eyes, appearance of the body, texture of the coat, and so on. Only cats that come up to the standards set for their breed can hope to do well in a cat show.

But a cat does not have to be pedigreed to make a good pet. Whether you choose an alley cat or a pedigreed cat as your pet, you must be sure that you get it from a clean place and that it does not appear to be sick. Then, as soon as possible, take your cat to a veterinarian and have it examined. The veterinarian will inoculate it against feline enteritis (cat flu).

▶ **MAKING A HOME FOR YOUR CAT**

A bed is not necessary for your cat. It can curl up almost anywhere and be comfortable. But if you want it to have a bed, a box with a piece of old clothing in it will do very well.

It is important for a cat to have a litter box in order to be housebroken. This can be a square plastic pan about 40 centimeters (15 inches) on a side, filled with a clay product called litter. You can buy litter at supermarkets, grocery stores, or pet shops. Your cat will learn to use the litter box when it is 3 weeks old. The litter absorbs the odor and may have to be changed only once or twice a week.

Your cat should have an exercise post. Some people call this a scratching post. They think that the cat sharpens its nails on the post. Actually, the cat stretches its muscles as it pulls at the post.

▶ WATERING AND FEEDING YOUR CAT

Your cat should have a bowl of clean water at all times. Its diet should consist mostly of raw food. For the cat, as for most animals who eat raw meat, the best parts are organs, such as kidney and heart. Your cat must also have some fish, which should be cooked. A balanced diet for the week includes: beef kidney three times; fish twice; a variety of other foods once; at bedtime, a raw egg yolk slightly beaten with a little water (never the white of the egg).

If you have a female cat, she may have kittens when she is old enough. They will get milk from their mother. When they are 4 weeks old, they will start to look for more solid food. This is called weaning time. A

FACTS ABOUT CATS

The cat was one of the most sacred of the Egyptian sacred animals. The cat-headed goddess, named Ubastet, represented to the Egyptians the life-producing power of the sun.

In Egypt, thousands of bodies of embalmed cats have been found in excavated cat temples and cat cemeteries.

In the Middle Ages people believed that witches could turn themselves into cats. For this reason cats were often burned to death.

Many people still believe that black cats are an omen of bad luck.

Cats have been the subject of many nursery rhymes, stories, and film cartoons. In his *Just So Stories*, Rudyard Kipling wrote "The Cat Who Walked by Himself."

Early Norsemen had great reverence for the cat. Their goddess of love, Freyja, traveled in a chariot pulled by two cats.

In China and Japan, cats have been used for centuries to protect the silkworm cocoons from rats.

A cat named Champion Tom was for many years the official mouser in the Post Office building in Washington, D. C.

BREEDS OF CATS

PERSIAN. The Persian has fine, long, glossy fur, which fluffs up all over its body. The Persian may be pure white, black, red, blue, or cream. It may be solid, tipped, or parti-colored. A good Persian has a broad chest and is rather low on sturdy legs. The head is round and massive, the neck short, and the forehead wide. The full tail should be short and straight.

RUSSIAN BLUE. The Russian Blue is best known for its heavy, bluish coat, which stands away from its body instead of lying smoothly against it. This breed is fine-boned and has a long, graceful body and long legs. The head is large, and the eyes should be a vivid green, set wide apart.

BURMESE. The Burmese has a dark, sable-brown coat and glowing, golden eyes. The face is round, with a blunt nose. Medium in size and strongly muscled, the Burmese presents a compact appearance. Its back should be level from shoulder to tail.

MANX. The Manx has no tail. Where the tail would be there is only a dimple. This cat has a double coat of fur, which may be one color or a combination of colors or stripes. It has a large, round head, prominent cheekbones, a broad muzzle (jaws and nose), and large, round eyes. The Manx's body is compact, with high hindquarters and a short back. Because of this, the cat has a loping gait (way of moving), rather like a rabbit's hop.

DOMESTIC SHORTHAIR. The Domestic Shorthair is the most familiar household cat. Its body is well-knit and strong, and its round, full eyes are set wide apart to show the breadth of its nose. The muzzle is rather square.

ABYSSINIAN. The Abyssinian, said to be the sacred cat of ancient Egypt, has a soft, thick coat. The hair is apricot-colored at the base and is "ticked," or banded, with darker shades of brown or black. The result is a ruddy-brown appearance. This cat has a triangular-shaped face and glowing gold, green, or hazel eyes. It is even more powerfully built than the Burmese.

SIAMESE. The Siamese has a pale fawn or cream coat, set off by "points"—dark areas on its face, ears, feet, and tail. Its eyes are a rich sapphire blue. They are almond-shaped and slant toward the nose. The Siamese is named according to the shade of the points. The chocolate point has milk-chocolate points and has a paler coat than the seal point. The blue point has soft, bluish-gray points and a coat that is almost white. The Siamese's coat is glossy and fine and lies flat on its body. Its legs are slim and taper down to oval paws. Its head and tail are long and tapered.

HIMALAYAN. The Himalayan was originally produced by crossbreeding the Persian with the Siamese. So it is a long-haired cat with the coloring and points of a Siamese. In build it is more like the Persian than the Siamese, but its eyes are a deep blue.

Copper-eyed Persian

Burmese

Russian Blue

Manx

Domestic Shorthair

Abyssinian

Seal-point Siamese

Himalayan

good food for weaning is a cup of baby cereal mixed with evaporated milk and a couple of drops of egg yolk. Put this in a flat dish, bring the kittens to it, and put a little on the end of their noses. They will lick it and look for more. Then put a teaspoon of the food near their mouths. They will probably lap it up. When they are 5 weeks old, you can start mixing small amounts of kidney or fish with their cereal. Before long the kittens will be on the same diet as their mother.

▶ HOW TO PROTECT YOUR CAT

Toys that can be ripped apart, chewed, or swallowed should be kept from your cat. Some plants are very dangerous. Ivy has proven fatal to many cats. Open windows are a source of danger, for cats are not aware of great heights and can injure or kill themselves if they fall.

It is unwise to let your cat roam the neighborhood unattended. Cats allowed to roam rarely reach 9 years of age. A cat properly cared for and kept in the house can live as long as 17 years. Your cat does not need to go outside if it is given proper care and attention. It won't want to be anywhere except in your house and will be happy purring away in your lap for the rest of its life.

MILAN J. GREER
Author, *The Fabulous Feline*

CATTLE AND OTHER LIVESTOCK

People have depended in some way on animals for millions of years. They have needed animals for meat, hides, or milk. Thousands of years ago people hunted and killed wild animals to obtain these things. As civilization developed, people discovered that they could raise and keep some animals. These animals are known as livestock. They include cattle, swine, sheep, and goats.

In addition to meat, milk, and hides, other uses for livestock were discovered. Primitive people found that if they let their animals into their huts at night, heat from the animals' bodies helped warm the dwelling. Later it was learned that animal fat could be used to make soap. In more recent times animal glands have been used as sources for certain medicines. Glue is made from hides, hooves, bones, and skins of animals.

▶ HISTORY OF LIVESTOCK RAISING

In ancient times cattle were regarded both as a source of wealth and as sacred animals. Cattle were sacrificed on altars to gods, given as gifts to kings, and traded for other goods by the poor.

The early Egyptians worshiped a bull known as Apis, a black bull with a white triangle on his forehead. The bull was allowed to live 25 years. Then the priests drowned him and chose another bull.

Today in Africa and India some people still consider cattle as sacred beings. The Dinka tribe of Africa never kills cows except in special ceremonies. Hindus in India do not permit cows to be slaughtered, and they allow the cows to run free.

In Biblical times sheep and other livestock were very much a part of life. Young calves and lambs were offered as sacrifices to the gods. Abraham prospered because of his great flocks and herds. In the book of Genesis, Adam and Eve's son Abel is referred to as a keeper of sheep. The shepherds on the hills with their flocks were the first people to see the star over Bethlehem when Jesus was born.

Most of the references to swine in the Old Testament concern the taboo against eating the flesh of the hog. These animals are still considered "unclean" by Jews and Muslims. The New Testament tells of Jesus transferring the "unclean spirits" from man to a herd of swine.

Nomads let their cattle, sheep, and goats wander freely to find grass and water. The nomads followed wherever the animals roamed, just as the Indians used to follow the bison on the plains to hunt them.

Cattle were important to the people of the ancient world. Laws were made by Hindus and Hebrews to protect cattle. Oxen were not to be worked too hard in the fields, and they were to have plenty of water. To hurt or be cruel to an animal was a punishable crime.

The Romans were interested in good wool, and they did much to improve the breeds of sheep they had. Much of the credit for the development of the Spanish merino breed of sheep could go to the Romans. They imported large numbers of sheep into Spain

Brahman cattle (*left*), developed by interbreeding cattle of India, and Watusi (*right*) cattle of tropical Africa. Both can withstand heat and are resistant to disease.

when that country was part of the Roman Empire. By about the 1st century A.D., the Spanish merino breed had developed.

During the Middle Ages in Europe, livestock became more important than ever. Next to bread, pork was probably the chief food of the time. Pigs were kept in wooded areas near villages, where they could eat roots, acorns, and nuts. Cattle and sheep were allowed to graze on the fields after the crops were harvested. While the crops were growing, the animals grazed in grassy meadows.

Livestock also played an important part in the development of the New World. None of the domesticated livestock was native to the New World, however. They had to be imported.

Columbus took cattle, pigs, sheep, and goats to the West Indies in 1493, on his second voyage. In the 1500's the Spanish brought merino sheep and small black Andalusian cattle to Mexico. English breeds of cattle were introduced to the American continent about 1623.

The American colonists used their cattle more for work and milk production than they did for meat. Instead of beef the colonists usually ate salt pork and wild game. Raising cattle for beef began when there were more cattle than were needed for work. The extra ones were killed at an earlier age than usual, and people found that the young beef was quite good. More and more people wanted the meat. The raising of beef cattle began to grow into an industry.

In the western United States there was a great amount of range space in which cattle could roam. There were already some cattle there—the descendants of the Andalusian cattle brought into Mexico by the Spanish in the 16th century. Some of these cattle were wild, and some were kept on the scattered ranches of the Southwest. Settlers coming in from the East brought their cattle with them. The crossing of these cattle with the cattle already there produced the Texas longhorn breed.

The longhorn was an awkward-looking creature. It had thin legs and a pair of huge, spreading horns that often measured 2 meters (6½ feet) or more from tip to tip. The longhorns came in a great variety of colors—red, black, yellow, tan, or a mixture of these. Al-though they were not much to look at and were stubborn and dangerous at times, the longhorns helped make the West one of the leading cattle areas of the world. By 1850 Texas was the foremost cattle state in the country. Only the hides and tallow (fat) of the half-wild longhorns were used at first. There was no way of getting the meat to market before it spoiled. There were no railroad connections between the Texas ranches and the parts of the country where the meat could be sold. Sending live cattle by boat would have been too slow and too risky. Many of the cattle might die on such a long journey. Hides and tallow, however, could make the long boat trip without spoiling.

The era of the cowboy really began after the Civil War. During the war the Texas cattle had roamed undisturbed in the wilds, breeding freely and greatly increasing in number. By the end of the war, Texas was full of wild cattle.

The people in the mushrooming cities of the East and Middle West wanted more meat. Local farmers could not keep up with the demand. The Texas cattle raisers discovered that there was a good market for their beef in the cities of the North. The only problem was how to get the cattle there.

The best way to get the cattle to the northern meat-packing plants was to walk them to the nearest railroad shipping point. Many railroads were being built in the West after the Civil War. The railroad owners were eager to get the business of hauling the ranchers' cattle. Thus began the famous cattle drives. Usually the cattle were walked for hundreds of kilometers to shipping points such as Sedalia, Missouri, and Abilene, Kansas. From there the cattle were carried in freight cars to processing plants in Chicago and St. Louis. Cattle drives were also made to New Orleans.

The cattle drive was a large-scale operation in the old West. First came the roundup of the cattle. The ones to be sold were taken out of the herds, roped, and branded, or marked with the owner's sign. Cattle from several herds were usually grouped together to make up the trail herd that was to go on the drive. The average size of the trail herd was about 3,000 cattle.

The drive was directed by the trail boss.

Under him worked the "ramrod," or foreman, the cook with his chuck wagon, the horse wrangler with his *remuda* (a herd of extra saddle horses), and the riders—the cowboys who herded the cattle and kept them moving along.

Facing the hazards of river crossings, tornadoes, stampedes, Indians, and outlaws, these men set out on the trail with the cattle. Before the drive was over, they would probably lose some cattle, and perhaps some men would die. When they reached their destination, the men would be paid off. Then they could go back to the cattle country and sign on with another drive. The excitement of the cattle drive has never been forgotten. It is often relived in the Western novel and the television Western.

Some workers still watch over the cattle on Western ranges and round them up in the spring and the fall. But long cattle drives are a thing of the past. During the last years of the 19th century, railroad branch lines were built into every part of the cattle country, so that no ranch was more than a few days' journey from a railroad track.

Gradually, better breeds of beef cattle took the place of the longhorns. Today the only longhorns that remain are in small, private herds at a few ranches and outdoor museums. But recently there has been renewed interest in the longhorns because of their hardiness and resistance to disease.

Livestock raising today is mechanized and scientific. Feed lots, where thousands of cattle are fed by machines, are becoming common in the Middle Western and western United States. The ability of cattle, hogs, and sheep to produce meat is now tested scientifically. Chemical sprays and dips protect the animals against parasites. Vaccines and antibiotics save thousands of animals from disease. The livestock industry today is very little like the one the cowboys knew.

▶ **CATTLE**

Cattle belong to a great family called Bovidae, along with the sheep, goat, water buffalo, American bison, and antelope. The animals in this family are ruminants, or cud chewers. They partly chew their food and swallow it. Later they bring it up and chew it thoroughly, swallow it again, and digest it.

Texas cattle are loaded into a boxcar to be shipped north for marketing.

Female cattle are called cows, and males are called bulls. Steers are males that have been deprived of the ability to reproduce. Steers used as work animals are called oxen.

Modern breeds of cattle can be divided into three types. These are beef, dairy, and dual-purpose cattle.

Beef cattle are raised especially to provide high-quality meat. They usually are more muscular than other kinds of cattle and are thicker through the shoulders and hindquarters. The major breeds of beef cattle in the United States and Canada include Hereford, Aberdeen Angus, and Shorthorn.

Dairy cattle are less fleshy than beef cattle. They eat the same kind of feed but use it more for the production of milk than for muscle or fat. The more popular breeds of dairy cattle are Holstein, Jersey, Guernsey, Brown Swiss, and Ayrshire.

Ankole cattle, found in Uganda and the adjoining areas of Africa, are known for their long horns.

Dual-purpose cattle are used to produce either milk or meat. They are not as specialized as beef cattle or dairy cattle.

There are several steps in raising beef cattle. Usually each step takes place on a different farm or ranch. Baby calves are raised until they are old enough to be weaned, or given solid food instead of their mother's milk. Calves are weaned when they are six to eight months old. At this point they weigh 180 to 225 kilograms (400 to 500 pounds). Most calf-breeding herds are located in areas where grain cannot be grown profitably but where there is a lot of pasture and hay. This is because breeding herds do not need to be fattened on grain. In the United States these areas include the plains of the Southwest and the hill regions of the northern Middle West and Southeast.

After the calves are weaned, they are moved to areas where grain is more abundant. There they are raised either to be used in a breeding herd or to be fattened for slaughter. They are fed on hay and grain, and they grow rapidly in size and weight.

Finishing is the last step in beef production. The calves are fattened rapidly in feedlots. When they are beefy enough, the young cattle are slaughtered for meat. Since the late 1950's many large feedlots have been built in the Southwest and on the West Coast. These feedlots have machines to feed the cattle and machines that clean the animals' pens. Many of the lots have meat-processing plants next door. When the cattle are ready for slaughtering and processing, they are taken from the feedlot to the plant.

Specialized branches of the beef cattle industry include the raising of purebreds, baby beef, and fat calves.

Purebreds are high quality beef cattle that are produced by mating the best bulls and cows in each breed. **Baby beef** comes from fat young calves that have been fed grain and slaughtered when they are between 8 and 15 months old. **Fat calves** are fattened on pasture grass and mother's milk instead of on grain. They are slaughtered at about 8 or 9 months of age.

Both dairy and beef cows are used for meat when they are no longer productive. This meat is called **cow beef**. It is used mostly

Hereford and Black Angus cattle are raised for beef.

as ground beef or as processed meats such as canned beef and sausages. Veal comes chiefly from male dairy calves that weigh between 45 and 90 kilograms (100 and 200 pounds) at the time they are slaughtered. Female calves are usually kept for milk production instead of being killed for meat.

Raising dairy cattle differs somewhat from beef cattle production. Dairy cows must be milked at least twice a day. They need abundant pasture. Dairy farms are located near cities, where the demand for milk is great.

Unlike many beef cattle farms, dairy farms are often fairly small, with herds of 30 to 50 cows. Because dairy cows must be milked daily, keeping more than this number of cows is impractical for many smaller dairies. Standards of cleanliness are very high on dairy farms. The milk produced must be as pure as possible. Government health regulations are strict.

Groups of dairy farmers sometimes hire drivers to haul their milk to the dairy plants in large tank trucks or in large cans. Many dairy farmers keep their milk in special refrigerated vats until the tank trucks come

to pick it up. The milk is piped out from the vat directly into the tank trucks. At the dairy plants the milk and cream are put into containers or are processed into cheese, butter, and other dairy products.

People who raise cattle face many problems in their business. One of the biggest problems is the weather. Much of the cattle country in western North America has long periods of dry weather. Without rain, the grass dries up, and the cattle lose weight. In northern areas the cattle must be protected from the severe cold of winter. Hay and grain must be stored in barns or silos to feed the cattle during winter. In warm, wet areas of the southern United States, cattle are bothered by flies and worms that threaten their health.

Cattle diseases are another problem. One disease, brucellosis (also called Bang's disease), used to kill thousands of unborn calves each year. Vaccination makes this disease less of a problem now. Tuberculosis also used to be a killer of cattle, but it too is being effectively controlled. Cattle with tuberculosis must be destroyed according to state laws. Other cattle diseases the livestock raiser must

Above: Driving sheep through mountainous Colorado. Below left: Spotted Poland China pigs crowd into the feeding trough for a meal scientifically planned to fatten them quickly. Below right: Farm animals in Dorset, England.

guard against are blackleg, anthrax, and foot-and-mouth disease. Blackleg and anthrax are caused by bacteria. Foot-and-mouth disease is caused by a virus. Parasites, such as cattle ticks, annoy and weaken the cattle. They may also carry dangerous diseases, such as tick fever and anaplasmosis. The parasite-borne diseases are controlled by bathing cattle in chemical solutions that kill the parasites.

▶ HOGS

Swine are often referred to as hogs or pigs. In the animal kingdom, they belong to the family called Suidae. The family includes the European wild boar, from which most domesticated swine are descended.

Swine are raised for lard, pork, or bacon. The hides are turned into leather, and their stiff, bristly hair is made into brushes. Swine raising is well suited to the small, family-size farm. Pigs do not have to graze, although pasture is especially good for breeding stock. Pigs often are grown for market in pens with concrete floors. The most common feed for swine is corn. They also eat wheat, barley, and oats. Very often meat scraps or fish meal are included in the feed.

People who raise swine must be very careful with the baby pigs. They are sensitive to cold temperatures and often are kept warm under heat lamps just after they are born.

At about eight weeks of age the pigs are weaned from the mother pig, or sow. After they are weaned, the pigs are fed as much as they can eat so that they will gain weight rapidly. It is not unusual for a pig to weigh about 90 kilograms (200 pounds) by the time it is five months old.

On the basis of body types, the two varieties of swine are bacon-type and meat-type hogs. Bacon-type hogs have long bodies because the bacon is cut from the sides of the hog. Meat-type hogs are usually not as long, but have fuller, fleshier bodies.

Some of the most common breeds of pigs in the United States and Canada are Duroc, Hampshire, Poland China, Berkshire, Chester White, Spotted Poland China, and Yorkshire.

Pigs are raised in all parts of the United States. The great center of pig production is the corn belt, where feed is cheapest.

▶ SHEEP

Domestic sheep are descendants of the wild sheep of Europe and Asia. Today there are more than 200 breeds of sheep throughout the world. But only 30 or 40 breeds are of major importance.

The breeds of sheep most common in the United States can best be classified according to the kind of wool they produce. The breeds are grouped as fine-wool, medium-wool, long-wool, and crossbred-wool sheep.

Sheep are raised for wool and meat. Meat from sheep less than a year old is called lamb. Meat from older sheep is called mutton. Medium-wool and long-wool sheep are used more for meat than for wool. In the United States they are raised chiefly in the East and the Middle West.

In Texas and the mountain states of the West, more emphasis is placed on wool. Western sheep ranches often are very large. They may have as many as 4,000 hectares (10,000 acres) of land and 1,000 or 2,000 sheep. The sheep ranges must be large because in the dry parts of the West there is not much grass on each hectare of land. A large range area is needed to give the sheep enough grass. The sheep eat grass right down to the roots, and time must be allowed for the grass to grow back where they have grazed. Thus they must be moved to other grazing areas fairly often. In the past, flocks of sheep were taken by shepherds into the wilds to graze. Now the usual practice is to graze the sheep on fenced-in pastureland. Sheep are often taken to pasture in trucks.

Lambs are generally born in the spring and stay with their mothers until fall, when they are weaned at four to five months of age. The sheep are shorn in the spring, either just before or just after lambing.

▶ GOATS

Goats belong to the same family as sheep and cattle. There are over 60 breeds of goats in the world, but only a few of these are common in North America.

The breeds can be divided into two groups —mohair goats and milk goats. The mohair group includes the Angora goat. Its hair is used as a material for sweaters. Breeds of milk goats include the Toggenburg, Saanen, Nubian, French-Alpine, and LaMancha.

Texas is the leading goat-producing state. The goat-raising area of Texas is the south-central region known as the Edwards Plateau. This is rugged grazing land, thinly covered by grass, cedar, and small oak trees, with a large amount of brush. The brush is of no value as food for other livestock, but goats thrive on it. Because goats can live on relatively poor pastureland, many people think that goats can live on almost anything, including trash and tin cans. This is not true. To be healthy and productive, goats must have proper nourishment just like other animals.

Goat's milk is similar to cow's milk, but it is naturally homogenized and is easier to digest. Many kinds of cheese are made from goat's milk.

Milk goats are popular dairy animals in many countries. Switzerland, Italy, France, Spain, and Germany lead in the production of goat's milk. The main centers of Angora-goat raising are Turkey, South Africa, and the southwestern United States. In India, China, and parts of Africa, goats are slaughtered for their meat.

▶ IMPORTANCE OF THE LIVESTOCK INDUSTRY

The raising of livestock provides the basis of many other industries and services. These include industries that pack meat, process dairy products, manufacture leather and woolen goods, and produce livestock feeds and farm equipment. Much of the success of the livestock industry depends on veterinary and scientific research services. As individuals, we also benefit from the livestock industry. Meat, milk, butter, and cheese make up an important part of our food supply.

DUANE C. KRAEMER
Texas A & M University

See also AGRICULTURE; DAIRYING AND DAIRY PRODUCTS; FOOD PRESERVATION AND PROCESSING; HOOFED MAMMALS; MEAT-PACKING.

CAVES AND CAVERNS

Jim White, a New Mexican cowboy, was galloping through the foothills of the Guadalupe Mountains late one afternoon in the summer of 1901. Suddenly he reined in his horse. Dead ahead of him a dark, funnel-shaped cloud was rising from the ground. As Jim drew closer he saw that the cloud was really a column of bats. Thousands, perhaps millions, of bats were spiraling upward from the sandy hillside.

Where were they coming from? Crawling on hands and knees, Jim found a yawning hole in the ground. Returning the next day with a rope ladder and kerosene lantern, Jim climbed down into the bats' hole. Deep inside the mountain the hole was far more than a hole. There were tunnels leading off to the left and right. When Jim followed the left-hand tunnel, he discovered the bats' roosting place.

The floor of the bats' room was slippery with their droppings. Backing out cautiously, Jim tried the other passageway. When he looked ahead, all he could see was his own wavy shadow.

Once he shouted to break the silence. His voice boomed back in echo. Once his light sputtered and went out. With shaking fingers he relit the lamp and walked on.

The passageway widened abruptly. Great stone "icicles" hung from the ceiling of an enormous room. Huge columns rose from its floor. In the flickering light of the lantern, Jim could see slender poles, wavy curtains, and frozen waterfalls of stone. In a far corner there was a pool with stone "lily pads" floating on the water.

Jim's scalp prickled. He felt as if he were dreaming. He had never read about caves for the very good reason that he didn't know how to read. But when he returned to the Triple X Ranch that night, he was determined to learn all that he could about the strange, silent world he had discovered.

No one in the bunkhouse would believe Jim's story. Some of the cowboys had heard of a bat cave, but they laughed at Jim's description of underground rooms filled with giant sculptures of stone. Only a 15-year-old Mexican known as the Kid was willing to go with him to the cave. With kerosene torches in their hands, Jim and the Kid explored miles of passageways. Wherever they wandered, they

The biggest room in the caverns in Carlsbad Caverns National Park, New Mexico. This room is 1.25 kilometers (about ¾ mile) long. The ceiling is covered with "icicles" of limestone.

found bigger and bigger rooms and more beautiful rock formations.

As the years passed, Jim was able to convince a few local business people that there was treasure of a sort in his cave. The bats' droppings, known as guano, were a valuable fertilizer. Jim became supervisor of a mining crew that dug the guano and brought it up to the surface of the mountain.

The guano mine petered out. The Kid drifted away. But Jim continued to spend his spare hours in the cave. He was sure that people would some day flock to see the wonders of his underground rooms.

At last, in 1922, two travelers asked Jim to guide them through the cave. A photographer went with them. When he printed his pictures, the cowboys on the ranch and the people in nearby Carlsbad begged for a guided tour, too.

Jim lowered these first sightseers, two at a time, in an iron bucket left over from the guano mine days. This time the news of the cave spread quickly. Jim White had discovered Carlsbad Caverns, the most spectacular system of caverns in North America, if not in the whole world. This natural wonder is preserved in Carlsbad Caverns National Park, established in 1930.

Today tourists can enter Jim's cave by elevator. The twisting trails are paved, and electric lights shine on the sculptured stone. But the cave has not changed. The visitors who wander through the rooms inside the mountain are as dazzled by what they see as Jim was long ago.

▶ **A CAVE IS BORN**

Carlsbad Caverns had its beginnings some 60,000,000 years ago, long before two-legged creatures walked on earth. As rains poured down and rivers flowed, the solid rock of the cave-to-be was slowly eaten away.

The special kind of rock in Carlsbad is limestone. Limestone is a fairly soft rock. It can also be dissolved by a weak acid. The acid that dissolves away limestone comes from rainwater. Falling drops of rain pick up carbon dioxide from the air and from the soil. This carbon dioxide changes the rainwater into carbonic acid. (Whenever you drink ginger

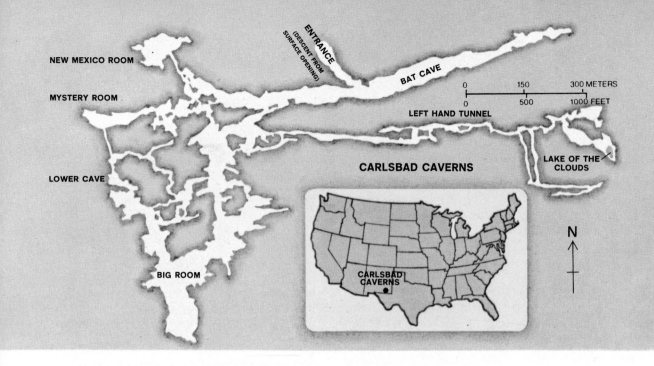

CARLSBAD CAVERNS

ale or soda, you are drinking carbonic acid. The fizzy bubbles contain carbon dioxide.)

Sixty million years ago, then, acid rainwater fell on a bed of limestone in what is now New Mexico. It nibbled away at the rock until hair-thin cracks began to appear. More rain fell. The water trickled down, enlarging the cracks. It found new paths between the layers of stone. The paths widened into tunnels. The tunnels crisscrossed and grew into rooms.

Over millions of years Carlsbad Caverns took shape. As long as water filled its tunnels and flowed through its rock-walled rooms, it grew bigger and bigger.

It is hard to imagine just how big a cave can be. Some of the rooms in Carlsbad are about 300 meters (1,000 feet) under the ground. The cave's largest room could hold ten football fields. In one place its ceiling is as high as a 30-story office building.

When nothing stops the acid rainwater, it can devour vast areas of limestone. In parts of Indiana and Kentucky—specially in the neighborhood of Mammoth Cave in Kentucky —the ground is pitted with **sinkholes**. These are huge sunken bowls that lead to underground rooms and waterways. There are 160,000 kilometers (100,000 miles) of caves in that part of the United States.

But at Carlsbad the work of the acid rainwater was brought to a halt. The earth's crust wrinkled and folded. The bed of limestone tilted up and became part of a mountain range. The water that filled the tunnels and flowed through the rock-walled rooms slowly drained away.

Carlsbad Caverns was born, but it did not look as it does today. No stone "icicles" hung from its ceilings. No columns rose from its floors. But as raindrops trickled down to the empty cave rooms, something new began to happen. Water started to decorate the cave.

▶ **DECORATING THE CAVE**

About 1,000,000 years ago a single drop of rainwater clung to the ceiling of Carlsbad's Big Room. As the water dripped, a tiny ring of lime crystallized on the ceiling. A second drop—and a third, a fourth, a fifth—left lime in the same place. As time passed, the rings of lime formed a little stone "icicle." It kept on growing.

Another drop of water dripped to the floor of the cave. Again the lime was left behind. As time passed, thousands of drops fell on the same spot. The specks of lime formed what looked like a stubby stone candle. The "candle" kept on growing.

The icicle of stone on the ceiling is called a **stalactite**. The stubby candle on the floor is a **stalagmite**. (Think of the c in stalactite as standing for ceiling and the g in stalagmite as standing for ground. This will help you to remember which is which.)

Each stalactite and stalagmite grows at a different rate, depending on the wetness of the cave, the temperature of the room, and the thickness of the limestone bed above it. Some stalactites grow a few centimeters a year. Others take 100 years to grow that much.

Often the stalagmites thrusting upward meet the stalactites that grow down. They form columns. The largest column in Carlsbad is about 30 meters (100 feet) high.

Stalactites, stalagmites, and columns are not the only cave formations. Lime-laden water covers cave walls with rippling **flowstone**. It forms curtains of **dripstone** when it oozes from cracks in the ceiling. It builds a border of **rimstone** when it evaporates from a pool on the floor. It coats sand grains with layer after layer of lime until each grain is transformed into a **cave pearl**.

The ceilings of some caves are covered with short, hollow stalactites that look like soda straws. Others have glittering stone needles on their walls or stone pincushions bristling from the floor. There are delicate cave feathers, graceful cave flowers, and a strange stalac-tite (called a **helictite**) that grows sideways and up as well as down. No one is sure how and why the helictites grow in corkscrew twists and turns.

In Carlsbad these weird and beautiful stone shapes stopped growing when the climate changed. Rains fell less often. Rivers grew shallow. Water seldom reached the rooms deep under the ground. Today the great cave is almost unchanging. Scientists speak of it as "dead."

▶ CAVES THAT ARE NOT CAVERNS

Although no two caves look alike, all of the really big caves in the world were formed in the same way. They were hollowed out of limestone (or related rocks like gypsum and marble) by acid water. They are called **solution caves**. A more familiar word for them is **caverns**.

Caverns are not the only kind of cave. For example, there are **sea caves**, those favorite hangouts of pirates and smugglers. Sea caves are formed by the steady pounding of waves on the rocky cliffs along the shore. The waves

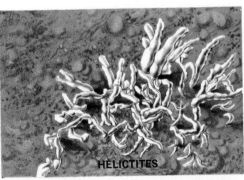
HELICTITES

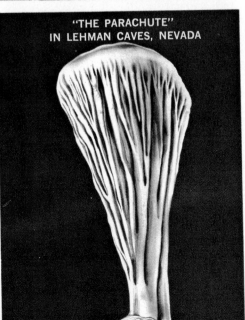
"THE PARACHUTE" IN LEHMAN CAVES, NEVADA

DRIPSTONE CURTAIN

CAVE FLOWERS

STALACTITES

STALAGMITES

Currents of warm air have hollowed out this glacial ice cave. Such caves are usually too dangerous to explore.

do not dissolve the rock. They dig it out, grinding away at it year after year with pebbles and fine sand. The best-known sea caves are the Blue Grotto in Italy's island of Capri (grotto is still another word for cave) and Fingal's Cave in the Scottish Hebrides. After the composer Felix Mendelssohn visited the Hebrides, he wrote a piece of music called *Fingal's Cave*. Listen to it, and you can hear the sounds of wind and wave beating against the cave's walls.

North America's largest sea cave is Sea Lion Cave in Oregon. Herds of sea lions raise their families in the cave's big room. Other sea caves are scattered along the Atlantic and Pacific coasts, as well as on the shores of the Great Lakes and the Bay of Fundy. There is even a sea cave in the Utah desert, 110 meters (360 feet) above Great Salt Lake. Can you figure out how it got there?

In the western part of the United States and on the volcanic islands of Hawaii there are hundreds of **lava caves**. These formed after hot, melted rock welled up from deep inside the earth. Rivers of the liquid rock, called lava, flowed above ground. Even when the surfaces of the lava rivers cooled, forming a hard crust, their fiery interiors traveled on. The hollow, hardened tubes they left behind are lava caves.

Lava caves are usually unbranched tunnels only a meter or so under the ground. Lava stalactites hang from their ceilings. And their floors are covered with ripple marks made by the fiery rivers that formed them.

Some lava caves contain huge beds of ice—ice that does not melt on the hottest summer day. Ages ago cold air from the surface entered the cave. The tube-shaped cave became a trap for the cold air. When rain or snow carried water to the cave, the water froze, making the porous lava rock still colder. The thicker the ice became, the less likelihood there was of its melting. Even in the Arizona and New Mexico desert, there are caves with perpetual ice.

In Canada and the northwestern United States there are also **glacial ice caves**. Hollowed out of glaciers, these caves have roofs and walls of ice. They grow bigger when warm air reaches them and smaller when it is cold. As they grow, blocks of ice often tumble from ceilings and walls. For this reason, glacial caves are usually too dangerous to explore.

During the Ice Age, when great glaciers covered large parts of North America, still another kind of cave was born. In the path of a glacier, boulders were split off from rocky hillsides. After the ice sheet melted, streams tumbled the boulders about and enlarged the openings in the hills. These openings, which never became very big, are **splitrock** or **boul-**

Stalactites hang from the ceiling of this cave in southwestern France, producing interesting reflections in the lake below.

der caves. They are found chiefly in New England.

WHAT LIVES IN CAVES?

Almost every cave is inhabited. Birds build nests near the entrance. Skunks use caves as a nursery in which to rear babies. Snakes sleep in caves in winter. So do many insects.

But the birds and skunks and snakes and moths are not true cave dwellers. They shelter in the cave only when they cannot find anything better. They never settle there permanently or visit the rooms far within.

The real cave dwellers are the creatures that live deep inside the cave. Some, like rats and bats, leave the cave to find food. But there are insects, fishes, and salamanders that spend their whole lives in black cave rooms. A long line of their ancestors lived in the same place. During centuries of darkness the bodies of these creatures have changed. They have lost their coloring, becoming white or pale pink or so transparent that you can see through them. Many are now blind, making up for eyesight with better hearing or a sharper sense of touch or smell.

The pale cave cricket has overlong feelers that help it to find food. So does the pearly white crayfish that lives in cave pools. The blind and wingless cave beetle is covered with fine hairs. The ghostly blindfish that swim in underground streams are unusually sensitive to vibrations. Even the gentlest tapping sends them scurrying.

Blind cave salamanders are rarer than the blindfish. Some kinds can see when they are born, although their eyelids grow together later on. Scientists have experimented with a big salamander found in European caves. When it was kept under a red light (the kind used in photographic darkrooms), its white skin darkened and its eyes started to grow. After years under the red light, the blind salamander regained its sight.

While these animals are able to adapt to cave life, few plants can. Molds and mushrooms flourish in the damp, dark underground rooms, but green plants cannot live without light. Only in caves that have been wired for electricity will you see greenery. There, on rocky ledges above the lights, gardens of green moss and feathery ferns are able to grow.

HUMAN CAVE DWELLERS

Long before people chopped down trees with stone axes or made tents of animal skins, they took shelter in caves. Now scientists are piecing together the story of their lives from remains found on cave floors—bits of charcoal from long-dead fires, stone knives and grinding bowls, bones of animals, and the skulls and teeth and hip bones of these ancient people.

Above: Blindfish (shown life-size), found in several North American caves, can detect even the slightest movement in water. Below: Texas blind salamander (also life-size), one of the world's rarest cave animals.

In a cave in Altamira, Spain, in 1879, a little girl made a most exciting discovery—a rough rock ceiling covered with paintings of animals. There were horses and deer and a great, charging bison. The paintings were richly colored, lifelike pictures drawn by primitive hunters.

Since that discovery painted caves have been found not only in Spain but in France, Africa, Canada, and the United States as well. These underground art galleries contain paintings of mammoths and rhinoceroses, long-legged birds and water buffalo. The pictures in American caves were painted by Indians. Some of them are 1,500 years old.

▶ FINDING A CAVE

How do you go about finding a cave? **Speleologists**, the scientists who study caves, are learning to locate them by examining rock formations and following the paths of underground streams. After careful study they figure out just where a cave ought to be.

Most American caves were found by accident, however. It was a cow named Millicent that pointed out the entrance of Howe Caverns in New York. On summer afternoons she was found enjoying a cool breeze in her rocky pasture. It came from a crack in a ledge of limestone—a crack that led deep underground. A wounded bear brought a hunter to the mouth of Mammoth Cave. A horse stumbling into a hole tossed its rider into Lehman Cave in Nevada. A rabbit hiding under a rock showed two boys the way to Endless Caverns in Virginia.

Only a small number of the 30,000 caves in North America have ever been visited. Speleologists and **spelunkers**, the men and women who enjoy caving as a sport, are slowly finding and exploring these "wild" caves. However, the sport can be dangerous.

The best caves for boys and girls are the commercial caves, with guides and lighted pathways. There are commercial caves in every section of the United States and in several Canadian provinces.

If you visit a cave, you will notice that the air seems purer and the temperature milder than above ground. Cave temperatures scarcely change throughout the year. In winter they are warmer than the land above them. In summer they are cooler.

The best part of a cave tour can come when the guide turns out the lights. The jet blackness is darker than anything you have experienced before. It is a world where the sun never shines. You can hear a bat overhead and a drop of water splashing on the rock floor. For a few seconds time rolls backward, and you can picture the ancient beginnings of caves and the people who used to live in them.

DOROTHY STERLING
Author, *The Story of Caves*

See also BATS; PREHISTORIC ART; PREHISTORIC PEOPLE; SPELUNKING.

CELL

Almost all living things are made of cells. Some tiny forms of life consist of only one cell. Larger forms of life are built of many cells. That is why cells are called the basic units of life.

The human body is made of billions upon billions of cells. That tells you something about cells—they are tiny. Most cells are so small that they can be seen only with a microscope.

The smallest cells are probably the bacteria. These one-celled forms of life can barely be seen even with a microscope. Nerve cells are probably the largest cells. Some of them are more than 3 feet long.

The microscope has shown that all cells have three main parts: the cell membrane, the cytoplasm, and the nucleus. The cell membrane is the outside surface of the cell. Inside the membrane is the cytoplasm. This is a mass of colorless material, which holds many other tiny cell parts. The nucleus is usually near the center of the cell. It is somewhat round in shape and has an outer membrane of its own.

There are many kinds of cells. Usually each kind does one special job. For example, in animals some cells expand and contract; these are muscle cells. Other cells are sensitive to light; these cells form the retina of the eye.

Modern microscopes show that cells are far from simple. They contain many complicated structures. And there is constant activity going on in cells.

Food and oxygen pass steadily into the cell through the membrane. The cell changes them into energy. It uses the energy to do various kinds of work. The cell also makes new cell material—more living matter. Some waste matter is left over from these processes. It passes out of the cell through the membrane. So do worn-out cell materials.

One of the most remarkable cell activities is division. Most kinds of cells can divide into two new cells. Both the new cells are exactly like the original cell.

With few exceptions, a single cell does not live very long. But if it divides, the two new cells start life afresh. That is, instead of aging and dying, the old cell becomes two new cells.

Plants and animals grow because of cell division. When they are fully grown, the cell division continues. New cells replace old or worn-out cells. As cell division slows, the body ages.

Although plant and animal cells differ from each other in some ways, in a broad sense they are alike. And so we say that the cell is the unit of life.

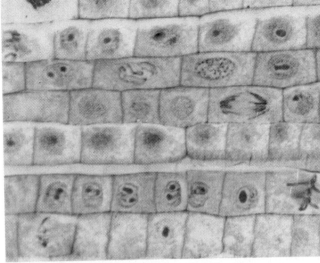

Tip of onion root, magnified 1,500 times. Cells have been stained. Cytoplasm is blue; nucleus is pink.

Animals and plants that are large enough to be seen without a microscope are made up mainly of living construction units called cells, just as a brick wall is made of bricks. Other materials are usually present as well, filling in between the cells, just as the bricks of a building are joined together by cement. Although cells make up the tissues of most organisms, there are a few exceptions. In some forms of life, such as mushrooms, the cell as the unit of construction is not present. Nevertheless, the cell must be looked on as the basic unit of life. A microscopic animal or plant may consist of only one free-living cell. Larger forms consist of many cells united together.

Cork cells drawn in 1665 by English scientist Robert Hooke. Using a microscope, he was the first to see cells.

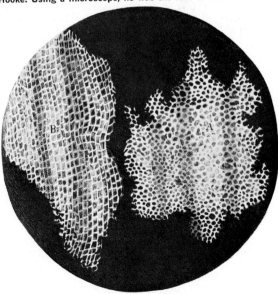

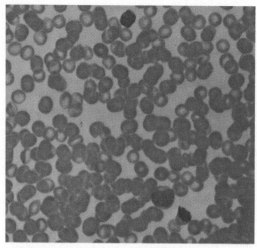

A stained slide of mouse blood, magnified 600 times. Red blood cells stain pink; white cells stain purple.

Most cells are so small that they can be seen only with the aid of the microscope. In fact, the existence of cells became known only after the microscope was invented. They were first noticed in plant tissues. This is not surprising, since plant cells are larger than animal cells; also, the walls of plant cells are readily seen. With better and new kinds of microscopes, more and more has been discovered about cells. There are many kinds, but they all have a great deal in common. So, to

Diagram of a typical cell, showing three main parts.

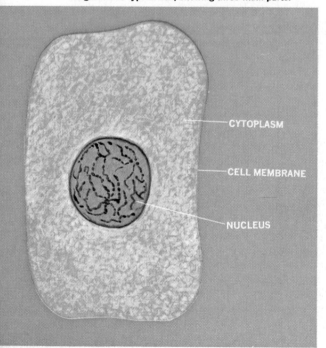

CYTOPLASM

CELL MEMBRANE

NUCLEUS

begin with, we can give a general description of a cell that will hold true for all cells.

▶ THE MAIN PARTS OF A CELL

A single cell consists of three main parts. The outermost surface consists of the **cell membrane**. Inside this is a mass of colorless material within which are many smaller structures of different kinds. This inner matter is called the **cytoplasm**. Inside the cytoplasm, usually near the center of the cell, is the **nucleus**. It is a roundish or oval structure; a membrane separates its own inner substance from the cytoplasm.

The cell membrane, cytoplasm, and nucleus work together. All three are necessary to the life of the cell. Together, they constitute what is called **protoplasm.**

The Cell Membrane

The cell membrane is the boundary separating the interior of the cell from the outside. Everything that enters or leaves the cell must pass through it by some means. Water, salts, oxygen, and food substances in some form must enter. Carbon dioxide, waste substances, and also water and salts must leave. There is a continual traffic through the membrane in both directions.

The Cytoplasm

The cytoplasm is the region where most of the chemical work of the cell is conducted. New cell materials are manufactured here, and old materials are broken down and passed out. Organic (carbon-containing) compounds from food substances are used. They are built up into new cell structures or are used for the stored energy they contain. Oxygen is needed to keep these processes going; carbon dioxide, water, and excess heat are produced as unwanted products.

A cell is therefore in the process of constant change. A continual stream of substances enters through the cell membrane. The substances are either built up into new cell substance or used as a kind of fuel. As fuel they supply the energy necessary either for the growth of cell substances or for the activity of cell structures. There is also a continuous outflow of the final products of fuel combustion and the breakdown of worn-out cell structures.

The cell is something like a candle flame. A flame has certain characteristics such as shape, color, and temperature; a cell has characteristics such as shape, size, and a molasses-like consistency. In both cases something happens as the result of an inflow and outflow of material. With the candle anything that cuts off either the supply of oxygen or the organic material (the paraffin) cuts off the flame. With the cell anything that cuts off either the supply of oxygen or the organic material (the food substances) cuts off the life. The cell is not only a unit of structure, it is the unit of life. Life is an activity, or a process, forever changing, even though the appearance may remain the same. This is one of the most important ideas in biology.

The Cell Nucleus

The nucleus is more concerned with controlling the nature of the cell than it is with the kind of cell activity just described. It contains threadlike material called **chromatin.** When a cell is about to divide into two, this material groups together into a number of slender, bent rods called **chromosomes.** The chromosome substance consists mainly of a very complex chemical called a **nucleic acid.** It is known as deoxyribonucleic acid, or DNA for short. In the nucleus DNA occurs as fine, spirally coiled threads that in turn coil around one another, like a twisted ladder. The chromosome material is confined within the nucleus, except when a cell is in the process of division. The chromosome material seems to be the most stable substance present in the cell. This is in keeping with the importance of the nucleus as the controller of cell growth and cell character.

Small, round bodies called **nucleoli** are also found in the nucleus. They contain another kind of nucleic acid—ribonucleic acid, or RNA.

The Nucleus and Cytoplasm

Both the cytoplasm and the nucleus have their own kinds of work to do. But they work together, and each is necessary to the cell's normal existence. (The one exception is the red blood cells of mammals, in which the nucleus disappears.) If the nucleus is removed from a cell, the cell life is shortened; on the other hand, a nucleus that has been removed from a cell can do nothing. The relationship between the nucleus and cytoplasm may be likened to that of a professional pianist and his piano—neither can work without the other. The nucleus and cytoplasm of a cell form a partnership.

New cell substance is continually manufactured close to the nucleus and under the influence of the nucleus. And this substance moves steadily toward the cell surface.

Structures in the Cytoplasm

The cytoplasm, lying between the cell membrane and the nuclear membrane, contains various special structures. These are part of the chemical machinery responsible for the production of energy and of new living material. One kind consists of minute, sausage-shaped bodies called **mitochondria.** These

Mitochondria in heart-muscle cell, magnified 30,000 times. These small, sausage-shaped bodies produce energy for the entire cell.

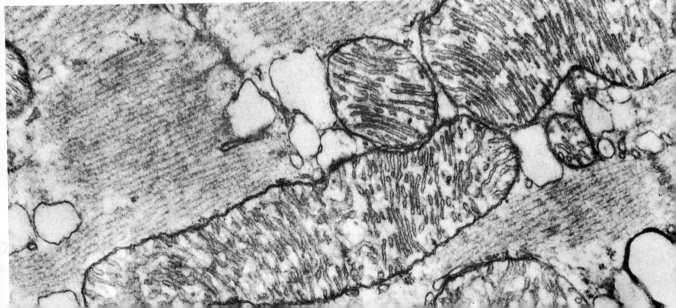

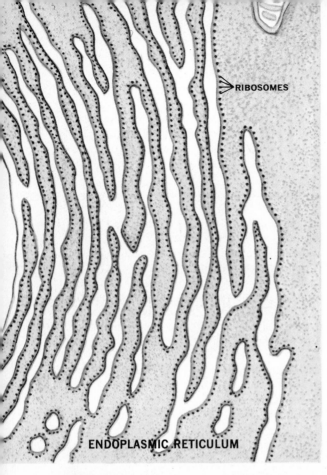

RIBOSOMES

ENDOPLASMIC RETICULUM

Above: Granules (ribosomes) along folds of endoplasmic reticulum (shown here greatly enlarged) produce new living material. Below: Structures in typical plant and animal cells. Main difference is that plant cell contains chloroplasts, structures essential for making food.

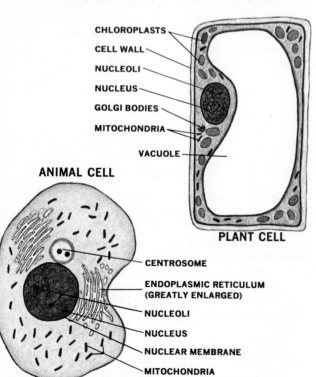

CHLOROPLASTS
CELL WALL
NUCLEOLI
NUCLEUS
GOLGI BODIES
MITOCHONDRIA
VACUOLE

PLANT CELL

ANIMAL CELL

CENTROSOME
ENDOPLASMIC RETICULUM (GREATLY ENLARGED)
NUCLEOLI
NUCLEUS
NUCLEAR MEMBRANE
MITOCHONDRIA

have a complex internal structure in spite of their small size. These small bodies have been called the powerhouse of the cell. They are responsible for converting simple organic substances such as sugar into a high-powered form of energy that the cell can use to perform work of various kinds. Another kind of structure consists of very extensive double membranes; in some cells these extend, layer after layer, all the way from the nucleus to the cell surface. This structure has the imposing name of **endoplasmic reticulum**. Along the reticulum are enormous numbers of minute granules called **ribosomes**. These structures are very important, for it is here that proteins are made. Proteins are complex chemical substances continually required by the cell.

The cytoplasm also contains structures called **Golgi bodies**. They are involved in the secretion of cell products.

The structures discussed so far are present in both animal and plant cells. However, in certain ways animal and plant cells differ from one another.

▶ **ANIMAL CELLS AND PLANT CELLS**

Both animal cells and plant cells require water and mineral salts. And both require organic substances—complex carbon-containing substances such as sugar. These substances supply the energy needed for growth and activity of the cell. However, animal cells cannot manufacture these organic substances themselves—they must obtain them from outside sources. Animal cells require atmospheric oxygen, whereas most of the time plant cells do not.

Most plant cells can manufacture their own sugars and other basic substances. They do this by using the energy obtained from light, together with water, carbon dioxide, and certain other raw materials. This manufacturing process is called **photosynthesis**. In photosynthesis, water is split into hydrogen and oxygen by means of light energy. The oxygen is passed into the atmosphere, where it is available for use by animal cells. The hydrogen combines with carbon dioxide, in a series of complicated steps, to produce the simple sugar, glucose.

Light is absorbed by the green pigment **chlorophyll**. Chlorophyll is confined in small, round, green discs called **chloroplasts**.

Each chloroplast represents a small factory for photosynthesis.

Most plant cells are also distinguished by having a large internal sac of fluid called the **vacuole**. This contains a salt solution important to the life of the cell. And a cell possesses a strengthening wall of **cellulose** outside the living cell membrane. Plant cells tend to become boxed in by their rigid external walls. Much of the strength and toughness of a plant comes from that.

Animal cells are more exposed. And their surface membrane is generally more active. Animal cells take in water, dissolved salts, and other substances by a process of **diffusion** through the invisible pores of the membrane. In addition, many kinds of animal cells take in these substances and even particles by a process of cell drinking called **pinocytosis.** In this process the membrane pushes out or folds in here and there. It does so in such a way that small droplets of water or particles of food substances are captured and passed into the cell interior.

Most of the physical activity of the animal cell is conducted at or close to the cell membrane. The membrane controls the passage of substances in and out of the cell. The outermost region of the cell produces active structures. For example, it produces intricately constructed hairlike structures extending from the cell surface. These show a regularly beating, whiplike movement. They either move the cell through the external fluid or move the fluid past the cell. Also part of this outer region are the very fine fibrils (little fibers) that cause a cell to contract and expand, as in muscle cells. The long, drawn-out extensions of certain cells, which we call nerve fibers, are also part of the same region. Altogether, this outer region is strikingly sensitive and responsive to influences from outside.

KINDS OF CELLS

Cells are of many different kinds. Each kind, as a rule, specializes in one particular activity. One kind may be especially sensitive to light; it serves as a retinal cell in the eye. Another may be exceptionally sensitive to chemicals in the air or water; it serves for smell or for taste. Another may be one of several kinds of muscle cells. Other cells may

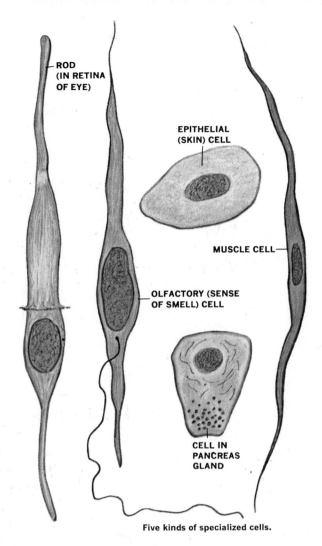

Five kinds of specialized cells.

produce and give off material of some sort; these are known as secretory cells. Still others are unspecialized and serve in a general way. For example, they may form a reserve from which other kinds of cells are produced.

CELL DIVISION

One of the most remarkable things a cell can do is become two cells. Most kinds of cells can divide into two cells exactly like the original. In doing so they go through a complicated process called **mitosis.** During mitosis, chromosomes in the cell nucleus divide and separate. In most animal cells the process is set in motion by a pair of small bodies called **centrioles**, which lie close to the nucleus. (Strictly speaking, "mitosis" refers only to the division of the nucleus of a cell. However, it is sometimes used to mean division of the entire cell.)

Each centriole becomes a center from which fibers grow in all directions, forming a radiating or star-shaped pattern known as an **aster**. Between the two centers the fibers run together, forming a bridgelike structure called the **spindle**. The two asters and their spindle become steadily larger. And in effect the two centers push each other apart. Finally, a furrow appears at the cell surface around the middle of the cell. The furrow deepens and divides the whole cell in two. Then each centriole, if it has not already done so, divides into two. And each new pair is ready to bring about division of the new cell when needed. (In some animals and in some plants, although a spindle can be seen, centrioles have not been detected.)

During all this time the nucleus is undergoing a division process of its own, which requires assistance from the mitotic apparatus. To begin with, the long, threadlike chromosomes become shorter and wider while the nuclear membrane disappears. Each chromosome, already duplicated, separates lengthwise so that each chromosome has now formed a pair. The duplicated chromosomes move to the equator of the spindle. From there the two sets of chromosomes are pulled apart by special spindle fibers. So each of the two cells about to be formed receives a complete set of chromosomes. From this set a new nucleus is reconstructed, exactly like the original nucleus. Each new cell resulting from division is consequently an exact copy of the old cell.

The importance of cell division is very great indeed. The life of an individual cell is generally short. The cell ages and dies. If it undergoes division, however, each new cell starts life afresh. So, as long as divisions continue, aging and death is postponed. Also, as cells multiply in this way, the body they compose continues to grow. Anything that stops cell multiplication stops growth. Even when the body is fully grown, many kinds of cells are continually dying and have to be replaced by new cells. As the body grows older cell replacement becomes slower, and the body ages.

One type of cell can develop into a complete new body. This cell, a fertilized egg cell, divides by the process of mitosis. The new cells divide again and again until a whole body is formed.

N. J. BERRILL
McGill University

See also AGING; BODY, HUMAN; EGGS AND EMBRYOS; GENETICS; PLANTS.

CELLOPHANE. See PLASTICS.

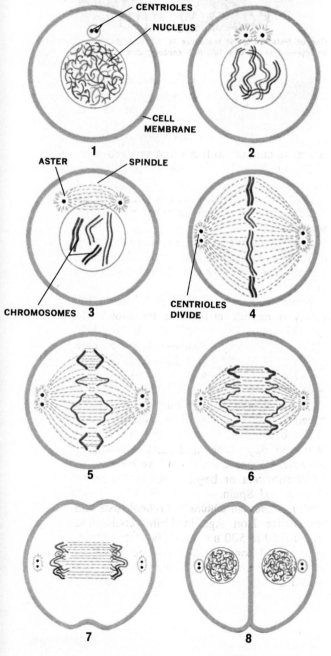

Animal cell dividing by mitosis. Figures 1–3: Centrioles begin moving to opposite sides of nucleus; spindle fibers start to form. Tangled chromosome threads coil up into tight strands, then nuclear membrane starts breaking down; each centriole divides in two. Figure 4: Chromosomes move midway between the 2 asters. Figures 5 and 6: Pairs of chromosomes pulled apart as spindles lengthen. Figures 7 and 8: Nuclear membrane forms about each group of chromosomes. Finally, new cell membrane appears. Mitosis is complete.

CENTRIOLES
NUCLEUS
CELL MEMBRANE
1
2
ASTER
SPINDLE
CHROMOSOMES 3
CENTRIOLES DIVIDE 4
5
6
7
8

CELTS

Evidence of the Celts (or Kelts) in Europe dates from long before the days of the Roman Empire. We owe to them many stirring tales of gods and goddesses and of heroes such as King Arthur and the Knights of the Round Table. To the Celts, calendar festivals were of great importance. We still celebrate their Samain, the eve of November 1, a time when humans could go into the otherworld and the divine inhabitants of that world could come into ours. Today we call it Halloween.

The classical writers tell us that the people we call Celts knew themselves by this name. The different groups of Celts were closely linked by language, religion, and culture. At the height of their power, about 300 B.C., they occupied all the land between the Baltic and Mediterranean seas and between the Black Sea and the Atlantic coast. Most of them were brought under Roman rule by the 1st century B.C.

The ancient Celts left few written records. They never formed a great empire, as the Romans did. Yet they created an important civilization in Europe north of the Alps, where they introduced the use of iron. With their superb skill in fashioning weapons and tools of this metal, they created one of Europe's major revolutions in technology. They carried on trade far beyond their own settlements.

The Celts produced works of art—beautifully decorated weapons, personal ornaments, ceramics, glass, and coins—quite different from anything else in the ancient world.

How We Have Learned About the Celts. The Celts built dwellings and other buildings such as shops and stables. The defenses of their forts—in both wood and stone, according to the material available—and many of their stone buildings survive today. But the Celts preferred to pass on their culture by word of mouth rather than by written records.

We know about the Celts partly through archeology and partly through the writings of their Greek and Roman conquerors, especially Julius Caesar. We have also learned about the ancient Celts from peoples who are their descendants and who still speak Celtic languages. These are a small and diminishing number among the Welsh, the Bretons of northwestern France, the Scots, and the Irish.

One of Ireland's great treasures is the Ardagh chalice, or cup—an example of late (8th century) Celtic art.

Celtic groups lived in present-day Great Britain and Ireland long before the Romans began their conquest of Britain in 55 B.C. The Romans remained there for 400 years. But they never entered Ireland or conquered the mountainous northern and western parts of Britain. The Celts in those areas kept their way of life and their pagan Celtic religion until they were converted to Christianity about A.D. 450. Later, monks, poets, and scribes carefully wrote down the great heroic tales and preserved the poetry and mythology that their ancestors, the pagan Celts, had passed down through the ages by word of mouth.

Where the Celts Lived. The Celts had a highly developed civilization by about 800 or 700 B.C. Their heartland was probably the small area in present-day Switzerland and West Germany where three great rivers—the Rhine, the Rhone, and the Danube—begin. Along these and other rivers, Celtic groups expanded until they reached their height between 500 and 50 B.C. The Gauls were one of the best-known Celtic groups. They lived in present-day France and parts of adjoining countries. Other Celts spread as far east as Czechoslovakia or beyond and as far south as Italy and Spain.

Way of Life and Culture. Archeologists call the earlier Iron Age in Celtic civilization (about 800 to 500 B.C.) the Hallstatt culture. It is named for a Celtic settlement discovered at Hallstatt, Austria. The culture of the later Iron Age (500 to 50 B.C.) is named

La Tène, for a site called La Tène (The Shallows) at the Lake of Neuchâtel, in Switzerland.

Finds made at the Hallstatt site in the mid-1800's show that the Celts had a large settlement there. They mined salt and traded with other peoples. There are hundreds of graves where noble Celts were buried in wooden chambers under mounds of earth. In the chambers were many objects made by Celtic artisans—swords and shields, metal drinking vessels, four-wheeled wagons and horse bridles. The Celts believed in a life after death. Warriors would need all this equipment, along with joints of wild boar (a favorite food), on their long journey to the otherworld.

La Tène was one of the Celts' many holy places, for they worshiped water whether in the form of lake, river, or spring. To such places they brought gifts for their deities and threw these offerings into the water. This was the origin of the wishing well. Many objects made by the Celts have been found at La Tène since excavations began there in the 1880's. These objects are richly decorated with fanciful birds and animals and elaborate designs composed of circles, swirls, and curves. The designs are often imitated by modern artists.

We know that many of the Celts were farmers. They grew wheat and other grains and raised cattle, sheep, and hogs. Sometimes they lived in large hilltop villages defended by huge walls of timber and stone. Inside, everything was well planned. There were small dwellings for the people and a large building where the chief, or king, lived and held feasts for the noble warriors. The smiths had their metal-working shops in one place, and huge quantities of grain were stored in another part of the village.

Other persons besides kings and warriors held a high place in Celtic society. These were the bards, who composed and recited verses about gods and heroes and their deeds; the smiths, who were thought to have magic powers; and the druids, who performed religious ceremonies and administered Celtic law.

Celtic women dressed in long tunics or loose trousers and wore hair ornaments, bracelets, rings, and pins. The men washed their hair with lime to stiffen and lighten it. They wore tunics, trousers, and great blanketlike cloaks. Their jewelry included torques (neck rings), armlets, and ornamental belt buckles. For war, the Celts carried spears, wore swords, and dodged enemy blows behind tall, oblong shields. When they killed an enemy, they cut off the head and carried it proudly home to keep as proof of their courage and skill.

The Celts worshiped many gods and goddesses. They enjoyed festivals, feasting and drinking, hunting, fighting, and cattle raiding. They admired courage, fine appearance, good speaking, generosity, and hospitality. Archeology and research are constantly turning up new information about the Celts and their contributions to the world.

ANNE ROSS
Author, *Everyday Life of the Pagan Celts*

See also ARTHUR, KING; ENGLISH ART AND ARCHITECTURE; FRANCE; IRELAND; LANGUAGES; SCOTLAND; WALES.

The Celts carved this gigantic horse on a chalk hill near Uffington, England.

CEMENT AND CONCRETE

Cement is one of the most useful materials in modern building. By itself it is a soft powder. But when it is mixed with water and allowed to harden, cement can bind sand or gravel into a hard, solid mass.

Cement is used chiefly as an ingredient of mortar and concrete. **Mortar** is a mixture of cement, sand, and water. **Concrete** is the same mixture with gravel or broken stone added to it.

Mortar is too weak to be used by itself as a material for building. It can, however, be used to bind together bricks or stones into masonry. Mortar is also used to make a protective coating called stucco, which is put on the outer walls of buildings. Sometimes it is used for interior decoration.

Concrete is very strong because of the gravel and stone mixed in it. When concrete is poured into molds, or forms, and allowed to harden, it will stand by itself. Concrete is often used to make walls, floors, and many other parts of buildings and bridges. It is a fairly cheap building material because the cement, sand, and gravel from which it is made are not costly. Because it is poured while still soft, concrete can be molded into odd shapes that would be impossible to make with other materials. For this reason modern architects often use concrete for the buildings they design.

▸ HOW IS CEMENT MADE?

Modern cement is made by heating a mixture of limestone and clay or slag to a very high temperature. This mixture is heated until large, glassy cinders called clinkers are formed. The clinkers are then ground to powder. When water is added to the cement powder, a very complicated chemical reaction takes place. The result is a durable artificial stone that will not dissolve in water. In fact, this type of cement will actually harden under water. For this reason it is called hydraulic cement, from the Greek word *hydor,* meaning "water."

Before hydraulic cement was discovered, cement was made from lime alone. Lime is a white, powdery substance that is made by heating limestone. Plain lime cement hardened very slowly in the air. It would not

A highway bridge gets a skeleton of steel reinforcing rods before the concrete is poured.

harden at all under water. It was not as strong as hydraulic cement.

The Romans discovered how to make a type of hydraulic cement in the 2nd or 3rd century B.C. by mixing volcanic ash with their lime. This discovery is still ranked as one of Rome's greatest achievements. Later, hydraulic cement was also made from cement rock, a naturally occurring kind of limestone that contains clay.

Soon after the Romans had learned how to make their cement, they used it to make concrete. Many of their most impressive structures were built of concrete. Some of these are still standing today.

After the Roman Empire fell, the knowledge of hydraulic cement was lost for centuries. Not until the 16th century did Europeans rediscover the secret of how to make this cement.

It was not always possible to get volcanic ashes or cement rock to make hydraulic cement; so men began to try to make it artificially. By the early 19th century several French and English builders had succeeded in this task. The best of these cements was made by an English bricklayer named Joseph Aspdin. In 1824 Aspdin invented a cement that he called Portland cement. He gave it this name because it looked like an English stone called Portland stone. The name has been used ever since.

Since the end of the 19th century all building cement has been made artificially. Cement manufacturers no longer have to depend on supplies of natural cement rock or volcanic ash. By preparing their own mixtures, the manufacturers can make cements that are specially suited to almost any use.

Along with the secret of Roman cement, the knowledge of how to make concrete had been lost. From the end of the Roman Empire until the late 18th century, there is no record of building with concrete. Aspdin's invention of Portland cement sparked a revival of building with concrete. During much of the 19th century, builders used concrete in the same way as stone. It was poured into solid masses for walls, arches, and vaults. It was also cast into blocks and laid like stone or brick masonry. Concrete block is still used in some small buildings.

One difficulty with concrete is that it is porous; that is, it is easily penetrated by water. Water can get into small holes or cracks in the concrete and then freeze, expand, and crack the concrete. When concrete is used where there might be a problem with water (for instance, in underground foundations or in structures that are exposed to sea water), the concrete is often coated with tar or waterproofing paint.

Reinforced Concrete

Like brick and stone, concrete has high compressive strength. That is, it can stand forces that press directly on it. But it has little tensile strength, which is the ability to resist being pulled apart. To overcome this weakness, engineers have developed ways to reinforce concrete with steel bars. The bars are put into the concrete at places where it might pull apart under normal loads.

For example, a concrete beam or floor slab tends to be pulled apart on the bottom and pushed together at the top. The steel bars are located near the bottom of the beam or slab, where the extra strength is needed.

Columns that have to support shifting loads, such as columns that hold up a bridge, may be subjected to bending in any direction. To counteract these bending forces, steel bars are set in the concrete column. The bars are linked by steel hoops so that a sort of cage is formed inside the concrete. This steel cage gives the column added strength.

Prestressing is a method for making reinforced concrete even stronger. Steel cables are stretched by powerful machinery while the concrete is being poured around them. When the concrete has hardened, the steel cables are released. The cables contract like a stretched spring that has been released. The contraction helps pull the concrete together and prevents it from being stretched by tension. This makes it more able to stand heavy loads. Prestressed concrete is used where very heavy loads must be carried, as in the beams of highway bridges.

The invention of reinforced concrete in the late 19th century, and the later invention of prestressed concrete, have allowed engineers to use concrete in many more ways than they could in the past. Concrete is now used in building everything from the thin, curving walls of modern buildings to huge, massive dams or bridge piers. Because it can be used in so many ways and costs relatively little, concrete has become a very popular building material. Along with steel, it is now the most widely used material in all types of construction.

Besides its usefulness as a structural material, concrete serves well as a decoration for buildings. Crushed glass or colored stone can be mixed into concrete to create beautiful floors and walls. Bits of crushed marble or granite are set in concrete to form a type of flooring called **terrazzo**. Terrazzo floors are often used in large public buildings and museums, as well as on patios adjoining private houses.

CARL W. CONDIT
Co-editor, *Technology and Culture*

See also BRICKS AND MASONRY; BUILDING CONSTRUCTION.

CENSUS

Usually, people think of a census as an official count of the population of a country. This kind of census, called a population census, has been taken since ancient times. "Census" comes from the Latin word *censere,* meaning "to assess, or tax." The Romans took the most complete censuses in the ancient world, beginning in the 500's B.C. Government officials, called censors, made a register of people and their property. One purpose was to identify persons for military service. The other was to place a value on property so that taxes could be collected.

▶ MODERN CENSUSES AROUND THE WORLD

Today almost every country takes an official population census, usually once every five or ten years. And most countries take other kinds of censuses, such as censuses of agriculture, industry, trade, and government. These censuses are scientifically designed to provide the statistics (facts and figures) that the people of a country need in studying economic and social conditions. Such statistics provide the basis for good government, economic progress, conservation of natural resources, and the welfare of all the people. This kind of census taking began to be developed in European countries in the 18th and 19th centuries.

After World War II, the United Nations and other international organizations set up programs to co-ordinate the timing of censuses in countries around the world, as well as the kinds of information that the various countries gathered. As a result, census reports have become more uniform. And the number of countries gathering statistics about agriculture, business and industry, trade, education, housing, and the like has increased steadily. This information has become increasingly valuable for economic and social planning, especially in the developing countries of the world.

Many countries have special agencies that are responsible for their censuses. In Canada, for example, censuses are taken by Statistics Canada, an agency of the Department of Industry, Trade, and Commerce. The Bureau of the Census of the Department of Commerce takes United States censuses.

How is the U.S. population census taken?

The 1980 population census was taken chiefly by mail. Four out of every five metropolitan households received a census form to be filled out and mailed back. This form asked a number of questions about every person in the household (such as age, sex, married or single, education), as well as numerous questions about the house or apartment (number of rooms, plumbing facilities, heating equipment, and the like). Every fifth household received a longer, more detailed questionnaire. These forms were also to be filled out and mailed back. If the form was not returned or was not properly filled out, an employee of the Bureau of the Census, called a census enumerator, visited the household to gather the information.

In rural areas, the shorter forms were delivered by letter carriers and picked up by census enumerators. Every fifth household was then asked the questions on the longer form.

Questionnaires from the district offices were collected for microfilming (storage on film). At the Bureau of the Census headquarters, the microfilm was converted into magnetic tape. This was fed into computers, which then produced the information desired.

▶ UNITED STATES CENSUSES

The Constitution requires a population census every ten years, and such a census has been taken regularly since 1790. At first, this was a simple count to provide a basis for apportioning the membership of the U.S. House of Representatives among the states. Later, Congress authorized the gathering of a great deal of information about each person. These statistics are used in many ways. For example, the amount of government aid given to a school district is based partly on the number of school-age children that the census shows to be living there.

During the years, Congress has requested that many other kinds of censuses be taken at regular times. These include censuses of manufacturing, mining, agriculture, fisheries, employment, construction, foreign trade, and energy sources. All census information is available to the public in a wide variety of publications, such as *The Statistical Abstract of the United States.*

ROBERT E. KENNEDY, JR.
University of Minnesota

See also POPULATION.

CENTIPEDES AND MILLIPEDES

Centipedes and millipedes are small animals with wormlike bodies and many legs. Although they are often confused with each other, it is easy to tell them apart. A centipede's body is slightly flattened, and each segment (joint) has only one pair of legs. A millipede's body is more rounded, and each segment has two pairs of legs.

These many-legged animals look as if they might be spiders or insects, but they are not. They are close relatives of spiders and insects, but they are classified separately. The many kinds of centipedes form a class by themselves; the many kinds of millipedes form another class.

Above: Centipedes are nocturnal creatures. They hunt for food only at night and hide from light during the day. Below: This millipede can roll its slender body into a ball to protect itself from danger.

HOW THEY ARE ALIKE

However, centipedes and millipedes share several features. Both have a great many legs, as their names indicate. (Centipede means "hundred feet or legs" and millipede means "thousand feet or legs.") The number ranges from 15 pairs to about 200 pairs, depending on the kind. In both classes the animals have long, slender bodies, made up of many segments. A few are born with their full number of segments and legs, but most grow new segments as they age. The last segment divides in two, and then the new last segment divides again. Such division continues until the animal has its adult number of segments.

The heads of centipedes and millipedes have antennae—long feelers like those of insects. Some kinds have simple eyes, but others are blind. They have tiny insectlike mouths.

Centipedes and millipedes have hard outer shells enclosing their muscles and body organs. These shells serve as skeletons. The shell's outer layer is shed from time to time, thus allowing an increase in size. Many of the body segments have air pores, which connect to an internal system of tiny tubes. These tubes allow air to reach parts of the body.

Centipedes and millipedes have a nerve center in the head—a kind of simple brain. A nerve cord runs along the lower part of the body, with smaller nerve centers in each body segment.

The digestive system consists of a tube that goes from the mouth through the body. Wastes are given off through an opening at the end of the body.

The blood-circulation system is simple. It consists of a tubelike heart, which pumps the blood from one end of the body to the other.

CENTIPEDES

Most of the common centipedes have 15 pairs of legs. The two front legs are fangs. They are connected to glands that secrete (give off) a poisonous fluid.

Centipedes use the poison to kill their

prey—usually slugs, earthworms, and insects. Sometimes centipedes kill and eat each other. (Only a few species are plant eaters.) The poison also helps them to digest their prey by dissolving its body tissues. Although the poison can cause intense pain and swelling, a centipede's bite is not fatal to human beings.

Centipedes live in damp places almost everywhere, but they are most common in warm, tropical regions. They hide during the day and become active at night. Their flattened bodies enable them to lie protected in cracks, under boards or stones, or in rotten logs.

Probably the most common variety is the house centipede, *Scutigera forceps,* often found in human dwellings. About 5 centimeters (2 inches) long, these creatures have 15 pairs of long, bent legs, which make them look like many-legged spiders. They feed on small insects and rarely bother human beings. But their bites can cause some pain.

The largest centipede, *Scolopendra gigas,* lives on an island in the West Indies. It may grow to a length of 30 centimeters (12 inches). It feeds mostly on insects but sometimes captures and eats mice and lizards.

There are a few centipedes that light up in the dark. One of these, the *Geophilus electricus,* is blind. The function of its light may be to attract prey.

Some centipedes bear their young alive. Most of the others lay eggs that hatch without help from the female. In a few species, the female guards her eggs until they hatch.

▶ **MILLIPEDES**

Millipedes vary in length from about 1.5 to 300 millimeters ($\frac{1}{16}$ inch to 12 inches). The larger kinds are found in warm countries. Most have about 35 segments. Millipedes feed on decaying vegetation. In damp weather they may eat living plants, especially the roots. A few of the tropical millipedes feed on dead animal matter.

Millipedes have no poison fangs. When disturbed, they defend themselves by coiling up like watchsprings or rolling into balls. Many kinds have poison or stink glands along the sides of their bodies. The substance given off by these glands repels insects and other enemies. Some millipedes give off a poison that can kill insects.

Female centipede protects eggs by coiling body around them. Few species protect their eggs.

Millipedes are slow-moving animals. Their numerous legs move one after the other in wavelike motions along each side of the body. They can usually be found in damp places under logs or leaves.

Most millipedes become active at night. And for a long time it was believed that they responded to the changes in temperature and light. Then scientists experimented by keeping millipedes in unchanging conditions. In theory, this should have confused the animals, but it did not. The millipedes kept up their regular daily cycle of activities. It seems that millipedes are governed by built-in "clocks," which cause them to leave their hiding places at certain times and crawl about.

A common millipede found in the eastern United States is *Spirobolus marginatus.* It is 10 centimeters (about 4 inches) long and about as thick as a pencil. Its color ranges from reddish brown to black. A variety of millipede found in California—the *Luminodesmus sequoiae*—lights up.

Millipedes lay their eggs in groups of 25 to 50. Among some kinds, the females cement bits of earth together with saliva to form dome-shaped nests within which the eggs are laid.

Ross E. Hutchins
Author, *Insects*

See also Bioluminescence; Insects; Spiders and Their Relatives.

CENTRAL AFRICAN REPUBLIC

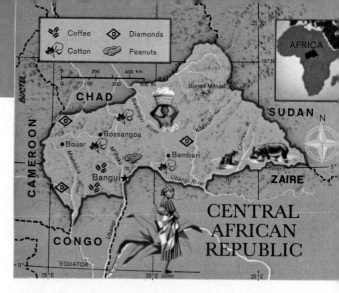

The Central African Republic is a land-locked country lying in the heart of Africa. At one time a French colony, it became independent in 1960. From 1976 until 1979, it was known as the Central African Empire.

▶ THE PEOPLE

The people of the Central African Republic belong to many different ethnic groups. The largest groups are the Banda, the Baya, and the Mandjia. Most Central Africans are farmers who live in small villages governed by traditional chiefs. Their square houses are made of mud bricks or mud-covered branches. The steep roofs are thatched with reeds.

At the end of the dry season, everyone gathers outside the villages to burn the surrounding fields and brush. This clears and fertilizes the land for the new crops. While the adults work, the children trap the small animals that scurry out of the burning grass.

Years ago the men spent most of their time fishing or hunting game and protecting themselves against neighboring communities. Today they grow cotton, coffee, and peanuts for export. The women cultivate manioc (a starchy root plant) and millet (a grain), which are

dried and pounded into flour. This is cooked into a stiff porridge and is eaten with meat or fish sauce and very hot pepper.

Each family owns a few chickens and, occasionally, some pigs. But there are few cattle, horses, or sheep because the tsetse fly, which thrives in this hot, damp climate, spreads disease among these animals. As a result, fish caught in the Ubangi River and its tributaries are more plentiful than meat. When there is fruit or other food to spare, the women carry it in baskets on their heads to a village market. At the market, entertainers in colorful costumes dance and chant to the beat of the big drums.

Most men now wear European clothes. Many women wear European dresses or long, bright wraparounds with gay head kerchiefs.

Children in the towns and in many of the villages attend elementary school. Lessons are conducted in French, which is commonly spoken along with Sango in all the communities. Many children go on to high school, and some go to universities in France or to the University of Bangui, founded in 1969. But most of the children in the villages start to work in the fields when they are quite young.

▶ THE LAND

Like much of Africa, the Central African Republic is a vast plateau, largely covered by rolling grassland. In the southwest are tropical rain forests and in the northeast, barren hills. The climate of the country is tropical. The heaviest rains fall from July to October, with lighter rain from March to June.

The Ubangi River, a major tributary of the Congo River, is the only river in the country

---

FACTS AND FIGURES

CENTRAL AFRICAN REPUBLIC is the official name of the country.

CAPITAL: Bangui.

LOCATION: Central Equatorial Africa. **Latitude**—2° 16′ N to 11° 20′ N. **Longitude**—14° 20′ E to 27° 45′ E.

AREA: 622,984 km² (240,535 sq mi).

POPULATION: 2,400,000 (estimate).

LANGUAGE: French (official), Sango.

GOVERNMENT: Republic (under military rule). **Head of government**—chairman, Military Committee for National Recovery. **International co-operation**—United Nations, Organization of African Unity (OAU).

NATIONAL ANTHEM: *La Renaissance* ("The Revival").

ECONOMY: Agricultural products—cotton, coffee, peanuts, manioc, millet, fruits and vegetables, poultry. **Minerals** —diamonds, gold, uranium. **Industries and products**— food and wood processing, textiles, consumer goods, jewelry. **Chief exports**—cotton, coffee, diamonds, lumber. **Chief imports**—machinery, motor vehicles, chemicals. **Monetary unit**—franc CFA (African Financial Community).

Gold mined in the country is made into jewelry by goldsmiths.

that is navigable for any important distance. The country's southern rivers flow into the Ubangi. The northern rivers, including the Shari, drain northward into Lake Chad.

Many tropical plants, including oil palms and giant kapok trees, are found in the country. Bananas, mangoes, and papayas are grown near most of the villages.

Elephants, buffaloes, lions, leopards, antelopes, and monkeys live in the bush—the grassy plateau region. In the north are large game reserves, where animals are protected from hunters. Crocodiles and hippopotamuses are found in the Ubangi and Shari rivers. Brightly colored birds, reptiles, and insects abound, and termites build castles of red earth 3 meters (10 feet) in height.

▶ THE ECONOMY

Cotton, coffee, and peanuts are the chief export crops. Trucks carry them to Bangui, the capital and major port on the Ubangi River. Here they are exported by river to Brazzaville and then by railroad to the ocean. The lumber industry is expanding, and timber processing is becoming an important industry. But the country still lacks the money to develop industries and depends on French help.

Fairly large quantities of diamonds and gold are mined. There are also deposits of iron, copper, lead, tin, and zinc. Uranium was discovered recently. Development of mineral resources has been hampered by the high cost of transporting them to market.

▶ HISTORY

Little is known about the history of the Central African Republic before the Europeans arrived at the end of the 19th century. If Europeans visited the country before that time, they left no written records; and the local peoples have few legends of their past. We do know that this area was once a center for Muslim slave traders from Sudan and East Africa. They transported their captives across the Nile River to the slave markets on the island of Zanzibar. Communities from the south and west also raided this region for slaves to be sold for work in the New World.

In 1898 the French set up a trading post at Bangui. Five years later they created the territory of Ubangi-Chari. In 1910 Ubangi-Chari and the three neighboring French colonies of Chad, Congo, and Gabon were joined to form French Equatorial Africa. In 1960, Ubangi-Chari, now called Central African Republic, was granted full independence, with David Dacko as president. Following a military coup in 1966, the constitution was abolished, and General Jean Bedel Bokassa became president. In 1976 he changed the name of the country to the Central African Empire and named himself emperor. Bokassa was accused of violating human rights and destroying the economy. He was overthrown in 1979. Since then the country has again been called the Central African Republic.

JOHN A. BALLARD
University of Ibadan (Nigeria)

Guatemala City is the largest city in Central America. The buildings in the civic center combine traditional designs with present-day architecture.

CENTRAL AMERICA

Central America is an isthmus (a narrow bridge of land) at the southern tip of the North American continent. It stretches from the southern boundary of Mexico to Colombia on the continent of South America. Central America stands at a key crossroads of the world, with coasts on both the Pacific Ocean and the Caribbean Sea (an arm of the Atlantic Ocean). The Panama Canal, which connects these two oceans, is an important route for world trade.

Central Americans usually apply the term "Central America" to the five republics of Guatemala, Honduras, El Salvador, Nicaragua, and Costa Rica. This is because these countries were once joined in a federation and they share a common history. Geographically, Panama and Belize are also included in Central America.

▶THE PEOPLE

About 25,000,000 people live in Central America. They belong to many ethnic groups. Guatemala is a largely Indian nation. Its citizens are the heirs of the Maya civilization, which flourished in the region before the coming of the Europeans. Honduras, El Salvador, and Nicaragua also have a strong Indian heritage, although their people are mainly mestizo (of mixed Indian and European ancestry). The population of Costa Rica is largely Spanish in origin. Many people in Belize are descended from black African slaves brought there from the West Indies. Panama contains a mixture of all these different groups.

Spanish is the major language in all the Central American countries except Belize, where English is spoken. Some of the Indians still speak their ancient languages. Most Central Americans are Roman Catholics.

The population of most Central American countries has long been divided into wealthy landowners and poor *campesinos* (peasants). Land ownership is the chief form of wealth in Central America and the main source of political power. Most of the people depend on the big landowners for their living. Some *campesinos* can find only seasonal work. Others toil on the big estates in return for the right to grow food for themselves on a small patch of ground. In the mountains, the Indians and other groups often grow food crops on plots too small to support their families.

▶THE LAND

Central America covers an area of about 523,000 square kilometers (202,000 square miles). The main feature is steep mountains,

An outdoor market in Central America. The bright blankets are woven in traditional Indian patterns.

CENTRAL AMERICA

which extend almost from ocean to ocean. There are many volcanoes, some of which are still active. Earthquakes are common, and some cities have been destroyed by earthquakes more than once.

There are two main breaks in the mountains —one in Nicaragua and one in Panama. These two countries are mostly low-lying. They are tropical in climate and have areas of dense jungle. Northern Guatemala and much of Belize are also jungle lowland. Most of the people of Guatemala, Costa Rica, Honduras, and El Salvador live in the highlands, where the climate is moderate. Most large cities, such as Guatemala City, San Salvador, Tegucigalpa, and San José, are also in the highlands.

The mountains are so steep that few rivers in Central America are navigable. The rugged land has also made it hard to build railroads and highways except along the narrow coastal plains. The most important highway is the Inter-American Highway, which extends from the Mexico-Guatemala border to southern Panama.

▶ THE ECONOMY

Central America is mainly an agricultural region. The chief crops are grown for export on large plantations or estates (*latifundia* or *fincas*). These plantations, which occupy most

of the best farmland, are owned by a small group of wealthy families and some foreign (mostly United States) corporations. In the highlands the chief crop is coffee—the leading export of Guatemala, El Salvador, and Costa Rica. In the coastal tropical areas, bananas and cotton are the main crops. Sugarcane and rice also flourish along the coast, and some fruits and vegetables are grown in the valleys. Hemp (used in making rope) and chicle (used in chewing gum) are important products of the jungle regions. Areas that are too mountainous for farming are used for forestry and the raising of livestock.

Central America supplies other countries of the world with large amounts of certain agricultural products. But the Central American countries must import most of the things they need, including grain and some other foods. Because they depend on a few major exports, they may lose millions of dollars when the price of a bag of coffee or a bunch of bananas drops only a few cents on the world market. When export prices fall, the governments have less money to pay for imports and for the services their people need.

Mining is not very important in much of the region. Small quantities of minerals such as gold, silver, lead, copper, and zinc are exported. Production of nickel has become significant in Guatemala, where oil has also been found in the remote northern jungles. Hydroelectric power is the only readily available source of energy. The cost of importing oil has caused economic difficulties for many countries.

There is some industry, particularly in El Salvador, Guatemala, and Costa Rica. But in-

Left: Sheep often graze high in the mountains where the land is not suitable for farming. Center and right: Bananas and coffee beans are two of Central America's leading exports.

dustry employs only a small part of the labor force, and it is not expanding very rapidly. Fishing is important along the coast. Panama derives much of its income from fees paid by ships using the Panama Canal.

Some landless peasants move to the cities in search of work. They find that jobs are scarce, especially for the uneducated and unskilled. Most of them exchange rural poverty for the bleak life of an urban slum. They often leave the city at harvesttime to toil for low wages on the large estates. Many families hope that education—more available in the cities—will lead to a better life for their children.

▶HISTORY

Maya-speaking peoples have lived in the northern part of Central America for about 3,000 years. Maya civilization reached its height from about A.D. 325 to 975. The ruins of huge Maya temples and monuments can still be seen at places like Piedras Negras and Tikal, in Guatemala, and Copán, in Honduras. Several other Indian groups settled in Central America south of Honduras.

Christopher Columbus sailed along the coast of Central America in 1502. The Spanish explorer Vasco Núñez de Balboa crossed the Isthmus of Panama in 1513. The Spanish gradually moved into the rest of the region from Panama and Mexico. The Spanish conquered the Indians, established plantations,

and forced the Indians to work on the plantations under conditions of virtual slavery.

In 1821, Guatemala, El Salvador, Honduras, Nicaragua, and Costa Rica declared their independence from Spain. They briefly became part of the Mexican empire led by Agustín de Iturbide and then formed their own federation, the United Provinces of Central America. But the federation did not last because the widely separated settlements had different interests. Panama did not gain its independence from Colombia until 1903. Belize (formerly British Honduras) remained a British colony until 1981.

During the 1800's, much of Central America was torn by political struggles between liberal and conservative groups. The conservatives wanted to continue the Spanish system. This system included an official state religion, a society in which social position was determined by birth, and a strong central government run by members of high-ranking families and church officials. The liberals wanted a more open society, the expansion of agriculture to grow crops for export, and less control of the economy and local affairs by the church and the central government. But neither group thought that the people were ready for self-government, and neither showed any concern for the problems of the poor. The disputes between liberals and conservatives often led to civil wars, and sometimes even to invasions of neighboring countries. The liberals, who were mostly landowners, benefited when the cultivation of coffee began in the late 1800's. The value of the land increased rapidly. So did the power and income of the landowners.

In the early 1900's, the tradition of government by powerful leaders continued. Some of these leaders were dictators who held office for long periods of time. Many people admired them because they were strong enough to bring the stability needed for economic growth. The army also grew powerful because it was able to keep order and control the armed bands that supported various political leaders. The army generally took the side of the wealthy landowners and opposed those who wanted land and wealth to be more equally divided. Yet the dictators and the military did promote agricultural expansion and the building of roads and railroads. This helped people of all classes by promoting economic growth and the creation of jobs.

Since World War II, there have been several revolutions in Central America led by people seeking social and economic change. In Costa Rica, a brief civil war in 1948 led to a middle-class reform movement that increased social services and restored a tradition of democracy and free elections. In Guatemala, leaders who wanted to improve the life of the poor held power from 1944 until they were overthrown in 1954. In Nicaragua, widespread discontent with the family—the Somozas—that had ruled the nation since the 1930's led to a bloody civil war. This war was won by leftist guerrillas in 1979. Leftist guerrillas also sought power in El Salvador.

The nations of Central America have had their differences. El Salvador fought a short but bitter war with neighboring Honduras in 1969, for example, and Guatemala claims Belize. But Central Americans have also tried to co-operate in ways that would benefit their region as a whole. All the Central American countries except Belize are members of the Organization of American States. In 1960, Costa Rica, El Salvador, Guatemala, Honduras, and Nicaragua formed the Central American Common Market. This organization helped to improve economic conditions and eliminate trade barriers in Central America.

Many Central Americans have viewed the United States presence in the region—espe-

Ruins of the Maya center of Copán, in Honduras. Maya culture flourished in northern Central America.

cially in Panama—as a kind of colonialism. The ratification of the Panama Canal treaties in 1978 marked an important attempt to improve the relationship between the United States and its neighbors to the south.

▶ THE FUTURE

Central America has limited resources and one of the highest population growth rates in the world. As more land is used to grow crops for export, there is less on which to grow food for the expanding population. Industry cannot provide enough jobs for the landless, and falling prices for many exports make it harder for governments to meet the needs of their peoples. Demands for reform have increased, but wealth and power in most countries are still concentrated in the hands of a few people. Modern weapons make civil war a more destructive way to settle political differences than it once was. The involvement of foreign nations—the United States, Cuba, and other countries—in Central American affairs has created further complications. For these reasons, the economic and social problems of the region are hard to solve.

KENNETH J. GRIEB
University of Wisconsin—Oshkosh

See also LATIN AMERICA; NORTH AMERICA; PANAMA CANAL AND ZONE; INDIANS OF NORTH AMERICA; articles on individual Central American countries.

CENTRIFUGAL FORCE. See EARTH, OUR HOME PLANET.

Ceramic products cover a wide range. Left and above: a Peruvian pottery jug (before A.D. 600) and a Chinese vase (1100's or 1300's). Right: Ceramic tiles are attached to the U.S. space shuttle.

CERAMICS

As strange as it may seem, the china plate you use at dinner has something in common with the U.S. space shuttle orbiter Columbia. The dinner plate is a ceramic product. And when Columbia re-enters the earth's atmosphere, it is protected from fiery heat by a skin of custom-made ceramic tiles.

Traditional ceramics are made from earthy materials—clay, sand, or ground rock—that have been subjected to high temperatures. Heat binds the materials together and hardens them. Most ceramics share certain qualities. They resist heat, pressure, corrosion, and moisture. But they have low tensile strength —they will break if they are pulled or bent.

The word "ceramics" comes from the Greek word *keramos,* meaning potter's clay or pottery. Pottery is the oldest form of ceramics, and potterymaking is one of the oldest crafts. Pieces of pottery have been found that were made before the beginning of recorded history. Bricks and glass are other early ceramic products.

Ceramics today include pottery, whiteware (china and porcelain), construction products such as bricks and pipes, glass, enamels, cement, and abrasives. In recent times, engineers and scientists have developed many new ceramic products for use in industry.

▶HOW CERAMICS ARE MADE

Most ceramics are made of minerals called silicates. These minerals include clay minerals, feldspar, quartz, and talc. They form 90 percent of the earth's crust, and they are found in various forms—rock, sand, and clay.

Clay is formed from rocks that are gradually broken up by weather. Most clay contains varying amounts of several minerals, and several kinds of clay are used in making ceramics. Common clays, which contain many impurities, are used chiefly in brickmaking. Kaolin clay is the purest type of clay. It is used to make fine china and porcelain. When fired, it turns a pure white. Fireclays have a slightly different mineral composition. They can withstand high temperatures.

Manufacturers often mix powdered minerals into clay to produce specific qualities in their products. The clay and other materials are then mixed with water. Just the right amount of water must be added—if there is too much, the clay will be too soft to hold its shape. If there is too little, the clay will be stiff and difficult to shape.

Individual pieces of pottery can be shaped by hand on a potter's wheel. But manufacturers use several methods to make many copies of the same object. In **slip casting,** a mixture of clay and water is poured into a plaster mold of the object. The mold absorbs the water and retains a thin coating of clay on the inside. More and more of the mixture is poured in, and the clay coating becomes thicker. When the coating is thick enough, it is allowed to harden. Then it is lifted out of the mold and trimmed, or **fettled.** Large ceramic pieces, such as porcelain washbasins, are cast in this way.

Another method of forming ceramics is **jiggering.** In this method a plaster mold is used to shape one surface of the article—for instance, the upper surface of a plate or the outside surface of a cup or bowl. The mold rotates, just as a potter's wheel does. Clay is forced down onto the spinning mold, so that it takes the shape of the mold on one surface. The other surface is shaped by a tool mounted on a lever.

A third method of shaping clay ceramics is to press the clay directly into a mold. Ceramic pipes and bricks are formed by a fourth method, **extrusion.** In this method, the clay is forced through the opening of a die (shaping tool).

After the piece has been formed, it is trimmed and dried. It is then ready for firing. This is done in a **kiln**—a special furnace for heating and hardening ceramics. High temperatures are needed, ranging from about 650 to 1800°C (1200 to 3270°F). The length of firing is just as important as the temperature. The clay is fired for varying periods of time depending on its ingredients and on the product being made.

Glazes are transparent, glassy coatings that are applied to the surfaces of many ceramic products after firing. They do two things— they beautify the object, and they prevent it from absorbing liquids. After the glaze is applied, the article is fired again.

Not all ceramic products are made of clay. For glass, silica (sand) is the essential ingredient. Cement consists of other minerals.

▶ CERAMIC PRODUCTS

Ceramic materials are used to make a wide range of products. Descriptions of some of these products follow.

Dinnerware and decorative ceramics. Because ceramics can hold liquid and resist extreme temperatures, they make excellent dinnerware. Porcelain, which is very hard and translucent, is the finest dinnerware. It is often called china, after the country that first produced it. Stoneware is another popular kind of dinnerware. It is strong and very resistant to heat and cold. And because clay can be shaped into many forms, ceramics are often used in figurines and decorative objects.

Construction Materials. Porcelain is also used to make sinks, bathtubs, and similar building fixtures. But many other ceramic materials are used in construction. They include brick and cement for walls and foundations; tiles for roofs, floors, and bathroom walls;

Ceramic insulators for electrical lines are rolled into huge kilns to be fired.

Machines are used to apply the decoration to factory-produced ceramic dinnerware.

drainpipes; gypsum for plaster walls and ceilings; glass for windows; and fiberglass for insulation.

Abrasives. Very hard ceramic materials are used in grinding, polishing, and sanding. These materials include sand, aluminum oxide, and silicon carbide.

Electrical Products. Some ceramics, such as porcelain, will not conduct electricity. They are used as insulation in high-voltage power lines and in products that range from automobile spark plugs to sophisticated electrical circuits. Other ceramic materials develop an electrical charge under pressure. They are used in phonographs, sonar, and ultrasonic devices.

Heat-Resistant Ceramics. Ceramics that can hold up under extremely high temperatures are called **refractories.** Refractories have many uses today—as linings in steelmaking furnaces, in nose cones for rockets and protection for other spacecraft, and in tail pipes for rocket and jet engines.

Special Products. Special ceramics are used in many industries. The fuel elements in most nuclear power plants are made of a ceramic material, as are many of the reactors' structural parts. Magnetic ceramics are used in computer memory cores and telecommunications equipment. Ceramics are also used in lasers. In medicine, special porcelains are used to make dentures and artificial joints.

Sometimes ceramics are combined with other materials. For example, glass fibers are used to reinforce plastics. And ceramics are combined with metals to make materials called **cermets.** Cermets combine the qualities of ceramics with the tensile strength of metals.

Reviewed by HANS NOWOTNY
University of Connecticut

See also BRICKS AND MASONRY; CEMENT AND CONCRETE; ENAMELING; GLASS; POTTERY.

CEREALS. See GRAIN AND GRAIN PRODUCTS.
CEREBRAL PALSY. See DISEASES.

CERVANTES SAAVEDRA, MIGUEL DE (1547–1616)

Spain's greatest writer was Miguel de Cervantes—the creator of Don Quixote, one of the best-known characters in world literature. Cervantes was born in 1547, probably on September 29, in Alcalá de Henares, near Madrid. His father was a poor barber-surgeon who moved his family from town to town in search of a practice.

Little is known of Cervantes' early life, but his writings show that he must have acquired a good education in one way or another. In 1569 he went to Italy, where he served briefly in the household of Giulio (later Cardinal) Acquaviva in Rome. He then joined a company of the Spanish army stationed there.

Cervantes fought bravely in the naval battle of Lepanto (off the coast of Greece). In this battle an allied Christian force, under the command of Don Juan of Austria, defeated the Muslim Turkish navy, on October 7, 1571. Cervantes was wounded and lost the use of his left hand. In 1575 he sailed for Spain, but he was kidnapped by pirates and taken to Algiers as a slave. He made several unsuccessful attempts to escape before he was ransomed by his family five years later.

Cervantes returned to Spain and tried to earn his living by writing plays. But his marriage in 1584 and his father's death in 1585 added to his responsibilities. In 1587 he went to Seville, where preparations for a Spanish attack on England were under way. He was hired to gather military provisions for the Armada, the invading fleet. Later he had a job collecting taxes, but he was imprisoned twice as a result of his irregular accounts.

After he left government service in 1597, Cervantes wrote short stories and began his masterpiece, *Don Quixote.* The first part of this book was published in 1605. It described the adventures, many based on Cervantes' own, of the mad knight, Don Quixote of La Mancha. The novel presented a brilliant picture of Spanish society and was an immediate success. The second part appeared in 1615. Cervantes' other works include a pastoral novel, *The Galatea* (1585), and a collection of short stories, *Exemplary Novels* (1613). He died on April 23, 1616, in Madrid.

Reviewed by MELVEENA MCKENDRICK
Author, *Cervantes*

See also DON QUIXOTE.

CÉZANNE, PAUL (1839–1906)

The study of modern painting often begins with the work of the painter Paul Cézanne. His paintings had so great an influence on modern art that the artist Georges Braque said, "We all start from Cézanne."

Cézanne was born in Aix-en-Provence, in southern France, on January 19, 1839. Although he spent much of his adult life in Paris, the town drew him back time and time again. There, as boys, he and his school friend Émile Zola wandered through the hills, reciting poetry. Together they dreamed of fame and success in Paris.

Cézanne's father, a wealthy banker, wanted his son to be a success in business or law. But in 1861 he finally permitted Cézanne to go to Paris. He hoped his son's paintings would be accepted by the Paris Salon, the exhibition sponsored by the French Academy of Fine Arts. Cézanne did not like the kind of paintings shown at the Salon. But he craved recognition, and he submitted a painting. When it was rejected, he was deeply hurt.

Because he was drawn naturally to country life, Cézanne disliked Paris. He neither combed his beard nor cared how much paint covered his coat. He was gloomy, awkward, and hot-tempered, and he had few friends.

In 1886, Zola wrote a book about a painter who was a failure. Everyone thought that Cézanne was the model for the artist in the book. Cézanne was so hurt that he never again spoke to his one close friend.

During the same year his father died and left Cézanne a rich man with enough money for himself, his wife (Hortense Fiquet), and their son, Paul.

Throughout the last 20 years of his life, Cézanne isolated himself from people and devoted himself entirely to his work. He died in Aix on October 22, 1906.

It took years of searching for Cézanne to find the way to express his ideas. In his mature paintings he tried to show the geometric forms—cylinders, cones, spheres—that he saw in nature. By using blocks of color he built up the appearance of solid shapes. To emphasize volume—the roundness of an apple or the thickness of a stone—he changed the actual appearance of objects. This distortion of shapes led directly to the style of painting called cubism.

Only ten years before his death, a small group of painters recognized Cézanne's genius. But even they did not foresee his impact on the painting of the 20th century.

Reviewed by FRANK GETLEIN
Author, *The French Impressionists*

Mount Sainte-Victoire with Tall Pine (1886–88), by Cézanne.

CHAD

The Republic of Chad extends from the center of the vast Sahara to the savanna regions of tropical Africa. It is a landlocked country deep in the heart of Africa. Chad's area is twice that of France.

▶THE PEOPLE

Only about 2 percent of the people of Chad live in the northern desert, although this region makes up nearly half of the total area of the country. Most of the northern people are Arab nomads. They live in scattered oases where thickets of date palms supply food, shade, and fuel.

The central grasslands provide grazing for cattle, sheep, goats, camels, donkeys, and horses. People in this area usually tend large herds of animals and do some farming. They are generally of mixed descent. Most of them are Muslims because of the strong North African (Arab) influence in the area.

More than half of the people live near Lake Chad and in the Logone and Shari river valleys. The chief group in this area is the Sara. They are Christians or followers of traditional beliefs. People in southern Chad live in groups of round mud houses with cone-shaped roofs. They grow their own food—grain, vegetables, peanuts, and a variety of spices, which are used generously for seasoning. Cotton is the main crop grown for export. Fish, which are plentiful in Lake Chad and in the rivers, are an important part of the diet.

Life in this largely desert country is not easy. Locusts and drought threaten crops and livestock. Few people live in cities or towns, and often all the members of a family must work to help feed themselves.

There are few schools in Chad, and children usually herd the family cattle or work in the fields. There is a university in N'Djemena, the capital. But many young people seeking higher education have studied at universities in France.

Life in Chad has also been affected by years of civil war. Towns and villages have been destroyed, trade has been disrupted, and many people have abandoned their homes and fled into neighboring countries.

▶THE LAND

All of Chad is usually very hot, and most of it is extremely dry. The country has three land regions—the savanna of the southern river valleys, the central grasslands, and the northern desert.

The grassy savanna is dotted with clumps of thorn forests and acacia trees. All the rain comes in summer and early autumn. Rainfall on the savanna is moderate. There is less and less rainfall to the north, where Chad becomes open grassland with no trees. In the far north the Sahara begins.

The chief body of water is Lake Chad, from which the country takes its name. The principal Chad rivers flowing into the lake are the Shari and the Logone. Both rivers flood their low-lying valleys every year during the rainy season, but they are mere trickles during the dry winter. Lake Chad's size varies with the seasons—from almost 26,000 square kilometers (about 10,000 square miles) to half that area.

▶THE ECONOMY

Most people in Chad earn their living by fishing, farming, or raising livestock. The

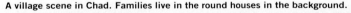
A village scene in Chad. Families live in the round houses in the background.

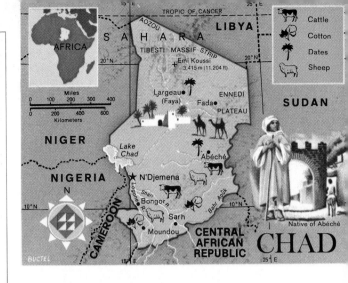

Native of Abéché

CHAD

FACTS AND FIGURES

REPUBLIC OF CHAD is the official name of the country.

LOCATION: North central Africa. **Latitude**—8° N to 23° N. **Longitude**—14° E to 24° E.

CAPITAL: N'Djemena.

AREA: 1,284,000 km² (495,754 sq mi).

POPULATION: 4,100,000 (estimate).

LANGUAGE: French (official).

GOVERNMENT: Republic. **Head of state**—president. **Head of government**—prime minister. **International co-operation**—United Nations, Organization of African Unity (OAU).

NATIONAL ANTHEM: *La Tchadienne* ("Chad").

ECONOMY: Agricultural products—cotton, millet, sorghum, dates, sweet potatoes, yams, peanuts. **Chief industries**—cotton and rice processing, processing of livestock products, fishing. **Chief exports**—cotton, livestock. **Chief imports**—manufactured goods, clothing. **Monetary unit**—franc CFA (African Financial Community).

raising of livestock is the chief occupation in the northern part of the country. The capital city and most of Chad's few large towns are in the south. Farmers there grow crops that can be exported.

Fishing is an important industry in Chad. There is little manufacturing except for the processing of rice, cotton, and livestock products.

Traces of tungsten and other rare ores have been found in the north, and oil deposits were discovered near Lake Chad. An area in northern Chad called the Aozou strip is believed to contain uranium. But it has been occupied by Libya since 1973. A long civil war has slowed exploration for minerals and has kept people from leading normal working lives.

The lack of suitable transportation also holds back development. Most waterways are navigable for only part of the year. There are no railroads and few good roads. Because travel on the ground is difficult, local air service is being expanded.

▶ **HISTORY AND GOVERNMENT**

For hundreds of years strong African empires—such as the Baguirmi, Kanem, Bornu, and Wadai—flourished around Lake Chad. Arab conquerors from North Africa brought the Muslim religion to this area in the 11th century, when they began hunting for slaves. The Sao, a black people who once occupied Chad, are remembered for their 200-year struggle against the Kanem empire. They were finally absorbed by the Bornu empire at the end of the 16th century. When the first French explorers reached the area in the 1890's, the local African empires were declining. By 1913 the French controlled the whole area. On August 26, 1940, immediately following the German occupation of France, Chad became the first French African territory to rally to the support of the Free French. This action had the effect of preventing outright German takeover of the French African territories. During World War II, Chad was an Allied supply base.

After World War II, Chad gradually took control of its own government by agreement with France. It gained independence in 1960.

In 1965, civil war broke out between the Muslims in the north and the Christians in the south who controlled the government. At various times, France sent troops to aid the government. A provisional government representing all of Chad's ethnic and religious groups was finally formed in 1979.

But the fighting soon resumed. This time, the struggle was between the nation's two most powerful Muslim leaders. In 1980, President Goukouni Oueddei defeated his rival with the help of Libyan arms and troops. Libya and Chad then announced plans to merge. But there were strong protests from France and several African nations. The Libyan forces soon withdrew, at Oueddei's request. A peace-keeping force sent by the Organization of African Unity did not stop the fighting. Oueddei was overthrown in 1982, and a lasting peace still seemed far away.

ANN E. LARIMORE
Michigan State University

Marc Chagall's painting *I and the Village* (1911) is based on memories of his childhood. The Museum of Modern Art, New York.

CHAGALL, MARC (1887–)

A soldier the size of a teacup and a fish playing a violin make perfect sense in a dream. They also make sense in the paintings of Marc Chagall, where dreams and fantasy are real, past and present are one, and the laws of gravity do not exist.

Marc Chagall was born on July 7, 1887, of a poor family in the Jewish ghetto of Vitebsk, Russia. Memories of early childhood—happy and sad—fill his pictures, as do themes from the Bible and folklore.

At the age of 20, Chagall went to St. Petersburg (now Leningrad) and studied scenery design. In 1910 the young artist left for Paris, where he lived until 1914. He returned to Russia for a visit. But World War I broke out, and Chagall stayed in Vitebsk.

During the Russian Revolution of 1917, he became commissar of fine arts for Vitebsk and set up an art school there. With his wife, Bella, he moved to Berlin in 1922 and to Paris the following year. In 1941 they left France to escape the conquering Nazis. Bella died in the United States in 1944. Chagall later returned to Paris, where he remarried.

The art of Marc Chagall is expressed in many forms. His oil paintings and watercolors hang in museums all over the world. His panels and ceiling murals decorate opera houses in Paris and New York City. His work in stained glass includes twelve windows in a synagogue in Jerusalem representing the twelve tribes of Israel. Among his other works are stage settings and costumes for operas and book illustrations. In 1973, the French Government honored Chagall by opening a museum in the city of Nice devoted exclusively to his work. It is called the National Museum of the Marc Chagall Biblical Message.

Reviewed by HAROLD SPENCER
University of Connecticut

See also MODERN ART; STAINED-GLASS WINDOWS.

CHAIN REACTION. See NUCLEAR ENERGY.
CHAIN STORES. See RETAIL STORES.

CHAMBER MUSIC

Chamber music is music written to be performed by a small number of players. There must be more than one but fewer than a dozen. There should be only one player to each written part. Usually there is no conductor. Chamber music is best heard in an ordinary room or a small hall. It can be performed at home for the players' own pleasure or in a concert for everyone's pleasure.

Any combination of instruments can be used in chamber music. The most popular are the stringed and woodwind instruments and the piano. A piece for two players is called a duo. Three players make a trio, and four make a quartet. There are quintets (five players), sextets (six), septets (seven), and octets (eight). Pieces for more than eight players are rare. A piece for three stringed instruments alone is a string trio; for four, a string quartet, and so on. If a piano or woodwind is used in place of one of the strings, the piece becomes a piano trio, or oboe quartet, or clarinet quintet, and so on.

The Juilliard String Quartet, famous for their concerts and their recordings of chamber music. A string quartet is made up of two violins, a cello, and a viola.

There are also pieces for woodwinds alone and for woodwinds and piano.

How did chamber music come about? From medieval times through the 18th century, musicians in Europe had two employers—the church and the nobility. When they were not performing in church services, musicians were hired to provide musical entertainment in a chamber of a noble's palace. This is how chamber music got its name. Old King Cole's fiddlers three were no doubt chamber musicians. Though they were friendly with the nobility, their position was not much better than that of servants.

Early chamber music used early instruments like the recorder, harpsichord, and viol. The viols were an important family of stringed instruments in the 16th and 17th centuries. There were treble (high), tenor (middle), and bass (low) viols, just as today we have violins, violas, and cellos. In England a set of these instruments (usually six) was called a chest of viols because they were kept in a chest, or cupboard. A family wealthy enough to own a chest of viols often played chamber music after dinner. During Queen Elizabeth's reign there were many fine composers of chamber music. Two of the best known were William Byrd (1543?–1623) and Orlando Gibbons (1583–1625). A very popular form of vocal chamber music was the madrigal. It was a short piece sung by voices often accompanied by instruments.

During the latter part of the 17th century and first half of the 18th, the trio sonata was the most important form of chamber music. A typical trio sonata was played by two violins, cello, and a keyboard instrument, which doubled the cello part and added harmonies. Important composers of these pieces include Henry Purcell (1659–95), Arcangelo Corelli (1653–1713), Johann Sebastian Bach (1685–1750), and George Frederick Handel (1685–1759).

CHAMBER MUSIC'S GOLDEN AGE

Most of the chamber music we hear today has been written since the middle of the 18th century. By then the viols had given way to the more brilliant-sounding violins, and the piano was replacing the harpsichord. Composers began to write pieces made up of three or four movements, or separate sections. A typical first movement was long, serious, and full of contrast and development. An expressive slow movement usually followed. Then came a minuet (dance) or a very fast scherzo ("joke"), which sometimes preceded the slow movement. The last movement was usually fast and full of high spirits.

Among the greatest chamber music composers were Franz Joseph Haydn (1732–1809), Wolfgang Amadeus Mozart (1756–91), Ludwig van Beethoven (1770–1827), and Franz Schubert (1797–1828). Haydn was mainly responsible for the early development of the string quartet (two violins, viola, and cello). He wrote 83 such works. Mozart, who wrote 25 string quartets, claimed he learned how to write them from Haydn. Beethoven, through his independent character and imagination, changed the course of chamber music history. First, he treated his noble patrons as his equals, not as his employers. Second, he wrote such difficult music that a great many rehearsals were needed to play it. Beethoven, with Schubert, led the way that chamber music was to follow for over 100 years.

All over Europe musicians composed and performed chamber works. Luigi Boccherini (1743–1805) alone wrote over 100 quartets, 155 quintets, 60 trios, and many other pieces. Chamber music was a part of early colonial life in America. Even Thomas Jefferson played chamber music.

Most of the important 19th century composers wrote chamber music: Felix Mendelssohn (1809–47), Robert Schumann (1810–56), Johannes Brahms (1833–97), Antonín Dvořák (1841–1904), and many others.

THE STRING QUARTET

Something about the sound of two violins, viola, and cello has appealed to nearly all composers of the last 200 years. The largest amount of chamber music has been written for string quartet. As a result, most professional chamber music groups have been string quartets. During the 19th century these ensembles began traveling from city to city giving concerts. They thus freed themselves from the role of servants to the nobility.

Early in the 1900's the Flonzaley Quartet became the first great chamber ensemble to give concerts all over the world. Many other outstanding ensembles have followed their example. Today string quartets from many countries perform everywhere.

STRANGE, EXCITING NEW SOUNDS

Chamber music composers in the 20th century began to explore ways of making new sounds. Claude Debussy (1862–1918) and Maurice Ravel (1875–1937) created shimmering, colorful musical impressions. Béla Bartók (1881–1945), Anton Webern (1883–1945), and Alban Berg (1885–1935) invented new sound effects with stringed instruments. Arnold Schoenberg (1874–1951) and Paul Hindemith (1895–1963) wrote pieces for unusual combinations of instruments. New chamber music works continue to be written today.

CHAMBER MUSIC REQUIRES TEAMWORK

Playing chamber music demands the alertness and spirit of a fine athletic team. All the players are equally important, and each one must know at all times what every other one is doing. Because of this, chamber music is the most democratic way of making music. It is also the most sociable and satisfying way. Even professional musicians love nothing more than to play this music at home with friends.

CHAMBER MUSIC IS FOR EVERYBODY

Millions of new listeners are discovering the exciting experience of hearing chamber music. They hear it at concerts, in private homes, and on many fine recordings. Chamber music concerts for young people are given in schools. Universities and special groups present more and more professional chamber music concerts. Some of the most beautiful and exciting sounds that man has ever created are found in chamber music.

ROBERT MANN
Juilliard String Quartet

CHAMELEONS. See LIZARDS AND CHAMELEONS.

CHAMPLAIN, SAMUEL DE (1567?–1635)

Samuel de Champlain was the founder of Quebec and the most famous explorer in Canadian history. Much of his life was spent exploring and mapping parts of the Atlantic coast, Ontario, and northern New York.

Champlain was born about 1567, at Brouage, France. He went to sea early in life and later became a soldier. Between 1599 and 1601 Champlain voyaged to the West Indies with a Spanish expedition. On his return to France, he was appointed royal geographer to King Henry IV. Champlain first visited Canada in 1603, sailing up the St. Lawrence River as far as Montreal. The following year he returned with an expedition sponsored by French fur-trading companies. King Henry hoped that French colonies in Canada would result from the expedition. Settlements were begun at St. Croix (on the present-day border of Maine and New Brunswick), and at Port Royal, in Nova Scotia.

For two years, Champlain was busy mapping the Atlantic coast as far south as Cape Cod. In 1608, he was sent to establish a fur-trading post at Quebec—the Indian name for "the place where the waters narrow." To build up the fur trade, Champlain made alliances with the Algonkin and Huron Indians against their enemies, the Iroquois. In 1609, while traveling with an Indian war party, he discovered the lake that bears his name. The rival Indian nations met in battle on the lakeshore, and Champlain helped defeat the Iroquois by shooting two of their chiefs with his musket. The Iroquois never forgave the French and became their bitter enemies.

Champlain then turned his attention westward. In 1613 he explored far up the Ottawa River in search of new lands and more furs. Two years later he again traveled up the Ottawa, crossing Lake Nipissing to Georgian Bay, an arm of Lake Huron. Then he journeyed southeast, across Lake Ontario into New York State. He was the first person to record explorations of these regions.

The fur companies had appointed Champlain governor of Quebec in 1612, and he hoped that the tiny settlement would grow into a strong colony. But the companies were interested only in profits and did not care about colonizing. In 1628, while England and

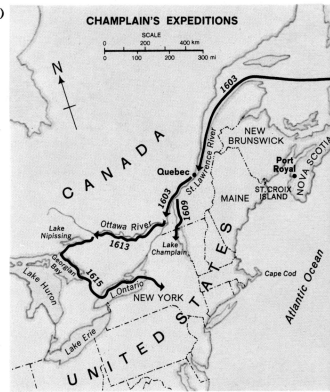

CHAMPLAIN'S EXPEDITIONS

France were at war, English ships blockaded Quebec. Champlain refused to give up his fort. But when the English returned the next spring, the settlers were near starvation, and Champlain was forced to surrender.

In 1633 Champlain returned to Quebec to find the settlement partly in ruins. He at once began to rebuild the colony. The next year he started a new settlement up the St. Lawrence, at Trois Rivières. On December 25, 1635, Champlain died at Quebec, the village he had built in the wilderness.

Champlain left behind him the beginnings of the colony of New France. Under his guidance settlement had begun and the fur trade had become very valuable. Champlain's books, especially the *Voyages,* give a vivid picture of Indian life, travel, and discovery in New France. His work as colonizer, explorer, and map maker truly earned him the title Father of New France.

JOHN S. MOIR
University of Toronto

See also EXPLORATION AND DISCOVERY.

CHANUKAH. See HANUKKAH.

CHAPLIN, CHARLIE (1889–1977)

Did you ever think about what makes you laugh? Charlie Chaplin found the secret to making people laugh, and it worked wherever his films were shown. With his funny little derby hat, cane, baggy pants, and tiny mustache, Chaplin created the famed Little Tramp of silent films. No movie character has ever been more widely enjoyed. Chaplin portrayed his tramp as an insecure fellow, constantly running into trouble but always coming out of each situation with his pride intact. People still laugh at the little man's struggles with authority or with people bigger than he. Chaplin also knew how to bring a tear to the eye with just the right amount of sadness.

Charles Spencer Chaplin was born on April 16, 1889, in London. His childhood was one of extreme poverty. But Charlie showed an early gift for performing and longed to be an actor. He went to the United States for the first time in 1910 as part of a vaudeville troupe. In 1913, the troupe toured the United States, and Chaplain came in contact with film producer Mack Sennett. His first short film, *Making a Living,* was made in 1914 for Sennett. By 1915, Chaplin was internationally famous and was earning $1,250 a week.

His talent was extraordinary. He wrote, directed, and produced most of the films in which he appeared. He even composed the music for those with sound. A short man, he could move with amazing quickness and ease. He invented comic situations that became classics, such as the feeding machine in *Modern Times* (1936). In this film, a worker is fed by a machine to save time on the assembly line. The machine goes out of control, and the worker is unable to stop it. Chaplin's comic ideas were brilliant. In *The Gold Rush* (1925), the starving tramp makes an enjoyable meal of his shoe.

Of the 80 films that Chaplin made, the best known include *The Kid* (1921), *City Lights* (1931), and *The Great Dictator* (1940). In *The Great Dictator,* Chaplin used his first speaking role to satirize the political views of Adolf Hitler.

After World War II, Chaplin was determined not to rest on his previous successes. He abandoned the Little Tramp character and tried to grow as an artist. He made *Monsieur Verdoux* (1947), about a man who murders women for their money, and *Limelight* (1952), about an aging vaudeville performer. *A King in New York* (1957) criticized a time in United States history when many people were unjustly accused of being Communists. His last film, *A Countess from Hong Kong* (1967), was a love story. A rediscovered masterpiece, *Woman of Paris* (1923), which Chaplin directed but did not act in, was released again in 1978.

Chaplin had good business sense and became quite wealthy. But controversy surrounded him. He was criticized for not

In this scene from *The Gold Rush*, the Little Tramp fends off the hunger-crazed Big Jim.

186b

Chaplin satirized Adolf Hitler in *The Great Dictator.*

becoming an American citizen, for his friendships with women, and for his political views, which some people thought leaned toward Communism. In 1952, when Chaplin sailed for England, the U.S. attorney general ordered that he not be allowed back into the United States without an investigation of his political views.

Chaplin settled in Switzerland with his fourth wife, Oona O'Neill, daughter of playwright Eugene O'Neill. They had been married in 1943. They had a large family—five daughters and three sons. (Chaplin also had two sons from a previous marriage.) In 1972, Chaplin revisited the United States for the first time, to accept honors from the film community. He was knighted by Queen Elizabeth II in 1975. When he died in Switzerland on December 25, 1977, the world mourned one of the greatest creative artists of the 20th century.

WILLIAM WOLF
Film Critic, *Cue* magazine

CHARADES

Charades is a guessing game in which every syllable of a word or an entire phrase is acted out. The game originated in France and takes its name from an old French word meaning "talk." This may seem strange, because the actor in a game of charades is not allowed to speak at all. The "talking" in charades is entirely in pantomime—actions and gestures in place of words.

To play charades, a group divides into two teams. Each team takes turns at acting and at guessing a word or words within a set time limit. If time is called before the word is guessed, the actors must stop. The audience team tries to guess the word before time is called because the team having the lowest time score at the end of the game wins. Charades may be played in either of two ways—simple charades and "The Game."

▶ SIMPLE CHARADES

In simple charades, several people on a team act out the different syllables of one word. The group is divided into two teams. One team leaves the room to choose a word to act out. The word must have two or more syllables, each of which can be acted as a shorter word. If, for example, the word "decorate" is chosen, the team might first act out the word "deck," then "oar," and then "ate." The last step is to act out the entire word in one pantomime scene. When a word is guessed or time is called, the other team takes its turn in acting out a word. The game may continue as long as the players wish.

▶ "THE GAME"

The other version of charades is so popular that it is sometimes just called "The Game." In this game, only one person does the acting. The actor pantomimes entire phrases for members of his or her own team. Sometimes the actor portrays the titles of songs, books, or movies. Nursery rhymes and well-known proverbs are other good subjects.

The two teams gather in separate groups, and each team selects several phrases for the other team to act. Each phrase is written on a slip of paper. The person who is going to be the first actor gets a slip from the opposing team and reads it. Actors are timed from the moment they say they are ready to begin. The other members of the team may ask questions, but the actor may answer only with actions. When the actor is finished, a person from the other team draws a phrase and begins to act. The game continues until each player has had a turn as actor.

▶ SIGNALS

Certain signals have become standard in charades. The first step is to show the category of the phrase. If the phrase is a book title or a song title, the actor pretends to read a book or pretends to sing. The actor then shows the number of words in the phrase by holding up the correct number of fingers.

The actor may pantomime the words in any order but should first show the team which word is to be acted. The actor may act parts of a single word by first showing which word has been chosen and then making a chopping motion on the arm. Then the actor shows which syllable of the word will be acted by holding up the correct number of fingers.

A rhyming word may be shown by cupping the ear with the hand. A short word is shown by holding two fingers close together. A long word is shown by holding the arms wide apart. The players will find other signals to use as the game progresses.

Members of the guessing team can help the player who is acting out a word if they speak aloud all the ideas that the pantomime suggests to them. Often victory depends just as much on imaginative guessing by the team as it does on clever acting by the person presenting the word.

The actor may encourage teammates by motioning inward with the hands when the team is "warm" and by pushing the hands out, palms toward the team, when the team is "cold." When a player on the team guesses the right word, the actor should point at that person and nod.

Some of the rules for playing charades may be different from group to group. Some people, for example, permit the actor to make sounds, such as whistling or groaning, as long as the word itself is not mentioned. However it is played, the game of charades adds fun and laughter to many friendly gatherings.

CHARCOAL.   See FUELS.

CHARLEMAGNE (742?–814)

In the 5th century, the once-powerful Roman Empire in the west came to an end. With the fall of its empire, the law and order that Rome had imposed on western Europe steadily declined. There was no strong central government to protect the widely separated towns and villages. With the Roman soldiers gone, tribes of wild barbarians from the north and east swarmed over the land. Learning and education slowly began to wane.

In Gaul (approximately the France, Netherlands, and Belgium of today), a Germanic tribe called the Franks was slowly building a kingdom. Under Charles Martel and his son Pepin the Short, their kingdom grew to include almost the whole of Gaul.

About 742, Pepin's wife, Bertrada, bore a son. This boy—who became Charles I but is better known as Charlemagne or Charles the Great—was to become one of the greatest kings of the Middle Ages. At the age of 26 he inherited half of his father's kingdom. The other half went to his brother, Carloman. When Carloman died four years later, Charles became sole ruler of the Franks.

Charles was different in many ways from the kings who had gone before him. His mother had encouraged her son to learn to read, a rare accomplishment then—even for kings. She instilled in him a love for learning that lasted all his life. Even as an old man, he slept with writing tools under his pillow so that he could practice the alphabet during wakeful nights. He never learned to write, though, and signed his name by making a cross and the letters "KRLS."

Much of what we know about Charlemagne comes from the writings of a member of his court, a monk named Einhard. Einhard says that at 13 Charles was brave and strong. When he grew to manhood, he was very tall. His hair and mustache were blond, and he had a long nose. His expression was good-natured but could become stern. Charles was fond of hunting and swimming. He liked to eat and drink, and at mealtimes he enjoyed listening to music and stories.

▶ CHARLEMAGNE'S REIGN

Soon after he became king, Charles received a plea for help from Pope Adrian I. The Lombards in northern Italy had seized church lands. Charles led his Franks against them and restored the lands to the Pope. He married Desiderata, daughter of the Lombard king, and became king of the Lombards.

In northern Germany lived the Saxons, a warlike, pagan people. For 30 years Charles fought bloody wars against them. He offered them a choice of Christianity or death by the sword. They resisted fiercely. Finally their leader, Wittekind, submitted to baptism. The Saxons then accepted Christianity as their religion and Charles as their ruler.

Charles preferred peace to war, but battles took up most of his 43-year reign. To unite his kingdom and protect its borders, he conquered the Slavs of central Europe. The Avars, who lived along the Danube River, were also defeated. And the powerful dukes of Bavaria were forced to submit to his rule.

The Legend of Roland. Of all Charlemagne's battles, the best remembered is a minor one that became a legend. In 778, he led his soldiers against the Muslim Saracens, conquerors of Spain. On their way home the Franks were attacked by Basques, who lived in the Pyrenees mountains. At Roncesvalles the entire rear guard of the army was killed. One of the slain officers was Count Hruodland. Three centuries later, he was to become famous as Roland, the hero of France's greatest epic poem, the *Song of Roland*.

▶ CHARLEMAGNE'S KINGDOM

By 800, Charles ruled supreme in western Europe. His kingdom covered most of what is today France, Belgium, the Netherlands, Switzerland, Austria, western Germany, northern Italy, and parts of Spain, Yugoslavia, and Czechoslovakia.

Charles divided his kingdom into counties. In each he assigned a count as governor. Bishops were placed in charge of church matters. Ambassadors traveled throughout the

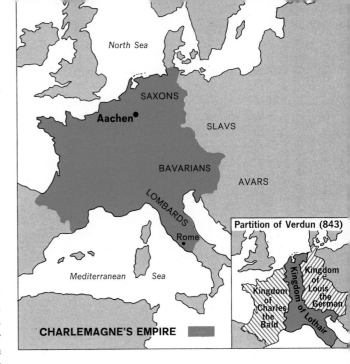

CHARLEMAGNE'S EMPIRE

Partition of Verdun (843)

huge kingdom. They saw to it that the king's orders were obeyed, and they listened to any complaints the people had. Farming, commerce, education, and religion were encouraged. A rough code of laws was developed. Some of these laws were harsh, but many were generous. The poor received charity.

Charles brought scholars and monks to his capital at Aachen (in Germany). A palace school was created, and its most eager pupil was the king himself. Free monastery schools were built, which were attended by the sons of serfs, as well as nobles.

▶ EMPEROR

In 800, Charles made a journey to Rome. On Christmas Day, as he prayed at the altar of St. Peter's Church, Pope Leo III placed a jeweled crown on Charles's head and declared him emperor of the Romans.

Charles ruled as emperor until his death in 814. His only surviving son, Louis the Pious, inherited the great empire. But unlike his father, Louis was a weak ruler. Under his grandsons the empire was divided into three separate kingdoms. From these kingdoms eventually came the modern nations of western Europe.

Reviewed by KENNETH S. COOPER
George Peabody College

See also HOLY ROMAN EMPIRE.

The 14th-century pilgrims pictured above entertained one another with stories on their way to the shrine of Thomas à Becket at Canterbury in England. This illustration is from an early manuscript of the *Canterbury Tales*, the most famous work of Geoffrey Chaucer (*right*).

CHAUCER, GEOFFREY (1340?–1400)

The greatest figure of medieval English literature—and one of the first great humorists of modern Europe—was Geoffrey Chaucer, the son of a London wine merchant. His most famous work, the *Canterbury Tales,* gives a vivid picture of life in 14th-century England.

Little is known about Chaucer's early years. In 1356 he became a page in the household of Prince Lionel, a son of Edward III. Three years later he took part in a military expedition to France and was taken prisoner. King Edward paid part of his ransom, and Chaucer returned to England in 1360. In the years that followed, he married one of the queen's attendants and held a number of government posts, including that of controller of customs in London. He made several trips to France and to Italy, where he may have met the Italian writers Petrarch and Boccaccio.

Chaucer wrote throughout his life. His first long poem was *The Book of the Duchess* (1369), written on the death of Lady Blanche, the first wife of John of Gaunt. It follows the style of the elegant French verse then popular. Italian literature influenced a later work, *Troilus and Criseyde.*

In the *Canterbury Tales,* Chaucer wrote about a group of pilgrims traveling to a shrine at Canterbury in England. Each pilgrim is a colorful and unique character, and each tells a story along the way. Chaucer himself was so skillful a storyteller that his account of their pilgrimage is as entertaining as the individual tales. He borrowed the design of the work from Boccaccio's *Decameron,* and he took the plots of the tales from many sources. But he wrote in an entirely original way—with robust humor and deep insight.

Chaucer's last official post was as a forester, in 1391. He died on October 25, 1400, in a small house he had rented on the grounds of Westminster Abbey, in London. His burial spot at the abbey is known as Poets' Corner.

Reviewed by GEORGIA DUNBAR
Hofstra University

See also ENGLISH LITERATURE.

CHECKERS

Checkers, or draughts, as it is known in England, is a board game for two people. A checkerboard is identical to the board used in playing chess. But the objects of the two games are not the same. In chess the object of the game is to capture the other player's king. The object of checkers is to make the other player unable to move. Usually this is done by capturing all the player's men.

Because the rules of checkers are not hard to learn, it is a favorite children's game. But it can also be a real test of skill between experts. Many players study it as they would a science, and learn hundreds of special moves for beginning and ending games.

In English-speaking countries one set of rules is followed. In other countries slightly different forms of the game, such as German, Spanish, or Turkish checkers, may be played.

How Old Is the Game of Checkers?

Some historians believe that the game was known in ancient Egypt. Boards very much like checkerboards have been found in tombs. But other experts point out that no one knows if the game played on those ancient boards was like our modern checkers. No one is certain, either, whether chess or checkers came first.

But we are certain that checkers as we know it has been played for at least 400 years. In 1547 the first description of it appeared in a book written in Spain by Antonio Torquemada. From Spain, it is believed, the game spread to other European countries.

In some countries checkers was called a game for women. This may have been because it was considered simpler than chess. In France it was *jeu des dames* and in Germany, *Damenspiel*. These names are still used.

In the 19th century there was great interest in checkers as a tournament game. Today it is played mainly as a pastime, although tournaments are sometimes held. In the United States these are sponsored by the American Checker Federation.

▶ HOW THE GAME IS PLAYED

American checkers, or British draughts, is played on a board marked off into 64 squares. Half of the squares are dark and half are light in color. The board is arranged so that each dark square is next to a light one.

Each player is given 12 round checkers, or men. These are often made of wood. One player's checkers are dark and the other's are light. Many checkerboards and checkers are black and red or black and white, but other colors are used, too. (In this explanation of the game, dark checkers and squares will be called black, and light checkers and squares will be called white.)

The players sit facing each other with the board between them. The board is placed so that a black square is in the left-hand corner of each player's section of the board. Each person places his 12 men on the black squares of the three rows of the board nearest him. The two center rows are left empty.

Each player tries to move his men into the other player's part of the board and either capture the other player's men or keep him from being able to move them.

The player who has the black checkers begins the game. (Players exchange checkers at the end of each game.) The person who plays first moves one man one space in the direction of the other player. All play must be on black squares, so the player cannot move straight ahead, but must move forward diagonally. He lands either on the black square to his left or the black square to his right in the row ahead.

The player who has the white checkers then moves one of his men in the same way. The game continues with each person moving in turn.

Jumping

After each player has made some moves into the other's territory, the checkers may be in such a position that one player is able to capture one of his opponent's men. This is done in the following way. Let us imagine that the player who has black checkers is ready to move forward, but in one of the black squares

nearest him there is a white checker. Just beyond the white checker there is an empty black square. The player who has the black checker jumps his man over the white one that is blocking him and lands in the empty square. He then removes the white checker from the board. This is called a single jump.

It is also possible for a player to jump over two or more checkers if they are blocking him and there is an empty square beyond each checker. In this case the player may make all of his jumps in one direction, or he may jump over a checker blocking him on one side, land on an empty square, then change direction and jump over another checker blocking him on the other side. A player must jump whenever possible. If more than one jump is possible, he may choose the one he wishes to make.

Kings

When a player's checker reaches the row of squares nearest the other player, this checker becomes known as a king and is given special power. It can be moved backward as well as forward. A checker is crowned a king in the following way. Let us imagine that a black checker is moved into the row nearest the player using white checkers. (The row nearest each player is called his king row.) The player using white checkers must take one checker from the pile of black checkers he has captured and place it on top of the black checker that has reached his king row. From that time on, the two checkers are played as a single man. A player's turn ends when he has had a checker crowned king.

A game ends when one player has captured all of the men of the other player or when one player has made it impossible for the other player to move any of his men.

Other Rules

When checkers is played according to the official rules, a 5-minute limit is placed on the time a player may take to think before he makes a move. At the end of 5 minutes, he is warned and then given 1 minute more. If he has not moved by the end of the extra minute, he loses the game.

The official rules also say that if a player touches a checker, he must move it. If he starts to move a checker in a certain direction, he must finish the move in that direction.

See also CHESS.

CHECKING ACCOUNT.   See BANKS AND BANKING.

CHEESE

The origin of cheesemaking is unknown, but references to it date back many centuries. One account claims that an Arab merchant tried milk that had curdled in a goatskin bag. The cheese curd pleased him, and man had found a new food.

The Bible mentions cheese as well as milk. In Chapter 17 of First Samuel, David is instructed by his father to "carry these ten cheeses to the captain of their thousand." Homer in Book Nine of the Odyssey described Ulysses' discovery of cheese made from goat's milk in the cave of the dreadful one-eyed cyclops. Other Greek and Roman scholars wrote about the manufacture of cheese as it was carried out over 2,000 years ago.

From this ancient background hundreds of different kinds of cheese have been developed throughout the world. There are several reasons why so many varieties of cheese can be made.

First, milk—the basis of cheese—comes from other animals besides the cow. Camels, goats, sheep, and water buffalo each yield cheese with a different flavor. Krutt is a cheese made in the Asiatic steppes from camel's milk by drying the curd in the sun until it is very hard. Roquefort is a famous French cheese made from sheep's milk. Goat cheese is a standard food in mountainous countries. Surati is a cheese made in India from buffalo's milk. The curd is drained in baskets and can be eaten fresh. Even if just one kind of milk is used, different processes and curing methods will produce different cheeses. Cheesemaking is described step by step in the article DAIRY-ING AND DAIRY PRODUCTS.

NORMAN F. OLSON
University of Wisconsin

See also MILK.

CHEMICAL INDUSTRY

In our daily lives we use a great many things that are made entirely or partly from chemicals. We are not often aware of this, because most chemical products do not reach us in the form of chemicals. Instead, they are used to manufacture such products as drugs, durable-press fabrics, fertilizer, plastic pens, photographic film, and detergents for washing dishes or laundry. For all these useful things and many others, we depend on the chemical industry.

The chemical industry has many branches. Besides making an endless variety of synthetic materials, it changes raw materials found in nature into thousands of useful products.

▶FROM ANCIENT CRAFT TO MODERN INDUSTRY

The chemical industry has ancient beginnings. Though their methods were crude and unscientific, ancient Egyptian and Mesopotamian chemists made such chemical products as pigments for paints, dyes that could be used to stain cloth and leather, medicines and cosmetics, alkali for glassmaking, and various glazes for pottery. Jewelry workers also developed ways of coloring gemstones and making colored metal alloys. Greek, Roman, and Arab chemists added improvements of their own.

Alchemists, who were magicians more than scientists, flourished from the early Christian era to the end of the 17th century. Their two main concerns were to find the secret of turning ordinary metals into gold and to discover the elixir of life. This was a mysterious liquid that was supposed to cure all sickness and even to prevent old age.

Of course the alchemists never succeeded in discovering either of these things. But in their experiments they did discover many chemicals on which the modern chemical industry depends. Among these were alcohol, nitric acid, hydrochloric acid, and sulfuric acid. The alchemists also developed better ways of preparing and purifying chemicals. Most important, the alchemists kept records of their experiments, which were later passed on to chemists. These chemists were interested in science rather than magic, but they put some of the alchemists' knowledge to good use.

During the Middle Ages, many industries used chemistry in a crude way. Production was usually limited, but a few products were turned out in fairly large quantities. These included saltpeter for gunpowder, alum for tanning

In this chemical technique, certain pollutants are removed from wastewater and converted into an energy-rich gas.

hides, potash for soap and glassmaking, and lime for mortar. As yet there was no separate chemical industry. Dyers, glassmakers, and druggists usually prepared their own chemicals.

Scientific researchers of the 17th and 18th centuries made the first big steps toward the development of a modern chemical industry. Among the pioneers were Robert Boyle (1627–91), Henry Cavendish (1731–1810), Joseph Priestly (1733–1804), Antoine Lavoisier (1743–94), and John Dalton (1766–1844). They discovered some of the chemical elements of which all matter is made. They learned to prepare chemicals that were purer than the chemicals made in the past. They studied the reactions that took place when one chemical was mixed with another. This study made them able to predict the result of a chemical process. Such ability was necessary if chemicals were to be useful at all.

In the late 18th century, the Industrial Revolution brought a great demand for chemical products. For example, more and better dyes were needed for the cloth that the new textile mills were turning out. Textile manufacturers also needed chemical bleaches to whiten cloth. Coal gas was developed to light factories and city streets.

The Industrial Revolution did more than create a need for chemical products. It also greatly changed the chemical industry. Machines replaced hand labor for many tasks. Chemicals were produced in great quantities instead of a small amount at a time. Some manufacturers began to specialize in making

Synthetic fibers, shown on rolls in this chemical plant, are plastics in the form of long, thin strands.

chemicals for such industries as dyeing and glassmaking. The foundations of the modern chemical industry were being laid.

▶ THE INDUSTRY TODAY

The modern chemical industry is quite different from the medieval workshops where the first chemicals were made. Today, the industry depends on the latest advances in science and engineering. Huge chemical plants, with their long piping systems and enormous tanks, turn out large amounts of chemicals a day. Research scientists seek ways to develop new products. Other trained people check the purity of raw materials and the quality of the final products. Engineers of every kind plan, construct, and maintain the plants. Complicated instruments keep track of pressures and temperatures during the chemical processes. Every step of the manufacturing process is closely controlled. The chemical industry is now highly automated. One worker at a control panel may handle an entire complicated process.

▶ MANUFACTURES

Chemicals may be classified in several ways. One of the oldest divisions is into organic and inorganic chemicals. Organic chemicals are those that contain carbon atoms. They are used to make such products as dyes, medicines, cosmetics, plastics, paints, synthetic fabrics, and building materials. Ethyl alcohol is an organic chemical. So are many of the new superstrong glues.

Inorganic chemicals do not usually contain carbon. But some substances that do contain carbon are classed as inorganic because of long-standing custom. Sulfuric acid—which is used in making fertilizer, in cleaning metal plates, and in other ways—is an inorganic chemical. So is hydrogen peroxide, which is used to bleach textiles and paper pulp.

Chemicals may also be classified as fine and heavy chemicals. Fine chemicals are refined to very high purity. They are usually made and used in small quantities. Synthetic flavorings, drugs, dyes, and gasoline additives are examples of fine chemicals.

Heavy chemicals are the "workhorses" of the chemical industry. They are produced in large quantities, totaling hundreds of thousands of tons each year. They are often not purified as much as fine chemicals. Some well-known heavy chemicals are sulfuric acid, nitric acid, ammonia, caustic soda (sodium hydroxide), benzene, and chlorine. In all there are about 25 heavy chemicals. The leading producers of chemicals are the United States, West Germany, Britain, Japan, and the Soviet Union.

RESEARCH AND DEVELOPMENT

Research is the heart of the chemical industry. Chemical companies depend on their researchers to develop new and better ways of making chemicals. There are two kinds of research. **Basic research** tries to find new facts and ideas, regardless of whether these facts and ideas can be turned at once into useful products. Synthetic rubber was discovered through basic research. **Applied research** is the practical side of research. Researchers start with the goal of making a certain product. In their work, they may use substances and ideas that are already known.

Synthetic rubber is one of the valuable products made possible through chemical research. For a century before World War I, chemists had been studying natural rubber. They tried to duplicate it in the laboratory. If they could do this, it would not be necessary to make long trips to distant countries to get natural rubber. They knew that if war broke out, the sources of supply might be cut off.

Chemists started with coke, a by-product of the distillation of coal. Using coke, limestone, and water, they made acetylene, a gas. By another process they were able to convert the acetylene into a new material—chloroprene. In all these processes they were rearranging the atoms and molecules of substances in an attempt to make a substitute for a material found in nature. Finally, in the 1930's, they found a way to change chloroprene into a rubberlike material that was similar to natural rubber.

Synthetic rubber has proved to be superior in many ways. One kind, neoprene, is resistant to oils, grease, and fire. Polyurethane rubber is very strong and wears well. These two kinds of synthetic rubber have been useful for making such things as conveyer belts for factories and tires for many kinds of vehicles.

A laboratory where gases are distilled (turned into liquids). This technique is used to purify chemicals.

Silicone rubber is the material used to make some kinds of artificial body parts, especially artificial heart valves.

THE FUTURE

The chemical industry is rapidly developing and changing. Many important chemicals can be made from many raw materials by different processes. New products and new processes can quickly make a plant's equipment out-of-date. The industry needs many scientists and engineers to develop new products and production methods. As the industry becomes more automated, there will probably be less need for unskilled and semi-skilled workers. There will be more need for highly skilled and trained technicians to set up equipment, keep it in operating condition, and assist research scientists.

Important new projects are under way in the chemical industry. Researchers are now perfecting the techniques for making synthetic fuels ("synfuels"), the new superstrong glassy metals, and the many new materials needed by the electronics industry. Plans are being made to study chemical production in space, where near-vacuum conditions are ideal for certain processes.

WILLIAM E. CHACE
Manufacturing Chemists Association

See also CHEMISTRY; DRUG INDUSTRY; NYLON AND OTHER SYNTHETIC FIBERS; RUBBER.

CHEMISTRY

Chemistry is the science that deals with the makeup of all the different substances in the world and with how that makeup can be changed.

All objects are made up of tiny particles far too small to be seen, even with the best microscopes. These tiny particles are called **atoms**. Everything—glass, brick, iron, water, the stars in the sky, and your own body—is made up of atoms.

There are many kinds of atoms. So far we know of 105 different kinds. But most of them are quite rare. Only about a dozen kinds of atoms are really common here on the earth.

Then how can there be so many different things on the earth? The answer is that atoms are like the letters of the alphabet—all the words in the English language are built out of only 26 letters. A particular kind of material, or **substance**, is formed when atoms combine. Even just a few kinds of atoms can combine in a large number of different arrangements. And each new arrangement makes up a different substance.

Sometimes a substance is made up of combinations of only one kind of atom. Such a substance is called an **element**. Iron is made up of one kind of atom. So are sulfur and aluminum. These are examples of elements. We can speak of the iron atom, meaning the kind of atom one finds in iron. Or we can speak of sulfur atoms, aluminum atoms, and so on.

When a substance is made up of combinations of more than one kind of atom, it is a **compound**. There is a blackish compound named ferrous sulfide that is made up of pairs of atoms. Each pair consists of one iron atom and one sulfur atom.

A group of atoms tightly bound together is called a **molecule**. We can say, for instance, that a molecule of ferrous sulfide is made up of one iron atom and one sulfur atom. Or the atoms in a molecule may be of the same kind. An oxygen molecule is made up of two oxygen atoms.

All this is part of chemistry. Chemistry is concerned with finding out what kinds of atoms make up a particular substance and how those atoms are arranged in molecules. This part of chemistry is called **analysis**.

▶ CHEMICAL CHANGE

Chemistry also deals with ways of changing the arrangement of atoms in a substance. And this is a particular kind of change. There are other changes that do not alter the arrangement of atoms, and these changes are not part of chemistry, but of **physics**.

For instance, you can break up a bar of iron into tiny pieces. Each tiny piece is still iron, for the atom arrangement has not been changed. This is a **physical change**. You can magnetize a piece of iron. You can let an electric current pass through it. Or you can heat it red hot. These, too, are physical changes.

You can mix iron with something else without changing the atom arrangement. Suppose you mix powdered iron with powdered sulfur. In this mixture each little grain of iron is still iron. And each little grain of sulfur is still sulfur.

You can easily separate the mixture again, since iron and sulfur behave differently. That is, they have different **properties**. A magnet passed through the mixture will attract the iron and leave the sulfur behind. A liquid called carbon disulfide will soak out the sulfur and leave the iron behind.

But what if you heated the mixture of powdered iron and sulfur? That would bring about a different kind of change. A blackish material would form, in which you could no longer see separate little bits of grayish iron or yellow sulfur.

The new material would have a new set of properties, unlike those of either iron or sulfur. The new substance would not be attracted by a magnet. It would not dissolve in carbon disulfide.

You would now have a substance called ferrous sulfide. In the heating each sulfur atom combined with an iron atom, forming molecules of ferrous sulfide. That is, a new arrangement of atoms was formed. And it made up a new substance with new properties. This is an example of a **chemical change**, which is also called a **chemical reaction**.

Chemical changes go on all about us. Whenever coal or oil burns, that is a chemical change. The rusting of iron is a chemical change. When food is cooked it goes through many chemical changes. And there are chemical changes going on inside the body at all

FIGURE 1

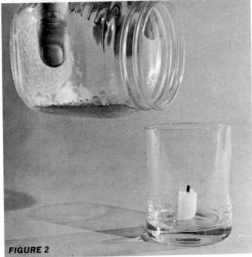

FIGURE 2

A CHEMICAL REACTION
   When a chemical reaction occurs, new substances are formed. You can see this easily by adding a tablespoon of baking soda to a jar containing a tablespoon of vinegar (Fig. 1). As you stir the solution you can see bubbles of the new substance forming. The bubbles are a gas called carbon dioxide.
   Now place a candle in a glass and light the candle (Fig. 2). Tilt the jar slightly over the candle so that the carbon dioxide flows but not the liquid. The carbon dioxide puts out the candle.

ALPHABETICAL TABLE OF ELEMENTS

ELEMENT	SYMBOL	ELEMENT	SYMBOL
Actinium	Ac	Manganese	Mn
Aluminum	Al	Mendelevium	Md
Americium	Am	Mercury	Hg
Antimony	Sb	Molybdenum	Mo
Argon	Ar	Neodymium	Nd
Arsenic	As	Neon	Ne
Astatine	At	Neptunium	Np
Barium	Ba	Nickel	Ni
Berkelium	Bk	Niobium	Nb
Beryllium	Be	Nitrogen	N
Bismuth	Bi	Nobelium	No
Boron	B	Osmium	Os
Bromine	Br	Oxygen	O
Cadmium	Cd	Palladium	Pd
Calcium	Ca	Phosphorus	P
Californium	Cf	Platinum	Pt
Carbon	C	Plutonium	Pu
Cerium	Ce	Polonium	Po
Cesium	Cs	Potassium	K
Chlorine	Cl	Praseodymium	Pr
Chromium	Cr	Promethium	Pm
Cobalt	Co	Protactinium	Pa
Copper	Cu	Radium	Ra
Curium	Cm	Radon	Rn
Dysprosium	Dy	Rhenium	Re
		Rhodium	Rh
Einsteinium	Es	Rubidium	Rb
Erbium	Er	Ruthenium	Ru
Europium	Eu	Rutherfordium	Rf
Fermium	Fm	Samarium	Sm
Fluorine	F	Scandium	Sc
Francium	Fr	Selenium	Se
		Silicon	Si
Gadolinium	Gd	Silver	Ag
Gallium	Ga	Sodium	Na
Germanium	Ge	Strontium	Sr
Gold	Au	Sulfur	S
Hafnium	Hf	Tantalum	Ta
Hahnium	Ha	Technetium	Tc
Helium	He	Tellurium	Te
Holmium	Ho	Terbium	Tb
Hydrogen	H	Thallium	Tl
		Thorium	Th
Indium	In	Thulium	Tm
Iodine	I	Tin	Sn
Iridium	Ir	Titanium	Ti
Iron	Fe	Tungsten	W
Krypton	Kr	Uranium	U
		Vanadium	V
Lanthanum	La	Xenon	Xe
Lawrencium	Lr		
Lead	Pb	Ytterbium	Yb
Lithium	Li	Yttrium	Y
Lutetium	Lu	Zinc	Zn
Magnesium	Mg	Zirconium	Zr

times. These are the changes that the chemist is interested in.

▶ SYMBOLS, FORMULAS, AND EQUATIONS

   The chemist often speaks of the different elements and of the compounds they form. He does this so often that a special shorthand language has been worked out. Each element is represented by one or two letters taken from its name. This is the **chemical symbol** of the element.

Often the chemical symbol is just the initial letter of the element. For instance, the chemical symbol of sulfur is S. Sometimes it is the initial letter plus one more. The symbol for aluminum is Al.

A few of the elements have been known since ancient times, when they were called by Latin names. In those few cases the chemical symbol is taken from the Latin names. For instance, the Latin name for iron is *ferrum*. And so the symbol for iron is Fe.

Symbols can be used to show the atomic makeup of a molecule. The ferrous sulfide molecule contains one iron atom and one sulfur atom. So the molecule is written FeS. This is an example of a **chemical formula**, a way of showing the atomic makeup of a molecule by means of symbols.

Whenever a chemical reaction takes place, atoms are rearranged. Therefore the details of the reaction can be shown in chemical symbols. When iron and sulfur are mixed and heated, ferrous sulfide forms. To put this quickly, we can write:

$$Fe + S \xrightarrow{\triangle} FeS$$

That is a **chemical equation**. It says that an atom of iron combines with an atom of sulfur to form a molecule of ferrous sulfide. The little triangle over the arrow stands for heat. It means that the mixture has to be heated before the chemical reaction takes place.

When a symbol is written by itself it stands for one atom of a particular element. What if a molecule contains more than one atom of that element? Suppose we consider the air all about us in this connection.

Air is a gas made up chiefly of two kinds of atoms, nitrogen (N) and oxygen (O). These atoms make up two kinds of molecules. One consists of a pair of nitrogen atoms. The other consists of a pair of oxygen atoms. The formula of the first molecule is N_2, and that of the second is O_2.

There is also a gas made up of atoms of hydrogen (H). Only traces of this occur in air, but the gas can be prepared by chemists. It also has a molecule made up of a pair of atoms, and its formula is H_2.

Hydrogen is flammable. That is, a jet of hydrogen gas in the open air can be lighted and made to burn. The hydrogen then undergoes a chemical change. It reacts with the oxygen in the air (but not with the nitrogen), forming a new molecule. The new molecule contains both hydrogen and oxygen atoms. It contains 2 hydrogen atoms and 1 oxygen atom. So its formula is H_2O. Water is the familiar compound represented by that formula.

The chemical reaction in which hydrogen and oxygen combine to form water cannot be written $H_2 + O_2 \xrightarrow{\triangle} H_2O$. This would say that 2 hydrogen atoms combine with 2 oxygen atoms to form a molecule of water. But the molecule of water contains 2 hydrogen atoms and only 1 oxygen atom. What happened to the other oxygen atom?

The reaction must be written:

$$2H_2 + O_2 \xrightarrow{\triangle} 2H_2O$$

O_2, you remember, stands for 2 oxygen atoms or 1 oxygen molecule. H_2 stands for 2 hydrogen atoms or 1 hydrogen molecule. So $2H_2$ stands for 2 hydrogen molecules (or 4 atoms). Therefore the equation shows that 2 hydrogen molecules and 1 oxygen molecule combine to form 2 molecules of water. The two molecules of water are made up of 4

One atom of oxygen and two atoms of hydrogen form a water molecule. A sulfur atom and an iron atom form ferrous sulfide.

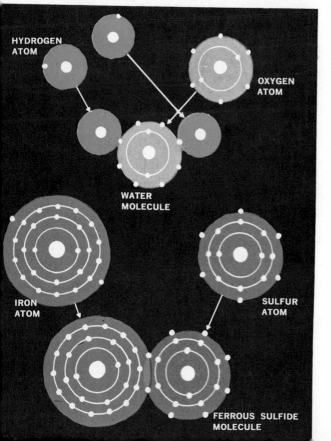

HYDROGEN ATOM

OXYGEN ATOM

WATER MOLECULE

IRON ATOM

SULFUR ATOM

FERROUS SULFIDE MOLECULE

hydrogen atoms and 2 oxygen atoms altogether. All the atoms are accounted for, and the result is a **balanced chemical equation**.

▶ CATALYSTS

Heat is not the only method for bringing about chemical changes. There are other ways, too.

The element chlorine (Cl) is a poisonous green gas. It forms molecules made up of a pair of atoms (Cl_2). If chlorine and hydrogen are mixed in the dark, nothing happens. If sunlight is allowed to shine on the mixture, the two gases combine with a loud explosion. The compound hydrogen chloride (HCl) is formed.

$$H_2 + Cl_2 \xrightarrow{\text{(light)}} 2HCl$$

Another common way of bringing about a chemical reaction is using an electric current. If a chemist passes an electric current through water, he breaks the water molecules into hydrogen and oxygen.

Heat, light, and electricity are different forms of energy. But chemical reactions can also be brought about, or at least made to go faster, by the use of special chemicals.

To explain this, let's start with a white substance called potassium chlorate. The molecule of potassium chlorate contains 1 atom of potassium, 1 atom of chlorine, and 3 atoms of oxygen. The symbol for potassium is K (from *kalium*, the Latin name for it). The formula of the compound is therefore $KClO_3$.

If potassium chlorate is heated, the oxygen atoms break away and become molecules of oxygen gas. What is left is potassium chloride. Its molecule is made up of an atom of potassium and an atom of chlorine. The chemical equation looks like this:

$$2KClO_3 \xrightarrow{\triangle} 2KCl + 3O_2$$

This says that 2 molecules of potassium chlorate (containing 6 atoms of oxygen altogether) lose the oxygen and become 2 molecules of potassium chloride. The 6 oxygen atoms become 3 oxygen molecules.

Quite a lot of heat has to be added to the potassium chlorate. And even then the oxygen gas bubbles off slowly. However, chemists found that the process could be speeded up if a blackish powder named manganese dioxide was added to the potassium chlorate before heating. Manganese dioxide has a molecule made up of 1 atom of manganese (Mn) and 2 atoms of oxygen. So its formula is MnO_2.

When the manganese dioxide is added to the $KClO_3$, oxygen comes off rapidly, even with only gentle heat. None of the oxygen comes from the manganese dioxide. Its oxygen is still there after all the potassium chlorate has broken up. The manganese dioxide doesn't seem to be changed.

Any substance that makes a reaction go faster, without itself seeming to be changed, is called a **catalyst**. The catalyst does not perform any magic, however. It actually takes part in the reaction. But then it re-forms as it was before.

Thus the potassium chlorate first combines with manganese dioxide. This combined molecule loses oxygen from the potassium chlorate part much more easily and quickly than potassium chlorate alone does. Once the oxygen is gone, the combined molecule breaks up into separate molecules of potassium chloride and manganese dioxide. The manganese dioxide is there to start with and at the end. It looks as though it has done nothing at all—but this is not so.

A number of substances can be used as catalysts to speed up reactions. A well-known catalyst is powdered platinum. It can speed up combinations of many substances with hydrogen.

Catalysts are particularly important in the body. Inside our bodies there is no light and very little heat or electricity. Here very complicated molecules are the catalysts. The body catalysts are called **enzymes**. Every different reaction in the body has its own enzyme. The way in which the different chemical changes take place depends on which enzymes are present and on the amount of each.

▶ STRUCTURAL FORMULAS

When different atoms combine to form a molecule, they follow certain rules. For instance, a single hydrogen atom can combine with only one other atom. A single oxygen atom, however, can combine with two other atoms. A single nitrogen atom can combine with three other atoms.

This combining power is called **valence**.

Hydrogen has a valence of one; oxygen, a valence of two; and nitrogen, a valence of three.

Sometimes formulas are written so as to show the valence. It is shown by little dashes between the atoms. The molecules of hydrogen, oxygen, and nitrogen can be written: H—H, O=O, N≡N. The hydrogen atoms are shown held together by a **single bond**; the oxygen atoms, by a **double bond**; and the nitrogen atoms, by a **triple bond**.

The formula of water (H_2O) can be written H—O—H. Here each bond of the oxygen atom is shown to be holding one of the hydrogen atoms. A molecule of a gas called ammonia (NH_3) can be shown with the three valence bonds of the nitrogen atom each connected to a hydrogen atom:

$$H—\overset{\displaystyle H}{\underset{|}{N}}—H.$$

Such formulas show the exact way in which the different atoms of the molecule are connected by bonds. They are called **structural formulas**. These are particularly important in compounds containing atoms of the element carbon (C).

Carbon atoms have an unusual ability. In combining, they can form long chains (often branched) and complicated rings. Molecules containing carbon atoms are therefore usually much larger and more complicated than molecules without carbon atoms. For instance, the important compounds of the body are made up of complicated molecules containing many carbon atoms. That is why chemists are particularly interested in carbon compounds. Carbon has a valence of four. In compounds of the sort found in the body, carbon combines mostly with hydrogen, oxygen, and nitrogen.

Structural formulas are particularly important to chemists dealing with carbon compounds. For it often happens that the atoms within the molecule can be arranged in more than one way. Each different arrangement is a different compound.

As an example, imagine a molecule made up of 2 carbon atoms, 6 hydrogen atoms, and 1 oxygen atom. These can be put together in two different ways:

In both compounds all the carbon atoms have four valence bonds. The oxygen atom has two. And the hydrogen atoms have one. In each compound the number of each kind of atom is the same. But the arrangement is different.

The compound with the molecule shown on the left is ethyl alcohol. It is the alcohol that is found in beer and wine. The compound with the molecule shown on the right is dimethyl ether. Its properties are completely different from those of ethyl alcohol. Ethyl alcohol is a clear liquid with a rather pleasant, sweetish smell. Dimethyl ether is a gas with a much sharper smell. If a small piece of the metal sodium is added to ethyl alcohol, a chemical reaction takes place. Bubbles of hydrogen gas are given off. If sodium is exposed to dimethyl ether, nothing happens.

So you have two different substances with molecules made up of the same atoms in different arrangements. Such substances are called **isomers**. The larger a molecule, the greater the number of isomers that can be built up out of its atoms.

There are giant molecules in the body, made up of thousands upon thousands of atoms. Examples are the proteins and the nucleic acids. Enzymes are one kind of protein molecule. The nucleic acids manufacture the enzymes and control the body chemistry.

Bonds (dashes between the atoms) show the valences of the atoms in a structural formula. Structural formulas show how atoms are combined.

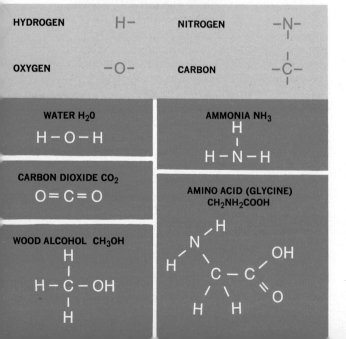

HYDROGEN H-	**NITROGEN** −N−
OXYGEN −O−	**CARBON** −C−

WATER H_2O
H − O − H

AMMONIA NH_3
H − N − H (with H above N)

CARBON DIOXIDE CO_2
O = C = O

AMINO ACID (GLYCINE)
CH_2NH_2COOH

WOOD ALCOHOL CH_3OH
H − C − OH (with H above and below C)

The number of different arrangements possible in giant molecules is too great to describe. But the number explains why there are so many different kinds of plants and animals.

THE ATOM

To understand something about why atoms combine, let's take a look at the way they are built.

The atom is made up of still smaller particles. There are three types of particles inside the atom: the **proton**, the **neutron**, and the **electron**. The protons and the neutrons are heavy particles that are located at the very center of the atom. They form the atomic nucleus. The electrons are very light particles. They are spread throughout the outer regions of the atom and orbit the nucleus.

The proton and the electron both carry an electric charge. All protons are charged the same way, and this charge is said to be **positive**. All electrons are charged in another way, **negative**. The neutrons have no electric charge at all.

The atomic nucleus contains all the protons of the atom. And so the nucleus has a positive charge. Each proton has a charge equal to +1. If the nucleus contains 2 protons it has a charge of +2; if it contains 5 protons it has a charge of +5; if it contains 100 protons it has a charge of +100. The number of protons in the nucleus is said to be the **atomic number** of that atom.

The electric charge on the electron is exactly as large as the electric charge on the proton. The electron's charge is negative, however. So we call it −1.

Each atom has exactly enough electrons to balance the protons. An atom with 1 proton in the nucleus has 1 electron outside. An atom with 5 protons possesses 5 electrons. One with 100 protons possesses 100 electrons. The negative electric charges of the electrons balance the positive electric charges of the protons. The atom as a whole is electrically **neutral**.

When two atoms collide it is their electrons that take part in the collision. The protons and neutrons are not touched. During such a collision the electrons may undergo changes in position or condition. It is these changes that make a chemical reaction.

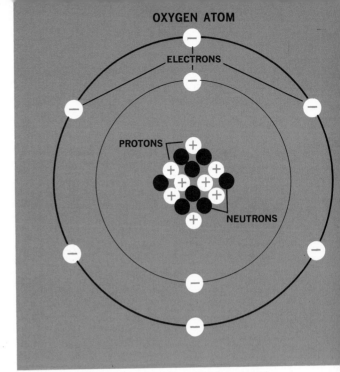

OXYGEN ATOM

This oxygen atom is neutral (has no electrical charge) because it has the same number of protons as electrons.

The way a particular atom reacts with other atoms depends on how many electrons it possesses. An atom with 5 electrons will behave differently from an atom with 6 electrons. But all atoms with 5 electrons will behave in the same way.

Now, the number of electrons in an atom is equal to the number of protons in its nucleus. And the number of protons in the nucleus is the atomic number. So all atoms with the same atomic number behave exactly alike. They take part in the same chemical reactions.

All hydrogen atoms behave alike, and so all must have the same atomic number. All oxygen atoms have the same atomic number. So do all sulfur atoms and all iron atoms. In fact, each element has its own atomic number.

The atomic number of hydrogen is 1; the atomic number of oxygen is 8; the atomic number of iron is 26; the atomic number of uranium is 92. This usually indicates that every hydrogen atom possesses one electron. Every oxygen atom has 8. Every iron atom has 26. And every uranium atom has 92.

The Periodic Table

Chemists know and have studied elements with every atomic number from 1 to 105. If the elements are arranged by atomic number, it can be seen that the valence changes in an orderly fashion. Look, for example, at the first 20 elements:

atomic number	element	valence
1	hydrogen	+1
2	helium	0
3	lithium	+1
4	beryllium	+2
5	boron	+3
6	carbon	+ or −4
7	nitrogen	−3
8	oxygen	−2
9	fluorine	−1
10	neon	0
11	sodium	+1
12	magnesium	+2
13	aluminum	+3
14	silicon	+ or −4
15	phosphorus	−3
16	sulfur	−2
17	chlorine	−1
18	argon	0
19	potassium	+1
20	calcium	+2

(Elements that lose electrons in a chemical reaction have a + valence. Those that attract electrons have a − valence.)

It is possible to arrange the elements in rows in such a way that elements with the same valences and very similar properties fall into the same column.

For instance, helium, neon, argon, krypton, and xenon are **inert gases.** "Inert" means that they are not chemically active and seldom combine with other chemicals. Each has a valence of zero. All have very similar properties. And all fall into the same column.

Lithium, sodium, potassium, rubidium, and cesium are all very active. They have a valence of 1 and very similar properties. And they fall into the same column.

Fluorine, chlorine, bromine, and iodine all have a valence of 1 and similar properties, and fall into the same column.

Elements form families when grouped by their valence.

VALENCES	+1	+2	+3	±4	−3	−2	−1	0
ROW 1	H 1							He 2
ROW 2	Li 3	Be 4	B 5	C 6	N 7	O 8	F 9	Ne 10
ROW 3	Na 11	Mg 12	Al 13	Si 14	P 15	S 16	Cl 17	A 18
ROW 4	K 19	Ca 20						

Such a table, called a **periodic table,** is in Volume E, page 156.

Electron Shells

Elements with similar properties must have similar electron arrangements. For it is the electrons that are responsible for the way in which atoms react.

Electrons are arranged in groups referred to as **electron shells.** Lithium, with an atomic number of 3, has its 3 electrons arranged in two shells: 2 in the inner shell and 1 in the outer. Its arrangment is 2, 1. Sodium, with an atomic number of 11, has three electron shells; the arrangement is 2, 8, 1. Potassium, with an atomic number of 19, has 4 electron shells, and the arrangement is 2, 8, 8, 1. Rubidium (atomic number 37) has the arrangement 2, 8, 18, 8, 1. Cesium (atomic number 55) has the arrangement 2, 8, 18, 18, 8, 1.

In that family each atom has a single electron in the outermost shell. And it is the outermost shell that takes the brunt of the collision between atoms. Therefore the outermost shell is most important in chemical reactions.

Consider the electron arrangements in another family. In fluorine it is 2, 7; in chlorine it is 2, 8, 7; in bromine it is 2, 8, 18, 7; in iodine it is 2, 8, 18, 18, 7. In each case there are 7 electrons in the outermost shells. Or take the inert gases. All have 8 electrons in the outermost shell (except helium, which has 2 electrons in its only shell).

Ions

An atom tends to rearrange its electrons so that its outermost shell holds 8 electrons. (However, the innermost electron shell can hold only 2 electrons at most. So atoms like hydrogen or helium, with only one electron shell, are exceptions to the rule of 8.)

A sodium atom, with its electrons arranged 2, 8, 1, can easily lose one electron. Its second shell, with 8 electrons, becomes the outermost shell. A chlorine atom, with its electrons arranged 2, 8, 7, can easily gain one electron. Its outermost shell then has 8 electrons.

If a sodium atom collides with a chlorine atom, an electron passes from the former to the latter.

The sodium atom, with an electron gone,

SOME ALKALI METALS	SOME HALOGENS	SOME INERT GASES

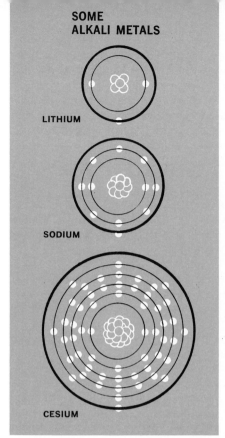

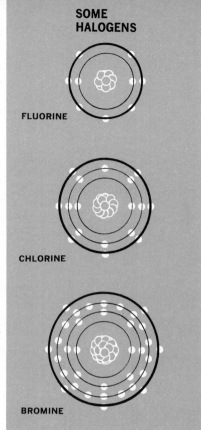

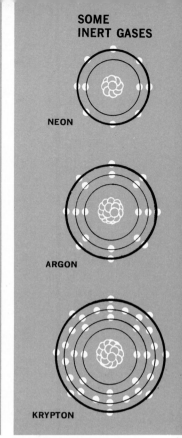

Elements with similar properties have similar electron arrangements. Alkali metals have only one electron in the outer shell and can easily lose it. The halogens have seven electrons in the outer shell and can attract the one needed to fill the shell. Inert gases have a full outer shell of eight electrons, so do not gain or lose them.

now has only 10 electrons to balance the 11 protons in the nucleus. There is one positive charge left over. And so the sodium atom now has a charge of +1.

An atom with an electric charge is called an **ion**. Instead of a sodium atom we have a sodium ion. The sodium atom has the symbol Na (from its Latin name, *natrium*), and the sodium ion has the symbol Na⁺.

The chlorine atom, with an electron gained, now has 18 electrons but only 17 protons in the nucleus. It has one negative charge too many. So it, too, is an ion. But it is a negatively charged one. Its symbol is Cl⁻.

The properties of ions are different from those of neutral atoms. Sodium is a poisonous metal, and chlorine is a poisonous gas. But their ions are mild and gentle. When sodium and chlorine react together, they form ions. The ions in turn form crystals called sodium chloride. This is ordinary table salt.

When two chlorine atoms collide, something different happens. Each can pick up an electron, but neither is likely to give one up.

Instead, each contributes an electron to be shared with the other. The two atoms combine, sharing a pair of electrons. They form the molecule Cl_2. Here a chemical reaction takes place without the forming of ions.

The number of electrons transferred or shared depends on the arrangement of the electrons in the atom. It depends especially on the number of electrons in the outermost shell. Each atom can transfer or share a particular number of electrons. (That is, each element has a valence.)

Isotopes

All the atoms of a particular element have the same atomic number. But they may not all be completely alike. In addition to the protons in the nucleus, there are neutrons as well. And the neutrons may vary in number.

For instance, all chlorine atoms have 17 protons in the nucleus, and all have the atomic number of 17. Some chlorine atoms, however, have 18 neutrons in the nucleus, while some have 20.

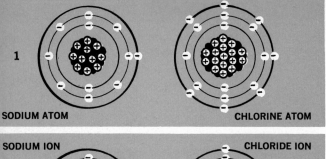

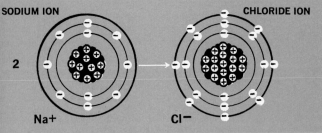

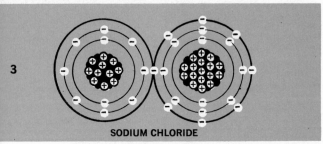

Above: (1) Sodium and chlorine atoms. (2) An atom of sodium easily loses an electron to chlorine, making them both ions. (3) The positive charge of the sodium ion attracts the negative charge of the chloride ion. The attraction binds the two together to form sodium chloride (table salt). Below: (A) Two atoms of chlorine form (B) a molecule of chlorine. Each atom can easily gain an electron, but will not give one up. Each shares one electron with the other atom.

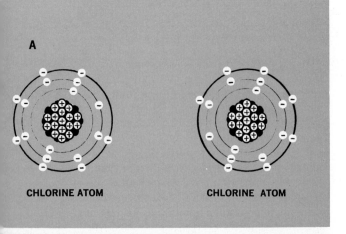

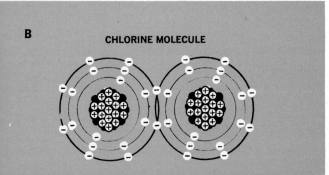

Protons all have the same mass. All neutrons have the same mass, too. And one proton is just about as massive as one neutron. Suppose you consider the mass of one neutron or one proton to be 1. Then you can work out the mass of an entire atom just by adding up the number of protons and neutrons in its nucleus. (The electrons are so light that they can be ignored.)

Chlorine atoms with 17 protons and 18 neutrons in the nucleus have a **mass number** of 35. Those with 17 protons and 20 neutrons in the nucleus have a mass number of 37. These two varieties of chlorine atom can be written as chlorine–35 and chlorine–37. Their symbols are Cl^{35} and Cl^{37}.

Both varieties have 17 electrons outside the nucleus to balance the 17 protons inside. (The neutrons have no electric charge and don't have to be balanced.) This means that both types of atom undergo the same chemical reactions. So they can be considered varieties of the same element. However, the more massive Cl^{37} is a little slower in its reactions than is the Cl^{35} atom. (Delicate instruments can tell one variety from the other.)

Atoms of the same element that differ only in their number of neutrons are called **isotopes**. In other words, Cl^{35} and Cl^{37} are two isotopes of chlorine.

These isotopes are well mixed throughout nature. For that reason, whenever a chemist prepares chlorine gas out of various chemicals, he ends with a mixture of these two isotopes. In this mixture there are three atoms of Cl^{35} for each atom of Cl^{37}. For that reason the average mass of the chlorine atoms in an actual sample of chlorine gas is about $35\frac{1}{2}$, and that is said to be the **atomic weight** of chlorine.

Some elements are made up of only a single variety of atom. Or they may have several varieties, but with one common and the others very rare. In that case the atomic weight of the element is just about the atomic weight of the common variety. The atomic weight is then just about a whole number. Thus the atomic

A chemical symbol contains many facts about an atom.

weight of hydrogen is just about 1; the atomic weight of helium is 4; that of oxygen is 16; of sodium 23; and so on.

▶ OTHER BRANCHES OF CHEMISTRY

This article lists just a few of the subjects that interest chemists. Actually, chemists' interests are spread so wide that chemistry overlaps other sciences.

For instance, the chemist can't help but be interested in some of the physical changes that chemicals undergo. He wants to know just what happens when water turns to steam—how much heat is taken up? What happens under pressure? How fast do reactions go, and what can be done to change the speed?

What happens when salt dissolves in water? And in what fashion does such a salt solution carry an electric current? The chemist studies all these subjects and many more by methods similar to those used by physicists. This branch of chemistry is called **physical chemistry**.

Chemistry also pushes in the direction of biology. Biologists are interested in living things. A chemist is interested in the study of the chemical reactions that go on in living creatures. This is **biochemistry**.

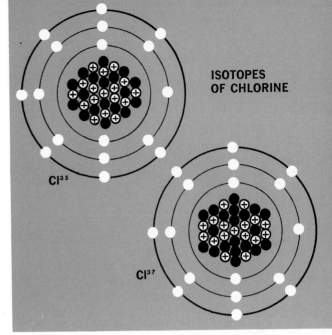

ISOTOPES OF CHLORINE

The Cl³⁷ isotope has two more neutrons than the Cl³⁵.

In fact, the range of subjects that interest chemists are so many and so various that it is almost impossible to describe them all.

ISAAC ASIMOV
Boston University School of Medicine

See also ATOMS; BIOCHEMISTRY; BODY CHEMISTRY; ELEMENTS.

CHEMISTRY, HISTORY OF

Long before the beginning of history, mankind was making use of chemical changes. Fire is the product of a chemical change—the burning of wood or other fuel in air. As soon as primitive man learned to start a fire, he was making use of a chemical change. With fire, he brought about more chemical changes. He cooked food and baked pottery. He heated sand and other substances into glass. He also brought about some chemical changes without fire. For example, fruit juice left standing in a warm, dark place changed into wine.

Somewhere in the Near East, perhaps around 4000 B.C., men discovered another kind of chemical change. They found that when certain types of rock were heated in a wood fire, shiny drops of copper were produced. Copper could be beaten into shape and made into ornaments and other objects.

Later a rock that produced tin was dis-

covered. When it was heated with copper ore, a copper-tin mixture—or alloy—formed. The alloy was bronze, and it was much harder than copper. A bronze shield was far better protection than a leather one. And a bronze-tipped spear was a better weapon than a stone-tipped one.

About 1400 B.C., methods for producing iron from ore were developed in Asia Minor. Iron weapons were even better than bronze ones.

Metal tools were useful in peacetime, too. They made it easier to construct buildings, to fight off wild beasts, and to fashion all sorts of laborsaving devices.

Meanwhile ancient peoples had worked out ways to get dyes from plants. They had also learned to make leather and to make cosmetics.

However, none of these ancient peoples

understood the chemical changes they were bringing about. By following a "recipe" they could get a certain result. But they never knew why the recipes worked.

▶ GREEK SCIENCE

The Greeks were the first people who tried to make sense out of chemical changes. They were the first to approach chemistry as a science. They studied what matter was made of. They studied how one kind of matter could be changed to another.

What was the earth made of—what were its elements? That question fascinated Greek men of science. Around 600 B.C. a Greek named Thales put forward his idea. He thought the whole world was made up of different forms of water. Earth, he said, was hardened water. Air was thinned-out water. This was the first chemical theory in history.

Other Greeks did not agree. For many years they argued. Then around 450 B.C. Empedocles suggested a different theory. He thought that there were four elements: earth, water, air, and fire. This seemed to be right, and the argument stopped.

About 100 years later Aristotle decided that these four elements made up only the earth itself. He said that the heavens were made up of a fifth element. He called it aether. Belief in these elements of the Greeks lasted over 2,000 years.

But what were elements made of? Around 400 B.C. Democritus had suggested that everything was made up of tiny particles. These particles were so tiny that they could not be divided up into smaller pieces. So he called them atoms, from a Greek word meaning "something that cannot be cut." Each element, he said, had atoms of a particular shape. Substances were made up of combinations of these atoms. How did one substance change

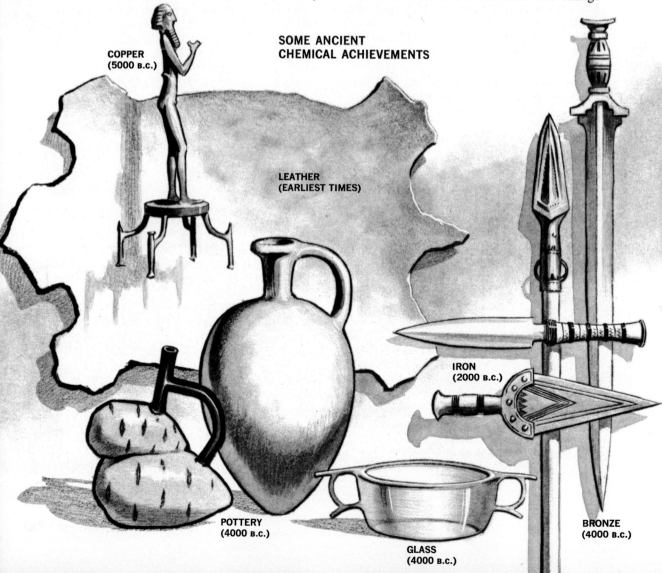

SOME ANCIENT
CHEMICAL ACHIEVEMENTS

COPPER
(5000 B.C.)

LEATHER
(EARLIEST TIMES)

IRON
(2000 B.C.)

POTTERY
(4000 B.C.)

GLASS
(4000 B.C.)

BRONZE
(4000 B.C.)

to another? It changed when the atoms were pulled apart and put together in another arrangement.

Democritus was on the right track. But most of the ancient Greeks didn't believe him. Aristotle thought atoms could not exist, and his arguments won out. However, men never entirely forgot Democritus' ideas. And more than 2,000 years later the idea of atoms was to rise again.

▶ ALCHEMY

In the time of Aristotle, Greeks spread into Egypt and Mesopotamia. And so, in the centuries that followed, the knowledge of those regions met and mixed with Greek theories.

For instance, Egyptian metalworkers knew how to make imitation gold by mixing copper with other metals. The mixture wasn't gold, of course, but it had the color of gold. However, a Greek theory said that gold and copper were really made of the same matter. They differed only in their "form." So it followed that one could make gold from copper or even from lead.

Naturally metalworkers began to try to make real gold. This was probably the beginning of a study called *chemia*. Exactly where this word comes from no one knows, but it is the root of our word "chemistry."

For many centuries the students of *chemia* tried to make gold out of other metals. But since this was impossible by the methods they used, they always failed.

As time passed, the Arabs became great conquerors. They won control of Mesopotamia and Egypt and much more. And they took up the study of *chemia*, which they called *al chemia* (*al* is Arabic for "the"). This expression has come down to us as "alchemy."

The most important Arabian alchemist was Jābir ibn-Hayyān. He lived about A.D. 750 and is also known by the Latin form of his name, Geber. He seems to have made a number of discoveries about ways to prepare chemicals. And it was he who started the search for a certain dry powder that came to be called the philosopher's stone. Alchemists

Each of these Greek thinkers had a different theory about the elements that make up the earth. Only Democritus believed matter was made of atoms.

THALES

WATER

EMPEDOCLES

FIRE

AIR

EARTH

WATER

ARISTOTLE

AETHER

THE EARTH

DEMOCRITUS

ATOMS

believed that it would turn other metals into gold. And they searched for it during hundreds of years.

Arabian alchemists did discover some important new chemical substances. Among these were ammonium chloride and certain strong alkalies. Most of their time, however, was spent searching for the philosopher's stone. And after the year 1000, Arabian alchemy came to an end.

However, by the 1100's Arabian books were reaching Europe. Books on alchemy (and many others) were translated into Latin. Europeans then began to search for the philosopher's stone.

European alchemists made some important discoveries, too. They learned to prepare pure alcohol. They prepared strong acids, such as sulfuric acid and nitric acid. These were much stronger than vinegar, which was the strongest acid used by the ancients and the Arabs. The strong acids could be used to bring about chemical changes never known before.

New materials were also studied. Arsenic was described around the year 1200. Later antimony, bismuth, and zinc were separated from minerals. But European alchemy also bogged down in the search for gold. In fact, so many people pretended they could make gold that "alchemist" came to be another word for "faker."

Fortunately by the 1500's a new spirit was on the rise.

▶ THE NEW SPIRIT

In the early 1500's there was a Swiss doctor who called himself Paracelsus. Paracelsus was an alchemist but not an ordinary one. He didn't think it was at all important to find methods for making gold. He thought that

While trying to change metals into gold, alchemists discovered important chemicals.

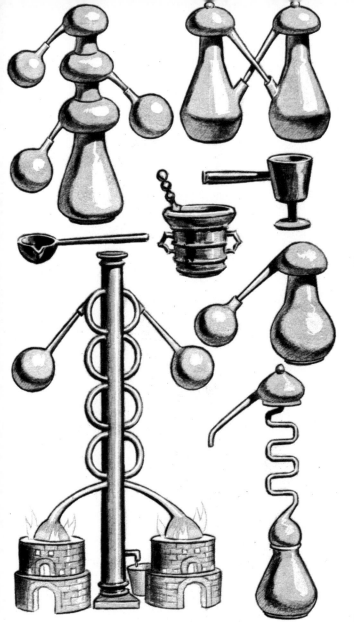

AIR —

MERCURY —

Robert Boyle measured pressure and volume of gases.

Left: Alchemists used odd-looking pieces of apparatus.

alchemists should search for medicines to cure sickness. He believed that ancient books on medicine were all wrong. So he gathered a few and burned them in the market place.

Paracelsus has a special value to the history of chemistry. He was not a great scientist, and some of his ideas were entirely wrong. But he wanted to put an end to ancient beliefs and start over. There he was right. He was also right in wanting to test ideas by experiments.

The experimental view slowly took hold. Paracelsus inspired men in his own field. And in other sciences great forward steps were being taken.

Beginning in the 1580's an Italian scientist named Galileo showed that it was very important to make accurate measurements. More could be learned in this way than in any other. His work in physics and astronomy helped to establish modern science.

In England a scientist named Robert Boyle greatly admired Galileo and his methods. Boyle tried to set up experiments that would measure the materials of alchemy.

For instance, one of Galileo's assistants, Torricelli, had shown that air has weight. Boyle trapped some air and put it under pressure. If he doubled the pressure, the air was forced into half its original space (or volume). If he tripled the pressure, the volume was reduced to a third. This discovery is still called Boyle's law, and with it exact measurement entered the world of chemistry.

Boyle published a book in 1661. In it he exploded the old Greek idea of four or five elements. He offered a new idea based on experiment. If a substance could be broken up into simpler substances, it was not an element. If it could not be broken up into simpler substances, it was an element. One could find out only by trying to break up the substance. Boyle's book was called *The Sceptical Chymist*. His book did much to establish modern chemistry.

Phlogiston

The most useful branch of European alchemy had been the heating of ore to obtain metal. For that reason the new chemists were very interested in finding out what happened when wood or coal burned. They were equally interested in what happened when rocky ores turned into shiny metals.

A German chemist named Georg E. Stahl had an idea, which he advanced around 1700. His idea centered on something that he called phlogiston. Anything, he said, that was full of phlogiston could burn. Wood and coal were full of phlogiston, and so they burned. As they burned, the phlogiston passed out into the air. The ashes that were left behind lacked phlogiston and could burn no more.

Stahl also thought that metals were full of phlogiston. When they rusted, they lost phlogiston to the air. So the rust that was produced lacked phlogiston.

The phlogiston theory seemed to explain how metals were obtained from ore. The phlogiston from burning wood or coal passed into the ore, which is a kind of metal rust. As the phlogiston left the coal or wood, that became ash. As the phlogiston entered the ore, that became metal.

This theory was important all through the 1700's. And it was used when chemists tried to explain the behavior of air.

One of the last of the alchemists was a Belgian named Jan Baptista van Helmont. He had discovered that there were several kinds of airlike materials. He was the first to study carbon dioxide (one kind of airlike material)

and to show that candles wouldn't burn in it. He invented the word "gas" for all airlike vapors.

When chemists came to study the air itself, they found that they could change its properties. In 1772 a Scottish chemist named Daniel Rutherford carried out this experiment. He burned a candle in a trapped volume of air until it went out. The candle would burn no more in the air. It would not burn even after the carbon dioxide formed during the burning had been removed by chemicals. Rutherford thought the air had taken up so much phlogiston while the candle was burning that it could hold no more. That was why the candle would no longer burn in it, he decided.

In 1774 a British chemist named Joseph Priestley heated a red powder that is now called mercuric oxide. From this he obtained a gas in which wood burned furiously. He thought the gas was air that had been emptied of all its phlogiston. Therefore it accepted phlogiston readily and made things burn quickly. Meanwhile another British chemist, Henry Cavendish, was studying a very light gas. It burned so easily that he thought it was phlogiston itself.

The Father of Chemistry

It was a French chemist, Antoine L. Lavoisier, who made sense out of the phlogiston mystery in the 1700's. He insisted that one must measure things as Galileo had done and as Boyle had done. For instance, when wood burned and supposedly lost phlogiston, it lost weight. When metal rusted and lost phlogiston, it gained weight. How could phlogiston bring about a loss sometimes and a gain at other times? Something had to be wrong. The only way to straighten things out was to measure.

Lavoisier heated metal in a closed container. Although the metal rusted, the container and metal did not change in weight. If the metal gained weight as it rusted, then something else in the container must have lost just enough weight to balance the gain. The something else had to be the air in the container. In other words, a metal wasn't losing phlogiston when it rusted. It was gaining something from the air.

Lavoisier decided that phlogiston could not be involved. Instead, air must be made up of two different gases. Priestley's gas, in which

Left: Joseph Priestley discovered oxygen in 1774. Above: Henry Cavendish discovered hydrogen in 1766.

In 1775 Antoine Lavoisier burned tin and found that it grew heavier as the air volume decreased. This showed that burning materials combine with oxygen.

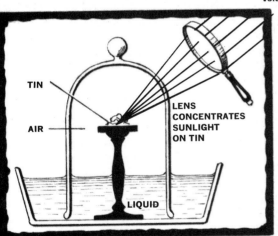

TIN

AIR

LENS CONCENTRATES SUNLIGHT ON TIN

LIQUID

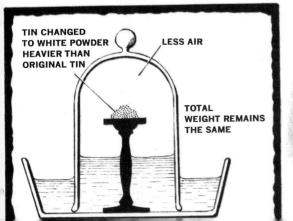

TIN CHANGED TO WHITE POWDER HEAVIER THAN ORIGINAL TIN

LESS AIR

TOTAL WEIGHT REMAINS THE SAME

things burned well, he called oxygen. Rutherford's gas, in which things didn't burn at all, was called nitrogen. Since a candle used up one fifth of the air before it went out, the air was one-fifth oxygen and four-fifths nitrogen.

Cavendish had found that his light gas burned in air to form water. Lavoisier at once called the gas hydrogen (water-former).

If a candle burned, Lavoisier explained, it didn't really disappear. The carbon and hydrogen in it combined with the oxygen of the air. They formed carbon dioxide gas and water vapor. If the candle burned in a closed vessel, the weight of the candle and vessel did not change.

Lavoisier argued that matter is never created or destroyed. It only changes its form. This is the law of conservation of matter.

Lavoisier went on to write the first modern textbook of chemistry. He, along with several others, made up a system for naming chemicals that is still used. The system finally made it possible for chemists to understand each other. For all these deeds Lavoisier has been called the father of chemistry.

▶ THE ATOMIC THEORY

By Lavoisier's time some new theory was needed to account for the discoveries being made by chemists. Look, for example, at the problem raised by Boyle's new definition of an element.

In the middle 1600's a German alchemist named Hennig Brand was looking for the secret of long life. He happened on a waxy substance that glowed in the dark. He called it phosphorus (light-bearer). It proved to be a new element, according to Boyle's definition, for it could not be broken down into simpler substances. It was the first element known to be discovered by a particular man at a particular time.

During the 1700's more elements were discovered. Some were metals such as cobalt, nickel, molybdenum, and manganese. The gases called oxygen, nitrogen, and hydrogen were also elements. By 1800 some 30 different elements were known. And this raised a problem.

Chemists had to explain why elements remained different. Iron and nickel, for instance, were very similar in some ways. Yet one could not be changed entirely into the other. They always stayed a little different. For one thing, iron formed a flaky red-brown rust, and nickel did not.

Then, too, Boyle had shown that air could be squeezed into a smaller volume. And that started chemists thinking about atoms again. If air could be squeezed together, it must consist of particles with empty space between.

In the late 1700's chemists began to measure more and more things accurately. They found that two elements always combined in definite proportions. For instance, 1 ounce of hydrogen always combines with 8 ounces of oxygen to form water. But the amount must be 8 ounces—it cannot be $7\frac{1}{2}$, $8\frac{1}{2}$, or any other amount.

In 1803 the British chemist John Dalton advanced an atomic theory. The theory was something like the one put forward by Democritus over 2,000 years before. But Democritus had only guessed. Dalton had carried out experiments and made measurements.

Dalton said that everything was made of atoms. Each element was made up of a different kind of atom. And one kind of atom could not be changed into another. That was why iron could not be changed into nickel, or lead into gold. All four were elements. Each had its own special kind of atom.

The atoms of different elements, Dalton said, had different weights. For instance, suppose 1 atom of hydrogen combined with 1 atom of oxygen to form water. And suppose the oxygen atom was 8 times as heavy as the hydrogen atom. Then 1 ounce of hydrogen would combine with exactly 8 ounces of oxygen, no more and no less.

Dalton tried to work out the different weights of the atoms (atomic weights), starting with hydrogen as 1.

However, he made some mistakes. For example, certain electrical experiments showed that 2 hydrogen atoms combined with 1 oxygen atom to form water. This meant that the oxygen atom was eight times as heavy as 2 hydrogen atoms together. That is, it was 16 times as heavy as a single hydrogen atom.

In the 1820's a Swedish chemist, Jöns Jakob Berzelius, analyzed many substances carefully. He measured exactly how much of each element was present in each substance. From such experiments he calculated quite accurate atomic weights.

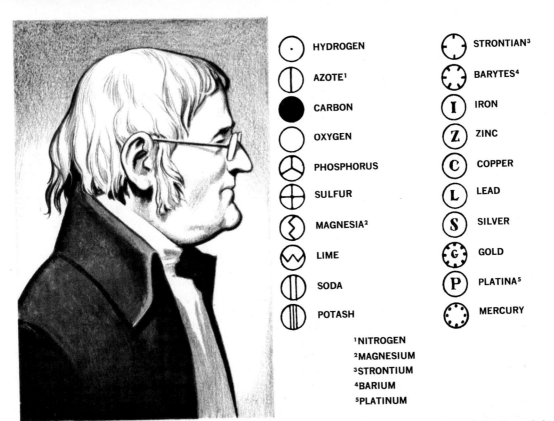

⊙	HYDROGEN	⊕	STRONTIAN[3]
⊘	AZOTE[1]	⊕	BARYTES[4]
●	CARBON	Ⓘ	IRON
○	OXYGEN	Ⓩ	ZINC
⊛	PHOSPHORUS	Ⓒ	COPPER
⊕	SULFUR	Ⓛ	LEAD
⊗	MAGNESIA[2]	Ⓢ	SILVER
⊗	LIME	Ⓖ	GOLD
⊕	SODA	Ⓟ	PLATINA[5]
⊕	POTASH	⊛	MERCURY

[1]NITROGEN
[2]MAGNESIUM
[3]STRONTIUM
[4]BARIUM
[5]PLATINUM

In 1803 John Dalton proposed the atomic theory and made a chart of atomic symbols.

Berzelius also suggested that each element be given a chemical symbol. This was usually the initial letter of the name of the element; sometimes a second letter was used, too. That is, the symbol of oxygen is O, while the symbol of aluminum is Al. These symbols could be used to write the formulas of substances. A formula told what atoms combined to make up a particular substance.

The Periodic Table

While this was going on chemists found new tools with which to sharpen their search for more elements. For example, in 1800 an Italian scientist, Alessandro Volta, had invented the chemical cell (battery). He discovered he could arrange two metals in such a way as to start an electric current flowing. Chemists quickly made a discovery. By passing an electric current through water, they could tear apart the water molecule. (A molecule is a tightly bound combination of atoms.) Hydrogen and oxygen were produced.

Chemists were sure that certain substances contained atoms of unknown metals. However, these metal atoms could not be pried loose from oxygen atoms. In 1807 the British chemist Humphry Davy melted such substances. Then he passed an electric current through the hot liquid. This, separated the atoms. And he discovered new metallic elements, such as sodium, potassium, calcium, and magnesium.

More elements were discovered by other methods. Aluminum was discovered. So were bromine, iodine, selenium, and others. By the 1860's about 60 different elements were known. And there was no sign of an end. How could chemists make sense out of all these elements? Some were metals, and some were gases. Some were hard to combine with other elements, while some were easy. Some were heavy, and some were light.

Chemists tried to arrange the elements in the order of their atomic weights. Perhaps then they could make sense out of the list. The most successful arranger was a Russian chemist, Dmitri I. Mendeleev. In 1869 he arranged the elements in rows and columns. In his arrangement all the elements in a group had similar properties. This is called a periodic table.

To make the elements fit properly, Mendeleev had to leave some empty places. He announced that these empty places contained elements that had not yet been discovered. He picked three such elements in particular. And then he figured out what their properties would have to be. In the 1870's and 1880's those three elements were discovered. They matched Mendeleev's predictions exactly. At last the elements were beginning to make sense.

ORGANIC CHEMISTRY

Meanwhile chemists had come to realize that chemical substances could be divided into two chief classes. Some, such as salt and water, could be heated and neither burn nor change their nature. They might melt or boil, but if cooled down, they were their original selves again. However, substances like sugar and olive oil changed. If heated, they either burned or else charred and gave off vapors. In either case, even gentle heating changed their nature.

Substances like sugar and olive oil came from living or once-living organisms. So in 1807 Berzelius suggested they be called organic. Substances like salt and water came from the nonliving world. They were inorganic.

At first chemists believed that organic chemicals could be formed only within living creatures. However, in 1828 a German chemist named Friedrich Wöhler showed this was not true. He formed urea (an organic substance) from ammonium cyanate (an inorganic substance). And he did it in a test tube. Through the 1830's and 1840's other organic substances were formed in this way. Some of them turned out not to be present in organisms at all but were so similar to ordinary organic substances that they had to be classified with them. Such a discovery was made in 1856 by an 18-year-old English chemist named William H. Perkin. He formed an organic substance that could be used as a dye. It was a synthetic dye (one made in the laboratory). It was not found in nature, and it was better than any dye that was found in nature.

The trouble at first was that chemists working with organic chemicals were in the dark in some ways. Molecules of organic substances were more complicated than molecules of inorganic ones. Even a simple organic molecule might contain a couple of dozen atoms.

And chemists didn't know enough about how these atoms might be arranged.

In 1852, however, a British chemist named Edward Frankland had worked out a theory of valence. It dealt with the bonds that hold atoms together. During the 1860's the German chemist Friedrich A. Kekulé began to write formulas in which valences were shown. In 1875 the Dutch chemist Jacobus H. van't Hoff explained how valence bonds should be thought of. They were not flat, as shown on paper. Rather, they had three dimensions.

These advances clarified the thinking of chemists. The arrangements of the atoms within a molecule were worked out. And methods for changing those arrangements were discovered.

From 1860 on organic chemists began to put atoms together in many ways. They learned to manufacture all sorts of new compounds. Some could be used for dyes, others for explosives, medicines, plastics, fibers—indeed, for almost anything.

Organic chemistry no longer concentrated on compounds formed by living organisms. After all, thousands upon thousands of organic compounds were being formed and studied. And these were never found in living creatures. Organic chemists were content to deal with any compound that contained carbon. Inorganic chemists dealt with all other compounds—those that did not contain carbon.

However, life-chemistry did not lose its importance. A new branch of chemistry was developing. Its interest centered mainly on the chemical changes in living creatures. This was **biochemistry** (life-chemistry).

PHYSICAL CHEMISTRY

As chemistry had been developing so had the science of physics. Physics deals with various forms of energy, such as heat, light, electricity, and magnetism. From about 1850 on, chemists began to apply the findings of physics to chemistry. In this way physical chemistry was developed.

For instance, physicists knew what happened if sunlight passed through a prism. It broke up into a series of colors, called a spectrum. In 1859 a German chemist, Gustav R. Kirchhoff, made an interesting discovery. He showed that each element, when heated red hot, produced a spectrum made up of separate lines of color. An instrument called the spectroscope allowed the light of a glowing mineral to shine through a narrow slit. The light was passed through a prism. And then the exact location of the different color lines was measured. Each element had its own pattern of lines. This meant that the different elements in the mineral could be detected.

Unknown elements were located by this method—that is, their color lines revealed them. In 1868, for example, the element helium was located in the sun by a study of the lines in the sun's spectrum. It was not located on earth until 1895.

A number of chemists began studying the heat involved in certain chemical changes. During the 1870's an American chemist, Josiah W. Gibbs, worked out a theory known as chemical thermodynamics. Through it chemists began to understand a great deal about why chemicals behaved as they did.

Physical chemistry also concerned itself with the relationship between electricity and chemistry. An electric current will pass through some solutions but not others. Why? A Swedish chemist, Svante A. Arrhenius, made a suggestion in 1884 about the molecules of certain substances, such as salt. When these substances dissolved in water, their molecules broke up into atoms or groups of atoms. These atoms carried electric charges. Such charged atoms are called ions. Ions can be made to move in a solution by an electric current. The movement allows the electric current to pass through the solution. If a substance does not break up into ions when it dissolves, the solution will not carry an electric current.

Each of these scientists discovered something about the structure of the atom. All their discoveries put together give us an idea of what the atom looks like.

ANTOINE HENRI BECQUEREL

J. J. THOMSON

MARIE CURIE

ERNEST RUTHERFORD

NIELS BOHR

215

Two important discoveries made in the late 1800's provided clues to the structure of the atom. In 1896 a French scientist, Antoine Henri Becquerel, discovered that the element uranium gave off a constant stream of electrons and other kinds of intense energy. This energy became known as radioactivity. In 1898 the Polish-born French scientist Marie Curie discovered two more radioactive elements, polonium and radium. The work of Becquerel and Curie seemed to show that atoms might be made of smaller particles, some of which were electrons.

▶CHEMISTRY IN THE TWENTIETH CENTURY

In 1909 the new picture of the structure of the atom fell into place. The British scientist Ernest Rutherford found that each atom had a nucleus, containing positively charged particles called protons. Circling the nucleus were electrons that were negatively charged. Then in 1914 another British scientist, Henry G. J. Moseley, found that the atoms of each element had a special number of protons in the nucleus. In 1913 Danish scientist Niels Bohr had discovered that the electrons of each atom were arranged in layers. These electron layers determined the valence of the atom.

In 1919, Rutherford discovered that atoms could be changed by blasting them with speeding particles from radioactive elements. If the particle made a solid hit on the nucleus of the atom, the atom could change into a different atom. Using such nuclear reactions, chemists were able to make the atoms of new elements not found on earth.

In the 1940's and 1950's, techniques were found to tap the energy within the nucleus of the atom. This intense nuclear energy was found to be useful both for weapons and for producing electricity. In the late 1960's, scientists began looking more carefully at the energy in the atom. They theorized that a particle smaller than the proton, called the quark, might be the atom's energy source.

In the mid-20th century scientists found ways to make very pure chemical crystals of germanium and silicon. These crystals had valuable qualities. The crystals could conduct electricity, making it possible to build tiny electronic devices such as pocket calculators and very small television sets. Silicon crystals and other forms of silicon were found to be useful for changing the sun's energy into badly needed electricity.

Biochemistry became more and more important as its vital role in physiology became known. Newer instruments and techniques enabled scientists to determine the structure of large complicated protein molecules. Once they knew the structure of these molecules, biochemists could make many chemicals that until then were produced only by living organisms. They were able to make chemicals such as insulin, needed by diabetics, and one kind of globulin, needed by persons with low resistance to infection.

Similar work provided the structure of DNA (deoxyribonucleic acid), the complex protein in the nucleus of the cell that directs all the activities of the cell. This understanding of the chemistry of the cell's control center opened many new frontiers for 20th-century chemists and biologists.

ISAAC ASIMOV
Boston University School of Medicine
See also ATOMS; BIOCHEMISTRY; ELEMENTS; NUCLEAR ENERGY; PHYSICS.

CHEMISTRY, SOME TERMS OF

ACID: A substance that releases hydrogen ions when dissolved in water. The more hydrogen ions formed, the stronger the acid. Some very strong acids are hydrochloric acid (HCl), nitric acid (HNO_3), and sulfuric acid (H_2SO_4). The sour taste of lemons, vinegar, and some other foods is caused by the weak acids they contain.

ALCOHOL: An organic substance with a molecule that contains an oxygen and hydrogen atom in combination (–OH). The most common alcohol is ethyl alcohol (C_2H_5OH), which is found in beer and wine.

ALKALI: A strong base. That is, it has a strong tendency to combine with hydrogen ions. Two examples are sodium hydroxide ($NaOH$) and potassium hydroxide (KOH).

ALKALI METALS: A family of soft, silvery-

RED CABBAGE AS AN ACID-BASE INDICATOR

With some red-cabbage water you can test a chemical to see if it is an acid or a base.

Above: Boil a red cabbage in a quart of water for 15 minutes. Allow it to cool. Right: Strain the water into a large jar.

Above: Place 2 tablespoons of cabbage water in a jar and add a teaspoon of lemon juice. Left: The color change from purple to red shows lemon is acid.

Above: Add a tablespoon of ammonia to half a glass of cabbage water. Left: The color will change from purple to blue, showing that ammonia is a base.

white metals that react very readily with other substances. They have a strong tendency to give up electrons in chemical reactions. Lithium, sodium, and potassium are alkali metals.

ALLOTROPES: Different forms of a particular element. The element carbon, for instance, can occur as graphite or diamond. These are allotropes of carbon.

ALLOY: A mixture of metals. Bronze is an alloy of copper and tin. Brass is an alloy of copper and zinc. Steel is an alloy of iron with a variety of other elements.

AMALGAM: An alloy containing mercury. The "silver" used in filling teeth is really a silver amalgam.

ANALYSIS: Testing to find out what a substance is made of—what atoms or groups of atoms make up its molecules. When salt is analyzed, it is found to contain the elements sodium and chlorine. When the exact amount of each element present is determined, the testing is called **quantitative analysis**.

ATOM: The smallest particle that can take part in a chemical reaction. All substances are made up of atoms. Each element is made up of a particular kind of atom.

ATOMIC NUMBER: The number of protons in each atom of an element. Each element has its own particular atomic number. The atomic number of hydrogen, for instance, is 1; the atomic number of oxygen is 8; and the atomic number of uranium is 92.

ATOMIC WEIGHT: The average weight of the atoms of a particular element. Such weight is not absolute, but relative to the most common type of carbon atom. This atom is given a weight of exactly 12. Then the atomic weight of hydrogen, for example, is 1.00797; the atomic weight of oxygen is 15.9994; and the atomic weight of uranium is 238.03. (On the carbon-equals-12 basis, the protons and neutrons each have a mass of about 1. Atomic weight is sometimes calculated by adding the protons and the neutrons of the nucleus. The result of this addition is sometimes called the mass number.)

BASE: Any substance with a molecule that will combine with hydrogen ions. A base is the opposite of an acid, which gives off hydrogen ions. In solution a base will neutralize an acid, and the combination is neither acid nor base. Ammonia (NH_3) is a rather weak base. A strong base is also called an alkali.

BOND: The force holding two neighboring atoms together; occurs when atoms share electrons or when electrons are transferred from one atom to another.

CATALYST: A substance that increases the speed of a chemical reaction. The catalyst is not used up in the course of the reaction; therefore only a small quantity is needed. **Catalysis** is the name of the process.

COMBUSTION: A chemical reaction that produces heat and usually light as well. The combination of coal or oil with the oxygen of the air is the most common form of combustion.

COMPOUND: A substance made up of molecules containing atoms of two or more elements. Examples are water (H_2O), sodium bicarbonate ($NaHCO_3$), and salt ($NaCl$).

COVALENT BOND: The type of linkage between two neighboring atoms that is produced when pairs of electrons are shared. The linkage in molecules such as those of carbon dioxide (CO_2) and chloroform ($CHCl_3$) is covalent.

CRYSTAL: A solid body with a definite, regular shape and flat sides. This shape results from the orderly arrangement of the atoms or molecules making up the solid. Substances such as salt and sugar form crystals.

DISTILLATION: The process of turning a liquid to vapor by careful boiling and then cooling the vapor so that it becomes liquid again. The liquid may thus be separated from salts or other impurities that will not turn to vapor. Thus if ocean water is boiled, only the water will form a vapor while the salt remains behind. The vapor can be cooled to form pure water without salt. In this way distillation can produce fresh water from sea water.

ELECTROLYTE: A substance that, when it is dissolved, can carry an electric current. Examples are sodium chloride, potassium nitrate, sulfuric acid. A solution of sugar will not carry an electric current; so sugar is a "nonelectrolyte."

ELECTRON: An atomic particle that carries a negative electric charge. It is found in the outer regions of the atom.

ELECTROVALENT BOND: The type of linkage between two neighboring atoms that is produced when electrons are transferred from one atom to another. The atom losing the electrons becomes a positively charged ion. The one gaining the electrons becomes a negatively charged ion. The two ions are held together by the attraction of the opposite charges. The atoms in sodium chloride (NaCl), for instance, are ions held together by an electrovalent bond.

ELEMENT: A substance made up of atoms that all have the same atomic number. Examples are oxygen, hydrogen, iron, copper, gold, and radium.

EQUATION, CHEMICAL: An expression of the way in which a chemical change takes place, making use of the symbols of the elements. For instance, hydrogen and oxygen combine to form water, and this may be shown by the equation $2H_2 + O_2 \rightarrow 2H_2O$.

FORMULA, CHEMICAL: An expression of the makeup of a substance, using the symbols of the elements. The formula of sulfuric acid is H_2SO_4. This means its molecule contains 2 atoms of hydrogen, 1 atom of sulfur, and 4 atoms of oxygen.

GAS: A form of matter in which the atoms or molecules are so far apart that they hardly affect each other. Each atom or molecule moves in its own fashion. A gas has no definite shape and does not take up a definite amount of space. The most common gas is air.

HALOGENS: A family of colored nonmetallic elements that react very readily with other substances. They have a strong tendency to gain electrons in chemical reactions.

INERT: Describes a substance that does not easily combine with other substances. Gold, platinum, nitrogen, neon, and glass are all inert substances. A substance that does combine easily is "active." Oxygen and sodium are active substances.

INORGANIC SUBSTANCE: One that does not contain carbon atoms as part of its main structure. Water, salt, and glass are examples of inorganic substances.

ION: Any atom or group of atoms that carries either a positive or a negative electric charge. Examples are sodium ion (Na^+), chloride ion (Cl^-), and sulfate ion ($SO_4^=$). A negatively charged ion may be called an **anion**; a postitively charged ion, a **cation**.

ISOMERS: Two or more substances with molecules containing the same types of atoms in the same numbers but in a different arrangement. Examples are ethyl alcohol (C_2H_5OH) and dimethyl ether (CH_3OCH_3); each has 2 carbon atoms, 6 hydrogen atoms, and 1 oxygen atom, but they are arranged differently.

ISOTOPES: Two or more types of atoms with the same atomic number but different mass numbers. Isotopes have different numbers of neutrons in their nuclei but the same number of protons. Chlorine, for example, is made up of two isotopes, Cl^{35} and Cl^{37}.

LIQUID: A form of matter in which the atoms or molecules are close together. So a particular quantity of liquid takes up a definite amount of space. However, the atoms or molecules in a liquid are not held tightly together but can move freely. For that reason, liquids have no definite shape. The most common liquid is water.

MASS: A simple way of describing mass is to say that it is the quantity of matter in any object. If two objects are weighed under the same conditions, the object with the greater mass weighs more.

MASS NUMBER: The number of neutrons plus the number of protons in the nucleus of an atom. The fluorine atom, for instance, has 9 protons and 10 neutrons in its nucleus. It has an atomic number of 9 and a mass number of 19.

MATTER: Anything that occupies space and has mass.

METAL: An element or mixture of elements that has the following special properties: it possesses a particular kind of shine called metallic luster; it can be beaten into shape without breaking; it can be drawn out into wires; it will carry an electric current; it will conduct heat easily. Examples of metals are silver, copper, chromium, iron, and aluminum. Substances that are "nonmetals" are, for example, sulfur, glass, water, and salt.

MINERAL: A substance that occurs in nature, that has a particular crystal form, and that is made up of particular elements in a definite proportion. Hematite, a common iron ore, is an example of a mineral.

MOLECULAR WEIGHT: The weight of a molecule as determined by adding the atomic weights of the various atoms making it up. Since the atomic weight of hydrogen is about 1 and the atomic weight of oxygen is about 16, the molecular weight of water (H_2O) is 1 plus 1 plus 16—18.

MOLECULE: A group of atoms that remain together and act as a unit. The molecule of oxygen is O_2 and of water is H_2O.

NEUTRAL: (1) Neither acid nor base. Water is neutral because it is neither acid nor base. (2) Carrying neither a positive electric charge nor a negative one. An iron atom is neutral because it carries neither a positive nor a negative charge.

NEUTRON: An atomic particle found in the nuclei of all atoms except the common variety of hydrogen atom. It carries no electric charge. It is much smaller in size than the smallest atom (hydrogen) but has about the same weight.

NUCLEUS, ATOMIC: A tiny central region of the atom. It contains all the protons and neutrons of the atom. Almost all the mass of the atom is in the nucleus.

ORGANIC SUBSTANCE: One that contains carbon atoms as a main part of its structure. The first substances of this type that were studied had been formed by living organisms. That is how the name arose.

PERIODIC TABLE: An arrangement of the elements in order of atomic number, placed in rows and columns in such a way that the elements having similar properties are grouped together.

PLASTIC: Any material that, while soft, can be molded to some desired shape; allowed to harden, it will keep the shape. Glass is an inorganic plastic. Bakelite is an organic plastic.

POLYMER: A substance composed of large molecules built up of a number of small units strung together. Rubber is a polymer; so are nylon, Bakelite, and other fibers and plastics.

PRECIPITATE: A solid formed in a solvent in which it will not dissolve; it settles out as fine particles. If a solution of barium nitrate $(Ba(NO_3)_2)$ is added to a solution of sodium sulfate (Na_2SO_4), barium sulfate $(BaSO_4)$ is formed. Barium sulfate is insoluble in water, and it settles out as a precipitate.

PROTON: An atomic particle found in the nuclei of all atoms. It carries a positive electric charge. It is much smaller in size than the smallest atom (hydrogen) but has about the same weight.

REACTION, CHEMICAL: Any chemical change.

SALT: A compound that is formed when an acid reacts with a base. When hydrochloric acid (HCl) reacts with the base sodium hydroxide (NaOH), sodium chloride (NaCl) is formed. Sodium chloride is ordinary table salt and gives its name to all other substances formed in this way.

SOLID: A form of matter in which the atoms or molecules are close together, as in liquids, but are held tightly in place as well. For this reason, a solid does not change its shape easily. The most common solids are the rocks that make up the earth's crust.

SOLUTION: A liquid (or **solvent**) that contains a solid, a gas, or another liquid (a **solute**) thoroughly mixed with it; they are so thoroughly mixed that the solute is present as separate atoms or molecules. The most common solvent is water. Solids such as salt or sugar, liquids such as alcohol, and gases such as ammonia all easily dissolve in water.

STRUCTURAL FORMULA: A formula that shows the arrangement of atoms in a molecule. The structural formula of ethyl alcohol is:

$$\begin{array}{ccc} & H & H \\ & | & | \\ H- & C- & C-O-H \\ & | & | \\ & H & H \end{array}$$

SYMBOL, CHEMICAL: A sign used to represent an element or its atom. These usually consist of the initial letter of the element; sometimes a second letter is also used. Examples are C for carbon, Cl for chlorine, N for nitrogen, Ne for neon, Fe for iron (from its Latin name, *ferrum*), and so on.

SYNTHESIS: The combining of simple molecules by chemists in such a way as to produce more complicated molecules. For instance, the giant molecule nylon can be synthesized by starting with a number of two different kinds of small molecules; these are treated in such a way that they hook together into long chains.

VALENCE: The number of bonds by which an atom of a particular element usually combines with other atoms; this occurs when atoms either transfer electrons or share them. For example, the valence of carbon is four, that of nitrogen is three, that of oxygen is two, and that of hydrogen is one.

Isaac Asimov
Boston University School of Medicine

CHERRY. See PEACH, PLUM, AND CHERRY.

CHESS

Chess is the most popular war game ever invented. The kings and queens who lead the two chess armies must face all kinds of dangerous situations. They are attacked and defended by castles, bishops, knights on horseback, and common soldiers. Eventually one of the kings is trapped and he must surrender to the other army. Every new game of chess is a different battle, and the two players are the generals who plan the battle.

Since its origin in India and Persia more than 13 centuries ago, chess, the "royal game," has provided many exciting hours of play for both children and adults.

The word "chess" is derived from the Persian word *shah,* which means "king." The term "checkmate," signifying that the enemy king is threatened and cannot be saved, can be traced to an Arabic phrase, *shah mat,* which means "the king is dead."

Many English words that are used in the game of chess, like "checkmate," "stalemate," "pawn," and "gambit," have become important words in our everyday language. You will find them used often by television commentators and newspaper columnists in describing political or military struggles.

Chess is extremely popular in the Soviet Union; chess heroes there are as famous as baseball heroes are in the United States. Russian masters have won many world championships since the end of World War II.

Even though many people think that chess is very complicated, its rules are really easier to learn than the rules of many other indoor games. Almost all the world's great players—the international grandmasters of chess—learned the moves and were strong players before they were 16. Bobby Fischer, an international grandmaster and world champion, won his first title as United States champion when he was only 14 years old and just entering high school.

Chess can be played at a variety of speeds. Youngsters as well as masters often enjoy playing at "lightning" speed, allowing only 1 to 10 seconds for each move. Under these regulations most games are completed within 15 minutes. Friendly games between amateurs of equal strength, played with no specific time limit, usually last about an hour. In inter-

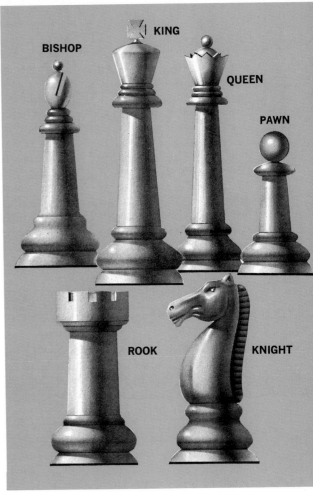

BISHOP · KING · QUEEN · PAWN · ROOK · KNIGHT

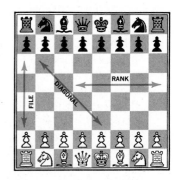

Chessboard set up for play (*left*). At right, the board, showing file, rank, and diagonal.

national and world title competition, there are automatic clocks that control the amount of time taken by each player. These serious matches normally last about 4 hours—which means an average of 3 or 4 minutes a move.

The Fédération Internationale des Echecs (FIDE) is the world-wide organization of chess players. It has members from more than 65 countries, as far apart as Australia and Iceland, or the Philippines and Tunisia. The United States Chess Federation (USCF) controls chess rules and activities in the United States.

There are tournaments in different sections of the United States and Canada almost every weekend. These events are ordinarily open to anyone who wishes to play, regardless of age or playing experience. Most of these tournaments are rated by the USCF according to a numerical system, and everyone who enters such a tournament receives a national rating that depends on his performance in that tournament. Thousands of active chess players hold national USCF ratings, and every year hundreds of newcomers are added to the list. Usually there are about 150 players who hold the rank of either senior master or master. Many more players have lower ratings, which range from expert down to classes A,B,C, etc.

▶ **THE RULES OF CHESS**

The rules of chess have been a subject for special study by mathematicians, military strategists, psychologists, and even by designers of modern electronic computers.

The Pieces

There are two opposing sides in chess, one consisting of light-colored (white) pieces and the other of dark-colored (black) pieces.

Each side has 16 pieces. The eight more important of these pieces are the king, the queen, two rooks (or castles), two bishops, and two knights. The other eight pieces in each army are the pawns.

The Board

The chessboard is the same as the checkerboard. It has 64 squares, 32 light-colored (white) and 32 dark-colored (black). All 64 squares are used in playing chess.

The board is always placed so that the first row ends with a white square on each player's right. The eight rows that run vertically between the two players are called **files.** The eight horizontal rows that run from left to right are called **ranks.** Straight lines of the same-colored squares running in a slantwise direction are called **diagonals.**

Setting Up the Board

At the start of a game, the two rooks occupy the extreme right and left squares of the first rank; the two knights stand next to the rooks; the two bishops are placed next to the knights; the queen is "on her color" (that is, the white queen on a white square and the black queen on a black square); and the king stands on the one remaining square along the first rank. When you set up the pieces in this way, the white queen will be on the same file as the black queen, and the white king on the same file as the black king. The pawns are then lined up in the rank directly in front of the more important pieces.

The Moves of the Pieces

Much of the variety and excitement of chess is due to the fact that each type of piece moves in a different manner. Each piece has a real personality of its own. You should become very familiar with the moves of each piece before you try to play an actual game.

The King. Although the king is the most important piece in chess and must always be protected from capture, he is not the most powerful and active piece on the board. The king may move only to a square that touches the one on which he stands. Thus, in the diagram the king on square A can move to any one of eight different squares, whereas the king on square B can only move to one of three different squares.

The Rook. The chess castle can move any number of squares left or right along an unblocked rank or up and down an unblocked file. In the diagram the rook on square C can move to and stop on any one of 14 different squares. The rook on square D, however, has a choice among only 12, since the white pawn blocks its movement further along the file.

The Bishop. The bishop may move any number of squares along an unblocked diagonal. Therefore, a bishop that starts a game on a black square will remain on the black squares throughout the game. In the diagram the bishop on square E can move to any one of 13 squares and the bishop on square F to any one of seven.

The Queen. The queen is the most powerful of all the pieces. She can move horizontally, vertically, or diagonally any number of squares along a line that is not blocked. In other words the queen combines the moves of the rook and bishop. In the diagram the queen on square G can move to any one of 25 squares.

The Knight. The horse-shaped knight is the favorite piece of many players because of its very mysterious way of moving. The knight's move will remind you of the letter L: it moves two squares in either a horizontal or vertical direction and then one square in the other direction. The knight on square H in the diagram can move to any one of eight squares; the knight on square I to only one of two. A knight standing on a white square always ends up on a black square after its move, and vice versa. Unlike the other pieces the knight can jump over pieces between its original square and the square to which it moves. However, it can only capture enemy pieces that are standing on the square it finally lands on.

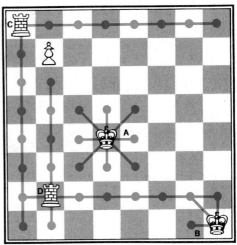

Moves of king and rook.

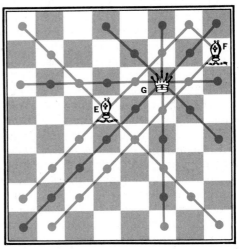

Moves of bishop and queen.

Moves of knight and pawn. The "V" capture.

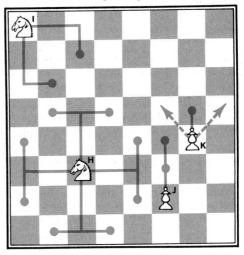

The Pawn. Because pawns are so weak, you may not pay much attention to them. But they are really very important. A lowly pawn may often rise to higher rank in the chess army.

The pawn may move one or two squares straight ahead on its first move, as illustrated by the pawn on square J in the diagram. Once it has made its first move, however, it can advance only one square at a time. The pawn, unlike the other pieces, can only move forward. Also, unlike the other pieces, which capture enemy men in the same way as they regularly move, a pawn may only capture an enemy piece that stands one square in front of it in a diagonal direction (the V-shaped capture), as shown by the pawn on square K.

If two opposing pawns block each other's advance on the same file, neither pawn can move or capture the other. If a pawn manages to reach the other side of the board (the eighth rank), it must be promoted immediately (as part of the same move) to any stronger piece except the king. Since the queen is the most powerful of the pieces, pawns that reach the eighth rank are almost always replaced by queens. It is therefore possible for a player to have nine queens at the same time—the original queen and eight others resulting from pawn promotions—but of course this does not happen very often.

Capturing

A chess piece captures an enemy piece by moving onto the square occupied by that enemy piece. The enemy piece is removed from the board, and the capturing piece replaces it on that square. Two pieces can never occupy the same square. A player is not forced to capture an enemy piece unless there is no other legal move for him to make.

Play and the Object of the Game

White always starts the game by moving one of his men—usually a pawn, in order to open up diagonals and files for the stronger pieces behind the pawns. Then black makes a move. From then on the players continue to alternate moves until the game is over. No player is permitted to let his turn pass. He must make some move, even if it is not a good one.

The goal of the game is to trap the opponent's king so that he cannot avoid capture.

Lower left, stalemate. At right, checkmate.

Whenever one of the players threatens to capture his opponent's king, he calls "Check!" A king that is checked must be guarded from this threat at once in one of three ways: (1) by moving the king to another square where he cannot be captured by any enemy man, (2) by capturing the piece that threatens the king, or (3) by placing another piece between the king and the enemy piece that is giving check. It is against the rules to ignore a check or to place a king where he can be captured. Therefore, a king is never really captured, and always remains on the board until the game ends. The game ends when a king is in check and there is no way for him to avoid capture. This is called **checkmate**, and it means victory for the other player.

When one player has secured a large advantage—for example, he has captured his opponent's queen without losing an important piece in exchange—it usually will be easy for him to corner the opponent's king and eventually checkmate him. That is why many players will resign (surrender before checkmate) if they are far behind in pieces or in position. Among grandmasters it is not uncommon for a player to resign when he is only a pawn behind.

Drawn Games

A game is called a draw (tie) if any one of the following occurs: (1) Both players agree to a draw during the game (in some competitions the players must each make at least 30 moves before they may agree to draw). (2) Neither player has enough pieces left for a possible checkmate (for example, only the

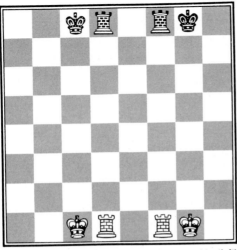

Castling kingside (*right*); queenside (*left*).

En passant.

two kings remain on the board or one player has a king and a bishop or knight against his opponent's king). (3) One player, whose turn it is to play, has no legal move and is not in check. This is called **stalemate** (note the difference between checkmate and stalemate—after checkmate the player also has no legal move, but his king is in check). (4) The same position is repeated three times during a game, with the same player about to move. (5) One player can prove that he can check the opponent's king endlessly (perpetual check); this rule usually reduces to rule (4) above, where the same position is repeated three times or more. (6) Neither side has made a capture or moved a pawn for the last 50 moves.

Special Rules

Castling. There is only one situation in chess when you can move two pieces simultaneously. This is a special move involving only the king and rook. If (1) the king and a rook have not yet moved during the game, and (2) the squares between the king and this rook are unoccupied, and (3) the king is not in check, and (4) the king will not have to move across a square threatened by an enemy piece, then the king may be moved two squares toward the rook, and the rook (as part of the same move) placed on the square directly on the other side of the king. It is possible to castle on the kingside (where only two squares separate the king and rook) or on the queenside (where three squares separate the king and rook). Each player can castle only once during a single game. Castling normally occurs

early in the game, and it is usually done to place the king in a safer position.

En Passant. *En passant* (French for "in passing") is a special way of capturing with a pawn. It occurs very rarely. If a pawn has reached its fifth rank, and an enemy pawn advancing two squares on its first move passes a square on which it could have been captured in the usual V-shaped way by the pawn on the fifth rank, then the pawn on the fifth rank may capture the advancing pawn as if it had moved only one square forward on its first move. This capture must be made on the very next move. If not taken advantage of immediately, the opportunity to capture *en passant* is lost.

▶ CHESS NOTATION

Every game of chess can be recorded in the form of a code, so that after the game is over it can be studied by the players or by other interested people. World-championship games are often published in newspapers in this code, and all chess books use it to record the moves. You will need to know chess notation if you decide to read some of the many books written about chess strategy and chess heroes.

In this code every piece has a letter symbol: K—king, Q—queen, R—rook, N—knight (Kt is sometimes used as the symbol for knight, but since it can be confused with K, N is preferred), B—bishop, and P—pawn. The pieces on the kingside of the board at the start of a game are called the KR (king's rook), KN (king's knight), and KB (king's bishop). Those on the queenside are the QR (queen's rook), QN (queen's knight), and QB (queen's bishop). Each pawn is identified by the piece that stands behind it at the start of the game (KP is the king's pawn, QRP the queen's rook pawn). The files are also given the name of the piece that stands on that file at the beginning of the game (for example, the QR file). The ranks are numbered 1 through 8. Rank 1 for white is rank 8 for black, and vice versa. Each square is identified by its rank and file. For example, the first square on the queen's rook file, from white's side of the board, is called QR1 for white and QR8 for black. The diagram shows the numbering of the squares from white's side of the board.

A move is recorded by identifying the piece moved (K,Q,R,N,B, or P), following it with a hyphen (-), and then naming the square on which it has been placed. Thus, "P-QR4" means "a pawn has moved to the fourth square on the queen's rook file," and "R-Q4" means "a rook has moved to the fourth square on the queen file." A capture is noted by "x"; therefore "RxB" means "rook captures bishop." Castling kingside is written "O-O," and castling queenside, "O-O-O." *En passant* is written "PxP e.p." "Check" is usually abbreviated "ch."

Here are two very short games of chess. See if you can replay these games using the code described above. First set up the pieces in their starting positions and then make the following moves. Don't forget that white always moves first. To determine who plays white, one person hides a white pawn in one fist and a black pawn in the other. His opponent chooses one fist and plays that color. The number of the move is given before each notation of white and black moves.

GAME 1

MOVE NUMBER	WHITE	BLACK
1.	P-KN4	P-K4
2.	P-KB4	Q-R5 chmate

GAME 2

MOVE NUMBER	WHITE	BLACK
1.	P-K4	P-K4
2.	B-QB4	B-QB4
3.	Q-R5	N-KB3
4.	QxKBP chmate	

▶ **OTHER SUGGESTIONS AND RULES**

The queen is the most powerful piece and is about nine times stronger than a pawn. If the queen is given the value of 9, then the next strongest piece (the rook) is worth about 5.

QR8	QN8	QB8	Q8	K8	KB8	KN8	KR8
QR7	QN7	QB7	Q7	K7	KB7	KN7	KR7
QR6	QN6	QB6	Q6	K6	KB6	KN6	KR6
QR5	QN5	QB5	Q5	K5	KB5	KN5	KR5
QR4	QN4	QB4	Q4	K4	KB4	KN4	KR4
QR3	QN3	QB3	Q3	K3	KB3	KN3	KR3
QR2	QN2	QB2	Q2	K2	KB2	KN2	KR2
QR1	QN1	QB1	Q1	K1	KB1	KN1	KR1

Chess notation from white's side only.

The bishops and knights are worth about 3½ each. The pawn is worth only 1. From these figures you can see that two bishops (7 points) are worth more than a rook (5 points), and that two rooks (10 points) are worth more than a queen (9 points). You should always calculate these values before exchanging any of your pieces for one of your opponent's. Incidentally, the king isn't given a numerical value, because the king can never be captured or exchanged.

If you touch a piece without having stated beforehand that you are only adjusting its position on a square (by saying "I adjust," or the French phrase *"J'adoube"*), then you must move it. If you touch an enemy man, then you must capture it if you can do so legally. You cannot take back a legal move and make another once you have removed your hand from the piece. It is a good idea to follow these rules strictly because you will learn much faster if you do not take moves back. Also, your opponent will not like it very much if you take back a move after he has made his next move and given away his plan.

As soon as you have learned the moves and played a few games, it would be a good idea to join a chess club in your town or school. You can improve in chess most quickly by playing with opponents who are equal to or better than you, so do not play only with those whom you always beat.

ELIOT HEARST
Captain, 1962 U.S. Chess Olympiad Team

Reviewed by BOBBY FISCHER
International Grandmaster
and World Chess Champion

CHIANG KAI-SHEK (1887–1975)

Chiang Kai-shek, one of the most important if controversial Asian leaders of modern times, led the Chinese people through 8 years of war with Japan. He was elected China's first constitutional president in 1948.

Chiang was born into a merchant family in Chekiang Province, China, in 1887. He received military training, and at the age of 20 joined Sun Yat-sen's revolutionary party, the Kuomintang. Chiang participated in the 1911 revolution that overthrew the 250-year-old Manchu dynasty and established the Chinese Republic. In 1923 he became head of the Whampoa Military Academy.

The revolutionary government called on Chiang to form and train an army in order to rid the country of warlords. In 1925 this army, the Northern Expeditionary Force, began its campaign, which lasted 3 years. Under Chiang's command it was finally able to unify China. A new government was formed in Nanking with Chiang as premier. Meanwhile, Chiang had married Mayling Soong, a sister-in-law of Sun Yat-sen.

Soon after Chiang became premier, he had to deal with the Chinese Communists who had revolted against the government and established a military base in South China. In 1932 and 1933 Chiang himself took command of the army and successfully attacked the Communist stronghold.

In 1937 Japan invaded North China and the Sino-Japanese War began. Under Chiang's leadership China was able to fight on alone for the next 4 years. After Japan attacked Pearl Harbor in December, 1941, China became one of the Allies, and Chiang was appointed Supreme Commander of the Allied Air and Land Forces in China. Chiang's attendance at the Cairo Conference with President Roosevelt and Prime Minister Churchill in 1943 indicated the importance of his (and China's) place in world affairs.

At the end of World War II the Communists controlled a large area of the Chinese countryside. After failing at the negotiation table, Chiang tried to defeat the Communists by force of arms but soon found himself fighting a losing battle. In 1949 Chiang and the Nationalist government retreated to Taiwan (Formosa). He served as president until his death in Taipei, Taiwan, on April 5, 1975.

CHICAGO

Chicago, the second largest city in the United States, is situated at the southwestern tip of Lake Michigan, in northeastern Illinois. Chicago has been called the Windy City because great gusts of wind sometimes blow across Lake Michigan. Carl Sandburg, who was born in Illinois, provided a memorable description of the city in his poem "Chicago":

> Hog Butcher for the World,
> Tool Maker, Stacker of Wheat,
> Player with Railroads and the Nation's
>   Freight Handler;
> Stormy, husky, brawling,
> City of the Big Shoulders.

Boston, New York City, and Philadelphia were already flourishing towns when the site of Chicago was nothing but swampland. But Chicago grew and prospered because of its location. It is near the center of the North American continent and near the agricultural heart of the nation.

▶ **CHICAGO TODAY**

Today Chicago ranks among the major cities of the world in population, industry and commerce, and educational and cultural institutions. It is the only inland city in the United States that is connected by water to both the Atlantic Ocean and the Gulf of Mexico. Chicago itself has a population of some 3,000,000. More than twice that number live in its metropolitan area, which includes surrounding counties.

The city is divided into the North Side, South Side, and West Side by the Chicago River and its tributaries. This river flows backward. To stop sewage from entering Lake Michigan, engineers reversed the river's flow into Chicago's canal system in 1900.

Downtown Chicago has two well-known sections, the Lake Shore area and the Loop. The Lake Shore was created by filling in portions of Lake Michigan. It has many lovely parks and impressive buildings. Three of the nation's tallest buildings—the Sears Tower, the Standard Oil Building, and the John Hancock Center—are among the skyscrapers that rise almost like a wall just beyond the lakefront. The Loop, the commercial heart of the city, is so named because elevated trains follow a rectangular "loop" of tracks within the area.

The population of the Chicago metropolitan area represents an ethnic and cultural cross section of the nation and the world. Many Chicagoans were born in other countries. The largest foreign-born groups today include Poles, Spanish-speaking peoples, Italians, and Germans. Black Americans make up about

This wood engraving shows people fleeing from the flames of the Chicago fire of 1871.

one third of the population of the central city. Some 8,000 American Indians live in Chicago. About one third of them were born in Illinois. Most of the remainder came from nearby states. There are also many Asians and people of Asian descent.

The Chicago metropolitan area is the nation's most important manufacturing center. The leading products are electrical and other kinds of machinery. Other major industries include petroleum refining, production of chemicals, printing and publishing, and the manufacture of clothing and transportation equipment.

Food products, too, are a source of income for Chicago's wholesalers. But the meat-packing industry, which once was centered in Chicago, has moved westward. The famous stockyards to which the livestock was shipped no longer exist.

The Chicago area has the largest capacity in the world for producing steel. The industry includes iron and steel mills, forging plants, and foundries. Most of the iron and steel mills are in east and south Chicago and along the lakefront in nearby Indiana.

Chicago is also a great commercial center. The Midwest Stock Exchange is located there. The Chicago Federal Reserve Bank ranks next to the Federal Reserve Bank in New York City in importance. Much of the wholesale trade of the Midwest originates in Chicago. The Board of Trade Building is the center of grain-trading activities. The Chicago Mercantile Exchange is the largest exchange for perishable goods, such as eggs and cattle, in the world. Chicago is the home of the nation's largest mail-order houses.

Transportation has been one of the most important factors in the growth and economic development of Chicago. The city is the heart of a vast network of railroads, highways, waterways, and airlines.

Chicago is one of the world's largest and busiest railroad and trucking centers. A huge volume of freight passes through the area each day. Commuter railroads and bus lines carry thousands of people between the city and suburbs.

Planes from all over the world land at O'Hare International Airport, the world's busiest air terminal. Chicago Midway Airport and Meigs Field also handle air traffic.

The John Hancock Center dominates this view of the Chicago skyline.

A large steel sculpture by the artist Pablo Picasso stands in Daley Plaza.

The completion of the St. Lawrence Seaway in 1959 opened the city to oceangoing ships. Vessels from the Atlantic Ocean now pass through the St. Lawrence River and the Great Lakes into Chicago to load and unload cargo. Barges from the Gulf coast can also reach Chicago by way of the Mississippi River, the Illinois Waterway, and the Chicago Canal System.

Chicago has long been a leader in education. The city supports a two-year college system and is the home of a number of well-known colleges and universities. Some of these are the University of Chicago, the Illinois Institute of Technology, Chicago State University, and the Chicago campuses of the University of Illinois. DePaul University and Loyola University of Chicago are both well-known Roman Catholic schools in the city. Northwestern University is in suburban Evanston. The first laboratory-produced nuclear chain reaction of atomic energy occurred in 1942 on the campus of the University of Chicago. Several of the universities have large medical schools and hospitals.

Chicagoans have access to a great variety of cultural activities and institutions, including music, theater, and museums. The Chicago Symphony Orchestra is one of the finest in the world. The Art Institute of Chicago, in Grant Park, houses a world-famous collection of 19th- and 20th-century French paintings. The School of the Art

Institute of Chicago–Goodman School of Drama grants teacher preparatory and professional degrees. Also in Grant Park are the John G. Shedd Aquarium, the Adler Planetarium, the Field Museum of Natural History, and an outdoor band shell where free concerts are held in summer. The Museum of Science and Industry, in Jackson Park, has exhibits carefully planned to help people understand the basic principles of science and the uses of science in industry.

There are many recreational facilities. Chicago has professional baseball, football, hockey, and basketball teams. Sandy beaches border the shores of Lake Michigan. Few large cities have a forested area to equal Cook County Forest Preserve, which extends around the city in a broken arc. Several parks line Chicago's Lake Shore area. Burnham Park, Jackson Park, and Grant Park are among the best known. Lincoln Park, the largest of the parks, includes beaches, playgrounds, sports facilities, and the noted Lincoln Park Zoo.

Chicago's location makes it an ideal convention city. Large convention halls and hotels accommodate the many trade and business conventions held there each year.

▶ **HISTORY**

In 1673 two French explorers, Father Jacques Marquette and Louis Jolliet, paddled down the Chicago River into Lake

Children viewing a miniature apothecary shop at the Museum of Science and Industry.

Michigan. They were the first white persons to pass through the area now called Chicago.

A small French trading post was in existence at the southern end of Lake Michigan throughout the 1700's. In 1795 the Potawatomi Indians gave a tract of land near the mouth of the Chicago River to the newly formed United States. Captain John Whistler was sent by the United States Government to take charge of the new land. He built Fort Dearborn in 1803. But in 1812 it was destroyed, and the settlers were killed in an Indian uprising. Fort Dearborn was rebuilt four years later.

Chicago was incorporated as a town in 1833, with a population of a few hundred. Within four years the population had grown to over 4,000, and Chicago became a small city. Farmers in the eastern United States and immigrants from Europe were flocking to the wide prairies of northern Illinois and southern Wisconsin. Wheat, cattle, and lumber began to pour into Chicago.

In 1848 the Illinois and Michigan Canal was completed. This connected the Illinois River with the Chicago River and Lake Michigan. The first train entered Chicago in the same year. Canals and railroads ensured the future growth of the city. By the 1850's, Chicago had become the railroad center of the country and the largest market for grain, cattle, and lumber in the United States.

A great fire started on the night of October 8, 1871, and burned for 27 hours. More than 17,000 buildings were destroyed, and thousands of people were left homeless. But Chicago was almost entirely rebuilt within two years. There is a legend that the fire was started when Mrs. O'Leary's cow kicked over a kerosene lantern. But the actual cause of the fire is unknown.

For the next 20 years, industry expanded rapidly. By 1890, Chicago was second only to New York City as the largest manufacturing city in the United States. Two world's fairs were held in Chicago—the World's Columbian Exposition in 1893 and the Century of Progress Exposition in 1933–34.

JAMES E. PATTERSON
Illinois State University

See also ILLINOIS.

CHICKEN POX. See DISEASES.

CHICKENS. See POULTRY.

CHILD DEVELOPMENT

"The Child is father of the Man," said William Wordsworth. This line of poetry expresses one of the major principles of the study of child development. It is believed that the beginnings of adult qualities are present in the child and that these qualities develop with time and with the child's experiences and activities.

Because of this view there is an active interest today in studying both the natural qualities of children and their experiences and activities. There is particular interest in understanding how a child's natural qualities and his experiences act together to help or hold back his development.

Working with children, studying them, and educating them occupy a large number of people in our society. Many psychologists, educators, and other specialists in the fields of science and social science are especially interested in children's growth and development.

As a field, child development is concerned mainly with the development of the child into a thinking, feeling, sometimes creative human being, aware of other human beings.

The areas studied by specialists in child development include children's relationships to their parents and to other children, the development and control of emotions, the development of an individual's attitudes toward others and toward himself, the ways people learn, and the best ways of teaching children.

▶ HOW DEVELOPMENT IS INFLUENCED

The qualities that make a person the particular individual he is are called his characteristics. Each person's characteristics depend partly on physical traits that have been passed on to him from his parents and partly on the conditions in which he lives and the experiences he has.

The passing on of traits from parents to children is called heredity. The conditions in which a person lives are his environment.

For a long time scientists argued about which was more important in deciding what a person was like and could be—heredity or environment. Now we realize that heredity and environment influence one another and overlap in deciding what a person will be.

A person may inherit a tendency to be tall, for example. But the foods he eats, the diseases he may have, and his physical activities will all have an influence on his reaching his full growth.

Other human characteristics, such as emotions (feelings) and intelligence, tend to reflect very closely the influences of environment. Most of the children of the world live under unfavorable social conditions. For these children, characteristics that are influenced by the environment cannot develop as fully as possible.

In many countries, for example, most children have a poor diet and live in crowded, often unsanitary homes. There are not enough schools, hospitals, and doctors. In other societies, where there may be enough schools and good health care, children may be treated unfairly because of the color of their skin or because of their religion. This kind of treatment, called bias or discrimination, becomes an important part of the environment. All of these unfavorable conditions tend to limit the fullest possible development of each individual child.

▶ WHAT IS NORMAL DEVELOPMENT?

Physical, mental, and social growth are all part of a child's development.

Physical Growth

The individual begins with the union, in the mother's body, of a cell from the mother and a cell from the father. This union is called conception. The two tiny cells that combine at conception multiply until, at adulthood, the individual's body is made up of approximately 26,000,000,000 (billion) cells.

The process of growth goes on for 9 months in the mother's body before the baby is born. Growth then continues for about 20 years, until the individual reaches his full adult size and proportions.

Different parts of the body grow at different times and rates. A newborn baby's head is much bigger in relation to his body than the head of an adult in relation to his body. This is because during the growth of the baby before birth, the head grows faster than the rest of the body.

During early childhood all parts of the body grow, but the arms and legs grow a bit faster than the trunk and head.

Another kind of physical development is the growth of muscles, organs, nerves, and brain. This growth is reflected in the way the child behaves and in the things he is able to do. Most babies, for example, walk when they are 12 to 14 months old. They are able to walk then because their leg muscles have become strong enough. Their nervous systems have also developed enough to allow them to use together the different sets of muscles needed for walking.

Measuring the ages at which babies can make certain movements and do certain things gives an indication of how fast they are developing. Not all babies are able to do the same things at the same ages, but for every individual certain skills come before certain other skills. For example, a baby is able to hold his head up before he is able to sit without being supported. He is able to sit before he can crawl, and he is able to crawl before he can walk. While this development of abilities is based partly on physical growth, it depends also on the ability to use muscles and nerves together. Understandably, this is harder at first and becomes easier with growth and practice. So a baby who is just learning to walk looks awkward and falls often, and he sometimes seems to give up and go back to crawling. At other times of life, when people are trying to learn to do something new, like riding a bicycle, they may look awkward at first, too.

In general, the muscles responsible for moving the larger parts of the body develop first. These are also the larger muscles. This means that control of arms and legs is developed before control of hands and fingers. Walking and waving, pushing and pulling, are easier than hammering a nail, sewing, or writing.

There are great individual differences, however, in the ages at which children develop various abilities. Some children are relatively fast in learning to walk and slower in learning to talk. Others are just the opposite. Unless the slowness is extreme (such as being unable to walk by the age of 3), these differences do not point out anything about the child's intelligence or general ability.

At the same time that the baby's muscles are developing and he is learning to control their use, the baby's senses and his awareness of the world around him are also developing. In the beginning he cannot focus his eyes. Then he learns to focus on something that does not move. Next he is able to follow a moving object with his eyes and turn his head to keep it in sight. Also, his reactions to his mother's voice begin to differ from his reactions to other voices. By the time the baby is about 6 months old, he is aware enough to know whether he is being held by his parents or by a stranger.

As the baby grows, he also stays awake for longer and longer periods. Thus he has time for activities that allow him to see, hear, smell, and feel many different things.

Mental Growth

The ability to speak and to describe things, experiences, and ideas is something that human beings alone have. Language is used in solving problems, in making wants known, and in learning from others. Therefore, one of the most important developments for the child is the growth of language.

A child understands language sooner than he can use it well himself. When he does begin to use it, he can understand more difficult sentences than he can form himself. Between the ages of a year and a year and a half, a child who cannot yet say words can follow commands, such as "Bring the paper to Daddy"

Different parts of the body grow at different times and rates.

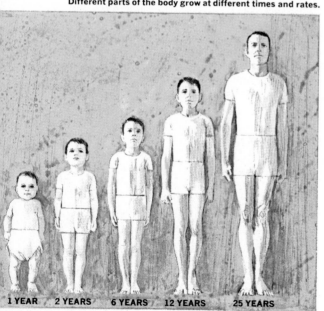

1 YEAR 2 YEARS 6 YEARS 12 YEARS 25 YEARS

or "Go look out the window." Usually between a year and a half and 2 years a child is able to name some things himself when he is asked to. At about 2 he begins to make his ideas known to others in language.

At first the child cannot express himself exactly. He does not know many words, and he knows even less about stringing them together in sentences. He does not yet have a good understanding of many of the aspects of the world around him, so he cannot use accurately the language that describes those aspects.

For example, the young child really lives in the present. He may remember books or toys or places, but he does not develop a real idea of time until later. "Tomorrow" or "next month" or "yesterday" have little meaning for the young child. Yet in language we use different words to describe something we are doing now, something we did before, and something we are going to do. The child who does not yet understand time differences does not know the differences between these words. When he says "Baby go," it can mean anything from "I want to go over there now" to "I have just gone over there and am now here."

Space is another aspect of the world of which a child has little understanding. At first a child does not use words such as "under" or "to the left" or "behind," because these words express ideas that he does not yet understand. Gradually, as the child comes to understand height and depth and width, he uses the words that express these ideas. It is also thought that learning the words for ideas helps the child learn about the ideas themselves.

Another way the child learns is by handling objects and by moving his body around. At first, the space that the child lives in and is aware of is his crib or playpen. He can reach out and touch the sides. He can also touch himself and see his arms and legs move. Gradually, by seeing and feeling his own body move and by touching walls and floors and the sides of his bed, the child learns something about the space he lives in.

By piling blocks and playing with other objects, the child realizes that objects can exist in particular relationships to one another. The blue block can be on top of the red one. The yellow one can be behind the black one.

Beginning with the moving around of his

MUSCULAR DEVELOPMENT

AGE OF CHILD   **ACTIVITY**

3 months   Can hold head up for short time.
Can roll from side to back.

6 months   Can sit with only slight support.
Can roll from stomach to back and back to stomach.

9 months   Can sit alone for a short time.
Can crawl a little forward or backward, using hands and feet.

12 months   Can pull self up to standing position.
Can walk when held and led (a few can walk alone).

15 months   Can walk alone and climb up stairs.
Can kneel.

18 months   Can walk backward.
Can climb into chair.

2 years   Can walk up and down stairs with help.

3 years   Can jump with both feet off ground.
Can walk tiptoe.

Kindergarten children can dance and keep time to music.

own body and of things he can see and touch, the child builds up an understanding of the space around him. From this early understanding he later develops a more advanced knowledge of space and of things he cannot see or touch, such as the movement of the earth around the sun.

Thought is believed to develop as this kind of understanding develops, from objects that can be touched to ideas that cannot be touched or seen. Thought is said to advance from the concrete to the abstract. The concrete is an idea represented in a thing that can be seen or heard or felt. The abstract is an idea that cannot be related to objects. A child has a concrete understanding of space, for example, before he has an abstract understanding of it. He understands what size peg can fit into what size hole before he can understand about the distance around the earth.

Because of the development of thought from the concrete to the abstract, it is felt that giving children real objects to play with and move around will help them develop abstract understanding later. It is thought that a child who has played at putting different-size pegs in different-size holes will later find it easier to understand why a table 5 feet wide will not fit through a doorway 4 feet wide. This kind of understanding, in turn, will help him understand ideas in mathematics and logic (the science of reasoning).

Experience with things in the world is believed to be very important in developing an understanding of things and ideas and the ability to talk and think about them. This point

is made especially by the Swiss psychologist Jean Piaget (1896–1980). Piaget's observations and theories have had great influence on present thinking in child development.

Social Growth

A child depends on his parents, his teachers, and other adults for learning how to use language. He also depends on them for learning how to act in the world.

We learn from other people by having them tell us certain things in words. We also learn by watching them and following their example. In these ways we learn how to use a fork and knife, how to ride on trains and buses, and how to walk from home to school. We also learn the less concrete things, such as manners, how to take turns, how to act in school, and how to talk to people so that they will listen and understand. The gradual learning of all these things is called socialization. It goes on all through life, but most of it takes place in childhood.

Since the infant and young child spend most of their time with their parents and other members of their family, the beginnings of socialization are mostly the result of the family's influence.

As the child gets older and goes to school, other people have an influence on his socialization. Usually the first person outside the family who has this kind of influence is the teacher. Sometimes the teacher will teach the child to do things in a way that is different from the way his parents taught. This may make the child uncomfortable, but it forces him to begin to develop his own ways. It is a step on his road to individuality and independence.

By the time a child becomes an adult, his ways of doing things are a combination of what he has learned from his parents, teachers, and friends and all the other people who have had an influence on him. These are the ways he will teach his children.

MARTIN DEUTSCH, PH.D.
Director, Institute for Developmental Studies
Professor of Early Childhood Education
New York University

CYNTHIA P. DEUTSCH, PH.D.
Institute for Developmental Studies
New York University

See also BABY; PSYCHOLOGY.

CHILD LABOR

A child with a factory job in 1815 might work from sunrise to sunset, 6 days a week, to earn a dollar. Many children began working before they were 7 years old. Some toiled as many as 18 hours a day in damp, dark, dirty buildings. They tended machines in spinning mills, hauled heavy loads, or dug coal underground. With no time to play and little time to rest, children often became ill.

Children had always worked, especially in farming. In the Middle Ages they were apprentices in the guild system (trade associations). In colonial America they worked at home, on the family farm, or in the shop. When the factory system began in the United States about 1800, the new power-driven machinery did not require adult strength. Children could work the machines, and they could be hired for less money than adults.

Samuel Slater started one of the first American cotton mills in Pawtucket, Rhode Island, in 1790. By 1801 he was using 100 children aged 4 to 10 to run his spinning machines. By 1832 two out of every five New England mill laborers were children.

As factories spread and grew, more children went to work. By 1810 about 2,000,000 school-age children were working 50- to 70-hour weeks. A glass factory in Massachusetts was fenced with barbed wire. The foreman said this was "to keep the young imps inside." The "young imps" were boys under 12 who carried loads of hot glass from 5:30 P.M. to 3:30 A.M., over a distance of about 22 miles, for a nightly wage of 40 cents to $1.10.

Church groups, labor leaders, teachers, and other public-spirited groups were horrified by this cruelty. But it took them many years to outlaw it. Connecticut passed a law in 1813 saying that working children must have some schooling. A Massachusetts law (1836) required children under 15 to go to school 3 months a year. The Knights of Labor, a nationwide industrial union, helped push 10 states into passing child labor laws in the period from 1885 to 1889. The Knights of Labor also called for a national child labor law in the 1880's. Its successor, the American Federation of Labor (AFL), at its first convention in 1881, called on all states to outlaw the employment of children. The AFL later be-came one of the strongest supporters of a federal child labor law. By 1899 a total of 28 states had passed laws regulating child labor.

Many efforts were made to pass a national child labor law. President Theodore Roosevelt urged Congress to enact such a law. Congress passed two laws, but the United States Supreme Court declared them both unconstitutional (1918, 1922). In 1924 Congress proposed a constitutional amendment banning child labor, but the states refused to ratify it. Rules against child labor were part of the National Industrial Recovery Act (1933), which the Supreme Court also declared unconstitutional. Not until 1936 did the United States pass the Walsh-Healey Public Contracts Act, the first federal law to regulate child labor that was not declared unconstitutional. It forbade firms with government contracts of over $10,000 to hire boys under 16 and girls under 18. This was followed by the most important law of all, the Fair Labor Standards Act (1936). It fixed a minimum age of 16 years for work during school hours, 14 for certain jobs after school, and 18 for dangerous occupations.

Today all the states and the federal government have laws regulating child labor. These laws have cured the worst evils of children's working in factories. In 1900 about 25 per cent of the southern cotton mill workers were children under 16. Today there are very few children of that age working in factories.

But certain kinds of work are not yet regulated by law. In these jobs there are still child workers employed long hours, sometimes in dangerous work. Children of migrant workers, for instance, have no legal protection. These children pick fruit or cotton in the fields and move around from place to place, so that they get very little schooling. Farmers may legally employ children outside of school hours. Many farm states still permit children under 16 to be excused from school to do farm work. However, the increasing automation of farms has led to a general decrease in the number of working children. In addition, federal, state, and local agencies are working together to meet the special educational needs of the children of migrant workers.

Reviewed by MILTON FRIED
Research Director
Amalgamated Clothing Workers of America

CHILDREN'S LITERATURE

For most people the word literature means books and reading. But there was a time when there were almost no books because there were no printing presses. And because there were so few books, not many people could read.

But people heard the tales of good storytellers and later retold the same tales—with a few trimmings of their own. They sang the folk songs they had learned by ear. Mothers sang old lullabies to their babies and repeated old nursery rhymes—the same ones their mothers had taught them. At work, men and women chanted old songs that paced the rhythm of their hoeing or woodchopping or rowing.

These tales, rhymes, and songs made up the literature of people who had few books. Theirs was an oral literature—that is, a literature that is spoken or sung.

In the days before printed books—long before radio and television—the human voice was the chief instrument for the spread of literature. In one household, the grandmother might be the one who entertained with the old tales as she remembered them. In another, it might be a visitor from a nearby town who brought news and told stories as he had heard them in his community.

Wandering storytellers or minstrels would gather stories and songs as they went about the countryside. Then, in a village square or the yard of an inn, they would put on their entertainment for young and old. Often the tales and songs had repeated lines that the audience would chime in on. And someone might suggest a new line or a new stanza for a song, added like a new link to an old chain.

Children were part of these singing and storytelling sessions at home and in the village. They took over the parts that appealed to them—the song with a dozen stanzas and a chorus that imitated various animals, the tales of the little person who outsmarted bigger people, the nonsense rhymes and singing games, the riddles and tongue twisters.

Even today, literature for children begins as oral literature—the songs a baby hears, the singing games the toddler learns, the nursery rhymes and tales. All are forms of oral literature that most people learn long before they are old enough to read.

▶ THE FIRST PRINTED LITERATURE

Until the mid-1400's, books were lettered by hand or were printed from woodcuts. Both required slow, painstaking work. Books were few in number and so costly that only the great monasteries and universities could have them. The people were without books. Then, a German inventor, Johann Gutenberg, developed a printing press with movable type that revolutionized printing. It produced printed literature for thousands of people who had previously relied only on oral literature.

Years passed before books were printed especially for children. In 1484, an English printer, William Caxton, brought out an edition of Aesop's *Fables*. He intended the book to be read by adults, but children may have enjoyed the lively woodcuts that illustrated the *Fables*.

One of the first picture books for children was a textbook in Latin called *Orbis Sensualium Pictus* (*The Visible World in Pictures*). It was written in 1658 by John Amos Comenius, a Czech educator and bishop. It was translated into English in 1659.

But printed books were too expensive for many children to use, even for their lessons. A low-cost substitute, called a hornbook, was widely used in England and in the British colonies of North America. The hornbook looked

Hornbooks were first used in the late 16th century.

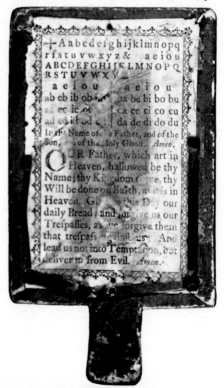

nothing like a book. It was a small wooden paddle on which was pasted a lesson sheet of paper or parchment. A transparent covering of horn protected the sheet. Usually the horn-book lesson began with the sign of the cross, followed by the alphabet and groups of syllables, sometimes the numbers, and finally the Lord's Prayer.

In the same period, printers were turning out quantities of newssheets, ballads, and booklets that were unbound and often unstitched. These were sold by street vendors and peddlers, called chapmen. The little booklets were commonly called chapbooks or penny histories, since they were sold for a penny each, along with a toy or trinket. Some chapbooks had as few as 4 pages and some as many as 24.

Most chapbooks were published for adults, but many were adventure tales that appealed to children. Chapbooks were sold by the thousand. In many homes, they may have been the only reading matter besides the Bible.

In the 1600's, strong religious feelings were building up in England and New England. Books published for children at this time warned of sin, death, and eternal punishment. *The New England Primer,* printed about 1690, contained the alphabet, spelling words, the catechism, and verses for religious training. A book for adults—*Pilgrim's Progress* (1678) by the English writer and preacher John Bunyan—grew out of this same religious climate. But Bunyan, who had been a reader of the chapbooks himself, knew how to tell a good story, and many children enjoyed his book.

▶ **THE SPIRIT OF THE FAIRY TALES**

The first change in this stern scene came with an amazing little collection of eight stories published in France in 1697. It included "Cinderella," "Puss in Boots," "The Sleeping Beauty," and "Little Red Riding Hood." All were told simply, gracefully—even joyously—with no heavy threat of gloom or doom and no religious teaching.

The title of the book, translated from the French, was *Stories or Tales of Long Ago with Morals.* No author was named in the first edition. But Charles Perrault, a member of the French Academy, is believed to be the one who retold the old stories. What is most interesting is the light touch that marks these stories and the brief moral following each one.

RULES *for* BEHAVIOUR. 101

BEHAVIOUR *at the* TABLE.

1 COME not to the Table without having your Hands and Face wafh-ed, and your Head combed.
2 Sit not down until thou art bidden by thy Parents or other Superiours.
3 Be fure thou never fitteft down until a Bleffing be defired, and then in thy due Place.

A page from Newbery's *Little Pretty Pocket-Book.*

The picture at the beginning of the book shows an old woman before an open fire telling stories to young listeners. On the door behind her is a sign: "Contes de ma mère l'Oye," which means "Tales of My Mother the Goose." In 1729, this little collection of stories was brought out in English with the title *Tales of Mother Goose.* It sparked a movement to bring beauty and delight to children through books created especially for them.

One of the pioneers in this development was John Newbery, a London printer, publisher, writer, and merchant. Newbery was evidently a keen businessman, who saw a market in these children who had been reading the chapbooks and now the *Tales of Mother Goose.*

In 1744, Newbery published his first children's book, *A Little Pretty Pocket-Book,* in covers of gilt and flowered paper, "for the instruction and amusement" of children. The tiny *Pocket-Book* included fables, rhymed directions for games, a few poems, letters from Jack the Giant-Killer, and rules for children's behavior.

The book was so successful that Newbery brought out more and more books for children.

One of the most popular was *The History of Little Goody Two-Shoes* (1765). It is probably the first book of fiction written for children and with illustrations drawn especially for the story.

Before this, printers used any woodcuts they had on hand to illustrate the chapbooks for children. One old chapbook used the picture of a sailboat on the page facing a poem about a good child saying his prayers. Because the woodcut was too wide to show the boat sailing across the page, the printer turned it on end to sail straight up the page.

One of the first artists to become an illustrator of children's books was Thomas Bewick, an engraver who worked in wood. The first book he designed and illustrated for children was *Tommy Trip's History of Beasts and Birds* (1779). Bewick pictured the beasts and birds in exquisite detail.

After John Newbery's death in 1767, his publishing house continued to bring out children's books that were charming and entertaining. One of these was *Mother Goose's Melody; or, Sonnets for the Cradle*. It did not include any of the stories from Perrault's *Tales of Mother Goose*. Instead, it brought together 52 old English nursery rhymes plus 16 songs from Shakespeare—all in the Newbery covers of flowers and gilt. Since 1922, the work of John Newbery has been commemorated through the Newbery award, which is presented to the most distinguished children's book published each year in the United States.

While Newbery and, later, his heirs were bringing out charming books for children in England, several American printers and publishers were following his lead. Frequently, they duplicated the English book without giving credit to the source. In 1785, Isaiah Thomas of Worcester, Massachusetts, brought out an American edition of *Mother Goose's Melody*—a direct copy from Newbery.

Yet these books for children's pleasure were the exception rather than the rule in both England and the United States. There were still many religious books for young readers. In the late 1700's, there began a flood of instructional stories as well. But children have a way of finding adventure tales, too. One way has always been to turn to books published for adults. Two adult books of those times became children's classics. *Robinson Crusoe* (1719), by Daniel Defoe, was about a person who had been shipwrecked on an uninhabited island. A part of *Gulliver's Travels* (1726), by Jonathan Swift, told of adventures in a land of Lilliputians (tiny people). Defoe's story was loaded with moralizing, and Swift's with political satire. Evidently, children skipped the heavy parts and enjoyed the adventures. Since then, both books have been published in shortened form with dramatic illustrations for children to enjoy.

▶ IMAGINATION AND LAUGHTER FOR CHILDREN

The 1800's brought a number of new books that bore no trace of the preaching or teaching that had been in most children's books. One of these came from Germany—the folktales collected by Jacob and Wilhelm Grimm, two university scholars. The Grimm brothers recorded the tales just as they had heard them from storytellers in the countryside. Here were stories of talking beasts and dancing princesses, of elves and dwarfs, and even of a princess who slept for a hundred years. The tales were recorded in the rhythmical language of the storyteller and with the same buildup of suspense that had held listeners spellbound for centuries. They were first published in 1812 in Germany. In 1823, these tales were brought out in England, where they became known as *Grimm's Fairy Tales*.

Another of the new books came from Denmark, where Hans Christian Andersen, following the lead of the Grimms, also turned to folktales. But unlike the Grimms, Andersen retold the old stories in his own way. He also added new stories that he created on the old folktale pattern. Andersen's *Fairy Tales and Stories* was translated for English publication in 1846.

That same year a nonsensical and very funny book for children was published in England. This was Edward Lear's *Book of Nonsense,* a collection of limericks (humorous five-line poems with a special rhythm and rhyme). The book contained exaggerated cartoons drawn by Lear, who was a famous illustrator of books on natural history. It is probably the first children's book to be created for real-life children, whom Lear consulted on every limerick and drawing. Lear's next book, *Nonsense Songs, Stories, Botany and Alphabets* (1871), included humorous verse and story poems.

Part of the humor springs from Lear's made-up words, tongue twisters, and absurd drawings. The Lear books were in sharp contrast to *The New England Primer,* which began, "In Adam's fall/We sinned all." For Lear, there was no sinning for children—only nonsense and laughter.

In much the same spirit, Charles Dodgson, a distinguished mathematician and university scholar, began telling stories to three little girls, one of them named Alice. These stories were published in 1865 as *Alice's Adventures in Wonderland* under the pen name Lewis Carroll. Alice goes down a rabbit hole, where she shrinks to the height of a flower, meets the Cheshire cat, nearly drowns in her own tears, and takes part in a mad tea party. Nonsense is spoken with great seriousness, and foolish doings multiply. Alice's adventures were continued in *Through the Looking-Glass,* published in 1872. This book contains the nonsense poem "Jabberwocky."

Both books were illustrated by Sir John Tenniel, a cartoonist for *Punch,* London's magazine of humor. For most readers, the Tenniel drawings are inseparable from the droll nonsense of Lewis Carroll's story.

▶ COLOR COMES TO THE PICTURE BOOKS

The illustrations of Lear and Tenniel were black-and-white line drawings. The artists used pen and ink to make clear, sharp lines that could be easily printed. Almost all books of that day were printed in black and white only. Some of the chapbooks were colored by hand with crude swashes of paint that swept beyond the black guidelines.

In the 1860's, Edmund Evans, an English printer, became interested in bringing out inexpensive children's books with fine color illustrations. Evans planned them for very young children—the nursery-school age. The first of these "toy books," as Evans called them, were nursery rhymes illustrated by Walter Crane, a fine wood engraver. Crane used flat colors and bold black lines. *The House That Jack Built, Dame Trot and Her Comical Cat,* and the *History of Cock Robin and Jenny Wren*

The mad tea party, drawn by Sir John Tenniel for *Alice's Adventures in Wonderland*.

were the first of many nursery picture books illustrated by Crane and printed by Evans in the 1860's and 1870's.

Another artist whom Edmund Evans worked with was Kate Greenaway. She had illustrated several children's books, but they were all rather poorly printed. Evans knew he could do better by her work. In 1878 he brought out a book of her verses, *Under the Window,* with her delightful color drawings. The Kate Greenaway drawings had a style of their own—sweet children in quaint old-fashioned clothes, with birds and blossoms surrounding them—all in soft pastels. Many Kate Greenaway books for children followed—birthday books, almanacs, a painting book, and her illustrated edition of Robert Browning's *Pied Piper of Hamelin,* among others.

At the same time, Randolph Caldecott was becoming known for his cartoons and sketches in English magazines and newspapers. Edmund Evans added Caldecott to his team of artists, and more "toy books" were under way. Caldecott spent part of his youth in the country, where he absorbed the sights and sounds of fox hunts, cattle fairs, and countryfolk. All of these show up in his drawings, which are done in simple, vigorous lines suggesting movement and sly humor.

The best-loved Caldecott books are the nursery rhymes, such as *Hey-Diddle-Diddle, Sing a Song of Sixpence,* and *Baby Bunting.* In tribute to the artist, the Caldecott Medal is awarded each year for the most distinguished picture book for children published in the United States.

▶ **THE BEGINNINGS OF REALISM**

Randolph Caldecott's people looked like real people. This was part of a trend to greater realism in books for children. The new authors did not write about children who were as stiff as wood and either too good to be true or too bad. Instead, they began to create flesh-and-blood characters who had their strong points and their weak points, who laughed and cried, loved and hated, as living people do.

The landmark in this development was Louisa May Alcott's *Little Women,* published in two volumes (1868 and 1869) in Boston. The story tells of the everyday ups and downs of the four teenage March sisters. This heart-warming book was based on the author's experiences in the genteel Alcott family—whose members, in spite of their poverty, lived lives rich in imagination and individuality.

Realism in children's books went even further when Mark Twain's *Adventures of Tom*

For *Under the Window,* Kate Greenaway drew pictures of children dressed in quaint clothing.

Randolph Caldecott drew this illustration for the ballad "The Diverting History of John Gilpin" by the English poet William Cowper. Caldecott's humorous touches added to the hilarity of the tale of John Gilpin and his runaway horse.

Sawyer was published in 1876. Poor folk and strange, shady characters from "across town" lived in Tom's world. Tom was from a "respectable" family, but his best friend Huck was the son of the town drunkard. The boys had some strange experiences. They witnessed a grave robbery and saw a murder being committed. They even attended their own funeral. These adventures were not the kind previously found in books for children. The sequel, *The Adventures of Huckleberry Finn,* was told in the rough river-town language of Huck himself. Both books give details of the rugged Mississippi River life as it was in those days. After Kate Greenaway's flower gardens and Lewis Carroll's Wonderland, the world of Tom and Huck seemed bold, harsh, and thrilling.

▶ TRENDS IN EARLY POETRY

Poetry for children has gone through changes, too. The earliest poems were rhyming verses with a definite moral purpose. Then came the teaching poems—"For a Bad Boy," "For a Selfish Child," and the like—again in rhyming verse with heavy-handed lessons.

Then, in 1789, came a book of truly lyric poetry singing the joys of childhood in a world sustained by love. This was *Songs of Innocence* by the great English poet William Blake. These poems are still widely read, usually more by adults than by children.

Almost 100 years later *A Child's Garden of Verses* (1885) by Robert Louis Stevenson appeared. The children in Stevenson's poems climb trees, play with their shadows, go up in swings, and have a joyous time. There are no morals in these poems and no dire warnings— only the invitation to enjoy each moment to the fullest.

▶ 20TH-CENTURY LITERATURE FOR CHILDREN

Children's literature has grown and expanded dramatically in the 1900's. Paperback publishing has expanded greatly, too. Millions of paperbacks are made available to children each year through school book clubs, supermarket racks, and library loans.

As children's literature has expanded, certain early trends have continued to develop. Among these are the popularity of the picture book, the growing realism of the stories, and the appeal of imaginative literature or fantasy.

The Popularity of the Picture Book

In most of the earliest books for children, the illustrations were an afterthought. But in the Caldecott "toy books," the pictures were as important as the few lines of copy, and they occupied far more space. One can almost read the nursery rhyme from the dramatic action of the pictures.

Walter Crane and Randolph Caldecott created their picture-book drawings for well-known fables, songs, and nursery rhymes. Somewhat later, Beatrix Potter wrote an original story for which she painted watercolor illustrations. The result was *The Tale of Peter Rabbit,* published in England in 1901. This is one of the most loved of all picture books. It would be difficult to imagine Peter without his blue jacket or to think of his sisters without their quaint little capes. The pictures and the words are inseparable.

Wanda Gág created story and pictures for *Millions of Cats,* published in the United States in 1928. With the rhythm of an old folktale, suspense builds up and the cats increase until there are "millions and billions and trillions."

The next 50 years saw publication of hundreds of highly successful picture books in which text and illustrations go together perfectly. Often one person is both author and artist—Hardie Gramatky, of *Little Toot;* John Burningham, of *Mr. Gumpy's Outing;* and Uri Shulevitz, of *One Monday Morning,* to name only a few. Many equally successful picture books have been produced by an author-artist team, as in *The Story About Ping,* written by Marjorie Flack and illustrated by Kurt Wiese; *The Happy Lion,* written by Louise Fatio and illustrated by Roger Duvoisin; and *Why Mosquitoes Buzz in People's Ears,* written by Verna Aardema and illustrated by Leo and Diane Dillon.

In this period, improved color printing made it possible for artists to experiment with many art techniques and materials. For illustrations in *The Snowy Day,* Ezra Jack Keats used collage made from bits of patterned paper. Nicolas Sidjakov used a felt-tip pen on clear plastic for his drawings in *Baboushka and the Three Kings.* For *Sam, Bangs & Moonshine,* Evaline Ness experimented with silk-screen textures to form montages. For *Don't You Turn Back,* a collection of poetry by Langston Hughes, Ann Grifalconi used bold woodcuts.

Unlike his sisters, Peter Rabbit disobeys his mother.

In this period the "wordless picture book" was also developed. This kind of picture book is now a popular form with young children, who are encouraged to talk about the way the pictures tell the story. Mercer Mayer, Eric Carle, and John S. Goodall are among the artists who are known for their brilliantly illustrated stories without words.

Growing Realism

Realism, which began to come into children's books in the 1870's, has become bolder and more probing. *Apartment Three,* written and illustrated by Ezra Jack Keats, tells of two lonely boys and a blind man in an ugly tenement—all in picture-book format with superb illustrations. In another picture book, *Annie and the Old One,* written by Miska Miles and illustrated by Peter Parnall, a little Navajo girl makes a futile effort to postpone the death of her aged grandmother. In *Bridge to Terabithia* by Katherine Paterson, death is central to the plot.

Divorce, seen from a child's viewpoint, is handled in *Emily and the Klunky Baby and the Next-Door Dog,* a very easy book by Joan Lexau with drawings by Martha Alexander. For older readers, Judy Blume tackles the same subject in *It's Not the End of the World.*

The struggle to protect a mentally retarded sister or brother is the theme for *Me Too* by Vera and Bill Cleaver and *The Summer of the Swans* by Betsy Byars. A little girl crippled by cerebral palsy is the central figure in *Mine for Keeps* by Jean Little.

There are stories about the lonely child—*Play with Me* by Marie Hall Ets, for example—and about the middle child who wants the privileges of being grown-up without the responsibilities, as in . . . *And Now Miguel* by Joseph Krumgold.

For some children, parents are a problem, too, especially those parents whose plans and expectations put the child in an unhappy situation. Manolo, the son of a famous Spanish bullfighter, is in that predicament in *Shadow of a Bull* by Maia Wojciechowska. Few children are expected to become famous bullfighters. But children see that Manolo's problem parallels their own, and they admire his revolt against adult demands.

In *Freaky Friday* by Mary Rodgers, a 13-year-old wakes up one Friday to find she is her own mother, saddled with the problems common to all mothers. Parent-child conflicts are seen from a new perspective.

Despite the growing realism in children's books, few reflected the truth about the multi-racial society in the United States before the early 1960's. When American Indians were part of the story, they often were pictured with war paint and tomahawks, out to scalp innocent white settlers. Black Americans were almost always shown as smiling servants dependent on their white masters. In text and art, Asians and Mexican-Americans were often pictured as ignorant and inferior.

Illustration by Donna Diamond for *Bridge to Terabithia.*

Jerry Pinkney's drawing for *Roll of Thunder, Hear My Cry.* This book by Mildred D. Taylor won a Newbery award.

In the 1950's and 1960's, though, the movement for racial equality began to gather force in the United States. Partly in response to this movement, the all-white world of children's books began to give way to a world where people of all races and economic levels were pictured realistically and sympathetically.

The Snowy Day (1962) by Ezra Jack Keats, *Stevie* (1969) by John Steptoe, and *Some of the Days of Everett Anderson* (1970) by Lucille Clifton are picture-book stories of black children in the city. They are warmly real, lovable children with humor, curiosity, and wisdom—qualities previously reserved for white children.

For middle-grade readers, *Roosevelt Grady* (1963) by Louisa R. Shotwell introduced a family of black migrant workers struggling against prejudice and poverty. *Sounder* (1969) by William H. Armstrong is the bittersweet story of a black sharecropper family. And in *Roll of Thunder, Hear My Cry* (1976) Mildred Taylor tells of a black Mississippi family's fight against economic exploitation and racial violence during the Depression.

In many instances, the stories of minority groups are tragic, the settings ugly. For some adults, this is not subject matter for children. Yet it is the world many children grow up in and the one shown vividly on television.

At the Same Time—Imagination

Despite the surge of realism in children's literature in the later 1900's, fantasy has persisted. Familiar folktales have been re-issued in new formats and with new illustrations. More tales have been published in countries where literature once was mainly oral.

A number of modern writers have created new fairy tales on the old patterns. Among these tales are *The Practical Princess* and *The Good-for-Nothing Prince* by Jay Williams, *The Emperor and the Kite* by Jane Yolen, and *The Truthful Harp* by Lloyd Alexander.

Some of the most popular books for children are modern fantasies taking place in a realistic setting. *Charlotte's Web,* by E. B. White, tells of a talking pig, a spider who can write messages in her web, and a little girl who understands it all. *Pippi Longstocking,* by Astrid Lindgren of Sweden, tells of a little girl who walks a tightrope in a circus and picks up two policemen by their belts and drops them over the fence. In both stories the impossible seems possible, the unreal seems real, and children revel in the experience.

Several very popular fantasies are British. Good examples are *The Borrowers* (1953) by Mary Norton, *The Children of Green Knowe* (1955) by L. M. Boston, and *Emma in Winter* (1960) by Penelope Farmer.

Strange worlds and imaginary kingdoms seem completely real in many of the modern fantasies. Lloyd Alexander created the land of Prydain for a cycle of five books that have won a loyal following among young listeners and readers. The imaginary land of Narnia was created by the British author C. S. Lewis for a series of seven fantasies. The best known of these fantasies is *The Lion, the Witch, and the Wardrobe.*

Poetry Reflects Every Trend

A few people have said that modern children are not poetry lovers. But the number of books of poetry for children has soared. Poets working in various elementary schools have proved that poetry can be a living form of literature. Impromptu choral reading and dramatization, dance and body movement, painting and sculpture—all tie in with the reading and writing of poetry.

The published books of poetry for children are direct extensions of the trends springing up in the late 1800's and early 1900's. The picture-book format is used again and again as the appropriate background for poetry for children. Several leading artists have selected poems for illustrations done by them—*Poetry of Earth,* selected and illustrated by Adrienne Adams, *Amelia Mixed the Mustard and Other Poems,* selected and illustrated by Evaline Ness, and many others. Twenty-five poems by David McCord make up a picture book entitled *Every Time I Climb A Tree,* illustrated by Marc Simont. Several of Aileen Fisher's story poems have been made into one-poem picture books. These include *Going Barefoot,* illustrated by Adrienne Adams, and *Listen, Rabbit,* illustrated by Symeon Shimin.

The realism that has marked many of the outstanding books of fiction shows up in poetry, too. There are poems about littered streets and boarded-up storefronts, about prejudice and poverty, about loneliness and insecurity. To some young readers, poetry about city streets may seem more real and more directly appealing than a poem about "a host of golden daffodils."

The titles of some of the newer books of poetry for children show the changes—*Some Haystacks Don't Even Have Any Needle,* selected by Stephen Dunning and others; *Garbage Delight,* poems by Dennis Lee, a Canadian; and *My Black Me: A Beginning Book of Black Poetry,* edited by Arnold Adoff.

▶ IDENTIFYING WITH BOOKS

It is involvement with the subject that most children seem to want when they select a book, be it poetry or prose, fiction or nonfiction. They hang onto every word of *Charlotte's Web* because they identify emotionally with the characters—laughing, sighing, weeping as the story unfolds. Judy Blume's books are completely different in character, setting, and plot, but they touch young readers' emotions and pierce their inner thoughts.

When this happens, children keep reading. As Daniel Fader, the writer and educator, puts it, they are "hooked on books."

NANCY LARRICK
Author, *A Parent's Guide to Children's Reading*

"Bonjour, Madame." The happy lion nodded again
when he caught up with Madame Pinson near the grocery store.
"Oo la la . . . !" cried Madame Pinson,

and threw her shopping bag full of vegetables into the lion's face.
"A-a-a-a-choooooo," sneezed the lion.
"People in this town are foolish, as I begin to see."

Roger Duvoisin illustrated *The Happy Lion*, by Louise Fatio.

Thousands of children's books are in print in the United States and Canada alone. Each year many more are published. A number of those published in the past 50 years have become modern classics, which children say are "too good to miss." The following lists include a selection of these favorite books, along with some classics from earlier times.

The books are grouped by theme or purpose. Within each group, titles are listed alphabetically. Each title is followed by the name of the author or editor, the name of the illustrator, and the name of the publisher.

To indicate the age level to which each book is most likely to appeal, the following key is used:

N—Nursery school and kindergarten (age 5 and under)

P—Primary grades (ages 6 to 8)

I—Intermediate grades (ages 9 to 11)

A—Advanced readers (ages 10 to 13)

▶ **NURSERY RHYMES, GOOD-NIGHT BOOKS, AND SONGBOOKS**

The Baby's Song Book, selected and arranged by Elizabeth Porter. Ill. by William Stobbs. Crowell. Traditional nursery songs with piano arrangements. N–P

Brian Wildsmith's Mother Goose. Watts. Eighty-six rhymes with brilliant illustrations. N–P

Bruno Munari's ABC by Bruno Munari. Collins-World. Fascinating ABC book to look at again and again. N

A Child's Goodnight Book by Margaret Wise Brown. Ill. by Jean Charlot. Addison-Wesley. Bedtime picture story of animals getting ready for bed. N

The Fireside Book of Children's Songs, edited by Marie Winn and Allan Miller. Ill. by John Alcorn. Simon. Over 100 songs for all moods, all ages.

Goodnight Moon by Margaret Wise Brown. Ill. by Clement Hurd. Harper. Delightful bedtime story. N

Hi Diddle Diddle: A Book of Mother Goose Rhymes. Ill. by Nola Langner. Scholastic paperback. Forty-two of the simplest rhymes. N

The Mother Goose Treasury, edited and ill. by Raymond Briggs. Coward. Over 400 rhymes with brilliant pictures. N–P

The Tall Book of Mother Goose. Ill. by Feodor Rojankovsky. Harper. One hundred favorites with appealing illustrations. N–P

▶ **PICTURE BOOKS**

And to Think That I Saw It on Mulberry Street, written and ill. by Dr. Seuss. Vanguard. A small boy's story gets bigger and bigger as he nears home. N–P

Andy and the Lion, written and ill. by James Daugherty. Penguin. How Andy saved the lion and the lion saved Andy. P

Are You My Mother?, written and ill. by P. D. Eastman. Random. A baby bird searches for its mother in a story with vocabulary limited to 100 words. N–P

Bedtime for Frances by Russell Hoban. Ill. by Garth Williams. Harper. A lovable little badger maneuvers to postpone bedtime. N

The Biggest Bear, written and ill. by Lynd Ward. Hough-

One winter morning Peter woke up and looked out the window. Snow had fallen during the night. It covered everything as far as he could see.

6

Ezra Jack Keats won a Caldecott Medal for *The Snowy Day*.

ton. How a bear cub grows into a problem. N–P

Blueberries for Sal, written and ill. by Robert McCloskey. Viking. Sal and her mother go blueberrying in Maine with Little Bear and his mother. N–P

The Cat in the Hat, written and ill. by Dr. Seuss. Random. Hilarious story easy enough for first-graders to read on their own very quickly. P

Chicken Pox and *Hide and Seek* by Ginette Anfousse. New Canada Publications. Colorful picture books about a little girl called Jo Jo. N–P

Curious George, written and ill. by H. A. Rey. Houghton. Adventures of a monkey with great curiosity. N–P

Evan's Corner by Elizabeth Starr Hill. Ill. by Nancy Grossman. Holt. How a small boy finds privacy in a two-room apartment occupied by a family of seven. P

Frog and Toad Are Friends, written and ill. by Arnold Lobel. Harper. Warm friendliness pervades these five gentle stories. N–P

Frog, Where Are You? by Mercer Mayer. Dial. Picture story without words. N

The Happy Lion by Louise Fatio. Ill. by Roger Duvoisin. McGraw. Adventures of a lion who escapes from a French zoo. N–P

Harry the Dirty Dog by Gene Zion. Ill. by Margaret B. Graham. Harper. Harry finally realizes that getting dirty means losing friends. N–P

How Summer Came to Canada by William Toye. Ill. by Elizabeth Cleaver. Oxford. A brightly colored picture book recounting a story from the Micmac Indians. P–I

Leo the Late Bloomer by Robert Kraus. Ill. by José Aruego. Dutton. The slow learner finally catches up with the other animals and becomes a hero. N–P

Little Bear by Else Holmelund Minarik. Ill. by Maurice Sendak. Harper. Four tender stories about the adventures of Little Bear that can be read by many first- and second-graders. P

The Little House, written and ill. by Virginia Lee Burton. Houghton. A city surrounds a house that was once in the country. P

Little Toot, written and ill. by Hardie Gramatky. Putnam. How a mischievous little tugboat becomes a hero. P

Look Again! photos by Tana Hoban. Macmillan. Dramatic photographs invite conversation with a child. N

Lyle, Lyle Crocodile, written and ill. by Bernard Waber. Houghton. Adventures of a pet crocodile and the family he adopts. P

Madeline, written and ill. by Ludwig Bemelmans. Viking. How little girls in a French school follow their leader. P

Make Way for Ducklings, written and ill. by Robert McCloskey. Viking. A family of mallard ducks that lived in the Public Garden in Boston. P

Mike Mulligan and His Steam Shovel, written and ill. by Virginia Lee Burton. Houghton. Success story of the steam shovel Mary Anne. P

Mr. Gumpy's Outing, written and ill. by John Burningham. Holt. Children and farm animals, on a boat ride, are warned, "Don't flap about," but they forget. P

Noah's Ark, with ill. by Peter Spier. Doubleday. Fascinating details in every picture make this a book to pore over. N–P

Petunia, written and ill. by Roger Duvoisin. Knopf. The amusing story of a goose who loved books. N–P

Play with Me, written and ill. by Marie Hall Ets. Viking. A little girl learns to win friends. Simple text; exquisite pictures. N–P

Sam, Bangs & Moonshine, written and ill. by Evaline Ness. Holt. The exquisite story of a lonely little girl and the tales of her mermaid mother. P

The Snowy Day, written and ill. by Ezra Jack Keats. Viking. Peter's adventures in city snow, with brilliant pictures. N–P

Above: Mr. Gumpy has a lot of passengers in *Mr. Gumpy's Outing*, by John Burningham. Right: Noah has a similar problem in *Noah's Ark*, a picture book by Peter Spier, which won a Caldecott Medal. Below: Robert McCloskey's *Make Way for Ducklings* was another Caldecott winner.

Inside the gate they all turned round to say thank you to the policemen. The policemen smiled and waved good-by.

"Thank you, Gum baby," said the fairy.
But the doll did not answer.

"Don't you reply when I thank you?"
cried the angered fairy.
The doll did not stir.

A Story, A Story, an African folk tale adapted and illustrated by Gail E. Haley, won a Caldecott Medal.

The Story About Ping by Marjorie Flack. Ill. by Kurt Wiese. Viking. A Chinese duckling's adventures away from his riverboat home. N–P

The Story of Babar by Jean de Brunhoff. Random. A little elephant becomes king of the jungle elephants. His story is continued in other Babar books. P

Sylvester and the Magic Pebble, written and ill. by William Steig. Simon. How a young donkey finds a magic pebble that assures every wish. N–P

The Two Reds by Will Lipkind and Nicolas Mordvinoff. Harcourt. Adventures of a boy and a cat in a big city. P

Where the Wild Things Are, written and ill. by Maurice Sendak. Harper. When Max is sent to his room, he visits the wild things and has a marvelous time. N–P

Who, Said Sue, Said Whoo?, written and ill. by Ellen Raskin. Atheneum. Like an old cumulative tale, this hilarious story repeats and repeats to a beautiful surprise ending. N–P

▶ **POETRY BOOKS**

Alligator Pie by Dennis Lee. Houghton of Canada. Nonsense rhymes mostly about familiar Canadian people and places. P

City in All Directions, edited by Arnold Adoff. Ill. by Donald Carrick. Macmillan. Poems about cities and city life. I–A

Don't You Turn Back by Langston Hughes; poems selected by Lee Bennett Hopkins. Ill. by Ann Grifalconi. Knopf. Forty-six poems by the great black poet, with dramatic illustrations. I–A

Early Moon by Carl Sandburg. Ill. by James Daugherty. Harcourt. A sparkling collection. I–A

Every Time I Climb a Tree by David McCord. Ill. by Marc Simont. Little. Twenty-five poems for the very young in picture-book format. P

Four-Way Stop and Other Poems by Myra Cohn Livingston. Ill. by James F. Spanfeller. Atheneum. Poems of many moods related to experiences and concerns of young readers. I–A

Hailstones and Halibut Bones by Mary O'Neill. Ill. by Leonard Weisgard. Doubleday. Each poem is about a different color—its variations, implications, and appeal. A model for children's observations and creativity. I–A

Hey, Bug! and Other Poems About Little Things, selected by Elizabeth M. Itse. Ill. by Susan Carlton Smith. American Heritage. Thirty poems about bugs, mice, frogs, fireflies, and other small creatures, with exquisite illustrations. I

How to Eat a Poem & Other Morsels: A Collection of Food Poems for Children, selected by Rose H. Agree. Pantheon. Humorous verse about foods and those who love them. I–A

Hurry, Hurry, Mary Dear! and Other Nonsense Poems, written and ill. by N. M. Bodecker. Atheneum. Poems full of imagination and "illogical logic." I–A

I Am the Darker Brother, edited by Arnold Adoff. Ill. by Benny Andrews. Macmillan. Modern poems by black Americans. A

It Doesn't Always Have to Rhyme by Eve Merriam; ill. by Malcolm Spooner. Atheneum. Modern free verse that is both witty and wise. I–A

Listen, Rabbit by Aileen Fisher. Ill. by Symeon Shimin. Crowell. Story poem about a boy who discovers a nest of rabbits. P–I

Oh, What Nonsense! edited by William Cole. Ill. by Tomi Ungerer. Viking. Fifty poems, silly and ridiculous, old and new. P–I

One at a Time by David McCord. Little. Crisp, vivid, humorous poems. I–A

Piping Down the Valleys Wild, edited by Nancy Larrick.

Ill. by Ellen Raskin. Delacorte. More than 200 poems with great appeal for those under 12. I–A

The Poetry Troupe: Poems to Read Aloud, compiled by Isabel Wilner. Scribner. More than 200 poems ideal for getting children involved through impromptu chanting, dramatization, and choral reading. I–A

Prayers from the Ark by Carmen Bernos de Gasztold; translated from the French by Rumer Godden. Ill. by Jean Primrose. Penguin. Animals at sea on Noah's Ark offer their prayers with humor and gentle pathos. A favorite of all ages. P–I

Reflections on a Gift of Watermelon Pickle and Other Modern Verse, edited by Stephen Dunning and others. Lothrop. Modern poems that appeal to young readers. A

Songs of the Dream People, edited and ill. by James Houston. Atheneum. These chants and images from Indians and Eskimo of North America have wonderful rhythm and a special beauty. I–A

When We Were Very Young and *Now We Are Six* by A. A. Milne. Ill. by E. H. Shepard. Dutton. Delightfully simple and childlike. N–P

Where the Sidewalk Ends, poems and drawings by Shel Silverstein. Harper. Wonderfully appealing to modern youngsters. P–I–A

You Come Too by Robert Frost. Holt. Fifty-two favorite poems selected for young readers. A

You Read to Me, I'll Read to You by John Ciardi. Ill. by Edward Gorey. Lippincott. Humorous poems for parent and child to read to each other. P–I

▶ **FOLKTALES**

Aesop's Fables, retold by Anne Terry White. Ill. by Helen Siegl. Random. Spirited retelling of the old fables. P–I

Always Room for One More by Sorche Nic Leodhas. Ill. by Nonny Hogrogian. Holt. Old Scottish folktale. P

Baboushka and the Three Kings by Ruth Robbins. Ill. by Nicolas Sidjakov. Parnassus. Russian folktale of the old woman too busy to join the Three Kings in search of the Christ Child. P

Call It Courage by Armstrong Sperry. Macmillan. A Polynesian legend full of harrowing adventures. I

Caps for Sale written and ill. by Esphyr Slobodkina. Addison-Wesley. How a troupe of monkeys teases a cap peddler. P

The Fairy Tale Treasury, selected by Virginia Haviland. Ill. by Raymond Briggs. Coward. Thirty-two folktales from around the world, with brilliant illustrations. N–P–I

John Henry: An American Legend, written and ill. by Ezra Jack Keats. Pantheon. Simplified story of the black superman and his hammer, with bold illustrations. I

Millions of Cats, written and ill. by Wanda Gág. Coward. A modern folktale full of rhythm and repetition that is great for reading aloud. N–P

The Mitten by Alvin R. Tresselt. Ill. by Yaroslava Mills. Lothrop. An old Ukrainian folktale about animals that live in a boy's lost mitten. P

The Shoemaker and the Elves by the Brothers Grimm. Ill. by Adrienne Adams. Scribner. Exquisite picture story

Leo and Diane Dillon drew the pictures for Verna Aardema's book, *Why Mosquitoes Buzz in People's Ears.*

of the poor shoemaker and the elves who help him.
P–I

Stone Soup, retold and ill. by Marcia Brown. Scribner. Humorous old tale of soup made with stones. P–I

A Story, A Story: An African Tale, written and ill. by Gail E. Haley. Atheneum. The old tale of Anansi, the spider, with brilliant woodcuts. P–I

The Three Billy Goats Gruff, edited and ill. by Marcia Brown. Harcourt. How three frisky billy goats outsmart the ugly troll. N–P

Tikki Tikki Tembo, retold by Arlene Mosel. Ill. by Blair Lent. Holt. Humor and repetition mark this tongue-twisting tale from old China. P–I

The Time-Ago Tales of Jahdu by Virginia Hamilton. Ill. by Nonny Hogrogian. Macmillan. Four African tales as told to a small black boy in Harlem. I–A

Why Mosquitoes Buzz in People's Ears: A West African Tale, retold by Verna Aardema. Ill. by Leo and Diane Dillon. Dial. Wonderful rhythm and repetition with stunning illustrations. I

Zlateh the Goat and Other Stories by Isaac Bashevis Singer. Ill. by Maurice Sendak. Harper. Yiddish folktales retold with warmth and humor. I–A

▶ FANTASY AND ADVENTURE

Bambi by Felix Salten. Ill. by Kurt Wiese. Grosset. Classic story of a deer, followed by *Bambi's Children.* I–A

The Borrowers by Mary Norton. Ill. by Beth and Joe Krush. Harcourt. Delightful story of miniature people who live by borrowing what they need. I–A

The Cat Who Wished to Be a Man by Lloyd Alexander. Dutton. Action, good dialogue, and comedy mark the adventures of the cat who suddenly had to cope with the ways and problems of human beings. I

Charlotte's Web by E. B. White. Ill. by Garth Williams. Harper. The tender story of a talking pig, a spider who can write messages in her web, and a little girl who understands them perfectly. P–I

Illustration from *The Little Prince* by Antoine de Saint-Exupéry. The story is beautiful and sentimental.

Chitty-Chitty-Bang-Bang by Ian Fleming. Ill. by John Burningham. Random. An old racing car develops the power to swim, fly, and communicate. I

The City Under Ground by Suzanne Martel. Archway. Science fiction about Montreal. I

The Cricket in Times Square by George Selden. Ill. by Garth Williams. Farrar. A country cricket takes over at a subway newsstand in New York City. I–A

Crictor, written and ill. by Tomi Ungerer. Harper. An elderly French schoolmistress and her pet boa constrictor create a hilarious story. P

The Enormous Egg by Oliver Butterworth. Ill. by Louis Darling. Little. When Nate Twitchell's old hen lays an egg that hatches a dinosaur, his adventures are just beginning. I–A

Half Magic by Edward Eager. Ill. by N. M. Bodecker. Harcourt. A mysterious coin grants only half a wish at a time, but children learn to manipulate it for great adventures. I–A

The Hobbit, written and ill. by J. R. R. Tolkien. Houghton. The marvelous adventures of Bilbo Baggins, who went in search of treasure. I–A

Jacob Two-Two Meets the Hooded Fang by Mordecai Richler. Knopf. An amusing fantasy about a little boy who says everything twice. I

The Lion, the Witch, and the Wardrobe by C. S. Lewis. Macmillan. English children visit the mysterious land of Narnia beyond the wardrobe. I

The Little Prince by Antoine de Saint-Exupéry. Harcourt. The story of a little prince who lives on a planet that has only one flower. I–A

The Marvelous Misadventures of Sebastian by Lloyd Alexander. Dutton. Fast-paced adventure story in an 18th-century fantasy land. I

Mary Poppins by Pamela L. Travers. Harcourt. When you know that Mary Poppins can slide up the bannister, you know anything can happen—and it does. P–I

Mr. Popper's Penguins by Richard and Florence Atwater. Ill. by Robert Lawson. Hilarious story of a family of penguins who monopolize the Popper household. P–I

The Mouse and the Motorcycle by Beverly Cleary. Ill. by Louis Darling. Morrow. How an ingenious mouse drives a miniature motorcycle and triumphs over all. I

Pippi Longstocking by Astrid Lindgren. Viking. A daredevil 9-year-old girl creates a sensation with the greatest ease. P–I

Rabbit Hill, written and ill. by Robert Lawson. Viking. When a new family moves in, they meet the animals that have taken over. I–A

The Wind in the Willows by Kenneth Grahame. Ill. by E. H. Shepard. Scribner. Classic story of animals who live along the Thames River and talk and act like English country gentlemen. P–I

The World of Pooh (*Winnie-the-Pooh* and *The House at Pooh Corner*) by A. A. Milne. Ill. by E. H. Shepard. Dutton. About 6-year-old Christopher Robin and his toy pets. N–P

A Wrinkle in Time by Madeleine L'Engle. Farrar. Science fiction of the most intriguing sort. A

▶ REALISTIC STORIES

Alexander and the Terrible, Horrible, No Good, Very Bad Day by Judith Viorst. Ill. by Ray Cruz. Atheneum. A small boy's comical recital of his difficulties on a single day. P–I

I went to sleep with gum in my mouth and now there's gum in my hair and when I got out of bed this morning I tripped on the skateboard and by mistake I dropped my sweater in the sink while the water was running and I could tell it was going to be a terrible, horrible, no good, very bad day.

From Alexander and the Terrible, Horrible, No Good, Very Bad Day by Judith Viorst.

. . . *And Now Miguel* by Joseph Krumgold. Ill. by Jean Charlot. Crowell. The middle son of New Mexican sheepherders longs to be accepted as a man. I–A

Anne of Green Gables by Lucy Maud Montgomery. Bantam. Probably Canada's most famous story for children—about a high-spirited girl adopted by an elderly couple in Prince Edward Island. I–A

Blue Willow by Doris Gates. Ill. by Paul Lantz. Viking. How Janey Larkin and her family, migratory workers, conquer great difficulties. I–A

The Case of the Scaredy Cats, written and ill. by Crosby Bonsall. Harper. An easy-reading mystery. P

A Certain Small Shepherd by Rebecca Caudill. Ill. by William Pene Du Bois. Holt. The Christmas miracle of a small mute boy in Appalachia. P

Chancy and the Grand Rascal by Sid Fleischman. Ill. by Eric Von Schmidt. Little. Ohio River adventures of a boy and his Uncle Will, the grand rascal. I–A

Crow Boy, written and ill. by Taro Yashima. Viking. Japanese schoolchildren learn to appreciate the one who is different. P

Danny Dunn and the Homework Machine by Jay Williams and Ray Abrashkin. McGraw. An enterprising schoolboy lets the computer handle his homework. I–A

Don't Take Teddy by Babbis Friis-Baastad. Archway. First-person story of a boy trying to protect his mentally retarded older brother. A

The Egypt Game by Zilpha Keatley Snyder. Ill. by Alton Raible. Atheneum. City children take over an abandoned junkyard for their dramatic games. I–A

Ellen Grae by Vera and Bill Cleaver. Ill. by Ellen Raskin. Lippincott. The child of divorced parents shows deep hurt. I

The Family Under the Bridge by Natalie Savage Carlson. Ill. by Garth Williams. Harper. A charming Paris hobo adopts a forlorn little family and gives them a real Christmas. I

From the Mixed-Up Files of Mrs. Basil E. Frankweiler by E. L. Konigsburg. Atheneum. How two children run away from their suburban homes and live in the Metropolitan Museum. I–A

Harriet the Spy, written and ill. by Louise Fitzhugh. Harper. Harriet, the loner, becomes a self-appointed spy with notebooks that cause trouble. I

Henry Huggins by Beverly Cleary. Ill. by Louis Darling. Morrow. Henry's adventures are always humorous and always real. P–I

Homer Price, written and ill. by Robert McCloskey. Viking. Hilarious adventures of an enterprising boy in Ohio. I–A

The Hundred Dresses by Eleanor Estes. Ill. by Louis Slobodkin. Harcourt. A little Polish girl who says she has 100 dresses finally wins the approval of her peers. I

Island of the Blue Dolphins by Scott O'Dell. Houghton.

Illustration by N. C. Wyeth for *The Yearling*, by Marjorie Kinnan Rawlings.

Moving story of an Indian girl who lived alone for 18 years on an island off the coast of California. A

Julie of the Wolves by Jean Craighead George. Harper. Arctic wolves protect a 13-year-old girl on the North Slope of Alaska. A

Lost in the Barrens by Farley Mowat. Little. An engrossing story of two boys' fight for survival in Canada's northland. A

Maxie by Mildred Kantrowitz. Ill. by Emily A. McCully. Parents. Humorous and touching picture story of the old lady who is befriended by the whole apartment house. P–I

Misty of Chincoteague by Marguerite Henry. Ill. by Wesley Dennis. Rand. Two children adopt a pony from the spring roundup on Chincoteague Island. A favorite of horse lovers. I

My Mother Is the Most Beautiful Woman in the World by Becky Reyher. Ill. by Ruth Gannett. Lothrop. A Russian folktale of a little lost girl's search for her mother. P

My Side of the Mountain, written and ill. by Jean George. Dutton. First-person narrative of a city boy who spends the winter living in the hollow of a great hemlock in the Catskills. A

Queenie Peavy by Robert Burch. Ill. by Jerry Lazare. Viking. Thirteen-year-old Queenie, whose father is in prison, fights her way through ridicule, poverty, and insecurity. A

Roosevelt Grady by Louisa R. Shotwell. Ill. by Peter Burchard. Collins-World. Black migrant workers struggle to get a home where they can "stay put." I–A

Sounder by William H. Armstrong. Ill. by James Barkley. Harper. A story of black sharecroppers. I–A

Stevie, written and ill. by John Steptoe. Harper. A small boy in Harlem tells of the crybaby in his family. P

Tales of a Fourth Grade Nothing by Judy Blume. Ill. by Roy Doty. Dutton. A 9-year-old's troubles with a younger brother make up this humorous tale. I–A

Tell Me a Mitzi by Lore Segal. Ill. by Harriet Pincus. Farrar. Three charming family stories of city children. P–I

The Yearling by Marjorie Kinnan Rawlings. Ill. by N. C. Wyeth. Scribner. The story of a boy, his pet fawn, and the problems of growing up. A

Zeely by Virginia Hamilton. Ill. by Symeon Shimin. Macmillan. Six-and-a-half-foot Zeely becomes a queen in the eyes of a small black girl from the city. A

▸ HISTORY IN MANY FORMS

Amos Fortune, Free Man by Elizabeth Yates. Ill. by Nora Unwin. Dutton. True story of the black slave who bought his freedom after 40 years. A

And Then What Happened, Paul Revere? by Jean Fritz. Ill. by Margot Tomes. Coward. Humorous, fast-paced, and historically accurate. I

The Bears on Hemlock Mountain by Alice Dalgliesh. Ill. by Helen Sewell. Scribner. On an errand for his mother, an 8-year-old encounters bears. P

Carry On, Mr. Bowditch by Jean Lee Latham. Houghton. Life story of a boy who became famous in maritime history. A

The Courage of Sarah Noble by Alice Dalgliesh. Ill. by Leonard Weisgard. Scribner. In the early 1700's, an 8-year-old assumes adult responsibilities in the Connecticut wilderness. P–I

Daniel Boone, written and ill. by James Daugherty. Viking. Life story of Daniel Boone in strong, rhythmical language. A

Freedom Train: The Story of Harriet Tubman by Dorothy Sterling. Doubleday. A

The House of Dies Drear by Virginia Hamilton. Ill. by Eros Keith. Macmillan. Ghosts from the Underground Railroad shadow the house that a black family moves into. A

Johnny Tremain by Esther Forbes. Ill. by Lynd Ward. Houghton. Story of a silversmith's apprentice in Boston in the days of Paul Revere. A

Little House on the Prairie by Laura Ingalls Wilder. Ill. by Garth Williams. Harper. The life story of a pioneer family in Wisconsin in the 1870's. I

North to Freedom by Anne S. Holm. Translated from the Danish. Harcourt. The story of a boy who escaped from a World War II concentration camp. A

Paddle-to-the-Sea written and ill. by Holling C. Holling. Houghton. The journey of an Indian boy's tiny canoe to the Atlantic by way of the St. Lawrence River. P

Thy Friend, Obadiah, written and ill. by Brinton Turkle. Viking. The story of a Quaker lad on Nantucket and his sea gull.

Tituba of Salem Village by Ann Petry. Crowell. The story of a black from Barbados who was drawn into the Salem witchcraft trials. A

Underground to Canada by Barbara Smucker. Clarke-Irwin. An exciting story of the Underground Railway that smuggled slaves from the United States into Canada before the Civil War. A

The Witch of Blackbird Pond by Elizabeth Speare. Houghton. A vivid tale of the hysteria of the great witch-hunt in Connecticut. A

CHILE

Chile is like a long, narrow shelf on the western coast of South America, isolated by geography from the rest of the continent. On the east the world's highest mountain chain, the Andes, divides Chile from Argentina. A barren desert in the north separates Chile from Peru and Bolivia. To the west, Chile faces the deep waters of the Pacific Ocean. Southern Chile ends at stormy Cape Horn, facing icy Antarctica.

▶ THE PEOPLE

The Chilean people are mainly of mixed Indian, Spanish, and other European descent. The faces of many Chileans today reflect their Indian heritage. But the remaining true Indians number only about 500,000. Most of them are known as Araucanians, or *Mapuche*. *Mapuche* means "people of the land," but the Indians lost most of their land to the Spanish settlers who arrived in the 1500's. The Araucanians now live on poor reservations in southern Chile. They survive by fishing, farming, and making handicrafts. Chilean culture today is based largely on Spanish customs. Spanish is the national language, and most of the people are Roman Catholics. There are smaller numbers of Jews and Protestants.

During the 1800's small numbers of newcomers from Peru, Bolivia, Germany, Yugoslavia, Syria, Lebanon, Ireland, and Britain arrived in Chile. Many of them were successful in business, agriculture, and politics. Germans and Yugoslavs, for example, established farms and ranches in southern Chile.

Way of Life

In Chile today, a huge gap still separates the few rich from the many poor. Wealthy Chileans own the factories, banks, and large farms and ranches. They live mainly in the capital city of Santiago or on the great estates surrounding it. The wealthy usually have large families, and their big houses contain many rooms and servants.

When cities began to grow in the early 1900's, a middle class developed there. The members of this group include doctors, teachers, clerks, merchants, mechanics, agricultural technicians, engineers, and soldiers.

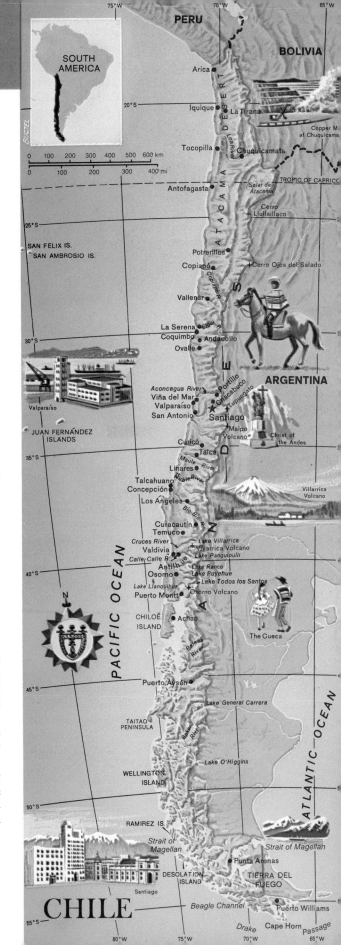

Often both husband and wife work outside the home, while a maid takes care of the house and children.

Poor Chileans are mostly mestizos, whose ancestors combined European and Indian blood. They try to earn a living as farmhands, miners, factory workers, and common laborers. But as many as one fourth of all Chileans have no jobs. Many live in shacks on the great estates or in city slums. The urban poor are called *rotos* ("broken ones"). The rural poor are known as *huasos* ("cowboys"). The rural poor toil in the fields from dawn to dusk. The *huasos* seen by tourists and at rodeos are actually wealthy landowners wearing fancy flat-topped hats, pointed silver spurs, and ponchos and sashes colored red, white, and blue to match the national flag.

Food and Drink. Many wealthy and middle-income Chileans eat four meals a day. For breakfast they usually have just a roll and coffee. Lunch is large and lengthy. Teatime at the end of the afternoon includes breads and pastry. Dinner often is not served until ten o'clock at night.

The most common national dishes are *empanadas* (meat pies filled with onions, raisins, and olives), chicken soup, fish stew, noodles, and steak with fried eggs on top. Chilean food, unlike Mexican food, is not spicy. Even children drink the local wines with their meals.

Entertainment. Chileans enjoy many sports. Whatever their income, they follow the national pastime of soccer, called *futbol*. Some Chileans play basketball, polo, golf, tennis, and cricket. Boxing and horse racing are also very popular, and livestock shows and rodeos draw big crowds outside the capital city. People enjoy swimming and fishing in the lakes and the ocean. Ski centers in the mountains attract wealthy Chileans and tourists. Almost everyone gambles on lotteries, which contribute to charitable causes.

Chileans also attend movies, plays, and operas and other musical events. The International Song Festival takes place each year in the seaside resort of Viña del Mar. Folk music and dancing are popular forms of entertainment, especially in rural areas. The *cueca*, the national dance, is a fast-moving, stomping courtship dance between a man and a woman in peasant costumes. The dancers flirt and wave handkerchiefs.

Chileans celebrate traditional Roman Catholic holidays. The July Feast of the Virgin of Carmen, the patron saint of the armed forces, attracts much attention. Christmas and New Year are also important holidays. At harvesttime many rural villages hold wine and food festivals. The biggest national holiday is Independence Day, September 18.

Education

In the 1850's only 14 percent of all Chileans could read and write, but nearly 90 percent can do so today. Some preschools now provide extra instruction, along with meals, for the poor. Schooling is required for all children from ages 6 to 14. But most Chileans do not go beyond the fifth grade because they must work. Only about one third of those who complete primary school attend secondary school. Most young people in high school take technical training—for example, in accounting, agricultural management, and mechanics—and enter the growing middle class. Only a few prepare for college.

The University of Chile, the leading public university, was founded in 1738 by the king of Spain. It was reorganized by the Venezuelan scholar Andrés Bello and reopened in 1843. Both the University of Chile and the major private university, the Catholic University of Chile, are in Santiago. These universities provide professional and cultural training. But very few Chileans—mainly the sons and daughters of the wealthy—complete a college education.

The Arts

Chilean crafts include colorful weavings, rugs, ponchos, black pottery, and copper sculptures. Many handcrafted items are sold to tourists. In rural Chile, folk songs, creative folk tales, and legends are handed down from generation to generation.

For a small country, Chile has made an important contribution to world literature. Two Chilean poets won Nobel prizes for literature —Gabriela Mistral (Lucila Godoy de Alcayaga) in 1945 and Pablo Neruda in 1971. Novelist Joaquín Edwards Bello gained fame in the 1920's for his book about the Chilean *roto*. Several Chilean authors became well known during the international boom in Latin-American novels that began in the 1960's, especially

Osorno Volcano towers over Lake Todos los Santos in the Chilean lake district, south of Temuco. Chileans and tourists come to this region to swim, sail, fish, and ski.

José Donoso. Many Chilean artists left the country after the military took control of the government in the 1970's.

Chile has also inspired writers from other countries. The British author Daniel Defoe based his story *Robinson Crusoe* on the adventures of a Scotsman stranded on one of Chile's islands in the early 1700's. The British scientist-author Charles Darwin formed some of his ideas about evolution during a visit to Chile in the 1800's.

▶ THE LAND

Chile stretches more than 4,120 kilometers (2,600 miles) from north to south but averages only 160 kilometers (100 miles) in width. It is like the west coast of the United States turned upside down, with the colder, rainy zone in the south and the hot, dry part in the north.

Northern Chile

In parts of the Atacama Desert in what is called the Great North, no rainfall has ever been recorded. Although harsh, this region attracts settlers because of its rich mineral deposits. Over the centuries it has been a source of gold, silver, nitrates, iodine, iron, and copper. Peru and Bolivia controlled the Great North until a war won by Chile in the 1880's. The area has a long history of boom towns, mining camps, violence, and bandits. Chile's highest mountain peak, Cerro Ojos del Salado, is located here. It rises to about 6,875 meters (22,550 feet) on the border with Argentina.

Below the Great North is a region called the Little North. It is a mixed zone of mining and farming. Not very many people live in either the Little North or the Great North.

Middle Chile

Until the late 1800's, the Chilean government really controlled only the middle of the country. The heart of this region is known as the Central Valley because it lies between the Andes and a range of coastal mountains. This fertile region extends from the Aconcagua River in the north to the Bío-Bío River in the south. The climate is mild, much like that of central California. Over two thirds of the people live in this region, mainly in the cities of Santiago and Valparaíso. Three fourths of Chile's industry is located in the Central Valley, as are most of the rich farms and great estates.

Southern Chile

This frontier region was held by the Araucanian Indians until they were defeated by the national army in the 1880's. The region is for-

Copper is Chile's leading export. Chuquicamata, shown above, is one of the world's largest copper mining and smelting centers. Another well-known Chilean export is wine, which comes from grapes grown in vineyards like the one pictured at the left.

ested and rainy, much like the Pacific Northwest in the United States. The manufacturing city of Concepción is situated here, but southern Chile is mainly an agricultural region. Snow-capped volcanoes and many rushing rivers and mountain lakes add to the scenic beauty of the area, which is sometimes rocked by earthquakes.

Few people live in the far south, which reaches down to the Antarctic Circle. Chile claims part of frozen Antarctica, but claims to Antarctica are not recognized internationally. The official boundaries of the nation stop at windswept Cape Horn. Before the Panama Canal was opened in 1914, ships from all over the world went through the Drake Strait or the Strait of Magellan in southern Chile to cross between the Atlantic and Pacific oceans.

Chile and Argentina have nearly gone to war over conflicting claims to three small islands in the Beagle Channel near Cape Horn. The two countries share the island called

Tierra del Fuego ("Land of Fire"). It seems odd that such a cold, wet island should have this name. But early explorers passing by saw Indians burning fires along the coast.

Chile owns other important islands off its west coast, including the Juan Fernández Islands. The most famous of these rocky outposts in the Pacific is Easter Island, which is known for the great stone heads that people there carved long ago. The origins of these statues continue to puzzle archeologists.

▶ THE ECONOMY

For centuries, more Chileans worked at agriculture than anything else. Many of them lived on the great estates, called *fundos,* where they worked the property of the wealthy landowners in exchange for low wages and small pieces of land on which to grow food for themselves. These tenant farmers were known as *inquilinos.* Other poor Chileans owned tiny plots of their own or traveled from farm to farm looking for work. Since the 1930's the government has discouraged farming while encouraging the growth of business and industry in the cities. As a result, most Chileans now live and work in urban areas. Mining does not employ large numbers of people, but it is very important to the economy.

Agriculture

Chilean farms still produce abundant crops. Sheep and goats graze on pastures in the Little North. In the fertile Central Valley, corn, beans, wheat, fruits, tobacco, sunflowers, and hemp flourish. There are also many excellent vineyards and some cattle ranches in this region. Farms in the south are not as huge as those in the Central Valley. Cereals and potatoes are the leading crops, and ranchers raise sheep and cattle.

Mineral Industries and Manufacturing

Under Spanish rule and in the early 1800's, silver and copper were Chile's chief mineral exports. By the late 1800's, nitrates had become the leading item sold abroad. The nitrates were used for making gunpowder and fertilizer. In more recent times, the economy has depended greatly on copper sales overseas. Chileans today say that "copper is the salary of Chile." Chuquicamata, high in the Andes, is one of the largest copper mines in the world. This mine and other large mines were owned by U.S. companies until the 1970's. Then Chile took them over because of their importance to the economic strength of the country. Iron ore, molybdenum, gold, and silver are other major metals. Iodine and boron are important by-products of nitrate mining. Coal, sulfur, and petroleum are also produced.

In the 1800's the Chilean government began to encourage the development of local industries so that the country would not have to import the manufactured goods it needed. From that time into the 1960's, Chilean manufacturing expanded rapidly. Factories produced processed foodstuffs, beer, textiles, paper, leather goods, glass, cement, and iron and steel. Wood products and fish meal became important exports. But industry declined after the military took control of the government in 1973.

Service Industries

As agriculture and industry became less important, Chile developed more of what is known as a service economy. Increasing numbers of people work at jobs that provide services. They are teachers, clerks, waiters, maids, shoeshiners, and the like. Many of them do not hold steady jobs.

▶CITIES

Chile's cities have been growing rapidly. In the 1830's, three fourths of all Chileans lived in rural communities. By the 1970's, three fourths lived in urban areas.

The capital city, Santiago, dominates all the other cities. One third of all Chileans live in this metropolis, which sprawls over a wide plain along the Mapocho River. The city is dotted with green parks, modern suburbs, and old and new slums. Some of these poorer neighborhoods are created by new arrivals from the countryside. Because these squatter communities often pop up overnight, they are called "mushrooms." An article on Santiago appears in Volume S.

The second largest city, Valparaíso, is Chile's major Pacific port. Built on steep hills encircling a bay, it reminds visitors of San Francisco in California. Cable cars carry passengers up the steep hillsides. Adjoining Valparaíso is the beach resort of Viña del Mar. Another large Chilean city is Concepción, which was founded in 1550. It grew from a frontier outpost to a regional industrial center.

▶HISTORY AND GOVERNMENT

Indians lived in Chile for thousands of years before the Spanish conquest. There were small tribes at the southern tip of the country and in the northern desert. The tribes in the north, who made their living by fishing and by farming on the oases, came under the control of the Incas of Peru in the second half of the 1400's. Like the Spanish who came later, the Incas built forts in central and southern Chile. Also like the Spanish, they were unable to defeat the Araucanians living there.

The many Araucanian groups developed different ways of life to adapt to Chile's different regions. But all of them shared a common language, even though they had no writing. They lived in family groups and in small villages. They hunted game, gathered fruits and vegetables, caught fish, and traded with other Indians. They were also involved in many tribal wars.

Colonial Times

The first Spanish people went to Chile from Peru. To get the Spanish to leave Peru, the Indians there told them wild tales about precious metals in Chile. Diego de Almagro be-

Santa Lucia Hill, in Santiago, has been called one of the most attractive urban parks in the world. It is located on the south bank of the Mapocho River near the downtown business district.

lieved the Peruvian Indian tales and went to Chile in 1535. He found no riches in the Central Valley, and many of his soldiers died. Pedro de Valdivia launched an expedition to Chile in 1540. Valdivia established permanent Spanish rule over the Central Valley, but he was killed in an Araucanian rebellion led by his former Indian groom, Lautaro.

The Araucanians in southern Chile continued to struggle against the Spanish during the first two centuries of colonial occupation. Because the Araucanians had no powerful central government, the Spanish could not simply capture their top ruler, as they did with the Incas in Peru and the Aztecs in Mexico. The mobile Araucanians adopted Spanish weapons and techniques of warfare, including the use of horses in battle. Those who were captured by the Spanish were enslaved by their conquerors and forced to work in the mines or on the farms. Fighting and disease reduced the number of Araucanians by two thirds during the first 100 years of Spanish occupation.

Under Spanish rule, Chile was a frontier colony held for defense against the Indians and coastal pirates. It was governed by the Spanish king through the viceroy in Peru. Because Chile lacked the mineral wealth of Peru or Mexico, many Spaniards created great estates worked by Indians and mestizos. They exported some agricultural products and handicrafts, as well as a little copper.

Many Chileans grew increasingly dissatisfied with Spanish rule. The Spanish king's hold over Spanish America was broken by a French invasion of Spain in 1808. When the French removed the Spanish king from his throne, Chileans refused to obey the French, the Spanish, or the Peruvians. Instead, they founded their own government on September 18, 1810. Some Chileans were simply waiting for the king to return to power in Spain. But others sought full independence.

Independence and Later Times

Bernardo O'Higgins became the most important leader of the fight for independence. The Spanish drove him to Argentina, where he joined forces with José de San Martín. The two led an army back over the Andes to defeat the Spanish in 1817. After other battles, Chile declared its national independence in 1818.

Following the victory over Spain, Chileans fought one another for control of the new government. O'Higgins served as supreme director until 1823, when he was forced to resign and go into exile in Peru. (A biography of O'Higgins appears in Volume O.) Civil wars raged until 1830.

From 1830 to 1891, Chile built a stable republic with a democratic, civilian government. Diego Portales, a cabinet minister, established order and helped create the Constitution of 1833, which lasted until 1925. The landowning families, the merchants, and the Roman Catholic Church ran the country. Only 1 percent of the people voted in elections. The government obtained money from increased exports of silver, copper, and wheat. Then Chile took the northern nitrate fields away from Peru and Bolivia in the War of the Pacific (1879–83). Afterward, President José Manuel Balmaceda tried to reduce the control of British companies over the nitrates. He also tried to strengthen the presidency at the expense of the legislature. British investors and the legislature supported the overthrow of Balmaceda by the military in 1891.

From 1891 to 1925, Chile was a parliamentary republic. Congress was very strong, and the president was very weak. Nitrate exports made the country prosperous, but the middle class and the workers wanted a larger share of the national income. During World War I, the development of artificial nitrates in Europe hurt Chile's exports. Many Chileans were displeased with the weak president and the weak economy. Arturo Alessandri Palma, who became president in 1920, promised to represent the middle and working classes. He helped write the Constitution of 1925, which lasted

until 1973. This constitution created a strong presidency and included many rights for labor.

Between 1925 and 1973, most adult Chileans won the right to vote. New parties speaking for the common people took office. From the 1930's through the 1950's, these reform parties encouraged the growth of industry and improved education, health care, and housing for people in the cities. From 1964 to 1970, President Eduardo Frei Montalva led the most reformist government yet. He extended higher pay, better working conditions, and more land to the poor in the countryside and city shantytowns. President Salvador Allende Gossens pushed reforms even further after his election in 1970. Allende was the first Marxist ever chosen by popular vote to head a government in Latin America. During his administration the government took over the banks and the copper mines and other industries that had been owned by foreigners and rich Chileans. Allende initially gave to the poor much money and property that had belonged to the wealthy. But production fell, and inflation soared. There were nationwide strikes and economic chaos. In 1973 the Chilean military overthrew Allende, who died during the coup.

The military government headed by General Augusto Pinochet Ugarte brought democracy to an end. The armed forces committed serious violations of human rights. Most of the factories and farmlands were returned to their former owners. The new government was successful in lowering the rate of inflation, which fell from 500 percent in 1974 to 31 percent in 1980. In 1980, Pinochet called a referendum to approve a new constitution. This constitution came into effect in 1981. It gave great powers to the president and provided for at least eight more years of military rule.

After growing from 1977 to 1980, the Chilean economy collapsed in 1982. Chile was burdened by huge foreign debts and affected by the worldwide recession, the rising cost of imports, and a reduced demand for copper. Some people continued to support Pinochet because he kept order. But most Chileans apparently wanted an end to dictatorship. The nation's economic problems increased the demands for a return to democratic rule.

PAUL W. DRAKE
University of Illinois, Urbana–Champaign

FACTS AND FIGURES

Republic of Chile is the official name of the country.

Capital: Santiago.

Location: Southwestern coast of South America.

Latitude—18° S to 56° S. **Longitude**—about 67° W to 75° W.

Physical Features: Area—756,945 km² (292,257 sq mi). **Highest point**—Cerra Ojos del Salado, about 6,875 m (22,550 ft), second highest peak in the Western Hemisphere. **Lowest point**—sea level. **Chief rivers**—Bío-Bío, Maipo, Maule, Aysén, Ñuble, Palena, Baker. **Chief mountain peaks**—Cerra Ojos del Salado, Cerro Llullaillaco, Tupungato, Maipo Volcano, Osorno Volcano.

Population: 11,400,000 (estimate).

Language: Spanish.

Government: Republic (under military rule). **Head of government**—president. **International co-operation**—Organization of American States (OAS), United Nations, Latin American Free Trade Association (LAFTA).

National Anthem: *Canción Nacional* ("National Song"). The first line is *Dulce patria, recibe los votos* ("Sweet fatherland, receive our vows").

Economy: Agricultural products—corn, beans, wheat, potatoes, fruits, tobacco, sunflowers, hemp, livestock. **Industries and products**—metals and metal products, foodstuffs, wine, fishing, fish processing, forestry products, beer, leather goods, textiles, glass, cement. **Chief minerals**—copper, iron ore, nitrates, coal, petroleum, iodine, molybdenum, gold, silver, boron, sulfur. **Chief exports**—copper, iron ore, nitrates, molybdenum, textiles, wine, fish meal, fruits, forestry products, livestock. **Chief imports**—industrial machinery, crude petroleum, foodstuffs, transportation equipment. **Monetary unit**—peso.

CHINA

More than 400 years ago, a Portuguese trader visited China and wrote a description of that country. Two things impressed him deeply—"the hugeness of the kingdom" and "the multitude of people." Almost everyone who has written about China during the last 400 years has noted these same facts. China is one of the biggest countries on earth, and it has more people than any other country.

Since the time of the Portuguese trader, China's size has stayed about the same, but the population has kept growing. When the Portuguese wrote of "the multitude of people," the Chinese probably numbered about 60,000,000 persons. Since then, especially in the last 50 years, China's population has grown greatly. In 1955 a geographer wrote a book on China entitled *Land of the 500 Million*. If he had written the book today, he might have called it *Land of the One Billion*. One fourth of all the people on earth live in China.

The country where these millions of Chinese live is the third largest in the world in land area. It is only slightly larger than the United States. But more than four times as many people live in China. Only the Soviet Union and Canada are larger than China, but they have fewer people.

If China's many millions could be spread over all parts of this large country, they would not be particularly crowded. But this is impossible. About two thirds of China is so mountainous or so dry that few people can live there. Much of the country is almost empty of people.

Almost all the people are in the eastern part of the country. They live along the coast, on the plains, and in the basins drained by the great rivers. The greatest concentration of people is in the land that stretches north from the Yangtze River to the city of Peking. South of the Yangtze most of the people live near the coast because much of the interior of the country is mountainous.

The Great Wall extends from the North China coast to the deserts of Central Asia.

The great Tibetan plateau fills much of the western part of China. Very few people can live on this high, frozen desert. North of the plateau lies a vast, nearly uninhabited region of mountains and deserts. Within this region is part of the Gobi, one of the world's largest deserts.

▶ **THE PEOPLE**

China is an old country. It has been China for thousands of years, and the Chinese are proud of their long past. But this does not mean that the Chinese have not seen great changes. They have had civil wars that changed not only governments but ways of living. Some of the greatest changes came after a Communist government under Mao Tse-tung took over all of China except the island province of Taiwan in 1949.

The Family

For hundreds of years, the Chinese taught their children that duty to the family came first. It was the chief loyalty. A Chinese family might include a man, his wife, his mother, his unmarried sisters and aunts, his sons and their wives, his unmarried daughters, and his sons' children. In the past the father, as the head of the family, made all important decisions. All family members were supposed to obey him, although he usually talked over important matters with the other adults.

The members of the old-fashioned Chinese family owned the land or business from which they made their living. There was only one family purse, and everyone shared whatever there was. The family decided about the children's education, and it decided when and whom a young man should marry. After all, this was a family affair because the bride became a member of the family.

The family in the old days was supposed to take care of its own. A man who became ill or suffered some other misfortune counted on his family to take care of him. He knew that he would not lack necessities so long as the family had anything. He knew that if he should die, his brothers and cousins would take care of his wife and children.

Families are still important in China, but the civil war and Communist takeover have brought changes. Families no longer own most of the land. They are not supposed to arrange marriages. Many women work outside the home on large farms or in industries. Child-care centers have taken over some of the family's duties. People are advised to marry late and to have no more than two children. Between 1967 and 1978, the birth rate in China declined by nearly half.

Children learn needlepoint at a day-care center in Shanghai.

Chinese Languages—Written and Spoken

If a person from Canton and a person from Peking met, they might not understand each other. Each would speak a different form of Chinese. These different forms are called dialects. The two people would often use different words. But even if they used the same words, they would pronounce them differently. Both would use different tones, for in Chinese the meaning of a word may depend upon its tone. A word said in a high tone has one meaning. The same word said in a low tone has another meaning. The person from Canton would use nine tones. The person from Peking would use only four. Far more Chinese understand the Pekingese dialect than the Cantonese. The Chinese call the Pekingese dialect the national language. It is also known as Mandarin.

The different dialects do not keep the Chinese from communicating through writing. If the person from Canton wrote a letter to the person from Peking, the latter could read it without any difficulty. Chinese writing is not based on the sounds of the spoken language. Each word has its own special sign, called a character. A person from Canton can use the same character for the word "bright" as does a person from Peking, even though they pronounce the word differently.

Because there are many thousands of words, there are many thousands of Chinese characters. Learning to read and write involves a tremendous amount of memorization. There are more than 40,000 different written characters, although most of them are rarely used. Even so, a person must understand 3,000 or 4,000 characters to be able to read a newspaper.

The Communist government has tried to make writing simpler. It has adopted an official system that uses fewer and simpler characters. The official system also makes use of an alphabet much like that used in writing

English. Alphabetic writing is based on the sound of the spoken national language. Children in school learn both the character for a word and the alphabetic spelling of its pronunciation. The alphabet has not replaced the characters at this time. This is impossible when people speak different dialects.

But some leaders have said that once everyone speaks the national language, the characters will no longer be used. This would be both an advantage and a disadvantage. It would be easier for large numbers of people to learn to read. But they could read only newly published books and newspapers. They could not read the writings of the past unless these were translated into the new writing. Some Chinese fear that the old books would seldom be read.

Education

The most famous Chinese in history was a teacher, Confucius, or K'ung Fu-tzu (551–479 B.C.). This tells one important thing about the Chinese way of life. For at least 2,500 years the Chinese have had a great respect for education and learning. Chinese families often made great sacrifices so that one of the bright boys might become a scholar. An old story

---

THE PINYIN SYSTEM

For many years, Chinese words were reproduced in English according to a system known as the Wade-Giles system. In the 1950's, the Chinese Government developed a new system of writing Chinese in Roman characters that came closer to the actual sound of spoken Chinese. This system, called the Pinyin system, was adopted by the United Nations and the United States Government in 1979. Here are some examples of familiar names and places:

Wade-Giles	Pinyin
Hua Kuo-feng	Hua Guofeng
Mao Tse-tung	Mao Zedong
Teng Hsiao-ping	Deng Xiaoping
Tientsin	Tianjin
Szechwan	Sichuan
Sinkiang	Xinjiang

CHINESE WRITING

Chinese writing is made up of hundreds of characters that stand for one-syllable root words. Here are some examples:

MAN	人	MOUNTAIN	山
SUN	日	TIGER	虎
MOON	月	TREE	木

These basic characters can be combined in many ways to form other words or to express ideas:

FOREST	林	[TWO TREES]
BRIGHT	明	[SUN AND MOON]
WIFE	婦	[WOMAN AND BROOM]
GOOD	好	[WOMAN AND CHILD]

tells of a poor farmer who did all of the work in the fields so that a younger brother who loved to read books might be free to study.

The emperors in past times chose their officials from among scholars who had passed examinations in history, poetry, and the writings of respected wise men. They particularly studied the writings of Confucius. A young man wishing to become an official would study for many years. He would take the first examination in his home district. If he passed this test, he could take the examination in his province. Those who passed this second test could then take national examinations in the capital. Sometimes the national examinations were supervised by the emperor himself.

Those who passed the examinations received special titles or degrees. Not all who received degrees were given official positions. Yet it was an honor to pass the examinations even if one never received any other reward.

Great changes have taken place in Chinese education during the last century. In the 1890's, a group of leaders came to believe that China needed new kinds of schools. It was no longer enough to know the old books. The leaders believed that the Chinese should study the mathematics and sciences brought from Europe and America. During the following 20 years, numerous modern schools were opened all over the country.

The Communist leaders also encouraged education after they came to power. Government-run schools are used as a means of spreading Communist ideas and showing Communism in a favorable light. But the campaign for education has taught millions of people to read. Education today is not just for children or for the privileged few. Adult factory workers, soldiers, and peasants have had to attend "spare-time schools."

Since the death of Mao Tse-tung, increasing emphasis has been placed on scientific and technical education. Special schools for the gifted have been established, and bright students no longer need to spend a period of time working in fields or factories before they are allowed to enter the universities. Millions of Chinese are learning English as a second language in classrooms and through English-language lessons on television. Many Chinese scholars study at universities in the United States and Europe.

A pedicab school bus (*above*) carries children to school. Student rally (*below*) in Peking.

Religion

The Chinese have a saying: "The Way has more than one name. There is more than one wise man." This saying tells much about the Chinese view of religion. China has several religions, and the Chinese have not thought that any one of them was the only way of truth.

The Chinese worshiped a great number of gods, or spirits, in ancient times. There were spirits of the rain, wind, thunder, trees, rivers, and mountains. There was a spirit of the kitchen and another spirit in charge of marriage. The spirit of Heaven was usually thought of as the greatest spirit. People believed that it was necessary to perform certain ceremonies in order to live on good terms with the spirits.

Two of China's great religions took over much of the old spirit worship. Confucius taught little about the spirits, but he did insist that a wise man perform the ancient ceremonies properly. The Chinese do not regard Confucianism as a religion. Confucius was mainly concerned with teaching people how to live together. But Confucius did teach ancestor worship, which is sometimes considered a form of religious practice.

The Chinese have heard differing views of Confucius since the Communists came to power. Sometimes leaders have quoted him as a wise man, a friend of the poor, and the greatest Chinese teacher. At other times, leaders have said that Confucius' teachings were wrong and that he favored the upper classes.

The Taoists, like the followers of Confucius, took over many old rituals and beliefs. Lao-tzu (604–531? B.C.), who is the supposed founder of Taoism ("the Way"), said very little about spirits or gods. But his followers of later times worshiped a vast number of them. Taoist priests claim magical powers for the ceremonies that they perform.

Buddhism began in India. But the Chinese adopted it nearly 1,900 years ago, when travelers brought the teachings of Buddha from India. Chinese Buddhists worship many gods. In addition to followers of these three main religions, China also has Muslims, Christians, and Jews.

Most Chinese in the past did not belong to any one religion. They would study the teachings of Confucius. They might go to a Buddhist temple for one purpose and to a Taoist temple for another. Buddhist and Taoist priests might both take part in a funeral.

When the Communist leaders came to power, they said that people were free to follow any religion. Government leaders state that China has Christians, Buddhists, Muslims, and atheists—people who do not believe in any religion. The Communist government was in fact hard on religious organizations. Most religious buildings were taken over for other uses, although the government kept a few temples as museums. Most priests and monks were forced to find other occupations.

▶ THE LAND

China is so large that, even within its eastern third, the climate differs greatly. Manchuria, in the northeast, has long, cold winters and short summers somewhat like Saskatchewan in Canada. On the other hand, South China has a moist, tropical climate. Canton's climate resembles that of southern Florida. The island of Hainan in the far south is a land of coconuts, rubber, and pineapples.

North China—Land of the Hwang Ho

The Hwang Ho is the great river of North China. The name of this river tells an important fact about it. *Hwang* is a Chinese word for "yellow," and *ho* is one of the words for "river." Hwang Ho simply means Yellow River. The Hwang has a muddy yellow color because of the yellow soil that washes down from the hills and plains of the west.

The Hwang Ho begins high on the Tibetan plateau. If you follow its course on the map, you will find that it flows in almost every direction at one place or another. It takes a long time for this river to reach the sea. The Hwang Ho is one of the longest rivers in the world.

The soil washed down by the Hwang Ho during many centuries has built up a great yellow plain along its lower course. You can judge how much soil the river has deposited by noting that at one time the Shantung peninsula was an island. All of the large, flat plain reaching from the Shantung peninsula to Peking has been filled in by the Hwang Ho and several smaller rivers.

This low, flat plain built up by the river is easily flooded whenever the Hwang Ho rises. For hundreds of years, the Chinese have built

The mighty Yangtze River flows through a series of gorges in south central China.

dikes along the river in an effort to hold back the floods. It has been necessary to build these dikes higher and higher. The river is now higher than the surrounding countryside. Whenever the river breaks through, it floods.

In spite of the floods, millions of people live on this great plain. Many of them are farmers who grow such grains as wheat, millet, and kaoliang, a sorghum. There are several great cities in North China, although neither of the two most important is on the Hwang Ho. Peking is on the northern edge of the plain. Tientsin, the great port of the north, lies north of the Hwang Ho.

Winters in North China are cold and dry. Winds from the deserts to the northwest blow clouds of fine yellow dust over the land. Summers are short, but the days are often hot. Rain comes chiefly in summer.

The Lands Along the Yangtze River

A very large number of Chinese live within the Yangtze basin—the land drained by China's greatest river, the Yangtze. It is sometimes known as the Yangtze Kiang, for *kiang* is another word for "river."

Terraced rice fields in Szechwan province, one of China's major farming regions.

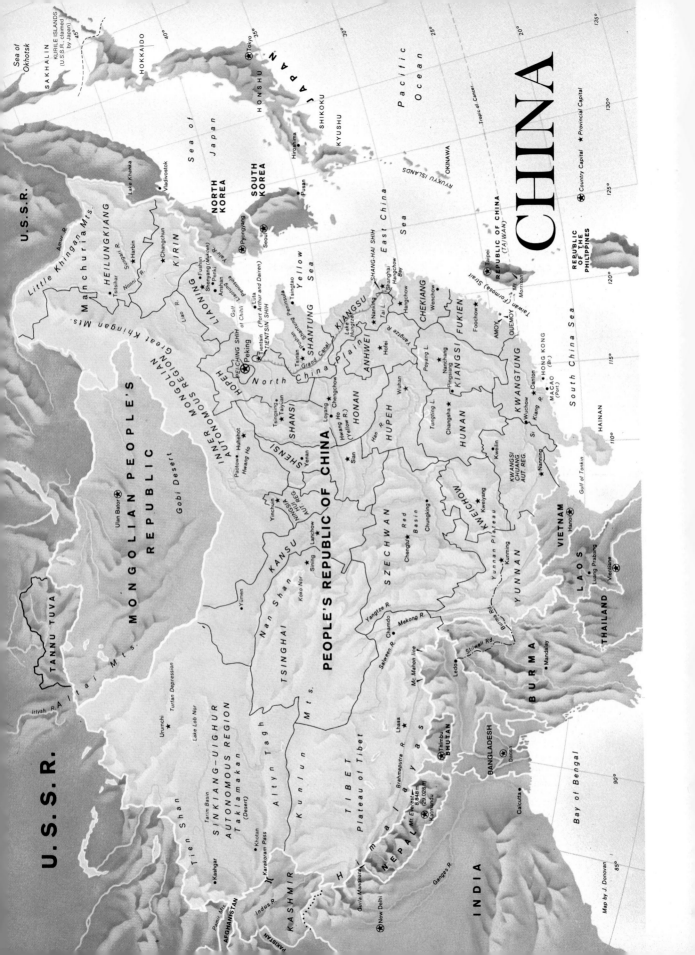

The Yangtze is the third longest river in the world, after the Nile and the Amazon. It rises in western Tsinghai province and flows swiftly for great distances through deep mountain gorges and canyons.

About halfway to the sea, the valley along the Yangtze broadens into a basin. This is called the Szechwan Basin—*sze* means "four" and *chwan* is another Chinese word for "river," and there are four large rivers in the basin. Chungking and Chengtu are the most important cities in Szechwan.

The mountains that surround the basin protect it from the worst of the cold winter winds. Temperatures do not often go below freezing, and rainfall is plentiful. The millions of farmers who live in the basin make the most of this. They not only plant the lowlands but also terrace and cultivate the hillsides.

The lower Yangtze becomes very large, and it has been called China's main street. Ocean-going ships can sail up the Yangtze as far as Hankow (part of the tri-city of Wuhan, which also includes Wuchang and Hanyang).

The Yangtze, like the Hwang Ho, has built up a flat plain near its mouth. Thousands of canals crisscross the plain. Small boats carry people and goods on the canals and small streams. People also fish in the canals, and farmers use the water to irrigate rice fields.

The climate along the lower Yangtze is damp and warm, although at times winter temperatures dip below freezing. Many cities are located on the Yangtze plain. They include Shanghai, which is China's largest city and its most important port, and Nanking, China's capital for many years.

The South China Coast

There are no broad river plains in China south of the Yangtze. Much of the land is hilly and mountainous. Most of the people live along the coast in the narrow river valleys and on the deltas. The sea furnishes the people with much of their food, and many of them earn their living by fishing.

The Si Kiang is the largest of South China's rivers, and millions live on the Si delta. Hong Kong, a British colony, is located near the mouth of the Si Kiang. The Portuguese colony of Macao lies across the bay from Hong Kong. City streets swarm with people who live and work in close quarters. People live almost everywhere—on steep hillsides and on the thousands of boats that fill the streams and bays. Some of the boat people earn their living by fishing or transporting goods. Others have jobs on land but come home at night to their boats. Living on boats has its problems, especially for those with small children. Frequently parents tie large pieces of bamboo on the children's backs. In case one falls overboard, the bamboo will keep the child afloat until someone comes to the rescue.

People in South China rarely see snow or frost except on high mountains. The warm climate and plentiful rain keep this region green throughout the year.

FACTS AND FIGURES

PEOPLE'S REPUBLIC OF CHINA is the official name of the country. It is called Chung Hua Jen Min Kung Ho Kuo in Chinese.

CAPITAL: Peking.

LOCATION: Central part of eastern Asia. **Latitude**—21° 09' N to 53° 54' N. **Longitude**—73° 37' E to 135° 05' E.

PHYSICAL FEATURES: Area—9,596,961 km² (3,705,390 sq mi). **Highest point**—Mt. Everest, 8,848 m (29,028 ft). **Lowest point**—Turfan depression (below sea level). **Chief mountain peaks**—Mt. Everest, Gurla Mandhata, Namcha Barwa, Minya Konka. **Chief rivers**—Yangtze, Hwang Ho, Si Kiang, Amur.

POPULATION: 1,008,000,000 (estimate).

LANGUAGE: Chinese (Mandarin, official; Shanghai; Cantonese; and other dialects).

RELIGION: Confucianism, Buddhism, Islam, Taoism, and Christianity.

GOVERNMENT: Communist republic. **Head of state**—president. **Head of government**—premier and chairman of Central Committee of the Communist Party. **International co-operation**—United Nations.

NATIONAL ANTHEM: "The March of the Volunteers."

ECONOMY: Agricultural products—wheat, rice, maize, cane sugar, soybeans, cotton, groundnuts, tobacco, tea, potatoes, green vegetables. **Industries and products**—iron and steel, textiles, cement, paper, cotton yarn, chemical fertilizer, chemicals, sugar, timber, tung oil. **Chief minerals**—coal, crude petroleum, salt, antimony, mercury, tin, tungsten. **Chief exports**—cotton, hog products, tea, silk, tobacco, petroleum, tung oil, machinery, mercury, tungsten. **Chief imports**—machinery and industrial equipment. **Monetary unit**—people's bank dollar, or *jen min piao* (usually known by its old name of yuan).

Parades mark the celebration of Taiwan's national holiday, held on the tenth day of the tenth moon.

FACTS AND FIGURES

REPUBLIC OF CHINA is the official name of Nationalist China. It is called Chung Hua Min Kuo in Chinese. Taiwan, which means "terraced bay," is the name of the island province. The island is also called Formosa, "beautiful island."

CAPITAL: Taipei.

LOCATION: Islands about 160 km (100 m) off the southeastern coast of the Chinese mainland. **Latitude**—21° 54' to 25° 18' N. **Longitude**—120° 03' E to 122° E.

PHYSICAL FEATURES: Area—35,961 km² (13,885 sq mi), not including islands of Quemoy and Matsu. **Highest point**—Sinkao Shan (Mt. Morrison), 3,997 m (13,113 ft). **Lowest point**—sea level.

POPULATION: 16,800,000 (estimate).

LANGUAGE: Chinese (Mandarin—official, Amoy, Swatow, and Hakka dialects).

RELIGION: Confucianism, Buddhism, Taoism, Islam, and Christianity.

GOVERNMENT: Republic. **Head of government**—president.

NATIONAL ANTHEM: *San Min Chu I* ("Three Principles of the People").

ECONOMY: Agricultural products—rice, cane sugar, sweet potatoes, pineapples, bananas, citrus fruits, tea, citronella oil, camphor, soybeans, jute, sisal, flax, ramie. **Industries and products**—food products, sugar, pineapples, tea, textiles, cement, fertilizer. **Chief minerals**—coal, limestone, salt, pyrites, sulfur, copper, gold, silver, crude petroleum, natural gas. **Chief exports**—sugar, rice, canned pineapple, tea, bananas, cement, citronella oil, camphor. **Chief imports**—machinery and tools, ores and metals, chemical fertilizer, vessels and parts, beans, peas. **Monetary unit**—new Taiwan dollar (yuan).

Taiwan—The Island Also Called Formosa

There are many islands along the South China coast. Taiwan, the largest, is larger than some countries in Europe. It is about 145 kilometers (90 miles) from the mainland. Taiwan is the Chinese name for the island. Almost 400 years ago, the Portuguese named it Formosa, a word that means "beautiful island" in their language. The Chinese prefer their own name for it.

The eastern two thirds of Taiwan is rough and mountainous. Most of the land suitable for farming lies on the western side. As you would expect, most people live where the good land is. Taipei, the capital, is in the northern part of Taiwan.

The Nationalist government, which lost control of mainland China in 1949, established itself on Taiwan and considers itself the true government of China. In 1979 the United States became the last major power to recognize the People's Republic as the legal government of all China, including Taiwan.

The Borderlands—Manchuria, Sinkiang, Tibet

Manchuria, in the northeast, has a rich, fertile plain. It is less crowded than the other great farming regions. Deposits of iron ore and coal have led to the development of heavy industry, such as steelmaking, in this region. Shenyang and Harbin are the largest cities in Manchuria.

Sinkiang, the northwest borderland, is mostly desert. Most of its people are herders who move with their flocks across the dry pastures. Some farmers live on oases on or near the mountain slopes. Sinkiang has deposits of minerals, including one of China's most important oil fields.

Tibet is truly the "roof" of China. Streams draining off this highland are the sources of several of China's great rivers. Few people live on this high, cold desert. Some herders manage to live by keeping sheep, goats, and yaks, the long-haired mountain oxen. Tibet's only farmers live in the sheltered valleys cut by rivers into the southern part of the plateau. Lhasa is the principal city.

▶ THE ECONOMY

China is a vast nation with many natural resources and a large work force. But much must be done before the nation's economy expands to match its size and population.

Agriculture. Because so much of China is dry and mountainous, the good farmland is very crowded. As the population has grown, the land has had to produce more and still more food. The Chinese farmers have great skill, but it takes more than skill to produce crops on frozen plateaus and deserts. The Chinese have had to grow most of their food on about one sixth of their land. Virtually all this farmland lies in the eastern third of the country.

Farming has always been important in China. Most Chinese in the past were farmers. Most still are. About three out of every four Chinese spend their lives plowing, planting, and harvesting. They have learned to make use of almost every bit of land. Because cropland is limited, the average farmer before 1949 had very little land. Whole families lived on farms smaller than a football field.

Chinese farmers know how to get the most out of their fields. They grow two or even three crops each year on the same land. Farmers in South China grow two rice crops a year. In North China, farmers plant wheat in the fall and harvest it in early summer. They then plant a summer crop such as soybeans or sweet potatoes. Land must be heavily fertilized when it is used so intensively.

The Communist government brought about a series of changes in agriculture. When the Communists first came to power, they took land away from landlords and divided it among those who had rented it. Each family worked its own small plot independently.

The government then decided that the many small farms would not increase production. The tiny plots were so small that the owners could not afford to buy new equipment or use it efficiently. It was hard to get millions of individual owners to try new methods.

In the 1950's, the government forced the farmers to merge their small plots into very large ones called **communes**. In the communes, thousands of farmers worked together under the management of government officials. The farmers were organized into work units somewhat like units in an army. The people in some communes lived in barracks and ate together in large dining halls. Small children were cared for in nurseries so that their mothers could work. The government told the farmers what to grow and how much they were expected to produce.

At first the communes did not produce as much as was expected. China had to import large amounts of food to feed its people. The government then made more changes. The communes were made smaller. There was less direct control by government officials. Farmers were again permitted to work small plots for their own use. But the communes still held the large fields. Under this new arrangement, Chinese farmers did increase the production of such basic crops as wheat, potatoes, green vegetables, and rice.

Farmers harvest wheat in Sinkiang (*left*). Apartments line a street in Shanghai (*right*).

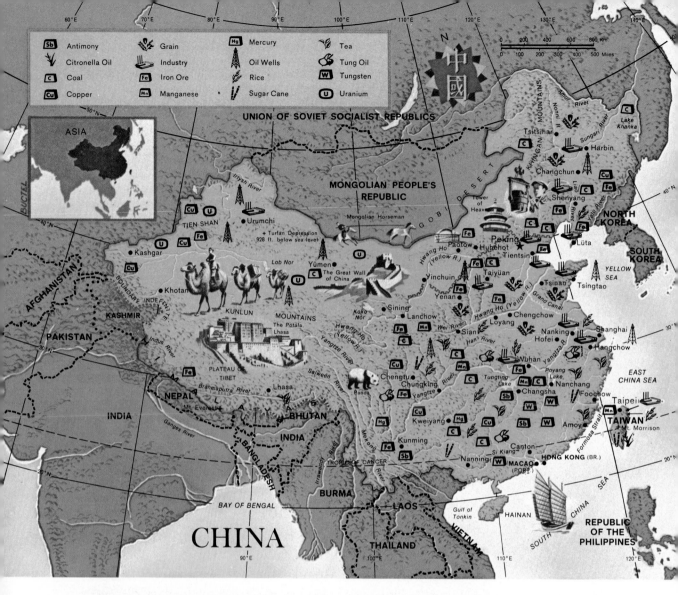

CHINA

There truly is a lot of rice in China. The country leads the world in rice production. Chinese farmers also grow maize, sugarcane, soybeans, cotton, groundnuts, tobacco, and tea. Good land is too scarce to be used for grazing many cattle or sheep. But there are many pigs and chickens. Fish is an important part of the Chinese diet. Fish not only are caught in the rivers and the sea but are raised in special ponds. Timber and tung oil—an oil from the seeds of the tung tree, used in making paints and varnishes—are products exported from China.

Mineral Resources. China is one of the world's leading coal producers. It also produces more oil than it uses. No one knows just how much oil there may be in China be- cause the Chinese have just begun to look for it. China also has substantial salt deposits. Other important minerals include antimony, mercury, tin, and tungsten.

Industries. China's leaders plan to make their country one of the world's leading industrial nations. They have made some progress in that direction. Steel mills, chemical plants, and various kinds of factories have been built. But many of China's industries are inefficient and use outmoded equipment. The Chinese have signed agreements with many nations to help them build modern factories, exploit their mineral resources, and train technical experts. Workers who produce more are being rewarded for their greater ability and effort.

▶GOVERNMENT

The Chinese were once taught that the emperor was "the father of the people." They owed the emperor the same respect and obedience that children owed their parents.

The emperor had complete power over the people but was supposed to rule them by setting a good example rather than by using force. The ruler was also supposed to enlighten them through education and to teach them generosity by giving aid in time of flood, drought, or other disaster.

The Chinese believed that if an emperor ruled badly, Heaven would show its displeasure. According to the teachings of the Confucian school, the people had the right to overthrow a bad ruler.

The overthrow of the last emperor, in 1912, brought with it new ideas about government. Sun Yat-sen, one of the new leaders, said that government belongs to the people. This did not mean that the people would actually run the government. Sun said that the people were like those who owned cars but could not drive. They had to employ a driver. The people must choose someone able to govern.

When the Nationalist Party first came to power, Sun Yat-sen did not believe that the people were ready to choose their own government. The Nationalist Party would have to govern until the people could learn the ways of democracy. Sun thought that this would take about six years, but the Nationalists ruled far longer than that.

When the Nationalist government moved to Taiwan, it continued to follow the ideas of Sun Yat-sen. The people of Taiwan elected representatives who made laws and others who elected the president. The president was given great powers. Chiang Kai-shek, who had become the leader of the Nationalists in 1927, served as president of the Nationalist government until his death in 1975. His son Chiang Ching-kuo was elected president in 1978.

The constitution of the People's Republic of China says that China is a socialist state, under the dictatorship of the working class. But it also says that workers must exercise their power through the Communist Party, the only political party. The National People's Congress, or parliament, does not really debate and decide issues. Mainly it listens to reports from Communist Party leaders and approves what they have done. Under a constitution adopted in 1982, a president serves as head of state.

Real power is held by the Communist Party, but titles do not always determine which party leaders are the most powerful. From 1945 until his death in 1976, Mao Tse-tung was chairman of the Central Committee. Since 1982, the Central Committee has been headed by a general secretary. There are other important groups within the party. A politburo and its standing committee set broad guidelines that are put into effect by a secretariat. A military affairs committee directs the army, and an advisory commission advises party leaders.

Portraits of Mao Tse-tung and his successor, Hua Kuo-feng, were once seen all over China.

People have lived in North China for a very long time. Not far from Peking, scientists have found the bones and stone tools of people who lived probably 500,000 years ago. We do not know much about the Peking people, but crude stone scrapers and spearpoints tell us that they made and used tools and weapons. Bits of soot-blackened stones and bones seem to show that they used fire.

The earliest farmers of China also lived in the north. They lived on the level delta land near the mouths of streams that flow into the Hwang Ho. There they grew vegetables and millet, a grain still grown in China. They also kept goats, cattle, and pigs. The Chinese farmers have long known the value of pigs. Pigs eat almost anything and grow rapidly.

Farmers in North China 5,000 years ago had no metal tools. They made their hoes, spades, and scrapers from sticks and stones. They cut grain with highly polished, thin stone knives that probably cut fairly well. The farming people also made beautiful pottery.

The Mighty Shang and Their Bronze Weapons

About 4,000 years ago, some people in North China learned to make bronze weapons. Metal weapons brought great changes to China, just as they did in other places. Soldiers who wore bronze helmets in battle and fought with bronze knives and battle-axes had an advantage over those who had only sticks and stones. As a result, the people with bronze weapons conquered their neighbors.

About 1523 B.C., one of the warrior peoples, the Shang, won control of most of North China. The warlike Shang ruled the land of the Hwang Ho for more than six centuries.

The Shang people knew how to write. We still have some of their writings on pieces of animal bone and tortoiseshell. People of that time believed that it was possible to learn the future through certain magical ceremonies. A priest would write a question on a bone or shell about going to war, hunting, health, or even the weather. One question actually reads: "Rain or not?" Evidence shows that after writing on the bone or shell, the priest pressed a hot bronze point against it, causing it to crack. Then the priest interpreted the cracks much as fortune-tellers today profess to read the lines in the palm of a person's hand. We do not know whether the Shang people learned much about the future from the fortune-telling shells, but we do know that scholars today learn much about the past from these ancient Chinese writings.

The Time of the Chou Kings and Philosophers

West of North China, along the Wei River, lived the Chou people. In the 11th century B.C. a king of the Chou led his people east across the Hwang Ho and defeated the Shang armies. The Chou went on to conquer both North China and the Yangtze plain.

The Chou king divided this large realm among his relatives and followers. Each was made the lord over a district. For a time this worked well enough, but later the great lords warred among themselves.

Some of the early Chou kings were great rulers. But the persons best remembered and honored were the teachers and philosophers, such as Confucius, who taught how the land could be peaceful and well governed. The people, they said, must begin with themselves. If each person practiced self-control, each family would be well governed. Then the whole country would be well governed.

Shih Huang Ti, Builder of the Empire

One group of philosophers taught that there could be peace in China only if the whole land was under a single, strong ruler. The lord of Ch'in, one of the states in the west, listened eagerly to those who said that a single warlike lord might conquer the other lords as easily as "sweeping off the dust from a kitchen stove."

The Ch'in ruler followed this advice. In 246 B.C. he made war against the other states. One old Chinese history says that he "rolled up the empire like a mat." In 221 B.C., when his armies had conquered the other states, he proclaimed himself Shih Huang Ti, which means "first emperor."

Shih Huang Ti made sure that no one could cause him trouble. He destroyed the walls of the cities he conquered and collected all weapons. He appointed his own followers to govern but kept a close watch on them. Those who served him well were richly rewarded. Those who bungled were severely punished.

Shih Huang Ti ordered that there be but

IMPORTANT DATES

1994–1523 B.C.	Hsia dynasty: silk making; use of wheels on vehicles; use of bronze weapons; growing of wheat.		907	Third division of the empire.
1523–1028 B.C.	Shang dynasty: early form of Chinese writing.		960–1279	Sung dynasties (Northern and Southern): Central and South China reunited; use of gunpowder in war; literature and painting flourished; use of abacus.
1028–256 B.C.	Chou dynasty: feudal period; earliest philosophers, poets, and historians; Confucius (551–479 B.C.), greatest teacher; first part of the Grand Canal built; first part of Great Wall built; coinage; astronomy.		1260–1368	Yüan, or Mongol, dynasty: China conquered by Kublai Khan; Marco Polo visited China.
			1368–1644	Ming dynasty: Mongols driven from power.
			1644–1912	Ch'ing, or Manchu, dynasty: 150 years of peace and prosperity.
221–207 B.C.	Ch'in dynasty: centralization of government; empire established.		1839–42	Opium war; China forced to open ports to foreign trade.
202 B.C.–A.D. 220	Han dynasties (Western and Eastern): empire became nearly as large as Roman Empire in Europe; supremacy of Confucianism established; Buddhism introduced from India; adoption of legal code; invention of paper making.		1900	Boxer Rebellion.
			1912	Republic established.
			1937–45	War with Japan.
			1945–49	Civil war.
			1949	Communists gain control of mainland China. Nationalists establish themselves in Taiwan.
220–265	The Three Kingdoms: empire broken up into three parts, each with a separate dynasty.		1950	People's Republic enters Korean War.
265–420	Chin dynasty (Western and Eastern).		1964	People's Republic detonates nuclear bomb.
479	Second division of the empire.		1966–69	Great Proletarian Cultural Revolution.
581–618	Sui dynasty: China reunited into a single empire; first printing of books from wooden blocks.		1971	People's Republic enters the United Nations.
			1976	Mao Tse-tung dies.
618–906	T'ang dynasty: prosperous period; expansion of empire; great art and poetry.		1979	United States recognizes People's Republic as sole legal government of all China.
			1982	People's Republic adopts new constitution.

one set of laws and rules throughout his empire. Everybody had to use the same weights and measures. All scholars had to write with the same script. All farmers had to put the wheels on their carts the same distance apart, so that all wheels could use the same ruts in the roads.

To protect North China from raids by tribes from the grasslands, Shih Huang Ti forced thousands of people to build the Great Wall. Today it extends from the seacoast into the deserts of Central Asia.

The Rise and Fall of Dynasties

Shih Huang Ti believed that his empire would last for 10,000 generations. But his family did not rule for long. Within four years after Shih Huang Ti's death, a revolt drove his son from the palace, and another man became emperor.

There were many such revolts during the next 2,000 years. They occurred when an emperor was either unusually weak or unusually harsh. A weak emperor could not force people to obey, and a harsh ruler so angered people that they revolted. The Chinese said that when a ruling family, or dynasty, was overthrown, it had lost "the support of Heaven."

More than 20 dynasties ruled China during these 2,000 years. The Han, T'ang, Sung, and Ming are the best known because they were in power longer than the other dynasties. The Han dynasty, which replaced the Ch'in in 202 B.C., lasted over 400 years. Under the Han, China became a great empire. Chinese power began to expand into Korea in the east and Central Asia in the west.

The Chinese consider the 300 years of T'ang rule the most glorious period of their country's history. At the height of its power, the T'ang was able to extend its influence over the entire continent of Asia, from Korea in the northeast to India in the southwest. The Chinese are so proud of the T'ang period that even to this day some of them call themselves "people of T'ang."

Although the Sung rulers controlled China for 300 years, they were militarily weak. The Sung foot soldiers were no match for the horsemen who invaded from the north. But the Sung period was China's golden age of arts and sciences. The invention of movable type made possible the printing of huge encyclopedias. Literature and landscape painting flourished. Gunpowder was first used for wars, and the magnetic compass was applied to navigation.

In the middle of the 13th century, the Mongols of Central Asia became the first foreign invaders to conquer China. By then the hardriding Mongol tribes, under their great ruler

Emperor T'ang T'ai. The T'ang dynasty ruled China from A.D. 618 to 906.

An artist's interpretation of a Mongol victory over the Chinese.

Ghenghis Khan, had already conquered much of Asia and eastern Europe. His grandson, Kublai Khan, completed the invasion of China and became emperor in 1260.

Kublai Khan conquered the Chinese, but he admired Chinese ways and tried to live like a Chinese emperor. He built his capital at Peking and supported Confucian colleges. He employed many Chinese officials, although he made use of foreigners, too. It happened that an Italian merchant named Marco Polo was in China in the days of Kublai Khan. He lived in China for many years and later wrote a famous account of his travels.

One hundred years of foreign rule were all the Chinese could tolerate. They rebelled against the Mongols in 1368 and established the Ming dynasty. Under its able emperor, Yung Lo, the Ming army chased the Mongols all the way to Siberia. The powerful Ming navy roamed the South Seas and reached the shores of Africa.

In 1644 the Manchu invasion brought an end to the three centuries of Ming rule. Although they were foreigners who came from north of the Great Wall, the Manchus respected Chinese culture and tradition. They quickly adopted Chinese ways of living. Under the early Manchu emperors, China enjoyed 150 years of peace and prosperity. During this time the Chinese empire became even larger than it had been in the famous T'ang period. The Manchus continued to rule until a republic was established in 1912, but their power steadily declined.

Europeans Who Sought Colonies in China

Although some Europeans, like Marco Polo, journeyed overland to China, only a few came before the discovery of the sea route around Africa. A Portuguese ship reached the South China coast in 1514.

The crews of the early ships were a rough lot. It is hard to say whether they should be called traders or pirates. The Chinese officials had many difficulties with the Portuguese, although the Chinese finally agreed to let them trade at Macao, a small peninsula near Canton. Even then the Chinese put a guarded wall across the peninsula to keep the Portuguese out of the rest of the kingdom.

Shortly after the traders reached China, a few Christian missionaries came, too. The missionaries finally got permission to live in places other than Macao. In 1601 an Italian priest named Matteo Ricci founded a mission in Peking, where he lived for the last nine years of his life. Father Ricci won the respect of the Chinese because he showed respect for them and their ways. He learned the Chinese language and dressed as a Chinese scholar.

Perhaps if all Europeans had been as wise as Father Ricci, the Chinese would have welcomed more Europeans, but such was not the case. With good reason, the Chinese feared that the Europeans planned to make a colony of China, just as they had done in India and the Philippines. So the Chinese made trade very difficult.

The Europeans disliked the restraints upon trade. They wanted to come and go freely in China's cities. They wanted to buy China's silk, tea, and porcelain, which they called chinaware. Chinese efforts to enforce the laws, especially those laws against the selling of opium, led to quarrels, and the quarrels led to wars. The Europeans had better weapons, and they won easy victories. The British defeated the Chinese in a war in 1842 and forced China to open certain ports to trade. The Chinese also had to give the British the barren island of Hong Kong, where the British built a great trading port.

Other countries demanded the same privileges as those enjoyed by Britain. France, Germany, and Russia gained control over large areas called spheres of influence. Even China's Asian neighbor Japan made war and defeated the Chinese in 1895. Some of the Chinese so hated the outsiders that they tried to drive them from the country. An organization known as the Boxers attacked foreign merchants, missionaries, and diplomats in 1900. They set fire to foreign-owned buildings, but this only made matters worse. The foreign countries again sent troops into China and so ended the short but savage Boxer Rebellion.

Indian soldiers attack the fortifications of Peking during the Boxer Rebellion.

Sun Yat-Sen and the Founding of the Republic

A government that could not defend China from the outsiders could not defend itself. In 1911 a revolution broke out, and early the next year the last of the emperors gave up all claim to power. China was declared a republic.

It was easy to topple the old government, but it was not easy to establish a new one. For a number of years China was torn by civil war. The real rulers of the country were military leaders called warlords, who forced the people in their localities to pay them taxes. During this time of civil war, one leader, Sun Yat-sen, said that the Chinese were no longer a nation but had become "just a heap of loose sand."

Sun Yat-sen (1866–1925) spent much of his youth in foreign countries. He left China when he was 12 to live with a brother in Hawaii. Later he traveled throughout Europe and America to raise money for the revolution. When he returned to China, he carried back a belief that his country must rid itself of foreign domination and establish a democratic government. He also thought that the Chinese should have a higher standard of living. After the revolution, he organized the National People's Party, or Kuomintang, usually called the Nationalist Party.

Sun's party became important in China. It was the only group that might make the republic work. When Sun died in 1925, one of his followers, Chiang Kai-shek, became the

Nationalist leader. Chiang was a military man, and he began a campaign to conquer the warlords. Chiang's army won victories, but Chiang realized that there were other enemies. The Communists whom Sun had let into the Nationalist Party were working to take over the country, too. In an effort to prevent this, Chiang expelled them from the party.

Chiang won victories over the Communists, but he was not able to defeat them completely. The Communists kept control in some rural areas. Mao Tse-tung, one of the principal leaders, believed that the Communists could bring about a second revolution if they could win the support of the poor people.

The Nationalists finally conquered the territory held by the Communist forces in the south, but Mao's army and leaders escaped. Mao led them on the Long March, a 9,700-kilometer (6,000-mile) trek to the borders of Tibet and then northeast to the valley of Yenan. There, in 1936, they established a Communist government.

While China was divided by the struggle between the Nationalists and the Communists, Japan invaded the country. Both groups opposed the Japanese, but neither trusted the other. After the defeat of Japan in World War II, civil war in China began again. The Communist forces grew increasingly stronger and won one area after another of the war-weary land. By 1949 the Communists controlled all of the mainland. The Communist leader Mao Tse-tung proclaimed the formation of a new government, the People's Republic of China.

The Nationalists held but one province, the island of Taiwan. They established their government there. China's political history then became that of "two Chinas," with the Nationalist Republic of China and the Communist People's Republic of China each claiming to be the legal government of the whole country.

Since the Civil War

The Chinese Communists set about to do away with any who might oppose their rule. No one knows how many people the revolutionists killed or sentenced to hard labor. But it is sure to have been millions. And the creation of the People's Republic did not end the struggle for power. There was a struggle

During the Great Cultural Revolution, Red Guards hold up books containing the thoughts of Mao Tse-tung.

between Communist factions. One group, called the pragmatists (practical people), thought that the revolution was over. They wanted the Chinese to devote their attention to the economic development of the country. They thought it was more important to make China strong than to carry out every Communist ideal. Another group, called the radicals, thought that the most important thing was to keep the revolutionary spirit alive.

Mao Tse-tung shared the radicals' views. In 1966 he launched the Great Proletarian Cultural Revolution. The radicals organized thousands of young people into groups called the Red Guards and encouraged them to demonstrate against officials who had supposedly lost the revolutionary spirit. At first the Red Guards only insulted their opponents, but later they beat and killed them. Once again China faced serious disorder. Schools were closed, and industry was disrupted. The situation grew so bad that Mao finally joined with the army to put a stop to the movement.

The struggle between the pragmatists and the radicals then continued behind the scenes. It was difficult for outsiders to know who really held power. When Mao Tse-tung died in 1976, many thought that the radicals would take over. Yet within a month four radical leaders—including Mao's widow, Chiang Ching—were under arrest. The "gang of four," as they were called, were charged with all sorts of crimes. The new government, led by Communist Party Chairman Hua Kuo-feng and First Deputy Premier Teng Hsiao-ping, believed that China's political revolution was over. They wanted to lead an economic revolution that would modernize the nation's economy by the end of the 20th century. Teng was a pragmatist whom the radicals had twice driven from office. He told the Chinese:

"There must be less empty talk and more hard work."

Foreign Affairs

The Soviet Union signed a treaty of friendship with the People's Republic soon after the Communist government came into power. But relations between the world's two largest Communist nations worsened. There were armed clashes along border regions claimed by both countries. There were also clashes between the People's Republic and India, again over disputed territory. In 1950, Chinese troops occupied Tibet.

The People's Republic supported the North Koreans with troops during the Korean War (1950–53). It also aided Communist governments in Southeast Asia during the Vietnam War. In 1979, China invaded Vietnam after Vietnamese troops had invaded China's ally, Cambodia.

The United States refused to recognize the People's Republic as the rightful government of China in 1949. Instead, it supported the claims of the Nationalists. By a treaty signed in 1954, the United States promised that it would act to "meet the common danger" if Taiwan should be attacked. From time to time the Communists bombarded the islands of Quemoy and Matsu, close to the mainland, but the Nationalists held firmly to these outposts.

The United States also gave the Nationalists financial aid, which helped raise the standard of living on Taiwan. The Nationalists built many schools, hospitals, sewers, water-supply systems, roads, canals, and dikes. They helped farmers who rented land to buy the farms they worked. Agricultural, livestock, and fishery production increased dramatically. The Nationalist government also helped establish new industries, in such fields as electronics, plastics, textiles, and chemicals. And it encouraged trade with other countries. The standard of living on Taiwan became one of the highest in Asia.

In the years after 1949, most of the nations of the world recognized the People's Republic as the sole legal government of all China. In 1971, the People's Republic was admitted to the United Nations, taking the seat formerly held by the Nationalists. In 1972, President Richard Nixon became the first U.S. president to visit the People's Republic.

Since then, visitors from many countries have had opportunities to visit mainland China, which was virtually closed off to most outsiders for some years after the civil war. They found cities that were drab but clean and bustling. In the parts of China seen by visitors, everyone had enough to eat, there were no slums, and there was little crime. The government had a great deal of control over people's lives, and wages were low. But food cost little, rents were low, and medical care and other welfare benefits were free.

Recent Events

The new leaders of the People's Republic sought assistance from the industrialized nations of the world to carry out a program they called the Four Modernizations. Their goal was to modernize agriculture, industry, science and technology, and the military by the year 2000. The Chinese encouraged Western companies to develop offshore oil deposits and build hotels, factories, and steel mills in China, using Western machinery and know-how and inexpensive Chinese labor. In 1978, China signed a peace treaty and economic agreements with Japan.

Late in 1978, President Jimmy Carter announced that the United States had agreed to recognize the People's Republic as the sole legal government of all China, including Taiwan. The two countries established full diplomatic relations in 1979, and formal diplomatic relations between the United States and Taiwan were ended. Economic and cultural ties between the United States and Taiwan continued on an unofficial level.

In 1981, the pragmatists showed that they had won full control of the government. Hua Kuo-feng, an old friend of Mao, resigned as Communist Party chairman. And for the first time, the Communist Party said that Mao had made many mistakes while he ruled China.

KENNETH S. COOPER
George Peabody College, Vanderbilt University

See also ASIA; CHIANG KAI-SHEK; CONFUCIUS; MAO TSE-TUNG; PEKING; SHANGHAI; SHENYANG; TAIWAN; TIBET; YANGTZE RIVER.

CHINESE ART. See ORIENTAL ART AND ARCHITECTURE.

CHIVALRY. See KNIGHTS, KNIGHTHOOD, AND CHIVALRY.

CHLOROPHYLL. See PHOTOSYNTHESIS.

CHOCOLATE AND COCOA

Christopher Columbus found Central American Indians using cacao beans for money, but he failed to discover the real treasure hidden in the dark-brown, almond-shaped beans. This was left to the Spanish explorer Hernando Cortes.

When Cortes and his men conquered the Aztec Empire in Mexico in 1519, they found the Indians using the cacao beans to make a beverage called *chocolatl,* the favorite drink of the Aztec ruler Montezuma. Montezuma gave Cortes and his men golden goblets filled with foamy *chocolatl.* This early form of chocolate was very bitter, and the Spaniards didn't like the drink until they sweetened it with sugarcane.

Cortes took cacao beans back with him to Spain, where chocolate became the special drink of the aristocracy. The Spaniards experimented with new flavorings, such as vanilla or cinnamon. Meanwhile the art of chocolate-making itself was kept a closely guarded Spanish secret.

Another 100 years passed before the other courts of Europe were introduced to the exotic drink. The elegant court of France adopted it at once. In England chocolate made its appearance in 1657 at the first "chocolate house," which soon became a fashionable meeting place.

Chocolate was too expensive for any but the very wealthy, since the beans had to be ground by hand. In 1730 the invention of a machine that speeded up the grinding process lowered the price.

In 1828 C. J. Van Houten, a Netherlander, revolutionized the chocolate industry by inventing a press that squeezed the rich cocoa butter out of the cacao beans. He ground the remaining chocolate into powder. This chocolate powder, or cocoa, made a smoother, less rich drink than the thick chocolate of the 18th century. Even more revolutionary, the cocoa butter that had been squeezed out was added to a sugar and chocolate combination and molded into bars. People began to eat chocolate as well as drink it.

But the chocolate was still coarse and bitter. In 1876 M. D. Peter, of Vevey, Switzerland, put milk into his chocolate and produced a new flavor. A few years later a final refinement turned chocolate into the smooth-grained, velvety candy of today.

▶CULTIVATION

The cacao tree originated in South or Central America. Spanish and Portuguese colonists planted the tree throughout the tropics, but the best growing areas lie within 20 degrees north and south of the equator.

A cacao plantation is full of unexpected color. Orchids and many-colored mosses grow close to the tree's tiny white or pink five-petaled blossoms. The blossoms are followed by green or maroon seed pods that ripen into a greenish, scarlet, or golden hue. The leaves of new young shoots gradually turn from red to green as the shoots and branches mature.

Cacao trees may cross-pollinate freely, and mixed varieties are common. This actually helps the chocolate grower. Superior new varieties have been found among these crossed, or hybrid, seedlings. Three basic types—Criollo, Forastero, and Trinitario—or crosses between them are generally raised. Improved crops can be grown by planting seeds from carefully selected parent trees. Plantation owners are also developing special hybrids to improve the quality of the bean and reduce damage from diseases and pests.

Wild trees may grow as high as 18 meters (about 60 feet) and live for 200 years. Cultivated trees are pruned to a height of between 5 and 8 meters (about 15 to 25 feet) and usually are replaced after 20 to 30 years. The young seedlings often are planted under

New Guinea workers scoop out the tiny cacao beans from their pods. There are about 20 to 50 beans in each pod.

larger trees, such as banana, breadfruit, or rubber. Without shade the delicate cacao tree is easily damaged by hot sun and wind.

A young tree may begin to bear pods when it is about 3 years old. The pods may be produced the year round in regions where rain falls throughout the year. In some climates with regular wet and dry seasons, a main crop and a smaller midseason crop are produced. The *tumbadors,* or pickers, must slice the melon-shaped pods off without bruising the soft bark. The pickers cannot climb the trees because the trees would break under their weight. They use long-handled, mitten-shaped knives for the high pods and machetes for pods growing on the trunk. The pickers must be careful to pick only ripe pods.

Other workers gather the pods and scoop out their pulpy insides. The beans, still covered with pulp, are heaped into baskets to ferment. Sometimes the beans are placed in covered piles or in wooden bins. The high temperature of the fermenting beans kills the seeds and allows the substances that give chocolate its flavor to form. When the beans turn a rich brown, fermentation is complete and drying begins. It takes about three to eight days for the beans to ferment. About 900 dried beans make up a kilogram.

At the shipping centers buyers cut some of the beans open to see if they are purple or slate-colored inside. Purple or slate-colored centers indicate that the beans have been incompletely fermented, and buyers will reject the crop. Good crops are shipped at once before the moisture of the tropical regions can damage their flavor.

▶ **MANUFACTURE**

Chocolate-making is still an art. Most manufacturers have their own secrets, just as the Spanish did.

The beans are sorted by type and origin and stored away from factory odors. The beans absorb odors easily, and their flavor may be ruined by an unpleasant odor. They are cleaned and roasted to a dark brown as they are needed. The roasted beans are cracked and the shell removed, leaving the nib, or meat, of the bean. Nibs from different types of beans are mixed together according to each manufacturer's special formula.

The nibs are crushed in mills between large grinding stones or heavy steel discs. Under the friction of grinding, the fat in the nibs melts, and "chocolate liquor" is formed. Chocolate liquor is the base for chocolate and cocoa products. Hardened, it is sold as unsweetened or bitter chocolate for baking and other uses.

The fat called cocoa butter makes up about 54 percent of the bean. It can be stored for years without oxidizing or becoming rancid. There are many by-products of cocoa butter, such as healing creams for burns and scars.

To make cocoa, chocolate liquor is put under pressure in giant presses. Most of the cocoa butter is squeezed out through metallic screens. The cake that is left is cooled, pulverized, and sifted into cocoa powder. Cocoa used in homes or as a flavor by dairies, bakeries, and candy manufacturers may have 10 percent or more cocoa butter content. Breakfast cocoa, a richer type, must have at least 22 percent cocoa butter. The darker and somewhat differently flavored "Dutch" cocoa has a small amount of alkali used in its processing.

While cocoa butter is removed in making cocoa, it is added in making eating chocolate. This is true with all eating chocolate, whether it is sweet chocolate or milk chocolate. Sweet chocolate, which may be dark, light, or bitter-sweet, is a combination of chocolate liquor, sugar, cocoa butter, and perhaps a little vanilla or other added flavor. Milk chocolate, of course, contains milk as well as these other ingredients.

The chocolate mixture is ground into a smooth paste. It is now ready for "conching." This process is named after the shell-shaped machine, or "conche," originally used. During conching the paste is kneaded under heavy rollers. Conching improves the flavor of the chocolate, and the amount of conching is another manufacturer's secret. After conching, the chocolate is molded. Finally automatic machines wrap it faster than human hands could.

Chocolate is a source of carbohydrates, fat, protein, riboflavin, calcium, and iron. Because of its sugar content, it satisfies the most demanding "sweet tooth."

Reviewed by RICHARD T. O'CONNELL
Chocolate Manufacturers Association of U.S.A.

See also CANDY AND CANDYMAKING.

CHOPIN, FRÉDÉRIC (1810–1849)

Frédéric François Chopin, one of the greatest composers for the piano, was born near Warsaw, Poland, on February 22, 1810. His mother was Polish, and his father was a Frenchman who taught French to the sons of Polish nobles. Chopin grew up among his father's pupils, and in the process became something of an aristocrat himself.

Chopin early showed an amazing talent as a pianist; he played a difficult concerto in public when he was only 8. He took lessons in composition, too, and published his first work at the age of 15.

In 1829 Chopin began a concert tour that included Vienna, Munich, and Paris. His playing won such high praise in Paris that he decided to settle there for life. He never returned to Poland. In Paris Chopin played at concerts and also gave piano lessons. He was a capable and a very fashionable teacher. Young French and Polish aristocrats begged him to take them as pupils.

But above all Chopin composed. Soon he was recognized by all as the greatest piano composer of his time. Though he wrote two concertos for piano and orchestra, his best works are short compositions for piano alone—preludes, études, nocturnes, waltzes, and, reflecting his Polish heritage, polonaises and mazurkas.

In his thirties Chopin developed tuberculosis. In spite of this he carried on with his concerts and teaching but finally retired. He died on October 17, 1849, when he was only 39 years old.

CHORAL MUSIC

Music meant to be sung by a chorus or a choir is called choral music. Choral singing has had a very long history. It was heard in Sumerian temples as early as 3000 B.C. In ancient Greece children were taught singing in school, where there were choral competitions as there are in schools today.

The Hebrews of Palestine developed a special kind of choral singing in their synagogues. Often the whole congregation sang together. A solo singer, or cantor, led the singing. The chorus was often divided into separate groups. Each group took turns singing responses in answer to the cantor's chants. The words used were from the Bible, mostly from the book of Psalms.

The earliest Christians used many Hebrew melodies in their services. Slowly a new style of singing developed. Toward the end of the 6th century, a great number of Christian chants were collected together. Pope Gregory I, who reigned from A.D. 590 to 604, ordered that they be sung on certain days of the Christian church year. This music is therefore often called Gregorian chant, after the name of that music-loving pope. Today it is still the official music of the Catholic Church.

Gregorian chant is monophonic music, which means music having only one melodic line. But beginning in about the 9th century, a new kind of music, called polyphony, began to develop. Polyphony is music having several melodies that sound together. By the late 12th century, pieces were written that combined all the musical elements of melody, rhythm, harmony, and polyphony. They were joyful pieces composed for the Christmas season by the French organist Perotin. They were performed by a chorus, solo singers, wind and stringed instruments, bells, cymbals, drums, and perhaps an organ.

The most important choral work of the 14th century is the famous *Notre Dame Mass*. It was written by the French composer and poet Guillaume de Machaut (1300?–77). A mass is a musical setting of the prayers from the main service of the Catholic Church. It became one of the chief forms of music in the 15th and 16th centuries. Machaut's mass was performed by voices and instruments.

▶ GOLDEN AGE OF CHORAL MUSIC

The period of the Renaissance (roughly from 1450 to 1600) is sometimes called the Golden Age of Music. It is also known as music's a cappella period; but this term is misleading. "A cappella" means choral music without instruments. It was once believed that all Renaissance choral music was of this kind. But scholars have discovered that instruments were often used to support the voices in performing this music. So it is not really correct to call it a cappella music.

Renaissance choral music is polyphonic. That is, it is music with two or more melodies sung together. Each melody is called a part. The parts are usually written to fit different voices, from the highest to the lowest. The highest children's and women's voice is called the **soprano,** the lowest the **alto.** In between lies the **mezzo-soprano** part. The highest men's voice is called the **tenor,** the lowest the **bass.** In between the tenor and bass parts is the **baritone.** The number of voice parts in a piece varied from two to six or more. But four or five were most often used. Many pieces were written for two or three choirs totaling eight or twelve voice parts. A famous piece by the English composer Thomas Tallis calls for eight choirs of five voice parts each.

Choral music in Renaissance style first developed in northern France in about the middle of the 15th century. Its first great composer was Guillaume Dufay (1400?–74), of Burgundy. Dufay wrote many masses, chansons (French songs), and motets. Renaissance motets were choral pieces based on Bible texts and sung in Latin. Netherlands composers such as Jean d'Ockeghem (1430?–95), Jacob Obrecht (1452–1505), and Heinrich Isaac (1450?–1517), developed a richer kind of choral music.

But the best Renaissance choral music was composed by Josquin des Prez (1450?–1521), one of the greatest musicians who ever lived. Like many other composers of his time, Josquin wrote motets, masses, psalms, hymns, chansons, and ballads. He influenced choral music style for generations.

With Josquin began one of the most remarkable centuries in the history of music. A great many composers of fine choral music came from almost every country in Europe. In Italy there were Giovanni Pierluigi da Palestrina (1525?–94), Andrea Gabrieli (1520?–86), and his nephew Giovanni Gabrieli (1557–1612). From the Netherlands came Nicolas Gombert (1490?–1556), Clemens non Papa (1510?–56?), and Roland de Lassus (1532–94). Spain produced Cristóbal de Morales (1500?–53) and Tomás Luis de Victoria (1549?–1611). French composers included Clement Janequin (1485?–1560) and Claude Le Jeune (1528–1600). In England were Thomas Tallis (1505?–85) and William Byrd (1543?–1623). These were only the most important composers among a great many others. Although they came from many different countries, they all composed in the same basic musical style.

Nearly all church music of the 16th century was choral music. The favorite form of church music was the motet. Outside the church the most popular form of music was the madrigal. Madrigals were vocal pieces having up to six or more sung parts. They were usually about love and were most often performed with only one singer to a part. Often a few instruments supported the voices. Today, however, madrigals are frequently sung by a chorus.

▶ FROM MONTEVERDI TO BEETHOVEN

In the 17th century it became the common practice to include instrumental parts in choral compositions. New forms of choral music were invented. Among the most important were the church cantata and the oratorio. Oratorios were musical settings of stories from the Bible. They were composed for chorus, soloists, and instruments. Almost always they were performed without action or scenery. A church cantata is like a short oratorio, but it can be performed by a smaller group of musicians. Masses and motets also were now composed for soloists, chorus, and orchestra.

Claudio Monteverdi (1567–1643) is admired chiefly for his madrigals and operas. But he also wrote important choral works, such as his famous setting of the vespers, or evening service. In his *Vespers* (1610) Monteverdi combined solo, choral, and instrumental groups in many different ways. The result is a composition of wonderful variety.

The German composer Heinrich Schütz (1585–1672) wrote many psalms, motets, oratorios, and Passions. A Passion is a musical setting of the story of Christ's death according to the Gospels. Both chorus and soloists take part in telling the dramatic story. Schütz's Passions are thought to be the finest works of their kind before the time of Bach. Unlike Bach, Schütz used no instruments in his Passion music.

Two of the greatest of all composers of choral music were Johann Sebastian Bach (1685–1750) and George Frederick Handel (1685–1759). Bach's wonderful cantatas, Passions, and B-minor Mass are milestones in the history of music. It has become a custom in many churches today to perform Bach's *St. Matthew* Passion every year before Easter.

One of the best-loved and most widely performed works in music literature is Handel's oratorio *Messiah*. It can be heard at Christmas or Easter time almost anywhere in the world where choral music is sung. Besides his *Messiah* Handel composed many other wonderful oratorios, such as *Solomon, Judas Maccabaeus,* and *Israel in Egypt*. In most of the great choral works of Bach and Handel, the orchestra and solo instruments play a very important part.

The composers of the period following Bach and Handel are known best for their instrumental music and operas. However, some of them wrote very important choral works, too. They tried to put more drama and variety into their choral music than did earlier composers. And they gave the orchestra an even bigger part to play.

In his 14 masses and three oratorios, Franz Joseph Haydn (1732–1809) composed some of his most stirring music. His oratorios *The Creation* and *The Seasons* match those of Handel in size and dramatic power. In both of these works there are lovely musical pictures of nature. Another great 18th-century choral work was the very last composition of Wolfgang Amadeus Mozart (1756–91), his beautiful *Requiem* (Mass for the dead). It was left unfinished at his death, yet it has become Mozart's most frequently performed choral work. Mozart's operas also contain many fine choral passages, as do those of Christopher Willibald Gluck (1714–87).

The choral writing of Ludwig van Beethoven (1770–1827) is very dramatic. In fact his finest choral work, the *Missa Solemnis,* is as powerful and exciting as any of his symphonies. The orchestra seems almost more important than the chorus and soloists. In his Ninth Symphony Beethoven used a chorus in the finale, or last part. Thus it is known as the Choral Symphony.

▶ 19TH-CENTURY CHORAL MUSIC

Until the end of the 18th century, choirs and choruses were usually quite small. Rarely did they consist of more than about 12 to 16 singers, who were, however, highly trained musicians. But during the 19th century concert choruses of 100 or more singers became widely popular. By 1850 large amateur choral societies had been started in almost every large city in Europe and the United States. The reason for their success is clear. Singing in a chorus gives the music lover a chance to take part in a musical performance of high quality. A large group of untrained singers can be made to sound very good under a skillful conductor. (The same is not true of an orchestra made up of untrained instrumentalists.) Thus a serious amateur chorus can be a strong influence in the musical growth of a community.

Many composers of the 19th century wrote outstanding choral works. Those by Franz Schubert (1797–1828) include six masses that follow the models of Haydn and Beethoven. In addition Schubert wrote a number of short nonreligious choral pieces of great beauty. Interest in choral music grew after Felix Mendelssohn (1809–47) conducted a performance of Bach's *St. Matthew* Passion, in 1829. Like most of Bach's great choral music, it had been almost completely forgotten for a century. Mendelssohn's own best-known composition for chorus, soloists, and orchestra is the oratorio *Elijah*. It was first performed in England in 1846.

Enormous compositions for several choruses, a huge orchestra, and soloists were written by Hector Berlioz (1803–69). His highly original works include the *Requiem, Te Deum,* and *Damnation of Faust.* One of the most popular choral works of the 19th century is the *Requiem* by Giuseppe Verdi (1813–1901). Verdi composed it in memory of his friend the great Italian writer Alessandro Manzoni.

Anton Bruckner (1824–96) wrote three great masses and many smaller choral pieces before he started composing symphonies. Later in life he produced his most famous work for chorus, orchestra, and soloists—the *Te Deum.* It is Bruckner's most deeply felt hymn of praise to God. *A German Requiem,* by Johannes Brahms (1833–97), is one of that composer's best-loved works. The text consists of passages from the Bible chosen by the composer. Brahms composed it in memory of his mother.

Other important 19th-century choral works are *A Faust Symphony,* by Franz Liszt (1811–86), *The Beatitudes,* by César Franck (1822–90), and the lovely *Requiem* of Gabriel Fauré (1845–1924).

▶ **CHORAL MUSIC OF THE 20TH CENTURY**

Many of the leading 20th-century composers have written excellent choral music. Probably the best known is Igor Stravinsky (1882–1971). Some of his most successful works are for chorus and instruments: a mass, *Symphony of Psalms,* and *Threni.* The *Gurre-Lieder* ("Songs of Gurra"), by Arnold Schoenberg (1874–1951), was composed for three male choruses, one mixed chorus, soloists, and a gigantic orchestra. Ralph Vaughan Williams (1872–1958) wrote a great deal of choral music, including a fine setting of the Mass. The *Lamentatio Jeremiae Prophetae* (*Lamentations of Jeremiah*) by Ernst Krenek (1900–) is an outstanding work for unaccompanied chorus.

Important 20th-century choral music has been composed also by Charles Ives (1874–1954), Béla Bartók (1881–1945), Zoltán Kodály (1882–1967), Arthur Honegger (1892–1955), Paul Hindemith (1895–1963), Ernst Lévy (1895–), Carl Orff (1895–1982), Sir William Walton (1902–83), and Benjamin Britten (1913–76).

PAUL BOEPPLE
Former conductor, Dessoff Choirs, Inc.

CHRISTIANITY, HISTORY OF

"Ye shall be witnesses unto me both in Jerusalem, and in all Judaea, and in Samaria, and unto the uttermost part of the earth." In the Acts of the Apostles (1:8) these are reported as the last words spoken by Jesus Christ before he returned to heaven. The mission that Christ entrusted to his followers would not be completed until they had carried the "good news" (or gospel) he had taught them to the ends of the world.

This enormous task was partly completed during the lifetime of the original Christians. The New Testament tells of the spread of Christianity from Jerusalem, where the disciples were instructed by Christ, through the towns of Judaea and Samaria and then out to the chief cities of the Mediterranean world.

Christianity came to Antioch, Athens, Corinth, and Ephesus, and to Rome, the center and capital of the empire.

In the beginning it was largely carried out by the disciples, who had been taught by Jesus Christ during his lifetime, notably by Saint Peter and Saint John. The good news was passed on and soon won many converts. At first the converts were men and women who, like the original Apostles, had been Jews before their conversion.

The most important of the early converts was Saint Paul. Paul had been suddenly converted during a journey to Damascus by seeing Christ in a vision. He inspired people with his own missionary zeal and formed groups of Christian converts in the many

cities where he preached. There is a clear picture of all this early missionary work in two books in the New Testament: the Acts of the Apostles, probably written by Saint Paul's friend Saint Luke; and Saint Paul's own letters, which are called the Epistles. The Epistles are full of interest because (like all genuine letters) they were not written as formal essays. They discussed practical day-to-day problems as they arose. In his later years Saint Paul made his way to Rome. He was shipwrecked on the Mediterranean island of Malta on the way. When he finally arrived at Rome, he was welcomed by a Christian community that had already been established, according to tradition, by Saint Peter. It is more likely, however, that the community was founded by Christian missionaries whose names have been lost.

For the years after the record in Acts ends, evidence for the history of the Christian Church becomes more scanty. There began to be passing references to it in pagan writers. These writers make it seem likely that the Roman Emperor Nero blamed the Christians for the burning of the city of Rome in A.D. 64. It is also very likely that Saint Peter and Saint Paul were put to death at Rome at about this

Above, the newborn Jesus Christ (*The Nativity*, by Gerard David, 16th century). Below, Christ chooses two of his disciples, Peter and Andrew, who were fishermen (Duccio di Buoninsegna, 1308–11).

time. Another landmark in the history of the early Church was the destruction of Jerusalem by the Roman armies in the year 70. In the earliest years Christians would have seemed to the outsider to be a group of Jews who differed from other Jews only because they held special beliefs about Jesus Christ. But after the fall of Jerusalem the religious differences between Christians and Jews became much clearer.

In the later years of the 1st century (70–100), many of the books of the New Testament were written, including almost certainly the Gospels of Saint Matthew and Saint John and perhaps (though these may be even earlier than A.D. 70) those of Saint Mark and Saint Luke.

▶ THE AGE OF PERSECUTIONS

By the end of the New Testament period the Church was firmly established. The next stage in the Church's life is from about A.D. 100 down to the year 313.

This period was a time of rapid expansion of Christianity. An ever-growing number of people heard about Christianity and found in it inspiration and faith. The pagan religions they knew had lost their vitality. Even pagan priests did not seem to take their gods seriously. Many people tried to find religious help in the mystery religions. These religions came from the East (Egypt, Asia Minor, Persia, Babylonia). They promised eternal life to those people who were willing to practice elaborate religious and magical rites. But the mysteries lacked something important that Christianity had—a moral code by which people could live. It gave them a clear challenge. It put before them a body of definite beliefs. Its worship was a spiritual form of devotion that reached its highest point every Sunday in the sacred meal of the Eucharist, or Holy Communion. What is more, Christianity from the first stressed the importance of morality. It had inherited from the Jews a strict moral code, including the Ten Commandments. This moral teaching had been set forth and expanded by Jesus Christ in the Sermon on the Mount and elsewhere in the Gospels.

And so Christianity spread. Around A.D. 200 a Christian writer named Tertullian wrote that in his day there were Christians in almost every town. It has been estimated that 100 years later nearly half the population of Asia Minor was Christian.

The organization of the Church developed in this period. Christianity at first was a missionary religion, directed by the original Apostles. They traveled from place to place and left behind them small groups of Christians in the towns where they preached. When the original Apostles died, the leadership of the Church was taken over by local pastors, known as bishops. Under them were ministers of lower rank, known as the presbyters and deacons. The Church organized the area of the Roman Empire into provinces. The bishops at the head of the Christian communities in the large cities such as Rome, Antioch, Alexandria, and Carthage ranked highest. At first the Christians assembled for their weekly worship in private houses. However, as time went on it became necessary to build churches in the larger cities.

During this period the Church was frequently persecuted. As Christ had predicted, discipleship was to be a hard (and sometimes dangerous) path to follow. Since traditional pagan religion was part of the accepted way of life of the people, refusal to take part in pagan ceremonies aroused suspicion. This suspicion was made stronger by the apparent secrecy of the Christian rites. Since only those people baptized as Christians could join in Christian worship, rumors started. Christians were said to be superstitious and immoral. Some people even said that they were cannibals. Men and women, boys and girls, too, suffered imprisonment and even death for their Christian belief. The two worst persecutions of Christians took place in the 3rd century, when Christianity was gaining more and more converts. Paganism tried to make a final stand. Under the Roman emperor Decius (249–251) an edict was put out in January, 250, requiring all citizens to make sacrifices in the pagan temples in honor of the emperor. Many thousands of Christians, including Pope Fabian of Rome, were put to death for refusing to take part in the pagan rituals. The worst of the persecutions, however, broke out in 303 in the reigns of the Emperor Diocletian (284–305) and his successors. A series of edicts brought to death a very large number of Christian martyrs.

In this 12th- or 13th-century Italian fresco (*above*), Constantine, the champion of Christianity, leads Pope Sylvester I (on horseback) into Rome. St. Augustine of Hippo (*below*), the great writer of the early Christian Church, at his desk (Sandro Botticelli, 1480).

▶ THE PERIOD OF THE FATHERS (313–800)

The new era in the history of Christianity began with the Roman Emperor Constantine (280–337). Constantine, who reversed the policy of earlier Roman emperors, became a supporter of Christianity. In the West this change dates from A.D. 313. After Constantine had made himself ruler of the whole civilized world in 324 at the Battle of Chrysopolis, he also established Christianity in the East. He introduced laws supporting Christian moral teachings. He also supported the observance of Sunday as a Christian holy day. The Christian bishops and other ministers, who had always been in danger of persecution, were given special privileges and honors. Constantine bestowed lavish gifts on the Church and erected fine churches at several of the leading Christian shrines. These included major churches, called basilicas, that were built over the tombs of the apostles Saint Peter and Saint Paul in Rome.

Under these new conditions pagans were converted to Christianity in large numbers. At first no one was forced to convert. Although Christians held privileged positions, their religion was still only one faith among many. But later, by the time of the emperor Theodosius the Great (346?–395), Christianity became the one official religion of the Roman Empire. Not only paganism, but also unorthodox forms of Christianity were forbidden. The new faith was taught in the universities and schools. Large numbers of books were written dealing with the relation of Christianity to the leading ideas of the day. The only emperor in the 4th century who tried to stop the spread of the new faith and keep pagan beliefs alive was Julian the Apostate (331–363). But his efforts failed.

In the 5th century the Barbarian people of northern Europe began attacking the Roman Empire. The Vandals and the Visigoths were two of the strongest of these Barbarian tribes. In 476 the Roman Empire finally came to an end. In a period when the political outlook was dark, hope and inspiration came from the Church alone. Moreover, some of the Barbarian leaders had already accepted Christianity. In the next 200 or 300 years Christianity became generally accepted throughout western Europe.

A notable development in this period was the building of monasteries. A monastery is a community of men who live and work together and devote their lives to prayer. These men are called monks. Already in the 3rd century large numbers of Christians had become monks. Some monks had even gone into the desert to get away from the world. The earliest settlements of monks were in Egypt. Later came the communities of Saint Basil (330?–379) in Cappadocia in Asia Minor and of John Cassian (360?–435?) in the south of France. At the end of the 4th century many devout and well-to-do Christians at Rome, weary of the luxury and corruption of life in the Western capital, decided to go to Palestine. There they helped the poor and the ever-growing number of Christian pilgrims who came to see the holy places of their religion. In Celtic lands and especially in Ireland the monasteries played an important role in the development of the Church from the first. In the middle of the 6th century Saint Benedict drew up a new "rule," a set of regulations for the life of a monk and the running of monasteries. The Rule of Saint Benedict and the way of life it helped to bring about were to be the inspiration of much that was best in Western Christianity for the following 1,000 years.

Another mark of the 3rd century was the rise of the great heresies. From the first, Christianity required that all of its members believe specific things about Christ and his Church. The basic beliefs of the Church were not understood. Some men made up their own distorted versions of these beliefs. These distortions were called heresies. In some ways the most dangerous heresy was the theory of Arius, who refused to accept the full divinity (godliness) of Jesus Christ. He produced a version of Christianity that was enough like the basic Christian creed to be believed by Christians. Arianism, as the heresy of Arius is called, was able to win over some of the most noted thinkers of the day. It was this heresy that was the chief matter in dispute at the first General Council of the Church, which met in 325 at Nicaea in Asia Minor. The council was sponsored by the Emperor Constantine. Although almost all the approximately 350 bishops who met at Nicaea rejected Arianism, this heresy continued to trouble the Church. It was finally condemned at the second General Council, held at Constantinople in 381.

The Church had the support of Christian rulers in crushing heresies. Those who refused to give up their heretical ideas were banished from the empire. Their exile led indirectly to the spread of Christianity, for the heretics were still Christians even though their beliefs differed from orthodox Christian doctrine. They introduced their versions of the Christian religion wherever they went in exile. Christian missionaries also spread the religion. Some of them reached India as early as the 5th century and China by the 7th century.

It was largely to defend itself against these heresies that the Church developed her own body of teaching, known as theology. The men who wrote the accepted theology of the Church became known as the Fathers. Most wrote in Greek or Latin. Among the leading Greek Fathers were Saint Athanasius (293?–373), Saint Gregory of Nazianzus (329?–389), and Saint Gregory of Nyssa (331?–395?); among the Latins, Saint Ambrose of Milan (340?–397), Saint Jerome (340?–420) and Saint Gregory the Great (540?–604). Most important of all was Saint Augustine of Hippo, who lived in North Africa in the 5th century. Saint Augustine was the greatest Christian theologian since the New Testament times. Among his many books two are very well known—the *Confessions* and the *City of God*. In his *Confessions* he gives a vivid picture of his early life and of the struggles by which he came to accept Christianity. In the *City of God* he gives a splendid description of what man's life in heaven will be like, contrasting it with the passing pleasures of earthly life.

We do not know how or when Christianity first reached the British Isles. Three British bishops took part in a council at Arles in the south of France in 314, so it must have been well established by the beginning of the 4th century. Conversions of the people from paganism to Christianity first took place on a large scale in Ireland under Saint Patrick (389?–461?), called the Apostle of Ireland. Before long Irish missionaries made their way into Scotland and the northern and western parts of England. The conversion of the Anglo-Saxons in the southeastern part of England, however, was not begun until the last years of the 6th century. Pope Gregory the Great sent Saint Augustine of Canterbury (?–604), the Apostle of the English, to England with a small band of Benedictine monks. Nearly 100 years after that the English Church was organized, largely through the efforts of Archbishop Theodore of Tarsus (602?–690). Two well-known Christian leaders of the next generation were English. Saint Boniface (680–754), called the Apostle of Germany, was a native of Devon. He carried the Christian faith from England through Holland and the south of Germany and after a life of many hardships was killed by pagans. The Venerable Bede (673?–735), another great English Christian leader of the period, lived in the monastery of Jarrow, near Durham. He lived a life of holiness, devoting himself to the study of the Scriptures and Christian learning. Among his many writings is a history of the early English Church.

▶ THE MIDDLE AGES

The next stage in the history of Christianity begins on Christmas Day in the year 800. On this day Charlemagne, King of the Franks, was crowned first Holy Roman Emperor by Pope Leo III. The influence of this alliance between the pope and the greatest political leader in Europe was immense.

Charlemagne wanted to build a civilization guided by Christian principles. When he conquered the pagan tribes in Saxony and elsewhere, he forced them to be baptized as Christians. Moreover, he loved everything Roman. He used Roman law in the lands he ruled and ordered the use of the Roman form of Christian religious worship. He invited the most learned and devoted scholars of the age to his court. By encouraging the founding of new schools, especially in the monasteries, he increased the Church's support of learning and education. This enthusiastic support continued through the Middle Ages.

Christianity thus became the framework for life in Europe. Countless Gothic cathedrals and parish churches all over Europe still stand as examples of the strong faith that inspired their building. The painting, sculpture, and books of the period also show the great influence of the Church and its teaching on the people. Beautiful objects of religious art show the labor and skill that men and women used in making things to be used in their religious services. In the later Middle Ages, especially after Pope Urban IV had instituted the Feast of Corpus Christi (the Body of Christ) in 1264, Christian services centered increasingly on the Sacrament of the Eucharist (Holy Communion).

Throughout the Middle Ages the clergy and the religious orders of monks had great influence on the people and their government. Many of the most important governmental offices were filled by bishops. Monks were to be found everywhere. New orders of monks and new reforms of the older orders came into being to meet new needs. In the earlier part of the period, these reforms usually followed more or less closely the Rule of Saint Benedict; the best known of them were the Cluniacs, the Cistercians, and the Carthusians. Later in the Middle Ages came the Friars (from the Latin word *fratres,* which means brothers), whose work consisted largely, though not entirely, in preaching and helping the poor and sick in the cities. Saint Francis of Assisi (1182–1226), with his devotion to the "Lady Poverty" and his love of the simple life and of animals, was the most famous of the friars. Saint Dominic (1170–1221) was known for his defense of Christianity against heretics. Among the men inspired by Saint Dominic was Saint Thomas Aquinas (1225–74), one of the greatest of all Christian writers and philosophers.

▶ THE AGE OF REFORMATION (1517–1648)

By the 15th century the medieval system had largely lost its vigor and was showing signs of breaking up. One reason was the growth of what was called the New Learning. The Christian Church of the East—of Greece especially—had awakened an interest in the classical age of ancient Greek culture. Men began to study the Greek classic literature and learned of the freedom of ancient Greece and the glories of its art. The improvement of printing in Europe in the 15th century enabled many more men to read. Countless new books were available. And, most important of all to Christians, the Bible could be printed. As a result of reading and learning, people were not as willing to believe without question everything their religious leaders told them. A fresh view of human nature was taken by such brilliant men as the painter and inventor Leonardo da Vinci (1452–1519) and the famous scholar Desiderius Erasmus (1466?–1536). These humanists, as they were called, led men and women to question many traditional religious practices accepted in the medieval Church. Moreover, people were unhappy with the finances of the Church. There were many instances of graft and corruption in the handling of money contributed by the people to the Church. Money intended to help the poor and the sick sometimes ended up in the pockets of high church officials. Large sums of money were collected by means of indulgences. An indulgence was the way the Church had of releasing a person from the punishments of a sin. This meant that a person who had committed a sin could have his penance (punishment) shortened or removed by an indulgence. His penance might be one placed on him while he was living on earth. It could also be a penance that was to be suffered by his soul after death. Sometimes an indulgence was granted if prayers were said. At other times an indulgence might be gained by making a contribution to the Church. Indulgences were widely resented, especially as the money that was sometimes paid for them passed into the papal treasury in Rome. Above all, the grow-

Life in a monastery today is much the same as it was for monks in the Middle Ages.

ing spirit of nationalism (interest in one's own country) was present in a large part of Europe. Some countries began to want freedom from Rome. The movement in which some countries broke away from Roman religious control and formed their own churches was called the Reformation. The Reformation was largely a nationalist movement. From the beginning it took different forms under its different leaders in the various countries where it was established.

The event that brought the Reformation to Germany took place on October 31, 1517, when Martin Luther, a former Augustinian monk and Roman Catholic priest, posted on the church door at Wittenberg a set of 95 propositions attacking the system of indulgences set up by the Church. Luther tried to show that the whole medieval system of indulgences was wrong. The system rested on the belief that what the Christian faith demanded of its disciples was good works. But such a doctrine, Luther said, was contrary to the teaching of Saint Paul. According to Saint Paul, what justifies a man in the sight of God is not good works, but simply faith in Jesus Christ. Luther soon won over a number of the princes in Germany, who were glad of this opportunity to free themselves from Rome. He also gained great influence among the people through his splendid German translation of the Bible. Hitherto the Scriptures had been available only in Latin. And only a small educated group in Europe knew Latin. The medieval services, including the Mass, were abolished in favor of others that Luther believed to follow the teaching of the New Testament more closely.

In northern Switzerland another Protestant movement was led by Huldreich Zwingli, Pastor of Zurich from 1519. In France the Reformation found its leader in John Calvin (1509–64), who, though a very different man from Luther and Zwingli, also left the mark of his personality on the movement that he began. Calvin, a native of Picardy, in the north of France, was a great organizer, a great disciplinarian, a great Biblical commentator, and a great theologian. In 1536 he set out his doctrines in a book known in the English-speaking world as the *Institutes*. This work, a book about Christian life, discusses the Ten Commandments, the Apostles' Creed,

Martin Luther, still wearing his monk's habit, nails the 95 propositions to the church door in Wittenberg (pen-and-ink sketch done around 1850).

the Lord's Prayer, the Sacraments, and church government. In 1541 Calvin established his authority at Geneva, where his religious principles were strictly enforced, and from 1555 on Calvinism was supreme there. One of the chief marks of Calvinism was the importance attached to the government of the church by elders, or presbyters, who were to replace bishops. Another was the belief that God had determined the destiny of every human soul; men had no power to save themselves. Calvin's system of discipline and belief became a model for large numbers of Protestants.

In England the Reformation took an independent course. Here its beginnings were less theological. Henry VIII (who reigned from 1509 to 1547) wished to end his marriage with Catherine of Aragon in order to marry Anne Boleyn. He asked Pope Clement VII for a divorce from Catherine. The Pope refused. Henry decided that the simplest way to get what he wanted was to reject the authority of the Pope in England and put himself at the head of the Church of England. Henry got Parliament to agree to his plan. At the same time England's wealthy monasteries were dissolved. In 1532 Thomas Cranmer became the new archbishop of Canterbury, the most important position other than the king's in the independent Church of England.

Unlike the European reformers, Henry VIII wanted little change in the Church of England. In his early years he had even written a treatise against Martin Luther. And though in middle age he had shown a certain sympathy with some of the new doctrines, later he definitely rejected them. In 1539 he promoted an act (called the Whip with Six Strings) to stop further changing of the services of the Church of England. It was only after his death that Protestantism became the official policy of the Church of England.

After an attempt to carry the principles of the Reformation to extremes under the boy-king Edward VI (1547–53) and a strong return to Catholicism under Mary I (1553–58), the Reformation in England reached a compromise in the long reign of Elizabeth I. Members of the Church of England and the other Anglican or Episcopal churches throughout the world believe that their Church is at once Catholic and Protestant.

A memorial in Geneva, Switzerland, to the Protestant Reformation.

They feel that it follows a middle path between Roman Catholicism and Protestantism. This has been possible because no single theologian such as Luther or Calvin ever dominated the English Church. While retaining bishops, priests, and deacons, the Church of England rejected other elements of the medieval Church and the authority of the pope. The Church of England also encouraged the study of the Scriptures and in 1611 issued a famous new version of the Bible, known as the King James Version.

The Reformation was accepted only in the north of Europe. Most countries nearer Rome continued faithful to the papacy. In fact, the Reformation brought fresh life into the Roman Catholic Church in many lands. This renewal came to be known as the Counter-Reformation. It arose partly through a new awareness in the Roman Catholic Church of a need to reform itself, partly in reaction to the Protestant movements in the north. Abuses were corrected, and a new religious spirit swept both the clergy and the people. The Roman Catholic clergy accepted a stricter discipline in their private lives, the service books were revised, and countless other reforms were made. At the head of this reforming movement was the Society of Jesus (Jesuits) founded by the Spanish priest and former soldier Saint Ignatius of Loyola, who died in 1556. Another important step in the Counter-Reformation was the General Council of Trent (1545–63). Though it had to face many difficulties and though it failed to bring the Protestants back into the Church, the Council helped greatly to form the basis for modern Roman Catholicism.

▶ MODERN MOVEMENTS (SINCE 1648)

The Peace of Westphalia (1648), which closed the great conflict known as the Thirty Years War, ended many of the struggles started by the Reformation. The peace divided Europe between Catholics and Protestants and left it almost as it is still divided today. Italy, France, Spain, Austria, South Germany, and Poland were the main countries and regions that remained Roman Catholic. Britain, North Germany, North Holland, and the Scandinavian countries were Protestant. The Orthodox Church in the East continued until quite recent times to stand apart from Roman Catholicism and Protestantism.

The Growth of Toleration

The modern world may be said to date from the later 1600's. It was marked by the rapid growth of the ideal of toleration. Before this time people had thought that it was the duty of the Christian state to uphold religious truth and to punish those who refused to conform to Christian beliefs. The Reformation did not immediately change this view, which continued to be held by Catholics and Protestants alike.

But after the Thirty Years War—under the influence of such thinkers as Voltaire, John Locke, and Wilhelm Leibniz—more liberal ideas began to take over. Religious beliefs came to be regarded as a private matter between God and each individual, not as a concern of the state. People began to question whether a nation ought to have an official state church. In many countries the ties between Christianity and the government were loosened or completely dissolved.

A modern Christian church rises above an Arizona canyon.

One of the effects of this freedom was the growth of independent Christian sects. It is true that in England the Church of England continued to have a privileged place. Its bishops continued to sit in the House of Lords, and it was the religion of the king. But toleration was granted to other Protestant bodies in 1689. The Congregationalists, the Baptists, and the Presbyterians enjoyed a new liberty and began to develop into the large bodies that they are today. The Roman Catholics were not granted this freedom until 1829. Because of English toleration for Protestant groups, the great Methodist leaders John Wesley (1703–91) and Charles Wesley (1707–88) were able to carry their religious ideas to the people. Their preaching would have been impossible 100 years earlier.

Christianity in the New World

Until the 1600's, most Christians were Europeans. But the expansion of European peoples all over the world spread Christianity. The growth has happened in two ways. When European settlers went to countries with few or no inhabitants, they tried to set up in their new lands the church organization and forms of worship that they had known at home. When they went to lands that were already populated, they tried to convert the population to Christianity.

North America. Many of the early settlers of North America, such as the Pilgrims, came from minority groups. They sought religious freedom in the New World. In general, the churches in America were liberal, and most of the early colonies adopted a Congregational form of church government. New York was originally the seat of a Dutch Reformed Church, but Anglicanism was introduced by the British in 1664. The only colony founded by Roman Catholics was Maryland, and it became officially Anglican in 1702. The Declaration of Independence (1776) did not set up an official Christian church, although it assumes belief in God.

Since 1776 the history of Christianity in the United States has closely followed the history of the nation. The Anglican Church (officially known as the Protestant Episcopal Church) was soon established on a firm basis. The first American bishop was Samuel Seabury, who was consecrated at Aberdeen, Scotland, in 1784. In the 19th century, the large immigration from Ireland, Poland, and Italy brought many Roman Catholic settlers. The following century saw a huge influx of Hispanic peoples from Mexico, Puerto Rico, and other Latin-American countries, adding to the number of Catholics. As a result, the Roman Catholic Church is now the largest single Christian body in the United States.

In Canada, Christianity came originally with the first French settlement of 1534 and was at first almost entirely Roman Catholic. The first bishop of Quebec was appointed in 1674. English colonists did not arrive until much later, and the first Anglican bishop was appointed in 1787. As the population increased, the churches grew in number and influence, and other denominations were established. The largest of these Protestant groups were the Methodists, the Presbyterians, the Baptists, and the Congregationalists. In 1925 the Methodists, Congregationalists, and most of the Presbyterians formed the new United Church of Canada. This is now the largest single Protestant church in Canada. At the present time over 40 percent of the Canadian population is Roman Catholic.

For many years, revivals (periods of renewed religious interest) have played a part in Christianity's continuing influence in the Western World, especially in North America. A return to fundamentalism—literal interpretation of the Bible as fundamental to Christian life and teaching—has been evident in Protestant movements. Often they are led by evangelists (ministers or others who preach at special services), such as Dwight Lyman Moody (1837–99) and William Franklin (Billy) Graham (1918–   ). The evangelists preach a modified fundamentalism and urge all who hear them to repent and be saved. Protestants and Catholics in the United States take part in the revival, or evangelical, movements.

Latin America. Latin America, which was colonized by the Spanish and the Portuguese, is about 90 percent Roman Catholic today. This area was a feudal, largely agricultural society until well into the 20th century. Many Latin Americans must still struggle to survive on low incomes. In the past, the Church was largely conservative and did little to help better the lot of the poor. But by the middle of the 20th century, some changes were beginning to appear. A "theology of liberation" was developed in the 1960's. In this theology, the work of Christ is seen as a mission to liberate all people from ignorance, hunger, misery, and oppression—to free them from injustice and hatred. A large number of priests and bishops are now solidly behind the efforts for social justice for all the people of Latin America.

The Ecumenical Movement

Throughout the history of Christianity, there have been many conflicts and divisions. But the past century has seen a trend toward unity. Missionary movements brought cooperation among Protestant churches and led to the World Missionary Conference of Edinburgh (Scotland) in 1910. This conference may be said to be the beginning of the movement toward worldwide Christian unity, later called the ecumenical movement.

In 1948 many Protestant churches joined to form the World Council of Churches. The World Council grew to include more than 200 member churches. The Orthodox Eastern churches joined in 1961. The Roman Catholic Church is not a member of the council, but it now participates actively in this movement toward unity.

One of the most important events in the ecumenical movement was the second Vatican Council, summoned by Pope John XXIII in 1962. The council examined the relations of the Catholic Church with other churches and non-Christian groups, and a program for the promotion of Christian unity was developed.

Many Christians now disregard the particular groups to which they belong and form alliances with one another. They have taken stands in major political and social concerns of the modern world, such as war, poverty, civil rights for minorities, and the ordination of women as members of the clergy. Great differences still exist among the followers of Jesus Christ, but the trend toward ecumenism continues today.

F. L. CROSS
Editor, *Oxford Dictionary of the
Christian Church*

See also APOSTLES, THE; BIBLE; BIBLE STORIES; CRUSADES; DEAD SEA SCROLLS; INQUISITION; JESUS CHRIST; ORTHODOX EASTERN CHURCHES; PROTESTANTISM; REFORMATION; RELIGIONS OF THE WORLD; ROMAN CATHOLIC CHURCH; and names of popes, saints, and other Christian leaders.

CHRISTMAS CUSTOMS AROUND THE WORLD

December 25 is a Christian festival and is observed as the anniversary of the birth of Christ. In early times this day was not one of the feasts of the Christian Church. In fact, church leaders thought the celebration of birthdays to be a heathen custom. It is believed that Christmas was not celebrated until some 300 years after the birth of Christ.

No one is certain why December 25 was chosen. There is nothing in the New Testament to indicate that this is the date of the Nativity. It is believed that the efforts of the early Christians in Rome to change pagan customs into Christian rites led, in the 4th century A.D., to the adoption of December 25 as the date of the Christ Mass, or feast, in honor of the birth of Christ. This day was probably chosen because, according to the calendar then in use, December 25 was the winter solstice, the time when days begin to grow longer in the Northern Hemisphere. The sun-worshiping pagans had celebrated this day as the promise of spring.

Actually very few of the customs associated with Christmas have their origin in church festivals. The exception is the crèche, or Christmas crib, ceremony. It is held on Christmas Eve and tells the story of the Magi bringing gifts to the infant Christ. Saint Francis of Assisi set up a Nativity scene at Greccio, Italy, in 1223, which popularized the re-enactment of the birth. Today these displays of the Holy Family and the adoration of the Wise Men are assembled in churches and Catholic homes all over the world.

In Italy the Christmas crib ceremony in churches is called the *presepe,* meaning "manger." It is called the *crèche,* or "crib," in France. In Germany it is known as the *Krippe,* and has the same meaning. In Spain and among Spanish-speaking South Americans, it is called the *nacimiento,* or "birth." The custom was introduced into England and America but never has been as popular as it is in Catholic countries.

▶ CHRISTMAS MUSIC

Christmas music is loved by all who hear and sing it every year. It includes some of the greatest compositions ever written for chorus and orchestra as well as the joyful melodies of the familiar Christmas carols. Carols, bells, and merry music have been a part of Christmas for centuries.

Many of the early carols were based on dance tunes and refrains from ballads and folk songs. Later, during the Reformation, the carols became gloomy, reflecting the dim view that the Puritans held regarding Christmas. This view came about because in England from the 11th to the 17th century, Christmas had become more and more a wild celebration of feasting and merrymaking that lasted for weeks, sometimes from mid-December until January. Because these feasts held in the great houses of England had little or no connection with the true meaning of Christmas, the Puritans outlawed Christmas. The observance of Christmas was forbidden by an act of Parliament in 1644. After the restoration of the monarchy in 1660, Charles II revived the custom. With the return of Christmas, the art of carol making and singing began anew. It is as popular today as it was in the 14th century.

All over the world the ringing of bells is a part of the Christmas tradition. For hundreds of years Zurich, Switzerland, has been famous for its beautiful bells. Every Christmas Eve the bells sound loud and clear to call families to church services. This ceremony is echoed in thousands of cities where cathedral chimes and church bells ring out at midnight. Bells are used as decorations on Christmas wreaths and as ornaments on trees to add a gay, tinkling note to Christmas gift wrappings. And as everyone knows, the most famous sleigh bells in the world belong to Santa Claus. It is said that Clement Moore, a professor at the General Theological Seminary in New York, was inspired to write *A Visit from Saint Nicholas* after listening to the merry jingle of the bells on his horses' harness as he drove along on a frosty winter night.

▶EVERGREENS, HOLLY, MISTLETOE, FLOWERS

The Christmas tree is the symbol of the spirit of the Yuletide in many homes. The custom came from Germany and dates to long ago when primitive people revered trees—particularly evergreens. These trees did not die or fade in winter and seemed to be a sign of immortality. The Christians changed the custom into one honoring Christ.

The northern peoples of Denmark, Sweden, and Norway, where the forests are plentiful, adopted the custom of bringing small trees into their homes at Christmastime.

Trees were not used in English homes until a German prince, Albert of Saxe-Coburg-Gotha, married Queen Victoria. Prince Albert had the first decorated Christmas tree set up at Windsor Castle in 1841.

The first Christmas trees in the New World were introduced by Hessian soldiers in 1776, during the Revolutionary War. Later, German immigrants brought the tradition into wider use in the United States.

The custom of decorating a community tree for outdoor display began in the early 1900's and is a favorite custom all over America today. Since 1933, Rockefeller Plaza, in New York City, has put up a giant tree, beautifully decorated with glittering ornaments and dazzling lights. Trees approximately 30 meters (100 feet) tall have towered over the plaza. Some 7,000 colored lights have been used to light them. Each year at Washington, D.C., there is a national tree lighting ceremony. The President of the United States pulls the switch that lights the brightly decorated new community Christmas tree on the White House lawn.

Many other Christmas decorations used today were once pagan symbols. The Romans used flowers and leafy boughs in their rites. Records show that the Saxons used holly, ivy, and bay in their religious observances. The Druids gave the world the tradition of hanging the mistletoe in the house. These ancient Celtic priests believed the plant to be a sign of hope and peace. When two enemies met under a sprig of mistletoe they would drop their weapons and embrace in friendship. It is thought that the modern custom of young men and women kissing under the mistletoe comes from this old ritual.

While Joel R. Poinsett was serving as United States minister to Mexico, he discovered the gay red-and-green tropical plant that has since been named for him. In 1828 he sent a cutting of the plant to a friend in the United States. Interested growers helped start the poinsettia in the United States, where it now flourishes as the favorite houseplant of the Christmas season.

▶PRESENTS AND MERRYMAKING

Some families open their presents on Christmas Eve; others wait for the next morning. Some boys' and girls' presents are placed in stockings and hung from the fireplace mantel or at the foot of their beds; others find their gifts under the Christmas tree. In France, Mexico, and the South American countries of Argentina and Brazil children find their presents in their shoes. In Catholic countries the Christmas crib rather than the tree becomes the center of the celebration.

Latin-American children have a Christmas party that includes the *piñata*. This is an earthenware jug or sometimes a small papier-mâché figure of a donkey or another little animal that is filled with candies and small toys. The piñata swings from a rope attached to the ceiling or the branch of a tree if the game is played out-of-doors. One of the children is blindfolded and given a stick and three chances to hit the piñata and break it. If the first child misses, the next in turn tries, until at last someone succeeds in shattering the jug or toy animal and the sweets and presents tumble down for all to share and enjoy.

In the Netherlands, Belgium, and parts of Germany, children receive their presents on December 6. This is the feast of Saint Nicholas, patron saint of children. Saint Nicholas was Bishop of Myra in Asia Minor in the 4th century A.D. and was famous for his generosity. In England he is called Father Christmas; in the Netherlands he is known as Sinter Klaas. It was this name the Dutch settlers brought to America. But to the ears of the English children in the colonies, Sinter Klaas sounded like Santa Claus, and that became his name in the New World. Pictures show that at that time Santa wore a wide-brimmed hat, short Dutch breeches, and smoked a long clay pipe. In 1863, the cartoonist Thomas Nast pictured a fat and jolly Santa wearing a red velvet fur-trimmed suit and still smoking a pipe.

Children in France welcome the visit of Père Noël at Christmastime. In Germany it is Kriss Kringle who brings gifts.

In Sweden Christmas Eve presents are brought by Jultomte, a fat man dressed in red. His helpers, who are like elves and sometimes help good people throughout the year, are called the *tomtar*.

Not all the Christmas patrons of children are men. In Italy the childrens' presents are brought by a woman who is named La Befana. Good children receive presents from her, but Italian mothers tell their babies that La Befana will punish them by leaving ashes for them if they are bad.

In Switzerland Saint Lucy and Father Christmas give presents. In Greece Saint Basil brings the gifts. In Poland gifts are believed to come from Father Frost, and in Hungary they are thought to come from the angels.

▶ **FAMILY GATHERINGS**

Christmas is a family day, and feasting is a part of the celebration. Foods of the season include turkey, goose, duck, fish, roast beef, and an abundance of the other good things people enjoy when they eat, drink, and are merry. In some European countries the old custom of serving a roast suckling pig with an apple in its mouth is still observed.

In Germany and the Netherlands the favorite dish is roast goose prepared with a delicious stuffing of prunes or apples. Turkey is the favorite food of the day in France, as it is in many English speaking countries. The southern Italians are fond of *capitone,* a dish of fried eels. For their main course they eat a fowl, usually stuffed turkey. In many other lands fish dishes are served at Christmas. In Austria and Czechoslovakia Christmas dinners feature baked carp or some other fish. In Norway and Sweden the meal may begin with codfish served with a cream sauce and boiled potatoes. In Spain the Christmas meal includes a meat stew called a *puchero olla.*

Of all Christmas desserts, perhaps the most popular ones in England and America are plum pudding and mince pie. Superstition says that eating mince pie on Christmas brings good luck. In many lands specially baked cakes are traditional, particularly rich cookies, fruitcake, and plum pudding. Preparation of these wonderful treats is begun weeks ahead of Christmas dinner. And the scent of tempting cakes and fancy cookies and candies drifts toward eager noses and gives away the secret of some of the surprises yet to come.

▶ **GREETING CARDS BEGAN IN ENGLAND**

One of the first artists to design and send a Christmas card was John C. Horsley, a member of the Royal Academy in London. He was commissioned by Sir Henry Cole in 1843 to design a card. The cards were lithographed in

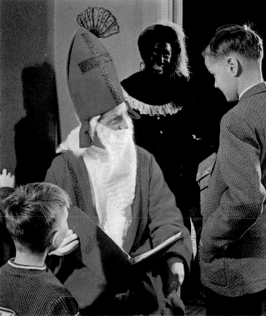

Above, Chinese Santa Claus gives children a ride on a toy merry-go-round. Above right, Nigerian children with "Father Christmas." Right, Sinter Klaas talks to a Dutch boy, while Black Peter, his Moorish servant, looks on. Below, a Mexican girl is about to swing at the gift-filled piñata.

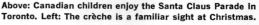
Above: Canadian children enjoy the Santa Claus Parade in Toronto. Left: The crèche is a familiar sight at Christmas.

black and white and colored by hand. About 1,000 of them were sold in London that year. At about the same time, another English artist, William Egley, designed a card and had it printed. He sent it to his friend with the now familiar message "A Merry Christmas and a Happy New Year."

A German emigrant printer, Louis Prang, designed and sold colored Christmas cards in Roxbury, Massachusetts, in 1874. In less than 10 years his shop was turning out 5,000,000 cards a year.

Today greeting cards have become a major industry, and literally billions of cards are sent all over the world every Christmas. Whatever language the greetings are written in, the message is the same—a wish for peace and goodwill among all people.

Reviewed by ETHNA SHEEHAN
Former Coordinator of Children's Services
Queens Borough Public Library (New York)

"A Visit from St. Nicholas" has been a part of Christmas in America since 1823, the year it was published. Clement C. Moore wrote it for his family on Christmas Eve, 1822.

A VISIT FROM ST. NICHOLAS

'Twas the night before Christmas, when all
    through the house
Not a creature was stirring, not even a mouse;
The stockings were hung by the chimney with
    care,
In hopes that St. Nicholas soon would be there;
The children were nestled all snug in their beds
While visions of sugar-plums danced in their
    heads;
And Mamma in her 'kerchief, and I in my cap,
Had just settled our brains for a long winter's
    nap,
When out on the lawn there arose such a clatter,
I sprang from my bed to see what was the
    matter.
Away to the window I flew like a flash,
Tore open the shutters and threw up the sash.
The moon on the breast of the new-fallen snow
Gave a lustre of midday to objects below,
When, what to my wondering eyes did appear,
But a miniature sleigh and eight tiny reindeer,
With a little old driver, so lively and quick,
I knew in a moment it must be St. Nick.
More rapid than eagles his coursers they came,
And he whistled, and shouted, and called them
    by name:
"Now, Dasher! now, Dancer! now, Prancer and
    Vixen!
On, Comet! on, Cupid! on, Donder and Blitzen!
To the top of the porch! to the top of the wall!
Now dash away! dash away! dash away, all!"
As dry leaves that before the wild hurricane fly,
When they meet with an obstacle, mount to the
    sky,
So up to the housetop the coursers they flew,

With the sleigh full of toys, and St. Nicholas too.
And then, in a twinkling, I heard on the roof
The prancing and pawing of each little hoof.
As I drew in my head, and was turning around,
Down the chimney St. Nicholas came with a
    bound.
He was dressed all in fur, from his head to his
    foot,
And his clothes were all tarnished with ashes
    and soot;
A bundle of toys he had flung on his back,
And he looked like a peddler just opening his
    pack.
His eyes—how they twinkled! his dimples, how
    merry!
His cheeks were like roses, his nose like a cherry!
His droll little mouth was drawn up like a bow,
And the beard on his chin was as white as the
    snow;
The stump of a pipe he held tight in his teeth,
And the smoke, it encircled his head like a
    wreath;
He had a broad face and a little round belly
That shook, when he laughed, like a bowl full of
    jelly.
He was chubby and plump, a right jolly old elf,
And I laughed when I saw him, in spite of my-
    self;
A wink of his eye and a twist of his head,
Soon gave me to know I had nothing to dread;
He spoke not a word, but went straight to his
    work,
And filled all the stockings; then turned with a
    jerk,
And laying his finger aside of his nose,
And giving a nod, up the chimney he rose.
He sprang to his sleigh, to his team gave a
    whistle,
And away they all flew like the down of a thistle.
But I heard him exclaim, ere he drove out of
    sight,
"HAPPY CHRISTMAS TO ALL,
AND TO ALL A GOOD-NIGHT!"

CHROMIUM

In 1797 a French chemist named Louis Vauquelin was examining some strange crystals. The crystals were **crocoite**, a rare mineral that had been discovered in the Ural Mountains of Russia. Vauquelin found that the crocoite contained lead and an unknown substance that changed color when different chemicals were added. A year later Vauquelin was able to break down this mysterious, color-changing substance and obtain a pure metal. He named this newly discovered metal chromium, from the Greek word *chroma* ("color"). At about the same time, the German chemist Martin Klaproth discovered chromium independently.

▶ PROPERTY AND USES

Chromium is a hard, brittle metal that is highly resistant to corrosion. It is silvery-white and when polished takes on a shiny luster. It is a poor conductor of electricity and heat.

Although chromium is probably best known as the shiny plating on automobile bumpers and other metal objects, its most important use is in steel alloys. Adding a small amount of chromium makes steel stronger, harder, and more resistant to corrosion. Chromium is a vital part of stainless steel. Stainless steel has hundreds of uses where resistance to corrosion is important. Knives, forks, and spoons; pots and pans; kitchen sinks and counter tops; engine valves and turbine blades; tools; dairy equipment; and surgical instruments are a few examples.

Other types of chromium steels are used where resistance to wear is important, as in ball bearings, railroad car wheels, and dies for stamping metal parts.

Stellite—an alloy composed of chromium, cobalt, tungsten, vanadium, and carbon—is extremely hard and heat-resistant. It is used for metal-working tools and oil-well drilling bits because it keeps a sharp edge even when it is red-hot.

Another chromium alloy, Nichrome, is used for the heating coils of electric stoves, toasters, water heaters, and room heaters. Nichrome is made of chromium and nickel.

Chromium metal is used to produce a shiny protective coating on metal objects. This coating is applied by a process called electroplating. Chromium plating was first used to decorate and protect watches, jewelry, and household appliances. Automobile makers began to use chromium plating on automobile bumpers and trim about 1925. The automobile industry is now the largest user of chromium plating.

Machine parts that must stand a great deal of wear and rubbing together, such as gears and bearing surfaces, are often chromium-plated. Such chromium-plated moving parts can actually be run without oil or grease.

Chromium's usefulness does not end here. Chromium salts are used to tan leather and in dyes for cloth. Many brightly colored chromium compounds are used in paints. A chromium-containing mineral called chromite goes into heat-resistant linings for furnaces used in making steel, glass, and cement.

▶ OCCURRENCE

Chromium is never found as a metal in nature. It occurs in a number of minerals, most of which are brightly colored. However, the metal is extracted from only one. This is the heavy black mineral called chromite. The Republic of South Africa, the Soviet Union, the Philippines, Rhodesia, and Malawi are the world's largest producers of chromite ore. Nations with smaller deposits include Cuba, India, Yugoslavia, and the United States.

Reviewed by Taylor Lyman
American Society for Metals

See also Alloys; Iron and Steel; Metals and Metallurgy.

CHROMOSOMES. See Genetics.

FACTS ABOUT CHROMIUM

CHEMICAL SYMBOL: Cr

ATOMIC WEIGHT: 51.996

SPECIFIC GRAVITY: 6.92 (almost seven times as heavy as water).

COLOR: silvery-white, with a bluish tinge.

PROPERTIES: hard and brittle, difficult to shape; poor conductor of electricity and heat (about $\frac{1}{7}$ as good as copper); forms brightly colored compounds; resists attack by oxygen, salt water, and many acids.

OCCURRENCE: never found in nature as a pure metal; occurs combined with other elements to form minerals.

CHIEF ORE: chromite (a combination of iron oxide, chromic oxide, and various impurities).

CHURCHILL, SIR WINSTON (1874–1965)

A biography of Sir Winston Churchill is almost a history of 20th-century England. Churchill was involved in every important event of his country from the Boer War to World War II. He served six British monarchs, from Queen Victoria to Elizabeth II. Statesman, soldier, author, journalist, and twice prime minister, Churchill's career has no parallel in modern history.

Winston Leonard Spencer Churchill was born at Blenheim Palace in Oxfordshire, England, on November 30, 1874. His father, Lord Randolph Churchill, was a brilliant Conservative politician. His American mother was the beautiful Jennie Jerome. One of his ancestors was John Churchill, Duke of Marlborough, a great military hero.

But Winston Churchill himself showed no early signs of greatness. He was a stubborn, red-haired boy and a poor student. He spent 4 years at Harrow, one of England's finest schools, at the very bottom of his class. However, he was fascinated by military subjects and did much better at Sandhurst, the Royal Military Academy. Young Churchill graduated eighth in his class and in 1895 joined the British Army. He served in Cuba, India, and the Sudan.

While in India Churchill took part in a military expedition against the fierce Pathans. Out of this experience came his first book, *The Story of the Malakand Field Force.* In 1899 he gave up his military career to enter politics, but was defeated for a seat in Parliament. He then left for South Africa to cover the Boer War as a newspaper reporter.

Although he was not there as a soldier, Churchill insisted on taking part in the fighting and was captured by the Boers. A month later he made a daring escape, crossing hundreds of miles of enemy territory to reach the British lines. When he returned to England, he was a hero. He ran again for Parliament as a Conservative and won.

▶HIS EARLY POLITICAL CAREER

Churchill disagreed with the Conservatives in 1904 and joined the Liberal Party. In 1905 he was appointed to his first political office, undersecretary for the colonies. He received his first Cabinet post, president of

the Board of Trade, in 1908. That same year he married Clementine Hozier.

In 1911 Churchill became first lord of the Admiralty. Foreseeing the possibility of German aggression, he immediately began a program to increase England's naval strength. Thus the Royal Navy was better prepared than any other military branch when World War I broke out in 1914.

Churchill faced his greatest political disaster in 1915. With typical daring he had launched a campaign against the Turkish peninsula of Gallipoli. His idea was to force the Dardanelles, thus opening a supply line to Russia. But the plan was badly carried out. Many British soldiers were killed, and Churchill was forced to resign. He rejoined the Army and left for the fighting in France.

In 1916 Churchill returned to Parliament. The following year he was appointed minister of munitions. He rejoined the Conservative Party in 1924 and was appointed chancellor of the exchequer, a post his father once held. But money matters bored him. He served for 5 years, but was not a success.

Churchill spent the next 10 years in what he described as the "wilderness." Although still a member of Parliament, he held no important office and disagreed with his own party. During the middle 1930's Prime Minister Neville Chamberlain gave in to Nazi Germany's aggressive demands in order to avoid war. Churchill opposed this policy of appeasement. He spoke out vigorously against Hitler. But not until 1939, when Germany invaded Poland, were Englishmen ready to listen to him. When World War II began, Churchill again became first lord of the Admiralty. Chamberlain was forced to resign in 1940, and Winston Churchill became prime minister. Six weeks later France fell, and England faced Germany alone.

▶A GREAT WARTIME LEADER

Churchill was an inspiring orator, and his confidence rallied the British people during the difficult early days of the war. We will never surrender, and we will win, he told them. Every day the people saw him, grim as a bulldog, a big cigar clamped firmly between his teeth, and his hand raised in the famous V for victory sign. Nothing seemed to disturb him, not even the bombs falling in the London streets.

But no sooner was the war in Europe over than the British people felt it was time for a change. On July 26, 1945, the Labour Party won the elections, and Clement Atlee replaced Churchill as prime minister.

▶THE LATER YEARS

Churchill's fighting spirit continued even out of office. He denounced the Soviet Union's policies and coined the term "Iron Curtain." He urged the unification of Europe. He also spoke warmly of an English-speaking union joining Great Britain and the United States. During these years out of office, Churchill wrote his memoirs, published under the title *The Second World War*.

In 1951 at the age of 77, Churchill again became prime minister. He finally accepted knighthood, the Order of the Garter—one of England's highest honors—in 1953. That same year he received the Nobel prize for literature. In 1963 Churchill was made an honorary citizen of the United States. He died on January 24, 1965, at the age of 90.

Reviewed by J. M. S. CARELESS
University of Toronto

CICERO, MARCUS TULLIUS (106–43 B.C.)

Marcus Tullius Cicero was the greatest orator Rome produced. Born at Arpinum in 106 B.C., he spent his boyhood in Arpinum and Rome, where he studied law, philosophy, and public speaking. When he was 25, Cicero began practicing law at Rome and soon made a name for himself. Then poor health forced him to put aside his legal practice for 2 years. He made good use of his misfortune by going to Greece for further study.

When Cicero returned to Rome, he married and resumed his career. In 70 B.C. he won great public acclaim by successfully prosecuting a government official named Verres for his dishonest rule over the island of Sicily. Cicero's popularity grew, and in the year 63 B.C. he reached the pinnacle of his career by winning an election for the consulship—the Roman Republic's highest office.

Cicero's chief opponent in the election was Catiline, a revolutionary with a large following among the Roman mob. Catiline denounced the election as unfair. He gathered some other dangerous men and made secret plans for murdering Cicero and seizing power by force.

Cicero, however, discovered the plot just in time. In the senate, before all the leading men of Rome, he denounced Catiline in a stinging, powerful speech. Catiline, who was present, fled to his army in nearby Etruria. He died in battle a few months later, early in 62 B.C.

In the next years Julius Caesar rose to supreme power in Rome. Cicero opposed this development, seeing in Caesar an ambitious politician bent on destroying the republican system of government that Cicero loved. Consequently Cicero applauded Caesar's assassination (44 B.C.), though he himself took no part in the plot.

Then Mark Antony, Caesar's chief lieutenant, gained power. In a series of brilliantly scathing speeches Cicero opposed Antony's plans for dictatorship, but he was at last killed by Antony's soldiers in 43 B.C.

Cicero was a great master of Latin prose. Of his work over 50 speeches, nearly 800 letters, and many essays have survived.

Reviewed by GILBERT HIGHET
Formerly, Columbia University

CIPHERS. See CODES AND CIPHERS.

When the circus comes to town, the elephants are always one of the greatest attractions.

CIRCUS

"The circus is coming to town!" This news long has heralded one of the most exciting events of childhood. Each year the people of almost every city and large town could look forward to at least one big-top show. Many circuses traveled the length and breadth of the land during the months of warm weather. Some were small one-ring shows. Today large shows, such as the famous Ringling Bros. and Barnum and Bailey Circus, visit many major U.S. cities each year, offering a breathtaking performance in each of their rings at the same time.

The circus has changed in looks and form over the years. But its appeal is ageless and never changing. People like to see amusing acts that will make them laugh, and they like to see colorful exhibitions that require skill and daring. The circus is entertainment in its purest form.

Every age has contributed to the circus we know today. Pottery and wall drawings found in ancient ruins show acrobats and jugglers. The word "circus" comes from a Roman

THE GREAT FOREPAUGH & SELLS BROTHERS SHOWS COMBINED

ALL EARTH'S AERIAL CHAMPIONS: THE WORLD FAMED HANLON TROUPE INTREPID GYMNASTS EXTRAORDINARY IN THE MOST ASTONISHING MID-AIR ACHIEVEMENTS EVER ACCOMPLISHED.

This poster from the early 1900's beckoned crowds to the excitement of the circus.

arena, the Circus Maximus. In Latin, *circus* means circle or ring. In the Circus Maximus there were feats of skill and daring, such as exciting chariot races. Two forerunners of the modern circus clown were Arlecchino (Harlequin) and Pulcinella (Pierrot) of the 16th-century Italian *commedia dell' arte*. The trained bear, the town juggler, the court jester of medieval times all have their counterparts in the circus today.

The circus as we know it dates from the late 18th century. In 1770, Philip Astley opened a riding school in England. In the morning he taught horsemanship. In the afternoon he put on a show that included skillful riding, acrobatics, wire walking, and acts by trained dogs.

In 1792, John Ricketts established the first circus in the United States. George Washington was one of the many people who attended Ricketts' circus in Philadelphia. There are earlier reports of circus acts in North America, but this was the first circus in which an entire and varied performance was given.

▶ **WINTER QUARTERS**

Every circus in the world has its winter quarters. This is its home base, where it takes a much-needed rest after the travel season. There are storage barns and practice buildings. An outdoor arena is scaled to the size of the big top (tent) or arenas where the show will play during the season. Many circus people have homes there.

In winter quarters all the equipment is repaired and repainted. New acts are put together, new tricks are learned, and new costumes are made. Talent scouts tour the world, looking for new attractions. The search goes on all year. The owners select the performers and help the producer put the show together. They decide where each act will be in the program.

There is a basic similarity among all shows. For example, there is always a big parade, called a spec (for spectacle). This may come at the beginning of the show or anywhere the management decides it fits best. The spec is mainly seen in North America, where it is

A bear rides a bike around the ring.

One of the favorite circus acts is performed by the tiger who leaps from stand to stand through a flaming hoop held by his trainer.

Aerial acts are a breathtaking part of the circus. Balancing is developed to a fine art in acts like the one shown above.

Clown Paul Wenzel holds his oversized watch during a performance of Ringling Bros. and Barnum & Bailey Circus.

more highly developed as part of the show than it is in Europe. It centers around a theme, such as Mother Goose or the Arabian Nights. All the performers take part. Colorful floats reflect the theme, as do the costumes of the performers. If it is an Arabian Nights theme, for instance, you may see Aladdin and his magic lamp or Ali Baba and the forty thieves. Even Sinbad the Sailor may appear.

The performance may be planned to last for an hour or two—or even longer. The Ringling Bros. and Barnum & Bailey performance is three hours long. There are clowns, wild-animal acts, trapeze performers, tightwire artists, and a host of other performers and acts. There may be an aerial ballet, with dancers performing on ropes and ladders, and a trained-elephant or horse number. In the finale all the performers and animals pass in review before the audience.

Some of the shows are kept very simple. Others, such as Ringling Bros. and Barnum & Bailey or the Circus Krone in Germany, build up full productions with special music and dancing.

The bandleader knows the acts in every show. The background music is arranged according to the tempo of each act. For example, the bareback-riding act requires a tempo different from that for the aerialists, elephants, or jugglers. The bandleader combines popular and classical music, old-time circus music, and music for parades.

▶ THE NEW SHOW ON THE ROAD

The show spends a month or several months in winter quarters. A new program is arranged and production numbers are set. The music is orchestrated, dances are choreographed, the wardrobe is designed and sewn, and the equipment is repaired and repainted. Routes are set, and permits obtained. Then the circus leaves its winter home for the first engagement.

Every circus has a crew skilled in loading and unloading equipment. The general manager supervises all the physical equipment and those who care for it. A number of people working in other departments—animal handlers, truck drivers, mechanics, cookhouse workers—are also needed to help move the circus.

Press agents travel ahead of the show to advertise and publicize it as it approaches each town. Other agents go ahead of the show to buy food for the animals and the circus people. If the circus is playing in a tent, they mark off the lot and set up flares to guide the truck drivers as they come into town. Movements from place to place are usually made late at night so that as little time as possible is lost during the day.

Many circuses today, as in earlier times, play outdoors—that is, in tents on open lots. Some in North America and Europe play to audiences in indoor areas. Among these are the famous Cirque d'Hiver (Winter Circus) in Paris and the Moscow Circus. Even when it traveled with its big canvas top, Ringling Bros. and Barnum & Bailey appeared for many years in New York's Madison Square Garden and in other big indoor arenas. Since 1956 this circus has used only permanent buildings. Shows that play arenas can tour during any time of year, regardless of the weather. But in a building a circus may be cramped. There is not so much space backstage—or "backyard," in circus language—as there is outdoors. Floats have to be lined up in corridors. Animals are quartered in the best way that can be arranged. With the large number of performers, dressing rooms and wardrobes are usually crowded.

Let us assume that we are looking on as preparations are made for an outdoor show. There may be as many as ten tops, as all tents are called. With them are the canvas side walls, the stakes, and the tools needed to raise and repair the tops.

The central feature is the big top, or main tent, where the big show is given. It may have one or three rings and seats for 3,000 to 5,000 spectators.

The life of the circus revolves around the big top. This tent divides the grounds into two sections. One is the front yard, where the midway and tents for the sideshow and menagerie are placed and where the audience comes in. The other is the backyard. In it are the dressing and wardrobe tops, the cookhouse (dining tent) and kitchen, and the ringstock (for horses) and elephant tops. There are also the cages of performing lions and tigers. Wagons are used as offices. The circus lot is sometimes very dusty or muddy. When wagons and trucks become stuck in the mud, elephants are brought out to the spot to push or pull the vehicle.

The size of the tent determines the number of center poles. Around each pole is a heavy bale ring. The canvas is unfolded, spread out on the ground, laced together, and attached to these rings. Then elephants slowly raise the tent. The boss of the canvas crew watches very closely.

Inside, quarter poles are set against the canvas and secured. Poles are also set in place to hold the edge of the canvas. Workers begin guying out (tightening) the whole tent with heavy ropes. Once the tent is up, the riggers and property crew hang the trapezes, ropes, and wires.

Ringling Bros. and Barnum & Bailey has a rigging system specially designed for indoor arenas. Over each ring there is a square frame hung by pulleys and ropes from the top of the arena. The workers can hang all the aerial equipment on the frame at ground level and then pull the frame up. This saves time.

While the riggers are putting up the trapezes, other workers wire the spotlights and set the curbs that form the rings where all of the acts take place. Each is almost 13 meters (42 feet) in diameter.

In tent shows, workers assigned to the elephants and other animals set up their tops, and by midmorning the animals have been fed. Sideshow and menagerie tops are set up. Wardrobe tops are also put up and are quickly filled with costumes.

Every piece of equipment must be made of materials that will last in spite of constant wear and tear. The costumes, sparkling with sequins and spangles, are made of heavy fabrics, designed to take constant wear and cleaning. Trappings for the elephants and horses are often made of heavy leather, sometimes with solid brass fittings. Trapezes are made of rope with chrome crossbars. Wires are of heavy cable wrapped securely with friction tape. Most frames and riggings are of steel. Such equipment is very expensive.

▶ ANIMAL AND AERIAL ACTS

Along with clowns, animals are the basis of a circus. Trained-animal acts are popular among circusgoers. People have always been amazed by a trainer's ability to make an animal perform on command.

A hushed audience watches as these tigers respond to their trainer's commands.

Carrot-topped Popov, a leading performer with the Moscow Circus, is an acrobat, mime, musician, and clown.

A daring performer juggles high in midair—hanging by her hair.

Most animals are trained with patience and discipline. Dogs are particularly responsive to love and training and make good performers. Dog and pony acts are a major part of the circus. There are liberty horses (those that work without a lead rein and take direction from the trainer), rosinbacks (so called because their backs are rubbed with rosin to help keep standing bareback riders from slipping), and saddle horses for fancy and trick riding.

The menagerie has always been popular because people like to look at wild animals. In many towns the menagerie animals may be the first of their kind that most people have seen. Some circusgoers enjoy wild-animal acts because of the element of danger that is present. A wild animal is trained but never tamed.

One of the most famous animals in circus history was the elephant Jumbo. He was bought from a London zoo in 1882 by P.T. Barnum. Standing 350 centimeters (11 feet 6 inches) at the shoulder and weighing about 6 metric tons, Jumbo was billed by Barnum as the biggest of all elephants.

Another famous circus animal was Gargantua, a gorilla. He was the monarch of the Ringling Bros. and Barnum & Bailey menagerie for eleven years. Throngs of people came to stare at him in his air-conditioned cage. Gargantua stood 170 centimeters (5 feet 7 inches) tall and weighed about 250 kilograms (550 pounds). He had the remarkable strength of 20 men.

The most popular acts, apart from those with trained animals, are the aerial and cannon acts. Timing is the all-important element in these most difficult stunts. Aerial acts include the cloud swing (with ropes and ladders), the trapeze, and high-wire walking. With its special tricks of cycling and human pyramiding, wire walking is a very difficult art to master.

All these acts are dangerous. An untrained person who tried to perform them would be risking serious injury or death. The first step in becoming either a trapeze flyer or a human cannonball is learning how to fall into the net correctly. This takes many days of practice. Circus people must stay in excellent physical condition to avoid injuries. They must always be alert and must concentrate on what they are doing. But their work is second nature to them and, from their point of view, is no more dangerous than any other job. Wire walkers feel the wire under them in the same way that a typist feels the keys of the typewriter.

▶ PEOPLE OF THE CIRCUS

The people of a circus work and live together, and they are a closely knit group. Most of them come from old circus families. Children from these families often follow in their parents' footsteps and may excel in an act before they graduate from high school. Many performers marry within the circus or into other circus families.

The members of a family group can do all kinds of acts, not only those they happen to be doing in one show. For instance, the Nerveless Nocks, who can trace their family back several hundred years in circus history, specialize in tricks at the top of sway poles. But they can also swing from a trapeze, walk a wire, juggle, and ride unicycles.

With any circus, no matter how big or small, people work hard and do many jobs. In some shows the performers not only work in the acts but also sew costumes, help set up seats, and take care of animals. Life on the road can be very difficult. But circus people have a great zest for living, and there is a bond of friendship among them that is hard to find anywhere else.

C. P. Fox
Ringling Bros. and Barnum & Bailey

See also CARNIVALS.

The Ginza, a shopping district in Tokyo, one of the world's most modern cities.

CITIES

Cities are the largest communities where people live and work. Whenever people are living together in one place, they form a community. Communities can generally be divided into three classes—farming villages; small towns, including the suburbs of large cities; and cities.

Have you ever wondered why great numbers of people choose to live in cities? Today about half of the people of North America, somewhat more than one third of the people of South America and Europe, and one tenth of the people of Africa and Asia live in cities of at least 100,000 people. People live in cities because they find something there that they want or need.

Throughout history, cities have been centers of activity and development. Some—like ancient Jerusalem and modern Salt Lake City —have been centers for religion. People gathered there originally to build a temple or shrine. Other cities have been centers of government, as Rome and Athens were in ancient times and London, Paris, Peking, and Moscow are today. Others are cultural, financial, and manufacturing centers—such as Rio de Janeiro, Chicago, and Toronto. Many cities have grown up around universities. Cities contain the world's greatest museums and libraries. It is not simply its size that makes a city important. It is what the city offers the people who live there.

It may seem that people who want to be at the center of cultural, intellectual, or political life would naturally live in cities. One might also imagine that those who dislike crowds and prefer open spaces and outdoor activities would choose to live in suburbs or in farming villages. But people do not always live where they want to live. Often they must live in places where they can find work. And often, work is found in cities. People select the community in which they live largely because it meets their needs.

▶HOW CITIES DIFFER FROM OTHER COMMUNITIES

One of the most important differences between the three kinds of communities is their crowdedness, or population density. Farming communities are the least crowded; cities, the most crowded. We can find the population density of a community by dividing the total number of residents by the area.

How crowded a city is helps determine its individual character. For example, New York

Above: An apartment building in a densely populated area of New York City. Below: Row houses in London. A less crowded city than New York, London has many one-family homes.

City and London have about the same population. But London occupies more land area than New York. New York has about 9,700 people to each square kilometer (25,000 people to each square mile). London, on the other hand, has only about half that many people to each square kilometer. For this reason, the typical Londoner can live in a small one-family house, while the typical New Yorker lives in an apartment.

Density can vary greatly. One of the most crowded cities in the world is Calcutta, a port city on the east coast of India. Calcutta has about three times as many people to each square kilometer as New York City. One of the least crowded cities is Flagstaff, Arizona. It has about 170 people to each square kilometer (440 people per square mile).

The crowdedness of cities is both good and bad. When a city is overcrowded, there is not enough room for parks and play areas. Streets are congested, with dangerous intersections. Apartments are small, crowded, and dark, especially for families with little money. But if people are widely scattered, the result is isolation—without shops, schools, hospitals, and cultural institutions nearby.

Density alone does not define a city. Another important characteristic is diversity. This term describes the variety that is part of city life. People of many different races and nationalities mingle in cities. Diversity cannot be measured mathematically, as density can. Hospitals, theaters, clubs, shops, hotels, railroad stations, schools, and government buildings are located in cities. And cities attract people with all the skills necessary to operate these institutions.

The diversity of peoples is especially noticeable in port cities such as San Francisco, Hong Kong, and the French port of Marseilles. The different groups often start neighborhoods in cities that reflect and continue their national traditions. Chinese, Italian, Hispanic (Spanish-speaking), and other communities can be found in cities around the world. London is dotted with Pakistani and Cypriot neighborhoods. Paris has many Algerians and people from other parts of Africa.

Neighborhoods in cities offer their residents certain advantages. These include a feeling of stability and safety, a sense of belonging to a group, and the experience of

An art museum.

Cities offer a wide variety of cultural, educational, and recreational activities. Above: Students visiting an art museum get an introduction to sculpture. Right: People crowd the streets of New York City's Chinatown for the Chinese New Year celebration. Below: Children and adults enjoy a pleasant day in the reconstructed Benjamin Franklin Court in Philadelphia.

New York City's Chinatown.

Benjamin Franklin Court in Philadelphia.

neighborliness that is said to be characteristic of small towns. But neighborhoods in cities can also have disadvantages. Sometimes they discourage new residents, who differ from the people already there in race, religion, or national origin. And they may prevent immigrants from mixing with the society of their new country.

▶ THE HISTORY OF CITIES

The development of cities has been influenced by many factors. These include social or political organization, economic conditions, advancements in technology, and the general history of the areas in which the cities are located.

Development of Cities

People could not live in cities—or help to build cities—until the surrounding area produced enough food to make city life possible. People in cities produced neither grain nor meat. They made goods such as cloth and pottery and offered services such as protection from enemy invaders. The people who lived outside the city were willing to trade some of the food they produced for these goods and services.

After people had learned to plant and harvest crops, permanent settlements began in areas where surplus food was produced. Often these settlements grew up in locations that could be easily defended. And they were usually near a source of water that could be used for transportation as well as drinking. Cities grew up where trade routes crossed and around shrines erected to gods.

Cities of the Ancient World

Archeologists have discovered traces of cities in Mesopotamia that existed as early as 5000 B.C. Other early cities were founded in Egypt and China.

Mesopotamia. Mesopotamia was the land between the Tigris and Euphrates rivers, in southwestern Asia. Some of the earliest cities—Ur, Babylon, and Nineveh—grew up there. The fertile land around these cities pro-

Athens, Greece, as it may have appeared in ancient times.

vided a good supply of food for city dwellers. After 3500 B.C., the cities of Mesopotamia became centers of trade, politics, religion, military command, and government administration. The people built houses and city walls, developed written alphabets, and founded legal systems. Often the cities became centers of science, learning, and the arts.

The years from 2000 to 1000 B.C. were marked by wars in Mesopotamia and elsewhere in the Middle East. Many of the cities fell under the rule of the Hittite, Mycenaean, or Egyptian empires. But at the end of this period, new city-states developed in the Middle East and especially in Greece.

Greek City-States. A city-state is a self-governing unit that includes the city proper and the surrounding countryside. After 1000 B.C., a number of such states developed in Greece. In these city-states, the idea of government based on a specific constitutional and legal framework took hold. Various forms of government developed. The first rulers were kings, followed later by the richest and most powerful citizens. In Athens, the most renowned of the city-states, democracy ruled for two centuries. Athens also became famous as a center of learning and art.

The Greek city-states were rivals in trade, and from time to time they fought one another. In the 4th century B.C., most of them were conquered by Macedonia, to the north. Later they were ruled by Rome.

Rome. The greatest ancient city was Rome. Advances in technology—such as good roads and aqueducts to carry water—eventually enabled the city to spread well beyond the original settlement by the Tiber River. During the reign of the emperor Augustus (27 B.C. to A.D. 14), Rome's population reached 800,000.

Roman armies conquered a vast empire, bringing political stability and a system of justice. In return, Rome took the treasures of the countries it ruled. These treasures included furs and leathers, metals, precious jewels, and art. They could be used to buy the food that Rome's large population needed.

The Roman Empire needed fortified cities other than Rome, located in strategic sites in all the countries occupied by Roman armies. Some of these cities, such as Jerusalem and Ephesus, were already famous in the ancient world. Others were founded by the Romans and have remained important in the modern world. These include Massilia (Marseilles, the great French port on the Mediterranean Sea) and a small settlement on the Seine River in northern France called Lutetia, which we now know as Paris. London, too, first became important under Roman rule.

In the 3rd century, the empire was divided. Rome ruled the western part. The eastern part was ruled from the city of Byzantium (later Constantinople) for more than 1,000 years.

Centuries Without Cities

By 500 A.D., Rome was occupied by invading Germanic tribes. They could not and did not try to keep up the elaborate military and political structure that Rome had created.

In Europe, the period known in western history as the Dark Ages followed. People who lived in later years called the period from about 500 to 1000 A.D. "dark" because so few examples of human accomplishment, such as literature and works of art and architecture, were left behind.

These years could also be described as the "centuries without cities" in the Western world. With the collapse of Roman organization and the Roman system of justice, cities faded out—perhaps not completely, but in great part. Invaders destroyed many of them. People had to find food for themselves. A few fortresses remained, as did a few monasteries and other religious communities.

In the 10th century, with the rebirth of trade, settlements of traders began to rise near fortresses and monasteries. Life began to flicker again on the sites of ancient cities. Within a few hundred years, the medieval cities of Europe had grown up. They were different from those of the ancient world, although technically they had not made much progress.

But during this same period, Asian cities in Japan and China had been flourishing. When Marco Polo traveled from Venice to China around 1275, he saw cities far greater than any in Europe. He described Asian cities of paved streets and magnificent buildings. European cities of that period had mud or cobblestone streets, and no buildings except cathedrals could be called beautiful.

This painting from the 15th century shows peasants working in the fields outside the walls of a town.

The Middle Ages

As in the ancient cities of Mesopotamia, the outstanding characteristic of the medieval city was its walls. The walls surrounded the city and provided protection from invaders. But they kept even small populations living in crowded conditions. A few cities in Europe still have walls standing very much as they did in the late Middle Ages. Carcassonne, in France, is a well-known example of a medieval walled city that has changed little over the centuries.

Usually the cathedral was the largest building in the medieval city. In front of the cathedral there was often a large marketplace. There trade was conducted, and religious fairs and celebrations were held. City streets were extremely narrow.

The walls, the cathedral, the marketplace—representing military power, religious faith, and commerce—gave the residents of the medieval city a sense of unity. They wor-shiped in a single church. They owed their political allegiance to one ruler. And they bought and sold what they needed in a single place. These qualities of city life helped the residents to feel secure in the face of dangers like famine, war, and disease.

Life was difficult in the medieval city. The water supply came from wells, easily contaminated with germs and filth. The streets of the city were its sewer and garbage disposal system. Unsanitary conditions spread disease, and plagues killed many people.

The growth of trade turned some medieval cities into specialized workshops. From the 11th to the 15th centuries, guilds (associations of people who do the same kind of work, such as weavers or merchants) were formed. Guilds for teachers and students aided in the formation of the university system. Some highly specialized medieval cities—such as Bruges, Belgium, a center of woolen manufacture—have survived to modern times almost unchanged in their basic design.

In the 1300's, trade began to thrive. More land was farmed, manufacturing increased, and trade based on money rather than barter became the rule. New towns were founded at strategic rivers, harbors, and crossroads. London and Paris became important cities. But in many respects—water supply and roads, for example—the medieval cities were not as advanced as those built by the Romans more than a thousand years earlier.

In the 15th century, the use of gunpowder made feudal walls and castles less effective as defenses. And the printing press revolutionized communications and stimulated the growth of universities. The universities, in turn, attracted more people to cities. Gradually cities began to spread outside their high walls.

Most cities suffered during the 14th and 15th centuries from wars among European nations. Financing these wars placed a heavy strain on the cities. Merchants came to resent this. Over a period of years they helped to form a strong middle class that demanded and obtained important changes in trade regulations and political processes.

In addition, new social patterns were evolving. For example, in Germany, members of the rising class of merchants were devising modern city governments of councillors

The important seaport of Lisbon, Portugal, during the 16th century.

and mayors. As they became more powerful, the merchants wanted to govern themselves. They were able to purchase the independence of the towns from their rulers. This trend toward self-government encouraged the growth of individual freedom.

Later, merchants played a key role in the cities of eastern Asia. For example, in Japan, merchants rose from the bottom of the social scale in the 17th century to dominate the economy and the arts in the 19th century.

The Renaissance

The Renaissance in Europe, which began in the 14th century and extended into the 17th century, was a time of vigorous trade. This trade stimulated the growth of cities and of city-states. In Italy, important cities included Venice, which was the main port of the Renaissance, and Milan, which was located where important trade routes crossed. Powerful city-states also developed in Germany. Hamburg and Cologne are two such cities that remain important today. To protect their interests, the German city-states formed an association called the Hanseatic League.

Renaissance interest in the past—especially in classical Greece and Rome—brought new ideas about cities. Ideal cities were designed, with vast open spaces and spacious streets radiating from a central square. Many of these designs remained only plans. But the Renaissance was a time of great building in cities, especially in those such as Paris that were centers of royal power.

During this period, city life was flourishing in the Western Hemisphere. In 1519, the Spanish explorer Hernando Cortes was dazzled by the cities of the Aztecs in Mexico. The city of Tenochtitlán (now Mexico City) was built over a lake. It was joined to the land by long causeways that were perhaps beyond European engineering skills.

The Industrial Age

If you happened to live in the United States in 1789, when George Washington became its first president, you would probably have been living in a farming village, as did most people in the 18th century. If you had been alive when Franklin D. Roosevelt became president in 1933—144 years later—you very

A 19th-century lithograph of Pella, Iowa. Such factory towns developed during the Industrial Revolution.

likely would have been living in a city. In the early 1930's, more people of the United States lived in cities than in suburbs or on farms. Today the suburbs are more likely to be your home. More people live in the suburbs than in the cities, and many more than in farming villages.

The Industrial Revolution in the late 18th and early 19th centuries drastically changed cities. Factories developed with the invention of machines to do work that previously had been done by hand. They became the centers of industrial cities. People left rural areas to seek work in the cities.

The Industrial Revolution marked the beginning of immense growth in population, especially in cities of the English-speaking world such as London, Birmingham, Manchester, Glasgow, and New York. It has been estimated that in 1800 under 3 percent of the world's population lived in cities of 20,000 people or more. Today about 25 percent of the world's population lives in areas of 20,000 people or more.

Improvements in transportation speeded industrial development and the growth of urban areas. Improvements in oceangoing carriers encouraged migration to cities. These ships also brought raw materials to be used in the factories and took factory products to be sold all over the world.

Industrial cities expanded in all directions.

Expansion carried some built-in problems, especially in the areas of housing and traffic congestion. In the early 1800's, cities concentrated on building factories, railroads, and bridges. Often there was not enough labor or materials for housing construction. Cheaply constructed, ugly tenements or row houses were built. There were problems of water, sanitation, and congestion. City death rates were far higher than those of rural areas.

By the middle of the 1800's, a social reform movement was working to ease these problems. Frederick Olmstead (1822–1903) designed parks such as New York City's Central Park, which brought sunlight, fresh air, and green space into the center of overcrowded cities. Jacob Riis (1849–1914), a Danish immigrant to New York, wrote about New York's slums, stimulating housing reform. Ebenezer Howard (1850–1928) started a movement in England to build "garden cities" outside the big cities. Inspired by his idea, the British Government financed "new towns" in England, Scotland, and Wales.

Few people did more to help the cities than the engineers, designers, and politicians who developed and fought for sewage systems, water supply systems, and transportation systems. These systems relieved some of the problems of urban life. The advent of cheap electric power, rapid transit, new building materials, and rising incomes also helped.

▶ MODERN CITIES

Today every continent is dotted with giant cities. Some are growing larger, others are in a state of decline, and some are being rebuilt. Each city has its own individual characteristics, but there are some problems that are shared by cities all over the globe.

Sometimes geography influences the character of a city, as well as the problems it faces. Two examples are New York, which is built largely on islands, and Rio de Janeiro, which is hemmed in by mountains and the sea. These cities have limited land area. They have expanded upward, with skyscrapers. Los Angeles, California, has had room to spread out. But its location between the Pacific Ocean and the Santa Monica Mountains has given it other problems—the mountains frequently trap polluted air over the city, and the area is subject to earthquakes.

History has also played a part in shaping modern cities. Cities such as Rome can tell their own histories through many ancient buildings that remain. But other cities have been almost totally destroyed and then rebuilt. An example is Tokyo, which was struck by a severe earthquake in 1923 and was bombed during World War II. Today it is one of the most modern of the world's large cities. Many European cities also suffered damage from bombing during World War II.

Some cities face unusual problems—Mexico City, for example, has difficulty providing water to its growing population. But there are certain problems that are shared by most modern cities.

With little room to expand outward, Rio de Janeiro, in Brazil, has grown upward—with skyscrapers.

Problems Shared by Cities

In general, modern cities are suffering from the effects of too much industrialization and too rapid urbanization. Often buildings that were built hastily in response to urgent need are now decaying. Crime and drug addiction continue to be serious problems for city residents. Poverty and crowded conditions contribute to these problems.

The diversity of city populations has sometimes brought racial conflict. Since World

Children play among conditions of poverty, overcrowding, and poor housing in New York City's Harlem.

Traffic jams are a problem in all large cities. Below, a street leading to St. Peter's Basilica in Rome.

War II, cities in North America and Europe have received large numbers of people from tropical and subtropical rural areas. Most of these migrants have had little chance in their original homes to learn the ways of an industrial urban society. It is difficult for present-day cities to provide employment and services for many of these people.

Traffic and Pollution. The automobile has been a mixed blessing for the city. It has helped relieve some of the crowdedness of cities because it allows people to live in suburban areas and commute to work. Suburban areas in some cases have grown to such an extent that it is difficult to tell where one metropolitan region ends and another begins.

But the automobile contributes to two of the worst problems a city must face—traffic congestion and pollution. Thousands of cars clog city streets during peak travel hours. In older cities such as Rome the problem is compounded by narrow streets that were never intended for automobiles. But even in modern cities such as Tokyo—which has an excellent transportation system of trains, subways, and monorails—traffic is a problem.

Pollution from automobile exhaust adds to pollution caused by industry. The effects of air pollution on the health of city residents cannot be calculated.

Another serious crisis for many cities is disposal of the waste products of city life. These include garbage and sewage, as well as the many chemicals used in industry. Often the rivers and lakes surrounding large cities are polluted with these wastes.

Housing. Many cities lack adequate housing, particularly for low-income residents. This problem is perhaps most severe in the cities of Africa and Asia that are receiving the greatest influx of people from rural areas. But few cities are without slum areas.

Financial Problems. Many cities must charge their residents high taxes to pay for services such as police and fire protection and waste disposal. In some cases, high taxes have contributed to the cities' decline. The high costs of doing business in a city—in taxes, salaries, and the like—have caused many firms to move to rural or suburban areas. This means that there are fewer jobs in the city. And the residents who remain must bear the full cost of providing services.

New York City, for example, must struggle to repay money it borrowed in the 1960's to build housing for middle-income families. The high taxes needed to repay the borrowed money have discouraged manufacturers and other businesses. The city's large public university system and large municipal hospitals were intended to help serve new residents. Workers in the city's factories and offices were expected to earn enough to carry the tax burden. Instead, manufacturing employment dropped. This meant that many city residents had no opportunity to work and earn money. Thus, in the 1970's a smaller working population struggled to carry the debts, as well as the high cost of supporting those who could not find work.

Urban Decline

New York is only one example of a city that, in a time of growth, made commitments that weakened its ability to adjust to later problems of decline. Industrial cities of Europe such as Birmingham, Liverpool, Glasgow, Turin, Milan, and the German cities on the Ruhr River have had similar problems. In the United States, decline has been most marked in the older cities of the northeastern and north central states.

Some people argue that the decline of cities cannot be prevented. They point to new inventions that threaten cities. Television and the telephone make it possible for people to exchange information without actually meeting. Diesel trucks and public highways now handle more freight than railroads. This means that it is no longer necessary to have factories located near the railroad yards of cities so that goods can be shipped by rail. Increased air travel and transportation reduce the importance of seaports, except for certain types of heavy freight that must travel on cargo vessels. Universities are often located in towns or small cities rather than big cities. The effect of these changes, it is argued, is that new locations—away from the older cities and their many problems—are becoming more attractive.

Hope for Cities

In recent years, some government programs have had dramatic success in bringing the economies of cities back to life. In the United

Lagos, Nigeria

New York
Quebec

States, for example, the Model Cities Program provided large sums of money for job training and improvement of schools. Other programs have concentrated on housing, sewage treatment, caring for the aged, helping members of minority groups, elimination of slums, and the planning of city development. European regional development programs have also had some measure of success in Britain, Scandinavia, Germany, and the Netherlands. The Spanish seaport of Barcelona contains an old section with many medieval buildings and a new section that is a fine example of city planning. And new cities in such widely scattered areas as South America, India, and Israel show the widespread concern of city planners about the future of the city.

Dallas, Texas, is an example of a city that has enjoyed renewed growth. In 1967 a program called Goals for Dallas was started. Its purpose was to reverse the loss of population and retail trade to the city's growing suburbs. With public and private funds, a new airport and several downtown retail projects were built. These projects brought new health to the city's economy.

People who believe that there is a future for cities argue that governments will provide financial aid for several reasons. One reason is that cities can be good savers of energy. Electric power can be distributed economically in cities. People save energy when they use the public transportation of cities instead of private cars. City buses and subways—and elevators, traveling from floor to floor—take the place of highways and cars that are needed outside cities to move people over greater distances to their homes.

People also say that the city must be understood in relation to the economy and culture of the entire country. The city provides a place where contact among people generates ideas. This face-to-face exchange of ideas cannot be replaced by long-distance telephone circuits. It enables the citizens of great cities to move in new directions. It has made city life interesting to novelists, playwrights, and artists throughout history.

▶ THE FUTURE OF CITIES

Each person who thinks about cities leans to one side or the other in the endless argument about their future. Some believe that cities will become more like one another as modern technology leads to rapid exchange of ideas and information. Skyscraper office buildings were built in New York because Manhattan, New York's central borough, is an island of limited area. Skyscrapers soon spread to other cities because they had become a symbol of the up-and-coming commercial city. Now they are found in such places as Sydney, Australia, and Warsaw, Poland.

Yet a contrary movement has been developing. It is based on the desire to retain traces of each city's past. Older, pre-skyscraper buildings differ from city to city. They make people remember their city's traditions. Some people demand that they be protected from demolition and decay. When old buildings are declared landmarks, they cannot be demolished or changed.

Many people believe that the city of the future will be the **megalopolis**. This is a word sometimes used to describe a "super city." It is a combination of two Greek words—*megas,* which means "large," and *polis,* which means "city." The megalopolis is a natural extension of the spread of urban areas, as cities and their surrounding suburbs expand into one another.

The densely populated area between Boston and Washington, D.C., is often called a megalopolis. It includes about 40,000,000 people. Similar areas in North America have developed along the Great Lakes and around Los Angeles and San Francisco, Houston and Dallas, and Miami. Megalopolises in Europe include the area around London and the Midlands, Paris and its surroundings, central Belgium, parts of the Netherlands, and the industrial basin around the Ruhr in northwestern Germany. In Japan, the Tokyo-Osaka area is also considered a megalopolis.

Whatever the city of the future is like, it probably will be different from the city of today. Throughout history, cities have adapted to new ways of life. Because they have done so, such cities as Rome, Paris, London, and Moscow remain living symbols of history. To a great extent, the history of cities is a record of civilization.

ROGER STARR
Editorial Board, New York *Times*

See also URBAN PLANNING; articles on individual cities.

CITIZENSHIP

A citizen is a member of a political community. Citizenship is gained by meeting the legal requirements of a national, state, or local government. A nation grants certain rights and privileges to its citizens. Protection while traveling or living abroad is one of these rights. In return, citizens are expected to be loyal to their country and to perform certain duties for it. The value of citizenship changes from nation to nation. In some nations, for example, citizenship gives people the right to vote in free elections when they reach a certain age. In other nations, where there are no free elections, different privileges are granted to citizens.

In general, living in a nation does not make a person a citizen of that nation. Some people are known as aliens or noncitizen nationals. An **alien** is a citizen of one nation who is living in another nation. Aliens must obey the laws of the country in which they are living. Their rights and duties are set by treaties and by the laws of the countries in which they stay.

In the United States, aliens must obey laws and pay taxes just as citizens do. They are entitled to protection under the law and to use of the courts. They may also own property, carry on business, and attend public schools. But aliens cannot vote or hold government office. In some states they are not allowed to practice certain professions until they become citizens.

A noncitizen national, under United States law, is a person who is neither a citizen nor an alien but who owes permanent loyalty to the United States. People in this category have some but not all of the rights of citizens. For example, inhabitants of a United States territory may not have the right to vote. Noncitizen nationals of the United States include those people on the Pacific islands of American Samoa who were born after the territory was taken over by the United States.

▶ HISTORY OF CITIZENSHIP

The idea of citizenship came into being many centuries ago. In the ancient city-state of Athens, citizenship was granted to males of many classes. Citizenship was also granted to a few foreigners and freed slaves. Citizenship meant that a person could vote, hold office,

serve on committees and juries, and give military service. He was also expected to share the work of government. But only some of the people of Athens could become citizens. A large part of the population was made up of slaves. These people, as well as women and practically all foreigners, were protected under the law but had few of the rights and privileges of Athenian citizens.

Citizenship was also important to the people of ancient Rome. Roman citizens often took part in their government. They even carried the rights of Roman citizenship with them when they settled in conquered lands as colonists. In the days of the empire, Roman citizenship was extended to foreign soldiers serving in the army. It was also extended to men of the conquered lands. By A.D. 212 almost all of the men in the provinces, except slaves, were citizens.

After the fall of the Roman Empire, in the 5th century, the idea of citizenship became less important for many years. The feudal system spread through western Europe in the Middle Ages. This system was based on services and loyalty to a higher person in exchange for his protection. Millions of serfs worked the land for lords. The lords owed their allegiance to overlords. The overlords in turn were controlled by the king. In this system the king and nobles, rather than any government independent of these, gave the people rights and privileges.

By the 17th century some kings had made many small states into nations. The common people no longer owed allegiance to nobles. Their first allegiance, or loyalty, was to the king. They began to take pride in their whole country. They also began to feel that they should have a voice in their country's government. As these changes took place, people started thinking of themselves as citizens of a nation as well as the loyal subjects of their king.

▶ CITIZENSHIP IN MODERN TIMES

In modern times every nation provides ways of becoming a citizen. For most people citizenship is a matter of birth. For others it may be acquired through a process known as naturalization.

Two rules are used to determine citizenship by birth: (1) *jus sanguinis,* law of the blood;

and (2) *jus soli,* law of the soil. Under *jus sanguinis,* children take their parents' nationality regardless of where they are born. For example, a child born to Italian parents in Britain is a citizen of Italy. On the other hand, the rule of *jus soli* says that children are citizens of the nation in which they are born, no matter what the parents' nationality is. Thus a child born to Italian parents in Britain is also a citizen of Britain. Since most nations apply both of these rules, a person can become a citizen of two nations. This is called dual citizenship.

In the case of U.S. citizens, dual citizenship is not recognized by the laws of the United States. The U.S. State Department may make exceptions in special cases.

Dual citizenship can result from naturalization, which is the legal way in which people change their citizenship. Internal law protects naturalized citizens as long as they live in their new country. But they may lose their new citizenship if they return to the country of their birth and remain for a long time. In wartime, a serious problem could arise if both countries demand their services in the armed forces.

Of the countries in the Commonwealth of Nations, Canada was the first to enact naturalization laws separate from those of Britain. The Canadian Citizenship Act of 1947 made the concept of a Canadian citizen distinct from that of a British subject. It was replaced by the Citizenship Act in 1977.

▶CITIZENSHIP UNDER THE U.S. CONSTITUTION

The United States Constitution, drafted in 1787, did not explain citizenship. It did, however, mention "citizens of the States" and "a citizen of the United States." Thus the Constitution does mention double citizenship. The founders of the country believed that any person who was a citizen of a state was also a citizen of the United States.

Since the young United States followed British common law, it accepted the rule of *jus soli,* or place of birth. As early as 1790 Congress recognized the rule of *jus sanguinis,* or blood relationship, by passing laws giving citizenship to a child born in a foreign country if the father was a citizen of the United States. In the same year, Congress passed the first of a series of naturalization laws.

The Fourteenth Amendment to the Constitution (1868) included the first official written explanation of citizenship in the United States. Section 1 of this amendment declares that "All persons born or naturalized in the United States, and subject to the jurisdiction thereof, are citizens of the United States and of the State wherein they reside." This amendment keeps the idea of double citizenship but places national citizenship before state citizenship. In other words, a person is first a citizen of the United States and then a citizen of one of the states. This prevents the states from denying U.S. citizenship to those who desire it. New citizens are entitled to the rights granted by both the national government and their own state governments.

The same amendment also made the rule of *jus soli,* or place of birth, a law for all U.S. citizens. This means that any child born in the United States becomes a citizen at birth. Only a few people are not affected by this law. Children born to foreign diplomats or United Nations officials are citizens of their parents' country. But children of some other representatives of foreign governments become citizens of the United States at birth. The rule of *jus soli* applies to children born in the United States even if their parents are aliens.

The Fourteenth Amendment does not include *jus sanguinis.* American citizenship acquired at birth in a foreign nation is usually determined by the law which is in effect at the time the child is born. The Immigration and Nationality Act of 1952, amended in 1965, 1976, and 1978, gives the requirements.

▶CITIZENSHIP BY NATURALIZATION

The U.S. Constitution gives Congress the power to make naturalization laws for the United States. No state can give citizenship to aliens.

A person can become a naturalized citizen of the United States individually or as part of a group. Generally any person who has come into the United States as an immigrant may become a naturalized citizen. To do so, the person must give up all loyalty to the nation of his or her birth and meet other conditions decided by Congress.

Group naturalization can be granted by the president's treaty-making power or through an act of Congress. It has usually been granted when the United States gains a new territory. For example, all the people of the present states of Louisiana, Florida, Texas, Hawaii, and Alaska were naturalized when these territories became part of the United States.

Some of the requirements for Canadian citizenship are legal admission to Canada, three years' residence, knowledge of the Canadian political system, and knowledge of one of the country's two official languages. Other requirements are given in the Citizenship Act of 1977.

▶ LOSS OF CITIZENSHIP

Most nations permit individuals to give up their citizenship. This act, known as **expatriation**, means that a person no longer wants the rights and responsibilities of citizenship in a particular country. Such a person may then become a citizen of another country or may become a stateless person (one without a country). If U.S. citizens wish to give up their citizenship, they must declare this on a form provided by the secretary of state.

A citizen of the United States loses U.S. citizenship by becoming a citizen of a foreign country unless a special exception is made by the State Department. A person can also lose U.S. citizenship for serving in the armed forces of, or holding office in, a foreign government. U.S. citizenship can also be taken away from people who have been convicted of a major federal crime, such as treason. But people cannot lose their citizenship for something they were forced to do. A person who is forced to serve in a foreign army, for example, will not lose U.S. citizenship.

Most people place a high value on their citizenship. They know that they owe loyalty to their country, and they are willing to fulfill specific obligations. In return they are granted many rights and privileges.

WARD WHIPPLE
Editor, *Civic Leader*

See also ALIENS; IMMIGRATION; NATURALIZATION.

CITRUS FRUIT. See LEMON AND LIME; ORANGE AND GRAPEFRUIT.
CIVETS. See GENETS, CIVETS, MONGOOSES, AND THEIR RELATIVES.

CIVIL LIBERTIES AND CIVIL RIGHTS

Civil liberties and civil rights are freedoms, protections, and benefits that are guaranteed to people by law or tradition. In the broadest sense, these phrases refer to the historical and natural desire of all people to achieve freedom, equality, and justice. In a more strictly legal sense, civil liberties are a person's basic rights, such as freedom of speech and assembly, and the protection of these rights against government interference. Civil rights refer to guarantees by law of equal treatment and equal opportunity for all people. As one example, the government may pass laws that protect a person seeking a job or wishing to vote in an election from discrimination (unfair and unequal treatment) because of race, religion, age, sex, or personal beliefs. In recent years, the phrase "human rights" has often been used to describe all these liberties and protections.

Historical Origins

Throughout history, people have struggled to gain and hold on to certain basic freedoms and liberties. Sometimes they have fought wars or made revolutions to achieve or protect these rights. Often men and women with new ideas about religion and politics, or who challenged the old way of doing things, have been imprisoned, exiled, or killed by repressive governments and rulers. The early Christians, for example, were persecuted (made to suffer for their beliefs) by the Romans and many were condemned to death for denying the Roman gods. In the Middle Ages, people who spoke out against the established Church were brought before a special court (inquisition) for trial and punishment. The most notorious of these courts was the Spanish Inquisition in the 15th century, which punished people by torture and death for spreading ideas considered dangerous by the government as well as the Church.

But even in those days of all-powerful kings and rulers, the basic idea of human rights already had a long history. In fact, the origins of civil rights and civil liberties may be traced to Biblical times. For instance, the idea of equal justice for all is stated in the

Speakers' Corner in London's Hyde Park is an open-air forum where citizens may speak freely on any subject.

Old Testament (Leviticus 19:15): "Ye shall do no unrighteousness in judgment; thou shalt not respect the person of the poor, nor honor the person of the mighty; but in righteousness shalt thou judge thy neighbor." During the period of the Roman Empire, a system of law was developed that protected the rights of Roman citizens. Roman law later became the basis for nearly all European legal systems.

Arguments for Human Rights. The modern idea of civil rights and civil liberties in the Western world has grown out of three main schools of thought. One school of philosophers argued that people have certain basic rights simply because they are human beings created by God or nature. This is known as the theory of natural law. The idea of natural rights was included in the American Declaration of Independence of 1776. It states that "all men are created equal" and are "endowed by their Creator with certain unalienable Rights."

A second school held that human rights were useful (utilitarian) because society benefited from the free and open exchange of ideas. One of the leaders of this school of thought was the English philosopher John Stuart Mill (1806–73). Mill believed that freedom was good for both society and the individual. Freedom made people think and act for themselves, and in Mill's view this made them better people.

The third school took the position that rights and liberties came from the political state or society to which a person belonged. According to this group of thinkers, a person living in a "state of nature" (outside of organized society) had no rights except the right of self-defense. Therefore, it was argued that only a government with the power to enforce the law can protect the rights of an individual. In order to have rights a person must accept society's rule.

Bills of Rights. Many nations have drawn up legal documents listing the rights and liberties guaranteed to their citizens. The earliest in Western history was the Magna Carta (1215), which forced the king of England to grant certain rights, mainly to his nobles. In 1689 the English Parliament passed a law that included a "bill of rights." The law provided that Parliament would be more powerful than the king and that the people would have certain basic liberties. A century later (after the American Revolution), when the first United States Congress was held in 1789, a bill of rights similar to the English one was proposed. The American Bill of Rights—the first 10 amendments to the United States Constitution—became a reality in 1791. Like the English Bill of Rights, it guarantees freedom of speech and the right to petition the government about grievances. It also provides for a free press, trial by jury, and freedom of religion; and it protects the citizen against cruel and unjust punishment, and against unlawful searches and seizures.

During the French Revolution (1789), a document stating the rights of the French people was issued. It was called the Declaration of the Rights of Man and of the Citizen, and it listed many of the same liberties included in the U.S. and English bills of rights. Many nations that have been formed since the late 1800's have bills of rights in their constitutions. Canada's bill of rights, adopted in 1960, confirmed the rights that Canadians had enjoyed under unwritten law.

When the United Nations was formed at the end of World War II (1945), an attempt was made to write a bill of rights that would be followed by the whole world. The Universal Declaration of Human Rights was adopted in 1948. It is a long document, listing over 70 items concerning the rights of all people, regardless of race, sex, nationality, or political belief. The United Nations declaration includes the basic individual liberties set forth in earlier bills of rights. But it also calls for certain social rights as well. According to the

United Nations document, people are entitled to an education, a job of their choice, decent living conditions, and the right to participate in cultural activities.

However, the United Nations has no way of forcing governments to live up to these principles. It can only request a member state to act in accordance with the ideals of the declaration. Many have done so; others have not. A number of countries have also signed various international agreements that protect special rights, including those of women, children, workers, and racial minorities, and that eliminate slavery and forced labor. In 1949 a group of European countries set up the European Commission on Human Rights. The commission has a special court that hears and judges complaints. Its decisions are above those of national courts. It is the first such court in modern history. Many countries also have government agencies or private organizations that aim to protect civil rights and civil liberties.

After years of struggle, civil rights and liberties now have more legal safeguards than ever before in history. But there are still violations of these rights. Some countries are dictatorships. That is, they are ruled by one party, the army, or a single political leader. In these countries, the rights of the people usually are limited. They may not be allowed to vote freely or to publish whatever they wish. Often they are not permitted to complain about bad social conditions or government actions. Even in democracies, the government sometimes tries to limit individual liberties. Governments and private groups alike may try to censor radio and television programs, books, and motion pictures. The struggle for human rights is far from over.

Recent Trends and Events

The 20th century has been a time of revolutionary change all over the world. During this period, nearly all of the peoples who formerly were under European colonial rule have gained their freedom. In the past, the rights and liberties of these peoples were strictly controlled by colonial rulers such as the British, French, Dutch, Spanish, and Portuguese. But now these emerging nations in Africa, Asia, and Latin America have the freedom to do as they wish; to form governments of their own choice; and to establish their own laws to protect citizens' rights. Nearly all these newly independent nations are members of the United Nations. The addition of these new states has changed the United Nations from a small organization of fewer than 60 countries in 1945 to over 150 independent nations in 1980. As a result, the United Nations now represents most of the peoples of the world. It therefore has a greater opportunity to strengthen and protect human rights everywhere.

Women's Liberation. The past few decades have also been a time of new freedom for women. Until the end of World War II, women were permitted to vote in only a few countries. Today only a few countries still deny women the right to vote. In 1971, Switzerland became the last of the Western democracies to grant voting rights to women in national elections. In the late 1960's, feminists (people who support women's rights) began to rally under the slogan "women's liberation." The women's liberation movement began in the United States. It quickly spread to other parts of the world. Women's liberation seeks full political rights and equal job opportunities for all women. In the United States, feminists support the passage of the Equal Rights Amendment (ERA) to the U.S. Constitution. It prohibits discrimination on the basis of sex. Feminists also support different social roles for women so that they are not limited to traditionally female occupations, such as homemaking.

Racial and Religious Conflicts. Great changes have been taking place in the world in recent times. Two examples are travel by jet plane and instant communication by television. Because of these and other changes, there is probably greater tolerance now than in the past—as least in parts of the world—of differences among religions, nationalities, and racial or ethnic groups. In the past, religious intolerance and feelings of racial or national superiority have led to the enslavement of peoples, wars, and brutal atrocities. One of the great horrors of history occurred from 1933 to 1945, when Germany was ruled by the ruthless dictator Adolf Hitler and his Nazi followers. Claiming racial superiority for the German people, the Nazis attempted to destroy all of Europe's Jews as well as other peoples whom they regarded as members of "inferior races." It was largely due to this tragic experience that the United Nations made the protection of human rights one of its major goals. One of the earliest actions by United Nations members was the adoption in 1948 of an agreement to outlaw and punish crimes of genocide—the attempt to destroy an entire people because of their race, religion, or culture.

History is full of examples of racial and religious intolerance leading to bloody conflict. During the religious wars of Europe in the 16th and 17th centuries, both Catholics and Protestants were guilty of cruelty and persecution. The Jews have suffered persecution throughout their history and today still suffer discrimination in the Soviet Union and other countries. Although there has been much progress towards religious and racial tolerance in recent years, the world is still plagued by such conflicts. Muslims and Hindus fought bitterly when India and Pakistan became separate states in 1947. Tens of thousands were slaughtered in bloody massacres. More recently, in the late 1970's, hundreds of thousands of Chinese living in Vietnam were forced by the government to flee the country. Many died at sea in open boats.

In the United States, the struggle by black people for racial equality resulted in violent clashes and riots during the 1960's. There were also serious racial battles between Malays and Chinese after the 1969 elections in Malaysia. Bitterness between the Catholic minority and the Protestant majority in Northern Ireland (a part of the United Kingdom) erupted in serious violence in 1969. British troops were sent in to control the situation, but violence continued. The United Nations and other international organizations cannot directly intervene in such cases. But world public opinion and protest, along with diplomacy, now play an increasing role in restraining these conflicts.

The Spread of Human Rights. The idea that people everywhere have the right not only to express their own views but also to learn what others are saying and doing has been helped by modern communication. With radio and television, news flashes to all corners of the globe. Someone who lives in Asia can learn about an event of importance in Europe or Africa hours or even minutes after it has happened. Governments may try to hide unfavorable news, but the newspapers, radio, and television usually defeat any efforts at concealment. When the United States Government tried to stop publication of confidential documents about the Vietnam War, the United States Supreme Court ruled (1971) that this was a violation of the right of a free press. Newspapers were then permitted to publish the documents.

In a dictatorship, of course, there are censors whose job it is to screen the news and keep certain information from becoming known to the people. But sooner or later the news spreads. Foreign books and newspapers may be smuggled into such a country, and the people can tune in foreign radio broadcasts. Eventually, as people throughout the world become better informed, they will be better able to judge what is good and what is bad for a society. The spread of human rights and liberties will then be aided by the force of world opinion.

Governments sometimes restrict civil liberties for reasons of national security or because they fear war. But today most governments at least claim to support human rights. The United Nations, the governments of democratic countries, and private organizations such as Amnesty International use their influence in the most serious cases of injustice. But it is difficult to judge the effects of this influence on the many countries that are dictatorships.

Will the law of human rights become universal? It exists already in democracies. Dictatorships appear to be influenced more and more by the views of their people and by ideas from other countries. It is hoped that in time all nations will adopt laws protecting their citizens' rights.

Equal rights and justice for all are difficult goals to achieve in any country. They are even more difficult to accomplish worldwide. Yet for the first time in history this is being seriously attempted. If people can set aside their differences and prevent wars, there is hope for a peaceful future in which the liberties and rights of all can be realities.

ROGER N. BALDWIN
Adviser, International Affairs
American Civil Liberties Union

CIVIL SERVICE

Civil servants deliver mail, collect taxes, plan roads, give advice to farmers, keep statistics, build dams, type letters, argue cases in court. The list is almost endless. All the people who work for the government other than elected officials, judges, and members of the armed forces are civil servants.

History

Today 3,000,000 people work for the United States Government. Nine out of 10 of these people were hired through the **merit system**. This means that they got their jobs by proving that they were qualified for them. They cannot be hired or fired because of their politics. But things were not always that way. For a long time there was no merit system. Presidents could fire almost any government workers and fill the jobs with their own political supporters. This was known as the **spoils system**. Government jobs were considered spoils (prizes of war). After every election jobs were given to members of the winning party. Andrew Jackson, in his 8 years as president, replaced 2,000 of the 11,000 people working for the government.

The spoils system did not work too badly when the government was very small. But as it grew larger, the problems increased. Abraham Lincoln complained that so much of his time was taken up with people asking for government jobs that he hardly had time to read the reports from the Civil War battlefront. Still, no effective reform was passed until a disappointed job seeker assassinated President James A. Garfield in July, 1881. In 1883, with demands for reform louder than ever, Congress passed the Pendleton Act. This act, which was strongly supported by President Chester A. Arthur, was the beginning of modern United States Civil Service. A three-member Civil Service Commission was formed to administer a merit system, hold examinations, and advise the president on how to put the act into effect.

Civil Service Today

Today any citizen of the United States can apply for a federal, state, or local government job through civil service. Applicants for most jobs are given written examinations. For jobs requiring a specific skill, such as typing, a practical examination is given as well. For some professional jobs there are no formal tests. The applicants are rated on the basis of interviews and their background in the field.

After a civil service test is given, a list is made up of the people who passed it. Those with the highest marks are at the top of the list and get jobs first. Those lower on the list may have to wait some time until an opening occurs. Everyone has the same chance to pass, except that veterans (people who fought in wars) are granted certain advantages. Since 1947, applicants have had to pledge their loyalty to the United States system of government.

As in 1883, the Civil Service Commission is charged with the overall administration of the United States Civil Service. The commission is headed by three members appointed by the president for 6-year terms. No more than two of them may be from the same political party. Much of the day-to-day administration of civil service workers has been taken over by the personnel departments of the various government bureaus in which they work.

More civil servants work for state and local governments than work for the federal government. They number about 6,000,000 (not counting teachers). The first state to establish a civil service merit system was New York, in 1883. Massachusetts followed the next year. Today the merit system covers at least some of the jobs in all state governments, since a federal law requires that all officials administering federal funds be under a merit system. In many states all other government workers are still under a spoils system.

Other Countries

In Canada about 280,000 people are civil servants in the federal, provincial, and municipal governments. Canada's federal civil service was created by the Civil Service Act of 1918. This act established a Civil Service Commission and put most jobs under a merit system.

Many other countries in all parts of the world have civil service systems, too. France and England, for instance, have civil service systems employing thousands of workers, many of whom are hired under very highly developed merit systems.

Reviewed by ISIDORE STARR
Formerly, Queens College (New York)

The Confederate bombardment of Fort Sumter in April, 1861, started the Civil War.

CIVIL WAR, UNITED STATES

At 4:30 A.M. Friday, April 12, 1861, a signal rocket rose high above the harbor of Charleston, South Carolina, and exploded in flame. Other rockets followed, lighting the sky and revealing the dark outlines of Fort Sumter on an island in the wide harbor. After the rockets came a barrage of shells from batteries of artillery ringing the shoreline. Fort Sumter was soon shrouded in the smoke of exploding missiles. The United States Civil War had begun.

The order to fire on Fort Sumter had been given by Confederate General Pierre G. T. de Beauregard at the direction of Jefferson Davis, the Confederate president. Major Robert Anderson, who commanded Fort Sumter, surrendered after a 34-hour bombardment. The flag of the United States was lowered, and the red and blue Confederate flag was raised in its place.

Eighty-five years after the Declaration of Independence had announced that Americans were free of English rule, the United States itself was battling for survival in the grip of civil war.

▶ BACKGROUND OF THE WAR

What had brought the rich, powerful, and growing United States to such a pass? The reasons were many. In the early 1800's the Northern states, especially those in New England, turned from farming to manufacturing.

But in the South, farming remained the most important way of making a living. Southern planters found cotton and tobacco to be their most profitable crops, and they used black slaves to work their fields.

Slavery was introduced into what is now the United States in 1619, when a Dutch merchant ship brought 20 black Africans to Jamestown, Virginia, and sold them to the colonists. For years the whole country practiced black slavery, but it soon disappeared in the North. One reason was that the Africans could not stand harsh winters in the North. Another was the high price of slaves. A sturdy field hand cost up to $1,800. Such labor was too expensive for Northern farmers. Finally, as the North turned toward industry, mechanics and not farmhands were needed.

Conditions were different in the South. To meet a rising worldwide demand for cotton and tobacco, the planters farmed large areas of land. Slave labor seemed best suited for producing these crops, and the number of black slaves increased.

Slavery Becomes an Issue

As slavery spread, sentiment against it began to grow. People felt it was morally wrong for one human being to own another. In 1808 the United States Government passed a law forbidding the slave trade. This meant that captains of ships could no longer haul cargoes of black Africans to Southern ports in the United States and sell them at auction.

THE UNION and THE CONFEDERACY
1861

THE UNION

THE CONFEDERACY

BORDER STATES

TERRITORIES

WASH. TERR.

OREGON

DAKOTA TERRITORY

NEVADA TERR.

CALIFORNIA

UTAH TERR.

NEBRASKA TERR.

COLORADO TERR.

NEW MEXICO TERRITORY

INDIAN TERR.

0   400 km
0   300 mi

MINNESOTA

DAKOTA TERRITORY

WISCONSIN

MICHIGAN

MAINE

VT.

N.H.

NEW YORK

MASS.

CONN.

R.I

NEBRASKA TERRITORY

IOWA

PENNSYLVANIA

N.J.

THE

MD.

DEL.

KANSAS

MISSOURI

ILLINOIS   INDIANA   OHIO

WEST VIRGINIA
(Joined Union 1863)

UNION

N

Public Land Strip

KENTUCKY

VIRGINIA

INDIAN TERRITORY

ARKANSAS

TENNESSEE

NORTH CAROLINA

THE

MISS.   ALABAMA

SOUTH CAROLINA

Atlantic Ocean

CONFEDERATE STATES

GEORGIA

OF AMERICA

TEXAS

LOUISIANA

FLORIDA

Gulf of Mexico

0   100   200   300   400 km
0   100   200   300 mi

However, this law did not affect slaves already in the country, and slavery continued to flourish in the South. But by the 1840's a widespread movement to abolish slavery had taken root in the North. The people who supported this movement were called abolitionists.

The Missouri Compromise

As the United States expanded westward the slavery problem grew worse. New states were carved out of the territories west of the Mississippi and admitted to the Union. At first an uneasy balance was kept between "slave" and "free" states. To satisfy both North and South, a free state was brought into the Union for every slave state.

Then in 1820 Maine, which had been part of Massachusetts, applied for admission to the Union as a free state. Missouri, the next territory seeking statehood, should have come in on the slavery side. But Missourians were themselves divided on slavery. Some favored it; others opposed it. Violence broke out between the two camps.

Congress enacted the Missouri Compromise to prevent more serious trouble. This law allowed Missouri to enter as a slave state and Maine to enter as a free state. But slavery in any new state to be formed on a line north of the 36th parallel was prohibited.

Abolitionist Feeling Grows

The Missouri Compromise worked well enough until 1845, when Texas was admitted as a slave state. The Mexican War followed the annexation of Texas, and vast regions were opened to slavery. The North protested vigorously at the prospect that the balance of power would be broken.

In 1852, public feeling against slavery was increased by the publication of Harriet Beecher Stowe's novel *Uncle Tom's Cabin*. Picturing slavery at its worst, the book caused thousands of people to join the abolitionists.

To help slaves escape to Canada, where they would be free, the abolitionists created the Underground Railroad. This railroad was actually a string of hiding places for fleeing slaves. It reached from the South to the Canadian border. Homes, barns, cellars, and stables were the hideouts, or stations, on the railroad. Escaping slaves moved secretly from one station to another until they reached Canada and freedom.

Angry Southerners demanded justice, claiming that the abolitionists were stealing their property. But nothing was done to stop the Underground Railroad, and bad feelings between North and South rose even higher.

Trouble in Kansas

Affairs came to a boil in Kansas Territory, where a guerrilla war broke out between free-state people, called jawhawkers, and pro-slavery people, known as bushwhackers. This situation was brought about by the Kansas-Nebraska Act, passed in 1854. This law replaced the Missouri Compromise. The law required that a new state be admitted free or slave according to the will of the people who lived in it, regardless of its boundary lines.

The Kansas-Nebraska Act succeeded only in stirring savage conflict in Kansas. The jayhawkers received abolitionist backing. Rifles were shipped to them from the East in crates marked "Bibles." Because this idea had originated with the Reverend Henry Ward Beecher, brother of Harriet Beecher Stowe, the rifles were called Beecher's Bibles.

The ugly Kansas war brought attention to John Brown, an abolitionist fanatic who believed that he had been chosen by God to free the slaves. Brown and his followers attacked proslavery settlers in Kansas and massacred a number of them at a place called Pottawatomie Creek. In January, 1861, Kansas voted to enter the Union as a free state. The United States flag now bore 34 stars.

The Dred Scott Case

Still more heat was added to the slavery issue by the Dred Scott case. Dred Scott was a slave who traveled with his master into free Wisconsin Territory. Scott sued for his freedom, claiming that once he had left slave territory, he was no longer a slave.

In 1857 the United States Supreme Court ruled against Scott. According to Chief Justice Roger Taney, Congress had no right under the Constitution to forbid slavery in the territories. Scott's position, therefore, had not been altered by entering Minnesota. Angered by Taney's decision, Northern antislavery groups swore to keep slavery out of the territories at any price—even war, if necessary.

States' Rights

Not only slavery but also the question of states' rights had long caused problems within the United States. Did the federal government have the power under the Constitution to control the states in all matters?

"No!" roared the South.

Southerners wanted no interference by the federal government in their state affairs. They reserved the right to reject any federal laws they didn't like.

In 1832 South Carolina had disapproved a federal tariff law and refused to obey it. When the government insisted, the fiery Carolinians prepared to secede from the Union. But it all came to nothing when President Andrew Jackson threatened to use military force against South Carolina and secession talk ended.

▶ THE NATION MOVES CLOSER TO WAR

Thus, because of slavery and states' rights, a wide rift developed between North and South. It yawned dangerously in October, 1859, when John Brown and a devoted band of followers captured the United States Arsenal at Harper's Ferry, Virginia. Brown called upon the slaves in the surrounding countryside "to rise up and destroy" their masters.

Brown's insurrection was crushed by United States marines under Colonel Robert E. Lee. Brown was convicted of treason against Virginia and was hanged.

But John Brown's cause did not die with him. Abolitionists began to sing that although "John Brown's body lies a-mold'ring in the grave," his truth "goes marching on!" They hailed Brown as a martyr, while Southerners regarded him as an archvillain. The nation was more divided than ever.

The Election of 1860

In 1860 the Republican Party picked as its candidate for president a lanky lawyer from Illinois, Abraham Lincoln. Hannibal Hamlin of Maine was Lincoln's running mate.

Although he was not an abolitionist, Lincoln had spoken against the spread of slavery into the territories. Since it was known that Lincoln opposed the spread of slavery, Southerners thought this meant he would abolish it. They looked upon Lincoln as an enemy.

But slavery advocates found no comfort in the Democratic candidate, Stephen Douglas,

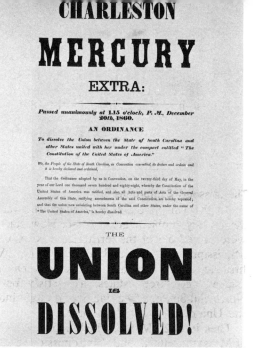

A South Carolina paper carries news of Southern states leaving the Union after Lincoln's election in 1860.

who also objected to the extension of slavery into the territories. As a result, Southern Democrats nominated John C. Breckinridge of Kentucky for president. A fourth candidate, John Bell, ran on an independent ticket.

Leading Southerners announced that they would demand secession from the Union if Lincoln won the election. On November 6, 1860, the voters chose Abraham Lincoln to succeed James Buchanan in the White House.

Secession

Secessionists proved true to their threat. South Carolina seceded in December, 1860. Mississippi, Florida, Alabama, Georgia, Louisiana, and Texas followed South Carolina in leaving the Union. These states claimed to have a legal right to secede from the Union. They had voluntarily joined it, and the Constitution did not specifically prohibit withdrawing from the Union. They established a new nation, the Confederate States of America, with its capital at Montgomery, Alabama. (The Confederate capital was moved to Richmond, Virginia, in May, 1861.)

On February 4, 1861, delegates met at Montgomery to draw up a Confederate constitution and appoint a president and a vice-president. The convention chose Jefferson Davis for president and Alexander Stephens for vice-president.

The original Confederate states were later joined by Virginia, Arkansas, Tennessee, and North Carolina, while in the border states of Kentucky and Missouri, Unionists and Secessionists fought for control.

The Firing on Fort Sumter

As each state seceded it would seize all federal properties within its borders. This included forts, posts, camps, arsenals, customs houses, and post offices. Most United States military establishments would surrender without resistance. But in December, 1860, Major Robert Anderson, commanding Fort Moultrie at Charleston, South Carolina, refused to give in. Instead he moved his garrison, which included only 68 fighting men, from Fort Moultrie to nearby Fort Sumter, a more defensible position in Charleston's harbor. After long negotiations, during which President Buchanan did little to help Anderson, the War Department decided that Fort Sumter must hold out as long as possible.

Anderson held grimly to his post in the face of growing Confederate forces. Lincoln was inaugurated on March 4, 1861. Five weeks later he sent ships to supply Anderson with rations since the fort's food supply was almost gone. The relief fleet was due to arrive at Charleston on April 12. Just before it reached the harbor mouth, the Confederates opened fire and forced Anderson's surrender.

The Confederates had committed an act of war that Lincoln could not ignore. The President of the United States took immediate action. He called 75,000 men to the colors and ordered a blockade of Southern ports. If the South wanted war, it would have it.

▶ 1861: THE WAR BEGINS

Although there were military preparations throughout the land and some clashes in Missouri and western Virginia, no major engagement was fought until July, 1861. Then Federal forces under General Irvin McDowell clashed with a Confederate army commanded by General Pierre G. T. de Beauregard at Manassas, Virginia, on the banks of a stream called Bull Run.

This battle, fought by untrained armies totaling about 70,000 men, ended in a rout of the Northern forces. However, nothing decisive resulted from it.

The Rise of General McClellan

After the Battle of Manassas (Bull Run), General George B. McClellan was placed in command of all Northern forces in Virginia and Washington, D.C. He did a brilliant job of reorganizing what was now called the Army of the Potomac. McClellan built his troops into a fighting machine—but fought no battles. He wanted to make sure they were ready before he moved. The only action during this time took place in August, when Federal soldiers captured Fort Hatteras and Fort Clark on the North Carolina coast.

In October McClellan marched at last, only to lose a bloody battle at Ball's Bluff, Virginia. The aged commander in chief of the Northern army, Lieutenant General Winfield Scott (hero of the Mexican War), resigned in November, and George B. McClellan replaced him. McClellan now commanded all the Union armies as well as his own Army of the Potomac.

Trouble with Britain

The year closed with an event that nearly triggered a war between the United States and Great Britain. On November 28 a blockading Union warship, the U.S.S. *San Jacinto,* halted a British vessel, the *Trent,* in mid-ocean. A boarding party from the *San Jacinto* seized James M. Mason and John Slidell, the Confederate envoys to Great Britain and France.

The British protested the act as a violation of the freedom of the seas. For a time it looked as though the British ruler, Queen Victoria, would declare war. But Lincoln wisely prevented this on December 26 by having Secretary of State William Seward release Mason and Slidell.

▶ 1862: THE FIGHTING QUICKENS

The war that had stalled after Bull Run flared again in 1862. Battles raged in Kentucky and Tennessee. The Union won stunning victories at Mill Springs, Kentucky, and took Fort Henry and Fort Donelson, key posts guarding the approaches to Tennessee.

The capture of Fort Henry and Fort Donelson marked the rise of a short, bearded, cigar-smoking Union general, Ulysses S. Grant. It was Grant who coined the phrase "unconditional surrender" when asked for terms by Fort Donelson's commander.

The battle between the *Monitor*, left, and the *Merrimack* took place in March, 1862.

The Ironclads

The year 1862 saw the first battle ever fought by ironclad warships. On March 8 the Confederate ironclad *Virginia,* also known as the *Merrimack,* sailed out of Norfolk, Virginia, and attacked the wooden ships blockading Hampton Roads, the entrance of Norfolk harbor. The *Virginia* spread dismay throughout the North by sinking or damaging several of the big wooden frigates. Only the coming of darkness kept it from destroying the entire Union fleet.

However, the *Virginia*'s career ended suddenly. When it sailed forth on March 9 to finish off the remaining Federal ships, its path was blocked by a strange-looking foe. This was the U.S.S. *Monitor,* an armored gunboat described as a "cheesebox on a raft." The two ironclads blasted each other for hours without a decision. At last the *Virginia* withdrew, never to fight again. When Union troops captured Norfolk on May 10, the retreating Confederates blew up the *Virginia*.

The battle between the ironclads made all the wooden navies of the world old-fashioned. It opened a new era in naval warfare.

Union Armies Push Toward Richmond

The pace of the conflict quickened. On April 6–7 Grant fought a costly battle at a place called Shiloh in Tennessee. The North won after a two-day battle that caused more than 23,000 to be killed and wounded in both armies.

Later during the same month a Federal flotilla led by Admiral David Farragut captured New Orleans, Louisiana, at the mouth of the Mississippi River—a shocking loss for the Confederates.

Meanwhile in Virginia, McClellan, who had been relieved as commander in chief on March 11, finally began his long-awaited offensive. A massive effort to capture Richmond with 100,000 splendidly trained and equipped men was begun. The campaign saw furious fighting on the Virginia peninsula. McClellan came to within 8 kilometers (5 miles) of Richmond but failed to capture the enemy's capital. At the Battle of Fair Oaks (Seven Pines), Federal troops actually entered the city's outskirts but had to fall back.

During the fighting around Fair Oaks the Confederate commander, General Joseph E. Johnston, was wounded. General Robert E. Lee (who had captured John Brown) took over from Johnston. The Confederate Army of Northern Virginia and Virginia's great military leader were at last united.

Lee Pushes Back

Lee drove McClellan back in a week of combat called the Seven Days' Battles. McClellan retreated from Richmond, and the peninsular campaign ended when the Army of the Potomac was withdrawn to its old lines around Washington.

The new commander in chief of the Union armies, General Henry W. Halleck, took several regiments from McClellan and formed the Army of Virginia under General John Pope, with orders to march on Richmond. Pope fought a series of disastrous battles against Lee and Stonewall Jackson between August 28 and September 1. The worst defeat took place on the old Bull Run battlefield. Pope's army fled to Washington in disorder. Halleck disbanded the Army of Virginia and returned the men to McClellan's command.

UNION SOLDIER

The Battle of Gettysburg was the turning point of the Civil War. From then on,

The Battle of Antietam

McClellan proved his worth as an organizer once more. The army regained its spirit, and when Lee crossed the Potomac River to invade Northern soil for the first time in the war, McClellan was able to meet the test.

The Army of the Potomac and the Army of Northern Virginia clashed near the village of Sharpsburg, Maryland, on the banks of rambling Antietam Creek. They fought for 14 hours on September 17. After both armies had lost a total of 24,000 men, Lee retreated across the Potomac River. McClellan, relieved at beating off the attack, did not pursue.

The Emancipation Proclamation

While the battle of Antietam brought no clear-cut victory to the North, Lincoln used its results as a springboard to strike a blow against slavery.

It was generally agreed that something had to be done about the plight of the black slaves. Some Northern officers had already acted. In August, 1861, General John Charles Frémont freed all slaves in Missouri, only to have the order revoked by Lincoln, who did not want to lose the support of slave-holding Missouri Unionists.

Slavery was abolished in the District of Columbia during April, 1862, because the government felt it was wrong for slavery to flourish on its own doorstep. By September, 1862, Lincoln felt the nation was ready for a strong step against slavery. The President announced to the nation on September 22 that effective January 1, 1863, "all persons held as slaves within any State or designated part of a State . . . in rebellion against the United States shall be then, thenceforward, and forever free."

The abolitionists were displeased by the Emancipation Proclamation. They felt it did not go far enough. On the other hand, Lincoln's words infuriated proslavery people and enraged the South.

Still, for all its shortcomings, the Emancipation Proclamation was a giant stride toward the abolition of slavery in the United States.

More Bloodshed

Following the battle of Antietam neither army launched any major offensive. McClellan began an advance in October, but his progress was so tedious that Lincoln relieved him of command, remarking, "He has got the slows."

CONFEDERATE SOLDIER

the Union forces grew in strength while those of the Confederacy declined.

McClellan's successor, General Ambrose Burnside, was no improvement. Burnside fought one battle at Fredericksburg, Virginia, in December, 1862. The year ended with mourning in thousands of Northern homes for the men who fell on the heights before Fredericksburg.

On the last day of 1862 a fierce battle started at Stones River near Murfreesboro, Tennessee. It lasted until January 3, 1863, without decisive results, although both sides lost heavily.

▶ KEY VICTORIES FOR THE NORTH

Early in 1863 General Burnside was relieved of his command of the Army of the Potomac. His successor was General Joseph Hooker, nicknamed Fighting Joe. Hooker took the field in April in a campaign he vowed would finally succeed in crushing the army of the Confederacy.

Instead Hooker suffered a serious defeat at Chancellorsville, Virginia, on May 2–4. Although Chancellorsville ended as a Confederate victory, Southern joy was dampened by the wounding of Stonewall Jackson, who died a few weeks later. Lee grieved, "I have lost my right arm."

Gettysburg

Shortly after Chancellorsville, Lee started another invasion of Northern territory. He crossed the Potomac River and marched up through Maryland toward Harrisburg, Pennsylvania. Even as Lee marched with his veteran army of 90,000 men, the Army of the Potomac had another change of commanders. Fighting Joe Hooker was replaced by stubborn General George Meade. Meade's army fought Lee at Gettysburg, Pennsylvania. The battle lasted from July 1 to 3, 1863. The casualties sickened the nation and shocked the world. More than 28,000 Confederates and 23,000 Union soldiers were killed, wounded, or missing.

Lee managed, somehow, to bring his shattered troops back into Virginia. Never again would the Army of Northern Virginia invade the North.

Meanwhile Vicksburg, the Confederate stronghold on the Mississippi River, had been under attack by Union forces since December, 1862. The Confederate garrison commanded by General John Pemberton was hopelessly trapped, but the city still held out.

At almost the same time that Lee's gallant legions met defeat at Gettysburg, the Confederates surrendered Vicksburg, on Saturday, July 4, 1863. This triumph won control of the Mississippi River for the North, and Lincoln could write: "The Father of Waters again goes unvexed to the sea. . . ."

Draft Riots

But Northern victory celebrations were marred by 5-day-long rioting (July 13–17) in New York City. The riots began when violent crowds protested a law to draft men for the army. The disorders were aimed at a clause in the law that permitted a man to buy his way out of the draft by paying the United States government $300. This angered the people who could not afford to pay that sum.

New York City had never known such ugly disturbances as the so-called Draft Riots. More than 1,000 persons were killed or wounded. Blacks were lynched, and houses and stores were looted and burned. Only after eleven regiments were rushed to the city from Gettysburg was the rioting finally put down.

Fighting near Chattanooga

As Meade and Lee jockeyed for position in Virginia, Confederate and Union forces fought for control of Tennessee. Despite losses at Vicksburg and Gettysburg, the Confederates fought on. They won a battle at Chickamauga, in the northwest corner of Georgia, near Union-held Chattanooga, Tennessee. General Braxton Bragg defeated Union General William Rosecrans. The Union Army was forced to flee. They would have been crushed completely before they reached the safety of Chattanooga if it hadn't been for the stand made by Union troops under General George Thomas. Thomas won the title "the Rock of Chickamauga."

The last major fighting of the year occurred outside of Chattanooga. There the Union Army practically destroyed Bragg's forces. Fighting Joe Hooker made up for his Chancellorsville failure by storming Lookout Mountain and smashing the center of Bragg's lines. This Confederate defeat ended any serious Southern military threat in Tennessee.

▶ 1864–65: TRIUMPH AND TRAGEDY

Both sides knew great events would take place in 1864, which was the year that a presidential election would be held in the

North. On March 9 President Lincoln summoned General Grant, promoted him to the rank of lieutenant general, and made him commander in chief of all the Union armies. Grant prepared an all-out offensive in Virginia and the West.

Grant in the Wilderness

On May 4 the Army of the Potomac crossed the Rapidan River in Virginia and headed for Richmond through an area known as The Wilderness. At the same time General William T. Sherman started a large army marching from Chattanooga through the heartland of the South to Atlanta, Georgia.

Grant kept moving forward despite terrible losses in the Wilderness campaign. But though he lost many men, Grant inflicted heavy casualties on Lee. The Southerners could not replace their losses. The war in Virginia settled down to a grim game of "pounding away." Out west Sherman pressed on, fighting engagements almost daily against forces led by General Joseph Johnston.

So the war ground along with its strings of victories and defeats. In June the Republicans renominated Lincoln and for vice-president chose Andrew Johnson of Tennessee.

The North Pushes for Victory

In Virginia, Grant placed Petersburg under siege. Grant knew that Lee could no longer maneuver at will. If Lee moved out of Petersburg, Richmond had to fall, for Petersburg was the key to the Confederate capital.

Grant knew he had only to keep Lee cooped up in Petersburg and the long-sought victory would be his. But the country was impatient and demanded a quick victory. Criticism against Grant and Lincoln mounted.

Not even the capture of Alabama's Mobile Bay by Union naval forces under Admiral David Farragut satisfied the Northerners. Lincoln's supporters were worried about the outcome of his re-election. On August 29 optimistic northern Democrats nominated General George B. McClellan as their presidential candidate.

On September 1–2 Sherman captured Atlanta. Almost overnight the national mood changed. Lincoln was returned to office on November 8 by a substantial vote. One week later Sherman, after burning Atlanta, began his famous March to the Sea, cutting across Georgia to Savannah, which he took on December 21. To climax a triumphant year, General Thomas scattered a Confederate army at Nashville, Tennessee.

Surrender

As 1865 came on, the feel of victory was in the Northern air. At the end of January, Congress passed the Thirteenth Amendment to the Constitution, abolishing slavery at once and prohibiting it forever in the United States.

Sherman marched out of Savannah on February 1 and headed north through the Carolinas. City after city fell to the rugged Union troops as Sherman moved northward. By mid-February Charleston, South Carolina, was in Union hands, and the Stars and Stripes again flew over Fort Sumter.

Abraham Lincoln was sworn in for a second term on March 4. In his inaugural address he called for a peace "with malice toward none, with charity for all . . . ."

A month later peace seemed close indeed. On April 2 Petersburg fell. The next day Federal soldiers entered Richmond. A week later General Lee surrendered to General Grant at Appomattox Court House, Virginia.

▶ THE BITTER AFTERMATH

And so the Civil War was over. In a way it was the last of a type of war—the war of the individual fighting man. Not that men would not fight with skill and bravery in later wars. But always they would be dwarfed by the vast machinery of warfare—the huge armies, the poison gases, the tanks, bombs, and planes.

But if the Civil War was the last of one kind of war, it was the first of another. Never before had there been so much slaughter and suffering in a war. Everywhere the story was the same—on the battlefield, where as many as 24,000 men died in a single day; in the countryside, where thousands of acres of beautiful land were ravaged; in the crude, understaffed field hospitals, where the sick and wounded suffered horribly; in the prisoner-of-war camps, where men turned into living skeletons. More Americans—Union and Confederate—died in this war than in the two World Wars combined.

Union drummer boys sounded daily camp calls.

Yet even the ending of the war did not bring real peace. On Good Friday, April 14, 11 days after Union troops had entered Richmond, an actor named John Wilkes Booth assassinated Lincoln as the President watched a play from his box in Ford's Theater, Washington, D.C. The one man who might have brought about a just peace was dead.

Results

The Civil War solved some old problems for the United States. But it created some new problems as well.

Slavery was gone from the United States forever. The Emancipation Proclamation and the Thirteenth Amendment to the Constitution had ended slavery in the United States. The old problem of secession was also solved. Never again could the states try to separate themselves from the Union. Many of the problems involving states' rights were also settled. The federal government had become the supreme authority in the United States.

Before the Civil War the development of industry and transportation had been slow. During the grim years of the war, American industry learned new ways of manufacturing weapons and more efficient methods of transporting people and supplies.

The United States faced three great new problems after the Civil War. First, the Southern economy had collapsed. Plantations were destroyed, and farmland was ruined. Many Southern cities and towns were devastated, and the people of the South were poor. Second, at the end of the war, the Southern states found themselves without governments. These states had to be re-admitted to the Union. But they could not be re-admitted until they had legal governments. Finally, the thousands of former black slaves had to start new lives as free people. Few slaves had been taught to read and write, and few blacks had

been taught a useful trade. A great problem lay ahead.

Many of the problems created by the Civil War have been solved. Towns have been rebuilt, new industries flourish, and new schools have been erected. Most of the damage of war has long been repaired. But many of the human problems still remain.

IRVING WERSTEIN
Author, *The Many Faces of the Civil War*

See also COMPROMISE OF 1850; CONFEDERATE STATES OF AMERICA; DRED SCOTT DECISION; EMANCIPATION PROCLAMATION; KANSAS-NEBRASKA ACT; MISSOURI COMPROMISE; RECONSTRUCTION PERIOD; SLAVERY; and names of individual generals and other leaders.

A CIVIL WAR CHRONOLOGY

1861
March 4: Abraham Lincoln inaugurated president of the United States.

April 12–13: Confederate guns fire on Fort Sumter.

April 15: Lincoln calls for 75,000 Union volunteers.

May 8: Richmond, Virginia, made capital of Confederacy.

May 24: Northern troops occupy Alexandria, Virginia.

June 10: Battle of Big Bethel, Virginia.

July 21: First Bull Run (or battle of Manassas), Virginia.

October 21: Union troops badly defeated at Ball's Bluff, Virginia.

November 1: General Winfield Scott resigns as commander in chief of Union armies; is succeeded by McClellan.

November 8: Confederate envoys Mason and Slidell removed from British steamer *Trent*. Crisis with England.

1862
January 19: Union troops defeat Confederates at Mill Springs, Kentucky.

February 6: Union forces under General U.S. Grant capture Fort Henry, Tennessee.

March 8–9: Sea battle between *Monitor* and *Merrimac*.

April 4: McClellan launches Peninsular Campaign.

April 6–7: Battle of Shiloh, Tennessee. A Union victory.

April 25: New Orleans captured by United States Navy.

May 5: Battle of Williamsburg, Virginia.

May 31–June 1: Battle of Fair Oaks (Seven Pines) on Peninsula.

June 26–July 2: General Robert E. Lee attacks McClellan, launching battles of the Seven Days.

July 17: Congress authorizes acceptance of blacks into United States Army and Navy.

August 28–30: Battle of Groveton followed by Union defeat at Second Bull Run.

September 17: Battle of Antietam (Sharpsburg).

September 22: Lincoln issues preliminary Emancipation Proclamation.

December 13: Battle of Fredericksburg, Virginia.

December 31: Lincoln signs bill admitting West Virginia to the Union.

1863
January 1: Emancipation Proclamation goes into effect.

May 2–4: Battle of Chancellorsville, Virginia.

May 22: Siege of Vicksburg starts.

June 15–26: Lee invades Pennsylvania.

July 1–3: Battle of Gettysburg.

July 4: General Ulysses S. Grant accepts surrender of Vicksburg, Mississippi.

July 8: Port Hudson, Louisiana, falls to Union.

July 13–17: Draft Riots in New York City.

September 19–20: Union defeat at Chickamauga.

November 23–25: Northern victory at Chattanooga, Tennessee.

1864
March 12: Grant made commander in chief of all Union armies.

May 5–6: Battle of The Wilderness, Virginia.

June 3: Battle of Cold Harbor, Virginia.

June 16–18: Grant starts siege of Petersburg, Virginia.

June 19: Confederate commerce raider *Alabama* sunk by U.S.S. *Kearsage* off Cherbourg, France.

July 20–28: Fighting before Atlanta, Georgia.

September 2: General William Tecumseh Sherman enters Atlanta.

September 19–22: General Phil Sheridan, Union cavalry leader, defeats General Jubal Early at Winchester and Fishers Hill, Virginia.

October 19: Sheridan beats Early at Cedar Creek, Virginia.

November 8: Lincoln re-elected president.

November 15: Sherman begins the March to the Sea.

December 15–16: Confederates defeated at Nashville, Tennessee.

December 21: Sherman takes Savannah, Georgia.

1865
February 1: Thirteenth Amendment to the United States Constitution, abolishing slavery, is proposed to Congress.

February 18: Charleston, South Carolina, is abandoned by Confederates.

February 22: Union forces take Wilmington, North Carolina.

March 4: Lincoln's second inauguration.

April 2: Petersburg captured by Union forces.

April 3: Richmond falls to Union.

April 9: General Lee surrenders to General Grant at Appomattox Court House, Virginia.

CLARINET

The clarinet is a wind instrument usually made of wood. It has a cylinder-shaped body with a single-reed mouthpiece at one end and a bell-shaped opening at the other. One of the most popular woodwind instruments, the clarinet is also one of the most versatile. It is equally at home in the symphony orchestra, in military and dance bands, and in jazz and chamber music. It is often used as a solo instrument.

The single reed and the shape of its body give the clarinet a rich, mellow tone, which contrasts strongly with the sharp, nasal sound of its close cousin, the oboe. The reed is made of cane, a kind of coarse grass, carefully shaved until its tip is as thin as paper. This thin tip vibrates when the player blows through the mouthpiece. The vibrations make the clarinet sound. Different notes are played by opening or closing the holes along the body of the instrument. When all the holes are closed, the sound is low in pitch. As the holes are opened one at a time the pitch rises from one note to the next.

In early clarinets most of the holes were covered by the player's fingers. Only nine holes could be covered at a time. Keys were added one by one over the years to cover more holes. This made it possible to play higher and lower notes, so that today the clarinet has a range of some 40 notes or more.

The clarinet is the youngest woodwind instrument. Yet less is known about its early history than that of other instruments hundreds of years older. According to legend Johann Denner invented it around 1690. Almost nothing is known about Denner except that he was a German flute maker, and not one of his clarinets still exists.

The great composers did not begin to write music for the clarinet until many years after its invention. The first to use it often was Mozart. It was one of his favorite instruments. He liked its wide range and variety of tone quality—from lush, creamy, low notes to piercing high notes—and he wrote some of his most beautiful music for it. Nearly every great composer since Mozart has given the clarinet an important place in the orchestra. In the modern band it is more important still, playing the leading part, as do the strings in

Jazz musician Benny Goodman plays classical and popular music as well as jazz on the clarinet.

the symphony orchestra. In jazz, as well as in classical music, the clarinet is a brilliant solo instrument.

The clarinet most often used for these solo parts is the B-flat clarinet, which is about 65 centimeters (26 inches) long. But it is only one of a large family. Some clarinets are only 40 centimeters (16 inches) long. Others are much larger. These include the alto and bass clarinets and the great contrabass.

Most early clarinets were made of boxwood, a yellow wood that looks like ivory. But for about the past 50 years clarinets have usually been made of granadilla, an African wood like ebony. This unusual wood is so heavy that it will not float; it is almost as hard as iron. It is also rare and costly. Clarinet makers have tried other materials, such as metal and hard rubber, but granadilla is still the best. Plastic clarinets are now used in many school bands and orchestras because well-made plastic clarinets are excellent musical instruments and are less expensive.

BENNY GOODMAN
Clarinetist

See also WIND INSTRUMENTS.

CLARK, CHARLES JOSEPH (1939–)

Charles Joseph (Joe) Clark was elected prime minister of Canada in 1979, as leader of the Progressive Conservative Party. He succeeded Pierre Trudeau, the Liberal Party leader, who had governed for eleven years.

The son of Charles and Grace Clark, Joe Clark was born on June 5, 1939, in High River, Alberta. He worked at his father's newspaper, the High River *Times,* and at several other newspapers. A visit to the House of Commons in 1956 inspired him to enter politics. Over the next ten years, he held various posts in the Progressive Conservative Party in Alberta. He also obtained a B.A. in history and an M.A. in political science, both from the University of Alberta. In 1967 he ran unsuccessfully for the Alberta legislature. He then worked as a speech writer and executive assistant to Robert Stanfield, the federal Progressive Conservative leader.

In 1972, Clark won election to Parliament as the member from Rocky Mountain, Alberta.

He was re-elected in 1974. In Parliament, his work focused on youth matters and the environment, and his debating skills won attention. Clark married Maureen McTeer in 1973. She retained her surname and pursued an independent career as a lawyer.

Clark became party leader in 1976. He was viewed as a candidate who could bring together different factions of the party. The party's popularity rose and fell during the next two years. But in the fall of 1978, the party won 10 of 15 by-elections (special elections held to fill vacant seats).

The 1979 election was fought on two main issues—the economy and national unity. Clark maintained that the Liberal government lacked economic leadership and had contributed to unemployment and inflation. He said also that Trudeau's attitude toward Canada's various regions was inflexible and had led to disunity. His party won the election in May. But it was defeated in December on budget measures that called for higher energy prices. In elections held in 1980, the Liberals regained power.

CLARK, WILLIAM. See LEWIS AND CLARK EXPEDITION.

CLASSICAL AGE IN MUSIC

In the history of music, the period from about 1760 to about 1825 is usually called the classical era. We call a work classical if it is of the highest quality, or class. Thus, we speak of a "classical example" or a "classic in its field." It must have lasting value and be a model worthy of our study. The word "classical" is used also to indicate formal perfection, as when we say a work has classical form. Musical works of classical value have been created in most periods of music history. But the classical age in music produced so many that it well deserves its name.

The music of the classical age includes the works of four of the world's greatest composers: Franz Joseph Haydn (1732–1809), Wolfgang Amadeus Mozart (1756–91), Ludwig van Beethoven (1770–1827), and Franz Schubert (1797–1828).

One of the characteristics of 18th-century musicians was that they liked to write treatises, or textbooks, about music. Musical dictionaries, encyclopedias, and books on music theory and instrument playing appeared in great abundance. Everything that could be known about music seemed to be explained in these scholarly books. One that is still famous today is *Essay on the True Art of Playing Keyboard Instruments,* by Johann Sebastian Bach's son Karl Philipp Emanuel (1714–88). Mozart's father, Leopold (1719–87), wrote a similar book on violin playing. Because of these scholarly works, musicians felt that all the rules of their art were clearly defined and understandable.

A great deal of the music of the classical age was understood and appreciated for itself alone. It was not dependent on the dance, drama, poetry, or religious ceremonies as earlier music usually had been. Music was enjoyed for its own sake simply as pure music.

Concerts as we know them today are a result of this approach to music. Today many people go to concerts to listen to music played by orchestras or soloists. Other people have concerts at home on the radio or the phonograph. Music is listened to for its own sake and not because it is part of a dance, story, or picture. The new audiences of the classical era supported concerts. They played instruments in their homes, and bought new music for their children to practice.

▶ NEW INSTRUMENTAL GROUPS

In the classical age the orchestra played on the concert stage as well as in the opera pit and the ballroom. The classical orchestra was built on a foundation of stringed instruments: first and second violins, violas, cellos, and double basses. The piano was new in the 18th century but soon replaced the harpsichord. It had a big tone and did not require the constant tuning of the older keyboard instruments. It became the leading solo instrument in concerts. The combination of piano and violin became a familiar duet team. The piano trio came to be the standard grouping of piano, violin, and cello. The string quartet—two violins, viola, and cello—began its exciting development.

▶ CLASSICAL MUSICAL FORMS

New ideas about music and the new instrumental groupings led composers to develop new musical forms. The classical forms were closely related to the classical sonata. The word "sonata" is very old and has been used in a variety of ways. In the music of the classical age, it has a special meaning and importance.

Sonata Form

Today we distinguish between music meant to be played on instruments and music for voices. This distinction was not always clear. It began to be clear in the baroque era. Instrumentalists developed the ability to play things that singers could not imitate. This development took place mainly in Italy. Hence Italian words were used to describe what musicians were doing. Thus, the word "cantata" comes from the Italian *cantare,* "to sing." In the same way, the word "sonata" comes from *sonare,* "to play." Before the classical age any piece of instrumental music could be called a sonata. Many of them were.

When baroque composers began writing long instrumental works of several parts, they called them sonatas. When they imitated re-ligious music, they called the work a church sonata, a *sonata da chièsa.* When they imitated dance pieces, they called the result a living-room sonata, a *sonata da camera.* These were the first sonatas consisting of several movements. (A movement is a section of a composition that is divided into separate contrasting sections, or parts.) Many of them are still played today.

Classical composers invented new forms for the sonata. It continued to be an instrumental piece with several movements. But the church and chamber styles were discarded. The structure of the first movement in a classical sonata came to be called sonata form. This is the special and important meaning of the word "sonata." It is the name for the most important musical form of the classical age.

Sonata form has three main parts: exposition, development, and recapitulation. The exposition presents the themes, or subject matter, of the movement. It consists of usually two or three main themes of contrasting character. The development section works out, or develops, the themes of the exposition. It is a test for the composer's musical imagination. He tries to vary the melodies and rhythms in the most interesting way he can. The development may be short or long. It may use only one or all of the themes given in the exposition. It usually moves rapidly through several different keys. It ends with a return to the main theme, which begins the recapitulation. The recapitulation repeats the exposition, often with important changes, and concludes the movement.

In the sonata form the composer seems to be saying to us: "These are the subjects I will talk about" (exposition); "Now I discuss them" (development); "This is what I have tried to tell you" (recapitulation).

The sonata form proved so useful that composers used it in many pieces not called sonatas. It was used in opera overtures, chamber music, and symphonies. Thus, a symphony is really a sonata for orchestra. A string quartet is a sonata for four stringed instruments. Sonata form was also used for movements other than the first. Sometimes it was used two or three times in the same work. All four movements of Beethoven's great Seventh String Quartet are in sonata form.

Sonata form has been used as a model by

almost every composer since the 18th century. It represents the most important and characteristic heritage of the classical age in music. It is one of the great achievements of man's genius for organization.

Minuet-Trio, Theme and Variations, and Rondo

In addition to sonata form, other classical forms included the minuet-trio, the theme-and-variations form, and the rondo. The minuet-trio came from the ballroom, court ballet, and the opera. It is in a three-part, or A–B–A, form. The minuet is a short piece, the trio another. After they are both played, the minuet is repeated, thus completing the piece. The theme-and-variations form consists of a theme, or melody, followed by a series of variations on the theme. Each variation is a repeat of the theme but with some aspect of the music changed. In a rondo the main melody alternates with a number of contrasting sections, or episodes. The chief feature of a rondo is the constant return of the first melody.

All these forms show endless possibilities for contrast and variety. A true understanding of them is possible only through an acquaintance with the music itself. Here are easily available examples of each form:

Sonata form:	Mozart: Symphony No. 40 in G minor (K. 550), first, second, and fourth movements.
	Beethoven: Piano Sonata No. 1 in F minor, Opus 2, No. 1, first and fourth movements.
Minuet-trio:	Mozart: Piano Sonata No. 11 in A major (K. 331), second movement.
	Mozart: String Quartet No. 14 in G major (K. 387), second movement.
Rondo:	Beethoven: Two rondos for piano, Opus 51.
	Beethoven: Piano Sonata No. 8 in C minor, Opus 13 (*Pathétique*), third movement.
Theme and variations:	Haydn: Symphony No. 94 in G major (*Surprise*), second movement.
	Schubert: String Quartet No. 14 in D minor (*Death and the Maiden*), second movement.

OPERA IN THE CLASSICAL AGE

Long before the classical age people had begun to tire of the old-style opera. It was thought to be too artificial. The stories were not lifelike and were often rather silly and complicated. The music and the action did not blend well. The dissatisfaction with this kind of opera came to a climax at the beginning of the classical age.

Christoph Willibald Gluck (1714–87) decided to reform the opera. He began his reforms with *Orpheus and Eurydice* (1762). Gluck gave the opera nobility and dramatic life. He made the music closely follow the action of the story. The music is simple and natural. The singers seem like real people with real feelings and passions. All these qualities are found in the great operas by Gluck, which include *Alceste* (1767), *Iphigenia in Aulis* (1774), and *Iphigenia in Tauris* (1779). Gluck's reforms attracted worldwide attention and strongly influenced opera composers who came after him.

The development of *opera buffa,* or comic opera, contributed to operatic reform. *Opera buffa* used contemporary stories and characters that came alive on the stage. The increasing use of native languages in opera also aided the reform. Most earlier operas were sung in Italian.

Hundreds of operas were written in the classical age. Those by Mozart are most characteristic of the period. *The Marriage of Figaro, Don Giovanni, Così fan tutte,* and *The Magic Flute* are Mozart's finest and most famous operas. The first three have Italian texts, and the stories contain strong comic elements. *The Magic Flute* is in German and also features broad comic scenes. All four operas made biting comments on the weaknesses and ideals of the people in the audience.

After Mozart, opera began to lose some of its classical qualities. Some of the characteristics of later Italian opera appear in the operas of Domenico Cimarosa (1749–1801) and Gioacchino Rossini (1792–1868). During the Revolutionary and Napoleonic eras, French opera was represented by the works of André Grétry (1741–1813) and Luigi Cherubini (1760–1842). Beethoven's only opera, *Fidelio* (1805), is a unique masterpiece. It has a German text with spoken dialogue. Carl Maria von Weber (1786–

1826) wrote three important operas during the classical age. But his *Der Freischütz* (1821), *Euryanthe* (1823), and *Oberon* (1826) already showed characteristics of the music of the following period.

▶ THE LIED

One of the important developments in the classical age was the appearance in Germany and Austria of the lied. A lied is a song with piano accompaniment that reflects the meaning and feeling of the poem being sung. The expressive capabilities of the piano made it well suited for this type of song. The flowering of the short lyrical poem in German literature at the time aided the development of the lied. Franz Schubert was the greatest composer of this kind of song. He inspired a succession of great song composers that flourished until late in the 19th century. A great number of Schubert's songs are classical examples of the lied. However, they expressed some of the musical ideals of the period that followed.

▶ THE VIENNESE CLASSICAL COMPOSERS

Haydn, Mozart, Beethoven, and Schubert were the greatest composers of the classical era. Mozart was a pupil of Haydn's brother and a friend of Haydn himself. Beethoven went to Vienna to study with Mozart. He played for him, but was then called back to Bonn by his mother's illness and death. When Beethoven returned to Vienna, Mozart was dead, so he took lessons from Haydn. Schubert spent his life in Vienna, where Beethoven lived. He served as a torchbearer at Beethoven's funeral. By Beethoven's and Schubert's time, Vienna had become the center of the musical world. Vienna was the city in which all four of these composers worked. Thus, they are often called the Viennese classical composers.

These four great men were surrounded by hundreds of active but lesser composers. The orchestra at Mannheim, Germany, was a laboratory for experimenting with the symphony. The composers in Mannheim helped to lay the foundations for the works of Haydn and Mozart. Johann Stamitz (1717–57), his two sons, and his pupil Christian Cannabich (1731–98) spread the fame of Mannheim all over Europe. At least two sons of the great Bach, Karl Philipp Emanuel and Johann Christian (1735–82), were important composers. Their music for keyboard had a strong influence on the piano music of both Haydn and Mozart.

Haydn is often called the father of the string quartet and the symphony. His 83 string quartets and at least 104 symphonies make him the great originator of all such music.

In his short life Mozart composed well over 600 works. With this great genius the classical period reached its highest perfection. Mozart's later operas, the *Requiem,* the last 10 string quartets, several quintets, many of the piano concertos, and at least the last four symphonies are among the great treasures of our culture.

Beethoven began in the classical tradition. He mastered all the technical and formal elements of the music of Haydn and Mozart. But in Beethoven's hands classical music began to show some of the characteristics of a later musical style.

With Beethoven the development of the piano sonata reached its highest point. His 32 sonatas showed new possibilities for the piano. The length and difficulty of the later sonatas set a new standard for this form. Beethoven also enlarged the symphony and made it express his own personality. His 16 string quartets are the core of chamber music literature.

Franz Schubert was one of music's greatest melodists. Much of his music seems to have been directly inspired by poetry. Many of his songs are masterpieces of extraordinary beauty. Most of Schubert's great instrumental music received very little attention during his short lifetime. The music lovers of Vienna appreciated Beethoven, but they did not recognize the masterpieces that came from Schubert's pen: the Ninth Symphony, the string quartets, the String Quintet in C, the Piano Trio in B flat, and many others. They were composed in the classical forms. But, like Beethoven's music, they already showed some of the characteristics of the music of the romantic age, the period that followed the classical.

THEODORE M. FINNEY
University of Pittsburgh

See also ROMANTIC AGE IN MUSIC.

CLASSICAL ART. See GREEK ART AND ARCHITECTURE; ROMAN ART AND ARCHITECTURE.

CLASSICS IN LITERATURE

Very often, in school and out, you will hear well-read people refer to "the classics." If you ask them what they mean, it may take them a long time to explain. Actually, they mean a great many things. What they call a classic is a piece of writing that has unusual value and is expected to last for a long time. It is a book that scholars would name if they were asked to list the best books. It is a book that is sometimes studied in school but much more often read willingly outside school by people who love to read and have excellent taste. It can be any kind of book—a novel, like *Anna Karenina;* a book of ideas, like Sir Thomas More's *Utopia;* a collection of poems, like those of Tennyson; a play by Shakespeare or Molière; or a children's book, like *Alice in Wonderland*. It can come from any time in man's history, like the great epic of Homer, the *Iliad,* or the essays of Charles Lamb. It can come from any part of the world, like the Bible, written in Palestine and Rome and the cities of the Near East, or the poems of Po Chü-i, written in China. There is only one thing that all classics have in common, and that is that they are believed to be of the highest class, as their name implies.

Literary opinions do not, of course, remain the same from one generation to another. It is hard for us to believe that in the 1700's Shakespeare was somewhat out of fashion, or that some critics had great enthusiasm and high praise for a book like *Uncle Tom's Cabin,* which we look at now as a kind of period piece. Yet, even though classics go off the list and sometimes come back onto it again, the list in general remains fairly stable. Most of the books considered classics a hundred years ago are still classics today.

Classics are by no means ancient books. Some have been written and recognized as classics during the last 50 years. The poems of Robert Frost, for instance, are generally considered worthy to go on the list, and so are the best works of Faulkner and Hemingway.

The first list of classics was compiled by monks and other scholars of the Middle Ages. At that time people were more intensely concerned with religion than they are today, and Latin reading matter was divided into two kinds: sacred reading, which meant the Bible and sermons and other writings of the great religious teachers, and classical literature, the worldly writings that had come down from the Greeks and Romans. There was a long argument in the Church as to whether classics, in this sense of the word, should be read at all. Greek and Roman classics had a great deal in them about pagan gods and heroes, and the Church repeatedly tried to ban such writings or at least to keep the monks from growing so fond of them that the pagan spirit drove out the Christian one. "Dye your wool once in that purple," Saint Jerome had said, "and it will never be white." He meant that once you have steeped your mind in the rich and colorful literature of the ancient world, you will never be free from its influence again.

But later, during the Renaissance, all opposition to the Greek and Roman classics was dropped. Luckily for us, they became a part of our reading heritage.

The printing press was invented, books became more plentiful, and people read everything they could get from the ancient world. There was a great increase in the number of classics available in Europe when the Turks took Constantinople (Istanbul) in 1453. It was the city where Greek and Roman literature had chiefly been preserved, and when the scholars of Constantinople fled to Europe, they took their books with them and made many translations. In that way much of what had been written in ancient Greece and Rome became part of the delight and learning of Europe and, through Europe, passed on to us.

But it must be repeated that classics are not all ancient books. A book being written in your own town at this very moment may become a classic. Classics have deep and fascinating things to say. They are always exciting if we give them our careful attention.

In a word, then, a classic is a piece of writing of any sort, written anywhere, made popular by any means, that captures people's imaginations and promises to last because it includes the best that writing can offer: excitement, knowledge, a deeper insight into human life, a richer picture of the world.

GLADYS SCHMITT
Author, *David the King*
The Heroic Deeds of Beowulf

CLASSIFICATION OF LIVING THINGS. See TAXONOMY.

CLAY, HENRY (1777–1852)

Henry Clay was one of America's great statesmen during the troubled years before the Civil War. He was born on April 12, 1777, on a frontier farm in Virginia. His father, a minister, died when Henry was 4, and the boy received only a few years of formal schooling. At the age of 15, Clay found work as a clerk in a Richmond court. He studied law in his spare time and became a lawyer in 1797.

Attracted by the opportunities of the west, the 20-year-old Clay moved to Kentucky. The tall, gangling young lawyer was popular and a skillful orator. He soon became one of the best-known lawyers in the state and in 1803 was elected to the Kentucky legislature. Debates there were often heated. One time a dispute became so violent that Clay challenged his opponent to a duel. Both were wounded.

Clay first entered the United States Senate in 1806 to fill a 1-year unexpired term. (He was to spend a total of 19 years in the Senate during his career.) He was not yet 30 years old, the required age for senators. In spite of this, the new member was allowed to take his seat.

In 1811 Clay was elected to the House of Representatives. On his first day he was chosen Speaker of the House. In this important position Clay became leader of a group of young congressmen called the war hawks. The United States and Great Britain were then quarreling over American naval rights. The war hawks urged President James Madison to declare war. But the War of 1812 was not the success they had expected. Clay was one of the commissioners sent to sign the Treaty of Ghent in 1814.

With the coming of peace, the United States began to grow. In Congress Clay developed what he called his American System. He urged federal aid in building roads and canals to link different parts of the country. He favored a national bank. And to protect the new industries of the North, he proposed a high tariff, or tax on imports.

Clay's lifelong ambition was to be elected president of the United States. He ran for the presidency three times. In 1824 both Andrew Jackson and John Quincy Adams received more votes than Clay. But since neither Jackson nor Adams received a majority of the

Henry Clay—the Great Compromiser.

electoral votes, the election was decided by the House of Representatives. Clay, now out of the contest, gave his support to Adams. When Adams was elected, he appointed Clay secretary of state. Jackson unjustly accused Clay of making a dishonest bargain with Adams. In 1832 Clay ran against Jackson and was defeated again. In 1844 he lost to James K. Polk. When told that one of his speeches had hurt his chances for the presidency, he replied: "I would rather be right than be president."

As the United States grew, sectional quarrels became more intense. The question of slavery and the problem of the tariff separated North and South. Clay, though a slaveowner himself, favored freedom for the slaves. But he was determined, above all, to preserve the Union. He said: "I know no North, no South, no East, no West . . . ." In 1820 he helped pass the Missouri Compromise, which admitted Missouri into the Union as a slave state so that Maine could enter as a free state. In 1832 South Carolina threatened to secede because of a tariff that it considered unjust—the "Tariff of Abominations.' Clay, then in the Senate, proposed a compromise tariff that prevented war.

In 1850 Clay, now old and ill, was once again able to prevent the United States from splitting into two armed camps. The Compromise of 1850 was his greatest achievement. Two years later, on June 29, 1852, he died, mourned by the whole nation as the Great Compromiser.

Reviewed by RICHARD B. MORRIS
Columbia University

See also COMPROMISE OF 1850; MISSOURI COMPROMISE; WAR OF 1812.

CLAY MODELING

Almost everyone has handled modeling clay at one time or another. One kind of clay, often called plasticine, contains oil. Therefore it will not harden and can be used over and over again. Squeeze a lump of clay with your hands, and make any shape or form you wish. Your imagination is the only limit to the objects you create.

An animal, a human figure, a mask, a puppet, a toy—anything can be made in clay. You can work at home, at school, at camp, indoors or outdoors.

If you make things that resemble objects in real life, you are doing realistic clay modeling. If you create something weird or fantastic, the result may be surrealistic. If you make geometric figures using curves and blocks, you are modeling abstract designs. It is always more fun to make something original than to copy another's work.

Modeling clay that will not harden usually comes in pound packages. Buy it in an art supply store or department store. This clay is indestructible. You can cut it, twist it, bend it, tear it, squeeze it, make a mistake and repair it. You may take pieces off and add pieces time and time again.

The simplest way to model a figure is to roll the clay in your hands into simple shapes. An egg shape can be the body; a ball of clay, the head; cigar shapes, the arms and legs. But if you want to model a figure showing action, you must have a framework to support the

clay. This framework is called an armature. It can be made of bell wire or coat-hanger wire. Twist the wire into a simple skeletal form. Staple the feet to a board so the armature will stand up. Now you are ready to add clay in small pieces to build up the figure. In making the figure, break off pieces of clay from the big lump and squeeze the pieces onto the armature.

Make a rough figure at first. Then by using your fingers, smooth and shape the form so that you can get some action into it and the object begins to assume some recognizable form.

To put in details, you will need some simple tools. A large paper clip, opened up and fastened to a pencil with scotch tape, makes a good tool for getting into corners. Of course you can use a small kitchen knife for cutting clay, or a small flat stick like a tongue depressor to cut and scrape the clay.

Would you like to make a mask? Cover the table with a sheet or plastic cloth or aluminum foil to keep the clay from soiling the table surface. Use a small, shallow, round pan or dish as the base of your mask. Turn it upside down on the table and cover the pan with a thin layer of clay so that it begins to take the shape of a face. Add small lumps for the eyes, nose, mouth, ears, and cheekbones. Use your simple tools to carve out the features. The tools will enable you to get into corners too small for your fingers.

If you want your mask to be a permanent decoration, you will need to make a cast. The simplest cast is made of papier-mâché.

Cover the clay mask with small, overlapping strips of paper that have been soaked in water. Smooth each piece with a brush dipped in library paste. First apply a layer of newspaper strips, then a layer of brown bag-paper strips. Alternate the layers until you have covered the mask six times.

After several days the paper will be thoroughly dry. Remove the cast from the clay model. Trim the mask with scissors and finish the edges with another layer of wet brown paper and paste. When dry, your mask will be light, firm, and strong. Paint it with brightly colored poster paints to suit your imagination.

Objects made of modeling clay are soft and not permanent. If you want to make something permanent, you must use self-hardening clay. Once you have formed your object with this type of clay, you can let it dry naturally or place it in an oven to harden more rapidly.

You model with this clay as you would with plasticine. But you must be careful to keep the clay moist so that it will not dry before you finish. Cover your clay model with a wet cloth when you are not working on it. Place the unused clay in a tightly covered tin can. This keeps the moisture in the clay from evaporating. If you do this, you can work on your object for days. Once it is finished and dried, you will have a permanent clay model. This can be decorated with special paints designed for use on self-hardening clay. With care your clay figure can last a long time.

SENECA FURMAN
Art Chairman, Board of Education
City of New York

See also PAPIER-MACHÉ.

CLEMENCEAU, GEORGES (1841–1929)

Georges Clemenceau was premier of France during the worst days of World War I. His fighting spirit and fierce manner earned him the nickname "The Tiger."

Clemenceau was born at Mouilleron-en-Pareds, Vendée, France, on September 28, 1841. He studied medicine, but his main interests were journalism and politics. In 1865 he visited the United States, where he spent 4 years writing, traveling, and teaching. He married an American girl, Mary Plummer.

When Clemenceau returned to France, he was elected mayor of the Montmartre district of Paris. In 1876 he was elected to the Chamber of Deputies. For years Clemenceau led the Radicals. He stood for strong democratic government and separation of church and state. But he did not win high office, because he was too independent. Instead he fought for his ideas as a newspaper editor and publisher.

Finally in 1906 Clemenceau was appointed minister of the interior. He became premier that same year but resigned in 1909.

When World War I broke out in 1914, Clemenceau urged an all-out war effort. In 1917 he became both premier and minister of war. He visited soldiers at the front to encourage them, and he roused the war-weary French people to fight on. After the war was won in 1918, he helped write the Versailles Peace Treaty. Clemenceau left office in 1920 and made a second tour of the United States. He died in Paris on November 24, 1929.

CLEVELAND

Cleveland has come a long way since its day as a frontier outpost in the Western Reserve (the name given to Connecticut's lands in the Ohio country). Cleveland has grown into Ohio's largest city, one of the nation's most important industrial centers, and a major port on the southern shore of Lake Erie. It is the center of a metropolitan area of approximately 2,000,000 people.

In 1796, Moses Cleaveland surveyed the lakeshore at the mouth of the Cuyahoga River and drew plans for a town. A village, named for him, slowly grew at the site. By 1820, Cleaveland (the name later became Cleveland through a spelling error) had only about 600 settlers.

The city today would astound Moses Cleaveland. Public buildings rise along a mall that extends from Lake Erie to the downtown area. Public Square, where the major avenues meet, is dominated by the 52-story Terminal Tower. Nearby is the Erieview urban renewal project. Recently a justice center and office towers for the state government and private business have been built, and a number of older buildings have been renovated.

Location was the key to Cleveland's growth. In 1825 the city was chosen as the Great Lakes terminus of the Ohio and Erie Canal. It became a shipping headquarters and attracted many businesses. One of the world's major oil companies, the Standard Oil Company, was founded there in 1870 by John D. Rockefeller.

Cleveland remained an important shipping point. Today more iron ore is brought to Cleveland than to any other port on the lower Great Lakes. Limestone, sulfur, wood pulp, bauxite, and coal also pass through its docks.

Cleveland is a major steel manufacturing center and one of the largest producers of automobile parts in the United States. Its factories also produce machine tools, precision machinery, aircraft parts, plastics, paints, and other items.

But Cleveland is more than an industrial city. Its well-known educational institutions include Case Western Reserve University and Cleveland State University. The Cleveland Museum of Art, the Cleveland Health Museum, and the Salvadore Dali Museum are major cultural attractions. The world-famous Cleveland Orchestra performs in Severance Hall at the University Circle cultural center. For sports enthusiasts, Cleveland has professional teams in baseball, football, basketball, and hockey. Lake Erie and the many parks in and around the city provide Cleveland's residents with fine recreational opportunities.

JOHN H. LATHE, JR.
President, Greater Cleveland Growth Association
See also OHIO.

An aerial view of downtown Cleveland.

GROVER CLEVELAND (1837–1908)

22ND AND 24TH PRESIDENT OF THE UNITED STATES

CLEVELAND, STEPHEN GROVER. Grover Cleveland was one man, but he is counted as two presidents. In 1884 Cleveland was elected the 22nd president. He ran again in 1888 but lost to Benjamin Harrison, who became the 23rd president. However, in 1892 Cleveland came back and beat Harrison. Then came the question, "Was Cleveland the 24th president, or was he still the 22nd?" The State Department answered that he was both. That is why Lyndon B. Johnson, who became president after the assassination of President John F. Kennedy in 1963, is the 36th president, although only 34 men had held the office before him.

▶ **EARLY LIFE**

Stephen Grover Cleveland was born on March 18, 1837, in Caldwell, New Jersey. He was the fifth of nine children. His father, the Reverend Richard Falley Cleveland, was minister of the Presbyterian church in Caldwell. When Grover was 4, the family moved to Fayetteville, New York. Here Cleveland lived until he was 13, so it was the first home that he remembered clearly.

Though he was named Stephen Grover, he was always called Grover. He was chubby and round-faced, with blue eyes and sandy hair. By the time he was 13, "Grove" could out-swim and out-wrestle most of the other boys of his age. At Green Lake, near Fayetteville, he learned to fish, and that remained his favorite sport all his life.

Until he was 11 Grover attended school in a one-room, one-teacher schoolhouse. However, in 1850 the family moved to Clinton, New York, where Grover attended the Liberal Institute (a sort of high school). He was a good student, but more because he worked hard than because he was unusually bright.

Grover Cleveland was not very different from millions of other American schoolboys. As a minister's son he had to do more churchgoing than most. But like most boys, he sometimes got into mischief. There are stories about Grover's rigging up a device to ring the school bell at midnight, and helping to carry off garden gates on Halloween.

The Clevelands had a large family but not very much money. So when he was 14, Grover went to work as a clerk in a store at Fayetteville at a salary of $50 a year. Here he learned something about bookkeeping, and here, too, his true character began to

WHEN GROVER CLEVELAND WAS PRESIDENT
The Kodak box camera was developed by George Eastman in 1888. The Statue of Liberty was dedicated in 1886 by President Cleveland. The first electric trolley cars were placed in commercial service in Baltimore, Md., in 1885. Gold was discovered in the Klondike in Alaska in 1896. Henry Ford's first automobile appeared in 1896 in Detroit, Michigan. Cleveland's birthplace was in Caldwell, N.J.

Photograph of President Grover Cleveland.

Frances Folsom Cleveland, the President's wife.

show. The clerks in the Fayetteville stores often entertained each other at ham-and-eggs suppers by filching the refreshments from the stores. Cleveland refused to attend any party unless everything was paid for. This made enemies of some of the clerks. But it was the only honest thing to do, and he was brave enough to do it.

▶ HIS FATHER DIES

In 1853, when Grover was 16, his father died suddenly. Grover had hoped to go to college to study law, but now, with four young children for Mrs. Cleveland to take care of, there was no money for college. One of his older brothers was a teacher at a school for the blind in New York City, and Grover got a job there as an assistant instructor. But after a year in the school, he made up his mind to go someplace where a young man's chances were better. He decided on the city of Cleveland, Ohio.

On the way he stopped to visit an uncle who had a fine herd of dairy cattle near Buffalo, New York. His uncle made Grover an offer. If he would stay and help him, he would pay Grover $50 and would also try to find him a permanent job as clerk in a lawyer's office. Cleveland accepted the offer, and his real career began in Buffalo.

▶ LAW AND POLITICS

At that time there were few regular law schools. Most young men gained their training for the bar by working as clerks for lawyers and studying law in their offices. Cleveland worked and studied hard. Less than 10 years after he came to Buffalo, he had not only been admitted to the bar but had also been made assistant district attorney for Erie County.

Cleveland's record of honesty and fairness in the district attorney's office led to his election as sheriff of Erie County. And in 1881, when the city government had become so corrupt that it disgusted many voters, the Democrats nominated Cleveland for mayor. As mayor he threw out the dishonest politicians and their friends and broke up their deals ruthlessly. This made Cleveland many enemies, but honest men liked him.

Then in 1882 the reform Democrats nominated the young mayor of Buffalo for governor of New York, and he was elected. As governor, Cleveland followed the same course of strict honesty and was hated equally by dishonest Democrats and dishonest Republicans.

Cleveland was the perfect presidential candidate for the Democrats in 1884. In that year the country was rocked by scandals in

Washington, and the Republican candidate, James G. Blaine, had been involved in some of them. The Democrats had not elected a president since James Buchanan in 1856. It was plainly good politics for them to name a man famous for his honesty. The speaker who seconded Cleveland's nomination explained, "We love him most for the enemies he has made."

The campaign was dirty. The Democrats tried to prove that Blaine was a thief, which he was not. And the Republicans, since they could not attack Cleveland's honesty, tried to prove that he was immoral and a Confederate sympathizer. But many reform Republicans, called Mugwumps, disliked Blaine. They deserted their party and supported Cleveland. Near the end of the campaign, one of Blaine's friends called the Democrats the party of "Rum, Romanism and Rebellion." This so offended the Irish Catholics in New York that many of them voted for Cleveland. By carrying New York he won a majority of the electoral votes, though he beat Blaine by only a small number of popular votes.

▶ HIS FIRST TERM

In winning the presidency Cleveland also won a great deal of trouble. The Democrats had elected a majority in the House of Representatives. But the Senate remained Republican, and was not inclined to do anything that would help a Democratic president. More than that, after 24 years out of office the Democrats naturally wanted to put their own men in every federal job. Some of

---

IMPORTANT DATES IN THE LIFE OF GROVER CLEVELAND

1837	Born at Caldwell, New Jersey, March 18.
1855	Arrived in Buffalo, New York.
1859	Admitted to the bar.
1863–1865	Assistant district attorney for Erie County, New York.
1871–1873	Sheriff of Erie County.
1882	Elected mayor of Buffalo.
1883–1885	Governor of New York.
1885–1889	22nd president of the United States. (Defeated for re-election in 1888 by Benjamin Harrison.)
1893–1897	24th president of the United States.
1908	Died at Princeton, New Jersey, June 24.

---

the party leaders recommended men who were useful to them but not fit for the job. Cleveland refused to appoint such men, which made the leaders furious.

One of the most difficult issues that faced Cleveland was the long-unsolved problem of the tariff (the tax on goods imported into the United States). The high tariff was causing an unhealthy surplus of money in the treasury as well as high prices on some products. Though Cleveland asked Congress to reduce the tariff, the tariff bill that resulted was a failure.

Another problem was the flood of pension bills for Union veterans of the Civil War that Congress sent to the President for his signature. Many of the pension claims were false. Although it angered the veterans, Cleveland vetoed many of the bills.

The one bit of really good fortune that came to Cleveland during this term was his marriage, on June 2, 1886, to Frances Folsom, daughter of one of his former law partners. The wedding ceremony was performed in the White House, the only time a president has been married there.

▶ HARRISON DEFEATS HIM

In the election of 1888 the Republicans nominated Benjamin Harrison, a grandson of President William Henry Harrison. Cleveland seemed likely to win. But just before the election, the British minister in Washington, D.C., made the mistake of writing a letter stating that the British government hoped to see Cleveland re-elected. This was regarded as foreign interference in American affairs. It so infuriated many anti-British people that Cleveland lost New York and with it the electoral vote, even though he got 95,000 more popular votes than Harrison.

Cleveland retired to New York, where he spent 4 years contentedly practicing law and going fishing with friends. He would have been satisfied to stay there the rest of his life, but the party needed him. Harrison got into trouble with Republican leaders. And by 1892 it was fairly plain that Cleveland, but probably no other Democrat, could beat him. So Cleveland was nominated for the presidency again. This time he received over 350,000 more votes than Harrison and won easily.

IN DARKEST CONGRESS.

A cartoon showing Cleveland as a missionary, trying to convert congressmen ("Indians") to his policies.

▶ HIS SECOND TERM

Cleveland had hardly taken office when the great business panic of 1893 broke and was followed by a long depression. Cleveland called a special session of Congress and asked for repeal of the Sherman Silver Purchase Act of 1890. Under this act the government was required to buy a set amount of silver each month and coin it into money. This caused a drain on the gold supply in the treasury. Cleveland favored a "hard," or gold, currency and felt that silver money would cause wild inflation. The repeal of the Silver Purchase Act antagonized many western Democrats—silver mine owners and farmers who favored silver. It caused a split in the Democratic Party that was to lead to its defeat in the election of 1896.

There were other problems, too. During the campaign Cleveland had promised to lower the tariff. However, conservative Democrats combined with the Republicans to pass a tariff bill so bad that Cleveland called it "party perfidy and party dishonor." During a railroad strike in Chicago, Cleveland sent in federal soldiers, although the governor of Illinois said they were not needed. So the President was out of favor with his own party because of the silver question, the tariff, and his use of federal troops.

Problems in Hawaii and Latin America

During President Harrison's administration American sugar planters in Hawaii had staged a revolution against the native king. A treaty to annex the islands had been sent to the Senate. But Cleveland felt that the United States had taken advantage of a weak country and withdrew the treaty.

A revolution also broke out in Cuba, which was then a Spanish colony, and some Americans tried to help the Cubans. Since this was against international law, Cleveland stopped them.

A more serious dispute arose between Venezuela and Great Britain over the boundary of British Guiana. When Great Britain extended her claims into Venezuelan territory, Cleveland told the British that this was a violation of the Monroe Doctrine. He did so in such blunt terms that there was almost a declaration of war.

In each case Cleveland did what he believed was the honest thing, but in each case he angered some powerful group in his own party. So in 1896 the Democrats turned away from Cleveland and chose as their candidate William Jennings Bryan, who was defeated by Republican William McKinley.

Cleveland retired to Princeton, New Jersey, where he lived until his death on June 24, 1908.

For a time Cleveland was ignored by politicians and almost forgotten by the public. But as the years passed, men began to realize how often his decisions, though unpopular, were wise and right. Slowly it became clear that even when he was mistaken it was an honest mistake. He asked no favors. At the height of the panic of 1893, doctors told Cleveland that he had cancer of the mouth. He went secretly on board a ship, where an operation was performed. He had recovered and was back at work before the country learned that he had been ill.

Grover Cleveland was not one of the great presidents, but for courage, honesty, and patriotism he has never been surpassed.

GERALD W. JOHNSON
Author, *The Presidency*

CLIMATE

Climate is the total of weather in a region over a long period of time. The weather at a certain place may be cold and rainy on a particular day. But that place may have a warm, dry, sunny climate. This is because weather and climate are not the same. Weather comes from the temporary conditions in the atmosphere. Climate is the combination of temperature, moisture, wind, and sunshine at a place over a period of years. Scientists learn about the climate of a place by studying its weather from season to season and year to year. These scientists are called **climatologists.** The study of climate is known as **climatology.**

Temperature and precipitation (moisture that falls to the ground, such as rain or snow) are the two most important factors that determine the climate of a place. Others are humidity (moisture that stays in the air), cloudiness, fog, sunshine, wind, storms, and air pressure.

▶ CLIMATE AND PEOPLE

Climate influences people's comfort, well-being, and activities in many ways. Most people do not work as well in a hot, moist climate as in a cooler, drier climate. Extremely high or low temperatures are uncomfortable. Certain diseases are more common in some climates than in others. But it is difficult to determine what is the best or ideal climate for human beings. People differ in their reactions to climate. Those who have grown up in a tropical climate, for example, may feel cold if they move to the middle latitudes. Young people usually adjust more easily to a different climate than older people.

The amount and kind of clothing people wear is determined partly by climate. Clothing for cold climates gives protection against wind and cold. Less clothing is needed in warm climates. There are many types of special clothing for wind, cold, sun, rain, and snow.

People build houses mainly for shelter from the climatic elements. Carefully planned houses take advantage of sunlight, wind direction, and other factors to obtain a maximum of comfort as well as protection. The amount of heating or air conditioning needed in a building depends on the construction of the building as well as the outside climate. The local climate also helps to determine whether

The Micronesian family above lives in a thatched house on a coral atoll in the Pacific Ocean. The Eskimo (Inuit) family below lives in a tent pitched on the Arctic ice. One family is dressed for a warm climate, the other for a cold one. Can you see other ways in which climate influences how people live?

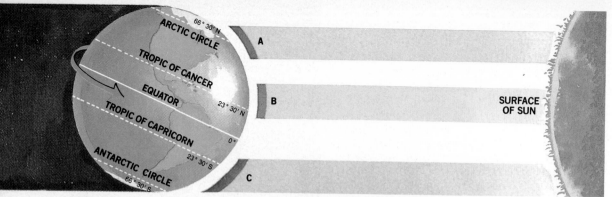

The sun's rays hit the earth most directly at the equator. Places near the equator are warm all year. The North and South Pole receive no sun at all for six months a year.

the sun and wind can be used to provide heat and power. Many modern inventions have made it possible for people to live and work comfortably in any kind of climate. Some huge buildings have their own indoor climates.

Climate affects the food supply by setting limits for gainful production of crops and animals. Wheat and potatoes grow well in cool areas, but bananas and sugarcane require warm, wet conditions. Climate influences cattle raising and forestry because it determines where grasslands and forests will grow.

Climate may also affect transportation. In the dense tropical rain forests, it is hard to build and maintain roads. Rivers are often the major highways. In polar climates, people often travel on skis and by sled or snowmobile.

▶ CAUSES OF DIFFERENT CLIMATES

What makes one place hot all year long while another place is cold, one place a desert and another a rain forest, one place sunny and another cloudy? The differences in climate from place to place are caused by **climatic controls.** The major climatic controls are latitude, altitude, land and water bodies, ocean currents, prevailing winds, pressure centers, and mountains.

Latitude

The main factor that determines the climate of any place is its distance from the equator. This distance is measured in degrees of latitude. At the equator (0 degrees latitude), the sun is never very far from being directly overhead at noon. The North Pole (90 degrees north latitude) and the South Pole (90 degrees south latitude) do not get any sunlight at all for six months of the year. Regions close to the equator remain warm throughout the year.

At high latitudes, far away from the equator, there are cold climates. In the middle latitudes, the sun is high in the sky in summer and low in winter. So in places like Portland, Maine (about 45 degrees north latitude), there are warm summers and cold winters.

Altitude

Altitude affects climate because temperatures decrease as the height above sea level increases. At high altitudes the air is less dense, and it does not absorb and hold as much heat. On the average, the temperature drops about 2 Celsius degrees for each 300 meters of altitude (about 3.5 Fahrenheit degrees for each 1,000 feet). Thus snow can stay on a mountain when nearby lowlands are warm.

Land and Water Bodies

Land warms up rapidly when the air is warm and cools off rapidly when the temperature drops. But large bodies of water change temperature more slowly. Islands and seacoasts usually have milder winters and cooler summers than mid-continental places because of the effect of water surfaces nearby.

Ocean Currents

Ocean currents are great streams of water moving in the oceans. Some currents carry warm water to cool regions. Others carry cool water to warm regions. These currents affect climate in many parts of the world. The Gulf Stream, for example, is a warm ocean current. It carries warm water from the tropical Atlantic toward the coasts of northwestern Europe. As a result, winters in western France are warmer than winters in the state of Maine in the United States, even though both are in about the same latitude.

Prevailing Winds

Winds affect climate because they carry heat and moisture. Winds that blow from the same direction most of the time are called prevailing winds. The southeastern United States has prevailing south winds (winds that blow from the south). These carry moisture and warm air from the Gulf of Mexico and help give the southeast a mild, moist climate.

In southern Asia, winds called **monsoons** change direction with the seasons. In the summer these winds blow from the ocean and bring heavy rains and cloudy skies. In the winter, when they shift around and blow from the land, the skies clear and temperatures fall. So southern Asia has two kinds of climate—rainy for half the year and dry for the other half—all because of the prevailing winds.

Pressure Centers

Pressure centers are large parts of the atmosphere where the pressure is much lower or much higher than in surrounding areas. Low pressure centers, or cyclones, usually cause stormy weather. High pressure centers usually bring clear, sunny weather. If low or high pressure centers tend to form over an area at certain times of the year, this weather pattern helps determine the climate of that area. Heavy rains in warm belts of low pressure near the equator create a tropical rain forest climate. Dense tropical forests grow well in this climate. High pressure centers are the primary cause of tropical desert climates like those of central Australia or the Sahara in northern Africa.

Mountain Barriers

Mountains form barriers that slow the movement of prevailing winds and air masses

Vegetation can tell a lot about climate. On a barren polar ice cap, temperatures are below freezing year round. Tropical rain forests like the one below are found in areas of high temperature and heavy rainfall.

Much of Utah has a cool desert climate because mountains block out rainfall. The mountains in the background remain snowcapped because of the effects of altitude.

and force them to rise. They also hold back large bodies of cold air. More rain falls on the **windward** side of mountains (the side against which the wind blows) than on the **leeward** side (the side protected from the wind). This is because air cools as it rises up the windward slopes of mountains. Water vapor in the cooled air condenses to form clouds and precipitation (rain or snow). A clear example is the two different climates on the mountainous island of Viti Levu in Fiji. The southeast side of the island gets most of the wind and rain. It looks like a storybook jungle, with palm trees, huge jungle ferns, and lots of shrubbery. The northwest side is protected from the winds by mountains. It has plenty of open fields, is rather dry, and looks a little like the coastal plain of California.

▶CHANGES IN CLIMATE

Climates have not remained constant throughout the history of the earth. From their study of rocks, fossils, and glaciers, scientists have discovered clues to climates of long ago. About 500,000,000 years ago, for example, the earth was warmer and wetter than it is now. But there also have been periods of geologic time that were drier and cooler. At different times in the past, thick sheets of ice spread over large parts of the continents. During one of these ice ages, a continental glacier reached as far south as the Missouri and Ohio rivers in what is now the United States.

Landforms and vegetation give other evidence of changing climates. By studying the sediments in river valleys or at the bottom of lakes, scientists learn about rainfall and temperatures in the past. Decayed plants in deep layers of soil tell what kinds of vegetation grew at a place at different times. The annual growth rings in trees make a record of years when conditions were different from the average. Tree rings usually are thicker in years with favorable growing seasons.

Written human history and ruins of past civilizations also help in the study of climatic

TYPES OF CLIMATE

There are many different types of climate on earth. Climates of the world can be classified according to their latitudes and the plants that grow there. Because different kinds of plants need different amounts of heat and moisture for growth, the vegetation of a region tells us about temperature and rainfall conditions over a long period of time.

Tropical Climates

Tropical climates are found in regions between 35 degrees north and 35 degrees south latitude. In a **tropical rain forest** climate (nearest the equator), conditions are warm and rainy all year long, and there is a thick cover of trees. Places farther north and south of the equator have a **tropical savanna** climate. There the forests are not so dense, and many trees lose their leaves in the dry season. Tall grasses and scattered trees grow in the **tropical savannas**, where the climate is too dry for forests. A **tropical steppe** climate is still drier and supports only short grasses. Along the tropics of Cancer and Capricorn, there are vast regions of **tropical desert** climate, where very little vegetation can grow.

Subtropical Climates

Subtropical climates are usually found between 30 and 40 degrees north and south latitude. The subtropical western coasts of the continents have a **Mediterranean** climate. Summers are hot and dry; winters are mild and wet. Scrub forests grow in this climate. On the subtropical eastern coasts of continents, the climate is **humid subtropical**. Summers are hot, and winters are mild. There is enough rainfall in all seasons for forests.

Mid-latitude Climates

Mid-latitude climates occur between 40 and 60 degrees north and south latitude. Prevailing westerly winds blow in the mid-latitudes. The west coast of North America has a **marine west coast** climate, which is mild and rainy most of the year. It helps the growth of fine timber forests. Some places in the mid-latitudes do not receive moisture because of mountain barriers or their distance from the oceans. Such places have **cool steppe** or **cool desert** climates. **Humid continental** climates cover large mid-latitude areas in eastern parts of the continents. They are forest climates with cold winters and warm summers. Most of the rainfall occurs in the summer.

High-latitude Climates

High-latitude climates occur from 60 degrees to the poles, north and south. In the high latitudes, temperatures are very low in winter and summers are cool. The **taiga** climate extends in a wide zone across northern Canada, northern Europe, and Siberia. North of the taiga is the **tundra**, where the climate is too cold for trees. Only grasses, mosses, and lichens can grow. Greenland and Antarctica have a **polar** climate, where great ice caps exist because of year-round temperatures below freezing.

High-altitude Climates

Highland climates are cooler than the climates of the surrounding lowlands because of the effects of altitude. Highland climates are found on the high mountains of the world, even on the equator. In the mid-latitudes and tropics, different kinds of vegetation grow in zones up the slopes of mountains to the permanent snowfields.

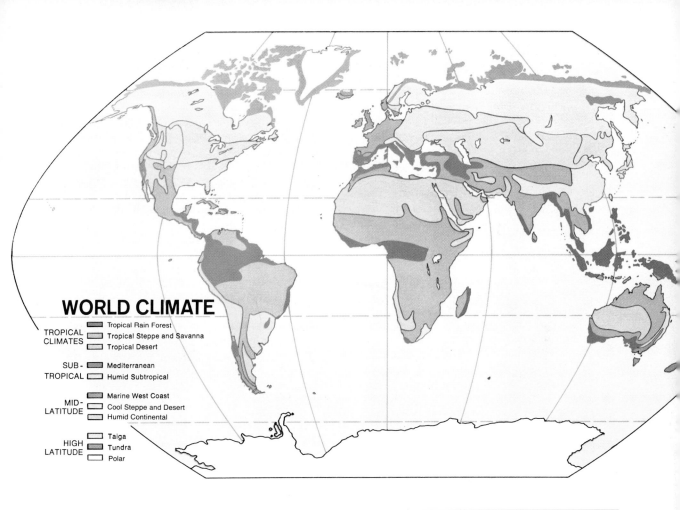

WORLD CLIMATE

TROPICAL CLIMATES
- Tropical Rain Forest
- Tropical Steppe and Savanna
- Tropical Desert

SUB-TROPICAL
- Mediterranean
- Humid Subtropical

MID-LATITUDE
- Marine West Coast
- Cool Steppe and Desert
- Humid Continental

HIGH LATITUDE
- Taiga
- Tundra
- Polar

changes over the past few thousand years. Colder or drier years may have caused people to move to lands with a better climate.

In this century, scientists have been keeping detailed records of actual weather observations. These records show small fluctuations in temperature, rainfall, and storminess. Average temperatures in the United States rose by 1 or 2 degrees between 1900 and 1950. But they fell again by about a degree between 1950 and 1970. Climatologists do not agree on whether the earth will cool or warm during the next century.

Many theories attempt to explain climatic changes. Among the possible causes are changes in the amount of energy put out by the sun, changes in the earth's orbit around the sun, or changes in the tilt of the earth on its axis. Some scientists believe that dark patches on the face of the sun, known as sunspots, cause cycles of drought over parts of the earth.

Dust and gases in the atmosphere can lower the amount of solar energy that reaches the

DISCOVERING MICROCLIMATES

The combinations of climatic elements in very small areas are called **microclimates**. Features of the land such as swamps, narrow valleys, or steep hillsides create their own miniature climates. Buildings and trees also can cause local differences in temperature, moisture, or wind. By observing conditions at several places around your home or school you may be able to discover some microclimates.

Here are some of the kinds of places to observe and compare:

A grassy lawn and a parking lot

The opposite sides of a wall or hedge

The surface of a small lake and the surrounding shore

The opposite sides of a city street

The top and bottom of a large plant leaf

Look for evidence of differences in sunshine, temperature, moisture, or the speed and direction of air movement. Can you think of reasons for the microclimatic differences? Can you find any other examples of microclimates?

earth's surface. They also influence the rate at which the earth loses heat to outer space. Volcanic eruptions like those of Mount St. Helens in the state of Washington in 1980 and El Chichón in Mexico in 1982 pushed ash and gases into the stratosphere. Some scientists believed that these clouds of volcanic dust might cause the temperature of the earth to drop slightly.

The burning of coal and oil in homes and factories produces carbon dioxide, water vapor, and smoke. Carbon dioxide traps part of the earth's heat that otherwise would be radiated beyond the atmosphere. This is known as the **greenhouse effect** because the carbon dioxide in the atmosphere acts somewhat like a very large glass greenhouse. An increase in the amount of carbon dioxide in the atmosphere could lead to global warming. Carbon monoxide, nitrous oxide, and ozone trap the sun's heat in a similar way. Methane is another gas that may cause the greenhouse effect. It is generated by the decay of organic matter in jungles, swamps, and farmlands.

Still other gases cause chemical changes in the makeup of the atmosphere.

Changes in the land and oceans are other possible causes of climatic change. Geologists have found evidence of shifts in the earth's crust. The movement of continents to different latitudes might explain why fossils of tropical plants are found at middle and high latitudes today. The building up and wearing down of mountains would change temperature, rainfall, and winds over large areas. A difference in the strength or direction of ocean currents could also be a factor in widespread changes of climate.

Several factors probably have acted together to change climates during the earth's history. Climatologists are still searching for complete explanations. If they can learn more about how climates change, people may be able to plan for climatic changes in the future.

HOWARD J. CRITCHFIELD
Western Washington University

See also WEATHER.

CLOCKS. See WATCHES AND CLOCKS.

CLOTHING

Like you, most people living in developed countries have a variety of clothes. Some clothes are for wet or snowy weather; others are for fair weather, warm or cold. Some are for school or work, others for play. Some are worn for swimming, others for sleeping, and so on.

What you wear and when you wear it often has as much to do with appearance as with usefulness. Even in ancient times, people wanted to improve their appearance. They put on animal skins and hung strings of beads and stones around their necks. Bark, leaves, straw, feathers, or whatever material was closest at hand was turned into clothing.

For ancient peoples, clothing also may have had magical qualities. Perhaps they believed that an animal skin worn during a hunt gave the hunter the animal's cunning. Perhaps wrapping oneself in a certain skin kept away evil spirits. By wearing the skins of powerful beasts, certain persons may have shown that they were group leaders or good hunters.

Judging by the tools used by prehistoric people more than 50,000 years ago, animal furs were first scraped. Then holes were pierced in the skins. Strips of leather or animal tendons were drawn through the holes to tie the pieces of fur together and to help keep them on the body. Red, yellow, and black mineral colorings found with the tools were probably used to apply decorative patterns to the skins.

Gradually, people learned to make the skins softer and more supple. A key tool for making clothes was the sewing needle, which was invented about 40,000 to 50,000 years ago. Like many other inventions, the sewing needle was independently discovered in widely scattered areas of the earth.

After people began to settle in communities, they learned how to weave. They discovered how to twist vines and, later, wool and animal hair together into long strands. The early Egyptians wove fabrics out of flax and cotton. Other ancient peoples spun wool into yarn for robes and tunics.

These early textiles unraveled easily. Therefore, for clothing, people draped pieces of fabric around their bodies instead of shaping

TRADITIONAL
NATIONAL COSTUMES

JAPANESE

ESKIMO

**DUTCH
(VOLENDAM)**

**NORWEGIAN
(HARDANGER)**

**GERMAN
(BAVARIAN)**

RUSSIAN

TURKISH

INDIAN

SWISS
(APPENZELL)

SCOTTISH

SPANISH
(ANDALUSIAN)

CZECHOSLOVAKIAN

the material by cutting it up. The more difficult job of putting separate pieces together by sewing was not necessary, as it was with furs. Instead, people experimented with different methods of draping material. Men and women on the islands in the South Seas wrapped long pieces of cloth around themselves, thus inventing the sarong. A Roman made a toga by winding a piece of material across the left shoulder. The burnoose worn by Arabs was a cloaklike garment with a hood, woven in one piece. It was designed to cover both the neck and shoulders. People also tried their skill at decorating. They embroidered geometric patterns and sewed precious objects on the material to make the draped folds more attractive.

In the colder climates, clothes covered all of the body as a protection against the elements. Because of cold weather, closer-fitting clothes were more typical. Trousers, tunics, and warm, protective cloaks came from these areas.

The weather usually influences the kind of clothes people wear, but there are exceptions. Charles Darwin discovered in the early 1830's that natives of Tierra del Fuego, at the tip of South America, wore no clothes in spite of the cold climate. Early travelers in the American West reported seeing Indians without a stitch on playing outdoor winter games. On the other hand, Arabs, in the midst of the desert heat, are a fully clothed people.

As communication improved between the sections of the globe, styles from different regions began to influence each other. The draped coverings of the southern areas were combined with the tailored clothes of the colder areas. The trousers found by Romans in northern Europe were thus gradually adopted farther south.

New materials and styles were discovered by the crusaders in the rich city of Constantinople. They brought back richly embroidered heavy silk and cotton materials. The jeweled and patterned Oriental gowns from this fabulous city influenced medieval and then Renaissance dress. Bit by bit, cutting and fitting became more of a skill, and clothes began to take on new shapes. The introduction of buttons and other fastening devices helped in the creation of new styles.

From the earliest days, different kinds of costumes were worn by different social groups. The clothes of the lower classes were looser and easier to work in. The dress of wealthier people emphasized the fact that they did no manual work. For instance, the Roman toga, looped over the left shoulder of a senator, left his right arm free for gestures. But his left arm was wrapped in so much fabric that it was almost useless to him. His slave, on the other hand, was dressed in a simple tunic that gave him full use of his arms.

Often the emphasis on richness of dress was made at the cost of comfort and convenience. Sometimes styles were designed to create an artificial shape of some part of the body. Padding at first simply gave extra warmth in the winter and protection during battle. During the 16th century, the Spanish turned padding into a mark of style. Arms, legs, and chests were puffed out by padding or by using stiff fabrics. Huge ruff collars held up by wires made it difficult for people to turn their heads. Women's skirts were made to stand out by fastening metal or whalebone hoops around the bottom of the hem. The most fashionable women wore heavy brocade dresses encrusted with pearls and other precious stones over several linen petticoats. A wide drum-shaped metal frame was fastened around the waist to exaggerate the hips even more. Men wore balloon-shaped trunks. Both men and women laced their waists so tightly it was painful.

The more amazing the style, the more people debated about whether or not it was proper. Early Christian writers during the first century A.D. criticized the vanity and folly of paying too much attention to cleanliness, style of clothes, and even changing clothes too often. Laws were passed during the days of the Roman Empire stating exactly what each class should wear. Purple togas were the exclusive right of emperors, generals, and magistrates. Ordinary free citizens had to wear plain white togas. Slaves were not allowed to wear togas at all.

Similar laws were passed by other rulers in later times. A statute passed in 1292 in the reign of the French King, Philippe le Bel, listed the number of garments as well as the kind of material allowed to each class. Ermine was limited to the nobility. Ordinary people were not allowed to wear it. Neither were they permitted to wear gold or precious stones.

Wives of the richer dukes, earls, and barons could have only four new dresses a year. Knights and their ladies had to get along with only two new robes per year. A limit was even placed on the value of fabrics out of which clothes were made. The poorer people could not spend more than 12 sous per yard, while the wives of barons were allowed to spend up to 25 sous per yard.

It was reported that Queen Elizabeth I had 3,000 dresses in her wardrobe. But she, too, passed laws about the material and style of clothes her subjects wore. Since velvet was a traditional sign of high rank, the middle class could put velvet facings only on their sleeves. Some of Elizabeth's laws were made to control outlandish styles by restricting the use of great ruff collars and by checking the use of elaborate designs on men's balloon-shaped trunks and long stockings. To help the wool trade in England, the Queen also encouraged her subjects to use fabrics made of English wool instead of imported materials.

By and large these laws were ineffective. In spite of the criticism of political and religious leaders, people continued to dress the way they wanted to.

The French Revolution had a great effect on clothing extravagance. The revolutionists adopted a simple costume as a sign that the influence of the aristocracy had really been destroyed. Since the king and his court had worn silk and velvet knee breeches called **culottes,** the patriots refused to wear them. Instead, they chose to wear long trousers (called pantaloons) and were called the **sans-culottes** ("without knee breeches").

The rise of democracy made men's clothes plainer everywhere, and they have remained so ever since. Women's clothes have also become simpler, although they change in fashion and style more often than men's.

Clothes Today

Present-day clothing designers take many of their ideas from the study of costumes through the ages. Chiffon evening gowns that fall in graceful pleats are adapted from the form of ancient Greek dress. Some women's coats, such as the coachman or chesterfield, are adaptations of coats worn by men in the last century.

People in the public eye influence styles, too. When Baron Raglan, a British officer, lost his arm at the battle of Waterloo, his tailor designed a special wide-type sleeve for him, setting it at the neckline instead of the armhole. The raglan sleeve has been in and out of fashion ever since.

Fabrics made entirely of natural fibers—cotton, wool, silk, or flax—have been used in making clothes for centuries. In this century, people have learned how to make synthetic fibers. By the mid-1960's, the development of permanent-press fabrics and polyester fiber caused clothing manufacturers to shift rapidly from fabrics made completely of natural fibers to blends of natural and synthetic fibers—and to 100-percent synthetic fabrics. Permanent-press fabrics need little or no ironing. Clothing made from synthetic fibers is crease-resistant and lightweight. And few synthetic fabrics shrink.

Fabrics made of natural fibers probably will never be totally replaced by synthetics. Many people prefer the comfort of natural fibers, which synthetic fibers have not yet achieved. And there have been developments that have improved the quality of natural fibers. For example, researchers have developed washable wool fiber and permanent-press cotton fabrics.

Because of the wide variety of fabrics and clothing, deciding what to wear can be a problem for people. But this is not always true. In many countries what a person wears for certain occasions is governed by tradition. Many people still wear national or traditional costumes to celebrate a special event or a holiday. Some of the most famous national costumes are those of the Dutch. The Dutch costume for men is blue, balloon-shaped trousers, a short jacket, and wooden shoes. The women wear striped full skirts, aprons, and high peaked caps. In Scotland, a wool skirt called a kilt is worn by both men and women. Each family's kilt is woven into a special plaid, or tartan, and no one outside the family is supposed to wear a kilt of that design. People in many provinces of France also wear distinctive costumes on special occasions. The Japanese sometimes wear loose ceremonial robes known as kimonos, which may be richly decorated with exquisite embroideries.

There are special clothes for some jobs, too—for example, soldiers' and sailors' uniforms. By looking at the uniform, you can tell the nationality, the rank, and the branch of service to which the wearer belongs. Other kinds of uniforms are worn by police officers, airline flight attendants, chefs, waiters, athletes, and so on. Some jobs require protective clothing, such as a fire fighter's asbestos suit, a detective's bulletproof vest, a construction worker's hard hat, or a doctor's sterile operating grown. Some clothing, such as a judge's robe, is a symbol of an office.

▶ THE CLOTHING INDUSTRY IN AMERICA

Around 1725, a woman in Northfield, Massachusetts, made shirts for the Indians. This is the first recorded case of ready-to-wear production in colonial America. Most garments, however, were made for the family by women in the households. On southern plantations clothing was made by slaves. Elsewhere the wealthier people eagerly awaited the arrival of traveling tailors with the latest fashion news.

Gradually tailors began to open shops in larger cities. Customers brought their own fabrics to be turned into fashionable coats and gowns. Soon cloth merchants began to provide a tailor service as well as material. Their customers bought fabrics in one section of the store and took them to another section to be made into clothes.

By the 1820's clothing manufacture was firmly on the way. This early start began with sailors whose stay in port was limited. They came from their ships with worn-out clothes on their backs and cash in their pockets for replacements. Ready-to-wear clothes could be bought first in the port town of Boston and then later in New York and Philadelphia. In 1849 people began to follow the gold rush to California. They needed clothes that could withstand the long trip and the wear and tear of mining, and they needed them at once. More and more shops selling ready-mades sprang up.

In 1849 about 43,000 establishments employed over 97,000 men and women to make men's and boys' wear. The factories were different from those we know today. They were really places where fabrics were cut, bundled, and handed out to workers. The sewing was done mostly by workers in their own homes.

The invention of the sewing machine revolutionized garment production. One of the earliest machines was patented by Elias Howe in 1846. Unfortunately, the machines were cumbersome to operate, and this slowed down their use in the factories. The worker had to crank the wheel with one hand to make it go. At the same time the material had to be guided with the other hand. The invention of the foot-treadle machine by Isaac M. Singer a few years later freed both hands of the operator for sewing. After further improvements, the treadle machine sewed 900 stitches a minute as compared with only 30 or 40 stitches by hand. Present-day machines powered by electricity can sew over 5,000 stitches a minute.

The first real test of the sewing machine came during the Civil War. Military uniforms were in great demand. However, hand sewers, working in factories or in their own homes, could not turn them out fast enough. Production increased when factories began to use sewing machines. Managers discovered that when each operator was given the same section to do repeatedly, even unskilled workers could sew faster.

With the rise in mass production, it was noticed that certain measurements came up over and over again. It became possible to work out a system of standard sizes and patterns for apparel. But it was many years before manufacturers could make ready-to-wear clothes that fit well.

The development of apparel manufacturing in the United States was influenced by the use of sweatshops. These establishments, usually small shops, were located in the poor sections of large Eastern cities. Manufacturers cut out the different parts of garments and sent them in bundles to these shops. In turn, these shops distributed the parts to people in the neighborhood, to be sewn in their homes. As time passed, more of the sewing was done in the shops themselves.

The name "sweatshop" tells us how hard this system was on the workers. People who worked in the shop had to bring their own machines, or else they had to rent them at the shop. They had to pay for the chairs they sat on, the thread they used, and the ice water they drank. Even children were caught in this system. Whole families had to work from early morning until far into the night just to earn enough to survive.

It took many years to do away with the evils of the sweatshops. Some work still is farmed out to homes, but laws have been passed to regulate and control work done at home. The labor unions—the International Ladies' Garment Workers' Union and the Amalgamated Clothing Workers of America—played a major role in the decline of these shops in the clothing industry.

THE CLOTHING INDUSTRY TODAY

From their very beginning, typical clothing factories were small. Plants employing several hundred workers exist, but the average clothing factory today employs fewer than 100 workers.

Three basic types of firms operate in this industry. Some are **manufacturers**. They purchase raw material and decide what kind of garments will be produced. The styles are designed and the fabric is cut and sewn in their own factories. The finished garments are then shipped to retailers.

Some firms are known as **jobbers**. Jobbers decide what styles they are going to produce. Then they send the specifications and the cut or uncut fabrics to contractors. **Contractors** produce the clothes and send them back to the jobbers for sale and shipment to retailers.

In the United States, New York City is the single most important area for clothing design and marketing. Manufacturing takes place there as well as in many other parts of the country. The United States, Canada, and Western Europe import much clothing from Asia, particularly from Hong Kong, Taiwan, and Korea. Other countries that are important in the production of apparel for export are the Philippines, Thailand, India, and China. In the Western Hemisphere, Mexico, Brazil, Haiti, and the Dominican Republic are expanding their exports of apparel.

Apparel manufacturers are not the only sources of clothing. Many people make their own clothes. In the United States, the home sewing market is very large. About 850,000,000 square meters (1,000,000,000 square yards) of fabric are sold over the counter each year. About half of this is used to make women's and children's clothing. Most of the rest is used for household furnishings.

HOW CLOTHING IS MADE

Factory production of clothing begins in the design rooms of the different firms. **Designers** work in advance of each season. They must try to guess correctly which colors and general shapes are going to be popular. Some designers produce only styles that will be sold at high prices. Other designers specialize in styles that can be made cheaply in large quantities for sale at popular prices.

Each designer works in an individual way. Some sketch their ideas on paper. Others work out their designs by draping and pinning material on a dressmaker's dummy. They must be familiar with different kinds of material in order to tell how their designs will look when those designs are made up in the fabric they select for final manufacture.

Sample makers are the work arm of the designers. They translate a designer's rough sketches or pinned-up models into actual garments to be produced. Like designers, sample makers are artists. They know where to place the seams and how to bring out the best lines of the design. The garments made by sample makers (called samples) are used to decide whether the particular sample will be put into production.

The samples chosen by store buyers have a long manufacturing journey ahead of them. First, they go to the **patternmakers**, who study each garment and prepare paper or fiberboard patterns for each section in a standard size. Then **pattern graders** work out different sizes by changing the dimensions of the original pattern. Patterns made by individuals are still used to make clothing, but today patterns are being produced by computers as well. Patterns for each garment in each size are printed on paper that can be placed directly over a pile of fabric and cut.

The cutting of fabric takes place in the **cutting room**. But before they are cut, fabrics are checked for defects. In the cutting room, fabrics are spread on long tables, many layers high. Skilled **cutters** place the pattern pieces on top of the piles of material so carefully that very little fabric is wasted. With computer-developed patterns, the cutter places a long sheet of paper (on which the patterns are drawn) over the layers of fabric.

The cutting of fabric is a highly skilled job. A cutter uses electrically powered cutting

ARMY

NAVY

AIR FORCE

MARINES

SOME UNITED STATES MILITARY UNIFORMS

MAIL CARRIER

DOCTOR

FIRE FIGHTER

COMMUNITY SERVICES

NURSE

POLICE OFFICER

A cutter carefully guides the electric knife along the pattern.

machines to cut through as many as 200 layers of fabric at one time. The cutter cuts exactly on the pattern outlines.

The job of cutting is also being taken over by computers. There are two methods of automatic cutting. One method uses a laser beam to cut the pieces of the pattern. The laser is guided by a computer. The other cutting method uses a long, very thin, pointed knife that can cut through as many as 100 layers. Although the knife moves up and down through the fabric at a very high speed, it moves slowly along the lines of the pattern, like the regular cutting machine. This high-speed knife is also guided by a computer.

After all the garment parts are cut out, they are gathered into bundles and taken to the sewing machines. The person who works at a sewing machine is called an **operator**. If a dress is going to be manufactured in very large quantities, each dress may be sewn by many operators. Several operators sew the different basic seams. Another operator may set in the sleeves. A different operator may attach collars or join bodice and skirt. If only a few copies of a dress are to be produced or if designs are complex,

one person can sew the complete dress more efficiently than a group could. This operator must be able to assemble the entire garment according to the detailed instructions that are provided.

The sewing room may utilize many different kinds of sewing machines. At first glance, many of them look alike. Actually, different machines are used to make varied types of stitches. Machines are also designed to do specialized work, such as sewing on buttons, loops, snaps, or labels.

Some sewing is done by hand. In this case, **finishers** may be called on to baste or to attach buttons, loops, or facings by hand, mostly on the more expensive clothes. These higher priced garments sometimes go through another adjustment. They are placed on dressmakers' dummies and are pinned by **drapers** to assure a better fit. Operators or finishers then sew the parts that have been pinned together.

The garment is now virtually complete. Loose threads and spots are removed by **cleaners** and **inspectors**. The garments are then ironed by **pressers**, either with hand irons or on pressing machines. Then they go to the

A garment worker measures pieces of fabric to be sure they have been cut correctly.

stockroom or shipping room to be sent to the stores to be sold to the retail customer.

▶ CAREERS IN THE CLOTHING INDUSTRY

Many of the industry's workers are trained directly on the job. But there are many vocational schools that teach designing, cutting, grading, patternmaking, and sewing machine operation. Workers must possess good eyesight, finger dexterity, and eye-hand-foot coordination. They must be able to work at a relatively steady pace. There are colleges that offer advanced training for technical, executive, and administrative positions in the garment industry.

The clothing industry is one of the most competitive industries in the world. Not much capital is needed to start a business. As a result, many new firms come into the industry each year. Many of them cannot last in the strong competition, but others take their place. The final success or failure of a firm is governed by how well it satisfies the customers.

Reviewed by CARL H. PRIESTLAND
American Apparel Manufacturers Association

See also FASHION; GLOVES; HATS AND HATMAKING; SEWING; SHOES; TEXTILES.

In a city's garment district, racks of clothes are rolled through the streets from warehouses to stores.

CLOUDS

Clouds have their beginning on the surface of the earth. Day and night, surface waters of oceans, lakes, and rivers evaporate. This means that the water changes from a liquid to a gas, called water vapor. Water vapor, which becomes one of the gases in the air, is the stuff necessary for cloud formation. But before clouds can form, two things must happen. The air hovering above the earth's surface must be cooled. And tiny particles of dust and other matter must mix with it.

▶HOW THE AIR IS COOLED

The air is cooled in two ways. One is by rising. The higher you go, the colder it gets, at least for the first 11 kilometers (7 miles) or so. For every 90 meters (300 feet) of altitude, the temperature drops 1.8 Celsius degrees (1 Fahrenheit degree). So when the temperature on the ground at sea level is 27°C (80°F), it will be about 17°C (63°F) at an altitude of 1,500 meters (5,000 feet). When air near the ground is heated, it expands and becomes lighter than the colder air around it. Because it is lighter, the heavier surrounding air forces it to rise. As the warm air rises into the colder regions of the atmosphere, it becomes cool. This type of cooling is called **adiabatic cooling.**

During the cooling process, something happens to the parcel of air—it "loses" some of its water vapor. This happens because cool air cannot hold as much water vapor as warm air. Let's see how this works.

Suppose that the air in a room is 21°C (70°F) and contains all the water vapor that it can at that temperature. The air is said to be **saturated.** No matter how hard we try, we cannot add more water vapor to the air so long as it remains at that temperature. This point is called the **dew point,** or **saturation temperature.**

If we lower the temperature, the air is forced to give up some of its water vapor. You have often seen this happen. When you take a hot bath, the warm air in the bathroom becomes laden with invisible water vapor that comes from the hot water in the tub. If you

Warm air, carrying water vapor, cools as it rises. Cool air can hold less water vapor than warm air. Some of the water vapor collects around dust particles or other material in the air and changes into tiny drops of water. These drops form clouds.

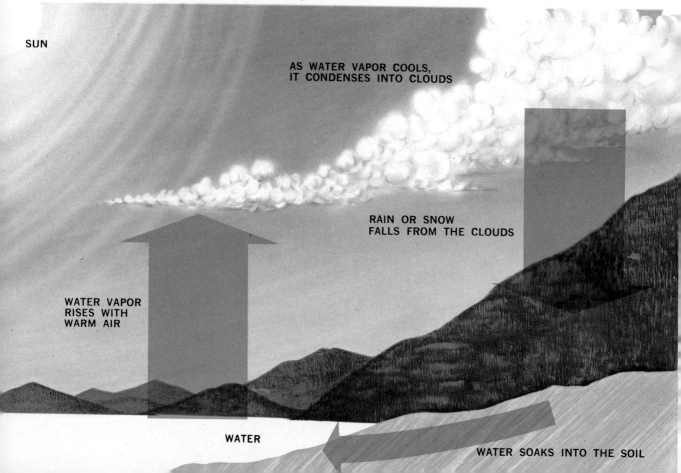

SUN

AS WATER VAPOR COOLS, IT CONDENSES INTO CLOUDS

RAIN OR SNOW FALLS FROM THE CLOUDS

WATER VAPOR RISES WITH WARM AIR

WATER

WATER SOAKS INTO THE SOIL

open a window and suddenly let cold air in, you lower the temperature, and the bathroom air is forced to give up some of its water vapor. What happens is that the invisible water vapor turns into visible water droplets and forms fog, or a cloud, in the bathroom. Drops of water also form on the walls and plumbing fixtures.

▶ HOW VAPOR CONDENSES

Like the air outside, the air in the bathroom contains billions upon billions of tiny dust particles. As the water vapor comes into contact with these particles, it collects around them and changes back into a liquid. This process is called **condensation.** Around each dust particle a tiny water droplet forms—in the shape of a sphere. It is these droplets, billions upon billions of them, that you see as the bathroom cloud.

Exactly the same thing happens when clouds are formed outdoors. Warm air laden with water vapor rises and cools. Its water vapor comes into contact with dust and other particles in the air. As this happens, the vapor condenses, and a droplet of liquid water forms around each tiny particle.

It has been estimated that 100,000,000 droplets may be needed to form one large raindrop. If this is so, it means that a typical cloud is made up of an enormous number of droplets. It would take more than a million million million droplets to make up a cloud 1 kilometer wide, 1 kilometer long, and 1 kilometer deep. Such a cloud may have about 800 tons of water in droplet (liquid) form and nearly 9,000 tons of water in water-vapor (gas) form.

The water vapor condenses into droplets around many kinds of particles. All such particles are called **condensation nuclei.** There are dust particles blown from deserts, dry topsoil, and volcanoes. There are tiny crystals of salt that have been sprayed into the air from the oceans. There are minute solid particles from the burning of soft coal and wood. And there are many other kinds of condensation nuclei.

▶ SUPERCOOLED CLOUDS AND ICE CRYSTAL CLOUDS

Some of the clouds we see on a cold winter day are made of supercooled water. This is water that does not turn to ice even though the temperature is below freezing. Water droplets have been known to stay in a liquid state in temperatures as low as −40°C (−40°F). The droplets making up supercooled clouds are formed in the same way as the droplets mentioned earlier. Exactly why these water droplets remain as water and do not freeze is not fully understood.

Thin, feathery clouds are sometimes seen very high in the atmosphere, where the temperature is well below freezing. These are made of ice crystals. Sometimes they are formed when droplets of supercooled water become so cold that they can no longer remain in the liquid state and turn into ice crystals. But these feathery clouds can also be formed in another way. Instead of turning into water droplets, the water vapor sometimes changes directly from a gas into a solid—ice crystals. This process is called **sublimation.** The ice crystals may remain suspended in the cloud by wind currents, or they may fall to the ground as snow. There is still much to learn about how snowflakes and ice-crystal clouds are formed. Special kind of nuclei, called sublimation nuclei, are needed. Although the best ones seem to be ice crystals themselves, tiny soil particles and certain particles produced by burning are known to work.

▶ CLOUDS FORM A HEAT BLANKET

The coldest winter days occur when there are no clouds in the sky. Why should this be so? The sun is constantly emitting many different kinds of radiation. Some of it we see as light. Some of it we feel as heat. And some of it (such as X rays and ultraviolet rays) we cannot sense at all.

If there is a cloud covering overhead, short-wave radiation from the sun penetrates the clouds and strikes the earth. The soil and ocean waters receive this radiation, are heated by it, and then radiate some of the heat back into the atmosphere. But this radiation is given back to the atmosphere in the form of long waves. They cannot penetrate up through the cloud layer. So they become trapped between the clouds and the ground. In this way, clouds act as a blanket, holding in heat. When the sky is cloudless, much more heat escapes.

TYPES OF CLOUDS

Nearly all clouds are found at altitudes of 1 to 11 kilometers (½ to 7 miles) above sea level. Sometimes clouds form on or near the ground. When they do, we call them fog.

Clouds take many different shapes. To the weather forecaster, their shapes are one clue to weather-in-the-making. Broadly speaking, there are three main forms of clouds—cumulus, stratus, and cirrus.

Cumulus. These clouds are fluffy and cauliflower-shaped, with broad, flat bases. Cumulus clouds usually form on top of rapidly rising currents of warm air and have sharp outlines. They resemble towers of cotton wool and move majestically across the sky in groups.

Stratus. In appearance these are perhaps the least interesting clouds. They can best be described as fog that has formed high above the ground. Usually they stretch across the sky in long, horizontal layers. Sometimes the layers are thick, while at other times they are thin. Unlike cumulus clouds, stratus clouds are a sign of a slow, large-scale rising of air.

Cirrus. These clouds are the "mares' tails" seen high in the atmosphere. They are made up entirely of ice crystals and are so thin that at night you can sometimes see the stars shining through them. Cirrus clouds are often the source of sublimation nuclei for snow clouds floating in the atmosphere at lower altitudes. The great height of cirrus clouds makes them appear to be hardly moving. Sometimes, however, they are moved by high winds at speeds of 160 to 320 kilometers (100 to 200 miles) an hour.

The three main groups of clouds can be further divided into subgroups.

Strato-cumulus. These clouds sometimes form an unbroken ceiling. Or they may be more loosely packed together. Different types of strato-cumulus clouds occur at different altitudes.

Alto-cumulus. These clouds look like strato-cumulus clouds. Cauliflower-shaped, they often parade across the sky in broken groups seen at different altitudes. The very thin edges of the alto-cumulus clouds provide a good way of identifying them. They may be seen at altitudes from about 2,000 to 6,000 meters (about 6,500 to 20,000 feet).

Cirro-cumulus. These clouds form high in the sky, from about 3,000 to 9,000 meters (about 10,000 to 30,000 feet). They are thin, ice-crystal clouds that look like fine sand ripples made by waves on a beach. The expression "mackerel sky" has long been used to describe cirro-cumulus clouds.

Alto-stratus. You can see these clouds between altitudes of about 2,000 to 6,000 meters. They form gray or bluish sheets. Sometimes they are thick enough to block out the moon or sun. At other times they are so thin that you can see the moon outlined through them.

Cirro-stratus. These are high-altitude clouds that cause us to see a halo around the moon or around the sun. One way to tell cirro-stratus clouds from alto-stratus clouds is by looking for shadows. The sun's light causes objects to cast shadows when it shines through the thin, white veils of cirro-stratus clouds. But no shadows are cast when it shines through alto-stratus clouds.

Nimbo-stratus. These clouds bring long spring rains. Their dark bases may be only 100 meters (330 feet) above the ground and are seldom higher than 1,000 meters (3,300 feet). Nimbo-stratus clouds are much thicker and darker than ordinary stratus clouds. You can see them develop when alto-stratus clouds grow thicker and sink lower as steady rain falls from them.

Cumulo-nimbus. Members of the cumulus family, these clouds are storm clouds. Thunder showers, sometimes accompanied by hail, burst forth from cumulo-nimbus clouds. On summer afternoons you can often see them building up from large cumulus clouds. The strong vertical wind currents within them cause these clouds to reach towering heights. At the top of a cumulo-nimbus cloud is an anvil-shaped cloud of ice crystals. The anvil is formed by the strong winds blowing near the top of these clouds. If you see cumulo-nimbus clouds forming in the morning, you can expect showers in the afternoon.

ROY A. GALLANT
Author, science books for young people
Reviewed by JEROME SPAR
Author, *The Way of the Weather*

See also ATMOSPHERE; FOG AND SMOG; RAIN, SNOW, SLEET, AND HAIL; THUNDER AND LIGHTNING; WEATHER.

Fair-weather cumulus clouds.

Cirro-cumulus clouds make a "mackerel sky."

Stratus clouds stretch across the sky in gray layers.

Gray or bluish sheets of alto-stratus clouds.

Thin, lacy cirrus clouds are made of ice crystals.

Cirro-stratus clouds cause a halo around the moon.

Above: Strato-cumulus clouds loosely packed. Below: Alto-cumulus clouds showing thin edges of the layers.

Above: Nimbo-stratus clouds are low, thick rain clouds. Below: Anvil-topped cumulo-nimbus are storm clouds.

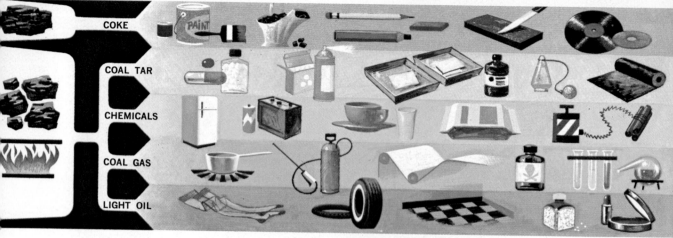

COKE
COAL TAR
CHEMICALS
COAL GAS
LIGHT OIL

Hundreds of useful materials are made from coal.

COAL AND COAL MINING

Coal is a rock, usually black but sometimes brown in color. It is one of the most useful minerals stored in the earth. Coal burns easily and gives off large amounts of heat. As a fuel, it has played an important part in the development of industry in many countries since the 1700's. And people have used it in their daily lives—to cook food and heat houses. In recent times it has been replaced for many purposes by fuel oil, natural gas, and electricity, which are easier and cleaner to use.

One of the most important uses of coal today is to run electric power plants. Another is in the making of steel. Coal is also turned into other kinds of fuel. And chemicals that come from coal are used to make hundreds of materials that we use every day, such as plastics, nylon, drugs, dyes, and fertilizers.

Simply by looking at coal, you would not be likely to guess that it was formed from plants. But like petroleum and natural gas, it is a **fossil fuel**—a fuel that comes from once-living things. It contains energy that has been stored underground for hundreds of millions of years.

Chemists tell us that coal is made up largely of the element carbon. It is much like the form of carbon known as graphite—the "lead" in ordinary pencils. But coal also contains hydrogen and small amounts of oxygen, nitrogen, sulfur, and other elements. In coal, these elements are combined into complex **hydrocarbons**, which are chemical compounds of carbon and hydrogen, and closely related substances.

▶ HOW COAL IS FORMED

The coal that is dug from the earth today began to be formed long before people appeared on the earth. Much of the earth then was covered by water. The land was low and swampy. Giant ferns, reeds, and primitive trees grew in the swamps.

When the plants died, they fell into the swamps and began to decay. New plants grew over them. Gradually a thick layer of partly decayed vegetation was built up. As the centuries passed, the dead plant material at the bottom was pressed tightly together by the weight of the material above it. Under this pressure it turned gradually into a brown, spongy material called peat.

More centuries passed, and the land sank in many places. The sea covered some of the peat swamps. Sand and mud settled over the masses of peat. When the mud piled up and reached the surface of the water, new plants began to grow. In some places this process was repeated over and over, and many layers of peat were formed.

How did soft, spongy peat become hard, black coal? The process was long and complicated. The weight of the mud and sand covering the peat beds pressed some of the moisture out of the spongy mass and made it harder. Under this pressure the peat turned to a rocklike substance. As the layers of mud grew thicker and heavier, they pressed harder on the material below. This great pressure, along with heat from within the earth, gradually turned much of the rocklike substance into a hard, black, brittle rock.

In places, forces within the earth's crust

caused the crust to buckle and fold. Huge mountain ranges and valleys were formed. This folding exerted great pressure on the underlying layers of rock and soil. Great heat also was produced. Some of the layers of black, brittle rock were caught in this folding of the earth's crust. Moisture and gas were squeezed and baked out of them until they turned to an even harder black rock.

Types of Coal

Coal deposits vary greatly. Unlike water or salt, coal has no definite chemical formula. Even the coal from parts of a single deposit may differ. These variations are caused by differences in the original plant material, the amount of time the material has been acted upon, and the kinds of processes it has undergone.

As a result, experts have developed a number of different ways of classifying and describing coal. One of these is the **rank** of the coal. The rank indicates chiefly the amount of change the coal has undergone. But the rank also gives a good indication of the composition of the coal and its suitability for certain uses.

The **peat** we find today—often in bogs—is the lowest ranking coal-like material. Usually it is not considered to be a true coal. It is much like the spongy brown plant substance that began the coal-making process long ages ago. Often peat must be dried out before it can be used. It is a poor fuel.

Lignite is on the borderline of being a true coal. It is sometimes called brown coal because of its color. It, too, often must be dried before use. It is soft and crumbly, and it produces little heat. Most of today's higher ranking coals probably went through an earlier lignite stage.

There are a number of different ranks of **bituminous** coal. This is the most abundant and most useful kind of coal. Usually called soft coal, it is a sooty, dull black rock that burns well and gives a good deal of heat. It is much used in industry. One of its most important properties is that it can be heated in a closed container to form **coke** (the nearly pure carbon used in making steel) and important chemical by-products.

The coal that has undergone the most change is **anthracite**, or hard coal. It is a shiny black material that can be polished and used for jewelry. It is the natural coal that is closest to pure carbon. It burns slowly with a clean flame and is good for heating houses.

Producers and users of coal have a number of ways of judging the quality of coal of the different ranks. One of the most important is the heat that can be obtained by burning a certain amount of the coal. Another way of judging the quality is the amount of **volatile matter** the coal contains. This is gaseous

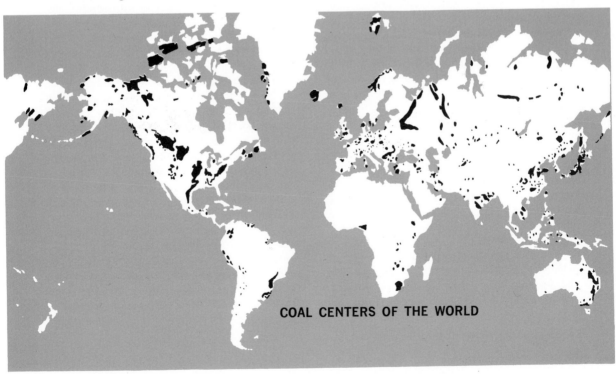

COAL CENTERS OF THE WORLD

matter that is easily driven off by heating. The harder the coal, the less volatile matter it contains.

For bituminous coal, the **coking properties** indicate how suitable it is for making coke. If coal is to be used in furnaces, it is important to know how easily the coal burns, or its **firing characteristics**. These depend on such things as the moisture content and the amount of inorganic matter (matter that did not come from living things) it contains.

The sulfur content of coal also is important. When coal burns, the sulfur it contains is converted to oxides of sulfur (and in the presence of moisture, to sulfuric acid). These are troublesome air pollutants.

The Location of Coalfields

As the coal-making processes went on, a great many coal beds were lost. Some were carried to the surface and weathered away. Others were swept deep into the earth, where they can never be reached. As a result of such activity, coal is not evenly distributed around the world. Every continent has some coal, but most of it is in the Northern Hemisphere. The United States has deposits estimated in the trillions of metric tons. Other countries or regions that are rich in coal are the Soviet Union, western Europe, and the People's Republic of China.

In the United States, northeastern Pennsylvania is the major anthracite center. The great Appalachian bituminous coalfield extends from Pennsylvania to Alabama. Large bituminous fields are also found in the central part of the country. The large coal beds in the West contain lignite or low-ranking bituminous coal. But they are valuable because the coal contains very little sulfur.

▶ THE USES OF COAL

The Chinese mined and used coal hundreds of years before the birth of Christ. An ancient Greek writer described coal in a book on rocks. Coal mining in western Europe is described in documents from the 12th century.

Uses in the Past

As a fuel, coal quickly became a competitor with wood. By the year 1688, England—then the leading coal center in the world—was producing 3,000,000 tons a year. With the de-velopment of the steam engine and the increasing use of this engine in ships, locomotives, and factories, coal came into wide use. By 1856, production in Britain had increased to 65,000,000 tons a year, and by 1900 to more than three times that amount.

In the United States, coal came into use more slowly because of the abundant supplies of wood. But the development of the iron and steel industry and the spread of railroads across the country brought ever-increasing demands. In 1850, coal replaced wood as the country's chief fuel. And by 1900, the United States produced more coal than Britain.

The peak years of coal use in the United States came in the late 1940's, when coal supplied 50 percent of the country's energy. But home owners turned increasingly to oil, gas, and electricity for heat. The railroads shifted to oil-burning diesel locomotives. Even electric generating plants began to use oil and gas. By 1950, coal was supplying only 36 percent of the country's energy, and by 1973, 17 percent. The long decline in the use of coal was reversed only in the late 1970's, when the cost of petroleum and natural gas increased rapidly and people became concerned about energy shortages.

Uses Today

Coal is still used to some extent to heat homes and industrial plants. But the main users of coal are now electric power companies and the iron and steel industry. Coal is also an important source of chemicals.

Electric Power Generation. More than half of all the electricity used in the United States is produced in coal-burning plants. In these plants, pulverized coal (coal in the form of powder, or dust) is blown into furnaces. There it is burned, and the resulting heat is used to heat water, converting it to steam. The pressure of the steam spins the great fanlike wheels of turbines. And these, in turn, spin the rotors of electric generators.

Steel Manufacture. Coal is used in the purification of many metals. In nature, most metals are combined with oxygen or other impurities. Coal is used to refine these ores— that is, to separate the impurities from the metal. The burning coal and the gases formed by the burning combine with the impurities, leaving the metal in its pure state.

This process is most important in the iron and steel industry. Almost all the iron and steel produced today is made with coal, usually in the form of coke. When steel is made from iron, some of the carbon in the coke is taken up by the iron to produce a chemical mixture, or **alloy**. This alloy of iron and carbon is steel.

Chemical Production. Many important chemicals are obtained as by-products when coke is made from coal. **Ammonia**, for example, is given off. It can be used to make fertilizers. Among the other chemicals produced are **naphthalene** (used in mothballs), **phenols** (such as carbolic acid), and **pyridine bases**. Most of these substances are used in the manufacture of dyes, plastics, drugs, explosives, paints, adhesives, and synthetic fibers. The coal tar produced can be converted to road-paving material.

▶ COAL MINING

Undoubtedly coal was first discovered in places where it had been carried to the surface by geological processes. Later, as people learned to follow the **seams** (layers of coal) deep into the earth, various methods for mining coal were developed.

Deep Mining

Deep, or underground, mining is the method that has been used for centuries. But modern machinery has greatly improved the process. It no longer is quite so dirty, dangerous, and backbreaking as it used to be.

Underground mines are of three types—**shaft**, **slope**, or **drift**. The type depends on the kind of opening that lets the miners in and out and permits the coal to be removed. In shaft mines, shafts are dug straight into the earth, and elevators are installed. In slope mines, the coal is reached by way of slanting tunnels. And in drift mines, there are horizontal tunnels—into the side of a hill, for example.

To get the coal out, miners used to chop away at the coal wall, or **face**, with pickaxes. Then they shoveled the loose coal into carts, in which it was hauled away.

Miners now use machinery to cut into and weaken the coal face. Then they set off explosions within the face. The coal that is knocked down by the blast is scooped up by

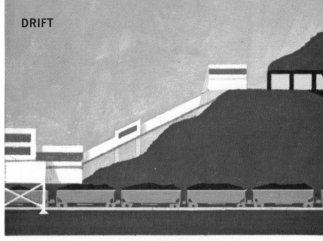

DRIFT

Drift mining is used when part of the coal seam is near the surface. The mine tunnel is dug directly into the side of the seam.

SURFACE

Above, strip mining is used when the entire coal seam is near the surface. The rock covering is removed, and the coal is mined with power shovels. Below, when the coal seam is too far below the surface, a passage must be dug in order to reach the coal. In slope mining, this passage is on an angle.

SLOPE

CLAY

ELEVATOR SHAFT

SANDSTONE AND SHALE

VENTILATION SHAFT

COAL SEAM

SHUTTLE CARS

SANDSTONE AND SHALE

COAL SEAM

DRILLING HOLES FOR BLASTING

SANDSTONE AND SHALE

CUTTING COAL BY MACHINE

COAL SEAM

Shaft mining is often the method used to reach deeply buried coal seams.

loading machines and deposited in shuttle cars or on conveyor belts to be carried out.

Another method, introduced in the 1940's, uses **continuous mining machines**. These continually cut and claw the coal from the face, rake it up, and load it into cars or onto conveyor belts. Such machines greatly increase the work that a single miner can do.

Two methods are used in attacking the coal face. The older one is called the **room-and-pillar** method. The coal is cut out in "rooms," leaving pillars of coal standing to support the roof. This is the preferred method in the United States.

European miners tend to use the **long-wall** method. They attack the coal face along a broad front, removing all the coal as they go. The roof is propped up directly over the miners but is allowed to collapse behind them as they move along.

Underground mines are dangerous for miners. They are also somewhat unproductive,

especially when pillars of coal are left standing. But there is no other way to reach deep seams.

Strip-mining

Strip-mining, or surface mining, is used where coal seams are close to the surface. The overlying soil and rock must first be removed to expose the coal. Giant power shovels and excavators dig away surface layers up to 60 meters (200 feet) thick. The uncovered coal is then broken loose—often with explosives—dug out with power shovels, and dumped into trucks for removal.

Strip-mining is cheaper than deep mining. It gets out more of the coal, and it is generally less dangerous for miners. But it destroys vegetation and can leave great piles of earth and rock, along with trenches where the coal has lain.

Until the early 1970's, only about one third of all the coal mined in the United States was produced by stripping. Now, with increased mining in the western states, where this method tends to be used, the amount is probably closer to one half.

Auger Mining

A third method uses giant augers, or drills, to bore into coal seams and bring out the coal. It is used for about 5 percent of the coal produced in the United States. Augers are used when the coal is too far below the surface to permit strip-mining but not far enough to demand underground mining. Auger mining is an easy method, and its use is increasing. It does not require many workers.

▶ PROCESSING COAL

As it comes from the mine, coal usually is not fit for immediate use. The lumps vary in size, and the coal is likely to contain rocks, soil, and other impurities. Various steps are taken to prepare the coal before it is sold to consumers. With anthracite, the first step is to crush the coal. And anthracite preparation plants are called **breakers**.

To sort the lumps by size, the coal is passed through screens with holes of different dimensions. It is purified by "washing" with water or air. Impurities that are lighter or heavier than the coal are separated from it during this treatment.

Transportation

About two thirds of the coal produced in the United States is carried from the mines by rail. A good part of the rest is moved by barge along inland canals and rivers. Giant freighters carry coal across the Great Lakes. And oceangoing coal ships, called **colliers**, carry coal between countries of the world.

Another way to transport coal is to crush it, mix it with water to form a **slurry**, and send the slurry through a pipeline. This method is not widely used. Slurry pipelines use a great deal of water and cannot be used in areas where water is scarce.

Coking

To produce coke, bituminous coal is heated in special ovens from which air is excluded. The process is called **carbonization**. Usually, it is carried out at high temperatures to produce the best quality coke, suitable for steel making. But low-temperature carbonization is also used to some extent. The coke oven is designed so that the chemicals given off during carbonization can easily be recovered.

Gasification and Liquefaction

Coal can be converted into a gas—mostly carbon monoxide and hydrogen—by burning it in the presence of oxygen and steam. This gas, called **town gas**, was extensively used as a fuel and for lighting in the 19th and early 20th centuries. But in much of the world, town gas has now been replaced by natural gas, which is a superior fuel.

In Germany during World War II, a process was developed to produce a synthetic natural gas from coal. This process was expensive. It is now being modified in the hope that large-scale gasification plants will soon convert coal into synthetic natural gas at a cost not far above that of natural gas.

Also being studied is liquefaction of coal—changing it into liquids that would serve as substitutes for petroleum. Coal would then be a source of both fuel oil and gasoline.

Gasoline, as well as a synthetic natural gas, was made from coal in Germany in World War II. A similar process is now being used in South Africa. In both cases, a method is used in which coal is treated with hydrogen to form petroleumlike hydrocarbons. Scientists also are studying the use of solvents to extract a fuel oil substitute from coal.

▶ PROBLEMS IN COAL PRODUCTION AND USE

The safety and health problems of coal miners have long been recognized. Explosions and fires from coal dust and gas are a constant problem. Many explosions once were set off by the lamps that miners carried. The safety lamp, invented in 1815, and today's electric lamps were important steps toward safer mines. Fans are used to sweep gases from the mines. Coal dust is kept down by spraying the walls and ceiling of the mine with powdered limestone—a process called **rock dusting**. A recent development in fighting fires in mines is the **foam plug technique**. A foam of air and water is used to fill the tunnel and blanket the fire.

Cave-ins are the greatest danger. Wooden and steel supports help prevent them. Another useful procedure is **roof bolting**. Long rods are inserted through the layers of rock that make up the ceiling of the mine. The rods help keep the ceiling from collapsing.

Constant breathing of coal dust in the mine leads to a serious and often fatal disease called **black lung**. Various efforts to combat dust in the mines have helped prevent this disease. It is also helpful for miners to wear masks when operating cutting, drilling, and loading machinery.

Environmental Disturbances

Underground mines can produce mountainous piles of waste, removed with the coal. Areas above old mines are likely to sink as rock and soil collapse into spaces emptied of coal. Open-pit mines can scar the landscape, destroy natural hills and mountains, and leave vast piles of stripped surface material. When high-sulfur coal is burned, the sulfur dioxide that is produced causes acid rains—rainwater made acid by the presence of sulfuric acid. In all these ways, the production and use of coal harm the environment.

But there are methods for dealing with these problems. Waste piles can be spread out and landscaped. Other surface damage can be repaired by careful restoration. **Scrubbers** or other devices in smokestacks remove sulfur dioxide before it gets into the atmosphere. These procedures are expensive, and they add to the cost of coal and the energy obtained from it. But as other fossil fuels become more and more expensive and as supplies decrease, the world will have to turn increasingly to coal to meet its energy needs.

DAVID M. LOCKE
University of Florida

See also CARBON; ENERGY SUPPLY; FUELS; GEOLOGY AND GEOPHYSICS; MINES AND MINING; ROCKS, MINERALS, AND ORES.

COAST GUARD. See UNITED STATES COAST GUARD.
COCOA. See CHOCOLATE AND COCOA.

COCONUT

A grinning face seemed to be peering at the Portuguese sailors as they peeled the husk from an unfamiliar nut. These 15th-century explorers called the nut *coco,* from their word for "grimace."

The face was made by three eyes, or undeveloped buds, on one end of the husked coconut, the fruit of the coconut palm. The coconut's outer fibrous husk cushions the inner seed, or nut, when it falls. The nut is 3 to 8 inches long. Just inside the hard, dark shell is a layer of dense white meat. The central cavity is filled with a watery liquid called coconut milk. When the coconut is planted in its husk, a new sprout pushes through one of the eyes. The palm usually bears fruit in about 8 years.

Coconuts are an important cash crop of the tropics. A mature coconut palm flowers throughout the year and almost always has a few ripe nuts. The flower clusters grow between the leaf bases in canoe-shaped sheaths, and after blooming develop into coconuts. It may take the nut a year or more to mature, depending on the place and variety. The average yearly production of a palm is 50 nuts.

The single bare trunk of the palm shoots from 20 to 90 feet in the air and is crowned with a tuft of long, feathery leaves. Each 10- to 20-foot leaf consists of a stout midrib (vein) with many leaflets in two opposite rows.

Coconuts can be grown at elevations as high as 3,000 feet above sea level, but they are planted more often at lower elevations.

Unlike most trees, the coconut palm can stand salt water, but it does not require it. The palm grows near the sea because its shallow roots can find moisture there. The husk is not harmed by salt water either, and the nut can be carried many miles by the sea to land and take root on a far-away beach. It is thought, however, that man spread the coconut by carrying nuts with him. No truly wild coconut has been found or its origins discovered.

Coconuts are harvested by climbing the palms and cutting off the cluster of nuts or by gathering ripe nuts from the ground. The husk is removed by hand after splitting it on a sharp iron or wooden stake driven into the ground. Large plantations may use machines.

Uses of Coconuts

For centuries the coconut has supplied the people of the Pacific islands with food, drink, shelter, and most of their other needs. The roots furnish a dye; the trunks are used for posts in buildings; and the harder outer part is cut into boards called porcupine wood.

Coconut meat is eaten in a variety of ways. Bowls are made from coconut shells, and cooking is done over a fire of either the husks or the shells. The coconut cream used in native cooking is prepared by grating coconut meat into a little water and sifting out the coarse particles. The liquid inside a green coconut is a refreshing drink. The sap drained from the palm by slicing the unopened flower clusters is made into vinegar, sugar, or the alcoholic beverage called arrack.

Thatching, mats, hats, baskets, and rope are made out of the leaves, midrib, and a fiber from the husks called coir. Coir is exported to other countries to make matting.

The most important commercial product of the coconut is **copra** and the oil pressed from it. Copra is the dried meat of coconuts. One hundred nuts will produce 50 pounds of copra, which in turn will yield as much as 60 per cent oil. After pressing out the edible oil, the leftover copra cake and meal make good cattle feed because of their high protein, sugar, and vitamin content.

The major uses of coconut oil are in soaps and margarines. The oil is also widely used in bakery products. Other uses include candles, cosmetics, and printing ink.

Another important product is dried coconut meat. This is widely used in candies, cakes, cookies, and pies.

Leading coconut producers and exporters are the Philippines, Indonesia, Ceylon, and the Federation of Malaysia. Ceylon and the Philippines are the leading producers of dried coconut used in pastry. The fresh coconuts that are sold in North America come from Puerto Rico and Central and South America.

HAROLD F. WINTERS
U.S. Department of Agriculture

See also NUTS.

COCOONS.   See BUTTERFLIES AND MOTHS.

COD.   See FISHING INDUSTRY.

CODES AND CIPHERS

If you and your friends wish to share a secret, you can write it in code, and no one else will be able to read it. Codes are one way of writing in secret. Ciphers are another. In a code each word is written as a secret code word or code number. In a cipher each letter is changed. Secret writing that uses codes and ciphers is called cryptography.

Codes and ciphers have played an important part in the history of the world. Julius Caesar, the Roman ruler who conquered almost all of Europe about 2,000 years ago, used a cipher when he sent secret messages to his generals. During the American Revolution George Washington's spies used a code to send him information about the enemy. In World War II the Americans "broke," or figured out, Japan's most important naval code and got enough information to destroy a powerful Japanese fleet.

Storekeepers use codes to mark their goods. The codes show how much was paid for the goods or when they were added to the stock. Businessmen use codes to hide plans from competitors. Sometimes personal letters or diaries are written in code. Many people enjoy working out codes and ciphers simply as a hobby.

In the 16th century, codes and ciphers were very popular among scientists. They wrote messages to each other in code so that no one else would learn their secrets. Geronimo Cardano, an Italian astrologer, mathematician, and doctor, invented the trellis cipher. He took two sheets of stiff paper and cut identical holes in each one. Then he sent one sheet, which he called a trellis, to a friend and kept the other for himself. Whenever he wanted to write a message, he put his trellis over a clean sheet of paper and wrote the secret message through the holes. Then he removed the trellis and filled up the rest of the paper with words that would make some sense. When Cardano's friend received the letter, he put his trellis over the writing and read the secret message.

Giambattista della Porta, another 16th-century Italian scientist, wrote a book about codes. He is sometimes called the father of modern cryptography. Galileo Galilei, the famous Italian astronomer and physicist, recorded his discovery of the phases of the planet Venus in a kind of cipher.

▸ TRANSPOSITION CIPHERS

Ciphers are divided into two types: transposition and substitution. In transposition ciphers the letters of the message are jumbled.

To construct a simple transposition cipher, write the "clear," or original, message in horizontal lines containing an equal number of letters in each line. The message MEET ME AT FOUR TOMORROW might look like this:

MEET
MEAT
FOUR
TOMO
RROW

Decide on some route to follow, such as up and down the columns, and copy the letters in that order. If you start at the upper left-hand corner and go down the first column and up the next, the message will read MMFT RROO EEEA UMOW ORTT.

The person receiving the jumbled message must know or must figure out what route was followed. Then he can reconstruct the message.

▸ SUBSTITUTION CIPHERS

In a substitution cipher the letters of the message do not change their order. Instead, other letters are substituted for the message letters. Every R in the message might be replaced by a T, every P by a B, and so on. To put a message into a simple substitution cipher, write out the alphabet. Then underneath it, write down the 26 letters of the alphabet in any order you wish. Substitute the letter in the bottom line for the letter in the top line whenever it appears in the message.

If the person receiving the secret message does not know the key—which letter was substituted for which—he may still be able to decipher the message. He will try different letters of the alphabet, beginning with the ones most often used. In English the letter E is used most often, so E would be tried in place of the letter that appears most frequently in the cipher. The letter T is the next most used, so it would be tried for the next most frequent letter in the cipher, and so forth.

Here is a simple cryptogram, or secret message, based on a substitution cipher:

XOPPS OBE YTLE MQOSLE CB YCT QXC EOSM

And here is the solution:

Wally and Fred stayed on for two days.

Numbers can also be used to replace letters. If 1 is substituted for A, 2 for B, and so on, the message MEET ME AT THE LIBRARY would appear:

**13–5–5–20 13–5 1–20 20–8–5
12–9–2–18–1–18–25**

You may also count backwards, so that Z is 1, Y is 2, and so on.

Simple substitution ciphers play an important part in two famous stories—Edgar Allan Poe's *Gold Bug* and Arthur Conan Doyle's *Adventure of the Dancing Men*. The substitution cipher used by Julius Caesar about 58 B.C., and later named after him, replaces each message letter with the letter that follows it in the alphabet. So the message COME AT SIX would read DPNF BU TJY.

Dear Robert,

Have you ever made the trip to Malaza this time of year? I went for Easter last year and found lots of action everywhere! The city is a lively one. I should like to return now and see the dances For me, they are the best part of the spring festivals.

Best regards,
Nancy

Codes are worked word by word instead of letter by letter. Because it would be very difficult to learn a code by heart, a code book must be used. When George Washington set up his spy system during the American Revolution, he had his spies use a code book that listed numbers for all the words they might need. The messages were written and decoded according to the numbers given in the book.

Of course, if a code book is lost or stolen, its code system loses its value. The finder or thief could decode any secret messages sent in that code. For example, the captain of a naval vessel during wartime must have a code book for sending and receiving messages about the enemy. If his ship is about to be captured by the enemy, he must destroy his code book.

Secret codes that are spoken rather than written are called jargon codes. They are particularly useful to people like air force pilots. In jargon codes important words are replaced by other words that seem to make sense when put together in a sentence. For instance, a list of code words may show that the jargon word LIBRARY stands for JACK'S HOUSE, MEET stands for GO, and ALWAYS stands for NOT. The sentence WE ALWAYS MEET AT THE LIBRARY would be decoded as DO NOT GO TO JACK'S HOUSE.

Secret languages like pig Latin are a form of jargon code. They follow one simple rule. In pig Latin the rule is to move the first letter of each word to the end of the word and add the letters AY. DOG becomes OGDAY. CATCHER becomes ATCHERCAY.

The ciphers and codes used by governments are far more complicated than any described here, but the basic methods are the same. It takes years of training and practice to become an expert at making and breaking codes, but anyone can have fun using simple ciphers and solving the mysteries of a coded message.

Reviewed by SAM AND BERYL EPSTEIN
Authors, *The First Book of Codes and Ciphers*

CODY, WILLIAM FREDERICK. See BUFFALO BILL.

COELENTERATES. See JELLYFISHES AND OTHER COELENTERATES.

COFFEE

When coffee was first introduced to Western Europe, around 1615, it raised a hue and cry. Some people said it was intoxicating. Some thought it was poisonous. But bit by bit coffee was accepted. Coffee houses became centers of gossip and social life. In England King Charles II was afraid plots against the government were being hatched in the coffee houses. He ordered them closed. But by this time coffee was so popular that he was forced to open them again.

No one knows exactly how coffee was discovered. The first coffee plants probably grew in Kaffa, a province of southwestern Ethiopia. This province may have given coffee its name.

According to one legend a goatherd learned of the use of coffee by accident. While he was guarding his flock of goats in the mountains, he saw to his surprise that they were jumping and playing in the hot sun. He watched the animals more closely. Each time they ate the berries of a certain wild plant, they became very lively. The goatherd sampled the berries, and he, too, felt wide awake and stimulated.

Whether or not this story is true, before A.D. 575 the Persian armies knew about the effect of coffee seeds and probably carried them to Yemen, on the Arabian Peninsula. There the Arabs tried brewing the bitter seeds into a drink to make them taste better. Soon the new beverage spread to Turkey and Europe.

By the beginning of the 17th century, so much coffee was passing through the Arabian port of Mocha that Mocha became another word for coffee.

The traders took coffee seeds to India and Ceylon, where they started coffee plantations. Toward the end of the 17th century and during the 18th century, coffee culture spread to Java (an island in the Netherlands East Indies), to other parts of southeast Asia, and to the New World. The Netherlands East Indies, now called Indonesia, dominated the world market for nearly a century. The coffee rust disease, followed by a series of insect pests, destroyed the Dutch plantings in 1888. All that was left of the famous coffee region was the name it had given coffee—Java.

Brazil took over the leading position in

Young coffee trees grow on a plantation in the highlands of Colombia.

Above, ripe coffee beans cluster near the white flowers of the coffee plant. Below, an electronic machine sorts coffee beans by color. Hundreds of beans are sorted each minute.

coffee-growing and has held it for many decades. Colombia and other South and Central American countries and the West Indies also produce large quantities of coffee.

The Coffee Plant

Coffee is produced by several related small evergreen trees native to tropical Africa. Almost all of the coffee that is raised, however, comes from one kind of coffee plant. This plant is called the Arabian coffee plant, although it is grown in coffee regions all over the world.

Arabian coffee plants are woody shrubs or small trees. A mature coffee plant can be a dwarf 5 to 6 feet tall or a vigorous bush as tall as 18 feet. The dark, waxy leaves are pointed like a lance and stay on the plant all year round. If the weather is very dry, some of the leaves may be shed.

The time of flowering is influenced by the climate. In areas having definite wet and dry seasons each year, coffee begins to flower toward the end of the dry period. Coffee flowering is repeated several times at 3- to 4-week intervals during the change of seasons. The plants are dotted with pure-white flowers, which cluster on short stalks between the leaves. Each time the plants bloom, a delicate perfume fills the surrounding countryside. Not all the flowers develop into the berries that are the fruit of the coffee plant.

It takes 5 to 7 months for the blossoms to turn into ripe fruit. The berries are bunched in clumps between the leaves. Since they are bright red when they are ripe, they are commonly called cherries in English and *cerezas* ("cherries") in Spanish.

The berries are ½ to ¾ inches long. Each berry contains two seeds. A layer of sweet, sticky pulp lies between the seeds and the outside skin. A thin, parchmentlike covering and a silvery inner skin further protect the seeds. After much preparation they become the "coffee beans" of commerce.

Cultivation

Coffee grows best in the tropical highlands, where lower temperatures and slow ripening produce a mild coffee. The plants thrive in well-drained, volcanic soils.

Coffee is by nature a shade-loving plant. Cultivated trees are commonly sheltered by leaving some of the natural tree cover when clearing a plantation, or by planting selected shade trees. Where the soil is good and the air humid, less shade is needed. At high elevations coffee can be grown in direct sunlight. Even at some lower elevations, as in Brazil and Hawaii, shade is not always needed because of the humidity.

Most coffee plants are raised from seeds planted in special nursery beds. The beds are located on the best land available and near a source of water. Bamboo strips or palm leaves attached to an overhead frame protect the seedlings from the hot sun. In 6 to 8 months, the plants are ready for transplanting to the permanent field location.

The plants bear their first fruits in 2 to 4 years, but do not come into full production for 6 to 7 years. The productive life of a planting varies from 15 to 30 years, depending on the variety, climate, soil, and care. An annual yield of 1,000 pounds of dry coffee beans per acre is considered a good crop.

Coffee's Enemies. Coffee is subject to several rather serious diseases and insect pests. Coffee in Africa and Indonesia has been struck hard by coffee rust, but this disease has not spread to the New World. Chemical sprays are only partly effective against this menace. The most common insects causing damage to coffee plantations are leaf miners, ants, green scale insects, and various beetles.

Harvesting the Berries

Because the plants flower in several flushes, the coffee beans do not ripen evenly. Berries of different ages are on the same tree at the same time. Since only fully ripe coffee berries produce a high-quality beverage, they are usually picked as they ripen.

In those countries where the plants only bloom a few times, the entire crop, both green and ripe, is harvested as soon as the berries show color. Coffee beans picked this way are lower in quality, but fewer berries are lost by shattering or by birds and animals eating them.

Harvesting has remained largely a hand operation, but changing the berries into "coffee beans" is done by machine.

In drier regions, and in Brazil, the **dry method** is used to prepare the berries for market. The berries are first dried. Then the pulp, parchment shell, and silver skin are removed, and the gray-green coffee beans appear. Many small plantations only dry the beans and then ship them to centers, where machines strip off the coverings.

The **wet method** is thought to give coffee a better flavor. The berries are put through a machine that removes the outer skin and as much of the pulp as possible. The seeds are then fermented in tanks of water until the pulp loosens and can be washed away. The clean seeds are dried for several days in the sun or in a mechanical hot-air drier before peeling off the parchment coat and silver skin.

At this stage the beans are known in international trade as green, or unroasted, coffee. To the coffee farmer, however, green coffee means coffee made from berries that were harvested before they were completely ripe.

Coffee is shipped to market in coarse bags made of jute, sisal, or other fibers. A bag of coffee beans weighs about 132 pounds. Dry coffee properly stored can be held for several years without losing its quality. In fact, aging is sometimes deliberately practiced to improve the quality of harsh-flavored varieties.

Manufacturing Coffee

Green coffee has little flavor, but roasting the beans brings out the characteristic coffee tang and aroma. Every coffee variety and every region produces a slightly different-tasting coffee bean. The only way to discover what the bean's taste will be is to select and roast a test batch from each variety. Skilled coffee tasters sample the brews and judge their quality. They decide which flavors go well together and recommend the amount of time to roast each mixture of beans.

After the outside shells are cracked off, the roasted beans are ground into different grades of fineness. The standard grades are drip, regular, and fine. Each grade is meant to be brewed in a different kind of pot.

In many European countries the root of the chicory plant is roasted with the coffee beans. People first added chicory because coffee beans were too expensive to use alone. Chicory gives the coffee bulk. At the same time it makes the coffee's color darker and its taste more bitter.

The quick cup of coffee that busy people make is often instant coffee. Instant coffee is actually coffee made twice. The manufacturer first brewed a strong coffee and then dried it into powder in a vacuum. The powder turns into coffee again when hot water is mixed with it.

Manufacturers have developed a special kind of coffee without caffeine. The coffee bean contains from 1 to 2 per cent caffeine. Caffeine is a stimulant that keeps some people from sleeping or makes them nervous. Caffeine is removed by soaking the unroasted beans in a chemical solvent.

One of the most important steps in coffee processing is careful and rapid packaging. Once coffee has been roasted it loses its flavor unless it is sealed away from the air. Vacuum-sealed coffee cans and jars keep the coffee fresh until it can be used.

Coffee is a popular drink in almost every country. The United States is the world's largest consumer, even though the continental United States does not have the proper tropical climate to grow coffee.

Harold F. Winters
U.S. Department of Agriculture

See also TEA.

COINS AND COIN COLLECTING

Coin collecting—referred to as **numismatics**—is one of the oldest known hobbies. In the past it was often enjoyed by kings and scholars. It is also a pleasant and profitable way of saving. The word "numismatics" comes from the Greek word *nomisma* and the Latin word *numisma,* meaning a coin. People who collect coins are called **numismatists**.

The designs on coins tell many stories. The coins of a country often are a record of its history and geography. Some ancient coins tell us all we know about a country or a period of history. They bring us portraits of rulers who would be otherwise unknown. Coins tell us about the art, mythology, religion, dress, and hairstyles of people who lived long ago.

A great variety of things were used as money before coins were invented. Among them were salt, grains, and animals. Sometimes objects of silver, gold, copper, or iron were used. Tobacco and **wampum** (beads made of shells) were used for trading by American colonists and their Indian neighbors.

Almost 3,000 years ago the Chinese had a form of money made from metal. But the first coin with a fixed value was not struck until the 7th century B.C. in Lydia (today Turkey). Ever since, coins have helped the world to carry on its trade and commerce.

▶ STARTING A COLLECTION

Your special interests will help you decide the kind of coin collection you would like to

| Greek coin (525–430 B.C.). | United States cent (1787). | Roman coin of the 1st century A.D. |

assemble. You may wish to collect the coins of one country or one part of the world. Or you may want your collection to contain coins from all over the world but limited to a certain period of time. Coins that illustrate one period of history or coins struck (made or minted) under a single ruler or head of state make an interesting collection.

Some people choose to collect the coins of their own country, while others are interested in ancient Greek and Roman coins. Many ancient coins are quite easy to obtain. Small ancient bronze pieces in average condition can often be bought for just a few dollars. A collection of present-day coins from countries forming the United Nations is not costly and is worldwide in scope. Coins that visitors bring back from foreign countries can be the beginning of a collection.

Another way to start a collection is to select the best examples of coins now in use. You may be able to assemble an interesting series of United States coins with different dates and mintmarks. Special mint sets and proof sets of United States coins are available from time to time. For information, write to the Office of the Director of the Mint, Treasury Department, Washington, D.C. 20220.

For a worthwhile collection, numismatists advise that you choose the coin in the best condition; choose a series and build it up; choose artistic pieces that please you and illustrate your historical knowledge.

UNITED STATES COINS

The first coins of the United States were authorized by the Mint Act of April 2, 1792, signed by President George Washington. By 1793 the Mint in Philadelphia was issuing gold, silver, and copper coins. The gold coins were eagles with the value of ten dollars. There were also half eagles and quarter eagles. The silver coins were dollars, half-dollars, dimes, and half dimes. The copper coins were cents and half cents.

Since then there have been many changes in coins and the laws governing coinage. Among the coins no longer made or issued are half dimes, half cents, and gold coins. The 5-cent coin appeared in 1886. No silver dollars were coined from 1935, and none issued from 1964 until 1971, when the first silver-clad Eisenhower dollars were minted. In 1978, Congress authorized the minting of a new dollar coin, dedicated to Susan B. Anthony for her efforts to gain women the right to vote.

A coin's design may not be changed more than once in 25 years, except by an act of Congress. In 1965, Congress passed a law making the first major change in United States coinage in over 100 years. Because of the shortage of silver, this metal was left out of the dime and quarter. Silver in half-dollars was reduced in 1965 and stopped altogether after 1970.

CARE OF YOUR COLLECTION

There are many ways to arrange coin collections. Some collectors keep their coins in small square envelopes. A complete description of the coins should be written on the outside of the envelopes. These envelopes are arranged in cardboard boxes. Envelopes and boxes may be bought at any coin store.

You can also use transparent envelopes and album pages made of plastic materials, which can be mounted in three-ring binders. Various other holders may be found in coin stores.

Never clean a coin unless it is caked with dirt. Remove the dirt by washing the coin gently with soap and warm water. Do not use scouring powder, metal polish, or steel wool. This will damage both the looks and value of the coin.

STUDY YOUR HOBBY

To get the most enjoyment from your hobby of coin collecting, read as much as you can on the subject. Try to form a group of collector friends. Visit special exhibitions and have a reliable dealer through whom you can buy your coins. If you have an old or foreign coin, find out where and when it was made, its name and value, and what you could have bought with it when it was in use.

Nearly every American city has at least one numismatic club. Many of these clubs belong to the American Numismatic Association. For information about the clubs, write the Executive Secretary, P.O. Box 2366, Colorado Springs, Colorado 80901.

Many thousands of books and publications are concerned with descriptions, histories, and other facts about coins. Your public library probably has many books on coin collecting. Of interest to the collector of modern coins are these catalog-type works: *A Guide Book of United States Coins,* R. S. Yeoman, Racine, Wisconsin (published annually); *A Catalog of Modern World Coins,* R. S. Yeoman, Racine, Wisconsin; *Standard Catalogue of Canadian Coins, Tokens, and Paper Money,* J. E. Charlton, Racine, Wisconsin (published annually).

Among the monthly magazines is *The Numismatist,* official publication of the American Numismatic Association in Colorado Springs, Colorado. Many notes of interest may also be found in weekly journals such as *Coin World,* published at Sidney, Ohio, and *Numismatic News,* Iola, Wisconsin.

For answers to your coin collecting problems, write the Division of Numismatics, Smithsonian Institution, Washington, D.C. The Smithsonian, however, will not advise on the money value of coins. Consult a coin dealer for this kind of information.

V. CLAIN-STEFANELLI
Curator, Division of Numismatics
Smithsonian Institution

COKE. See FUELS.

COLD, COMMON. See DISEASES.

COLLAGE

A collage is a picture made by pasting pieces of cloth or paper on cardboard, wood, or canvas. Some artists make collages by adding various kinds of paper and fabric to their paintings. Others, such as the French artist Henri Matisse (1896–1954), have used nothing but colored paper and glue to create outstanding works of art.

Collages are easily made at home. All that you need are such ordinary materials as old newspapers and magazines, theater or bus tickets, some rags, and perhaps a package of colored tissue or construction paper. A pair of scissors is helpful, but a piece of paper can often be more interesting when its edges have been torn rather than cut. Contrasting textures may be added to your collage with bits of a burlap bag or sandpaper. The most important

Above: *Clarinet* (1913), a collage by Georges Braque, is in a private collection in New York. Left: *Nuit de Noël* (*Christmas Night*) (1952), by Henri Matisse, is a collage design for a stained-glass window. Museum of Modern Art, New York. Below: *City*, a collage made by a 7th-grade student.

tools, however, are paste (*collage* is a French word for "pasting") and your own imagination.

Your first collage may be something simple—a birthday or Christmas card, for example. With a little more work, you can make pictures of a street on which children play, a barnyard with animals and a farm family, or a still life with a bowl of fruit and a vase of flowers.

One of the most interesting kinds of collage that you can make is an abstract design—one that does not depict a lifelike scene. To create such a collage, cut and tear your paper and fabric into shapes that do not resemble real objects. When you paste them onto your cardboard, try to contrast the shapes and textures.

The best collages will result from experiments. Colored tissue paper, when pasted flatly with rubber cement, is transparent (you can see through it); and countless effects can be created by pasting tissue on top of newspaper, sandpaper, or cloth. On the other hand, it is often effective to wrinkle the tissue when pasting it down. Some of whatever is underneath then shows through, while other parts do not. Another way to achieve interest-

ing effects is to sprinkle sand, coffee grounds, or uncooked rice over an area that you have covered with glue. The grains stick to the glue, and this creates unusual and varied textures.

A collage may be made quickly, with no planning at all, or it may be made with painstaking detail after a great deal of planning and thought. The way you make yours depends on how you like to work, but as a beginner it is best to try both. Make one collage by quickly tearing, cutting, and pasting shapes onto the cardboard. Your thinking will be done while you work. Then try planning a second collage. Cut out all the shapes you plan to use and lay them on the cardboard. Add more shapes, take some away, or change the form of others as you think necessary. When you are satisfied, draw pencil lines on the cardboard around each shape. Then remove the shapes, coat them one by one with paste, and replace them within their proper guidelines.

GIUSEPPI BAGGI

See also DESIGN AND COLOR; MODERN ART.

COLLECTIVE BARGAINING. See LABOR AND MANAGEMENT.

COLLEGES AND UNIVERSITIES. See UNIVERSITIES AND COLLEGES.

COLOMBIA

Colombia is the only country in South America with a coastline on both sides of the continent. It is bordered by the Pacific Ocean on the west, and by the Caribbean Sea on the Atlantic side.

Colombia is a large country, larger than France and Spain combined. It is fourth in size among the countries of South America—after Brazil, Argentina, and Peru. It is also a country of great contrasts. Three parallel mountain ranges lie between Bogotá—the capital—and the Pacific. These ranges run north to south and are separated by narrow valleys. Most Colombians live in these high valleys, cut off from each other by still higher mountains. The mountains drop to the Caribbean Sea on the north. Here are Barranquilla, Santa Marta, and Cartagena—the country's chief port cities and Colombia's stepping-stones to the mountains. To the east and south of Bogotá are the *llanos,* or grassy plains, and the jungle lowlands of the Amazon Basin, where almost no one lives.

Mountains, high valleys, seacoasts, grass and jungle lowlands—this geography of contrasts affects everything Colombians do and have done. Distances from one place to another and different climates and soils have made for different ways of life. Food, dress, houses, and recreation differ from one place to another in Colombia. This fact gives the country variety. But it also creates serious economic and political problems. The history of Colombia has been the struggle to unite the country, economically and politically. This unity is its triumph.

▶ **THE PEOPLE**

Colombia's people represent a variety of ethnic groups. About 20 percent are of European descent, mostly Spanish. About 5 percent are blacks, who live mostly in the coastal areas. About 7 percent of the people are pure-blooded Indians, who live near the Colombia-Ecuador border. Most Colombians—about 68 percent of the total population—are mestizos, or persons of mixed European and Indian descent.

The early Spanish explorers found several groups of Indians in Colombia. Most of them were wanderers. But one group, the Chibchas, who lived on the plateau of Bogotá, were settled farmers. They grew corn and potatoes, but had no domestic animals except dogs. They made fine pottery and cloth, and gold and emerald jewelry. The Chibchas survived the Spanish conquest, but the languages they spoke had disappeared by the 19th century.

Language and Religion. Colombians have kept many Spanish traditions. They speak the oldest and purest Spanish in Latin America. This can be explained by the disappearance of the Chibcha languages, the absence of immigrants who spoke other languages, and the long lack of exchange between one city and another. Colombians are

---

FACTS AND FIGURES

REPUBLIC OF COLOMBIA is the official name of the country.

CAPITAL: Bogotá.

LOCATION: Northwest South America. **Latitude—** 12° 24′ N to 4° 30′ S. **Longitude—**67° W to 79° W.

PHYSICAL FEATURES: Area—1,138,916 km² (439,736 sq mi). **Highest point—**Pico Cristóbal Colon, 5,776 m (18,950 ft). **Lowest point—**sea level. **Chief rivers—** Magdalena, San Juan, Atrato, Cauca. **Chief mountain peaks—**Pico Cristóbal Colon, Sierra Nevada de Cocuy, Nevado del Huila, Nevado del Ruiz.

POPULATION: 25,000,000 (estimate).

LANGUAGE: Spanish.

RELIGION: Roman Catholic.

GOVERNMENT: Republic. **Head of government—** president. **International co-operation—**United Nations, Organization of American States (OAS), Latin American Free Trade Association (LAFTA).

NATIONAL ANTHEM: *Himno Nacional* (National Anthem). The first line: *O gloria inmarcesible!* ("O glory unfading!").

ECONOMY: Agricultural products—coffee, cattle, plantain, cotton, sugarcane, corn, tobacco, yucca, potatoes, rice, wheat, cocoa. **Industries and products—** textiles, food processing and packaging, iron and steel, paper mills, light consumer industries, rubber, hardwood, medicinal plants, lubricants, cement, glass, chemicals, fertilizers, leather. **Chief minerals—** petroleum, silver, platinum, salt, emeralds, gold, iron, coal, manganese, copper, mercury, lead, mica. **Chief exports—**coffee, cotton, bananas, sugar, platinum, gold, tobacco, emeralds. **Chief imports—** machinery and electrical equipment, chemical products, metals and metal products, textiles, transport equipment, cereals. **Monetary unit—**Colombian peso.

devout Catholics. The Church affects the lives of nearly all Colombians—at baptism, marriage, and death. The celebration of Holy Week in the southern city of Popayán is similar to that in Seville, Spain. Sacred images are carried in candlelit processions through the streets. Businesses close on many religious holidays. Until 1942 the Church was entitled to some control over text books and studies. Religious instruction is required in all public schools.

Education. Many schools are supported by the national government; some by local governments. Boys and girls usually go to separate schools. There are some large, modern school buildings in the cities, but most are simple; in the country, many have only one or two classrooms.

It is estimated that four out of ten Colombians cannot read or write. For this reason the government is training teachers and building schools. For this reason, too, Colombia was the first country in South America to use radio for education. A group of Catholic priests began the experiment in order to teach the country people who live beyond the reach of schools. Old and young gather around a radio or television set, usually in a store or a church, to hear lessons in reading,

Bogotá, Colombia's capital, is a great center of commerce. Indian farmers from the surrounding region flock into the city to offer their goods for sale on its streets.

writing, mathematics, and hygiene. The experiment is being copied in other South American countries.

There are no fewer than 28 national and state universities, both public and private, in Bogotá, Medellín, Popayán, Cartagena, and Cali. The largest is the National University, at Bogotá.

Literature. Among educated people in Colombia the love of books is a family tradition, handed down from parent to child. There are well-stocked bookshops in most cities. Often they serve as art galleries as well. Colombia, sometimes called "the land of poets," has produced many fine writers. It is not unusual for business people or politicians to publish volumes of poems. The best-known Colombian writer is Jorge Isaacs. His romantic novel *María,* written in 1867, is still widely read.

Newspapers are excellent and very influential. *El Tiempo* of Bogotá is one of the best-known newspapers in the Americas. Its publisher, Eduardo Santos, was president of Colombia from 1938 to 1942; a former editor, Alberto Lleras Camargo, was president from 1958 to 1962.

Country Life. There are many small family farms in Colombia, especially in the coffee zones. Coffeegrowing is a family occupation. It requires a great deal of hand labor, so the whole family helps, even the small children. Frequently the coffee farm grows with the family. More trees are set out when a son is born.

Some country customs have been adopted in the cities and have become typically national. The *ruana,* or Colombian poncho, is even worn by fashionable women in Bogotá. It is a woolen square about 1 meter on each side, with a slit in the center for the head. The *ruana* hangs from the shoulders to slightly below the waist. People in the hot coastal regions sometimes wear a bright-colored *ruana* of cotton.

Hand-woven fiber hats, called *jipas,* are popular. So are fiber shoes, or *alpargatas.* The *arrieros,* or "muleteers," and the coffee-growers wear a shoulder bag of calfskin, called a *carriel.* It has many partitions, for carrying money and a most varied assortment of personal articles, including amulets.

Recreation. A country dance called the *Bambuco* is the national dance of Colombia. The *merengue,* a dance of the coast, has become popular outside of Colombia. The *tiple,* a kind of guitar, is the typical instrument for playing folk music.

Soccer (*futbol* in Spanish) is the favorite sport of the Colombian people, and the game most often played in the schools. There are tournaments between schools in tennis and basketball. *Tejo,* a Chibcha game similar to discus throwing, is a typical field event. Bicycle racing is popular.

The Magdalena River is vital for the transport of goods from the mountains to the coast.

Barley is grown in a high valley of Nariño, near Ecuador. The small, Indian-owned plots are farmed according to ancient traditions. The scythe is still common at harvest.

Baseball, played by the children of the Caribbean coast, is becoming equally popular in the interior. Big crowds turn out to see bullfights and cockfights as well as horse races and polo matches.

▶ THE LAND

The Andes mountains are not quite so high in Colombia as they are in Peru. They are divided into three ranges that reach like fingers from south to north. Most of the cities lie between these mountain fingers. Because of the mountains there are few highways or railroads. Until the airplane was invented, it was hard to go from one valley to another. In 1919 Colombia became the first American country to establish a commercial airline. Most travel today is by plane. Colombia, some people say, is held together by air.

A main artery of travel in Colombia has always been the broad Magdalena River. It flows for about 1,600 kilometers (1,000 miles) between the two easternmost fingers of the Andes and empties into the Caribbean. But river travel is uncertain in the dry season when the water is low. In 1961 a railroad was completed along the river, between the coast and the capital city, Bogotá.

Further west is the beautiful Cauca River, a branch of the Magdalena. Its valley is Colombia's richest farming area. The Cauca is shallower than the Magdalena, and it is broken by rapids. This makes it less useful for shipping. The government, using the Tennessee Valley Authority in the United States as a model, has harnessed the Cauca with dams to provide electric power. Flood control and irrigation have increased agricultural production.

On the border with Panama, in the northwest, is the Darien, a dense jungle area. Engineers are planning a road through the Darien that will someday join Panama and Colombia.

Climate

Like most countries close to the Equator, Colombia does not have hot and cold seasons. Temperature depends on the height of the land above sea level. At a given altitude, there is almost no difference in temperature between July and December.

Instead of winter and summer, most Colombians speak of rainy and dry seasons. These come at different times in different parts of the country. From December through

February it is generally dry in the highlands. On most of the Pacific coast it rains in the afternoon nearly every day of the year.

Agricultural Products

The crops a farmer can grow depend on altitude. In places up to 900 meters (3,000 feet) the temperature averages about 25°C (77°F). Tropical products grow well here. These include rice, sugarcane, bananas, cotton, cacao, tobacco, and tropical fruits. Bananas are shipped from the north coast to many countries. On the *llanos* of eastern Colombia there are big cattle ranches. The forests of the Amazon basin provide valuable lumber and also medicinal plants. Scientists collect and study the medicines of people who live in the jungle.

The "mild" Colombian coffee grows at altitudes ranging from 900 to 2,000 meters (3,000 to 6,500 feet). Colombia is second only to Brazil as a producer and exporter of coffee. Coffee accounts for over half of Colombia's foreign earnings.

The Palace of the Inquisition in Cartagena, Colombia, is an example of Spanish colonial architecture.

At the same altitudes, farmers can grow corn, beans, sisal, and citrus fruits. Plantain, a kind of starchy banana, is a popular food that is cooked like a potato.

At altitudes from about 2,000 to 3,000 meters (6,500 to 10,000 feet), the temperature rarely goes above 18°C (65°F). Here farmers grow barley, wheat, apples, and potatoes. Higher still are the cold, treeless *páramos,* or "meadows." These make good pasture for sheep.

Minerals

Colombia is rich in the gold and precious stones that lured Spanish adventurers to the New World. For many years explorers looked for the land of El Dorado. According to an Indian legend, the "Gilded One" was a native prince so rich that on special occasions his subjects gilded his body with gold dust. Then he bathed in a sacred lake and washed off the gold as an offering to the gods.

No one ever found El Dorado. But the museums of Colombia have priceless collections of gold objects made and worn by early Colombian Indians. In the Bank of the Republic, in Bogotá, there is a display of gold vases, rings, breastplates, and necklaces. Some were made as early as the year A.D. 300. Indian artisans used methods that are still used by goldsmiths today. Colombia remains the largest producer of gold in South America.

Almost all of the world's emeralds come from around Muzo, northwest of Bogotá. The Muzo Indians mined this rich green gem before the Spanish came.

Colombia is the only country in South America where platinum is found. This precious metal is mined and dredged in the Atrato and San Juan rivers in western Colombia. In the department of Santander, north of Bogotá, uranium began to be refined in 1959. Coal and iron are mined and used in the production of steel at Paz del Río and Medellín. Formerly, Colombia produced enough oil for its own needs and for export. But production has declined, and since 1976, Colombia has had to import oil.

At Zipaquirá, just north of Bogotá, there is a giant salt mine that could supply the whole world for 100 years or more. Workers have carved out a vast underground cathedral in the mine. Its dark galleries of rock salt are lit with electric lamps. Zipaquirá, besides providing Colombians with salt for their tables, is now a tourist attraction.

CITIES

Colombia's four major cities are very different from one another. The capital, Bogotá, is quiet and conservative. It is situated on a plateau high in the mountains. The climate is cool, and there is a great deal of rain. *Bogotanos* hurry about their business dressed in dark clothing and often carrying rolled umbrellas. Bogotá is Colombia's largest city and is growing rapidly. It is the nation's center of business, education, and culture.

Around Plaza Bolívar, in the center of Bogotá, the Spanish built a beautiful cathedral and government buildings. At night the buildings are lit by floodlights. Very old churches—such as San Francisco, Santa Clara, and San Agustín—still stand next to modern office buildings. Many people walk into these churches at any hour of the day. During holidays the altars are ablaze with candles placed there by the faithful.

The National Capitol, built a century ago, is still the most famous public building in the country. The church of Monserrate—which rises high above the city and is reached by cable car—offers a splendid view of the city and its surroundings.

Steep, narrow streets climb into the old section of Bogotá. Here the houses have barred windows, carved doorways, and broad tile roofs that extend over the street. Still farther up is a section with crowded streets, teeming with activity. Crumbling houses of whitewashed adobe line the cobbled streets. An article on Bogotá is included in Volume B.

Medellín, the second largest city, is the capital of the department of Antioquia. It is lower in elevation than Bogotá but still in the mountains. Medellín is Colombia's industrial, coffee, and mining center. There are many large, modern textile factories. Some of these industries have music and sports clubs and even museums that add to the life of the city. Most colonial buildings have disappeared. The city is neat and modern. Cattle are raised in the nearby countryside. There is a cattle auction in Medellín every week.

Barranquilla, on the north coast, is the main port of Colombia. It is a modern city, famous

Bogotá is a city surrounded by mountains.

for its gay carnival celebration. The nearby port of Cartagena is a very old city. It is still surrounded by the walls that were built in the 17th century. Nearby hills have been mined for over a thousand years.

Cali is the chief city of the Cauca Valley and one of the most beautiful in Colombia. It lies high above sea level, but it has a mild tropical climate. Sugar is an important crop in the area. Every December a sugarcane festival is held. Throughout the city there is dancing and music, and the world's best bullfighters perform in the Cali bullring. Today the city is attracting industries. Textiles, paper, soap, and plastics are made there.

GOVERNMENT

For generations each Colombian city was the center of a region that was cut off from the rest of the country. Each region had its own way of life. At times Colombia was a loose confederation of city-states. Today the Republic of Colombia has a strong central government, operating under the constitution of 1886, which has been amended a number of times.

The president is elected for a 4-year term and cannot serve two terms in succession. The legislature, called the Congress, consists of the Senate and the House of Representatives. Members are elected for 4-year terms at the same time as the president.

The country is divided into 22 departments. Each has a governor appointed by the president. Governors appoint the mayors of cities. Some distant areas, where few people live, have not yet become departments. They are called intendancies and commissaries.

▶ HISTORY

The first permanent settlement in Colombia was at Santa Marta, on the Caribbean coast, in 1525. The conquistador Gonzalo Jiménez de Quesada journeyed up the Magdalena River and found the plateau of Bogotá in 1538.

The name "Colombia" is taken from the name of Christopher Columbus, discoverer of the New World. This was not always the name of the country. The Spanish called it New Granada and its seat of government Santa Fe de Bogotá. The name Colombia was first used after independence was won.

Colombian Independence Day, July 20, commemorates the day in 1810 when patriots set up the first free Colombian government. But it was nine years before the country was really free of Spanish rule. During that time the battle for independence was led by a Venezuelan, Simón Bolívar, "The Liberator." After his victory at Boyacá in 1819, Bolívar became president of the Republic of Gran (Greater) Colombia. This included the present nations of Panama, Ecuador, Venezuela, and Colombia.

Bolívar spent most of his time on the march, helping to liberate countries to the south. The real leader of Gran Colombia was Francisco de Paula Santander, the vice-president. In 1830, Venezuela and Ecuador broke away from Gran Colombia. (Panama remained part of Colombia until 1903.) Bolívar died soon after. Santander became the president of what was then called the Republic of New Granada.

Two competing political parties had developed in the country, the Conservatives and the Liberals. The Conservatives wanted a strong central government, allied to the upper classes, the army, and the Catholic Church. The Liberals wanted a loose confederation of states and wished to take away the great power of the church and its control over education. The political struggles between the two parties continued throughout the 19th century. They finally erupted into a violent civil war in 1899.

An agreement between the two parties brought an end to the civil war in 1902. Colombia enjoyed democratic elections and industrial growth. In the early decades of the 20th century, the Conservatives held power. In 1930 the Liberals won election, and they controlled the government for the next 16 years. During this period labor unions were made legal and other social reforms were begun.

In 1948 a well-known Liberal leader, Jorge Gaitán, was assassinated. Colombia was again plunged into violence as guerrilla bands killed thousands of people. In 1953 the desperate Colombians turned to General Gustavo Rojas Pinilla, who ruled as a military dictator for four years. Finally, the Liberals and Conservatives joined forces and deposed Rojas. In an effort to end the political turmoil, the two parties agreed, in 1957, to share in running the government. Under this plan, called the National Front, the presidency was to alternate between Liberals and Conservatives every four years.

Recent Events. The National Front alliance brought a measure of political stability and economic progress to Colombia. Gradually, this system was phased out. In the elections in 1974, several political parties competed freely, although the Liberals and Conservatives remained dominant. In 1978, Julio César Turbay Ayala, a Liberal, was narrowly elected president. He was faced with a number of problems, including inflation, unemployment, illegal drug traffic, and demands for social and economic change. Belisario Betancur Cuartas, a Conservative who was elected president in 1982, pledged to improve the economy. He also sought peace with the left-wing terrorists who had been fighting the government and the army for more than 30 years.

J. DAVID BOWEN
Author, *Hello, South America*

COLONIAL LIFE IN AMERICA

The first Englishmen who settled at Jamestown in 1607 did not know how to live in the wilderness. George Percy, one of the settlers, wrote of life in those early times, "There were never Englishmen left in a foreign county in such misery as we were in this newly discovered Virginia." The settlers suffered from hunger, exposure, and disease. When the food they brought from England ran out, many died. They did not know how to hunt in the American forests even though the forests were filled with game. They might have planted gardens, but every man strong enough to work had to help fortify the town and build houses. Also they wasted time looking for gold. Since the Englishmen did not know how to build log cabins, they constructed mud and frame houses like those built by poor farmers in England. It took them a long time to learn to live in the forest.

People faced these same problems in almost every new settlement. The Plymouth settlers, sick and hungry, lived most of their first winter on board the *Mayflower*. The few men who were well spent their time building a storehouse and simple homes. In Massachusetts the first Puritan settlers spent a winter in wigwams and sailcloth tents. Over

200 of about 1,000 settlers died before February, 1631, when a vessel arrived from England with fresh supplies.

In time, though, Englishmen began to learn how to live in the wilderness. By the 18th century small cities and towns were well established. The fear of starving was over, and the colonists began planning a future for themselves, their children, and their grandchildren. They now built permanent homes and public buildings. The new land was becoming their homeland.

▶ FAMILY LIFE IN COLONIAL AMERICA

When Benjamin Franklin was a boy in Boston, he could look across the dinner table and count as many as 13 brothers and sisters. He might also see his Uncle Benjamin, his parents, and a neighborhood friend. In his home he might listen as his elders talked about local affairs or sang or played the fiddle. Sometimes the congregation of Boston's Old South Church held prayer services in the Franklin home. Franklin learned to read at home long before his father decided to send him to school. He went to school at 8 but was only allowed to stay 2 years. Then, at 10, young Ben began learning his father's trade of candle and soap making. He watched his elder brothers and sisters marry and leave home. Then, when he was 12 years old, he too left to become his brother's apprentice in the printing trade.

Benjamin Franklin's family was not unusual. Most families did not have as many children as the Franklins, but the birth rate in colonial America was very high. Half the people of colonial America were less than 16 years old.

Life in colonial America centered around the family. Most people worked, played, learned, and worshiped at home within the family circle. Their relatives and friends lived nearby. It was quite common for someone to live his entire life without moving outside the circle of family and friends.

Servants and Slaves

Most well-to-do town families had servants, often country girls who came to town to work. Some colonists in the North as well as in the South owned Negro slaves. Farm families in New England usually had hired men who helped with the farm work. Young servants lived as members of the family, except in the wealthiest homes.

Some servants were called indentured servants. They were poor immigrants who bound themselves to work for masters who paid the costs of the expensive journey to America. In Pennsylvania, Maryland, and Virginia their term of service was frequently 4 years, and in New England 7 years. While in service,

Main street in a colonial seaport, such as New York or Philadelphia, probably looked like this.

they were fed, clothed, and cared for within the family. The master had the same authority over them that he had over his own children. For example, they could not marry without his consent. When their time of indenture (service) was up, the master gave them money, clothing, and tools to start them on their way as free citizens.

Farmers in the South bought slaves to help with crops that required a great deal of labor. The farmers fed and clothed the slaves, and cared for them when they were sick. Slaves labored at every kind of job that needed to be done without any hope of freedom.

▶ HOW PEOPLE EARNED A LIVING

Colonial families used money less than people do today. They made many things for themselves that we buy in stores. Even so, every family had to have some way to earn money. Most Americans were farmers, but there were craftsmen who made such things as furniture and shoes. Some men worked as miners, millers, shipbuilders, shopkeepers, or merchants. In every colony there were also teachers and preachers, lawyers, doctors, and government workers. A well-to-do man often earned his money in more than one way. He might be a farmer, a lawyer, and a government official; or a merchant, a manufacturer of rope, and a shipbuilder. But most men made their living by one kind of work that could be done at home.

Farming

Farm families worked very hard. The women cared for the vegetable gardens and the dairy. The farmer, his sons, and his servants plowed the fields, split rails for fences, and cleared new land. Work went on all during the year, from the spring planting of crops to the making and repairing of tools in midwinter.

A farmer's work never ended, but he was busiest at harvest time. On a Pennsylvania farm when hay was ready to be mowed, the farmer's family got up at dawn. The farmer and his boys sharpened sickles until breakfast time. By then, neighboring farm families began to arrive to help in the fields, for these farmers helped one another with major jobs, such as harvesting wheat or building barns. By six o'clock, 15 or 20 men, women, and boys were in the fields, mowing the hay with the sharp, curved sickles. After a stop at ten o'clock for lunch, they raked and hauled hay to the barns until late afternoon, when they stopped again for supper. Then, starting in again, they mowed until dark.

New England farms were smaller than those elsewhere. The farmers did not have any one large crop they could sell for much money. The farmer planted and harvested some wheat, corn, and hay. He also raised a few cattle and often kept sheep for their wool. Farmers who lived near the forests of Maine or western Massachusetts spent much of their time cutting timber and making the lumber for which New England became famous. New England farm families made and sold wooden pegs, wooden bowls, pitch, tar, and turpentine. Those farmers who lived near the sea were often fishermen who farmed only enough to get food for their families.

Large farms in the South were called plantations. Southern planters used slaves to help with the work. Tobacco was grown in the best fields because the plant required rich soil. Within 6 or 7 years, tobacco would exhaust the soil and the planter would have to clear new land. Clearing fields, growing tobacco, cutting timber to make hogsheads (barrels) in which the tobacco was packed to be shipped to England, and growing the family's food kept the planter and his workers very busy. But growing rice called for even more labor. The rice plantations of South Carolina could not operate without large numbers of slaves. Rice planters frequently chose to live in Charleston during the hot summers, leaving overseers in charge of their inland plantations.

Crafts, Manufacturing, and Business

Craftsmen were skilled workers. Cobblers made shoes, stonemasons built chimneys, and millers ground flour. Every town had its carpenters, cabinetmakers, tailors, printers, hatmakers, wigmakers, and saddlemakers. There were also bakers, tallow chandlers (candlemakers), cutlers (knife repairers), wheelwrights, coopers (barrelmakers), and apothecaries (pharmacists). The craftsman's house was often behind his shop, which made it convenient for his family to help with the work. Behind the house were the family

The house above was typical of the homes in colonial New England in the 17th century.

In the Middle Colonies, Dutch homes like the one above were popular. Below, the home of a wealthy planter in Virginia is modeled after an English manor house.

garden and pens for the pigs and chickens.

A few Americans ran businesses. Some operated iron furnaces and forges, while others were merchants who imported supplies from Great Britain and sold American goods overseas. These men often worked in partnership with relatives in England or America. Very few had enough money or credit to establish a large business by themselves.

In the colonies a young man often learned a trade by serving as an apprentice. Apprentices began living in their masters' households when they were about 14 years old. They were legally bound to their masters for 6 or 8 years. The master fed, clothed, and housed his apprentices. He taught them his craft and to read and write. Sometimes the master was paid for his trouble. The son of a prosperous family might be sent to England to learn about business from a great merchant.

Many lawyers and doctors in colonial America also learned their professions by serving as apprentices. Law was not taught in any American college until 1755, and the first medical college was not established until 1765. The only way a young man could learn these professions was by assisting a colonial doctor or lawyer at his work.

COLONIAL HOUSES

The first settlers in America built very crude kinds of shelters, wanting only to get a roof over their heads as quickly as possible. In Jamestown the settlers built one-room thatch and mud huts, with a hole in the roof to let out smoke. The homes of the first Massachusetts settlers resembled the wigwams of the local Indians. In Plymouth the earliest shelters were merely holes dug into hills and covered over by a bark roof supported by poles. These English settlers were unfamiliar with the one-room log cabin that later became so common on the American frontier. It was the Swedes who introduced the log cabin to America in their settlements on the lower Delaware.

Later the colonists began to build plain wooden houses that were sturdy but not large or elaborate. Usually the house was a box-shaped frame of heavy beams covered with rough hand-split boards or shingles. These were left unpainted to weather a silver gray. The upstairs had three or four small,

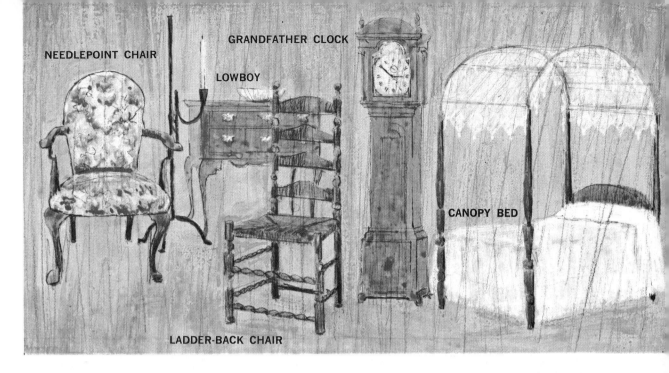

NEEDLEPOINT CHAIR

GRANDFATHER CLOCK

LOWBOY

CANOPY BED

LADDER-BACK CHAIR

square bedrooms with low ceilings. The downstairs was divided into rooms where the family ate and worked. Sometimes, especially in the South, the kitchen was a separate building.

New Englanders built many houses that were one and a half stories high in the front and only one story in the back. Their roofs sloped steeply from front to back. These were called salt-box houses because they looked like the wooden boxes in which the colonists stored salt. In New York the end of the house faced the street, so that the house appeared to be high and narrow. In the South a house might have brick chimneys at each end and a central hallway through the middle. The chimney was built in the center of the house in New England.

The interior walls of most colonial houses were made of wooden planks that were sometimes plastered. Windows were small, and few had glass panes. Wooden shutters kept out the cold and rain. In New England floors were made of hand-packed dirt sprinkled daily with fresh sand. Later floors were made of wide boards left unpainted. Furniture was plain and consisted of unpainted chairs, stools, beds, and tables made of oak, maple, or pine. Most rooms had large cupboards, for there were no clothes closets.

In the 17th century even the large houses of the well-to-do had low ceilings and dark,

plain interiors. These houses were sometimes built of brick and had diamond-shaped windowpanes. The lady of the house often cherished a few pieces of silver and some fine chairs of polished oak, which had been made in England.

Then in the 18th century a great change took place in the style of American homes. Well-to-do Americans built elegant houses similar to those in England. Three-story frame mansions topped with graceful walks and cupolas (small domes or towers) dotted the New England coast. Fine stone or brick houses made Philadelphia a handsome city; and on southern plantations there were brick houses and well-arranged groups of service buildings. Furniture imported from England and fine pieces of brass and pewter began to brighten the rooms of most houses. Inside 18th-century mansions walls were paneled in wood or covered with wallpaper imported

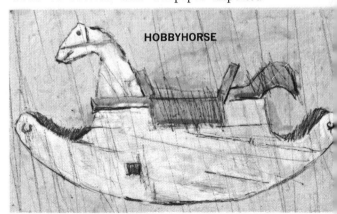

HOBBYHORSE

Brewis, crusts cut from a loaf of thick, hard bread, and stewed in milk or other fluids.

Dumbfish, codfish which has gone through a curing process called dumbing or dunning.

Jerky, beef cut into strips and dried before a fire.

Nocake, parched corn pounded into powder. In winter the parched corn was mixed with snow, and in summer it was mixed with water.

Pompion, an affectionate nickname for pumpkin.

"Rye-an' injun," a loaf of bread made with equal parts of rye flour and corn meal.

Samp, corn pounded into a coarse powder and eaten with milk and butter. Roger Williams called it "a diet exceedingly wholesome for English bodies."

Suppawn, or **hasty pudding,** corn meal boiled with milk into a thick porridge.

from France or England. Persian rugs, mahogany tables and chairs, damask and silk draperies, portraits, gilt mirrors, and gleaming silver urns and teapots blended to create homes as beautiful as America has ever known.

▶ **CLOTHING AND FEEDING THE FAMILY**

A group of ladies and gentlemen attending a banquet in New York in the 1740's dressed brilliantly. They ordered the very latest English fashions from London, and only the finest silks or wools pleased them. A man might wear a green silk coat trimmed with lace, a brilliant yellow waistcoat, buff knee breeches, and white silk stockings. He usually carried a sword at his side. Or he might wear a coat of satin or silk in shades of scarlet, sky blue, or maroon. The ladies in their silk dresses matched the men in color and splendor. And the food at a New York banquet was as elegant as the dress of the guests. Imported oranges, olives, raisins, anchovies, and Madeira wine added interest to the platters of beef, fowl, fish, and garden vegetables.

The great majority of the colonists, however, did not dine or dress elegantly at all. Most families bought long-wearing linen or flannel for their clothing. In rural New England and on the distant frontier, people often made their own cloth. Day after day the women sat at home sewing the dull green, brown, or mottled gray material. They also patched and altered clothing as long as there

was any wear left. Laboring men often wore tough leather breeches.

Even more time went into keeping the family fed. Where labor was scarce, a garden might have only cabbages, beans, corn, and pumpkins. Potatoes became common some time after the 1720's. More prosperous gardeners grew carrots, beets, turnips, onions, leeks, radishes, and melons. Apples, plums, cherries, peaches, and pears came from the orchards. As for meat, flocks of chickens and ducks were to be found in farmyards, and the woods were teeming with wild game. Stories have come down to us from colonial times of great herds of 200 deer and of flocks of 100 wild turkeys. Deer were so plentiful that some frontier families lived on venison for 9 months a year. William Penn wrote that a 30-pound wild turkey could be bought for a shilling (then worth about 25 cents) in Pennsylvania. Pheasant, partridge, woodcock, and quail were hunted in large numbers. There were so many pigeons that flocks would darken the sky and break the limbs of trees on which they perched. Squirrels were so numerous that they became a problem, and many towns began paying a bounty for their heads. In 1749, in Pennsylvania, over 600,000 squirrels were killed for bounties. Perch and trout were caught in the streams, and fish, clams, lobsters, turtles, and oysters were gathered from the sea.

Although they had no refrigeration and did not know how to can, colonial families had ways of preserving their food. They dried beans and fruit, hung strings of onions in high, dry places, and pickled sauerkraut in large crocks. They salted, spiced, and smoked meats of all kinds. Many farmers made their own beverages—cider, beer, and even brandy.

▶ **BRINGING UP CHILDREN**

One of the hardest jobs a parent had in colonial times was keeping his newborn children alive. Shocking numbers of young children died of diphtheria, smallpox, scarlet fever, and measles. In Hingham, Massachusetts, where records were kept, one death out of five in the community was of an infant less than 2 years old. The famous Massachusetts clergyman Cotton Mather saw nine of his children die before their second birth-

Clothing in colonial times ranged from very elegant dress clothes to simple everyday working-clothes.

days. Tragedies like this were common. The few doctors in the colonies in those days had very limited medical knowledge. One remedy, for example, was to give a sick child a mixture of roots, rum, and water.

Like parents today, colonial parents wanted their children to grow up to be useful and responsible adults. To many parents in colonial times, bringing up a child properly sometimes meant being strict. Colonial parents expected their children to be obedient, prompt, and polite. Their children were about as well behaved as children today. Some were polite. A few were rude. Colonial children usually learned about the adult world by doing things the way their parents did.

Colonial children were expected to help with a good share of the family's work. Self-reliance was emphasized. In the South it was common for a father to hand his young son a gun and send him out alone into the woods. Thomas Jefferson's father did this when his son was 10, although all young Tom managed to kill was a wild turkey that he found trapped in a pen.

Young girls too did a great deal of work. Four-year-old girls could knit stockings. One young girl in New Hampshire became so

The schoolmaster looks on as a pupil recites his lesson from a slate.

Parties on Virginia plantations featured the minuet, a dance popular in Europe.

skilled that she knitted the whole alphabet and a verse of poetry into a single pair of mittens.

As for formal schooling, most children in early colonial times never saw the inside of a schoolhouse. Some well-to-do families sent their daughters to dancing masters or to music teachers. A few of the richer families hired private tutors, who then set up a little school for all the young people of the family. And there were some neighborhood schools in New England and most towns and cities. A great many children learned to read at home, too.

By the time they were 14, most children were already considered adults. Boys would soon do a man's work at home or leave home to be an apprentice. Girls learned to manage a house, and expected to marry early, probably by the time they were 16 and surely before they were 20.

▶ FAMILY AMUSEMENTS

Colonial children played many of the same games children play today. Little girls cared for their pets and played with dolls. Boys shot marbles, pitched pennies, and went fishing. Colonial children played games like tag and blindman's buff.

Adults too managed to take time out from their work to enjoy themselves. Most country people loved to dance, and at weddings the dancing and card playing often lasted all night. On militia days men drank beer or rum punch together and swapped tall tales after they finished their drilling and marching. Men and boys sometimes came from all over a rural countryside to watch a famous cockfight or to race their fastest horses.

Everyone looked forward to fairs, when countryfolk would come to town from miles around to sell their produce and have a good time. There were races, prizes, dancing, puppet shows, and magicians. A prize was offered to the man who could catch a greased pig or climb a greased pole, or whistle a tune without laughing.

In the towns there were always things to do. Taverns had billiard tables, skittle tables, and shuffleboards. Many had bowling greens outside. A public race track ran around Beaver Pond on Long Island, and most towns south of New York had at least one track for horse racing. There were public dances in the towns and elegant parties in the ballrooms of the great mansions. In the 17th century, racing, dancing, and gaming were prohibited in New England, but during the 18th century, Boston had dancing schools, and stableboys matched pennies in the streets. By the middle of the 18th century, there were theaters and musical clubs that

In New England the ducking stool was the punishment for women who gossiped in public.

gave concerts of violin, flute, and organ music.

▶ LIFE IN THE NEW ENGLAND COLONIES

In colonial America, as in all civilized places, there were schools, churches, markets, and governments. But ways of living differed from colony to colony. New England in the 18th century was a land of tidy fields and villages. Many towns were built around a common (village square). The church, the school, and sometimes a town hall were built on the common.

Religion in New England

The Puritans who came to New England in the 17th century were a strongly religious people. Everything in the New England Puritan communities centered around the church. In fact, one of the main reasons these people lived so close to villages was so that they could be near their church. They believed that God had chosen them to be an example for others of the good Christian life. Therefore their most important duty was to worship God and spread the Puritan religion.

On Saturday afternoon all activities came to a halt in the Puritan towns. The preparations for Sunday began. On Sunday everyone had to go to church services. The services began in the morning and lasted well into the afternoon, with one intermission around noon. Sermons lasted for 2 or 3 hours, and prayers for 1 or 2. Psalm singing would sometimes stretch out for a half hour. The deacon read aloud while the congregation stood and sang after him, usually off-key. In winter the people had to bundle up warmly, for the churches were unheated until late in the 17th century.

The church was also the center of the political life of the Puritan community. Town meetings were held in the church, and the Puritan ministers were respected leaders in the communities. Justice was closely bound up with religion. A man might be punished for an offense against his religion, such as getting drunk, or fishing on Sunday, or not working hard enough. A man who got drunk might have to wear a sign with a D on it around his neck so that everyone would know why he was being punished. There were more severe punishments in New England, too, such as whipping or branding with a hot iron. Such punishments were customary in Europe and other colonies as well.

The Puritans came to America to gain religious freedom. But the religious freedom they sought was for themselves and not for others. The Puritan leaders believed that dissenters (people who disagreed with their religious ideas) would have a bad effect on

Puritans. Therefore, they not only failed to practice religious toleration but thought it dangerous. People like Roger Williams and Anne Hutchinson, who were dissenters, were forced to go to other colonies. Quaker missionaries who tried to make converts among the Puritans in the 1650's were imprisoned and put to death.

Superstition was also a part of life in New England. To the Puritans, as to other people of the 17th century, the world was a battleground where good and evil forces fought. Devils and witches were everywhere, causing thunderstorms, strangling infants in their cradles, making people sick, sinking ships, and ruining crops. The Puritans believed that the devil sometimes won people over to his side and made them witches.

There were two periods of witch-hunting in New England in the 17th century. Between 1647 and 1663 hundreds of people in Massachusetts and Connecticut were accused of witchcraft and 14 were actually executed. Later, from 1688 to 1693, there was another witch hunt, in Salem, Massachusetts, during which 19 people were hanged. In the end the witch-hunt frenzy became so bad that even the leaders of communities were accused of being witches. It was then that the power of the witch-hunters was broken. They had gone too far.

By the early part of the 18th century many people with less religious zeal than the early Puritan settlers were moving into the colonies. Puritan ministers in the 18th century no longer played such active roles in town affairs.

New England Schools

To the Bible-reading Puritans of New England, education was important. Puritans had to be educated so that they could read the Bible and understand their ministers' sermons. An even better education had to be provided for young men who wanted to become ministers. Schooling was so important to the Puritans that the government in Massachusetts passed laws requiring towns to have schools. New England had more schools than any other region of colonial America. The Boston Latin School, founded in 1635, carefully prepared its boys for entrance to college. Most other schools taught little more than reading, writing, and arithmetic. A few schools were also provided to teach Indian children.

In 1636 Massachusetts set up Harvard College, the first college in the colonies. Before the end of the colonial period there were three more New England colleges—Yale, Brown, and Dartmouth.

The New England colleges tried to keep alive a spirit of learning. Latin, Greek, science, and philosophy took up most of the students' time. They also learned to debate and to write well. Those who graduated became the clergymen, lawyers, doctors, and leaders in their communities, even though they were not trained for any particular profession. They often got their special training by serving as apprentices.

New England Books and Newspapers

New England was the center for the printing of books and newspapers. The first American printing press began operation in 1638. By 1715 New England had six busy presses. The Boston *News Letter,* founded in 1704, was the first newspaper printed in the colonies. The printers also published copies of English books, sermons, pamphlets, and government documents. Newspapers and almanacs became popular with readers in every colony.

Public Affairs in New England

The first New England leaders believed that their government had the special approval of God. They debated among themselves to decide what God's will was. Thus a tradition of public debate and discussion began. Leading citizens debated town problems as well as religion. Everyone could join in the town-meeting debate. New England voters could vote for more public officials than most other colonists.

The New England Economy

New England grew most of its own food, made much of its own clothing, and produced many of its supplies. But New Englanders had to buy cloth and tools and almost all their luxury items from England. New England had few things it could ship to England in return. The furs, lumber, and ships that were sent were not worth as much as the

The tradition of the New England town meeting began in colonial days. Everyone could attend these meetings and debate church and town matters.

goods bought in England. So the New Englanders found other ways of earning the money they needed. They caught, salted, and preserved codfish, halibut, and mackerel in great quantities. They sold the best of their catch in Spain and Portugal, and the rest in the West Indies as food for slaves. They also engaged in a rather complicated trade involving molasses, rum, and slaves. The New Englanders would take dried fish and supplies to the West Indies, and bring home molasses. From molasses they made rum, which they sold in the colonies or hauled to the coasts of Africa to buy Negro slaves. Then they sold the slaves in the West Indies or in the southern colonies. New England traders also made money by selling iron pots, kettles, and tools in other colonies and by hauling goods from colony to colony.

▶ LIFE IN THE MIDDLE COLONIES

Living side by side in New York, New Jersey, and Pennsylvania were people who spoke different languages and worshiped in different ways. In Albany and New York City, ministers preached in Dutch to their Dutch Reformed congregations for a hundred years after the colony became an English possession. Though leading Englishmen in New York were Anglicans (members of the Church of England), many Englishmen and Scots were Presbyterians. There were also Baptists, Jews, and Roman Catholics in New York City.

The English who named and settled Pennsylvania were Quakers. They hoped Pennsylvania would be a place where they could worship simply and live peacefully. Several German religious groups also came to Pennsylvania. Among these were Mennonites, Moravians, Dunkers, and Schwenkfelders. Lutherans and German Reformed groups as well as Scottish and Irish Presbyterians and Anglicans became active in Pennsylvania affairs.

Philadelphia had more civic, social, and

religious organizations than any other city. Unlike a New England villager, a man living in Philadelphia in the middle of the 18th century expected to see separate schools run by the Quakers, Baptists, Lutherans, and Moravians, among others. There were many different clubs and societies. Some were to help the poor; others supported libraries; and one kept alive the songs and legends of Ireland. There were insurance companies, fire companies, and organizations of merchants or artisans. One group of doctors opened a hospital. Philadelphia and New York bustled with the activity of citizens meeting, planning, and doing things together.

The Economy of the Middle Colonies

The Middle Colonies, like the New England Colonies, produced many things. Farmers raised more than enough food for the growing population. Pennsylvania was a center for iron mining and making iron tools,

nails, and pots and pans. The Philadelphia craftsmen were known throughout America for their fine furniture and well-designed silver. But colonial workmen could not make cloth as cheaply as English or European workers, for colonial wages were high. The Middle Colonies imported cloth, manufactured goods, and luxuries.

What could they sell abroad? Mainly wheat, flour, barley, and oats. Flour milling was a major industry, and millers of Pennsylvania and New York competed for the reputation of making the best flour in America. Merchant millers sometimes built bakehouses and made hard bread to be sold abroad. Pennsylvania butchers bought cattle from as far away as North Carolina, and sold thousands of barrels of salted beef and pork each year to other colonies and to Europe. The best markets for wheat and flour were in Spain and Portugal. The West Indies offered good markets for all types of

Ferryboats were a common form of transportation in colonial days.

food. Less important exports were flaxseed sent to Ireland and iron ore and ships to Great Britain. Trade was so brisk that the Middle Colonies became very prosperous.

▶ LIFE IN THE SOUTHERN COLONIES

It took a long time for a man to travel by land from Savannah, Georgia, to Baltimore, Maryland, in the 18th century. The roads were often only paths through the woods, and there were no signs to point out the way to the traveler. He could easily get lost. But on the other hand he could travel for hundreds of miles without having to spend much money. Travelers were rare, so farmers along the way gave them food and a place to sleep in exchange for their company and news of public events.

A Savannah-to-Baltimore traveler passed through Charleston, the one large town in the South. He rode through the shadowy pine forests of the Carolinas. He had to ford dozens of slow-moving streams, and ferry across the broad James River to Williamsburg, the small but handsome capital of Virginia. Then he traveled on through the Chesapeake country to Baltimore. On this trip the traveler could see the finest tobacco fields in all America, and perhaps some great plantation houses. But even then he could not say he had seen the South, for the South was large and its people were scattered. The distance from Savannah to Baltimore is close to 600 miles, but a traveler in those days stayed along the eastern coast, where most traveling was done. By the 18th century the colonial South extended as far as 350 miles inland, past the Piedmont and Blue Ridge Mountains all the way to the Appalachians. The people who lived in the western mountain country or in the Great Valley of Virginia in western Virginia had little contact with the eastern communities. They had their own way of life.

Charleston and the Chesapeake Country

During much of the 18th century, life in Charleston was similar to that of Philadelphia and New York. Most of the white people were English, but there were some Scots and a number of French Protestants called Huguenots. The Anglican Church was strong, and there were few congregations of other religious groups. Negro slaves made up a large part of the population and did most of the manual labor. More often than in New York or Boston, the Charleston merchants were agents of British firms. Charleston was famous for its clubs and societies and its gay parties. Its Library Society was known by booklovers everywhere.

Most of the people in the Chesapeake country lived on farms and plantations. About half of them were Negro slaves; most of the rest were English. There were a few Irish workmen and, in the villages, some Scottish storekeepers and traders. Two towns, Norfolk and Baltimore, began to grow as trading centers just before the American Revolution. Families in the Chesapeake area lived too far apart to take part in many community activities. There were few schools and churches except in the villages. William and Mary College, founded in 1693 at Williamsburg, was the only college in the South.

Life on a Southern plantation was leisurely and gracious for the planter and his family.

Public affairs were in the hands of the county court and the colonial government. The vestry was the governing body of the parish church. Vestrymen looked after the church and cared for orphans and the poor. The county court heard legal disputes and cases involving law violations. It also was in charge of issuing licenses to tavern keepers and seeing to it that roads were built and repaired. Members of the county court were appointed by the colonial governor. The most important local occasion came when the county court met. Lawyers came to try cases. Merchants were there to buy crops and to collect debts. Farmers came to do business and just to see one another. For a day or so the little villages were as crowded as larger towns. Everyone was so busy having fun that this became a traditional time for slaves who wanted freedom to escape from their masters.

The Southern Economy

The people of the Chesapeake area grew large crops of tobacco, corn, and wheat. The planters of South Carolina grew rice and indigo. The cakes of valuable blue dye made from the indigo plant were much sought after by cloth manufacturers. From the pine trees of Carolina and Virginia, farmers made pitch, tar, and turpentine. Upland farmers herded cattle and hogs. A few Virginia mines yielded iron ore.

Unlike the New Englanders the Southern colonists produced many things wanted in England. Tobacco was the most valuable colonial export to England. (As yet little cotton was raised.) When prices were high, Southerners could make good money from farming. As a result, they manufactured less and imported more tools and household goods than the colonists of the North. Few Southerners became merchants. English and Scottish merchants brought them most of their goods and bought their tobacco and rice. But when the land became worn or when prices went down, the farmer's crops would not sell for enough money to buy the things he needed. Then, unless he could get new land and find a cheaper way to grow his crops, he faced financial ruin.

Southerners loved to farm and loved the country life. They said proudly that Virginia

How did the American colonists make candles?

Candles were made of tallow, bayberry wax, or beeswax. Candle dipping was generally done in the same iron pot used for making soap. Animal fat (tallow) was melted and then allowed to cool slightly. Six or eight wick strings, made of hemp or cotton, were hung on sticks called candle rods. These wicks were dipped in and out of the tallow again and again until the candles reached the desired thickness. It was a long and tiresome process. Between each dipping there was a wait for the tallow to harden.

In more prosperous homes candles were made in moulds of pewter or sheet iron (called tin). In some towns traveling candlemakers, called chandlers, went from house to house carrying their moulds with them. Benjamin Franklin's father was a tallow and wax chandler.

The New England colonists learned that the waxy substance of the grayish-white bayberry was excellent for candle making. The berries were tossed into a kettle of boiling water. The wax in the berries floated to the surface and was skimmed off. This wax was allowed to harden and then was melted down again. The process was repeated several times until the wax acquired a transparent green color. Candles made from bayberry wax gave a clearer light and also had an agreeable fragrance.

A few candles were made of beeswax. These candles were shaped by hand by pressing bits of heated wax around a wick. Hives of bees were kept by farmers as much for their wax as for their honey.

was the largest and wealthiest of the colonies. They counted on their land and their skill as farmers to keep Virginia prosperous.

▶ THE FRONTIER

In 1670, when the first American colonies were fairly well settled, the population was about 115,000. A hundred years later, a few years before the Revolutionary War, it was nearly 2,250,000. Colonial America was no longer a number of settlements on the Atlantic coast. Now it was a great stretch of land reaching hundreds of miles inland and being pushed farther west by pioneers every day. People in the earliest settlements had their established patterns of living, but the pioneers were facing the wilderness just as the first American settlers had.

By the 18th century colonial pioneers like James Robertson and Ethan Allen lived deep in the wilderness far from the coast. New Englanders began moving westward into central Massachusetts and northward up the Connecticut River Valley. By the 1760's they were settling Vermont and western New Hampshire, and pushing back the frontiers of Maine. To the south, pioneers settled western New York, Pennsylvania, western Maryland and Virginia, and the Piedmont region of North and South Carolina. Some of the pioneers came from the colonies that had already been established on the Atlantic coast. Others were new immigrants to America—mainly Germans and Scotch-Irish, Scots who had earlier migrated to Northern Ireland. Before the American Revolution, pioneers had begun crossing the Cumberland Gap into eastern Kentucky and clearing fields in the valleys of eastern Tennessee.

ROBERT POLK THOMSON
George Peabody College

See also AMERICAN COLONIES; JAMESTOWN; PLYMOUTH COLONY.

COLOR. See DESIGN AND COLOR; LIGHT.

COLORADO

The burro was a familiar sight on the mining trails of the Old West. It plodded along, carrying a pack of mining equipment—picks, hammers, washing pans, shovels—and sacks of "grub." Beside the burro walked the prospector, dreaming of shining gold.

In the town of Fairplay, Colorado, high in the Rocky Mountains, there is a monument to a burro whose name was Prunes. For years Prunes worked faithfully, hauling ore and carrying supplies up and down lonely mountain trails. Everybody knew him and liked him. When Prunes died, the townspeople put up a monument for him. Buried near him is his last owner, an old prospector.

The voice of the burro is most unmusical—a roaring "heehaw." Westerners laughingly called the little animals Colorado Mocking Birds or Rocky Mountain Canaries. These "canaries" did their share in the winning of the West. The monument to Prunes is a tribute to all of them.

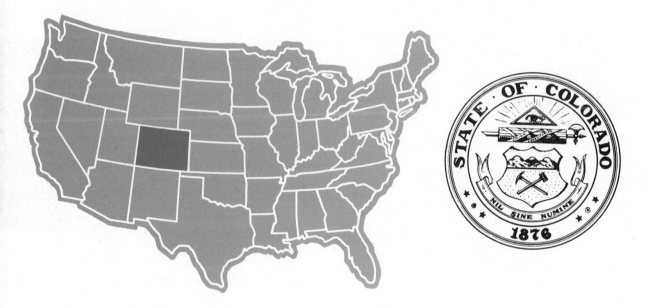

Mountains make the difference between Colorado's story and that of most other states. Gold from the mountains, washed down by mountain streams, brought the first rush of settlers to Denver in 1859. All during the 1860's, prospectors worked their way into the mountains, panning for the fine specks of gold. When surface gold gave out, they took to hard-rock mining and filled the mountainsides with holes and tunnels. Mountain towns sprang into being near the mines and the mills. And cities, in turn, grew up as supply points.

Loggers worked the pine forests of the mountains for railroad ties, bridge timbers, mine props, and boards for buildings. All this activity stimulated the growth of a supporting agriculture of farms and ranches.

Rainfall is light in much of Colorado. It does not permit farming like that of the grain-producing states. But the mountains comb rain and snow from the sky. Great snowbanks and reservoirs hold the water needed for cities and for irrigated farming. Mountains and high plateaus also provide the livestock industry with much of its grassland.

Coal has been of great importance to the economy of Colorado. Coal is mined in many parts of the state—on the plains, in the foot-hills, and in the mountains.

Last, but very important, the mountains are

the main playground for an army of vacationers. In the summer, people from all parts of the nation travel the high mountain passes, fish the trout streams, climb the peaks, and run the rapid rivers with their kayaks.

Then, in the fall, the mountains and plateaus fill up with brightly dressed hunters of deer and elk. In the winter, people flock by the thousands to the mountain slopes to ski. Skiing has revived several old mountain towns—Aspen, Telluride and Steamboat Springs—and created at least one new town, Vail.

The mountains have been a great challenge, too. The early wagons had to climb over steep, rocky passes. The railroads were forced to go through rock cuts and tunnels and over trestles—and to make long detours on their climbs over the high passes. The building of today's wide highways requires blasting and moving huge quantities of rock.

▶ THE LAND

Colorado is one of the group of states called Mountain States because they include parts of the great Rocky Mountain system of North America. Colorado's Rockies are known as the Southern Rocky Mountains.

Colorado is the "Top of the Nation"—the highest of all the states. Its average elevation is about 2,070 meters (6,800 feet).

STATE FLAG.

STATE TREE: Colorado blue spruce.

STATE BIRD: Lark bunting.

STATE FLOWER: Rocky Mountain columbine.

COLORADO

CAPITAL: Denver.

STATEHOOD: August 1, 1876; the 38th state.

SIZE: 269,595 km² (104,091 sq mi); rank, 8th.

POPULATION: 2,889,735 (1980 census); rank, 28th.

ORIGIN OF NAME: From the Spanish word *colorado,* meaning "red" or "reddish colored." The name was first given to the Colorado River and then to the state.

ABBREVIATIONS: Colo.; CO.

NICKNAME: Centennial State because Colorado was admitted to the Union 100 years after the signing of the Declaration of Independence.

STATE SONG: "Where the Columbines Grow," by A. J. Fynn.

STATE MOTTO: *Nil sine numine* (Nothing without the divine will).

STATE SEAL: At the top, in a triangle, is the "all-seeing" eye of God. Under the eye are fasces (a bundle of rods containing an ax), a symbol of authority from ancient Roman times. The words "Union and Constitution" appear on the band around the fasces. On the shield below the fasces are mountains and a miner's sledgehammer and pick.

STATE FLAG: The three stripes—blue, white, and blue —represent the blue of the sky and the white of snow-capped mountains. The golden disk inside the letter C represents gold, the early source of mineral wealth. The red C stands for Colorado.

Snow-covered Pikes Peak rises on the rim of the Rockies.

Landforms

The rectangle of Colorado is divided into three main landforms—mountains, plains, and plateaus. The Southern Rocky Mountains occupy a broad north-south strip in the west central part of the state. To the east of the mountains lie the Great Plains. On the west the mountains give way to tablelands called the Colorado Plateau. Besides these main divisions, there is another region—a small section of the Wyoming Basin—in the northwestern part of the state.

Mountains. The Rocky Mountains rise abruptly from the plains. Some of the mountains, like Pikes Peak, stand alone, with foothills around them. More often the mountains occur in ranges. The usual range is a long, irregular line of peaks, like saw teeth. The Sangre de Cristo Mountains, in south central Colorado, are of this type. The San Juan Mountains, in the southwest, make up a vast domed area where volcanic rock has been eroded into a jumble of peaks and ridges.

Altogether there are more than 2,000 mountains in Colorado. Many of them are not even named. Scattered among them are more than 50 with summits higher than 4,300 meters (14,000 feet) above sea level. They are called fourteeners. Mountain climbers often make

a goal of climbing all of them. The highest is Mount Elbert, in the Sawatch Mountains southwest of Denver. Others in the vicinity of Mount Elbert are named for well-known universities—Mount Harvard, Mount Yale, and Mount Princeton.

Pikes Peak, rising to 4,301 meters (14,110 feet) west of Colorado Springs, became best known in early days because it was the easternmost sentinel for the whole mountain region. Gold seekers of 1859 painted "Pikes Peak or Bust" on their wagons. And now, every day in the summer, hundreds of people reach the top of Pikes Peak by the cog railway or the winding highway or by trail.

In the Rockies snow begins in the autumn. Through the winter and spring it continues to whiten the mountains with a deepening reservoir of moisture. Rotary plows are used to keep the passes open. Dynamite is used on certain slopes to avalanche the snow before it gets dangerously deep above the roads. Only skiers and snowshoers can get around in the mountains at this time of the year, and they usually keep to the ski-tow areas, where the trails are packed for easy running and are patrolled for safety. Melting begins in the spring. It swells the streams through June and early July, turning the mountains into a vast patchwork of white spots, which all but disappear by September.

The mountains show the marks of long centuries of snow, which once packed into deep ice, forming glaciers. These slow rivers of ice scoured great circular "armchairs," called cirques, at the heads of the valleys. The valleys are U-shaped instead of V-shaped, as are valleys cut by water. The deposits left by the glaciers often dam up little blue and green lakes. The Rocky Mountain National Park, in north central Colorado, is a concentrated area of such ice carvings and glacial lakes.

Within the mountain region of Colorado,

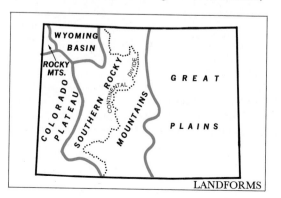

LANDFORMS

there are broad, level valleys, called mountain parks. The San Luis Valley, lying west of the Sangre de Cristo Mountains, is such a park. Three other inland valleys of this kind are North Park, along the North Platte River; Middle Park, through which the upper Colorado flows; and South Park, headwater region of the South Platte. All these areas have an abundance of grass. Bordering them are the summer grazing lands in the mountainous national forests.

The Great Plains. East of the Rockies lie the Great Plains. The valleys of this region are shallow and generally flat. They are used for irrigated farming. Between the valleys are rolling hills, which are usually treeless and grass-covered. Land of this kind is used for pasture or, where there is enough moisture, for the growing of wheat.

The Colorado Plateau. West of the Rockies the rivers run down between high tablelands, which they have cut up into mesas—small, high plateaus with steep sides. Some of these mesas are extensions of the mountain highland. The Blue Mesa, south of the Gunnison River, is of this kind. Others, such as the White River Plateau and the Mesa Verde, are separate formations.

The mesas receive moisture in proportion to their height. The lower ones—those up to 1,800 and 2,100 meters (6,000 and 7,000 feet) in elevation—are dry. The Mesa Verde is of this sort. It has little plant life. In a few cases the lower mesas can be irrigated by water from the mountain streams and can be farmed. The highest mesas—those between 2,400 and 3,000 meters (8,000 and 10,000 feet) in elevation—catch enough rain and snow to support forests and meadows. When cleared, they are suitable for the growing of small grains. Some of the mesas taper off smoothly into lower country. More often they are bordered by steep rimrock, or cliffs. It was in the rimrock that the cliff dwellers of the Mesa Verde built their fortress homes.

The Wyoming Basin. This small section extends into Colorado from Wyoming. It is an area of rolling hills and plateaus surrounded by mountains.

Rivers and Lakes

The great snow pile of winter and the rains of summer combine to build up four river systems that start in Colorado—the Colorado, the Platte, the Arkansas, and the Rio Grande. The high ridge of the Rocky Mountains separates rivers flowing toward the Pacific Ocean from those flowing toward the Atlantic. This ridge is known as the Continental Divide. In Colorado the Continental Divide follows a line shaped somewhat like a great reverse S, with an upper bulge to the east and a lower bulge to the west.

The rivers that rise east of the Continental Divide are the North Platte and the South Platte, which drain into the Missouri; the Arkansas, which squeezes out through the Royal Gorge and heads for the Mississippi; and the Rio Grande, which rises in the great western loop of the S and flows out to the

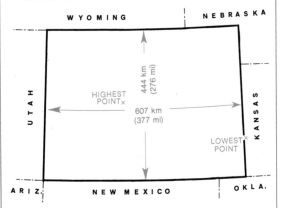

THE LAND

LOCATION: Latitude—37° N to 41° N. **Longitude**—102° 03' W to 109° 03' W.
Wyoming and Nebraska to the north, Utah on the west, New Mexico and Oklahoma to the south, Kansas and Nebraska on the east.

ELEVATION: Highest—Mount Elbert, 4,399 m (14,433 ft). **Lowest**—On the Arkansas River at Colorado-Kansas border, 1,022 m (3,350 ft).

LANDFORMS: Great Plains in the east, Southern Rocky Mountains in west central part of state, Colorado Plateau in the west, Wyoming Basin and Rocky Mountains in the northwest.

SURFACE WATERS: Major rivers—Colorado, North Platte, South Platte, Arkansas, Rio Grande. **Major artificial lakes**—John Martin, Granby, Green Mountain, Dillon, Blue Mesa.

CLIMATE: Temperature—Denver region, yearly average, 10°C (50.4°F), January average −1°C (30°F), July average 23°C (73.4°F). **Precipitation**—Rainfall average statewide, about 430 mm (17 in); varies from 250 mm (10 in) to 640 mm (25 in). Snowfall, from 10 cm (4 in) in desert areas to over 900 cm (30 ft) on some mountain crests. **Growing season**—Statewide average, 120 days.

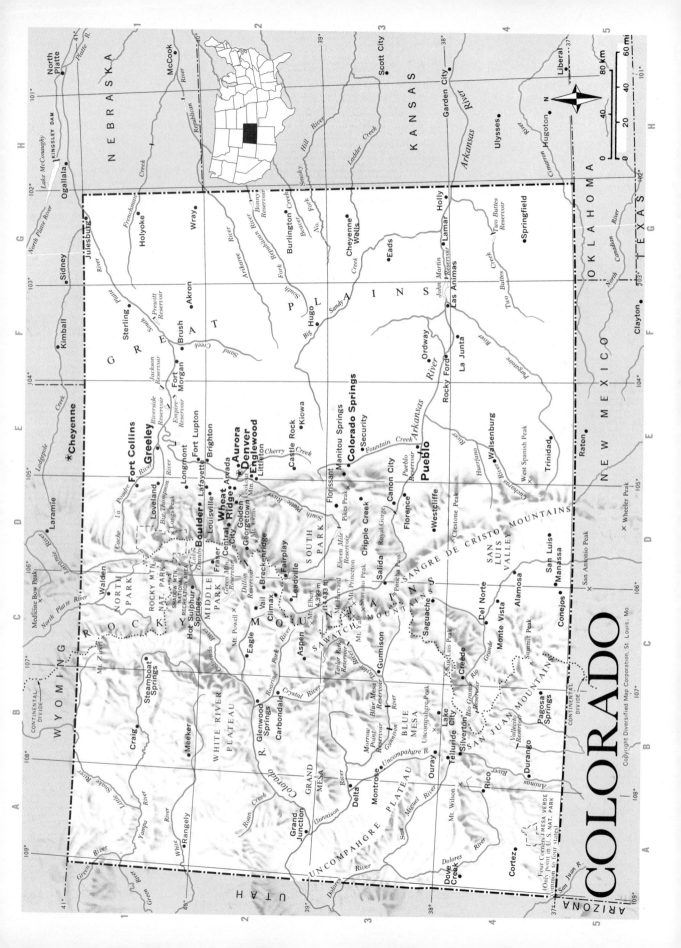

INDEX TO COLORADO MAP

• County Seat   Counties in parentheses   ★ State Capital

POPULATION

TOTAL: 2,889,735 (1980 census). **Density**—10.8 persons to each square kilometer (27.9 persons to each square mile).

GROWTH SINCE 1870

Year	Population	Year	Population
1870	39,864	1960	1,753,947
1900	539,700	1970	2,209,596
1920	939,629	1980	2,889,735

Gain between 1970 and 1980—30.8 percent.

CITIES: Population of Colorado's 10 largest cities according to the 1980 census.

Denver	492,365	Arvada	84,576
Colorado Springs	214,821	Boulder	76,685
Aurora	158,588	Fort Collins	65,092
Lakewood	113,808	Greeley	53,006
Pueblo	101,686	Westminster	50,211

south through New Mexico. The Colorado is the great river that rises west of the Continental Divide. It is fed by several branch rivers that also rise in Colorado.

In the mountains and on the higher plateaus there are hundreds of beautiful natural lakes. Dams have been built in some of the lakes and in the major rivers to form reservoirs.

Complex systems of ditches, reservoirs, and tunnels bring water from west of the Continental Divide to the farms and cities of the plains area. The largest of these projects are the Colorado–Big Thompson Project for the Denver area and the Fryingpan-Arkansas Project for southern Colorado.

Water is in heavy demand, not only for farming and the lawns, parks, and domestic requirements of the growing cities but also for many industrial processes. The steel mill at Pueblo, for example, uses a large conduit to obtain water from the Arkansas River.

Climate

In general Colorado's climate is dry, cool, and sunny. But there are great differences within the state, for mountains have much to say about the climate of Colorado.

Temperature and the Mountains. In the first place, the mountains tend to cause eddies in the main air currents, and these eddies may contribute to sudden changes in temperature. Occasionally, in winter, there are warm west winds, called chinooks, that devour snowbanks and can cause temperatures to rise sharply overnight. On summer's hottest day, black clouds may pour forth hail, which beats crops and gardens to pulp in minutes.

In the second place, the mountains make cool summers for all towns near them. Elevation is the main cause, since high elevations tend to be cool both day and night. Cities such as Denver and Colorado Springs may have summer daytime temperatures of 32°C (90°F). But at night people reach for their blankets. Towns at lower elevations, farther from the mountains, may be much warmer.

Precipitation. The mountains cause enormous differences in precipitation. Desert regions on the western slope of the Rockies receive under 250 millimeters (10 inches) of rainfall a year. The crests of the Rockies receive much more moisture.

Growing Season. Much of Colorado's farming is done within a growing season of 120 days, bounded by May 21 and September 21. But there are wide variations. Parts of the Great Plains, as well as areas on the Colorado Plateau, have growing seasons of 160 days or longer. A few other areas, especially at high elevations, have much shorter seasons.

Natural Resources

Minerals, forests, and farmlands are major sources of Colorado's wealth. But any listing of natural resources would also include magnificent scenery and the many places for outdoor recreation that attract an increasing number of visitors to the state each year.

Minerals. Gold and silver have had great historic importance in Colorado. They are still available when the price makes them worth mining. But attention has turned to Colorado's supply of the nonprecious metals needed in the space age—molybdenum, vanadium, tungsten, and uranium.

Colorado has some petroleum, notably at the Rangely field in the northwest, and some natural gas. There is an abundance of coal. Soft, or bituminous, coal underlies both the foothills east of the mountains and some valleys of the western plateau country. A still softer coal, called lignite, is found in extensive underground fields east of Colorado Springs. North of Gunnison there are deposits of hard coal, called anthracite.

Some of the western mesas contain vast quantities of layered rock called oil shale. Oil has been extracted from it in pilot experiments. But the quantities of water required and the high cost of the process make it a doubtful asset for the near future.

Building materials are abundant in Colorado. These include marble, granite, limestone, sand and gravel, clay, and gypsum.

Soil. The soil that is most common east of the mountains and in the mountain valleys is a light or sandy soil with varying amounts of loam. A few areas are heavy with clay, or adobe, as Spanish-speaking people call it. Some soils are excellent, and others are managed in such a way that they produce fine crops.

Forests and Wildlife. The prairie tree is the cottonwood, which lines the river valleys and irrigation ditches. At higher elevations there is a series of different timber belts, beginning with the dry junipers and the small, gnarled piñon pines of the foothills and low mesas. Next, at 2,400 and 2,700 meters (8,000 and 9,000 feet), are forests of yellow, or ponderosa, pine. Higher, and on the northern slopes where there is more moisture, the pines are replaced by the soft green Douglas fir. Above the firs are blue and Engelmann spruces. In some places there are forests of tall, straight lodgepole pines, named for their use among the Indians. Many mountainsides are covered with white-barked aspen trees. Their leaves turn to a bright golden color before falling in the autumn.

The state stocks hundreds of lakes and creeks with rainbow trout, cutthroat trout, and other fish. Game animals include deer, elk, bighorn sheep, and antelope.

WHAT COLORADO PRODUCES

MANUFACTURED GOODS: Processed foods; precision instruments and related products; nonelectrical machinery; fabricated metal products; products of printing and publishing; transportation equipment, particularly aircraft; primary metals; rubber and plastic products; electric and electronic equipment.

AGRICULTURAL PRODUCTS: Cattle and calves (accounting for about two thirds of the total value of agricultural production), wheat, corn, milk, sheep and lambs, hay, greenhouse and nursery products.

MINERALS: Molybdenum, petroleum, bituminous coal, natural gas, cement, silver, sand and gravel, uranium, gold, vanadium, lead, tungsten.

▶ THE PEOPLE AND THEIR WORK

In 1870 there were approximately 40,000 people in Colorado. Most of them had been attracted by the gold rush. Thirty years later there were half a million, and by 1930 the population reached a million. Between 1930 and 1950 the rate of increase was low. Since 1950, Colorado has grown rapidly.

Over the years most of the large increases in population have come from people with eastern United States heritage. But in some of the southern counties there are many Spanish-speaking Americans. Ute Indians occupied western Colorado long before the Europeans arrived. Some of their descendants, together with Jicarilla Apache, live on reservations extending eastward from the Four Corners, along the New Mexico border. In recent years the Ute have received some compensation for the lands they lost to gold seekers and settlers.

Industries and Products

Colorado's first industry, mining, was surpassed almost from the earliest days by agricultural production. In the middle 1950's manufacturing stepped ahead of both.

Agriculture. Livestock—cattle and calves particularly—bring in far more income than do crops. Cattle are raised on the grassy hills of north central Colorado. They are fattened for market in pens called feedlots.

Irrigated farmlands in the Arkansas and the South Platte river valleys produce corn, potatoes, alfalfa, sugar beets, and beans and other vegetables. Rocky Ford, on the Arkansas River, is known for melons. Wheat is grown on the plains, usually without irrigation. Valleys in the Colorado Plateau produce vegetables, fruits, and grains. Carnations are a famous product of Colorado's greenhouses.

Manufacturing. Colorado's most important manufacturing industry is the processing of foods. This industry makes use of the agricultural products of the state. It includes meatpacking and canning of fruits and vegetables.

Quantities of metal goods are also produced. Pueblo has one of the largest steel plants west of the Mississippi. There is a flourishing tool industry, and a number of lesser industries produce everything from toys to turntables. A recent and fast-growing field of manufacture is electronics equipment. Another important industry is the manufacture

Ouray, one of the older mining towns, was settled in 1875, when silver was discovered nearby.

of transportation equipment, principally aircraft and aircraft parts.

Mining. Petroleum, natural gas, and metals needed in the space age have been among Colorado's most important mineral products during recent years. Petroleum is produced from wells in the Rangely field, in the northwestern part of the state, as well as in various other areas. Colorado is the nation's leading producer of molybdenum, and it ranks high in production of uranium. Molybdenum comes from mines at Climax, on the Continental Divide southwest of Denver. Space-age engineers need this metal to make a steel that can withstand the great heat of jet fuels and the impact of the atmosphere on high-speed rockets. Uranium comes from deposits in the dry mesa country west of the mountains.

Colorado's mines continue to produce coal and minerals such as zinc, lead, gold, and silver. The quarries produce limestone, sand and gravel, gypsum, and other materials needed in the building industries.

The ski center at Aspen is one of the many winter vacation spots in Colorado. Aspen is also well known for the festival of arts held there each summer.

Transportation and Communication

Several railroads enter Colorado from the east and climb to cities at the eastern base of the mountains. The Denver and Rio Grande Western Railroad sends lines across the mountains. Trains through scenic Colorado carry vista-dome cars, with glass-enclosed upper decks where passengers can see in all directions.

More than a dozen broad all-year highways climb the Continental Divide at elevations averaging more than 3,400 meters (11,000 feet). Many more cross the summer passes or run through the mountains from north to south. Where there are deep gorges, such as the Royal Gorge, the highways climb around them. The most-traveled route is the north-south interstate highway along the eastern base of the mountains. A similar east-west highway is being built.

The Denver airport has one of the busiest control towers in the United States. Planes provide nonstop flights to many of the nation's important cities. There is also regular air service to many small communities that cannot be reached easily in other ways because of the mountain barrier.

Colorado has more than 20 daily newspapers and five times that number of weeklies. The best-known newspapers are the Denver *Post,* founded in 1892, and the *Rocky Mountain News,* Colorado's first newspaper, which was started in 1859 by William N. Byers.

Colorado's first radio stations began operating in the early 1920's. Television began in Denver in 1952. The state has a dozen television stations and about 120 radio stations.

▶ EDUCATION

Colorado takes pride in its educational and cultural institutions. Its schools attract many students from other states. Summer visitors look forward to the music and drama festivals for which Colorado is well known.

Schools and Colleges

In the autumn of 1859, the gold-rush year, Colorado's first school was opened by O. J. Goldrick, who came from the East to the community that is now Denver. He wore a silk shirt and a top hat, and he had but 50 cents in his pocket on arrival. The community raised $250, and parents added a small tuition. Mr. Goldrick taught reading and 'riting and 'rithmetic, but there was nothing fancy, such as sorting the children into different grades. Other communities soon started schools, and in 1861 the first territorial legislature passed a school law. One provision of the law was that a certain part of every new vein of gold or silver was to be set aside as a school claim. Proceeds from these claims were to be used for education. The law was not enforced, and it produced no money for schools. But later on, government lands that were given to the state did produce school revenues. By the time Colorado became a state in 1876, an effective school law provided for free public education supported by taxation.

The largest state-supported institution of higher education, the University of Colorado, was founded at Boulder in 1861. Today it also has campuses at Colorado Springs and Denver. Other state universities and senior colleges are located at Alamosa, Denver, Durango, Fort Collins, Golden, Grand Junction, Greeley, Gunnison, and Pueblo. Community colleges have been established in all sections of the state.

The United States Air Force Academy, near Colorado Springs, attracts many visitors. Private institutions of higher learning include Colorado College, at Colorado Springs, and the University of Denver, Colorado Women's College, Regis College, and Loretto Heights College, all in or near Denver.

Libraries and Museums

Colorado has more than 120 public libraries. The central library in Denver, with its fine Western history department, is among the nation's best.

The state of Colorado has a museum adjacent to the Capitol in Denver, and the city of Denver has a natural history museum in one of its parks. These museums have dioramas and collections of weapons, costumes, tools, minerals, and many other items. Golden has a railroad museum with examples of the largest locomotives and cars from the age of steam. Many communities have historical museums that preserve old forts and homes, as well as the implements and furniture that went with them. Denver and Colorado Springs have large art museums, which school classes visit regularly. The Ute Indian Museum, south of Montrose, has many Ute Indian artifacts, paintings, and costumes.

Music and Drama

Music events of wide interest include summer festivals at Denver and Aspen. Denver's Center for the Performing Arts includes theaters and the home of the Denver Symphony Orchestra.

Elitch Gardens Theater, in Denver, has the longest continuous record for a stock theater in the United States. It opened in 1891. The Central City Opera House, in Central City, is an architectural gem left from gold-mining days. It opens every summer for a festival of operas and plays. The Koshare Indian dancers, a Boy Scouts organization at La Junta, have a museum of Indian art, a stockade, and a trading post. Their headquarters are in an underground ceremonial room.

▶ PLACES OF INTEREST

The mountains are all-important to visitors and Coloradans alike. Roads, lodges, and hundreds of campgrounds take care of the thousands who fish, hunt, climb the peaks, shoot the rapids, search for crystals, or simply enjoy themselves driving and hiking through Colorado's mountain playground. In winter, most of the skiers use the ski-tow areas. But many groups explore the gentler slopes on cross-country skis.

The mountain towns are the places most often visited. Among them are Central City, Cripple Creek, Aspen, Ouray, and Telluride.

National Areas

About a fifth of the state's total area lies within 12 national forests. Those most visited are in the eastern mountain ranges, near the larger cities—the Roosevelt, the Arapaho, the Pike, and the San Isabel. Grand Mesa National Forest is a lake-dotted plateau. The San Juan, the Gunnison, the Rio Grande, and the Uncompahgre cover the large San Juan uplift of

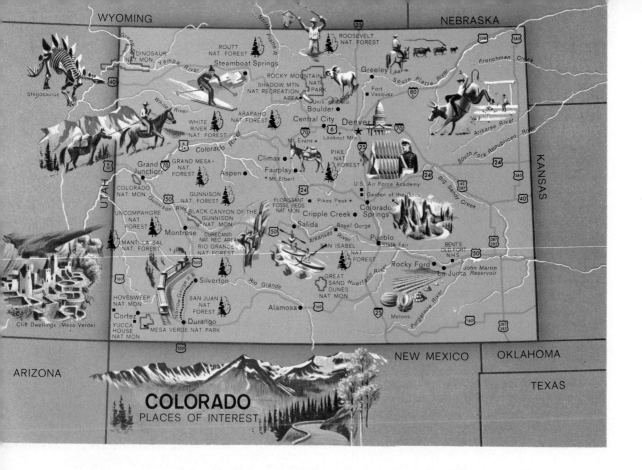

COLORADO
PLACES OF INTEREST

southwestern Colorado. Some of the national forests have particularly fine wilderness areas. Colorado shares the Manti–La Sal National Forest with Utah.

Shadow Mountain National Recreation Area, in the southwestern corner of Rocky Mountain National Park, includes Granby and Shadow Mountain lakes. The Curecanti National Recreation Area surrounds Blue Mesa and Morrow Point reservoirs on the Gunnison.

Other national areas preserve natural, archeological, and historical treasures:

Rocky Mountain National Park is a scenic mountain region straddling the Continental Divide northwest of Denver. Lakes, fishing streams, trails, and Longs Peak are the main attractions.

Mesa Verde National Park, in southwest Colorado, includes the Southwest's finest cliff dwellings.

Bent's Old Fort National Historic Site, near La Junta, preserves an early outpost for trappers that was later a center of the fur trade.

Black Canyon of the Gunnison National Monument, on the Gunnison River northeast of Montrose, includes several kilometers of Colorado's deepest and narrowest river gorge.

Colorado National Monument, near Grand Junction, is an area of rose-colored canyons and tall pillars sculptured by the wind.

Dinosaur National Monument, north of Grand Junction, is shared by Utah and Colorado. Deep river channels of the Green and the Yampa rivers and a variety of dinosaur skeletons are its important features.

Florissant Fossil Beds National Monument, near Florissant, preserves ancient fossil insects, seeds, and leaves in perfect detail, as well as petrified stumps of sequoias.

Great Sand Dunes National Monument, north of Alamosa, has dunes up to 180 meters (600 feet) high.

Hovenweep National Monument, west of Cortez on the Colorado-Utah border, includes groups of prehistoric pueblos and rock towers.

Yucca House National Monument, near Cortez, has pueblo ruins that are still awaiting excavation.

Other Places of Interest

Colorado abounds with scenic and recreational high spots and reminders of early days.

The Silverton Branch is the last of the steam-operated narrow-gauge railroads with

Above: The Garden of the Gods, a part of Colorado Springs' city park system, is noted for strange rock formations of vivid red sandstone. Below: Dunes sculptured by the wind in Great Sand Dunes National Monument.

Above: The falcon, mascot of the Cadet Wing, tops a monument at the United States Air Force Academy near Colorado Springs. The Cadet Chapel, with 17 towering aluminum spires, is in the background.

Royal Gorge of the Arkansas River, with railroad deep in the gorge and suspension bridge high above.

passenger service. In the summer it runs full trains daily between Durango and Silverton.

Mount Evans is reached by a beautiful side highway off U.S. 6, west of Denver. A laboratory for high-altitude studies occupies the summit.

Grand Mesa, east of Grand Junction, has scores of small lakes on a cool tableland high above the hot valleys surrounding it.

Fort Vasquez, on the South Platte River near Greeley, is a replica of a fur-trading post. It commemorates French trapping days.

Lookout Mountain, west of Denver, includes a scenic high drive and the grave of Buffalo Bill.

Annual Events

Colorado's annual events number several hundred. They include everything from grand opera to burro races and rodeos. The following brief list shows the variety:

January—Display of fireworks on summit of Pikes Peak to celebrate New Year.

June—International White-Water Kayak Race on the Arkansas River, Salida.

July—Automobile race on Pikes Peak highway, Independence Day.

August—Colorado State Fair, Pueblo.

September—Arkansas Valley Fair at Rocky Ford, first Thursday of the month, featuring Watermelon Day; Fall Color Days, Ouray.

▶ CITIES

Colorado's largest cities are at the eastern base of the mountains. They are located almost in a line north and south of Denver.

Denver

The state capital and largest city is the trade and transportation center for the state, as well as for the whole Rocky Mountain area. A water supply from the mountains gives Denver its fine system of parks and its beautiful lawns.

Denver began as a mining settlement in the late 1850's. In 1860 rival settlements were united with it. The first territorial legislature met at Denver in 1861. For a time afterward the legislature met at other places, but in 1867 the seat of government was transferred permanently to Denver. The capitol is domed with gold leaf, a memorial to early mining days.

The suburban area around Denver has grown rapidly. By 1980, it included four of the ten largest cities in the state—Aurora, Lakewood, Arvada, and Westminster. An article on Denver is included in Volume D.

Pueblo

Pueblo is an important industrial center. It is called the Pittsburgh of the West because of its steel mills. Its main industry is the Colorado Fuel and Iron Corporation. Other industries process foods from the Arkansas Valley and make such products as machine parts and building materials. The Arkansas River runs through Pueblo and provides water both for the city and for an irrigated farm area to the east.

Colorado Springs

Colorado's second largest city is a famous resort, located east of Pikes Peak. William J. Palmer, founder of Colorado's mountain railroad system, chose Colorado Springs as his residence and helped to develop the features that would make it a pleasing place for others to live in and visit. He planned a varied park system that includes the famous Garden of the Gods. He also helped found Colorado College. Recent growth of the city has centered around the manufacture of electronics and

Denver's Civic Center (*above*) includes the Bucking Bronco statue and the gold-domed state capitol. The cliff dwellings at Mesa Verde (*below*) were built by pre-Columbian Pueblo Indians more than 600 years ago.

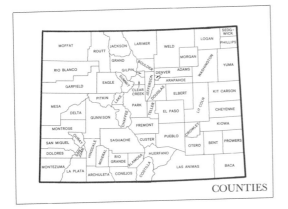

COUNTIES

precision instruments. Nearby are Fort Carson and the U.S. Air Force Academy.

Other Cities

Boulder, an important educational center, is also a nationally known center for scientific research and development. The National Bureau of Standards is among the many research agencies and organizations with offices in or near Boulder. Fort Collins and Greeley are also educational centers. Colorado State University is at Fort Collins, and the University of Northern Colorado is at Greeley. Both cities are in a rich agricultural area known especially for production of beef cattle.

Grand Junction is the largest city on the western slope of the mountains. Fruit, especially pears and peaches, and vegetables are among agricultural products of the irrigated area surrounding the city. Durango is the trade hub for a region producing coal, metals, and some petroleum. The San Juan Mountains to the north and the narrow-gauge railroad that connects it with Silverton make Durango a flourishing tourist center in southwestern Colorado.

▶ GOVERNMENT

Colorado became a territory in 1861 and a state in 1876. The constitution adopted in 1876 is still in force, although it has been amended many times.

The General Assembly, as the legislature is called, makes the laws of the state. It consists of the Senate and the House of Representatives.

The executive branch of the state government is headed by the governor and several other officials. They include the lieutenant governor, secretary of state, attorney general, and treasurer.

The state judicial system is headed by the

GOVERNMENT

Capital—Denver. Number of counties—63. Representation in Congress—U.S. senators, 2; U.S. representatives, 6. General Assembly—Senate, 35 members, 4-year terms; House of Representatives, 65 members, 2-year terms. Governor—4-year term; no limit on number of terms. Elections—General and state, Tuesday after first Monday in November of even-numbered years.

Supreme Court. It consists of seven justices appointed initially by the governor and later re-elected by the voters for 10-year terms. Colorado also has an intermediate court of appeals below the Supreme Court. The major trial courts are district courts. Lower courts include county and municipal courts.

▶ FAMOUS PEOPLE

Mountainous Colorado has been the home of many energetic leaders. The following persons are among those who have made notable contributions to the nation and to the building of Colorado's cities, roads, and business empires:

John Evans (1814–97) was born in Ohio. After a distinguished career in Chicago, he accepted President Lincoln's appointment as the second territorial governor of Colorado (1862–65). He promoted many of the railroad, banking, and other business projects that made Denver an important city. He was a founder of the University of Denver and other institutions of cultural life.

William J. Palmer (1836–1909), a Civil War soldier, was born in Delaware. After the war he came through Colorado to help survey for the Union Pacific Railroad, which was to cross the West. He remained to become president of the new Denver and Rio Grande Railroad. Besides building railroads he helped found several towns, including Colorado Springs, Alamosa, Durango, and Grand Junction. General Palmer was a shy person in early life, but after his retirement he liked to give grand parties. One of these was an annual Easter egg hunt for all the children of Colorado Springs who could walk or get a ride to his castle grounds.

Otto Mears (1840–1931), a Russian immigrant, came to Colorado by way of California and Santa Fe, New Mexico. He operated a saw mill, a general store, and a flour mill in the San Luis Valley. In crossing Poncha Pass on the way to mining camps, he spilled a load of wheat and so learned the value of roads. The toll roads that he built across the passes were preliminary steps in opening up the mountain country. He helped to negotiate the treaties by which the Ute Indians were induced to yield their lands to the gold seekers.

Florence Rena Sabin (1871–1953), born in Central City, was one of the nation's first women to receive medals and other honors in medicine. After distinguishing herself in the fields of public health and tuberculosis research in the East, Dr. Sabin returned to Colorado in

1938. She retired briefly and then took up work in the health organizations of the state.

Well-known persons who were born in Colorado include writer Gene Fowler (Denver), novelist Anne Parrish (Colorado Springs), musician Paul Whiteman (Denver), actor Douglas Fairbanks, Sr. (Denver), and television and radio entertainer Ralph Edwards (Merino).

William Harrison "Jack" Dempsey, winner of the world's heavyweight championship in 1919, was called the "Manassa Mauler" for Manassa, his birthplace in the San Luis Valley. Byron R. "Whizzer" White, an All-American football player at the University of Colorado in 1937, was appointed to the United States Supreme Court in 1962. He was born in Fort Collins. Astronaut Malcolm Scott Carpenter was born in Boulder.

▶ HISTORY

The cliff dwellers were among the prehistoric inhabitants of Colorado. The ruins of their culture can be seen at Mesa Verde National Park, as well as Canyon de Chelly National Monument in the northeastern corner of Arizona.

The Indians who traded and fought with the

Who were the cliff dwellers?

The cliff dwellers were the ancestors of the Pueblo Indians. They were called the Anasazi, an Indian word for "Ancient Ones." The Anasazi lived mainly in the area now known as Four Corners—the area where Colorado, New Mexico, Arizona, and Utah meet.

The cliff dwellers are remembered for their great stone villages built on the tops of mesas or on the terraced sides of cliffs. Some of these structures stood several stories high. Cliff Palace at Mesa Verde National Park in Colorado contained more than 100 rooms.

When Europeans first came to the Four Corners, they found the cliff dwellings uninhabited. What had happened to the Anasazi? Why had they abandoned the cliff dwellings? Disease, a major drought, and enemies who invaded from the north have all been suggested as possible answers. Or perhaps quarrels among the Anasazi led them to leave. Whatever the cause, the Anasazi disappeared from their cliff dwellings about the year A.D. 1300.

first white people belonged mainly to three tribes—the Arapaho, the Cheyenne, and the Ute. The Arapaho and the Cheyenne inhabited the plains, and the Ute lived in the mountains. The state bears many Ute names, such as Uncompahgre River.

Exploration and Early Settlement

Coronado may have crossed the southeast corner of Colorado searching for gold in 1541. In 1706 a Spanish expedition from New Mexico claimed the land for Spain. French fur traders had been coming into the area for some time, and France also claimed the land that is now Colorado, especially the eastern part. In 1762 France ceded all its claims west of the Mississippi River to Spain. In 1800 Spain gave the land back to France. Then, in 1803, the United States acquired eastern Colorado as part of the Louisiana Purchase.

Three years later, in 1806, the United States Government sent Zebulon M. Pike to explore the area. His assignment took him to the Rockies, western boundary of the newly enlarged United States. He saw the peak that bears his name, but he was unable to climb it. Soon other explorers and fur trappers and traders came into the area, and trading posts such as Bent's Fort were built. At the close of the Mexican War in 1848, Mexico ceded to

IMPORTANT DATES

1803	The United States acquired most of eastern Colorado as part of the Louisiana Purchase.
1806	Zebulon M. Pike explored Colorado and discovered the peak named for him.
1848	Mexico ceded western Colorado to the United States.
1858	Gold discovered near the site of Denver.
1861	Congress established Colorado territory.
1867	Denver chosen as permanent capital.
1870	Railroad connections established with the East.
1876	Colorado became the 38th state on August 1.
1899	First beet-sugar refinery began operating at Grand Junction.
1906	U.S. Mint at Denver issued its first coins.
1915	Rocky Mountain National Park established.
1927	The Moffat (railroad) Tunnel under Continental Divide completed.
1937	Beginning of Colorado–Big Thompson Project to bring water from the western slope of the state to the eastern slope.
1958	The U.S. Air Force Academy moved to its present site near Colorado Springs.
1973	Eisenhower Tunnel, the highest vehicular tunnel in the world and the longest in the United States, was opened through the Continental Divide on March 8.
1977	U.S. Olympic Committee Headquarters and Training Center established at Colorado Springs; Federal Solar Energy Research Institute, near Golden, went into operation.

the United States the rest of what is now Colorado. For a time it was part of Kansas territory.

Gold Strikes

The finding of gold near the present site of Denver in 1858 led to the great gold rush of 1859. During the years that followed, gold seekers settled in Denver and in the smaller towns. Some took to ranching and lumbering. Others developed the large-scale ore mining and milling that replaced panning. In 1861 Congress created Colorado territory. The railroads came in the 1870's and opened up quick travel and cheap freight to the mining areas.

Colorado Becomes a State

Gold mining prospered, and a growing population made statehood possible in 1876. The growing towns and the smelters needed coal, and coal mining increased into the 1920's, when petroleum began to replace coal.

Then, many small coal mines were shut down. And Colorado developed some petroleum and natural gas fields. Now, fewer—but very large —coal mines are being developed as oil and gas reserves dwindle and the nation's demand for energy increases. Molybdenum, vanadium, and uranium are now more in demand than gold or silver.

Agriculture has adapted to changing conditions and has profited by new methods of farming. Today dry farming has been developed in an area near the Four Corners that was once considered useless.

The Future

Colorado's attraction for tourists provides an incentive for the state to maintain high standards of conservation and environmental protection. Its coal, new industries, and the wealth in its mountains seem to ensure continued economic growth.

ROBERT M. ORMES
Formerly, Colorado College

COLUMBUS, CHRISTOPHER (1451?—1506)

When Columbus sailed into the unknown Atlantic Ocean in 1492, he was not trying to prove that the earth is round. Educated people already knew that. He was not trying to discover a New World. Few people dreamed that such a world existed. But Columbus was a man with a vision. He wanted to find a sea route to the gold, jewels, and spices of Asia. And he was possessed by the idea that he could reach Asia by sailing west.

Christopher Columbus (in Italian, Cristoforo Colombo) was born about 1451 in Genoa, Italy. His father was a weaver, and Christopher worked for his father, combing out wool. Genoa was a great seaport. Young Columbus was probably a dreamy, adventurous boy. He listened to sailors' yarns, and as soon as he could, he went sea.

When he was 14, he sailed along the coast of the Mediterranean Sea. Later he made trips to Greece and Portugal. Between voyages he studied mapmaking and geography.

About 1477, Columbus moved to Lisbon, Portugal, then a center for explorers. He married the daughter of a famous Portuguese sea captain. From his father-in-law's maps and charts Columbus obtained considerable information about the world. He read Marco Polo's story of his journey to Cathay (China) in 1275. In Cathay were spices, jewels, and silks.

In Columbus' time the only route to Asia was eastward across the Mediterranean Sea and then by caravan across thousands of kilometers of desert and mountains. Europeans were eager to find an easier route for their trading ships. Already Portuguese explorers were sailing south, hoping to find a way to the East around Africa. Columbus talked with geographers. He decided that Asia was on the other side of the Ocean Sea (the Atlantic). He would sail west to Japan.

For years Columbus tried to interest European rulers in his plan. Many people agreed that Asia lay to the west. But how far? No one knew. Columbus estimated that Japan must be about 4,000 kilometers (2,500 miles) due west of the Canary Islands. But he thought the earth was smaller than it is. Japan was over 16,000 kilometers (10,000 miles) away.

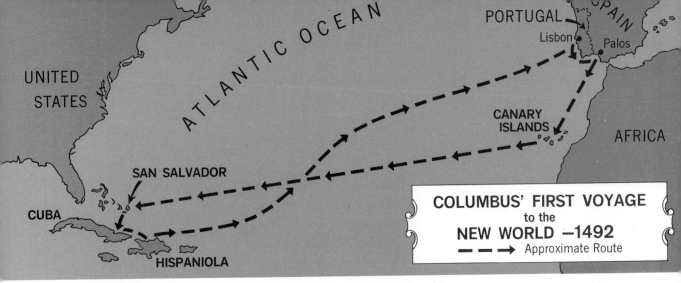

ATLANTIC OCEAN

UNITED STATES

PORTUGAL
Lisbon
Palos

CANARY ISLANDS

AFRICA

SAN SALVADOR

CUBA

HISPANIOLA

COLUMBUS' FIRST VOYAGE
to the
NEW WORLD —1492
- - - → Approximate Route

Finally in 1492 King Ferdinand and Queen Isabella of Spain agreed to outfit three ships for Columbus. They made him viceroy (governor) of any new lands he might acquire for Spain. But sailors were afraid of the unknown sea and it was difficult to recruit them for the voyage. At last a crew of about 90 men was gathered for the three ships—the *Niña,* the *Pinta,* and the *Santa María.*

On August 3, 1492, the tiny fleet set sail from Palos, Spain. The ships stopped at the Canary Islands to make repairs and take aboard fresh food. Then they headed out into the open Atlantic—the Sea of Darkness.

As they sailed west Columbus kept two logs (ships' diaries). In one he kept what he thought was a true record of the distance traveled. The other—for the crew to see—showed a much shorter distance. Columbus hoped that the men would be less frightened if they did not know how far from home they really were. Weeks went by, and still no land was sighted. The ships had already sailed about 4,800 kilometers (3,000 miles). The crew threatened mutiny. It is said that Columbus had agreed to turn back if land was not sighted soon. He had seen birds flying from the southwest, and he changed course to sail that way. At 2 A.M. on October 12 one of the *Pinta's* sailors shouted "Land! Land!" It was the New World.

The sailor had sighted one of the Bahama Islands near Florida. Columbus named it San Salvador. The island people were friendly. Columbus, believing he had found the East Indies, called them Indians.

Columbus sailed on, looking for the rich cities of Cathay and Cipango. He discovered Cuba and Hispaniola. Near Hispaniola the *Santa María* went aground. Helplessly Columbus watched the waves smash his best ship to pieces. Leaving some men behind to establish a fort, Columbus set sail for Spain in the *Niña.* Severe storms almost sank the tiny ship before they arrived safely back at Palos. The *Pinta* also reached port safely. The entire voyage had taken 224 days.

Ferdinand and Isabella were delighted with what Columbus had brought back—gold, parrots, strange plants, and several Indians.

Between 1493 and 1504 Columbus made three more trips to the Americas, still searching for the great cities Marco Polo had described. The men he had left on Hispaniola were all dead when he returned. Columbus started a new colony called Isabela.

But the colonists in Hispaniola did not find the golden palaces and jewels they had expected. Many blamed Columbus for unsatisfactory conditions in the colony and accused him of injustice. In 1500 he was sent back to Spain in chains. Queen Isabella sided with Columbus and set him free. But he was no longer viceroy.

Columbus returned to Spain from his fourth voyage in 1504, sick and disappointed. Columbus spent the last years of his life vainly seeking an audience with King Ferdinand. On May 20, 1506, Columbus died without knowing that he had discovered a New World.

Reviewed by DANIEL ROSELLE
Author, *Our Western Heritage*

See also EXPLORATION AND DISCOVERY.

COMBUSTION. See FIRE AND COMBUSTION.

Halley's comet, photographed in 1910. The comet was named after Edmund Halley, an English astronomer (1656–1742).

COMETS, METEORS, METEORITES, AND TEKTITES

From time to time moving lights appear in the night sky. Far and away the most common of these are the "shooting stars," which are really meteors. Anyone who watches the sky on a clear night is bound to see the streak of light that marks the passage of a meteor in the earth's atmosphere. At certain times of year, brilliant showers of meteors splash the sky. These showers occur when the earth passes through the remains of a comet. Comets are another of the moving lights in the night sky. But they are much rarer than meteors and are seldom seen. Most are so small and distant that their movement is not immediately apparent. To see that a comet moves, you must watch it over a period of weeks.

▶ COMETS

About three or four times a century, a comet passes so close to the sun that its bright, glowing tail can easily be seen. However, of the dozen or so comets that approach the sun each year, most can be seen only through a telescope. It is possible to see the others with the unaided eye only if one knows where to look for them.

In their trip around the sun, most comets travel very elongated orbits. That is, the path they take resembles the shape of a long, fat cigar, as shown. Their orbits may carry them as far as halfway to the nearest stars. A comet following such an orbit takes thousands of years to complete one trip.

Comets are strongly influenced by the gravitational pull of the planets. A few comets have been pulled out of their regular orbits and forced into shorter ones. Jupiter, for example, has collected a number of comets, each of which takes about 6 years to orbit the sun. Other comets have orbits that carry them just beyond Neptune. The most famous of the comets that travel regularly around the sun and Neptune is Halley's comet, which can be seen without a telescope whenever it appears. Halley's comet appears once every 75 to 77 years. Its last appearance was in 1910. It will appear again in April of 1986.

As seen through a telescope, a comet has a "head" and a "tail." The head is a large cloud of glowing gases called the "coma" of the comet. The coma may be more than 1,000,000 miles in diameter. Its gases are so light that the "wind" from the sun blows them. The tail of a comet forms when gases are blown back by the solar wind.

As a comet approaches the sun its tail grows larger and larger because the pressure of the solar wind is increasing. As the comet moves away from the sun into the coldness of space the pressure of the solar wind continues to blow against the gases. For this reason the tail of a comet always points away from the sun.

A small, shining point of light can sometimes be seen in the center of the coma. The point of light is called the "nucleus" of the comet. Astronomers think that the nucleus is like an enormous, dirty snowball—a mixture of ice and dust particles forming a ball about ½ mile in diameter.

Why a nucleus forms in the first place is something of a mystery. One theory is that when the solar system first came into being, there were many more particles of ice and dust floating in space than there are now. The particles gradually collected into "snowballs," each snowball forming the nucleus of a comet. Perhaps comets are still being formed in space out of ice and dust. Some astronomers think there may be millions of these gigantic snowballs traveling through the solar system.

We see a comet only when one happens to pass close to the sun. Then the heat of the sun changes the ice in the nucleus into gas. Radiation from the sun passing through these gases ionizes them and causes the gases to glow with light. That is how the coma is formed. (Something similar occurs inside a fluorescent tube, which glows with light when an electric current passes through the gas in the tube.)

In time, as the ice of the nucleus turns into gas, the solid particles of dust fall away and scatter around the comet. If the comet is small or if it makes several trips around the sun, all the ice evaporates. Nothing is left of the nucleus except the solid particles of dust. These continue to travel through space in the orbit of the former comet. If the earth passes through a swarm of this dust, a meteor shower occurs.

There is, in fact, an enormous amount of dust in the solar system, most of it being the remains of former comets. Most of the meteors that enter the earth's atmosphere originate from this dust.

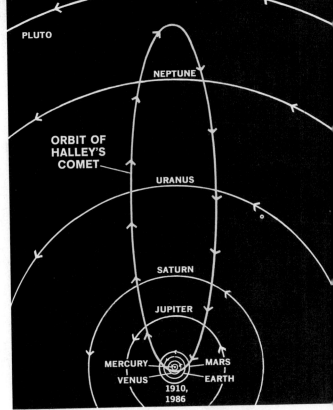

The orbit of Halley's comet. All known comets travel around the sun in long, oval-shaped paths. It takes years for a comet to complete its path.

▶ METEORS

Ninety million visible meteors enter our atmosphere every day. Meteors have been arriving in such numbers for millions of years, only to vaporize in the atmosphere. Their remains sink slowly toward the earth. Scientists estimate that several thousand tons of meteor dust fall to the earth every day.

How can a particle of dust cause the brilliant streak of light that is a shooting star? The answer lies in the speed at which the particle enters the earth's atmosphere.

The particle of dust is traveling through space at 26 to 30 miles a second. The earth is traveling through space at 18.5 miles a second. If the two meet head-on, the speed of the particle of dust through the earth's atmosphere will be 44.5 to 48.5 miles a second. Friction is generated between the particle of dust and the molecules of air. The friction causes the particle of dust to heat up so that it glows brightly. At the same time, the particle smashes against the molecules of air in its path, pushing them aside violently. These molecules in turn push violently against other molecules for several feet around. The force

These craters were made when meteorites hit the earth. Above: Deep Bay Crater in northern Canada is at least 60,000,000 years old. It is 6 miles across and 700 feet deep. Below: Meteorite Crater in Arizona is almost a mile across and 600 feet deep.

Tektites look like frozen drops of liquid rock. They were probably made by meteorites striking the earth.

of the collisions causes the air molecules to ionize and glow with light. Thus a shooting star is not just a tiny particle of dust. It is a glowing cylinder of air several feet in diameter, with a tiny glowing particle of dust in the center.

The larger the particle of dust is, the brighter the meteor. Particles as large as baseballs cause **fireballs**—meteors that are bright enough to light up the sky like a flash of heat lightning.

Sometimes the earth passes through a dense cloud of billions of dust particles, all that remains of the nucleus of a former comet. When this happens, the result is a **meteor shower,** or storm. The most brilliant display of this kind occurred on the night of November 12, 1833. This event was called the Leonid storm because the meteors appeared to originate from a point in the sky where the constellation Leo was. The sky was alive with meteors all night. Many people were panic-stricken, thinking that the end of the world had come.

The earth passes through several meteor showers every year, although none causes a spectacular display. The best-known yearly meteor shower seen in the Northern Hemisphere is called the Perseids. The Perseid shower occurs every year between August 10 and August 13. Its meteors seem to come from the direction of the constellation Perseus. Another meteor shower known as the Geminid shower occurs every year between December 10 and December 12. The Geminids seem to come from the direction of the constellation Gemini.

▶ **METEORITES**

Occasionally a large piece of matter flashes through the sky without completely burning up and strikes the earth. This is a meteorite.

The surface of the moon is pocked with craters. These craters may have been formed by meteorites. (Some scientists think that the craters were formed by volcanoes.) The moon has been bombarded by meteorites for millions of years. Since the airless moon has no weather, the craters remain unchanged. Wind and water have not worn them down.

Many of the earth's craters have been erased by weathering, but some large ones remain. Meteorite Crater in Arizona is almost

This meteorite, made of iron and nickel, weighs 36½ tons. It was found in Greenland.

CAPE YORK (Ahnighito)
Cape York, Greenland
Gift of Mrs. Morris K. Jesup
Found, 1894.

a mile in diameter and 600 feet deep. The Ashanti Crater in Africa is 6 miles in diameter and the Chubb Crater at Ungava in northern Canada is 2 miles in diameter. The biggest crater of all is the Vredefort Ring in South Africa. This crater is 130 miles in diameter. It was formed when an enormous meteorite struck the earth more than 250,000,000 years ago.

Meteorites are still falling on the earth. Scientists estimate that, on the average, a meteorite weighing 40,000 tons falls on the earth once every 1,000 years. Once in every 100 years or so, a meteorite weighing 4,000 tons falls on the earth. Every day three or four meteorites that each weigh at least 20 pounds fall to earth. Fortunately, since much of the earth is ocean, these meteorites seldom strike an inhabited area.

Most of the meteorites found on earth are made of an alloy of iron and nickel. Others are made of stone or mixtures of stone and metal.

No one knows for certain where meteorites come from. One theory is that meteorites are the pieces of two or more small planets that collided in space several billion years ago. Another theory is that meteorites are collections of rock and metallic dust that have come together in space.

Scientists examining meteorites have discovered very interesting things about them. The pieces of a meteorite that fell in Kentucky in 1950 were ground up and placed in a broth used for growing bacteria. After a few days the broth turned cloudy, and it was found to contain a kind of bacteria previously unknown. Other meteorites have yielded the kinds of chemicals that are necessary for life to exist. No one knows whether life does exist elsewhere in space, but these meteorites are a sign that it may.

▶ **TEKTITES**

Meteorites are probably responsible for the curious objects called tektites. Tektites are glassy stones with a yellowish-brown or greenish color. They look as if they were drops of liquid that had frozen solid while in midair. Tektites are found in many parts of the world, including the United States, North Africa, Indonesia, and Australia.

It was once thought that tektites were the remains of meteorites that melted as they passed through the earth's atmosphere and hardened again. A more recent theory is that tektites were formed when large meteorites struck the earth. The meteorites struck with such force that the rocks on which they fell became molten. Liquid drops of rock were splashed high into the air. While in the air they cooled into the stones called tektites.

Reviewed by GERALD S. HAWKINS
Boston University

COMIC BOOKS

Most people are familiar with comic books and comic strips. The **comic strip** is usually found in daily newspapers. It is made up of three or four picture panels telling a story with one or more characters. Some comic strips tell a different incident every day. In other comic strips the story continues from day to day until it is finished, and then a new story begins with the same main characters. The Sunday newspapers usually include sections of comic strips in which the story is told in a greater number of pictures and in color. The comic strips on Sunday often continue the stories carried in the daily paper during the week.

Comic books are extensions of comic strips into magazines. Each magazine is about one set of characters, and the pictures tell a complete story.

Generally comic books are printed in color. The words are printed in balloons over a speaker's head to indicate the person speaking. A few sentences may be used to bridge a gap in a story, but most of the plot is carried by direct conversation and by action in the pictures. Comic book covers are made of glossy paper, and there are generally the same number of pages—usually 32—in each book in a particular series. More than one story is included in each issue, and there is usually some advertising.

Comic books are published regularly, that is to say every month, every 2 months, or once a year. Because of their regular publication, they are often called comic magazines. Approximately 200 different titles are published. The exact number varies from month to month. Some people estimate that close to 500,000,000 copies of comic books are sold each year.

Different Kinds of Comic Books

Comic books or comic strips are not all humorous stories. The Comics Magazine Association of America lists these types of comic books: adventure, animal, biography, detective, fantasy-mystery, history, humor, military, religion, romance, satire, science-fiction, teen-age, "kiddie," and western. Some types, such as adventure and humor, sell better, so there are more of them. However, the popularity of comic books has led many kinds of groups to use them to tell a story. There are comic strips in some Sunday school papers, the Army uses the comic-strip technique in training soldiers, and many companies use comic books to tell the story behind a product or the history of their company.

How Comic Books Began

Comic strips began in newspapers as early as the 1870's. Comic books similar to those published today first appeared in the 1930's and were collections of comic strips previously printed. The next step in comic book history was the writing of stories for comic book use alone, using a single set of characters in two or three plots.

The development of animated cartoon movies led to comic books about the same characters, such as Mickey Mouse. Sometimes a comic book retells a plot from a movie or a popular old book. In at least one case—Superman—the comic strip and comic book character led to television and movie versions. Television shows that are popular with young people are often made the subject of comic

This seal on the cover of a comic book shows that the magazine has been approved for publication. Look for it when buying comic books.

Comic books today contain stories about real problems. Here Archie and a friend persuade a factory owner to find out why his paper mill causes water pollution.

books because the publishers know they will quickly find buyers.

Comic Books—Good or Bad?

Comic books increased in popularity very quickly, and soon there were many different kinds aimed at pleasing different age groups and interests. During World War II the comic book industry grew fast. Unscrupulous publishers began using themes of sadistic violence and sex. This brought the wrath of parents and organizations such as the P.T.A. against the whole comic book industry.

The improvement of comic books came about through the efforts of leading members in the comic book industry—the people who publish, print, and distribute comic books. In 1954 the Comics Magazine Association of America was organized for the purpose of setting up a code of approval for each comic magazine. The Code Authority covers the story content—text and artwork—and the advertisements used. Each comic book published by one of the member groups is carefully scrutinized before publication to see if it conforms to the code. When an issue of a comic magazine is cleared for publication, it may carry the Code Authority's seal on the upper right-hand corner.

Nearly all comic magazine publishers belong to the group that conforms to the code. However, some publishers do not belong, and some of their comic books still carry an unhealthy amount of sadistic violence or sex. People who buy comic books should shop carefully for the better kinds.

Most teachers and librarians are not too concerned about young people reading comic books that conform to the code unless that is the only type of outside reading the person ever does.

For years many of the most popular comic books contained stories of adventure or crime prevention. These were usually built around the exploits of a leading character of superhuman or exceptional powers. Other popular stories were in the realm of fantasy or science-fiction. But by the 1970's comic books were being read by a more sophisticated audience. This audience preferred heroes who coped with the real world. Thus comic books began to feature stories on such subjects as ecology, race relations, and women's rights.

The comic-book form is sometimes used to teach as well as entertain. Comic books are used to help explain complicated subjects. They are also useful tools to civic organizations in public information campaigns. A reference list of free and inexpensive materials will include many comic books such as those published by General Electric, Goodrich Company, or Swift and Company. Such material often contains valuable information. However, it is wise to keep in mind the source of the material if it is to be used in arguments. For instance, material from the American Railway Association will not tell about similar services performed by the national trucking industry.

Telling a story through pictures will probably continue to be popular for some time to come. However, comic books have changed a great deal since they first began. Other changes will very likely come in the future.

CONSTANCE CARR MCCUTCHEON
Author, *Substitutes for the Comics*
Reviewed by LELAND B. JACOBS
Columbia University

COMMERCE. See TRADE AND COMMERCE.

Record album cover with illustration by Jan Balet.

Photograph used as a magazine advertisement for Kodak.

1903

1918

1928

Package design is an important commercial art. The appearance of the Shredded Wheat box has been changed frequently to keep pace with changing styles.

Today

1944

COMMERCIAL ART

The term "commercial art" is usually used to mean art created for a business purpose. Unlike fine art, such as painting or sculpture, commercial art is made for reproduction. The illustrator often draws illustrations that will be reproduced in thousands of magazines or newspapers. Another commercial artist is the industrial designer. The industrial designer may design products intended to be mass produced and sold in quantity. The advertising industry probably uses more commercial artists than any other business.

There are many steps in planning a sales campaign, and commercial artists are involved in almost every step. A product must be designed, packaged, and displayed properly in order to make certain that people know about it. An advertising campaign calls attention to the product through magazine advertisements, television commercials, and posters.

The importance of commercial art can be seen by examining the sales campaign of a particular product. A breakfast cereal makes a good example because it is usually not the appearance of the cereal itself that makes us familiar with it. Instead it is the design of the box or the commercial on television that first introduces us to the cereal.

A good package must do more than hold the breakfast cereal and keep it fresh. It must be designed to catch the eye of shoppers in the market. Package designers usually choose large, bold, easy-to-read lettering for the name of the cereal. Bright colors and gay pictures are used to make the package interesting.

How the new cereal is displayed is also important. Commercial artists design posters and display cards to put on the shelves near the cereal. Displays are also planned for the windows of stores. The display artist must not only attract your attention but must also make you want to come into the store to buy the product.

▶ PRINTED ADVERTISING

To help sell the cereal, advertisements appear in magazines, newspapers, and other advertising media. These advertisements give the name of the cereal and tell what is new or special about it. A picture of how the cereal looks when served with fruit and cream may be shown. There may also be an illustration of a healthy girl or boy running or playing ball to show that the cereal is a good energy food. An imaginative commercial artist will think of many ways to illustrate the fact that the product is nutritious and good to eat.

Every advertising agency has an art director. The art director decides on the artwork that will be best for the advertising campaign. Suppose the art director decides that a magazine advertisement should show a young ball player in uniform eating breakfast on the morning of an important game. The purpose of the illustration will be to show that the player will do best after a good breakfast of the vitamin-filled cereal.

After deciding on the contents of an advertisement, the art director gives sketches to a layout person. The layout person arranges the various parts of the advertisement in an attractive and striking way. The rough layout is shown to the food manufacturer whose product is being advertised. If the layout is approved, a more detailed version is given to the artists who will complete the advertisement.

Advertising illustrators are often specialists in drawing certain subjects—children, animals, cars, and so forth. Sometimes a photograph is used as an illustration in an advertisement. The photographer who does this work is, in a way, a commercial artist, too.

The words in an advertisement or on a package design are either drawn by hand or

Trademarks of four well-known companies: Coca Cola, Volkswagen, Westinghouse, and Bovril.

Drawing for television safety film.

David Stone Martin's drawing was used to advertise Danny Kaye's television program for UNICEF.

printed. The commercial artist who draws letters is called a **letterer**. Lettering requires skill in drawing letters so that they have different effects. A diet cereal, for example, may have a package with tall, thin lettering (to suggest that anyone who eats the cereal may become slim). The person who chooses the style of printed type to be used is called a **typographer**. The typographer selects a type style that will go well with the hand lettering and the general idea of the advertisement. Often one person does both lettering and typography, as these jobs are so closely related.

Another important part of an advertisement or package is the trademark. Usually a trademark is made up of the name or initials of the manufacturer written in some special way. The trademark is used in all advertising and becomes familiar to the public. A good trademark is easily recognized and remembered.

When all of the different parts of an advertisement have been drawn by the artists, a paste-up is prepared. This means that everything is put in place on a piece of heavy paper. The paste-up shows exactly how the advertisement will look.

Every magazine has many advertisements —some with drawings, some with photographs. The kind of art technique used—such as pen and ink drawing or photography— often depends on where the advertisement will appear. The good quality of the paper in magazines allows complicated advertisements using color and great detail. Simpler advertisements must be planned for the rough, cheaper paper of a newspaper.

Another important kind of advertising that requires the skill of a specialized commercial artist is the outdoor poster. The picture must be very clear and the text short because the poster is often seen quickly and from a distance.

▶ TELEVISION COMMERCIALS

Commercial artists also work for television commercials. Since methods of advertising on television are different from methods of advertising in print, different skills are needed. Television commercials almost always show the real product. The cereal will be shown in its package and ready to eat in a bowl. Often the artist makes a simplified package because the television viewers cannot see the fine print and details on the real package. An artist sometimes draws sketches of the action as a guide to the camera crew and actors.

Commercials often use imaginary cartoon figures. Cartoonists are among the busiest commercial artists because they must make hundreds of drawings—it takes about 1,400 pictures to make a 1-minute cartoon.

The work of all these commercial artists in magazines, in newspapers, on television, and on billboards makes us familiar with the new product.

Reviewed by DAVID STONE MARTIN

Why are so many New York Times
reporters going to the summit?

Because it is there!

Advertisement by Tomi Ungerer.

Orange juice poster from Finland.

Jane Addams

Civilization
is a method
of living,
an attitude
of equal
respect
for all men.

Container Corporation of America

Container Corp. poster.

Poster for the London *Times*.

JAFFA

HARTWALL

THE TIMES

COMMON MARKET. See European Communities.

COMMONWEALTH OF NATIONS

The saying used to be "The sun never sets on the British Empire." Today the saying might be "The sun never sets on the Commonwealth of Nations." The Empire is no more, and many countries that were once colonies in the Empire have now become independent nations in the Commonwealth.

The Commonwealth is a group of nations and their dependencies that try to work together for their mutual benefit. Commonwealth nations co-operate to reduce tariffs. They work together on defense and exchange ideas on industry, farming, science, and education. But each of the Commonwealth members has complete control over its own affairs. Whatever each does as part of the Commonwealth, it does voluntarily.

Some Commonwealth nations, like Canada, are monarchies. They officially recognize Queen Elizabeth II as their sovereign, even though she has no real power in their affairs. Other nations, like India, are republics, but they recognize the Queen as head of the Commonwealth. A governor-general represents the Queen in each of the Commonwealth monarchies but, like her, has no real power.

The first step in organizing the Commonwealth as it exists today was taken at a conference in London in 1926. The **dominions** of the British Empire—the areas having the most independence—were recognized at that time as free and equal nations in the Commonwealth. Many other former British dependencies have since become independent members.

Another part of the Commonwealth is made up of the dependencies and associated states of various independent members. The amount of self-government that they have varies.

The dependencies of Australia and New Zealand are called **territories**. Each has an administrator chosen by the Australian or New Zealand government, which is responsible for defense and foreign relations. The administrator sometimes shares power with an elected assembly. Territories with complete self-government, such as the Cook Islands and Niue Island, control their internal affairs and can declare independence at any time.

In 1967, a group of British-connected states in the Caribbean formed the West Indies Associated States. They controlled their internal affairs as **associated states** of the United Kingdom, which was responsible for their foreign affairs. All but Anguilla, which broke away from St. Kitts–Nevis in 1969, had become independent members of the Commonwealth by 1983.

Some British dependencies never formally belonged to the United Kingdom and are not now joined to it for citizenship purposes. They have simply made treaties permitting the British government to manage their defense and foreign relations. Other dependencies are jointly administered by two nations.

Many British dependencies are overseas territories that are officially annexed or joined to the United Kingdom. They were formerly called **colonies** or **crown colonies**. Their people are citizens of the United Kingdom. In these dependencies, the highest official is a governor appointed by the British government.

Many dependencies have increasing self-government. They may one day become independent members of the Commonwealth.

Reviewed by Robert Bothwell
University of Toronto

COMMONWEALTH MEMBERS

Independent members of the Commonwealth: Antigua and Barbuda, Australia, Bahamas, Bangladesh, Barbados, Belize, Botswana, Canada, Cyprus, Dominica, Fiji, The Gambia, Ghana, Grenada, Guyana, India, Jamaica, Kenya, Kiribati, Lesotho, Malawi, Maldives, Malaysia, Malta, Mauritius, Nauru, New Zealand, Nigeria, Papua New Guinea, St. Kitts–Nevis, St. Lucia, St. Vincent and the Grenadines, Seychelles, Sierra Leone, Singapore, Solomon Islands, Sri Lanka (Ceylon), Swaziland, Tanzania, Tonga, Trinidad and Tobago, Tuvalu, Uganda, United Kingdom, Western Samoa, Vanuatu, Zambia, Zimbabwe (Rhodesia).

Dependencies and Associated States of the United Kingdom: Anguilla, Bermuda, British Antarctic Territory, British Indian Ocean Territory, British Virgin Islands, Brunei, Cayman Islands, Channel Islands, Falkland Islands and Dependencies, Gibraltar, Hong Kong, Isle of Man, Montserrat, Pitcairn Island group, St. Helena, Turks and Caicos Islands.

Dependencies of Australia: Australian Antarctic Territory, Christmas Island, Cocos Islands, Coral Sea Islands, Heard and McDonald Islands, Norfolk Island.

Dependencies of New Zealand: Cook Islands, Niue Island, Tokelau Islands, Ross Dependency.

COMMUNICATION

Communication means transmitting information, ideas, or feelings from one person to another. If you tell someone what you think or want, you are transferring that information from your mind to the mind of the other person. When you talk something over with a friend, you are both trading ideas. This is communication by speech. It is the earliest and still the most important way people communicate. But it is by no means the only way. We communicate also by a gesture, a look, or a picture, by written and printed language, and in many other ways.

The word "communicate" comes from the Latin *communicare,* which means "to share" or "to make common." Communication requires a message (the idea you want to communicate) and a means of giving it to someone else.

The chief means of communication are the brain and the senses. Human beings use mainly the senses of seeing and hearing. But they may use other senses, too. People who cannot see or hear sometimes learn to communicate by the sense of touch. Sightless people read by touching raised letters with their fingertips. People who cannot hear or speak but can see communicate by using a special hand language and finger alphabet.

Animals can communicate, too. Their brains are much simpler than human brains, but they use their senses very well. They cannot speak a language. They communicate by grunting, chirping, barking, and making other noises or movements. They can warn each other of danger, call their mates, or express fear, pain, and joy. A mother cat calls her kittens with a special sound when their eyes are not yet open to see her. Even insects can communicate. A honeybee that has found food tells the other bees where the food is and how far away. It does this by a special kind of "dancing."

Pet animals can also communicate with people. A dog barks, wags its tail, and jumps around the refrigerator. It is telling you that it wants food. It whines or scratches on the door when it wants to go out.

Many intelligent animals—apes, dogs, seals, dolphins—can communicate with human beings. They learn to do tricks in response to a trainer's signals.

But human beings have developed communication far beyond the animal or signal level. Speech, writing, printing, postal service, books, magazines, telegraph, telephone, radio, computers, and television—these and many more form the mighty web of communication today.

Communication makes it possible for people to share their knowledge, add to it, and pass it on to the next generation. By communicating, each person adds ideas to the pool of ideas for others to use. Imagine how it would be if there were no communication. People would have to find out everything themselves. They would have to make everything they used. Each person would have to start all over from the beginning.

The history of communication is the story of how our ancient Stone Age ancestors developed into modern people. How did it begin? How did it all come about?

SPEECH

People probably learned to talk hundreds of thousands of years ago. We have no way of finding out how speech began. Primitive people did not know how to write, so they could not keep records. Somehow primitive people learned to make others understand what their vocal sounds meant, and they learned to put the sounds together into language. But we can never really know how human beings invented speech. We can only wonder and guess.

In earlier times speech had two main drawbacks. The moment a word was spoken, it died away on the air. To hear what was said, you had to be near the person speaking. Neither drawback is true today. But in the past how could people send messages to others far away? How could they save important knowledge for people in the future?

Early groups of people tried to solve these problems with spoken words and memory. They could send a runner to tell the news to their friends far away. The messenger had to remember the words and repeat them.

Ancient tribes preserved their history in the form of spoken words and songs. People told the stories over and over, so listeners would remember them and tell them to their children. The stories changed in the telling because nobody remembers things exactly. Stories kept only the meanings that were most important to the people—including meanings about how life and death and earth and humanity were thought to have begun. So the stories became myths and legends.

For thousands of years only storytellers and singers preserved these legends. During the Middle Ages minstrels did what books and newspapers do today. They wandered from one court to another, giving listeners stories and news in the form of ballads.

Very early in history, people realized that words have great power. They used them to communicate with other people and with spirits and gods created by their imaginations. They even tried to communicate with the forces of nature. People thought that by using the right words they could even tame the spirits, bring rain, or prevent hurricanes. So they tried to get control over the frightening forces of nature by the power of words—by chanting charms, incantations, and magic spells. But the power of words was still limited as long as people could not put them down in written records and store them and so communicate beyond the reach of voice alone.

WRITING

Storytellers and messengers did not really solve the problems of saving knowledge for the future or communicating at a distance. For this, people needed written language. Yet they did not invent writing for thousands of years after they learned to speak.

In the Stone Age, people knew how to make a picture represent an object. Cave dwellers carved pictures of animals on the walls of their caves. So thousands of years later, these people still tell us what animals they hunted. This was not writing as we know it, but

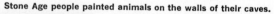

Stone Age people painted animals on the walls of their caves.

The ancient Egyptians left records of their daily life in hieroglyphic writing.

writing did grow out of picture making. Gradually the pictures became more and more complicated. They began to stand for ideas as well as for animals or objects.

American Indians had various forms of picture writing before the time of Columbus. The Maya in Central America had a highly developed written language of hieroglyphics—picture symbols that stand for things or ideas. Other American Indians told a story with pictures of men, women, animals, and spirits. Some, like the Kickapoos of the Middle West in North America, could make a mark on a prayer stick stand for a prayer or a mythical event. The North American Indians almost developed hieroglyphic writing.

People took a giant step toward inventing real writing when they learned to make a picture stand for a sound—a word in spoken language—instead of an object. The Sumerians in Mesopotamia (now Iraq) began to do this over 5,000 years ago. The ancient Egyptians and Mayas also wrote in pictures that meant words. The Chinese still use a very complicated form of picture writing today. In their language each written sign (called an ideograph) stands for a single one-syllable spoken word. So they need many thousand ideographs in order to write. Scholars have found the keys to some ancient languages, and we can read them today.

The next step was to invent a written language in which each sign stood for a single sound instead of for a whole word. The word "alphabet" comes from the first two letters of the Greek alphabet, *alpha* and *beta*. Mediterranean peoples, the Hebrews and the Phoenicians, were the first to use an alphabet. Since

the Phoenicians were great sea traders, they needed a simple, efficient way of writing to keep their business records. So about 3,000 years ago they developed a system of 22 pictures that stood for the sounds of the consonants in their language. This was much better than using a different picture to mean each word, because they could make any word they wanted from their 22 letter signs.

The Greeks, the Etruscans, and the Romans all based their writing on the Hebrew and Phoenician alphabet. The Greeks added signs that meant vowel sounds. Over 2,000 years ago the Romans developed the Roman alphabet, which we still use in the Western world.

When people learned to write, they had to have something to write on and something to write with. In ancient times people carved word pictures on stone or on trees. Later they used clay tablets or a tablet coated with soft wax. The Egyptians made a crude kind of paper from the papyrus plant, which grew along the banks of the Nile. Much later in medieval Europe people made parchment or vellum by splitting animal skins into thin layers. Sometimes they rolled these soft skins up on scrolls, like rolls of wallpaper today. The slang word for a modern college diploma is "sheepskin." The word comes from the old custom of writing on prepared animal skins.

In the Middle Ages few people knew how to read or write. Monks, living in secluded monasteries, were almost the only writers. Each monastery had a special room called a scriptorium, or writing room. Here the monks wrote on parchment with quills—goose or turkey feathers. They printed each letter carefully by hand and illustrated the pages with beautiful colored drawings. These were manuscript books. (The word "manuscript" comes from two Latin words meaning "written by hand.") Each book was a work of art. No one except a very rich bishop or feudal baron could afford such a book.

One of the reasons manuscript books were so rare and precious was that it took so much time and skill to make them. Another reason was that there was no inexpensive, lightweight material for people to write on. By the 2nd century A.D. the Chinese knew how to make paper from bamboo, silk, or linen. But there was very little communication between the Far East and Europe. Not until Marco Polo visited China in the 12th century did Europe learn about the invention of paper.

Once Europe learned about paper, the art of papermaking spread rapidly. William Rittenhouse, a Mennonite minister, built the first paper mill in the American colonies. He went there from the Netherlands in 1688 and built his factory in Pennsylvania in 1690. In those days paper was made from cloth rags.

Fine-quality paper is still made from rags. But we make far more paper from wood. In the early 1700's a French scientist, René de Réaumur, is supposed to have seen wasps chewing up wood to make a kind of paper for their nests. He experimented until he could also make paper from wood. Today paper mills turn forests into pulp in order to feed our huge appetite for newspapers, books, and magazines.

Writing tools have changed as much as writing material. The Romans used one of the oldest kinds—a sharp-pointed metal stylus. But Rome had to outlaw the metal stylus. Too many Romans, including schoolboys, were using it as a dagger. There is a record of students stabbing their schoolmaster with these writing instruments. So Romans had to change the stylus and make it out of less dangerous material. Sometimes they made it from the bones of birds or carved it from ivory. The blunt end of the stylus could smooth out mistakes on clay or wax much as a modern eraser does on paper.

The Egyptians and the Chinese were the first to use ink. Sometimes they made it of charcoal or of lampblack mixed with glue. The Chinese painted their picture words with brushes and ink. The Greeks and Romans made ink from the ink sac of the cuttlefish.

Medieval monks used quill pens. Later a British locksmith named Samuel Harrison learned how to make pen points of metal. English craftsmen made the first steel pens in 1819. In 1858 Richard Esterbrook, an Englishman, came to America. He saw a good market for pens in America. He wrote to his father, "Made in USA is having a great effect on the market place . . . suggest you consider coming here and bringing a small crew of skilled pen-makers. . . ." His father went to the United States, and together he and Richard opened a pen factory at Camden, New Jersey.

By the 8th century the Chinese were printing on paper with inked wood blocks.

In 1884, Lewis Edson Waterman patented the first fountain pen and opened a factory in New York. More recently, penmakers developed the popular ballpoint pen. It has become almost as inexpensive and useful as the lead pencil.

A lead pencil doesn't really write with lead, though the Egyptians did use lead for writing over 2,000 years ago. The modern pencil makes its marks with graphite, a form of carbon. As early as A.D. 1400 English peddlers were selling pieces of graphite for writing. It was breakable, almost like a stick of charcoal. Craftsmen learned to surround the graphite with wood to protect it. Now when the pencil point breaks, we just sharpen the pencil again.

Another step in the development of writing tools was the typewriter. In 1714 Queen Anne of England granted a British engineer, Henry Mill, a patent for making a writing machine. He did not produce a practical one. Neither did William Austin Burt, who made the first American typewriter. His machine was patented but never manufactured. Finally, in 1868, Christopher L. Sholes and three of his friends designed and patented the Type Writer, a machine something like the typewriter we use today. Other inventors improved it until now we have typewriters that are controlled by computers.

▶ **PRINTING**

Before the invention of printing the only way anyone could make several copies of a book was to copy it again and again, each time by hand. Every book was rare, unique, and expensive.

By the 8th century A.D., the Chinese knew how to make copies by block printing. Artisans carved pictures or picture words on blocks of wood. They carved them backwards (like the page you see if you hold a book up to a mirror) so that they would print the right way on pages. Then they coated the surface of the wood with ink, placed sheets of paper over the block, and rubbed it. People do a similar thing today with linoleum blocks. The Chinese printed entire books that way.

Of course each block printed only one particular page. The letters on the block could not be used to print anything else. In the 11th century another Chinese, Pi Sheng, made

A page from the famous Gutenberg Bible (1456).

separate clay type for each Chinese ideograph. These could be put together in different order to print different messages, and they could be used over and over. This was the first use of movable type.

But the Chinese language had thousands of characters, one for each word. So Pi Sheng's device wasn't as practical for Chinese as it would have been for the 26-letter alphabet of the Western world. Four hundred years after Pi Sheng's time, the news of his movable type had not yet reached Europe.

In the 15th century Johann Gutenberg of Mainz, Germany, perfected the first practical printing press using movable type. He had seen playing cards printed by using blocks of wood. Perhaps complete books could be printed this way. By 1440 Gutenberg was experimenting with movable type that could be rearranged in any order and used again and again. At first he carved letters on separate blocks of wood. He used a wooden hand press like a wine press to push the type against the paper. Later he invented molds for casting metal type.

The famous two-volume Gutenberg Bible

published in 1456 was his masterpiece. Gutenberg's press signaled the beginning of the age of printing.

Printing revolutionized communication and education. By using movable type and a letterpress system, it became possible to print books in large number. Many people could own copies of the same book. Ideas began to spread more rapidly.

Today newspapers are beginning to use the laser beam in the printing process. The Los Angeles *Times,* for example, uses lasers in production.

▶ PHOTOGRAPHY

Pictures communicate some ideas better than words do. Since the days of the cave people, artists have been drawing pictures. But early in the 19th century, people tried to invent a mechanical way of picturing an object just as it really was.

A French painter, Daguerre, first developed a camera in the 1830's. His pictures were called daguerreotypes. Pictures were taken on glass plates coated with chemicals. The photographer had to carry a huge, heavy camera. A wagonload of equipment was needed to take these pictures and process them. In spite of these hardships, photographers were able to record and publish pictures of the American Civil War in the 1860's. Mathew B. Brady made some of the most famous Civil War pictures. Since the early 19th century cameras have been used to photograph and thereby save the real look of people and events.

In 1889 George Eastman produced roll film and a simple, lightweight camera. Photographs could be taken and reproduced in minutes. It became possible to see pictures of people and places all over the world, as well as pictures taken from satellites showing how the earth looks. Rare old manuscripts and paintings could also be photographed. The camera copies them for libraries everywhere.

During the 1890's Thomas A. Edison and others invented a fascinating new communications tool—the motion picture camera. Photographers could then take pictures of events and people in action. They could photograph plays, and so entertain and inform an audience. From this invention the movie industry was born. During the 20th century movies have become a main source of amusement everywhere. Newsreel photographers record an important event so people everywhere can see exactly the way it happened.

▶ PHONOGRAPH AND TAPE RECORDER

Today we can save the spoken word on records or on tape. Thomas Edison invented the first practical phonograph in 1877. German scientists before him had experimented with recording sounds on tinfoil. Edison wrapped a sheet of tinfoil around a cylinder that could be rotated. When sound waves struck Edison's device and made it vibrate, a needle traced the pattern of the sound vibrations on the foil. The sounds could be played back. The first sounds Edison recorded were the verses of "Mary Had a Little Lamb."

Other inventors improved the phonograph. They coated the cylinders with wax instead of tinfoil. Then they began recording on disks instead of cylinders. The first phonographs were not electrical. The machine had to be wound up to make it play. But modern phonographs use electricity, both to record and to play records.

In the 1920's scientists began to record sounds on a roll of magnetic wire instead of on disks. Later they found that a thin, narrow strip of magnetic tape wound on a reel worked better.

By the 1940's they had developed a practical tape recorder. Today radio programs are recorded on tape and can be broadcast many times. The invention of videotape makes it possible to record pictures as well as sounds. Many TV programs are taped on videotape and broadcast all over the world.

Some people have their own home tape recorders. They can save the sound of a baby's first words or the sounds of a family celebrating Christmas or record a historic speech as it is broadcast over television.

In this way the actual sound of a famous voice can be saved. For example, people born years after President Franklin Delano Roosevelt died can listen to his recorded voice as he announced the attack on Pearl Harbor on December 7, 1941. But no one can hear the real voice of Lincoln reading the Gettysburg Address because there were no voice-recording devices in Lincoln's day. Until the 20th century there was no way to keep the

Over 2,000 years ago the Persians used a relay system of postriders.

sound of spoken words from vanishing like smoke.

▶ **POSTAL SERVICE**

Years ago people had no way to send messages quickly over vast distances. People in one country could not learn what others thousands of kilometers away had already known or invented. They had to invent each tool and develop each idea themselves. New knowledge passed slowly from place to place. It did not flash around the world in a few minutes, as it does today.

Even people of ancient times had to send messages from one place to another. At first, royal rulers were the only people who had postal service. They sent official messages by runners. A ruler 4,000 years ago might inscribe a message on a clay tile and send a runner speeding off to deliver it to another ruler.

After people learned to tame horses, postriders were used. Early Persians had developed a relay system of postriders. These riders were stationed at certain places. One would pick up the message and ride off with it to the next. Two thousand years later Americans used the same system in the West with the Pony Express (1860–61).

The Romans built roads and developed a good postal system. When Julius Caesar invaded Britain, messengers carried his letters to Cicero in Rome in a few weeks' time.

Pigeons and postriders were the forerunners of today's mail carriers. As long ago as 1000 B.C., King Solomon and the Queen of Sheba exchanged messages by carrier pigeon. This kind of pigeon will find its way home when it is released. Turkish sultans used pigeons

in the 11th century A.D. to fly long distances with tiny message capsules attached to their legs. During the French Revolution, generals sent war news to outlying districts by means of pigeons.

In the 16th century, during the reign of England's Queen Elizabeth I, postriders on horseback carried letters to and from her court. They carried horns and blew them at frequent intervals to herald their arrival. They rode at a speed of about 12 kilometers (7 miles) an hour.

Ancient postal service was only for royalty and very rich or important people. The messages had to be important to be worth the trouble. But in the 1500's, English rulers began to see that ordinary people needed to send messages, too. By 1683, the London penny post would deliver a letter anywhere in London for a penny.

During the very early days of the American colonies, letter writers had to depend on the good nature of travelers. A Bostonian would write a letter to a friend in another town and give it to someone who was going to that town. The traveler would leave the letter at an inn. With luck, the friend who was supposed to get the letter might come to that inn and pick the letter up.

Twenty years after the Pilgrims landed, the Massachusetts Bay Colony appointed a postmaster. This postmaster, Richard Fairbanks, received a penny for every letter he delivered. Much later, the colonies established regular mail services between important towns. There was one postrider a month between New York and Boston. This postrider took two weeks for the trip and traveled only by day.

When Benjamin Franklin became postmaster for all the colonies in 1753, he set up a chain of post stations from Maine to Georgia. Postriders made one trip a week between New York and Philadelphia, and had to ride by night as well as by day. Stagecoaches also carried mailbags, but riders were much faster. In colonial days the person receiving the mail paid the postage. It cost a shilling to send a letter from Boston to New York City.

This improved communication tied the colonies together. When the colonists began to have trouble with England in 1765, the Boston patriot Samuel Adams set up Committees of Correspondence. Leaders in each colony wrote letters telling people in all the other colonies what was going on in their region. In this way all the colonies shared news and views.

During the colonial period communication between the colonies and England was still very slow. Colonial governors gave sea captains important official messages to deliver in England. With good weather, sailing ships took several weeks to cross the Atlantic. If a storm blew up, it might be months.

The ship captain usually hung a sack in a tavern in the port town shortly before sailing. Ordinary citizens could drop letters in this sack. If their friends on the other side of the ocean thought to come down to the dock when the ship arrived, they would get their letters. The captain had no further responsibility once the ship docked.

When the American colonies began to quarrel with England in the 1760's, it took weeks or months for each side to know how the other side answered the latest argument. Slow, poor communication was one of the reasons that the English and Americans could not understand each other's point of view.

After the Revolutionary War, American leaders realized the vital importance of communication. Separate states and scattered frontier settlements had to be tied together into a single country. George Washington said: "Open all the communications which nature has afforded between the Atlantic States and the Western territories, and encourage the use of them to the utmost. . . . sure I am there is no other tie by which they will long form a link in the chain of Federal Union."

At first the pioneers in Kentucky or Ohio had very little communication with settled areas in the east. Travelers, peddlers, and circuit riders brought news occasionally to the isolated western villages. For some time rivers were the best highways. Towns sprang up along rivers, and riverboats carried letters and newspapers. But a pioneer in Kentucky probably knew less about what was going on in Washington, D.C., than today's schoolchild knows about Asia or Africa.

During the early 19th century inventors learned to harness steam engines to boats and railroad lines. Robert Fulton's steamboat the *Clermont* steamed successfully on the Hudson in 1807. Soon steamboats became common river carriers, and canals began to tie river systems into a great inland water network. By the 1830's steam locomotives proved practical. The government helped railroad builders with subsidies, and by the mid-19th century railroad lines linked the country as far west as the Mississippi River.

When people invented new means of communication, they did not always abandon the old ones. Sometimes old and new methods were used at the same time. For example, during the 20-year period from 1849 to 1869 five kinds of communication carried messages between the East Coast and California. Clipper ships carrying mail around the Horn took months to reach San Francisco, California. In 1858 the Butterfield Overland Stage began carrying transcontinental mail. A transcontinental railroad to transport freight and heavier mail was completed in 1869.

In 1860, Pony Express riders carried messages across the continent. They used a relay system not unlike that of the Persians 2,400 years earlier. Starting at St. Joseph, Missouri (the western end of the telegraph line), they could carry a message from New York to San Francisco in 9 to 12 days. But the Pony Express lasted only 18 months. In 1861, telegraph wires connected New York and San Francisco. As a result, a message could flash across the country in seconds, so the Pony Express riders went out of business. One of the newest methods of communication displaced one of the oldest in less than two years.

But while we no longer use Pony Express riders, the telegraph and telephone have not displaced postal service. People still write letters. Thanks to airmail, a letter can reach

Europe from the United States in hours instead of weeks or months, as was the case 200 years ago.

SIGNS, SIGNALS, GESTURES

Modern means of communication have not entirely taken the place of a very simple kind—communication by sign or signal. People often communicate without words—by a smile, a shake of the head, a wave of the hand. A driver signals for a turn. A traffic light turns from green to red, signaling "Stop." An alarm clock rings, meaning "It's time to get up."

Signals—messages that are communicated without written or spoken words—are of two kinds. There are sight signals—something you see, such as the police officer's hand waving you to cross the street. Or there are sound signals—something you hear, like the ringing of a schoolbell.

A signal may carry just one message. The doorbell ringing means that someone is at the door. Or signals may be combined into a complicated code, so that taken together, they relate a message that can be translated into words.

DRUMS, GUNS, AND BELLS

Thousands of years before the telegraph was invented, people knew that sound traveled faster than even the speediest runner or horse. Primitive peoples sent messages by beating out codes on drums or hollow logs. Each beat had a particular meaning. Far away on a hilltop, the next drummer would hear the message, answer it, and pass it on. A long chain of drummers might repeat the drumbeat, until the message traveled a long distance from its origin.

In pioneer days, Americans on the frontier sometimes used guns for signal communication. In a small town several revolver shots meant a fire alarm. People sent coded messages by horn blasts, gunshots, or ringing bells.

For centuries, people have used bells to ring out important news. Bells communicate by a sound signal, and everyone within hearing should understand the signal. Bells were used to ring the curfew hour (time to be indoors, off the streets) or announce that the town crier in the city square had something important to tell. Bells still ring in the new year and call people to church or to school. Telephone bells and doorbells signal that someone wants attention. The long, slow, sad tolling of the church bell tells of a death or a funeral.

The sound of a bell or a siren tells that a fire is near or that an ambulance is coming. In cities, cars stop when they hear the fire siren. During wartime, sirens signal air raids. Everyone takes shelter when the siren blows.

All these sound signals deliver short but very important messages. Even with all our modern electronic marvels of communication, a bell or a siren is still one of the quickest, surest ways of getting a vital warning to everyone within hearing.

SMOKE AND LIGHT SIGNALS

Sound signals are fast because sound travels at about 1,220 kilometers (760 miles) an hour. A loud sound communicates its meaning to everyone who hears it, whether or not the person is expecting the message. Signals that you see rather than hear are even faster because they travel by light waves. Light moves at about 300,000 kilometers (186,000 miles) a second. But the receiver has to be watching in the right direction.

Sight signals are sent by means of smoke, fire, or light beams. The American Indians sent messages by smoke signals. The sender waved a blanket over a fire, making the smoke puffs go up in a certain way to form a message. An Indian watching far away could read the puffs and understand the message.

American Indians used smoke signals to communicate.

The ancient Chinese, Egyptians, Greeks, and Persians all signaled by smoke or fire. Aeschylus, the Greek poet, records that the news of the fall of Troy was sent to Greece by means of a series of bonfires. The Greek historian Herodotus tells us that as early as the 5th century B.C. the Greeks signaled by reflecting sunlight in a polished metal mirror. This is called heliograph signaling. Until radio became practical in the 1920's, ships communicated with each other by a code of light flashes. In the daytime they used a pair of signal flags held in semaphoric positions. Later Samuel F. B. Morse used the idea of the semaphore code when he invented the Morse code.

Light signals, like bells, are still useful for simple warnings. The lighthouse tells ship captains to stay away from hidden rocky reefs. The stoplight in an automobile tells another motorist to slow down. Traffic lights signal stop and go.

But although light travels quickly, its signals have a serious disadvantage. The message can travel only as far as a person can see. At best light signals only travel a good distance at sea or on a level plain, where there are no mountains to get in the way. Even then light signals will be cut off by the curve of the earth before they have gone very far.

▶ TELEGRAPH

Electrical impulses move almost as fast as light waves and travel as far as power and equipment permit.

The age of electrical communication began when Samuel Morse invented the first practical telegraph. The Morse telegraph code was a system of long and short buzzer signals (dots and dashes) arranged to spell out the letters of the alphabet. In 1837 Morse demonstrated that he could make a wire carry a series of electrical signals and so spell out a message.

The first successful telegraph line was built

Samuel Morse sent his first telegraph message on this machine.

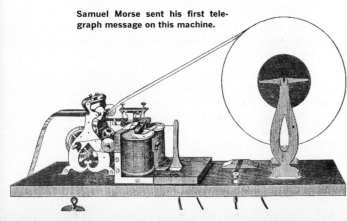

from Baltimore, Maryland, to Washington, D.C. Morse sent the first message on May 24, 1844. It has become one of the most famous messages in history: "What hath God wrought!"

In 1858 Cyrus W. Field and other engineers tried to lay an underwater telegraph cable between America and Europe. It worked for about three weeks and then went dead. During 1865 and 1866, Field chartered a steamship, the *Great Eastern,* and tried again to lay a transatlantic cable. There were already underwater cables tying Newfoundland to the mainland of North America and Ireland to England. Finally, after many heartbreaking setbacks, Field's company laid an underwater cable between Newfoundland and Valentia, Ireland—3,140 kilometers (1,950 miles) long. Telegraph wires linked the two continents.

Eventually, scientists invented a printing telegraph machine, called a teletypewriter or telegraph printer. It was no longer necessary for trained operators to send and decode Morse code messages. The sender merely typed the message on a teletypewriter in one place. Another machine typed the message mechanically at the receiving end. News services now use telegraph printing to send news stories from one place to another.

▶ THE TELEPHONE

The next step was to make the human voice travel by electricity along a wire. Alexander Graham Bell, a Scotsman who emigrated to Boston, was a teacher of the deaf. With an electrician friend, Thomas Watson, Bell experimented to see if a telegraph wire could transmit the sound of the human voice. Bell patented his telephone design in 1876. He sent the first telephone message by accident. Just as he was about to try out his transmitter he spilled acid on his clothes. He cried out, "Mr. Watson, come here. I want you." Through the receiver in another room, Watson heard Bell's voice come over the wire. The telephone worked.

Now most homes in the United States and Canada have telephones. People can pick up the telephone and dial directly. Almost at once they can be speaking to someone thousands of kilometers away.

The telephone connects people in many countries with other parts of the world. But

The shape of the telephone has changed many times since its invention, but its use has remained the same—an easy means of communication between people.

not until 1956 did a successful underwater telephone cable finally link the continents by telephone wires. Long before that, in 1927, another invention—the radio telephone—had started voices speaking across the sea. But storms often interfered with radio waves. Today a worldwide network of cables has greatly improved intercontinental telephone communication.

▶ RADIO

Radio waves travel at the speed of light. Since they go through the atmosphere, they need no wires. Therefore, radio communication can be used in airplanes and in ships or automobiles.

Radio waves can carry speech or electric signals. Guglielmo Marconi, the inventor of radio transmission, began with code signals similar to the Morse code. He first sent radio waves through the air in 1895. By 1901 Marconi was able to send his "wireless telegraph" signals across the Atlantic Ocean.

A year before that, in 1900, the American physicist Reginald A. Fessenden proved that voices also could travel on radio waves. In 1915 engineers managed to send a voice message from Arlington, Virginia, to Paris and to Hawaii. They proved that long distance radio-telephone communication was possible. Since almost everyone can understand voice sounds of one kind or another, radio communication was no longer limited to people who knew Morse code.

Because radio needs no wires, it is of tremendous help to ships and planes. All ships now keep in contact by voice radio. Radios in control towers of airfields "talk the pilot in"—that is, people on the ground direct the airplane pilot so that the craft is landed safely. Police cars have radios. Precinct captains can call police officers in cars and direct them to trouble spots. Many doctors and business people also have two-way car radios.

Citizens band (CB) radio communication has made it possible for motorists to exchange messages as they are driving in the same area. For the driver on a lonely road, this means company. Those who need assistance can ask for help over their two-way radios.

Public radio broadcasting began in November, 1920, when station KDKA in Pittsburgh, Pennsylvania, broadcast the presidential election returns: "Harding elected President." Radio rapidly became a favorite form of entertainment.

▶ TELEVISION

Once television became practical, people could sit in their living rooms and see as well as hear a play or a news broadcast. As far back as 1927 radio engineers had known that pictures, as well as sounds, could be sent by radio waves. But technical problems slowed their progress. TV broadcasting did not begin on a large scale until the late 1940's. Then it quickly became one of the world's most popular forms of communication and entertainment.

Television reaches millions of people. By a flick of the switch, viewers can enjoy a concert, a lecture, a play, or a comedy skit. News events can be seen as they happen. Television has become one of the most important mass communication tools.

▶ COMMUNICATIONS SATELLITES

Astronauts have journeyed off the planet earth and out into space. Ventures into space have led to the latest tool in long-distance communication—the communications satellite. The satellite is equipped with radio receivers and transmitters. Rockets boost it into orbit, and the force of gravity keeps it from flying off into space. The communications satellite is the earth's captive, circling the planet in space. The satellite acts as a television relay station. Engineers on the earth bounce television signals off it at an angle, and the signals come down at a different angle to receivers on another continent. Television

This communications satellite can carry color TV transmissions and telephone calls.

signals are blocked by mountains, by the earth's curvature, or sometimes even by buildings. Therefore, they have to be relayed from one transmitter to another in order to travel long distances.

In 1962, the first important United States communications satellite, **Telstar I**, was placed in orbit. Television engineers in Europe bounced a picture off Telstar, and viewers in the United States saw it. For the first time people sat at home in New York and watched something happening in London or Paris at the moment it took place.

In 1965 the United States launched Early Bird, the first commercial communications satellite, and the U.S.S.R. launched Molniya I. Today people in many parts of the world watch live television from other continents.

More recent communications satellites include Comstar D3, a U.S. telephone service satellite, and the U.S.S.R.'s Raduga 4. Both were orbited in 1978.

COMPUTERS AND LASERS

Computers are machines that are storehouses for all kinds of information. In recent years, small and large computers have kept many records relating to the lives and activities of citizens. Among such records are those dealing with school grades, social security, taxes, consumer credit, driving records, insurance policies, health and hospital treatments, bank deposits and loans, arrests and convictions, and memberships in organizations.

These records can be easily retrieved and reproduced. They are helpful in crime detection, as well as in national security matters. But such records can also be abused. Keeping all these records in centralized places may de-prive people of the right to privacy and may encourage surveillance of private individuals who have done no wrong.

Computer networks have been established over telephone lines. A central computer can send and receive information by telephone to or from a distant computer terminal. The terminal may be a typewriter-like device that can print out the central computer's information, or the terminal may have a video screen that displays the information.

Since the 1960's, the use of laser light has greatly improved the quantity and speed of storage and the retrieval of information. The laser is now being used in the publication of books and magazines. It has speeded up the printing process in many places.

MASS COMMUNICATION

The tools for mass communication are sometimes called mass media. Printing was the first such tool. With the development of printing, more and more books recorded ideas and spread them to more and more people. Many people, not just a few, could share information. Almost all knowledge is stored in books, just as food is stored in a freezer, ready for anyone who wants it. Within the last century, great public libraries have grown up. People can borrow books as well as buy them. People can read more books than they can afford to buy.

Publishers also began to print inexpensive paperback books. These books are sold in many supermarkets and drugstores as well as in bookstores.

Magazines reach even more people than do books. Over the past century, magazine publishing has grown into a giant industry. Millions of people read magazines. Because they appear regularly and often and are printed more rapidly than books, magazines can publish news more quickly and offer opinions on public affairs.

Newspapers move even more quickly than magazines to print news and opinions. And they are read by even more people. The United States and Canadian newspapers reach many millions of readers a day.

Magazines may appear every week or month, newspapers every day, and radio or television news may be broadcast every hour. All of them can take a single message—news or opinion or propaganda—and beam it like a powerful spotlight into millions of minds at once. So the mass media have the power to shape thoughts—power beyond the wildest dreams of any ancient ruler. This spotlight can throw light into dark corners, bringing people valuable information and helping them to be wiser citizens. Or it can blind people and harm them by spreading wrong information, false advertising, or dangerous propaganda.

The Rights and Responsibilities of the Media

The writers of the United States Constitution realized the importance of the public press, although they could not know how powerful the press would become. So the First Amendment to the Constitution guaranteed freedom of the press. That means that the government cannot decide what newspapers, magazines, radio, or television should say. It cannot stop people from writing, thinking, reading, and speaking. This is one of the most precious freedoms Americans have. It protects every person's right to disagree with the government or with any other authority, in public and in print.

In return for their freedom, newspapers have an obligation to the public. They must print news—facts—as well as opinion. The opinion part of the paper is the editorial section. There editors may say whatever they please. But editors are not supposed to distort or slant the news so that people are reading opinion when they think they are reading facts. Radio and television have the same obligation. Opinion is separated from news.

Newspapers and other mass media have a huge responsibility. They must keep people informed. They must decide which news is most

Information appears on the computer terminal's screen. The student responds, using the typewriter keyboard.

important. They must be sure it is accurate. And they must make wise use of their power to influence people's thoughts and attitudes through their editorial opinions.

One thing that helps readers in democratic countries retain their freedom of opinion is the custom of public disagreement and debate. Competition of ideas, like competition of products, is a tradition, and different newspapers represent many different opinions.

If law and custom did not keep our press free, one person or a group of people could use the power of the press to force a single line of propaganda upon a whole country. Confining the mass media to the expression of a single official propaganda line would end the competition of ideas.

Only a few laws regulate mass media. It is illegal to harm people by publishing false information about them. In the United States and many other countries, laws protect the public from false or misleading statements that are considered libelous, or harmful.

Mass media of communication often combine information with entertainment. A newspaper's main job is publishing news and opinion, but it also contains advertising and seeks to entertain its readers. Magazines, books, radio, television, and motion pictures provide entertainment. But they are forms of mass communication too.

ESTILL I. GREEN
Formerly, Engineering Management Consultant
Reviewed by ISIDORE STARR
City University of New York Queens College

COMMUNISM

As a political movement, Communism has been a powerful force in shaping the history of the 20th century. Its supporters and opponents are deeply divided. About one third of the world's people live in countries that are governed by Communist parties, and Communist groups are active in many other countries.

The term "communism" was first used to refer to any society in which property would be held in common (owned by everyone) rather than by individuals. This idea is very old. It was expressed—at least in part—by the Greek philosopher Plato in the 4th century B.C. and by the 15th-century English philosopher Thomas More.

The movement that we call Communism today is based on specific ideas about society, government, economics, and history. It is concerned mainly with changing countries from an agricultural to an industrial way of life. It was during a period of such change that the basic ideas of Communism were formed.

▶ THE BEGINNINGS OF COMMUNISM

In the early 1800's, industry grew rapidly in Western Europe. Privately owned factories and mills competed with one another, and the number of factories increased. (This kind of economic system, based on private ownership, is called capitalism.) But the people in these factories and mills often worked under dreadful conditions and suffered great hardships.

Some critics of the early industrial society thought that the hardships of workers would end if there was no private property. The burdens and benefits of society would then be shared equally by all. They called this type of system communism or socialism, using the terms interchangeably. The terms are still sometimes used that way. But strictly speaking, "Communism" refers to the programs of Communist parties, which grew from these early ideas.

Two beliefs in particular have played a role in the development of Communism. One is that all individuals are equal. This view can be traced back to the 16th and 17th centuries. It was a reaction to the division of European society into the privileged classes—including nobles, the clergy, and military officers—and those who lacked privileges. These were the tradespeople, artisans, and people who worked the land. The second belief is that the interests of the individual should come second to the interests of the community. This belief was held by people who thought that human freedom would come most quickly through common efforts.

The Theories of Karl Marx

These early beliefs were the basis for a theory of history developed by Karl Marx, a German thinker, in the mid-1800's. Marx thought that the goals of equality, freedom, and economic security would be reached through a new social order. He saw society as having developed from primitive communal life through various forms of oppression—slavery in ancient times, serfdom in the Middle Ages, and the harsh treatment of workers in his own time. Marx believed that society passed through these stages as a result of conflict between the privileged classes and those without privileges. At each stage, the oppressed overthrew the oppressors.

In the final stage, Marx thought, the workers

What are the differences between Communism and socialism?

"Communism" and "socialism" originally had the same meaning—public, rather than private, ownership of the means of production and distribution. But in the 19th and 20th centuries, these two terms have come to have different meanings.

"Socialism" is the more general term. The public ownership that is advocated by socialists may be by co-operatives, by cities, or by state or national governments. Socialist parties or governments may be democratic or may favor a one-party system. Socialist parties in democratic countries generally favor public ownership only of selected key elements of the economy—transportation and energy industries, for example. Some socialist parties are strongly opposed to Communism. "Communism" is most often used today to mean the program of the Communist parties. This program includes party control of government and of social activity, as well as of the economy. In most cases it also includes the goal of spreading Communism through violent revolution.

The countries governed by Communist parties use the terms somewhat differently. They consider themselves to be in a "socialist" stage of development, under firm party control. True "communism" will come later, when they have enough resources to meet the needs of all people, regardless of what the people contribute to society.

Karl Marx (*left*) and Friedrich Engels were founders of the modern Communist movement.

would overthrow capitalism and take power. They would then work to create a Communist state, in which all the people would own the means of production—factories, mills, farmlands, and the like. When the ideal had been reached, government would no longer be needed because there would no longer be conflict between privileged groups and those without privileges. Marx believed that Communism would combine the qualities of early communal life, in which all individuals were equal, with the benefits of modern industrial society.

Marx thought that this last revolution might take place in his own lifetime. The *Communist Manifesto,* written by Marx and his friend Friedrich Engels in 1848, was a call to revolt during a troubled period in European politics.

Marx did not expect the rest of the world to follow the pattern he foresaw for Europe. He realized that countries like Russia, India, and China did not have the same experience with capitalism as the countries of Western Europe. He believed that capitalism would have to spread to the rest of the world before these other countries could begin to develop toward Communism.

Socialist parties with Marxist ideas were established in most Western European countries in the 1800's, but they did not gain wide influence until after World War II.

The Rise of Lenin

The Russian socialist movement originated in the 1800's. The Russian Social Democratic Labor Party, of which Vladimir I. Lenin was leader, was founded in 1898. In 1903 it split into two branches. The Bolsheviks, who formed the majority branch, were led by Lenin. They wanted to form a disciplined party dedicated to overthrowing the government. The Mensheviks, the minority branch, favored a broadly based party and expected gradual development toward socialism.

In 1905 the Russian empire was shaken by its first modern revolution, triggered by defeat in its war with Japan. The socialists had their first opportunity for revolutionary action. They organized Soviets, or Councils, of Workers' Deputies, which prepared striking workers for action and co-operated with other groups that opposed the czar. This uprising was soon put down. Then, in March, 1917, the government suffered a more disastrous collapse because of the strains of World War I. Lenin had now become the most powerful of the socialist leaders. He headed the movement that brought the socialists to power in November, 1917, and his Bolshevik faction of the Social Democratic Party was in charge.

▶ THE SOVIET MODEL

In the first months after the revolution, Lenin established the program that has become known as Marxism-Leninism. It continues to characterize the Soviet form of Communism. In this program the government owns all means of production. The Communist Party controls the government and has charge of all policymaking. The party plans and directs the economy and all social and intellectual activity. The aim of this control is to organize skills and resources for rapid economic growth and large-scale social change. This type of system, which the Soviets call socialism, is supposed to be a stage in the development of an ideal Communist state. Social goals include universal education, equality for women, and an end to the old systems of class privileges.

Today, Lenin is still cited as the final au-

Lenin led the Communists to power in Russia and developed their basic programs. In this painting, he delivers an address to workers at a steel plant.

thority on all matters of principle. But there have also been many changes. Lenin died in 1924, before much progress had been made in changing Soviet society. After Lenin there was a struggle for control. Joseph V. Stalin was the victor, and he led the country until his death in 1953.

Under Stalin's administration, the Soviet Union was transformed from an agricultural to an industrial society. It became a major world power in 1945, after stopping a German invasion in World War II. These achievements were accompanied by large-scale purges, in which people who were considered disloyal were removed. Thousands of people were executed, and many more were sent to labor camps. The later administrations of Nikita S. Khrushchev and Leonid I. Brezhnev continued the policies of rapid economic growth and social change, but they did so with only moderate use of force.

Opinions of the developments in the Soviet Union vary. One of the positive achievements has been the rapid growth of industrial production. The Soviet Union has also gained leadership in some fields of science and technology. And it has made great progress in education and public health.

The feature of the Soviet system that has been most criticized has been its record on human rights. Stalin's purges were among the most severe suffered by any nation in peacetime. And the state, as an employer, has taken greater advantage of workers than do most factory owners elsewhere. Influential members of Soviet society lead very comfortable lives, but the life of the average citizen was harsh for many years. It began to improve only in the 1960's and 1970's. Emphasis on heavy industry has led to severe shortages in food and consumer goods.

The fact that the Communist Party, with about 16,000,000 members, makes all the decisions for a population of more than 260,000,000 is also criticized. This monopoly of power restricts not only political freedom but artistic and literary expression as well.

▶ THE EXPANSION OF COMMUNISM

Many people saw the 1917 revolution—and the later economic growth in the Soviet Union —as a striking example of a worldwide effort to replace the old order of privileged classes with a new order of rapid industrialization and social justice. But between World War I and World War II, the Soviet Government had difficulty in trying to project the image of a country leading the world toward the goals of Communism.

An association of Communist parties, called the Third International (Comintern), was established by Lenin in 1919. Like two earlier associations, it was formed to spread the idea of world revolution and to co-ordinate the Communist parties in other countries. In the 1920's, Communist uprisings were attempted in Germany, Finland, Estonia, Hungary, Poland, Bulgaria, Iran, and Java and Sumatra in the Netherlands East Indies. But only in Mongolia, which had been under Russian protection since 1912, did Communists come to power. The Comintern was dissolved in 1943.

In the 1930's, Stalin was more interested in the economic and social development of the Soviet Union than in the export of revolution. He used the Communist parties abroad to support Soviet foreign policy. The Soviets' rapid economic growth was impressive at a time when the West was undergoing an economic depression. Yet when the scope and the results of Stalin's purges became known, many people saw that what was happening in the Soviet Union did not have much to do with Marx's theories of socialism.

In 1940, the Soviet Union annexed the Baltic republics of Estonia, Latvia, and Lithuania. But Communism's greatest period of expansion came after World War II (1939–45). In the final year of the war, the Soviets overran Poland, Rumania, Bulgaria, Hungary, Czechoslovakia, eastern Germany, and northern Korea. Communist governments were set up in these areas after the war.

In a few other countries, the old governments were weakened by the strains of war. Communist parties were able to seize power there largely by their own efforts. This occurred in Yugoslavia and in Albania. In 1949, Mao Tse-tung declared the formation of the People's Republic of China. A Communist government was formed in North Vietnam in 1954. The North Vietnamese extended their control to South Vietnam in 1975. And in the same year, Communists came to power in neighboring Cambodia (renamed Kampuchea) and Laos. In 1961, the Cuban leader Fidel Castro proclaimed Cuba a Communist country.

Communist parties have also achieved successes in a number of elections in democratic countries. They have participated for brief periods in coalition governments in Finland, France, Italy, Iceland, Chile, and Guatemala. In the 1960's and 1970's, they were also active in supporting revolutionary governments in Yemen (Aden), Angola, Portugal, and Ethiopia. And in 1978 a Communist government came to power in Afghanistan.

The expansion of Communism was strongly opposed by capitalist, non-Communist countries, particularly the United States and its allies. From the late 1940's, the capitalist and Communist countries engaged in a struggle for economic and political influence that became known as the Cold War. Both the U.S.S.R. and the United States built up large stockpiles of nuclear weapons, increasing the strain between them. Tension reached its highest points during incidents such as the Soviet blockade of Berlin in 1949, the Korean War (1950–53), and the discovery in 1962 that the Soviets had placed missiles in Cuba.

In the 1970's, the United States and the Soviet Union expressed policies of détente, or easing of tensions. Trade and cultural exchanges between Communist and non-Communist countries increased, and important arms-control agreements were signed. But the Communist and non-Communist countries remained deeply opposed in principle, and tension remained between them.

COMMUNISM TODAY

The number of countries under Communist rule grew from 2 to 17 between 1945 and 1980. This growth was accompanied by increasing differences among the Communist parties of different countries. The Soviets liked to stress the unity of the Communist move-

Banners above a street in Rome urge Italians to vote for Communist and socialist parties.

ment. But in fact, various Communist parties became deeply divided. After 1945, Soviet troops were used only in Communist countries —East Germany (1953), Hungary (1956), Czechoslovakia (1968), and Afghanistan (since 1979)—and in border skirmishes with China. China fought both the Soviet Union and Vietnam. And Vietnam and Cambodia became engaged in a bitter war. It is important to distinguish between the common features of these Communist countries and the differences that have led them to intense conflict.

Two features especially are common to Communist countries. First, the Communist parties hold the power and make all decisions. No other points of view are permitted. The Communists exercise their power by controlling all appointments to leading positions in government, the economy, and society. Opposition to their policies is suppressed by police methods. The second common feature is that the main goal is rapid economic growth and social change. Communists give priority to industry, science and technology, education, and public health. They are less concerned with human rights and consumer goods.

The efforts of the Soviet Union to dominate, or control, other Communist countries have led to much of the conflict among them. Since the 1930's the Soviet leaders have been more interested in preserving the national security of their country than in revolutions in other countries. They feel most secure when all other Communist countries are under their control. But the other Communist countries vary in levels of development and in national traditions. Each wishes to develop the forms of socialism that best meet its needs. The only countries that the Soviet Union fully controls are East Germany, Poland, Czechoslovakia, Hungary, and Bulgaria. And these countries strongly resent Soviet control.

China has developed a very different form of Communism from the Soviet form. It places greater emphasis on the welfare of workers and on equal incomes. After the death of Mao Tsetung in 1976, China improved its relations with non-Communist countries and began a program of rapid industrial development.

The Chinese have successfully resisted efforts of the Soviet Union to control their policies. They resent the Soviet Union's refusal to return territories taken from China by the czars, and there have been several border clashes between the two countries. China is also concerned about Soviet influence in Southeast Asia. This has helped lead to its conflict with Vietnam, a Soviet ally.

There are Communist parties in most of the non-Communist countries of Western Europe. They are especially active in France, Greece, Italy, Spain, and Sweden. These parties have adopted a policy called Eurocommunism. As part of this policy, they have promised to seek and exercise power through democratic methods rather than by revolution. They gained strength generally in elections during the 1970's, but they remained minorities.

Today many countries are seeking rapid economic growth and social change. There are many ways to achieve these goals. Countries that have come under Communist leadership have on the whole been no more successful than others. Critics say that these countries have paid a much higher cost in human suffering. Communist-led countries have found cooperation very difficult and have been unable to agree on common policies. The Soviet Union had hoped that the Communist states would become allies, but often national differences have proved stronger than the bond of Communism.

CYRIL E. BLACK
Princeton University

See also SOCIALISM; CAPITALISM; MARX, KARL; LENIN, VLADIMIR ILICH.

COMPASS. See GEOMETRY AND GEOMETRIC FORMS; MECHANICAL DRAWING.
COMPASS, MAGNETIC. See DIRECTION; NAVIGATION.

COMMUNIST COUNTRIES TODAY

COUNTRY	DATE*	POPULATION (estimate)
U.S.S.R.	1917	268,000,000
Mongolia	1921	1,500,000
Yugoslavia	1945	22,600,000
Albania	1944	2,600,000
East Germany	1945	16,700,000
Poland	1945	35,900,000
Hungary	1945	10,700,000
Rumania	1945	22,000,000
Bulgaria	1945	9,000,000
North Korea	1945	17,900,000
Czechoslovakia	1948	15,300,000
China	1949	1,008,000,000
Vietnam	1954	53,700,000
Cuba	1961	9,500,000
Cambodia (Kampuchea)	1975	6,700,000
Laos	1975	3,500,000
Afghanistan	1978	15,500,000

*Date Communist leadership came to power

COMOROS

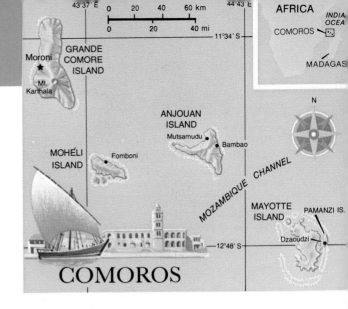

COMOROS

Comoros is made up of a group of volcanic islands, islets, and coral reefs. They lie in the northern entrance to the Mozambique Channel off the east coast of Africa. These little-known islands have been described as the lost pearls of the Indian Ocean.

▶ THE LAND

There are four main islands in the Comoro archipelago, or chain of islands. They are Grande Comore, Mayotte, Anjouan, and Mohéli. The largest island is Grande Comore, which has about half the country's population. The smallest and least populous is Mohéli. Moroni, on Grande Comore, is the capital and largest city.

The Comoros are mountainous and densely forested in many places. Most of the islands are volcanic in origin. Mount Karthala, on Grande Comore, is an active volcano. At 2,475 meters (8,120 feet), it is the highest point on the islands. Its crater is believed to be one of the largest in the world.

▶ THE PEOPLE AND THEIR WORK

The first inhabitants of Comoros are believed to have come from the African mainland. They were followed by people from Southeast Asia, by Arabs, and later by people from the nearby island of Madagascar. Arab influence remains strong today. Most Comorians are Muslims. Arabic and Swahili, a tongue of eastern Africa, are the chief languages.

Comorians grow many crops in the fertile black volcanic soil. Fish, plentiful in the waters surrounding the islands, are a major source of food. The chief export crops are vanilla, cloves, and plants used in making perfume. The perfume essences are shipped to France for use in the perfume industry. There are small sugar-refining, lumbering, and copra-processing industries.

▶ HISTORY AND GOVERNMENT

The history of Comoros goes back to earliest times. The Arabs gave the first detailed account of the islands and later ruled Comoros. The first Europeans visited the islands in the 16th century. Quarrels among the various rulers, who included Malagasy sultans, led to the ceding of the islands to France in the 19th century. They became a French colony in 1912 and an overseas territory of France in 1946. In 1968, they were granted internal self-government.

In 1974, the majority of the Comorians voted for independence. Mayotte rejected the vote and still considers itself part of France. Grande Comore, Anjouan, and Mohéli declared unilateral independence in 1975. They consider Mayotte part of Comoros.

Sheikh Ahmed Abdallah, the first president of Comoros, was quickly overthrown by Ali Soilih, who ruled as a dictator. The entire civil service was dismissed, public services fell into disarray, and French aid was cancelled. In 1978 a small group of foreign mercenaries restored Abdallah to the presidency.

Reviewed by HUGH C. BROOKS
St. John's University (New York)

FACTS AND FIGURES

COMORO STATE is the official name of the country.

CAPITAL: Moroni.

LOCATION: Indian Ocean off east coast of Africa.

AREA: 2,171 km² (838 sq mi).

POPULATION: 370,000 (estimate).

LANGUAGES: Arabic, Swahili, French.

GOVERNMENT: Republic. **Head of state**—president. **International co-operation**—United Nations, Organization of African Unity (OAU).

ECONOMY: Agricultural products—rice, cassava, corn, sweet potatoes, eggplant, vanilla, perfume plants, coconuts, spices, sisal, sugarcane, coffee. **Industries and products**—lumber, perfume distilling, food processing. **Chief exports**—vanilla, perfume essences, cloves. **Chief imports**—vehicles, petroleum products, rice. **Monetary unit**—CFA (African Financial Community) franc.

COMPOSITIONS

A composition is a group of sentences organized around a central theme or topic. There are several different kinds of compositions. A composition may tell a story, real or imaginary. It may be written or oral. It may describe or explain something. It may take the form of a letter. Whatever its form, a composition should express the writer's own thoughts, feelings, and ideas. Preparing a composition is one good way to organize thoughts and share knowledge with other people.

Choosing a Topic

Think of something that has happened to you, something that you have seen, heard, or felt, something that you know. If a particular thing has impressed you, the chances are that others will also find it interesting.

Any number of ideas for composition topics come from everyday happenings. For example, "The Alarm Clock," "How My Book Fell in the Mud," and "Late Again!" are topics that may suggest themselves if one thinks of things connected with an ordinary school day. Other parts of a routine day offer ideas for compositions: "Going to the Store for Mother," "Walking the Dog," and so on. If you use your imagination, it is easy to find topics to write about. Perhaps ideas will come from books, movies, or television programs. The most important thing about choosing a topic is this: have a point of view. Be certain that you have something to say.

Organizing Ideas

Some teachers ask students to write or talk on a certain topic. Whether the composition is to be oral or written, the first step is the same:

Step 1. Organize your ideas by preparing an outline. Jot down your main ideas. Under each of these important ideas, write a few words to remind you of what you want to include. These words, known as **key words,** will be very helpful.

Preparing an Oral Composition

To prepare an oral composition, practice talking from the outline. Try your talk out on a friend or a member of your family before you present it at school. Ask this person to listen carefully. If it is hard for him to hear you, or to understand you, or to keep his mind on what you are saying, then your teacher and your schoolmates may have the same difficulties. Time your talk, since you will probably be given a time limit.

After practicing your oral composition and talking it over with your listener, you will know whether it is interesting, whether you need more facts and details, whether it is too long or too short, and so on. Then you can add, take out, or change words, phrases, or sentences to improve the piece.

Preparing a Written Composition

If the assignment is a written composition, prepare an outline and then go on to the next steps:

Step 2. Reread the outline. Be sure to include all the ideas needed to cover the topic and to make yourself clear. Cross out any idea unrelated to the topic.

Step 3. Take the first main idea from the outline and put it in sentence form. This important sentence, known as the **topic sentence,** introduces the main idea. If it catches the reader's attention, it will make him want to read the sentences that follow. If the topic sentence is not interesting, the reader may stop reading or skip over the next few sentences.

Step 4. Go back to the outline. Look at the key words you have jotted down and write a sentence or two about each fact or idea the key words call to mind. These sentences together with the topic sentence will make a first paragraph.

Step 5. Write a topic sentence based on the outline's second main idea. Then fill in the details as you did for the first paragraph. Continue in this way, writing a paragraph for each important idea. (A helpful hint: After you have finished writing about each main idea, check it against the outline. This will ensure complete coverage of the main ideas.)

Step 6. Review the composition before handing it in. Reread it and check for:

Sentence sense. Do your sentences make sense to you? If not, they will also be unclear to others.

Correct spelling and punctuation. Use your dictionary to check the spelling of words you are unsure of. If corrections are necessary, draw a line through the misspelled word and rewrite it neatly above. Insert corrections in punctuation where they are needed.

Legibility. Can others read your handwriting? Give the composition to someone else to read. If that person has any difficulty, it is wise to recopy the piece entirely, instead of crossing out words and writing between the lines.

Repetition. Sometimes it is a good idea to repeat a word or a phrase to stress its importance or to give writing a certain rhythm. At other times repeating a word or phrase serves no good purpose. Repetition can even make writing too wordy and perhaps hard to understand.

Reread your composition carefully, looking for unnecessary words. If you feel that you should take out a sentence or word that adds nothing, or substitute a new word for a repeated one, draw a line through the words to be deleted or changed, making necessary corrections above. If numerous changes make the composition hard to read, recopy it. Check the clean copy to be sure that nothing has been left out.

REMINDERS FOR IMPROVING WRITTEN COMPOSITIONS

Select a topic you know about.

Organize your ideas around a central theme.

Prepare an outline and develop its main idea.

Use interesting topic sentences to catch the reader's attention.

Vary your vocabulary with synonyms and picture words.

Proofread the composition for spelling, punctuation, and complete sentences.

Reread your composition. Make sure you have said what you want to say in the best possible way.

Improving Your Compositions

Once you have mastered the fundamentals of writing a composition, there are still ways you can improve your papers. Here are some suggestions to follow:

"Paint a picture" with words. Use words that help readers to see a picture. If, for example, you are writing about a dog, tell whether it is big or little, shaggy or smooth, fierce or gentle, brown or white. Or, if you are writing about someone eating, words such as "gobbled," "gulped," or "swallowed" give more of a picture than the word "ate."

Use words that help readers to "hear." Some words describe sounds more accurately than others. For example, a dog may "bark," "yap," or "whimper." Each of these words will help your reader "hear" a different sound. Words that seem to imitate a sound often make compositions more interesting. Some of these words are "thump," "crunch," "swish," "buzz," and "hiss."

Use different kinds of sentences to express different moods and feelings. A sentence such as "How cold it was!" carries more feeling than "It was cold." The question "Was it a dog that stood behind him?" will probably arouse more interest than the statement "The dog stood behind him."

Juggle words around. Sometimes a writer gives his readers a better feeling of mood simply by rearranging the words in a sentence. For example, "Behind him stood a big brown dog" builds up more of a feeling of suspense than "The big brown dog stood behind him."

Keep to the topic. While one can write too little on a given topic, it is also possible to write too much. Ideas that do not belong to the topic will weaken a composition. Examine each idea to see whether it relates to the topic. If it does not add anything by way of explanation or description, omit it.

Add a personal touch. The writer's personality can add color to a composition. Keep in mind the necessity for correct spelling, punctuation, and organization. But remember also the importance of expressing personal feelings and ideas. A composition that is a copy of what someone else has written can never be as effective as one that is truly original.

RUTH LIEBERS
New York City Board of Education

See also OUTLINES; REPORTS.

COMPROMISE OF 1850

The Compromise of 1850 was an unsuccessful attempt to solve the problems of slavery and westward expansion in pre-Civil War America.

Victory in the Mexican War (1846–48) gave the United States a huge block of southwestern land stretching from the Texas shore of the Gulf of Mexico to the Pacific Ocean. The organization of this territory into states brought with it a serious problem. Should these new states be free or slave states?

Since 1820 southern senators had been fighting to keep the number of slave states equal to the number of free states. In 1849 California applied for admission as a state with a constitution forbidding slavery. If California were admitted as a free state, this would upset the balance between free and slave states. Southern congressmen feared slavery might also be prohibited in the Utah and New Mexico territories. Northern congressmen, on the other hand, were determined to halt the spread of slavery.

Several other problems were also involved. One was the Underground Railroad—a secret route of hiding places and back roads used by escaped slaves to reach freedom in the North or in Canada. Southerners demanded a stricter fugitive slave law. Another issue was the abolition of slavery and the slave trade in Washington, D.C., the nation's capital.

These questions threatened to split the Union. Senator Henry Clay, the Great Compromiser, tried to keep this from happening. He introduced eight resolutions into the Senate. He hoped these resolutions would persuade each side to trade something it wanted for a concession from the other side. Clay proposed that the South let California be admitted as a free state. Then the North should let the rest of the new territories decide the slavery question for themselves. Slave trade should be abolished in the District of Columbia, but slavery would be permitted there. A stricter fugitive slave law should be passed, but the future slave state Texas should give up some of its land to New Mexico.

Clay's proposals touched off a furious debate in the Senate. Northern radicals opposed even the possibility of slavery in the new land and denounced the fugitive slave law. Southerners, led by John C. Calhoun of South Carolina, also denounced Clay's proposals, saying the South could not compromise and still remain in the Union.

The brilliant orator Daniel Webster climaxed the great debate with his answer to Calhoun—the famous Seventh of March speech. Though he was a lifelong enemy of slavery, Webster said he spoke not as a Massachusetts man, but as an American. He begged the nation to accept Clay's compromise in order to save the Union. Many people, stirred by his speech, urged Congress to compromise. In September Congress passed five bills. Together these are called the Compromise of 1850.

▶ WHAT THE COMPROMISE SAID

(1) California was admitted to the Union as a free state.

(2) Texas, a slave state, gave up to New Mexico some of the land both claimed, and the federal government paid Texas $10,000,-000 for it.

(3) Slave trade, but not slavery, was abolished in the District of Columbia.

(4) When the territories of New Mexico and Utah asked for statehood, they could vote whether to be slave or free.

(5) A new fugitive slave law made it a crime for anyone to help an escaped slave.

▶ THE COMPROMISE IN ACTION

The compromise did not really settle the slavery controversy. The new fugitive slave law aroused fierce anger in the North. It imposed severe penalties on those found guilty of assisting an escaped slave. The abolitionists redoubled their efforts to abolish slavery. Their cause won many new supporters through *Uncle Tom's Cabin*—a powerful antislavery novel by Harriet Beecher Stowe. The northern radicals became convinced that slavery must be outlawed everywhere in America. Southerners found it increasingly unbearable to remain in the Union under such abuse.

The Compromise of 1850 brought the United States a little more than 10 years of official peace before the Civil War broke out. But it was an uneasy peace, marked by growing hostility and violence.

Reviewed by ISADORE STARR
Queens College (New York)

COMPUTERS

Computers are electronic machines that store, "remember," and process information automatically. A computer can do as many additions in one second as a person could do working 24 hours every day for 30 years. Computers can remember vast amounts of information, and they make very few mistakes. Since they were introduced only 40 years ago, electronic computers have become thousands of times more powerful, thousands of times smaller, and thousands of times less expensive. For these reasons, computers are widely used.

Businesses use computers in many ways. A computer can keep track of all the people who work for a company. It can calculate and print out their paychecks. The same computer can keep track of the company's sales and send bills to the company's customers.

In many factories, computers are used to run machine tools and industrial robots. Computers in textile factories control the operations of hundreds of high-speed looms. Many oil refineries and electrical generating stations are run almost entirely by computer.

Computers are used in all kinds of scientific work. They perform very delicate measurements with great accuracy, and they calculate complex mathematical problems quickly. Computers are used in medicine to diagnose diseases, to run very complicated machinery, and to keep track of the condition of patients.

Governments use computers to tabulate censuses, to calculate taxes owed and to run sophisticated military machinery and weapons.

Computers are widely used for other purposes. They keep track of reservations for seats on airplanes and at basketball games and theaters. They also print the tickets. Libraries use computers to locate references quickly.

Personal computers are used for many purposes. Farmers use them to forecast crop yields. Many people keep track of finances with them. They are used as teaching tools. And they are used to send and receive information over long distances. Exciting games can be played using computers, as well.

There are many kinds of computers, and they come in many sizes and shapes. Although personal computers are seen most often, very large and powerful computers, called **mainframes,** are used by government and industry. Very small computers, called **microcomputers,** are used as parts of other machines. No matter what their shape and size, computers today represent one of the great technological achievements in history.

▶**CALCULATORS AND COMPUTERS**

There are some very large computers, but many computers are small enough to fit on a desk. Even smaller are the pocket calculators

Children play a mathematical game on a home computer connected to a television set.

A computerized checkout counter. The machine automatically lists the items, totals them, and prints the bill. It also keeps track of all merchandise sold.

that are sold everywhere for office and personal use. But there is a big difference between calculators and computers of any size.

Calculators and computers both work with numbers, and both are very fast. But most calculators can do only one thing at a time, and you must keep telling them what to do by pressing various buttons.

For example, suppose that a teacher needs to find the average of the marks of each of 135 children in four school subjects. The four marks of the first pupil must be added together, and the sum divided by 4. The same steps must be repeated for each of the remaining 134 pupils.

A calculator can be used to do this work much faster than it can be done with pencil and paper. But the calculator stops each time it adds one number to the next. It must be told when to add again—and when to divide—for each of the 135 averages.

To do the same work, a computer would be given a series, or **sequence**, of instructions, called a **computer program**. The program would direct the computer to follow all the steps needed to find the 135 averages. If desired, the program could be set up so that the computer would provide other information. It might arrange the averages, in order, from the highest to the lowest. It might also make a list

of the above-average marks and another list of the below-average marks, make a list for the averages in each subject, and so on. Once given the program, the computer would do all this work automatically, without further instructions or help from the operator.

▶ YESTERDAY AND TODAY

In the past, machines that could do arithmetic were called computers, or computing machines. Today we usually call them "calculators." We use the word "computer" for machines that can do arithmetic, follow long programs, and make decisions.

The first calculator was the abacus. It was developed thousands of years ago, and it is still in use in many parts of the world. An early adding machine was built in the 1600's by Blaise Pascal, a French mathematician and philosopher. By the end of the 1800's, machines that could add, subtract, multiply, and divide had become popular.

Charles Babbage, an English mathematician of the 1800's, spent much of his life designing a machine he called an "analytical engine." The machine never worked, but some of Babbage's ideas for this early computer are used in the design and programming of modern computers.

A big step toward the automatic computer came in the late 1800's. Herman Hollerith, a United States statistician, developed machines to be used with special cards. Holes were punched into the cards. The positions of the holes represent letters of the alphabet or numbers. The Hollerith machines could sense, or "read," the numbers on the cards electrically. They added the numbers together or did whatever other arithmetic was needed. The results were printed out on paper or punched into new cards.

Hollerith's cards and machines were used in the United States Census of 1890. Besides helping to determine the population of the country, the cards proved useful in dealing with many other facts. The information on each individual's census card might give age, sex, income, occupation, and years of schooling, among other facts. The cards could be run through the machines over and over to process the information quickly in different ways. For example, it was possible to find out how the amount of money a person earned depended

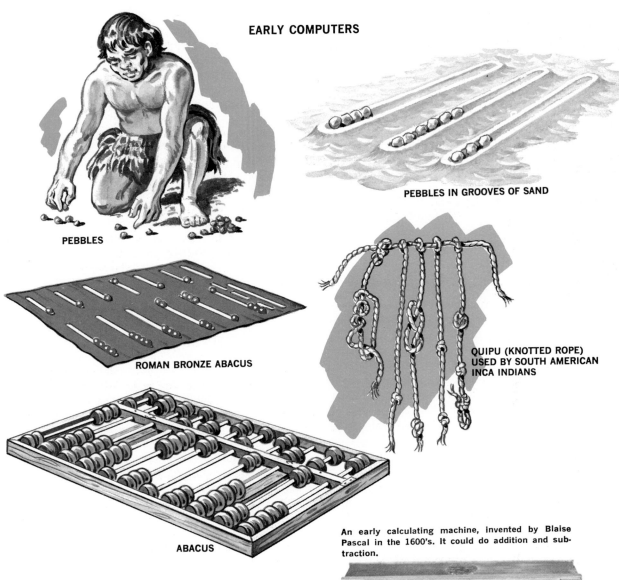

EARLY COMPUTERS

PEBBLES

PEBBLES IN GROOVES OF SAND

ROMAN BRONZE ABACUS

QUIPU (KNOTTED ROPE) USED BY SOUTH AMERICAN INCA INDIANS

ABACUS

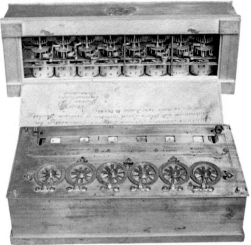

An early calculating machine, invented by Blaise Pascal in the 1600's. It could do addition and subtraction.

on the number of years of schooling that he or she had had. Or it could be learned how the average life span of people was related to their occupation or sex.

The first modern, or electronic, computers were built in the 1940's. Each of these computers needed thousands of vacuum tubes, which look somewhat like light bulbs. And like light bulbs, they burn out. The burnouts wasted a great deal of time. And the tubes used great amounts of electric power, producing much waste heat. These problems were overcome when computer designers began to use transistors in place of vacuum tubes. A transistor is only a fraction of the size of a tube. It uses very little electric power, and it lasts a very long time. Transistors made it possible to build computers that were small, reliable, and inexpensive to operate.

A new way of grouping large numbers of transistors in a tiny space was soon developed. Each group is an **integrated circuit,** or **I.C.**

An I.C. is a piece, or **chip,** of silicon. An I.C. only 5 or 6 millimeters (about ¼ inch) on a side and a fraction of a millimeter thick is made up of many thousands of transistors. The methods for making the chips improved rapidly, and they became fairly inexpensive. In turn, computers that made use of I.C.'s could be sold at low prices.

▶**HOW DOES A COMPUTER WORK?**

A computer stores and handles numbers. The numbers may be mathematical formulas or columns of figures. They may also be codes that stand for letters of the alphabet, words, or instructions to the computer. Most computers are actually **computer systems,** made up of **hardware** and **software. Hardware** refers to all of the machinery (electrical and mechanical devices) in the system. **Software** refers to the programs, or instructions, that tell the computer what to do.

All computers have three basic parts:

A video terminal is made up of a keyboard and a television-like screen that displays information. The information can be typed out by a printer (*right*).

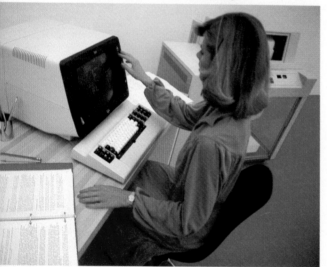

(1) **Input and output units** (abbreviation I/O). The input unit takes in the information and instructions that the computer works with. When the work has been done, the output unit gives the results.

(2) A **central processing unit,** or **CPU.** This unit does the actual work of computing.

(3) A **memory.** It stores or "remembers" the information and instructions that the CPU needs for doing the work.

Input and Output Units

You know what the letters H–A–T stand for, or what the number 12 means. A computer can work only with electrical signals. So there must be some way to "translate" letters and numbers into electrical signals that the computer can use. There must also be a way to change electrical signals back into letters and numbers so people can understand the results of the computer's work. These changes are made by the input and output units.

The input and output units are called **peripherals.** The peripherals make it possible for people to communicate with computers. Peripherals provide the way to **load** a computer —that is, to give it information and instructions. They also are the means by which information is obtained from the computer.

There are several kinds of peripherals. One common type is the **video terminal,** or computer terminal, which is really two peripherals in one. The first part is a typewriter-like keyboard. When you strike the A key, for example, a certain sequence of electrical signals is produced. The B key produces a different sequence of electrical signals, C still another, and so on. The computer can recognize the letters and numbers because it recognizes the different sequences of signals.

The second part of the video terminal is a television-like screen on which the output of the computer is seen as numbers, letters, words, or even graphs and pictures.

Video terminals are used a great deal in offices. Suppose an office clerk wants a list of people who have not paid their bills. The clerk types a request on the keyboard. The computer then flashes a list of names onto the screen. If a permanent record of the list is needed, the clerk uses another peripheral, the **printer,** to make the list. The printer is connected to the computer. The clerk types a certain number code, ordering the list. Then the printer, fed by information from the computer, types out the list at high speed.

Video terminals are also widely used to speed up the preparation of newspaper stories. The story is typed out on a terminal by a reporter. The editor reads the story as it is displayed on the television screen and makes any necessary changes. The story is then ready to be set by an automatic typesetting machine.

Another kind of input unit is used for reading printed numbers. Banks use units of this kind to identify and sort the checks written by their customers. Customers' account numbers are printed on their checks in magnetic ink. As a check is run through the reading unit, the magnetic ink sets up a pattern of electrical signals. The unit senses each customer's account number from this pattern.

Another important kind of peripheral is called a **storage device.** It is often used when more information must be stored than the computer's main memory can hold. Magnetic disks or magnetic tapes are used for this purpose. The disks or tapes store signals in the form of magnetic pulses, which the computer can turn into numbers or letters.

Many small computer systems use a type of disk called a **flexible,** or **floppy, disk.** Floppy disks look like very thin phonograph records but are usually only 5¼ inches or 8 inches in diameter. A **disk drive** is a machine that writes, or stores, information on the disk. It is also used to read the information on the disk and to load that information into the computer's memory.

Another important kind of peripheral is a **modem.** (*Modem* stands for *mo*dulator/*dem*odulator.) Modems translate computer signals into telephone signals. This allows a computer to "talk" to another computer thousands of kilometers away. It is very much like the way people communicate with long-distance telephone calls. A large company might use this form of **telecomputing** to send information to its branch offices located in another state.

The index of this encyclopedia is prepared with the help of peripherals. Each entry for the index is stored on magnetic tape. When the index is to be printed, the information on the tapes is loaded into the computer. Its output is typed out by a high-speed printer.

The Memory

Information from the input unit is stored in the computer's memory. The memory also stores the programmed instructions that the central processing unit is to follow. That unit gets new data and instructions from the memory at almost every stage of a calculation.

Most computers store only two numbers—0 and 1. Then how can they store numbers such as 3, 7, or 8,463? Computers use numbers in the **binary system.** This system is based on the number 2. The numbers we use ordinarily are in the **decimal system.** They are based on the number 10. A computer that uses binary numbers is much easier and less expensive to build than one that can work with decimal numbers. But it is easy to change decimal numbers to binary numbers before they are used in a computer. (The binary number system is explained later in this article.)

There are several kinds of memory units. The kind that is most widely used is made up of many integrated circuits. Each I.C., which is a tiny chip of silicon, contains more than 100,000 transistors, and it can store 256,000 binary digits, or **bits,** of information. The memory chips can supply the processing unit with millions of bits per second.

A standard group of bits (usually 8 or 16) are handled by the computer as a unit called a **byte.** Computer memories are often measured in thousands of bytes, or **kilobytes** (abbreviation K). The measurement is approximate. One kilobyte actually consists of 1,024 bytes. A computer said to have 64K of memory actually has 65,536 bytes.

The Central Processing Unit

The central processing unit is the part of the computer that does the actual work of computing. It is made up of many electronic circuits. A big computer may have as many as 200,000 circuits.

What Is in a Circuit?

A computer circuit is made up of transistors and other devices that control the flow of electricity. A transistor may strengthen electric currents flowing through it or change the path they follow. The transistors in a circuit, like those in the memory, are built into tiny chips of silicon. One such chip may hold thousands of circuits.

This tiny silicon chip is used in a computer. It can fit through the eye of the needle behind it.

The circuits must be tiny. The smaller a transistor is, the faster it works. The circuits work by means of electrical signals that reach them through wires. Such a signal takes one billionth of a second to travel about 15 centimeters (6 inches) along a wire. One billionth of a second may seem like a short time. But if the circuits were not tiny and very close together, the travel time of signals along the wires would be longer than the time needed for the circuit to do its job.

The job of each circuit is to perform a very simple operation in arithmetic.

Circuits Called AND

One group of circuits is especially suited for the work of multiplication. These are known as AND circuits. In every AND circuit, two wires lead in (the input wires) and one wire leads out (the output wire). If there is an electrical signal in each of the inputs, the AND circuit sends a certain type of signal through the output. If there is a signal in only one of the inputs, or in neither of them, the circuit sends a second kind of signal as its output. The AND circuit gets its name from the fact that it sends the first kind of output signal only if one input AND the other input carry signals.

Think of the first kind of output signal as representing a 1. The second kind of signal represents a 0. An AND circuit gives the output signal that represents 1 only if it is receiving a signal from each input. If either or both inputs carry no signal, the output is the second kind of signal, representing 0. Look at the rules for arithmetic in the Binary Number System. You will see that an AND circuit gives the answers for problems in binary multiplication. When each of its inputs is 1, it is receiving the problem $1 \times 1 = ?$ The circuit's output signal, 1, is the answer. If both of the inputs are 0, the problem is $0 \times 0 = ?$ If either input is 0, the circuit is receiving the problem $1 \times 0 = ?$ or $0 \times 1 = ?$ Whenever there is a 0 in the input, the circuit gives an output signal representing 0.

Circuits Called OR and NOR

Another type of computer circuit is the OR circuit. Such a circuit puts out a 1 if one OR the other of its inputs is a 1. It puts out a 0 if both inputs are 0. This circuit gives the answers in problems of binary addition.

A third type of circuit, the NOR circuit, puts out a 1 if neither one NOR the other of its inputs is 1. The NOR circuit is useful in subtraction and division.

You can see that each kind of circuit does only the simplest kind of arithmetic, never using more than a 0 and a 1. Yet computers do long, complicated problems at enormous speed. One reason that computers can work so fast is that they have so many circuits. A computer may contain 100,000 or more circuits. The time that a circuit takes to do its job is only a few billionths of a second. Then it is ready for the next problem.

Can Computers Reason?

A computer can be made to work in a way that resembles complicated reasoning. It can be instructed, or programmed, to work out the moves in checkers or chess games, for example. It can prove theorems in geometry and do many other things that require a series of steps in reasoning.

A computer can solve complicated mathematical problems by doing many simple arithmetical operations quickly. In somewhat the same way, the computer's "reasoning" ability is based on simple logical steps that its circuits can perform. In fact, the circuits are called AND, OR, and so on to show that they can do these logical steps.

Let's look at a simple problem in reasoning. You and your friend Jackie have planned to go on a hike. You awake early and look out at a downpour. What should you do? Forget about the hike? Go, even if the rain continues? Wait to hear what Jackie wants to do? Without realizing it, you use a series of simple logical steps as you try to decide what to do. If each step were given a code number for use in a computer, the steps might be written out this way:

(A) If the rain stops—code 1.
(B) If the rain continues—code 0.
(C) And if Jackie still wants to go—code 1.
(D) And if Jackie doesn't want to go—code 0.
(E) I will go—code 1.
(F) I won't go—code 0.

You might decide to go on the hike, using step A and step C to reach step E. If you expressed your thinking out loud, you might say, "If the rain stops and Jackie still wants to go, then I'll go." Or you might reach step F by using steps B and C, because you dislike getting wet.

A computer can deal with logical statements. But each statement must first be turned into a symbol the computer can use. For example, statements A and C each are represented by the symbol 1. If these two 1's are put through an AND circuit, its output will be a 1. (Remember that 1×1 is always 1.) In this case the output 1 means "I will go" (Step E).

Suppose the steps are to be "If the rain continues (0) and Jackie still wants to go (1), I will go (1). An OR circuit would do this reasoning. (0 plus 1 is 1.) What kind of circuit would carry out these steps? "If the rain continues (0) and Jackie still wants to go (1), I won't go."

Other problems can also be programmed into the computer: "If we go in the rain, we can take sandwiches, or we can try a cookout." If it is still raining when we leave, shall we take a bat and ball on the chance the weather may clear?" and so on. It may look as though the computer makes the decisions, but it is only following the program it was given.

"AND" CIRCUITS AT WORK

An AND circuit gives an output of 1 only in answer to the multiplication of 1 X 1. If a 0 is involved in the multiplication, the output is 0.

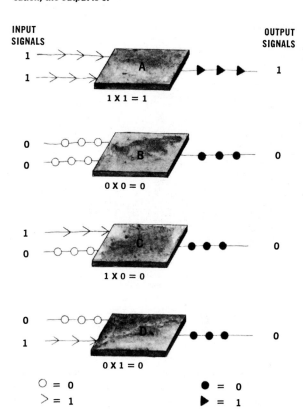

INPUT SIGNALS

OUTPUT SIGNALS

$1 \times 1 = 1$

$0 \times 0 = 0$

$1 \times 0 = 0$

$0 \times 1 = 0$

○ = 0
> = 1

● = 0
▶ = 1

Computer Programming

A computer by itself is like a car without a driver. It is useless without a person to guide it. People guide computers by writing programs for them. A program is a set of instructions that tell the machine how to solve a problem. The program sets up pathways through the circuits so that they will solve a particular problem.

The digital computer uses only 0's and 1's, so the program can contain only these two symbols. With the earliest computers a programmer had to write the instructions as a series of 1's and 0's. This was a very slow and difficult job because it is almost impossible to remember the long strings of symbols that represent various operations.

The first step in overcoming this problem

THE BINARY NUMBER SYSTEM

You can use a stack of coins to store numbers. Suppose that a coin lying head up represents a 1. A coin tail up represents a 0. These two arrangements, or "states" (heads and tails), are all that is needed to indicate a binary number. Binary numbers are made up of only two kinds of digits —1's and 0's. (Binary means "by twos.") A binary number such as 10110 can be shown with five coins.

Most computers work only with binary numbers. Of course no coins are used. Instead the two states may be shown by an "on" and an "off," like a light bulb. When an electric current flows through a bulb, it lights up. When no current flows, the bulb is off. In a computer the "on" state, when a current flows, may be used to represent a 1. Then the "off" state, when there is no current, represents a 0.

Turning a coin to change the state from a 1 to a 0 might take you a quarter of a second. But a change of state in a computer takes only a few billionths of a second. This is one reason why computers can work so fast.

How can the binary system, using only 1 and 0, show a number like 5, 9, or 147? The binary system, like the decimal system we use ordinarily, is a place-value system. Both systems are methods of writing numbers in a way that tells you the value of each digit. Thus, if you have $1,000,000, you are a millionaire. But if you have $0,000,001, you have only one dollar. The digits are the same, but their place makes all the difference.

In the decimal system, you multiply the value of a digit 10 times by moving it one place to the left. For example, a 1 by itself is just 1. Move it one place to the left, and it becomes 1 times 10, or 10. Move it another place to the left, and it is now 1 times 10 times 10, or 100. The 0's are put in to show how many places the 1 was moved.

In the binary system, moving a digit one place to the left multiplies its value only by two. Thus a 1 by itself is just 1. Move it one place to the left and it becomes 1 times 2, or 2. It is written in this way: 10. Move the 1 another place to the left, and it is now 1 times 2 times 2, or 4. This is written 100. The 0's show how many places the 1 was moved.

The binary system seems difficult at first, because it forces us to think of numbers in a new way. But the binary system has a great advantage for use in computers. A machine that uses only two numbers, 0 and 1, is easier and cheaper to build than a machine that can handle numbers from 0 to 9. Any number, no matter how big it may be, can be represented in the binary system.

Here are the first eleven numbers in the decimal and binary systems:

Decimal Number	Meaning	Binary Number	Meaning
0	Zero	0	Zero
1	One	1	One
2	Two	10	Two
3	Three	11	Two and one
4	Four	100	Four
5	Five	101	Four and one
6	Six	110	Four and two
7	Seven	111	Four and two and one
8	Eight	1000	Eight
9	Nine	1001	Eight and one
10	Ten	1010	Eight and two
11	Ten and one	1011	Eight and two and one

Try to work out the binary numbers from 12 to 20. The answers are printed below:

12-1100	15-1111	18-10010
13-1101	16-10000	19-10011
14-1110	17-10001	20-10100

The rules of arithmetic in the binary system are simple, because there are only two numbers.

The rules for addition are:

$$0 + 0 = 0$$
$$0 + 1 = 1$$
$$1 + 0 = 1$$
$$1 + 1 = 10 \quad \text{(Remember, this means } two \text{ in the binary system.)}$$

The rules for multiplication are:

$$0 \times 0 = 0$$
$$1 \times 0 = 0$$
$$0 \times 1 = 0$$
$$1 \times 1 = 1$$

These operations can be carried out by simple electronic circuits in only billionths of seconds.

Computers work with electrical signals representing numbers. However, there are special codes for changing letters into numbers in the binary system. When this is done, computers can work with letters, words, names, and addresses.

was the development of **sub-routines.** These instructions could be stored in the computer's memory. The programmer could then order a whole operation by name, such as "Add" or "Multiply." This is called **assembly language.** Assembly language was a big improvement in setting up programs. But programming was still slow work, and the programmer needed a great deal of training and experience.

A computer-user often has several different kinds of problems to solve. A large company that builds boats, for example, may need a computer to calculate and print the paychecks of the employees. The same computer may be used to save thousands of hours of calculations by engineers working on the design of a new type of boat. But each of these jobs requires a different program for the machine.

Instead of assembly language, one of the **high-level** languages may be used in writing the program. High-level languages are easier to use. Their instructions to the computer are not written out in as much detail as those of assembly language. Less detail in the program means that the computer takes somewhat longer to do its work. But a great deal of program-writing time is saved.

There are many high-level languages. Most of them were designed for the solution of particular kinds of problems. Thus the boatbuilding company might use COBOL (*co*mmon *b*usiness *o*riented *l*anguage) for its payroll work. COBOL is especially useful in solving problems connected with the operation of a business. For the calculations for the new boat design, the engineers might use FORTRAN (*for*mula *tran*slation), a high-level language set up for solving complicated mathematical formulas.

Most personal computers use BASIC (*b*eginner's *a*ll-purpose *s*ymbolic *i*nstruction *c*ode) and Pascal (named for the philosopher Blaise Pascal). PILOT (*p*rogrammed *i*nquiry, *l*earning, *or* *t*eaching) is a language developed specifically for computer-aided instruction. LOGO (or Logo) is a special language used to teach computer programming to children.

▶ RECENT DEVELOPMENTS

The development of the **microprocessor** (a computer processor on a single chip) has made low-cost **minicomputers** and **microcomputers**

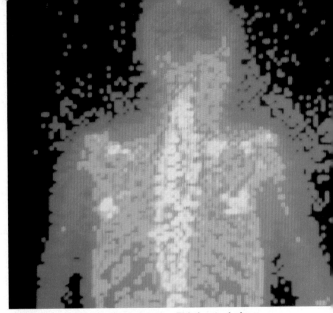

Computers are used in thermography. This is a technique in which various temperatures in parts of the body display as different colors on a video screen.

available to small businesses, schools, and individuals. Computer-aided instruction is now common in many schools, from the earliest grades through graduate level university courses. Portable computers small enough to carry in a briefcase let people on business trips communicate with their offices.

Computers are also making large amounts of information available in new and fast ways. Through **videotex** and **online** information retrieval systems, individuals and businesses can tap into large data bases stored on very large computers thousands of kilometers away. The type of information available is almost limitless and includes magazine and newspaper articles, sports scores, encyclopedia articles, travel and weather information, and much more.

Research is continuing to make even more powerful and efficient computers, and to find new uses for them. There seems to be no limit to the work that computers can do. And that work is transforming the lives of all of us.

RICHARD T. MILLER
IBM Research Division
Yorktown Heights, N.Y.

See also ABACUS; AUTOMATION; CALCULATORS; ELECTRONIC COMMUNICATIONS; ELECTRONICS; NUMERALS AND NUMERATION SYSTEMS.

CONCERTO. See MUSIC (Musical Forms).
CONCRETE. See CEMENT AND CONCRETE.
CONDENSATION. See CLOUDS; HEAT.
CONDIMENTS. See SPICES, HERBS, AND CONDIMENTS.

CONESTOGA WAGON

The Conestoga wagon was first used as a freight carrier in the colonies during the 18th century. It was named for the village of Conestoga in Pennsylvania, where Pennsylvania Dutch craftsmen first invented it about 1725. They built the back and front ends of the wagon higher than the middle so freight couldn't fall out, and they painted it bright blue and red. An arched hood made of white homespun and held up by hoops kept travelers and goods safe from rain. When Ohio was still the western frontier, the Conestoga wagon was used for the rough westward journey across the Alleghenies. Mountain roads were nothing but wagon tracks, so wide-rimmed wheels were used to keep the wagons from bogging down in the mud. A wagon carried from 4 to 8 tons of goods, and teams of 4 to 6 horses were needed to pull it.

The **prairie schooner**, which carried pioneers across the Great Plains and the Rocky Mountains in the 19th century, was a smaller version of the Conestoga wagon. It did not curve upward at the ends as sharply as the Conestoga. The prairie schooner was built to travel great distances—not to carry enormous loads. A family lived, ate, and slept in its prairie schooner for more than 3 months on the trails to the Far West. From 20 to 100 wagons traveled together for safety against Indian attack.

During the 18th and 19th centuries the wagons did the work now performed by trucks and freight trains.

CONFEDERATE STATES OF AMERICA

The Confederacy was born on December 20, 1860, when the state of South Carolina formally seceded—withdrew—from the Federal Union of the United States. A Charleston, South Carolina, newspaper brazenly proclaimed, "The Union is Dissolved!" Five other southern states—Georgia, Florida, Alabama, Louisiana, and Mississippi—quickly followed South Carolina's lead. The secession of these states came shortly after the election of Abraham Lincoln, a Republican, as President of the United States.

Delegates from the six seceding states met in Montgomery, Alabama, the Confederacy's first capital, on February 4, 1861. They drafted a constitution creating a new republic called the Confederate States of America, which was dedicated to the principles of states' rights and preservation of the institution of slavery. Kentucky-born Jefferson Davis, a former U.S. Senator and Secretary of War then living in Mississippi, was chosen to be president of the Confederacy. Alexander H. Stephens, a Georgian, was designated vice-president. (The capital of the Confederacy was later moved to Richmond, Virginia.)

Five other southern states subsequently joined the Confederacy. These were Texas, Virginia, Tennessee, Arkansas, and North Carolina. Several southern "border states"—Missouri, Kentucky, and Maryland—did not secede. They gave troops to both sides during the Civil War.

The Confederacy lasted only from 1861 to 1865. During most of that period, the Confederacy (South) fought the Union (North) in the American Civil War. When the war ended in a Union victory, the Confederacy was dissolved. Its member states were gradually readmitted to the Union during the Reconstruction Period.

President Jefferson Davis was in many ways an able leader. But he lacked the warm personal appeal, sense of humor, and gift for language of Abraham Lincoln. Davis was an aloof, austere man. He presided over a lost cause and suffered the humiliation of imprisonment after the war. Many Confederates blamed Davis for the failure of the southern cause, and by the end of the war he was resented throughout the South.

But Davis performed better than most of his contemporaries thought. A graduate of West Point and a man of military experience, he appointed able commanders to head the Confederate armies and chose a capable group of men to serve in his Cabinet.

Davis also adopted a flexible military strategy of offensive defense, which made the best use of Confederate strength while minimizing its many weaknesses. Although some historians might disagree, Davis showed strong character and grew in stature as a leader during the course of the war. His tough political, social, and military measures were disliked by many southerners but were necessary to keep the Confederacy alive.

▶ SOUTHERN RESOURCES

War between the North and South began on April 12, 1861, when Confederate troops bombarded the Federal garrison at Fort Sumter, in Charleston harbor. In almost every respect the South was at a disadvantage in resources when compared to the North. The South had a white population of about 6,000,000, as compared to the North's 21,000,000. However, the South also had 3,500,000 black slaves. While they were not used as soldiers until the very end of the war, they were a valuable military resource. They built fortifications, served as teamsters and farm workers, and performed other useful services. However, the full potential of black manpower was never used.

Financial resources were almost nonexistent. In all of the South there was only $27,000,000 in currency. Few factories, iron foundries, or other industrial plants existed. Southern railroads were inferior to those of the North. Cotton, land, and courage were the South's major assets.

The myth of "King Cotton" blinded the Confederacy to the realities of financing a modern war. Southerners believed that cotton was so vital to the textile-producing nations of Europe that these nations would become their allies. They thought that their abundant farmland would enable them to feed their armies and that the fighting ability of their soldiers would offset Northern superiority in weapons and manpower.

The South was proved wrong on all counts. European countries dependent on southern cotton found other sources. Much of the South's rich farmland fell to invading Union armies. Northern technology also proved decisive. The South could never match the North's ability to produce cannon, rifles, ships, and other war matériel.

▶ SOUTHERN DIPLOMACY

Failing to win peaceful secession through negotiation, southern diplomats tried to gain foreign recognition and support. Both the French and British governments favored the Confederate cause. But the people of these countries opposed war with the United States. Many English working people sympathized with the North, because they saw southern slavery as an evil institution. After Lincoln signed the Emancipation Proclamation, in 1863, the North won vastly increased international support. Even so, Great Britain came close to recognizing the Confederacy. But as southern military fortunes declined, hope for foreign intervention faded.

Faced with these problems, the Confederacy had to rely on other measures. Most southern war supplies had to be brought in from overseas, past the Union naval blockade. Fleets of fast blockade runners shuttled between southern ports and Nassau, Jamaica, Bermuda, and Cuba. The blockade runners carried cotton, which was exchanged for European shipments of rifles, cannon, and such items as coffee, lead, textiles, and medicines.

Lack of money was the Confederacy's greatest problem. The Confederacy was able to exist because loyal Southerners accepted promissory notes. But when the war seemed lost, Confederate money became worthless. Nevertheless, Jefferson Davis kept hopes alive by such stern measures as military conscription of all able-bodied white males and impressment—the seizure of goods without payment. Impressment was a desperate measure and a serious invasion of private rights. But without it southern armies could not have been fed, clothed, and sheltered.

▶ ON THE BATTLEFIELD

The Confederacy's survival for 4 years was mainly a tribute to the courage of its soldiers and the skill of its leading generals—men like Robert E. Lee, Thomas "Stonewall" Jackson, "Jeb" Stuart, and Nathan Bedford Forrest. In the early years of the war, Confederate armies won a string of victories—including First and Second Bull Run, the Seven Days' Battles, and Fredericksburg.

But as the war progressed, a new breed of Union general emerged. Among these generals were Ulysses S. Grant, William T. Sherman,

"Little Phil" Sheridan, and George H. Thomas. Helped by superior numbers and weakening southern morale, they began to turn the tide. In July, 1863, Lee's Army of Northern Virginia was beaten at the Battle of Gettysburg, and General Grant captured the Confederate citadel at Vicksburg, Mississippi. This victory gave the North complete control of the Mississippi River.

From then on, Confederate armies had to endure the pain of defeat. In 1864, Grant hammered away at Lee in Virginia, while Sherman captured Atlanta and began his "March to the Sea." At the same time, Sheridan defeated the Confederates in the Shenandoah Valley. The Union forces destroyed the crops growing on the rich farmlands of the valley—"the granary of the Confederacy."

The end came in April, 1865. After a long siege, Grant captured Petersburg, Virginia. Lee's army was forced to retreat, abandoning Richmond, the Confederate capital, to the Union forces. On April 9, 1865, cut off and surrounded, Lee surrendered his army to Grant at Appomattox Courthouse. A few weeks later, General Joseph E. Johnston surrendered his army to Sherman.

Military defeat meant the end of the Confederacy. The South was devastated and drained of able-bodied workers and resources. But in death, the Confederacy left an enduring legend of gallantry and heroism in defense of the "Lost Cause."

FRANK E. VANDIVER
Rice University
See also CIVIL WAR, UNITED STATES.

CONFUCIUS (551–479 B.C.)

Confucius was the greatest wise man of China. Because of his wisdom, Confucius has followers even today. Confucianism is not a religion. It does not teach about God, heaven, and life after death. It is a philosophy that teaches people a way to live life on earth wisely.

"Confucius" is the European form of the Chinese name K'ung Fu-tzu, or Master K'ung. The Chinese called him master because he was a great teacher. Many legends grew up about him. It was said that dragons guarded his mother when he was born.

K'ung was born in the state of Lu (now in Shantung). His father died when K'ung was very young. And as soon as he could the boy went to work to help his mother. Still he had time to study and to practice archery and music, which he loved. He desired order and grace in behavior, like the order and harmony of music.

When he was 22, K'ung became a teacher. Pupils came to his home to learn history, poetry, and manners. He taught by talking with them and making them think. He believed that "A person's character is formed by the Odes [poetry], developed by the Rites [ancient rules of courtesy and ceremony], and perfected by music."

K'ung's way to an orderly world was this: A man must start by being honest and brave, and learn how to behave courteously and truthfully. If he could do that, he could manage his family wisely. If every family were well managed, orderly, and moral, the government would be well ordered, too. So wisdom and good government begin at home.

Unlike most philosophers K'ung did not believe thinking and teaching were enough. He wanted most of all to put his ideas into practice. He held several offices. But when the ruler of Lu neglected his counsel, K'ung resigned. He went into exile with his disciples and wandered for 13 years.

K'ung spent his last years writing and teaching. He left behind him the Five Classics, which he edited and compiled, plus the *Analects* (conversations) put together by his pupils. Typical of Confucius' wisdom is his version of the Golden Rule: "Do not do to others what you would not have them do to you." But he did not believe in returning good for evil. He reasoned in this way: If you reward with kindness the person who hurts you, what do you have left to give to the person who is kind to you?

Reviewed by KENNETH S. COOPER
George Peabody College

CONGO

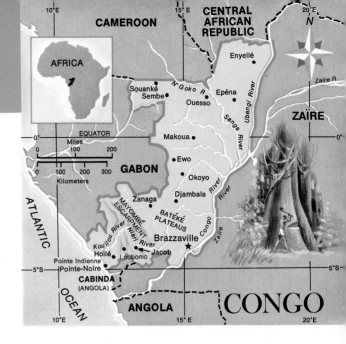

Several times a day white ferryboats make their way across the Congo River between Brazzaville, the capital of the Congo, and Kinshasa, the capital of the neighboring country of Zaïre. Its location on the Congo River has long been important to Brazzaville. During colonial times, Brazzaville was the administrative capital of French Equatorial Africa. The city is linked by the Congo-Ocean Railroad to the port of Pointe-Noire on the Atlantic Ocean. The Congo and its port thus serve as a gateway for the overseas trade of the surrounding countries.

▶ THE PEOPLE

The earliest settlers were the Pygmies, who originally lived throughout the area. Today they are found only in scattered valleys and swamps in the northeast of the country. The Pygmies were pushed into this region by the Bantu as the Bantu moved southward from the Cameroons about 1,000 years ago.

The Pygmies live by hunting and fishing and by collecting foods from the forest areas. They sometimes supplement their diet by trading meat and fish for agricultural products from their Bantu neighbors. The Bantu are unwilling to venture into the unknown forests and swamps where the Pygmies live. But this land supports and protects the Pygmies because they know how to use its resources.

Except for the relatively few Pygmies and a small number of Europeans, the people of the Congo are of Bantu stock. The Bantu are divided into many groups. The largest is the Bakongo (or Kongo), who are found chiefly in the Brazzaville area. In the southwest are the Batéké (or Téké), who excel in hunting and fishing. The Vili live along the coast, around Pointe-Noire. Farther inland are the M'Bochi (or Mbochi), who live along the Congo River, and the Sangha (or Sanga), who inhabit the northern forests. Many of the M'Bochi have moved to the cities, where they hold skilled jobs in industry and many of the civil service positions.

Several Bantu languages are spoken in the Congo, but French is the official language. Most of the European residents are French.

As a whole, the country is sparsely settled, averaging only about four persons to each square kilometer (fewer than eleven to each square mile). Many of the people still live in rural areas. But the number in the cities is increasing. People are being drawn to the cities in the hope of finding good jobs and a better way of life.

FACTS AND FIGURES

THE PEOPLE'S REPUBLIC OF THE CONGO is the official name of the country.

CAPITAL: Brazzaville.

LOCATION: Central Equatorial Africa. **Latitude—** 4° N to 5° S. **Longitude—**11° 7' to 18° 39' E.

AREA: 342,000 km² (132,047 sq mi).

POPULATION: 1,500,000 (estimate).

LANGUAGE: French (official), Bantu languages.

GOVERNMENT: Republic. **Head of state**—president. **Head of government**—prime minister. **International co-operation**—United Nations, Organization of African Unity (OAU).

NATIONAL ANTHEM: *Les Trois Glorieuses* ("Three Glorious Days").

ECONOMY: Agricultural Products—palm nuts, peanuts, coffee, tobacco, bananas, sugarcane, yams, cassava, maize (corn), rice. **Industrial products**—wood, potash fertilizer, sugar, cigarettes, soap, beer, palm oil. **Chief minerals**—potash, petroleum, lead, copper, gold, zinc. **Chief exports**—wood, potash, sugar, petroleum, coffee, palm oil, peanuts, palm kernels, tobacco. **Chief imports**—manufactured goods, machinery. **Monetary unit**—franc CFA (African Financial Community).

The harbor at Pointe-Noire, the Congo's chief seaport.

Education

Education was important under French rule. Today a considerable part of the Congo's budget is spent on education, which is free and compulsory for all children between the ages of 6 and 16. Almost all children attend primary school. This is rare in many African countries. The Center of Higher Education in Brazzaville was established as a national university in 1972. It is now called Marien Ngoubai University. There are several technical schools and institutes for the training of teachers.

Yet the country has serious educational problems. Not enough of the young Congolese go on to secondary schools, and too few of them graduate. Illiteracy is still high among adult Congolese. The government realizes the seriousness of this situation and is taking steps to improve education for all the people, whatever their age.

Religion

Missionaries, mostly from France and Scandinavia, went to the Congo in the early 18th century. But they did not reach the inland areas until late in the 19th century. Because of their efforts, the country is now almost half Christian (either Roman Catholic or Protestant). A little less than half of the people follow their traditional African religions. A small minority of Muslims live in the northeastern part of the country.

▶ THE LAND

The country lies astride the equator. It is long and narrow in shape. Most of the area consists of low plateaus with flat, swampy valleys divided by low hills. The land tends to decrease in elevation from north to south. The highest area, about 820 meters (2,700 feet), is in the Batéké plateaus. Several rivers, including the Kouilou, flow through deep valleys to the Atlantic Ocean, which forms the western border of the country. The Kouilou is known as the Niari River in its middle course. Other rivers, such as the Sanga and the Likouala, sweep sluggishly across the low-lying valley of the Congo and Ubangi rivers, creating a vast swamp.

Some distance inland from the Atlantic Ocean lies a range of high, steep hills known as the Mayombé Escarpment. These hills run in the same general direction as the coast and reach a height of over 790 meters (about 2,600 feet). They stand as a barrier between the coast and the Congo Basin area. Dense vegetation, which becomes a jungle in places, adds to the difficulty of traveling through the area. To cross this region, the French built the Congo-Ocean Railroad in 1904. It extends for a distance of 515 kilometers (320 miles), linking Pointe-Noire and Brazzaville.

Climate

The climate of the country is hot and humid. There is very little seasonal change throughout the year, generally less than 8 degrees between the warmest and the coolest months. Temperatures rarely rise above 32°C (90°F). About two out of every three days are cloudy, and the humidity averages more than 80 percent.

Rainfall tends to increase from the coast to areas in the interior of the country. At the port of Pointe-Noire it is over 1,200 millimeters (48 inches) each year. Brazzaville receives almost 1,500 millimeters (58 inches). At Makoua in the northeast over 1,750 millimeters (almost 70 inches) of rain are recorded. The dry season is confined largely to a few areas of the Batéké plateaus. Because of the year-round high temperatures, high hu-

The rapids of the Congo River swirl along the eastern border of the Republic of the Congo.

midity, and rainfall, some two thirds of the country is covered by rain forests or swamps. Only in the extreme north of the plateau area do the trees become scattered and grasslands appear. Along the coast, where rainfall is light, there are sand dunes.

Natural Resources

The Congo does not have large-scale mineral resources. It does have considerable deposits of potash and smaller quantities of gold, lead, zinc, copper, and bauxite. One of the largest potash mines in the world is located at Hollé, not far from Pointe-Noire. Petroleum was discovered offshore in 1972. Iron deposits have been found but have not yet been mined.

▶ THE ECONOMY

Most Congolese are still traditional farmers. They follow the same farming patterns found in most parts of Equatorial Africa. Cassava, sweet potatoes and yams, bananas, maize (corn), rice, and beans are the main food crops. Because of the heavy rains, much of the soil is poor, and yields are quite low. A good deal of the actual work is done by women. Farming is generally on a subsistence basis. People grow only enough food to meet their immediate needs.

The most modern and developed section of the country's farmland is in the Niari River valley. There, sugarcane plantations produce sugar for export. Other export crops are coffee, cocoa beans, peanuts, and palm kernels. Tobacco is also grown.

With more than half the land covered by forest, it is not surprising that the timber industry plays an important part in the nation's economy. Wood accounts for the largest proportion of the Congo's exports. One of the most important trees is the limba. Its wood is used in the making of fine furniture. Potash is exported for chemical fertilizer, and some gold, lead, zinc, and copper are mined. Petroleum is also exported. In time, petroleum may prove a valuable source of revenue.

Manufacturing is done on a fairly small scale. Some agricultural products are processed, and factories produce textiles, soap, cigarettes, beer and soft drinks, and cement.

▶ CITIES

Brazzaville, the capital and largest city, has about 300,000 people. It lies on the west bank of the Congo River. In the center of the city are wide, palm-lined boulevards. The city is named for the Italian-born French explorer, Pierre Savorgnan de Brazza, who founded the first settlement there. Brazzaville has grown

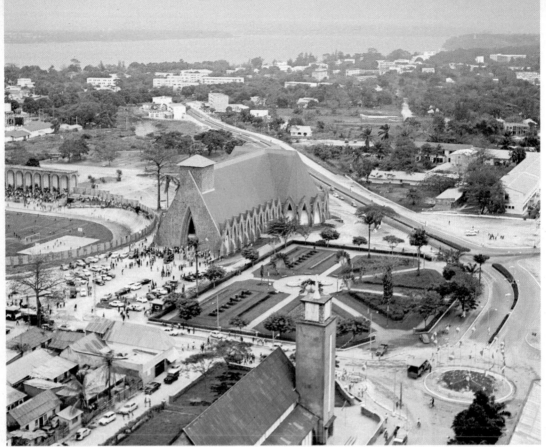
The city of Brazzaville stretches to the river front.

rapidly in recent years. It is the center of the country's manufacturing as well as the seat of government.

Pointe-Noire, the Congo's seaport, is the second largest city. It handles cargo for much of the equatorial region. Other important towns are Loubomo (formerly Dolisie) and Jacob.

▶ HISTORY AND GOVERNMENT

In the late 15th century the Portuguese explorer Diogo Cão discovered the mouth of the Congo River and visited the powerful Kongo people living on its banks. The area soon became a source of slaves. When slavery was outlawed by the Treaty of Vienna in 1815, the French navy began to patrol the area to stop slave ships.

The explorer Pierre Savorgnan de Brazza traveled up the Ogooué (Ogowe) River in 1875 and crossed into the Congo Basin. During a second expedition in 1880, he established a post that has since become the modern city of Brazzaville. The treaties he made with the Batéké rulers allowed the French to gain control over the entire area. In 1903, France gave territorial status and the name "Middle Congo" to the region. Middle Congo—along with the territories of Chad, Gabon, and Ubangi-Chari—became part of French Equatorial Africa in 1910.

French Equatorial Africa was dissolved in 1958, and the Congo became a self-governing member of the French Community. It won complete independence on August 15, 1960.

The Congo's first president was overthrown in 1963, and the country became a Marxist-socialist state. The Army took over the government in 1968. Marien Ngoubai, an army officer, was president from 1969 until 1977. After his assassination in 1977, the constitution was suspended and the National Assembly was dissolved. The Congo was governed by a military committee until 1979, when elections for the National People's Assembly were held and a new constitution was approved. The ruling political party appoints the president and Council of Ministers.

HUGH C. BROOKS
St. John's University (New York)

CONGO RIVER

A Portuguese navigator, Diogo Cão, discovered the mouth of the Congo River while sailing down the west coast of Africa in 1482. In the years that followed, many explorers managed to penetrate farther up the river. But it was not until 1874 that Henry Morton Stanley, the English explorer, began his journey down the entire length of the Congo River, from its headwaters to its mouth. Stanley's party included three white men and 300 Africans. The trip was completed in 1877, and more than half of his men died in the effort. From start to finish, the expedition took about 1,000 days.

Even today travel on the Congo River is an adventure. The navigable waters of the Congo stretch for many miles like a shining highway. But here and there are roaring waterfalls and rapids, bypassed by short railway lines.

Fuel- and wood-burning freighters load and unload cargo at the many river ports that dot the banks of the Congo. Tiny but powerful tugboats blow their horns. The sound is like the trumpeting of elephants, which are, in fact, not too far away from the shore.

Modern steamers with attractive cabins and wide decks ply the waters of the river between Kinshasa and Kisangani. Passengers catch exciting glimpses of African villages and wild animal life. At some places along the banks of the Congo, the dense jungle creeps right to the water's edge. Tangled masses of flowering vines, thick bushes, and tall trees grow along the shore.

A favorite sport of the river people is boat-racing. Daring boys stand upright in homemade dugouts. They paddle furiously, trying to outdistance the steamer. Children play in the shallow waters. They sail small hand-carved boats made from the wood of the umbrella or iroku tree. Near the reed-covered banks of the Congo sleepy crocodiles sun themselves. Herds of hippopotamuses lie submerged in the river; only their bulging eyes peer above water at the passing boats.

African deck boys, called depth-sounders, stand at the bow of the steamer. They test the depth of the river with long poles and guide the helmsman with cries of "mai moke" or "mai mingi" ("little water" or "much water"). Sometimes a siren blasts the air to greet a

Lisala is a small port on the Congo. The people trade fruit and smoked fish for other goods.

passing steamer, or as a salute to a river settlement. A stopping-off port is announced by the sound of a gong.

The Congo is the most important river of central Africa. It is over 4,600 kilometers (2,900 miles) long and drains an area of about 3,750,000 square kilometers (1,450,000 square miles). At one point the river is 14 kilometers (9 miles) wide. At some places the Congo is shallow and sluggish. At others there are rapids and waterfalls. Stanley Falls and Livingstone Falls are the most famous waterfalls.

Today the Congo River and its tributaries play an important part in the economic development of central Africa. They are being harnessed to furnish hydroelectric power for mining, smelting, and refining metals.

Reviewed by THE PERMANENT MISSION OF
THE PEOPLE'S REPUBLIC OF THE CONGO
TO THE UNITED NATIONS

CONGRESS, UNITED STATES. See UNITED STATES (History and Government of the United States).
CONJUNCTION. See PARTS OF SPEECH.

CONNECTICUT

A tablet in New Haven marks the site of Roger Sherman's house. There is good reason for remembering Roger Sherman.

He was born in Massachusetts in 1721. In his early years he was a shoemaker. When he moved to Connecticut in 1743, it is said that he walked the entire distance of 240 kilometers (150 miles), with his cobbler's tools on his back. He became a merchant, a lawyer, a surveyor, a writer of almanacs, and New Haven's first mayor.

Besides all this, Roger Sherman was a statesman, sometimes called the Shoemaker Statesman. He joined with George Washington, Thomas Jefferson, and other patriots in the struggle for freedom. In 1774 he signed the Articles of Association. Then, in 1776, he was one of the signers of the Declaration of Independence. In 1778 he signed the Articles of Confederation. When Roger Sherman put his name to the Constitution in 1787, he became the only person in United States history who had signed all four great documents of the Republic.

STATE FLAG.

STATE TREE: White oak.

STATE BIRD: American robin.

STATE FLOWER: Mountain laurel.

Connecticut is one of the smallest states in area. Only Rhode Island and Delaware are smaller. In shape it is a compact rectangle, about twice as long as it is wide.

The three grapevines on Connecticut's seal and flag stand for the three earliest settlements in Connecticut. The vines could also stand for three qualities that led this small, compact state to greatness. These qualities are independence, inventiveness, and industriousness.

From the earliest days the people of Connecticut were vigorously independent. In 1662 they received a charter that guaranteed their liberties and gave them the right to self-government. When the agents of the king arrived in Hartford 25 years later to take the charter away, the people of Connecticut de-

fended it in a very clever way. They hid it in a hollow oak tree, the famous Charter Oak. Then they said they could not give their charter up because it could not be found.

Many of the first settlers walked to Connecticut from Massachusetts, driving their cattle before them. There in the wilderness they needed many things that they did not have—firearms, pots and pans, buttons, and needles and pins. The western hills held deposits of iron. Before long the inventive people of Connecticut had found ways of manufacturing many different items. By the time of the Revolutionary War, Connecticut was able to provide the Continental Army with some of its cannons. Connecticut also provided cattle and grain to help feed the army. The Provision State was its nickname in those days— and rightly so.

By the early 1800's the Yankee citizens of Connecticut had established many small factories. To keep the factories going, they needed a market for their goods. They found this market in the growing seaports and on the frontier. Industrious peddlers filled their packs with assorted wares—pots and pans, clocks and guns, buttons and thread—and traveled far to the west and the south. Yankee peddlers live in history as the carriers of Connecticut's wares to the rest of the country. They live in legend as ones who occasionally sold wooden nutmegs to their eager customers. For this reason Connecticut came to be called the Nutmeg State. Whether such tales were true or not, Yankee peddlers found a welcome in other parts of the country and a market for Connecticut's goods. They brought back information about other kinds of manufactured products that were needed, and Connecticut's industries grew.

Over the years more patents were granted to residents of Connecticut, in proportion to population, than to residents of any other state. The city of New Haven alone claims such interesting firsts as the first clock, the first steel fishhooks, the first sulfur matches, and the first football tackling dummy.

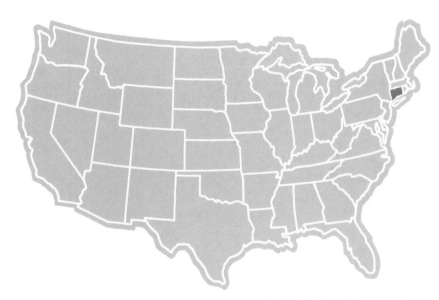

CONNECTICUT

CAPITAL: Hartford.

STATEHOOD: January 9, 1788; the 5th state.

SIZE: 12,997 km² (5,018 sq mi); rank, 48th.

POPULATION: 3,107,576 (1980 census); rank, 25th.

ORIGIN OF NAME: From the Indian expression *quinnitukq-ut,* meaning "At the long tidal river." The name was given to the river and then to the state.

ABBREVIATION: Conn.; CT.

NICKNAME: Constitution State (official); Land of Steady Habits; Nutmeg State.

STATE SONG: "Yankee Doodle."

STATE MOTTO: *Qui transtulit sustinet* (He who transplanted, sustains).

STATE SEAL: The seal shows three grapevines, supported and bearing fruit. The vines stand for the three original English settlements in the Connecticut Valley—Windsor, Wethersfield, and Hartford. The state motto appears on a streamer beneath the vines. The words of the motto indicate that the three colonies were transplanted from Massachusetts and that they grew and prospered.

STATE FLAG: The flag is azure blue. The three grapevines, in their natural colors, rest on a silver-white shield in the center of the flag. Beneath the shield, on a white streamer, is the state motto.

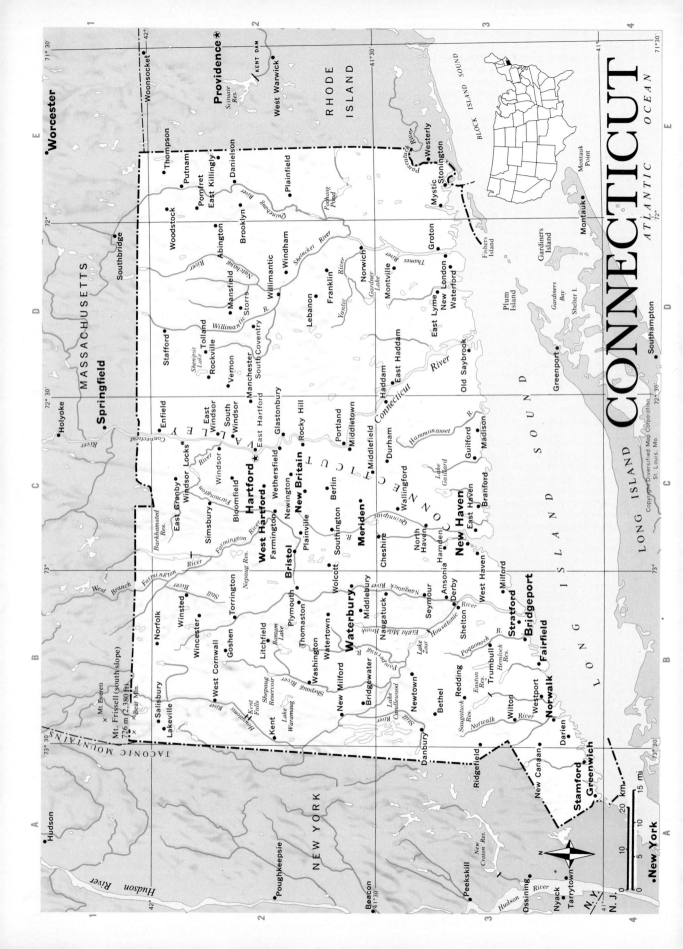

CONNECTICUT

ATLANTIC OCEAN

Copyright Diversified Map Corporation, St. Louis, Mo.

INDEX TO CONNECTICUT MAP

The Connecticut of today continues to be a leading producer of the nation's goods. It looks to the future, but the past is not forgotten. The stately buildings and the lovely village greens of colonial days are carefully preserved and cherished.

▶ THE LAND

Connecticut is one of the group of states known as New England States. It is the most southwesterly of the group. Two other New England States border on Connecticut. They are Massachusetts, to the north, and tiny Rhode Island, to the east. Long Island Sound, a sheltered arm of the Atlantic Ocean, forms all of Connecticut's southern border. Across the Sound is the island for which it was named, Long Island. This island is part of the state of New York, which adjoins Connecticut on the west.

Landforms

A small part of the Taconic Mountains enters the northwestern corner of Connecticut. All the rest of the state lies within a region known as the New England Upland. It may be divided into several parts—the Eastern and the Western uplands, the Coastal Lowland bordering each upland, and the Connecticut Valley Lowland.

The Eastern Upland is an area of rolling hills cut by swift streams that have eroded the land for millions of years. There are peaks of over 300 meters (1,000 feet) in the north, but hills are lower to the south.

The Connecticut Valley Lowland occupies a narrow strip of land between the Eastern and the Western uplands. It extends from Long Island Sound northward through the center of the state. The land is relatively flat, and the soil is fertile.

The Western Upland is a hilly region like

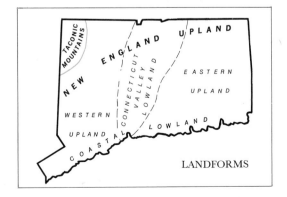

LANDFORMS

its twin in the eastern part of the state. But it is much higher along the northern border.

The Coastal Lowland is a sloping extension of the uplands. Along the Sound it becomes a low, almost flat plain. The mouths of the rivers in this coastal strip form harbors.

The Taconic region of Connecticut is made up of two different parts—the low valley of the Housatonic River and the sharply elevated Taconic Mountains. The highest point in the state is on the southern slope of Mount Frissell. The peak of this mountain is in Massachusetts.

THE LAND

LOCATION: Latitude—40° 57' N to 42° 03' N. **Longitude**—71° 46' W to 73° 44' W. Massachusetts to the north, New York to the west, Long Island Sound to the south, Rhode Island to the east.

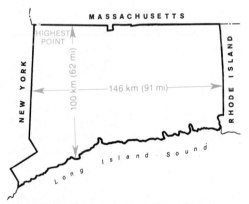

ELEVATION: Highest—On the south slope of Mount Frissell, 726 m (2,380 ft). **Lowest**—Sea level, on Long Island Sound.

LANDFORMS: Eastern Upland, Connecticut Valley Lowland, Western Upland, Coastal Lowland, Taconic Mountains.

SURFACE WATERS: Major rivers—Connecticut in central part of state, Thames River system in the east, Housatonic and Naugatuck in the west. **Major artificial lake**—Candlewood. **Largest natural lake**—Bantam.

CLIMATE: Temperature—Summer average, 21°C (70°F); winter average, −3°C (27°F). **Precipitation**—Yearly average, 1,140 mm (45 in). Snowfall varies from 64 cm (25 in) along the coast to 190 cm (75 in) in the northwest. **Growing season**—Varies from 190 days near Long Island Sound to 135 days in inland areas.

Rivers, Lakes, and Coastal Waters

Connecticut's rivers, lakes, and coastal waters attracted Indians and early colonists, and they continue to attract people today. The Connecticut River, longest in New England, divides the state almost in half. It is navigable between the coast and the Hartford area. Rivers of the Eastern Upland include the Willimantic, the Shetucket, the Quinebaug, and the Yantic. All these rivers join at various points to form the broad Thames, which empties into Long Island Sound between New London and Groton. The Housatonic and the Naugatuck are the major rivers that drain the Western Upland. These two rivers join at Derby and continue southward as the Housatonic, which flows into Long Island Sound at Stratford.

Like the rest of New England, Connecticut is dotted with small lakes. But the largest bodies of water in the state are artificial lakes rather than natural lakes. Lake Candlewood, Connecticut's largest reservoir, stretches through the rugged upland north of Danbury. It is important as a place of recreation, but its major purpose is to supply water to the power plants on the Housatonic River.

The shore of Long Island Sound is noted for its natural beauty, its many residential communities, and its beaches and harbors. The Sound is approximately 160 kilometers (100 miles) in length. Connecticut's total shoreline, counting the shores of all the inlets and islands, is 994 kilometers (618 miles) long.

Climate

Connecticut's climate is much like the climate of the New York City area. Winters are fairly mild, and summers tend to be warm and humid. Extremes of heat or cold are unusual.

Precipitation is somewhat higher in the uplands than in the Connecticut Valley. Snowfall is variable. The southeast receives much less than areas of the northwest.

It is not the average weather conditions that Connecticut must fear but the occasional excesses in wind and rain. Tropical hurricanes have brought destruction to areas along the Sound. Heavy rains in the hilly interior sometimes cause floods that destroy property near the rampaging streams and rivers.

Connecticut rarely has long droughts, but local areas may receive little or no moisture

Above: Boats of many kinds, piers, and waterside houses line the harbors of Long Island Sound. This scene is at Groton.

Below: Mystic Seaport recalls Connecticut's colorful seafaring past. A 19th-century fishing village has been restored, and an old whaling ship is on display.

for several weeks at a time. These dry spells may damage crops and force city dwellers and industries to reduce their use of water.

Natural Resources

Connecticut's soils, forests, and minerals were the source of its wealth in early days. But for more than 100 years factories have supplied its citizens with greater income than have these natural resources. The wooded valleys and hills and the coastal areas provide pleasant places for living and for recreation.

Like other states, Connecticut has established a department of environmental protection and has passed laws to help halt pollution and preserve the natural beauty of the countryside. Among the laws are clean-water and anti-litter acts. Steps also are being taken to protect agricultural land against loss to commercial or residential uses.

Soils. Connecticut's soils were deposited mainly by glaciers, and most of the land is rocky. It is only in the large river valleys that water-deposited soils are found in abundance. The best agricultural soils are the sandy loams in parts of the Connecticut Valley.

Forests. The woodlands of the state are largely hardwoods. They have been used continuously since the first white settlers arrived. All the virgin timber was cut down long ago, but more than two thirds of the state is still forested. Lumbering on a small scale is carried on in many areas.

Minerals. In early times Connecticut gained a certain fame for its minerals. Iron ore from the Salisbury area was used to make cannons, gun barrels, and chains during the Revolutionary War. Production of iron continued to be important in the 1800's and the early 1900's. Copper from the mines of East Granby went into the first minted coins in the United States.

Today the mining industry is concerned mainly with the quarrying of stone, especially for road building. Lime is made from local limestone and marble formations. Extensive supplies of sand and gravel are used in the construction industry.

Wildlife. The wooded areas of Connecticut shelter much small game, such as woodchuck, fox, rabbit, and squirrel. Deer are increasing in number, and occasionally black bears are seen. Pheasant, quail, wild turkey, duck, and other game birds live in great numbers in the state, which is also known for its songbirds.

▶ THE PEOPLE AND THEIR WORK

Connecticut was one of the original 13 colonies. The earliest European settlers came from neighboring Massachusetts or directly from England. After that time Connecticut shared in the vigorous tide of immigrants to the United States from other European countries. Today the population includes representatives of many parts of the world.

But when the Europeans arrived, Connecticut was the home of 16 separate Indian tribes. The best-known were the Pequots, centered in Groton and Stonington. Today some of their descendants live on small reservations in the same area. They have been overlooked in the past, but their needs are now being recognized. The state has established an office of Indian affairs, as well as a council on which representatives of the reservations serve.

Where the People Live

More than three fourths of Connecticut's people live in cities or in suburban areas. The main population centers extend from Greenwich eastward along the Sound to New Haven, and then northward to Hartford. Many people who live in the extreme southwest— in Greenwich, Stamford, and elsewhere— work in nearby New York City.

Manufacturing

About one third of the people who work in Connecticut are employed in manufacturing. There are several large industrial centers, but factories are widely spread through the state. Connecticut is well known for the many

POPULATION

TOTAL: 3,107,576 (1980 census). **Density**—246.3 persons to each square kilometer (637.8 persons to each square mile).

GROWTH SINCE 1790

Year	Population	Year	Population
1790	237,946	1900	908,420
1820	275,248	1920	1,380,631
1840	309,978	1960	2,535,234
1860	460,147	1970	3,032,217
1880	622,700	1980	3,107,576

Gain Between 1970 and 1980—2.5 percent

CITIES: Population of Connecticut's largest incorporated places (cities) according to the 1980 census.

Bridgeport	142,546	Norwalk	77,767
Hartford	136,392	New Britain	73,840
New Haven	126,109	Danbury	60,470
Waterbury	103,266	Bristol	57,370
Stamford	102,453	Meriden	57,118

useful items that were invented by its citizens and produced in its factories from early times. Its greatest contribution was the idea of interchangeable parts, which was developed by Eli Whitney in his gun factory in New Haven. Whitney's idea was to make the several parts of a gun by machines. Each trigger would be exactly like every other trigger. The same would be true for each of the other parts of a gun. If a trigger broke, the owner of the gun could buy a new one, and it would fit the gun. Before this time, the gunsmith had to make a special trigger to fit each gun, a slow and expensive process. Whitney's idea was applied to many other types of manufacturing. It reduced the cost of manufactured goods, and thus many more people could buy them.

Major Industries. Any listing of Connecticut's manufacturing industries would be long indeed. In recent times the transportation-equipment industry has been the leader. This industry turns out such highly specialized products as jet aircraft engines, helicopters, and nuclear submarines.

Other leading manufactures include firearms for sports and for military use, ball bearings, typewriters and other office machines, general hardware, and such household appliances as electric irons, vacuum cleaners, and sewing machines.

Brass and Silver. The brass industry in the United States began in Connecticut. In 1802, Porter and Company began making brass buttons in Waterbury. Waterbury's brass works flourished, and others sprang up in the area. Soon the Naugatuck Valley became a major center of brass production, and brass was used in making such products as clocks and watches. The modern silverware industry began in Hartford in 1847. Today Meriden and Wallingford are known for silverware.

Clocks. Clocks with wooden works were made in Connecticut before the Declaration of Independence was signed. Eli Terry, Chauncey Jerome, and Seth Thomas gave the state its early start in clock production. Because the wooden works were affected by humidity and temperature changes, the earliest clocks were not altogether dependable. After the year 1800 sheet brass was used to make brass cogs and wheels. The timepiece industry and the brass industry in central Connecticut expanded together, each depending on

The nuclear submarine *Triton* is launched at New London.

the other. Today Connecticut's clocks and watches are sold all over the world. Centers of production include Bristol, Middlebury, Waterbury, and Winsted.

Other Industries. Many of the older industries have disappeared or changed with changing times. In 1900 Danbury was the hat capital of the United States, and Connecticut as a whole was the center of industries that made men's hats. Danbury still makes hats, but its manufactures include many other products such as surgical instruments, lighting fixtures, and electronic equipment.

By 1845 New London, Connecticut, was second only to New Bedford, Massachusetts, as a whaling center. The whaling industry declined and disappeared. But the tradition continues in the modern ship-building industry of the New London area, including the nuclear submarine center at Groton. Here the first nuclear-powered submarine, the USS *Nautilus,* was launched in 1954.

Connecticut continues to produce needles and pins, as it did in the days of the Yankee peddler. Factories that make needles, pins, and fasteners are found in Shelton, Thomaston, Torrington, and elsewhere. Eastern Connecticut is still known for textiles. Manchester, Putnam, Danielson, and Willimantic are among the centers that manufacture silk, rayon, cotton, and woolen fabrics and yarns. Factories that make rubber products are

Winding roads and attractive farms adorn Connecticut's hilly countryside.

found in communities from Naugatuck to New Haven.

Agriculture

Well-kept farms dot the countryside, even though Connecticut is not an important agricultural state. At present dairying is the most important agricultural occupation. Dairy farms are found throughout the state, with the greatest number in the hilly sections of Litchfield County. Poultry production is especially important in the Eastern Upland. The northern Connecticut Valley specializes in truck farming and in the growing of tobacco. Connecticut's farm population is most heavily concentrated in this fertile area.

Transportation and Communication

Because it is located between the cities of New York and Boston, Connecticut lies on a main transportation route. It is well equipped for transporting people and goods by land, air, and water. Railroads provide freight service, as well as some passenger service.

Connecticut's beautiful Merritt Parkway was one of the earliest passenger express highways in the nation. Other major highways include the Wilbur Cross Parkway and the Connecticut Turnpike, which was opened in 1958. Bradley International Airport, at Windsor Locks, north of Hartford, is the major airport. The Connecticut River and the deepwater ports on Long Island Sound handle large quantities of freight.

Connecticut has more than 20 daily newspapers. The most famous of these is the Hartford *Courant,* which was established in 1764. The *Courant* and the New Haven *Journal-Courier* have the largest circulation. Connecticut has more than 50 local weeklies, representing every part of the state. There are approximately 60 radio stations and several television stations.

▶ GOVERNMENT

In 1639 the citizens of the three original settlements in Connecticut adopted a plan for governing themselves. They called this plan the Fundamental Orders. It is said to be one of the first written constitutions adopted by any government. Thus, Connecticut is sometimes called the Constitution State. In 1662 Connecticut received a charter from the English king. It remained in effect until 1818, when a new constitution was adopted. The state's present constitution dates from 1965.

The executive branch of the state government includes the governor and five other executive officers. All are elected for 4-year terms.

WHAT CONNECTICUT PRODUCES

MANUFACTURED GOODS: Transportation equipment; nonelectrical machinery, mainly industrial and metalworking machinery; fabricated metal products; electric and electronic equipment; chemicals and related products; instruments and related products; primary metals; products of printing and publishing; processed foods; rubber and plastic products.

AGRICULTURAL PRODUCTS: Milk, eggs, greenhouse and nursery products, tobacco, cattle and calves, apples, potatoes, sweet corn.

MINERALS: Stone, sand and gravel, feldspar, lime.

The legislative branch of the government is called the General Assembly. It is made up of the Senate and the House of Representatives. Senators and representatives are elected for 2-year terms. In 1970 the voters of Connecticut approved annual sessions of the General Assembly. Before that time sessions had been held every other year.

The judicial branch is made up of a series of courts. The Supreme Court is the highest court. Other state courts include the superior, circuit, and juvenile courts and the court of common pleas.

The entire state is divided into towns. In Connecticut and other New England states, the word "town" does not mean "village," as it does in other parts of the nation. It refers to a section of the state that has its own local government. Each town holds town meetings, at which all qualified voters may speak and vote. Every farm, woodland, village, or city is part of a town. Many of the towns include several villages with different names. The villages may have their own post offices and stores, but they do not have their own governments. They share in the town government. Altogether there are 169 towns. There are also 23 city governments. This means that 23 of the 169 towns have cities within their limits. In some cases the town and city are combined into one political unit.

The state is divided into 8 counties. But counties were never as important in Connecticut as in most other states. In 1959 the General Assembly voted to do away with county government, effective in 1960.

▶ **EDUCATION**

More than 100 years before the Revolutionary War, the laws of Connecticut stated that parents had to educate their children. Communities of more than 50 families were required to hire a schoolmaster. Through the years the state has maintained its tradition of respect for education.

Schools and Colleges

Connecticut's system of public education owes much to the noted educator Henry Barnard. In the 1830's Barnard introduced a bill in the General Assembly to provide for state supervision of public schools. At that time the common, or public, schools were very poor in comparison with the private schools. Most parents sent their children to private schools if they could afford to do so. Barnard insisted that all children should have a chance for excellent schooling. He traveled over the state. He wrote and lectured to help people understand the need for good public schools. He recommended that the state establish "higher schools"—later called high schools—to prepare young people for everyday living as well as for entrance to college. Barnard also worked to improve the training of teachers. Connecticut's first teachers' college was founded in 1849 at New Britain, with Barnard as the first principal.

Today almost all the public high schools offer some kind of vocational training. Because Connecticut's industries need a supply of skilled workers, the state also has established vocational-technical schools in the main industrial centers. In these schools young people and adults may complete apprenticeship training in the skilled trades. The state-supported institutions of higher learning are the University of Connecticut, at Storrs, and state universities at Danbury, New Britain, New Haven, and Willimantic. The state has also set up a number of two-year community colleges in the major cities.

Connecticut has long been known for its private schools and colleges. Famous preparatory schools include Choate, at Wallingford; Gunnery, at Washington; Hotchkiss, at Lakeville; Taft, at Watertown; and Miss Porter's, at Farmington. Yale University, New Haven, is the third oldest institution of higher learning in the United States. (The two older than Yale are Harvard University, at Cambridge, Massachusetts, founded in 1636; and the College of William and Mary, at Williamsburg, Virginia, founded in 1693.) Yale was chartered in 1701 under the name the Collegiate School. Later it became Yale College and then Yale University. Two other well-known Connecticut colleges are more than a century old. They are Trinity College, at Hartford,

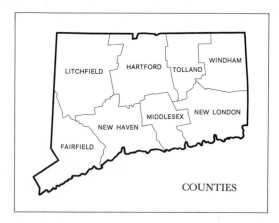

COUNTIES

Hill-Stead Museum, Farmington, consists of a fine old mansion with 19th-century furnishings and rare art.

Mystic Seaport and Marine Museum, Mystic, includes both indoor and outdoor exhibits. Visitors may wander through a restored whaling village, go aboard a wooden whaling ship, and see homes, shops, and hundreds of items from whaling days.

Peabody Museum of Natural History, a part of Yale University, is one of the great natural-history museums of the nation.

Whitfield House, Guilford, is often called the oldest stone house in New England. It is preserved as a state museum.

▶ **CITIES**

Connecticut's cities have their special attractions for visitors. Among points of interest are the insurance company buildings in Hartford, the fine parks in Bridgeport, and the campus of Yale University in New Haven.

Hartford

Hartford, the state capital, is centrally located on the Connecticut River. It was settled in the 1630's and was named for Hertford, England. For more than 150 years, Hartford was one of the two capitals of Connecticut. The other was New Haven. Meetings of the General Assembly alternated between the two. In 1873 the people voted to select a single capital. Hartford won, and from 1875 on it was the only seat of government.

Hartford has grown to be a great manufacturing and business center. Some of its well-known products are typewriters, brushes, revolvers, and airplane engines and parts. It was the home of the nation's first successful insurance companies. Today so many insurance companies have their headquarters in Hartford that it is known as the Insurance Capital of the United States. In 1962 Hartford won a national award for work that had been done to clear away slums and to renew parts of the city.

Bridgeport

Bridgeport is located on Long Island Sound at the mouth of the Poquonock River. It was named for the first drawbridge over the river. It has grown from a small shipping community to a large industrial center. Its many products include electrical appliances, firearms and

founded in 1823, and Wesleyan University, at Middletown, founded in 1831. Altogether Connecticut has more than 20 private universities and colleges. The United States Coast Guard Academy is located at New London.

Libraries and Museums

Connecticut's first library was established at Durham in 1733. Today most communities have public library service. The Connecticut Historical Society, in Hartford, maintains a library devoted especially to the history of the state, as does the Connecticut State Library, also in Hartford. Yale University's library collections are among the largest and the best in the nation. They total more than 4,000,000 volumes. At Groton there is an unusual library of books about submarines.

Connecticut has a wide variety of museums, both public and private. Important art museums include the Wadsworth Atheneum, at Hartford, the Museum of American Art, at New Britain, and the Yale University Art Gallery, at New Haven. The Connecticut Historical Society Museum and the Connecticut State Library Museum, both at Hartford, contain exhibits pertaining to the history of the state. Historical societies in many of the towns and cities have fine local-history museums. Some of these are historic homes, furnished as they were in early days. The following are a few of the other museums of special interest:

Branford Trolley Museum, East Haven, preserves old trolley cars. The cars are in operation for the public.

Bristol Clock Museum, Bristol, displays several hundred clocks and watches dating from the early 1700's.

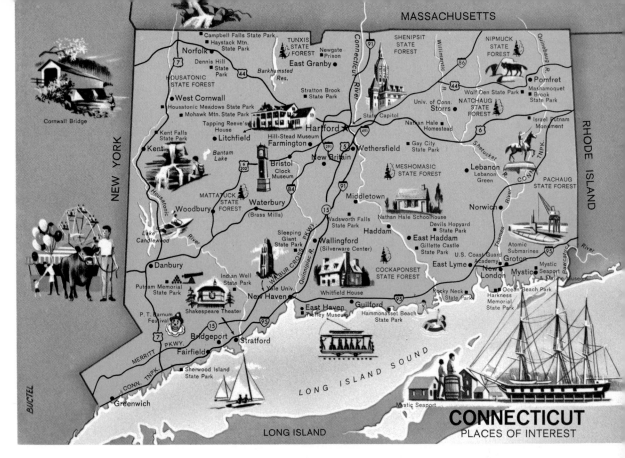

Map labels (Connecticut — Places of Interest):

MASSACHUSETTS

Campbell Falls State Park • Haystack Mtn. State Park • Norfolk • TUNXIS STATE FOREST • Newgate Prison • SHENIPSIT STATE FOREST • NIPMUCK STATE FOREST • Quinebaug R.

Dennis Hill State Park • East Granby • Connecticut River • 91 • Pomfret • Mashamoquet Brook State Park

HOUSATONIC STATE FOREST • 7 • 44 • Barkhamsted Res. • Stratton Brook State Park • Wolf Den State Park • 44 • Israel Putnam Monument

West Cornwall • Housatonic Meadows State Park • Mohawk Mtn. State Park • Tapping Reeve's House • State Capitol • Univ. of Conn. Storrs • NATCHAUG STATE FOREST

Cornwall Bridge • Kent Falls State Park • Litchfield • Hartford • 491 • Nathan Hale Homestead • 6

Kent • Farmington • Hill-Stead Museum • Wethersfield • Gay City State Park • Shetucket R. • RHODE ISLAND

NEW YORK • Bantam Lake • New Britain • 291 • 5 • Lebanon • Lebanon Green • PACHAUG STATE FOREST

Bristol Clock Museum • 6 202 • 84 • MESHOMASIC STATE FOREST • CONN. TNPK.

MATTATUCK STATE FOREST • Waterbury (Brass Mills) • 15 • Middletown • Norwich • Thames R.

Woodbury • Housatonic River • Wadsworth Falls State Park • Nathan Hale Schoolhouse • Devils Hopyard State Park • Atomic Submarines • 95

Lake Candlewood • Sleeping Giant State Park • Haddam • East Haddam • Gillette Castle State Park • U.S. Coast Guard Academy • Groton • Mystic

Danbury • WILBUR CROSS PKWY • Quinnipiac R. • Wallingford (Silverware Center) • COCKAPONSET STATE FOREST • East Lyme • New London • Mystic Seaport & Marine Museum

Putnam Memorial State Park • Indian Well State Park • Yale Univ. • Whitfield House • Rocky Neck State Park • Ocean Beach Park • Harkness Memorial State Park

P. T. Barnum Festival • Shakespeare Theater • New Haven • East Haven • Trolley Museum • Guilford • Hammonasset Beach State Park

7 • 15 PKWY • Bridgeport • Stratford • MERRITT PKWY • Fairfield • CONN. TNPK.

Sherwood Island State Park • LONG ISLAND SOUND

Greenwich • Mystic Seaport

LONG ISLAND

BUCTEL

CONNECTICUT
PLACES OF INTEREST

---

ammunition, jet-engine parts, and office machines. Because of its fine parks, Bridgeport is known as the City of Parks. It is also known as the home of P. T. Barnum, the great showman. Barnum was once mayor of Bridgeport. There are memorials to him throughout the city. Bridgeport's educational institutions include the University of Bridgeport.

New Haven

New Haven, on Long Island Sound near Bridgeport, is world famous as the home of Yale University. For many years New Haven was one of Connecticut's two state capitals. The city was founded in 1638. It was laid out in squares with a public square, or village green, in the center. The Green has been carefully preserved. It is much like a park, which thousands of people use and enjoy daily. In early days New Haven was an important port for whaling vessels and for clipper ships bringing the riches of the Far East to the New World. At the time of the Civil War, it was a busy manufacturing center. Today it is an industrial and trading center as well as a center of learning and culture.

PLACES OF INTEREST

In compact Connecticut one is never far from places for outdoor recreation and points of historic interest and scenic beauty. There are scores of well-marked historic sites, large areas set aside as state forests, more than 70 state parks, and long stretches of sandy beaches facing Long Island Sound. The following list shows the wide variety of places of interest in Connecticut:

American Shakespeare Festival Theater, Stratford, is famous for Shakespearean plays produced there each summer.

Cornwall Bridge, one of Connecticut's few remaining covered bridges, spans the Housatonic River at West Cornwall.

Gillette Castle State Park, on the Connecticut River at East Haddam, includes a beautiful woodland setting and an unusual stone castle, where the actor William Gillette once lived.

Harkness Memorial State Park, south of New London, includes a seaside mansion with beautiful formal gardens. In the mansion is a famous collection of paintings of American birds, by Rex Brasher.

Haystack Mountain State Park and **Dennis**

Hill State Park, both near Norfolk, offer mountain scenery, hiking, and picnicking.

Kent Falls State Park, near Kent, is noted for woodland trails and scenic waterfalls on the Housatonic River. Other state parks with beautiful waterfalls are Campbell Falls, north of Norfolk, and Wadsworth Falls, near Middletown.

Lebanon Green, Lebanon, is an excellent example of a village green almost unchanged from colonial times.

Nathan Hale Schoolhouse, East Haddam, is the country school where Nathan Hale, the famous American patriot, once taught. The Nathan Hale Homestead, South Coventry, is one of the historic homes in Connecticut open to the public.

Newgate Prison, East Granby, contains the grim ruins of a prison and of copper mines where the prisoners worked during Revolutionary War days.

Ocean Beach Park, owned by the city of New London, provides a beautiful modern public beach.

Old State House, Hartford, is considered a masterpiece of architecture. It was designed by the colonial architect Charles Bulfinch.

Rocky Neck State Park, East Lyme, has fine public beaches, as do Hammonasset Beach State Park, Madison, and Sherwood Island State Park, Westport.

Wolf Den State Park, near Pomfret, preserves a den where Israel Putnam is said to have killed a wolf that had brought terror to eastern Connecticut. Mashamoquet Brook State Park is nearby.

▶ FAMOUS PEOPLE

Connecticut has a long roll call of famous citizens. The list goes back to the very beginning of the nation's history.

Thomas Hooker (1586?–1647), a Puritan minister from England, is known as a founder of Connecticut. He and other Puritans left England because they were not allowed to worship as they pleased. Hooker arrived in Massachusetts in 1633. In 1636 he led a group of Puritans to Connecticut and settled in the Hartford area. Here he preached a famous sermon on government. Ideas from this sermon were used in the Fundamental Orders, the first constitution of Connecticut.

Tapping Reeve (1744–1823) was a teacher and a learned writer on law. He was born in New York and was educated at the College of New Jersey, now Princeton University. Reeve moved to Connecticut in 1771. He is best remembered as the founder of a famous law school at Litchfield in 1784. It was one of the first law schools in the United States. Reeve's house is one of the places of interest in present-day Litchfield.

Nathan Hale (1755–76), the Revolutionary War hero, was born near South Coventry. He is remembered especially for the statement "I only regret that I have but one life to lose for my country." A biography of Nathan Hale appears in Volume H.

Noah Webster (1758–1843) gained fame for his "Blue-backed Speller" and his dictionary of the English language. He was born in West Hartford. Volume W contains a biography of Noah Webster.

Charles Goodyear (1800–60), born at New Haven, worked for many years to discover a way to keep rubber from melting and sticking together in hot weather. In 1844 he patented the process known as vulcanizing. Goodyear's discovery made it possible for industries to manufacture many different products from rubber. A biography of Goodyear is included in Volume G.

Roger Sherman was the most famous of Connecticut's four signers of the Declaration of Independence. The others were Samuel

---

Who was Israel Putnam?

It was high noon, and the sun blazed down on the furrows. Soon, the Connecticut farmer thought, he would rest and eat his midday meal. But who was that, riding pell-mell along the dusty road? What news did he bring? "They're fighting at Lexington!" the rider shouted.

It is said that Israel Putnam left his plow in the furrow and started instantly for Massachusetts. Whether he started instantly or not, he did go to the scene of the fighting. "Old Put," as he was called, was already a popular hero, famous for bravery and deeds of daring, especially in the French and Indian War. Now in 1775, at the age of 57, he became a major general in the Continental Army. He fought at Bunker Hill and took part in campaigns in New York and Pennsylvania. Finally, after a severe illness, he returned in 1779 to his farm in a part of Pomfret, Connecticut, later known as Brooklyn.

Putnam was born in Salem Village (now Danvers), Massachusetts, in 1718. He died in Brooklyn in 1790. A state monument at Brooklyn includes his burial place and a statue of him. Putnam Memorial State Park in Redding, named for him, preserves Revolutionary War training grounds and war relics. Because of this, the Connecticut General Assembly designated it a Bicentennial Park.

Stratford's summer theater is modeled after the Globe Theater of Shakespeare's day.

The Congregational Church and parish house at Guilford face the village green.

Whitfield House in Guilford is said to be the oldest stone house in New England.

Huntington (Windham), William Williams (Lebanon), and Oliver Wolcott (Windsor). Inventors besides Charles Goodyear who were born in the state include John Fitch (Windsor), who invented a steamboat, and Samuel Colt (Hartford), who invented and manufactured the famous Colt revolver.

Well-known names in the arts include painter John Trumbull (Lebanon), composer Reginald De Koven (Middletown), opera singer Rosa Ponselle (Meriden), and actor William Gillette (Hartford).

Harriet Beecher Stowe, author of *Uncle Tom's Cabin,* was born in Litchfield. Mark Twain was born in Missouri, but he lived in Hartford for many years. The house that he built there attracts many visitors.

Connecticut was the birthplace also of the abolitionist John Brown (Torrington) and of Phineas T. Barnum (Bethel), creator of "The Greatest Show on Earth." Biographies of Barnum, John Brown, Harriet Beecher Stowe, and Mark Twain are included in Volumes B, S, and T.

Wilbur L. Cross (Mansfield) and Abraham A. Ribicoff (New Britain) are two well-known former governors of Connecticut. Ribicoff was also a United States Senator.

▶ HISTORY

The discovery of a stone spearhead near Washington, Connecticut, in 1977 showed that Indians had lived in the Shepaug Valley as long as 12,000 years ago. They were ancestors of the tribes that the English and Dutch met in the 1600's. All belonged to a group of North American Indians known as the Algonkins. They lived by hunting, fishing, and farming.

The first Europeans in Connecticut were probably Dutch traders who sailed out of New Amsterdam. In 1614 a crew under Adriaen Block explored Long Island Sound and then sailed up the Connecticut River. Almost 20 years later the Dutch returned and built a fort near what is now Hartford.

IMPORTANT DATES

1614	Adriaen Block, a Dutch explorer, sailed up the Connecticut River.
1633	The Dutch built a fort on the present site of Hartford.
1633–1635	English colonists from Massachusetts started first permanent settlements on the Connecticut River at Windsor, Wethersfield, and Hartford.
1638	Puritans from London settled New Haven.
1639	The three river towns drew up a document, called the Fundamental Orders, under which they were to be governed.
1662	Connecticut obtained a charter from King Charles II.
1701	Collegiate School founded, later to become Yale University.
1740	Manufacture of tinware began at Berlin.
1788	Connecticut admitted to Union on January 9, as 5th state.
1802	Brass industry began at Waterbury.
1807	Noah Webster published the first important English dictionary in the United States.
1810	Hartford Fire Insurance Company incorporated.
1818	State constitution adopted.
1836	Samuel Colt patented the Colt revolver.
1844	Charles Goodyear patented vulcanizing process for rubber; New York and New Haven Railroad chartered.
1873	Hartford selected as state capital.
1881	Storrs Agricultural School founded, later to be University of Connecticut.
1910	United States Coast Guard Academy moved to New London from Maryland.
1936	Floods caused great damage in Connecticut River Valley.
1954	The USS *Nautilus*, world's first nuclear-powered submarine, launched at Groton.
1965	New state constitution adopted.
1975	Ella T. Grasso took office as the nation's first woman governor who was not preceded in office by her husband.
1977	Archeological discovery showed that people had lived in Connecticut since about 10,000 B.C.
1980	Plans were made to bring the decommissioned *Nautilus* home to Groton.

Colonial Days

Connecticut's first white settlers were Puritans from nearby Massachusetts. They had heard of the fertile Connecticut Valley. In the early 1630's, they began to migrate in search of land. Some of them, such as the Reverend Thomas Hooker, were also looking for greater religious freedom than they enjoyed in Massachusetts. By 1637 they had built the three river towns of Windsor, Wethersfield, and Hartford. They had also defeated the feared Pequot Indians. In 1639 representatives of the three towns drew up the famous Fundamental Orders, by which they were all to be governed. Together they formed a colony that was commonly known as Connecticut.

In the meantime, settlements were being made along the coast of Long Island Sound. In 1638 a group of Puritans from London founded New Haven and other nearby towns. The New Haven colony had its own government. For more than 20 years it was entirely separate from the colony to the north known as Connecticut.

In 1661 the governor of Connecticut, John Winthrop, Jr., went to England to obtain a charter, or legal title, for the colony. Up to this time the settlers had never asked the king to recognize their right to own their land and govern themselves. Winthrop persuaded Charles II to grant the famous charter of 1662. It gave the people of Connecticut the right to elect their own governor and pass their own laws. It also gave the colony a wide stretch of territory that included the New Haven area.

Connecticut's unusual rights of local self-government were soon threatened. The next king of England, James II, wanted more control over the American colonies. He formed all the northern colonies into a unit called the Dominion of New England. He then appointed Edmund Andros, of New York, as governor. But the people of Connecticut refused to give up their right to govern themselves. They hid their charter when Andros came to Hartford to seize it in 1687. The Dominion of New England did not last very long. James II was overthrown in 1689, and Andros left the colonies. But only Connecticut and Rhode Island kept the right to complete self-government.

Constitution Plaza is the center of Hartford's urban renewal program.

Connecticut Becomes a State

When the Revolutionary War began, Connecticut joined the other colonies in the struggle for freedom. No great battles were fought on its soil. But General Washington could depend on his close friend Governor Jonathan Trumbull, of Connecticut, to provide war materials, food, and soldiers.

Connecticut's representatives took part in all the meetings that led to the formation of the Union. On January 9, 1788, Connecticut adopted the federal Constitution and became the fifth state to enter the Union.

During the early 1800's most of the people still made their living by farming. But Connecticut's inventors and its many small factories were busy laying the foundations for the great industries of the future.

The Growth of Manufacturing

Several events helped the growth of industries. One important event was the building of railroads in the 1830's and later. Connecticut did not have many of the raw materials necessary for manufacturing. Railroads were needed to bring in raw materials and to carry manufactured goods to markets. About this time immigrants were pouring into the United States from Europe. Many of them came to Connecticut, where factory workers were needed. Connecticut inventors developed methods of manufacturing by the use of interchangeable parts, and mass production became possible. At the time of the Civil War, the Union could depend on Connecticut not only for men but for great quantities of war materials and other manufactured goods. Connecticut's industrial centers continued to grow during the late 1800's and the 1900's. The farm population dwindled rapidly, but the state kept its rural loveliness.

The Future

Connecticut continues to be a leading manufacturing state. But, like other states, it faces several problems. Many of its larger cities have lost population. The growth of slums has forced people to move to suburbs. Some of the cities have carried out projects for rebuilding slum areas. Many more such projects are needed. Recently the state has faced the problem of flood control. More and better roads are needed to transport people and goods. These problems can be solved, and Connecticut, the Land of Steady Habits, looks to a bright future in swiftly changing times.

DELMAR C. MULTHAUF
Formerly of Western Connecticut State College

Reviewed by JOSEPH B. HOYT
Author, *The Connecticut Story*

CONRAD, JOSEPH (1857–1924)

Teodor Józef Konrad Korzeniowski, who spoke only Polish and French until he was 21 years old, grew up to become Joseph Conrad, one of the world's greatest writers in English. Joseph was born December 3, 1857, in the Ukraine, Russia, of Polish parents. His father, a writer and translator, was arrested during the Polish struggle for independence in 1863. The family went into exile in northern Russia. Joseph's mother died in 1865, his father in 1869. An uncle arranged for Joseph's education in Cracow, Poland.

A lonely youth, Joseph read a great many French and Polish books, and his reading made him dream of a life of adventure. In 1874 he left Poland for France and the sea, sailing from Marseilles to the West Indies. In 1877 he was involved in a political conspiracy, transporting guns and ammunition to the coast of Spain. He arrived in England in 1878, knowing hardly a word of English. Eight years later he became a British subject and passed difficult exams to become a master in the British Merchant Navy.

Injured in 1887 on a voyage to Southeast Asia, Conrad was hospitalized in Singapore. To fill the empty hours, he began to write about the people he had met. During the next years he wrote whenever he could while sailing ships between England and Australia. He made one unfortunate trip to Africa, where he picked up illnesses that plagued him all his life.

Conrad left the sea in 1894, settling in England. After finishing the book he had been working on for over 4 years—*Almayer's Folly,* about a man he had known in Borneo—he started *An Outcast of the Islands.* These two books and his later *Lord Jim* have the same setting. He wrote to earn a living, generally drawing on his past experiences.

Conrad's marriage in 1896 resulted in two sons, but he had to battle continually against poverty and sickness to support them. Although his books were praised by the critics, and a number of leading writers became his friends, general fame came late. He was an important literary figure by 1923, however, when he was warmly received in the United States. He died August 3, 1924.

CONSCRIPTION. See DRAFT, OR CONSCRIPTION.

CONSERVATION

Have you ever saved aluminum cans, bottles, or old newspapers and taken them to a collection point? Have you ever turned off the water while brushing your teeth? If so, you have practiced conservation.

The word conservation comes from a Latin word meaning "to keep" or "to guard." It once meant careful preservation and protection chiefly of forests and wildlife. Now we know that we must apply conservation to everything in our environment. We must include all the natural resources that our planet provides—air, water, soil, forests and grasslands, wildlife, and minerals, as well as the many products that are made from these resources.

The practice of conservation is really a way of life that avoids waste of our natural resources and finds ways to share the limited supplies. It means that we must not pollute the environment—or must clean up areas that are already polluted. Individuals, businesses, governments, and entire nations must learn to follow this way of life.

The challenge of conservation is perhaps the greatest challenge that people have ever faced. The world's population is growing faster than the supplies of food, drinking water, housing, and other necessities of life. We must plan now so that people of our generation and those of future generations will have the resources they need. People are a resource, too. If people lack food, housing, health care, and the chance to become productive members of society, there is great suffering, and human resources are wasted.

▶ **METHODS OF CONSERVATION**

There are many methods of conservation, and all of them are related. This is so because all the earth's resources—all the living and nonliving things in our surroundings—are linked together. (The story of this linkage is told in the article LIFE, WEBS OF, in

Three methods of conserving our resources. Above left: Children help sort metal cans at a center where cans are collected for recycling. Above right: Giant sequoia trees are protected in Sequoia National Park, California. Below: Contour plowing on hillsides is one important way of preventing soil erosion.

Here an oil spill at sea is being sprayed with chemically treated sand. The oil and sand mixture then sinks to the seafloor.

Volume L.) For this reason the conservation —or waste—of one resource directly affects another.

Water. Water is essential to life, but water must be clean to be of use. Often we use lakes and rivers—and especially the oceans— as sewers and dumping places for wastes of many kinds, some of them poisonous. Most bodies of water can absorb and recycle some wastes. But many have been overloaded, or polluted. Sewage treatment plants have helped in some cases, as have measures taken by industries to clean up waters that they have polluted. Accidental pollution from oil spills at sea is an increasing problem.

The best hope for conserving our lakes, rivers, and oceans seems to be informed and concerned citizens. They must take the lead, first in seeing that the waters of the world are protected by laws and then in seeing that the laws are obeyed.

There are many simple things that we as individuals can do to conserve water. We can turn off the tap while brushing our teeth. We can water lawns and gardens in the evening, when less moisture will evaporate. We can keep drinking water in the refrigerator so we will not have to run the faucet to get cold water. And we can fix leaky faucets. Untold quantities of water could be saved each year in these ways.

Soil. Perhaps our most important resource is soil. Topsoil, the uppermost layer of fertile soil, is the only type of soil that will produce high yields of food crops. It forms very slowly. As much as 100 years of careful management are needed to make 2.5 centimeters (1 inch) of good topsoil. Yet it can be quickly lost—eroded away by wind, rain, or flood. During the 1930's, overgrazing, poor farming practices, and years of drought stripped the grass from vast areas of the Great Plains in the United States. With no grass to hold it in place, precious topsoil was blown away. The area was known as the Dust Bowl until grass and trees were planted and reservoirs were built to hold water for irrigating the land.

Farmers can preserve soil in a number of ways. Contour plowing—plowing horizontally across slopes—helps prevent erosion by water. Planting of trees or bushes (hedgerows) between fields prevents erosion by wind. Planting different kinds of crops, rather than the same crop year after year, slows the loss of nutrients from soil.

Forests and Grasslands. Forests provide timber for building houses and making furniture, as well as wood for paper, chemicals, and many other products. As the population grows and demand for these things increases, forests are in danger of being overused.

Perhaps the most important forest conservation method is selective cutting. In selective cutting, only mature trees are cut down. Younger ones are left to grow, so that the forest can provide a continuous supply of timber. And individual large trees remain as homes for wildlife.

Grasslands provide food for livestock that are an important part of the world's food supply. When too many animals are permitted to graze in one area, the grass is devoured or trampled and never gets a chance to grow back. In the United States, federal agencies control the number of animals that are allowed to graze on public lands. In other parts of the world—particularly in Africa near the Sahara—the combination of overgrazing and drought has led to severe erosion and famine. The United Nations is helping African nations with conservation methods, including reseeding and land management.

Wildlife. The earth has more than 1,500,000 kinds, or species, of plants and animals. Part of the wildlife kingdom has already been lost, and a great many species are threatened. The

Threatened species. Above: The cheetah is nearly extinct in Asia. Below: Whooping cranes have become a symbol of the save-the-wildlife movement in North America.

Endangered Species List, started by the U.S. Government in 1969, contains about 600 animal species that are in danger of becoming extinct, or dying off. Once an animal or plant species is gone, it cannot be re-created. And we may never know what value it might have had in the web of life.

Uncontrolled killing, for profit or sport, was once the chief cause of extinction. Today laws regulate hunting and fishing in many countries. But other dangers to wildlife exist. As the population grows, more forests are cleared, and wildlife habitats are lost. New dams may threaten the existence of certain kinds of fish. A highway may cut some animals off from sources of food.

Conserving other natural resources helps to protect wildlife. If we use less paper, fewer trees will be cut down. If we use less electricity, fewer dams will be built. We can help to conserve wildlife directly, too— by obeying hunting and fishing laws, planting bushes and shrubs to provide food and shelter for wildlife, and putting out birdseed in winter and nesting boxes in spring.

Minerals. Many of the things we use—cars, bicycles, appliances—are made from metals. These metallic minerals took ages to form, and they are limited in supply.

In some cases, substitutes have been found for metals. For example, plastics are now used to make many things that were once made only of metal. Scientists are seeking ways to reduce waste in the processing of ores. Recycling also conserves minerals. If the metal in aluminum cans can be used again, less new ore will be mined.

The chief mineral fuels are the coal, oil, and gas that we burn to heat our homes, run our cars and factories, and provide electricity. Like the metals, they took millions of years to form, and supplies are limited. Some scientists think the world will run out of oil before alternate sources of energy can be developed. And as the population grows, the demand for energy increases.

There are many things that we can do to conserve energy. We can insulate our homes and regulate our thermostats to use less fuel. We can walk or bicycle to the store rather than ride in an automobile, and we can use trains and buses for longer trips. We can use fewer electric lights and no electric can openers or other gadgets. Such measures save energy without harming the quality of life.

Manufactured Goods. Think of all the manufactured items you use each day—furniture, baseballs, television sets, toys, books, clothes. It takes only a minute to make a long list. Manufactured goods must be conserved because they are the products of natural resources and energy. These resources are wasted when manufacturers make things that wear out quickly. Many containers, such as disposable soft drink bottles, are meant to be used once and then thrown away. In the United States, some states have banned disposable containers.

By repairing worn or broken articles, we could conserve the energy and resources needed to make new ones. We would also reduce the amount of garbage. Large cities create mountains of garbage each day, much of it unnecessarily. Many towns and cities have set up recycling centers where people bring bottles, aluminum cans, and newspapers, so that the materials they are made from can be reprocessed and used again.

▶ **CONSERVATION IN THE PAST**

Conservation is not a new concern of society. It has been an important part of civilization for many centuries. The farmers of China and Southeast Asia have used methods such as terrace farming for thousands of years to prevent soil erosion. The Romans realized that their coastal fisheries would be endangered if they drained the nearby wetlands where young fish were bred and grew.

In North America, the first conservationists were the Indians. They killed only the animals that they needed, and they wasted nothing. When European settlers came to North America, they found a continent of seemingly endless resources. They set out to use these resources to the fullest, and the new population grew and prospered. But many resources were overused and wasted.

Uncontrolled killing wiped out the Carolina parakeet, the passenger pigeon, and the Atlantic gray whale. By 1889 only a few hundred bison were left, compared to the millions a hundred years earlier. As cities and industries grew in the late 1800's, streams and rivers were dammed for waterpower or polluted by wastes.

By the early 1900's, many people in the United States were concerned about the waste of resources and the destruction of forests and places of scenic beauty or scientific or historic interest. Some conservationists and naturalists who were greatly concerned laid the foundations for the present system of national parks, forests, and wildlife refuges.

In the years that followed, many other countries established national parks. And conservation efforts of many kinds continued quietly until the 1960's and 1970's, when the growing population strained resources all over the world. The publicity given to massive oil spills from supertankers and to reports of the diminishing numbers of such animals as the tigers of India helped to increase interest in conservation.

▶ CONSERVATION TODAY

In spite of public concern about conservation, waste and pollution have continued. Population growth is only partly to blame. Technology has also played a part by enabling manufacturers to turn out an almost endless stream of products, from electric carving knives to snowmobiles. More wood, minerals, and energy are needed for increased production of manufactured goods. As a result, many countries have passed laws to conserve natural resources and protect the environment.

In the United States. The National Environmental Policy Act of 1969 requires the U.S. Government to prepare a study, called an environmental impact statement, before it begins any project. If the government wants to build a highway, for example, it must first study the effect that the highway will have on wildlife, soil, water, and other resources. Many state and local governments have passed similar laws. In 1977, Congress passed a law requiring strip-mine operators to restore the land that they mine to its original state.

These are only examples of specific governmental actions. Both the nation and the states long have had many special departments or agencies dealing with conservation. More recently, they have established environmental protection agencies to end or control pollution in the areas of air, water, solid wastes, noise, radiation, and poisonous substances.

A machine spreads and compacts rubbish, which will be covered with a layer of soil.

Elephants, long prized for their ivory tusks, are protected in Kenya, where big-game hunting is forbidden by law.

There are many private organizations that work to save threatened areas and conserve natural resources. One of the largest is the National Audubon Society, with over 400,000 members. Other private organizations include the American Forestry Association, Friends of the Earth, the National Wildlife Federation, and the Sierra Club.

Around the World. A number of United Nations agencies are co-ordinating conservation programs on a worldwide basis, and private conservation groups are active in many countries. The International Union for Conservation of Nature and Natural Resources is the oldest and largest such private organization. Its scientists research environmental problems in over a hundred countries.

Canada, like the United States, has a wide range of programs, agencies, and laws dealing with the management of natural resources and protection of the environment. Many areas of special beauty or interest are preserved in national and provincial parks.

Early settlers in Latin America wasted natural resources. But serious environmental problems did not occur until after World War II, when a tremendous growth in population strained natural resources. Many countries have since built irrigation projects to redevelop overused land. Countries in the Amazon region have agreed to protect part of the jungle by establishing parks.

Conservation treaties have been signed by many European countries. Nations that border the Mediterranean Sea have agreed to work together to clean up the water and prevent oil spills. Members of the European Economic Community have established pollution guidelines, and many countries have wildlife refuges. The countries of southern Europe, where many resources have been overused, are beginning conservation programs.

In southern Africa, several countries have developed programs to protect natural resources. South Africa and Kenya have systems of national parks, and Kenya has banned big-game hunting. In 1977 a U.N. conference on the spread of desert areas brought attention to northern Africa. Programs to stop this spread—including the planting of a "green belt" of trees in the northern Sahara—have been started. Egypt has begun to develop a series of parks along the banks of the Nile River.

In Asia, overgrazing, the cutting down of entire forests, and the killing of wildlife have left many countries with serious environmental problems. Conservation programs are difficult to enforce in some of these countries because the basic needs of their vast populations must often be met first. Some countries, such as Japan and India, have established national parks and wildlife refuges and are acting to conserve resources in various ways. In others, such as Cambodia, Thailand, and Vietnam, less has been done.

▶ **CAREERS IN CONSERVATION**

In the past, young people interested in careers in conservation were limited to forest, park, and wildlife management. Jobs in these fields are still available. But there are many other possibilities as well. There is a great need for specialists in the conservation of all forms of energy. Engineers are needed to develop new methods of recycling manufactured goods and using wastes. Soil conservationists are needed to study how soils are formed and how they can be made more productive. Lawyers are needed to help with the growing number of conservation regulations. Urban planners and landscape architects also contribute to conservation efforts.

A person who plans a career in conservation will find courses in basic science, mathematics, and ecology especially useful. A solid education is necessary because many conservation problems are very complex and highly technical.

GERARD A. BERTRAND
Chief, International Affairs
U.S. Fish and Wildlife Service

See also the articles listed in the Index under Conservation, Environment, and Pollution.

CONSTANTINE THE GREAT (280?–337)

The first Christian ruler of the ancient Roman Empire was Constantine I, who is known as Constantine the Great.

Constantine's full name was Flavius Valerius Aurelius Constantinus. He was born about A.D. 280 in the Roman province of Moesia (now part of Yugoslavia). His father, Constantius I, was a soldier and one of the rulers of the Roman Empire. As a boy young Constantine fought in Egypt and Persia. Later he joined his father's military campaign against the wild Picts of Britain. In 305 Constantius became emperor of the Western Roman Empire. When he died a year later, his soldiers acclaimed Constantine as the new western emperor.

But disputes arose over who was the legal emperor, and fighting broke out. Eventually two rivals were left—Constantine and Maxentius. In 312 Constantine marched on Rome to attack Maxentius. According to an ancient writer, on the night before the great battle, Constantine had a vision. He saw a flaming cross in the sky, and beneath it these words, in Latin: "By this sign thou shalt conquer."

Constantine accepted Christianity that night. The next day he defeated Maxentius and became emperor of the Western Roman Empire. A year later Constantine published the Edict of Milan, which gave all Romans religious freedom. Sunday became the day of worship. In 324 he defeated Licinius, emperor of the Eastern Roman Empire, becoming sole ruler of the Roman world.

In 325 Constantine ordered a meeting held at Nicaea, in Asia Minor, to settle a question that threatened to split the Christian Church: Was Jesus Christ actually divine? The Council of Nicaea decided that Christ was divine.

In 330 Constantine established a new capital in the East, Constantinople—"the city of Constantine." (Today the city is called Istanbul and is the largest city in Turkey.)

Constantine died in 337, and the Roman Empire was divided among his three sons, Constantine II, Constantius II, and Constans. Though the Western Empire fell to barbarian invaders in 410, the Eastern Empire, with Constantinople as its capital, lasted for over 1,000 years.

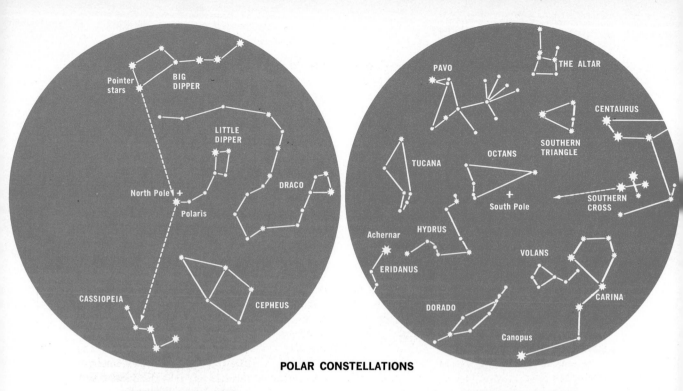

POLAR CONSTELLATIONS

NORTHERN HEMISPHERE   SOUTHERN HEMISPHERE

CONSTELLATIONS

To ancient peoples the earth was flat and the sky above their heads seemed an enormous dome. The sun moved across the dome by day and the moon moved across it by night. At night also, the inside surface of the dome was covered with stars. Many of the brightest stars were grouped in patterns. These groups are what we call **constellations,** a name that comes from a Latin word meaning "group of stars." In every ancient civilization men gave names to the constellations, calling them after gods and heroes, and after animals and familiar objects.

Very early, people noticed many other things about the stars.

For example, during the course of a year, the stars seemed to march in a great procession across the dome of heaven. Certain constellations always appeared above the eastern horizon in the spring of the year. These constellations were seen a little higher in the sky with every passing night. After several months they had traveled across the sky and disappeared below the western horizon. Spring constellations were followed by summer constellations. In the fall and winter, still other

constellations appeared in the sky. This great procession repeated itself year after year.

Within the procession 12 constellations were noticed in particular. The sun and the moon always rose and set within the part of the sky that held these 12. At the beginning of spring, for example, the sun rose in the part of the sky occupied by the constellation that we know as Aries, the Ram.

Also traveling among the stars of the 12 constellations were five moving lights known as the "wanderers." (We know these five wanderers as the planets Mercury, Venus, Mars, Jupiter, and Saturn. In fact, "planet" comes from a Greek word meaning "wanderer.")

Most of the 12 constellations were named for living things. And so the part of the sky through which the sun, the moon, and the planets traveled was named the **zodiac,** which meant "circle of living things" or "circle of animals." It was divided by the ancients into 12 sections, each named after one of the 12 constellations. We know these constellations as Taurus, the Bull; Aries, the Ram; Pisces,

... i-
... r-
... go,
... ab;

... the
... rent
... stern
... med

... of the
... miliar
... se 48
becaus... as the
"ancient" constellations. ... 's and
1600's, Europeans began to explore the earth.
To the south they discovered hundreds of
stars that had been unknown to the ancient
peoples. Later, astronomers grouped these
"new" stars into 40 constellations to which
they gave Latin names, since Latin was the
language of learning. These constellations are
known as the "modern" constellations. Thus,
all stars now belong to one constellation or
another.

Many of the brightest stars have names as
old as the names of the constellations them-
selves. Some of the stars were named by
Arabian astronomers who lived in ancient
Persia. A few of the stars with Arabic names
are Mizar, Hamal, and Deneb. Other stars
were given names by the ancient Greeks—Pol-
lux, Castor, and Procyon are three. We know
still others by their Latin names—Polaris,
Vega, Sirius, and Regulus are four.

All these bright stars were especially helpful
to early sailors and explorers. Today 57 of the
brightest stars in the sky are still used by sea
and air navigators.

▶ LOOKING AT THE CONSTELLATIONS

The ancients thought that the constellations
moved across the heavens. Actually it is the
earth that moves. But because we live on the
earth, we don't see its motions. What we see is
the **apparent movement** of the constellations
across the sky. Most of the constellations are
visible only during certain seasons of the year.
These are the seasonal constellations. Other
stars appear to circle over the North and
South poles throughout the year. These con-
stellations do not march from view. They are
called the polar constellations.

The Polar Constellations

There are three main polar constellations in
the Northern Hemisphere. Their names are
Ursa Major (meaning the "Great Bear"),
Ursa Minor (meaning the "Little Bear"), and
Cassiopeia, the Queen. If you can recognize
these constellations, you will then be able to
find all the others.

The best-known polar constellation in the
Northern Hemisphere is Ursa Major, which
contains the Big Dipper. If you know the Big
Dipper, you can find Polaris, the **North Star.**
Imagine a line drawn through two of the stars
that make up the cup of the Big Dipper (they
are called the "pointer stars") and extending
beyond them. The line will point to Polaris.

Polaris is the only star that does not appear
to move in the sky. This is because Polaris is
almost directly over the earth's axis.

Polaris is also part of the constellation
called Ursa Minor, known as the Little Dip-
per. Polaris is the star on the end of the handle
of the Little Dipper.

If the imaginary line from the pointer stars
is continued past Polaris, it leads to Cassio-
peia. Cassiopeia looks like the letter W.

People living in the Southern Hemisphere
see the polar constellations that circle over the
South Pole. The best known of these is Crux
Australis, the Southern Cross.

The Seasonal Constellations

Since at least two thirds of a hemisphere's
dome can be seen during the course of a night,
the seasonal constellations overlap. That is, a
winter constellation is also visible during late
fall and early spring.

The Winter Constellations.   The best-known
winter constellation is Orion, the Hunter. It is
one of the most easily recognized constella-
tions in the sky. Orion can be seen in the
southern part of the sky from most places in
the United States and Canada. It is readily
identified because of its line of the three bright
stars known as Orion's Belt. The three stars
are enclosed in a lopsided square made up of
four bright stars; the brighter two are called
Betelgeuse and Rigel.

If an imaginary line is drawn from the three
stars in Orion's Belt toward the west, it points
to the bright star called Aldebaran. Aldebaran
is part of the constellation named Taurus, the
Bull.

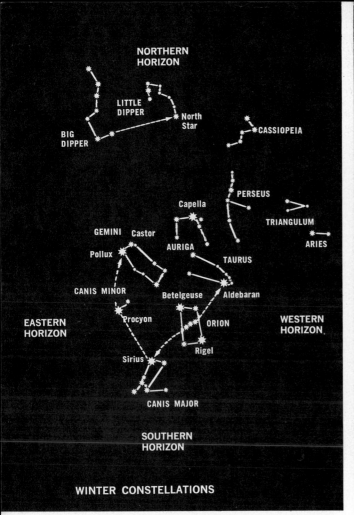

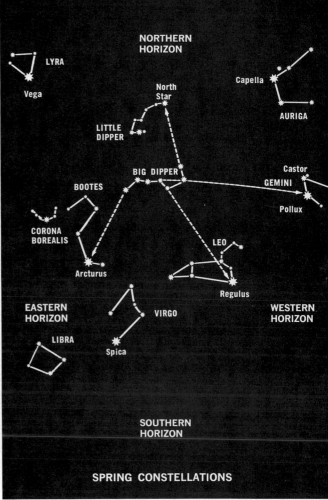

If the three stars in Orion's Belt are followed eastward, they point to a very bright star named Sirius, the Dog Star. Sirius is part of a constellation named Canis Major, which means the "Big Dog."

Follow an imaginary curved line from Sirius, and you will see two other bright stars, Procyon and Pollux. Procyon is part of a constellation named Canis Minor, which means "Little Dog." (The constellations Canis Major and Canis Minor are supposed to be the hunting dogs of Orion.) Pollux, farther to the northeast, belongs to the spring constellation named Gemini, the Twins.

The Spring Constellations. Gemini can be found in the spring by drawing an imaginary line from the two stars in the bowl of the Big Dipper. The two bright stars in Gemini are Pollux and Castor. Pollux is a little brighter than Castor.

The constellation that is best seen in the spring is Leo. Leo is easy to find because of the bright star, Regulus, in Leo's mane. To locate Regulus in the sky, draw an imaginary line from the two stars in the Big Dipper.

Another bright star in the spring sky is named Arcturus. Arcturus is part of the constellation Boötes, the Herdsman. The star can be found by drawing an imaginary line that continues the curve of the Big Dipper's handle.

Between Boötes and Leo, in the southern part of the sky, is the constellation Virgo. The bright star located in Virgo is called Spica.

The Summer Constellations. The brightest star in the summer sky is called Vega. Vega may be found by drawing an imaginary line from the two stars in the Big Dipper.

Vega is part of a constellation named Lyra, the Harp. Northeast of Vega is a constellation that resembles a cross; it is named Cygnus, the Swan. The bright star in Cygnus is called Deneb.

Just to the south of Lyra and Cygnus is a

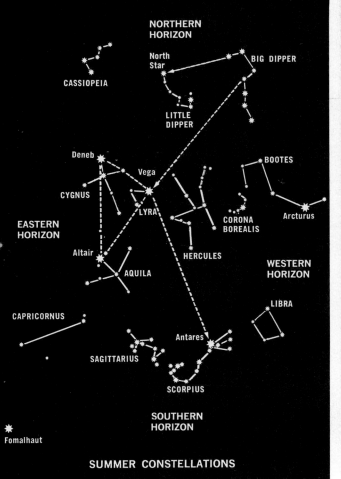

SUMMER CONSTELLATIONS

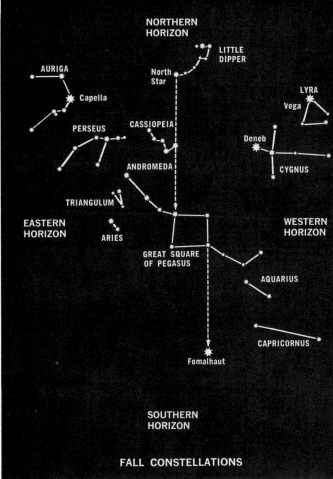

FALL CONSTELLATIONS

constellation named Aquila, the Eagle. The bright star in Aquila is called Altair.

These three stars—Vega, Deneb, and Altair—form a triangle. Once you have found this triangle in the sky, the rest of the summer stars will be easy to locate.

For example, if you draw an imaginary line southward from Deneb and Vega, you will find a bright, reddish star named Antares. Antares is part of the constellation Scorpius, which resembles a fishhook. The constellation is fairly low in the sky.

Although the Milky Way is visible throughout the year, it can be seen to the greatest advantage during the summer months. The Milky Way then appears overhead as a glowing band of light stretching from horizon to horizon.

The Fall Constellations. In the Northern Hemisphere fall is the poorest season of the year for viewing the sky. The summer constellations Lyra, Cygnus, and Aquila are still visible in the western sky, but the new constellations are not bright ones. There is only one new bright star, Fomalhaut. Fomalhaut can be located by drawing a line south from two of the stars that make up the Great Square of Pegasus.

Pegasus, the Winged Horse, is the best-known fall constellation. Its main feature, a square, can be found easily. Just draw an imaginary line from Polaris and through Cassiopeia. The line will point to one side of the square, called the Great Square of Pegasus.

The constellation Andromeda shares one of Pegasus' stars. Once Pegasus has been located, it is easy enough to find Andromeda.

Reviewed by GERALD S. HAWKINS
Center for Archeoastronomy
University of Maryland

See also ASTRONOMY; STARS.

CONSTITUTION, UNITED STATES. See UNITED STATES (Constitution of the United States of America).

CONSTRUCTION. See BUILDING CONSTRUCTION.

Consumer education helps people make wise choices when they are shopping.

CONSUMER EDUCATION

The main purpose of consumer education is to provide a better standard of living for all citizens. As working conditions improve and opportunities for employment increase, income levels rise. People have more money with which to buy the wide variety of products they need and want. Those interested in consumer problems are becoming more and more aware that there is a real need to teach shoppers how to use their money wisely in order to live well. In other words, consumer education is really a preparation for everyday living because it helps people to make intelligent choices. When consumers have proper knowledge and information, they are able to buy wisely, use money intelligently, and get greater satisfaction from their efforts.

There is another important reason for consumer education. As consumers, all citizens have certain rights as well as responsibilities, which they come to understand best through consumer education programs.

Only a few decades ago, there was little concern about consumers and their problems. The accepted attitude had generally been *caveat emptor,* which means "let the buyer beware." But great progress has been made in consumer education. Through special programs in the schools, as well as a vast body of new information, buyers of almost every kind of merchandise and service are learning how to make the best use of their money.

▶ WHAT IS A CONSUMER?

A consumer is anyone who buys or uses any kind of product. Consumers are important people, and they have real power. It is to their advantage to make use of this power to benefit themselves as well as for the welfare of all citizens.

Consumers buy things that are produced—automobiles, furniture, clothing, and food, for example. Consumers also make use of the skills of other people—plumbers, mechanics, teachers, and secretaries—all of whom provide the consumer with important services. These people receive payment for their services, and they, in turn, become consumers.

There are certain things that consumers should know about the purchasing process. First, they must understand what causes them to buy. Do they really need a particular product? Will it improve their standard of living or add to their pleasure? Are they buying it not so much because they really need it but because they have been persuaded by a skillful newspaper or television advertising campaign?

Once consumers have determined that they need a particular product, they should learn how to buy wisely. Before they shop, they should have a clear idea of the services they will expect the product to perform. By thinking of this in advance, they will be less likely to become victims of persuasive selling techniques. By studying the costs and the quality of various brands, they will be in a position to get the best value for the price they can pay.

Before making important purchases, consumers should follow a few simple rules. They should set up standards for the products they want to buy and then find out where to buy them at the best prices. They should make certain that they are not being misled by manufacturers' claims. Finally, they should go to dealers who are reliable and who are willing to stand behind their products.

It is a good policy for consumers to be cautious in all of their purchases. Greater caution may seem necessary if they are buying expensive items like automobiles and television sets. But wise buyers know that even in the purchase of their daily needs, they would do well to be informed and alert. Knowledge and care in shopping for household items can save them small sums that eventually add up to sizable amounts.

One of the ways in which consumers are likely to make mistakes is in choosing among packages (boxes or cans) of different sizes. Sometimes they are misled by labels such as "giant economy size." The contents of the large package actually may cost more per kilogram, or per unit, than the contents of the smaller packages of the same product. Shoppers tend to believe that large packages are always more economical. But this is not necessarily true. A wise shopper will find out the unit price of the product and then choose.

To help end the confusion caused by misleading labels and packaging, many stores have adopted unit-pricing systems. A shopper may decide that for convenience the large box is preferable, even though the price per unit is higher. But the shopper has all the facts needed to make an intelligent choice.

▶ THE GROWTH OF CONSUMER GROUPS

An important development is the tremendous growth of consumer groups all over the world. The largest of these groups is the International Organization of Consumers' Unions (IOCU), which was formed in 1960. The IOCU has member organizations throughout the world. Its purpose is to share ideas on subjects of interest to the consumer, from product testing to packaging and drug control. The IOCU also acts as consultant to agencies of the United Nations. Its headquarters are in The Hague.

Many groups operate on a national level. In the United States the Consumer Federation of America (CFA) and the group of organizations headed by consumer-rights advocate Ralph Nader work to bring the interests of consumers to the attention of government agencies. The Consumers Union of the United States is primarily a testing company. Its magazine, *Consumer Reports,* has close to 3,000,000 subscribers. The Consumers' Association of Great Britain publishes *Which?,* a magazine that has about 600,000 subscribers. There are similar organizations in Japan, West Germany, and many other countries. In some countries, consumer groups receive financial assistance from their governments.

▶ GOVERNMENTS AND THE CONSUMER

In many countries of the world, people are achieving a standard of living that enables them to buy more products. In some developing nations, where most people have been able to afford few products, incomes are rising, and new consumer markets are being created.

As a result of these steadily growing markets, governments are becoming more and more involved in consumers' problems. The huge numbers of items produced and offered to the public often make buying a confusing task. Many governments have set up special departments to reduce this confusion and guide and protect the consumer.

A number of federal, state, and local consumer agencies have been set up in the United States. Among the most important are divisions of the Department of Agriculture, the Federal Trade Commission, and the Department of Health and Human Services.

The meat inspection service of the Department of Agriculture seeks to prevent diseased meat from reaching the country's markets. Other services of the department include the grading of a wide variety of products and informing people about which foods are the most nutritious and least expensive.

The Federal Trade Commission in the United States guards against false advertising claims. It makes sure that labels are truthful and that no dangerous products are sold. The Federal Communications Commission monitors broadcasting practices.

Two divisions of the U.S. Department of Health and Human Services offer valuable aids. The Office of Consumer Affairs co-ordinates federal activities in the area of consumer protection. The Food and Drug Administration regulates the safety of foods, drugs, and cosmetics and controls chemical additives and pesticides. The Department of Education develops consumer education programs for use in the schools.

The U.S. Government publishes scores of books and pamphlets on consumer problems. These can be obtained by writing to the Superintendent of Documents, Washington, D.C., 20402.

In Canada, consumer affairs are handled on the federal level by the Department of Consumer and Corporate Affairs, which was established in 1968.

▶ **THE RESPONSIBILITY OF CONSUMERS**

As consumers, all citizens should be aware of their duties and their rights. They should encourage setting up programs on consumer education in the schools. They should report any improper practices that they are aware of. They should familiarize themselves with the various government agencies and consumer interest groups that can help them with their problems. And they should continually keep informed about current consumer information, so that they will always be able to make intelligent dollars-and-cents decisions.

ARTHUR A. NATELLA
Co-author, *The Consumer and His Dollars*

See also FOOD REGULATIONS AND LAWS.

CONTACT LENSES. See LENSES (Contact Lenses).

COOK, JAMES (1728–1779)

The sun had not yet come up in the morning of January 18, 1778, when the lookout on the British ship *Resolution* shouted "Land Ho!" He had spotted an island looming ahead, barely visible in the pale dawn light.

Captain James Cook, the *Resolution*'s commander, raised a telescope to his eye and took a closer look. Later that day, he wrote in his journal: "An island was discovered and soon after we saw more land . . . entirely detached from the first." The two islands Cook saw that day were Oahu and Kauai—part of the island chain we now know as Hawaii. And Captain Cook and his British sailors were the first Europeans known to have set foot there.

James Cook won fame and honor for his explorations and for his work as a navigator who used the latest scientific methods. Many consider him the greatest British explorer. Cook was born in Yorkshire, England, on October 27, 1728. His family was poor, and young James had to limit his education and go to work when he was only 12 years old. After serving as an apprentice for a shipping company, he joined the Royal Navy as an ordinary seaman. An intelligent and ambitious young

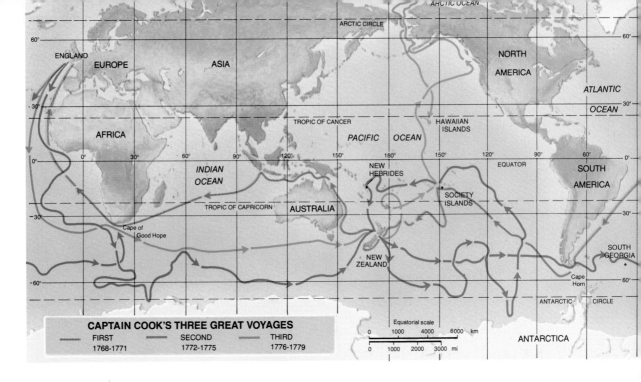

CAPTAIN COOK'S THREE GREAT VOYAGES

FIRST	SECOND	THIRD
1768-1771	1772-1775	1776-1779

Equatorial scale

0   1000   4000   6000   km

0   1000   2000   3000   mi

man, Cook was promoted quickly. By 1759, he was the master of his own ship.

Cook studied mathematics, astronomy, and geography in his spare time. Because of his scientific knowledge, he was chosen to lead an expedition to the Pacific. His mission was to observe the planet Venus passing between the earth and the sun, a rare occurrence. But Cook also carried secret orders to look for new lands in the South Pacific that could be settled as British colonies.

Cook's ship, H.M.S. *Endeavour,* left England in the summer of 1768, sailed around Cape Horn, and reached the island of Tahiti, in the Society Islands, a year later. Cook and the scientists who were with him observed the passage of Venus. Cook then went on to map and explore the coasts of New Zealand.

Early in 1770, Cook reached the previously uncharted east coast of Australia. He claimed the territory for Britain and named it New South Wales. When he returned to England, he won praise for his achievements and was promoted to captain.

Besides finding new lands, Cook helped to improve the lot of sailors. Their living quarters were often dirty and infested with rats. Cook required his men to bathe regularly and keep the ship clean. He had them eat fresh vegetables and fruit to prevent scurvy, a disease caused by lack of vitamin C.

In 1772, Cook once again put out to sea. His two ships, the *Resolution* and the *Adventure,* headed for the southern oceans where some scientists predicted an undiscovered continent would be found. There was no southern continent, as Cook proved by sailing into the frigid waters below the Antarctic Circle. But he discovered New Caledonia and Norfolk Island, south of New Hebrides. And his ships were the first to cross the Antarctic Circle.

Cook sailed on his third and final voyage in 1776. It was during this voyage that he came upon the Hawaiian Islands, which he named the Sandwich Islands in honor of his patron, the Earl of Sandwich. Cook claimed the islands for George III of England, although Polynesians had discovered them centuries earlier.

From Hawaii, Cook moved up the west coast of North America as far as the Bering Strait and the Arctic Ocean. Only when his way was blocked by solid ice did he turn back. Late in 1778, he returned to Hawaii. There, on February 14, 1779, he was killed during an argument with some islanders who he believed had stolen one of his small boats. It was a tragic ending to the life of one of the greatest seagoing explorers of all time.

HENRY I. KURTZ
Author, *John and Sebastian Cabot*

CALVIN COOLIDGE (1872–1933)

30TH PRESIDENT OF THE UNITED STATES

COOLIDGE, CALVIN. For Americans July 4 marks Independence Day. For John and Victoria Coolidge of Plymouth Notch, Vermont, July 4, 1872, also marked the birth of a son. Their son, John Calvin Coolidge, was to become the 30th president of the United States.

▸ THE COOLIDGES OF PLYMOUTH NOTCH

Calvin Coolidge's ancestors came to America from England in about 1630. The first Coolidge to live in Plymouth Notch was John Coolidge of Massachusetts, a soldier in the Revolutionary War, who settled there in the 1780's. The Coolidges were hard-working farmers and storekeepers. Some of Calvin's ancestors had been deacons in the community church and served in local political offices. Calvin's father had been elected to the Vermont legislature. Their ideals of honesty, thrift, and hard work were passed down from generation to generation. And young Calvin was brought up to believe in these ideals.

During the late 1870's and 1880's, the United States was rapidly changing into a nation of cities and factories. But these changes did not affect Plymouth Notch, which was nestled in the peaceful Green Mountains of Vermont. As late as 1923 Calvin's father's house had no electricity. When Calvin Coolidge took the oath of office as president there, he took it by the light of an oil lamp.

▸ "SILENT CAL"

Young Calvin helped with the chores on the farm and went to the one-room village school. When he was 13, he entered Black River Academy, at Ludlow, Vermont. In 1891 he was admitted to Amherst College, in Massachusetts.

Coolidge was not a brilliant student at Amherst, but he studied hard and in 1895 he was graduated with honors. He did well as a debater and public speaker, and was chosen as one of the speakers at his graduation. In private conversation, however, he was a man of few words. His nickname of "Silent Cal" was well earned. There is a story that a man once bet a friend that he could make Cal say at least *three* words in a conversation. When the man met Coolidge he told him of the bet. All Coolidge said was, "You lose."

After graduation Coolidge decided to become a lawyer. He went to work in a law office in Northampton, Massachusetts, and studied for the bar examination. Although 3 years of study were required, he passed the examination after less than 2 years.

In 1898, at the age of 25, Coolidge opened his own law office in Northampton. He kept a careful account of his earnings and noted that in his first year of practice he earned $500.

Coolidge's upbringing made him place great emphasis on thrift. He never owned an automobile and, until he retired from the presidency, he never owned his own home. In later years he liked to remark that there were two ways to be self-respecting: "To spend less than you make, and to make more than you spend." Coolidge always spent less than he made.

▶ EARLY POLITICAL CAREER

Coolidge had shown some interest in politics at college, and he soon began to take an active part in Northampton politics. He worked hard for the Republican Party, and in 1898 he was elected to his first office—city councilman.

In 1906 Coolidge was elected to the Massachusetts House of Representatives. He was a conservative in politics and did not trust reformers. But he did vote for two reform resolutions that later became amendments to the United States Constitution. One resolution called for the direct election of United States senators by the people (senators were then elected by the state legislatures). The other gave women the right to vote.

After two terms in the legislature, Coolidge returned to Northampton. In 1909 he was elected mayor. With his goal of thrifty government, Coolidge lowered taxes and reduced the city debt. At the same time he was able to raise the pay of many city employees.

While in Northampton, Coolidge met Grace Goodhue, a teacher at a school for the deaf. They were married in 1905 and had two sons. Mrs. Coolidge was gay and full of fun—just the opposite of her quiet, careful husband.

▶ GOVERNOR OF MASSACHUSETTS

In 1911 Coolidge returned to the legislature as a state senator. His re-election to a second and third term in the Senate made him an important figure in state politics. In 1915 he was elected lieutenant governor, and 3 years later he became governor of Massachusetts.

The Boston Police Strike. In 1919 an event occurred that made Governor Coolidge a national figure. On September 9, 1919, most of the Boston police force went on strike for higher pay. For 2 days there was rioting and robbery in the city of Boston. Finally, in response to the mayor's call for help, Coolidge called out the National Guard, and order was restored. In reply to a plea for sympathy for the striking policemen, Coolidge issued his

Left, Calvin Coolidge as a student at Amherst College in 1895. Right, as governor of Massachusetts, with Mrs. Coolidge and their sons, Calvin (*left*), and John (*right*).

President and Mrs. Coolidge on the way to his inauguration in 1925. Senator Charles Curtis is at right.

Above, President Coolidge opens the baseball season by throwing out the first ball. Below, the President celebrating a western-style Fourth of July at Rapid City, S.D.

famous statement: "There is no right to strike against the public safety by anybody, anywhere, any time." He became a national hero and a symbol of law and order.

In the 1920 Republican Party convention, Senator Warren G. Harding won the nomination as candidate for president. When one of the delegates suggested Coolidge's name for vice-president, the cry of "We want Coolidge" rang out through the convention hall. Coolidge became the vice-presidential candidate, and in the election of 1920 Harding and Coolidge won an overwhelming victory.

▶ PRESIDENT

On the morning of August 3, 1923, Vice-President Coolidge was in Plymouth, visiting his father, when the news of Harding's death reached him. Coolidge was now president of the United States. His father, a notary public, administered the oath of office to him.

Soon after Coolidge entered the White House, the scandals of Harding's administration came to public attention. The worst was the Teapot Dome oil scandal, which involved members of Harding's cabinet. Secretary of the Interior Albert B. Fall went to jail for his part in the affair, and Secretary of the Navy Edwin Denby was forced to resign. Attorney General Harry M. Daugherty was involved in another scandal and almost went to jail. Coolidge was never connected with the scandals, and his reputation helped to save the Republican Party from disgrace.

Coolidge was so popular that he had no trouble winning the election of 1924. His campaign slogan was "Keep Cool with Coolidge," and he received almost twice as many popular votes as his Democratic opponent, John W. Davis.

The Roaring 20's

Calvin Coolidge was president during one of the most colorful periods in American history. The 1920's are often called the Roaring 20's and the Jazz Age. It was the era of Prohibition. The Volstead Act, the 18th amendment to the Constitution, had made the sale of alcoholic beverages illegal. But many people ignored this highly unpopular law and purchased liquor from "bootleggers" or in "speakeasies." The most notorious of the bootleggers was a man who helped make the word "gangster" a part of the language—Al Capone.

But the 20's were more than an era of bootleg liquor and gangsters. The 19th amendment to the Constitution gave women throughout the United States the right to vote. Charles A. Lindbergh became the first man to fly nonstop and alone across the Atlantic Ocean. The first talking movie, *The Jazz Singer,* starring Al Jolson, was produced. It was a golden age of sports. Babe Ruth was hitting home runs, and Gene Tunney defeated Jack Dempsey for the heavyweight boxing championship of the world.

During the 1920's the population of the United States grew from less than 106,000,000 to almost 123,000,000. And for the first time in American history, more people lived in cities and towns than in rural areas. The country seemed prosperous, and everybody wanted to have a good time and not worry too much about tomorrow.

Coolidge's Popularity

Coolidge was popular because the people saw him as a symbol of the prosperous times. They also admired his old-fashioned virtues of thrift and common sense. As president he was conservative in his views on economics. He did not believe in government interference in private business. However, his support of a high protective tariff, or tax on goods imported into the United States, aided American business. With his respect for thrift, Coolidge worked to limit government spending, to reduce the national debt, and to lower taxes. But, though there was prosperity, not everybody shared in it. Many industrial workers were paid low wages, and farmers were hard hit by declining prices on their crops. A bill to raise the prices of farm products was vetoed by Coolidge.

Foreign Affairs

Coolidge took little interest in foreign affairs. He opposed the United States's joining the League of Nations, an organization similar to the United Nations. He did favor American membership in the World Court. But Congress' insistence on certain conditions before approving membership, and Coolidge's lack of real enthusiasm kept the United States out of the Court. The Kellogg-Briand Pact, an American and French plan to outlaw war, met with more success. It was signed by the United States and 14 other nations in 1928.

Coolidge showed more concern about Latin American matters. Revolutions in Nicaragua prompted him to send 5,000 marines to that country to protect American lives and business interests. When relations between Mexico and the United States became strained in a dispute over oil lands, the president appointed Dwight W. Morrow ambassador to Mexico. Morrow succeeded in improving relations between the two countries.

▶ COOLIDGE LEAVES THE WHITE HOUSE

Many people thought that Coolidge would run again for president. He surprised the nation when he said: "I do not choose to run for president in 1928." In the election of 1928, Herbert Hoover became president.

Some historians and economists have criticized Coolidge for a lack of forcefulness and political leadership. They say that his administration was partly responsible for the Great Depression that began in 1929, soon after President Hoover took office. However, during the 1920's most Americans supported Coolidge's policies.

After Coolidge left the White House, he returned to quiet Northampton, where he spent the remaining years of his life. He wrote articles for a newspaper, giving his opinion on current events and politics, and he published his autobiography. On January 5, 1933, he died suddenly of a heart attack.

DAVID M. REIMERS
Brooklyn College

IMPORTANT DATES IN THE LIFE OF CALVIN COOLIDGE

1872	Born in Plymouth Notch, Vermont, July 4.
1895	Graduated from Amherst College.
1897	Became a lawyer in Northampton, Massachusetts.
1898	Elected city councilman in Northampton.
1905	Married Grace Goodhue.
1907–1908	Served in the Massachusetts legislature.
1910–1911	Mayor of Northampton.
1912–1915	Massachusetts state senator.
1916–1918	Lieutenant governor of Massachusetts.
1919–1920	Governor of Massachusetts.
1920	Elected vice-president of the United States.
1923	Became 30th president of the United States upon the death of President Warren G. Harding, August 3.
1924	Elected to a full term as president.
1929	Retired from the presidency.
1933	Died in Northampton, Massachusetts, January 5.

COOPER, JAMES FENIMORE (1789–1851)

James Fenimore Cooper, the author of the first outstanding American novel, was born on September 15, 1789, in Burlington, New Jersey. He soon moved with his family to Cooperstown, New York, a settlement established by his father on the edge of the frontier.

James lived so close to the wilderness that he learned firsthand about the frontier and the life of the woods. He attended a village school and was tutored by a rector in Albany before he entered Yale in 1803. But he took his college studies so lightly that he was dismissed in his third year. He then went to sea and received a commission as midshipman. But after his marriage to Susan De Lancey, he resigned in 1811 to take up the life of a gentleman farmer.

One day when Cooper was reading a novel aloud to his wife, he said he could write a better one. She challenged him to do it. In 1820 he produced *Precaution,* a novel set in England. It was not successful, but Cooper tried again. He had read Sir Walter Scott's historical novels about England. He knew that American history could be just as exciting. In 1821 he wrote *The Spy,* a story of the American Revolution. It was an immediate success.

Cooper was also inspired by Scott to write *The Pilot* (1823), the first of his many novels about the sea. In 1839, he wrote *History of the Navy of the United States.*

But Cooper is best known for his wilderness scout Natty Bumppo, also called Hawkeye, who is introduced in *The Pioneers* (1823). Hawkeye's friend Uncas, a Mohican, is one of the heroes of *The Last of the Mohicans* (1826). It is among the most famous books in American literature. In *The Prairie* (1827), Hawkeye is an old man in the West. In *The Pathfinder* (1840), he is middle-aged. *The Deerslayer* (1841) tells of his first adventures. The five novels are known as the Leatherstocking Tales.

Cooper loved his country. But he feared that democracy would not work until everyone was better educated. He argued his unpopular ideas in his writings. He died in Cooperstown on September 14, 1851.

JEROME H. STERN
Florida State University

COOPER, PETER (1791–1883)

Peter Cooper was an inventor and manufacturer whose interest in new developments helped to start industry in the United States. He became very wealthy. Today he is remembered as a highly successful business leader, as well as a philanthropist—one who uses personal wealth to help other people.

Cooper was born in New York City on February 12, 1791. By the time he was 16, he had worked with his father as a hatter, a brewer, a store clerk, and a brickmaker. His only mechanical training came from working as an apprentice to a carriage maker and then in a factory that made cloth-cutting machines.

When Cooper was in his 20's, he bought a glue factory. Soon he supplied the glue for most of the United States. Later he became the owner of a number of iron and steel mills. The first iron for fireproofing buildings was rolled in Cooper's ironworks.

Cooper worked out the design of the first locomotive built in the United States. It was so small that it was called the "Tom Thumb." In 1830, the "Tom Thumb" was entered in a race against a horse. At first the machine puffed along in the lead. But mechanical trouble stopped the engine, and the horse won. Still, "Tom Thumb" had traveled at the surprisingly fast speed of 25 kilometers (15 miles) an hour. It helped prove that locomotives were practical.

Cooper was one of the early leaders in the fight for a public school system. He believed in education not just for the rich but for everyone. In 1859 he founded Cooper Union in New York City. This institution still provides free instruction in the arts and sciences.

In 1876 the Greenbacks, a reform party, made Cooper their candidate for president of the United States. This was a fitting tribute to his interest in the welfare of others. He died in New York City on April 4, 1883.

Reviewed by DAVID C. COOKE
Author, *Inventions That Made History*

CO-OPERATIVES

The word "co-operate" means "to work together." Sometimes people work together to buy or sell something or to solve a problem better and at less cost than they could separately. They form a business that is called a co-operative.

Co-operatives are all around you. The milk, eggs, meat, and fruit on your table may be marketed through a farmer co-operative. You may wear clothes made of wool or cotton woven by a co-operative. One co-operative makes denim for jeans. Your family may live in a co-operative apartment, shop at a co-operative store, or borrow money through a credit union.

▶ TYPES OF CO-OPERATIVES

Co-operatives formed to obtain goods or services are usually called consumer co-operatives. ("Consumer" means "user.") Many consumer co-operatives are organized to buy goods such as food or gasoline. Farmers often form co-operatives to obtain supplies.

In a housing co-operative, members jointly own an apartment building. Other consumer co-operatives are formed to obtain services, such as insurance. A medical co-operative is a plan under which members receive health care. In rural areas, people often form co-operatives to bring electric or telephone service to their homes. Credit unions are co-operatives that grant loans to members. Farmers obtain loans through farm credit associations.

When people join together to produce or sell something, they form producer or marketing co-operatives. Co-operative farms are common in some countries, such as Israel. Members share the work and divide the profits. In the United States and many other countries, farmers set up co-operatives to process or market what they produce individually.

▶ HOW CO-OPERATIVES WORK

Suppose that students at your school want to buy supplies at the lowest possible prices. They decide to set up a co-operative store. They sell membership shares to raise the money needed to start the store, and they elect a board of directors and agree on rules for the store. A manager is put in charge of the business. The store buys supplies in large quan-

A worker bags oats at a farmer co-operative. Farmers form co-operatives to buy supplies and sell products.

tities directly from the companies that make them. It pays wholesale prices. The supplies are resold, to members and nonmembers alike, at prices high enough to cover the cost of operating the store.

Most co-operatives have rules adapted from those set up in the 1800's by an early co-operative in Rochdale, England:

(1) Anyone may join, by buying shares in and making use of the co-operative. Members are also free to leave.
(2) Members control the co-operative by voting on issues and electing officers.
(3) Interest rates on the money that members have invested are limited.
(4) Earnings are used to improve the business or are returned to members. The earnings are divided among the members according to how much each has used the co-operative.

Other practices begun in Rochdale are also widely followed. For example, goods are sold at current market prices. And many co-operatives use some of their funds to tell the public about the co-operative movement.

▶HISTORY OF CO-OPERATIVES

The idea of working together to produce, sell, and obtain goods and services goes back to the earliest times. But co-operatives as we know them began to be formed in the 1700's. A group of Scottish weavers formed one of the first British co-operatives, in 1769, to obtain handicraft supplies. In the United States a co-operative creamery was formed in Connecticut in the early 1800's. Co-operative aid societies and fire insurance companies were also formed.

The Rochdale co-operative, formed in 1844, was most influential. Its members opened a co-operative store to obtain food at low prices. By 1860 there were several thousand members. Many co-operatives were soon formed elsewhere in Europe and in North America.

In the United States the number of farmer co-operatives increased greatly after 1900.

One reason was the passage of the Capper-Volstead Act, in 1922. This federal law recognized the farmers' right to form co-operatives. Today five out of six U.S. farmers use co-operatives to sell their products and obtain supplies, credit, and services. Farmer co-operatives have grown into large associations with thousands of members. Most of Canada's wheat is marketed through large co-operatives called wheat pools. And large U.S. co-operatives sell fruit, dairy products, and other goods under brand names known all over the country. The number of consumer co-operatives in towns and cities has also increased.

There are co-operatives in all parts of the world. They have been very successful in Europe, especially in Scandinavia and other parts of Western Europe. In Japan, India, and other Asian countries, many successful co-operatives have been formed in the fishing and handicraft industries, as well as in farming.

CAROL L. JAMES
Cooperative League of the USA

COPERNICUS, NICOLAUS (1473–1543)

Nicolaus Copernicus worked out a system of astronomy showing that the planets orbit the sun.

Nicolaus Copernicus is thought of as the founder of modern astronomy. He was born in Torun, Poland, on February 19, 1473. Little is known about his early life except that his father died when Nicolaus was 10 and he was adopted by an uncle, who was a Catholic bishop.

Copernicus went to the university in Cracow. There he studied such subjects as Latin, mathematics, and astronomy. It was probably at this time that he changed his Polish name, Niklas Koppernigk, to the Latin form of Nicolaus Copernicus.

In 1496, Copernicus went to Italy, where he spent the next ten years at various universities. He studied medicine, obtained a degree in canon (church) law, and pursued his interest in astronomy. While at Bologna, he found in Professor Domenico da Novara someone with whom he could discuss his growing doubt about the way in which the scholars of his time viewed the universe.

Copernicus questioned the system of astronomy that had been put forth 1,400 years earlier by Ptolemy of Alexandria and was still upheld not only by scholars but also by the Church. This system viewed the earth as the center of the universe, and all things—the sun, the stars, and the planets—were thought to be moving around the earth.

Using mathematics and logic, Copernicus concluded that Ptolemy's system was wrong. For one thing it could not account for the motion of the planets as they seemed to go back and forth across the sky. So Copernicus worked out a different system that accounted for their movements. It was his view that all of the planets, including the earth, move through space in orbits around the sun. He also concluded that while the earth is traveling through space, it is revolving on an axis once every 24 hours. This rotation accounts for the apparent movement of the sun and stars rising and setting each day.

Copernicus did not announce his findings because he did not want to quarrel with the official position of the Church. In fact, he was a staff member of the Cathedral of Frauenburg (now Frombork), a post he held until his death. Still, despite his dedication to the Church, he could not stop thinking about earth's place in the universe. So he submitted his ideas in unsigned, handwritten form to other scholars. Finally he allowed his work to be published. His great book, *On the Revolutions of the Heavenly Bodies,* appeared at the very end of his life. Legend says that Copernicus saw the first copy on the day he died, May 24, 1543.

Copernicus had expected his book to cause an uproar. But it caused none. Because the book was highly technical, almost no one could understand it. Still, some scholars did read the book, among them Galileo and Kepler. Its influence on them was great. They realized that Copernicus' view of the universe was the correct one, and they carried on his work. The theories Copernicus developed became the basis for the science of modern astronomy.

JOHN S. BOWMAN
Author and science editor

See also ASTRONOMY; SOLAR SYSTEM.

COPLAND, AARON (1900–   )

The composer Aaron Copland is known as a leading writer of 20th-century music. He has written successfully in many different styles and has helped to make American music known and respected abroad. He is also a pianist, teacher, conductor, and author of many articles and books about music.

Copland was born in Brooklyn, New York, on November 14, 1900, the son of Jewish immigrants. He learned to play the piano from an older sister. In high school he began to study harmony, counterpoint, and composition. At the age of 20, he went to Paris, for more advanced study of music.

Copland returned to New York in 1924. His first compositions reflected his European training. But he soon introduced American jazz elements into works such as *Music for the Theater* (1925). In the 1930's he became concerned about composing music that would appeal to a large public. He began to simplify his music and to adapt popular folk rhythms. *El Salón México* (1936), based on Mexican popular tunes, was an immediate success. His ballet scores—*Billy the Kid* (1938), *Rodeo* (1942), and *Appalachian Spring* (1944)—were even more popular. One of his best-known works on an American theme is *A Lincoln Portrait* (1942), based on the Gettysburg Address.

Copland reached a somewhat different audience with *The Second Hurricane* (1936), an opera for children, "with a chorus of parents." In the 1940's he wrote the scores for several films, including *The Red Pony* (1948). He later made use of the "twelve-tone method" of composition developed by Arnold Schoenberg. But his major works of this period, *Connotations* (1962) and *Inscape* (1967), were not so popular as his earlier works.

From 1940 to 1965, Copland taught composition at the Berkshire Music Center (Tanglewood) near Lenox, Massachusetts. He tried to encourage wider understanding of modern music through his writings. Later he devoted much of his time to conducting and helping younger musicians.

DIKA NEWLIN
Author, *Bruckner-Mahler-Schoenberg*

COPPER

Copper is one of our most plentiful metals and is used often in our daily lives. Copper wiring carries electricity for lights, radios, television sets, and air conditioners. Copper wire is also an important part of electric motors and generators. Copper tubing and pipe is used in plumbing. Many parts of airplanes, missiles, automobiles and satellites are made of copper. Copper sulfate is used in plant sprays and to keep algae from growing in swimming pools. It is used in electroplating and in some batteries. It can be combined with other metals to form alloys. The most common copper alloys are bronze (copper and tin) and brass (copper and zinc). Copper is also used in art.

Special qualities of copper make it a useful metal. It conducts heat and electricity better than any other metal except silver. It is very malleable (easy to shape) and ductile (easy to draw into wire). Copper is also durable. A piece of copper pipe used by the ancient Egyptians more than 5,000 years ago is still in good condition. Its resistance to corrosion makes copper an important metal for automobile brake systems and radiators, gas and oil lines, plumbing pipes, boiler tubing, and roof coverings.

Copper is found in nature in two forms—as "native copper" (the metal itself) and in mineral ores (combined with other elements). There are more than 160 known mineral ores that contain copper.

About half of the world's copper supply is found in a bright yellow mineral called **chalcopyrite.** This ore, which is often called copper pyrite, is a compound of copper, iron, and sulfur. It contains 34.5 percent copper. One of the richest copper ores is dark gray **chalcocite,** sometimes known as copper glance, which contains almost 80 percent copper. Other important and colorful copper ores are cuprite, malachite, and azurite.

Copper is used in greater amounts than any metal except iron and aluminum. Close to 1,500,000 tons of copper are used by U.S. industries every year. About half of this copper is used by the electrical industry.

Copper was given its name by the ancient Romans, who called it *aes Cyprium* ("metal of Cyprus"), and later *cuprum.* The island of Cyprus was the chief source of copper for the Romans.

The first Europeans who went to the New World found Indian people using copper for jewelry and decoration. Indian people got much of their copper from the region around Lake Superior.

The copper industry began early in the United States. A copper mine was established in Lynn, Massachusetts, in 1664. Many new deposits of copper were discovered in Michigan during the mid-19th century. Later, prospectors in search of gold in the West uncovered some of the richest veins of copper in the United States. These formed the basis of today's copper mining.

There are small deposits of copper scattered all over the world, but most of the world's copper comes from five main areas. These are the Rocky Mountain and Great Basin regions of the United States; the Andes mountains, in Peru and northern Chile; Zaïre and Zambia, in Africa; central Canada and northern Michigan; and the Ural Mountains, in the Soviet Union. In the United States about 95 percent of the copper deposits are located in six states—Arizona, Utah, Montana, Nevada, New Mexico, and Michigan.

About two thirds of the copper used each year in the United States comes from the mines. The rest is obtained by melting down scrap copper. Discarded copper objects and copper parts from buildings and worn-out machinery are sources for this "secondary" copper. The re-use of old copper helps assure an abundant supply of the metal.

ROBERT C. CARMODY
Copper and Brass Research Association

See also ALLOYS; BRONZE AND BRASS; METALS AND METALLURGY; TOOLS.

COPRA. See COCONUT.

FACTS ABOUT COPPER

CHEMICAL SYMBOL: Cu.

ATOMIC WEIGHT: 63.54.

SPECIFIC GRAVITY: 8.9 (nearly 9 times as heavy as water).

COLOR: reddish brown (pink when freshly made).

PROPERTIES: soft and easily shaped, becoming hard when cold-worked; good conductor of electricity and heat; forms compounds that are easily broken down; resists corrosion by atmosphere and sea water.

OCCURRENCE: sometimes found in nature as a metal; usually occurs in various bright-colored minerals in igneous rocks.

CHIEF ORE: chalcopyrite (a compound of copper, iron, and sulfur).

COPYRIGHT

Copyrights protect the rights of creative people. Writers, artists, filmmakers, composers of music, and developers of computer programs all hold copyrights on their works. This gives them the legal right to decide how and when their works should be published or performed. No one can reproduce the copyrighted works without their permission.

The United States has had copyright laws since 1790. In 1978 a new copyright law went into effect. Under it, the creator of a work can obtain a copyright without waiting for the work to be published. In most cases the copyright continues for 50 years after the creator's death. If the work was commissioned by an employer, the employer may hold the copyright. Such a copyright lasts for 75 years from the date of publication or for 100 years from the date of creation, whichever is shorter.

Permission to use a copyrighted work is usually granted on payment of a fee. Every time a disc jockey plays a song on the radio, the authors of the words and music must be paid. When a play is performed, the producer must pay the playwright. Authors of books receive payments for all copies of books that are sold. These payments are called royalties.

Using copyrighted material without permission is a form of stealing. The owner of the copyright can sue someone who does this. But there are exceptions to the law. Films and plays may be presented for educational purposes if tickets are not sold. Teachers may make a few copies of a work for class use, but whole books may not be copied in this way.

Many countries have copyright laws. But the laws of one country do not protect authors if their work is used in other countries. Two treaties provide such protection. They are the Bern Convention of 1891 and the Universal Copyright Convention of 1952.

The symbol © or the word "copyright" appears on all copies of a copyrighted work. In a book this notice is usually on the back of the title page. Look for it in this volume.

JESSICA DAVIDSON
Attorney

See also PATENTS; PUBLISHING; TRADEMARKS.

CORALS

A chunk of coral is made of the skeletons of tiny marine animals called coral polyps. The polyp's skeleton grows outside its body. Cup-shaped, it both protects and supports the polyp's body and grows as the animal grows. When the polyp dies, the skeleton is left. Coral reefs and islands are formed of billions upon billions of these tiny skeletons.

▶CORAL POLYPS

Coral polyps belong to a group of animals called coelenterates. The two main kinds of coelenterates are jellyfish and polyps. Jellyfish float freely; polyps live attached to the sea bottom, to rocks or to one another.

The coral polyp has a soft, hollow, tube-shaped body with an opening at the top. Around the opening are fingerlike tentacles, which can be drawn inside the cup or extended into the water. With its waving tentacles, the coral polyp captures small sea animals that drift within its reach. Each tentacle has poison stingers that paralyze the

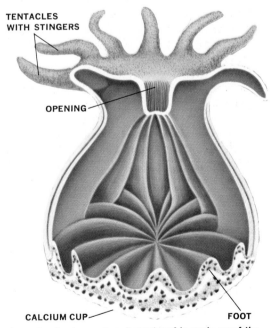

A coral animal, or polyp. A coral reef is made up of the skeletons (calcium cups) of billions of polyps.

prey as the tentacles push it into the opening. The waving tentacles look like flower blossoms. That is one reason why people long thought that corals were plants, not animals.

At the other end of the polyp's body is a round foot. It is anchored to the cup, or skeleton, into which the polyp can withdraw. The cup consists mainly of calcium, made and given off by the polyp's body, and is covered by living tissue. Food eaten by the polyp may cause the skeleton to be tinted pink or red.

Polyps hatch from eggs. They swim about briefly and then settle down, usually in a coral colony. When they join the colony, they start making their skeletons.

A coral colony consists of living corals. Each is attached to a solid base, such as a rock or the skeletons of earlier generations.

▶CORAL REEFS

Coral colonies are found in all the earth's seas. But reef-building coral polyps are found only in warm, shallow waters; a depth of about 46 meters (150 feet) is best for them. Yet in some parts of the world, coral reefs rise from great ocean depths.

How could those coral reefs have formed? The person who solved the riddle was Charles Darwin, the famous naturalist.

Darwin knew that the earth's surface changes. Mountains are forced up in one place; in another the earth's crust sinks. Studying coral reefs, he noted three kinds: fringing reefs, barrier reefs, and atolls (rings of coral). Putting all this information together, he worked out the following theory.

A volcanic island forms where an undersea volcano rises above the surface of the water. In the shallow waters of the island shores, corals build a fringing reef. As time passes the volcano becomes cold and dead; it begins to sink back into the sea. The fringing reef is now separated from the island by a wider channel, and it goes on growing; it has become a barrier reef. If the volcano sinks completely and vanishes, only the coral reef is left; it has become an atoll, a ring of coral surrounding a lagoon.

Today's scientists have broadened Darwin's theory. They know that island shores may rise or sink and ocean levels may rise or fall. All these changes help to explain the building of atolls, barrier reefs, and fringing reefs.

BARBARA LAND
Columbia Graduate School of Journalism
Reviewed by N. J. BERRILL
McGill University

See also JELLYFISHES AND OTHER COELENTERATES.

Formation of coral reefs: Ring of coral grows around top of undersea volcano, to form fringing reef. Later, volcano sinks as coral grows, leaving barrier reef. Still later, volcanic island sinks below ocean's surface. Coral ring and lake it encloses are called an atoll.

FRINGING REEF

BARRIER REEF

ATOLL

CORK

Cork has been used for many things, from shoe soles to hat linings. This useful material is the outer layer of bark of a tree called the cork oak.

The bark of the cork tree is made up of tiny cells with tough, elastic walls. In one cubic inch of cork there are about 200,000,000 of these minute cells called cork cells. The many tough cell walls make the cork springy and durable. The cell walls are lined with a wax-like material that keeps water and air from passing through. The hollow air spaces inside the cells make the cork light and spongy. In fact, over half the volume of cork is air.

Cork is used in life preservers and buoys because it floats well. Because it is tough and durable, it is a good material for floor and wall coverings. Cork conducts heat poorly, and it is not easily penetrated by air or water. This makes it useful for cold-storage insulation, bottle stoppers, and cap liners for food and beverage containers.

Depending on the job for which it is needed, cork can be used in its natural state or ground up. Ground cork can be mixed with adhesive binders and pressed into various shapes or sliced into sheets or blocks.

The cork oak tree grows mainly in Spain, Portugal, and North Africa. Attempts have been made to establish cork groves in the United States in the Far West and the Southwest. The tree will grow quite well there. But so far these attempts have not been successful economically. The tree grows to a height of 30 to 40 feet, with a trunk 3 to 4 feet thick. The tree can produce cork for about 150 years if properly cared for. The cork is usually thick enough to be stripped off for the first time when the tree is 20 to 25 years old.

When the cork is stripped, two cuts are made around the tree trunk, one near the ground and one just under the main branches. Cuts are then made up and down the tree trunk, and the cork is peeled off in sections. The cutting and stripping must be done very carefully. If the inner layer of bark, called the cork cambium, is damaged too much, the tree will die.

After the first stripping, cork can be taken from the tree every 8 to 10 years. The first cork cut from a tree, called virgin cork, is rough and of poor quality. After the third or fourth cutting, the cork is of much better quality and is called reproduction cork.

When the cork has been cut, it is dried and boiled. The boiling makes the cork more flexible so that it can be flattened and baled for shipment to the processing plant.

More than 2,000 years ago the ancient Romans used cork to keep their fishing nets and marker buoys afloat. The Romans also made shoe soles of cork.

Floats, shoe soles, and bottle stoppers were the chief uses of cork until early in this century, when many new uses for ground cork were discovered. New methods and machines were developed to grind the cork and make such products as automobile engine gaskets, inner soles for shoes, low-temperature insulation, and a wide variety of useful products.

The floor covering known as linoleum used to be made by mixing finely-ground cork "flour" with linseed oil and spreading the mixture on burlap. The so-called "battleship" linoleum is still made with cork flour.

During World War II, when the supply of cork was greatly reduced, attempts were made to develop cork substitutes by using synthetic materials or the bark of other kinds of trees, and even peanut shells. Synthetic materials are often cheaper than cork, and they can be made in large quantities. Most of them are made of glass or various types of plastics. These have replaced cork for many uses. But cork is still used for many products because of its distinctive qualities.

Reviewed by ARTHUR L. FAUBEL
President, Cork Institute of America

The bark of the cork oak tree is sliced and then carefully peeled off.

CORN

Corn, or maize, is one of the most useful plants. Scientists believe that it originated somewhere in Central America or South America. Prehistoric Indians probably selected seeds year after year from wild grasses, until after several centuries they had developed a plant very like the corn we know today. Corn is so much a creation of people that it cannot survive without their care. No wild plants that closely resemble corn are now known.

Indians had their own stories about the origin of corn. In one tale a young girl turned herself into a corn plant to give humanity a new grain. She left her hair on the plant as corn silks to remind people to take good care of her gift.

The Indians liked corn with blue, red, and black kernels. They gave their colorful corn to the Pilgrims to feed them during the first cold winter in America. The next year the Pilgrims shared their own harvest with the Indians. This was the first Thanksgiving.

Corn was first introduced to the Old World by Christopher Columbus as *maiz,* the Indian name for the grain. It has kept this name, spelled in a variety of ways, in most countries. Since the word "corn" in England meant any kind of grain, the Pilgrims called this new grain "Indian corn."

▶THE CORN PLANT

Corn is a member of the grass family, with large, coarse stalks and leaves. The plants are usually about 2 meters (6 feet) tall. But some types may range from 0.6 meters (2 feet) to ten times that height. There is a main stalk, or stem, and there may be other stems. The main stalk bears one or more ears, protected by husks. The ears grow on shanks, branches below the middle of the stalk.

A tassel that is full of pollen grows at the end of the cornstalk. The unformed kernels on the cobs send up long threads called corn silks, which end in a tuft above the husks. Wind shakes the pollen onto the silks. A fine tube grows from the pollen grain through the silk to the egg cell in the young kernel. The male cell from the pollen fuses with the egg. The egg develops into the embryo, or miniature new plant, inside the kernel. A ripe ear of corn is 7 to 45 centimeters (3 to 18 inches) long, and has 8 to 24 rows of kernels.

Most corn grown today is hybrid. This means that pollen from one carefully selected variety has pollinated the corn silks of another. The resulting hybrid seed produces a strong, high-yielding corn. Every year the farmer buys the kind of hybrid seed he wants to plant from special growers.

The kernels of different varieties may be white, yellow, red, or purple. Six kinds lead corn production. The most widely grown corn in the United States is called **dent corn** because it has a definite notch at the top of the kernel. **Flint corn** has hard kernels and withstands cold and disease. These two varieties are used to feed livestock and in industry.

Eating corn is usually **sweet corn, flour corn,** or **popcorn.** Sweet corn is high in sugar and can be recognized by clear kernels that wrinkle when they are ripe. The Indians in South America use flour corn, since the large amount of starch in the mealy kernels makes them easy to pound or chew. The familiar popcorn bursts from its small, hard-shelled

What makes popcorn pop?

Popcorn is different from other kinds of corn because its kernels have a hard, tough, waterproof covering. When popcorn kernels are heated, this covering keeps the natural moisture inside the kernels from escaping. If the kernels are heated enough, this moisture turns to steam and actually explodes the kernels. This makes the popcorn soft and puffed up.

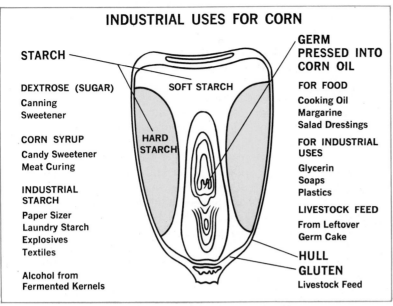

INDUSTRIAL USES FOR CORN

STARCH

DEXTROSE (SUGAR)
Canning
Sweetener

CORN SYRUP
Candy Sweetener
Meat Curing

INDUSTRIAL STARCH
Paper Sizer
Laundry Starch
Explosives
Textiles

Alcohol from
Fermented Kernels

SOFT STARCH

HARD STARCH

GERM PRESSED INTO CORN OIL

FOR FOOD
Cooking Oil
Margarine
Salad Dressings

FOR INDUSTRIAL USES
Glycerin
Soaps
Plastics

LIVESTOCK FEED
From Leftover
Germ Cake

HULL
GLUTEN
Livestock Feed

CORN KERNELS
Hominy
Corn Flour
Breakfast Food

COBS
Livestock Feed
Insulation
Fuel

STALKS
Paper
Wallboard
Rubber Substitute

kernels when heated. **Waxy** corn has a waxlike appearance when the kernel is broken open. It came into use during World War II as a substitute for tapioca in making adhesives and the stiffening in soft puddings.

▶ CULTURE

Corn grows best in rich loam, but it will also grow well in fertile sandy or clay soil. It needs warm weather and plentiful moisture. Planting is in the spring, when the soil temperature reaches 13°C (55°F) or higher, but young plants can be killed by a sudden freeze. The seeds are planted in rows about 1 meter apart. Several kernels are dropped in each hill or spot. These are spaced about half a meter to a meter apart in the row.

Weeds must be kept down so that they will not choke out the young corn plants. The weeds must be chopped and the soil loosened around the plants. This must be done three to five times during the growing season.

Most corn is ripe about 4 to 5 months after it is planted. The ears are snapped off the shanks by hand or machine. Corn for livestock feed must be husked and dried before storing. Snapping, husking, and shelling the corn in the field can be done in one rapid operation by machines. Such corn is still so damp that it must be dried under artificial heat.

▶ ENEMIES OF CORN

Corn smut, a harmful fungus, is a common disease. Locusts strip the plant's leaves. European corn borers and stem borers (larvae of certain moths) bore tunnels in the stalks and

ears, sometimes causing the stalks to break off. The corn earworm, another larva, devours the ripening kernels on the ears. Chemicals and proper cultural practices, such as crop rotation, and clearing the field of old stalks and leaves, partly control destruction. Breeding of hybrid varieties that can resist attack also helps prevent damage.

In Africa, Asia, southern Europe, and many Central American and South American countries, most of the corn is used for human food. The grain is ground to a meal in mills, between stones, or by hand pounding. Corn bread is baked from the meal. In Mexico two popular corn meal dishes are thin pancakes called tortillas, and tamales, made partly of cornmeal mush wrapped in corn husks. Mush, or cooked meal, is a staple in many diets.

Corn has become an important crop in southern Europe, Africa, and parts of Asia, but it is most important in the United States. In fact, the states ranging from Ohio to Nebraska are called the Corn Belt.

JOHN H. MARTIN
Formerly, U.S. Department of Agriculture

See also AGRICULTURE; GRAIN AND GRAIN PRODUCTS.

CORNET. See WIND INSTRUMENTS.

CORTES, HERNANDO (1485–1547)

For most of Europe, certainly for Spain, Columbus' discovery in 1492 of a new world was a wonder second only to the creation of the world itself. Many Spaniards left home to conquer and explore the new lands. One of the boldest of these Spaniards was Hernando Cortes, conqueror of Mexico.

Cortes was born in 1485 at Medellín, Spain. His father sent him to the University of Salamanca to study law. But 14-year-old Hernando, though quick of mind, was eager for action, and he left after 2 years. In 1504, at the age of 19, he sailed for America.

For 7 years Cortes was a planter on the island of Hispaniola (now Haiti and the Dominican Republic). In 1511 he took part in the conquest of Cuba. In 1519 Diego Velásquez, governor of Cuba, appointed Cortes to lead an expedition to Yucatán, Mexico, to verify news of great riches brought back by two earlier expeditions. Eagerly Cortes sold his land to help finance the expedition. But Velásquez became suspicious of Cortes' intentions and cancelled the expedition. Cortes disregarded his orders. He loaded 11 ships with over 500 soldiers, 16 horses, and some cannons and set off for Mexico.

Cortes landed in Yucatán, conquered Tabasco, and founded the port town of Veracruz. There he named himself captain general, and to prevent mutiny and escape, burned all but one of his ships. Steel armor and swords, his guns, and his horses gave him victory over the larger forces of Tlaxcalan and Cholulan Indians. With diplomatic skill and cunning Cortes recruited as allies these tribes, who were traditional enemies of the Aztecs. Cortes' army was now stronger and ready to march inland against Tenochtitlán (now Mexico City), the rich capital of the Aztec Empire. News of Cortes had already reached Montezuma II. The Aztec emperor thought the Spaniards might be messengers of Quetzalcoatl, the great white bearded god.

Within 3 months Cortes reached Tenochtitlán. It was a huge city of tall towers, palaces, and temples, built on an island in the middle of a lake. Montezuma, accompanied by many of his nobles, greeted Cortes and escorted the Spaniards into the city.

Cortes admired the wealth and culture of the Aztecs, but he disliked their religion. Statues of the Aztec gods were destroyed and replaced by crosses and pictures of the Virgin Mary. Cortes cleverly ruled through Montezuma, and the city came under his control.

Meanwhile Velásquez sent soldiers to arrest Cortes. Cortes rushed off toward the coast and defeated them. However, while he was away, his lieutenant, suspecting a revolt, killed many Aztec nobles. Cortes hurried back to Tenochtitlán and tried to use Montezuma to calm the people. When the emperor attempted to speak to them, the people stoned him as a traitor and revolted. (Montezuma died 2 days later.) Cortes fled, losing half his men.

In 1521 Cortes attacked Tenochtitlán with a new army of Spaniards and Indians. For 10 weeks the Aztecs held out. Finally, near starvation, their capital in ruins, and many of their people dead, they surrendered. Cortes had conquered an empire for Spain.

In 1527 Cortes was recalled to Spain to explain charges of misconduct. After clearing himself, Cortes returned to Mexico. He rebuilt Tenochtitlán, planted sugar, wheat, and fruit trees, bred mules and cattle, and built ships. However, the appointment of a royal governor limited Cortes' authority. He returned to Spain in 1539. On December 2, 1547, he died near Seville.

Reviewed by DANIEL ROSELLE
State University College (Fredonia, New York)

COSMETICS

Styles in cosmetics are continually changing. Men have often used more perfume, powder, and oils than women. Women painted their cheeks so brightly in the 18th century that the British Parliament passed a law about makeup. The law forbade using cosmetics to catch a husband. In the Victorian period all makeup was frowned upon.

Cosmetics today are used from head to toe and by people of all ages. There are three kinds of cosmetics. One kind can be seen, like lipstick, eye makeup, and nail polish. Another kind is rubbed in or hidden, like hand lotion, perfume, hair dressing, and antiperspirant. A third kind is used during a treatment and is then wiped, rinsed, or rubbed off. Examples are shaving cream, shampoo, mouthwash, and bathing preparations. Soap is not usually considered to be a cosmetic.

Manufacture of Cosmetics

Three types of ingredients, singly or in combination, are the basis of most cosmetics. Fats or oils form a base. Water or alcohol acts as the liquid. Vegetable gums and emulsifiers hold the mixture together. Colors, perfumes, and preservatives are added to make a cosmetic attractive and long-lasting.

Face powder is made by blending several different dry materials. Talc, a very soft mineral, is an important ingredient. Others include zinc oxide, chalk, and metallic stearates. These substances make the face powder spread evenly, stay on the skin, and reduce gloss. Mild perfumes are added to make the powder more pleasant to use.

The natural skin tones of face powder are made by combining a wide range of pastel colors. The color blender in the factory mixes huge batches of colored powder into the various tints that people buy. Some stores buy their powder unmixed. A cosmetic expert at the store mixes powder for customers right before their eyes. The expert blends a little blue, a little yellow, and perhaps some lavender and orange into a base of rose powder. This is exactly what the color blender in the factory does, but the expert at the store works with smaller amounts of powder.

Cake rouge is made in much the same way as powder. Gum or some other binder is added to hold the cake more tightly together. Liquid and cream rouge are also on the market. All types of rouge come in various shades of red.

Lipsticks come from a combination of castor oil and waxes, which are mixed by melting. Coloring is added by spreading dye or colored powder through the mixture with rollers or by stirring it in with special stirrers. Exact shading is a delicate job. Once the colors are mixed, the mass is reheated and poured into molds. The final step is placing the cooled lipsticks in metal or plastic holders.

From the earliest days people have not been able to resist painting the skin around their eyes in all sorts of different shades. Eye makeup is just as popular today. In drugstores and other kinds of stores, you will find mascara, eye shadow, eyeliner, and eyebrow pencil in an astonishing array of colors. Eye makeup usually has a base of beeswax or some other kind of wax. A fat such as lanolin or cocoa butter makes the eye cosmetics creamier and easier to put on. Special preservatives are added to help prevent eye infections.

Hand lotions and foundation creams often are called skin foods. They help to give back to the skin materials that have dried up or have been rubbed off by everyday exposure to air, wind, clothing, and sun. Many chemical ingredients go into these creams, but mixed in with the chemicals are some surprising natural oils. Avocado oil, raisin-seed oil, turtle oil, and cod-liver oil are some of the natural oils that help moisten and soften skin. The various ingredients are stirred evenly in large stainless steel or glass vats to make sure that the finished product is smooth.

Hair used to be held in place by solutions of gum in water, which left a flaky film on the hair, or by heavy greases. Present-day hair sprays are better for grooming the hair because the holding solutions are broken into tiny liquid parts, which are easier to apply. These solutions are based on transparent, nonflaking resins.

Toothpaste is prepared by putting large amounts of abrasives (hard, gritty substances) into solutions of detergents, moisturizers, and flavors, thickened with gum. Most toothpastes also contain fluorides, which reduce tooth cavities. A machine that looks like a dough mixer kneads the mixture until it is well blended. Air that was folded in during the blending must be removed by a vacuum. Otherwise, when the toothpaste is put into the tube, it will contain air pockets.

Cosmetic chemists work closely with physicians and dermatologists (skin doctors) to make products that will not harm skin or eyes, will not cause allergic reactions, and are not poisonous. In many cases drugs are added to cosmetics to give them a double action. Antiperspirants, special suntan lotions, hormone creams, and acne preparations are all products that contain drugs.

In the United States, the Food, Drug, and Cosmetic Act of 1938 brought government control into the manufacture and sale of cosmetics. New regulations are passed frequently to keep the act up-to-date. For example, one recent addition requires manufacturers of cosmetics to list all ingredients on the packages of their products, so that customers know what is in the cosmetic. Poisons, habit-forming drugs, and dirt cannot be put into cosmetics. The government inspects factories to see that conditions are sanitary and that only proper materials are used. Only approved colors, called certified dyes, can be used to tint cosmetics.

History of Cosmetics

The earliest cosmetics had religious uses. Incense and oils were used to anoint the living and the dead in religious services. The ointments and hair dressings were at first prepared by priests or slaves, according to temple or family recipes.

The Egyptian queen Cleopatra was famous for her beauty and her skill in using cosmetics. She bathed in milk to make her skin more beautiful, used strange perfumes, and painted her face in brilliant colors.

Where did pioneers get their cosmetics?

Pioneers in the United States and Canada found the materials for their cosmetics in the woods and fields near their homes. Creams for softening the skin were probably the most sought-after cosmetics. Pioneer women made these creams from a mixture of lanolin (fat from wool) or beeswax and oil and water. They scrubbed their faces with buttermilk to help remove freckles from their sunburned skin. Flour was used as face powder. To color their lips and cheeks, they used the juice from red berries.

In Rome the great public baths and the many barbershops supplied perfumes, oils, bleaches, dyes, and lotions. A fashionable man fresh from the barbershop would have dyed curls perfumed with cinnamon, makeup cream on his face, and patches of cloth stuck to his cheeks to hide defects. A fashionable woman would be made up, too, with a mixture of chalk and white lead on her brow and arms, dregs of wine staining her cheeks and her lips red, and ashes on her eyebrows.

In Europe, after the fall of Rome, cosmetics were a luxury that only a few people knew about and even fewer could afford. But when the Crusaders returned from the religious wars in the East, they brought back cosmetics and exotic perfumes. By the 16th century, commoners and royalty alike were experimenting with cosmetics. The subjects of Queen Elizabeth I copied her habit of rouging and painting her face. The extravagant use of cosmetics made many Elizabethan writers complain about the folly of using too much makeup.

For hundreds of years, materials for cosmetics were supplied by barbershops and pharmacies. In the early 19th century, a few peddlers tried mixing their own cosmetics and branding them with trade names. Soon people were buying the peddler's brand instead of making their cosmetics at home.

Just before the beginning of the 20th century, the United States manufacturing firm of Daggett and Ramsdell used mineral oil in their cold creams. The mineral oil replaced vegetable oils that rapidly became rancid. For the first time, long-lasting cosmetics could be made. One company after another introduced products that became nationally known.

Today cosmetics are an important part of careful grooming for men and women alike. Bottles, boxes, and jars of cosmetics crowd dressers and dressing tables in many homes. More bottles, jars, and sprays fill family medicine cabinets. This amazing collection can clean the skin and change a person's appearance in many ways. Many people today follow the latest trends in cosmetics as closely as they watch fashions in clothing.

RICHARD K. LEHNE
Contributor, *Cosmetics: Science and Technology*
See also BEAUTY CULTURE; PERFUMES.

COSMIC RAYS

From far out in space, atomic particles keep crashing into the earth's atmosphere. The atmosphere is itself made of atoms, some of which are broken up by the high-speed particles. In breaking up, the atoms themselves become particles. All these particles—those from outer space as well as those from the atmosphere—are called cosmic rays.

Cosmic rays are extremely energetic particles. They can penetrate (enter and pass through) almost all forms of matter. Every minute hundreds of them pass through everything on earth, including man. However, the particles are so small that we never feel or notice them.

Cosmic radiation was discovered in 1912 by the Austrian scientist Victor Hess. His instruments had indicated that some kind of radiation was always arriving in the laboratory, and he decided to investigate it. Taking his instruments with him, he rose in a balloon to a height of more than 3 miles. The instruments showed him that the higher he went, the more radiation there was. Hess then realized that the radiations must come from far out in space.

Since Hess's discovery cosmic rays have been studied by scientists all over the world. The study takes them to many different places. The penetrating radiation is found far down in mines and deep beneath the sea, although it is at its weakest in these places. Scientists who set up observing equipment on mountains find

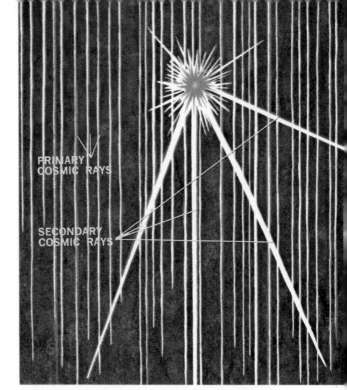

Primary cosmic rays bombard atoms in the atmosphere and break them up. Secondary cosmic rays are given off.

the radiation is much stronger than on the ground. And the strongest radiation is recorded by instruments sent high into space in balloons, rockets, and satellites.

▶ PRIMARY AND SECONDARY RAYS

The atomic particles from outer space are called **primary cosmic rays.** Most of them are the kind of particles called protons. However, sometimes a second kind of particle is involved. These are neutrons. Both protons and neutrons make up the nuclei (centers) of atoms.

When primary rays strike the earth's atmosphere, they break up some of its atoms. As a result, these atoms splinter and some particles are broken off. Some of these splintered atoms also send out rays. Together these rays and particles are known as **secondary cosmic rays.**

Secondary cosmic rays include three kinds of particles: protons, mesons, and electrons.

So far as is known, the protons do not play an important part as secondary cosmic rays.

Most of the cosmic rays that reach the earth are mesons. These atomic particles exist for only a few millionths of a second, but they move so quickly that many reach the ground. Some travel far into it before they break up.

The electrons play a very important part in

Victor Hess is the scientist who discovered cosmic rays.

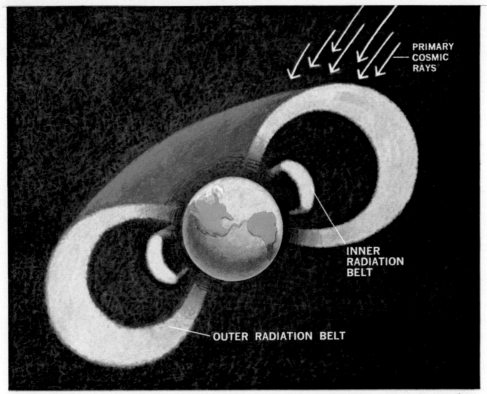

PRIMARY COSMIC RAYS

INNER RADIATION BELT

OUTER RADIATION BELT

Cosmic rays from outer space become trapped mainly in the outer radiation belt.

cosmic rays. They are themselves secondary cosmic rays. And, as high-speed particles, they bombard the atoms of the atmosphere, causing the atoms to give out electrons and rays. The rays are more powerful even than X rays. Both the rays and the electrons bombard other atoms, making still more cosmic rays.

Radiation Belt

Not all the secondary cosmic ray particles reach the ground. Some never even get very far into the atmosphere. Instead they are caught by the earth's magnetic field. The particles become trapped in a belt that lies about 2,000 miles above the middle region of the earth. This belt is called a radiation belt. (It is one of two such belts that surround the earth.) Particles escape only very slowly from the radiation belt. And as they do they are soon replaced by others.

Cosmic-ray tracks made on a photographic plate.

▶ HOW COSMIC RAYS ARE OBSERVED

Scientists have several ways of studying cosmic rays. One method is to use a **cloud chamber.** This is a box with a glass window; the box contains moist air. When secondary cosmic rays pass through the moist air, they leave a trail of tiny droplets of water. (This is like the droplets, called a vapor trail, that you sometimes see along the path of a high-flying airplane.) The cloud chamber trail is photographed and then studied in detail by scientists.

Another instrument for observing cosmic rays is a **Geiger counter.** This is a small tube with a gas inside. When a cosmic ray particle rushes through the gas, it causes the tube to give out an electric pulse. The pulse works a counting device that records the number of cosmic ray particles.

A third method of learning about cosmic rays is to use **photographic glass plates.** A pile of plates is fixed in a light-tight box, which is sent miles into the atmosphere by balloon. When the plates return they are developed, just as if they had been used for taking an ordinary photograph. Wherever a cosmic ray has crashed into the plates, its tracks are left behind on record.

Another instrument is called the **mass spectrograph.** This device makes use of the fact that protons and neutrons are heavy. It

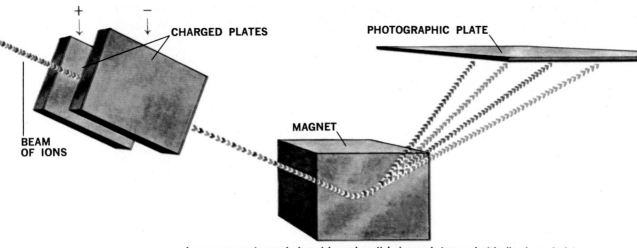

In a mass spectrograph, ions (charged particles) pass between electrically charged plates and on to a magnet, where they separate. They leave marks on a photographic plate.

spreads the nuclei out according to their mass (the amount of matter in them). Then it measures their different masses as well as their speed and number. Such instruments are carried in many satellites and space probes to measure cosmic rays.

WHERE COSMIC RAYS COME FROM

Scientists do not know exactly where the primary cosmic rays come from. But they think there are three possible sources.

One is the sun. The sun sends out an immense amount of light, heat, radio waves, X rays, and other radiations. It also shoots off atomic particles, especially at the time of solar "storms." Some of these particles are protons and neutrons, so it seems likely that some primary cosmic rays come from the sun. However, there are far more primary rays than the sun can supply.

A second source of primary cosmic rays could be the stars known as supernovae. These are stars that suddenly explode, blowing huge balls of hot, glowing gas into space. When this happens the star also shoots off protons and neutrons at high speeds. These may account for some of the cosmic rays that reach the earth's atmosphere.

Primary cosmic rays may also come from a third source—the dust and gas moving about far out in space among the stars. Scientists believe that many of the atoms of this dust and gas are rushing around in giant whirlpools. Some of the nuclei of these atoms may fly off from the whirlpools. Such nuclear particles are like the cosmic rays that crash into the earth's atmosphere.

WHY THE RAYS ARE STUDIED

Scientists study cosmic rays for many reasons.

For one thing, they are interested in finding out more about the rays themselves. They would like to know more about how and why the rays form.

Scientists are also interested in studying the effects of cosmic rays. For example, cosmic rays break up the atoms in the atmosphere. This provides scientists with special information about these atoms.

Then, too, cosmic rays affect life on the earth. The secondary rays make changes in the cells of living things. These changes, which are handed down from parents to young, have been going on since the beginning of life. Therefore modern studies give scientists information about the ways that plants and animals evolve.

Scientists also believe that a study of cosmic rays will give them a better picture of the stars, dust, and gas that exist in space. For example, cosmic rays from the sun tell something about what is happening to the sun's atoms. And because the sun is just one of many billions of stars, cosmic rays can teach much about other stars. If cosmic rays are proved to come from supernovae, scientists will understand more clearly the kind of explosion that takes place on such stars. Cosmic rays may also give information about the gas and dust in outer space, which is difficult to observe in any other way.

COLIN A. RONAN
Fellow of the Royal Astronomical Society
See also ATOMS; RADIATION; RADIATION BELTS.

Costa Rica is a country of active volcanoes.

Above: Costa Rica was the first country in Central America to grow bananas for export. Left: The country is also rich in other crops for domestic consumption: sugar, rice, beans, corn, vegetables, fruits, and tobacco.

Below left: Our Lady of the Angels is a shrine in Cartago for all Central Americans. Below right: Settlers from Andalusia, Spain, have made Costa Rica famous for its flowers.

COSTA RICA

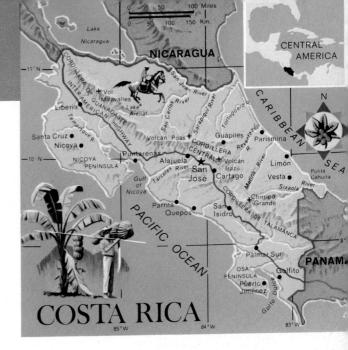

COSTA RICA

In September, 1502, Christopher Columbus landed on the forested, tropical coast of this tiny Central American country. Because the Indians wore gold earrings, Columbus thought the land must be rich in gold. It was probably he who named the area Costa Rica, Spanish for "rich coast." Though little gold was found, the name is suitable. Today Costa Rica is rich with tropical vegetation, flourishing banana and cacao plantations, and fertile mountain valleys dotted with thousands of small, prosperous farms.

▶ THE PEOPLE

The majority of the people of Costa Rica are the descendants of Spanish settlers who came to America during the 16th century. The Costa Ricans live mainly on the Meseta Central, or Central Plateau, where they own farms. Many black Costa Ricans live in the Caribbean province of Limón. Their ancestors were brought from Jamaica at the beginning of the 20th century to work on the banana plantations. Many of them still speak English instead of Spanish. There are almost no Indians left in Costa Rica, though a few tribes, especially the Chorotegas, have left relics of fine carved jade and multi-colored pottery.

Many Spanish traditions survive in Costa Rica. It is not usual for boys and girls to go out together without an older escort. In the late afternoon young people still meet in the central plaza for the *retreta* and the band concert. Girls walk together around the plaza in one direction and boys in the other. As they pass, the boys call out flowery compliments to the girls in the hope that the girls will remember them when they meet again. Around the edge of the plazas in each town are coffee shops, where people meet to chat and do important business.

Almost all Costa Ricans are Roman Catholics. Their most important religious festival takes place in Cartago, the former capital of the country. On August 2 the pilgrims come from all over Central America to the shrine of Our Lady of the Angels. Her tiny black stone statue was found by a country girl in the 17th century. On the day of the festival, the statue is carried in procession to other churches in Cartago.

At Christmastime city streets are lined with booths offering tiny figures of shepherds, animals, and the Holy Family. These figures are used in the nativity scene, or *portal,* that each family sets up in the house. Some *portales* are so large they fill a whole room.

Costa Ricans are proud of their modern schools and well-trained teachers. In fact, the first three women ever elected to the Congress in Costa Rica were schoolteachers. Almost every village has a school, and all children between 7 and 14 years old are required to attend. Boys and girls usually go to separate schools. Classes begin early in March and continue through November. December, January, and February are harvest time, and the children are expected to help their parents pick coffee beans. Costa Rica has a beautiful new free university near San José.

Costa Ricans love color. In the city and the country, houses are painted in gay pinks, greens, and blues. Colorful flowers bloom all year round. There are artisans who specialize in decorating the farmers' oxcarts in dazzling designs. Each cart has its own design, in the manner of a coat of arms. Each cart has its own sound, too, as its wheels creak on their axles. By listening to the "song" of a cart, country people say they can tell who is passing. Nowadays most farmers take their

Many housing projects like this one have been built for Costa Rica's growing population.

The University of Costa Rica receives government funding, but it is run by a board of professors and students.

products to market in trucks and jeeps instead of by oxcart.

Costa Rican *sabaneros* (cowboys) herd cattle on broad plains of the "Wild West" in Guanacaste Province, on the north Pacific coast. Each *sabanero* carries a machete, or broad-bladed knife, in a leather holster. The knife is used for everything from cutting rope to opening cans.

The people of Guanacaste are especially fond of music and fun. They celebrate their own holiday on July 25, with outdoor barbecues and guitar and marimba music. Their lively dance, the Punto Guanacasteco, has become Costa Rica's national dance.

The national sport of Costa Rica is soccer, called *futbol*. Basketball is played also. Bullfights are particularly popular at festivals, but the bull is never killed.

▶ **THE LAND**

Costa Rica is on the narrow Central American isthmus that connects North and South America. To the north is Nicaragua. To the south is Panama. Costa Rica is one of the smallest countries in the Americas. On a clear day Costa Rica's Caribbean and Pacific coasts can be seen from the top of Irazú volcano, which rises to 3,434 meters (11,263 feet) above sea level. There are still a few active volcanoes in the mountain ranges that run the length of the country.

The Meseta Central has rich volcanic soil and a pleasant climate. It lies at an average

elevation of 900 to 1,200 meters (3,000 to 4,000 feet) above sea level and has spring-like weather all through the year. The capital city of San José and most of the other important towns are on this plateau.

Along Costa Rica's coastal lowlands, the weather is quite hot. The Caribbean coast receives a great deal of rain, and there are many swamps and great forests. Huge green sea turtles lumber onto the beaches north of the port of Limón to lay their eggs. The people of this region like to eat turtle eggs and turtle meat.

Costa Rica's Pacific coast is much longer than its Caribbean coast. The ocean teems with fish, especially sharks and tuna, lobster and shrimp.

Costa Rica has limited mineral resources. The most important are gold, bauxite (aluminum ore), sulfur, and limestone.

▶ **THE ECONOMY**

Costa Rica is basically an agricultural country. Coffee has been its most important product since early in the 19th century. The coffee plantations are found mainly in the Meseta Central. Bananas are the second most important export. Other commercial crops include sugarcane, tobacco, cotton, cacao, coconuts, fruit, and abaca fiber, which is used in making rope. The raising of beef cattle for export and for meat has been developed in recent years.

With help from the government, Costa Rica has increased its industrial output. Processed foods, textiles, drugs, chemicals, and wood products are among the leading manufactured goods. The fishing industry is important, and sharkskins and shark-liver oil are valuable exports.

Railroads, buses, and airlines connect Costa Rica's principal cities. The narrow-gauge Northern Railway connects San José to Limón. It follows an exciting 160-kilometer (100-mile) route along the gorge of the Reventazón River. The railroad was built between 1871 and 1890 by Minor C. Keith, an adventurous North American. More than 4,000 people died of malaria, yellow fever, and other diseases while building it. Keith introduced banana growing to Costa Rica in order to have freight for his railroad. Another railroad runs from San José to Puntarenas on the Pacific coast.

Costa Rica has an international airline, LACSA, and several local airlines. Jet planes land at the airport of El Coco, near San José. The Inter-American Highway connects Costa Rica with its neighbors to the north and south.

▶CITIES

San José, the capital, is no longer a sleepy colonial town. More than 400,000 people live in the city and its suburbs. It was founded in 1737, but most of its old buildings have been replaced by newer ones of concrete and glass. One of the most beautiful buildings in San José is the National Theater. It has marble stairways and statues, gold-framed mirrors, and paintings. The contemporary government buildings stand out in sharp contrast to the buildings dating from colonial times.

Puntarenas is a port and popular beach resort in the central part of the Pacific coast. Golfito is a port to the south that is used by big agricultural companies for exporting bananas. Limón is the only major port on the Caribbean coast.

▶GOVERNMENT

Costa Rica is a republic with a government divided into three branches—executive, legislative, and judicial. Costa Ricans are proud of their democratic institutions. Theirs is one of the few countries in Latin America where democratic elections for civilian presidents are held regularly. Political campaigns are financed by the government. An independent electoral court oversees elections to prevent fraud. There is universal suffrage.

The president serves as head of state and government and appoints cabinet members and provincial governors. The president and two vice-presidents are elected for 4-year terms. A president must wait two terms before seeking re-election. Members of the legislature are elected for 4-year terms and cannot serve successive terms. The judiciary consists of a supreme court and lower courts.

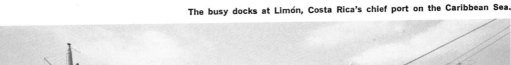

The busy docks at Limón, Costa Rica's chief port on the Caribbean Sea.

Under its constitution, Costa Rica is prevented from establishing a permanent army. Its only legal peacekeeping body is a police force, and its people are proud of this fact.

▶HISTORY

The original Indian peoples of Costa Rica were living in small, scattered settlements when Christopher Columbus landed on the Caribbean coast in 1502. The Spanish did not settle in the area until the 1560's. The Indians refused to work for the Spanish. They fled to the mountains or, if caught, were shipped to Panama or the mines of Peru. The Spanish therefore lacked Indian labor for large estates and began to cultivate their own small plots. Costa Rica became a land of small farmers of mostly Spanish origin, cut off from the outside world by high mountains.

Costa Rica was ruled from Guatemala as part of the Viceroyalty of New Spain (Mexico) for nearly 300 years. When Mexico rebelled against Spain in 1821, the Central American countries of Costa Rica, Guatemala, El Salvador, Nicaragua, and Honduras also declared their independence. They joined the short-lived Mexican Empire led by Agustín de Iturbide, but they soon broke away and formed a union of their own. This federation did not last, and Costa Rica became a separate republic in 1838.

From 1838 to 1889, Costa Rica prospered as the export of coffee began to bring money into the country. Public schools and railroads were built. Several dictators came to power during this period, but only one lasted long— Tomás Guardia, who ruled from 1870 to 1882. The most serious threat to the nation came in 1856, when William Walker, an ambitious adventurer from the United States, seized control of neighboring Nicaragua. He threatened Costa Rica, too. Central American forces united against him and made him withdraw. During the Battle of Rivas, on April 11, 1856, a peasant drummer boy, Juan Santamaría, lost his life setting fire to a building that Walker had occupied. Santamaría became a national hero. The anniversary of the battle is a national holiday.

In 1889, Costa Rica held what has been called the first truly free election in Central America. This established a pattern of democratic elections that has been broken only twice. From 1917 to 1919, Federico Tinoco Granados ruled the country as a dictator. And in 1948 a coalition of Communists and Conservatives tried to prevent President-elect Otilio Ulate Blanco from taking office. A brief civil war erupted. José Figueres Ferrer raised a militia of the people and overthrew the government. For 18 months, Figueres served as president of a temporary government, called the Founding Junta of the Second Republic. When peace was restored, Ulate took office. Figueres was elected president in 1953 and again in 1970. He founded the National Liberation Party, one of Costa Rica's leading political parties. Under Figueres the government took control of the banking system. It enacted many social reforms, including social security and medical care programs.

During the early 1980's, Costa Rica faced serious economic problems. But its democratic traditions continue, and its literacy rate and income per person are among the highest in all Latin America. Costa Rica has been little affected by the violence that has swept much of Central America. It has been a haven for exiles of many political views.

J. DAVID BOWEN
Author, *Hello, South America*
Reviewed by JOSÉ FIGUERES FERRER
Former President of Costa Rica

COSTUME. See CLOTHING.

FACTS AND FIGURES

REPUBLIC OF COSTA RICA is the official name of the country. Costa Rica means "rich coast" in Spanish.

CAPITAL: San José.

LOCATION: Central America. **Latitude**—8° N to 11° 15′ N. **Longitude**—82° 30′ W to 86° W.

AREA: 50,700 km² (19,575 sq mi).

POPULATION: 2,300,000 (estimate).

LANGUAGE: Spanish.

GOVERNMENT: Republic. **Head of state and government**—president. **International co-operation**—United Nations, Organization of American States (OAS), Central American Common Market (CACM).

NATIONAL ANTHEM: *Noble patria, tu hermosa bandera* ("Noble country, your beautiful flag").

ECONOMY: Agricultural products—coffee, bananas, tobacco, sugarcane, rice, beans, cotton, cacao, abaca fiber, livestock, coconuts, fruits. **Industries and products**—food processing, textiles, drugs, chemicals, wood products.
Chief minerals—gold, bauxite, sulfur, limestone.
Chief exports—coffee, bananas, cocoa, beef cattle, abaca.
Chief imports—machinery and transportation equipment, petroleum and lubricants, foodstuffs (wheat flour, dairy cattle, milk), chemicals. **Monetary unit**—colón.

COTTON

Cotton is one of the world's most important and abundant natural textile fibers. It is made into many kinds of cloth for clothes and household fabrics. Even the seeds of cotton are turned into useful products.

THE COTTON PLANT

Cotton is a warm-weather plant that belongs to the mallow family. Its relatives include okra, hollyhock, hibiscus, and rose of Sharon. When it grows wild, a cotton plant may live for many years and grow to the size of a small tree. When grown by farmers as a cultivated plant, cotton plants are like small shrubs, growing to a height of 0.5 to 2 meters (1½ to 6½ feet).

The plant has cream-colored or yellow flowers, which turn red the day after they open. Around the flowers are leaves that remain after the flowers fall off the plant. These leaves hold seed pods, called **cotton bolls**. Inside the bolls are the cotton seeds and fibers. Cotton fibers are actually hairs that grow on the cotton seeds, protecting them while they ripen. A cotton fiber looks like a flattened, twisted tube. The many little twists in the fiber are important. They help hold the fibers together when they are spun into yarn or thread. A cotton fiber is actually as strong as a steel wire of the same thickness.

▶ HISTORY

Archeological evidence indicates that cotton was cultivated in Mexico some 7,000 years ago. Written records found in India indicate that it was used there as long ago as 3000 B.C.

(1) A cotton plant starts life as a tiny seedling.

(3) After about two months, blossoms open.

(2) In a few weeks it becomes a sturdy bush.

(4) Blossoms ripen into silky white bolls.

Europe first heard of cotton through the Greek historian Herodotus, who lived in the 5th century B.C. Herodotus described the cotton plant as a kind of natural wonder—a tree that bore wool instead of fruit. The "wool," of course, was actually cotton.

Arab merchants probably brought cotton into the Mediterranean world over the trade routes from India. The English word "cotton" comes from the Arab word *qutun*.

During the Middle Ages the use of cotton spread throughout Europe. Cotton arrived in England some time before the 13th century. At that time coarse woolen cloth was often called cotton, so it is difficult to know just when cotton really began to be used. Cotton was used mainly for candlewicks, embroidery yarn, and clothing. The popularity of cotton grew because cotton cloth was easy to wash and the printed cottons imported from India were beautiful. Wool merchants and sheep farmers became alarmed because cotton was hurting the wool business. In the early 18th century, the wool merchants got Parliament to pass laws against trading in cotton. The trade was not stopped, however. The public wanted cotton, and the cotton merchants wanted to make money.

Cotton goods continued to be imported into England by the famous East India Company, and domestic production of cotton goods continued. The cotton manufacturers became so powerful that they eventually had the restrictions lifted on cotton cloth that was woven in England. Imports of cotton cloth from India were still restricted.

The growth of England's cotton industry was greatly helped by a series of inventions in the 18th and 19th centuries. John Kay invented the fly shuttle, an attachment to the weaver's loom that speeded up the weaving of cloth. Cloth could be made so much faster with Kay's new shuttle that a way had to be found to spin yarn more quickly to feed the looms. The old spinning wheel could not produce yarn fast enough to keep up with the weavers. Several machines to spin yarn were soon invented. James Hargreaves made the spinning jenny. Richard Arkwright invented the spinning frame, also called the water frame, a machine run by waterpower that twisted cotton yarn and wound it on spools. Samuel Crompton made the spinning mule, a mechanical spinning machine that combined some of the ideas of the earlier machines.

The first power loom for weaving cotton cloth was made in 1785 by Edmund Cartwright. This machine did not work very well, however. The movement of the shuttle was often too violent. The shuttle sometimes broke the yarn and sometimes even flew off, giving the weaver a nasty blow.

Better power looms were invented later. These machines worked so well that they put some weavers out of jobs. When the unemployed weavers rioted in 1812, much of their anger was directed against the power looms. Despite the troubles, the machines and methods developed by the English inventors made England a world leader in cotton production.

Cotton in the New World. When the Spanish conquistadors came to the New World, they found the Indians growing cotton in many places. The Incas, in Peru, the Aztecs, in Mexico, and some of the farming tribes in what is now the southwestern United States made excellent cloth from this native cotton. The Spanish are said to have planted their own varieties of cotton in Florida in 1536. English colonists in Virginia were growing cotton on a small scale by 1619. But cotton growing was far from being an industry for some years. The colonists grew cotton for their own use. Exports of cotton to England's factories began in the 18th century.

During the American Revolution the supply of cotton cloth from England was cut off. This spurred the development of the cotton textile industry in America. In 1793 the first large cotton mill was built at Pawtucket, Rhode Island, by Samuel Slater, who had once worked in the cotton mills in England.

The Cotton Gin. One problem held back the American cotton industry for years. It was difficult to separate the fibers of American cotton from the seeds. Most of the cotton grown in 18th-century America was, as it is today, the short-fibered kind. The tightly curled fibers of this kind of cotton cling firmly to the hairy seeds. Picking the seeds out of the fibers had to be done by hand. This was slow work. One worker could clean only about 0.5 kilogram (1 pound) of cotton a day.

Growers of long-fibered cotton, such as grew in India, did not face this problem. Long-

Eli Whitney's original hand-cranked cotton gin (*left*) and its giant modern descendant (*right*).

fibered cotton was easy to separate from its seeds. The cotton had only to be passed between rollers that resembled an old-fashioned clothes wringer. The silky, white fibers would go through the rollers, but the smooth, black seeds were caught and squeezed loose. The machine used for cleaning this long-fibered cotton was called a **roller gin**. ("Gin" is short for "engine.")

Unfortunately for American cotton planters, long-fibered cotton would not grow well on the North American mainland. They had to grow short-fibered cotton or none at all.

But if a cheap, fast way to clean out the seeds could be found, enormous quantities of American cotton could be sold to England's textile mills. With their new machines the English mills were able to spin and weave cotton at amazing speed. The mills could handle all the cotton that growers could sell to them.

The person who solved the problem of getting the seeds out of American cotton was Eli Whitney. His invention of a machine to extract the seeds started the American cotton industry on its way to becoming the largest in the world.

Basically, the cotton gin that Whitney per-

fected in 1793 was made of three parts—a revolving cylinder with stiff wire hooks, a metal plate with slots in it, and a brush. When the cylinder turned, the wire hooks, which looked like rows of saw teeth, went through the slots, snagged the cotton fiber, and pulled it down through the slots. The seeds, which were too large to go through the slots, caught on the metal plate and snapped off. As the cylinder turned past the brush, the fiber was brushed off the hooks and fell in a heap at the bottom of the gin. If the cylinder was turned by a hand crank, almost 5 kilograms (about 10 pounds) of cotton could be ginned a day. Using a horse or waterpower to turn the crank increased production to at least five times as much. Whitney's cotton gin was simple but so efficient that the basic idea of the original cotton gin has never been changed.

Now that its seeds could be removed easily and rapidly, American cotton was usable on a large scale. The spinning and weaving of cotton cloth increased enormously in the United States. Within 10 years the value of cotton increased more than 50 times. To meet the great demand, growers in the South started large cotton plantations, where slaves were used to plant and harvest the crops. The cotton plantations were for years the basis of the way of life in the South.

After the Civil War, Southerners began building their own textile mills. Until that time, most of the mills had been in New England. Today the U.S. cotton textile industry is located almost entirely in the South. By building mills in the South, textile manufacturers were close to the cotton fields. This saved the cost of shipping the cotton long distances to the mills. And labor in the South was cheaper than in other parts of the country.

The cotton-growing area of the United States is called the cotton belt. It includes 18 states stretching from the Atlantic to the Pacific.

The Boll Weevil. Until the 1920's cotton was not grown outside the old South. Then a little beetle from Mexico caused many changes. This beetle was the boll weevil, which entered Texas from Mexico in 1892. The boll weevil uses its long, sharp snout to pierce a hole in the young cotton boll. Then it lays its eggs inside. The eggs quickly hatch into grubs that devour the developing seeds and fibers. By the 1920's this destructive pest had overrun the entire South.

But the boll weevil does not thrive in a dry climate. Cotton growers began pushing westward into the High Plains of western Texas, and on into New Mexico, Arizona, and southern California. The discovery of large supplies of underground water in the Southwest that could be used for irrigating cotton was another reason for the westward move in cotton growing. A third reason was that the soil in the old South was badly eroded and the plant foods in the soil were used up from long years of growing the same crop.

Mechanical planters dig a number of small furrows at a time, plant the seeds, and cover them.

COTTON GROWING TODAY

About 80 nations in the world grow cotton. The leading producers are the United States, the Soviet Union, China, India, Egypt, Mexico, Brazil, and Pakistan. The United States grows about one fifth of the world's cotton.

Different kinds of cotton are classed according to the staple, or length, of their fibers. Longer fibers are more valuable because they can be made into finer products. Most of the cotton grown in the United States and elsewhere in the world is **American upland** cotton, which has a fiber length of about 25 millimeters (1 inch). This is short-staple cotton. **Egyptian** cotton, which actually originated in Peru, has fibers over 30 millimeters (about 1¼ inch) long and is known as long-staple cotton. **Pima** cotton, which is a popular long-staple type grown in the United States, is the result of crossing Egyptian and American cotton plants.

Care of the Crop

The methods of growing cotton have changed greatly in the past 25 years. Mules used to pull plows to cultivate the soil before planting; now tractors do the cultivating. Chemicals are used to fight weeds and diseases and parasites that harm the plants. The use of irrigation and fertilizers has increased. As a result of these changes, the yield of cotton per unit of land has almost doubled.

One of the most serious problems faced by cotton growers is insects. The boll weevil and other insects destroy about one bale of cotton out of every five or six bales grown each year. Cotton farmers spend large amounts of money for spraying and dusting their plants with insecticides (insect-killing chemicals).

Mechanical harvesters of the picker type move through a cotton field.

Weeds are another problem for the cotton grower. Weeds are usually removed by machine and by the use of herbicides (weed-killing chemicals). Herbicides may be put into the ground at the time of planting, or they may be applied after the cotton plants are growing.

Sometimes cotton growers drive flocks of geese onto the fields to eat the weeds. The geese do not bother the cotton plants because they prefer the weeds. Or flamethrowers (devices that expel a burning stream of fuel from a nozzle) may be used to burn off the weeds. These are used after the plants have grown a tough bark, so that the flames will not damage them.

Farmers must also control diseases that attack the cotton plant. Crop rotation, trash disposal, and chemical treatment of the soil are some of the ways that plant diseases are fought.

Cotton plants need food just as the human body does. The main ingredients of cotton fertilizers are nitrogen, phosphorus, and potassium. Fertilizers are applied before planting. For extra nourishment fertilizer is sometimes given to the young cotton plants after they have begun to grow.

Irrigation is a common practice in the dry areas of the western cotton belt, in Texas, Oklahoma, New Mexico, Arizona, and California. The land is usually watered before planting so that the cotton seeds will have moist earth to sprout in. Growing plants are watered as they need it.

When the leaves drop off, the cotton bolls are exposed to sunlight and air. This exposure helps to keep the cotton fiber from rotting and allows the boll to ripen and burst open quickly. For machine harvesting the leaves are re- moved by spraying the plants with chemicals called defoliants. Removal of the leaves also makes picking easier and cuts down on the amount of trash gathered with the cotton.

The time for planting cotton varies with the area of the country. In southern Texas the seeds are planted around the beginning of February. Farther north—in North Carolina, Tennessee, and Missouri, for instance—planting begins in May. The total time from planting to harvesting is usually 130 to 140 days.

From 7 to 10 days after planting, young sprouts push their way through the soil. Within about 2 months blossoms have formed on the plants. In another 2 months the cotton bolls have ripened. The bolls are shaped something like giant green raindrops. They are about 40 millimeters (1½ inches) long and 25 millimeters (1 inch) thick. When the bolls burst open, revealing the white, fluffy cotton fiber inside, the cotton is ready to be picked.

Harvesting

Cotton is now harvested mainly by machine. In the past all the harvesting was done by hand. Field-workers pulled the cotton fiber and seeds from the bolls and put it into long sacks hanging from their shoulders. Harvesting cotton by hand is laborious and expensive. For years people tried to invent a machine that would do the work. Several types of machine harvesters were tried during the 19th century, but large-scale machine harvesting did not really get started until the 1940's.

There are two kinds of machine harvesters —the picker and the stripper. The picker has revolving shafts that catch and pull the cotton fiber out of the bolls and throw it into large storage baskets. The stripper pulls the entire boll from the plant, and the fiber is removed from the bolls later. Today more than 95 percent of the crop is harvested by machine.

After harvesting, the cotton is taken to the cotton gin. The original gin invented by Eli Whitney could produce about 22 kilograms (50 pounds) of cotton fiber a day. A modern gin can turn out ten times as much in only six or eight minutes. After the seeds have been removed, the fiber (which is also called **lint**) is compressed into bales, wrapped in cloth, and tied with steel bands. An average bale weighs about 225 kilograms (500 pounds).

Cotton from the harvester is loaded into a container. It is then taken to the gin.

Cleaned cotton in large rolls, called laps (*left*), is ready for carding. When carding is finished, the cotton has been formed into a ropelike strand called a sliver (*right*).

From the cotton gin, the fiber and the other parts of the cotton plant go their separate ways. Linters, the short fuzzy hairs on the seeds, are removed and used in making ammunition, camera film, phonograph records, lacquer, and dynamite. The seeds are crushed, yielding cottonseed oil, which is used in shortening, cooking oils, margarine, salad oil, and dressings. After the oil has been removed, the dry seed is ground up into meal and used as livestock feed. The seed hulls (the outer husks of the seeds) are used for livestock feed as well as in the manufacture of plastics. The bales of cotton fiber are taken to textile mills, where the cotton is made into fabric.

From Fiber to Fabric

Raw cotton goes through a long series of processes before it is finally woven into fabric. The cotton is first cleaned and formed into large rolls, called **laps**. The laps are fed into machines that straighten and smooth the tangled fibers and remove any remaining impurities. This process is called **carding**. By the time carding is finished, the cotton has been formed into a ropelike strand called a **sliver**. The sliver (pronounced "slyver") is about as thick as a grown man's finger.

If the cotton is to be made into high-grade fabric, it will be combed as well as carded. Combing straightens out the fibers and sepa-rates the long fibers from the short ones. A yarn made entirely of long fibers is smoother and more even than one made with mixed long and short fibers. Combed yarns thus make the best fabrics.

A sliver of cotton is really only a loose strand of cotton fibers. To make this strand into yarn strong enough for weaving, it must be pulled and twisted so that the fibers form a tight, thin thread. The pulling, or drawing out, is done on a machine called a **drawing frame**. This operation is repeated several times, drawing out the fibers into finer and tighter strands. The cotton is finally spun into yarn on spools, called bobbins. These bobbins of yarn are then taken to the weaving room, where the cloth is made.

After the cloth has been woven, it may be dyed in various colors. Colors and designs can also be printed on the cloth by huge presses similar to those used to print newspapers.

Fabrics made with cotton include broadcloth, calico, cheesecloth, corduroy, denim, gabardine, and terry cloth.

Cotton cloth is used for many articles of clothing. Dresses, shirts, trousers, and underwear are often made entirely of cotton or have some cotton in them. Large quantities of cotton go into making such household fabrics as drapes, sheets, rugs, and bedspreads.

About one fifth of the cotton produced

The slivers are pulled and twisted into thinner strands (*left*). Then they are spun into yarn. Warp (lengthwise) yarns are wound (*right*) onto a loom for weaving.

each year is made into things other than clothing and household fabrics. Cotton is used to insulate electric cords. Special sturdy cotton cloth is used to cover books and suitcases. Cotton is also turned chemically into plastics, synthetic fibers, and artificial leather.

▶ **NEW DEVELOPMENTS**

Since the 1930's synthetic materials such as rayon, nylon, and fiberglass have challenged cotton's position as the leading textile fiber. To meet this competition, cotton manufacturers are constantly looking for ways to improve their products. One example is the development of stretch fabrics, which give with body movements and are ideal for ski and other sports clothing. Chemicals can be added to cottons so that they do not wrinkle and need little or no ironing after washing. Other chemicals added to cotton make it resistant to fire, water, and mildew. One of the most popular chemical treatments makes cotton resistant to spots and stains.

Cotton farmers and manufacturers put money into a central fund for research to find better ways of growing and harvesting cotton, to find ways of improving the quality of the cotton fiber, and to find new uses for cotton.

EMMETT E. ROBINSON
National Cotton Council of America

See also FIBERS; TEXTILES; WHITNEY, ELI.

A loom produces woven cloth by interlacing warp yarns and filling (crosswise) yarns.

COUNTRY AND WESTERN MUSIC

Country and western is a native American music. Its origins lie in the folk songs of the English, Scottish, and Irish people who settled the southeastern United States. By the early 1800's, the sentiments and rhythms of their songs had changed to suit the rugged, challenging country in which they lived.

In its early stages, this music was called hillbilly music—a reference to the "hill country" of the Appalachian Mountains. Songs were passed from family to family and friend to friend. But for the most part, the music remained within its own community. In small towns and among close-knit families, it was one of the main sources of entertainment. Often small bands made up of two fiddlers and two guitarists played very fast, complex, and delicate melodies for lyrics that were sung in high, close harmonies. This style came to be called bluegrass music. Over the years it was blended with other styles—blues, jazz, and the sentimental ballads of the southwest—until it became what we know as country and western.

From the beginning, country and western was a music of struggle and determination. The songs celebrated hard work and good fun, and they told tales of romantic and financial troubles.

▶ **EARLY COUNTRY AND WESTERN STARS**

The entertainment business thrived in the 1930's and 1940's. It was during this time that the popularity of country and western music began to spread all over the United States.

The first wide exposure given to country and western performers came from two main sources—the radio and the Grand Ole Opry, in Nashville, Tennessee. On radio, such singers as Jimmie Rodgers, Roy Acuff, and Ernest Tubb could reach many more listeners than they could in person. The Grand Ole Opry—a huge, barn-shaped music hall—presented country and western shows every Saturday night. It made Nashville the center of country and western music. Many of the country and western performers of the time made their homes there, and recording studios were built in the area.

Western movies also contributed to the rise of country and western music. Popular heroes such as Gene Autry and Tex Ritter displayed

Johnny Cash.

the musical talents that had started them in show business.

By the late 1940's, there was a large, devoted audience for country and western music, and many popular singers recorded hit records. Country and western became a recognized form of music, as had rhythm and blues before it. Country and western stars and their bands crisscrossed the country in buses, playing hundreds of one-night shows.

One of the first major stars of country and western was Hank Williams. He was an important figure not only because he was an exciting performer but also because he wrote many of his songs. Before Williams, most country and western singers either adapted traditional folk and country songs or used songs written by professional songwriters. Williams wrote songs about loneliness and isolation as well as about good times. Most of his songs were either slow, mournful ballads or fast, jumping tunes that were accompanied by piano. These fast-paced songs came to be known as honky-tonk music. Other performers who specialized in honky-tonk were Lefty Frizzell, Webb Pierce, and Ray Price.

As country and western grew in popularity throughout the 1950's, some radio stations began broadcasting only country and western music. It offered new kinds of songs—songs that told exciting stories about heroes and common people and were sung with sincerity. Johnny Cash's "I Walk the Line," Johnny Horton's "Battle of New Orleans," and Marty

Dolly Parton.

Willie Nelson.

Chet Atkins.

Robbins' "El Paso" were among the most popular of this type of song. The 1950's also saw the rise of women as important country and western performers. Kitty Wells and Wanda Jackson were among the leading female singers of the time.

▶ PROGRESSIVE COUNTRY MUSIC

During the 1960's, country and western took full advantage of the newest technology of the recording industry. Performers used orchestral string sections and brass instruments such as trumpets, saxophones, and even French horns. Oddly enough, it was a guitarist who pioneered these changes. Chet Atkins, who had accompanied nearly every country and western performer, became Nashville's most acclaimed record producer. His elaborately orchestrated records sold in the millions. This new sound was called "progressive country."

The key to the success of the progressive sound was smoothness and polish. Many older performers thought this new sound was an undignified attempt to appeal to the large pop music audience. But young artists like Charlie Pride—country and western's first black star —and Buck Owens recorded strings of hit songs using the new methods.

▶ COUNTRY AND THE "OUTLAWS"

The progressive sound continued to be popular throughout the 1960's and 1970's. Singers such as Tanya Tucker and Bill Anderson recorded popular story-songs by writers such as Tom T. Hall. Many leading singers—Dolly Parton, for example—wrote much of their own material. Around this time, the popularity of country and western began to spread throughout the world. Often it was called simply country music. Olivia Newton-John, an Australian, became well known as a performer. Enormous enthusiasm developed in Japan.

As happens with any vital, growing musical form, there were those who disagreed with the main trends. Some younger performers believed that much of country's original strength had been in its rough energy and lack of restraint. They felt that the calm, progressive sound denied the music this sort of energy. These young performers also enjoyed rock music, and rock's loud volume and beat began to find its way into the new country music.

These dissenting artists were referred to as "outlaws" because they made their music outside the usual Nashville recording studios. The most prominent outlaws included Waylon Jennings and Willie Nelson, a veteran Nashville songwriter who became a singer.

Country and western music in all its various forms—from bluegrass to progressive country to the outlaws' country rock—continues to evolve and flourish. And the number of people who are attracted to it is increasing all the time.

KEN TUCKER
Music Critic
Los Angeles *Herald Examiner*

TRIAL BY ORDEAL

COLD WATER

HOT WATER

HOT IRON

THE MORSEL

COURTS

Wherever people live together in communities, disputes are bound to arise. Among animals, conflicts result in victory for the stronger or quicker. But human beings believe that in an argument the one who is right should win. Sometimes an argument can be settled quickly. But sometimes the problem is more complicated and can be settled only in a court.

A court is a forum, or meeting place, established by the government for the just and peaceful settlement of disputes and the enforcement of laws. Courts and methods of carrying out justice have changed as society has changed. Over the centuries the changes have been enormous.

Europeans in the Middle Ages often settled disputes in ways that seem extremely crude and unfair to us today. One method was called trial by ordeal. There were four forms of ordeal—"cold water," "hot water," "hot iron," and the "morsel." In the cold water ordeal, the accused person was tied and lowered into water. If he sank, he was declared innocent. If he floated, he was considered guilty and was punished. In ordeal by hot water, the accused plunged his hand into boiling water and pulled out a stone. If his hand showed no injury after 3 days, he was considered innocent. In the hot iron ordeal, the accused had to carry a red-hot iron bar 9 feet. As in the boiling water ordeal, his hands were inspected 3 days later to determine guilt. The morsel ordeal, although not so painful, was as hard to pass as the other three. The accused had to swallow a big piece of food without choking on it.

Trial by ordeal was a typical way of doing justice in the Middle Ages. From these crude and unreliable procedures, there developed through the centuries our present system of trials in courts of law. We will skip this interesting history and see what procedure was devised by the great minds of several nations through many eras as the best way to settle serious disputes in the courts.

▶ CIVIL AND CRIMINAL SUITS

Courts handle two kinds of disputes: civil and criminal. It is not always easy to tell the difference between the two, and some disputes may be either criminal or civil. In general, though, a civil case is a dispute between two private citizens. The court must decide which one is right. A criminal case is a dispute between an individual and the whole community. The community's representative —usually a policeman—claims that the individual has broken a law or committed a crime that harms the community. The court must decide if the person is guilty of this crime.

Civil law has to do with the things people have a legal right to expect of one another. For example, when one man signs his name to a promise to pay money to another, the second man has a right to expect payment. When one man promises to deliver goods, the other man has a right to expect delivery. Otherwise he cannot run his business. If the first man fails to keep his promise, the second man may sue him in civil court.

Other civil suits arise from accidents. Often the people involved in an accident disagree about whose fault it was. The civil court must decide. The "plaintiff" claims money in compensation (payment) for damage that he accuses the "defendant" of having done to him.

Criminal law, on the other hand, is a public matter. Here the injury is thought to be to the community as a whole. For instance, if a thief breaks into a man's store and steals money or jewelry, his action not only hurts the man but breaks one of the vital rules set up for the peace and safety of everyone. Therefore it is a case for the criminal courts. Men are sent to jail fairly often in criminal cases, but only rarely in civil cases.

▶ **HOW COURTS WORK TO SETTLE DISPUTES**

In a civil case one person sues another. The one who sues is the plaintiff. He complains that the other has "injured" him. A lawyer writes out the complaint and files it with the court. This piece of paper, the "complaint," tells what the argument is about. The filing of the complaint by the plaintiff's lawyer starts the case.

Next, the lawyer for the defendant prepares an "answer" and files it with the court. The complaint, answer, and similar papers are called "pleadings" because they are requests, or pleas, to the court. The lawyers may make various motions, or claims, concerning the pleadings until the dispute is clearly stated. Then "the issue is joined." That means it is ready to be decided by the court.

A criminal case, on the other hand, starts when a policeman arrests someone (the defendant) for breaking the law. For some crimes the policeman must see the man breaking the law in order to arrest him. For others he may make the arrest when a witness tells him about it. Then the policeman takes the arrested person to court as soon as possible.

In court a complaint is drawn up. In the criminal complaint the policeman or the victim accuses the defendant of doing certain things which amount to a crime. The complaint (accusation) is read to the defendant. But he need not answer it yet. He has a right to have a lawyer defend him. He is given time to prepare his defense. In the meantime the accused probably will not have to stay in jail. Instead he can put up some money to assure the court that he will return to answer the charges. This money is called bail.

The next step in a criminal case is for the prosecutor (usually called a district attorney) to prepare formal written charges. In many cases the prosecutor must call his witnesses before a group of citizens known as a grand jury. They decide whether to make an accusation. If they vote to accuse the defendant of a crime, their charge or accusation is called an indictment. If they feel there is not enough evidence, they may dismiss the charge, and that ends it.

Sometimes witnesses are called and evidence presented to a grand jury before anyone is arrested. In such a case the defendant is arrested only after he has been indicted. Where there is no grand jury or where the crime is not serious, the formal accusation is made by the district attorney. This is sometimes called an information.

The defendant may be charged with a serious crime (a "felony") or a less serious one (a "misdemeanor"). After the accusation is filed with the court, the defendant is called in with his lawyer to answer it. This is the "arraignment." When he is arraigned, the defendant is asked: "How do you plead?" He may admit the truth of the charge by pleading guilty. He may deny the accusation or simply refuse to admit guilt by pleading not

A trial in a typical American county courtroom. The jury of 12 men and women and the judge listen as the lawyer questions a witness.

guilty. If he pleads not guilty, the case is ready for the court. The court trial will decide whether or not he is guilty.

▶THE TRIAL

A trial is frequently called a search for truth, and that is what it should be. It is not supposed to be a battle of wits, or an appeal to sympathy. It is meant to be an effort by two opposing sides to arrive at the truth by reason, logic, and good sense. Sometimes the decision is in the hands of one fact finder, a judge. More often, in serious cases, a jury of 12 citizens decides. Either way it is the job of the fact finders to decide what really happened. For example, did the accused man break into a store with the intention of stealing from the safe?

The lawyer for the defense and the lawyer for the prosecution each presents evidence to prove his side is right. That evidence may be the testimony of "witnesses," people who know something about the case from their own observation. A witness may be the taxi-driver who saw the defendant hurrying away from the store, the expert who found his fingerprints on the safe, or a friend who heard the defendant say he needed the money. A witness for the defense might say the man was home with him at the time and could not have stolen the money.

In addition to firsthand accounts by witnesses, evidence may include physical objects —the stolen jewels found in the defendant's pocket when he was arrested, or the jimmy used to force open the window of the store. These items are the "exhibits."

What can be used as evidence and how it is

Are British and American courts different?

There is a strong family resemblance between American courts and the courts of the United Kingdom. This is not surprising, for the British system of justice prevailed on American shores for 150 years. When the United States became an independent nation, the American court system took many ideas about justice from the British court system.

Today if an American walked into a British court, he would find that it did not look much like an American courtroom. The lawyers, called barristers in the United Kingdom, wear black robes and small, curled, white wigs. They call the judge "My Lord" rather than "Your Honor" as Americans do. A British trial usually seems to go more smoothly than an American trial, for there are fewer interruptions and rarely does anyone raise his voice. Usually trials are shorter in Britain, too, although a difficult case may last several weeks. Relatively few cases in Britain are reviewed by another court after the trial is over.

There are many reasons for the differences between British and American courts. First of all, the British system is the older system and has had more time to settle down. Then, too, there are many fewer barristers in Britain than there are trial lawyers in the United States. Many of the barristers know each other and the judges. They eat lunch together and are a sort of club or legal fraternity. They do not disagree as violently in court as lawyers often do in the United States. Another reason for the difference is that in the United Kingdom a case is more firmly set before the trial in court begins. Most witnesses have made statements in writing which the barristers have examined, and the case has been prepared by a different kind of British lawyer called a solicitor. The barrister almost never talks to his client or to the witnesses before they appear in court.

But fundamentally the two systems are the same. In both countries, the court is a place

BRITISH CRIMINAL COURT

1 ACCUSED IN DOCK
2 POLICE ESCORT
3 BARRISTERS
4 JUDGE
5 CLERKS OF THE COURT

where a jury of ordinary citizens decides the facts of a past event. The jury hears witnesses under oath tell their stories about the event and examines objects and documents that have a bearing on what happened. They listen to the way the witnesses answer questions that the lawyers ask. The whole proceeding is supervised by a judge who sees to it that rules are followed to keep the trial on its proper course.

to be considered by the jury are legal questions. The law governing evidence is based on fairness, on "materiality" (which means helpfulness in deciding the issue). When the lawyer for one side or the other thinks certain testimony should not be considered by the jury, he objects. He may think the evidence has nothing to do with the question. He may think it would create unfair prejudice. Then the judge must decide the legal question of whether or not to admit that evidence.

Witnesses at the trial give testimony under oath. That means they swear (promise) to tell the truth. Sometimes they may fail to keep

their promise, or they may be honestly mistaken, or they may have forgotten what happened and be mixed up. So one of the most important and difficult jobs for the fact finders is to determine whether the witness is accurate and whether he is telling the truth. The law has set down certain guides to help the jury decide these questions. For one thing, they are allowed to consider the witness' "demeanor"—how he behaves on the witness stand, his tone of voice, his attitude. If the witness gave a different story in the past, the jury may be told of it. They may also consider the interest the witness may have in the outcome of the case or any other prejudice that might affect his testimony. They may take into account bad character shown by previous criminal or immoral acts.

But the best way of testing the truthfulness and reliability of a witness is cross-examination. When a lawyer asks questions of a witness whose answers will help his side of the case, that is called direct examination. When the lawyer on the other side questions the same witness, it is called cross-examination. If there is anything wrong with the witness' story, the lawyer hopes to find it out.

▶ REACHING A VERDICT

After the jury has heard all the evidence, the judge instructs the jury. He explains the law that applies in the case. This is called the court's "charge" to the jury. In a jury trial these 12 citizens become judges for that case. They are the ones who must decide what happened. But they must also know some law in order to hand down a "verdict"—either guilty or not guilty in a criminal case, or an award of money as "damages" in a civil case. In his charge the judge tells them all the law necessary for that particular case.

After the charge, the jury leaves the courtroom. Alone in the jury room, they talk over the case, make up their minds, and try to reach a verdict. They must remember that in the United States a man is considered innocent until proven guilty. As long as a juror has a reasonable doubt about a defendant's guilt, he must return a verdict of not guilty.

In a criminal case everybody on the jury has to agree. In a civil case a strong majority is enough. Sometimes jurors reach a verdict in minutes. Sometimes it takes days. If the jurors never can agree, we say that the jury is "hung," or deadlocked. Then the case must be tried over again, before a different jury.

When the verdict is returned, the court— that is, the judge—makes it final by giving a "judgment" based on the verdict. This is usually done at a later date. If the verdict is guilty in a criminal case, the judge sentences the defendant—says what his punishment shall be. The more serious the crime, the longer the jail sentence that the judge may impose. To a large extent it is up to the judge to do justice in the case. Usually he will do one of three things: send the defendant to jail for a specified time, fine him money, or release him on "probation"—that is, on condition that he behave himself well in the future.

To help the judge decide what is fair, he usually has a complete report on the defendant. What kind of person is he? What sort of life has he led? What were the circumstances of the crime? Justice may depend on special circumstances. A sentence that would be fair in one case might be too easy or too harsh in another.

▶ APPEALS

After judgment is pronounced, the trial court's work is over. But frequently the case is not. The trial may have been unfair. Perhaps the judge made mistakes in his ruling. So there are higher courts that may review the judgment of the trial court. This review is called an appeal. In a civil case either side or both may appeal. In a criminal case usually only the convicted defendant can appeal.

There are no juries, witnesses, or evidence in the appeal case. Instead of one judge, as in the trial court, the higher (or appellate) court has three, five, seven, or even nine judges. They hear the appeal—the arguments of lawyers on both sides. Then they decide whether the trial court's verdict was right or wrong. If they decide it was right, they "affirm" it. If they think it was wrong, they "reverse" it. The case is then either "dismissed" (ended) or sent back to a lower court for a new trial. Sometimes these judges write opinions to accompany their decision. These opinions express the judges' interpretations of the law and may themselves become law for future cases.

After a review by an appellate court, lawyers may appeal the case further, to a still higher court. In rare instances there is a final review by the Supreme Court of the United States, the highest court of the land.

H. Richard Uviller
Assistant District Attorney in Charge of
Appeals Bureau (New York City)

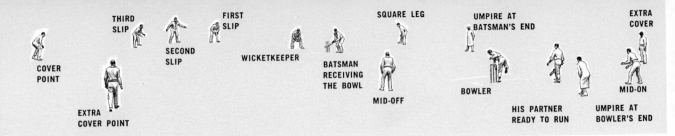

CRICKET

Cricket is one of the most popular games in England, Australia, India, and Pakistan. It is played in all English-speaking nations, including the United States and Canada.

In England in the late Middle Ages, there was a game known as stoolball. The object was for a player with a stick to keep an upturned three-legged stool from being hit with a ball thrown by another player. From stoolball has developed the boys' and men's game cricket. The name "cricket" probably comes from an early word that meant "stick" or "bat."

▶ THE PLAYING FIELD AND EQUIPMENT

Cricket is played with a ball and bat on a large field by two teams of 11 players each. The ball is about the size of a baseball. It has a cork center that is bound tightly with twine and covered with leather. The bat, no longer than 38 inches, has a flat striking surface up to 4¼ inches wide.

The center of the grass field is called the pitch. On it are two wickets, 22 yards apart. A wicket consists of three stumps (stakes) that stand close together in the ground. Small sticks, or bails, fit into grooves in the tops of the stumps. Boundary lines must be agreed upon before the match. The playing field varies between 3 and 20 acres in extent.

▶ BOWLING, BATTING, AND SCORING

The object of the game is for a team to score the most runs during its innings, or turn at bat. While one team has its innings, the 11 players of the other team take positions in the field, from which they try to put out the batsmen.

Play begins with a batsman at each wicket. A player of the fielding team, called the bowler, delivers the ball to the batsman at the opposite end of the pitch. With his bat the batsman must keep the ball from hitting the wicket and knocking off a bail, in which case he would be "bowled out." He is also out if any part of his body except his hand obstructs a bowled ball that the umpire decides would have hit the wicket; if he knocks a bail off the wicket with his bat or body; if he crosses the popping crease (a line 4 feet in front of the wicket), does not hit the ball, and fails to return behind the line before the wicket keeper catches the ball and knocks off a bail; or if he hits the ball and it is caught by a fieldsman before it touches the ground.

A batsman may stroke the ball forward, or deflect it in any direction. There is no foul ball in cricket. If a batted ball rolls across the boundary line, four runs are scored. If it goes over the boundary line before touching the ground, six runs count.

The batsman may also score a run if he and his batting partner at the other wicket can run to opposite ends of the pitch safely. They need not run at all, but if they do, either batsman may be put out if he fails to reach the popping crease toward which he is running before a fielder upsets the wicket at that end with the ball. The batsmen may score runs on one play as many times as they safely exchange ends.

The bowler must deliver the ball with straight overarm or underarm action and with at least one foot behind his bowling crease (a line even with the wicket). A well-bowled ball will land on the pitch and bounce in such a way as to confuse the batsman.

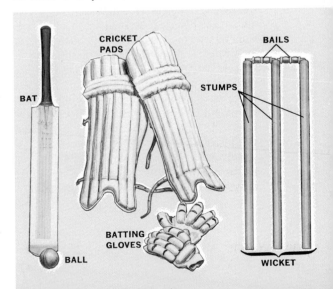

BAT

CRICKET PADS

BAILS

STUMPS

BATTING GLOVES

BALL

WICKET

Batsman is out if he fails to reach the popping crease before the wicket-keeper upsets the wicket with the ball.

Batsman is out if he crosses the popping crease, doesn't hit the ball, and fails to get back of the line before the wicketkeeper catches the ball and knocks out a bail.

Batsman is out when he knocks a bail from the wicket with his bat or body.

Finger spin may be used to make the ball change direction after having alighted on the pitch. It is also possible to make the ball swerve in the air before reaching the batsman.

A penalty run is added to the score of the batting side if the umpire calls a "no ball" (one bowled with an illegal action) or a "wide ball" (one delivered out of the batsman's reach), only if no runs result otherwise from the bowled ball. A bowler delivers six bowls for an "over." Then another bowler at the other end of the pitch bowls six balls to the batsman at the wicket opposite him. They alternate bowling until 10 batsmen have been put out, ending the innings.

▶ INNINGS AND MATCHES

Each team has one or two innings, as agreed on in advance. Games of a single innings are usually played in one day. Games of two innings, such as international (test) matches, usually last several days. Play usually begins at 11:30 A.M. and finishes at 6:30 P.M. with time out for meals. A scoring rate of 50 runs per hour is considered reasonable under normal circumstances. If the side that bats second is behind when the time allotted for the match has run out, neither team is the winner.

The two umpires usually wear long white coats. One stands behind the wicket at the bowler's end, calls bowling infractions, and makes decisions on plays at his end of the pitch. The other—the "square leg" umpire—stands on line with the popping crease at the batsman's end. Arguing with an umpire's decision is not allowed under any circumstances.

DONALD KING
Canadian Cricket Association

CRIME AND CRIMINOLOGY

A crime is an act that is forbidden by law because it it harmful—to a person, to property, or to society in general. Criminology is the study of crime. It is concerned with the different kinds of crimes, the persons who commit crimes, and ways of preventing and correcting crime.

Crime of some kind has existed ever since people began to live together in groups. People in the earliest societies were as much concerned as we are today with such harmful acts as stealing and killing. They realized, as we do, that respect for life and property is essential to the survival of any society.

Most societies today have written laws that define certain acts as crimes and set punishments for those acts. Before people had written languages, they defined crimes and set punishments through what we call tradition. For example, if a goat or sheep was missing and the owner thought it had been stolen, the elders of the tribe or village would meet to investigate what had happened. They would find out who was guilty of the theft, and they would set the punishment. It might be the same punishment that had been used in their society for centuries. This tradition, or way of dealing with crime, was passed on orally from parents to children, down through the generations. The story of how people have developed systems of law, from earliest times to the present, is told in the article LAW AND LAW ENFORCEMENT in Volume L.

Some acts forbidden by law today were unknown until modern times. For example, before the air age, there was no need for laws against the hijacking of planes. And there is no exact agreement today about all the many kinds of acts that may be defined as crimes. Laws vary from country to country. Some acts that are considered basic rights in a democracy—criticizing the government, for example—are considered crimes in societies that do not value individual freedom. And just as people disagree about which actions are crimes, they disagree about the causes of crime and how society should deal with it.

▶ KINDS OF CRIME

In spite of differences of opinion, certain acts are considered crimes, or criminal of-fenses, in most modern societies. They can be grouped, or classified, in several ways.

Felonies and Misdemeanors

Crimes can be classified according to their seriousness, or the amount of harm they cause. Few people would say that making false statements on an income tax return is as harmful as killing a human being. Yet both acts are crimes. Under the laws of the United States and of many other countries, crimes are classified in two broad groups—felonies and misdemeanors. Whether an act is a felony or a misdemeanor helps to determine the penalty, or punishment, attached to it.

A felony is a form of crime that is considered extremely serious and a real danger to society. Felonies include such acts as murder (also called homicide), robbery, rape (sexual attack), kidnapping, arson (intentionally setting fire to a building), and assault (physical attack). A person who commits a felony is called a felon.

Misdemeanors are less serious forms of crime—a traffic violation, for example, or theft of an item with very little value. A person who commits a misdemeanor is called a misdemeanant.

In general, there is widespread agreement about which acts should be regarded as felonies and which as misdemeanors. But it is important to realize that these definitions may change as a society's values change. And in the United States, an act that is legally defined as a felony in one state may be a misdemeanor in another. For example, having any amount of the drug marijuana is a felony in some states. But in other states, possession of a small amount is a misdemeanor.

Other Classifications of Crime

In terms of the victims or the objects of criminal acts, crimes are often classified as **crimes against persons** or **crimes against property**. Crimes against persons—such as murder, kidnapping, assault, and sexual attack—usually bring severe penalties. Crimes against property—robbery, burglary, arson, vandalism, automobile theft, and the like—generally bring less severe punishment than crimes against persons.

Some acts do not visibly harm persons or property but instead threaten the order of so-

A counselor works with a juvenile offender. Juvenile offenses are a serious aspect of crime today.

ciety or offend its moral code. These acts—drunkenness, gambling, and various crimes of vice—are often called **victimless crimes**. The "victims" are the persons performing the acts or are willing participants.

Crimes are also classified according to the methods used to carry them out or the background of the persons who commit the crimes. Many serious crimes are committed by individuals or small groups, often with very little planning. These crimes are sometimes called **street crimes**. Assaults, muggings, and other violent crimes against persons are the most feared street crimes.

Organized crime is carried out by people who have banded together for the sole purpose of committing crime. Organized criminals are involved in large-scale operations in the United States, as well as in many other countries. They usually avoid crimes such as robbery and assault. Instead, they concentrate on crimes that will yield a high profit. Organized criminals import huge amounts of heroin and other illegal drugs, run illegal gambling operations, lend money

at illegal rates of interest, and bribe public officials in an attempt to increase their control of government. Some persons involved in organized crime are also business and community leaders. Organized crime is a serious threat to society because its operations are largely invisible.

White-collar crime is committed by people who violate the law in the course of everyday business activities. A person who lies about business profits in order to reduce the amount of taxes owed would fall into this category, as would a person who hires an arsonist to burn down a failing factory in order to collect insurance money. Other examples of white-collar crime are charging illegal prices for merchandise, polluting the air with factory smoke, and selling unsafe products. But unlike organized criminals, white-collar criminals are not persons who have banded together for the purpose of committing crimes.

Juvenile offenses are acts committed by young people, usually under the age of 18. Some such acts—running away from home or skipping school, for example—do not qualify as crimes. But others involve robbery, auto theft, or even murder. In most years, more young people than adults are arrested for street crimes. And many juvenile offenders later commit criminal acts. For these reasons, juvenile offenses are among the most serious aspects of the modern crime problem.

▶CAUSES OF CRIME

No one knows exactly what causes crime, although many scientific theories seek to explain it. It may be that different forms of crime have different causes. For example, a person who becomes angry during an argument and attacks another person is probably not influenced by the same motives that lead a bank teller to steal from a bank.

Some scientists think that the causes of crime are physical, or **biological**. This is a very old point of view. Some of the earliest researchers believed that people who committed crimes were different from other people in such things as their body builds or the shapes of their heads. Most modern scientists reject this theory. But some research is being done today to discover if some aspects of the criminal's body chemistry are different from those of other people.

Other scientists think that the causes of crime are **social**. These scientists attach importance to such things as poverty, unemployment, and poor housing. Lack of education or job training and a broken or deprived home are among factors that these researchers believe may lead to crime.

Still other scientists believe that the causes of crime are largely **psychological**. They view the criminal as someone who is driven by mental forces—forces that are often thought to be beyond the criminal's control. In this theory, crime is viewed as a symptom of some problem—fear, anger, or perhaps deep sorrow—that has led to mental illness. Researchers who take this view often think that a criminal is someone to be helped rather than punished.

▶ CRIME RATES

Statistics compiled by the Federal Bureau of Investigation show that the crime rate more than doubled in the United States during the 1960's and 1970's. Violent crime skyrocketed. The number of robberies increased more than 250 percent; the number of assaults, more than 150 percent; and the number of murders, more than 100 percent.

High crime rates appear to be closely linked with such problems as poverty, overcrowding in large cities, and unemployment. Countries with these and other problems have crime rates very similar to those of the United States. In general, countries that have a great deal of material wealth—cars, television sets, and the like—have serious problems with theft. Less wealthy nations, on the other hand, may have a murder rate many times that of the United States.

Violent crimes have increased sharply in Europe in recent years, although they are still somewhat below U.S. levels. In some European and South American countries, there has been an increase in the number of politically motivated crimes—kidnappings and assassinations, for example. But Japan, which has strict laws controlling the possession of guns, reports comparatively few murders. In recent years Tokyo has reported fewer than 200 murders, while New York City, with a smaller population, has reported about eight times that number.

But it is difficult to compare the crime rates of different countries because their methods of reporting crimes and even their definitions of crime vary a great deal. Many Communist countries do not publish crime statistics regularly.

Even when statistics are available, it is difficult to know how much crime there really is in a country. Many crimes—even serious ones—are never reported to the police and therefore are not included in official estimates of the extent of crime. In the United States, the government conducted a survey asking citizens if they had been victims of crimes and if they had reported those crimes to the police. The survey showed that there may well be more than twice as much crime as official estimates indicate.

▶ HOW SOCIETY DEALS WITH CRIME

There are many specialized agencies that have been set up to deal with crime and criminals. Together, they form the **criminal justice system**. Some, such as police departments, detect crimes, collect evidence, and arrest suspects. Courts determine guilt or innocence and assign penalties.

In addition to punishing those who have committed crimes, society usually seeks ways to help them become law-abiding citizens. And researchers try to discover the causes of crime and find ways to prevent it.

Crime Detection

Some crimes are fairly easy to detect and solve, while others are more difficult. Violent crimes are often easier than crimes involving property because most violent crimes are sudden and unplanned and involve strong emotions. Very often the criminal and the victim know one another—a person strikes a fellow worker during a heated argument on the job, for example. In such situations, there may be witnesses or physical evidence of the crime.

Burglary, auto theft, and other crimes against property are a different matter. These crimes are usually committed against total strangers and often involve careful planning. Little, if any, evidence is left for the police. The rate of success in solving crimes against property is often only 20 percent, compared to as much as 80 percent for murder, a violent crime.

Penalties

When a court finds that a person has committed a criminal offense, it assigns a penalty, or punishment. The seriousness of the crime and the background of the offender—including whether or not the person has committed other crimes in the past—affect the penalty given. A court may simply place some offenders on probation. Probation is a warning. These persons may remain free only as long as they do not commit any further crimes. Usually they must report to probation officers from time to time, so that the court can keep track of them.

A person who commits a misdemeanor must pay a fine or spend time in **jail**. A jail is a place where people who have committed criminal offenses are kept for short periods of time, usually less than a year.

Felons generally are placed in **prisons**—places designed to hold prisoners for longer periods of time. Prison terms range from one year to the life of the prisoner. In some areas, certain felonies may be punished by death, or **capital punishment**.

Offenders who show in prison that they are capable of good behavior are often released on **parole**. They return to society but are subject to certain restrictions.

Crime Prevention

More and more attention has been given in recent years to ways of preventing crime. Many people feel that crime will be reduced when some of the social factors that seem to be closely linked with it are improved.

There are many things that people can do to lessen the chances that they will become the victims of crime. Police often meet with neighborhood and citizen groups to make them aware of these things.

For example, people learn which types of locks are most secure. They are urged to record the serial numbers of television sets, stereo equipment, and other possessions to improve the chances of recovering these things if they are stolen.

In many areas, people who have citizens band radio equipment work with the police by reporting suspicious situations. There are special police programs aimed at helping certain groups, such as the elderly, guard themselves against crime. Through these and similar measures, people are becoming more aware that the prevention of crime is everybody's business, not just a matter for the police.

▶ CRIMINOLOGY

Criminology involves the study of crime and criminal offenders in many different settings and from many different points of view. In a sense, everyone in the criminal justice system is a criminologist—a police officer cruising a beat must be as concerned with understanding crime and criminals as is a judge in a courtroom. The field of criminology offers a great many opportunities for interesting careers.

One type of criminologist, the **criminalist**, is trained in the laboratory analysis of physical evidence—footprints, fingerprints, bloodstains, and the like. Police officers, detectives, and investigators are also considered criminologists, as are the assistant district attorneys who prosecute cases in the courts.

Penology is another branch of criminology. It covers the measures applied to persons who have been convicted of crimes—jails, prisons, probation, and parole. Careers in penology include those of the corrections officer, who works in a state or federal prison; the parole officer, who supervises persons recently released from prison; and the probation officer, who is appointed by a court.

There has been a steady increase in the educational and training requirements for all careers in criminology. At one time, one could become a police officer without a high school diploma. Now most police agencies require two- or four-year college degrees.

Requirements for other careers vary. A criminology professor at a university may hold a doctorate. An assistant district attorney may hold a law degree; a laboratory criminalist, a master's degree; and a parole officer, a four-year college degree. But every career in criminology demands integrity, intelligence, and dedication to the goal of improving society.

GEORGE L. KIRKHAM
Florida State University
ALAN A. MALINCHAK
University of South Dakota

See also COURTS; FEDERAL BUREAU OF INVESTIGATION; JURY; JUVENILE DELINQUENCY; LAW AND LAW ENFORCEMENT; LAWYERS; POLICE; PRISONS.

CROCHETING. See KNITTING AND CROCHETING.

CROCKETT, DAVY (1786–1836)

Davy Crockett was a colorful figure who loved to tell tall tales. In fact, his neighbors were so impressed by Crockett's stories that they elected him to Congress. Later he went off to fight for Texas independence and died a hero at the battle of the Alamo.

David Crockett was born in the backwoods of Tennessee on August 17, 1786. He had only four days of schooling before he ran away from home at the age of 13. After a few years of roaming, he returned home. Although still in his teens, he was as tall and strong as a grown man. He went to work to pay off a $76 debt owed by his father. With some extra money he earned, Davy bought a rifle and soon became an expert shot. His skill as a hunter became legendary.

When he was 18, Davy fell in love. To win the girl, he was even willing to go back to school. He stayed six months. When the girl married someone else, Davy left school forever. He married Polly Findlay, borrowed $15, and settled down as a farmer. Although he was a good hunter, he was a bad farmer. During the next nine years, he moved from place to place, often depending on his rifle to keep his family well fed.

In 1813, Crockett fought under Andrew Jackson against the Creek Indians. Two years later Polly Crockett died. Davy Crockett married again and moved farther west in Tennessee. He was appointed a judge and elected to the state legislature.

Crockett delighted Tennessee voters with fanciful accounts of his hunting skill. One story was about a raccoon in a tree. The animal, recognizing the great Davy, cried, "You needn't take no further trubble, for I may as well cum down without another word."

Crockett was elected to Congress three times. He was easy to recognize in Washington, D.C., for he often wore clothing from his frontier days. Eventually he was defeated for re-election because of his opposition to President Jackson. Disappointed, Crockett resolved not to return to Tennessee. When he heard of the Texans' revolt against Mexico, he traveled to San Antonio to join the fight.

On March 6, 1836, more than 5,000 Mexican soldiers stormed the Alamo, a mission turned into a fort. Crockett and the 186 other Americans in the Alamo were all killed.

CROCODILES AND ALLIGATORS

Crocodiles and alligators are reptiles, a major class of animals that also includes the snakes, lizards, and turtles. All the living reptiles are descended from animals that roamed the earth about 250,000,000 years ago. Today some 25 species of reptiles belong to a group called the crocodilians. It includes the caymans and gavials, as well as the more familiar crocodiles and alligators.

All crocodilians look much alike. They have long tails and large jaws. Their skin, or hide, consists of many small bony plates and scales that are like hard leather. But there are ways of telling one crocodilian from another. The snout of the true crocodile is long and tapering, and the head has an almost triangular shape. Then, too, the teeth of this animal meet in such a way that it appears to be grinning. The snout of the alligator is broad and rounded, as is that of the cayman. The gavial's snout is extremely long and thin.

Crocodilians spend their lives in or close to water. Most of them frequent freshwater lakes, rivers, or swamps, but some are found in coastal waters. They are all good swimmers. They swim with twisting strokes of the powerful tail. The legs are held close to the body. On land they run only for short stretches. Sometimes they travel overland to get from one waterway to another. They also leave the water to sun, to rest, and to wait for prey.

Most crocodilians are found in the tropics. But some inhabit the warm, moist regions of the temperate zones. Various species of the true crocodiles live in parts of North and South America, Australia, Africa, and Asia. Except for one alligator native to a small area of eastern China, the alligators are restricted to the Americas. They frequent the coastal areas of the southern United States, the West Indies, Central America, Colombia, and Ecuador. Caymans are found in South

NILE CROCODILE

SPECTACLED CAYMAN

INDIAN GAVIAL

MARSH CROCODILE

AUSTRALIAN CROCODILE

AMERICAN CROCODILE

America, mostly in the rivers of eastern Brazil. The gavials live only in India and parts of southeastern Asia.

The crocodilians are egg-laying animals. The number of eggs in one clutch varies from 20 to 90, depending on the species and the crocodilian's size. The eggs of most crocodilians are long, white, and shiny, and have a hard, thick shell. Some crocodilians lay their clutch of eggs in a hole scooped out of a stream or riverbank. Others make a nest of plant materials in which they deposit their eggs.

Upon hatching, the young feed on fishes, water insects, and shellfish. The mother alligator is one of the few reptiles that guards her offspring. But the young soon leave the nest and go off on their own.

Adult crocodilians feed on fishes, birds, or almost any other animal they can catch—including their own relatives. Sometimes a crocodilian waits just beneath the surface to snap up a duck, muskrat, or other water animal. At other times a crocodilian uses its powerful tail to knock its prey from a stream bank into the water. The crocodilian also waits near a watering hole to seize an animal that comes to drink. With its strong jaws a crocodilian can grip animals as large as deer and cattle. Once the prey is in the water, the crocodilian—twisting and turning—drags it beneath the surface to drown. Some crocodilians attack people, and all are dangerous when cornered or wounded.

The crocodilian is well adapted for swimming or floating at the water's surface. Eyes, ears, and nostrils are on the top of the head and snout; they remain above the waterline while the crocodilian floats, with the eyes acting as periscopes. Although its jaws are not watertight, its throat can be blocked off by a valve of flesh. This keeps water from flowing down the throat when the crocodilian is submerged. An air passage goes from the nostrils to an opening behind the throat valve. The nostrils also have valves that close when the crocodilian dives. It is reported that crocodilians can stay under water for at least two hours and perhaps as long as five hours. Their bodies automatically ration the supply of oxygen to the important organs and tissues.

As a group, crocodilians are fairly long-lived. Ages of 20 or 30 years for those in

Note broad, rounded snout of this American alligator.

captivity are not uncommon. Alligators are less active than their crocodile cousins and tend to live longer. The oldest alligators on record have lived more than 50 years.

The crocodilians are also among the heaviest reptiles. An adult American alligator weighs about 225 kilograms (500 pounds). And an American crocodile was reported to weigh about 610 kilograms (1,350 pounds).

Crocodilians make all kinds of booming, barking, croaking, and grunting noises. But there are times when they remain silent. If there is a long period of hot, dry weather, the crocodilian buries itself deep in the mud. There the animal goes into a state of estivation (deep summer sleep). If the weather becomes too cold, the crocodilian goes into hibernation (deep winter sleep). During such periods its bodily processes slow down until the animal is barely alive.

The crocodilians have some value for people. The American alligator roots plants out of waterways, making a better habitat for fish and waterfowl. In many regions crocodilian flesh is eaten. The hides are used to make shoes and other leather articles. This practice has brought these reptiles close to extinction in some places. As a result, some governments have passed laws to protect the crocodilians.

WILL BARKER
Author, *Familiar Reptiles
and Amphibians of America*

See also REPTILES.

CROMWELL, OLIVER (1599–1658)

For one short period in history, England had no king or queen. After the English Civil War (1642–49), the nation was governed by a commoner. He was Oliver Cromwell, who was given the title Lord Protector.

Cromwell was born in Huntingdon, England, on April 25, 1599. He attended Cambridge University, where he was influenced by the Puritans. Their religious ideas affected his actions all his life.

In 1628 Cromwell was elected to Parliament. At that time King Charles I wanted to rule without interference and quarreled bitterly with Parliament. In 1642 a civil war broke out between the Cavaliers and the Roundheads. The Cavaliers were supporters of the King. The Roundheads, so called because they wore their hair short, opposed the King. The war finally ended in 1649 with the execution of Charles I on a charge of treason.

Oliver Cromwell had been one of the leaders of the Roundheads in the rebellion against the King. After Charles's death Cromwell became the actual ruler of the English Commonwealth. He later became Lord Protector of England and ruled as a dictator.

Cromwell, too, had his problems with Parliament. In one argument he stormed into the hall followed by a group of soldiers. He insulted the members of Parliament and ordered them removed. Cromwell himself locked the door of the chamber and put the key in his pocket.

Cromwell believed he was doing God's work. He was often very harsh. He forbade swearing and drinking and closed the theaters. When rebellions broke out in Scotland and Ireland, Cromwell was cruel in suppressing them.

Cromwell granted religious freedom to the Puritans and Quakers. He allowed the outcast Jews to build a temple in London.

He was a simple and direct man. To the artist who painted his portrait he said: ". . . paint my picture truly like me . . . pimples, warts, and everything . . ."

Cromwell died on September 3, 1658. His son, Richard, who was a weak ruler, followed him as Lord Protector. In 1660 Charles's son was recalled from exile and crowned King Charles II. The monarchy was restored, but never again would it be as strong as it was before Oliver Cromwell.

See also ENGLAND, HISTORY OF.

CROQUET

Croquet is a lawn game that everyone, young and old, can play. It can be played by two opponents or by two teams of two, three, or four players each. Croquet has a lot in common with billiards. Both developed from an old French game called *jeu du mail,* a ball game played with a mallet. Billiards became a table game, while croquet stayed on the ground.

The name croquet has been explained as a northern French way of saying *crochet.* This means "hooked stick." Such a stick was once used in the game.

▶ EQUIPMENT

Today lawn croquet is played with hardwood or hard rubber balls and wooden mallets. The course should be a level, grassy plot. It can be of any size up to about 40 by 70 feet.

The equipment includes as many as eight colored balls, and mallets striped to match. There are two stakes and nine wire wickets. The balls are $3\frac{3}{8}$ inches in diameter. The stakes and wickets are placed as you see them in the drawing. When set up, the field looks like a squared-off figure eight. For children, the wickets should be at least 5 inches wide.

▶ HOW TO PLAY

The object of the game is to hit a ball through nine wickets in correct order. The order is: wickets 1 through 7; hit turning stake; return through wickets 7,6,8,4,9,2, and 1; hit home (starting) stake. When two people play, the player who hits the home stake first wins the game. When teams play, all members of a team must touch home stake in order for the team to win.

Players take turns in shooting. Each time a player hits his ball through a wicket in correct order, he gets an extra stroke. Going through two wickets at once gives him two extra shots. Hitting the turning stake gives him one extra. But a player can never have more than two extra strokes after any one shot.

If your ball hits another ball (whether your opponent's or teammate's), you get two extra shots. You may use one shot to knock a rival's ball away or out of position. To do this, place your ball next to the ball you have just hit. Then place your foot on your ball and strike it sharply with your mallet. This drives the other ball away in the direction in which you aimed. Or you may take one shot to knock the two balls along at the same

time. You may then use your second shot to get through the next wicket. If you prefer, you may place your ball the length of a mallet head away from the ball you hit and use both extra shots as you please. The ball you hit is "dead" to you, and you may not get extra strokes for hitting it again until you have gone through a wicket or hit the turning stake in correct order.

When a player finishes the course but has not yet touched home stake, he can become a "rover." A rover may go anywhere on the course and hit any ball in each of his turns. If he has a partner, he can help his partner get home and keep the other side from doing so. When playing rover it is a good idea to stay within striking distance of the stake so your opponents cannot beat you to it.

CRUSADES

One November day in the year 1095 a large crowd gathered on an open field outside the French town of Clermont. Nobles, knights, and many common people stood listening to the words of Pope Urban II, who spoke to them from a platform high above the gathering. Pope Urban urged the crowd to arm and drive out the "wicked race" of Turks, who occupied the Christian lands of the East. Moved by the Pope's words, the crowd took up the cry "It is the will of God." Many vowed that they would march to the East and battle the Muslims.

Thus began the first of a long series of expeditions known as the **Crusades**—wars for the cross of Christianity. In the following years many groups of Western Christians from France, Germany, Italy, and England set out for the East. The eastern lands for which the Crusaders fought are now the modern countries of Israel, Turkey, Syria, Lebanon, Jordan, and Egypt.

At one time Christians had ruled all the Holy Land. Then the Muslims began their conquest of the East. By 1095 the Muslims held everything except the Christian Byzan-

tine Empire, ruled by Emperor Alexius at Constantinople. Alexius was at war with the Muslim Turks and needed more troops. He appealed to Pope Urban to urge Christians in western Europe to come and serve in his army.

Europeans were interested in the Holy Land because they wished to visit the places where Jesus had walked the earth. Journeys to such holy sites are called **pilgrimages.** For years the Muslims had permitted Christian pilgrims to come and go freely, but recently returning pilgrims had told of being mistreated by the Turks.

Religion was not the only thing that made men want to go on the Crusades. Many people, having heard of the East's great wealth, hoped to make their fortunes there. And some, no doubt, went for the adventure.

▶ THE FIRST CRUSADE, 1096–1099

The First Crusade began in 1096. This was a pilgrimage to the Holy Land as well as a military expedition. The first to set out were a large number of common people, led by the popular preacher Peter the Hermit. The people were of all sorts—unarmed men, priests, monks, and even women. Few had horses, so

The Crusaders attacked the Muslim-held city of Jerusalem in 1099. The Christian army used catapults to launch heavy missiles against the great walls of the city.

they went on foot. They had scarcely any supplies or money, so they had to depend on whatever they could get as they went along.

By the time they reached the outskirts of Constantinople, they were a ragged, sorry-looking crowd. Emperor Alexius was disappointed. He had asked for fighting men and instead had gotten a crowd of ragged, hungry pilgrims. The Byzantine Emperor gave them supplies and transported them across the water to Asia Minor. Then this strange crowd of pilgrims foolishly attacked the Turks and the Turks destroyed almost all of them.

Bands of knights also began to arrive at Constantinople in the summer of 1096. They too created a problem for Alexius. He had wanted men from Europe to come and fight under him. Instead armies came with their own leaders. The Byzantines suspected that some of the Western nobles had their eyes on the great wealth of Constantinople and even on the Emperor's throne. Alexius, therefore, did not allow the armies from the West to stay within the walled city of Constantinople. Only five or six knights at a time were admitted through the gates to go sight-seeing. Yet in spite of such mistrust, Alexius and the Crusaders were outwardly friendly. The Emperor gave them supplies and guides to help them on their way across Asia Minor.

The Crusaders faced many hardships as they marched into Asia. They crossed deserts and mountains. Many of their horses died, and they loaded their baggage on goats, dogs, and even hogs. Occasionally a knight who had lost his horse rode a lumbering ox. Tents rotted and wore out, and food and water ran short. The Westerners tried eating all sorts of fruits and plants that they found along the way. This was how they discovered sugar cane, a plant not known in Europe.

In spite of the hardships and even though the Muslims outnumbered them, the Crusaders won victories. They were helped by the fact that the Muslims were badly divided among themselves. In 1099 the Crusaders finally took Jerusalem. The men from Europe displayed great courage and skill in the bloody battle for Jerusalem. They also showed a fierce and greedy spirit once they had won the city, killing many of the people and looting.

The Crusaders' States in the East

The Crusade leaders divided the conquered lands into states for themselves, one of the most important being the Kingdom of Jerusalem. Since the Crusaders were so few in number, they wanted other people to come from the West and settle as colonists in these newly won lands. Some did come, but never a great number, and most of them came only as pilgrims.

The rulers of the Crusader states collected tribute from the conquered peoples, and they sometimes used brutal means to make them pay. Baldwin, the first man to take the title of king of Jerusalem, learned one day that a rich tribe of Arab Bedouins—wandering herders—was camped across the Jordan River. The king took a band of his men, attacked the camp at night, killed most of the Bedouin men, and carried away their treasure. After this, the nearby tribes and villages began sending "gifts" as tribute to Jerusalem. One city that did not bow to King Baldwin was attacked and looted by the victorious soldiers. But as long as the people paid tribute and did not revolt, the Crusade rulers did not greatly disturb them. They even allowed the Muslims to keep their own laws and religion.

The True Cross, made of wood from the Cross on which Christ was crucified, was the symbol of the Crusades.

Many of the Crusaders who stayed in the East adopted the customs and habits of the people they ruled, and some learned to speak Arabic. They furnished their houses in the Eastern fashion, sitting on carpets and cushions rather than chairs. They ate the food of the East. People from the West found the loose-fitting clothing of the East more comfortable in the hot climate than the tight-fitting garments they had brought from Europe. The Crusaders' ladies sometimes wore veils out of doors, as did the Muslim women. Pilgrims newly arrived from the West were sometimes shocked at the sight of Christian settlers living so like their Muslim neighbors.

Losses in the East and More Crusades

The Crusaders ruled only a narrow strip of land, mostly along the Mediterranean coast. Muslim rulers made war from time to time, trying to win back some of this territory, and the strip grew still narrower. In 1187 a great and powerful Muslim leader, Saladin, took Jerusalem.

News of these losses made people in Europe realize the seriousness of the Crusaders' plight. They launched the Second Crusade in 1145 and the Third Crusade in 1189. Kings and emperors took part in these Crusades, but they failed to recover the Holy City of Jerusalem.

One of the kings was England's famous Richard I, or Richard the Lion-Hearted. The Third Crusade, led by Richard, did keep Saladin from driving the Westerners from the East. Westerners still held a few port cities and the territory about them.

The Capture of Constantinople, 1204

The West did not stop sending Crusades to the East, but one of these, the Fourth Crusade (1202–1204), never reached the Holy Land. Instead it conquered Constantinople. It seems strange that Crusaders should have conquered the Byzantine capital, since the First Crusade had come to help the Byzantines. But there had been trouble between the Western and Eastern Christians from the very beginning. Neither group really trusted the other, and the distrust grew. By the time of the Fourth Crusade, the quarrel had grown so bitter that in 1204 the leaders of the Crusade decided to make themselves masters of Constantinople before going on to fight the Muslims. The great riches of Constantinople tempted the men from the West. When the city was taken, each man tried to get as much of the city's wealth as he could. Perhaps this is why the Fourth Crusade never reached the Holy Land.

The Children's Crusade

The Crusades stirred strange waves of excitement in the West. In 1212 bands of children and young people gathered in Germany and France, and called for the reconquest of Jerusalem. They marched from town to town, and those in Germany followed a boy named Nicholas across the Alps into Italy. According to one old tale the children expected the sea to open up so that they could walk to the Holy Land. Since this did not happen, the bands broke up. Some returned home; some were taken by merchants and sold as slaves. It is not known whether any of them reached the Holy Land.

Later Crusades

There were a number of later Crusades. One of them had some success. Frederick II, Holy Roman Emperor, King of Sicily, and leader of the Sixth Crusade, managed to get the Muslims to recognize him as the ruler of Jerusalem in 1229. But the Muslims regained control of the city within 15 years. By 1291 Muslims had conquered the last small Crusader state. The movement begun by Pope Urban II in 1095 was ended.

KENNETH S. COOPER
George Peabody College

CRUSTACEANS. See SHRIMPS, LOBSTERS, AND OTHER CRUSTACEANS.

A crystal of table salt seen through a microscope.

CRYSTALS

The word "crystal" probably makes you think of something that is hard, smooth, and glittering. The ancient Greeks must have thought the same thing. Our word "crystal" comes from the Greek *krystallos,* meaning "clear ice." The Greeks used *krystallos* to mean ice and also to mean quartz, a transparent mineral. They believed that when ice remained long frozen underneath mountains, it lost its ability to melt; it then became quartz. Thus they believed that mountain glaciers were made of quartz, rather than ice.

We know that ice does not become quartz. Ice and quartz are chemically different. However, both are crystalline—that is, both are made of particles of matter put together in a special way that is true of all crystals. Many other substances also are crystals; salt, sugar, rubies, diamonds, and aspirin are just a few. In fact, nearly all solid materials in the world are made up of crystals. Most rocks and minerals are crystalline. So are many parts of plants and animals. So are many synthetic products.

Plants contain the partly crystalline material cellulose. It is taken from trees as wood pulp and manufactured into paper; it is taken from cotton or flax plants as cotton or linen fibers and made into cloth. Our hair, teeth, and

bones are partly crystalline. The metals in automobiles contain crystals. So does the nylon in shirts and stockings.

From this you can see that crystals themselves may be made up of various different chemical elements. But crystals are alike in many ways. A true crystal is solid, and it has a definite, regular shape. Some crystals are shaped like boxes, some like pyramids, and some like a box with a pyramid at each end. Crystals can have other forms, too. But they are always regular in shape and have flat sides. For example, no crystal could be shaped like an orange or a tin can. Oranges and tin cans have regular shapes, but their sides are curved.

If all crystals have flat sides, how can something curved, like a tooth, be crystalline? The answer is that a tooth is not made of one big crystal. It contains thousands of crystals so small that they cannot be seen without a microscope. When many crystals are stacked in piles, the edges can form curved surfaces. You can demonstrate this effect with a deck of cards; hold it loosely in one hand and push gently against one end with a finger. A curve is formed when each crystal—or card—has its edge set back a little from the edge of the one below it.

The world is full of crystals. Most crystals are too small to see without a magnifier. But many familiar substances are made up of crystals. The fats and vitamins in our food are composed of crystals, as are snowflakes, sand grains, and some drugs, metals, and plastics.

▶ WHAT CRYSTALS ARE MADE OF

Why do crystals have certain shapes? To understand this it is necessary to learn something about how crystals are put together.

All matter is made up of atoms. Therefore we may think of atoms as the basic building blocks of which crystals are made.

A diamond crystal is made of atoms of carbon. The carbon atoms all have the same shape and size. They fit together in an orderly, regular pattern.

Sucrose (table sugar) is composed of atoms of carbon, hydrogen, and oxygen. These are chemically combined into groups of atoms called molecules. Sucrose molecules are all alike. And they are the building blocks of which sucrose crystals are made.

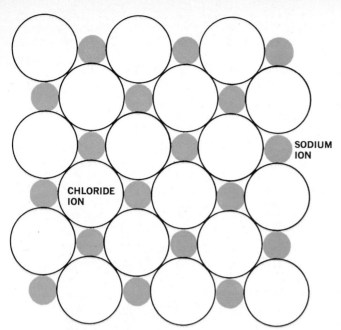

Figure 1A. Sodium and chloride ions in a salt crystal.

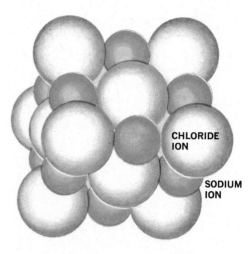

Figure 1B. Another view of the ions in salt crystal.

Since sucrose molecules are different in size and shape from carbon atoms, they fit together in a different orderly pattern. As a result, a sucrose crystal is shaped differently from a diamond crystal.

But every perfect sucrose crystal has the same shape as every other perfect sucrose crystal. And every perfect diamond crystal has the same shape as every other perfect diamond crystal. Some diamonds are larger than others, but the shape of a perfect crystal

Figure 2. The electron microscope shows bean virus particles in an orderly crystal structure.

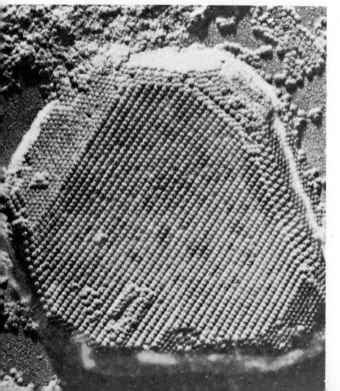

is always the same. (Diamonds used in jewelry seldom have the perfect crystal shape, which has only eight faces, or sides. When a diamond crystal is made into a gem, it is usually cut to a shape having many more faces so that it will sparkle more.)

Shake a few crystals of table salt onto a dark-colored surface. Look at them through a magnifying glass. You will see that the clearest crystals are cube-shaped and that some cubes are larger than others. Notice also that some of the particles are not cubes; these are imperfect crystals, which have formed too fast or which are not pure salt.

The chemical name for table salt is sodium chloride. Sodium chloride is built up of atoms called ions. Ions are atoms (or groups of atoms) with positive or negative charges. In sodium chloride, sodium ions and chloride ions are arranged in the regular pattern shown in Figure 1A. The colored circles represent sodium ions. The large circles represent chloride ions. Of course, the ions are really shaped like round balls, not flat circles. So Figure 1B gives a better picture of how the ions are put together in a small portion of a salt crystal. This picture is greatly magnified—an average-size crystal from a salt shaker contains at least 5,000,000,000,000,000,000 (quintillion) ions. The individual ions are much too small to be seen through a microscope. But scientists working with X rays have shown that these pictures are accurate.

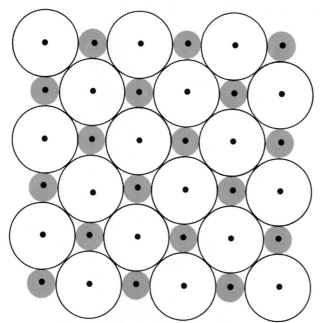

Figure 3A. To begin making a model of a crystal lattice, a dot is first placed in the center of each ion.

Figure 3B. The dots alone show the positions of the ions.

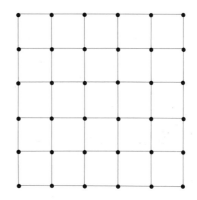

Figure 3C, above: Lines connect the centers of the ions. Figure 4, below: The dots are used as lattice points. The lattice points are connected to form a cube. This gives the framework, or lattice, of the salt crystal.

Some crystals are built of molecules large enough to be seen with a special instrument, called an electron microscope. For example, giant molecules of protein each contain thousands of atoms and are thousands of times larger than the ions in sodium chloride. Such molecules are the building blocks of certain viruses. The photograph (Fig. 2) shows a single crystal of a virus that causes a disease in bean plants. Each little ball is a virus particle, magnified 50,000 times by the electron microscope. Notice the orderly pattern in which they are arranged.

▶ CRYSTAL LATTICES

Look again at Figure 1A. If we place a dot at the center of each circle, we get Figure 3A. Erase the circles and we have Figure 3B, a pattern of dots. Each dot shows the position of the center of an ion. It is easy to see that the pattern of dots is regular and orderly. Now suppose we connect the dots with lines, as in Figure 3C. The drawing begins to look like a net, or lattice.

Now look back at Figure 1B, where the ions are shown as solid balls. Suppose we place a dot at the center of each ball and draw the same kind of picture as in Figure 3C. We then get the framework in space shown in Figure 4. Such a framework is called a **crystal lattice,** and the dots are called **lattice points.** This crystal lattice has the shape of a cube.

A substance like sodium chloride has ions

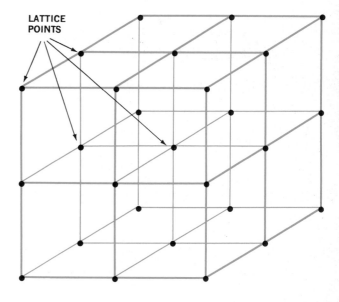

LATTICE POINTS

that fit the lattice, with the center of an ion at each lattice point. Therefore we should expect sodium chloride to form cube-shaped crystals. And it does. A salt crystal big enough to see would include millions upon millions of lattice points. We may imagine the salt crystal as made up of huge numbers of cubes like the one represented in Figure 4. These cubes are all alike, and all contain the same arrangement of lattice points. They fit together to form a pattern of lattice points. The pattern repeats itself, again and again, in all directions within the crystal.

Now you can see that our earlier idea of individual atoms or individual molecules as building blocks of crystals was too simplified. The true building blocks are small, identical groups of atoms or molecules that fit together to make certain shapes, such as the cube.

▶ CRYSTALS AND GLASSES

True crystals are the most orderly kind of matter in nature. They are solid, and their atoms occupy particular places defined by their crystal lattices. The arrangement of atoms is the same in one part of the crystal as in another. The atoms vibrate in their places. But they do not pass by each other to wander about inside the crystal.

By contrast, the atoms and molecules in liquids are not held in any special places. They are free to move past each other throughout the liquid. Atoms and molecules in gases are even freer. Thus liquids and gases are composed of atoms or molecules that are arranged in irregular patterns. Their atoms and molecules move constantly, forming other irregular and non-repeating patterns. That is why scientists call liquids and gases **disorderly.**

Not all solids are orderly. In solids called **glasses**, the atoms are arranged in irregular, or random, patterns. Figure 5A shows a regular crystal pattern. Figure 5B shows the random arrangement of atoms typical of a glass. The pattern in each part is a little different from the pattern in the next part. There are other glasses besides the familiar material of windows and mirrors. Lacquers, varnishes, the fine tableware called crystal, and the type of rock called obsidian are all glasses.

▶ LIQUID CRYSTALS

A few kinds of matter are more orderly than a true liquid but less orderly than a true crystal. Although their molecules are arranged in an orderly way, these kinds of matter flow like liquids. They are called **liquid crystals**.

Normally liquid crystals are transparent. They allow light to pass like clear window glass. But an electric current applied to these crystals re-arranges them, so that they change the direction of the light. Liquid crystal display (L.C.D.) watches and calculators make use of this property. The numerals in an L.C.D. contain liquid crystals. Electronic circuits in the watch or calculator send electric currents into some numerals but

Figure 5A. Atoms of a crystal are arranged in an orderly way.

Figure 5B. Atoms of glass are arranged at random.

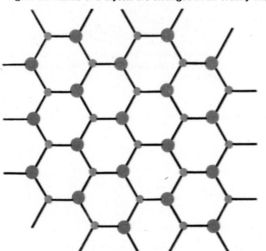

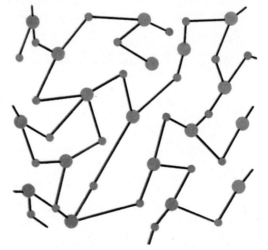

GROWING YOUR OWN CRYSTALS

1
Place a charcoal briquette in a glass bowl.

2
Next mix ¼ cup of laundry bluing, ¼ cup of water, ¼ cup of table salt, and 1 tablespoon of clear household ammonia. Stir well.

3
Pour this solution over the briquette. Leave the bowl uncovered, and let it stand for a few days.

4
Observe the crystals that form.

1
Pour ¼ cup of boiling water into a glass.

2
Slowly add copper sulfate to the water until no more dissolves.

3
Place the solution in a shallow bowl, and let it stand for a few days. Observe the blue crystals that form.

1
Add ¼ cup of Epsom salts to ¼ cup of boiling water, and stir well.

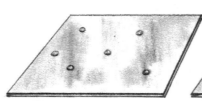

2
Put a few drops of this solution on a square of plastic floor tile.

3
Observe the long needle-like crystals that form as the water evaporates.

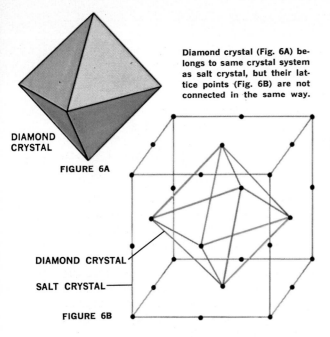

DIAMOND CRYSTAL

FIGURE 6A

Diamond crystal (Fig. 6A) belongs to same crystal system as salt crystal, but their lattice points (Fig. 6B) are not connected in the same way.

DIAMOND CRYSTAL

SALT CRYSTAL

FIGURE 6B

not into others. The numerals receiving the current can be seen because they change the direction of the light, while the other numerals remain clear and invisible.

Some liquid crystals also respond to heat. They show different colors at different temperatures. They are used in some thermometers. They are also used in detecting certain diseases. The crystals are spread out to coat a large screen, which is placed next to a patient's body. The crystals are affected by the body heat, so the screen becomes a kind of "map" of body temperatures. Areas that show as "hot spots" may indicate the presence of infections or tumors.

▶ CRYSTAL SYSTEMS AND CRYSTAL FORMS

There are only six different kinds of crystal lattices. All crystals whose atoms fit the same kind of lattice belong to the same **crystal system**. But these crystals are not necessarily identical.

For instance, diamonds belong to the same crystal system as sodium chloride. So they must have the same kind of crystal lattice. Yet a diamond crystal is not a cube, as a salt crystal is. A diamond crystal has the shape shown in Figure 6A. This shape is called an octahedron (from the Greek for "eight faces"). It is related to the cube and can form on the same lattice.

To show how that can happen, suppose we take the lattice shown in Figure 4 and connect

all the lattice points that lie in the middle of the six sides, or faces, of the cube. The result is an octahedron inside the original cube (Fig. 6B). Related shapes like the cube and the octahedron are called **crystal forms**.

▶ CRYSTAL GROWTH

In nature, most crystals are formed in one of the following ways:

When a gas or a liquid gets cold enough, it can crystallize. Snow crystals are formed from a gas (water vapor) in the air. Ice crystals form when liquid water freezes.

Hot, molten volcanic rock is a liquid. Quartz and other minerals crystallize from it as the liquid cools.

Crystals also can grow from solutions. Seawater is a solution. Salt and other minerals washed from the land are dissolved in it. When salt water evaporates, solid crystals of salt are left behind.

In nature, crystals form when conditions happen to be just right. To be perfect, crystals must grow slowly. In the controlled conditions of the laboratory, we can often grow crystals that are better than natural crystals.

Some crystals are hard for us to grow. Diamonds require tremendous heat and pressure for their formation. So we can grow only small ones, even in special laboratories. But some kinds of crystals can be grown easily, even at home. Instructions for growing crystals are given on the preceding page.

Today the growing of crystals for transistors is an important industry. Radios, television sets, computers, calculators, telephones, watches, and many other electronic devices make use of transistors.

Transistors are made from crystals of purified elements such as silicon and germanium. The crystals are grown slowly in laboratories under carefully controlled conditions. In order to work, transistors must contain extremely small amounts of other elements as impurities. These impurities are added as the crystals are grown.

LUCY B. MCCRONE
Research crystallographer
Walter C. McCrone Associates

See also ATOMS: EXPERIMENTS AND OTHER SCIENCE ACTIVITIES; GEMSTONES; IONS AND IONIZATION; METALS AND METALLURGY; ROCKS, MINERALS, AND ORES; TRANSISTORS AND INTEGRATED CIRCUITS.

CUBA

Cuba, the largest island in the Caribbean Sea, belongs to a group of islands called the Greater Antilles. It lies just below the Tropic of Cancer about 160 kilometers (100 miles) from the southern tip of Florida, in the United States.

Christopher Columbus reached the northern coast of Cuba in 1492, on his first voyage to the New World. He described the island as "the most beautiful land human eyes have ever seen."

The island remained a Spanish colony for about 400 years. The final struggle for independence began in the 1890's and involved help from the United States. A republic was established in 1902, but Cuba remained partly dependent on the United States. Dictators came to power in the country, which was divided between the few who were rich and the many who were very poor. In 1959, revolutionaries led by Fidel Castro overthrew the government, and almost everything in Cuba changed. The Castro government seized the land and property of the wealthy and began ambitious new programs to help the poor. Cuba became the first Communist nation in the Western Hemisphere.

▶ THE PEOPLE

Many of the people are of Spanish ancestry. Others are of African descent or of mixed ancestry. The original Indian inhabitants of the island died out after the Spanish conquest. In spite of its varied population, Cuba has known no racial conflict. The language of the country is Spanish. But the character and style of Cuban life is a mixture of Spanish and African elements.

Religion

The leading religion of Cuba is Roman Catholicism. In both the country and the city there are cults like *changó* and *yemayá* that combine worship of a Catholic saint with an African deity. From the beliefs and practices of the *ñáñigos,* or witch doctors, were created songs, legends, and stories that have become a part of the nation's folklore, opera, theater, painting, and literature.

Education and the Arts and Sciences

Santiago de Cuba had a college as early as 1523. Before the end of the 16th century, there were 20 colleges in Cuba.

All education is now state-controlled. Children have one year of kindergarten, followed by six years of elementary school. They then have three years of basic secondary school, which includes broad general education as well as pre-vocational or technical courses.

Afterward, students may elect three years of upper secondary education at one of the nation's commercial, fine arts, agricultural, industrial, technical, or teacher-training institutes. Finally, they may attend one of the national universities.

When education became compulsory in Cuba, many new schools like this one were built.

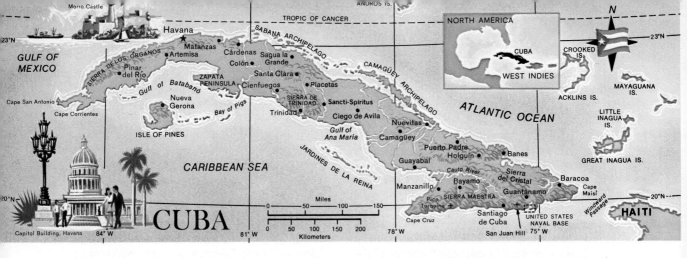

Morro Castle · Havana · TROPIC OF CANCER · ANDROS IS. · NORTH AMERICA · N · 23°N

GULF OF MEXICO · SABANA ARCHIPELAGO · CUBA · WEST INDIES · CROOKED IS. · ACKLINS IS. · MAYAGUANA IS.

Cape San Antonio · SIERRA DE LOS ÓRGANOS · Pinar del Río · Artemisa · Matanzas · Cárdenas · Sagua la Grande · Santa Clara · Colón · CAMAGÜEY ARCHIPELAGO · ATLANTIC OCEAN · LITTLE INAGUA IS.

Cape Corrientes · Gulf of Batabanó · ZAPATA PENINSULA · Cienfuegos · Santa Clara · Placetas · SIERRA DE TRINIDAD · Sancti-Spiritus · Ciego de Ávila · GREAT INAGUA IS.

Nueva Gerona · Bay of Pigs · Trinidad · Nuevitas · Camagüey · Puerto Padre · Holguín · Banes

ISLE OF PINES · Gulf of Ana María · Guayabal · Cauto River · Sierra del Cristal · Baracoa · Cape Maisí

CARIBBEAN SEA · JARDINES DE LA REINA · Manzanillo · Bayamo · Guantánamo · Windward Passage · HAITI

CUBA · Pico Turquino · SIERRA MAESTRA · Santiago de Cuba · UNITED STATES NAVAL BASE · San Juan Hill · Cape Cruz

Capitol Building, Havana · 84°W · 81°W · Miles · 78°W · 75°W · 20°N · Kilometers

A number of Cubans have made contributions to the arts and to science. José Enrique Varona was Cuba's foremost philosopher. José María de Heredia y Heredia and Julián del Casal were well-known poets. Wilfredo Lam was noted for his painting, and Moisés Simón for his music. Carlos Finlay was the first person to identify the specific mosquito that transmitted yellow fever. José Martí, a hero of Cuban independence, was both a poet and a political leader.

Food and Recreation

Traditional meals include *paella,* a delicious combination of chicken, pork sausages, clams, olives, tomatoes, and spices cooked together. Other popular Cuban foods are rice mixed with beans, fried sliced plantain (a kind of banana), and stewed meat, which is eaten almost every day. Tiny cups of strong, hot, sweet coffee are served after dinner.

The cockfight is the favorite amusement in the countryside. Like jai alai, often called the fastest game in the world, it is of Spanish origin. Baseball, another popular sport, comes from the United States. *Carnaval,* a month-long religious festival, is celebrated throughout the country.

▶ THE LAND

There are several low mountain ranges in Cuba—the Sierra de los Órganos, in the western part of the country; the Sierra de Trinidad, in central Cuba; and the rugged Sierra Maestra, in the east. Pico Turquino—which rises to 2,000 meters (6,560 feet) in the Sierra Maestra—is the highest point. The rest of Cuba consists of plateaus, valleys, and gentle, rolling hills.

Two river systems flow from the heart of Cuba, one toward the north and west; the other, toward the south. The Cauto, which is navigable for about a third of its length, is Cuba's only important river. But the coastline has many natural harbors.

Cuba has only two seasons—dry and rainy. The dry season is from November to the end of April, with an average temperature of 21°C (70°F). This is the season of the sugar harvest. The rainy season lasts from May to October, with a mean temperature of 27°C (81°F). Rainfall averages 1,370 millimeters (54 inches) a year. The trade winds cool Cuba's generally hot climate.

▶ THE ECONOMY

A semitropical climate, rolling land, and excellent soils have made Cuba an agricultural country. Sugarcane was first planted around Santiago in the early 16th century. During the 18th century, sugar became Cuba's basic crop.

Today Cuba is one of the world's leading producers and exporters of sugar. Much of the land is devoted to the cultivation of sugarcane, which is grown chiefly in the eastern provinces. From December to May hundreds of thousands of people labor in the sugar industry, producing sugar, as well as by-products—molasses, alcohol, rum, and brandy. This intensive labor is vital, for sugar is a mainstay of the Cuban economy. Exports of sugar and its by-products provide most of the country's income.

Before Fidel Castro came to power and the economy came under state control, private corporations controlled sugar production. The United States was then Cuba's major sugar market. Today government co-operatives run the sugar industry. Most of Cuba's sugar is now sold to Communist countries.

Tobacco was one of Cuba's leading crops for many years. Thousands of workers were engaged in the manufacture of cigarettes and world-famous Havana cigars. But a plant disease wiped out much of the tobacco harvest in the late 1970's, and many cigar factories were closed. Coffee, rice, and cotton are now more important crops. Oranges, pineapples, plantain, melons, mangoes, and other tropical fruits are also grown. There are large numbers of cattle and hogs. Horses, sheep, goats, and poultry are also raised.

Cuba's mineral resources include nickel, iron, chromium, manganese, copper, and asphalt. A small amount of petroleum has been found, but there is no coal. Cuba has one of the world's largest deposits of nickel and ranks among the leading producers of this metal. Nickel is the country's most important money-earner after sugar.

Other Cuban industries include the manufacture of cotton and rayon textiles, tires, soft drinks, soaps and detergents, and chemicals and drugs. Oil refineries process imported crude petroleum. The sea yields fish, lobsters, oysters, shrimps, and large sponges.

Cuba's transportation system, developed by United States investments in earlier years, is the best in the Caribbean. Railroads and highways connect the major cities. The island has a number of fine harbors. Cubana, the national airline, operates out of the international airport in Havana.

▶ CITIES

Havana is Cuba's capital and largest city. It has a metropolitan population of almost 2,000,000 and is considered among the most beautiful capital cities in the Caribbean. Before the Castro revolution, it was one of the liveliest cities in the Western Hemisphere. One of its interesting sights is the former capitol, which was modeled after the United States Capitol in Washington, D.C.

Santiago de Cuba is a manufacturing city, and Pinar del Río, a producer of fine tobacco. Cienfuegos and Matanzas are both sugar ports, and Camagüey is a cattle and sugar town. Trinidad and Sancti-Spíritus are rich in history. Holguín is one of the country's newest and fastest-growing cities.

▶ HISTORY AND GOVERNMENT

In 1508, 16 years after Cuba was discovered, Sebastián de Ocampo learned by sailing around the island that it was not part of the mainland, as Columbus had thought. From 1511 to 1515 the conquest and colonization of Cuba was carried out by Spain, under Captain Diego Velásquez. Some of the first cities were founded about this time.

Because Cuba had little gold, the Spanish went on to conquer and exploit other parts of America. Cuba served as a port of transit for troops, ships, and arms destined for the conquest and control of Mexico and Peru.

The Spanish *Flota,* or "Fleet," stopped at

Morro Castle, a famous fortress and tourist attraction, guards Havana's harbor.

Havana, the capital of Cuba, is the largest city in the Caribbean.

Cuba twice a year for supplies on its journey to and from Spain. Sugar and tobacco were cultivated from the 16th century. When the Indians died out, slaves were brought from Africa to work the plantations.

Efforts to gain independence from Spain began in the mid-19th century. The two heroes of Cuban independence were Carlos Manuel de Cespedes and José Martí. Martí led the final struggle, which began in 1895 and involved the United States in 1898. Complete independence was finally won in 1902. But an amendment to the Cuban constitution (the Platt Amendment) gave the United States the right to intervene in Cuba to protect U.S. citizens and property. This right was given up in 1934. The United States also secured exclusive use of a naval base at Guantánamo for 99 years.

Cuba's sugar plantations made some Cubans rich. Several United States business firms also profited from their investments in the country's agriculture, manufacturing, and transportation. But the majority of Cubans suffered from low wages, unemployment, and lack of schools, housing, and medical facilities. Cuba's political leaders were self-seeking and tyrannical. Two became dictators—Gerardo Machado, who governed from 1925 to 1933; and Fulgencio Batista, who was in and out of power between 1933 and 1959.

Most Cubans believed that Cuba needed several things. They wanted land to be distributed among the rural workers to offset the annual six-month unemployment after the sugar harvest. They also wanted more schools, houses, and medical clinics; honesty in government; gradual nationalization of industry; and an agriculture producing other crops to reduce the country's dependence on sugar.

Batista was overthrown in 1959 by Fidel Castro, a young revolutionary who promised these reforms. Castro did distribute some land among farm workers. He built housing and provided education and medical care for the poor. He nationalized industry and all foreign businesses. But he also made himself dictator of Cuba. He controlled all aspects of Cuban life and permitted no political opposition. The land was placed under state ownership, and the economy was regulated by the government. Under Castro, Cuba became a Communist country. It received economic and military assistance from the Soviet Union. Many Cubans—especially those from the middle-income groups, who had been among Castro's early supporters—fled the country.

In 1961 the United States broke diplomatic relations and cut off all trade with Cuba. That same year Cuban exile forces, trained by the United States, landed at the Bay of Pigs but failed in their attempt to overthrow Castro. In 1962, it was discovered that Soviet troops and missiles had been sent to the island. But under strong pressure from the United States, the missiles were removed.

Cuba supported revolutionary groups elsewhere in Latin America. In the 1970's, Cuba's Soviet-equipped army began to aid Marxist groups in Africa. Cuban troops fought in the civil war in Angola, helped the Ethiopian Government in its conflicts with rebel groups, and trained black nationalist guerrillas in southern Africa. Cuba's activities in Africa and Latin America were an obstacle to better relations with the United States. Relations between the two countries improved somewhat during the late 1970's but again became strained in the 1980's.

Life for Cuba's poor has improved since Castro came to power. Free education, modern medical care, and other social services are available. But Cuba has faced economic difficulties. Food and consumer goods are often rationed. And the country relies heavily on aid from the Soviet Union. The government restricts emigration. But at times the restrictions have been lifted briefly, and many Cubans have left in search of a different way of life. In the late 1960's and early 1970's, an airlift took thousands of Cubans to the United States. And in 1980, thousands more made the trip in small boats.

Cuba's government is based on the Constitution of 1976. The Communist Party is the only political party. The legislature is called the National Assembly of People's

FACTS AND FIGURES

REPUBLIC OF CUBA is the official name of the country.

CAPITAL: Havana.

LOCATION: Caribbean Sea. **Latitude**—19° 49′ N to 23° 17′ N. **Longitude**—74° 08′ W to 84° 57′ W.

AREA: 114,524 km² (44,218 sq mi).

POPULATION: 9,500,000 (estimate).

LANGUAGE: Spanish.

GOVERNMENT: Communist Republic. Head of state and government—president of the Council of Ministers. **International co-operation**—United Nations, Organization of American States (OAS) (active membership suspended in 1962), Council for Mutual Economic Assistance (COMECON).

NATIONAL ANTHEM: *Himno de Bayamo* (''Hymn of Bayamo'').

ECONOMY: Agricultural products—sugar, tobacco, coffee, rice, fruits, cattle, poultry, cotton. **Industries and products**—sugar refining and sugar by-products, oil refining, alcohol, leather goods, textiles, soap, chemicals and drugs. **Chief minerals**—nickel, iron, chrome, copper, manganese, asphalt. **Chief exports**—sugar, nickel, tobacco, fruits, fish, iron, chrome. **Chief imports**—machinery, crude oil, coal. **Monetary unit**—Cuban peso.

Power. Its members are elected for 5-year terms. They meet twice a year. When the legislature is not meeting, laws can be passed by a smaller body called the Council of State. The Council of State is selected by the legislature from among its members. The president of the Council of State appoints a Council of Ministers to run the government and handle foreign affairs. Fidel Castro serves as president of both the Council of State and the Council of Ministers. He is also the head of the Cuban Communist Party.

HUMBERTO PIÑERA
Formerly, New York University

Sugarcane is cut and piled on oxcarts at Bejucal.

Marie Curie worked and saved for 6 years to pay for her training as a physicist.

CURIE, MARIE (1867–1934) AND PIERRE (1859–1906)

Until the end of the 1800's, chemistry and physics were treated almost as separate sciences. Gradually the barriers between these fields came down, through the work of scientists like Marie and Pierre Curie. Together the Curies discovered the rare chemical element radium and helped to launch modern nuclear physics.

Marie Curie was born Marja Sklodowska in Warsaw, Poland, on November 7, 1867. Her father taught high-school physics and mathematics. Her mother had been director of a school for girls.

Marja was the youngest of five children, all good students. At 15 she was graduated from high school with a medal for excellence in studies. Since the family was far from rich, Marja went to work at 17 as a governess. In

her spare time she read and dreamed of going to a university. (At that time the University of Warsaw was closed to women.) By 1891 she had saved enough money to go to Paris. When she registered at the Sorbonne (part of the University of Paris), Marja changed her name to its French form, Marie. She found a bare, unheated room near the school and settled down to her studies.

Within 2 years Marie took the master's examination in physics and scored highest in the class. She was completely absorbed in science when, in 1894, she met the physicist who became her husband.

Pierre Curie, born on May 15, 1859, was the son of a French doctor and showed an early talent for science. While in his 20's Pierre, with his brother Jacques, discovered that an electric current can be produced by exerting pressure on quartz crystals. This was the beginning of a new field of research, piezoelectricity. Curie's Law is named after his later discovery about the relationship between magnetism and temperature.

At the age of 35, Pierre Curie was well known and respected as a physicist. Unmarried, he felt that women could not understand a scientist's need to devote himself to his work. Then he met Marie Sklodowska. She asked him questions about crystals, magnetic fields, and electricity. She was remarkable. She not only listened politely but also understood and appreciated Pierre's work.

In a year's time they were married. After bicycling through the French countryside on a wedding trip, they settled in a small apartment in Paris near the School of Physics and Chemistry, where they shared a laboratory. Pierre had just been named a professor, but his salary was small, and the Curies lived modestly. Since Marie had never cooked much, she secretly took cooking lessons from a sister who also lived in Paris. Soon she discovered that cooking did not matter. Neither she nor Pierre ever paid much attention to food.

The second year of their marriage brought a number of changes into the Curies' lives, for their first daughter, Irène, was born in September. Though money was scarce, they hired a nursemaid to take care of the baby while Marie was at the laboratory.

At first the young mother rushed home several times a day to see that all was well.

Then Pierre's father came to live with the couple. The family moved to a house at the edge of Paris. The child's grandfather helped take care of her and became her first teacher.

Meanwhile both Curies had become interested in the work of another French scientist, Antoine Henri Becquerel. In 1896 he had discovered that uranium gave off invisible radiations, which could "take a picture" on a photographic plate, even in total darkness. Marie wanted to find out what these radiations were.

Using a device invented by her husband, Madame Curie measured the radiations coming from pitchblende—an ore containing uranium. She discovered that there was far more radioactivity in the pitchblende than uranium alone could produce. Perhaps the ore contained another and unknown element. Pierre became so interested in Marie's work that he was soon spending all his non-teaching time on the pitchblende experiments.

During the next few years, the Curies made discoveries that have affected the work of scientists ever since. They were first to prove that the atoms of some elements are continually breaking down, all by themselves. In breaking down, such elements give off radiations that can pass through many other materials. The Curies called these elements—including Becquerel's uranium—radioactive.

In their search for the hidden element in pitchblende, the Curies discovered two new elements. The first was named polonium, in honor of Marie's native country. The second, a glowing element, was named radium.

The Curies announced the discovery of the new elements in 1898. It took 4 more years of hard work to get a sample of radium. Working in a drafty, leaky shed, the Curies patiently sifted and processed a ton of pitchblende. It was heavy, slow work. Bit by bit the Curies extracted a fraction of a gram of almost pure radium.

In 1903 the Curies and Becquerel won the Nobel prize in physics for their discovery of radioactive elements. Madame Curie was the first woman ever to receive that honor.

The following year their second daughter, Eve, was born. By then the Curies were already beginning to regret their fame. They had lost much of the privacy and time needed for their work. Then Pierre's work came to a sud- den end. In 1906 he was run over by a heavy cart and killed. Marie hid her grief in work, carrying on his classes in physics as well as her own research.

A second Nobel prize—this time in chemistry—was awarded to Marie Curie in 1911 for her discovery of radium and polonium. She was the first person to receive two Nobel awards in science.

Madame Curie received many other honors. She never again had to worry about money, but her health steadily declined. She continued to work long hours in her laboratory, forgetting to eat unless her daughters reminded her. She was at work on the isolation of a new element when she died on July 4, 1934. After her death it was discovered that her body tissue had been poisoned by exposure to too much radioactivity.

The Curie daughters achieved their own honors. In 1935, Irène and her husband, Frédéric Joliot-Curie, were awarded the Nobel prize for their work with synthetic radioactive elements. Eve became a musician and author whose best-known book is the story of her famous mother.

BARBARA LAND
Formerly, Columbia University

Three Curies, three Nobel prize-winners. Marie and Pierre Curie with older daughter Irène.

Left: Curler prepares to slide the stone toward the far end of the rink. Right: Players sweep a path ahead of a stone.

CURLING

Curling is a game something like bowling, played on a strip of ice. Instead of rolling balls, the players slide stones along the ice toward a target. Sweepers with brooms and brushes try to control the course of a stone and the distance it goes by sweeping the path ahead of it. Curling is rarely a sport for onlookers because almost everyone who is interested in it takes part in the game.

Curling was introduced into Canada and the United States from Scotland in the early 1800's. Until about 1900, before the growth of skiing and ice hockey, it was the most popular North American winter sport.

A curling team is composed of four members and is called a rink. Each player has a particular position and objective. The players are called the lead; the second; the third, or vice-skip; and the skip, or captain. Each player curls two stones, alternating with the player having the same position on the opposing team. The curlers may follow their stones and help with the sweeping.

The skips play last and direct the entire play of the other three members of their teams from the opposite end of the sheet.

The sheet is a strip of ice on which curling is played. It consists of starting blocks (hacks) and target areas (three-ringed bull's-eyes

called houses). Sets of hacks and houses are placed at opposite ends of the sheet, and play alternates between them. A tee line bisects each house. Water is sprinkled on curling ice to give it a pebbled surface.

Curling has been called the roaring game because of the sound of the stones gliding across the ice on a lake or pond. A curling stone is 30 centimeters (1 foot) across and has a maximum weight of 20 kilograms (44 pounds). The stones have metal handles, and the twist given these handles by the players as they deliver the stones gives the stones a spinning, curved sliding path, or "curl."

Between tee lines two members of the rink try to guide the course of the stone to its desired final position by sweeping the ice ahead of it. In some cases, sweeping makes a big difference in the distance the stone travels. Fast, rhythmic sweeping is the most interesting feature of curling. Rink members may sweep a stone only after it passes the tee line behind which it was delivered. Once the stone has passed the tee line at the other end of the sheet, only the skip or vice-skip may sweep. In the houses the skips and vice-skips may sweep their own team's stones, and behind the tee line they may also sweep the opponents' stones. If sweepers touch a stone delivered by a member of their own team while that stone is still in motion, it is called a burned stone and is at once removed from play.

The object of the game is to get a team's stones closer to the target center, or tee, than the opponent's stones. One point is scored for each stone of one side that is nearer the tee than any rival stone. The delivery of the last stone can decide the count. The chance to deliver this important stone goes to the team that did not score in the previous inning, or end. Ten ends usually constitute the game.

▶ THE STRATEGY OF CURLING

As the stones gather in the target area the strategy and the play become very complex. The ability of the skip to read the ice, decide on strategy, and call the shots, as well as the ability of the team to deliver the desired shots, makes curling an intense game.

In the strategy of placing the stones in the house, four shots are basic:

(1) The Draw: used to slide a stone into the position directed by the skip.

(2) The Strike: used to strike an opponent's stone and knock it out of the house.

(3) The Raise or Promotion: used by players to hit one of their own stones and move it into scoring position.

(4) The Guard: used to position a stone so that it protects or guards another stone from being knocked out of scoring position.

In throwing a stone (the delivery), the player gives a slight spin to it. If the spin is clockwise, it is called an in-turn. If it is counterclockwise, it is called an out-turn. This spin produces the desired arc, or curl, in the path of the stone as it continues down the sheet of ice and gives the name "curling" to this sport. Also important in the delivery are the player's stance in the hack and the method of delivery. Among the variations are the push delivery, the delivery with little slide, and the graceful swing-slide delivery much favored by the younger curlers. The stance and the method of delivery are important to accuracy and good results. A curler must also be able to judge the speed of the ice, which constantly changes as the game progresses or the temperature changes within the ice shed. It is up to the curlers to give proper direction and the right speed to their stones, which they must deliver before they reach the tee line.

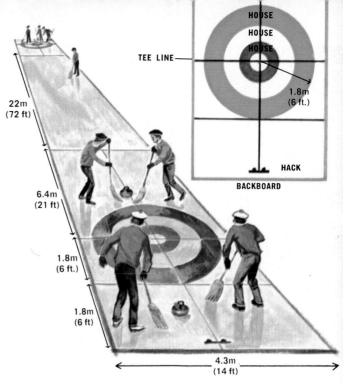

▶ ORGANIZED PLAY

The "world series" of Canadian curling is called the Macdonald's Brier. It was first played at the Granite Club in Toronto in 1927.

The first world championship curling match was in 1959; a yearly match has been played since then in Scotland. For several years only the United States, Canada, Scotland, and Sweden played, but now several other countries also compete for the trophy, a silver broom.

The oldest curling club today is the Dudingston Curling Society, organized in Edinburgh, Scotland, in 1795. But the most important club was formed in 1838. It received royal charter in 1842 and since then has been known as the Royal Caledonian Curling Club of Scotland.

One common event in organized curling is the bonspiel. It is a curling tournament with several competitions, each one being a play-off to produce a winner. Each play-off is a single event that may be either a knock-out, or sudden death, competition or a round robin series, where each team plays all the other teams at least once to determine which is the winner.

ROBERT W. HURD
Utica Curling Club

CURRICULUM. See EDUCATION.

CYCLONES. See HURRICANES AND TORNADOES.

CYMBAL. See PERCUSSION INSTRUMENTS.

CYPRUS

The island nation of Cyprus is situated in the northeastern corner of the Mediterranean Sea. It is so beautiful that the ancient Greeks believed Aphrodite, their goddess of love and beauty, was born there. Historically, Cyprus is closely associated with Greece. But for many centuries it was under the rule of Turkey, and it has a sizable number of people who speak Turkish. In recent times Cyprus has been torn by civil strife. This strife has left the country divided between its Greek and Turkish communities.

THE PEOPLE

About 80 percent of the Cypriot population speak Greek; most of the remainder speak Turkish. The Greeks are Christians who belong to the Greek Orthodox Church. The Turks are predominantly Muslims. There is a small Armenian-speaking group, which is Christian.

According to legend the first Greeks arrived several hundred years before the Trojan War—or about the 12th century B.C. The Turks came in the 16th century A.D. The other Cypriot groups are more recent arrivals.

Although the island's inhabitants differ in their languages and religions, they are much

A contrast of the new and the old in Cyprus: above, a luxury hotel on the beautiful waterfront at Famagusta beach. Below, water is drawn from underground wells in a small village.

alike in appearance and customs. The houses, clothes, and food of Greek-speaking Cypriots are very much the same as those of their Turkish-speaking neighbors.

Agriculture is the chief occupation of the Cypriots, and the amount of land that can be farmed is quite limited. For this reason many people have emigrated to neighboring Asian and African countries. But the population of the island has not shown any marked decrease.

Byzantine Church, Peristerona

CYPRUS

▶ THE LAND

The island of Cyprus is about 65 kilometers (40 miles) south of Turkey. Mountains border both the northern and southern coasts of the island. The Troodos Mountains in the south reach elevations of over 1,800 meters (6,000 feet). But they are less rugged than the lower Kyrenia range in the north. It is in the Troodos that most of the deposits of copper, iron, and asbestos are found. The mountains receive plenty of rain and snow. For this reason their higher slopes are covered with forests of pine and cedar. But most of the island's people live on the plain between the mountains. Because the plain is dry except after heavy rains, most settlements are located where irrigation water is available from mountain streams or underground wells.

The climate of Cyprus, like that of other Mediterranean areas, is mild, with rainy winters and hot, dry summers. In the mountains much of the precipitation falls in the form of snow, which lies on the ground for several months each year. In this season it is possible to go skiing in the mountains and bathing in the ocean in the same day. The winter snows are important as a source of water during the hot, dry summers. There are no lakes of any size on the island.

▶ THE ECONOMY

Despite the island's early importance as a mining center, most Cypriots today are farmers. They grow olives and carobs on the lower slopes of the mountains. The fruit of the carob tree is used chiefly as animal feed. Potatoes and vegetables are planted on the plains. Wheat is an important crop. Due to the mild winters, crops in Cyprus ripen early. As a result, Cyprus can sell much of its produce to Britain and other northern European countries before the crops of these countries are ready

for harvest. Oranges are grown near the southern coast, where some cotton is also planted. Vineyards are numerous, and wine is the chief beverage.

Nicosia, the capital, has a population of over 100,000 (metropolitan area) and is the island's business center. It has modern hotels, and there is a large international airport nearby. Famagusta, on the east coast, is the principal seaport. But trade also moves through Limassol and Larnaca. Other important cities are Kyrenia and Paphos.

One of the most famous industries of Cyprus is lacemaking. Cyprus exports iron

---

FACTS AND FIGURES

REPUBLIC OF CYPRUS is the official name of the country.

CAPITAL: Nicosia.

LOCATION: Island in the eastern Mediterranean Sea. Latitude—34° 33′ N to 35° 41′ N. Longitude—32° 17′ E 34° 35′ E.

AREA: 9,251 km² (3,572 sq mi).

POPULATION: 640,000 (estimate).

LANGUAGE: Greek and Turkish (official), English.

GOVERNMENT: Republic. **Head of government**—president. **International co-operation**—United Nations, Commonwealth of Nations, Council of Europe.

ECONOMY: Agricultural products—wheat, olives, grapes, potatoes, citrus fruits. **Industries and products**—lace, embroidery, pottery. **Chief minerals**—iron and copper pyrites, copper, gypsum, asbestos, chrome ore. **Chief exports**—iron pyrites, copper, citrus fruits, potatoes, vegetables, wine. **Chief imports**—machinery, textiles, petroleum, meat and dairy products, transportation equipment. **Monetary unit**—Cyprus pound.

View of Nicosia (*above*), located on the Messaoria plain with the Kyrenia Mountains in the background. Below, bread is baked by ancient methods.

pyrites, copper, oranges, potatoes, vegetables, and wine. This enables it to pay for imports of other foods, machinery, textiles, transportation equipment, and petroleum.

▶ HISTORY AND GOVERNMENT

Following its settlement by Greeks, Cyprus fell under the successive domination of the Assyrian, Egyptian, Persian, Roman, and Byzantine empires. The Greek-speaking Byzantines ruled the island for about 800 years. Between the late 12th century and the 15th century, it was a French kingdom. In 1489 it came under the control of the Venetians. The Turks conquered Cyprus in 1571 and ruled it for the next 300 years. In 1871 they ceded it to Britain, which formally annexed it in 1914.

Most Greek Cypriots had long desired union with Greece. The movement for union, called *enosis,* intensified in the 1950's into a guerrilla war against British rule. Turkish Cypriots feared domination by the Greek majority, and they sought partition of the island. In 1960, Cyprus was given independence under terms that forbade either *enosis* or partition. The constitution provided for a Greek Cypriot president and a Turkish Cypriot vice-president. Seats in the legislature, the House of Representatives, were allotted by population. Archbishop Makarios III, the head of the Orthodox Church in Cyprus, became the first president.

But mistrust between Greek and Turkish Cypriots remained. In 1963, when President Makarios attempted to change the constitution, fighting erupted between the two communities. United Nations peacekeeping forces brought about a truce. But in 1967, fighting broke out again and threatened to involve Greece and Turkey in war. In 1974, Greek Cypriots who favored *enosis,* led by Greek army officers, temporarily took over the government. Turkey cited the terms of the independence agreement and sent troops to Cyprus, occupying the northern part of the island. Almost 200,000 Greek Cypriots fled their homes for refuge in the south. In 1977, President Makarios died. He was succeeded by Spyros Kyprianou. A separate administration was established by the Turks in the 40 percent of the country they controlled. Little progress was made in attempts to reunite the country.

ALEXANDER MELAMID
New York University

CZECHOSLOVAKIA

A European map made before 1918 does not contain the name Czechoslovakia. Nor does it show the location of this small Central European country. Before 1918 Czechoslovakia was part of the old Austro-Hungarian empire. Present-day Czechoslovakia was formed from the Austro-Hungarian territories of Bohemia, Moravia, Slovakia, and part of Silesia.

▶THE PEOPLE

The name "Czechoslovakia" was coined from the names of the two most important peoples in the country—the Czechs and the Slovaks. Both are Slavic peoples and speak languages related to Polish and Russian. Like the Poles, but unlike the Russians, most Czechs and Slovaks belong to the Roman Catholic Church. Most city people work in factories, offices, and shops. In many families both parents have jobs. The young children are often cared for in government nurseries and day schools. When children reach the age of 6, they enter the basic school. This lasts for 9 years. Mathematics, Czechoslovakian languages and literature, and Russian receive the greatest emphasis. Physical education is also stressed. After school hours most young people take part in various government-

sponsored youth organizations. These organizations promote educational, cultural, and sports activities. Gymnastics, soccer, and track are the favorite sports. During the winter season children and adults are enthusiastic ice-hockey players.

At the end of the 9-year basic school, the Czechoslovakian student may continue in either a trade school or a general secondary school. Most young people go to the apprentice training centers and vocational schools to learn special skills for jobs in industry. Fewer young people go on to study in universities, art academies, and teacher-training institutes. Admission is on the basis of ability, and the government pays the cost of education.

In the cities the people go to art galleries and museums and attend plays, operas, and concerts. They go to the movies often to see the films that have made their country one of the leaders in movie production all over the world. They enjoy their famous puppet theaters and vaudeville shows, as well as regular dramatic performances. There are hotels, restaurants, and clubs with dance orchestras that play jazz. People listen to radio or watch television. There is a fairly rich cultural life. Most people work hard but do not earn much money. Very few can afford to own one of

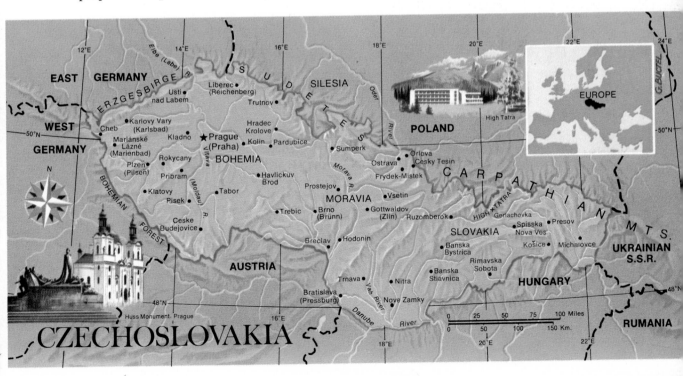

Prague, Czechoslovakia's capital and largest city, dates from the 9th century.

the expensive automobiles made in Czechoslovakia or in the Soviet Union.

Country people work chiefly on large, state-owned co-operative farms. Although they work long hours, few of the country people earn enough to buy good clothes or other luxuries. After long days in the fields, many farmers spend their evening hours cultivating little gardens around their cottages. Here they raise vegetables for themselves or for sale.

In the cities and in the villages many people still attend church services regularly even though the government does not encourage churchgoing.

▶ THE LAND

Czechoslovakia has three major landform regions: the Bohemian Plateau in the west; the Moravian Lowland in central Czechoslovakia; and the mountainous region in the east called Slovakia.

The Bohemian Plateau is a rolling land surrounded by low, forested mountains. Bohemia is the most productive and densely populated part of the country. Prague, the nation's capital, is located near its center. The Elbe River, rising in this region, provides land-locked Czechoslovakia with an all-water route to the North Sea.

The Moravian Lowland is a wide, rolling lowland that serves as a natural route between the plains of Poland and Hungary. Like Bohemia, it is an important farming and industrial region. Most of Moravia is drained by the Morava River, which flows southward into the Danube. The Danube gives Czechoslovakia another all-water route to the sea—in this case to the Black Sea. The Oder River drains Northern Moravia and provides still another all-water route to a sea—the Baltic.

In Slovakia, the rugged Carpathian Moun-

tains reach their greatest heights in the High Tatra. The Carpathians are well forested. Their lower slopes are clothed in broadleaf trees, with clearings for fields and meadows. Higher up the needle-leaf trees take over. At the tops of the mountains are only Alpine grasses or bare rock.

Climate

The climate of Czechoslovakia varies with the regions. In the lowlands of Bohemia and Moravia, summers are warm and sunny, and winters are rather mild. In the mountains of Slovakia, summer temperatures are cool, and winters are quite cold. Well over twice as much moisture falls in the highlands of Slovakia as in the lower, western regions.

Natural Resources

The most important of Czechoslovakia's mineral resources is coal, though many different metallic ores are mined as well. Czechoslovakia is one of the world's leading coal producers. Most of the coal, however, is lignite, a low-grade brown coal found chiefly in Bohemia. It is used mainly in the chemical industry. A better grade of coal, mined around Ostrava in Moravia, has given rise to a large steel industry.

Many minerals are found in the mountains of Czechoslovakia. Iron, uranium, copper, silver, graphite, garnets, rock salt, and aluminum are mined. Since this is one of the most richly wooded areas in Europe—one third of the country is forested—timber is an important resource. About one half of all the land, much of it very fertile, can be tilled. But the people of Czechoslovakia are its most important resource. They have a long tradition of being among the most skilled and industrious workers in Eastern Europe.

▶ INDUSTRIES AND PRODUCTS

Czechoslovakia is a highly industrialized nation. Manufacturing and mining employ about one third of all workers and account for about 70 percent of the country's income.

Since the government owns all industry, it decides what products shall be manufactured. The construction of machinery is now strongly emphasized. It accounts for over one third of the total industrial output. So much of this machinery is shipped to foreign lands that it ranks as the country's major export.

In order to manufacture machinery, the country produces great amounts of iron and steel. Czechoslovakia is one of the largest steel producers in Eastern Europe. Most of its production comes from the Ostrava area. A very large steel mill was opened near Košice in the eastern part of Slovakia in 1964.

Second in importance to machinery construction is the textile industry. In the past textiles were produced in hundreds of small, privately owned factories. Now that the government operates all industry, production is concentrated in fewer but larger modern plants. However, all of the raw cotton and most of the wool for this industry must be imported.

Other important industries are food-processing and the manufacture of building materials, chemicals, armaments, wood products, china, and glassware. Sugar, from sugar beets, and beer, from malt, hops, and grain, are important products. The Lenin (Skoda) firm in Pilsen is famous for guns and automobiles. The province of Bohemia has a long history of fine craftsmanship in porcelain and crystal.

Although industry is highly developed in Czechoslovakia, there have been serious economic problems. The country's economy is closely tied to that of the Soviet Union. All of Czechoslovakia's oil, most of its synthetic rubber, and most of the needed extra iron ore comes from the Soviet Union. In order to meet Soviet directives, Czechoslovakia had to stress production of iron and steel, armaments, and heavy machinery.

This emphasis on heavy industry had adverse effects. Little attention was given to the products for which Czechoslovakia is traditionally famous—glassware, china, shoes, and textiles. Production of goods for home consumption fell behind. The massive housing shortage was neglected. Recently, however, attention has been given to making better

A *Spartakiada*—gymnastics festival. Gymnastics are a favorite Czechoslovakian sport.

Wenceslas Square in Prague.

One of Prague's many outdoor cafés.

quality and better designed goods to increase sales in world markets.

About one fourth of Czechoslovakia's workers are now employed in agriculture. Farming has shown little improvement since the Communists seized power. In the days before World War II, the farmers were able to feed the nation and still export. Today the country needs to import grain, meat, butter, and animal feed.

The farm problem is chiefly due to the attitude of the farmers. More than 85 percent of the country's cropland was taken away from its former owners. Output fell off when the farmers were put to work on the large government-owned co-operative farms. Steps are now being taken to improve production. More fertilizer, better seeds, and more machinery are being made available. About half the farmland is used for growing grains. Wheat, rye, oats, and barley are the most important varieties. Potatoes are widely grown and used for both food and livestock feed.

All other branches of the economy are controlled by the government. It even runs the many health spas, such as the famous one at Carlsbad (Karlovy Vary), and maintains the most important of the more than 2,500 ancient castles that dot the countryside.

Cities

Today more than half the people live in cities. The largest and most important city is Prague (Praha), with over 1,000,000 people. In this ancient city is Charles University, one of the oldest and most famous universities in Europe. Prague is located on the banks of the Vltava River. On a hill overlooking the west bank of the river stands an imposing medieval castle and a magnificent cathedral. On the lower, eastern bank is the main business section of the city. But everywhere the medieval and the modern mingle. There are great baroque palaces, quaint fountains, and old churches across the street from modern office buildings of concrete and glass.

The next two largest cities are Brno and Bratislava. Brno is the country's textile center. Bratislava, on the Danube River, is the capital of Slovakia and the nation's chief river port. Other major cities include Košice, a transportation and commercial center; Ostrava, which produces steel; and Pilsen (Plzeň), famous for beer and armaments.

▶ HISTORY AND GOVERNMENT

In the 5th century A.D. many small tribes of Slavic peoples began to move into the area that we now call Czechoslovakia. Gradually these small tribes were united into larger groups called Czechs, Slovaks, and Moravians. For a time the Moravians were the most powerful of these peoples. But the most important role in the country's history has always been played by the Czechs.

Among the Czechs was a tribe known as the Bohemians, who were ruled by the Premysl family. This family became strong enough to unite all of the Czechs and Moravians and to establish the Kingdom of Bohemia around the year 900.

The second ruler of Bohemia was Vaclav I, who later became a saint. He is best known to most people as the Good King Wenceslaus of the Christmas carol. He is supposed to have ruled from 921 to 929.

Bohemia was a powerful kingdom in central Europe for several centuries. During its greatest period, its king was Charles IV (1316–78), a wise, far-sighted monarch, who ruled the Holy Roman Empire from Prague. The capital still has many landmarks of this period, during which its great university was founded and the Church Cathedral of St. Vitus was rebuilt. Charles introduced new agricultural methods, attempted to reform the laws, and protected the lower classes by giving them courts where they could sue the nobles. Then, in 1526, Austria gained control of Bohemia. From that time on the country began to decline in importance.

Throughout these many centuries Slovakia remained in the background of European history. It was conquered by the Magyars in 906 and was a part of Hungary until 1918.

The Czechs had long wanted their independence from the Austrians, just as the Slovaks wished to be freed from Hungarian rule. The defeat of Germany and its Austro-Hungarian ally in World War I gave them their opportunity. Czech and Slovak patriots, led by Tomáš Masaryk and Eduard Beneš, formed a provisional government in London. On October 18, 1918, they declared the independence of the Czechoslovak nation. Masaryk was elected as Czechoslovakia's first president. When he retired, Beneš was elected president.

Many people regarded the new country as one with a great future. It was a country with a well educated and hardworking population, led by outstanding statesmen. A very liberal democratic constitution was adopted. But the independence of the new country did not last very long. In 1938 Adolf Hitler, the dictator of Nazi Germany, demanded that Czechoslovakia surrender the Sudetes Mountains region. He based his demand on the fact that many Germans had remained living in the area after World War I. The leaders of the British and French governments met with Hitler in Munich in September of that year to discuss his demand. Rather than risk war they consented to let Germany annex the region.

But the annexation of the Sudetenland did not satisfy the Nazis. They described Czechoslovakia as "a dagger pointed at the heart of Germany"—a dagger which had to be re-

Farm machinery being used to sow crops on a state farm in central Bohemia.

moved. In 1939, German troops invaded the country. Since Soviet forces helped liberate Czechoslovakia in 1945, the Communist Party became a powerful force in the new government. In 1948 the Communists took complete control of Czechoslovakia.

The federal government of Czechoslovakia consists of a president, who is head of state, a premier, and a Federal Assembly. The Federal Assembly is composed of two houses, the Chamber of the People and the Chamber of the Nations. The Federal Assembly elects the president, who appoints the premier to act as head of the government. There are separate Czech and Slovak republics, each of which has its own national council. The national councils elect the members of the Chamber of the Nations.

But real power in Czechoslovakia rests with the Communist Party and its first secretary. In 1968, this office was taken over by Alexander Dubček. He succeeded Antonín Novotný, who had held that post since 1953. Opposition to Novotný had grown because of the rigid censorship, lack of personal freedom, and the economic stagnation of the country.

When Dubček came to power, he had the backing of most of the people. He immediately set about giving them the reforms they wanted. The laws of the country were rewritten to allow free speech, free press, and secret ballot. In eight months Czechoslovakia was transformed into one of the most liberal of the Communist countries.

The Soviet Union and its closest allies—East Germany, Poland, Hungary, and Bulgaria—became alarmed. At a meeting in July, 1968, at Cierna, Czechoslovakia, a tiny town near the Soviet border, the Soviet leaders demanded an end to the reform program. The Czechoslovak leaders stood firm. They were supported by Yugoslavia and Rumania as well as the Communist leaders in Western countries. At first the Soviet Union seemed to agree to let Czechoslovakia proceed with its reform program. But on August 20, 1968, troops of the Soviet Union and its four allies invaded Czechoslovakia and imprisoned its liberal leaders. In spite of this, the Czechoslovakian people remained unyielding. They met the invading tanks with signs pointing the way back to Moscow. Underground radios encouraged passive resistance. Members of the Federal Assembly met secretly and re-elected the imprisoned leaders.

All this proved of no use. Dubček and the other leaders were taken by force to Moscow, where the Soviets dictated the terms of an agreement to them. Dubček was permitted to return home, but in 1969 he was replaced as party leader by Gustáv Husák. Dubček's followers were removed from office. The liberal reforms were canceled, and the country's policies were brought back in line with those of the Soviet Union. In 1975, Husák became president. He remained the leader of the Communist Party. Like many other Communist nations in Eastern Europe, Czechoslovakia faced economic problems in the early 1980's.

JOSEPH A. FEKETE
State University of New York College at Buffalo

See also MASARYK, TOMÁŠ.

FACTS AND FIGURES

CZECHOSLOVAK SOCIALIST REPUBLIC is the official name of the country.

CAPITAL: Prague

LOCATION: East Central Europe. **Latitude**—47° 44′ N to 51° 03′ N. **Longitude**—12° 05′ E to 22° 34′ E.

PHYSICAL FEATURES: Area—127,869 km² (49,370 sq mi). **Highest point**—Gerlachovka Peak, 2,662 m (8,737 ft). **Lowest point**—163 m (535 ft). **Chief rivers**—Elbe, Danube, Oder, Vltava (Moldau).

POPULATION: 15,300,000 (estimate).

LANGUAGE: Czech, Slovak (official); also Hungarian (Magyar), German, Russian.

RELIGION: Roman Catholic.

GOVERNMENT: Communist Republic. **Head of state**—president. **Head of government**—premier. **International co-operation**—United Nations, Council for Mutual Economic Assistance (COMECON), Warsaw Pact.

NATIONAL ANTHEM: The first part is Czech: *Kde domov muj?* ("Where is my native land?"). The second part is Slovak: *Nad Tatrou sa blyska* ("It storms over the Tatra").

ECONOMY: Agricultural products—sugar beets, potatoes, wheat, barley, rye, oats, maize (corn), hops, livestock. **Industries and products**—tools, machinery, vehicles, engines, armaments, woodworking, chemicals, iron and steel, textiles, cement, glass and ceramics, paper, timber, beer. **Chief minerals**—coal, iron ore, lignite, uranium. **Chief exports**—machinery, tools and equipment, steel, minerals, foodstuffs (sugar, barley, malt, hops), glass, ceramics, shoes, textiles, timber and wood products. **Chief imports**—fuels and raw materials, food products (wheat, corn, lard, butter, pork), machinery, tools and equipment, consumer goods. **Monetary unit**—koruna.

C, third letter of the English alphabet **C** 1
See also Alphabet
C-14 see Carbon-14
Cab, of a truck **T** 296

Cabala (CAB-al-a) (or Kabbalah; Cbbala), mystical tradition in Judaism, attributing mystical significance to each word, letter, and number found in Scriptures. It was popular in many medieval Jewish communities, especially during 12th to 16th centuries. The tradition was subscribed to by Christians, who believed they could substantiate divinity of Christ and other Christian beliefs in the Cabala. The Zohar (Book of Splendor) is the most sacred book of Cabalists.

Caballero, Fernán (Cecilia Böhl de Faber), Spanish
   writer **S** 370
Cabaret, musical **M** 543
Cabbage, vegetable **V** 290
   Alaska produces, picture **A** 137
   leaves we eat **P** 307; picture **P** 306
Cabbage palmetto (Sabal palmetto), tree
   state tree of Florida, South Carolina, pictures
   F 259, **S** 296

Cabell (CAB-ell), **James Branch** (1879–1958), American author, b. Richmond, Va. He wrote a series of romantic novels set in fictional country of Poictesme. In this collection, known as the Biography of Manuel, characters often trace ancestry to historic Virginia. Cabell's best-known works are Jurgen, Smire, and Let Me Lie.

Cabeza de Vaca (ca-BAY-tha day BA-ca), **Álvar Núñez** (1490?–1557?), Spanish explorer and public official, b. Jerez de la Frontera. He was one of four survivors on the ill-fated Spanish expedition to Florida (1528) that ended on an island off Texas. After 8 years spent wandering and in captivity of Indians, he reached a Spanish settlement in Mexico. He told this story in Adventures in the Unknown Interior of America. He was later colonial governor of Paraguay (1540) and supreme court judge of Seville. **N** 194

Cabinda (ca-BIN-da), enclave district of Angola **A** 260
Cabinet, of the United States **P** 447–48
   flags **F** 230
Cabinetmaking **W** 230
Cabinet of Doctor Caligari, The, motion picture **M** 484
Cabinets, in government **P** 81–82
   Canada **C** 77, 78
   United States, presidential advisers **P** 447–48
Cable, George Washington, American novelist **A** 205;
   L 361
Cable cars
   San Francisco **S** 28; picture **S** 29
Cable logging **L** 374; **R** 331, 332
Cables, for transmitting electrical energy from one place
   to another
   telephone **T** 57, 59–60
Cables, submarine **T** 54
   communication, history of **C** 438, 439
   electronic communication, history of **E** 142d–142e
   Field, Cyrus, promoted first underwater transatlantic
   cable **F** 113
   first transatlantic cable **T** 52

Cable tool drilling, for petroleum **P** 172
Cable TV, device in electronic communication **E** 142c
   television, new industry in **T** 67, 70b–70c, 71
Cabochon (CAB-osh-on), cut of gemstones **G** 71
Cabooses (ca-BOO-ses), of freight trains **R** 83
Cabora Bassa Dam, Mozambique **M** 501
Cabot, George, American businessman and politician
   M 147
Cabot, John, Italian explorer for England **C** 2; **E** 384
   English claim to Canada **C** 68
   flag he carried **F** 228
Cabot, Sebastian, Italian explorer for England **C** 2
   how Argentina was named **A** 388
Cabot family, of Massachusetts **M** 147
Cabot Strait, Canada **N** 344a
Cabot Trail, on Cape Breton Island, Nova Scotia,
   Canada **N** 344g
Cabral, Amilcar, Guinea-Bissau patriot **G** 406b
Cabral, Luiz de Almeida, president of Guinea-Bissau
   G 406b
Cabral (ca-BROL), **Pedro Alvares,** Portuguese navigator
   B 372; **E** 384; **P** 403

Cabrillo (cab-RI-yo), **Juan Rodríguez** (?–1543), Portuguese navigator. He sailed to Mexico (1520) with Pánfilo de Narváez under Spanish flag and was with Hernando Cortés at capture of Mexico City (1521). He explored California coast (1542).
   California, history of **C** 27, 28

Cabrillo National Monument, Point Loma, California
   S 27

Cabrini (cob-RI-ni), **Saint Frances Xavier** (Mother Cabrini) (1850–1917), first U.S. citizen to be canonized, b. Sant'Angelo Lodigiano, Italy. She founded Missionary Sisters of the Sacred Heart in Codogno, Italy, and was then sent to United States (1889) to work among Italian immigrants. She became American citizen (1909) and traveled throughout United States, South America, and Europe establishing convents, schools, and hospitals. She was canonized (1946) by Pope Pius XII, who later named her patron saint of emigrants (1950).

Cabriole leg, of furniture **F** 507; picture **F** 508
Cacao (ca-CA-o), tree yielding chocolate and cocoa
   C 274–75
   cocoa butter **O** 76
Cachalots (CASH-a-lots) (sperm whales) **W** 147
CACM see Central American Common Market
Cacomistles (CAC-o-mistles), animals related to racoons
   R 26
Cactus, plant **C** 3–4; **A** 405
   adaptations of plants to surroundings, pictures
   L 215
   Burbank's spineless cactus, picture **B** 453
   desert plants, pictures **D** 125, 126
   desert terrarium, how to make **T** 104
   organ pipe cactus, Arizona **A** 414
   saguaro cactus, **A** 414; picture **A** 402
   used for food in Mexico **M** 242
Cactus wrens, birds, pictures **B** 234
   state bird of Arizona, picture **A** 402
Caddies, carriers of golf clubs **G** 260
   how to become a good golfer **G** 255

Caddis flies, insects I 279
Caddo confederacy, Indians of North America L 362
Cadeau, Le ("The Gift"), dadaist sculpture by Man Ray
    M 393; *picture* **M** 394
Cadence, in music **M** 532
Cadenza, in music **M** 533
Cadets, students at United States Military Academy
    U 168; *picture* **U** 167
Cadette (ca-DETT) **Girl Scouts G** 216

Cadillac, Sieur Antoine de la Mothe (1656?–1730),
French soldier and official in America, b. Gascony. He
went to America (1683) and was given command of post
at Mackinac (1694). He conceived plan to fortify Detroit
River, protecting French fur trade in region from English
and established settlement (1701) later called Detroit. He
was governor of Louisiana (1713–16).

Cadman, Charles Wakefield (1881–1946), American
composer and organist, b. Johnstown, Pa. His interest in
music of American Indians is reflected in such works as
operas *The Land of the Misty Water* and *Shanewis* and
song "From the Land of the Sky-Blue Water."

Cadmium, element **E** 154, 160
    acid rain **A** 8
Cadmus, legendary Phoenician prince **A** 172
Ca' d'Oro, palace in Venice, Italy
    restoration, *picture* **U** 87
Caduceus (ca-DU-ce-us), symbol of the doctor, *picture*
    M 208c
Cady, Hamilton Perkins, American chemist **K** 190
Caecilians (ce-CIL-ians), land-water animals **F** 476–77
Caedmon (CAD-mon), English poet **E** 246
Caernarvon Castle, Wales, *picture* **W** 4
Caesar (CE-zer), **Gaius Julius,** Roman general and
    statesman **C** 5–6, 298
    ciphers used in secret messages **C** 369, 370
    dictator of Roman Republic **R** 303
    England invaded by **E** 215
    Julius Caesar, play by Shakespeare **S** 135
    Mark Antony delivered his funeral oration **M** 100
    pictured on a Roman coin **A** 232
    place in Latin literature **L** 78–79
    quoted **B** 130; **Q** 20
    Roman calendar **C** 12
    Why were the Roman emperors called Caesars? **C** 6

Caesar (CE-zar), **Sid** (1922–), American comedian, b.
Yonkers, N.Y. Known as a master of pantomime, his TV
shows include *Your Show of Shows* with Imogene Coca and
Carl Reiner, *Caesar's Hour,* and *The Sid Caesar Show.* He
appeared on Broadway in *Little Me* (1962–63) and *Four
on a Garden* (1971). His autobiography, *Where Have I
Been?,* was published in 1982.

Caesar Augustus *see* Augustus
Cafeterias (ca-fet-ERE-i-as), restaurants **R** 186
Caffeine (ca-FENE), substance in coffee and tea
    C 374
    drugs as stimulants **D** 329–30
Cagayan (ca-ga-YON) **River,** Philippines **P** 186

Cage, John (1912–), American composer, b. Los Ange-
les, Calif. He is noted for his work in several experimental
forms. Two of these forms are aleatoric music (music
determined by an element of chance) and electronic mu-
sic. In 1938 he created the "prepared piano" by placing
objects between the piano's strings. This produced new,
percussionlike effects. Cage was awarded a Guggenheim

Fellowship in 1949 for his work. His books include *Empty
Words: Writings '73–'78* (1979).

Cagliavi, Paolo *see* Veronese, Paolo
Cagniard de la Tour (can-YAR d'la TOUR), **Charles,**
    French doctor **F** 90
Caguas, Puerto Rico **P** 522
Cahaba (ca-HA-ba), Alabama **A** 127
CAI *see* Computer-assisted instruction
Caicos Islands *see* Turks and Caicos Islands
Caiman (or cayman), kind of crocodile, *picture* **C** 534
    kinds of reptiles **R** 180–81

Cain and Abel, in the Old Testament (Genesis 4), sons of
Adam and Eve. Abel was a sheep herder, Cain a tiller of the
ground. Cain killed his brother when God favored Abel's
offering. For his sin Cain was condemned by God to a life
of wandering.

Cairn terrier, a small breed of working terrier, developed on
the Isle of Skye in Scotland. This playful dog was called a
cairn terrier because it could root under *cairns,* or piles of
stones, in pursuit of foxes and badgers. The cairn terrier
stands about 25 cm (10 in) at the shoulder and weighs
about 6 kg (13 lb). Its harsh outercoat and soft, furry
undercoat may be any color except white.

Cairo (KIRE-o), capital of Egypt **C** 7–8; **E** 90f, 91
    Nile River, at Cairo, *picture* **E** 90f
    tomb-mosque of Sultan Hasan, *picture* **I** 417
Cairo, University of, Egypt **E** 90c
Caisson disease *see* Bends, the
Caissons, watertight chambers for construction work
    D 81
    building construction **B** 401, 434
Caisson Song, by Edmund L. Gruber **N** 25
Caius, Saint, pope **R** 296
Cajuns (CAY-juns), French Canadian settlers in
    Louisiana **L** 349, 353
Cakewalk, dance **J** 57

Calabash gourd (bottle gourd), a hard-shelled fruit that
grows on tropical vines. The shells are used as bowls,
cups, water dippers, and other utensils. Calabash gourds
range in size from 7.5 to 90 cm (3 in to 3 ft). The calabash
tree grows a large fruit that is similar to the calabash
gourd. The shells of this fruit are also used as bowls and as
pots for cooking.

Caladium (ka-LA-dee-um), a tropical American plant with
colorful, triangular leaves. The caladium's leaves have
deep veins that appear against a background of red, green,
yellow, or green and yellow. Caladiums are grown outdoors
or as house plants.

Calamity Jane (Martha Jane Burke) (1852?–1903),
American frontier personality, b. near Princeton, Mo. She
grew up in Montana mining camps, where she became
expert sharpshooter and rider. She dressed and acted like
a man. Her nickname came from legend that calamity fol-
lowed her constantly. She often rode with frontiersman
Wild Bill Hickok during her days in Deadwood, South
Dakota.

Calamus root (sweet flag), plant
    plant remedy **P** 314; *picture* **P** 315
Calcars, spurs, of bats, *picture* **B** 92
Calcite, form of calcium carbonate **R** 267; *picture*
    R 265
Calcium, element **E** 154, 160

coral polyp content **C** 504
lime needed for plant growth **F** 96
nutrition, use in **N** 416
Calculators, machines for solving mathematical
problems **C** 9; **O** 55–57; *pictures* **C** 451
automation **A** 532–33
compared with computers **C** 449–50
See also Computers
Calculus (CAL-cu-lus), branch of mathematics **M** 157
Leibniz, Gottfried Wilhelm von **L** 136
Newton, Isaac **N** 206
Calcutta (cal-CUT-ta), India **C** 10–11; **I** 122; *picture*
I 128
population density **C** 306

Caldecott (CALL-de-cott), **Randolph** (1846–86), English
artist and illustrator, b. Chester, England. Still honored by
the award that bears his name, given each year to the artist
of the most distinguished American picture book, Calde-
cott pursued an art career throughout his life. His sketches
appeared in England and the United States. He also mod-
eled in clay and worked in oil. Hoping to improve his del-
icate health and, at the same time, to sketch the American
scene, he went to Florida in 1886. There he died of tuber-
culosis at the height of a distinguished career. Among the
many books he illustrated are *The Diverting Story of John
Gilpin* and *The Three Jovial Huntsmen.*
children's literature, history of **C** 240, 242
illustration for the ballad "The Diverting History of
John Gilpin," *picture* **C** 241

Caldecott Medal, book award **B** 309–310b; **C** 240
Calder (CALL-der), **Alexander,** American sculptor
U 116
mobiles, *pictures* **D** 137, **N** 42
modern art **M** 397
sculpture of forms in motion **S** 105
Seven Foot Beastie, sculpture, *picture* **A** 438e
Steel Fish, sculpture, *picture* **S** 104
Two-Faced-Guy, A, sculpture, *picture* **M** 398
Calder, Alexander S., American sculptor **P** 143
Caldera, caved-in summits of ancient volcanos
Crater Lake, Oregon **O** 192
Valles Caldera, New Mexico **N** 182
Calderón de la Barca (cal-der-ON day la BAR-ca), **Pedro,**
Spanish dramatist **D** 296; **S** 369, 372–73

Caldwell, Sarah (1928–   ), American opera director
and conductor, b. Maryville, Mo. In 1976, she became the
first woman to conduct a performance of the Metropolitan
Opera in New York City. Caldwell showed an unusual apti-
tude for music and mathematics at a very young age. A
founder of the Opera Company of Boston (1957), she is
known for her novel approach in integrating the theatrical
and musical aspects of opera.

Calendar Islands, Maine **M** 44
Calendars C 11–13
ancient Egyptian **A** 220
Aztec calendar stone, *pictures* **I** 195; **W** 220
biological calendars of plants and animals **L** 247–
50
Caesar, Julius **C** 6
Easter, how the date falls **E** 35
folklore of calendar customs **F** 305
international date line **I** 314
measuring time by moon and sun **T** 193–94
moon's phases shown on July, 1969, calendar
M 447
New Year's Day around the world **N** 208

religious holidays by different calendars **R** 153
science and society **S** 78
tree-ring calendars **T** 286–87
Calenders, machines with heavy rollers
calendered paper **P** 53
plastics and rubber **P** 330; **R** 347
use in textile manufacturing, *picture* **T** 142
Calfskin leather L 107
Calgary (CAL-ga-ry), Alberta, Canada **A** 146f; **C** 67
Calgary Exhibition and Stampede, Canadian rodeo
A 146f; *picture* **A** 146g
Calhoun (cal-HOON), **John C.,** American statesman
C 13
as vice-president, *picture* **V** 326
Compromise of 1850 opposed by **C** 448
Jackson opposes his states' rights theories **J** 6
Cali (CA-li), Colombia **C** 383
Calibers, diameters of gun bores **G** 419; **R** 231
Calico, cloth, how named **E** 387
Calico scallop, mollusk
shell, *picture* **S** 147
California C 14–30
Apollo tracking antenna at Goldstone **S** 340g
Bear Flag, 1846 **F** 228
Compromise of 1850 **C** 448
Death Valley, *pictures* **D** 131, **P** 284
earth's crust of moving plates produces faults
G 117
gold discoveries **G** 250–51
Lassen Peak, *picture* **V** 380
lemon growing **L** 137
local color in American literature **A** 205
logging near Mount Shasta, *picture* **N** 293
Los Angeles **L** 344–47
Mexican War **M** 239
olive trees **O** 101, 102
orange industry **O** 177
San Andreas fault, *picture* **E** 27
San Diego **S** 26b–27
San Francisco **S** 28–29
Shasta Dam, *picture* **D** 17
Yosemite National Park **Y** 352–53
California, University of C 23
campus at Los Angeles, *picture* **U** 102
California Aqueduct A 344; **C** 19
California condor, endangered species of bird **B** 232;
E 197
California gold rush M 320
California laurel, tree, *picture* **T** 278
California poppies, flowers, *picture* **W** 170
California sea lions W 6
California State University and College System C 23
California Test of Personality, sample **T** 119
California Trail O 263–65
Pony Express **P** 392
California Water Project C 19
Californium (cal-i-FOR-ni-um), element **E** 154, 160

Caligula (ca-LIG-u-la) (A.D. 12–41) (Gaius Caesar), Ro-
man emperor, b. probably Antium, Italy. He was a son of
Germanicus and Agrippina. Raised in army camps, he
gained the nickname Caligula, or "Little Boots." He suc-
ceeded Emperor Tiberius in 37, beginning his reign with
acts of generosity and justice. Following recovery from an
illness that possibly affected his mind, he became increas-
ingly cruel and capricious and demanded to be worshiped.
Assassinated by Praetorian Guards, he was succeeded by
his uncle Claudius.

Caliper, instrument for measuring distance between two points, such as thickness or diameter of pipes. It consists of two thin metal legs that can be opened or closed by turning screw joining them.

measuring tools, *picture* **T** 216

Calisthenics (cal-is-THEN-ics), floor exercises **G** 429–30, 432

conditioning exercises **P** 226–29; *picture* **P** 224

Caliver, Ambrose (1894–1962), American educator, b. Saltville, Va. After serving as head of the manual arts department (1918–25), he became assistant dean (1925–27), and then dean (1927–30) of Fisk University, Nashville, Tenn. He was appointed education specialist (1930) and black higher education specialist (1946) in the U.S. Office of Education in Washington, D.C. He became assistant to the Commissioner of Education, Federal Security Agency (1950). Instrumental in establishing Adult Education section of Office of Education, he was appointed head at its formation (1955).

Calixtus III, antipope **R** 297
Calixtus I, Saint, pope **R** 296
Calixtus II, pope **R** 297
Calixtus III, pope **R** 297
Callaghan, Morley, Canadian writer **C** 64

Callas (CA-las), **Maria Meneghini** (1923–77), operatic soprano, b. New York, N.Y. She was known for the dramatic power she brought to her roles. Of Greek background, she studied in Athens and made her debut with the National Opera of Greece (1938). She made her American debut in Chicago (1954) in *Tosca.* She went on, in a brilliant and controversial career, to sing leading roles in most of the world's great opera houses, including the Metropolitan Opera House in New York and La Scala in Milan. She gave her last public opera performance at the Metropolitan (1965) in *Tosca.* However, she made a worldwide concert tour (1973–74).

Callaway Gardens, Pine Mountain, Georgia **G** 142
Callers, for square dancing **F** 299

Callicrates (cal-LIC-ra-tese), Athenian architect and sculptor who lived during 5th century B.C. He was designer, with Ictinus, of Parthenon and temple of Athena Nike, both on Acropolis in Athens.

Callières Bonnevue (cal-YARE bon-VUE), **Louis Hector de** (1646–1703), French army officer and colonial governor in French Canada, b. Cherbourg. Appointed governor of Montreal (1684), he attempted unsuccessfully to obtain support from French King in launching offensive against English in New York. He led reinforcements from Montreal to defend Quebec from attack by English (1690). He was appointed governor of Canada (1699) at death of Frontenac, and he concluded peace treaty with Iroquois Indians (1701).

Calligraphy (cal-LIG-raphy), art of beautiful writing **H** 33; *pictures* **W** 320, 321

Chinese art **A** 461; **B** 318; **O** 215
Chinese literature **O** 220b
illuminated manuscripts of Islam **I** 88
illustration of scrolls and manuscripts **I** 88
Islamic art **I** 417
Japan **J** 28
monks in Middle Ages **M** 297

Callimachus (cal-LIM-ac-us), Greek scholar and librarian **G** 355
Calling of Saint Matthew, painting by Caravaggio **I** 472

Calliope (ca-LY-o-pi), goddess of epic poetry in Greek mythology. She and her eight sisters, the daughters of Zeus and Mnemosyne, were the muses, or patrons of the arts and sciences. She was the wife of Apollo and the mother of Orpheus. Her name was given to the musical instrument whose gay sound is often heard at fairs and circuses. Operated by forcing steam through a series of whistles on a keyboard, the calliope is sometimes called a steam organ or steam piano.

See also Muses

Callisto (ca-LIST-o), satellite of Jupiter **P** 275
Call letters, of radio stations **R** 54
Call number, of books **L** 184
Call of the Wild, The, book by Jack London **A** 208
Callot (cal-LO), **Jacques,** French artist
Two Clowns, etching **G** 304

Calloway, Cab (Cabell Calloway) (1907–), American bandleader and singer, known as the "Hi-de-ho man," b. Rochester, N.Y. His orchestra played alternately with Duke Ellington's at Cotton Club in New York (1929–39). Songs "Minnie the Moocher" and "St. James Infirmary Blues" became his trademarks. He played in all-black casts of film *Stormy Weather* and play *Hello, Dolly!*

Calonne (cal-LONNE), **Charles de,** French statesman **F** 464
Caloric (ca-LOR-ic) **theory,** of heat **H** 86d–87
Calories (CAL-o-ries), heat units **E** 199; **H** 91; **W** 117
nutrition **N** 415–16
Calorimeter (cal-or-IM-et-er), instrument for measuring specific heats **H** 91
Calotype, photographic process **P** 215
Calpurnia (cal-PUR-nia), wife of Julius Caesar **C** 6
Calumet, peace pipe **I** 196
used by Bison and Wild Rice area Indians **I** 167, 178
Calumet region, Indiana **I** 142, 148–49; *picture* **I** 143
Calusas (ca-LU-sas), Indians native to Florida **F** 272
Calvary, place of Jesus Christ's crucifixion **J** 86
Calvert, Cecil, 2nd Lord Baltimore **M** 129
named American colony Maryland **A** 192
Calvert, George, 1st Lord Baltimore **A** 192; **M** 129
Calvert, Leonard, first governor of Maryland colony **A** 192; **M** 128, 130
Calves, young cattle **C** 148, 149
dairying **D** 4
roped at rodeos **R** 281–82
young of moose, elk, and caribou called calves **D** 83
Calvin, John, French theologian and Reformation leader **C** 30, 286; *pictures* **P** 483, **R** 131
English psalter, of hymns **H** 311–12
Protestantism **P** 482
Reformation **R** 132

Calvin, Melvin (1911–), American chemist, b. Saint Paul, Minn. He was awarded Nobel prize (1961) in chemistry for finding number and order of chemical reactions in photosynthesis (process by which plants make sugar from water and carbon dioxide). The plants used in his research were one-celled algae. Radioactive atoms helped trace path of chemical elements involved.

Calving (CAV-ing), detachment of icebergs from glaciers I 7, 25
Calvinism, religious belief C 286; P 483; R 132
Calvino, Italo, Italian writer I 481
Calypso (ca-LIP-so), Greek goddess O 53
Calypso music F 321
Cam, Diogo *see* Cão, Diogo
Camagüey, Cuba C 549
Camargo (ca-MAR-go), **Marie,** Belgian-born French ballerina B 24; D 25
Camas, plant
    Camas Area Indians of North America I 175–77
Cambio, Arnolfo di *see* Arnolfo di Cambio
Cambium layer, of plant growth P 290–91
    how tree rings are formed T 286
    trunks of trees T 280; W 225
Cambodia (Kampuchea) C 31–34
    Angkor Thom, *picture* S 335
    dance, *picture* D 31
    flag F 239
    Vietnam, history of V 334c
Cambrian period, in geology E 23; F 383, 384; *picture* F 385
Cambridge, Alexander A.F.W.A.G. *see* Athlone, 1st Earl of
Cambridge (CAME-bridge) **University,** England U 68; *picture* E 73
Camellia (cam-E-lia), flower
    state flower of Alabama A 113
Camelot (CAM-el-ot), court of King Arthur A 442, 444
    ...al play
                                    ... 248

                    ...ortation A 65
                    ... transportation A 402
                    ... A 451
                    ...es H 213
                    ...n, *pictures* D 126, 129
                    ... H 212
                    ..., *picture* S 506
                    ... 307
                    ...l distribution L 237
                    ...ure P 408

                    ... A 99
                    ...*picture* S 449
                    ...*picture* A 467
                    ...ng loaded on camels, *picture*

                    ...(em-bair), cheese D 13
                    ...s), carved gemstones J 93; *picture*

                    ...art G 348
    a...ent ...an art, *picture* A 230
Camera hunting H 290
Camera obscura, cameralike device P 214
Camera operators, for motion pictures M 481
Cameras P 200–20
    camera terms used in motion picture production M 487
    communication advanced by C 434
    Eastman, George E 44
    lenses used in L 147–48
    motion picture photography P 214
    pinhole camera, how to make E 366
    telescopes used as camera lenses O 11; T 63
    television cameras T 65–70
    underwater, *pictures* O 41, 43
    use in astronomy A 476a

Cameron, Eleanor (1912–), American author of children's books, b. Canada. She won a National Book Award in 1974 for *The Court of the Stone Children.* A number of her books for young readers, including her first, *The Wonderful Flight to the Mushroom Planet* (1954), have been Junior Literary Guild selections.

Cameroon (cam-er-OON) C 35–36
    flag F 235
    homes, *picture* H 169
    literature A 76b, 76c, 76d
Cameroon, Northern *see* Nigeria
Cameroon Mountains, western Africa A 49
Camille (ca-MELE), play by Alexandre Dumas *fils* D 342
Camino Real (ca-ME-no ray-OL), El, "The Royal Highway," historic trail in California C 23
Camoëns (CAM-o-ens), **Luis Vaz de,** Portuguese poet E 389
Camouflage (CAM-o-flodge) L 219–20
    demonstration of camouflage L 220
    fishes F 193; *pictures* F 192
    insects use for protection I 274
    optical illusion helps animals to survive O 164
    snakes, diamond-back rattler, *picture* S 210
    See also Protective coloration

Camp, Walter Chauncey (1859–1925), "The Father of American Football," b. New Britain, Conn. An outstanding undergraduate athlete at Yale, where he became athletic director (1888), he helped alter English rugby to approximate form of today's American football by decreasing number of players from 15 to 11, initiating position of quarterback, and putting ball in play under control of single player by means of scrimmage. He began choosing All-American football team (1889) and developed exercises known as "daily dozen."

Campanella, Roy (1921–), American baseball player, b. Homestead, Pa. As catcher for the Brooklyn Dodgers (1948–57), he was three times voted Most Valuable Player of the National League. His career was ended by serious automobile accident (1958). He was one of first blacks in major league baseball and was elected to Baseball Hall of Fame in 1969.

Campaniles (cam-pa-NE-lese), bell towers I 460

Campbell, Sir Alexander (1822–92), Canadian statesman, b. Yorkshire, England. He was elected Liberal-Conservative member of Legislative Council of Canada (1858) and was leader of Conservative opposition party in senate (1873–78). He served as postmaster general (1867–73, 1879–80, 1880–81, 1885–87), minister of justice (1881–85), and lieutenant governor of Ontario (1887–92).

Campbell, Alexander, Irish-born American founder of the Disciples of Christ W 138
    Protestantism, history of P 484
Campbell, Donald, English speedboat racing champion B 264

Campbell, Earl (1955–), American football player, b. Tyler, Texas. A running back for the Houston Oilers of the National Football League (NFL), he is known especially for his strength and running power. In his first four years in the NFL (1977–81), Campbell rushed for 6,457 yards, a league record for a four-year span. After the 1982 season, he was tenth on the NFL career rushing list. As a

Campbell, Earl (continued)
senior at the University of Texas, he won the 1977 Heisman Trophy, which is awarded to the nation's best college football player.

Campbell, John W., Jr., author and editor **S** 85
Campbell, Sir Malcolm, English automobile racer
    A 540

Campbell, Mrs. Patrick (Beatrice Stella Tanner) (1867–1940), English actress, b. London. She is noted primarily for her roles in relatively modern dramas. She played in Henrik Ibsen's *Little Eyolf* and *Hedda Gabler* and is identified with title roles in *Magda* and *The Second Mrs. Tanqueray.* She originated the role of Eliza Doolittle in George Bernard Shaw's *Pygmalion,* which he wrote expressly for her.
    Shaw's love for her **S** 144

Campbell, Robert (1808–94), Canadian fur trader and explorer, b. Glenlyon, Scotland. As agent for Hudson's Bay Company (1832–71), he explored Mackenzie River district of northwest Canada. He discovered Pelly River (1840) and its source, the Yukon River, and later helped to map the region.
    first trading post in Yukon **Y** 365

Campbellton, New Brunswick, Canada **N** 138f
Camp David accords, between Egypt and Israel **I** 322
Camp Fire, youth organization **C** 37–39
Campfires, how to build **C** 43–44

Camphor ($C_{10}H_{16}O$), white resin of *Cinnamomum camphora,* evergreen tree native to Taiwan. It is also made synthetically. Camphor is used in manufacture of plastics, drugs, disinfectants, explosives, and chemicals.

Campin, Robert *see* Flémalle, Master of
Campiña, Enrique Granados *see* Granados, Enrique
Campinas, Brazil **S** 36
Campine region *see* Kempen region
Camping **C** 40–46
    Camp Fire, Inc. **C** 37–39
    equipment to be carried in boats **B** 263–64
    Girls Clubs of America **G** 220
    Girl Scouts **G** 217–18
    organized *see* Camping, organized
    vacations and travel **V** 258
Camping, organized **C** 47
    boys' camp, *picture* **U** 101
    for diabetic children, *picture* **D** 194
    vacations **V** 258
Campion, Thomas, English poet and composer **E** 270
Camp meetings, for religious services **H** 315
Campobello (cam-po-BEL-lo) **Island,** New Brunswick
    M 43
    Roosevelt Campobello International Park **N** 138f
Campo Formio, Treaty of, 1797 **N** 10
Camps *see* Camping; Camping, organized
Camus, Albert, French author **F** 443
Canaan (CANE-an), ancient region corresponding to
    Palestine, now Jordan and Israel **I** 444; **P** 40a
    Promised Land **A** 6b; **B** 154; **M** 468
Canada **C** 48–67
    acid rain **A** 8
    agriculture **A** 88–92, 93–95
    aliens **A** 166
    art **C** 65
    automobiles **A** 550
    ballet **B** 28b; **C** 63

    Banff National Park **B** 42
    banks and banking **B** 50–51
    Boy Scouts **B** 357, 360
    census taken by Statistics Canada **C** 169
    citizenship **C** 312, 313
    conservation programs **C** 488
    Consumer and Corporate Affairs, Department of
        C 494b
    co-operatives **C** 500
    Dominion Day **H** 152
    education **C** 62
    emigration to the United States **I** 100, 102
    Eskimos (Inuit) **E** 284–91
    ethnic groups **E** 302
    favorite foods **F** 339
    flag **F** 241
    football **F** 366
    foundations **F** 390
    4-H clubs **F** 396a
    fur trade in North America **F** 520–23
    gold discoveries **G** 253
    government *see* Canadian government
    history *see* Canadian history
    holidays **H** 149, 152
    ice hockey originated **I** 33
    immigration **I** 102–03
    income tax **I** 111
    Indian dwellers of Caribou Area **I** 169–72
    Jasper National Park **J** 54–55
    literature *see* Canadian literature
    lumber and lumbering **L** 372
    music **C** 63
    music festivals **M** 552
    national anthem **N** 21
    National Ballet of Canada, *picture* **D** 32
    National Gallery of Canada **N** 43–44
    Niagara River, Horseshoe Falls **N** 243–44
    occupational health and safety **O** 17
    Ottawa, capital of Canada **O** 124, 236f–239
    paper industry **P** 56
    patriotic songs **N** 27
    police **P** 374, 375, 377
    political parties **P** 381, 382
    public-assistance programs **W** 120
    religion **C** 289
    Royal Canadian Mint **M** 338
    Saint Lawrence River and Seaway **S** 16–17
    social insurance programs **S** 222
    taiga **T** 10–11
    territorial settlements with United States **T** 105,
        108
    theater **C** 63
    United States, military co-operation with **C** 82
    universities and colleges **U** 208–208a
    See also names of provinces, territories, and
        principal cities

Canada, United Church of, union of Methodist, Congregationalist, and some Presbyterian churches formed by United Church of Canada Act (1924). The membership makes up approximately 20 percent of total Canadian population.
C 289; **P** 484

Canada Act, 1982 **B** 180; **C** 76
Canada Council, government foundation **C** 62; **F** 390
    Massey Commission **M** 150
Canada Deposits Insurance Corporation **B** 51
Canada Games, amateur sporting events **C** 67
Canada Institute for Scientific and Technical Information
    L 177

Canada lynxes (LINX-es) C 139
Canada Pension Plan, social insurance program S 222
Canada thistle, *picture* W 105
Canadian Amateur Hockey Association C 67; I 33, 35
Canadian Armed Forces C 79–82
Canadian Association of Children's Librarians
    book awards B 309
Canadian Broadcasting Corporation (CBC) C 61; O 122
Canadian Confederation C 73; P 456f–456g
Canadian Department of Transport B 262
Canadian Football League C 67
Canadian government C 76–78
    civil service C 317
    history C 72–73
Canadian Group of Painters C 65
Canadian Guards Band, *picture* B 41
Canadian history C 68–75
    Bill of Rights B 180
    Borden, Sir Robert Laird B 336
    boundary and territorial settlements with United
        States T 105, 108
    Cartier, Jacques C 124d
    confederation fathered by George Brown B 411
    Diefenbaker, John George D 165
    King, William Lyon Mackenzie K 248
    Laurier, Sir Wilfrid L 85
    Macdonald, Sir John A. M 3–4
    Mackenzie, Sir Alexander M 4a
    Mackenzie, William Lyon M 4a
    Massey, Vincent M 150
    Pearson, Lester P 115
    Revolutionary War, American R 201
    Saint Lawrence River S 16–17
    Seven Years War (French and Indian War) F 458–
        62
    Trudeau, Pierre T 297
    War of 1812 W 9–11
    See also history section of province articles
Canadian Home and School and Parent-Teacher
    Federation P 67
Canadian Kennel Club D 259
Canadian Labour Congress (C.L.C.) L 10
Canadian Library Association (Association Canadienne
    des Bibliothèques), joint committees with
    American Library Association L 191, 192
Canadian literature C 64
    Book of the Year for Children Medal B 309
Canadian National Railways (CNR) C 58; *picture* C 60
    Macdonald's National Policy helps build M 4
Canadian Professional Boxing Federation B 352
Canadian Rockies N 284
Canadian Shield, North America N 285, 288
    Canada, landforms and mineral resources of C 50,
        56
    Labrador N 140
    Michigan, Upper Peninsula of M 260
    Ontario section O 119
    Prairie Provinces section A 146a; M 76, 77, 79;
        S 38a
    Quebec section Q 10
    Yukon and Northwest Territories section Y 361
Canadian Skateboard Association S 184b
Canal (ca-NAL) boats E 278–80
Canal du Midi (Languedoc Canal), France E 208
Canaletto, Antonio, Italian painter I 473
Canals C 83–86
    Amsterdam, the Netherlands N 118
    Bruges, Belgium, *picture* B 127
    Canada O 121
    Chesapeake and Ohio Canal M 125–26

Erie Canal E 276–80
Florida's system F 262
Grand Canal, Venice, *picture* E 304
Jakarta, Indonesia J 13
Mars, none shown on M 104–05
new sea-level canal considered for Panama P 47
Nicaragua considered for canal N 246
Ohio O 66
Panama Canal P 46–49
Saint Lawrence Seaway S 17
Saulte Sainte Marie (Soo) Canals M 266; *picture*
    G 326
Suez Canal S 450–52
Thailand klong, *picture* T 148
transportation, importance to T 261
tunnels T 314
United States U 110–11
Venice, Italy V 300, 301
Wabash and Erie Canal I 144
Which canal took its boats over a mountain by rail?
    C 86
Canals, of ear B 287–88; *diagram* B 285
Canal Zone *see* Panama Canal Zone
Canaries, birds B 245–46; P 181; *picture* B 247
    animal learning, *picture* A 284
Canaries Current G 411
Canary Islands, off northwest Africa I 427–28; S 356
Canasta (can-AS-ta), card game C 113–14
Canaveral, Cape, Florida F 258, 272; *picture* F 266
Canberra (CAN-ber-ra), capital of Australia C 87–88;
    picture A 495
    Apollo tracking antenna S 340g
    Australia's cities A 514
Cancer, constellation C 491

Cancer (the crab), fourth sign of the zodiac. Cancerians
are people born between June 21 and July 22. They are
said to be ruled by the moon, which astrologers consider a
planet, and their moods vary with the phases of the moon.
They can be crabby and hard to get along with, but they are
also gentle and sensitive. Cancer is a water sign.
    sign of, *picture* S 245

Cancer, Tropic of *see* Tropic of Cancer
Cancer and cancer research C 89–95
    cancer cells, *picture* D 192
    diseases, research problems in D 192–93, 218
    food additives may produce cancer-causing agents
        F 348
    fund established by Mildred Zaharias Z 366
    hypnosis relieves side effects of chemotherapy
        H 317
    interferon G 91
    leukemia, disease D 199
    occupational health and diseases O 16, 17
    Public Health Service testing programs P 504
    saccharin, dangers of S 456
    smoking and cancer S 203
    virus study V 367, 370–370a
Cancer epidemiology, study of the occurrence of cancer
    in different groups of people C 92
Candellilla (cand-el-LI-ya) wax W 76
Candide (con-DEDE), book by Voltaire V 388
    European novels N 348
    satire H 280
Candid photography P 211, 216
Candlefish torch, *picture* L 280
Candlemas Day R 155
    known as a Witches' Sabbath W 208
Candlenut tree

Candlenut tree (continued)
    state tree of Hawaii, *picture* **H** 56
    torch, *picture* **L** 280
Candlepins, a bowling game **B** 349
Candles **C** 96–97
    Easter symbol **E** 35
    lighting **L** 280–81
    light intensity (brightness) measured in foot candles
        L 265
    made by American colonists **C** 399
    riddle "Little Nanny Etticoat" **J** 133
    smoke candles for search parties **F** 156
Candlewood, Lake, Connecticut **C** 470
Candling, egg *see* Egg candling
Candy and candymaking **C** 98–99
    chocolate **C** 274, 275
    recipes **R** 115, 116
Canes, walking sticks
    symbol of furrier trade **F** 515
    technique of use by the blind **B** 254
Cane sugar **S** 454
    sugarcane **G** 319; *picture* **G** 318
Canidae (CAN-id-e), dog family **D** 243
Canis (CAY-nis), dog genus **D** 243
Canis Major (Big Dog), constellation **C** 492
Canis Minor (Little Dog), constellation **C** 492
Cankerworms **P** 289; *picture* **P** 288
Cannae (CAN-ne), **Battle of,** 216 B.C. **H** 34
Cannas, flowers **G** 41
Canned foods
    grades and can sizes **M** 101
Canneries
    first successful cannery in United States **F** 346
    floating canneries of Japan **A** 462
Cannibalism (CAN-ni-bal-ism), practice of eating one's
    own kind
    animals' eating habits **A** 266
    early custom of Fijians **F** 122
    former custom of Carib Indians **I** 210

Canning, George (1770–1828), English statesman, b. London. He entered Parliament (1794) as supporter of Prime Minister William Pitt. He was undersecretary for foreign affairs (1796–99) and foreign secretary (1807–09) and leader of House of Commons (1822), and he succeeded Liverpool as prime minister (1827). Canning is noted for acknowledging independence of Spanish colonies in New World, promoting nonintervention policy, encouraging liberal and nationalist movements in Europe, and advocating emancipation of Roman Catholics in England. He established Great Britain's independence of Holy Alliance.

Canning and preserving **F** 345–46
    baked goods, canned **B** 388a
    botulism, poisoning, how to guard against **F** 354
    developed by Nicholas Appert **F** 345

Cannon, Annie Jump (1863–1941), American astronomer, b. Dover, Del. A long-time curator at Harvard Observatory, she was in charge of photographs of stars and other celestial bodies. She introduced best modern method of classifying stars according to surface temperatures, as shown by kind of light they give off. Cannon discovered five new stars and was first to show changes in brightness for 300 other stars. **D** 99

Cannonball express, railroad train **T** 74
Cannon bone, of the feet of animals **F** 81, 82;
    diagram **F** 80

Cannon Mountain (Profile Mountain), New Hampshire
    N 148, 157; *picture* **N** 150
Cannons **G** 414–26
Canoes (ca-NOOS) **and canoeing** **C** 100a; **S** 155
    earliest type of ships **S** 155
    hosteling **H** 254–55
    Indians of North America, *pictures* **I** 171, 179,
        182, 186
    Olympic events **O** 108
Canon, books accepted as Holy Scriptures **B** 152
Canon, musical form **M** 535

Canonicus (ca-NON-ic-us) (1565?–1647), American Indian chief of Narragansett tribe. He ceded to Roger Williams land on which state of Rhode Island was founded (1636). Through Williams' influence, he remained friendly with English and signed a treaty acknowledging their sovereignty (1644).

Canonization, the final process whereby a person is declared to be a saint. This occurs when at least two miracles are declared to have been brought about by the intercession of a person already beatified, or blessed. Miracles are not required in the case of a person who has died a martyr.

Canon law **L** 87
Canopy bed, *picture* **C** 389
Canova (ca-NO-va), **Antonio,** Italian sculptor **I** 473
    neoclassic sculpture **S** 101–02
    Tomb of the Countess Maria Christina, sculpture
        S 102
Canso, Strait of, Canada **N** 344a
Cantabrian Mountains, Spain **S** 352
Cantaloupes (CAN-ta-lopes), melons **M** 216
Cantata (can-TA-ta), musical form **B** 64–65; **M** 535
    choral music **C** 277–78
Canter, gait of a horse, *picture* **H** 230

Canterbury, Archbishop of, Primate of All England, bishop of diocese, or region, of Canterbury, and spiritual and symbolic authority of Anglican Communion. He presides at Lambeth Conferences of Anglican (Episcopal) bishops throughout the world. Augustine was consecrated first archbishop of Canterbury (597) by Pope Gregory. British Reformation Parliament (1529–36) under King Henry VIII severed all ties with Catholic Church in Rome, and British monarch replaced pope as secular head of Church of England, with archbishop of Canterbury as spiritual head. Robert Runcie was appointed archbishop of Canterbury in 1979.

Canterbury Cathedral, England **E** 235; *picture* **E** 234
Canterbury Tales, by Geoffrey Chaucer **C** 190; **E** 249;
    picture **E** 248
Cantilever (CAN-til-e-ver) **bridges** **B** 399
Canton (cant-ON), China **C** 260
Canton (CANT-on), of a flag **F** 226
Canton, Ohio **O** 72

Canton and Enderbury islands, coral atolls in the central Pacific Ocean once administered jointly by the United States and Britain (1939–79). Canton was used as an airline base and a satellite tracking station. Both islands are now part of Kiribati.

Cantor, leader of musical services in synagogues
    J 119
    choral music **C** 276

Canute (994?–1035), king of Denmark and first Danish king of England. He invaded England and became king in 1016. He then returned to Denmark to strengthen his hold there and reigned from 1020 to 1035. Legend relates that to discourage belief in his limitless power, he took his courtiers to edge of sea and ordered waters to halt; his limitations were proved when the tide continued to come in.

Danish Vikings' invasion of England **E** 217; **V** 340

Canvas-back duck, *picture* **B** 222
Canyon de Chelly National Monument, Arizona **A** 414
Canyonlands, Utah **U** 242
Canyonlands National Park, Utah **U** 250
Canyons, deep valleys **M** 493, 495
Mars **M** 109
Cão (CAUN), **Diogo**, Portuguese navigator **C** 464, 465
Angola **A** 261
Capacitance (ca-PAS-it-ance), in electricity **E** 126–27
Capacitors (ca-PAS-it-ers), devices for storing electrical
energy **E** 126–27
semiconductors **E** 148
Capacity (ca-PAS-ity), volume **M** 236a
measurement **W** 113, 117
Cape, for the geographic feature *see* name of cape as
Canaveral, Cape
Cape Breton Island, Nova Scotia **I** 429; **N** 344a,
344b, 344g
Cape buffalo, of Africa **B** 428, 429 **M** 148
Cape Cod, Massachusetts **M** 136–37
Cape Cod Bay, Massachusetts **M** 138
Cape Cod Girls, folk song **F** 323
Cape Cod National Seashore, Massachusetts **M** 144
Cape Coloureds *see* Coloureds
Cape Columbia, northernmost point in Canada **Y** 361
Cape Hatteras National Seashore **N** 316
Cape hunting dogs **D** 250; *picture* **D** 251
Cape Lookout National Seashore, North Carolina
N 316
Čapek (CHA-pek), **Karel**, Czech playwright **D** 298;
R 252
Capella (ca-PEL-la), **Martianus**, Latin scholar **T** 139
Cape of Good Hope Province, South Africa **C** 100b
Capetian (ca-PE-tian) **kings**, of France **F** 415
Cape Town, legislative capital of South Africa
C 100b–101; **S** 270, 271; *picture* **S** 272
Cape Verde (VERD) **C** 102–03; **G** 406b
flag **F** 235
Cap-Haïtien (cape HAI-shen), Haiti **H** 9
Capillaries, tiny blood vessels **B** 275; **H** 86
digestive function **B** 276–77
Capillary action **L** 310
Capistrano, swallows of *see* San Juan Capistrano
Capital
bookkeeping **B** 312
capital goods, productive factor in trade **T** 242
cattle, early form of money **M** 410
economics **E** 46
labor and capital **L** 2–3
stocks and bonds **S** 427–33
Capitalism **C** 104–05; **E** 46–47, 49–50; **S** 220
Marx's analysis of **C** 443; **M** 114
poverty, cures for **P** 424b
trust and monopoly regulation **T** 305
See also Socialism
Capitalization (cap-it-al-i-ZAY-tion) **P** 532–33

Capital punishment, the execution (killing) of a person found guilty of a serious crime. For centuries, capital punishment was used for a great number of offenses. Today, it is carried out almost solely for the crime of murder. Many people are against capital punishment because they feel it is cruel or immoral. Those who favor it say it helps to prevent crime. In 1972 the U.S. Supreme Court ruled that the death penalty, as it was then enforced, was "cruel and unusual punishment." But in 1976 the Court ruled that capital punishment is constitutional under certain circumstances. States were then free to impose the death penalty according to the Court's guidelines. Some states have done away with capital punishment. Others greatly limit its use. Many nations have officially abolished capital punishment, including Canada (1976) and Britain (1969). **C** 532d; **L** 88, 89

Capitals, letters of the alphabet **A** 173
punctuation **P** 532–33
Capitals, of columns
three Greek orders **G** 346, 348; *pictures* **G** 347
Capitol, Washington, D.C. **W** 28–29
American classical architecture **U** 123
Capitol pages, for the members of Congress and the
Supreme Court **U** 142
Capitol Reef National Park, Utah **U** 250
Capone (ca-PONE), **Al** **C** 497
Capote (cap-O-te), **Truman**, American novelist **A** 214

Capp, Al (Alfred Gerald Caplin) (1909–79), American cartoonist, b. New Haven, Conn. Capp was the creator of the popular comic strip *Li'l Abner,* which he drew from 1934 until 1977. It depicted the life of the Yokums, a hillbilly family in the imaginary town of Dogpatch. Capp frequently satirized modern life and American politics in the comic strip.

Capper, Arthur, American editor and public official
K 190
Capper-Volstead Act, 1922 **C** 500
Capri (CA-pri), island at entrance to Bay of Naples
I 429; *picture* **I** 428
Capriccio, musical composition **M** 533
Capricorn, constellation **C** 491

Capricorn (the goat), 10th sign of the zodiac. According to astrologers, Capricorns (born December 22–January 19) are serious and do not have a strong sense of humor. They are ambitious and enjoy a challenge. They are slow to form relationships, but they are loyal friends. Capricorn is an earth sign, ruled by the planet Saturn.
sign of, *picture* **S** 244

Capricorn, Tropic of *see* Tropic of Capricorn
Caprification (cap-ri-fi-CAY-tion), pollination of fig tree
flowers **F** 117
Capri figs **F** 117
Capsule, of a spacecraft *see* Command module
Captain, chief officer of a ship **O** 22
Capuchins, monkeys **M** 420

Capulets, 13th-century Italian political group. The name adopted by Luigi da Porto in story of feud between Capulet and Montague families of Verona, which in a later version is the basis of Shakespeare's *Romeo and Juliet.*

Capybara (capy-BA-ra), rodent of South America
R 280
Carabiner (car-a-BI-ner), snap link used in mountain
climbing **M** 490
Carabinieri (ca-ra-bin-IER-ee), Italian police **P** 374;
picture **P** 373

Caracalla, Baths of
model for Pennsylvania Station **U** 123
Caracals, lynxlike wild cats **C** 139
Caracas (ca-RA-cos), capital of Venezuela **V** 296, 299;
pictures **L** 58, **V** 298
Simón Bolívar Center, *picture* **S** 284
Caracci (ca-RA-chi), **Annibale,** Italian painter **P** 23
Caramanlis, Constantine *see* Karamanlis, Constantine
Caramels, candy **C** 98
Carapace, shell on the back of some animals
crustaceans **S** 169
turtles **T** 331–32
Carats, units for measuring gemstones **J** 92, 93
See also Karats
Caravaggio (ca-ra-VA-jo), **Michelangelo Merisi da,** Italian
painter **C** 105; **I** 473
art of the artist **A** 438f
baroque art **B** 56–57
Calling of St. Matthew, painting **I** 472
Conversion of Saint Paul, The, picture **B** 57
Entombment, painting, *picture* **C** 105
Musicians, The, painting **A** 438c
nature copied faithfully **P** 23
Caravans, companies of travelers, *picture* **S** 8
Caravans, houses on wheels **H** 175, 177
Caravel (CA-ra-vel), sailing vessel **E** 374–75

Caraway, Hattie Wyatt (1878–1950), first woman elected
to the U.S. Senate, b. Bakerville, Tenn. After being
elected (1932) to fill the seat of her late husband, Thad-
deus H. Caraway, she was re-elected senator from Arkan-
sas (1933–44). She was appointed by President Roose-
velt to the U.S. Employees Compensation Commission
(1945).

Caraway seed **S** 382
Carbines, guns **G** 423; *picture* **G** 418
Carbohydrates (car-bo-HY-drates)
body chemistry of **B** 289–90
bread is an important source **B** 385
nutrition, needs in **N** 416
starch **S** 401
sugar **S** 453
Carbon, element **C** 106; **E** 153–54, 160
alloys **A** 168
atomic structure, model **A** 487
atomic symbol, *picture* **D** 15
batteries **B** 97
coal, chief ingredient of **C** 362
diamonds **D** 153
importance to fuels, especially coal **F** 487
lamp filaments **L** 284
rings and chains, structural formulas **C** 200
spectrum, *picture* **L** 267
Carbon-14, radioactive variety of carbon
dating by use of radioactive carbon **R** 65–66
for ice age dating **I** 22–23
use in archeology **A** 361
Carbon arc lamps **L** 285
Carbon black **R** 347
Carbon cycle, fusion reaction on the sun **S** 463–64
Carbon cycle, in ecosystems **E** 44
Carbon dioxide (dy-OX-ide) **C** 106
acid rain **A** 8
action to keep air warm **I** 24
atmosphere contains **A** 479
blood carries **B** 255, 256, 275, 277
carbon and oxygen cycles in ecosystems **E** 44
chemical reaction, how to show, *picture* **C** 197
earth's history, **E** 20, 22

fermentation **F** 90
fire extinguishers, use in **F** 136, 137
first studies by Helmont **C** 210
gases **G** 59
greenhouse effect **C** 348
human body's waste product **B** 278
Mars **M** 108, 110
photosynthesis **P** 222–23
wells in New Mexico **N** 187
See also Dry ice
Carbon disulfide (dy-SUL-fide) **C** 196
Carbonic (car-BON-ic) **acid** **A** 8
cave formations **C** 153–54
Carboniferous (car-bon-IF-er-ous) **period,** in geology
fossils **F** 384; *picture* **F** 386
Carbonization, chemical process **C** 367
Carbon monoxide (mon-OX-ide), poisonous gas **G** 59
acid rain **A** 8
air pollution **A** 110
catalytic converter **A** 111
greenhouse effect **C** 348
hyperbaric chambers used in cases of poisoning
M 210
low-pollution automobiles being developed **E** 272g
poisoning **P** 357
Priestley's discovery **P** 456

Carbon paper, thin paper coated on one side with a waxy
ink. Pressure from uncoated side results in reproduction of
impression on paper placed under the carbon paper.

Carbon tetrachloride (CCl_4), colorless, nonflammable
heavy liquid used as a fire extinguisher, insect extermina-
tor, spot remover, or dry-cleaning solvent. It is made from
carbon disulfide and chlorine in the presence of a cata-
lyst.
first aid for poison victims **P** 356

Carbon tissue, transfer material **P** 467
Carborundum (car-bor-UN-dum), abrasive **G** 388–89
Carburetors (CAR-bu-raters), of internal-combustion
engines **I** 310, 313
use principle of the venturi tube **A** 37
Carcassonne (car-cas-SONN), France, *picture* **M** 289
Carcinogens (car-CIN-o-gens), cancer-causing agents
C 91, 93
Carcinomas (car-ci-NO-mas), cancers **C** 89–90
Cardamom seed, spice **S** 382; *picture* **S** 381
chief export of Sikkim **S** 177
Cardano (car-DA-no), **Girolamo** (or Geronimo), Italian
mathematician **M** 156
codes and ciphers **C** 369
Cardboard **P** 53
book matches cut from **M** 153
Card catalogs, in libraries **L** 185–86
Cárdenas (CAR-they-nos), **García López de,** Spanish
explorer, first European to see Grand Canyon
G 290

Cárdenas (CAR-day-nas), **Lázaro** (1895–1970), Mexican
political leader and president, b. Jiquilpán de Juárez,
Michoacán. He supported Mexico's revolutionary move-
ments between 1915 and 1929 and served as governor of
his native Michoacán (1928–32) and as president of the
country (1934–40). His term was marked by a 6-year
reform plan including redistribution of land to peasants,
development of rural education, and expropriation of for-
eign-owned oil properties.
Mexico, history of **M** 251

Card games C 107–15
Cardiac patients H 86c
Cardiff, capital of Wales U 77; W 4
Cardiff giant, famous hoax I 360
Cardinal Albert of Brandenburg as St. Jerome in His Study, painting by Lucas Cranach G 167
Cardinals, birds B 220; *picture* B 234
    Illinois, state bird of, *picture* I 71
    Indiana, state bird of, *picture* I 137
    Kentucky, state bird of, *picture* K 213
    North Carolina, state bird of, *picture* N 307
    Ohio, state bird of, *picture* O 61
    Virginia, state bird of, *picture* V 344
    West Virginia, state bird of, *picture* W 127

Cardinals, Sacred College of, advisory body of Roman Catholic cardinals appointed by pope as his cabinet. College directs Curia Romana, or papal administration, and has sole responsibility for election of pope. It was formed under Alexander III (12th cent.). The red hat (galero) that was associated with the office was eliminated by Pope Paul VI (1969) to simplify dress.

Cardinal virtues, chief virtues considered by the Roman Catholic Church as the main types of all possible excellences. The early Christians borrowed four—prudence, fortitude, temperance, and justice—from Greek philosophy and added three—faith, hope, and love.

Carding, of fibers
    cotton C 524
    wool W 235
Cardiopulmonary resuscitation, first aid technique
    F 157–58

Cardozo (card-O-zo), **Benjamin Nathan** (1870–1938), American jurist, b. New York, N.Y. He was appointed by President Hoover to the U.S. Supreme Court in 1932. There he played an important role with his liberal interpretation of the Constitution. Earlier, Cardozo had served on the New York State Court of Appeals. His writings include *The Nature of the Judicial Process.*

Card tricks M 19–20; T 288
Carducci (car-DU-chi), **Giosuè,** Italian poet I 480
CARE *see* Cooperative for American Relief Everywhere
Careers *see* Vocations

Carew, Rod (Rodney Cline Carew) (1945–), American baseball player, b. Gaton, Panama. As an infielder for the Minnesota Twins (1967–78), he won seven batting titles. In his best season, 1977, he hit .388 and won the American League's Most Valuable Player Award. He was traded to the California Angels before the 1979 baseball season. *picture* B 76

Carey, James Barron (1911–73), American labor leader, b. Philadelphia, Pa. He was president of United Electrical, Radio, and Machine Workers (UE) (1936–41) but lost position because of his stand barring Communists from holding union offices. When UE was expelled from CIO on charges of Communist domination, he became president (1950–65) of newly formed International Union of Electrical, Radio, and Machine Workers (IUE). He was elected a vice-president of AFL-CIO in 1955.

Cargo cults, Pacific islands M 564
Cargo ships S 158
Carib (CARR-ib), Indians of South America I 209
    Caribbean islands C 116

Dominica D 279
Grenada G 374b, 375
Puerto Rico P 516
St. Lucia S 18b
St. Vincent and the Grenadines S 18c, 18d
Trinidad T 292

Caribbean Community and Common Market (CARICOM), an organization of states, formed in 1973 to promote unity in the Caribbean region. The community works to co-ordinate the economic development, trade, and foreign policies of its members. Headquarters are in Georgetown, Guyana. S 18b

Caribbean (ca-rib-E-an or ca-RIB-e-an) **Sea and islands**
    C 116–19
    Antigua and Barbuda A 316b
    Cuba C 547–51
    dances D 30
    Dominica D 279
    Dominican Republic D 280–83
    emigration to the United States I 100
    Haiti H 7–11
    Indian tribes I 207–08, 209
    industries and products N 302
    Jamaica J 14–18
    life in Latin America L 47–61
    outlying areas of the United States U 100
    Saint Kitts-Nevis S 15
    St. Lucia S 18a–18b
    St. Vincent and the Grenadines S 18c–18d
    Trinidad and Tobago T 290–92
    Turks and Caicos Islands T 329
Cariboo Road, British Columbia, Canada B 405
Caribou (CARR-i-boo), hoofed mammals H 214;
    pictures H 186, 216
    Alaska A 135; *picture* A 134
    Eskimo groups, essential for E 286–87
    Indians of the Caribou Area, northern Canada
    I 169–72
Caricatures (CARR-i-ca-tures), drawings C 125
    Daumier, Honoré D 43
Caries (CARE-eez), disease of the teeth T 48
Carillons (CA-rill-ons), sets of bells for ringing tunes
    B 137–38
    Bok Singing Tower, Florida F 269
    keyboard instruments K 240
    tower at University of Wisconsin, *picture* W 203
Cariocas, people of Rio de Janeiro B 375; R 235
Carissimi (ca-RI-si-mi), **Giacomo,** Italian composer
    I 484
    baroque music B 64

Carl XVI Gustaf (1946–), king of Sweden, b. Stockholm. He became king in 1973, succeeding his grandfather, Gustaf VI Adolf. His father, Crown Prince Gustaf Adolf, was killed in an airplane crash in 1947. Carl Gustaf served in the Swedish armed forces for two years. He also spent two years studying Sweden's government agencies in preparation for becoming king. He married a West German commoner, now Queen Silvia, in 1976.

Carleton, Sir Guy, British army officer and colonial
    governor Q 13
    Canada, history of C 71
Carleton, Mount, highest point in New Brunswick,
    Canada N 138
Carleton University, Ottawa, Canada O 238

Carlin, John (1940–   ), governor of Kansas, Democrat, b. Salina. Carlin was elected governor in 1978 and re-elected in 1982. Before he became governor, he was a member of the state House of Representatives for eight years. During that time, he served as minority leader (1975–77) and as speaker (1977–79).

Carlisle, Anthony, English scientist **E** 129

Carlota (kar-LO-ta) (1840–1927), empress of Mexico (1864–67), b. Laeken, Belgium. Only daughter of Leopold I of Belgium, she married (1857) Maximilian, Archduke of Austria, and accompanied him to Mexico (1864) when he was made emperor of Mexico by Napoleon III of France. After Maximilian was deposed, she returned to Belgium.
   Mexico, history of **M** 249

Carl Sandburg Home National Historic Site, North
   Carolina **N** 316
Carlsbad, health spa in Czechoslovakia **C** 562
Carlsbad Caverns, New Mexico **C** 153–55
Carlsbad Caverns National Park, New Mexico **N** 189

Carlson, Natalie Savage (1906–   ), American author of children's books, b. Winchester, Va. Her numerous books include *Alphonse, That Bearded One, The Talking Cat and Other Stories of French Canada, The Happy Orpheline,* and *Sashes Red and Blue.*

Carlton, Steve (Stephen Norman Carlton) (1944–   ), American baseball player, b. Miami, Fla. In 1983 he became the 16th pitcher in baeball history to win 300 games. In that same year, Carlton, a left-hander, surpassed Walter Johnson's career record of 3,508 strikeouts; he finished the season with 3,709. Carlton pitched for the St. Louis Cardinals (1965–71) and the Philadelphia Phillies (1972–   ). He is the only pitcher to have won four Cy Young Awards (1972, 1977, 1980, 1982), given each season to the best pitcher in each of the major leagues.

Carlyle, Thomas, Scottish historian, critic, and
   philosopher **E** 262

Carman, Bliss (William Bliss Carmens) (1861–1929), Canadian poet and journalist, b. Fredericton, New Brunswick. He wrote primarily romantic poems and ballads describing nature. He was literary editor of New York *Independent* (1890–92) and held editorial position on *Atlantic Monthly* magazine. He served as editor of *Oxford Book of American Verse* (1927) and was poet laureate of Canada (1928). Collections of his poems include *Low Tide on Grand Pré* and *Sappho.* **N** 138g

Carmen, opera by Georges Bizet **O** 142

Carmichael, Hoagy (Hoagland Howard Carmichael) (1899–1981), American songwriter and pianist, b. Bloomington, Ind. Carmichael abandoned a law career to compose popular songs, such as "Stardust," "Lazy Bones," "Georgia on My Mind," and "In the Cool, Cool, Cool of the Evening," which won an Academy Award in 1951. He had his own radio and TV programs and acted in films.

Carmichael, Stokely (1941–   ), American civil rights leader, b. Port of Spain, Trinidad. He attended public schools in New York City and was graduated from Howard University in 1964. In his work for civil rights, he took part in freedom rides and voter registration drives among blacks in the South. As chairman of the Student Nonviolent Coordinating Committee (SNCC) from 1966 to 1967, he helped popularize the slogan "black power," which urged black people to work for political power. Carmichael was prime minister (1967–69) of the Black Panther Party, a militant black power organization. With Charles Hamilton, he wrote the book *Black Power* (1967).

Carmona (car-MO-na), **António Oscar de Fragoso,**
   president of Portugal **P** 403
Carnation, flower
   state flower of Ohio, *picture* **O** 61
Carnauba (car-na-U-ba), wax palm tree of Brazil
   B 378; **W** 76
Carné, Marcel, French motion picture director **M** 487
Carnegie, Andrew, Scottish-born American industrialist
   and philanthropist **C** 119
   libraries **L** 200
   peace movements **P** 105

Carnegie, Dale (1888–1955), American author and lecturer, b. Maryville, Mo. He began giving courses in public speaking (1912) and later broadened these to include study of success in all aspects of life. His book *How to Win Friends and Influence People* was followed by a series of radio lectures of same name. He also wrote *How to Stop Worrying and Start Living.*

Carnegie Corporation **F** 390
Carnegie Endowment for International Peace **P** 105

Carnegie Foundation for the Advancement of Teaching, organization established (1905) by Andrew Carnegie with a gift of $10,000,000, to provide retirement pensions for professors in field of higher education in the United States and Canada. It provides research funds for educational problems and consulting services on higher education.

Carnegie Hero Fund Commission, organization endowed (1904) by Andrew Carnegie with $5,000,000, to recognize civil heroes otherwise little appreciated. It awards the Carnegie medal to persons performing heroic deeds in saving or attempting to save human lives and gives financial aid to injured heroes or their survivors.

Carnegie Institute, Pittsburgh, Pennsylvania **C** 119
Carnegie Medal, book award **B** 310
Carnegie Peace Palace, The Hague **P** 105
Carnelian (car-NE-lian), chalcedony quartz **Q** 7
Carnera, Primo, Italian boxer **B** 353
Carnival of the Animals, The, music **F** 446
Carnivals **C** 120–21
   Brazil's Carnival **B** 375; *picture* **B** 374
   Latin-American celebrations **L** 50
Carnivores, meat-eating animals **A** 266; **M** 65–66
   balance of nature **L** 258–59
   bears **B** 104
   cats **C** 134–41
   communities of living things **K** 258–59
   dinosaurs **D** 173–75
   dog family **D** 242–51
   food chains **E** 43
   mammals, orders of **M** 62, 69
   pinnipeds **W** 5–8
   snakes **S** 212
   teeth **M** 65–66
Carnivorous (car-NIV-or-ous) **plants** **P** 317–18;
   pictures **P** 316

Carnot (car-NO), **Sadi** (Nicolas Léonard Sadi Carnot) (1796–1832), French physicist, b. Paris. The most important of his ideas led to science of thermodynamics (study of relation of heat to energy of motion—for example, a steam engine or any engine can work only if heat is passed from a warmer to a colder body).

Caro, Anthony, English sculptor **E** 242
Carob (CARR-ob) **tree C** 557
Carol I, king of Rumania **R** 358
Carol II, king of Rumania **R** 358–59
Carolina, colony of A 193
Carolina Bay lakes N 309; **S** 298
Carolina cuckoo, bird
    bill, *picture* **B** 223
Carolina jessamine, flower
    state flower of South Carolina, *picture* **S** 296
Carolina parakeets, extinct birds **B** 232
Carolina parrot, bird
    bill, *picture* **B** 223
Carolina wren, bird
    state bird of South Carolina, *picture* **S** 296
Caroline Islands, Pacific Ocean **P** 6
    Belau, Republic of **P** 6
    Micronesia, Federated States of **P** 7
Carolingian kings of France F 415
Carols, songs **C** 122
    Christmas customs **C** 290–91
    folk carols **F** 303
    folk songs **F** 325
    hymns for special occasions **H** 313
Carom billiards B 176
Carotene, substance convertible to vitamin A **V** 370c
    leaves **T** 282
    milk **M** 309
Carothers, Wallace H., American scientist **N** 428
Carp, fish **F** 187
    baits **F** 206
    habitat, feeding habits, uses **F** 216

Carpaccio (car-PARCH-o), **Vittore** (1455?–1523?), Italian Renaissance artist, b. Venice. He is noted for historical and sacred works painted for Venetian religious orders. His paintings include a series of pictures entitled *History of St. Ursula* and *Life of St. George.*

Carpathian (car-PATHE-ian) **Mountains,** Europe **P** 359
    Czechoslovakia **C** 560
    Rumania **R** 356

Carpentaria, Gulf of, large inlet of the Arafura Sea along the northern Australian coast. It contains Sir Edward Pellew Islands, Groote Eylandt, and Wellesley Island. Explored by the Dutch seaman Abel Tasman (1644), it was probably named for Dutch official Pieter Carpentier.

Carpenter, John Alden, American composer **M** 402

Carpenter, Scott (Malcom Scott Carpenter) (1925–   ), former American astronaut, b. Boulder, Colo. Carpenter was one of seven pilots chosen for the U.S. space program called Project Mercury. On May 24, 1962, he became the second American and the fourth person to orbit the earth. He left the space program in 1967 to become a Navy aquanaut and work in oceanographic research. He retired from the Navy in 1969 and later entered private industry.

Carpenter ants A 329; *pictures* **A** 328, **I** 270, 281
Carpenter bees B 123

Carpenters' Hall, Philadelphia **P** 182
Carpentry W 230
    building construction, *pictures* **B** 436, **W** 212
Carpetbaggers, Northerners in the South after the Civil War **R** 120
Carpetbag rule *see* Reconstruction Period
Carpet beetles, insects **H** 262; *pictures* **H** 263
Carpets *see* Rugs and carpets
Carpi, Ugo da, Italian artist
    Diogenes, woodcut **G** 304
Carr, Emily, Canadian artist **B** 406d; **C** 65
Carr, Gerald P., American astronaut **S** 340k
Carr, Mary Jane, American writer **O** 206
Carranza, Venustiano, Mexican statesman **M** 250
Carré (car-RAY), **Ferdinand,** French inventor **R** 135

Carrel (car-REL), **Alexis** (1873–1944), French zoologist and surgeon, b. Sainte-Foy-lès-Lyon. He was awarded Nobel prize (1912) in physiology and medicine for method of repairing broken blood vessels and for techniques in keeping tissues alive outside the body. He was first to keep whole organs, such as heart and kidney, alive outside the body.

Carreño, Maria Terese, Venezuelan pianist **R** 123
Carriages *see* Wagons, carts, carriages, and coaches

Carrier, Willis Haviland (1876–1950), American inventor, b. Angola, N.Y. He developed first scientific air-conditioning system (1902). Air conditioning was used mainly in industry until the early 1920's, when Carrier produced a machine using a safe cooling material. Machine was introduced into theaters and railroad cars. He founded Carrier Engineering Corp., later Carrier Corp., (1915).

    called father of air conditioning **A** 102
Carriers of disease *see* Vectors
Carrier transmission, in electronic communication
    telegraph **T** 53–54
    telephone **E** 142d; **T** 59–60
Carroll, Charles, American Revolutionary War leader
    M 128

Carroll, Daniel (1730–96), American statesman, b. Upper Marlboro, Md. He was a member of Continental Congress (1780–84), a delegate to Constitutional Convention (1787), a representative from Maryland to first U.S. Congress (1789–91), and commissioner of District of Columbia (1791–95).

Carroll, Diahann, American singer and actress **M** 488c

Carroll, John (1735–1815), American Roman Catholic prelate, b. Upper Marlboro, Md. Carroll was ordained a Jesuit priest in France, but, in 1774, after the suppression of the Jesuit order in that country, he returned to the United States. In 1789, Carroll, named first bishop of Baltimore by Pope Pius VI, became the first Roman Catholic bishop in the United States. As bishop and later (1808) archbishop of Baltimore, he founded many Catholic educational institutions in Maryland.

Carroll, Lewis, pen name of Charles Lutwidge Dodgson, English mathematics professor and writer
    C 123, 239; **E** 265
    Alice's Adventures in Wonderland, book, *excerpt* **A** 164–65
    "Jabberwocky," poem **N** 272–73
    Through the Looking-Glass, book, *excerpt* **A** 165
Carrots V 290

Carrots (continued)
    roots we eat **P** 307; *picture* **P** 306
    supposed medicinal powers **F** 335
Carryl (CARR-il), **Charles E.**, American author **N** 275
Cars, motor *see* Automobiles
Cars, of railroad trains **R** 80–81

Carson, Johnny (John William Carson) (1925–   ),
American comedian, b. Corning, Iowa. Carson is host of
U.S. television's most successful talk show, "Tonight."
He is known for his rapport with his audience and for the
comic monologue with which he opens the show. As a
child, Carson put on his own magic shows. After graduat-
ing from the University of Nebraska, he worked in radio.
He moved to California in 1951 and performed on several
television shows before taking over "Tonight" in 1962.
N 95

Carson, Kit (Christopher Carson), American frontiersman
    C 123; **N** 193, 195
    Navajo moved to Fort Sumner **I** 193
Carson, Rachel, American writer **A** 214a
    quoted on the environment **E** 272h
Carson City, capital of Nevada **N** 133
Carstensz, Mount, New Guinea *see* Puncak Jaya
Cartagena (car-ta-GE-na), Colombia **C** 383
    Palace of the Inquisition, *picture* **C** 382
Cartagena, Spain **S** 351
Cartago (car-TA-go), Costa Rica **C** 515; *picture* **C** 514
Carte, Richard D'Oyly *see* D'Oyly Carte, Richard
Cartels (car-TELS), international monopolies **T** 306
Carter, Amy, daughter of President Carter **C** 124a;
    picture **C** 124b
Carter, James Earl, Jr., 39th president of United States
    C 124–124c; *pictures* **G** 273; **I** 318
    black Americans helped to elect **B** 250q
    Egyptian-Israeli peace talks **I** 445
Carter, Lillian Gordy, mother of James E. Carter **C** 124
Carter, Rosalynn Smith, wife of James E. Carter
    F 180b; **C** 124a; *picture* **C** 124b

Carteret, Sir George (1610?–80), English naval officer, b.
Jersey, Channel Islands. Appointed lieutenant governor of
Jersey (1643), he gave military assistance to Royalists and
granted asylum to Royalist exiles during the English civil
war. After surrendering to the Commonwealth (1651), he
received a commission in the French Navy. After the Res-
toration he served as treasurer of the navy (1661–67) but
was banished from House of Commons for mismanaging
funds (1669). A Carolina proprietor, he and Berkeley
received land, named New Jersey in his honor.

Carteret, Philip (1639–82), English colonial governor, b.
Jersey, Channel Islands. The first governor of New Jersey,
he was appointed by English Lords Proprietors of colony.
He became involved in dispute with New York over cus-
toms jurisdiction.

Cartesianism, philosophy of Descartes **D** 123; **P** 192
Carthage, ancient city on northwestern coast of Africa
    Hannibal and the Punic Wars **H** 34; **P** 533
    settlements in Spain and Tunisia **S** 351; **T** 309,
    311
Carthusians (car-THU-sians), monks **C** 284
Cartier (car-ti-AY), **Sir George Etienne,** Canadian
    statesman **Q** 13
Cartier, Jacques, French explorer **C** 124d
    discovers cure for scurvy **P** 310
    early history of Canada **C** 68
    exploration of the New World **E** 385
    Quebec **Q** 14
    Saint Lawrence River, discoverer of **S** 16

Cartier-Bresson (car-ti-AY bre-SON), **Henri** (1908–   ),
French photographer, b. Chanteloup, France. First trained
as a painter, he turned to photography in 1930. After
World War II, in which he served in the French under-
ground following his escape from the Nazis, he used his
camera increasingly to secure candid photographs of dra-
matic events. He is the author of *The Decisive Moment.*
His work has been exhibited in the Museum of Modern Art,
New York, and in the Louvre, Paris.
    photograph of Seville, Spain, in the 1930's, *picture*
    P 217

Cartilage (CAR-ti-lage), tough animal tissue **S** 140

Cartland, Barbara (1901–   ), British writer. Cart-
land's hundreds of romance novels have made her one of
the world's best-selling authors. Her stories usually have
an exotic historical setting and always hava a happy end-
ing. Cartland began writing at 17 when her father was
killed in World War I, leaving the family with little income.
Today she dictates her novels to a secretary, completing
one in about two weeks. She is interested in charitable
causes and is an advocate of good nutrition.

Cartography (car-TOG-raphy), map making **M** 88–95
    branch of geography **G** 108
    photogrammetry used in map making **O** 171–72
    surveying, use in **S** 479
Cartoon, drawing guide **D** 301
    designs for tapestries **T** 23
Cartoons **C** 125–28
    Thurber cartoon, *picture* **A** 214b
    See also Comic books
Cartoons, animated *see* Animated cartoons
Cartoons, political **C** 125–27
    Arthur, Chester Alan, cartoons **A** 439, 440
    Cleveland, Grover, cartoon **C** 342
    Daumier, Honoré **C** 125; **D** 43
    Garfield and Crédit Mobilier scandal, cartoon **G** 55
    Harrison, Benjamin, cartoon **H** 46
    Jackson, Andrew, cartoon **J** 6
    McKinley tariff bill, cartoon **M** 188
    Nast, Thomas **C** 126
    Pulitzer prize for editorial cartooning **P** 524
    Roosevelt, Theodore, cartoon **R** 329
    Tilden-Hayes election, cartoon by Nast **H** 80
Cartridges, ammunition for guns **G** 417, 418, 419
Cartridges, tape recorders **T** 21
Cartridge television *see* Video cassettes
Carts *see* Wagons, carts, carriages, and coaches
Cartwright, Alexander J., American promoter of baseball
    B 69–70
Cartwright, Edmund, English inventor **C** 520; **I** 235

Cartwright, John Robert (1895–   ), Canadian judge, b.
Toronto. He served in the Army during World War I (1914–
19). After practicing law in Toronto, he was appointed
(1949) justice of the Canadian Supreme Court. He was
Chief Justice from 1967 to 1970.

Caruso, Enrico (1873–1921), Italian tenor, b. Naples.
His unusual vocal power and control made him a legendary
figure even during his lifetime. He sang at opera houses
throughout the world and was leading tenor with Metropol-
itan Opera Company (1903–21). Caruso sang over 40
leading roles, those in *Rigoletto, Tosca,* and *I Pagliacci*
being among the most famous.

as the Duke in *Rigoletto, picture* **O** 135
recording for the phonograph, history of **R** 123

Caruthers (car-OTHERS), **William Alexander,** American
novelist **A** 200
Carver, George Washington, American botanist and
educator **C** 128–29
peanuts, research on **P** 110
research at Tuskegee Institute, Alabama **A** 125
statue, as a boy **M** 377
Carver, John, governor of Plymouth Colony **P** 344

Carver, Jonathan (1710–80), American explorer, b. Wey-
mouth, Mass. He explored parts of Wisconsin and Minne-
sota and the shores of Lake Superior (1766–68) in an
attempt to find the Northwest Passage. He wrote *Travels
Through the Interior Parts of North America in the Years
1766, 1767, and 1768.*
his book a best seller in Europe **M** 336

Carver Research Foundation C 129
Carving, in sculpture **S** 90
Eskimo (Inuit) handicrafts **E** 288; *picture* **E** 291
Carving, meat
cuts of beef, pork, and veal, *pictures* **M** 193–94
Carving, wood *see* Wood carving
Cary, Alice and **Phoebe,** American poets **O** 73

Cary's Rebellion (1711), colonial uprising in North Caroli-
na. Quakers, angered by discriminating restrictions bar-
ring them from voting or holding office and by naming
Church of England official church, had governor Thomas
Cary removed from office. Cary then led an unsuccessful
revolt against the new governor.

Casaba (ca-SA-ba) **melons M** 216
Casablanca (ca-sa-BLON-ca), Morocco **M** 458, 461

Casablanca Conference, World War II meeting of President
Roosevelt, Prime Minister Churchill, and leaders of Free
French. Held at Casablanca, Morocco, (Jan. 14–24,
1943) to co-ordinate British and American war policy, the
conference resulted in decision to demand "unconditional
surrender" of Axis powers. It also appointed General
Eisenhower supreme commander of Allied forces.
World War II **W** 297

Casa Grande National Monument, Arizona **A** 414
Casal, Julián del, Cuban poet **C** 548

Casals (ca-SOLS), **Pablo** (1876–1973), Spanish cellist,
conductor, and composer, b. Vendrell. He lived in self-
imposed exile in France and later in Puerto Rico in protest
against Franco's regime. Considered a master of the cello,
he organized annual music festivals at Prades, France
(1950), and Puerto Rico (1957).
Casals Festivals **M** 551
Sardana melodies for folk dancing **F** 299

Casamance (ca-za-MONCE), region of Senegal **S** 120

Casanova, Giovanni (Giovanni Jacopo Casanova de Sein-
galt) (1725–98), Italian adventurer of dubious repute, b.
Venice. He excelled as gambler, violinist, preacher, dra-
matist, spy, and rogue. While in exile in Bohemia (1785–
98), he wrote his famous *Mémoires,* highly colored
account of his romantic and adventurous life. His name
has come to describe person who uses his charms to
unscrupulous ends.
duels in literature **D** 341

Casbah
Morocco, old quarter, *picture* **M** 459
Muslim section of Algiers **A** 160, 163
Cascade, small fall of water **W** 62
Cascades, mountain range, North America **U** 92
California **C** 16
Crater Lake, *picture* **L** 29
Oregon **O** 194, 196, 197
Washington **W** 13, 14, 15, 22
Cascara, drug **P** 314
Casein (case-EEN), protein in milk **M** 309–10
glue **G** 243
Case Western Reserve University, Cleveland, Ohio
C 338

Cash, Johnny (1932–   ), American singer and com-
poser, b. Kingsland, Ark. He is an internationally known
star of country and western music. His songs, such as
Folsom Prison Blues, and his rich baritone voice made him
a popular performer and recording artist. He has acted in
several films. His autobiography is entitled *Man in Black*
(1975). *picture* **C** 524b

Cash crops A 88
Cashews, nuts **N** 421
Cashmere, hair of an Asian goat **F** 107
Cash registers O 58
Casimir III, Polish king **P** 361
Casing, glass process **G** 229
Casing, pipe that lines wells **P** 177
water wells **W** 122
Casino (ca-SI-no), at Monte Carlo, Monaco **M** 406
Caslon (CAS-lon), **William,** English type designer
T 345
Casper, Wyoming **W** 335
Caspian Sea L 27; **U** 33
Cass, Lewis, American lawyer and statesman **M** 270–
71
Taylor and Cass **T** 35

Cassandra (Alexandra), in Greek mythology, a daughter of
King Priam and Queen Hecuba of Troy. She received the
gift of prophecy from Apollo, who later cursed her so that
no one would place faith in her prophecies. She foretold
the destruction of Troy at the hands of Greeks. Enslaved by
Agamemnon, she predicted his death and subsequent
revenge by his son Orestes. The name today signifies any-
one who continually predicts disaster.

Cassatt, Mary, American painter **C** 129
Mother About to Wash Her Sleepy Child, picture
C 129
Cassava (cas-SA-va) (manioc), plant from which tapioca
is made
African dish *gari* prepared from **A** 61
Brazil **B** 376
Cassegrain, N., French scientist **T** 62
Cassettes, tape recorders **T** 21
Cassia, genus of legumes
senna **P** 314; *picture* **P** 298
Cassian (CASH-ian), **John,** monk, promoted
monasticism in southern France **C** 283

Cassini (ca-SI-ni) **family,** French astronomers for four gen-
erations, each of whom became director of Paris Observa-
tory. **Jean Dominique** (1625–1712) first accurately mea-
sured distance of sun from earth. He discovered four
moons of Saturn and large gap in Saturn's ring. **Jacques**
(1677–1756) studied shape of earth. **César François**
(1714–84) made first accurate map of a region of earth

Cassini family (continued)
(most of France). **Jacques Dominique**, Count de Cassini
(1748–1845), completed father's map of France and
wrote history of family (1810).
> map making, history of   **M** 94

Cassiodorus (cas-si-o-DOR-us), **Flavius Magnus Aurelius**,
> Roman nobleman and librarian   **L** 195–96
> scriptoria, writing rooms   **B** 319

Cassiopeia (cas-si-o-PE-a), polar constellation   **C** 491
Cassiterite (cas-SIT-or-ite), mineral   **T** 195
Cassoni (ca-SO-ni), wooden chests   **D** 75
Cassowaries (CAS-uh-weries), flightless birds   **O** 236c;
> *picture* **O** 236b
> Australian wildlife   **A** 506

Castagno (cast-ON-yo), **Andrea del** (1421?–57), Floren-
tine painter, b. Castagno. Noted primarily for frescoes
characterized by spontaneity and monumentality of style,
he influenced 15th-century Florentine, Venetian, and
Paduan painters through effects of foreshortening and pre-
cise draftsmanship. His works include frescoes *Last Sup-
per* and *Famous Men and Women*.

Castanets (cas-ta-NETS), musical instruments   **P** 152–
53

Castelo-Branco, Camillo, Visconde de Correia Botelho
(1826–90), Portuguese writer, b. Lisbon. A prolific au-
thor, he wrote poetry, plays, and criticism but was most
famous for his novels. Castelo-Branco's best-known nov-
els, written in a romantic, ornate, and poetic style, include
Amor de Perdição, Amor de Salvação, and *Os Misterios de
Lisboa*.

Castes, system of social division
> ants   **A** 322–23
> Hinduism   **H** 130, 132
> poverty in India and Pakistan   **P** 424a
> segregation in India   **I** 120, 121; **S** 114
Castiglione (ca-stil-YO-nay), **Baldassare**, Italian writer
> Renaissance man   **R** 162
Castile (cas-TELE), former kingdom in Spain
> Ferdinand and Isabella   **F** 88
> Spanish language and literature   **S** 366
Castilian (cas-TIL-ian) **Spanish**, official language of
> Spain   **S** 366
> dialect of Castile   **D** 152; **S** 352
Castilla (cas-STI-ya), **Ramón**, president of Peru   **P** 166
Casting, in fishing   **F** 208–09, 211
Casting, shaping of substances
> bronze   **D** 70
> continuous casting, steel process   **I** 406
> die casting   **D** 166
> jewelry making   **J** 100
> metallurgy   **M** 230
> sculpture   **S** 91–92
Cast iron   **I** 404–05
> building material   **B** 435, 438
> wrought iron and cast iron plows   **F** 57
Castle, Vernon and **Irene**, American dancers   **D** 27
Castles   **F** 375; *pictures* **F** 99
> Alcazar, in Segovia, Spain, *picture*   **S** 359
> architecture   **A** 379–80
> built by Crusaders in Syria, *picture*   **S** 506
> Caernarvon Castle, Wales, *picture*   **W** 4
> Carcassonne, France, *picture*   **B** 394
> English architecture   **E** 234
> homes, types of   **H** 178–79

Kronborg, at Helsingor, is scene of *Hamlet*, *picture*
> **D** 113
> Luttrellstown Castle near Dublin, *picture*   **I** 388
> Luxembourg, land of haunted castles   **L** 379
> Neuschwanstein, *picture*   **G** 148
> Nijo Castle, Kyoto, Japan   **K** 311
> Olavinlinna, Finland, *picture*   **F** 135
> Osaka, Japan   **O** 231–32
Castles in the air, saying   **M** 342
Castor, multiple star   **S** 409
> spring constellations   **C** 492

Castor and **Pollux**, in Greek mythology, sons of Zeus and
Leda. The mortal Castor, a skilled horseman, was killed in
battle. Pollux, though immortal, asked to join Castor in the
heavens. His wish was granted, and they became two stars
(Alpha and Beta) in the constellation Gemini, worshiped
as patrons of travelers and athletes.

Castor beans, plants   **P** 322
> plant remedy   **P** 314; *picture* **P** 315
Castor oil   **O** 76
> extracted from herb bean   **D** 327
Castries, capital of St. Lucia   **S** 18a
Castro, Cipriano, Venezuelan president   **V** 300
Castro, Fidel, president of Cuba   **C** 130, 550, 551
Casualty insurance *see* Insurance, casualty
Caswell (CAZ-well), **Richard**, American statesman
> **N** 319
Cat *see* Cats
CAT, X–ray technique   **M** 208c, 208h; **X** 341

Catacombs, underground burial places. The most famous
and extensive are the Christian catacombs outside Rome.
These were dug as tombs during a period of Christian per-
secution from the 1st to the 4th century. They later served
as shrines for the worship of saints. They were abandoned
from the 800's to the 1500's, when they were rediscov-
ered. The Roman catacombs have yielded art objects and
information about Christian symbolism.

Catalan, language   **L** 39; **S** 352
> Andorra   **A** 254
Catalogs, for libraries   **L** 185–86
> catalog cards, *picture*   **L** 184
> indexes on cards   **I** 115
Catalogs, of galaxies   **U** 199–200
Catalpa, tree
> leaves, *diagram*   **L** 115
Catalysts (CAT-al-ists) **and catalysis** (ca-TAL-i-sis), in
> chemistry   **C** 199, 218
> body catalysts, enzymes   **B** 293–94
> enzymes in metabolism   **K** 253–54
> petroleum refining   **P** 175
> photosynthesis   **P** 222
> vitamins, building blocks for enzymes   **V** 370b
Catalytic converter, device to prevent air pollution
> **A** 111, 552; **I** 313
Catalytic (cat-al-IT-ic) **cracking**, breaking down
> hydrocarbons of petroleum   **P** 175
Catamaran, raft-like boat, *picture*   **T** 262
Catamounts, mountain lions   **C** 139
Cat and rat, circle game   **G** 16
Catapults, devices for hurling or launching, *picture*
> **C** 538
> developed by Alexander the Great   **A** 151
Cataract, large fall of water   **W** 62
Cataracts, eye conditions causing blindness   **B** 251
> contact lenses may be worn after cataract operations
> **L** 151

Catastrophe theory, branch of mathematics **M** 163, 164

Catbird, any one of several brown and gray birds found in North and South America. They feed on insects, fruits, and berries. They are all songbirds and have a catlike call, from which they derive their name. The green catbird of Australia and white-throated catbird of New Guinea belong to a different family but also have a mewing call and similar feeding habits. *picture* **B** 234

Catboat, *pictures* **S** 9
Catbrier, weed, *picture* **W** 105
Catcher, in baseball **B** 74

Catechism, a question-and-answer method of religious instruction used in Christian churches. Although most widely known as a means of teaching the young, catechisms of various kinds are also used to instruct teachers and members of the clergy. Among the first catechisms were those of Martin Luther (1520; 1529) and a Jesuit named Peter Canisius (1556). The word, from the Greek meaning "oral instruction," is sometimes used to describe the teaching of non-religious subjects.

Categories (CAT-e-go-ries) (Guggenheim), word game **W** 238
Catel (ca-TEL), **Charles Simon,** French bandmaster and composer **B** 39
Caterpillars, larvae of butterflies and moths **B** 468, 470, 472
    adaptations with camouflage **L** 219; *picture* **L** 218
    how insects develop **I** 264–65
    jumping beans contain **J** 150–51
    plant pests **P** 289
    royal walnut moth, caterpillar of, *picture* **I** 275
Caterpillar Tractor Company **B** 446
Cat family **C** 134–41
    See also Cats
Cat Fanciers' Association **C** 141

Catfish, a large group of toothed, scaleless fishes found throughout world, usually in fresh waters. Generally dark-colored, with long feelers around mouth, they may have either sharp spines or poison glands on fins. Their diet includes plants, insects, and sometimes other fish.
    aquarium scavengers **A** 343
    baits, habitat, feeding habits, uses **F** 206, 216
    white catfish, *picture* **F** 209

Cat has nine lives, A, saying **S** 475

Cathay, a name for China used by Europeans in medieval times. The word comes from Khitan, the name of a Mongolian people who founded the Liao dynasty (947–1125) in northern China. European travelers in China, including Marco Polo, called the land Khitai, or Cathay. The name "Cathay" is still used poetically.

Cathedral Gorge State Park, Nevada, *picture* **N** 132
Cathedral of the Dormition, Moscow, *picture* **U** 55
Cathedrals **C** 131–33
    architecture, history of **A** 378
    art as a record **A** 438e
    Cathedral of the Assumption, Mexico City, *picture* **L** 47
    English architecture **E** 235; *pictures* **E** 234, 235, 237
    Gothic architecture **G** 264–72
    Italian architecture **I** 463; *pictures* **I** 460, 462

    Marie-Reine-du-Monde, *picture* **C** 65
    Middle Ages, architecture of the **C** 308b; **M** 297
    Moscow, Russian church architecture, *picture* **U** 55
    Notre Dame, Paris, *picture* **A** 379
    Orvieto, Italy, *picture* **G** 267
    Saint Basil's Cathedral, Moscow, *picture* **U** 27
    Saint Isaac's Cathedral, Leningrad, *picture* **L** 140
    Salisbury, England, *picture* **U** 65
    stained-glass windows **S** 393–95
Cathedral schools (Bishops' schools) **M** 295
Cather, Willa Sibert, American novelist **N** 95
    American literature, place in **A** 207
    regional novels **N** 349
Catherine de Médicis, Italian-born queen of France
    origin of ballet **B** 23; **D** 25
Catherine of Aragon, first queen of Henry VIII of England **E** 220; **H** 109
    beginnings of the Reformation in England **C** 286
Catherine of Siena, Saint **R** 293

Catherine of Valois (1401–37), English queen, b. Paris, France. A daughter of Charles VI of France, she married Henry V of England (1420) and became the mother of Henry VI (1421). After the death of Henry V she retired from public life, marrying a Welshman, Owen Tudor. Their son, Edmund, was made Earl of Richmond (1453) by his half brother Henry VI, and was father of Henry VII.

Catherine the Great, empress of Russia **U** 49
    architecture, neoclassical **U** 53
    Hermitage Museum **H** 119
    Jewish repression **J** 110

Cathode, metallic rod or plate that acts as source of electrons (small particles with negative electric charge). In a battery the cathode (also called negative electrode) is the source of electric current. In an X-ray tube a stream of electrons given off by heated cathodes strikes a metal surface and causes it to give off X rays. In radio tubes, fluorescent light bulbs, and electron microscopes, such streams of electrons have other effects.

Cathode rays **E** 145; **X** 339–40
    how X rays are made **X** 339–40
Cathode-ray tubes, electron tubes **E** 148
    how X rays are made **X** 339–40
    word processing systems **O** 58
Catholic Association, Ireland **O** 49
Catholic Church *see* Roman Catholic Church
Catholic Library Association **L** 192
Catholic University of Chile **S** 34
Catiline, Roman politician
    Cicero's denunciation of **C** 298
Cat in the Hat, The, book by Dr. Seuss **S** 128
Catkins, of trees **T** 284
Catlin, George, American artist **U** 120–21
    A Bird's Eye View of the Mandan Village, painting, *picture* **U** 119
Cato (CAY-to), **Marcus Porcius,** Roman statesman and writer **L** 77
Catoctin (ca-TOC-tin) **Mountain Park,** Maryland **M** 125
Cats **C** 134–41
    domestic *see* Cats, domestic
    endangered species **E** 195
    leopards **L** 155
    lions **L** 307
    tigers **T** 186
    tracks, *picture* **A** 271
Cats, domestic **C** 141–44

Cats, domestic (continued)
    animal problem box test **A** 284
    dominance orders **A** 280
    fleas **H** 260
    pets **P** 179
    scratch fever **I** 286
    superstitions about **S** 475
Cats, musical **E** 177
Cats and Bats and Things with Wings, book by Conrad Aiken
    Milton Glaser illustration **I** 97
Cat's-eyes, gemstones **G** 69–70, 75
Catskill Mountains **N** 211, 212, 213
Cat's paw, knot **K** 292

Catt, Carrie Lane Chapman (1859–1947), American reformer who helped secure women's right to vote, b. Ripon, Wis. Catt was president of the National American Woman Suffrage Association from 1900 to 1904 and from 1915 to 1920. In her second term, she organized the campaign that led to the ratification in 1920 of the 19th Amendment, giving women the right to vote. She later helped found the League of Women Voters and became active in the world peace movement. A graduate of Iowa State College, she had worked as a school administrator in Iowa before beginning her work for woman suffrage in 1887. **W** 212b

Cattle **C** 145–49, 151
    Africa **A** 62; *pictures* **C** 145, 148
    African songs about **A** 78
    anthrax **I** 287
    Argentina **A** 395–96
    Australian outback **A** 498
    Bernese Alps, *pictures* **S** 497
    dairy *see* Dairy cattle
    dolphins and porpoises related to **D** 272, 273
    Hawaii's famous ranch **H** 64
    herds, *pictures* **A** 90, **M** 434
    hides, source of leather **L** 107
    hoofed mammals **H** 217, 221
    Kirghiz crossbreed **U** 46
    meat-packing **M** 192
    Paraguay, Chaco region, *picture* **P** 65
    raising and marketing cattle **M** 192
    ranch life **R** 102–05
    roundups, *picture* **A** 409
    ruminants, or cud-chewing animals **H** 209
    stomach of cud-chewing animals **H** 209
    Texas **T** 122
    whales related to cattle **W** 150
    wild cattle **H** 221
    world distribution **W** 264; *diagram* **W** 265
Cattle drives **C** 146–47
    Goodnight-Loving Trail in New Mexico **N** 188
    Wyoming **W** 328–29
Cattle wars
    Wyoming **W** 337
Catton, Bruce, American writer **A** 214a; **M** 272
Catullus (ca-TULL-us), **Gaius Valerius,** Roman poet **L** 78
CATV *see* Cable TV
Cauca (CA-uca) **River,** Colombia **C** 381
Caucasian languages **L** 40; **U** 27–28
Caucasoid (CAU-ca-soid) **race**
    Africa **A** 55
Caucasus (CAU-ca-sus), mountain range in Soviet Europe **E** 309
    folk dance **D** 30
    Transcaucasian Republics **U** 44–46

Caucus, a meeting of leaders of a group to discuss internal affairs. The term, possibly from the Algonkian Indian *caucauasu,* meaning "adviser," was used in colonial Boston to denote factional political meetings. Congressional caucuses were used to select presidential candidates (1796–1824). Today caucuses are held locally to select candidates for offices or elect convention delegates. In Congress they are called to choose candidates for Senate and House positions, to assign members to committees, and to draft party policy.
    organization in U. S. Congress **U** 144

Caudill, Rebecca (1899–   ), American author of children's books, b. Harlan County, Ky. She lived in the woods of Kentucky, from which she derived much of the material for her books, including *Happy Little Family* and *Schoolhouse in the Woods.* Her books for younger children include *Barrie and Daughter* and *Tree of Freedom.*

Caudillo, strong political leader in South American countries **L** 61; **S** 294
Cauliflower, vege*table* **V** 290
    flowers we eat **P** 307–08; *picture* **P** 309

Caulkins, Tracy (1963–   ), American swimmer, b. Nashville, Tenn. In 1982, Caulkins won her 37th United States national individual swimming championship and thus broke the record of 36 held by Johnny Weissmuller. Caulkins won her first championship in 1977. An extremely versatile swimmer, she has won titles in freestyle, backstroke, breaststroke, butterfly, and individual medley races.

Causeways, roads raised over water
    Lake Pontchartrain, Louisiana **L** 33
Cauto (CA-ut-o), major river in Cuba **C** 548
Cauvery Falls, India **W** 63
Cauvery River, India **I** 125
Cavalier of the Rose, The (*Der Rosenkavalier*), opera by Richard Strauss **O** 153
Cavalier poets, in English literature **E** 254
Cavaliers, Royalists in English Civil War **C** 536
Cavalleria Rusticana, opera by Pietro Mascagni **O** 142
    based on story by Verga **I** 480
Cave, Edward (Sylvanus Urban), English printer and publisher **M** 14
Caveat emptor ("let the buyer beware") **C** 494
Cave bears
    fire repelled **F** 140
Cave drawings **P** 14–15
    art as a record **A** 438
    communication method of Stone Age **C** 430–31
    prehistoric art **P** 439–41
Cave dwellers **C** 157–58
    art as a record **A** 438, 438b; **C** 430–31
    fire and early peoples **F** 139–40
    painting, earliest artists **P** 14–15
    prehistoric art **P** 439–41
Cave flowers **C** 155
Cavelier, Robert, French explorer *see* La Salle, Robert Cavelier, Sieur de

Cavell (CAV-ell), **Edith Louise** (1865–1915), English nurse, b. Swardeston, Norfolk. She ran a hospital in Belgium (1914–15) for wounded soldiers in World War I. She helped Allied soldiers return to battlefields and aided Belgian men in escaping from the Germans. She was captured by the Germans (1915) and tried and executed, despite intervention of Allied governments on her behalf. There is a monument to her in London.

Cavemen *see* Cave dwellers
Cavendish, Henry, British chemist C 210; E 127;
S 72; *picture* C 211

Cavendish (Candish), **Thomas** (1560?–92), English navigator and privateer, b. Suffolk. The third navigator to circle globe (1586–88), he returned home by way of Cape of Good Hope, after looting Spanish towns on western coast of South America.

Caves and caverns C 152–58
   art as a record A 438
   Ash Cave entrance, Ohio, *picture* O 71
   bats B 93; *picture* B 95
   homes of the past H 177
   ice cave, *picture* I 12
   Lascaux Cave, France, *picture* W 217
   Lewis and Clark Cavern, *picture* M 439
   painting, earliest artists P 14–15
   paintings found in France, *picture* A 354
   prehistoric art P 439–41
   spelunking S 380

Caviar, roe (eggs) of sturgeon and other large fish, such as tunney and mullet, that has been processed and salted. It is served as an hors d'oeuvre.

Cavies (CAVE-ies), rodents R 280
   See also Guinea pigs
Cavill, Richard, Australian swimmer S 490
Caving, method used to remove ore deposits M 318
Cavities (tooth decay) T 48
Cavour (ca-VOOR), **Camillo di,** Italian leader I 457
Cawley, Evonne Goolagong, *see* Goolagong, Evonne
Caxton, William, English printer P 457
   early ads A 33–34
   first printing of children's books C 236
   printed *Morte D'Arthur* A 445
Cayenne (ca-YEN), capital of French Guiana G 396

Cayley, Arthur (1821–95), English mathematician, b. Richmond, Surrey. He originated many new fields of mathematics—some important in work on theory of relativity and quantum theory.

Cayley, Sir George, English inventor A 568

Cayman Islands, island group of the West Indies made up of Grand Cayman, Little Cayman, and Cayman Brac. Discovered by Columbus (1503) and first colonized in the 18th century by the English, they were a dependency of Jamaica (until 1962) but are now administered by the British Colonial Office. The capital of the islands is Georgetown, Grand Cayman. Principal industries include tourism and turtle farming.

Caymans, reptiles C 533–35; R 181
Cayuga (cay-U-ga), Indians of North America I 184
Cayuga, Lake, New York L 28
CBC *see* Canadian Broadcasting Corporation
CBI *see* Cumulative Book Index
CB radio *see* Citizens band radio
CBS Building, New York City U 125
CCC *see* Civilian Conservation Corps
C clef, in musical notation M 526
CCMS *see* Committee on the Challenges of Modern Society

Ceauşescu (chou-SHES-ku), **Nicolae** (1918–   ), Rumanian political leader, b. Scorniceşti, in the lower Olt River region. He became head of the Rumanian Communist Party in 1965 and president of the country in 1967. Ceauşescu furthered industrial development and worked for closer relations with western countries and China, while keeping Rumania within the Soviet bloc. R 360

Cebu City (say-BU city), Philippines P 186, 188, 189
Cebus (CE-bus) **monkeys,** *picture* A 287

Cecil (CES-il), **Robert,** 1st Earl of Salisbury and 1st Viscount Cranborne ("the crooked-backed earl") (1563?–1612), English statesman, b. probably Westminster, London. The son of William Cecil, he was appointed secretary of state under Queen Elizabeth I (1596). Aiding James VI of Scotland to succeed to the English throne as James I (1603), he continued as secretary of state until appointed lord treasurer (1608).

Cecil, William, 1st Baron Burghley (1520–98), English statesman, b. Bourn. As chief secretary of state (1558–72) and lord high treasurer (1572–98) to Queen Elizabeth I, he held great power. To counteract possible plots against the throne, he formed a network of informers and he had Mary Queen of Scots executed (1587). E 178

Cecilia, Saint (2nd or 3rd century), one of most venerated martyrs of early Christian Church. She converted to Christianity her pagan husband, Valerian, and his brother Tiburtius, who were martyred before her. Patroness of music, she is usually portrayed with a musical instrument. Her feast day is November 22.

Cecropia (ce-CRO-pia) **moth**
   cocoon, *picture* I 265
   metamorphosis, *picture* M 235
Cedar Rapids, Iowa I 369
Cedar trees, conifers T 284
   of Lebanon L 122
   uses of the wood and its grain, *picture* W 223
Cedar waxwings, birds B 216; *picture* B 234
Ceiba (SAI-ba) (silk-cotton tree), yields kapok fibers K 193
Céilis, Irish musical entertainments I 385
Cela (THAY-la), **Camilo José,** Spanish author S 372
Celadon, Korean porcelains K 299
   wine pot, *picture* K 300
Celaque, Sierra de, mountains, Honduras H 196
Celebes (CEL-eb-ese) (Sulawesi), island in Indonesia I 219
Celebrated Jumping Frog of Calaveras County, The, story by Mark Twain T 336
   Jumping Frog Jubilee, Angels Camp, California C 26
Celery, vegetable V 290
   leaf stalks we eat P 307; *picture* P 306
   supposed medicinal powers F 335
Celery seed, spice S 382; *picture* S 381
Celesta (ce-LES-ta), keyboard instrument K 240; M 550
   orchestra seating plan O 186

Celeste, Richard F. (1937–   ), governor of Ohio, Democrat, b. Lakewood. After serving two terms in the Ohio legislature, Celeste was elected lieutenant governor in 1974. He made an unsuccessful bid for the office of governor in 1978. The following year he was appointed director of the Peace Corps by President Carter. He was elected governor in 1982.

Celestial navigation, of airplanes **A** 562
Celestial poles, of the celestial sphere **S** 109
Celestial sphere **S** 109
Celestine II, antipope **R** 297
Celestine I, Saint, pope **R** 296
Celestine II, pope **R** 297
Celestine III, pope **R** 297
Celestine IV, pope **R** 297
Celestine V, Saint, pope **R** 297
Cell, voltaic see Voltaic cell
Cella, inner chamber of Greek temple **A** 374
Cellini (chell-E-ni), **Benvenuto,** Italian sculptor **I** 472
   autobiography **I** 478
   decorative saltcellar **D** 74
   Perseus, statue **I** 469
Cello, musical instrument, *picture* **M** 545
   orchestra seating plan **O** 186
Cellophane, transparent material **P** 331
Cells, basic units of life **C** 159–64; **L** 211
   aging **A** 84
   animal and plant cells, compared, *diagram* **K** 250
   blood corpuscles **B** 256–57
   body chemistry, composition of cells **B** 289–97
   cancer and cancer research **C** 89–95
   cell-killing viruses **V** 367, 368
   cell membrane in body chemistry **B** 269, 293
   cell theory, in biology **B** 193; **S** 73
   cork cells **C** 505
   egg cell division to become an embryo **E** 90
   functions in the human body **B** 267
   fungi **F** 496
   gene splicing of bacteria **G** 89, 90
   genetics **G** 77–78, 80–81, 82–83
   microscope, how to look at body cells through a **M** 285
   nerve cells of the brain **B** 363–65
   nutrition **N** 415
   one-celled organisms **M** 277
   osmosis **O** 234–35
   reproduction **R** 176
   steps in division, *diagram* **B** 267
   unit structure of living things, *picture* **K** 250
   See also Eggs; Embryos
Cells, electric see Electric batteries
Celluloid, plastic material **P** 324
   early example of applied research **R** 183
   substitute for ivory **I** 488
Cellulose
   cellophane **P** 331
   crystalline material **C** 541
   fibers **N** 424, 427
   paper making **P** 51
Cellulose nitrate (guncotton explosive) **E** 392, 393–94
Celsius, Anders, Swedish scientist **H** 89; **M** 236a
Celsius scale, temperature scale **M** 236a; **T** 165; **W** 116
   conversion to Fahrenheit **H** 89
   heat **H** 89
Celsus, Roman writer **M** 204
Celtic art and architecture **C** 165, 166
   Ardagh chalice, *picture* **C** 165
   carving of horse, *picture* **C** 166
   crosses **E** 233–34
   Stonehenge **E** 233
Celtic languages **C** 165
Celtic literature **C** 165
Celts (SELTS or KELTS), people **C** 165–66
   Arthur, King **A** 445
   France **F** 403
   handball, origin of **H** 22

   Ireland **I** 384, 390
   mistletoe ceremony **C** 291
   Spain **S** 351
   Wales **W** 3, 4
Cement **C** 167–68
   adhesives **G** 242
   masonry **B** 391–93
Cement truck **T** 296
Cementum, bonelike material of teeth **T** 48
Cemeteries
   national cemeteries of the United States **N** 28–30
     See also Funeral and burial customs
Cenerentola (chay-nay-RAIN-to-la), **La,** opera by Gioacchino Rossini **O** 142
Cenozoic era, in geology **E** 25; **F** 383, 389; **P** 438

Censorship, a restriction of the freedoms of speech and the press. Governments impose censorship to keep certain information from becoming known. They may prevent the information from being broadcast on radio or television or from appearing in films or in books, newspapers, and other publications. They may seize films and publications in which it appears, and sometimes they inspect private mail. Dictatorships practice censorship to keep opposing views from being heard. Democracies sometimes censor obscenities or information that would harm national security.
   civil liberties, violations of **C** 315, 316
   motion picture industry **M** 488a–488b, 488c
   television production **T** 70b, 70c, 70d–71

Census, official count of people and property **C** 169
   automation used for data **A** 532
   Domesday Book **W** 173
   Hollerith cards and machines used in the census of 1980 **C** 450
   How is the U.S. population census taken? **C** 169
Census, Bureau of the see United States Bureau of the Census

Centaurs (SEN-tors), creatures in Greek mythology that were half human and half horse. They are said to have lived in areas of northern Greece, especially on Mt. Pelion in Thessaly. Most were drunken and wild. But Chiron, a centaur who taught Achilles, Heracles (Hercules), and Jason, was unusually good and wise.

Centenary International Philatelic Exhibition, 1947 **F** 12
Centennial State, nickname for Colorado **C** 401
Center for UFO Studies, Northfield, Illinois **F** 287
Centigrade scale see Celsius scale
Centigram, unit of weight **M** 236a
Centimeter, measure of length **W** 111–12
Centipedes, many-legged animals **C** 170–71
   compared to insects, *picture* **I** 263
Central African Republic **C** 172–73
   flag **F** 235
Central America **C** 174–77
   agriculture **N** 298
   Caribbean Sea and islands **C** 116–19
   flags **F** 242
   Indian art **I** 152–57
   industries and products **N** 301–02
   Inter-American Highway **P** 50
   life in Latin America **L** 47–61
   Monroe Doctrine and Roosevelt Corollary **M** 425, 426–27; **R** 329
   Organization of American States **O** 210
   Panama Canal and Zone **P** 46–49
   See also names of individual countries.

Central American Common Market (CACM), economic group originally made up of Costa Rica, El Salvador, Guatemala, Honduras, and Nicaragua. Established (1960) through a series of treaties beginning in 1951, its purposes are to remove tariffs and customs duties on products of member nations and to establish a common tariff on goods of non-member nations. The Common Market promotes development of industries that, to function efficiently, require markets larger than any one Central American country can offer. **C** 177

Central Arizona Project **A** 407
Central Asia *see* Inner Asia
Central Bank for Co-operatives **B** 47
Central heating **H** 98–99

Central Intelligence Agency (CIA), U.S. Government agency established (1947) under National Security Act in order to co-ordinate intelligence activities of several government agencies and departments. The agency advises and makes recommendations to National Security Council. Its headquarters are in Washington, D.C. **S** 390

Central Lowland, North America **U** 90
Central nervous system **C** 282–83; *diagram* **B** 281
Central Park, New York City **N** 234; **P** 77; *pictures* **M** 479, **N** 234, **P** 76
Central Park Carrousel, collage-sculpture by Joseph Cornell **U** 116

Central Powers, nations that fought against Allied Powers during World War I. These countries were Austria-Hungary, Bulgaria, Germany, and Turkey.
World War I **W** 274, 275, 276

Central processing unit, of computers **C** 453–54
Central University, Caracas, Venezuela **V** 295
Central Valley Project, irrigation system, California **C** 19
Centrifugal (cen-TRIF-u-gal) **casting**, of metals **M** 231
Centrifugal force
earth's spin acts against gravity **G** 323
Centrifugal pumps **P** 530
Centrifuge, *picture* **V** 367
uranium 235 separated from uranium 238 **U** 231
Centrioles (CENT-ri-oles), of cell **C** 163; *picture* **C** 164
Century plant, Mexican agave **I** 194
Cephalopods (CEPH-al-o-pods), mollusks **O** 276–77
Cephalothorax (ceph-a-luh-THO-rax), head-chest section of crustacea and arachnids **S** 169, 170, 383
Cepheid (CE-phe-id) **variables**, stars **A** 475, 476d; **S** 408
Ceramics **C** 178–80
folk art **F** 295–96
Islamic art **I** 422; *picture* **I** 418
pottery, ceramic vessels **P** 413–19
Ceratopsia (cer-a-TOP-sia), dinosaurs **D** 180
Ceratosaurs (cer-AT-o-saurs), dinosaurs **D** 174
Cerberus (CER-ber-us), watchdog in Greek mythology **G** 357, 363–64
Cerci (CER-ci), feelers of some insects **I** 263
Cereal grasses **G** 317
Cereals, grain **G** 280–87
cereal grasses **G** 317
corn **C** 506–07
food production of high yielding cereals and population growth **F** 343
living standards judged by cereal consumption **F** 332
nutrition, need in **N** 417

oats **O** 4
rye **R** 364
wheat **W** 154–56
See also Grain and grain products
Cereals, prepared **G** 285
Cerebellum (cer-eb-ELL-um), part of the brain **B** 366
function in body control **B** 282
Cerebral (ce-RE-bral) **cortex**, of the brain **B** 366, 367–68
Cerebral palsy (CER-eb-ral POL-sy), disorder of the nervous system **D** 193; **H** 27
occupational therapy **O** 18
Cerebrum (cer-E-brum), part of the brain **B** 366; *picture* **B** 364
function in body control **B** 282
Ceres (CE-rese), asteroid **A** 473
solar system **S** 243
Ceres, Roman goddess **G** 359–60
origin of word "cereal" **F** 332; **G** 281
Cereus (CE-re-us), night-blooming cactus **C** 4
Cerium, element **E** 154, 160
Cermets, materials that combine the qualities of ceramics with the tensile strength of metals **C** 180
Cernan, Eugene, American astronaut **S** 340j, 340k
Cerro, geographic term *see* mountains by name, as Punta, Cerro de
Certificates of deposit, in banking **B** 45
Certification, of teachers **T** 42
Certified Public Accountant (C.P.A.) **B** 314
Certosino (chair-to-SI-no), ivory inlay **D** 75
Cervantes Saavedra, Miguel de, Spanish writer **C** 180; **N** 345
Don Quixote, excerpt **D** 285–86
Don Quixote, quotation from **Q** 20
duels in literature **D** 341
golden age of Spanish literature **S** 368–69
monument in Madrid, *pictures* **M** 12, **S** 354
satire **H** 280
Cervera y Topete (thair-VAIR-a e to-PAY-tay), **Pascual**, Spanish admiral **S** 375
Césaire, Aimé, West Indian poet **A** 76c–76d
Cesium (CE-zi-um), element **E** 154, 160
ion-drive for spaceships **I** 351
Cespedes, Carlos Manuel de, Cuban revolutionary **C** 550
Cesta, basket to catch the ball in the sport jai alai **J** 11
Cestus, leather covering for Greek and Roman boxers' hands **B** 353
CETA *see* Comprehensive Employment and Training Act of 1973
Cetaceans (cet-A-tians), marine mammals
dolphins and porpoises **D** 270, 272–73
mammals, orders of **M** 62, 64, 68
whales **W** 147–51
Cetology (ce-TOL-ogy), study of whales **D** 272
Ceuta (ce-U-ta), Spanish enclave in Morocco **S** 356
Ceylon *see* Sri Lanka
Cézanne (sai-ZANNE), **Paul**, French painter **C** 181
French art **F** 431
Kitchen Table, painting **P** 28
modern art **M** 388
Mount Sainte-Victoire with Tall Pine, painting, *picture* **C** 181
Picasso and Cézanne **P** 243
Pines and Rocks, painting **F** 429
Rocky Landscape, painting **M** 389
style of his still-life painting **P** 29
Chacabuco (cha-ca-BU-co), **Battle of**, 1817 **S** 33

Chaco (CHA-co), region of South America **S** 277, 280
Argentina **A** 388, 391–92, 393
Paraguay **P** 62, 64, 66
Chaconne, musical form **M** 535
Chad C 182–83
children, *picture* **A** 54
flag **F** 235
Chad, Lake, north central Africa **L** 27
Africa, lakes of **A** 50
Chad **C** 182, 183
Chadds Ford, Pennsylvania **P** 140–41
Chadwick, Edwin, English reformer **M** 208

Chadwick, Florence (1918–), American long-distance
swimmer, b. San Diego, Calif. She set the women's record
when she swam the English Channel from France to
England in 13 hours, 20 minutes (1950). The first woman
to swim the Channel from England to France (1951), she
also swam the Dardanelles, the Bosporus, and the Strait of
Gibraltar.

Chadwick, French Ensor, American naval officer
W 139

Chadwick, Sir James (1891–1974), English physicist, b.
Manchester. He was awarded Nobel prize in physics
(1935) for discovery of the neutron, one of two types of
particles in nucleus of atom.

Chaff, of grain **F** 60
Chagall (sha-GOL), **Marc,** Russian painter **C** 184
I and the Village, painting, *picture* **C** 184
Over Vitebsk, painting **U** 57
stained-glass windows for synagogue, *picture*
S 394
Chagga (CHA-ga), a people of Africa **T** 16
Chagos Archipelago *see* British Indian Ocean Territory
Chagres River (CHA-grace), Panama Canal Zone **P** 47
Chaillot, Palais de, Paris **P** 70
Chain, Ernst, English scientist **A** 312; *picture* **A** 315
Chain dance D 28
Chained books, in early libraries **L** 196; *picture* **L** 195
Chain lightning T 172
Chain mail, armor **A** 433
Chain newspapers N 200
Chain reactions, of atoms **N** 360–63
What is "atom smashing"? **A** 489
Chain stores S 468
retail stores **R** 188
Chairs
colonial, *pictures* **C** 389
Mies van der Rohe's Barcelona chair, *picture* **D** 76
mountain "settin' chair" **T** 74
plastic, *picture* **F** 502
Robert Adam chair, *picture* **D** 67
upholstery **U** 227
Chaitanya, Indian poet **O** 220e
Chakri dynasty, Thailand **B** 43; **T** 151
Chalcedony (cal-CED-ony), quartz **Q** 7
gemstones **G** 75
Chalcocite, (copper glance), copper ore **C** 502
Chalcopyrite (cal-co-PY-rite), mineral **G** 249
copper, ore of **C** 502
Chaldean (cal-DE-an) (Neo-Babylonian) **Empire,** of
Mesopotamia **A** 241
ancient art **A** 241–42; *picture* **A** 243
Chalets (sha-LAYS), houses **H** 169
Gsteig, Switzerland, *picture* **E** 314

Chaliapin (or shul-YAH-pin), **Feodor Ivanovich** (1873–
1938), Russian operatic bass, b. Kazan. Known for his
character acting as well as his great voice, he toured Rus-
sia and United States (1898–1915). He was a leading
singer at New York's Metropolitan Opera (1921–35), be-
coming famous for title roles in *Boris Godunov, Ivan the
Terrible, Mefistofele,* and *Don Quichotte.*
as Boris Godunov, *picture* **O** 137

Chalice, cup used at a Communion service, *picture*
G 227
Byzantine, *picture* **D** 72
Chalk, form of limestone **R** 267
drawing materials **D** 301, 303
white cliffs of Dover, England **E** 213
Challenger, space shuttle orbiter **S** 340k, 345

Challenger expedition, scientific expedition on H.M.S.
Challenger (1872–76) sponsored by British Royal Society
under direction of Scottish naturalist Charles Thomson.
Members traveled around the world investigating aspects
of the seas, including temperature and composition of
water, currents, depth, and marine life. Findings were
published in 50-volume *Challenger Report.*

Châlons (shol-ON), **Battle of,** 451 **B** 100
Chama foxes C 250
Chambered (pearly) **nautilus,** mollusk **O** 277; **S** 149
Chambered Nautilus, The, poem by Oliver Wendel
Holmes **H** 159

Chamberlain, Joseph (1836–1914), English statesman,
b. London. He was father of statesmen Neville and Sir
Austen Chamberlain. As mayor of Birmingham (1873–
76), he advocated slum-clearance plans and educational
reforms. As colonial secretary (1895), he worked for closer
union of Britain with its self-governing colonies. He gained
passage of Workmen's Compensation Act (1897) and
Commonwealth of Australia Bill (1900) and was first
chancellor of Birmingham University (1901).

Chamberlain, Joshua Lawrence (1828–1914), American
soldier and educator, b. Brewer, Maine. He served in 20th
Maine Infantry (1862–66) in Civil War. He was awarded
Medal of Honor at Gettysburg and made brigadier general
on the field for gallantry by General Grant (1864). Cham-
berlain was governor of Maine (1866–70) and president of
Bowdoin College, Maine (1871–83), and he wrote *Maine:
Her Place in History.*

Chamberlain, Neville (Arthur Neville Chamberlain)
(1869–1940), British statesman, b. Birmingham. As
prime minister (1937–40), he negotiated treaty recogniz-
ing Italy's Ethiopian conquest (1938) and signed Munich
Pact with Italy, France, and Germany (1938), giving Hitler
part of Czechoslovakia to "keep peace in our time." He
declared war on Germany when Hitler invaded Poland
(1939) but resigned post as prime minister largely be-
cause of criticism of his war policies.
Churchill opposes appeasement policies in events
leading to World War II **C** 297–98; **W** 286
England, history of **E** 231

Chamberlain, Owen (1920–), American nuclear physi-
cist, b. San Francisco, Calif. He worked on development of
atomic bomb (1942–46). With physicist Emilio Segrè he
discovered the antiproton. They shared the Nobel prize in
physics (1959) for this discovery.

Chamberlain, Wilt (Wilton Norman Chamberlain) (1936–
), American basketball player, b. East Philadelphia, Pa.

Chamberlain—nicknamed Wilt the Stilt because of his 216-centimeter (7-foot 1-inch) height—became the leading scorer and rebounder in the history of the National Basketball Association (NBA). A center, he played for the University of Kansas (1955–58) and joined the Philadelphia (now Golden State) Warriors in 1959. He was named NBA Rookie of the Year and Most Valuable Player (MVP) in 1960. Later, he played for the Philadelphia 76ers and the Los Angeles Lakers and was named MVP for three consecutive years (1966–68). He retired from the game in 1973 and was elected to the Basketball Hall of Fame in 1979.

dunking the ball, *picture* **B** 90a

Chamberlain's Men, an acting company **S** 131

Chamberland (cham-ber-LAN), **Charles Edouard** (1851–1908), French bacteriologist, b. Chilly-le-Vignoble, France. He is best known for his filter of unglazed porcelain, which permits liquids but not bacteria to pass through. With Pasteur and Roux he made studies of the cause of rabies and was first to use preparations of weakened bacteria in the treatment of disease.

Chamberlin, Thomas Chrowder (1843–1928), American geologist, b. Mattoon, Ill. He was professor of geology and director of Walker Museum at University of Chicago (1892–1928). His significant contributions to science include research on glacial phenomena and investigations of climates during geological periods. He formulated "planetesimal," or spiral-nebula, hypothesis, which advanced theory that our solar system resulted from near collision of sun with passing star, drawing off masses of gas, which then orbited sun. Chamberlin's writings include *The Origin of the Earth* and *The Two Solar Families.*

planetesimal theory **S** 246–47

Chamber music **C** 184–86
basic record library **R** 125
chamber orchestras **O** 182
English music for viols **E** 270
festivals **M** 551, 552
musical forms, definitions of **M** 535–38

Chamber of commerce, association of business people—on community, state, or national level—whose purpose is to promote commercial and industrial interests.

Chamber orchestra **O** 182
chamber music **C** 184–86
Chameleons (ca-ME-le-ons), lizards **L** 318–19

Chamizal (cha-mi-SAL), **El,** a tract of land involved for over a century in a Mexican-U.S. border dispute. It was named *El Chamizal* after the Spanish word for the thickets that cover the land. The dispute came about because of an 1848 treaty that fixed the Rio Grande River as the boundary between the U.S. and Mexico. However, the river changed its course, transferring hundreds of acres of land to the U. S. side. In 1963 the U.S. Government agreed to hand El Chamizal back to Mexico. The ceremonies marking the formal transfer of the land were held in 1967.

Chamizal National Memorial, Texas **T** 133

Chamois (SHAM-ee), brownish, mountain-dwelling animal with short, hollow horns that are hooked at the end and are carried by both sexes. Found in Europe and Asia, it feeds on herbs, flowers, and pine shoots. It is related to sheep and goats. *picture* **H** 220

Champagne (sham-PANE) **W** 189
Why are ships christened with champagne? **S** 160
Champions, in sports
characteristics of **B** 15
Champlain (sham-PLAIN), **Lake,** United States **L** 27
Champlain, Samuel de, French explorer **C** 186a
Canada **C** 68–69, 79
exploration of the New World **E** 386
Great Lakes **G** 327–28
Nova Scotia **N** 344g
Quebec **Q** 14
Saint Lawrence River, settlements near **S** 16
Champlain Valley, Vermont **V** 308
Champlevé (shon-lev-AY), enameling technique **E** 188; *picture* **E** 189
decorative arts **D** 72

Champollion (shon-pall-YON), **Jean François** (1790–1832), French archeologist, b. Figeac. One of founders of science of Egyptology, he used Rosetta Stone to find solution to translation of Egyptian hieroglyphics. He is most famous for book about his discoveries, *Précis du Système Hiéroglyphique des Anciens Egyptiens.*

Champs-Elysées (shons-ay-le-ZAY), **Avenue des,** Paris, *picture* **P** 71
Chance, science of *see* Probability

Chancellor, Richard (?–1556), English navigator. He reached Moscow (1553) while on expedition to find northeast passage to India, and obtained trade concessions from Russian emperor Ivan IV, leading to formation of Muscovy Company (1554). He was shipwrecked and lost returning from second voyage to Russia (1555–56).

Chancellorsville, Battle of, 1863, Civil War **C** 325
Jackson, Stonewall **J** 8
Chan-Chan, city of ancient Peru **P** 165
Chandidas, Indian poet **O** 220e
Chandigarh, India
planned by Le Corbusier **A** 386a
Chandni Chowk (Street of Silver), Delhi, India **D** 101–02
Chandragupta Maurya (chan-dra-GUP-ta MA-ur-ya), king of Magadha (modern Bihar), India **I** 131

Chandrasekhar (chun-dra-SHAY-khar), **Subrahmanyan** (1910–), American astronomer, b. Lahore, India (now Pakistan). He developed many equations and theories regarding, among other things, the densities of stars and the relation of their color to their temperature.

Chanel (shan-ELL), **Coco** (Gabrielle Chanel) (1883–1971), fashion designer and creator of Chanel No. 5 perfume, b. Auvergne, France. In 1919 she introduced the "Chanel look" in fashion. This youthful style emphasized comfort and was characterized by shorter skirts, straight-lined cardigans, and long pearl necklaces worn with jersey suits. The style remains popular.
Chanel suit, *picture* **F** 69

Chaney, Lon, American actor **M** 473
Chang, John, Korean statesman **K** 304
Changan, China *see* Sian
Ch'angan Boulevard, Peking, People's Republic of China, *picture* **P** 119

Change, adaptations to **L** 216–17
Changpai, volcano, Korea and Manchuria *see* Paektu-san
Channel Islands, Great Britain **I** 429; **U** 79
Channel Islands National Park, California **C** 24
Channels, television **T** 66–67
Chansons (shon-SON), French songs **F** 444; **M** 538
Chantilly (shan-TILLY) **lace** **L** 19
Chants, in church music
   choral music **C** 276
Chanukah *see* Hanukkah
Chanute, Octave, American engineer **G** 239–40

Chao Phraya (CHOW pra-YA) **River** (Menam), Thailand's main river. It drains the northern and central regions of the country, flowing approximately 260 kilometers (160 miles) before it empties into the Gulf of Siam. The river irrigates one of Asia's most important rice-producing areas.

Chaos (CAY-os), in Greek mythology **G** 356
Chapala, Lake, Mexico **N** 289

Chaparral (shap-a-RAL), the name for thick vegetation made up of bushes, shrub plants, and small trees. It is found in the southwestern United States and in Mexico. Chaparral plants include shrub oak, sage, and mesquite. Chaparral grows in areas with little rainfall and often contributes to the rapid spread of fires.

Chaparral birds (roadrunners)
   state bird of New Mexico, *picture* **N** 181
Chapbooks, early paperbacks **P** 58
   ballads **B** 22
   children's literature **C** 238
Chaplin, Charlie, English actor **C** 186b–187; **M** 473
   as the Little Tramp, *picture* **M** 473

Chapman, George (1559?–1634), English poet and dramatist, b. near Hitchin, Hertfordshire. He is famous for his translations of Homer's *Iliad* and *Odyssey*. The latter inspired John Keats's famous sonnet *On First Looking into Chapman's Homer.* Chapman also wrote poem "The Shadow of Night" and plays, including *The Blind Beggar of Alexandria* and *All Fools.*

Chapman, John *see* Appleseed, Johnny
Chapultepec (cha-POOL-tep-ec), **Battle of,** 1847 **M** 239
Chapultepec Park, Mexico City **M** 252–53
Character bottles **A** 319
Characters, literary
   heroes of fiction **F** 109–12
   in novels **N** 345
   short stories **S** 166
Characters of Chinese words *see* Chinese writing
Character witnesses, in law cases **J** 159
Charades (sha-RADES) **C** 187–88
Charbonneau, Toussaint, interpreter for Lewis and Clark expedition **I** 66
Charcoal **C** 106
   deodorizing property **D** 117
   drawing material **D** 301
   fuel **F** 487
   outdoor cooking uses **O** 247

Charcot (shar-CO), **Jean Baptiste Etienne Auguste** (1867–1936), French physician and explorer, b. Neuilly-sur-Seine. He headed the Clinic of the Faculty of Medicine at the University of Paris (1896–98) and led Antarctic expeditions (1903–05, 1908–10), on which he mapped the western side of the Antarctic Peninsula and discovered the island named for him.

Charcot, Jean Martin (1825–93), French physician, b. Paris. He organized the study of nervous diseases and was first to describe many nervous ailments. His studies of hypnosis influenced Freud's theories on treating the mentally ill.
   Freud and Charcot **F** 469

Chardin (shar-DAN), **Jean Baptiste Simeon,** French painter **F** 425; **P** 24
   Bowl of Plums, painting **F** 424
Chardonnet (shar-duh-NAY), **Hilaire, Count de,** French inventor **N** 427
   textiles **T** 142
Chares (CARE-ese) **of Lindos,** Greek craftsman **W** 216
Charge accounts **I** 289
   department stores allow **D** 119
   interest **I** 297
Charges, electric *see* Electric charges
Charging, of storage cells in batteries **B** 99
Chariot, sculpture by Alberto Giacometti **M** 395
Charioteer, statue **G** 345
Chariot races
   women drivers, *picture* **O** 104
Chariots, ancient wheeled vehicles **W** 157, 158
Chari River, central Africa **C** 173, 182
Charities
   foundations **F** 390
   income tax deduction **I** 110
Charlemagne (SHAR-l'mane) (Charles I or Charles the Great), ruler of the Franks **C** 188–89
   architecture **A** 377; **M** 296
   art as a record **A** 438e
   Austria's founder **A** 518
   Christianity, history of **C** 284
   education furthered by **E** 66
   founded Germany's First Reich **G** 158–59
   France, history of **F** 415
   Holy Roman Empire **H** 160
   jury system **J** 159
   legends based on actual deeds **L** 129–30
   Middle Ages (Dark Ages) not so dark **M** 290
   religious reform by force **R** 291
   signature reproduced **A** 527

Charles I (1226–85), count of Anjou and Provence. He was the son of Louis VIII of France. After defeating Manfred (1266), king of Naples and Conradin (1268), contender for the throne of Naples, he reigned as king of Two Sicilies (1266–85). He influenced the election of French pope Martin IV (1281).

Charles, Ezzard, American boxer **B** 353
Charles II, Holy Roman Emperor (Charles I, king of France, called Charles the Bald) **F** 99
Charles V, Holy Roman Emperor (Charles I, king of Spain) **H** 163
   keeps Reformation from Italy **I** 456
Charles VI, Holy Roman Emperor **A** 524–25
Charles, Jacques, French balloonist **B** 31; **G** 57
   aviation history **A** 568
Charles I, king of England **C** 536
   clashes with the Puritans **E** 222–23
Charles II, king of England **E** 224
   beginning of Whigs and Tories (political parties) in Great Britain **P** 378

Charles VII (Charles the Victorious) (1403–61), king of France (1422–61), b. Paris. When he succeeded his father, Charles VI, to throne, northern and part of southwestern France was under English rule. Aided by Joan of Arc, he captured Orleans (1429) and was crowned at Reims (1429). He concluded a treaty with the Duke of Burgundy (1435) and entered Paris (1436). During his reign he effected a tax reform, formed the first standing army of France, and declared the Pragmatic Sanction of Bourges (1438) to restrict papal power over the church in France.

Joan of Arc and Charles VII **J** 120a

Charles X (before accession, Charles Philippe, comte d'Artois) (1757–1836), king of France (1824–30), b. Versailles. After the outbreak of the French revolution, he joined royalist exodus to England (1789). At the restoration (1815) he returned to France and led the ultraroyalist faction. He succeeded his brother Louis XVIII (1824) and tried to establish an absolute monarchy. Faced with mounting opposition, he dismissed Chamber of Deputies (1830) and issued "July ordinances" curbing freedom of press and declaring new election methods. He was forced by the July Revolution (1830) to abdicate. **F** 417

Charles II (1661–1700), king of Spain (1665–1700). He succeeded his father, Phillip IV, to throne under regency (until 1675) of queen mother Mariana de Austria. His reign was marked by weakness and corruption. He joined a coalition that declared war against French king Louis XIV, resulting in Peace of Ryswick (1697). Charles had no children and was forced to choose Philip of Anjou, grandson of Louis XIV, as successor. His death sparked War of the Spanish Succession.

Charles IV (1748–1819), king of Spain (1788–1808), b. Naples, Italy. He succeeded his father, Charles III, to the throne (1788). He yielded Louisiana to France (1800) and joined Napoleonic France in war against England, resulting in destruction of Spanish fleet by England at Trafalgar (1805). A weak monarch, he was dominated by his wife, Maria Louisa, and his incompetent prime minister, Manuel Godoy. Following French invasion of Spain, he abdicated (1808) in favor of his son Ferdinand, who was supplanted by Joseph Bonaparte.

Charles XII, king of Sweden **S** 486

Charles, Mary Eugenia (1919–   ), prime minister of Dominica, b. Pointe Michel. In 1980 she became the first woman prime minister in the Caribbean. Charles, a lawyer, helped found the Dominica Freedom Party in 1968 and was appointed to parliament in 1970. She served as leader of the opposition (1975–80) before becoming prime minister and minister of foreign affairs, finance, and development. She was president of the Organization of Eastern Caribbean States (OECS) when that organization obtained U.S. help in invading Grenada in 1983 to restore democratic rule there. **D** 279

Charles III, prince of Monaco **M** 406

Charles, Prince of Wales (Charles Philip Arthur George) (1948–   ), son of Queen Elizabeth II and heir to the British throne, b. Buckingham Palace. He was educated at schools in England, Scotland, and Australia and entered Cambridge University in 1967. He became heir to the throne in 1952 and prince of Wales in 1958. He was invested as prince of Wales (1969) in colorful ceremonies at Caernarvon Castle, Wales. In 1981, Charles married Lady Diana Spencer, who became Princess of Wales. A son, Prince William, was born to them in 1982. **E** 232

Elizabeth II **E** 179

Charles, Ray (Ray Charles Robinson) (1932–   ), American singer, composer, and pianist, b. Albany, Ga. He has been highly successful in several fields of music, including jazz, rhythm and blues, and country and western. Charles lost his sight as a small boy and learned to play the piano at a school for the blind. Among his best-selling recordings are *I Got a Woman* and *Georgia on My Mind*. He has received many Grammy Awards from the National Academy of Recording Arts and Sciences.

Charles XIV John, king of Sweden and Norway **S** 487
Charles' law, on gases **G** 57

Charles Martel (Charles the Hammer) (689?–741), grandfather of Charlemagne. His historic defeat of the Arabs at the Battle of Tours (Poitiers) in 732 stopped the Islamic advance into western Europe. His son, Pepin the Short, became the first Carolingian king of France. **C** 188

Carolingian kings of France and the Roman Catholic Church **F** 415; **R** 291

Charles River, Massachusetts, *picture* **M** 139
Charles the Bald *see* Charles II, Holy Roman Emperor (Charles I, king of France)
Charles the Bold, Duke of Burgundy **D** 363
Switzerland, attempt to conquer **S** 502
Charles the Great *see* Charlemagne
Charles the Simple, king of France **V** 339
Charleston, capital of West Virginia **W** 137; *pictures* **W** 132, 138
Charleston, dance **D** 27
Charleston, South Carolina **S** 302, 307
colonial life **C** 397–98
Charles Town, West Virginia **W** 136–37
Charles University, Czechoslovakia **C** 562, 563

Charlevoix (sharl-ev-WA), **Pierre François Xavier de** (1682–1761), French Jesuit historian, b. St. Quentin. He taught in missions of Quebec, Canada (1705–09), and traveled (1720–22) through French colonies and down Mississippi to New Orleans in search of "Western Sea." He was author of a history of New France.

Charlie Is My Darling, folk song **F** 327
Charlotte, North Carolina **N** 318
Charlotte Amalie, capital of the Virgin Islands **U** 100
Charlottesville, Virginia **V** 357
Charlotte's Web, book by E. B. White **C** 244; *excerpt* **W** 161
Charlottetown, capital of Prince Edward Island, Canada **P** 456f, 456h; *picture* **P** 456c
Charm bracelets, jewelry **J** 99
Charnock, Job, English founder of Calcutta **C** 11
Charon (CARE-on), boatman in Greek mythology **G** 357
Charon, satellite of Pluto **P** 278
Charpentier, Jean de, Swiss scientist **I** 18
Charpentier, Marc Antoine, French composer **F** 445
Charter airlines **A** 566
Charter Oak, historic landmark in Hartford, Connecticut **C** 466
Charter of Rights and Freedoms, Canadian bill of rights **B** 180
Charters, laws of municipal government **M** 503

Chartres (SHART-ra), **Cathedral of**, France, *picture*
G 268
pipe organ, *picture* O 208
rose window, *picture* D 73
Charybdis (ca-RIB-dis), in Greek mythology O 54
Chase (frame), for printing type P 461–62

Chase, Salmon Portland (1808–73), chief justice of the United States during Reconstruction, b. Cornish, N.H. Chase was appointed chief justice in 1864 by President Abraham Lincoln after having served as secretary of the treasury (1861–64) in Lincoln's Civil War cabinet. As chief justice (1864–73), Chase was known for his fairness in dealing with problems of Reconstruction and in presiding at the impeachment trial of President Andrew Johnson in 1868. Chase long was a resident of Ohio, where he served as governor (1856–60) and as a U.S. senator. He made several unsuccessful attempts to gain the presidential nomination. N 161

Chase, Samuel (1741–1811), American Revolutionary leader and Supreme Court justice, b. Somerset County, Md. He signed Declaration of Independence but opposed ratification of Constitution. Appointed Supreme Court justice (1796) by President Washington, he was impeached (1804) for disregard of law, but he was acquitted (1805).
impeachment not a weapon for removing political enemies I 108

Chasing, art of ornamenting metal surfaces D 74
Chassis (SHAS-sy), of automobiles A 543, 549–50
Chateaubriand (sha-to-bri-ON), **François René, Vicomte de**, French novelist F 439
Château Frontenac, Quebec City Q 16; *picture* Q 17
Château-Thierry (sha-TO-ti-AER-ry), **Battle of**, 1918 W 280
Châteaus (or châteaux), large country houses F 406
Blois, France F 421; *picture* F 422
Chenonceaux, *picture* F 414
Renaissance architecture A 381
Chatham, New Brunswick, Canada N 138f
Chatham Islands, New Zealand N 237
Chatoyancy (sha-TOY-ancy), cat's-eye effect in gemstones G 69–70
Chattahoochee National Forest, Georgia G 139
Chattahoochee River, United States A 115, 120
Chattanooga, Tennessee T 86, 89; *picture* T 87
Civil War campaigns C 326
Chatterton, Thomas, English poet E 259
Chaucer, Geoffrey, English poet C 190
beginnings of English literature E 249
Middle English, the language of Chaucer E 244
Chaudière Falls, Ontario, Canada O 236f, 238
Chaulmoogra, tree P 313; *picture* P 312
Chautauqua (sha-TAU-qua) **Institution**, New York M 552
Chávez (CHA-base), **Carlos**, Mexican composer L 75

Chavez, Cesar Estrada (1927–), American labor organizer, b. Yuma, Ariz. Son of a migrant worker, Chavez has devoted himself to bettering working conditions of Mexican-American farm laborers. In 1965 his association joined others in striking California grape growers. His group became affiliated with AFL-CIO. The workers' plight gained much sympathy and support and the growers began signing labor contracts with the unions in 1970. In the 1980's, Chavez worked to form a "Chicago lobby" to represent the needs of urban Hispanics and farm workers.

Chavez (SHA-vez), **Dennis**, American senator N 193
Chavin (cha-VEEN), early civilization of Andes I 155

Chayefsky (cha-YEF-skee), **Paddy** (Sidney Chayefsky) (1923–81), American playwright, b. New York, N.Y. He was known especially for his sympathetic portrayals of ordinary people and his ability to reveal their characters in a single bit of dialogue. He wrote for stage and television but gained his greatest fame as a screenwriter. He won Academy Awards for his screenplays for *Marty*, in 1956; *The Hospital*, in 1972; and *Network*, in 1977.

Checkers, game C 191–92
How old is the game of checkers? C 191
See also Chess
Checking accounts, at banks B 44d, 45
Checkmate, chess term C 224
Checkoff, of labor union dues L 9, 16
Checks, at banks B 44d, 45, 46
Checks and balances, system of government
division of power of U.S. Government U 139
United States Congress U 142
Check truncation, banking system B 46
Check valves V 270
Cheddar cheese D 13
Cheese C 192–93
Danish blue cheese, *picture* D 110
Edam cheese, *picture* N 117
how cheese is made D 12–13
legend of its origin F 334
nutrition, food planning with dairy products N 417
outdoor snack O 248
Cheetahs, wild cats C 139; M 63; *pictures* C 138, 485
endangered species E 195

Cheever, John (1912–82), American writer, b. Quincy, Mass. Cheever drew on his observations of upper middle-class New England life for his sophisticated, satirical novels and short stories. His novels include *The Wapshot Chronicle* (1957) and *The Wapshot Scandal* (1964), *Bullet Park* (1969), and *Falconer* (1977). Many of his more than 200 short stories were collected in *The Stories of John Cheever*, which won the Pulitzer prize for literature in 1979.

Chehalis, Indians of North America I 180
Chekhov (CHEK-off), **Anton**, Russian writer S 165
poetic realism in the drama D 298
Russian literature U 61
Chelan, Lake, Washington W 15, 23
Chemical bonding, adhesive process G 242
Chemical carcinogens (car-CIN-o-gens), cancer-causing agents C 91
Chemical changes of matter M 177
Chemical coatings P 33
Chemical elements *see* Elements, chemical
Chemical energy E 199, 202; P 234–35
food a source of E 201
nuclear energy N 352–71
Chemical engineering E 206
Chemical fertilizers F 97
Chemical industry C 193–95
Delaware D 87, 93
hydrogen gas used in G 61
industrial importance I 247
New Jersey N 170–71
salt, uses in S 21
synthetic dyes D 370–72
wood products W 227
Chemical oceanography O 33–34

Chemicals, products of the chemical industry **C** 193–95
    air pollution **A** 109
    chemical control of harmful insects **I** 257
    chemical pollution of the environment endangers species **E** 196
    chemicals that cure disease **D** 216
    drug industry **D** 323
    first aid for chemical burns **F** 162
    first aid for poisoning by caustic chemicals **P** 356
    food contamination **F** 355
    food preservation and processing **F** 348
    gene splicing, products of **G** 91
    occupational diseases **O** 17
    poisons found in the home **P** 356
    toxic chemical wastes **S** 30, 31
    water pollution **W** 64, 65, 66–67, 68
Chemical symbols, of elements **E** 155, 156–57; **C** 220
    alphabetical table of elements **C** 197–98
    periodic table **C** 213

Chemical warfare, warfare in which chemicals other than explosives are used. The term applies particularly to the use of gases. Some gases irritate or burn, disabling the enemy. Others affect the nervous system, producing severe damage or death. Chemical warfare also includes the use of defoliants to clear jungle or forest areas, often by causing rapid burning on contact.

Chemical waste
    air pollution **A** 109
    sanitation problem **S** 30, 31
Chemise (shem-ESE), (sack dress) **F** 65
Chemistry **C** 196–205
    applied to agriculture **A** 100
    atoms **A** 483–89; **C** 196
    batteries **B** 97–99
    biochemistry **B** 181–84
    body chemistry **B** 289–97
    branches of **C** 205
    catalysts **C** 199
    compounds **C** 196
    crystals **C** 541–46
    dyes and dyeing **D** 366–72
    electrolysis **E** 129
    elements **E** 153–65
    equations, balanced **C** 198–99
    experiments in chemistry and physics **E** 364–67
    explosives **E** 390–96
    fermentation **F** 89–92
    fibers **F** 105, 108
    fine and heavy chemicals **C** 194–95
    fire and combustion **F** 136–37
    food chains and chemical cycles in ecosystems **E** 43–44
    formulas **C** 197–200
    history *see* Chemistry, history of
    inorganic *see* Chemistry, inorganic
    iodines and other halogens **I** 349
    ions and ionization **I** 354–55
    matter, chemical changes in **M** 177–78
    Nobel prizes **N** 268a–269
    oils and fats **O** 76–79
    organic *see* Chemistry, organic
    origin of the word **C** 207
    oxygen and oxidation **O** 270–72
    periodic table, of chemical elements **C** 202
    petrochemistry, chemistry of petroleum **P** 176–77
    physics and chemistry compared **C** 196

    reactions (changes) **C** 196–97, 199, 201
    spectrochemical analysis **L** 267–68
    symbols, chemical **C** 220; **E** 155, 156–57; Dalton's chart of atomic symbols **C** 213
    terms of **C** 216–20
    valence **C** 199–200
    See also Atoms; Biochemistry; Chemical industry; Crystals; Ions and ionization; Microchemistry; Nuclear energy; and names of elements and chief compounds
Chemistry, history of **C** 205–16; **S** 71–72
    Curie, Marie and Pierre **C** 552–53
    Faraday, Michael **F** 47
    Lavoisier's contributions **L** 86
    radioactive elements **R** 67–68
Chemistry, inorganic
    chemical industry **C** 194
    how chemistry led to biochemistry **B** 181–82
Chemistry, organic **C** 214
    chemical industry **C** 194
    contributions to biology **B** 193–94
    new branch of chemistry **S** 74
    origins of biochemistry **B** 181–82
    plastics **P** 324–31
Chemistry, physiological *see* Body chemistry
Chemotheraphy (kem-o-THER-apy), treatment of diseases with chemicals **B** 182
    cancer treatment **C** 95
    hypnosis relieves side effects **H** 317
Chengtu (cheng-DU), China **C** 263

Chennault (shen-NOLT), **Claire Lee** (1890–1958), American aviator, b. Commerce, Tex. He pioneered in use of paratroops and in parachute landing of supplies. Chennault became air adviser to Chinese commander Chiang Kai-shek (1937) and organized American Volunteer Group ("The Flying Tigers") to aid China against Japanese aggression (1941–42). He was chief of U.S. air operations in China (1942). He wrote *The Role of Defensive Pursuit.*
    See also Flying Tigers

Cheops (KE-ops), king of ancient Egypt **W** 214
    Great Pyramid of **A** 220; **E** 96
Chephren (KEPH-ren), king of ancient Egypt **E** 96
    Great Sphinx and pyramid of, *picture* **E** 93
Cherokee, Indians of North America **I** 213
    Georgia's Cherokee nation **G** 147
    Indians of the Southeastern Maize Area **I** 187–88
    North Carolina **N** 310
    removed from Alabama **A** 127
    Sequoya **S** 124
    Unto These Hills, outdoor drama **N** 315
    Why was Sam Houston called the Raven? **H** 271
Cherokee National Forest, Tennessee **T** 82
Cherokee Outlet, Oklahoma **O** 86
Cherokee rose, flower
    state flower of Georgia, *picture* **G** 133
Cherrapunji (churra-POON-ji), India
    rainfall heaviest in the world **I** 126; **R** 94
Cherry **P** 107, 108–09
Cherry blossom festivals
    Japanese celebration **J** 31
Cherrystone (hard clam), shellfish **R** 215

Cherub, one of the cherubim, a rank of angels. Cherubs are part of the Jewish, Christian, and Islamic religious traditions. Holy books often speak of them as winged creatures with both human and animal features. They possess great knowledge. During the Renaissance, Christian artists

Cherub (continued)
painted cherubs as winged children. Because of this, people with chubby faces and rosy cheeks, especially small children, are sometimes called cherubs.

Cherubini (care-u-BI-ni), **Luigi,** Italian composer **F** 445
opera **O** 134
Chesapeake and Delaware Canal, Maryland **M** 124, 131
Chesapeake and Ohio Canal, Maryland **M** 125–26
Chesapeake Bay, eastern United States **V** 347
colonial life **C** 397–98
Maryland **M** 118, 119, 122, 124
Chesapeake Bay Bridge-Tunnel B 399; **M** 119; **V** 350
famous tunnels **T** 318
Chesapeake Bay retriever, dog
state dog of Maryland **M** 116

Cheshire cat, fictional cat with a wide grin, said to have been created by Lewis Carroll in *Alice's Adventures in Wonderland.* The cat was able to vanish, leaving only its grin. Carroll's character may have been inspired by pictures of lions rampant on signs above many inns in Cheshire, England.

Chesnutt, Charles Waddell (1858–1932), American author, b. Cleveland, Ohio. He was principal of Fayetteville, N.C., state normal school and was subsequently admitted to the bar (1887). He is famous for *The Conjure Woman,* series of humorous stories related by fictional Uncle Julius. Many of his novels depict struggles of black Americans as he knew them growing up in North Carolina.

Chess, the "royal" game **C** 221–26
Union of Soviet Socialist Republics **U** 31
Chester, Pennsylvania **P** 142
Chester, song by William Billings **N** 23
Chester Dale Collection, of art **N** 41

Chesterfield, 4th Earl of (Philip Dormer Stanhope) (1694–1773), British politician and man of letters, b. London. He was ambassador to The Hague, the Netherlands (1728–32, 1744). Lord high steward until dismissed for opposing bill favored by Sir Robert Walpole (1733), he attacked government of George II in letters signed "Geffery Broadbottom" (1743). He was lord lieutenant of Ireland (1745–46) and secretary of state (1746–48). His name became a synonym for gallant manners and worldliness. Chesterfield is best known for *Letters to His Son* and *Letters to His Godson.*

Chesterton, Gilbert Keith, English author **E** 266
essays **E** 292
the "inverted" detective story **M** 555
Chestnut blight, bark disease **N** 421
Chestnuts N 421; *picture* **P** 298
Chetniks, Yugoslav faction **Y** 358
Chevrolet, automobile model, *picture* **A** 535
Chevrotains (SHEV-ro-tains) (mouse deer) **H** 212; *picture* **H** 213
Chewing gum R 185
stain removal **L** 84
Chewing insects P 284
Chewinks (CHE-winks) (towhees), birds **B** 220; *picture* **B** 236
Cheyenne (shy-ENNE), capital of Wyoming **W** 334–35
Chiang Ching, wife of Mao Tse-tung **M** 86

Chiang Ching-kuo (jahng jing GWO) (1910?–   ), president of the Chinese Nationalist Government on Taiwan, b.

Chekiang Province. The eldest son of Chiang Kai-shek, he became the political leader of Taiwan after his father's death in 1975. He was elected president in 1978. Chiang received his university education in the Soviet Union. He returned to China in 1937 and went into government service. In 1949, after the Communist takeover of China, the Chinese Nationalists moved to Taiwan. Chiang became minister of defense (1965–69), deputy prime minister (1969–72), and prime minister (1972–78) of the Nationalist Government. **C** 267; **T** 13

Chiang Kai-shek (CHANG ky-SHEK), Chinese general and president of Nationalist China **C** 227, 267, 271–72; **T** 13
Mao Tse-tung and Chiang Kai-shek **M** 86
Chiari, Roberto, president of Panama **P** 46
Chiaroscuro (ke-ar-os-CU-ro), painting technique
L 153; **R** 156
Night Watch, by Rembrandt **R** 156
Chibchas (CHEEB-chas), Indians of South America
Colombia **B** 299; **C** 378
Chicago, Illinois **C** 227–30; **I** 77, 78–79, 83, 86; *pictures* **I** 79, 82
expressway, *picture* **U** 111
hotel, *picture* **H** 258
places of interest in black history **B** 250d
writers group **A** 207
Chicago, poem by Carl Sandburg, *excerpt* **C** 227
Chicago, University of, Chicago, Ill. **C** 229
Chicago Defender, black newspaper **B** 250h
Chicago Fire, 1871 **C** 230
Chicago Portage National Historic Site, Illinois **I** 81

Chicano, an American of Mexican descent. The term probably developed as a short form of *Mexicano,* the Spanish word for Mexican. In the 1960's, young militant Mexican-Americans gave the term a new meaning that suggested racial and cultural pride.

Chichén Itzá (chi-CHAIN e-TZA), Mexico **I** 198
ruins, *picture* **I** 153

Chichester, Sir Francis (1901–72), British pilot and yachtsman, b. North Devon, England. An aviator before turning to sailing, he won first singlehanded Transatlantic Yacht Race (1960), and set record (1962) for solo east-west Atlantic crossing. In 1966–67 he solo circumnavigated the globe in his boat, *Gypsy Moth IV.* He wrote *The Lonely Sea and the Sky,* and *Gypsy Moth Circles the World.* He was knighted in 1967. In 1971 he sailed solo across the Atlantic in 22 days.

Chichewa, language **M** 48
Chichón, El, volcano, Mexico
dust resulting from 1982 eruption **D** 347
Chickadees, birds, *picture* **B** 233
Maine, state bird of, *picture* **M** 32
Massachusetts, state bird of, *picture* **M** 134
Chickamauga (chick-a-MAU-ga), Georgia **C** 326
Chickamauga and Chattanooga National Military Park
Georgia **G** 139, 141
Tennessee **T** 83
Chickasaw, Indians of North America **I** 187
Chicken in every pot, campaign slogan **H** 223
Chicken pox, virus disease **D** 193
Chickens, poultry **P** 420–23
hatching process **B** 215
pets **B** 248; **P** 180
rous sarcoma virus **V** 369
Chickering, Jonas, American piano builder **P** 242

Chickweed W 104; *picture* W 105
Chicle, juice of sapodilla trees R 185
   Guatemala produces G 392
Chicory, plant, *picture* W 168
   coffee C 373
Chief justices, of the United States S 476
   trials of impeached presidents I 108
Chiggers (red bugs) I 284
   harvest mites S 388
Chignecto, Isthmus of, Canada N 138, 344a, 344b

Chihuahua (chih-WAH-wah), the smallest breed of dog. It is about 13 cm (5 in) high and weighs from 0.5 to 2.7 kg (1 to 6 lb). There are two varieties, smooth-coated and long-coated. Colors range from white to black. The chihuahua has large, batlike ears and an alert manner. It is believed to be descended from the Techichi, a dog of the Toltecs, an ancient Mexican people. Popular pets, chihuahuas are often seen resting in their owners' arms. D 259, 261; *picture* D 256

Chihuahuan (chi-HUA-huan) **Desert,** Mexico, *picture* D 125
Chikamatsu, Monzaemon, Japanese dramatist D 293; O 220d
Chik T'Sun, champion Pekingese dog D 261
Chilam Balam, book describing ancient Mayan religious beliefs G 391
Child, Francis James, American philologist and collector of ballads B 22

Child abuse, physical mistreatment of children by their parents or other caretakers. Examples of child abuse include severe beatings and starvation. Often, people who abuse children suffer from emotional problems and were themselves abused or neglected as children. Many cases of child abuse are not reported, but some estimates place the number of cases in the United States at 2,000,000 a year. A federal agency, the National Center on Child Abuse and Neglect, was established in 1974 to study the problem and to support programs to combat child abuse. State laws require physicians and social workers to report suspected cases.

Childbirth R 180
   nurse midwives N 409
Child development C 231–34
   baby B 3, 4
   family group F 37–45
   progressive education K 243–44
   society teaches girls and boys their roles W 211
   television programs T 71
   women, role of W 211
   See also Adolescence
Childe Harold's Pilgrimage, by Lord Byron E 260; *excerpt* B 481–82
Child is father of the Man, the, quotation from Wordsworth C 231
Child labor C 235
   early factories of the Industrial Revolution I 238
   government regulation L 14
Child Labor Act, 1916 W 179
Child Protection and Toy Safety Acts, 1966, 1969 F 352
Child psychology *see* Child development
Children
   adoption A·25–26
   baby B 2–4
   Christmas patrons around the world C 292
   colonial America C 390–92

development *see* Child development
   divorce, problems involving D 236–236a
   Do children pay income taxes? I 111
   educating the blind B 252
   family group F 37–45
   fashion modeling M 385
   first aid F 157–63
   foster-family care O 227
   games G 10–24
   handicapped, rehabilitation of the H 27–30
   indoor activities for rainy days I 223–26
   juvenile delinquency J 162–64
   kindergarten and nursery schools K 242–46
   libraries L 170–72, 175–76
   literature for children C 236–248d
   museums for M 520
   orphanages and foster-family care O 227
   percentage in populations P 395–96
   pioneer life P 256; *pictures* P 257
   playgrounds P 77–78
   poverty, chance to break cycle of P 424b
   public assistance W 119–20
   reform schools P 470
   retardation, mental R 190–91
   safety S 3–7
   society teaches girls and boys their roles W 211
   storytelling S 434–36
   toys T 230–35
   women, role of W 211
   See also Child labor

Children's Book Council (CBC), nonprofit organization that aims to encourage children to read better books. It sponsors National Children's Book Week, updates booklist and award information, and maintains a library. It was founded in 1945, has its headquarters in New York, N.Y., and publishes *Children's Book Council Calendar.*

Children's Crusade C 540
Children's Day H 158
   Japan H 158; K 266b
Children's Games, painting by Pieter Brueghel D 354
Children's literature C 236–248d
   book awards B 309–310b
   figures of speech F 119–20
   German forerunners of comic strips G 178
   illustration of children's books I 97
   libraries, children's services L 170–72, 180–88
   magazines M 16
   Newbery, John N 137
   nursery rhymes N 402–08
   poetry P 349–55
   See also Fables; Fairy tales; Folklore; Nursery rhymes; Storytelling; names of authors
Children's Museum of Indianapolis, Indiana I 145
Children's zoos Z 379

Childs Cup, trophy awarded for victory in Childs Cup rowing race. Established by George W. Childs (1879), publisher of Philadelphia *Public Ledger,* for competition among Columbia, Princeton, and Pennsylvania universities, it is oldest trophy for sprint, or short-distance, racing.

Child's Garden of Verses, A, by Robert Louis Stevenson, poems from S 424
   children's literature, history of C 241
Child welfare W 119–20
   adoption A 25–26

Child welfare (continued)
    orphanages and foster-family care **O** 227
    social work with child welfare agencies **S** 225
Child with a Dove, painting by Picasso, *picture* **P** 243
Chile (CHIL-e) **C** 249–55
    Easter Island **I** 430
    flag **F** 242
    life in Latin America **L** 47–61; *picture* **S** 289
    national anthem **N** 21
    O'Higgins, Bernardo **O** 59
    open-pit copper mine, *pictures* **S** 275, 292
    San Martín, José de, early fighter for freedom **S** 33
    Santiago **S** 34
    special stamp, *picture* **S** 399
Chile, University of, Santiago **C** 250; **S** 34
Chili powder, blend of spices **S** 382
Chilkat, Indians of North America **I** 180

Chilkat Pass, route from Haines, Alaska, to the Yukon, located 80 km (50 mi) west-northwest of Skagway. Used during the Klondike gold rush of the 1890's, it is now crossed by the Alaska Highway.

Chilkoot Pass, pass through Coast Mts. on border between Alaska and British Columbia, Canada. It was used by Indians, fur traders, and particularly prospectors during gold rush in Klondike (1896) as shortest way to Yukon Territory. It stretches 47 km (29 mi) from former village of Dyea, Alaska, to Lake Bennett, Canada, at approximate elevation of 1,067m (3,500 ft) much of it being dangerous canyons and perpendicular walls. Travel lessened through pass after Yukon Railroad was built through White Pass (1900).

Chimborazo (chim-bo-RA-zo), inactive volcano in Ecuador **E** 54
Chime clocks **W** 50
Chimera (kim-ER-a), monster in Greek mythology **G** 364
    age chimera **A** 87
Chimes, sets of bells, *picture* **M** 548
    jade stones make musical chimes **J** 10
Chimney Rock National Historic Site, Nebraska, **N** 92; *picture* **N** 93
Chimney swifts, birds **B** 220
Chimpanzees **M** 419
    animal intelligence tests **A** 287–88; *pictures* **A** 285, 288
    feet and hands **F** 83
    learning experiments, *picture* **L** 101
Chimp-O-Mat tests, used to study chimpanzees' intelligence **A** 288
Chimu (CHI-mu), ancient Indian empire in Peru **I** 207
    crafts, *pictures* **I** 203, 205
China **C** 256–73
    acupuncture **M** 208a, 208b
    art *see* Chinese art
    Asia, history of **A** 468
    Asia dominated by **A** 448–49
    Asia's population **A** 452–53
    Boxer Rebellion **B** 350
    bridges, admired by Marco Polo **B** 397–98
    Buddhism and Confucianism **B** 425
    canal system **C** 83, 84
    Confucius **C** 460
    dialects **D** 152
    drama **D** 292
    dynasties **C** 269–70
    education in the Orient **E** 62
    emigration **I** 100, 101, 103

    evidence of early cooking fires **F** 139
    explosives, invention of **E** 391
    fans **F** 46
    fireworks **F** 156
    flags, origin of those made of cloth **F** 225
    food, typical meals **F** 333, 339
    funeral and burial customs **F** 492; *picture* **F** 493
    Great Wall, *picture* **W** 219
    holidays **H** 148
    ideographic writing **C** 431, 433
    India ink first made in **I** 255
    Kites' Day **K** 266b
    largest encyclopedia **E** 190
    literature **O** 220–220b
    Manchuria **C** 260, 264
    Marco Polo's travels in **E** 373; **P** 389–90
    marriage rites **W** 103
    missiles invented by Chinese in 13th century **M** 343
    Mongolia **M** 416
    music **O** 220d–221
    Open-Door policy **M** 189–90
    paper **C** 432; **P** 56
    paper for accordion-folded books **B** 318
    porcelain first produced **C** 179
    relations with Hong Kong **H** 205
    rice eaten mainly in south China **G** 282
    San Men Dam foundations, *picture* **D** 20
    silk **S** 178
    Sun Yat-sen **S** 467
    theater **T** 163
    Truman's policy toward **T** 303
    Vietnam **V** 334b
    What are chopsticks and how are they used? **K** 287
    Yangtze River **Y** 343
    See also names of major cities
China, People's Republic of **C** 267, 272–73
    Chiang Kai-shek's struggle against **C** 227
    Communism **C** 445, 446
    education **E** 80
    flag **F** 239
    international relations **A** 469
    Kashmir **K** 199
    Korean War **K** 306
    Mao Tse-tung **M** 86
    modern factory, *picture* **A** 463
    moviemaking, *picture* **M** 480
    national anthem **N** 21
    Peking **P** 117–19
    population largest in the world **P** 396
    primary school children, *picture* **A** 2
    relations with India **I** 135
    Shanghai **S** 138–39
    Shenyang **S** 150
    Tibet, autonomous territory of China **T** 175–78
    Tientsin **T** 185
    USSR, relations with the **U** 51
China, Republic of **C** 264, 267, 272, 273; **T** 12–13
    Chiang Kai-shek, first president **C** 227
    flag **F** 239
China Sea **O** 46–47
Chinatown, Los Angeles, *picture* **I** 98
Chinatown, motion picture **M** 488c
Chinatown, New York City, *picture* **C** 307
Chinatown, San Francisco, California **S** 28
Chinatown, Washington, D.C. **W** 34
Chinaware **A** 319; *pictures* **A** 318, 319
    dolls made of **D** 265

Chinchillas (chin-CHIL-las), rodents **R** 280; **F** 518
   native to the Andes **A** 253
Chinchona see Cinchona, tree
Chincoteague (CHINC-o-teag) **National Wildlife Refuge**
   V 348
Chincoteague ponies **V** 344
Ch'in dynasty, ancient rule of China **C** 268–69
Chinese Americans, ethnic group **I** 100; picture **I** 98
Chinese art **O** 215–17; pictures **O** 214, 220
   art as a record **A** 438f
   bronze vase, picture **D** 69
   carpet **D** 66
   decorative arts **D** 68–69
   jade carvings **J** 9–10
   lacquerwork, picture **D** 69
   porcelain **D** 69; **P** 414, 417; pictures **D** 67,
     P 415
   rosewood bed, picture **D** 76
   vase, Shang dynasty, picture **A** 360
   woodcut from the Diamond Sutra **G** 302
Chinese chestnuts, picture **P** 298

Chinese crested dog, a dog that is hairless except for a growth of long, silky hair on its head, a plume on its tail, and little "socks" of hair on its feet. Its smooth skin may be dark colored, pinkish, or have flesh-toned patches on a dark background. The Chinese crested dog stands 30 cm (12 in) at the shoulder and weighs about 7 kg (15 lb). Because Chinese crested dogs do not have a natural coat, their owners must cover them warmly in cold weather. **D** 261; picture **D** 260

Chinese drama **D** 292
Chinese Exclusion Act, 1882 **I** 101
   policies of the Arthur administration **A** 441
Chinese insect wax **W** 76
Chinese language **C** 258; **O** 220
Chinese literature **O** 220–220b
Chinese music **O** 220d–221
Chinese Shar-Pei, dog **D** 261
Chinese theater **T** 163
   dance **D** 32
Chinese water deer **H** 217; picture **H** 215
Chinese writing **C** 258, 269
   communication by ideographs **C** 431, 433; **W** 318

Ch'ing (Manchu) **dynasty** (1644–1912), last Chinese imperial dynasty. Its rulers, the Manchus, invaded China from Manchuria. They governed through Chinese officials and brought a period of peace and prosperity. (More books were published in China during this time than in all the rest of the world.) Powerful rulers, they extended the Chinese empire into Tibet, Mongolia, Nepal, and Korea, up to founding of Chinese Republic (1912).
   China and Mongolia, history of **C** 270; **M** 416
   Shenyang (Mukden), capital **S** 150

Chinoiserie (she-nua-zer-E), Chinese influence on
   decorative arts **D** 77
Chinook (shin-OOK), warm, dry wind **G** 100
   Colorado **C** 405
   Prairie Provinces **A** 146c; **C** 55
   snow-eater **R** 95
   Wyoming **W** 327
   See also Foehn
Chinstrap penguins **P** 124
Chip, computer **C** 452, 453; picture **C** 454
Chipewyan, Indians of North America **I** 164, 170
Chipmunks **L** 252–53
   each organism has its own niche **L** 222

rodents **R** 276; pictures **R** 275, 277
   why small animals hibernate **H** 124
Chippendale, Thomas, English furniture designer
   F 507
   antiques **A** 317
Chippewa, Indians of North America **I** 178–79, 200b
   See also Ojibway
Chipping sparrows, birds **B** 219
Chiricahua National Monument, Arizona **A** 414
Chiricahuas (chi-ri-CA-huas), Indians of North America
   G 189
Chirico (KE-ri-co), **Giorgio di,** Italian surrealist painter
   I 473; **M** 395
   Melancholy and Mystery of a Street, painting **I** 472

Chiropody (kir-OP-ody) (from combination of Greek words cheir, "hand," and pous, "foot"), branch of medicine dealing with the care and treatment of the human foot. It is also called podiatry.

Chiropractic (KY-ro-prac-tic) (from Greek cheir, meaning "hand," and praktikos, meaning "efficient," "practical," or "operative"), system of healing based on premise that irregularity in the nervous system causes disease. Treatment involves manipulation of the body structures, especially of the spinal column, by hand.

Chiroptera, order of mammals **B** 92; **M** 62, 69
Chisels, tools **T** 213
   woodworking **W** 230

Chisholm, Shirley (1925–), American legislator, b. Brooklyn, N.Y. A former teacher, she became interested in politics and served in the New York state legislature. In 1968 she became the first black woman elected to the U.S. House of Representatives. She served seven terms in the House, retiring in 1982. picture **B** 250p

Chisholm Trail **O** 266–67
   Oklahoma **O** 88
   Wichita, Kansas, early trading post **K** 188
Chitarrone (ki-tar-RO-nay), musical instrument, picture
   S 438
Chitons (KI-tons), mollusks **O** 278; **S** 149
Chittagong, Bangladesh **B** 44b
Chivalry (SHIV-al-ry), knight's code of behavior
   K 274–75, 277
   early French literature **F** 435
   King Arthur, legends of **A** 442–45
   medals and decorations **M** 198
Chives, plants of onion family **O** 118
Chloramphenicol, antibiotic **D** 211
Chlorella, alga, food source **A** 157
Chlorine (CLOR-ine), element **G** 59
   action of catalysts **C** 199
   elements, some facts about **E** 154, 160
   iodine and other halogens **I** 349
   ions and isotopes **C** 203; diagrams **C** 204, 205
   waste-water treatment **S** 30
   water desalting **W** 60–61
Chloroform, used as anesthetic **A** 258
Chlorophyll (CLOR-o-phyll), in plants **P** 221–22
   algae **A** 155
   cell functions **C** 162
   food chain, exchange of forms of energy in **E** 202
   fungi lack **F** 496
   leaves of odd and interesting plants **P** 318
   leaves of trees and their function **T** 281
   plant plankton **P** 279–80
   term adopted by Liebig **B** 194

Chlorophyta, division of plant kingdom **P** 292
Chloroplasts, in plant cells **P** 294; *picture* **B** 183
   cell structure **C** 162
   photosynthesis **P** 221
Chloroprene (CLOR-o-prene), chemical **C** 195
Chmielnicki (hm-yel-NEET-ski), **Bogdan,** Cossack hero
   U 9

Choate (CHOAT), **Rufus** (1799–1859), American lawyer,
b. Hog Island, Mass. He served in the U.S. House of Rep-
resentatives (1831–34) and Senate (1841–45). An orga-
nizer of the Massachusetts Whigs, he opposed the emer-
gence of the Republican Party.

Chocolate **C** 274–75
   candymaking **C** 99
   Hershey, Pennsylvania, the Chocolate Capital
     P 142
   stain removal **L** 84
Choctaw, Indians of North America **A** 126; **I** 187
Choibalsan (CHOI-bol-son), Mongolia **M** 415
Choirs (KWIRES), music
   ancient Hebrew **A** 246
   hymns, sung by professional choirs **H** 309
   training in Flemish and French schools **D** 363
   See also Choral music; Choruses
Choke, valve on a carburetor **I** 310
Choking on foreign bodies
   first aid **F** 159–60

Cholera (COL-er-a), **Asiatic,** disease caused by certain
bacteria that enter digestive system. It causes loss of body
fluids through vomiting and diarrhea and is treated by
replacement of fluids. It occurs in epidemic form where
water supply is contaminated by bacteria, chiefly in Far
East. Vaccination prevents it for short time.

Cholesterol (co-LES-ter-ol), chemical found in all animal
tissues and fluids. Necessary for life, though its role is not
well understood, it can be changed by body into other
chemicals needed for proper functioning—for example,
vitamin D in humans. It has been cited as a contributing
factor in heart disease.
   body chemistry, lipids in **B** 293
   hardening of the arteries **D** 195
   special diets **N** 418
   vitamin D **V** 370d–371

Cholla (CHOLE-ya), cactus, *picture* **C** 3
Cholon (cho-LUN), Vietnam **V** 334b
Cholos, mestizos that live in Peru **P** 160
Choltitz, Dietrich von, German general **P** 75
Chomedey, Paul de *see* Maisonneuve, Paul de
   Chomedey
Chomolungma (cho-mo-LUNG-ma), Tibetan name for
   Mount Everest **E** 336
Chondokyo, native Korean religion **K** 296
Chong Son, Korean painter **K** 299
Chopin (SHO-pan), **Frédéric,** Polish pianist and
   composer **C** 276
   French music **F** 446
   nocturnes **R** 311
Chops, meat, outdoor cooking **O** 247
Chopsticks, eating tool most commonly used in eastern
   Asia **K** 287
Chop suey, food **F** 339
Chorale, musical form **M** 535
Chorales (co-RALS), German hymns **H** 311
   religious music in Germany **G** 182
Choral (COR-al) **music** **C** 276–79

   ancient Hebrew **A** 246
   basic record library **R** 125
   black spirituals **H** 314
   English **E** 269, 271
   festivals **M** 551, 552
   German **G** 182
   hymns **H** 309–15
   Mass as musical form **D** 363
Choral Symphony (Ninth Symphony), by Beethoven
   C 278; **G** 185
Chord (CORD), of airplane wing **A** 554
Chords, in music **M** 529, 533
   for guitar **G** 410
   rock music **R** 262c
Chords, of circles **G** 127
Choreography (cor-e-OG-raphy), arrangement of dances
   D 22
   avant-garde dancers **D** 34
   ballet **B** 23–29
   dance music development **D** 36–37
Choreomanias (cor-e-o-MANE-ias), dance manias of
   Middle Ages **D** 24
Chores
   for pioneer children, *pictures* **P** 257
   on the farm **F** 52–53
Choruses, music
   ancient Greece **A** 247
   See also Choirs
Chorus Line, A, musical **M** 543
Choson ("Land of Morning Calm"), Koreans' name for
   their country **K** 296
Chota Nagpur plateau, India **I** 126
Chotts (or shotts), salt lakes **A** 160; **T** 309
Chouart, Médart *see* Groseilliers, Médart Chouart

Chou (JO) **Dynasty,** third and longest ruling house in Chi-
nese history (about 1028–256 B.C.). Begun by Wu Wang
(rulers took title *Wang*, meaning "King"), it controlled
most of China north of Yellow River during Western Chou
period, but was forced to flee from barbarians later and
moved eastward during the Eastern Chou period. It was
characterized by advanced knowledge and craftsmanship.
The three most important Chinese philosophers, Lao-tzu,
Confucius, and Mencius, wrote during this period and laid
foundation of Chinese thought. **C** 268
   transportation advances **T** 258

Chou En-lai (JO en-LIE) (1898–1976), Chinese Commu-
nist leader, b. Kiangsu province. He served under Chiang
Kai-shek, leader of Kuomintang (Nationalist Party), during
First United Front, a period of co-operation with Chinese
Communists (1924–27). He was Political Commissar of
First Army (1926). After Chiang Kai-shek's purge of Com-
munists from Kuomintang (1927), Chou joined with Chu
Teh, head of Red Army. During Second United Front
(1937–45), when China and Japan were at war, he acted
as adviser to Chiang Kai-shek's government. With procla-
mation (1949) of People's Republic of China, he became
foreign minister (until 1958) and premier (1949–76)
under Mao Tse-tung.

Choupique, fish **L** 353
Chouteau (shoot-O), **René Auguste,** American fur trader
   M 379
   Saint Louis, Missouri **S** 18
Chouteau family, fur dynasty **F** 522
   Chouteau Trading Post Marker, Oklahoma **O** 91

Chow Chow, a powerful, square-bodied, muscular dog that
is the only breed in the world with a blue-black tongue.

Popular in China for centuries, the Chow Chow is often said to resemble a lion. It has small, erect ears, straight hind legs, a broad head, and a thick ruff of hair around its neck. Chow Chows may be any of a number of colors. They are loyal to their owners, but they dislike being approached by strangers. **D** 261

Chow mein, food **F** 339
Chowringhee Road, street in Calcutta **C** 11
Chrétien de Troyes (cret-YEN d'TRWA), French poet **F** 436
    Arthurian legends **A** 445
Christ see Jesus Christ
Christchurch, New Zealand **N** 241
Christ Church, Philadelphia **P** 182
Christi, John, English organ manufacturer **M** 550
Christian, Charlie, American musician **J** 60
Christian art, Early
    decorative arts **D** 72
    Italy **I** 458
    sculpture **S** 96

Christian Brothers (Brothers of the Christian Schools), an order of Roman Catholic Brothers who devote their lives to educating the young. The order was founded in 1680 in France by St. Jean Baptiste de la Salle. Their innovations in child education helped bring about general primary education in Europe. Schools and colleges conducted by Christian Brothers are found throughout the world.

Christian Church (Disciples of Christ) **P** 484

Christian Endeavor, International Society of (ISCE), Christian organization for young people in the United States, Canada, and Mexico. The society aims to promote Christian life among its members and to train them for church work. It sponsors citizenship projects and contests and Youth Week. It was founded in 1881 and has headquarters in Columbus, Ohio. It publishes *Christian Endeavor World.*

Christiania, Norway see Oslo, Norway
Christianity **C** 279–89
    Abraham honored by **A** 6b
    Africa **A** 56
    Anglo-Saxon England becomes Christian **E** 216
    Apostles, The **A** 332–33
    Armenia **U** 44
    art as a record **A** 438b
    Asia, chief religions of **A** 460
    Augustine, Saint **A** 494
    Bible **B** 152–62
    Byzantine art and architecture **B** 483–90
    Byzantine church **B** 492
    Christmas customs **C** 290–94
    Constantine the Great, first Christian ruler **C** 489
    Coptic Church **A** 56
    Crusades **C** 538–40; **E** 372
    dance a part of worship in the early church **D** 24
    decorative arts of early Christians **D** 72
    divorce **D** 236
    early Christian art **I** 458
    Easter **E** 35–36
    funeral customs **F** 494, 495
    historical writings **H** 134–35
    hymns **H** 310–15
    Inquisition **I** 256
    Japan **J** 44, 46
    Jerusalem **J** 78–82
    Jesus Christ **J** 83–87
    Lebanese civil war **L** 121, 123–24
    Middle Ages **M** 293–95
    Middle East, religions of the **M** 305
    Orthodox Eastern churches **O** 228–30
    Palestine, history of **P** 40b
    Patrick, Saint **P** 98
    persecutions of Christians by Nero **N** 114
    Peter, Saint **P** 167
    Protestantism **P** 482–86
    Reformation **R** 130–33
    religions of the world **R** 149–50
    religious holidays **R** 153–55
    Roman Catholic Church **R** 287–302
    Roman Empire **R** 307–08
    sculpture of early Christians **S** 96
    Southeast Asia **S** 331
    Ten Commandments **T** 72–73
    wedding customs **W** 100–02
    See also names of saints, popes, Christian leaders
Christian names **N** 7
Christians and Jews, National Conference of see National Conference of Christians and Jews
Christian Science Monitor, newspaper **N** 200
Christian Scientists (Church of Christ, Scientist) **P** 484
Christianshaab, Greenland, *picture* **G** 367

Christie, Dame Agatha (Agatha Mary Clarissa Miller Christie Mallowan) (1890–1976), English novelist and playwright, b. Torquay. She is best known for detective stories, many of which feature Belgian detective Hercule Poirot or English sleuth Jane Marple. She also wrote romantic novels (under the name Mary Westmacott) and several successful plays. In 1971 she was made a Dame Commander of the Order of the British Empire.

Christmas at Home, painting by Grandma Moses, *picture* **F** 40
Christmas cards **C** 292, 294; **G** 372–74
    how to make a Christmas card **G** 374
Christmas Carol, A, book by Charles Dickens **D** 159
Christmas carols **C** 290–91
Christmas customs around the world **C** 290–94
    Advent **R** 155, 290
    Australia and Vermont, *pictures* **S** 111
    carols **C** 122
    crib, or manger, scene begun by St. Francis **F** 449
    folk music **F** 325
    holy month of December **D** 56
    Latin America **L** 51
    mistletoe **P** 318
    toys **T** 233
    Visit from St. Nicholas, A, by Clement Moore **C** 295
    Yuletide and Yule log, pagan Norse customs **N** 277
Christmas Island, isolated island in Indian Ocean **A** 495
Christmas Island, one of the Line Islands, Kiribati **K** 266, 266a; **P** 6
Christmas Night (*Nuit de Noël*), collage by Henri Matisse, *picture* **F** 376
Christmas trees **C** 291
Christmas trees, collections of valves and controls on oil derricks **P** 173–74

Christophe (chris-TOPHE), **Henri** (1767–1820), king of Haiti, b. Grenada, British West Indies. He participated in first Haitian revolt (1791) against French. He joined second uprising (1803–04) of Jean Jacques Dessalines, upon whose death in ambush (1806) he made himself King Henri I of northern Haiti. His rule became oppressive

Christophe, Henri (continued)
and caused rebellion (1818–20) and his suicide. He built palace of Sans Souci and fortress of the Citadelle.
> Citadelle or Citadel, *pictures* **H** 11, **W** 217
> history of Haiti **H** 10

Christopher, antipope **R** 296

Christopher, Saint, legendary Christian martyr and patron of travelers. He is said to have been a giant who carried travelers across a stream on his shoulders. Once he carried the Christ child in this way. The St. Christopher medal, often seen in automobiles, usually depicts this scene. In 1969, St. Christopher's feast was removed from the calendar of the Roman Catholic Church because of doubts about his existence.

Christopher Robin, character in A. A. Milne's stories and poems **M** 310, 311

Christophers, The, three kings of Denmark. **Christopher I** (1219–59) reigned (1252–59) through period of conflict with archbishop of Lund. **Christopher II** (1276–1332) was considered incompetent ruler, and Denmark was divided during his reign (1320–26, 1330–32). **Christopher III** (1418–48), known as "Christopher of Bavaria," king of Denmark and Sweden (1440–48) and Norway (1442–48), made Copenhagen official royal residence (1443).

Christus, Petrus, Flemish painter **D** 351
Christy, Howard, American artist **O** 73
Chromatic (cro-MAT-ic) **aberration,** defects of lenses **L** 148–49
Chromatic scales, in music **M** 529, 533
> modern music **M** 399

Chromatin (CRO-ma-tin), of cell nucleus **C** 161
Chromatography (cro-ma-TOG-raphy), in chemistry, for qualitative analysis of elements and compounds
> do an experiment in paper chromatography **E** 367

Chromatophores (cro-MAT-a-phores), color cells in skin of fishes **F** 194
Chrome-tanning, leather process **L** 109, 111
Chromite (CRO-mite), mineral **C** 296
> leather tanning agent **L** 110

Chromium, metallic element **C** 296
> alloys **A** 168
> elements, some facts about **E** 154, 160
> lasers **L** 46b–46c
> metals, chart of ores, location, properties, uses **M** 227
> stainless steel contains **I** 396

Chromosomes (CRO-mos-omes), in nuclei of cells, determining heredity **G** 77, 82–83
> analyzing and counting (karyotyping), a medical laboratory test **M** 202
> cell structure **C** 161, 164
> division of the cell, *diagram* **K** 255
> mutation theory of cancer **C** 94–95
> X–ray damage, *picture* **C** 92

Chromosphere, layer of the sun's photosphere **S** 461–62
Chronic bronchitis **D** 192
> emphysema **D** 194

Chronic diseases **D** 186
> old age ailments **O** 97

Chronicles, I and II, books of Bible, Old Testament **B** 156
Chronographs, timers **W** 50
Chronometers (cro-NOM-eters), highly accurate timepieces **W** 47, 50

invention of **I** 346
navigation **N** 66
Chrysalis (CRIS-a-lis), butterfly pupa **I** 264–65
Chrysanthemums, flowers **G** 51; *picture* **G** 50
> Japanese festival **J** 31–32

Chrysler, Walter Percy (1875–1940), American automobile manufacturer, founder and president of the Chrysler Corporation, b. Wamego, Kan. He was assistant manager of the American Locomotive Company (1910) and president and general manager of the Buick Motor Company (1916–19). In 1919 he became a vice-president of General Motors and later executive vice-president of the Willys-Overland Company (1920–22). He founded the Chrysler Corporation in 1924 and was responsible for the construction of Chrysler Building in New York, N.Y. **K** 190

Chrysoberyl (CRIS-o-beryl), gem mineral **G** 70, 75
Chrysolite, gem mineral **G** 76
Chrysopolis (cris-OP-o-lis) **Battle of,** A.D. 324, **C** 282
Chrysoprase (CRIS-o-prase), chalcedony quartz **Q** 7
Chuang Tzu, Chinese philosopher **O** 220a
Chubb, Jeremiah, English inventor **L** 324
Chubb Crater, Ungava, Canada **C** 421
Chuck wagons
> ranch life, *picture* **R** 102

Chuckwallas, lizards **L** 319, 321
Chugach (CHU-gack) **National Forest,** Alaska **A** 140
Chukchi (CHOOK-chi) **Sea** **O** 47
Chulalongkorn (chu-la-LONG-korn), king of Thailand **T** 151
Chun Doo Hwan, president of Korea **K** 304
Chungking, China **C** 263
Chuquicamata, copper mine, Chile **C** 253; *pictures* **C** 252; **S** 275, 292
Church, Frank, American senator **I** 67
Church and state
> Christianity in modern times **C** 287–88
> divorce **D** 236
> education and the battle for the common school **E** 70–71, 75
> England, Church of **E** 220–21
> freedom of religion **F** 457
> Jefferson's reforms in Virginia **J** 64
> separation of, origin of the principle in Jefferson's interpretation of the Constitution **F** 457

Church architecture **A** 376–79, 382–83
> art, the meanings of **A** 438
> art as a record **A** 438e
> basilica **I** 458
> Byzantine **A** 377; **B** 483–90
> cathedrals **C** 131–33
> English architecture **E** 234–35
> France, development in **F** 421
> Gothic architecture **G** 270
> Italian architecture **I** 458, 463; *pictures* **I** 459–60
> Latin America in 16th century **L** 62
> Middle Ages **M** 296–97
> mission churches of the Southwest **U** 122–23
> modern Swedish church, *picture* **R** 149
> mosaics used in **M** 463
> Renaissance **A** 381; **R** 167
> Russian architecture **U** 52–53
> Spanish architecture **S** 363
> stained-glass windows **S** 393–95

Church councils
> Arles, 314 **C** 284
> Constantinople, 381 **C** 283
> Nicaea, 325 **C** 283, 489

Trent, Council of **C** 287; **G** 374a
Vatican Council II **C** 289; **R** 298

Churches of the Nazarene, union of several small church groups as part of Holiness Movement started after the American Civil War. It follows doctrines of holiness and sanctification as taught by the 18th-century evangelist John Wesley. The union was founded in 1908 in Pilot Point, Texas.

Churchill, John *see* Marlborough, 1st Duke of
Churchill, Lord Randolph, British statesman, father of Sir Winston Churchill **C** 297
Churchill, Sir Winston, British statesman and author **C** 297–98; **E** 231, 268; *pictures* **C** 297, **P** 456a
   coined the phrase "Iron Curtain" **I** 320; **M** 375
   description of Uganda **U** 4
   oratory **O** 181
   Teheran Conference, 1943, *picture* **W** 298
   visits Coventry Cathedral, *picture* **E** 230
   with Stalin and Roosevelt at Yalta, *picture* **R** 324
Churchill Downs, race track in Louisville, Kentucky **H** 232–33; *picture* **K** 220
Churchill Falls (formerly Grand Falls), Newfoundland **N** 143, 144
Churchill River (formerly Hamilton River), Labrador **C** 57; **N** 144
Churchill River, western Canada **M** 76; **S** 38c
Church music
   ars antiqua of French music **F** 444
   baroque period **B** 64; *picture* **B** 65
   choral music **C** 276–79
   Dutch and Flemish music **D** 363–64
   early use of plainsong in Italy **I** 482
   hymns **H** 309–15
   Middle Ages **M** 298–99
   musical forms **M** 535–37
   Palestrina **P** 41
Church of Christ, Scientist (Christian Scientists) **P** 484
Church of England *see* England, Church of

Church of God, name used by many small Protestant denominations in United States. Sects were organized in 1903 by Bishop A. J. Tomlinson.

Church of Jesus Christ of Latter-day Saints *see* Mormons
Church of the Holy Family (Sagrada Familia), Barcelona, by Antonio Gaudí **S** 365
Churn, vessel for making butter **B** 467
Churriguera (chu-ri-GAY-ra), **José,** Spanish architect **S** 363
   decorative arts **D** 75
Churrigueresque (chu-rig-er-ESK), baroque style of art and architecture **D** 75
   Latin-American architecture **L** 63
   Spanish architecture **S** 363

Chute, Marchette (1909–   ), American author, b. Waycata, Minn. She is noted for biographies and literary histories, such as *Shakespeare of London, Ben Jonson of Westminster,* and *Geoffrey Chaucer of England.* Her books of poetry include *Rhymes About the Country.*

Ch'ü Yüan, Chinese poet **O** 220a
CIA *see* Central Intelligence Agency

Ciardi (CHAR-di), **John** (1916–   ), American poet and author, b. Boston, Mass. He taught at Harvard University (1946–53) and at Rutgers University (1953–61) and was poetry editor of *Saturday Review* magazine (1956–72). His works include a translation of Dante's *Inferno,* a guide to poetry *How Does a Poem Mean?* and *The Monster Den,* poems for children.
   "The Reason for the Pelican," nonsense rhyme **N** 274

Cíbola (CI-bo-la), **Seven Cities of,** seven fabled Zuni (Pueblo Indian) towns in northern Mexico, purported to be cities of gold. Riches were found to be only legendary by Spanish explorer Francisco Vásquez de Coronado (1540) on the expedition during which he discovered the Grand Canyon.
   Zuni Indians **I** 192

Cicadas (ci-CAY-das), insects **I** 268; *picture* **I** 281
   animal homes, *pictures* **A** 273
   sucking insects **P** 285
Cicero (CIS-er-o), **Marcus Tullius,** Roman orator and statesman **C** 298
   disapproved of dancing **D** 23
   oratory **O** 180–81
   place in Latin literature **L** 78
Cichlids (CICK-lids), common aquarium fishes **F** 201
Cicutoxin (cic-u-TOX-in), plant poison **P** 321
Cid, El, Spanish national hero **L** 130
   beginnings of Spanish literature **S** 366–67
   bullfighting **B** 449
Cid, Le, play by Pierre Corneille **D** 296
Cider, apple beverage **A** 333
Cienfuegos, Cuba **C** 549
Cierna, Czechoslovakia
   conference of Soviet leaders, 1968 **C** 564
Cierpinski, Waldemar, East German athlete **O** 116b
Cierva (thee-AIR-va), **Juan de la,** Spanish aeronautical engineer **H** 104
Cigarettes
   bronchitis and emphysema **D** 192, 194; **S** 203
   cancer research **C** 91–92
   smoking and cancer **S** 203
   tobacco **T** 200–01
Cigar-store Indian, sculpture **U** 117
Cilia (CIL-ia), hairlike threads on some cells **M** 276
   animal movement in water **A** 266
Ciliates (CIL-i-ates), micro-organisms **M** 276
Cimabue (chi-ma-BU-ay), **Giovanni,** Florentine painter **P** 18
   humanism of the late Middle Ages **I** 463
Cimarron (CIM-a-ron) **River,** United States
   Cimarron Cutoff, part of Santa Fe Trail **O** 257
Cinchona (cin-CO-na), tree **P** 313; *pictures* **D** 327, **P** 312
   bark is a source of quinine **D** 323
Cincinnati, Ohio **O** 65, 68, 71; *picture* **O** 72
   civic fountain **F** 395

Cincinnati, Society of the, American fraternal and patriotic organization founded in 1783 by Revolutionary War officers, and later including their male descendants and kinsmen. The organization was named after the Roman statesman Lucius Quinctius Cincinnatus. Its first president was George Washington. Until 1792 it had a branch in France. Headquarters are in Washington, D.C.

Cincinnati Turngemeinde *see* Turnverein

Cincinnatus of the West, Lord Byron's epithet for George Washington in *Ode to Napoleon Buonaparte.* The term was

Cincinnatus of the West (continued)
probably taken from legendary Roman statesman Lucius Quinctius Cincinnatus, whose name came to represent simplicity, ability, and virtue.

Cinder cones, of volcanoes **V** 383
Cinderella, most loved folktale **F** 302–03
    Perrault's version of the story **F** 305–08
    La Cenerentola, opera by Rossini **O** 142
    scene from animated movie **A** 298
Cinema *see* Motion picture industry
Cinemascope, motion picture projection system **M** 478
    The Robe, first Cinemascope film **M** 487
Cinerama, motion picture projection system **M** 477–78
Cinnabar, mercury ore, *picture* **R** 272
Cinnamon, spice **S** 382; *picture* **S** 381

Cinque, Joseph (1811–52), b. Africa, leader of Amistad Revolt. Sold into slavery in Havana, Cuba, he was purchased by Spaniards who put him with 38 other slaves on the schooner *Amistad* to be shipped to Príncipe Island, off coast of Africa. Cinque led the slaves in revolt. The ship landed in Connecticut, where the slaves were imprisoned. New England Abolitionists defended them, and finally the U.S. Supreme Court freed them and allowed them to return to Africa.

CIO *see* Congress of Industrial Organizations
Ciphers (CY-phers), method of secret writing **C** 369–71
Circassians (cir-CAS-sians), non-Arab Muslim people of Jordan **J** 136
Circe, in Greek mythology **O** 54
Circle dances **D** 28; **F** 297, 299
    Middle Ages, *picture* **D** 24
Circle games (ring games) **G** 13–16
Circle graphs (pie charts) **G** 313
Circle of Fire (Ring of Fire), volcanoes **M** 499
Circles, in geometry **G** 127
Circle strideball, circle game **C** 15
Circuit riders **P** 259
Circuits, electronic, of computers **C** 452, 453–54
Circular saws, tools **T** 218
Circulation (circ-u-LAY-tion), of blood **B** 275–77
    heart, function of **H** 86–86c
Circulation, of newspapers **N** 200, 204
Circulatory (CIR-cu-la-tory) **system,** of blood
    body, human **B** 275–77
    effects of jogging and running on **J** 120b
    fish, amphibian, bird, *diagrams* **B** 202, **F** 186
    hardening of the arteries **D** 195
    heart, function of **H** 86–86c
Circum-Caribbean (cir-cum-ca-ribb-E-an) **Indians** **I** 207–08
Circumference, of a circle **G** 127
Circus **C** 299–304
    circus building in Bulgaria, *picture* **B** 441
    Circus World Museum, Baraboo, Wisconsin **W** 201
    elephants **E** 171
    toy circus, *picture* **T** 235
    See also Carnivals
Circus, The, poem by Elizabeth Madox Roberts **P** 35
Circus Maximus, in ancient Rome **C** 300
Cire perdue, lost wax casting **D** 70, 74
Cirques (CIRKS), formed by glaciers, *picture* **I** 16
Cirro-cumulus (cirro-CU-mu-lus) **clouds** **C** 360; *picture* **C** 361
Cirro-stratus clouds **C** 360; *picture* **C** 361
Cirrus clouds **C** 360; *picture* **C** 361

Cistercians (cis-TER-cians), religious order **C** 284; **R** 292
Citadel, fortress in Quebec City, Canada **Q** 16
Citadel, Haiti, *pictures* **H** 11, **W** 217
Cithara (CITH-a-ra) (or kithara), ancient musical instrument **A** 247; *picture* **A** 246
Citicorp, building, New York City, *picture* **A** 387
Cities **C** 305–10
    Africa, chief cities of **A** 65
    air pollution **A** 108–11; **E** 272f–272g
    ancient civilizations **A** 217–19, 221–23, 224
    Asia, chief cities of **A** 452, 453
    buses **B** 465–66
    city-states of Italy **I** 455
    desert cities **D** 127
    environment, problems of **E** 272a–272h
    Europe **E** 327, 329–30
    family **F** 39, 41
    fires and fire fighting **F** 146, 148, 150–51
    growth with Industrial Revolution **I** 239–40
    homes in the city **H** 182–84
    island cities **I** 425
    juvenile delinquency **J** 163
    Latin America **L** 56–59
    libraries for urban centers **L** 174
    Metro Toronto, union of Toronto and suburbs **T** 227
    Middle Ages sees their growth **M** 292–93
    municipal government **M** 503–08
    North America **N** 304
    Oklahoma City, "built in a day" **O** 92
    parks and playgrounds **P** 76–78
    police force **P** 372–77
    port cities **H** 37
    poverty **P** 424, 424a
    problems of black mayors **B** 250q
    public utilities **P** 510–13
    Roman Empire, city life in **R** 306
    sanitation **S** 30–31
    state governments and cities **S** 415
    traffic control **T** 247–48
    transportation **T** 264
    urban landscape in New England **N** 138h
    urban planning **U** 232–34
    zoning plans to control floods **F** 257
    See also Federal cities; Urban planning; country, province, and state articles; and names of cities
Citizen Kane, motion picture **M** 485
Citizen King, Louis Philippe of France **F** 417
Citizens' action groups
    television, influence of **T** 70d
Citizens Band Radio, type of amateur radio **C** 439; **E** 142c; **R** 63
Citizenship **C** 311–13
    American Indians granted citizenship **I** 215
    democracy **D** 104–05
    education for **S** 223
    geography for **G** 104, 107
    income tax, citizens' duty to pay **I** 111
    jury duty **J** 159–60
    naturalization **N** 65
    qualification for voting **E** 113
    See also Aliens; Naturalization
Citiric acid **A** 7
Citrine, quartz gemstone **G** 71, 75; **Q** 7
Citron, citrus fruit **L** 136, 138

Citronella oil, a yellowish green oil with sharp odor, used as an insect repellent and as perfume in soap. The source of the oil is citronella grass, which grows in Sri Lanka, India, the Malay Peninsula, and Java.

Citrus fruits
    citric acid **A** 7
    citron **L** 138
    Huascarán Valley, Peru, *picture* **S** 290
    lemon and lime **L** 136–38
    orange and grapefruit **O** 176–79
    orange groves, Florida, *pictures* **F** 260, 265
    subtropical fruits **F** 481, 484
    vitamins, discovery of **V** 370a
City editors, on newspapers **N** 202
City of Brotherly Love, name for Philadelphia **P** 182
City of Light, Paris **P** 68
City of Refuge National Historical Park, Hawaii **H** 66
City of Roses, Portland, Oregon **P** 398
City planning *see* Urban planning
City-states **C** 308a
    ancient Greece **G** 338
    Italy during the Renaissance **R** 157
City University of New York System **N** 232
Ciudad Bolívar, Venezuela **V** 300
Ciudad Guayana, Venezuela *see* Santo Tomé de Guayana
Civets, catlike animals **G** 92, 93, 94, 95
Civic Repertory Theater, New York City **T** 161
Civics, study of government and laws **S** 224

Civil Aeronautics Board (CAB), U.S. Government agency that supervises civilian aviation. Its five members are appointed by the president for 6-year terms. According to the Air Transportation Deregulation Act (1978), CAB authority over domestic routes was ended in 1981, and over domestic fares, mergers, and acquisitions in 1983. CAB itself is to be abolished by 1985.
    interstate regulatory agencies **I** 332

Civil Air Patrol (CAP), a civilian auxiliary of the U.S. Air Force, with membership comprised of high school cadets and adults. The CAP participates in search and rescue missions, operates nationwide radio network, provides educational services, books, films, and workshops. Many members are licensed pilots. It was founded in 1941, and has headquarters at Maxwell Air Force Base, Alabama.

Civil defense, refers to federal, state, and local programs for protecting life and property against enemy attack or natural disaster. The United States Office of Civil Defense operates a vast communications system, offers emergency financial aid to state and local governments, and provides medical aid for survivors of a disaster. Interest in civil defense reached its height in the 1950's and early 1960's, when there was widespread fear of atomic attack.

Civil disobedience
    Gandhi leads India's movement for self-rule **G** 24
    Indian national movement **I** 133
    Martin Luther King's philosophy **K** 247
    struggle for black civil rights **B** 250n
Civil Disobedience, essay by Henry David Thoreau **A** 201
Civil engineering **E** 204–05
    canals **C** 83–86
    dams **D** 16–21
    road building **R** 249–50
    tunnels **T** 313–18

Civilian Conservation Corps (CCC), relief program **R** 322
Civilizations, ancient *see* Ancient civilizations
Civil law
    courts **C** 526–30
    jury trials **J** 159–60
Civil liberties and civil rights **C** 313–16
    beliefs of the founders of the United States **F** 393
    black history **B** 250g–250q
    censorship in wartime *see* Censorship
    Civil Rights Acts, 1964, 1968 **B** 250o, 250p
    courts **C** 526–30
    Declaration of Independence **D** 61, 63
    democratic privileges **D** 105
    disabled people's civil rights, laws to protect **H** 30
    Four Freedoms of Franklin Roosevelt **R** 324
    Fourteenth Amendment **J** 125
    freedom of religion, speech, and press **F** 457
    Human Rights, Universal Declaration of **U** 84, 88
    international law **I** 315, 317, 324
    Johnson, Andrew, and Reconstruction **J** 125
    jury, trial by **J** 159–60
    King, Martin Luther **K** 247
    Magna Carta **M** 22
    Plessy v. *Ferguson,* Supreme Court ruling on separate but equal facilities **B** 250g
    Reconstruction in the South **R** 118
    segregation in the United States **S** 115
    Soviet system's record on human rights **C** 444
    Supreme Court rulings **S** 477
    women, role of **W** 212a–213
    See also Freedom of assembly; Freedom of petition; Freedom of religion; Freedom of speech; Freedom of the press; Habeas corpus
Civil rights *see* Civil liberties and civil rights
Civil Rights, President's Committee on *see* President's Committee on Civil Rights
Civil Rights, United States Commission on *see* United States Commission on Civil Rights
Civil Rights Act, 1866 **B** 250g
Civil Rights Act, 1875 **B** 250g
Civil Rights Act, 1964 **B** 250o, 250p; **S** 115
Civil Rights Act, 1968 **B** 250p; **S** 115
Civil service **C** 317
    council-manager form of municipal government **M** 506
    Pendleton Act, 1883 **A** 441; **C** 317
    Roman Empire **R** 304
    state governments **S** 414–15
    See also Spoils system

Civil Service Commission, federal personnel organization established by the Pendleton Act of 1883. To appoint civil servants on the basis of their ability rather than of religious or political association, a bipartisan board of three members was formed and a system of examinations devised for selection of government employees. Further legislation has increased efficiency in recruiting, selecting, and promoting civil servants.

Civil War, English, 1642–49 **E** 223
    Cromwell, Oliver **C** 536
    English literature, effect on **E** 255
    Milton given post in Cromwell's government **M** 312
    Puritan Revolution **P** 343–44
Civil war, in China **C** 272
Civil War, Spanish, 1936–39 **S** 358
Civil War, United States, 1861–65 **C** 318–28
    Alabama location of formation of Confederate States of America **A** 127

Civil War, United States (continued)
American literature   **A** 204
Barton, Clara   **B** 68
black history   **B** 250f–250g
Brady's photography   **C** 434
Brown, John   **B** 411–12
Buchanan, could he have prevented it?   **B** 420
clothing industry stimulated   **C** 353
Compromise of 1850   **C** 448
Confederate States   **C** 458–60
Davis, Jefferson   **D** 45
draft and conscription laws   **D** 289
Dred Scott decision   **D** 310–11
Emancipation Proclamation   **E** 185–86
first blood spilled in Baltimore, Maryland   **M** 131
Grant, Ulysses S.   **G** 294–95
Indian loyalties divided during   **I** 213–14
industrial expansion, result of the war   **U** 130
Jackson, "Stonewall," Confederate general   **J** 8
Kansas-Nebraska Act   **K** 192
Lee's campaigns   **L** 125–26
Lincoln, Abraham   **L** 295–97
Medal of Honor established   **M** 198
Missouri Compromise   **M** 382
New Mexico   **N** 195
northernmost action, St. Albans, Vermont   **V** 321
Reconstruction Period   **R** 117–20
Sherman, William Tecumseh, Union general   **S** 151
slavery   **S** 199
songs   **N** 24–25
submarine made first successful attack   **S** 445
Trent Affair, 1861   **C** 322
United States Marine Corps campaigns   **U** 178
United States Navy   **U** 186
Unknown Soldier, Tomb of the, Arlington National Cemetery   **N** 30
women spies   **S** 388–89
See also Reconstruction Period; Slavery; names of individual leaders

Civitan International, a service organization of business and professional men and women interested in promoting effective citizenship on local, national, and international levels. It sponsors essay contest and awards scholarships to winners. It was founded in 1920.

Claiborne (CLAI-borne), **William** (1587?–1677?), Virginia colonist, b. Westmorland, England. In 1621 he emigrated to Virginia, where he served as secretary of state (1625). A trading post he set up on Kent Island in Chesapeake Bay became the subject of a bitter ownership dispute between Virginia and Maryland and was finally settled in favor of Maryland (1638).

Claiborne, William Charles Coles, American lawyer   **L** 361
Claims adjusters, in insurance companies   **I** 296
Clair, René, French motion picture director   **M** 484
Clams, mollusks   **O** 274–75
bioluminescence experiment   **B** 197
fishing industry   **F** 220–21
giant clam of the tropics   **A** 265; **G** 200
nervous system, *diagram*   **B** 363
shells   **S** 148; *pictures* **S** 149
Clans and clan system   **A** 303
Albania   **A** 144
Australian aborigines   **A** 6a
Chippewa Indians   **I** 179
Creek Indians   **I** 188–89
Hopi Indians   **I** 191

Japan   **J** 43
totem poles   **I** 156; *pictures* **I** 182, 183
Zuni Indians   **I** 192
See also Family
Clapboard (CLAB-ard) **houses**   **H** 169
Clapperton, Hugh, Scottish explorer of Africa   **S** 8

Clare (or Clara) **of Assisi, Saint** (1194–1253), Italian nun, b. Assisi. After hearing Saint Francis of Assisi preach, she founded (1212) order of Franciscan nuns that became known as Order of Poor Ladies or Poor Clares. Living strictly by rule of poverty, she served as their abbess until her death. She was canonized in 1255.

Clarín (Leopoldo Alas), Spanish writer   **S** 371
Clarinet, collage by Georges Braque   **C** 376
Clarinet, musical instrument   **C** 329; **M** 549
ancient instrument   **A** 245
orchestra seating plan   **O** 186

Clark, Abraham (Congress Abraham) (1726–94), American political leader, b. Elizabethtown, N.J. An early supporter of the Revolution, he joined the New Jersey Committee of Safety (1774) and was a member of the New Jersey Provincial Congress (1775). He sat in the Continental Congress (1776–78, 1779–83), signed the Declaration of Independence (1776), and served in the U.S. House of Representatives (1791–94).

Clark, Ann Nolan (1898–   ), American author and educator, b. Las Vegas, N.Mex. She worked for the Bureau of Indian Affairs, concerning herself with the education of American Indians. She was a U.S. delegate to the UNESCO Conference in Brazil. Her works include *Secret of the Andes,* which won the Newbery medal (1952) and *In the Land of Small Dragon* (1979).

Clark, Champ, American statesman   **M** 380
Clark, Charles Badger, American poet   **S** 325
Clark, Charles Joseph, prime minister of Canada **C** 330, 75; **T** 297
Clark, George Rogers, American Revolutionary War leader and explorer   **K** 225
capture of Vincennes, 1779   **I** 150
Clark and his Long Knives win Illinois territory from British   **I** 85–86
Revolutionary War   **R** 204–05

Clark, Jimmy (James Clark) (1936–68), Scottish automobile racer, b. Fife Co., Scotland. He began driving junior cars in the 1950's. He won the Grand Prix Championship (1963, 1965), as well as the Indianapolis 500 (1965). He died in a crash at Hockenheim, W. Germany.

Clark, Kenneth Bancroft (1914–   ), American educator and psychologist, b. Panama Canal Zone. A professor at the College of the City of New York, he was a founder of the Northside Center for Child Development and of Harlem Youth Opportunities Unlimited (HARYOU). His book *Desegregation: An Appraisal of the Evidence,* about the effects of racial discrimination upon black and white children, was cited by the United States Supreme Court in its 1954 school desegregation ruling. His other books include *Prejudice and Your Child* and *Dark Ghetto.*

Clark, Sir Kenneth (MacKenzie) (1903–83), English art historian, author, and expert on Italian Renaissance art, b. London. Clark was director of the National Gallery, London (1934–45), a professor at Oxford (1946–50, 1961–62), and head of the Arts Council of Great Britain (1953–60).

His books include *The Nude: A Study in Ideal Form* (1956), *The Romantic Rebellion* (1974), and *Another Part of the Wood* (1975) and *The Other Half* (1978), his autobiography. The highly successful television series *Civilisation* confirmed his reputation as a leading authority on art and culture.

Clark, Mark Wayne (1896–   ), U.S. Army officer, b. Madison Barracks, N.Y. He commanded 5th Army Group, including all Allied fighting forces in Italy (1944–45). He was commander in chief, U.S. Occupation Forces in Austria (1945–47) and UN commander in Korea (1952–53), succeeding General Matthew B. Ridgway. He signed Korean peace treaty (1953). He was president of The Citadel (the Military College of South Carolina) (1954–65), and has written *Calculated Risk* and *From the Danube to the Yalu.*

Clark, Ron, American balloonist   **B** 32

Clark, Thomas Campbell (1899–1977), American Supreme Court justice, b. Dallas, Tex. He was the co-ordinator of alien enemy control in the Western Defense Command during World War II. After serving as U.S. attorney general from 1945 to 1949, he was a justice of the U.S. Supreme Court until 1967. He retired when his son, **Ramsey Clark** (1927–   ), became U.S. attorney general. Ramsey Clark held that post from 1967 to 1969 and then practiced law in New York City.   **T** 136

Clark, William, American explorer   **L** 162
   Idaho   **I** 54
   Missouri   **M** 379

Clarke, Arthur Charles (1917–   ), English astronomer and science-fiction writer, b. Minehead. He was one of the first persons to suggest the use of artificial satellites for international communication (1945). With a partner, Mike Wilson, he conducted undersea exploration of Australia's Great Barrier Reef. His books include nonfiction, such as *The Exploration of Space* and *Profiles of the Future*, and such fictional works as *Childhood's End, Rendezvous with Rama,* and the screenplay for the film *2001: A Space Odyssey.*

Clarke, Charles Cowden, English scholar   **K** 200
Clarke, Richard W. *see* Deadwood Dick
Clarksburg, West Virginia   **W** 132

Class action, a type of lawsuit in which a few persons represent a large group of people with the same legal problem. Class actions are often brought in consumer rights cases. The outcome of a class action affects all those who belong to the group.

Class distinction
   clothing   **C** 351–52
   France before the Revolution   **F** 462
   Marx's analysis of   **M** 114
Classes, divisions of biological classification   **T** 29
Classical Age, in Greek art   **G** 345–46
   art as a record   **A** 438b
Classical age in music   **C** 330–33
   German composers   **G** 184–85
   Mozart   **M** 502
   orchestra   **O** 184
   sonatas   **M** 539
   symphony   **M** 540
   See also Romantic age in music
Classical art *see* Greek art; Roman art

Classical conditioning, in learning   **L** 99
Classical literature *see* Greek literature; Latin literature
Classical mathematics   **M** 156
Classicism (CLASS-i-cism)
   French literature   **F** 437–38
Classics in literature   **C** 334
   paperback editions   **P** 58a
   types of literature   **L** 313–14
Classification (class-i-fi-CAY-tion), in biology   **B** 191
   insects, orders of, *chart*   **I** 280
   kingdoms of living things   **K** 249–52
   Linnaeus, Carolus   **L** 304
   mammals, orders of, *chart*   **M** 62
   races, human   **R** 29–32
   See also Taxonomy
Class numbers, of books in libraries   **L** 184
Classrooms
   kindergarten and nursery schools   **K** 245
   schools   **S** 55–58
Class struggle
   Communism, ideas of   **C** 442–43; **M** 114
Claudel (clo-DEL), **Paul,** French poet and dramatist   **D** 298; **F** 441
Claude Lorrain (CLODE lo-RAN) (Claude Gellée), French painter   **B** 60; **F** 442, 425
   Landscape with the Flight into Egypt, painting   **B** 58
   View of Harbor, painting   **F** 423
Claudius I, Roman emperor   **R** 304
   conquest of Britain   **E** 215
Claudius Caecus, Appius, Roman official   **E** 208

Clausius (CLOW-ze-us), **Rudolf Julius Emanuel** (1822–88), German physicist, b. Köslin, Germany (now Poland). Best known for his work on the different ways gas molecules can move, he founded the science of thermodynamics (the relation of the energy of motion to heat energy). He was the first to state the second law of thermodynamics: Heat cannot pass by itself from a colder to a hotter body. He was the first also to present a way to calculate entropy (the amount of energy no longer available for work in physical systems, such as steam engines).
   physics, history of   **P** 234

Claustrophobia, fear of enclosed places   **H** 318
Clavichord (CLAV-i-cord), keyboard instrument   **K** 237–38; **M** 547
Clavier, The Well-Tempered, by Bach   **B** 5

Clavilux (from Latin words *clavis,* meaning "key," and *lux,* meaning "light"), instrument exhibited (1922) by Thomas Wilfred for creating art form called lumia, or color music. A complex keyboard controls form, color, and motion of light, which is projected on screen in moving patterns. Compositions are sometimes performed to musical accompaniment.

Clavius (CLA-vi-us), **Christopher,** Bavarian astronomer   **C** 12; **M** 450
Claws
   bats   **B** 92
   cats   **C** 134
   crustacea   **S** 170, 171
Clay   **S** 231
   aluminum   **A** 176
   ancient cities built with clay   **A** 218
   archeological dating   **A** 362
   bricks   **B** 390–93, 430
   ceramics   **C** 178–80
   clay modeling   **C** 336–37

Clay (continued)
pottery clay **F** 142–43; **P** 413
sculptors' material **S** 90–91
tablets for writing **A** 218–19, 222
Clay, Cassius Marcellus, Jr. *see* Ali, Muhammad
Clay, Henry, American orator and statesman **C** 335
Adams, John Quincy, and Clay **A** 16
Compromise of 1850 **C** 448
Missouri Compromise **M** 382
nullification crisis **J** 7
opposes statehood for Texas **P** 384–85
personal and political feud with Tyler **T** 339, 341
slavery question **S** 199

Clay, Lucius DuBignon (1897–1978), American army officer, b. Marietta, Ga. He was military governor of the American Zone and commander of the U.S. Occupation Forces in Germany (1947–49), as well as commander in chief of the European Command (1947). He helped organize the Berlin Airlift, which counteracted the Soviet blockade of that city (1948–49), and helped draft the constitution of West Germany (1949). He wrote *Decision in Germany,* about the postwar years.

Clayburgh, Jill, American actress **M** 488c
Clay modeling C 336–37
See also Ceramics; Pottery
Clay pigeons, for trapshooting **T** 268
Clay tablets A 218–19, 222
libraries **L** 192–93
Clayton Antitrust Act, 1914 **T** 306
Wilson's domestic policies **W** 179
Clayton-Bulwer Treaty, 1850 **T** 36
Clean Air Acts, United States laws **A** 111
Cleanliness
baths and bathing **B** 91
hair **H** 3, 84–85
health **H** 82–85
Clean rooms, atmosphere-controlled areas for atomic technology **D** 339
Clean Water Act, 1977 **W** 69
Clear-cutting, of timber **L** 374
Clearinghouse, for checks in banking, *diagram* **B** 46
Clearing of land, by pioneers **P** 252
Clearstory, in architecture *see* Clerestory

Cleary, Beverly (1916–   ), American children's author, b. McMinnville, Oreg. She was a children's librarian before becoming a writer. Her first book, *Henry Huggins* (1950) was a great success. Her other books include *Fifteen* (1956), *Henry and the Clubhouse* (1962), *Runaway Ralph* (1970), and *Ramona and Her Mother,* which won an American Book Award in 1981. Cleary won the Laura Ingalls Wilder award in 1975 for her "lasting contribution to literature for children."

Cleavage, cell division **E** 90
Cleavage, of minerals **R** 270
Cleaveland, Moses, American pioneer, founded Cleveland, Ohio **C** 338
Cleaver, Bill and **Vera,** American authors **C** 242

Cleaver, Eldridge (Leroy Eldridge Cleaver) (1935–   ), American author and former Black Panther leader, b. Wabbaseka, Ark. He wrote his autobiography, *Soul on Ice,* while serving a prison term for assault. Paroled in 1966, he joined the Black Panthers (1967) and served as their minister of information. Following a new charge of attempted murder and assault, he fled to Cuba, then to Algeria and France. In 1975 he returned to the United States. He told of his years in exile and of his conversion to Christianity in *Soul on Fire* (1978).

Clefs, in musical notation **M** 524, 525, 533
Cleft palate (PAL-at), a mouth deformity **H** 27
Clemenceau (CLAI-mon-so), **Georges,** French publisher and statesman **C** 337; *pictures* **P** 456a, **W** 180, 270
France in World War I **F** 419
Paris Peace Conference, 1919 **W** 282
Clemens, Samuel Langhorne *see* Twain, Mark
Clement III (CLEM-ent), antipope **R** 297
Clement VII, antipope **R** 297

Clement I, Saint (Clement of Rome), pope (90?–99?), third successor to Saint Peter as bishop of Rome. He is believed to have been the Clement cited by Paul in Philippians (4:3). The only work definitely known as his is the first Epistle to the Corinthians. **R** 296

Clement II, pope **R** 297
Clement III, pope **R** 297
Clement IV, pope **R** 297
Clement V, pope **R** 293, 297
France held the papacy under Clement **F** 415
Clement VI, pope **R** 297

Clement VII (Giulio de' Medici) (1478–1534), pope (1523–34), b. Florence, Italy. An Avignon pope, he joined the Holy League of Cognac (1526) with France, Venice, and Milan against Charles V, but he crowned Charles emperor in 1530. He refused (1534) to sanction the divorce of Henry VIII of England, causing a split between the Church of England and Rome. **R** 297
Christianity, history of **C** 286

Clement VIII, pope **R** 297
Clement IX, pope **R** 297
Clement X, pope **R** 297
Clement XI, pope **R** 297
Clement XII, pope **R** 297
Clement XIII, pope **R** 297
Clement XIV, pope **R** 297
Clement, Rene, French motion picture director **M** 488

Clemente, Roberto (1934–72), American baseball player, b. Puerto Rico. Clemente, a star outfielder with the Pittsburgh Pirates and a national hero in his homeland, was the eleventh player in baseball history to get 3,000 hits. He was killed in an airplane that crashed while attempting to carry supplies to earthquake victims in Nicaragua. Clemente was elected to the National Baseball Hall of Fame in 1973. **B** 81

Clementi, Muzio, Italian composer **I** 485
Clements Mountain, Glacier National Park, Montana, *picture* **G** 222

Cleopatra (cle-o-PAT-ra) (69–30 B.C.), last Macedonian queen of Egypt, b. Alexandria. She ruled with Ptolemy XII, her brother and husband, and later with Ptolemy XIII, another brother whom she married. Cleopatra became favorite of Julius Caesar and Mark Antony, with whom she met defeat at Actium (31 B.C.). Rather than submit to victorious Octavian, she killed herself (according to legend, with an asp). She is heroine of Shakespeare's *Antony and Cleopatra.*
Caesar and Mark Antony **C** 6; **M** 100
cosmetics and perfumes **C** 510; **P** 154

motion pictures about **M** 488a; scenes, *pictures* **M** 477

Ptolemaic rulers of Egypt **E** 91

Cleopatra makeup, *picture* **P** 340

Cleopata's Needle, ancient Egyptian obelisk **O** 6

Egyptian art **E** 95

in London **L** 337

Clepsydras (water clocks) **W** 45

Clerestory (CLERE-story), part of a church **A** 376; **E** 234; *diagram* **A** 379

Clergy, persons ordained for religious service

kings versus clergy in English history **E** 219

Clermont, first steamboat **F** 491

Clervaux (clair-VO), Luxembourg, *picture* **L** 379

Cletus, Saint, pope **R** 296

Cleveland, Frances Folsom, wife of Grover Cleveland **F** 175; *pictures* **C** 340, **F** 174

Cleveland, Grover, 22nd and 24th president of the United States **C** 339–42

New York, governor of **N** 226

Cleveland, Mount, highest peak in Glacier National Park, Montana **G** 221

Cleveland, Ohio **C** 338; **O** 65, 68, 71

Cleveland, Rose, acting first lady in Cleveland's first administration **F** 175

Clewiston, Lake, Florida **F** 267

Cliburn (CLY-burn), **Van** (Harvey Lavan Cliburn, Jr.) (1934–), American pianist, b. Shreveport, La. In 1948 he made his Carnegie Hall debut as the winner of the National Music Festival Award. He gained world fame by winning the International Tchaikovsky Piano Competition in Moscow in 1958. Noted for his interpretations of the works of Romantic composers, he has made many concert tours. In 1962 he established the Van Cliburn International Piano Competition in Fort Worth, Texas.

Click beetles **P** 284–85

Cliff dwellers, ancestors of Pueblo Indians **C** 415

Arizona **A** 414, 415

Indian Cliff Palace, Mesa Verde, *pictures* **A** 353, **C** 413

Clifton, Lucille, American writer **C** 243

Climate **C** 343–48; **W** 89–90

altitude creates zones of climate **Z** 372–73

artificial in botanical gardens **Z** 379

atmosphere **A** 479–82

climatic barriers to spread of life **L** 235

climatology, study of world climate **G** 108

clothing and climate **C** 351

dinosaur's extinction is possibly the result of changes in **D** 180-81

effects of dust from volcanic eruptions **D** 347–48

equator areas **E** 272h

fruitgrowing **F** 481–82

gardening to suit climates **G** 30, 52

homes adapted to **H** 168–70

how shown on maps **W** 77–79; *picture* **M** 92

ice ages **I** 13–24

microclimates **C** 347

modified by lakes **L** 26

mountains influence climate **M** 497

ocean currents **G** 110; **O** 32–33; **W** 88

polar regions **P** 363–71

prairies **P** 430

rain forests **R** 99–100

seasons **S** 108–12

soils, effect on **S** 233

taiga **T** 10–11

trade winds **T** 246

tropics **T** 294

vegetables, cool- and warm-season crops **V** 287–88

weather and climate **W** 71, 87–89

winds and weather **W** 184–87

world climates and vegetation patterns, *diagram* **W** 256

world rainfall **R** 94–95

zones, a simple classification of climate **Z** 372–73

See also Weather; continent, country, province, and state articles

Climate maps **W** 77–79

Climatologists, scientists who study climate **C** 343

Climatology (cli-ma-TOL-ogy), study of climate **C** 343; **G** 108

Climatron, The, botanical garden, *picture* **Z** 373

Climax, Colorado

observatory **O** 9

Climbing

animals: locomotion **A** 294

snakes, concertina climbing **S** 211

Clingstone peach **P** 106

Clinical microscopy (my-CROSC-opy), division of a medical laboratory **M** 201

Clinton, De Witt, American statesman **N** 223

Erie Canal promoted by **E** 276–77

Clinton, George, vice-president, United States **N** 223; **V** 330; *picture* **V** 325

Clinton, Sir Henry, English military commander **R** 204, 206, 207; **W** 40

correspondence with Benedict Arnold **A** 436

Clinton, William J. (Bill) (1946–), governor of Arkansas, Democrat, b. Hope. Clinton was elected attorney general of Arkansas in 1976. In 1978 he was elected governor of the state, becoming the youngest governor in the nation. Before his election as attorney general, Clinton was on the staff of the University of Arkansas School of Law.

Clio (CLY-o), goddess in Greek mythology. She was the daughter of Zeus and Mnemosyne, and the muse of history. Led by Apollo, she and her sisters were the nine muses, or patrons of the arts and sciences. Her symbols were the laurel wreath and the scroll.

See also Muses

Clip, containers for cartridges **G** 422

Clipper ships (Yankee clippers), sailing ships **S** 159–60; *pictures* **S** 156, **T** 263

importance to transportation **T** 261

United States Merchant Marine **U** 183

Clips, as jewelry **J** 99

Clitellum (clit-EL-lum), section of a worm **W** 309

Clive, Robert (Baron Clive of Plassey) (1725–74), British soldier and colonial administrator, b. Styche, Shropshire. He went to Madras, India (1743), as writer for East India Company and distinguished himself in Britain's struggle for domination of India. Clive established British supremacy in Bengal in victory at Plassey (1757) over superior forces of nawab of Bengal and French auxiliaries. As governor of Bengal (1764–67), he instituted many reforms and strengthened British rule in India. He was attacked for corrupt practices upon his return to England and finally committed suicide.

East India Company and European penetration of India **E** 37; **I** 133

Cloaca Maxima (clo-A-ca MAX-im-a), sewer of Rome **M** 204

Clock-bells B 137
Clocks W 44–50
  astronomical clocks, *picture* O 9
  Big Ben, London L 335
  Bristol Clock Museum, Connecticut C 476
  built-in biological mechanisms L 247–50
  chronometers in navigation N 66
  Connecticut industry C 473
  correct time T 192–93
  early inventions I 346
  grandfather clock W 47; *pictures* C 389, W 46
  ormolu clock, *picture* D 75
  pendulum clocks W 46–47
  water clocks W 44, 45, 71
  See also Calendars
Clocks, biological *see* Biological clocks
Cloisonné (clwa-son-NAY), enameling technique
  E 188; *picture* E 189
  decorative arts D 72
Cloister, part of a monastery A 379
Cloisters, museum, New York City M 237

Clone, a group of living organisms produced from a single organism by cell division. Each member of a clone is identical to the parent. Many one-celled plants and animals reproduce by cell division, but higher animals and most higher plants reproduce through the union of male and female cells. Frogs have been cloned in scientific experiments, but attempts to clone higher forms of life have been largely unsuccessful.

Clontarf, Battle of, 1014 I 390
Closed shop *see* Open and closed shop
Close-up lenses, for cameras P 204, 205
Closure *see* Cloture
Cloth *see* Fabrics; Textiles
Clothes driers, electric E 120
Clothes moths, insects H 261; *picture* H 263
Clothing C 348–57
  air-cooled suit, *picture* A 101
  ancient invention I 347
  buttons B 478–80
  camping C 41, 43
  climate and clothing C 343
  colonial American C 390; *picture* C 391
  dressmaking D 311–15
  dry-cleaning process D 337–39
  dyes and dyeing D 366–72
  Easter symbols E 35–36
  Eskimo E 288
  fashion F 65–71
  fibers F 104–08
  furs, a sign of social importance F 511
  gaucho, or cowboy, of Argentina A 389; *picture* A 391
  gloves G 240–41
  hats and hat making H 53–55
  home economics training H 164–65
  ice-skating equipment I 46–47, 51
  laundry L 84–85
  Metropolitan Museum of Art Costume Institute M 237
  modeling, fashion M 384
  pioneer life P 256
  poverty means inadequate clothing P 424, 424a
  rubberizing process R 341
  sewing S 128a–128b
  shoes S 162–63
  textiles T 140–45
  wool clothing W 235

  See also Costume; Fans; Uniforms; people section of continent and country articles
Clothing industry C 353–54, 356
  Amalgamated Clothing Workers of America C 354
  computer-guided lasers cut through many layers of cloth, *picture* L 46d
  garment center, New York City N 231
  Industrial Revolution and new inventions I 233–41
  International Ladies' Garment Workers' Union C 354
  showroom modeling M 384–85
Clotting, of blood B 257
  vitamin K V 371
Cloture, limitation of debate in a legislative body by calling for a vote
  See also Filibuster
Cloud chamber, to detect radioactivity A 489
  cosmic rays C 512
  ions and ionization I 353
Clouded leopards L 155
  cat family C 138
Clouds C 358–61
  climate C 343
  dust affects formation of D 348
  fog and smog F 288–89
  hail-producing cumulonimbus clouds R 98
  mistaken for flying saucers, *pictures* F 285, 287
  thunder and lightning T 170–72
  Venus P 270, 271
  weather and climate W 76, 80
  See also Atmosphere; Rain and rainfall
Clouet (cloo-AY), Jean, French painter F 422
Clouzot, Henri-Georges, French motion picture director M 488
Clove (ratline) hitch, knot K 292
Cloven-hoofed animals F 82; H 206, 208–09; *picture* F 80
Clover, plant
  wonder crop in agriculture A 96
Cloverleaf crossings, on roads R 250; *picture* R 248
Cloves, spice S 382; *picture* S 381
  Zanzibar is world's leading producer T 18
Clovis I, king of the Franks F 415
Clown fish F 204
Clowns
  circus C 300; *pictures* C 301, 303
  rodeos R 281
Clowns, ballet, *picture* D 33
Club fungi F 498
Club mosses P 304; *picture* P 292
Clubs
  Boys' Clubs of America B 355
  Boy Scouts B 356–60
  Camp Fire, Inc. C 37–39
  4–H clubs F 396–396a
  Future Farmers of America F 524
  Girl Guides and Girl Scouts G 213–19
  Girls Clubs G 220
  Junior Achievement, Inc. J 157–58
  parliamentary procedure P 79–80
  reading clubs L 171–72; P 514
  Student Action for Education T 41–42
Clubs, golf implements G 254
Cluj (CLOOJ), Rumania R 357
Cluniacs, monks C 284
Cluny lace L 19
Cluster plan, of housing developments H 184
Clutch, coupling between parts of a mechanism
  transmissions T 255–56
Clydesdale horse, *picture* H 240

Clymer, George (1739–1813), American merchant and politician, b. Philadelphia, Pa. An active revolutionist, he sat in the Continental Congress, serving on war and treasury boards (1776–78, 1780–83), and signed the Declaration of Independence (1776) and U.S. Constitution (1788).

Clytie, in Greek mythology, a water nymph who loved Apollo, the sun god, in vain and daily watched his chariot cross the sky. The gods took pity on her and changed her into a sunflower that constantly turns toward the sun.

Cnossus see Knossos
CN Tower, Toronto, Canada **T** 227
Coaches, in sports
  famous college football coaches **F** 364–65
Coaches see Wagons, carts, carriages and coaches
Coahuiltecs (co-a-hu-EEL-tecs), Indians of North
    America **I** 177
Coal and coal mining **C** 362–68; **F** 487; *pictures*
    M 319, 320
  acid rain **A** 9
  atomic energy released in burning **A** 489
  blasting **E** 394, 395; *picture* **E** 393
  carbon, form of **C** 106
  China's anthracite deposits **A** 450
  coal barges, *picture* **G** 155
  coal-producing regions of North America **N** 294
  energy supply **E** 202a–202b
  English coal-mining town of 19th century, *picture*
    E 226
  Europe's resources **E** 311
  Germany's major resource **G** 155
  heating with stoves **H** 97
  importance to Industrial Revolution **I** 236–37
  kerosene obtained by gasification of **K** 235
  poverty in Appalachia **P** 424a–424b
  Union of Soviet Socialist Republics **U** 34
  United Kingdom **U** 72, 74
  world distribution **W** 261
  world distribution of coal is an evidence of
    continental drift **G** 111
Coalescence (co-a-LES-cence), of cloud droplets
  causes of precipitation **W** 76
Coal gas **F** 488–89
  fuel for early automobiles **A** 542
Coaling stations
  Pacific islands **T** 114
Coalition (co-al-ISH-on) **governments** **P** 382
  prime ministers **P** 456
Coal oil see Kerosene
Coalsack, nebula **N** 98
Coal tar, sticky black liquid left from distillation of coal
  cancer-causing agent **C** 91
  dyes made from **D** 370
Coastal Plain, North America **U** 89
Coaster car race see Soap Box Derby
Coast Guard see United States Coast Guard
Coast Guard Academy, New London, Connecticut
    U 176
Coast Guard Auxiliary **U** 176
Coast Mountains
  Alaska **A** 130–31
  Canada **C** 51
Coast Ranges, North America
  California **C** 16, 18
Coated abrasives **G** 387, 389
Coated steels **I** 402–03, 406
Coatings, chemical
  plastics **P** 330–31

Coatis (co-OT-is), animals related to raccoons **R** 26–27
Coat of many colors, given to Joseph **J** 140
Coats of arms **H** 115–18
  knights, knighthood, and chivalry **K** 272
  Washington's **F** 244

Coatsworth, Elizabeth (Elizabeth Coatsworth Beston) (1893–   ), American author of children's books, b. Buffalo, N.Y. She won the Newbery Medal (1931) for *The Cat Who Went to Heaven,* a story reflecting her interest in the life and legends of Buddha. She also wrote many stories set in New England, such as *Jock's Island.*

Coaxial (co-AX-ial) **cables** **E** 142d
  cable TV **E** 142c
  telephones **T** 59, 60
  television **T** 67
Cobalt (CO-balt), element **E** 154, 160
  metals, chart of ores, location, properties, uses
    M 227
  radioactive cobalt in cancer treatment **C** 91
  steel **I** 396
  Zaïre is world's principal supplier **A** 53

Cobb, Irvin Shrewsbury (1876–1944), American author and humorist, b. Paducah, Ky. As journalist, he worked on New York *World* (1905–11). *Saturday Evening Post* (1911–22), and *Cosmopolitan* magazine (1922–32). He also acted in films and was noted after-dinner speaker. Cobb won first O. Henry short-story award (1922).

Cobb, Ty (Tyrus Raymond Cobb) (1886–1961), American baseball player, b. Narrows, Ga. Cobb, who was nicknamed the Georgia Peach, was one of the greatest baseball players of all time. He had the most hits (4,191) and the highest lifetime batting average (.367) in baseball history. He led the American League in hitting 12 times and stole 892 bases during his career. Cobb was an outfielder for 24 seasons. During most of his career, he played for the Detroit Tigers (1905–26), but he spent his last two years (1927–28) with the Philadelphia Athletics. He was elected in 1936 as one of the five original members of the National Baseball Hall of Fame. *picture* **B** 81

Cobblers see Shoemakers
COBOL, language in computer programming **C** 457
Cobras (CO-bras), snakes **S** 207–08; *picture* **S** 206
  mongooses kill and eat **G** 95; *picture* **G** 94
  with snake charmer, *picture* **A** 275
Coca (CO-ca), shrub, leaves yielding cocaine **B** 303;
    picture **D** 327
  Peruvian Indians use **P** 161
Cocaine, drug **P** 314
  drugs as stimulants **D** 330
Coccus, bacterium **B** 10
Cochabamba (co-cha-BOM-ba), Bolivia **B** 306
Cochineal (COCH-in-eal), dye made from insects' bodies
    D 369
  cochineal insect, *picture* **D** 367

Cochise (?–1874), American Indian, chief of Chiricahua Apaches of southwestern United States. After he and other chiefs were captured while under flag of truce and tortured by U.S. Army officer, he campaigned to drive white men from territory. Cochise finally surrendered (1871) and lived on Chiricahua reservation established (1872) in Arizona. **I** 195

Cochlea (COC-le-a), inner ear **B** 285, 288

Cochran, Barbara, American skier **O** 115

Cochran (COCK-ran), **Jacqueline** (Jacqueline Cochran Odlum) (1910?–80), American flier and business leader, b. Pensacola, Fla. Jacqueline Cochran received her pilot's license in 1932 and became one of the best-known fliers of her time. She was the first woman to enter national and international air races, to ferry a bomber to England, and to fly faster than the speed of sound. In World War II she organized and headed the Women's Airforce Service Pilots (WASPs). She married the financier Floyd B. Odlum in 1936. In the business world, she headed a cosmetics firm named for her. She told the story of her life in *The Stars at Noon* (1954).

Cockatoo, bird **P** 85; *picture* **P** 84
Cockerels, young roosters, *picture* **P** 421

Cocker spaniel, a small bird-hunting dog named for its skill in hunting woodcocks. The breed is very old and was first shown in England in 1883. The American cocker spaniel stands about 40 cm (15 in) high at the shoulder. The English variety is slightly larger. The soft, curly coat may be black, buff, red, liver, black and white, black and tan, or tricolor. Cocker spaniels are popular as pets.
    sporting dogs, *picture* **D** 253

Cockfighting
    Cuba **C** 548
Cockle, mollusk, *picture* **S** 147
Cockneys, Londoners **L** 333–34
Cockroaches, insects **H** 262; *picture* **H** 263
    ant colony dwellers **A** 325
    conditioned responses **A** 283
Cocks, kind of valve **V** 269
Cockscomb Mountains, Belize **B** 132
Cocks-of-the-rock *see* Cotingas
Cocoa **C** 274–75
    Ghana **G** 195–96
    stain removal **L** 84
Cocoa butter **C** 274, 275
    oils and fats **O** 76
    use in cosmetics **C** 509
Coconut, fruit of the coconut palm **C** 368–69
    seed, cut section, *picture* **P** 298
    seed dispersal **F** 281
Coconut oil **O** 76
Coconut palm, tree, *pictures* **L** 234, **T** 276
    copra **C** 369; **P** 5
    Philippines, called tree of life in **P** 187
Cocoons (coc-OONS), of insects **I** 264–65, 279
    ants **A** 323
    bees **B** 123
    butterflies and moths **B** 470
    how made by silkworms **S** 179
Cocos Islands, Indian Ocean **A** 495

Cocteau (kok-TO), **Jean** (1889–1963), French writer and artist, b. Maisons-Laffitte. His work in drama, novels, films, and art was considered highly original. His plays *Antigone* (1922) and *La machine infernale* (1934) were based on ancient Greek legends. *Les enfants terribles* (1929), a story of troubled adolescents, is his best-known novel. His films, which often blend fantasy and reality, include *The Blood of a Poet* (1932) and *Beauty and the Beast* (1945). Cocteau was elected to the French Academy in 1955. Some of his autobiographical works were collected in *Professional Secrets* (1970). **F** 442

Cod, fish **F** 222–23

    egg laying of **E** 89
    fishing the Grand Banks **C** 57, 68
    habitat, feeding habits, uses **F** 213
    Massachusetts **M** 134
Coda (final section), in a sonata cycle **M** 533, 539

Coddington, William (1601–78), American colonial leader, b. Boston, England. He arrived in Massachusetts Bay colony (1630) and moved to Aquidneck (R.I.) (1638) after dispute with Massachusetts authorities regarding colony's lack of religious freedom. He founded Pocasset (Portsmouth) and then Newport. **R** 226

Codeine (CO-dene), narcotic drug **N** 12
Code Napoléon *see* Napoleonic code
Code of Terpsichore, by Carlo Blasis **D** 25
Codes, of honor
    knight's code **K** 274–75, 277
Codes, of law
    canon law **L** 87
    Hammurabi **A** 219; **L** 87; *picture* **A** 218
    Louisiana's legal system based on Napoleonic Code
        L 348–49
    Napoleonic Code **N** 10
    See also Justinian's Code
Codes, radio and telegraphic
    International Morse Code **R** 63
Codes, secret writing **C** 369–71
    coded legend used with the Ten Commandments
        E 1
Codex (CO-dex), early Roman book **B** 319; **L** 194; *picture* **B** 218
Codicils (COD-i-cils), additions to wills **W** 175
Codling moths **A** 335
C.O.D. mail delivery service **P** 410
Cod wars, conflict between Iceland and Great Britain
    over coastal fishing limits **I** 45
Cody, William Frederick *see* Buffalo Bill

Coe, Sebastian (1956–   ), British runner, b. London. Coe is an extremely talented and versatile middle-distance runner. Within 41 days during 1979, he set three world records—in the 800-meter run, the 1,500-meter run, and the mile. In the 1980 Olympics, he was the gold medalist at 1,500 meters and the silver medalist at 800 meters. At the end of 1983, Coe held the world record at 800 meters (1 min. 41.73 sec.), 1,000 meters (2 min. 12.18 sec.), and the mile (3 min. 47.33 sec.). **O** 116b; *picture* **O** 116c

Co-education
    universities and colleges **U** 205–24
Coelacanths (CE-la-canths), lobe-finned fishes **F** 183; *picture* **F** 182
Coelenterates (ce-LEN-ter-ates), jellyfishes **J** 70–75
    coral polyps **C** 503–04
Coelophysis (ce-LO-phis-is), genus of dinosaurs
    D 173–74
Coelostats (CE-lo-stats), for observing the sun **S** 466
Coenzyme (co-EN-zyme), in body chemistry **B** 294
Coetzee, Gerrie, South African boxer **B** 353

Co-existence, living together or at the same time. The word usually refers to nations that, in spite of widely differing beliefs and policies, manage to maintain diplomatic and trade relations and to refrain from outright conflict.

Coffee **C** 371–74; **E** 300
    Brazil, important crop in **B** 378, 383; **S** 36; *picture* **B** 382

Central American export crop **C** 175
Colombian farms **C** 380, 382; *picture* **C** 372
Costa Rican plantation workers, *picture* **A** 97
El Salvador's major export **E** 182
fruits we eat **P** 308; *picture* **P** 309
Guatemala **G** 392; *picture* **G** 394
northern African crop carried to Brazil and Indonesia
    A 100
Vienna's coffee **V** 332j
world distribution, *diagram* **W** 266
Coffeehouses **C** 371
Austria **A** 520
established in England **R** 186
Coffeepot, antique, *picture* **A** 319
Coffeepot, guessing game **I** 226
Coffee rust, disease of coffee plants **C** 371, 373
Coffee tree
Kentucky, state tree of, *picture* **K** 213
Cofferdams, temporary structures **D** 18
Coffin, Levi, American abolitionist **N** 320; **U** 12
abolitionist movement **B** 250f

Coffin, Robert Peter Tristram (1892–1955), American
writer, b. Brunswick, Maine. He wrote mainly about his
native state. His books of verse include *Strange Holiness,*
for which he was awarded a Pulitzer prize (1935), and
Primer for America.

Coghlan, Eamonn (A-mun COG-lin) (1952–   ), Irish
runner, b. Dublin. Known for his powerful kick—the final
sprint to the finish line—Coghlan ranks among the world's
best middle-distance and distance runners. He is particu-
larly effective running in indoor meets, and in 1983 he
became the first person in history to run the indoor mile in
less than 3 min. 50 sec., with a time of 3 min. 49.78 sec.
At the first World Track and Field Championships, held in
Helsinki, Finland, in 1983, Coghlan was the gold medalist
in the 5,000-meter run.

Cohan, George M., American actor-songwriter **R** 225
musical comedy **M** 542
national anthems and patriotic songs **N** 26
Cohen, Isidore, American violinist, *picture* **C** 185
Cohen, Leonard, Canadian writer and performer **C** 64
Coherent (co-HE-rent) **light** **P** 239
lasers **L** 46b, 46c
Cohesion (co-HE-sion), in physics **L** 310
discoveries of the properties of liquids **P** 233
Coils, induction **E** 131–32
electric generators **E** 121
Coimbra (co-EEM-bra), Portugal **P** 401
Coin bank, *picture* **A** 320
Coin laundries **L** 84
Coin-operated machines *see* Vending machines
Coins and coin collecting **C** 374–75
ancient Roman, *pictures* **A** 232
history of coins **M** 411
mint is place where money is coined **M** 338
nickel **N** 250
silver **S** 181–82
stamped out by coining dies **D** 166, 167
Why do people throw coins into fountains? **F** 395
Coin shift, trick **T** 288
Coir, fiber of coconut husk **C** 369; **F** 106
Coke **C** 363, 364, 367
carbon, form of **C** 106
fuel **F** 488
use in processing of iron and steel **I** 397, 404

Coke (COOK), **Sir Edward** (Lord Coke) (1552–1634), En-
glish jurist, b. Mileham, Norfolk. He was chief justice of
the Court of Common Pleas (1606) and chief justice of the
King's Bench (1613). His conflict with James I and Fran-
cis Bacon over royal prerogative resulted in his suspension
from council and loss of his right to exercise judicial duties
(1616). He is famous in legal history for having upheld
supremacy of law over royal power, thus laying the foun-
dation for the principle of constitutional supremacy in
democratic government.

Coker, David R., American plant specialist **S** 297
Coking properties **C** 364

Colbert (col-BARE), **Jean Baptiste** (1619–83), French
statesman, b. Rheims. Financial minister (1661–83) to
Louis XIV, he worked for France's economic independence
by encouraging industry, regulating tariffs, and developing
strong navy. He became unpopular when forced to
increase taxes to finance Louis XIV's extravagances. Col-
bert was a patron of the arts and sciences and founded
several academies, including the Académie des Inscrip-
tions and Académie des Sciences (1666).
set up state-owned Gobelins rug and tapestry work-
    shops **R** 351–52; **T** 24

Cold, common *see* Common cold
Cold, meaning "having little heat" **H** 86d
anthropological study of Alakaluf Indians **A** 306–07
body's sense of **B** 287
climate **C** 343–48
matter's reaction to cold **M** 177
refrigeration **R** 134–36
Cold-blooded animals **B** 259
dinosaurs **D** 172
fishes, temperature of **F** 187
hibernation **H** 123
reptiles **R** 180–81
snakes **S** 204–14
turtles **T** 334
Cold chisels, tools **T** 213
Cold cream, cosmetics **C** 510
invention of **B** 111
Cold drawing, steel process **I** 401
Cold front, in meteorology **W** 76; *diagram* **W** 77
Cold light *see* Bioluminescence
Cold-rolling, of metals
bronze and brass **B** 410
steel production **I** 402, 406
Cold storage of food *see* Cool storage of food
Cold type composition, in printing **N** 203–04; **P** 465
Cold War, in international relations **C** 445; **I** 325
disagreements over division of Germany **G** 163
Kennedy, John F. **K** 209–10
Stalin's seizure of lands in Eastern Europe **S** 395
Union of Soviet Socialist Republics **U** 51
Cold-water suits, for skin diving **S** 190

Cole, Nat "King" (Nathaniel Adams Coles) (1919–65),
American singer and pianist, b. Montgomery, Ala. He
began his career with King Cole Trio (1937–48) and spe-
cialized in soft ballads. His records include *Mona Lisa* and
Nature Boy. He played roles in such films as *Istanbul* and
Autumn Leaves.

Cole, Thomas, American painter **U** 121

Cole, William (1919–   ), American writer and anthol-
ogist of poetry books for children, b. Staten Island, N.Y.
Cole has edited many anthologies of children's poetry,

Cole, William (continued)
including *Oh, What Nonsense!* (1966) and *Oh, How Silly!* (1970). Two of his other anthologies, *I Went to the Animal Fair* (1958) and *Beastly Boys and Ghastly Girls* (1964), were named Notable Books by the American Library Association.

Colechurch, Peter, English clergyman **B** 395
Coleman, Ann, fiancée of James Buchanan, *picture* **B** 418

Coleman, Gary (1968–   ), American actor, b. Zion, Illinois. Coleman became a celebrity at age 10 for his performance in the television series *Diff'rent Strokes.* Although small for his age as a result of a kidney disease, he was a successful model at age 6. He has appeared in commercials and has acted in films. He owns his own film production company.

Coleman, Ornette, American jazz musician **J** 61
Coleridge, Samuel Taylor, English poet **E** 260
    odes **O** 52
    quotation from *The Rime of the Ancient Mariner* **Q** 20
    William and Mary Wordsworth **W** 242

Colette (Sidonie Gabrielle Claudine Colette)(1873–1954), French author, b. Saint-Sauveur-en-Puisaye. Considered France's leading woman writer during her lifetime, she published at least one novel a year. Her largely autobiographical works include *Cheri* and *Gigi.*

Coleus (CO-le-us), house plant, *picture* **H** 269

Colfax, Schuyler (1823–85), American politican, b. New York, N.Y. A resident of Indiana, he was elected to the U.S. House of Representatives (1855–69) and became speaker of the House (1863–69). He served one term as U.S. vice-president (1869–73).
    as vice-president, *picture* **V** 327

Collage (col-LODGE), in art **C** 376–77
    Braque, Georges **B** 371
    Central Park Carrousel, by Cornell **U** 116
    Grandmother, by Arthur Dove, *picture* **D** 142
    Le Courrier, by Braque, *picture* **D** 136
    modern art **M** 390–91
    Picasso **P** 243
    used by some 20th century painters **P** 30
    See also Assemblage
Collar cells, of sponges **S** 392
Collators (CO-lay-tors), office machines **O** 58
Collective bargaining **W** 253
    labor's position **L** 8, 12
    management's position **L** 12, 14, 15
Collective farms
    Albania and Bulgaria **A** 144; **B** 439
    Czechoslovakia **C** 562; *picture* **C** 563
    Israel **I** 443
    Rumania **R** 357
    Union of Soviet Socialist Republics **U** 36–37
Collective security, principle of international relations **L** 96
    United States **U** 138–39
Collections, of dresses **F** 70
Collector, in electronics **E** 146
Collectors and collecting
    antiques **A** 317–21
    autographs **A** 526–27

automobile models **A** 535–37
buttons **B** 479–80
coin collecting **C** 374–75
dolls **D** 263–69
leaves **L** 117
phonograph record collecting **R** 123–25
plankton **P** 280
prints **G** 308
rock and mineral collecting **R** 273
shells **S** 147–49
slime mold sporangia **F** 497–98
stamp collecting **S** 396–400
College Board examinations **E** 348–49
College Entrance Examination Board **E** 348
College Handbook, The **E** 348
Colleges see Universities and colleges; education section of country, state, province, and city articles
Collegium (col-LE-gi-um), group of college professors of Middle Ages **E** 67

Collie, a large breed of dog originally used for herding sheep. Males average about 65 cm (25 in) high at the shoulder. Females are slightly smaller. There are two varieties—smooth-coated (which is rare) and rough-coated. Colors include sable and white, tricolor, bluish gray, and white. The collie comes from the British Isles and is of ancient ancestry. *pictures* **D** 254; **G** 79

Collins, John S., American businessman **M** 254

Collins, Martha Layne (1936–   ), governor of Kentucky, Democrat, b. Bagdad. In 1983, Collins became the first woman to win election as governor of Kentucky. At that time, she held the office of lieutenant governor. From 1975 to 1979, she served as clerk of the state court of appeals (now the Supreme Court of Kentucky). Earlier she had been a teacher.

Collins, Michael (1930–   ), American astronaut, b. Rome, Italy. A graduate of the U.S. Military Academy, he became test pilot for the Air Force before joining the astronaut program. He was on Gemini 10 space flight (1966), and piloted the command module of Apollo 11 moon expedition. He orbited moon in July, 1969, while astronauts Armstrong and Aldrin descended to the moon's surface. Collins served as director of the National Air and Space Museum of the Smithsonian Institution (1971–78) and was appointed undersecretary of the Smithsonian Institution in 1978. **S** 340, 340j

Collins, William, English poet **E** 258
Collins, William Wilkie, English writer **E** 264
    mystery-suspense fiction **M** 554
Collip, James B., Canadian biochemist **B** 52
Collodi (co-LOD-i), **Carlo,** Italian writer **I** 480
Collodion process, in photography **P** 215–16

Colloids, particles or droplets of one substance, usually solid or liquid, suspended or floating in another substance. Fog and blood are two common examples. In fog, droplets of water are suspended in air, while in blood solids are suspended in liquid. Colloids are too small to be seen even with a microscope.
    dust particles **D** 347

Cologne (co-LONE), perfumed liquid **P** 154
Cologne, West Germany **G** 157
Cologne, Cathedral of **G** 157; *picture* **G** 165

Coloma (co-LO-ma), California
gold discovery at Sutter's mill **G** 250
Colombia (co-LUM-bia) **C** 378–84
Bogotá **B** 299
coffee plantation, *picture* **C** 372
emerald source **G** 71
flag **F** 242
life in Latin America **L** 47–61
national anthem **N** 21
Panama gains independence from **P** 45–46, 48
supermarket in Medellín, *picture* **L** 55
Colombo (co-LUM-bo), capital of Sri Lanka, *picture*
S 392b

Colombo Plan (The Colombo Plan for Cooperative Economic Development in South and Southeast Asia), a plan for financing economic projects in South and Southeast Asian countries with aid from various Western countries, including Britain and United States. The plan was inaugurated in 1951.

Colón (co-LONE), Panama **P** 44, 45
Colonial Dames of America *see* National Society Colonial
Dames XVII Century
Colonial history, United States *see* American colonies
Colonialism (co-LO-nial-ism), form of imperialism
I 109, 324
Asia **A** 468–69
civil liberties and civil rights, recent trends **C** 315
migration of people **I** 98
scramble for Africa **A** 69
Southeast Asia **S** 335
Colonial life in America **C** 385–99
architecture **U** 123
Conestoga wagon **C** 458
covered bridges **B** 400
education **E** 69–70
elections **E** 114
events preceding Revolutionary War **R** 194–98
expansion of the English language **W** 240
explosives **E** 391–92
fishing industry **F** 212, 217
furniture design **F** 509
glassmaking industry **G** 230
homemade soaps **D** 146
homes **H** 180–82
immigration **I** 99
inns **H** 257
kitchen in Williamsburg, *picture* **V** 355
libraries **L** 198
literature **A** 195–98
magazines, first **M** 14
newspapers **N** 198
slavery **B** 250c
textbooks used **T** 139
Thanksgiving Day **T** 152–54
theater **D** 299; **T** 162
transportation **T** 260
See also American colonies; Jamestown; Plymouth
Colony; Smith, John
Colonial National Historical Park, Virginia **V** 353
Colonial-style house, *picture* **H** 168
Colonies, American *see* American colonies
Colonies, British **C** 428
Colonnades (col-on-ADES), in architecture
Louvre **L** 367–68
Colons (co-LON), French settlers in Algeria **A** 160
Colons (CO-lons), punctuation marks **P** 531
Color **D** 138–43
atmosphere's effect on **A** 482

different flower colors attract different insects
F 278
dyes and dyeing **D** 366–72
experiment with color absorbing solar energy **E** 364
eye's reception of **B** 284–85
fashion **F** 66
gemstones **G** 69
gold changes with alloying **G** 248
graphics arts, color prints **G** 303–08
hair **H** 2
leaves of trees **T** 282
light wavelength determines **L** 265–67; **R** 42, 43
minerals identified by **R** 270
of lights of neon and other noble gases **N** 109,
110
optical illusions **O** 164
rainbow **R** 98
separations for book illustrations **B** 330
spectroscope **O** 173
star colors **S** 407
sunset through dust **D** 348
What causes the delicate colors of soap bubbles?
L 270
See also Dyes and dyeing
Color, of animals
animal communication, sight signals **A** 278
birds **B** 212, 237
butterflies, moths, and caterpillars **B** 470
fishes, protective coloration of **F** 193
mammals **M** 65
octopus **O** 276, 277
turtles **T** 332
See also Protective coloration
Colorado **C** 400–16
Denver, capital city **D** 116
gold discoveries **G** 251
harvesting sugar beets, *picture* **S** 456
Indian Cliff Palace, Mesa Verde, *picture* **A** 353
Rocky Mountains, peaks **R** 274
San Juan National Forest, *picture* **N** 36
sheep raising, *picture* **C** 150
Colorado, University of, Boulder, Colorado **C** 409
Colorado–Big Thompson Project **C** 405
Colorado blue spruce, state tree of Colorado, *picture*
C 401
Colorado River, United States **A** 404–05; **C** 405;
R 240; *pictures* **N** 284, **R** 241
California **C** 16, 19
Grand Canyon **G** 290–92
Hoover Dam **D** 20; *picture* **D** 17
Los Angeles, California, water source **L** 347
Colorado Springs, Colorado **C** 413–14
U.S. Air Force Academy Chapel, *picture* **U** 159
Coloraturas (col-or-a-TU-ras), musical term **B** 65;
M 533; **V** 375
Color balance, of photographic film **P** 207
Color blindness, inherited disease **D** 188
Daltonism **D** 15
Coloreds, people of mixed races in Africa *see* Coloureds
Color engraving **P** 458
Color filters **L** 267
Colorimeters (color-IM-et-ers), optical instruments
O 174
Color negative film, in photography **P** 206
Color photography **P** 207, 218
film **P** 206, 207
silent pictures **M** 474
Color reversal film, in photography **P** 206
Color television **T** 68–70
Color wheel **D** 139; *picture* **D** 138

Colosseum (col-os-SE-um), Roman arena **A** 231;
   R 286, 313; *pictures* **R** 312, **W** 217
   gladiators fighting, *pictures* **R** 305, **S** 196
Colossians (co-LOS-sians), book of the Bible **B** 161
Colossi of Memnon, statues, *picture* **E** 99
Colossus of Rhodes **W** 216
Coloureds, people of mixed races in Africa **A** 55
   Namibia **N** 8a
   South Africa **S** 268
   Zambia **Z** 367
   Zimbabwe **Z** 368b
Colt, Samuel, American inventor of guns **G** 421–22

Colter, John (1775?–1813), American explorer, b. near
Staunton, Va. He joined the Lewis and Clark expedition to
explore U.S. territory to the Pacific coast (1803) and
became the first white explorer to enter what is now the
Yellowstone National Park region. He fought with Crow
and Flathead Indians against the Blackfeet (1808 and
1809).
   exploration of Wyoming **N** 46; **W** 335

Coltrane, John (1926–67), American jazz musician, b.
Hamlet, N.C. A saxophonist, he played with various top
jazz bands and eventually formed his own quartet. His jazz
style, developed in the 1950's, has been described as
"sheets of sounds" and as having the "effect of an aural
battering ram." In 1965 he was named Jazzman of the
Year by *Down Beat* magazine. **J** 61

Colts, young horses **H** 243
Colubrids, family of snakes **S** 204, 207
Colugos, gliding mammals **M** 64; *picture* **M** 69
Columbanus (col-um-BAY-nus) **Saint,** Irish monk
   R 290
Columbia, Cape, northernmost tip of Canada **C** 51
Columbia, capital of South Carolina **S** 307
Columbia, United States space shuttle orbiter **A** 576;
   S 340k, 344–45; *picture* **S** 343
   ceramic tiles protect it from re-entry heat **C** 178
Columbia Basin Project, Washington **W** 20
Columbia Plateau, region of the United States
   Idaho **I** 57, 59; **V** 383
   Nevada **N** 124
   Oregon **O** 194–95
   Washington **W** 14–15
Columbia Presbyterian Medical Center, New York City,
   picture **H** 247
Columbia River, North America **R** 240; *picture* **R** 237
   dams **D** 19–20
   discovered by Captain Robert Gray **O** 192
   flood stage, *picture* **E** 283
   Lewis and Clark expedition **L** 162–63
   Washington **W** 15, 18, 20, 26
   waterway system in Oregon **O** 195, 197, 199, 203
Columbia River Basin, Washington **D** 19–20

Columbia Scholastic Press Association (CSPA), an organi-
zation to promote student writing by encouraging school
publications. The association holds annual conferences
for scholastic yearbook, magazine, and newspaper staffs.
It was founded in 1925, has headquarters in New York,
N.Y., and publishes *School Press Review.*

Columbia School of Journalism **P** 524
Columbia, the Gem of the Ocean, song **N** 24
Columbia University, New York City **N** 217, 232;
   picture **U** 206

Columbine, traditional character in Italian theater (*com-
media dell'arte*), usually daughter of Pantaloon and wife of
sweetheart of Harlequin. Columbine is also found in
French comic opera and English pantomime.

Columbines, flowers, *pictures* **G** 49, **W** 168
   state flower of Colorado **C** 401
Columbium *see* Niobium
Columbus, capital of Ohio **O** 65, 70–71; *picture* **O** 72
Columbus, Georgia **G** 144
Columbus, Bartolomé, Italian explorer **D** 282
Columbus, Christopher, discoverer of America **C** 416–
   17
   Caribbean Sea and islands **C** 118
   corn introduced to Europe **C** 506–07
   Costa Rica **C** 515
   Cuba **C** 547
   exploration of the New World **E** 377–78, 380
   Ferdinand and Isabella **F** 88
   flag of Spain, 1492 **F** 228
   holiday honoring **H** 151
   Honduras **H** 195
   Jamaica given to his family **J** 14
   Nicaragua, discovery of **N** 248
   spice trade between the New and Old World **F** 334
   tomb in Santo Domingo **D** 283
   towns and cities named for **E** 388
Columbus Circle, New York City, *picture* **N** 233
Columbus Day **H** 151
Columbus Theater, Buenos Aires, Argentina **A** 390
Columns, in architecture **A** 375; *diagram* **A** 376
   ancient Greek stone masonry **B** 394
   Greek orders **G** 346, 348; *pictures* **G** 347
   optical illusions used in building Greek columns,
   picture **O** 165
   Roman architecture **R** 286
Colville River, Alaska **A** 133
Coma (CO-ma), cloudlike head of the comet **A** 474;
   C 418–19
Comanche (co-MAN-che), cavalry horse **K** 176
Comanche, Indians of North America **I** 164
Comaneci, Nadia, Rumanian gymnast **G** 428b; **O** 116;
   picture **O** 116a
Combat, trial by **M** 291
Combat arms, of the United States Army **U** 168, 171
Combat Arms Regimental System **U** 173
Combative sports, in the Olympics **O** 108
Combat units, of the United States Army **U** 173
Combed yarns **C** 524
Combination locks **L** 326
Combination square, measuring tool **T** 216
Combined waste water (combined sewage) **S** 30
Combine paintings, of Robert Rauschenberg **M** 397
Combines, farm machinery **F** 60; **W** 155; *picture* **F** 61
   harvesting wheat, *picture* **A** 90–91
Comb jellies, ctenophores **J** 75; *picture* **J** 74
Combustion, burning **F** 137
   chemical reaction **C** 218
   explosives **E** 390
   internal-combustion engines **I** 308–13
   Lavoisier's explanation **L** 86
   provides energy for missles **M** 345
   rapid oxidation **O** 270
   See also Fuels; Heat
COMECON *see* Council for Mutual Economic Assistance

Comédie-Française, national theater of France. It per-
forms past masterpieces and highly selective contempo-
rary works. In 1680 Louis XIV consolidated the Comédiens
du Roi and the combined troupes of the Théâtre du Marais

and the company of Molière into what became known as the Comédie-Française. **P** 70; **T** 160

Comedy, form of drama **D** 293–94
  American **A** 215
  English **E** 256–57, 268
  Greek **G** 353
  motion pictures **M** 473, 474–75, 484, 485, 487, 488c
  musical comedy **M** 542–43
  origin of the word **D** 293–94
  slapstick and farce **H** 278
Comedy of Errors, The, play by Shakespeare **S** 134
Comedy of manners, in English drama **E** 256–57, 268
Comenius (co-ME-nius), **John Amos,** Czech educator and theologian **E** 68
  first picture book for children **C** 236
  kindergarten, origin of **K** 243
Comet Falls, Washington **W** 63
Comets **C** 418–19; **S** 245–46
  astronomy, history of **A** 473–74
  radar astronomy studies **R** 74
Comic books **C** 422–23
Comic opera see Opéra bouffe
Comics Magazine Association of America, The **C** 422, 423
Comic strips **C** 128
  animated cartoons compared to **A** 297
  German forerunners **G** 178
  made into comic books **C** 422
Comino, island, Malta **M** 59
Comintern, later Cominform see Third International

Commager, Henry Steele (1902–), American historian and educator b. Pittsburgh, Pa. History professor at Columbia U. (1939–56) and at Amherst College (since 1956), he has written a large number of historical books, most of them supporting his theory that absence of thought is the world's greatest threat. His works include *Documents of American History* (editor) and *Freedom, Loyalty, Dissent.*

Commander in chief, presidential powers **P** 452
Command module (CM), section of Apollo spacecraft **S** 340a, 340d; *pictures* **S** 340b, 340c

Commandos, small bands of men organized to pursue native cattle raiders during the early days of white settlement in South Africa. The name was later applied to Boer fighters in the Boer Wars (1881, 1889–1902). British shock troops, trained for hand-to-hand combat and other special operations, are also called commandos. These men carried out important missions in World War II. The U.S. Army's Special Forces employ commando-like units.

Commas, punctuation marks **P** 531
Commedia dell'arte (com-MAY-dia dell AR-tay), Italian company of character actors **D** 295
  forerunners of circus clowns **C** 300
Commemorative stamps **P** 409
Commentators, news service of radio broadcasting **R** 58
Commerce see International trade: Trade and commerce
Commerce, United States Department of **P** 448
  Merchant Marine Academy **U** 182
  Patent and Trademark Office **P** 97
Commercial art **C** 424–27
  illustration and illustrators **I** 92, 95

  industrial design **I** 229–32
  mechanical drawing **M** 197
  posters **P** 404
  See also Advertising; Posters
Commercial banks **B** 46–47, 48
Commercial property **R** 112d, 113
Commercials, in advertising **A** 28–29, 32
  television **T** 70b, 71
Commission, form of municipal government **M** 505
Commissioned officers, United States Army **U** 167
Commissions, fees for real estate brokers **R** 113
Committee for Original Peoples Entitlement, political group **E** 291
Committee of Public Safety, French Revolution **F** 467–68
Committee on the Challenges of Modern Society (CCMS), of the North Atlantic Treaty Organization **N** 305
Committees, of the United States Congress **U** 141, 144
Committees of Correspondence **A** 18
  communication in American colonies **C** 436
  events leading to Revolutionary War **R** 196–97
  political parties in colonial America **P** 379

Common Cause, a citizens' lobbying organization in the United States that works for political reforms and for legislation on national problems. It was founded in 1970 by John Gardner, a former secretary of the U.S. Department of Health, Education, and Welfare. Common Cause takes credit for having helped to lower the voting age to 18 and bring about reforms in political campaign financing. It has about 225,000 members. Headquarters are in Washington, D.C.

Common cold, virus disease **D** 193
Common Cormorant, The, nonsense rhyme **N** 272
Common law **L** 88
  origin in medieval England **E** 218
Common Market see European Economic Community
Common Market, Central American see Central American Common Market
Common nouns **P** 90
Commons (village greens) **P** 77; *picture* **N** 138h
Commons, House of, British Parliament **E** 219, 222–23; **U** 78
  growth of the parliamentary system **P** 81
Commons, House of, Canada **C** 77
Common schools **E** 70–71
Common Sense, pamphlet by Thomas Paine **P** 13
  how Declaration of Independence was adopted **D** 61
  literature of the American colonies **A** 198
Common stocks, shares in a company **S** 428
Commonwealth, English **E** 232a
  Cromwell, head of **C** 538

Commonwealth Fund, trust fund established (1918) by Mrs. Stephen V. Harkness to promote health through grants for medical education and health services.

Commonwealth of Nations **C** 428; **E** 232–232a
  Commonwealth Day **H** 152
  United Kingdom **U** 64, 65, 67
  See also United Kingdom of Great Britain and Northern Ireland; names of individual member nations
Commonwealths
  four states of the United States **P** 142
  Puerto Rico's status **P** 522–23; **U** 103
Commonwealth Trans-Antarctic Expedition **P** 370–71

Communes, China's government-run farms **C** 265
Communicable diseases (infectious diseases) **D** 186
Communication C 429–41
    advertising media **A** 27–34
    alphabet, origin of **A** 170–73
    animals **A** 275–80
    braille for the blind **B** 251–54
    cables **T** 52, 54
    civil and human rights ideas spread by modern
        communication **C** 316
    communications satellites **C** 439–40; **S** 42; **T** 67
    data communication **T** 54–55
    deaf, communication with **D** 50
    electronic communication **E** 142–142f
    geographical knowledge **G** 97
    handwriting **H** 31–33
    inventions advance **I** 338, 345–46
    journalism **J** 142–45
    language arts **L** 36
    letter writing **L** 157–60
    musical notation **M** 522–32
    newspapers **N** 197–205
    orchestra conducting technique **O** 191
    organization of scientific societies **S** 69–70
    paper **P** 51
    post office **P** 405–10
    printing **P** 457–67
    propaganda **P** 480–81
    public relations **P** 507–08
    public speaking **P** 508–10
    publishing **P** 513–15
    radio **R** 50–61
    satellites transmit radio signals **S** 41, 42; **T** 67
    speech **S** 376–78
    tape recorders **T** 20–21
    telegraph **T** 50–55
    telephone **T** 55–60
    television **T** 65–71
    universal languages **U** 194–95
    world pattern of communication **W** 267
    writing **W** 318–21
    See also Language and languages; country, province,
        and state articles
Communication among animals *see* Animals:
    communication
Communications satellites C 439–40; **S** 42; **T** 67
    Intelsat **E** 142e
    television **T** 69, 70, 71
Communion *see* Holy Communion
Communism C 442–46; **S** 220
    civil war in China **C** 272
    communes, government-run farms, China **C** 265
    economic system **E** 50
    education in China **C** 259
    Fascism and Communism in Italy **F** 63
    Hungary **H** 288
    international relations **I** 321, 324, 325
    Khrushchev, Nikita **K** 240–41
    Korean War **K** 305–06
    Lenin, Vladimir Ilich **L** 138
    Marx, Karl **M** 113–14
    Nazism **N** 80
    one-party system of politics **P** 382
    religion in China **C** 260
    Southeast Asia **S** 336
    Stalin and the Russian Communist Party **S** 395
    Union of Soviet Socialist Republics **U** 41–42, 50–
      51
    What are the differences between Communism and
        socialism? **C** 442

Communism, Mount, Union of Soviet Socialist
    Republics **U** 33
Communist China *see* China, People's Republic of
Communistic societies
    Amana colonies, Iowa **I** 367
    New Harmony, Indiana **I** 144
Communist Manifesto C 443; **M** 114
Communist Party, Albanian *see* Albanian Labor Party
Communist Party, Cambodian *see* Khmer Rouge
Communist Party, Chinese C 267
    Mao Tse-tung **M** 86
Communist Party, Cuban C 130, 550, 551
Communist Party, Czech C 564
Communist Party, East German G 152, 158
    East Berlin **B** 145
Communist Party, Mongolian M 413, 415
Communist Party, North Korean K 304
Communist Party, Polish P 361, 362
Communist Party, Rumanian R 357, 360
Communist Party, Vietnamese V 334b
Communist Party, Yugoslav C 445
    Tito **T** 199
Communities, of kingdoms of living things **K** 257–59
    complex web of life **L** 253–55
Community Antenna Television *see* Cable TV
Community centers
    nurses and nursing **N** 411
    parks and playgrounds **P** 76–78
    senior citizens' centers **O** 100

Community chest (United Fund), a general fund collected
from individual contributions and used for the communi-
ty's health, welfare, and recreation needs. The **United
Community Funds and Councils of America** (UCFC),
founded in 1918, with headquarters in New York, N.Y., is
the national association. It publishes the magazine *Com-
munity.*

Community college, a type of public two-year college.
Community colleges are supported by taxes and small
tuition fees. Programs prepare students for employment or
for transfer to a 4-year college and are often set up to
accommodate part-time students. In Canada, occupation-
al programs may last three years. U.S. community colleges
grant associate's degrees. **E** 73

Community foundations F 390
Community life
    colonial America **C** 385–99
    community services, uniforms, *pictures* **C** 355
    4-H clubs **F** 396–396a
    juvenile delinquency **J** 164
    parent-teacher associations **P** 66–67
    pioneers **P** 258
    social work **S** 225–26
    sociology, the study of **S** 227
Community theaters T 161–62
Commutative properties, of numbers **N** 387
Commutators, electric E 131
    electric generators **E** 121
    electric motors **E** 137
Commuter trains, of railroads **R** 80
Como (CO-mo), **Lake,** northern Italy **L** 27–28
Comoros, Indian Ocean **C** 446a
    flag, *picture* **F** 235
Compact 35 cameras P 204
Company, infantry troop unit **U** 172
Comparative advantage, production specialization of
    nations **I** 326–27
Comparative anatomy *see* Anatomy, comparative

Comparative religion see Religions
Comparators (contour projectors), optical instruments
    O 172
Compass, magnetic, navigation instrument N 66
    airplanes A 560
    effect on exploration E 374
    electricity, experiments with E 129, 130
    gyrocompass G 437
    history of, as a direction finder D 182
    magnetic poles M 24
    points of, named for Norse dwarf gods N 277
Compass, tool for drawing geometric figures G 130
    Greek geometry G 123
    mechanical drawing tool M 197
Compass jellyfish, picture J 72
Compensation see Workers' compensation
Competition
    change and development in industry I 244
    feature of capitalism C 104–05
    responsibilities of labor and management L 11
    sets pattern for interstate commerce I 332
    tariff T 25
    trusts and monopolies limit competition T 303
Competition, in sports
    golf G 260
    gymnastics G 432–33
    Olympic Games O 103–116c
Complementary colors D 139–40
Complex mountains M 496
Complex numbers N 387
Composed upon Westminster Bridge, sonnet by William
    Wordsworth S 255
Composers
    chart of names, dates, pictures M 522–23
Composing rooms, of newspapers N 203
Composing machine, for typesetting P 457
Composing stick, to hold type P 463
Composite numbers N 379
Composite volcanoes V 384
Composition, in photography P 211
    effects of changing camera lenses, pictures P 206
Composition, in printing P 465
Composition, music M 522–41
    baroque period B 65
    electronic music E 142g–142h
Composition, painting by Piet Mondrian D 362
Composition III, painting by Wassily Kandinsky M 391
Compositions, in writing and speaking C 446b–447
    bibliography B 170
    book reviews as compositions B 317
    essays E 292–93
    outlines O 250–51
    proofreading P 479
    report writing R 175–76
Composition sketch, preparatory drawing D 301
Compositors, typesetters for printing P 463
Compost, decayed organic material G 30
    fertilizers F 96
    solid-waste disposal S 31
Compound eye, eye made up of many separate lenses
    crustaceans S 170
Compound (open) fractures, broken bones
    first aid F 163
Compound interest I 297
Compound microscopes M 283–84, 288
    lenses L 146–47
Compounds, chemical C 196, 218
    atomic combinations A 485
    body chemistry, composition of cells B 289
    . structure of matter M 175

Comprehensive Employment and Training Act of 1973
(CETA), a U.S. law providing funds to state and local governments for job training and the creation of jobs for the unemployed. The law combined a number of employment programs that had been run by various agencies and placed them under the direction of the Department of Labor. In 1982 the federal government announced plans to reduce CETA programs and to give the states block grants for employment training instead.
    libraries L 178–79

Compressed air G 59
    atmospheric pressure compared to compressed air
      W 71–72
    deep-sea diving equipment D 79
    pneumatic devices P 347–48
    shock waves produced by airplanes S 470
Compressibility, property of a gas P 233
Compression ratio, of engines
    diesel engines D 171
    internal-combustion engines I 309
Compression refrigerating system R 134–35
Compression waves, of earthquakes E 27–28
Compression waves, of sound S 257
Compressors, for gases
    engines E 211
    jet engine J 88, 89
Compromise of 1850 C 448
    achievement of Fillmore's administration F 125
    black history B 250f; S 199
    Calhoun's protest C 13
    Clay, Henry C 335
    Zachary Taylor's opposition T 35–36

Compton, Arthur H. (1892–1962), American physicist, b. Wooster, Ohio. He is known for his work on first nuclear chain reaction and also for his discovery that X rays striking a surface at an angle have a longer wavelength on rebounding than they had on striking. For this discovery, called the Compton effect, he was awarded a Nobel prize (1927). O 73

Compton, John G. M., prime minister of Saint Lucia
    S 18b
Compulsory education E 69, 70
Compurgation, in law J 159, 160

Computer, personal, a computer for individual use. Personal computers are designed to be affordable and easy to use, so that they will appeal to people with little technical background. At the heart of the machine are electronic circuits printed on tiny silicon chips. These make up the computer's central processing unit, which performs arithmetic and supervises the system, and its memory, which stores information. Information and instructions are entered from a keyboard or from magnetic disks or tapes. The information can be displayed on a video screen or printed by a separate printer. Personal computers first appeared in 1975. By 1983, more than 1,000,000 were in use in the United States. C 449, 457

Computer-assisted instruction (CAI) C 457; P 476–77
Computer chip C 452, 453; picture C 454
Computerized axial tomography, X-ray technique see
    CAT
Computer programming see Programming, Computer
Computers C 449–57
    abacus A 2
    astronomy, use in A 476c
    automation A 530, 531–33; picture A 534

Computers (continued)
- automobile engines controlled by I 313
- aviation A 562, 576
- banks and banking B 45–46; *picture* B 51
- binary number system C 456; N 401
- CAT scanning in medicine M 208c
- clothing industry C 354, 356
- communication, advances in C 440
- computer center, *picture* E 204
- computer engineers E 206
- data communication system T 54–55
- dictionary production D 165
- digital recording of music H 127
- earthquake location E 29
- election results based on probability theories, *picture* P 474
- electronic devices to help conserve fuel A 552
- electronics in the future E 148
- first electronic computer, *picture* E 147
- guidance systems of rockets M 346–47; R 261
- library use for information storage and retrieval L 179, 190
- mathematics M 163, 164, 165–66, 168
- meteorological uses W 85
- music M 532
- navigation, uses in N 69
- newspapers N 202, 204
- newspaper videotext editions N 197
- observatories, use in O 12
- office machines O 58; *picture* O 56
- paper for cards, bleached bristols P 53
- police make use of P 376
- robots A 533–34; R 252–54
- spacecraft guidance S 340d–340e, 340g
- stock exchanges S 432
- teaching machines P 476–77
- telephone and the computer E 142b
- textile industry T 142
- traffic control system T 248
- transit system tool B 466
- typewriters, an essential part T 348
- *See also* Calculators

Computer simulation, form of computer-assisted instruction P 477
Comstar D3, U.S. telephone service satellite C 440
Comstock Lode, mining discovery in Nevada N 129
- fifty-niners gold rush G 251
Comte (CONT), **Auguste,** French philosopher S 227

Comus (CO-mus) (from greek *kōmos,* meaning "a revel"), in late Roman mythology, the god of gaiety, feasting, and drunken revelry. A companion of Dionysus, he and Momus were in charge of entertainment for the Olympians. Comus is represented as a youth dressed in white and wearing a crown of roses. He holds a lighted torch in his hand.

Comyn (COME-in), **John,** Scottish chieftain B 414
Conakry (CON-ak-ry), capital of Guinea G 405–06

Conant (CO-nant), **James Bryant** (1893–1978), American educator, b. Dorchester, Mass. Conant was president of Harvard University (1933–53) and U.S. ambassador to Germany (1955–57). He conducted studies on American public high schools and on education of American teachers that resulted in his best-known books, *Slum and Suburbs: A Commentary on Schools in Metropolitan Areas* and *The Education of American Teachers.*

Concave lenses T 61, 62
Concave mirrors L 262–63

Concentrating collectors, of solar energy S 236, 238–39
Concentration, in psychology S 440
Concentration, of ores M 227–28
- lead L 95

Concentration camps, prison camps often used for confinement of prisoners of war, political prisoners, or refugees. One of the first camps to which term was applied, in which Boer civilians of South Africa were "concentrated" to prevent their aiding Boer guerrillas (1900–02), was under English general Kitchener. Term also refers to Spanish general Weyler's camps during Cuba's war of independence (1896–97). Most infamous were concentration camps of Nazis, first established at Oranienburg and Dachau, Germany (1933), and gradually set up throughout occupied Europe. Approximately 7,000,000 people were killed in these camps because they were Jewish or "politically unreliable."
- Dachau memorial, *picture* N 81
- Nazism N 81

Concepción (cone-cep-ci-OHN), Chile C 252, 253
Conceptual art M 398
Concertina (con-cer-TI-na) F 330
Concerto grosso, form of orchestral composition M 535; O 184
Concertos (con-CHERT-ose), in music M 535–36
- baroque period B 66
- basic record library R 125
Conches, mollusks O 278; S 148
Conching, chocolate-making process C 275
Conchobar (con-CO-bar), legendary king of Ulster I 392
Conchology *see* Shells and shell collecting
Conciergerie (con-ci-airge-REE), **La,** Paris P 73
Concord, capital of New Hampshire N 159
Concord, Massachusetts M 144–45
- Alcott, Louisa May, home in A 149
- Emerson's home E 187, 188
- home of eminent American writers A 201
- Revolutionary War begins R 198
Concordat (con-CORD-at), kind of treaty
- Concordat of 1801 F 416, 418; N 10
- Concordat of Worms, 1122 R 291
Concorde, supersonic passenger plane N 270; S 472
Concorde, Place de la, Paris P 69–70
- obelisks brought from Egypt O 5–6
Concord grapes G 297
Concord Hymn, The, poem by Emerson E 187
Concrete C 167–68
- advantages of, as bridge material B 401
- architectural possibilities A 385, 386a, 386b, 386c
- building material B 430–31; *pictures* B 433
- dams D 16–21
- highway surfaces R 250
- homes H 175
- masonry B 393–94
- Roman architecture used A 376; R 285–86
- termite-proof house, *picture* A 302
Concrete arch dams D 16
Concurrent powers, in government U 139
Condensation H 93
- action of geysers G 193
- cloud formation C 359
- dew F 289
- distillation process D 224–25
- fog F 288–89
- insulation prevents I 290

rain **R** 93–95
　water, forms of **W** 52
　water desalting **W** 60
Condensed milk **D** 10
Condensers, devices for accumulating and holding
　　electrical energy **E** 127
Condensers, steam
　distilling equipment **D** 224
　Watt's invention **S** 420
Condiments *see* Spices and condiments
Conditioned reflexes, psychology **P** 496
　impulses to take drugs **N** 13
　learning **L** 99
　of animals **A** 282–83
　Pavlov, Ivan **P** 100
Conditioning exercises *see* Exercise

Condominium, joint control by two or more powers over
politically dependent territory. Example is principality of
Andorra, ruled by France and Spanish bishops of Urgel
(since 1278). In current use, joint ownership of property,
or property so owned, such as an apartment complex with
each unit bought and sold, without the approval of the
other owners. Each unit owner pays a service fee or "com-
mon charge" to cover the cost of maintaining the common
facilities.
　group housing **H** 183

Condon, Edward Uhler (1902–74), American physicist,
b. Alamogordo, N.Mex. He worked in the research project
responsible for the development of the atomic bomb. He
was a strong advocate of international atom bomb control.
He held high positions in the government and in scientific
research projects. Condon was co-author of *Quantum Me-
chanics.* **N** 194
　study of UFO sightings **F** 287

Condors, birds **B** 205, 226, 232
　California condor is an endangered species **E** 197
Conducting, of music **O** 188–91
　ancient music **A** 245
Conduction, movement of heat through matter **H** 94–
　　95, 96
Conductors, electric *see* Electric conductors
Conductors, on trains **R** 86
Conduits, pipes or tubes
　early plumbing systems **P** 342
Cone-bearing trees *see* Conifers
Cones, in geometry **G** 129, 131
Cones, of retina of the eye **B** 284–85
　birds **B** 204
Cone shell, *picture* **S** 147
Conestoga (con-es-TO-ga) **wagons** **C** 458; *pictures*
　　A 199, **P** 253, **T** 258
　designed to transport freight **T** 260
　Santa Fe Trail **O** 257–59
　originated in Pennsylvania **P** 136
　pioneer life **P** 253
Coneys *see* Pikas
Confectioners' sugar **S** 453
Confections **C** 98–99
Confederated Unions of America **L** 7
Confederate Memorial Day **H** 152
Confederate States of America **C** 458–60
　Benjamin, Judah P. **L** 361
　Civil War **C** 318–28
　Davis, Jefferson **D** 45
　flags **F** 248; *pictures* **F** 228
　Lee, Robert E. **L** 125–26
　Lincoln, Abraham **L** 295–97

map **C** 319
　Museum of the Confederacy, Richmond **V** 353
　Tyler, a representative of Confederate Provisional
　　Congress **T** 342
Confederation
　early government of United States **U** 134–35
　See also Articles of Confederation
Confederation Centre of the Arts, Charlottetown, Prince
　　Edward Island, Canada **P** 456f; *picture* **P** 456h
Confederation of Canada **C** 73
　"Birthplace of Canada," Prince Edward Island
　　P 456f–456g, 456h
Confederation of National Trade Unions (C.N.T.U.)
　　L 10
Confession, the "I'm sorry" prayer **P** 434–35
Confessions, branches of Christianity **O** 228
Confessions of Saint Augustine **A** 494
Confirmation, sacrament of Roman Catholic Church
　　R 301
Confucianism **C** 260, 460; **R** 147–48
　Chinese literature **O** 220a
　compared with religions of Asia **A** 460
　Korean state philosophy in the late 1300's **K** 296,
　　303
Confucius, Chinese philosopher **C** 460; **R** 147–48
　Chinese literature **O** 220a
　ideas on government **C** 267, 268
　national sage of China **C** 260
Congeners (CON-gen-ers), impurities in distilled
　　beverages **W** 159
Congenital diseases **D** 188
　blindness **B** 251
　deafness **D** 50
　heart disease present at birth **H** 86b
　syphilis **D** 208, 216
Congenital handicaps **H** 27
　blue babies **H** 86b
Conger eels **E** 85
Congestive heart failure **D** 196
Conglomerate (con-GLOM-er-ate), rock **R** 266; *picture*
　　R 267
Congo (People's Republic of the Congo) **C** 461–64
　flag **F** 235
Congo, Democratic Republic of the *see* Zaïre
Congo eels, land-water animals **F** 475–76
Congo (Zaïre) **River** **C** 465; *picture* **C** 463
　Africa, rivers of **A** 49
　fishing, *picture* **A** 301
　Zaïre **Z** 366b
Congregational Church, Groton, Massachusetts, *picture*
　　P 484
Congress, United States *see* United States Congress
Congressional districts **U** 142–43
Congressional Medal of Honor *see* Medal of Honor

Congressional Record, The, published account of proceed-
ings of U.S. Senate and House of Representatives, pub-
lished daily (since 1873). Similar records under different
names had been published previously.

Congress of Industrial Organizations (CIO) **L** 6
　Lewis, John L. **L** 161
Congress of Racial Equality (CORE) **B** 250L, 250n
Congress of Vienna *see* Vienna, Congress of
Congress Party, of India **I** 133
Congreve (CON-greve), **William,** English designer of
　　rockets **M** 343
Congreve, William, English dramatist **D** 297
Conic projection, of maps **M** 92–93

Conic section, any one of several curves obtained when a cone is cut through by a plane. Kind of curve depends on angle at which plane cuts through cone. Curves resulting are circle, hyperbola, parabola, and ellipse. All are useful in designing bridges and, in astronomy, for describing paths of planets and certain comets.

Conifers, trees **T** 284
 forests **F** 371
 gymnospermnae, *picture* **P** 292
 history of plants on land **P** 304
Conjugations, in Latin grammar **L** 76
Conjunctions, words that join words, phrases, or clauses **P** 92
 grammar **G** 289
Conkling, Roscoe, American politician **A** 439
 Hayes and Conkling **H** 81
Connally, John B., American public official **T** 135
Connally, Thomas T., American senator **T** 136
Connecticut C 466–81
 American colonies **A** 189
 colonial life in America **C** 385–99
 founders of the United States **F** 392
 Great Danbury State Fair, *picture* **F** 13
Connecticut, University of, at Storrs, Connecticut, **C** 475, 480
Connecticut River C 470
 Massachusetts **M** 137
 New Hampshire **N** 151

Connelly, Marc (Marcus Cook Connelly) (1890–1980), American playwright, b. McKeesport, Pa. Author, with George S. Kaufman, of *Beggar on Horseback,* he is best-known for his Pulitzer prize winning play (1930), *The Green Pastures,* which shows the Old Testament from the point of view of Southern blacks.

Connolly, James, American athlete **O** 109
Connolly, James, Irish patriot **I** 391

Connolly, Maureen Catherine (Little Mo) (1934–69), American tennis player, b. San Diego, Calif. She won U.S. women's singles championship at age 16 (1951) and was first woman to win a "grand slam"—all four major championships (U.S., French, English, and Australian) in one year (1953).

Connors, Jimmy (James Scott Connors) (1952–), American tennis player, b. East St. Louis, Ill. In 1974, he set modern records for percentage of games won (.960) and fewest losses (4). His major titles that year included the Australian, U.S., and Wimbledon singles. He won the U.S. singles title again in 1976, 1978, 1982, and 1983. He won a second Wimbledon singles title in 1982.

Connotation, of a word **S** 118
Conon, pope **R** 296
Conquian (CON-ki-an), Spanish card game **C** 112
Conrad, Charles, Jr., American astronaut **S** 340j, 340k
Conrad, Joseph, Polish-born English writer **C** 482; **E** 266
 themes of his novels **N** 347

Conscientious (con-chee-EN-tious) **objector,** one who is opposed to participation in military service. U.S. Supreme Court ruled in 1970 that the draft law exempts "all those whose consciences, spurred by deeply held moral, ethical, or religious beliefs, would give them no rest or peace if they allowed themselves to become a part of an instrument of war."

 draft exemptions and regulations with classifications **D** 289, 290; **P** 105

Conscription *see* Draft, or conscription
Conservation C 482–89
 Arizona's soil and water control **A** 407
 beavers' role in **B** 114
 communities of living things **K** 259
 dams, benefits of **D** 18–19
 ecological balance, problem of **E** 45
 endangered species **E** 195–97
 energy **C** 486; **E** 202d–203
 erosion, practices to halt **E** 281–82
 fishing industry **F** 217, 223–24
 forests, protection of **F** 372–74
 homebuilding **H** 184
 hunting, rules of sportsmanship in **H** 289–90
 insect control **I** 257–58
 irrigation **I** 408–10
 National Forest System **N** 32, 35–37
 petroleum **P** 178
 public lands **P** 507
 Roosevelt, Theodore, resources program **R** 329
 soils **S** 234
 tree-farming in Mississippi's forests **M** 355
 water pollution **W** 64–69
 water storage to control floods **F** 257
 Why should topsoil be conserved? **S** 233
 wild flowers **W** 171
 See also Environment; Natural resources; country, province, and state articles
Conservation of energy, first law of thermodynamics **E** 200; **M** 173
 definition of work **W** 245
 in nuclear reactions **N** 369
 studies in physics **P** 238
Conservation of matter P 237–38
 laws of **M** 172–73
Conservative Judaism J 118–19
Conservative Party, Canada **C** 77
Conservatives, British political party **P** 379
Conservatories, music schools **M** 524
Conshelf (Continental Shelf Station), underwater station **U** 17–18
Consolidated schools E 75
Consolidations and mergers, business
 newspapers **N** 199–200
Consonance, in music **M** 533
Consonants, speech sounds
 alphabet **A** 170, 173
 closed sound of letter B **B** 1
 double consonants in Welsh words **W** 3
 evolution of letter J from vowel **J** 1
 how named **D** 1
 Latin language **L** 76
 pronunciation **P** 478
 speech **S** 377–78
Constable, John, English painter **P** 27; **E** 240
 The Hay Wain, painting, *picture* **N** 39
Constables, police officers **P** 372
Constance, Lake of, West Germany **G** 154
Constans, son of Constantine the Great **C** 489
Constanta (cone-STON-tsa), Rumania **R** 357
Constantine, Algeria **A** 163
Constantine, antipope **R** 296
Constantine, Arch of, Rome, Italy, *picture* **A** 231
Constantine I, king of Greece **G** 339

Constantine II (1940–), former king of Greece, b. Athens. He succeeded his father, King Paul I. After a military junta seized power in 1967, Constantine fled Greece. In 1974 the junta was overthown, but the Greek people voted not to restore the monarchy. During his reign, Constantine won an Olympic gold medal in yachting. He married Princess Anne-Marie of Denmark in 1964.

Greece, history of **G** 339

Constantine, pope **R** 296
Constantine II, son of Constantine the Great **C** 489
Constantine the Great, Roman emperor **C** 489
   art as a record **A** 438b
   Byzantine art and architecture **B** 483
   Byzantine Empire **B** 491
   Christianity made state religion of Roman Empire **C** 282; **R** 308
   ended persecution of Christians **R** 288–89
Constantinople (formerly Byzantium, now Istanbul), Turkey **B** 491, 492; **C** 489; **R** 308; **T** 328
   art as a record **A** 438b
   Byzantine art and architecture **B** 483–85, 490
   captured by Crusaders, 1204 **C** 540
   Russian Vikings attack **V** 339
   See also Istanbul
Constantinople, Council of, 381 **R** 289
Constantius I, Roman emperor, father of Constantine the Great **C** 489
Constantius II, son of Constantine the Great **C** 489

Constellation, U.S. frigate built to subdue Barbary pirates, launched in 1797. In hostilities between United States and France it captured French ships *Insurgente* (1799) and *Vengeance* (1800), becoming first U.S. Navy ship to capture a foreign warship. Frigate is now a national shrine in Baltimore, Maryland.
   oldest warship afloat **B** 35

Constellations **C** 490–93
   ancient Egyptian sky map **A** 470
   Corvus, the crow, *picture* **R** 70
   galaxy clusters **U** 200
   how to make a planetarium to study stars **E** 363
   planetarium **P** 267–68
   twelve constellations of the zodiac **S** 243; *pictures* **S** 244–45
   See also Stars

Constitution, system of rules of nation, state, or body politic that defines the form of government, limits of governmental power, people's rights, and means of exercising governmental authority.
   state constitutions **S** 412

Constitution, American naval vessel **W** 10; *picture* **W** 9
   saved by Holmes's poem "Old Ironsides" **A** 203; **H** 159
Constitution, United States see United States Constitution
Constitution Act (formerly British North America Act), 1867, of Canada **C** 76
Constitution Act, 1982, of Canada **C** 76; **P** 82
Constitutional Convention, 1787 **U** 145–46
   delegates become the founders of the United States **F** 391, 393
   Washington, George, chosen its president **W** 41
Constitutional democracy **G** 274
Constitutional monarchies **G** 276
   Canada **C** 77
   government of the United Kingdom **U** 77–78
Constitutional-Union Party, United States **P** 381
Constitution Day, Japan **H** 152

Constitution Plaza, Hartford, Connecticut, *pictures* **C** 481, **U** 233
Constitution State, nickname for Connecticut **C** 474
Construction see Architecture; Building construction; Engineering
Construction engineering **E** 205; *picture* **E** 207
Constructivism, in art **M** 391, 392–93
   architecture **A** 386
   sculpture **S** 105
Consular service **F** 369
Consulates, headquarters of consular service **F** 369

Consumer Affairs, Office of, an agency of the U.S. Department of Health, Education and Welfare. Established in 1971, it receives complaints from consumers and refers them to the government agency that can provide assistance. It also studies existing federal consumer-protection programs and makes recommendations to improve them. **C** 494b

Consumer buying **C** 494–494b
   budgets, family **B** 425–26
   buying through co-operatives **C** 499–500
   consumer demand **T** 243
   "consumer propositions" in advertising **A** 30, 32
   economics **E** 49–50
   food regulations and laws **F** 350–52
   installment buying **I** 288–89
   marketing **M** 100–03
   opinion surveys **O** 159–60
Consumer co-operatives **C** 499–500
Consumer Credit Protection Act (1968) **I** 289
Consumer education **C** 494–494b
   experiments and other science activities **E** 368–69
   See also Food regulations and laws

Consumer Federation of America (CFA), U.S. consumer lobbying group. The CFA is made up of national, regional, state, and local consumer organizations. It supports legislation and promotes consumer rights in such areas as the pricing and quality of goods, service and guarantees, government regulation of industry, credit and insurance, and natural resource development. The CFA also conducts research into consumer issues. Its publications include the monthly *CFA News* and an annual record of congressional voting. Headquarters are in Washington, D.C. **C** 494a

Consumerism see Consumer education

Consumer Price Index, a measure of changes in the cost of living. In the United States the index is prepared by the Bureau of Labor Statistics, which keeps a check of changes in retail prices throughout the country. Since 1918, when it was started, the index has shown a steady increase in the cost of living, except during the Depression of the 1930's. The information is used by businesses and labor unions in establishing wage guidelines and by government as a guide for fiscal policy.

Consumer Product Safety Commission, a U.S. government regulatory agency. It was established by Congress in 1972 to protect consumers from unsafe manufactured items. The commission sets safety standards for most consumer products and has the power to ban those that are dangerous. It is headed by four commissioners and a chairman. They are appointed by the president, with the approval of the Senate, and serve 7-year terms.

Consumer Reports, magazine for testing agencies of
Consumers Union **C** 494a
Consumers League, National *see* National Consumers
League
Consumers' Unions, International Organization of
C 494a
Contact lenses L 151
Contact prints, in photography **P** 213
Contagious (cont-A-gious) **diseases D** 187
early studies of **M** 208
quarantine to prevent spread of disease **D** 221
whooping cough **D** 211
Containerboard P 53
Containers, paper P 51
Container ships S 161
Containment, policy in international relations **I** 325
Contamination of food *see* Food spoilage and
contamination

Contempt of court, term used in law courts to refer to an
act that embarrasses, hinders, or obstructs court proceed-
ings or lessens the dignity or authority of the court. The
term also refers to failure to comply with a court order.

Contests
Junior Achievement, Inc. **J** 158

Continent, one of the great, continuous land masses on
the earth's surface. The continents of the world are Asia,
Africa, North America, South America, Antarctica, Eu-
rope, and Australia. Physically, Europe and Asia are one
land mass, known as Eurasia, or the Eurasian continent.
But the two areas have been divided by tradition along the
Ural Mountains and are usually spoken of separately. Con-
tinents comprise about 29 percent of the earth's surface.
Continental shelves, the submerged edges of continents,
make up another 5 percent. **W** 254
continental drift **G** 111–12, 116–17
continental shelf **O** 28
earth's history **E** 19–20
land bridges form a world continent **L** 236–37;
N 282
See also names of continents

Continental Army, United States **U** 166
Continental Congress, First, 1774 **R** 197–98
events leading to Declaration of Independence
D 60
first government for United States **U** 134
Washington, George, a delegate **W** 38
Continental Congress, Second, 1775 **R** 200–01;
picture **A** 13
Adams, John, a delegate **A** 11
Declaration of Independence **D** 61
first government for United States **U** 134
flag design **F** 244; *picture* **F** 229
Halifax (North Carolina) Resolves, 1776 **N** 321
Jefferson, Thomas **J** 65
Washington, George, a delegate **W** 38
Continental Divide, North America **N** 284
Colorado **C** 403, 405
Glacier National Park **G** 222
Montana crossed by **M** 430
Rocky Mountains **R** 274
Wyoming **W** 324
Continental drift E 19–20; **G** 111–12, 116–17
climatic changes, sources of **C** 348
ice ages **I** 24
Continental glaciers G 223
ice ages **I** 20

Continentality, way land or water is arranged around an
area **W** 87–88
Continental Marines, first United States Marines
U 177
Continental Navy, first United States Navy **U** 185
Continental Navy Jack, flag, 1775 **F** 229
Continental paper money, *picture* **M** 410
Continental shelf, ocean floor off the coasts of
continents **O** 28
fishing industry **F** 218
life, distribution of plant and animal **L** 231
petroleum deposits **P** 170
Continental Shelf Station (Conshelf), underwater station
U 17–18
Continental System, of Napoleon **N** 11
Continually powered missiles M 343, 344, 349
Continuo (basso continuo), in music **M** 533
Continuous casting, in steelmaking *see* Strand casting
Continuous rolling mills, in steel production **I** 402,
406
Contour drawings D 305
Contour levels, crop planting **A** 93
Contour lines, on maps **G** 100; **M** 90; *diagram* **M** 91
Contour plowing, on contour levels **A** 93; **C** 485;
pictures **C** 483, **E** 282, **V** 349
Contour projectors, optical instruments **O** 172
Contract bridge, card game **C** 107–12
Contraction, in physics
cold causes **H** 94
Contractors, building B 434
Contracts
labor and management **L** 15, 16
Contra dances (longway sets) **F** 299
Contralto voice M 533; **V** 375
Contrast, of photographic film **P** 206–07
Control rods, of nuclear reactors **N** 363; *diagram*
N 362
Control tower, at airports **A** 564
Conundrums (con-UN-drums), riddles **J** 132
a section of folklore **F** 304
Convection, a mode of transmission of heat **H** 95
heating methods **H** 96
Convection currents H 95
continental drift, theory of **E** 19–20; **G** 112, 113
What makes the atmosphere move? **W** 73
Convention of 1818, boundary agreement **T** 109
Conventions, between nations *see* Treaties
Conventions, political P 382; *picture* **E** 112
national nominating convention originated with
Andrew Jackson **J** 6
Convents, dwellings of nuns **M** 294
Convergence, painting by Jackson Pollock **D** 135
Converging lenses L 144–45, 146–47, 149; *diagram*
L 143
Conversation
effective speaking, a language art **L** 36
new words, use of **V** 372
Samuel Johnson a brilliant conversationalist **J** 131
speech **S** 376
Conversion, in football **F** 361
Conversion of mass and energy M 174–75
Conversion of Saint Paul, The, painting by Caravaggio
B 57
Conversions
Christianity, history of **C** 279, 282
Conversion tables, to and from the metric system
W 112, 113
Converted rice R 230
Convex lenses T 61, 62
Convex mirrors L 262

Conveying machinery *see* Hoisting and loading machinery
Convolutions
of the brain **B** 366; *picture* **B** 367
Convulsions, (seizures)
epilepsy **D** 194

Conway, Thomas (1735–1800?), Irish soldier of fortune. He went to America (1777) and served in Continental Army. He is remembered for his part in conspiracy, "Conway Cabal," designed to have General Horatio Gates replace George Washington as commander in chief of Continental Army (1778). Conway resigned when conspiracy was discovered and left America to serve with French Army (1779–87). He was governor general of French possessions in India (1787).

Coober Pedy, Australia **A** 512
Cook, James, English navigator **C** 494b–494c
Australian exploration **A** 515
British Columbia **B** 407
introduced the word 'kangeroo' into other languages **K** 170
Washington **W** 26
Cook, Mount, New Zealand **N** 237; *picture* **M** 498
Cooke, John Esten, American novelist **A** 200

Cooke, Terence James, Cardinal (1921–83), American Roman Catholic churchman, b. New York, N.Y. Cooke was ordained in 1945 and taught social science at Fordham University. In 1968 he succeeded Francis, Cardinal Spellman as archbishop of New York. Pope Paul VI named him cardinal in March, 1969.

Cooke, William F., English inventor and engineer **T** 51
Cookies, food **B** 388b
recipes **R** 115, 116
Cooking
appliances **E** 118
bread and baking **B** 385–388b
camp meals **C** 44–45
candy and candymaking **C** 98–99
flour, kinds of **F** 274–75
food spoilage **F** 354–55
French **F** 405
metric conversions for the kitchen, *table* **W** 113
nutrition and balanced meals **N** 417
origin of, through use of fire **F** 140–41
outdoor cooking and picnics **O** 247–48
recipes **R** 114–16
recipes originating from limited food supply **F** 333
restaurant specialties **R** 187
terms **R** 114
See also Marketing
Cooking appliances **E** 118
Cook Inlet, Alaska **A** 135, 137
Cook Islands, Pacific Ocean **P** 6
Niue **P** 8
Cookworthy, William, English porcelain maker **P** 418
Coolant, fluid cooling agent
helium **H** 107, 108
Cooley, Charles H., American sociologist **S** 227

Cooley, Denton Arthur (1920–), American surgeon, b. Houston, Tex. As an intern at Johns Hopkins Hospital in 1944 he assisted in the first "blue baby" operation. A specialist in cardio-vascular surgery, he has since performed numerous heart transplants, including the first operation that utilized an artificial heart.

Cooley's anemia *see* Thalassemia
Coolgardie, Australia **A** 512
Coolidge, Calvin, 30th president of the United States **C** 494d–497
as vice-president, *picture* **V** 328
Harding cabinet member, *picture* **H** 40
Coolidge, Grace Goodhue, wife of Calvin Coolidge **F** 177–78; *pictures* **C** 495, 496

Coolidge, Olivia E. (1908–), American teacher and author of children's books, b. Buckinghamshire, England. A gifted storyteller, she has written many books on historical subjects, such as *Greek Myths* and *Legends of the North.*

Coolidge, William David, American physicist **I** 334
Coolidge Dam, Arizona **A** 407
Coolidge Festival, at the Library of Congress, Washington, D.C. **M** 552
Coolidge Homestead, Vermont, *picture* **V** 320
Cooling
air conditioning principle **A** 101–03
cooling system of an internal-combustion engine **I** 311
fog resulting from **F** 288
matter, changes in volume of **M** 172
refrigeration **R** 134–36
Cool storage, of food **F** 346–47
apples require **A** 337
refrigeration **R** 136

Cooney, Barbara (Barbara Cooney Porter) (1917–), American writer and illustrator of children's books, b. Brooklyn, N.Y. She wrote and illustrated *King of Wreck Island* and *Captain Pottle's House.* She illustrated *Chanticleer and the Fox,* for which she received the Caldecott medal in 1959. In 1980, she received the same honor for *Ox-Cart Man.* Cooney won an American Book Award in 1983 for her picture book *Miss Rumphius.*

Coonskin Library, Amesville, Ohio **O** 68
Cooper, Charlotte, British tennis player **O** 109

Cooper, Gary (Frank James Cooper) (1901–61), American film actor, b. Helena, Mont. He won Academy Award for *Sergeant York* (1941) and *High Noon* (1952). He was given a special Academy Award (1961). **M** 441

Cooper, Ivan, civil rights leader in Northern Ireland **U** 76
Cooper, James Fenimore, American novelist **C** 498; **N** 348
American literature **A** 200
Cooper, Kenneth, American physician **J** 120b
Cooper, L. Gordon, Jr., American astronaut **S** 340j
Cooper, Peter, American industrialist and philanthropist **C** 498
designed and raced the *Tom Thumb,* locomotive **L** 330
Co-operation, international *see* International co-operation
Co-operative apartments **H** 183
Co-operative communities
Rochdale Society, England **C** 499, 500
Zoar Village, Ohio **O** 70
See also Utopias
Co-operative Extension Service **A** 94
4-H clubs **F** 396a

Cooperative for American Relief Everywhere (CARE), nonprofit agency for the international assistance of needy people on a voluntary, personal basis. CARE provides food and

Cooperative for American Relief Everywhere (continued)
clothing, as well as educational, vocational, and agricultural equipment. Through MEDICO (Medical International Cooperation Organization) it provides medical treatment and training. Founded in 1945, it is sponsored by 26 American voluntary organizations.

Co-operatives C 499–500
Central Bank for Co-operatives **B** 47
Czechoslovakia **C** 560, 562
Danish farms **D** 110
El Salvador **E** 183
Germany **G** 155
Inuit, in Canada **Y** 364
Israel **I** 443
Korea **K** 302
Rumania **R** 357
Saskatchewan Wheat Pool **S** 38f
Shakespeare's acting company **S** 131
Vietnam **V** 344a
Cooperstown, New York, "Home of Baseball" **B** 80–81; **N** 220
Cooper Union, New York City, New York **C** 498
Lincoln's speech in 1860 **L** 295
Coosa River, Alabama **A** 115
Coos Bay, Oregon **O** 197
Copacabana (co-pa-ca-BA-na) **Beach,** Rio de Janeiro, Brazil, *picture* **B** 372
Copán (co-PON), Honduras **H** 198–99; *picture* **C** 177
Copenhagen (co-pen-HAIG-en), capital of Denmark **D** 106, 107, 112
Tivoli amusement park, *picture* **D** 106
Copepods (CO-pe-pods), very small crustaceans **S** 168; *picture* **L** 230
animal plankton **P** 280–81
insecticides, effect on **E** 272f
ocean life **O** 37
vectors **V** 283
Copernican (co-PER-nic-an) **system,** of astronomy **A** 471; **S** 240
Galileo developed **G** 6, 7
planets seen in belt of zodiac **S** 243
science, advances in **S** 66
Copernicus, lunar crater **M** 455; *picture* **M** 449
Copernicus (co-PER-nic-us), **Nicolaus,** Polish astronomer **C** 500–01
astronomy, history of **A** 471
Renaissance humanist **R** 160–61
Coping saws, tools **T** 213; *picture* **T** 212
Copland (COPE-land), **Aaron,** American composer **C** 501; **M** 402
dance music **D** 37
Copley, John Singleton, American painter **U** 116–17
Paul Revere, painting **U** 118
Copper C 502; **E** 154, 160
alchemy **C** 207
alloys **A** 168, 169
antiques **A** 321
beginnings of the history of chemistry **C** 205
brazing alloys **S** 249
bronze and brass **B** 409–10
Chilean economy dependent on **C** 253
cooking utensils, *picture* **M** 232
copper-producing regions **M** 314; **N** 293
metals, chart of ores, location, properties, uses **M** 227
open-pit mines, *pictures* **C** 252, **M** 314, **N** 67, 239, **S** 275, 292, **U** 97
ore, *picture* **R** 272

pyrite, "fool's gold," *picture* **R** 271
silver found in copper ores **S** 181
smelter, *picture* **A** 409
wire **W** 190a
world distribution, *diagram* **W** 260
Zambia is one of the world's leading producers **Z** 368
Copper-eyed Persian cats, *picture* **C** 143
Copper glance (chalcocite), copper ore **C** 502

Copperheads, Northern Democrats who, while not necessarily in sympathy with the Southern cause, opposed the U.S. Civil War in favor of negotiated peace. The name was taken from the copperhead snake, which strikes its victim without warning, and signified a surprise blow dealt Northerners from within their own ranks.

Copperheads, snakes **S** 209
animals harmful to people **I** 284
Copper River, Alaska **A** 133
Coppola, Francis Ford, American film director **M** 488b
Copra (CO-pra), dried meat of coconuts **C** 369
important cash crop of Pacific islands **P** 5; *picture* **P** 4
Seychelles **S** 129
Cops (coppers), name for American policemen **P** 373–74
Coptic Church A 56
Copy editors B 331
newspapers **N** 202
Copying machines O 57–58; *pictures* **O** 56
Copyright, to protect the rights of creative people **C** 503
copyright page of a book **B** 331
date of a book **L** 181
photocopying in libraries **L** 179
Webster, Noah, efforts to promote **W** 99
Copy writers, in advertising
book promotions **B** 334
Coquina (co-KI-na), type of limestone **R** 267
Coracle, small boat, *picture* **T** 262
Coracoid (COR-a-coid) **bone**
strongest in a bird's skeleton **B** 201
Coral Gables, part of Greater Miami, Florida **M** 254
Coralli, Jean, French choreographer **B** 25
Corals, marine animals or polyps **C** 503–04
earth's history **E** 23–24
ocean life **O** 38–39
organic gems **G** 76
polyps related to jellyfishes and other coelenterates **J** 74
Coral Sea O 47
Coral Sea, Battle of, 1942 **W** 294
Coral snakes S 208–09
Arizona coral king snake, *picture* **S** 205
harmful to people **I** 284, 285; *picture* **I** 282
Corbett, James John, American boxer **B** 353
Corbusier, Le *see* Le Corbusier
Cordgrasses, builders of land **G** 319
Cordilleras (cor-dil-AIR-as), groups of mountain systems **M** 499
Canada's westernmost landform **C** 51
North American **N** 282, 284
See also systems by name
Córdoba (CORD-o-ba), Argentina **A** 394
Córdoba, Spain **S** 352, 356
Cordobés, El, Spanish bullfighter **B** 450
Córdova, Francisco Hernández de
Mexico, history of **M** 247
Cordovan (CORD-o-van) **leather L** 110

Cormorants (COR-mor-ants), water birds found throughout
the world. The adult is a dark-colored bird that grows up to
1 m (3 ft) long. It has a slender hooked bill, short, strong
legs, and webbed toes. The throat-pouch and face parts
are usually bare of feathers and may be brightly colored.
Cormorants live in groups and fish for food, chiefly in salt
water.

Cornelia (lived about 150 B.C.), Roman matron, paragon
of virtue. She was the daughter of Scipio Africanus, wife of
Tiberius Sempronius Gracchus, and mother of the Grac-
chi, champions of democratic reforms. She refused to
remarry after her husband's death, and devoted herself to
the care and education of her sons. Legend says that she
once shamed a foolish woman who was inordinately fond
of jewels by pointing to her own children and saying,
"These are my jewels."

Cornell, Ezra (1807–74), American businessman and
philanthropist, b. Westchester Landing, N.Y. Assisting
Samuel Morse in construction of the Washington-Balti-
more telegraphic line, he developed a method of insulating
telegraph wire supported by poles. He established numer-
ous lines, including ones in New York, Vermont, Quebec,
and the Middle West. He merged his company with others,
forming the Western Union Telegraph Company. He
served as a director of this company (1855–74). He sat in
New York State Assembly (1861–63) and Senate (1863–
67) and with Andrew Dickson White founded Cornell Uni-
versity (1865).

Cornell, Katharine (1893–1974), American actress, b.
Berlin, Germany. She is well-known for her roles in *The
Barretts of Wimpole Street, Candida,* and *Romeo and
Juliet* and is the author of an autobiography, *I Wanted to
Be an Actress.*

Cornering the market, stock-market term for buying all or
most of the stock in a commodity in order to be able to
control its price. Today it is an infrequent manipulation.
Some of the most famous corners occurred in late 19th
and early 20th centuries. In the United States cornering
was prohibited by the Securities Exchange Act of 1934,
which prevents deception in sale of stocks. The term also
refers to a virtual monopoly in any area.

Cornstalk (1720?–77), Shawnee Indian chief who allied himself with French traders and led raid against English settlers in Virginia (1759). He raided settlements in western Virginia during Pontiac's War (1763) and formed a treaty with the governor of Virginia, Lord Dunmore, after his defeat (1774) at Point Pleasant. After 3 years of peace (1777) Cornstalk went to warn white settlers that the Shawnee, incited by the British, were about to attack them. He was held as hostage and was murdered.

Cornucopia, horn of plenty, *picture* **T** 153
Cornwallis (corn-WA-lis), **Charles, 1st Marquess,** British general **R** 202, 207–08
　Washington and Cornwallis **W** 40
　What was Guilford Courthouse? **N** 316
Cornwallis, Edward, English founder of Halifax **N** 344h
Cornwell, Dean, American illustrator and painter **I** 92
Coroebus of Elis, Greek athlete, first Olympic Games winner **O** 104
Corona (co-RO-na), luminous halo around the sun **E** 41–42; **S** 462–63
Coronado (cor-o-NA-do), **Francisco Vásquez de,** Spanish explorer in America **A** 416; **E** 386; **N** 96, 194
Coronagraphs (co-RO-na-graphs), special kind of telescope **S** 466–67
Coronary circulation of blood, in the heart **H** 86a
　heart disease **D** 196

Coronation (from Latin *coronare,* meaning "to wreathe" or "to crown"), act or ceremony of crowning a king, queen, or sovereign's consort.

Coronation of Napoleon, The, painting by David, detail, *picture* **N** 11
Coronation of the Virgin, painting by Fra Angelico **P** 20
Corot (cor-O), **Jean Baptiste,** French painter **F** 426; **P** 29
Corporal punishment **P** 468

Corporate state, system of government in which workers and employers in each industry are organized into corporations that assume jurisdiction over particular areas of the state's economic life. An attempt was made to form a corporate state in Italy (1925–39) under Mussolini, but the system was maintained only by dictatorship and police power.

Corporation for Public Broadcasting (CPB) **T** 70b
Corporations, in business and industry
　companies in industry **I** 242–51
　foundations **F** 390
　income tax on profits **I** 110
　Junior Achievement, Inc., miniature corporations **J** 157–58
　labor and management represented **L** 11
　stocks and bonds **S** 427–33
　trusts and monopolies **T** 303–06
Corps, army combat unit **U** 173
Corpus Christi (Body of Christ), **Feast of** **C** 284
　religious holiday **R** 154, 290
Corpuscles (COR-puscles), blood **B** 256–57
Correctional institutions, for imprisonment of convicted criminals **P** 468
Correggio (cor-REJ-o), **Antonio Allegri da,** Italian artist **I** 472
Corregidor, Philippines
　World War II **W** 293
Correlative conjunctions, in sentences **P** 92
Correspondence see Letter writing
Corridos (cor-RI-dose), Latin-American folk music **L** 74

Corrosion
　aluminum resists **A** 177
　anticorrosive paints **P** 32
　See also Rust
Corrugated paper **P** 53
Corsac foxes **D** 250
Corsairs, Barbary, pirates **P** 263
Corsica, island south of Genoa **I** 429
　birthplace of Napoleon I **N** 9
　French places of interest **F** 407
Corso, Gregory, American poet **A** 211
Cortes (COR-tes), **Hernando,** Spanish conqueror of Mexico **C** 508
　cacao beans (chocolate) introduced to Spain **C** 274
　exploration of the New World **E** 385
　factors important in helping Cortes conquer Mexico **M** 247
　myths of Aztecs helped Spanish conquest **M** 561–62
Cortex, of the brain **B** 366, 367–68
Corticosteroids, drugs **D** 191
Cortina d'Ampezzo, Italy
　Olympic Games, 1956 **O** 112
Cortisone, drug **P** 313

Cortot (cort-O), **Alfred Denis** (1877–1962), French pianist and conductor, b. Nyon, Switzerland. He is noted for interpretations of Richard Wagner's music. He formed a trio with violinist Jacques Thibaud and cellist Pablo Casals (1905) and founded (1919) and directed the École Normale de Musique in Paris.

Corundum (cor-UN-dum), aluminum oxide, gem mineral **G** 71
　abrasive for grinding and polishing **G** 387
Corvinus, Matthias see Matthias Corvinus
Corvus, constellation
　located by radio waves, *picture* **R** 70
Corydon, former capital of Indiana **I** 151
Cos, Greek island, home of Hippocrates **M** 203

Cosa (CO-sa), **Juan de la** (1460?–1510), Spanish navigator. He accompanied Christopher Columbus on his first voyage to America (1492) and in his exploration of Cuba (1498). Cosa also made voyages to the coast of South America and made the oldest known map of the New World (1500).

Cosby, Bill (1938–　　　), American comedian and actor, b. Philadelphia, Pa. A high school dropout, he joined the U.S. Navy and later attended Temple University on an athletic scholarship. He writes his own material, based mainly on his childhood experiences. He has played in numerous nightclubs, and his comedy albums have sold millions of copies. He was the first black entertainer to co-star in a weekly television series *(I Spy).* He has won 4 Emmy and 8 Grammy Awards.

Cosby, William, American colonial governor **Z** 368a
Cosi fan tutte (co-SI fon TU-tay), opera by Mozart **O** 143
Cosmetics **C** 509–10
　beauty culture **B** 110-111
　deodorants **D** 117
　makeup, theatrical **P** 341; **T** 156
　Where did pioneers get their cosmetics? **C** 510
　See also Perfumes
Cosmic rays **C** 511–13
　cloud chambers to detect radioactivity **A** 489
　ions and ionization **I** 353

radiation belts **R** 46–49
radioactive dating **R** 65
Cosmology (cos-MOL-ogy), the branch of metaphysics
that studies the structure of the universe **P** 192
relativity **R** 139–44
Cosmonauts, U.S.S.R. space explorers **S** 340
space flights and flight data **S** 340j–340k
See also Astronauts
Cosmos, flowers **G** 46
Cosmos, Soviet space probe **S** 346
Cosmos, term used for universe **U** 196–204

Cossacks (from Turkish for "freeman" or "adventurer"),
wild, warring tribes of czarist Russia. The Cossacks were
runaways, discontents, and adventurers who formed set-
tlements (16th century) on the Ukrainian frontier. They
gained a reputation as daring horsemen and served in the
czar's security police (19th century) in return for land.
Ukraine, history of **U** 9

Costa, Lucio, Brazilian architect **L** 67
Costa Brava ("Rugged Coast"), Spain, *picture* **S** 353
Cost accountants B 314

Costain, Thomas Bertram (1885–1965), American editor
and author, b. Brantford, Ontario, Canada. He was an edi-
tor with *Saturday Evening Post* (1920–34) and Doubleday
and Company (1939–45) but is best known for his novels,
The Silver Chalice and *The Black Rose.*

Costa Rica C 514–18
agriculture, *picture* **A** 97
banana crop, *picture* **B** 37
Central America **C** 174–77
flag **F** 242
life in Latin America **L** 47–61
national anthem **N** 21
Costa Rica, University of, *picture* **C** 516
Coster, Charles de, Belgian writer **B** 129
Cost of living *see* Standard of living
Costume
dolls of the world, *pictures* **D** 263–69
fashions through the centuries, *pictures* **F** 66–69
folk dancing **F** 300
hats from different parts of the world and from
history, *pictures* **H** 53, 55
national costumes, traditional, *pictures* **C** 349,
350
Pilgrim boy and girl **T** 152
plays **P** 341; *pictures* **P** 339, 340
shoes, historical survey of, *pictures* **S** 163
See also Academic dress; Clothing; Uniforms; and
people section of country articles
Costume designers, of plays **T** 158
motion pictures **M** 481
Costume jewelry J 92, 101
Coterie (CO-ter-rie), social unit, for animals **A** 281

Cotingas, birds of the Western Hemisphere, chiefly of trop-
ical forests. All cotingas are alike in structure of the vocal
organs, legs, and feet. But some are drab, while others are
brightly colored and ornamented by crests, beards, or
feathered tassels. Cotingas include the brilliantly colored
cock of the rock and the umbrella bird. On the umbrella
bird's head is a crest of feathers that it can expand like an
umbrella.

Cotman, John Sell, English painter **E** 241
Cotonou (co-ton-NU), Benin **B** 139, 140

Cotopaxi (co-to-PAX-i), active volcano in the Andes
A 252; **E** 54
Cotswold Hills, England
limestone cottages, *picture* **H** 174
Cottage cheese D 13; **M** 310
Cottage industries, supplanted by the Industrial
Revolution **I** 233–34
English thatched cottage, *picture* **A** 302
Cottage system, of reformatories **P** 470
Cotton C 519–524a
bales ready for shipment, *picture* **U** 105
boll weevils **P** 285
Confederate States of America **C** 459
cotton gin in Georgia **G** 132–33
experiment on heat loss **E** 351
fibers **F** 104, 105, 106
first grown in India **A** 223
flame cultivators **F** 59
guncotton, explosive **E** 392
harvesting, *picture* **N** 310
Industrial Revolution, America's contribution of the
cotton gin **I** 238–39
King Cotton economy, Alabama **A** 119–20, 127
rope **R** 333
stripping cotton, *picture* **N** 299
textile industry **T** 141
Whitney, Eli **W** 166
world distribution **W** 264
Cotton belt, cotton-growing area of United States
C 522
Cotton bolls C 519, 523
Cotton-boll weevils P 285
Cotton Bowl, Dallas, Texas, New Year's Day football
game **D** 14; **F** 365
Cotton Bowl Stadium, Dallas, Texas **D** 14
Cotton gin C 520–21, 523
early textile industry in America **T** 141
Whitney, Eli **W** 166
Cotton Kingdom, term applied to the southern United
States **S** 198
Industrial Revolution in America **I** 239
Cottonmouths (water moccasins), snakes **I** 284;
S 209; *pictures* **L** 218, **S** 210
Cotton picker C 523; *picture* **C** 522
Cottonseed oil C 524; **O** 76
Cottonseed products C 524
margarine and shortenings **O** 77, 79
Cotton stripper, machine used to harvest cotton
C 523; *picture* **N** 299
Cottontail rabbits R 22, 23
Cottonwood, tree, *picture* **T** 276
bud scales and leaf scar, *picture* **L** 119
Kansas, state tree of, *picture* **K** 177
male and female flowers, *picture* **P** 297
Nebraska, state tree of, *picture* **N** 83
Wyoming, state tree of, *picture* **W** 323
Cotyledons (cot-i-LE-dons), of seeds **F** 283; **P** 299
Coubertin (coo-ber-TAN), **Pierre de,** French businessman
and sportsman **O** 103, 105–06, 107
Cougars (COO-gars), mountain lions **C** 139
Coulees (COO-lees), steep-walled valleys **A** 146a;
M 325; **W** 14

Coulomb (coo-LOM), **Charles Augustin de** (1736–1806),
French physicist, b. Angoulême. He invented the torsion
balance and used it to discover the law named for him.
This law states that the attraction or repulsion of two elec-
trical charges or two magnetic poles is inversely propor-
tional to the square of the distance between them. The
coulomb, electrical unit, was also named for him.

Council for Mutual Economic Assistance (COMECON), an organization of countries allied with the Soviet Union. It was founded in 1949 to co-ordinate economic development and trade. COMECON also works to expand technology and industrialization and to improve the standard of living in member nations. Bulgaria, Cuba, Czechoslovakia, East Germany, Hungary, Mongolia, Poland, Rumania, the U.S.S.R., and Vietnam are members. A large part of each member's foreign trade is carried on with other member nations.

   trade in Eastern Europe   **E** 327; **I** 329; **U** 39

Council Grove, Kansas   **K** 186
Council-manager, form of municipal government
      M 506
Council of Economic Advisers, in the United States
      E 51

Council of Europe, an organization of European nations formed to promote social and economic progress and to uphold parliamentary democracy. It devotes particular attention to the rights of the individual. The organization was founded in 1949, and its membership has grown to 21. Headquarters are in Strasbourg, France.

Council of Jerusalem, A.D. 50   **R** 288
Council of Ministers, U.S.S.R.   **U** 42
Council of Nicaea *see* Nicaea, Council of, 325
Council of Trent *see* Trent, Council of
Councils, church *see* Church councils
Councils, ecumenical *see* Ecumenical councils
Counseling *see* Guidance; Social work; Vocations
Counselors at law *see* Lawyers
Countable sets, in mathematics   **M** 161
Countercurrents, of the ocean   **O** 33
Counterespionage (counter-ES-pi-o-nodge)   **S** 388
Counterpoint, in music   **M** 299, 533
      Bach's *Art of the Fugue*   **B** 5; **M** 536
Counter Reformation, of Roman Catholic Church
      C 287
Counterspies   **S** 389
Counties, major divisions of states   **M** 503–04
      See also county maps for each state
Counting, (natural) **numbers**   **N** 384
Count of Monte Cristo, The, novel by Dumas *père*
      D 342
Country and western music   **C** 524b–525; **R** 262a,
      262b
      Tennessee   **T** 82
Country Bedroom, The, poem by Frances Cornford
      P 355
Country dances   **D** 29
Country life *see* Farm life
County agent, adviser on agriculture   **A** 94, 95

Coup d'etat (coo d'et-TA) (from French, meaning literally "stroke of state"), sudden overthrow of existing government by unconstitutional and sometimes violent means. It differs from outright revolution in that there is no popular uprising and no prolonged fighting. Louis Napoleon produced a "coup d'etat" (1851) when he dismissed the popular assembly and had himself declared emperor of France.

Couperin (coo-PRAN), **François,** French composer
      F 445
Couple dances   **F** 299
Couplet (CUP-let), in poetry   **P** 353
      Dryden's use of heroic couplet   **E** 256

Coups (KOOZ), successful blows against an Indian
      enemy   **I** 167, 168, 196
Courbet (coor-BAY), **Gustave,** French painter   **F** 426
      modern art   **M** 386–87
      realism in painting   **P** 29
      Sleeping Spinner, painting   **F** 427
Coureurs de bois (COUR-er d'BWA), French-Canadian
      fur traders   **F** 520
Courrier, Le, collage by Georges Braque   **D** 136
Court, contempt of *see* Contempt of court

Court, Margaret Smith (1942–   ), Australian tennis player, b. Albury. Court won many titles in major tournaments. In 1970 she became the second woman (Maureen Connolly was first, in 1953) to achieve a Grand Slam—singles titles in the Australian, Wimbledon, French, and U.S. championships. In 1979 she was inducted into the Tennis Hall of Fame.

Courtly love
      French literature   **F** 436

Court-martial, military court comprised of commissioned officers responsible for trial of members of armed forces or those civilians who commit offenses against military or naval law in time of war or during military operations.

Court of Queen's Bench, Canada   **C** 78
Courts, of law   **C** 526–30
      adoption laws   **A** 26
      Are British and American courts different?   **C** 529
      Canada   **C** 77–78
      civil rights and civil liberties protected   **C** 316
      common law, origin of, in England   **E** 218
      divorce   **D** 236
      International Court of Justice (World Court)   **I** 317,
      322
      jury   **J** 159–60
      juvenile courts   **J** 164
      lawyer's work   **L** 92
      penalties for crimes   **C** 532d
      president of the United States, judicial powers
      P 454
      probate proceedings for wills   **W** 175
      state courts (the judiciary)   **S** 415
      Supreme Court of the United States   **S** 476–77
      See also Law and law enforcement; Lawyers; Prisons
Courtship
      Latin America   **L** 52
      See also Dating, a social custom
Courtship, of animals
      birds   **B** 212
      fishes   **F** 200
      snakes   **S** 213–14
Court tennis   **R** 34; **T** 100
      See also Tennis
Couscous, African dish made from semolina   **F** 339;
      T 311
Cousins, Robin, British figure skater   **O** 116c
Cousteau (coo-STO), **Jacques-Yves,** French inventor of
      the Aqualung   **S** 189–90
      filming his *World Without Sun,* picture   **M** 479
      oceanographic research   **O** 42
      underwater exploration   **U** 14

Cousy (KOO-zee), **Bob** (Robert Joseph Cousy) (1928–   ), American basketball player, b. New York, N.Y. He was one of the game's greatest players. A star of the Boston Celtics (1950–63), he led them to six National Basketball Association championships. He was chosen for the

All-Pro team ten years in a row. Later, he coached college and professional teams. He was named to the Basketball Hall of Fame in 1971. Cousy was commissioner of the American Soccer League from 1974 to 1979.

Couturiers (coo-TU-ri-ers), designers of high fashion **F** 70
Covalent (co-VALE-ent) **bond**, in chemistry **C** 218
Covent (CUV-ent) **Garden**, London, England **L** 337
Coventry, England
    cathedral, modern **C** 133
Cover crops A 93
    soil conservation **S** 232

Coverdale, Miles (1488?–1569), English ecclesiastic and reformer, b. Yorkshire. A priest and scholar, he made first English translation of entire Bible to be printed (1535). He superintended new English edition, called the Great Bible, and second edition, called Cranmer's Bible (1540). He left England (1540) after execution of Protestant reformer Thomas Cromwell and went to Germany. In 1548 he returned to England as chaplain to Edward VI and became bishop of Exeter in 1551. His religious views again forced him to leave England (1553) when Mary I became queen. He returned in 1559, when Elizabeth I came to throne.
    Bible in English, history of **B** 153

Covered bridges B 400
    Cornwall Bridge, Connecticut **C** 477
    longest in the world, Hartland, New Brunswick,
        picture **N** 138e
Covered wagons *see* Conestoga wagons
Coveys, of quail *see* Quail
Covington, Kentucky **K** 224
Coward, Noël, English actor and playwright **D** 298
    comedies of manners **E** 268
Cow beef C 148–49; **D** 4
Cowbirds, *picture* **B** 235
Cowboys C 146–47
    Argentina's gauchos **A** 388–89; *picture* **A** 391
    Arizona, *picture* **A** 413
    Chile **C** 250
    Costa Rica **C** 516
    folk songs **F** 311
    "Git Along, Little Dogies," folk song **F** 320
    Idaho, *picture* **I** 61
    llaneros of Venezuela **V** 296
    National Cowboy Hall of Fame and Western Heritage
        Center **O** 89
    Pecos Bill, cowboy hero **F** 316–17
    ranch life **R** 102–03; *picture* **R** 105
    rodeos **R** 281–82
    roping **R** 333–35
    work songs **F** 304
Cowcatcher, device to remove animals from railroad
        tracks **L** 330

Cowell, Henry Dixon (1897–1965), American composer, b. Menlo Park, Calif. He developed tone clusters by hitting keyboard with forearm, elbow, or fist; invented, with Leon Theremin, the Rhythmicon, device for mechanically producing rhythms and cross-rhythms; and founded *New Music Quarterly* (1927) for publication of ultramodern music. His compositions include *Dynamic Motion*, hymns and fuguing tunes, and the opera *O'Higgins of Chile*.

Cowish, herb with edible roots **I** 175, 176
Cowley, Abraham, English poet **O** 52

Cowling, protective covering
    bobsleds **B** 264–65

Cow pea, name for annual plant native to tropical areas of the Old and the New World. It has leaves in groups of three and seeds in long, thin pods. It is grown in the United States primarily as food for livestock.

Cowpens, Battle of, 1781 **R** 207; **S** 303
Cowpens National Battlefield, South Carolina **S** 303
Cowper (COO-per), **William**, English poet **E** 258
    illustration for "The Diverting History of John
        Gilpin," *picture* **C** 241
Cowpox, virus disease **D** 214; **M** 207
    Jenner's studies **J** 76
Cowries, mollusks **O** 278
Cows C 147, 149; **D** 3–8
    India, sacred animals **C** 145; *picture* **H** 132
    Jersey cow, *picture* **H** 218
    milk **M** 309
    spectrograms of animal sounds, *pictures* **A** 276

Cowslip, common name of many different kinds of plants. In the United States name refers to the Virginia cowslip, with trumpet-shaped, bluish flowers in clusters, and to the marsh marigold, with bright-yellow flowers. Cowslip mentioned by Shakespeare is a yellow-flowered plant native to England.

Cow towns, Kansas **K** 186–87, 188
Cox, David, English painter **E** 241

Coxey's Army, group of persons unemployed following Panic of 1893, led by Jacob Sechler Coxey in march to Washington, D.C. (1894). They presented petition to Congress urging allotment of funds to build new roads and make other public improvements that would give work to many of the unemployed. Known as the Commonweal of Christ, they were later joined by industrial groups from the Pacific coast.
    labor unrest in Ohio **O** 75

Coxswain (COX-in), steersman of racing boat **R** 338
Coyote Gulch, Utah, *picture* **P** 218
Coyotes (KY-otes) **D** 246–47
Coyote State, nickname for South Dakota **S** 313
Coypus (nutrias), South American rodents **R** 280
Cozzens (CUZZ-ens), **James Gould**, American novelist
    A 213
C.P.A. *see* Certified Public Accountant
CPB *see* Corporation for Public Broadcasting
CPR *see* Cardiopulmonary resuscitation
C.P.U., of computers *see* Central processing unit
Crab, constellation *see* Cancer
Crab apples A 333–34
    seedling, *picture* **G** 40
Crabgrass, *picture* **W** 105
Crab nebula, supernova **A** 476, 476c; **N** 98; **S** 409,
    410; *picture* **A** 475
    pulsars **Q** 8
Crabs, crustaceans **S** 168–71
    Chesapeake Bay fisheries, *picture* **M** 123
    crab fishing in the Bering Sea, *picture* **E** 286
    fiddler crabs measure time **L** 246–47
    horseshoe crab, related to crabs **H** 245
Crab's-eye bean, *picture* **P** 298
Crab spiders S 387; *picture* **S** 385
Crackers, food **B** 388b
Cracking, extracting gasoline from petroleum **G** 63
Cracow (CRA-cow), Poland **P** 360–61

Cradle, device for washing gold from sand   G 251;
    picture G 252
Cradle, harvesting tool   F 60
Cradleboards, for Indian babies   I 167, 196
Cradlesongs   F 303–04
Craft guilds   G 401–03
Crafts *see* Handicrafts
Crafts (trades) *see* Vocations
Craft unions   L 8–9
Craig, James, city planner of Edinburgh, Scotland
    U 233
Craigie House, Longfellow's home in Cambridge, Mass.
    L 342
Crampons, sharp spikes to fit on boots for mountain
    climbing   M 491
Cramps, menstrual   M 219b

Cranach (CRA-nock) (or Kranach; Kronach) (KRO-nock),
Lucas, the Elder (1472–1553), German artist, b. Kro-
nach. Noted primarily for religious pictures, portraits, and
classical subjects, he also engraved both wood and copper
and was court painter at Wittenburg (1504). His paintings
include *Crucifixion* and *Bathsheba at the Bath.*
    *Cardinal Albert of Brandenburg as St. Jerome in His
    Study,* painting   G 167

Cranberries   G 301; M 140; *picture* G 300
    New Jersey crop, *picture*   N 171
Cranberry bog, *picture*   G 300
Crane, Hart, American poet   A 210; O 73
Crane, Ichabod, character in *Legend of Sleepy Hollow,
The*   A 199–200
Crane, Stephen, American novelist   A 206, 208;
    N 178

Crane, Walter (1845–1915), English illustrator, b. Liver-
pool. Crane was one of the first illustrators to produce well-
designed, decorative picture books for children. His many
works include *Buckle My Shoe* and *Song of Sixpence.*
    book cover, *picture*   I 93
    children's literature, history of   C 239–40

Crane Memorial Library, Massachusetts, *picture*   U 124

Cranes, any one of a family of large, long-legged, migrating
birds that inhabit marshes and prairies of all continents
except South America. All have a long neck, head partly
bare of feathers, and a loud, distinctive call. They feed on
grain, fruits, some insects, and a few fish. The famous
whooping crane of North America is the tallest of American
birds.
    whooping cranes, *picture*   B 230

Cranes, machines   H 143–44
    shipbuilding, *picture*   S 161
Crankshaft, of the internal-combustion engine   I 308
Cranmer, Thomas, archbishop of Canterbury   E 221
    annulled marriage of Henry VIII and Catherine of
    Aragon   H 109
    Reformation in England   C 286
Crannogs, island refuges in lakes *see* Lake dwellers
Cranston, Rhode Island   R 224
Crappie, fish, *picture*   F 209
Crassus, Marcus Licinius, Roman statesman
    Caesar and Crassus   C 5
Crater Lake, Oregon   L 28; O 195; *pictures* L 29,
    O 202
    volcanic origin   O 192; V 382
Crater Lake National Park, Oregon   O 203
Craters, cup-shaped holes

Mars   M 107, 109; P 273
Mercury   P 270
meteors and meteorites   C 420–21
moon   M 449, 453, 455; *pictures* M 449, 452
Venus   P 270–71
volcanoes   V 383
Craters of the Moon National Monument, Idaho   I 63–
    64
Crawford, Robert, American teacher and poet   N 26
Crawford, Thomas, American sculptor   W 29
Crawford Notch, New Hampshire   N 157
Crawl, swimming stroke   S 490; *picture* S 492
Crawler tractor, construction machine   B 446
    "cat" train, *picture*   M 80
    farm machinery   F 55
Crayfish, crustaceans   S 168, 170, 171
    blood system, *diagram*   B 259
    fresh water creatures, *pictures*   L 257
    nervous system, *diagram*   B 363
Crayons, drawing materials   D 303

Crazy Horse (1849?–77), chief of Oglala Sioux Indians.
He led part of Sitting Bull's forces in battle of Little Big
Horn (1876), where Colonel George Armstrong Custer
made his famous "last stand." He surrendered (1877) at
Red Cloud agency in Nebraska. He was arrested when
army officers feared a planned uprising and was mortally
wounded as he resisted imprisonment.
    Indian Wars   I 169, 214; N 92

Crazy Horse Memorial, South Dakota   S 312
Cream, fat content of milk   B 467; M 309
    Babcock invented mechanical separator   B 467
Cream cheese   D 13
Cream of tartar *see* Tartar
Creams, cosmetics   C 509, 510
Creasy, Edward, English historian
    list of important battles   B 100–02

Creationism, a term for the belief that the world and
human beings were created solely by God. Many people
who hold this view identify themselves as creationists.
Because they do not believe that the creation of the world
can be explained scientifically, they do not accept the the-
ory of human evolution. They encourage educators to
present creationist beliefs along with the teaching of evo-
lution in science classes.

Creation of Adam, painting by Michelangelo   M 255
Creation of the world
    in Greek mythology   G 356
    in Norse mythology   N 277
    mythology   M 557–64
Creative writing *see* Writing (authorship)
Crèche (CRESH), French word for crib, Christmas
    Nativity   C 290; *picture* C 294
Crèche, name used for a group of penguin chicks
    P 123
Crécy (crai-CY), Battle of, 1346   H 281–82
    knights made warfare pay   K 274
Credit   I 288–89
    department store charge accounts   D 119
    in bookkeeping   B 312

Credit card, an identifying card authorizing a person or
organization to charge goods or services and be billed at a
later date. Issued by banks, petroleum companies, hotels,
department stores, or other large companies, they have
become very widely used.
    bank cards   B 45

Crédit Mobilier (cray-DI mo-bi-li-AY) **of America,** company involved in bribe scandal **G** 55

Credit union, co-operative association that finances small, short-term loans of members at low interest rates, the funds being raised by the members' buying shares in the union. These nonprofit organizations are chartered by the state or the federal government, and their profits are returned to members through dividends.
   banking **B** 47
   co-operatives **C** 499

Cree, Indians of North America **I** 170
Creek, Indians of North America **I** 188–89, 199
   Alabama **A** 112, 118, 126–27
   Florida **F** 273
   Horseshoe Bend, Battle of, 1814 **J** 4

Creepers, slender, small birds of forest regions throughout the cooler parts of the Northern Hemisphere. Of speckled and spotted brownish color, the creeper has a stiffened tail that it uses as a brace when climbing trees in search of insects. (Several birds of the nuthatch family are also called creepers but these birds do not use their tails as braces when climbing.) The brown creeper has the widest range of all the creepers. It is found from Alaska to Nicaragua in the New World and from Siberia to Japan in the Old World.
   brown creeper, *picture* **B** 222

Creeping, animal locomotion **A** 294
Creighton, Helen, Canadian folk music collector **C** 63
Cremation, of the dead **F** 493
Crenshaw melons **M** 216
Creole, language **L** 50
   Cape Verde **C** 102
   Haiti **H** 7
   Seychelles **S** 129
Creoles, people
   Belize **B** 132
   French Guiana **G** 396
   Louisiana **L** 353
   Sierra Leone **S** 174
   Surinam **S** 478b
Creole State, nickname for Louisiana **L** 349

Creosote, dark-brown to yellowish oily liquid with a smoky odor. It is made by distilling coal or wood tar and is used to preserve wood and as a disinfectant.

Creosote bush, plant **N** 123
Crepe (CRAPE) **rubber** **R** 345
Crerar (CRE-rar), **Henry Duncan Graham,** Canadian soldier **C** 80
Crescendo, musical term **M** 533
Crescent moon **M** 447
Cress Delahanty, novel by Jessamyn West **H** 278

Cressida, in Greek mythology, daughter of the Trojan priest Calchas. Cressida broke her vows to her Trojan lover, Troilus, and transferred her affections to the Greek hero Diomede. Chaucer and Shakespeare wrote versions of the legend.

Crests, in heraldry **H** 118
Crests, of a wave **T** 253–54
Cretaceous (cret-A-cious) **period,** in geology **E** 24; **F** 387
   dinosaurs **D** 172, 174–75, 180–81

fossil birds **B** 207, 209
water and land areas, *diagram* **E** 342
Crete, island southeast of Greece **I** 429–30
   ancient civilization **A** 226–27
   bull dancing in ancient Crete **B** 449
   clay calendar, *picture* **C** 12
   Greece, landforms of **G** 333
   Minoan architecture **A** 373–74
   Minoan art **A** 237–38
   painting at Knossos **P** 15–16
   ruins at Knossos, *picture* **A** 355
   water and drainage system **P** 342–43
   World War II **W** 290
Crevasses (cre-VASS-es), cracks
   glaciers **I** 7–8
Crèvecoeur (crev-CUR), **St. John de,** French-born American writer **A** 198

Crib death (sudden infant death syndrome, SIDS), the sudden and unexplained death of an apparently healthy baby. Crib death usually occurs among sleeping infants under 6 months of age. It is more frequent among premature babies, boy babies, and those in large cities. It happens most often during cold weather and at night. The specific causes of crib death are not known. It is thought that crib death is caused by a combination of factors. Some medical researchers feel that a defect in the central nervous system may be the cause. Others think that a viral infection of the respiratory tract (lungs) may be involved.

Criccieth, Wales, *picture* **U** 65

Crick, Francis H. C. (1916–   ), English biochemist, b. Northampton. Known for work on the large molecules making up all living things, he was awarded Nobel prize (1962) in medicine (with J. D. Watson and M. H. F. Wilkins) for showing the coiled structure of nucleic acids—the molecules that control heredity.
   science, history of **S** 77

Cricket, game **C** 531–32
   popular sport in the United Kingdom **U** 70
Crickets, insects
   ant colony dwellers **A** 325
   ears, *diagram* **I** 267
   leg, *diagram* **I** 273
Crime and criminology **C** 532a–532d
   arson **F** 153–54
   courts **C** 526–30
   Federal Bureau of Investigation **F** 76–77
   fingerprinting **F** 129
   jury **J** 159–60
   law and law enforcement **L** 87–89
   narcotics addicts **N** 13–14
   police **P** 372–77
   prisons **P** 468–70
   What are war crimes trials? **I** 318
Crime and Punishment, novel by Dostoevski **D** 287

Crimean (cri-ME-an) **War** (1854–56), armed conflict in which Russia was defeated by the combined armies of England, France, Sardinia, and Turkey. It was caused by Russia's effort to obtain control of Black Sea and eventual partition of Turkey. It was named after Crimean peninsula, where the war was fought, and was ended by the Treaty of Paris (1856).
   Nightingale, Florence **N** 259

Crimes against persons **C** 532a–532b, 532c

Crimes against property C 532a–532b, 532c
Crime stories *see* Mystery, detective, and suspense
    stories
Criminalist, person trained in the laboratory analysis of
    physical evidence C 532d
Criminal law L 87–88
    courts C 526–30
    jury J 160
    lawyers' work on criminal cases L 92
Criminals *see* Crime and criminology
Criminology *see* Crime and criminology
Criollos (cri-OLE-yos), Latin Americans of European
    descent L 48, 59, 61
    early Spanish settlers in Peru P 160, 161
    Mexico M 248
Crippen, Robert L., American astronaut S 340k

Crippled Children, Association for the Aid of (AACC), foun-
dation financing research on the causes, effects, and pre-
vention of conditions leading to crippling in children. The
organization was founded in 1900 and maintains head-
quarters in New York, N.Y.

Cristobal (cris-TO-bol), Panama Canal Zone
    adjoined to Colon P 45
Cristofori (cris-TOF-o-ri), **Bartolommeo,** Italian inventor
    of the piano P 241
    Italian music I 484
    keyboard instruments K 239
Critical size, in a chain reaction N 361–62
Criticism, literary *see* Literary criticism
Critics, literary L 312–13

Crivelli (cri-VEL-li), **Carlo** (1430–94?), Italian Renais-
sance artist, b. Venice. Associated with Venetian school of
art, he painted mostly madonnas. He was skilled in use of
tempera colors. His works include *Madonna della Candel-
etta* and *Coronation of the Virgin.*

Crizzling, of antique glass A 318

Croaker, any one of several long, flat fishes that produce
rumbling sound, which gives fish its name. Atlantic croak-
er is found in warm, shallow waters of the Atlantic. Brassy
in color, with dark spots, it is one of the main food fishes of
the middle Atlantic states.

Croatia (cro-A-sha), Yugoslav state Y 358
Croatoan Island, North Carolina A 181
Croce (CRO-chay), **Benedetto,** Italian philosopher and
    critic I 480
Crocheting (cro-SHAY-ing) K 281–84
Crockett, Davy, American frontiersman C 533
    folk hero tales F 311
Crocodiles C 533–35; R 180–81
Crocodilians (croc-o-DIL-ians), groups of reptiles
    C 533–35
Crocoite (CRO-co-ite), mineral C 296
Crocuses, flowers
    garden planting G 42; *picture* G 44
Crofton, Sir Walter, Irish prison reformer P 469
Crofts, Freeman Wills, Irish writer M 555
Croix de Guerre (crwa d'GAIR), French award, *picture*
    M 200
Cro-Magnon man, *picture* A 305
Crome, John, English painter E 240

Crompton (CRUMP-ton), **Samuel** (1753–1827), English
inventor, b. Firwood, near Bolton. He invented the spin-
ning mule (1779), which, with modifications, is used in

nearly all textile mills today. This machine produced finer,
smoother cloth by drawing, twisting, and winding cotton in
one operation. C 520

Cromwell, Oliver, Lord Protector of England C 536;
    E 223–24
    Irish crushed I 390
    Milton accepts post in his government M 312
Cromwell, Richard, Lord Protector of England, son of
    Oliver Cromwell C 536

Cronin (CRO-nin), **A. J.** (Archibald Joseph Cronin) (1896–
1980), English novelist and physician, b. Dumbarton-
shire, Scotland. He left the medical profession in 1930 to
devote his time to writing. His works include the novels
The Citadel and *The Keys of the Kingdom.*

Cronkite, Walter (1916–), American journalist and
commentator, b. St. Joseph, Mo. He was war correspon-
dent for United Press (1942–45) and chief correspondent
at the Nuremberg war crimes trials. Cronkite was a mem-
ber of the news staff of the Columbia Broadcasting System
from 1950 to 1981. He also anchored the news and was
managing editor of "CBS Evening News with Walter Cron-
kite."

Cronstedt (CROON-stet), **Axel,** Swedish scientist
    N 249
Cronus (CRO-nus), Greek god G 356

Crook, George (1829–90), American soldier, b. near Day-
ton, Ohio. Before the Civil War he served in Army as Indian
fighter and explorer of Northwest. As member of Union
Army, he fought in battles of South Mountain and Antie-
tam (1862) and in Chickamauga campaign (1863). He
commanded Union forces in West Virginia and led infantry
corps during General Sheridan's Shenandoah Valley cam-
paign (1864). After the war he played an important part in
Indian wars. He is known for fairness to Indians at a time
when they were often persecuted by white soldiers and
settlers.
    Indian Wars I 214

Crookes, Sir William (1832–1919), English scientist, b.
London. He discovered element thallium (1861), distin-
guished different forms of uranium, and invented Crookes
tube and radiometer for studies of electric discharges in
gases.
    cathode rays E 145

Crookston, Minnesota M 334
Crop, food storage chamber of birds' gullets B 202,
    221
Cropping, in photography P 213
Crops, farm A 88–89, 93, 96
    insect control by crop rotation I 258
    main crops of United States U 105, 108
    world distribution W 263–64
Croquet, (cro-KAY), game C 536–37
    See also Billiards

Crosby, Bing (Harry Lillis Crosby) (1904–77), American
singer and movie actor, b. Tacoma, Wash. He began his
singing career with Paul Whiteman's trio in 1927. He
starred in many films, among them *Going My Way* (for
which he received an Academy Award as best actor in
1944) and *White Christmas.*
    Gonzaga University library collection W 21

Cross, Mary Ann Evans *see* Eliot, George

Crossbar switching, in telephony **T** 58
Crossbills, birds **B** 209
Crossbreeding, of strains of plants and animals
    domestic dog, origin of the **D** 248
    genetic engineering **G** 88–89
Cross-country and road running, track events **T** 238–39
Cross-country skateboarding **S** 184b
Cross-country skiing **S** 184d, 184e; *picture* **S** 185
Crosscut saws, tools **T** 212
Cross examination, in law **C** 530
Crossing guards, for schools **S** 5–6
Crossing your fingers, superstition **S** 474
Cross matching, test for matching blood **M** 202
Cross of Gold, speech by William Jennings Bryan
    B 415–16
    oratory **O** 181
Cross-pollination, in botany
    flowers **F** 277–80
    fruitgrowing **F** 483
Cross-references, in indexes and in library catalogs
    I 114–15; **L** 186
Crossroads of America, motto of Indiana **I** 143
Crossroads of the East, nickname for Southeast Asia
    S 328
Cross staff (forestaff), navigation instrument **N** 64
Cross the T's, saying **T** 1
Crossword puzzles **W** 237
Cross your heart, superstition **S** 474
Croup (CROOP), acute form of laryngitis **D** 193
Crouse, Russel, American playwright **O** 73
Crow, constellation *see* Corvus
Crow, Indians of North America **I** 168
Crown, glassmaking process **G** 229
Crown, of teeth **T** 48
Crown gall tumor, in plants **C** 90

Crown jewels, emblems or insignia—often including crowns, scepters, and swords—inherited by monarchs when they ascend the throne. The crown jewels of Britain are displayed in a special jewel house within the Tower of London.
    famous diamonds, *pictures* **D** 156

Crowns, royalty
    French crown, *picture* **J** 97
    head coverings, *pictures* **H** 53, 55
    Kohinoor diamond **D** 156
Crows, birds **B** 220; *picture* **B** 235
    talking birds **P** 86; *picture* **P** 84
Crows and cranes, line game **G** 24
Crozat (craw-ZA), **Antoine,** French merchant **L** 362
CRT *see* Cathode-ray tubes
Crucifixion, of Jesus Christ **J** 83, 86–87
    Byzantine art depicting **B** 488–89
    detail from German carving depicting, *picture*
    G 166
Crucifixion, The, painting by Taddeo Gaddi, *picture*
    J 86
Crude oil **P** 169–70
    petroleum before being refined **F** 488
Cruelty, grounds for divorce **D** 236
Crufts dog show **D** 261
Cruikshank (CROOK-shank), **George,** English artist
    etching from *Oliver Twist* **I** 91

Cruise missile, a small, unpiloted, and very accurate type of missile. It was designed to have a range of 2,400 km (1,500 mi), flying at altitudes low enough to avoid detection by enemy radar. The missile was intended to replace expensive piloted bombers and to be capable of being launched from submarines, ships, aircraft, or the ground. **M** 347, 348, 349; *picture* **M** 343

Cruisers, United States Navy **U** 192
Cruise ships **O** 21
Crummell, Alexander, American clergyman **N** 250e
Crunden, John, English architect **E** 240
Crusades **C** 538–40; **R** 292
    building methods, effect on **A** 380
    Byzantine Empire weakened **B** 492
    castle built by Crusaders, *picture* **S** 506
    clothing, new types introduced to Europe **C** 351
    Constantinople captured, 1204 **B** 492
    cosmetics brought to Europe **C** 510
    exploration encouraged **E** 372–73
    Jews persecuted in Europe during **J** 108
    kettledrums used in battle **D** 336
    medals used to identify knights **M** 198
    Muslims versus Christians **I** 414
    Venetians destroy Byzantine art **B** 490
Crusoe, Robinson, hero of Defoe's *Robinson Crusoe,*
    picture **F** 111
    See also Selkirk, Alexander
Crust, of the earth **E** 19, 20; **G** 113–17; *diagram*
    G 112
    earthquakes **E** 27–34
    seismic waves picture earth's interior **E** 33
Crust, of the moon **M** 450, 453
Crustaceans (crust-A-ce-ans), large class of mostly
    aquatic animals **S** 168–71
    animal plankton **P** 280–81
Crustal plates *see* Plates, of the earth's crust
Crutchers, soap mixing machines **D** 147
Crux Australis (aus-TRAY-lis), Southern Cross,
    constellation **C** 491
Cruz (CROOSE), **Juana Inés de la,** Mexican poet **L** 70
Cruz, Ramón Ernesto, president of Honduras **H** 199
Cruzen, Richard, American naval officer **P** 368
Crwth (KRUTHE), musical instrument, *picture* **M** 548

Cryobiology, the study of the effects of extreme cold on living things. Rapid freezing can preserve some living tissues for an indefinite period of time. Liquid nitrogen is usually used because it can freeze living cells in a few seconds. In the cells, life processes stop. When thawed rapidly, the cells start to work again. Blood and blood components, sperm cells, and skin tissue can be frozen and thawed successfully. In cryosurgery, diseased cells in the body are destroyed by freezing.

Cryogenics (cry-o-GEN-ics), science of low temperatures
    H 90
    liquid oxygen and other liquid gases **L** 308
Cryolite (CRY-o-lite), mineral
    aluminum refining **A** 176
    Greenland, major source of **G** 369
Cryptography (cryp-TOG-raphy), secret writing using
    codes and ciphers **C** 369–71
Crystal glass **G** 230; *picture* **G** 236, 237
Crystalline lens, of the eye **L** 149
Crystallography, study of crystals **S** 251
    ways of identifying minerals **R** 272
Crystal Palace, International Exposition, 1851 **F** 13;
    picture **F** 14
Crystals **C** 541–46
    alloys **A** 168, 169
    diamond **D** 153, 154
    gemstones **G** 69
    how solids form **S** 251

Crystals (continued)
  ice crystal clouds **C** 359, 360
  piezoelectricity, a characteristic of quartz **Q** 6
  polarized light **L** 271–72
  polarizing microscopes used to study **M** 284
  quartz **Q** 6–7
  rocks and minerals **R** 264, 272
  snowflakes **R** 95–96
Ctenophores (TEN-o-phors), jellyfishlike animals **J** 75

Ctesibius (te-SIB-ius), Greek physicist and inventor who lived in Alexandria during the 2nd century B.C. He is credited with many mechanical inventions, including water clock and force pump.
  gear wheels **G** 65–66

Ctesiphon, Arch of, Iraq **I** 382
Ctesiphon II, painting by Frank Stella **M** 396b
Cuauhtémoc (cwow-TAY-moc), last Aztec emperor **M** 247
Cuba **C** 547–51
  Caribbean Sea and islands **C** 116, 118, 119
  Castro, Fidel **C** 130
  Columbus' discovery **C** 417
  Communism **C** 445
  flag **F** 241
  issue of imperialism for McKinley **M** 189
  Kennedy, John F., administration policies **K** 210
  life in Latin America **L** 47–61
  Monroe Doctrine and why it was not invoked in 1960 **M** 427
  national anthem **N** 21
  Ostend Manifesto and U.S. attempt to buy Cuba **B** 419; **P** 247
  refugees **R** 137
  schoolgirls, *picture* **L** 48
  Spanish-American War, 1898 **S** 374–76
  territorial expansion of the United States **T** 113–14
Cube, geometric figure
  crystals **C** 544
Cubi IX, steel sculpture by David Smith **S** 105
Cubic measure, of volume **W** 113
  matter measured by space occupied **M** 170
Cubism, modern art movement **F** 431–32; **M** 390
  art of the artist **A** 438g
  Braque, Georges **B** 371
  Cézanne's influence **C** 181
  Mondrian, Piet **M** 407
  painting in the 20th century **P** 30
  Picasso **P** 243
  planes, flat surfaces in design **D** 136
  sculpture of the 20th century **S** 104
Cubits, measures of length **W** 109
Cub Scouts **B** 357, 359
  uniform, salute, and badges, *pictures* **B** 358
  Wolf Cubs of Canada **B** 360
Cuchulain (cu-HUL-in), Irish hero **I** 392

Cuckoo (CU-koo), small, long-tailed, brownish bird with short bill curved downward. Cuckoos are found in most parts of world in forest areas. The name comes from mating call of male. Some species lay eggs in nests of other birds for care and feeding.
  adaptations in process of natural selection **L** 217
  black-billed cuckoo, *picture* **B** 233

Cuckoo clocks **W** 50; *picture* **W** 46
Cucumbers **V** 291

Cucurbit (cu-CUR-bit), gourd family
  melons **M** 216
Cud-chewers, animals **H** 209, 217, 221
Cue, billiards **B** 174
Cuer d'amours espris, Le (*The Heart of the Spirit of Love*), French medieval manuscript, page from **I** 87
Cuestas (CWES-tas), landforms **W** 323

Cuffe, Paul (1759–1817), American merchant and philanthropist, b. Cuttyhunk Island, Mass. He worked to improve position of blacks in America and was influential in passing Massachusetts law (1783) that gave blacks equal legal rights and privileges, including right to vote. He advocated settlement of blacks in Africa and financed voyages to Sierra Leone. **B** 250e

Cugnot (coon-YO), **Nicholas,** French engineer **A** 541; **T** 264
Cukor (CU-kor), **George,** American motion picture director, *picture* **M** 479

Culbertson, Ely (1893–1955), American writer and contract bridge expert, b. Poyana de Vervilao, Rumania. He was editor of *Bridge World Magazine,* captain of American team in international bridge tournaments, and author of *Contract Bridge Blue Book*.

Cullen, Countee (1903–46), American poet, b. New York, N.Y. He wrote lyrical poetry describing life of blacks. Cullen was assistant editor of *Opportunity: Journal of Negro Life* (1926–28). His works include *On These I Stand* and *Ballad of the Brown Girl*. **A** 210

Cullen, Michael, American supermarket owner **S** 468
Cullinan, diamond **D** 156
Culottes (cu-LOTTS), French knee breeches **C** 352
Culpepper Minutemen, flag, 1775 **F** 229
Cultivators and cultivation, of the soil **F** 58–59
  vegetable gardening **V** 288
Cultural anthropology **A** 300–05, 308, 309
  artifacts from past cultures compared **A** 360–61
  Mead, Margaret **M** 191
Cultural patterns, in geography **G** 104
Cultural Revolution, 1966–69, China **C** 272
  Mao Tse-tung and Chiang Ching **M** 86
Cultured milk products **D** 10
Cultured pearls **P** 114–15
Culture heroes **M** 560–61
Cultures, of bacteria **B** 11
  medical laboratory tests **M** 202, 209
  studies in microbiology **M** 275
Culverts, drainpipes **R** 249
Cumaná (cu-ma-NA), Venezuela **V** 300
Cumberland, Maryland **M** 127
Cumberland Gap, eastern United States **K** 214
  Wilderness Road **O** 255
Cumberland Gap National Historical Park
  Kentucky **K** 221
  Tennessee **T** 83
  Virginia **V** 353
Cumberland House, fur-trading post **F** 521
Cumberland Island National Seashore, Georgia **G** 141
Cumberland Narrows, natural gorge, *picture* **M** 118
Cumberland River **T** 77
Cumberland Road (National Road) **O** 255, 267; **P** 260
  how transportation affects interstate commerce **I** 331
  Indiana **I** 143

Maryland **M** 123
Ohio **O** 66
West Virginia **W** 133
Cumin, spice product **S** 382
Cummings, Edward Estlin (e. e. cummings), American poet and painter **A** 210
Cumulative (CU-mu-la-tive) **Book Index I** 115
Cumulative stories and songs F 303, 322–23
Cumulonimbus (cum-mu-lo-NIM-bus), clouds **C** 360; *picture* **C** 361
hail-producing **R** 98
Cumulus clouds C 360; *picture* **C** 361
Cuna Indians, of Panama, *picture* **P** 43
Cuneiform (CU-ne-if-orm), ancient writing system
alphabet **A** 170
ancient civilizations **A** 218, 224–25
Eblaite civilization **A** 222
how numbers were written **N** 395; *picture* **N** 397
libraries on clay tablets **L** 192–93
Cuneni, Rumania, *picture* **R** 356
Cunha (COON-ya), **Euclides da,** Brazilian writer **B** 377
Cunningham, Glenn, American runner **K** 190

Cunningham, Merce (Mercier Cunningham) (1919–), American dancer and choreographer, b. Centralia, Wash. Cunningham is known for creating new forms of abstract dance movement. He began his career in 1940 with the Martha Graham dance company and also began a long collaboration with John Cage, one of the best-known composers of modern music. He formed his own company in the early 1950's and choreographed more than 50 works for it, including *Suite by Chance, Rune, Variations V,* and *Inlets.* In the 1970's he began composing dances especially for film and videotape. **D** 34

Cuomo, Mario M. (1932–), governor of New York, Democrat, b. Queens. Elected governor in 1982, Cuomo had served earlier as New York's secretary of state (1975–79) and as lieutenant governor (1979–83). In 1977, as the candidate of the Liberal Party, he ran unsuccessfully for the office of mayor of New York City.

Cup fungi F 498
Cupid (CU-pid), Roman god **G** 361
Valentines **V** 266
See also Eros
Cup plates, antique glass receptacles **A** 318
Cupronickel, copper and nickel alloy **A** 169
Cups and Balls, magic trick **M** 18

Curaçao (cu-ra-SA-o), the largest island of the Netherlands Antilles off the coast of Venezuela. Discovered (1499) by Alonso de Ojeda and Amerigo Vespucci and colonized by the Spanish (1527), it has been Dutch since 1634 except for British occupation during the Napoleonic Wars. The principal industry, refining and shipping Venezuelan oil, is centered at the capital, Willemstad.
Caribbean Sea and islands **C** 118, 119
physical fitness class, *picture* **E** 82
Willemstad, *picture* **C** 116

Curare (cu-RA-re), poison used as drug **D** 325
plants, medicinal **P** 314; *picture* **P** 315
Curds, of milk **D** 12–13; **M** 310
used in making cheese **C** 193

Curfew, an order setting a specific time in the evening when certain rules apply, such as that no one may be out-

side. Taken from the French, meaning "cover the fire," the curfew in medieval Europe signaled the time when fires should be put out.

Curie (cu-RIE), **Eve,** French musician and author **C** 553
Curie, Irène Joliot *see* Joliot-Curie, Jean-Frédéric and Irène
Curie, Jacques, French physicist **C** 552
Curie, Marie, Polish-born French physicist **C** 552–53
chemistry, history of **C** 216
radium, discovery of **U** 230
science, history of **S** 76
Curie, Pierre, French physicist **C** 552–53
radium, discovery of **U** 230
science, history of **S** 76
Curie's Law C 552
Curing, preservative process
cheese **D** 13
leather **L** 108
meat **M** 192
tobacco **T** 201
Curitiba (cu-ri-TI-ba), Brazil **B** 383
Curium (CU-ri-um), element **E** 154, 160
Curling, game **C** 554–55
a favorite sport in Canada **C** 67
Currants, berries **G** 52
Currency, money as a medium of exchange **M** 411
coins and coin collecting **C** 374–75
monetary units of countries *see* country articles
Current electricity E 123
Current-measuring buoys O 32–33
Current River, Missouri **M** 366; *picture* **M** 368
Currents, ocean *see* Ocean currents
Curriculum (cur-RIC-u-lum), course of study **E** 77–78

Currier & Ives, American lithographers whose prints, popular in the 19th century, included political cartoons, landscapes, and scenes that captured spirit of growing young nation. Nathaniel Currier (1813–88) went into lithography business (1834) and took artist James Merritt Ives (1824–95) into partnership (1857).
popular art distinguished from folk art **F** 292

Curry, Jabez Lamar Monroe (1825–1903), American educator and statesman, b. Lincoln County, Ga. He was member of U.S. House of Representatives (1857–61). During Civil War he was member of Confederate Congress (1861–63, 1864) and Confederate Army (1864–65). After war, Curry was president of Howard University in Alabama (1865–68) and U.S. minister to Spain (1885–88, 1902). As agent for Peabody and Slater Funds and supervising director of Southern Education Board, he worked in South to establish schools for both blacks and whites.

Curry, John, British figure skater **O** 116b

Curry, John Steuart (1897–1946), American painter, b. Dunavant, Kans. Famous for scenes of rough life, violent weather, and calm landscapes in Kansas farm country, such as *Line Storm, Baptism in Kansas,* and *Tornado over Kansas,* he also painted circus scenes, including *The Flying Codonas.* **K** 190

Curry powder, blend of spices **S** 382
Cursive writing H 31–33
Curtain walls, of buildings **B** 434; *picture* **B** 433
Curtin, Phyllis, American singer **W** 139
Curtis, Charles, American statesman **K** 189; **V** 331; *pictures* **C** 496, **V** 329

Curtis, Cyrus Hermann Kotzschmar (1850–1933), American publisher and philanthropist, b. Portland, Maine. He founded the Curtis Publishing Co. (1890), which acquired and published various newspapers and magazines, including *Ladies' Home Journal* (established by Curtis), *The Saturday Evening Post, Country Gentleman,* and the Philadelphia *Inquirer.* Generous with his wealth, he made donations to colleges, hospitals, and charities.

Curtis Cup, trophy awarded to winners of match between women's amateur golf teams of United States and Great Britain. It was donated by Harriot and Margaret Curtis and is awarded every other year (since 1930).

Curtiss, Glen Hammond (1878–1930), American inventor and pioneer aviator, b. Hammondsport, N.Y. He designed the airplane June Bug and piloted it for 1 kilometer in first public flight in United States (1908). During World War I his factories produced military planes for the Allies. His most important contribution was the invention of the aileron, a movable wing part that provides lateral control.

Curve ball, *picture* **B** 73
Curved mirrors **L** 262–63
Curves, geometric **G** 124

Curwood, James Oliver (1878–1927), American novelist, b. Owosso, Mich. He worked as reporter and editor for the Detroit *News-Tribune* (1900–07). His 2 years of writing for the Canadian Government in the northwest was a main source for his 26 novels about rugged people, wild animals, and outdoor life. His works include *The Grizzly King, The Valley of Silent Men,* and *Nomads of the North.* **M** 272

Mount Curwood, Michigan **M** 261

Cuscuses (CUS-cus-es), marsupials **K** 175

Cushing (COO-shing), **Harvey Williams** (1869–1939), American surgeon, b. Cleveland, Ohio. Cushing reduced death toll in brain operations through his techniques of controlling bleeding, cutting out tumors, and avoiding shock. He introduced continuous taking of blood pressure during surgery, a valuable method of detecting shock. Cushing first described the disease bearing his name, which he found to be associated with pituitary-gland tumor. He wrote several classics on brain structure and disease, including *Pituitary Body and Its Disorders* and Pulitzer-prize-winning biography of physician Sir William Osler. **O** 73

Cushing, Richard, Cardinal (1895–1970), Roman Catholic churchman, b. Boston, Mass. Ordained a priest in 1921, he served as pastor in Archdiocese of Boston (1921–39). He was active in Society for the Propagation of the Faith and became its director (1929). Archbishop of Boston (1944–70) and cardinal after 1958, he wrote many articles on social and ecclesiastical problems.

Cushions **U** 226, 227

Cushites, in Old Testament, the descendants of Cush, the son of Ham. The name generally refers to the inhabitants of the land of Cush, or Ethiopia. First dominated by Egypt (approximately 1991–1786 B.C.), they later established an Ethiopian, or Cushite, line of kings over Egypt (715–656 B.C.) but were forced by Assyria to return to their own land.

Cushitic (cush-IT-ic) **languages** **L** 39
spoken in Africa **A** 55
Cusimanses (cu-si-man-ses), animals related to mongooses **G** 95
Cuspids, teeth **T** 47
Custer, George Armstrong, American army officer **I** 214
coming of the white man **I** 168–69
Custer Battlefield National Monument, Montana **M** 438
Custer's Last Stand **I** 214; *picture* **I** 215
Teton Sioux Indians **I** 168–69
Custer State Park, South Dakota **S** 322–23
Custis-Lee Mansion, Virginia *see* Arlington House, The Robert E. Lee Mansion
Custody, of children in divorce **D** 236
Customary system, measurements *see* English system
Custom-made, production of goods **M** 151
glove making **G** 240–41
Customs *see* Tariffs
Customs, social *see* People, how they live and work; sections of continent, country, province, and state articles

Customs Service, United States, an agency of the U.S. Department of the Treasury. It sets and collects customs duties (taxes) on imported goods. It also checks goods and people coming into or going out of the country. This is done to prevent smuggling and to prevent anything harmful to health or agriculture from entering. Customs duties have been collected by federal law in the United States since 1789.

Cut-and-cover tunnels **T** 314–15
Cut glass **G** 230, 232
Cuthbert, Betty, Australian athlete **O** 112
Cutin (CU-tin), waxy substance of leaves **L** 120
Cutler, Manasseh, American clergyman **W** 143
Cutlery, different kinds of knives, scissors, and shears **K** 285–88
Cut-pile fabric **R** 352
Cutter, Charles Ammi, American librarian **L** 189
Cutter number, letter and number system used in libraries to represent authors' names **L** 189
Cutting, of gemstones **G** 71
Cuttings, from plants **H** 268–69
Cuttlefishes, mollusks **O** 277; *picture* **L** 230
ink made from ink sac **C** 432
Cutworms, caterpillars **P** 289
Cuvier (cu-vi-AY), **Georges,** French naturalist **F** 381
Cuvier and the correlation of parts **B** 191
early work in geology **G** 118
Cuza (CU-za), **Alexandru Ioan,** prince of Rumania **R** 358
Cuzco (CU-zco), Peru, capital of Inca Empire **I** 206; *picture* **P** 164
ancient Inca road **P** 165
Cyanide method, gold extracting process **G** 249
Cyanocobalamin, vitamin B_{12} **V** 370d

Cybernetics, comparative study of learning in animals and machines, including study of the way information is received and stored and the way problems are solved on basis of past experience. It was first treated as separate science in Norbert Wiener's book *Cybernetics* (1948).

Cycad trees, ancient tropical plants **D** 177
Cyclades (CIC-la-dese) **Islands,** southeast of Greece **I** 430; *picture* **I** 428

Cyclamate, an artificial sweetener used in various food products to replace sugar. In 1969, U.S. Secretary of Health, Education, and Welfare Robert H. Finch banned use of cyclamates in soft drinks and other foodstuffs. Ban was due to laboratory tests indicating a possibility that cyclamates might be a cause of some forms of cancer.
    chemicals that cause cancer **C** 91
    FDA tests and ban on **F** 351

Cyclamen (CIC-la-men), house plant, *picture* **H** 268
Cycles, miracle plays **M** 339
Cycling *see* Bicycles and bicycling
Cyclones, low-pressure areas in the atmosphere
    climatic control **C** 345
    highs and lows affecting weather **W** 74
    hurricanes and tornadoes **H** 293, 296, 298
    Pecos Bill ropes a cyclone, story **F** 316–17
    wind patterns **W** 187
Cyclopes (cy-CLO-peze), in Greek mythology
    cyclopean masonry **B** 394
    Odyssey **O** 53
Cyclopropane (cy-clo-PRO-pane), an anesthetic **A** 258
Cyclosporine, drug **H** 86c
Cyclotrons (CY-clo-trons), atom smashers **A** 489
    nuclear energy **N** 366
Cygnus (CIG-nus), constellation **C** 492
    astronomy, discoveries in **A** 476b
    black holes **S** 411
Cylinder, (CIL-in-der) geometric figure **G** 129
Cylinder presses, for printing **P** 461–62
Cylinder recordings, for the early phonograph **R** 123
Cylinders, of engines
    hydraulic machines **H** 301
    internal-combustion engines **I** 304, 305
    steam engines **S** 419
Cymbala, bell chime **B** 137
Cymbals, musical instruments **M** 550; *picture* **M** 548
    ancient music **A** 246
    percussion instruments **P** 152

Cymbeline, drama by William Shakespeare. The title is the name of an English king who ruled Britain from about A.D. 5 to 40, and the plot is based on a story about him from the collection Decameron by the Italian writer Giovanni Boccaccio. The tale involves a bet made by Iachimo that Imogen, Cymbeline's daughter, will not remain true to her husband, Posthumus. Iachimo steals a bracelet from Imogen as she sleeps and convinces Posthumus of her infidelity. Iachimo's treachery is finally revealed, and the couple is reunited.

Cynewulf (KIN-e-wolf), early English poet **E** 246

Cynics, members of philosophical school founded by Greek philosopher Antisthenes (445?–365? B.C.). Cynics believed in "the natural life," free from vanity and hypocrisy of social conventions, as means of achieving virtue. Most famous Cynic was Diogenes (412?–323 B.C.), who supposedly lived in a tub and carried a lantern in search for "an honest man." Cynics' contempt for civilized people and customs gave rise to their Greek name, *kynikós,* meaning "doglike," and to modern meaning of "cynic," someone who has no faith in human goodness or sincerity.

Cypress, evergreen tree found throughout the world. It has small, rounded cones and scalelike leaves. The wood, often fragrant, is used in making pencils, shingles, and boats. Unrelated trees called cypress include the bald cypress of the southern United States. This tree is large at the base, tapering toward the top. Its wood is used in mak-ing railroad ties and posts.
    bald cypress, *picture* **T** 276
    uses of the wood and its grain **W** 223

Cypress Gardens, near Charleston, South Carolina **S** 304

Cyprian, Saint (Thascius Caecilius Cyprianus) (200?–258), Christian martyr, b. Carthage. Converted to Christianity about 248, he labored for unity of Church and readmission of Christians who had renounced their religion under persecution. He was beheaded during Christian persecution under Emperor Valerian.

Cyprus (CY-prus) **C** 556–58; **T** 328
    considered part of Asia **A** 448
    flag **F** 239

Cyrano de Bergerac (ce-ra-NO d'bear-jer-OC), **Savinien de** (1619–55), French poet and soldier, b. Périgord. He served in the army (1637–40) and established a reputation as a poet and duelist. Forced to retire as a result of his wounds, he devoted the rest of his life to writing. Cyrano was immortalized in Edmond Rostand's play *Cyrano de Bergerac,* although the plot actually has little basis in fact.
    first science-fiction novel of space travel **S** 84

Cyril (CIR-il) and **Methodius, Saints**
    Kievan state of Eastern Slavs **U** 47
Cyrillic (ci-RIL-lic) **alphabet**
    Bulgarian language first to use **B** 440
    Russian language **U** 58
    Union of Soviet Socialist Republics **U** 47–48
Cyrus (CY-rus) **the Great,** king of Persia **A** 225; **I** 375

Cyrus the Younger (424?–401 B.C.), Persian prince, son of Darius Nothus. He plotted against his brother Artaxerxes II (401 B.C.) but was pardoned and restored as prince of Asia Minor. In command of Asiatic forces, he met Artaxerxes at Cunaxa in Babylonia, was defeated and killed. The subsequent Greek retreat (401–399 B.C.) was recorded in the *Anabasis* by Xenophon.

Cystic acne **D** 205

Cystic fibrosis, inherited disease affecting exocrine glands—those producing mucus, sweat, saliva. Disease results in improper functioning of many organs, including lungs, pancreas, and sometimes liver. **D** 198–99

Cysts (CISTS)
    crusts enclosing certain amoebas **M** 278–79
Cytology (cy-TOL-ogy), study of plant and animal cells **B** 190, 195–96
    medical laboratory tests **M** 202
Cytoplasm (CY-to-plasm), cell **C** 159, 160, 161; **M** 277
    how human body grows by cell division **B** 267
Czaczkes, Samuel Joseph *see* Agnon, Shmuel Yosef
Czar (ZAR), title of Russian rulers **C** 6
    Russian czars **U** 48–50
Czechoslovakia (chec-o-slo-VA-kia) **C** 559–64
    costumes, traditional, *picture* **C** 350
    flag **F** 237
    Hitler's takeover **W** 286; *picture* **W** 287
    Masaryk, Tomáš, first president **M** 133
    motion picture industry **M** 488a
    national anthem **N** 21
    national dance **D** 30

PHOTO CREDITS

The following list credits the sources of photos used in THE NEW BOOK OF KNOWLEDGE. Credits are listed, page by page, photo by photo—left to right, top to bottom. Wherever appropriate, the name of the photographer has been listed with the source, the two being separated by a dash. When two or more photos by different photographers appear on one page, their credits are separated by semicolons.

C

3– Hubert A. Lowman
4
7 George Holton—Photo Researchers
8 Birnback; C. Zachary—Egyptian State Tourist Administration.
9 Michel Combazard
10 Robert W. Young—Lenstour
12 Bettmann Archive
13 From *Les Tres Riches Heures du Duc de Berry*, Conde Museum, Chantilly, France; Giraudon—Rapho Guillumette.
14 Ronald Perkins; J. H. Atkinson—FPG; Bucky Reeves—National Audubon Society; California State Fish and Game Commission.
17 Ray Atkeson
18 Ray Manley—Shostal; C. W. Sorensen.
24 Ray Manley—Shostal; John S. Flannery—Alpha; Fred Lyon—Rapho.
27 Shostal; FPG.
33 Nat & Yanna Brandt—Photo Researchers; Ralph Gerstle—Photo Researchers; Van Bucher—Photo Researchers.
34 Cy La Tour
36 Marc & Evelyne Bernheim—Rapho
37– Camp Fire, Inc.
39
40 Winnebago Industries, Inc.
53 George Hunter; Malak; DPI; Malak.
59 Malak; Malak; Malak; George Hunter.
60 George Hunter
63 Miller Services Limited
64 National Gallery of Canada, Ottawa
65 George Hunter
68 By permission of the Huntington Library, San Marino, California
70 Anne S. K. Brown Military Collection, Brown University
72 Provincial Archives of Victoria, B.C., Canada
76 R. Curtis—Monkmeyer Press Photo
79 Public Affairs Office, Department of National Defense, Canada
81 ANI
83 Perceval
87 Jerry Cooke—Photo Researchers
88 Australian News & Information Bureau
89 Francis Delafield Hospital, New York City; Francis Delafield Hospital, New York City; American Cancer Society.
90 American Cancer Society
91 Courtesy of Pfizer Inc.
92 Brookhaven National Laboratory
93 American Cancer Society
94 Chas. Pfizer & Co.; National Institutes of Health, Public Health Service, U.S. Department of Health and Human Services.
97 Shell Oil Company
99 Clyde Smith—Alpha
100b Harrison Forman
101 South African Tourist Corp.
102 Graham Young—Photo Trends
105 Art Resource
116 Charles W. Herbert—Photo Trends; John G. Ross—Photo Researchers; Tom Hollyman—Photo Researchers.
117 Marc & Evelyne Bernheim—Rapho Guillumette; Allan J. Lity—DPI.
118 Marc & Evelyne Bernheim—Rapho Guillumette
121 C. W. Herbert—Photo Trends; Publix; Annan.
124b Charles M. Rafshoon
124c UPI; © 1978 David Hume Kennerly—Contact.
125 By special permission of *The Saturday Evening Post* © 1963 by the Curtis Publishing Co.

126 *Le Charavari*, August 15, 1845; Thomas Nast—Culver.
127 Drawing by Charles Addams © 1940, The New Yorker Magazine, Inc.; Ed Fisher—*Saturday Review*.
128 TM Reg. U.S. Pat. Office. All rights reserved © 1964 by United Features Syndicate, Inc.
129 Los Angeles County Museum of Art, Mrs. Fred Hathaway Bixby Bequest
130 © François Lochon—Gamma/Liaison
131 Jerry Cooke; Shostal Associates.
132 William G. Froelich, Jr.
133 Art Reference Bureau; British Travel and Holidays Association.
134 Tommy Lark—Photo Researchers
135 Jarrold
136 George Holton—Photo Researchers
137 South Africa Tourist Corporation; Marc & Evelyne Bernheim—Rapho Guillumette.
138 Ylla—Rapho Guillumette; Simon—Photo Researchers.
139 W. Suschitzky—Pix
140 Jarrold; Jewel Craig—National Audubon Society; Atlantic Press.
143 Guy Withers—Photo Trends; Walter Chandoha; W. Chandoha; W. Chandoha.
144 Walter Chandoha; E. L. Taylor—Annan; Walter Chandoha; E. L. Taylor—Annan.
145 Jacques Six; Boubat—*Réalités*.
147 Robert Davis—Photo Researchers
148 John & Bini Moss—Photo Researchers
149 Jack Zehrt—Shostal
150 Ray Manley—Shostal; Shostal; A. L. Goldman—Rapho Guillumette.
153 Copyright 1952 E. "Tex" Helm
156 R. Weininger—Editorial Photocolor Archives
157 Jacques Jolfe
158 National Park Concessions, photo by W. Ray Scott; Charles E. Mohr.
159 Brookhaven National Laboratory; Rare Book Room, The New York Public Library.
160 Institut de recherches scientifiques sur le cancer, Villejuif, France
161 Abbott Laboratories
165 Snark International—National Museum, Dublin
166 Dr. J. K. St. Joseph
167 William Graham—Photo Researchers
170 Jacques Six; Jacques Six.
171 Dr. Schremmer
173 Harrison Forman
174 Carl Frank
175 Luis Villota—The Stock Market
176 Bill Stanton—The Stock Market; Carl Frank; Harrison Forman.
177 Jerry Frank
178 Lisa Little, Museum of Primitive Art, New York; Metropolitan Museum of Art, bequest of Mary Stillman Harkness, 1950; NASA.
179 Bickley Furnaces; Syracuse China Corporation.
181 Giraudon—Courtauld Institute, London
182 Marc & Evelyne Bernheim—Rapho Guillumette
184 The Museum of Modern Art, New York, Mrs. Simon Guggenheim Fund
185 Don Hunstein—Columbia Records
186b The Museum of Modern Art, New York, Film Stills Archive
187 Culver Pictures
190 Trustees of the British Museum
193 Celanese
194 Courtesy of Rhodiaceta
195 Courtesy of Rhône-Poulenc
197 Fundamental Photographers
217 Fundamental Photo
221 Wide World
228 Historical Pictures Service, Inc.
229– Hedrich Blessing
230

234 Suquet—I.P.N.
236– Rare Book Division, New York Public Library
237
241 From *John Gilpin and Other Stories* by Randolph Caldecott, published by Frederick Warne & Co., Inc., New York and London
242 Reprinted by permission of Frederick Warne & Co. Ltd. from Beatrix Potter's *The Tale of Peter Rabbit*
243 Illustration by Donna Diamond from *Bridge to Terabithia* by Katherine Paterson, © 1977 by Katherine Paterson, by permission of Thomas Y. Crowell; frontispiece by Jerry Pinkney from *Roll of Thunder, Hear My Cry* by Mildred D. Taylor, © 1976 by the Dial Press, New York.
245 Reprinted by permission of McGraw-Hill Book Company from *The Happy Lion* by Louise Fatio, illustrated by Roger Duvoisin
246 From *The Snowy Day* by Ezra Jack Keats, © 1962 by Ezra Jack Keats. Reprinted by permission of the Viking Press, Inc.
247 From *Mr. Gumpy's Outing* by John Burningham, © 1970 by John Burningham. Reprinted by permission of Holt, Rinehart, and Winston; from *Noah's Ark* by Peter Spier, © 1977 by Peter Spier. Reprinted by permission of Doubleday and Company, Inc.; from *Make Way for Ducklings* by Robert McCloskey, © 1941, 1969 by Robert McCloskey. Reprinted by permission of the Viking Press.
248 From *A Story, A Story*, © 1970 by Gail E. Haley, by permission of Atheneum Publishers
248– Illustration by Leo and Diane Dillon from
248a *Why Mosquitoes Buzz in People's Ears: A West African Folktale*, retold by Verna Aardema, Dial Press.
248b Illustration from *The Little Prince* by Antoine de Saint-Exupéry, © 1943 by Harcourt Brace Jovanovich, Inc., renewed 1971 by Consuelo de Saint-Exupéry, reproduced by permission of the publishers
248c Used by permission of Atheneum Publishers from *Alexander and the Terrible, Horrible, No Good, Very Bad Day* by Judith Viorst, illustrated by Ray Cruz. Copyright © 1976 by Judith Viorst. Illustrations copyright © 1976 by Ray Cruz.
248d Reprinted by permission of Charles Scribner's Sons from *The Yearling* by Marjorie Kinnan Rawlings, illustrated by N. C. Wyeth.
251 Stockpile
252 Jerry Frank; Jacques Jangoux.
254 © Jonathan T. Wright—Bruce Coleman Inc.
256 Alan Vroom
257 © 1978 George Holton—Photo Researchers
259 Felix Green—FPG; Henri Cartier-Bresson—Magnum.
261 Henri Cartier-Bresson—Magnum; Marc Riboud—Magnum.
264 Harvey Lloyd—The Image Bank
265 Audrey Topping—Rapho-Photo Researchers; © 1979 George Holton—Photo Researchers.
267 © George Holton—Photo Researchers
270 National Palace Museum, Taipei, Taiwan; Mandel—Ziolo.
271 Cauboue—Bibliothèque des Arts décoratifs, Paris
272 Koch—Rapho
274 Stockpile
276 Scala
280 Metropolitan Museum of Art, The Jules S. Bache Collection, 1949; National Gallery of Art, Washington, D.C., Samuel M. Kress Collection.
282 Art Reference Bureau
285 J. Barnell—Shostal
286 Bettmann Archive
287 Swiss National Tourist Office
288 Arlene Ragsdale—FPG
290 © 1977 William Hubbell—Woodfin Camp

293 David J. Roads—Shostal; Marc & Evelyne Bernheim—Rapho Guillumette; Malak; Tom Mahnken—Photo Trends.
294 Katon's—Ireland Graphics Photography Limited; Jay Hoops—Photo Trends.
297 Karsh, Ottawa—Rapho Guillumette
299 Sue McCartney—Photo Researchers
300 Circus World Museum
301 Myles Adler; Myles Adler; Myles Adler; Myles Adler.
303 Jalibert; Pic.
304 Cordon
305 Amano—Ziolo
306 Lizabeth Corlett—DPI; Gerald Clyde—FPG.
307 Charbonnier—*Réalités*; Davis Overcash—Bruce Coleman Inc.; © 1976 Linda Bartlett—Photo Researchers.
308 Culver Pictures, Inc.
308b Bettmann Archive
308c Giraudon—Library of the Hydrographic Service of the Navy, Paris
308d Bettmann Archive
308e Claus C. Meyer—Black Star; Thomas—Photo Researchers; Eric Carle—Shostal Associates.
309 Shostal Associates; Charles Shapp; George Hunter—Publix.
310 George Daniell—Photo Researchers
314 J. Cron—Monkmeyer Press Photo Service
318 Culver
321 Rare Book Division, The New York Public Library
329 Popsie
330 Robert Conlan
335 Bettmann Archive
336 Arline Strong; Harold M. Lebow; Lois Lord.
338 Hastings-Willinger & Associates
340 Bettmann Archive; Bettmann Archive.
342 Bettmann Archive
343 © M. Devore III—Bruce Coleman Inc.; © Marcello Bertinetti—Photo Researchers.
345 Gene Klebe; Dennis Hallinan—Alpha; Chuck Abbott—Rapho Guillumette.
356 American Apparel Association
357 American Apparel Association; Louis Goldman—Rapho Guillumette.
361 Anthony Sas, University of South Carolina
372 Standard Oil Co. of New Jersey; Standard Oil Co. of New Jersey; Bob Yeargin—Mandrel Industries, Inc.
374 Chase Manhattan Bank, Money Museum; The American Numismatic Society; The American Numismatic Society.
376 Sandak, Copyright, The Museum of Modern Art, New York, 1962; Sandak; Lois Lord.
377 Hella Hammid
379 Dietar F. Grabitzky
380 Lillian Tonnaire—Taylor

381 Shostal
382 Colombia National Tourist Board
383 Mike Andrews—Camera Press-Pix
401 Color Illustration Inc.; Rutherford Platt; Colorado Department of Public Relations; Colorado Department of Public Relations.
402 Josef Muench
407 Ray Manley—Shostal
408 Margaret Durrance—Rapho Guillumette
411 Josef Muench
412 Josef Muench; Shostal.
413 Winston Pote—Shostal; Lawrence S. Williams—Rapho.
418 Yerkes Observatory, University of Chicago
420 Royal Canadian Air Force; Fairchild Aerial Surveys; Dr. Virgil E. Barnes.
421 American Museum of Natural History
422– National Periodicals Publications, Inc.
423
424 Courtesy of RCA Victor Co., R. M. Jones, Art Director, Jan Balet, Artist; W. S. Eberle, Zurich-Eastman Kodak Co.; Photos from National Biscuit Co. through Kenyon-Eckhart Advertising Agency.
425 Coca-Cola Co.; Volkswagen of America, Inc.; Westinghouse Electric Corp.; Bovril Ltd.; Distributed in America by Red Line Commercial Co.
426 New York City Department of Traffic; David Stone Martin.
427 Courtesy of *The New York Times*, BBDO Advertising Co.; Container Corp. of America; Hartwall Co.; The Times Publishing Company, Ltd.
433 The New York Public Library
438 From *Communication Through the Ages* by Alfred Still, published by Murray Hill Books, Inc.
440 NASA
441 Digital Equipment Corporation
443 Josse—Grolier
444 Launois—Rapho—Museum of the Revolution
445 Marc Garanger
449 Courtesy Regis McKenna
450 IBM
451 Snark International—Musée des Techniques, Paris
452 IBM
454 IBM
457 IBM
462 Naud—AAA Photo
463– Naud—De Wys, Inc.
464
465 W. D. Friedman—PIP
466 Color Illustration Inc.; J. Horace McFarland; Allan D. Cruickshank—National Audubon Society; J. Horace McFarland.
471 A. Griffin; P. Roll—Photo Researchers.
473 Jerry Cooke

474 Robert Tschirky—Annan
479 Robert Tschirky—Annan
481 Phoenix Mutual Life Insurance
483 Alcoa; Tom Hollyman—Photo Researchers; Josef Muench.
484 Shell Oil
485 Jarrold; Mark N. Boulton—National Audubon Society.
487 Paolo Koch—Rapho Guillumette
488 Byron Crader—Lenstour
494 Ray Ellis—Rapho Photo Researchers
494b National Maritime Museum, Greenwich Hospital Collection
495 Wide World Photos; Brown Brothers.
496 Bettmann Archive; Brown Brothers; Wide World Photos.
499 John Colwell—Grant Heilman
500 Hubert Josse—Musée de l'Observatoire, Paris
505 C. W. Sorenson
506 Alpha
511 Fordham University News Office
512 Brookhaven National Institute
514 Douglas Faulkner
516 Inter-American Development Bank; Jane Latta.
517 Fred Ward—Black Star
520 National Cotton Council
521 The New York Public Library; National Cotton Council.
522 Grant Heilman; Grant Heilman.
523 Webb Photos
524 National Cotton Council; National Cotton Council.
524a National Cotton Council; National Cotton Council; National Cotton Council.
524b Ken Regan—Camera Five
525 O. Franken—Sygma; Neil Leifer—Camera Five; Jodi Cobb—Woodfin Camp and Associates, Inc.
532b Bill Powers—*Corrections* magazine
535 Editorial Photocolor Archives
541 Walter Dawn
542 M. Pope; Professor Ralph W. G. Wyckof.
547 Henri Cartier-Bresson—Magnum Photos, Inc.
549 Cyr Agency
550 Shostal
551 Rene Burri—Magnum
552 Brown Brothers
553 Culver
554 R. Curtis—Monkmeyer; Perrin.
556 Robert Davis—Photo Researchers
558 Emil Brunner—Pix; Robert Davis—Photo Researchers.
561 Lomeo Bullaty—Nancy Palmer
562 Jerry Cooke; Martin Swithinbank—PIP.
563 Eastfoto